An Introduction to Canadian History

Edited by A.I. Silver

With Carl Berger,
Allan Greer,
Lori Chambers,
Danielle Hamelin,
Jane Harrison,
Leila Mitchell McKee,
and Kathryn Ridout

An Introduction to Canadian History

First published in 1991 by
Canadian Scholars' Press Inc.
339 Bloor Street West, Suite 220
Toronto, M5S 1W7
Canada

Copyright © Canadian Scholars' Press, 1991. No copy, reproduction or transmission of this material may be made without written permission.

Canadian Cataloguing in Publication Data

Main entry under title:

An Introduction to Canadian History

ISBN 0-921627-67-X

1. Canada - History. I. Silver, A.I. (Arthur Isaac), 1940-.

FC170.I57 1991   971   C91-094045-2   F1026.I57 1991

Printed and bound in Canada

Acknowledgements:

Bruce Trigger, "The French Presence in Huronia: The Structure of Franco-Huron Relations in the First Half of the 17th Century" is taken from pages 107-141 of *Canadian Historical Review*. Copyright © 1968 University of Toronto Press. Reprinted by permission of University of Toronto Press. Cornelius J. Jaenen, "French Sovereignty and Native Nationhood during the French Regime" is taken from pages 83-113 of *Native Studies Review*. Copyright © 1986 Native Studies Review, University of Saskatchewan. Reprinted by permission of Native Studies Review. W.J. Eccles, "The Social, Economic, and Political Significance of the Military Establishment in New France" is taken from pages 1-22 of *Canadian Historical Review*. Copyright © 1968 University of Toronto Press. Reprinted by permission of University of Toronto Press. John Bosher, "The Family in New France" is taken from pages 1-13 of Barry Gough, ed., *In Search of the Visible Past*. Copyright © 1991 Wilifrid Laurier University Press / CANCOPY. Reprinted by permission of CANCOPY. Michel Brunet, "The British Conquest and the Decline of the French-Canadian Bourgeoisie" is taken from *La presence anglaise et les Canadiens*. Copyright © 1958 Dale Miquelon, University of Saskatchewan. Reprinted by permission of Dale Miquelon. José Iguartua, "A Change in Climate: The Conquest and the Marchands of Montreal" is taken from 115-134 of *Historical Papers*. Copyright © 1974 Canadian Historical Association. Reprinted by permission of Canadian Historical Association. Neil MacKinnon, "Nova Scotia Loyalists, 1973-1985" is taken from pages 17-48 of *Histoire sociale / Social History*. Copyright © 1969 Histoire sociale/Social History. Reprinted by permission of Histoire sociale/Social History. S.F. Wise, "Sermon Literature and Canadian Intellectual History" is taken from pages 3-18 of *The Bulletin of the Committee on Archives of the United Church of Canada*. Copyright © 1965 The United Church of Canada. Reprinted by permission of The United Church Publishing House. Sylvia Van Kirk, "'Women in Between': Indian Women in Fur Trade Society in Western Canada" is taken from *Historical Papers*. Copyright © 1977 Canadian Historical Association. Reprinted by permission of Canadian Historical Association. Jennifer S.H. Brown, "Diverging Identities: The Presbyterian Métis of St. Gabriel Street, Montreal" is taken from pages 195-206 of Jacqueline Peters and Jennifer Brown, eds., *The New Peoples: Being and Becoming Métis in North America*. Copyright © 1985 University of Manitoba Press, Winnipeg. Reprinted by permission of University of Manitoba Press, Winnipeg. David Gagan, "Genesis: Settling Peel County" is taken from pages 20-37 of *Hopeful Travellers*. Copyright © 1981 University of Toronto Press. Reprinted by permission of University of Toronto Press. Michael S. Cross, "The Shiners' War: Social Violence in the Ottawa Valley in the 1830s" is taken from pages 1-26 of *Canadian Historical Review*. Copyright © 1973 University of Toronto Press. Reprinted by permission of University of Toronto Press. Lawrence A.H. Smith, "Le Canadien and the British Constitution, 1806-1810" is taken from pages 93-108 of *Canadian Historical Review*. Copyright © 1973 University of Toronto Press. Reprinted by permission of University of Toronto Press. Fernand Ouellet, "French-Canadian Nationalism: From its Origins to the Insurrection of 1837" is taken from pages 171-186 of Dale Miquelon, ed., *Society and Conquest*. Copyright © 1965 Dale Miquelon. Reprinted by permission of Dale Miquelon, University of Saskatchewan. Jacques Monet, "French-Canadian Nationalism and the Challenge of Ultramontanism" is taken from pages 41-55 of *Historical Papers*. Copyright © 1966 Jacques Monet / CANCOPY Reprinted by permission of Jacques Monet and CANCOPY. J.M.S. Careless, "Mid-Victorian Liberalism in Central Canadian Newspapers, 1850-67" is taken from pages 221-236 of *Canadian Historical Review*. Copyright © 1950 University of Toronto Press. Reprinted by permission of University of Toronto Press. Michael Katz, "The People of a Canadian City, 1851-2" is taken from pages 402-426 of *Canadian Historical Review*. Copyright © 1972 University of Toronto Press. Reprinted by permission of University of Toronto Press. Judith Fingard, "The Winter's Tale: The Seasonal Contours of Pre-Industrial Poverty in British North America, 1815-1860" is taken from pages 65-94 of *Canadian Historical Review*. Reprinted by permission of Judith Fingard, Dalhousie University. D.G.Creighton, "Confederation: The Use and Abuse of History" is taken from *Journal of*

Canadian Studies. Copyright © Journal of Canadian Studies. Robert Vipond, "Confederation and the Federal Principle" is taken from pages 15-45 of *Liberty and Community.* Copyright © State University of New York Press, Albany. Reprinted by permission of State University of New York Press, Albany. T.W. Acheson, "The National Policy and the Industrialization of the Maritimes, 1880-1910" is taken from pages 3-28 of *Acadiensis.* Copyright © 1972 Acadiensis, University of New Brunswick. Reprinted by permission of Acadiensis, University of New Brunswick. Michael Bliss, "Canadianizing American Business: The Roots of the Branch Plant" is taken from pages 26-42 of I. Lumsden, ed., *Close to the 49th Parallel.* Copyright © 1974 University of Toronto Press. Reprinted by permission of University of Toronto Press. Noel Dyck, "An Opportunity Lost: The Initiative of the Reserve Agricultural Programme in the Prairie West" is taken from pages 121-137 of L.F. Barron and J.B. Waldram, eds., *1885 and After.* Copyright © 1986 Canadian Plains Research Centre. Reprinted with the permission of the Canadian Plains Research Center, University of Regina. Thomas Flanagan, "Aboriginal Title" is taken form pages 75-100 of *Riel and the Rebellion: 1885 Reconsidered.* Copyright © 1983 Western Producer Prairie Books. Reprinted by permission of Western Producer Prairie Books, Saskatchewan. Gregory Kealey, "'The Honest Workingman' and Workers' Control: The Experience of Toronto Skilled Workers, 1860-1892" is taken from pages 32-68 of *Labour/Le Travailleur.* Copyright © 1976 Labour/Le Travailleur. Reprinted by permission of Labour/Le Travailleur. "The Fragmented Family: Family Strategies in the Face of Death, Illness, and Poverty, Montreal, 1860-1892" is taken from pages 109-128 of Joy Par, *Childhood and Family in Canadian History.* Copyright © 1991 McClelland and Stewart / CANCOPY. Reprinted by permission of CANCOPY. Donald Avery, "Canadian Immigration Policy and the 'Foreign' Navvy, 1896-1914" is taken from the *Canadian Historical Review.* Copyright © 1972 Canadian Historical Association. Reprinted by permission of the Canadian Historical Association and Donald Avery. John C. Lehr, "Government Perceptions of Ukrainian Immigrants to Western Canada, 1896-1902" is taken form pages 1-12 of *Canadian Ethnic Studies.* Copyright © 1987 Canadian Ethnic Studies. Reprinted by permission of Canadian Ethnic Studies. Robert Craig Brown, "Sir Robert Borden, the Great War, and Anglo-Canadian Relations" is taken from J.S. Moir, ed., *Character and Circumstance.* Copyright © 1970 Macmillan of Canada. Desmond Morton, "French Canada and War, 1868-1917: The Military Background to the Conscription Crisis of 1917" is taken from J.L. Granatstein and R.D. Cuff, eds., *War and Society in North America.* Copyright © 1971 Nelson Canada. Wendy Mitchinson, "The WCTU: 'For God, Home, and Native Land': A Study in 19th Century Feminism" is taken from pages 152-167 of Linda Kealey, *A Not Unreasonable Claim.* Copyright © 1979 The Women's Press, Toronto. Reprinted by permission of The Women's Press, Toronto. John H. Thompson, "'The Beginning of our Regeneration': The Great War and Western Canadian Reform Movements" is taken from *Historical Papers.* Copyright © Canadian Historical Association. Reprinted by permission of the Canadian Historical Association. James Struthers, "Two Depressions: Bennett, Trudeau, and the Unemployed" is taken from *Journal of Canadian Studies.* Copyright © 1979 Journal of Canadian Studies. Reprinted by permission of the Journal of Canadian Studies. Walter D. Young, The Great Depression and the CCF" is taken from *Democracy and Discontent.* Copyright © 1978 McGraw Hill, Ryerson. Reprinted by permission of McGraw Hill, Ryerson. H.B.Neatby, "Mackenzie King and National Unity" is taken from pages 54-70 of H.L. Dyck and H.P. Krosby, *Empire and Nations.* Copyright © 1969 University of Toronto Press. Reprinted by permission of University of Toronto Press and H.B. Neatby. J. L. Granatstein, "Staring into the Abyss" is taken from *How Britain's Weakness Forced Canada into the Arms of the United States.* Copyright © 1989 University of Toronto Press. Reprinted by permission of University of Toronto Press. Ramsey Cook, "Au Diable avec le Goupillon et la Tuque: The Quiet Revolution and the New Nationalism" is taken form *Canada, Quebec, and the Uses of Nationalism.* Copyright © 1986 McClelland and Stewart. Reprinted by permission of McClelland and Stewart. Richard Jones, "Politics and the Reinforcement of the French Language in the Province of Quebec, 1960-1986" is taken from Michael Behiels, ed., *Quebec Since 1945: Selected Readings.* Copyright © 1987 Copp Clark Pitman Ltd. Reprinted by permission of Copp Clark Pitman Ltd.

Table of Contents

Foreword vii

Section 1
French-Indian Relations in the 17th and 18th Centuries

a) Introduction 1
b) The French Presence in Huronia: The Structure of Franco-Huron Relations in the First Half of the Seventeenth Century 3
   Bruce Trigger
c) French Sovereignty and Native Nationhood During the French Regime 37
   Cornelius J. Jaenen

Section 2
The Society of New France

a) Introduction 56
b) The Social, Economic, and Political Significance of the Military Establishment in New France 57
   W.J. Eccles
c) The Family in New France 77
   John Bosher

Section 3
The Conquest

a) Introduction 88
b) The British Conquest and the Decline of the French-Canadian Bourgeoisie 89
   Michel Brunet
c) A Change in Climate: The Conquest and the Marchands of Montreal 112
   José Igartua

Section 4
Loyalism and Conservatism in Early British North America

a) Introduction 131
b) Nova Scotia Loyalists, 1783-1785 132
   Neil MacKinnon
c) Sermon Literature and Canadian Intellectual History 160
   S.F. Wise

Section 5
Fur Trade Society

a) Introduction 176
b) "Women in Between": Indian Women in Fur Trade Society
    in Western Canada 177
    Sylvia Van Kirk
c) Diverging Identities: The Presbyterian Métis
    of St. Gabriel Street, Montreal 194
    Jennifer S.H. Brown

Section 6
Settlement and Social Class in Upper Canada

a) Introduction 205
b) Genesis: Settling Peel County 206
    David Gagan
c) The Shiners' War: Social Violence in the Ottawa Valley
    in the 1830s 219
    Michael S. Cross

Section 7
Political, Economic, and National Conflict in Lower Canada

a) Introduction 243
b) *Le Canadien* and the British Constitution, 1806-1810 244
    Lawrence A.H. Smith
c) French-Canadian Nationalism: From its Origins
    to the Insurrection of 1837 258
    Fernand Ouellet

Section 8
Ideological Divergence under the Union

a) Introduction 271
b) French-Canadian Nationalism and the Challenge
    of Ultramontanism 272
    Jacques Monet
c) Mid-Victorian Liberalism in Central Canadian Newspapers,
    1850-67 286
    J.M.S. Careless

Section 9
Society in the Union Period

a) Introduction 299
b) The People of a Canadian City, 1851-2 300
    Michael Katz
c) The Winter's Tale: The Seasonal Contours of Pre-Industrial Poverty
    in British North America, 1815-1860 323
    Judith Fingard

Section 10
Confederation

a) Introduction 353
b) Confederation: The Use and Abuse of History 355
   D.G. Creighton
c) Confederation and the Federal Principle 367
   Robert Vipond

Section 11
National Development Policies

a) Introduction 396
b) The National Policy and the Industrialization of the Maritimes, 1880-1910 397
   T.W. Acheson
c) Canadianizing American Business: The Roots of the Branch Plant 423
   Michael Bliss

Section 12
The North-West Rebellion, 1885

a) Introduction 435
b) An Opportunity Lost: The Initiative of the Reserve Agricultural Programme in the Prairie West 437
   Noel Dyck
c) Aboriginal Title 454
   Thomas Flanagan

Section 13
Labour and Industrialisation

a) Introduction 480
b) "The Honest Workingman" and Workers' Control: The Experience of Toronto Skilled Workers, 1860-1892 481
   Gregory S. Kealey
c) The Fragmented Family: Family Strategies in the Face of Death, Illness, and Poverty, Montreal, 1860-1885 517
   Bettina Bradbury

Section 14
Immigration in the Laurier Period

a) Introduction 536
b) Canadian Immigration Policy and the "Foreign" Navvy, 1896-1914 538
   Donald Avery
c) Government Perceptions of Ukrainian Immigrants to Western Canada, 1896-1902 560
   John C. Lehr

Section 15
World War I

a) Introduction 574
b) Sir Robert Borden, the Great War,
   and Anglo-Canadian Relations...576
   Robert Craig Brown
c) French Canada and War, 1868-1917: The Military Background
   to the Conscription Crisis of 1917..596
   Desmond Morton

Section 16
Social Reform and the Great War

a) Introduction 611
b) The WCTU: "For God, Home, and Native Land":
   A Study in 19th-Century Feminism 612
   Wendy Mitchinson
c) "The Beginning of our Regeneration":
   The Great War and Western Canadian Reform Movements.................628
   John H. Thompson

Section 17
The Great Depression

a) Introduction 646
b) Two Depressions: Bennett, Trudeau, and the Unemployed.................647
   James Struthers
c) The Great Depression and the CCF..663
   Walter D. Young

Section 18
Foreign Relations and the Second World War

a) Introduction 678
b) Mackenzie King and National Unity 679
   H.B. Neatby
c) Staring into the Abyss...694
   J.L. Granatstein

Section 19
Modern Quebec

a) Introduction 711
b) "Au Diable avec le Goupillon et la Tuque":
   The Quiet Revolution and the New Nationalism 713
   Ramsay Cook
c) Politics and the Reinforcement of the French Language in Canada and
   Quebec, 1960-1986 730
   Richard Jones

Foreword

The essays in this book have been chosen to introduce students to a wide range of scholarly writing on Canadian history. They focus on specific topics or problems and should be read in conjunction with a course of lectures or a general textbook that can supply context and continuity.

Historical research has expanded tremendously in the past two decades. New questions have been asked about history, new sources of information have been examined, and new techniques of inquiry have been applied. Historians, long preoccupied by a fairly common body of concerns and methods, have struck out in new directions, come into contact with the work and methods of other disciplines, and become so diverse that it is sometimes hard to see the common element in what they do.

In this collection an attempt has been made to combine some older works with newer ones and to mix subjects of traditional but enduring importance with some of the subjects that have interested researchers in more recent years. It is hoped that this will give students a fair idea of the types of work that are being and have been done by historians of Canada as well as by scholars in related disciplines.

What kinds of questions do historians ask? Where do they look for answers? How do they come to their conclusions, and how do they attempt to convince their readers that those conclusions are sound? These are questions which students might keep in mind as they read the following essays. In this edition all notes are included with the text at the bottom of each page, so that readers can see more easily what sources historians use, how they find and use evidence, and how they construct their arguments.

French-Indian Relations in the 17th and 18th Centuries

Section 1

When the French arrived in North America, they found living here peoples whose customs, values, and social organisation were very different from their own, and who claimed exclusive rights over various regions of the continent. Despite technological advantages, the French found themselves in a position of relative weakness in dealing with these peoples. Because they were so few in North America and because the fur trade was so important to their colony, the French were not generally able to impose their rule or their way of life upon the Indians. On the contrary, it was essential for them to maintain friendly relations with Indian tribes and therefore to make concessions to Indian control of territory and to Indian customs and values. At the same time, the French were able to establish colonies of their own in Acadia and in Canada, and asserted a claim to vast tracts of Indian territory that was recognised by other European powers.

In the fur trade, the French naturally depended on Indian willingness to sell to them; but as Bruce Trigger argues in the first essay here, Indians would only trade on certain conditions. Why is it important for Trigger to show that an Indian trading system was aready well established before the French arrived? Why did trade among the Indians require the establishment of political, social, and family alliances as well as simple commercial contracts? How did this need affect the destiny of New France—and of the Hurons?

Trigger's argument requires him to find out about the customs, institutions, and beliefs of the Indians. But historians usually depend on written records to obtain that sort of information, and the Indians did not write. How does Trigger, an anthropologist, get around that difficulty?

In the second essay, Cornelius Jaenen, an historian, discusses French-Indian relations in the light of ideas that are very much in the news nowadays: nationhood and sovereignty—both ideas that will turn up again in these readings.

What is sovereignty? What did it mean to the French government in the 17th and 18th centuries? How could that government claim sovereignty over Indian territory when it couldn't impose its power over the Indians living there? What was the use of doing so? What right did the French think they had to claim sovereignty? In what sense could they see the Indians as French subjects and yet still self-governing? What does that show us about the idea of sovereignty? What was the Indian view of this relationship? What was the difference between French rule on the St Lawrence and French sovereignty in the interior?

Those wanting to read more on Indian-white relations in Canadian history might consult J.R. Miller, Skyscrapers Hide the Heavens: A History of Indian-White Relations in Canada.

The French Presence in Huronia: The Structure of Franco-Huron Relations in the First Half of the Seventeenth Century[1]

Bruce G. Trigger

Few studies of Canadian history in the first half of the seventeenth century credit sufficiently the decisive role played at that time by the country's native peoples. The success of European colonizers, traders, and missionaries depended to a greater degree than most of them cared to admit on their ability to understand and accommodate themselves not only to native customs but also to a network of political and economic relationships that was not of their own making. Traders and missionaries often were forced to treat Algonkins and Iroquoians as their equals and sometimes they had to acknowledge that the Indians had the upper hand. If the Europeans were astonished and revolted by many of the customs of these Indians (often, however, no more barbarous than their own), they also admired their political and economic sagacity.[2] Indeed, one Jesuit was of the opinion that the Huron were more intelligent than the rural inhabitants of his own country.[3] If the missionary or fur trader felt compelled to understand the customs of the Indians, the modern historian should feel no less obliged to do so.

In order to appreciate the role that the Indians played in the history of Canada in the first half of the seventeenth century, it is necessary to study their customs and behaviour and the things they valued. Because their way of life differed from that of the Europeans, the fur traders and missionaries who interacted with them frequently became amateur anthropologists, and some of them became very good ones. For some tribes the documentation amassed by these early contacts is extensive and of

---

[1] A shorter version of this paper was presented at the Seventeenth Conference on Iroquois Research held at Sagamore, New York, Oct. 21-23, 1966. This paper is based in part on research carried out with the assistance of Miss A. Elaine Clark during the academic year 1965-66. Miss Clark's assistance was made possible through a research grant provided by the French Canada Studies programme of McGill University.

[2] See, e.g., Samuel de Champlain's comment on the sagacity of the Indians in trade (H.P Biggar, ed., *The Works of Samuel de Champlain* (6 vol.; Toronto, 1922-36), II, 171), and Jean de Brébeuf, Gabriel Lalemant, and Francesco Bressani on the efficacy of Huron law (R.G. Thwaites, ed., *The Jesuit Relations and Allied Documents* (73 vols.; Cleveland, 1896-1901), X, 215; XXVIII, 49-51; XXXVIII, 277).

[3] Thwaites, ed., *Relations*, XVIII, 21. A similar statement is made by Paul Ragueneau (XXIX, 281).

high quality. For no tribe is this truer than for the Huron.[4] From the detailed picture of Huronia that emerges from these studies, it is possible to ascertain the motives that prompted the behaviour of particular Indians, or groups of Indians, in a manner no less detailed than our explanations of those which governed the behaviour of their European contemporaries. I might add, parenthetically, that historians are not alone to blame for the failure to utilize anthropological insights in the study of early Canadian history. Iroquoian ethnologists and archaeologists have tended to avoid historical or historiographic problems. Only a few individuals, such as George T. Hunt, have attempted to work in the no man's land between history and anthropology.

Two explanations have been used by anthropologists and historians to justify the existing cleavage between their respective studies. One of these maintains that when the Europeans arrived in eastern North America, the native tribes were engaged in a struggle, the origins and significance of which are lost in the mists of time and therefore wholly the concern of ethnohistorians. Because of this, there is no reason for the historian to try to work out in detail the causes of the conflicts and alliances that existed at that time.[5] Very often, however, the struggle between different groups is painted in crude, almost racist, terms (and in complete contradiction to the facts) as one between Algonkin- and Iroquoian-speaking peoples, the former being an indigenous population, mainly hunters, the latter a series of invading tribes growing corn and living in large villages. It should be noted that such a simplistic explanation of European history, even for the earliest periods, would now be laughed out of court by any competent historian. The alternative hypothesis suggests that European contact altered the life of the Indian, and above all the relationships among the different tribes, so quickly and completely that a knowledge of the aboriginal conditions is not necessary to understand events after 1600.[6] From an a priori point of view, this theory seems most unlikely. Old relationships have a habit of influencing events, even when economic and political conditions are being rapidly altered. Future studies must describe in detail how aboriginal cultures were disrupted

---

[4] Invariably, however, these early witnesses of Indian culture were interested in rather limited aspects of Indian life and tended to interpret Indian culture in terms of their own. Because of this, a valid assessment of these early records requires a comparative knowledge of Indian culture in later times. The groundwork for our understanding of seventeenth-century Huron culture is thus the work of several generations of ethnologists and ethnohistorians in Canada and the United States. The best résumé of Huron culture is Elisabeth Tooker, *An Ethnography of the Huron Indians, 1615-1649* (Washington 1964,). For a shorter and less complete synopsis see W.V. Kinietz, *The Indians of the Western Great Lakes, 1615-1760* (Ann Arbor, 1940).

[5] F. Parkman, *The Jesuits in North America in the Seventeenth Century.* (Centenary Edition: Boston, 1927), 3, 4, 435, 436; G.E.. Ellis, "Indians of North America," in J. Winsor, ed.., *Narrative and Critical History of America* (8 vols.; Boston and New York, 1884-89), I, 283.

[6] G.T. Hunt, *The Wars of the Iroquois: A Study in Intertribal Relations.*(Madison, 1940), 4, 19.

or altered by their contact with the Europeans, rather than assume that interaction between Indians and Europeans can be explained as a set of relationships that has little or no reference to the native culture.

We will begin by considering developments in Huronia prior to the start of the fur trade.

The Huron

When the Huron tribes were described for the first time in 1615,[7] they were living in the Penetanguishene Peninsula and the part of Simcoe County that runs along Matchedash Bay between Wasaga Beach and Lake Simcoe. The Huron probably numbered twenty to thirty thousand, and, according to the most reliable of the descriptions from the Jesuit missionaries,[8] they were divided into four tribes that formed a confederacy similar in its structure to the league of the Iroquois.[9] The Attignaouantan or Bear tribe, which included about half of the people of the confederacy, lived on the western extremity of Huronia. Next to them lived the Attingueenougnahak, or Cord tribe, and the Tahontaenrat or Deer tribe. Farthest east, near Lake Simcoe, were the Ahrendarrhonon or Rock nation. The Tionnontate, or Petun, who spoke the same language as the Huron and were very similar to them, inhabited the country west of Huronia near the Blue Mountain. The Petun, however, were not members of the Huron confederacy and prior to the arrival of the French, they and the Huron had been at war. Another Iroquoian confederacy, the Neutral, lived farther south between the Grand River and the Niagara frontier. Except for a few Algonkin bands that lived west of the Petun, there do not appear to have been any other Indians living in southern Ontario, except in the Ottawa Valley. The uninhabited portions of the province were the hunting territories of the Huron, Neutral, and Petun and also served as a buffer zone between these tribes and the Iroquois who lived south of Lake Ontario.

The Huron, like other Iroquoian tribes, grew corn, beans, and squash. These crops were planted and looked after by the women, who also gathered the firewood used for cooking and heating the houses. Contrary to popular notions the men also made an important contribution to the tribal economy, inasmuch as it was they who cleared the fields for planting (no small task when only stone axes were available) and who caught the fish which were an important source of nutrition. Because of the high population density, the areas close to Huronia appear to have been depleted of game

---

7 Biggar, ed., *Works of Champlain*, III, 49-51; IV, 238-44.
8 Thwaites, ed., *Relations*, XVI, 227.
9 L.H. Morgan, *League of the Ho-de-no-sau-nee, or Iroquois*, (Rochester, 1851; reprinted New Haven, 1954) For a briefer description, see Morgan's *Houses and House-life of the Indian Aborigines*, (Washington, 1881; reprinted with original pagination Chicago, 1965), 23-41.

and expeditions in search of deer had to travel far to the south and east.[10] In general, hunting appears to have been of little economic importance among the Huron.

Huron villages had up to several thousand inhabitants and the main ones were protected by palisades made of posts woven together with smaller branches. Inside large villages there were fifty or more longhouses, often 100 feet or more in length, made of bark attached to a light wooden frame. These houses were inhabited by eight to ten very closely related families. Families that traced themselves back to a common female ancestor formed a clan which was a political unit having its own civil chief and war leader. Each tribe in turn was made up of a number of such clans and the clan leaders served on the tribal and confederal councils.[11]

The events that led to the formation of the Huron confederacy are not well understood. The Huron themselves said that it began around AD 1400 with the union of the Bear and Cord tribes and grew thereafter through the addition of further lineages and tribes. Archaeologically it appears that, although one or more of the Huron tribes was indigenous to Simcoe County, other groups moved into historic Huronia from as far away as the Trent Valley, the Toronto region, and Huron and Grey counties to the west.[12] Two tribes, the Rock and the Deer, had been admitted to the confederacy not long before the arrival of the French.

Historians frequently have asserted that it was fear of the Iroquois that prompted the Huron to seek refuge in this remote and sheltered portion of Ontario.[13] While this may be why some groups moved into Huronia, it is clear that in prehistoric times the Huron outnumbered the Iroquois and probably were not at any military disadvantage. For this reason ethnologists have begun to seek other explanations to account for the heavy concentration of population in Huronia in historic times. An abundance of light, easily workable soil may be part of the answer. Since the Huron lacked the tools to work heavier soils, this advantage may have outweighed the tendency towards drought and the absence of certain trace minerals in the soil which now trouble farmers in that area.[14] Huronia also lay at the south end of the main canoe route that ran along the shores of Georgian Bay. North of there the soil was

---

[10] Meat remained largely a festive dish, commonest in winter and spring (G.M. Wrong, ed., *Sagard's Long Journey to the Country of the Hurons*, (Toronto, 1939), 82; Thwaites, *Relations*, XVII, 141-3).

[11] Thwaites, ed., *Relations*, XVI, 227-9. See also Elisabeth Tooker, "The Iroquois Defeat of the Huron: A Review of Causes," in *Pennsylvania Archaeologist*, XXXIII (1963), 115-23, especially 119, 120.

[12] J. V. Wright, *The Ontario Iroquois Tradition*, (Ottawa, 1966), 68-83. For information concerning the movements from the West I am indebted to a personal communication from Dr. Wright.

[13] See, for example, D. Jenness, *The Indians of Canada* (5th ed., 1960), Ottawa, 280.

[14] B.G. Trigger, "The Historic Location of the Hurons," in *Ontario History*, LIV (1962), 137-48. For physiographic conditions, see L.J. Chapman and D.F. Putnam, *The Physiography of Southern Ontario*(2nd ed., Toronto, 1966), 299-312.

poor and the growing season short, so that none of the tribes depended on agriculture. They engaged mainly in hunting and fishing and tribes from at least as far away as Lake Nipissing traded surplus skins, dried fish, and meat with the Huron in return for corn which they ate in the winter when other food was scarce.[15]

As early as 1615 the French noted that Huronia was the centre of a well-developed system of trade. Hunt, however, seems to have seriously overestimated both the extent of this network and the degree to which the Huron were dependent on it.[16] The main trade appears to have been with the hunting peoples to the north who happened to be Algonkin-speaking. The other Iroquoian tribes had economies similar to that of the Huron, so that with the exception of a few items, such as black squirrel skins, which came from the Neutral country, and tobacco from the Petun, trade with the other Iroquoian tribes was of little importance. Trade with the north, however, brought in supplies of dried meat, fish, skins, clothing, native copper, and "luxury items" such as charms which were obtained in exchange for corn, tobacco, fishing nets, Indian hemp, wampum, and squirrel skins.[17] Although manufactured goods, as well as natural products, flowed in both directions, the most important item the Huron had for export undoubtedly was corn. In 1635 Father Le Jeune described Huronia as the "granary of most of the Algonkians."[18]

Whole bands of northerners spent the winters living outside Huron villages, trading furs and dried meat with their hosts in return for corn. The Huron assumed a dominant position in these trading relationships and the Jesuits record that when the Algonkins had dealings with them, they did so in the Huron language since the latter did not bother to learn Algonkin.[19] The social implications of such linguistic behaviour cannot be lost on anyone living in present-day Quebec. In the French accounts the Algonkins appear to have been better friends of the Rock tribe than they were of the Bear.[20]

Considerable quantities of European trade goods that are believed to date between 1550 and 1575 have been found in Seneca sites in New York State.[21] Since both archaeological and historical evidence suggests that there was contact between the Huron and the tribes that lived along the St. Lawrence River in the sixteenth

---

15 Biggar, ed., *Works of Champlain*, III, 52, 53. On the importance of corn meal among the northern hunters see Wrong, ed., *Sagard's Long Journey*, p. 268.
16 Hunt, *Wars of the Iroquois*, 53-55.
17 For the reference to squirrel skins see Thwaites, ed., *Relations*, VII, 13; to nets, VI, 309.
18 Ibid., VIII, 15.
19 Wrong, ed., *Sagard's Long Journey*, 86.
20 For a hostile statement about the Bear by the Algonkins, see Thwaites, ed., *Relations*, X, 145.
21 C.F. Wray, and H.L. Schoff, "A Preliminary Report on the Seneca Sequence in Western New York State, 1550-1687," in *Pennsylvania Archaeologist*, XXIII (1953), 53-63.

century,[22] it is possible that trade goods were arriving in Huronia in limited quantities at this time as well. In any such trade the Algonkin tribes along the Ottawa River would almost certainly have been intermediaries. It is thus necessary to consider the possibility that trade between the Huron and the northern Algonkins originally developed as a result of the Huron desire to obtain European trade goods.

There are a number of reasons for doubting that trade with the northern tribes had a recent origin. For one thing, the rules governing trade were exceedingly elaborate. A particular trade route was recognized as the property of the Huron tribe or family that had pioneered it, and other people were authorized to trade along this route only if they had obtained permission from the group to which it belonged.[23] Thus, since the Rock were the first Huron tribe to establish relations with the French on the St. Lawrence, they alone were entitled by Huron law to trade with them.[24] Because of the importance of this trade, however, the Rock soon "shared" it with the more numerous and influential Bear, and with the other tribes of Huronia.[25] The control of trade was vested in a small number of chiefs, and other men had to have their permission before they were allowed to engage in it.[26] An even more important indication of the antiquity of Huron contact with the north is the archaeological evidence of the Huron influence on the native cultures of that region, which can be dated as early as AD 900 and is especially evident in pottery styles.[27] Taken together, these two lines of evidence provide considerable support for the hypothesis of an early trade.

In the historic period the Huron men left their villages to visit other tribes in the summers, while their women were working in the fields. Profit was not the only reason for undertaking long voyages. The Jesuits report that many travelled into distant regions to gamble or to see new sights—in short for adventure. Trading expeditions, like war, were a challenge for young men.[28] Trading between different

---

[22] Colonel James F. Pendergast (personal communication) reports finding considerable evidence of Huron influence in late Iroquoian sites along the St. Lawrence River. These probably date from the sixteenth century or only a little earlier. For the historical evidence of contacts between the St. Lawrence Iroquoians and the interior of Ontario, see H.P. Biggar, ed., *The Voyages of Jacques Cartier* (Ottawa, 1924), 170-1, 200-2.

[23] Thwaites, ed., *Relations*, X, 225.

[24] Ibid., XX, 19.

[25] Ibid. In 1640 Lalemant reported that the Rock still considered themselves the special allies of the French and were inclined to protect them. This attitude changed after the Jesuits became more active in the interior of Huronia.

[26] Wrong, ed., *Sagard's Long Journey*, 99. Sagard says that a special council decided each year the number of men who could go out from each village. For more on the control of trade by old and influential men, see Thwaites, ed., *Relations*, XIV, 39.

[27] J.V.Wright, A Regional Examination of Ojibwa culture History," in *Anthropologica*, N.S., VII, (1965), 189-227.

[28] Thwaites, ed., *Relations*, V, 241.

tribes was not always a safe and uncomplicated business and, for all they had to gain from trade during the historic period, the Huron frequently were hesitant to initiate trade with tribes of whom they had only slight acquaintance.

The dangers that beset intertribal contacts were largely products of another institution, as old, if not older than trade—the blood feud. If a man was slain by someone who was not his kinsman, his family, clan, or tribe (depending on how far removed the murderer was) felt obliged to avenge his death by slaying the killer or one of the killer's relatives. Such action could be averted only by reparations in the form of gifts paid by the group to which the murderer belonged to that of the murdered man. When an act of blood revenge actually was carried out, the injured group usually regarded it as a fresh injury; thus any killing, even an accidental one, might generate feuds that would go on for generations. This was especially true of intertribal feuds.[29]

The Huron and Five Nations had both suppressed blood feuds within their respective confederacies, but only with great difficulty. When quarrels arose between individuals from tribes not so united, they frequently gave rise to bloodshed and war. The chances of war were also increased because skill in raiding was a source of prestige for young men who therefore desired to pursue this activity.[30] If it were possible, prisoners captured in war were taken back to their captors' villages to be tortured to death, partly as an act of revenge, but also as a sacrifice to the sun or "god of war."[31] These three motives—revenge, individual prestige, and sacrifice—were common to all the Iroquoian-speaking peoples of the northeast and to many of their neighbours and generated and sustained intertribal wars over long periods of time. Indeed, where no close political ties existed, such as those within the Huron confederacy, and where there were no mutually profitable trading relationships, war between tribes appears to have been the rule. The Huron were almost invariably at war with one or more of the Five Nations, and prior to the development of the fur trade (when they started to carry French goods to the south and west) they appear to have been at war with the Neutral and Petun as well.[32]

On the other hand, when a trading relationship developed between the Huron and some neighbouring tribe, every effort was made to control feuds that might lead to

---

[29] The Huron claimed that their feud with the Iroquois had been going on fifty years prior to 1615 (Biggar, ed.), *Works of Champlain*, V, 78).

[30] Thwaites, ed., *Relations*, XXIII, 91.

[31] Wrong, ed., *Sagard's Long Journey*, 159-61. For comparative discussions of Iroquoian warfare see Nathaniel Knowles, "The Torture of Captives by the Indians of Eastern North America," in *Proceedings of the American Philosophical Society*, LXXXII, (1940),151-225; R.L. Rands and C.L. Riley, "Diffusion and Discontinuous Distribution," in *American Anthropologist*, LVIII,(1958), 274-97.

[32] For the wars with the Petun, see Thwaites, ed., *Relations*, XX, 43. Even at the time of Sagard's visit, there was a threat of war with the Neutral (Wrong, ed., *Sagard's Long Journey*, 151, 156, 157).

war between them. The payment that was made to settle a blood feud with the Algonkins was greater than that made to settle a feud inside the confederacy,[33] and the dearest payment on record was made to the French in 1648 to compensate them for a Jesuit *donné* murdered by some Huron chiefs.[34]

A second method of promoting stable relations between tribes that wished to be trading partners appears to have been the exchange of a few people both as a token of friendship and to assure each group that the other intended to behave properly. Very often, these hostages appear to have been children. Although this custom is never explicitly described by the early French writers, the evidence for its existence is clearcut. Huron, whose sons or nephews (sister's sons and therefore close relatives) were sent to the Jesuit seminary in Quebec, boasted that they were relatives of the French and for this reason hoped for preferential treatment when they went to trade on the St. Lawrence.[35] Others said they had "relatives" among the Neutral and Petun and one man is reported as leaving his daughter with these relatives.[36] The priests and lay visitors who came to Huronia in early times were treated as kinsmen by the Huron, and families and individuals were anxious to have them live with them,[37] no doubt because the Huron regarded these visitors as pledges of good faith whose association with a particular family would establish good relations between that family and the French officials and traders down river. The presentation of young children to Jacques Cartier at a number of villages along the St. Lawrence suggests, moreover, that this custom may have been an old one.[38]

The Huron thus not only traded with other tribes prior to the start of the fur trade, but also, in common with other tribes in the northeast, had developed a code or set of conventions that governed the manner in which this trade was conducted. Being a product of Indian culture, this code was designed to deal with specifically Indian problems. We will now turn to the French attempts to adapt themselves to the native trading patterns after Champlain's first encounter with the Indians in 1608.

---

[33] Thwaites, ed., *Relations*, XXXIII, 243.
[34] Ibid., XXXIII, 239-49.
[35] Ibid., XIII, 125. The Bear tribe wanted the French to participate in their Feast of the Dead so that they could thereby claim them as relatives (X, 311).
[36] Ibid., XXVII, 25; XX, 59.
[37] Chretien Le Clercq, *First Establishment of the Faith in New France*, trans. J.G. Shea (2 vols,; New York, 1881), I, 97; Wrong, ed., *Sagard's Long Journey*, 71.
[38] Biggar, ed., *Voyages of Cartier*, 132-3, 143. The custom of giving children to Cartier may have arisen, on the other hand, as a result of the Indians observing Cartier's predilection for kidnapping Indians. In 1534 he had seized the two sons of Donnoconna, the chief of Stadacona.

Early Franco-Huron Relations

In 1608, the year Champlain established a trading post at Quebec, he was visited by the representatives of some Algonkin tribes from the Ottawa Valley and, in order to win their respect for him as a warrior and to secure their goodwill, he agreed to accompany them the following year on a raid against their chief enemy, the Iroquois.[39] The regions to the north gave promise of more pelts and ones of better quality than did the Iroquois country to the south and fighting with a tribe alongside its enemies was an effective way of confirming an alliance.[40] Thus Champlain's actions seem to have been almost inevitable. At the same time he probably also hoped to drive Iroquois traders from the St. Lawrence Valley and to open the river as a valuable trade artery.[41]

When the Ottawa River Algonkin returned the next year, they were accompanied by a party of Huron warriors from the Rock tribe. In later times the Huron informed the Jesuits that they had first heard of the French from the Algonkins early in the seventeenth century, and as a result of this had decided to go down river to meet these newcomers for themselves.[42] Very likely Champlain's account and the Huron one refer to the same event. Some of the Ottawa River Algonkin, who were already probably in the habit of wintering in Huronia, may have tried to recruit Huron warriors for their forthcoming expedition against the Iroquois and the Huron, prompted by curiosity and a desire for adventure, may have agreed to accompany them to Quebec.

Champlain was keenly interested at this time both in exploring the interior and in making contacts with the people who lived there. Learning the size of the Huron confederacy and their good relations with the hunting (and potentially trapping) peoples to the north, Champlain realized their importance for the development of the fur trade and set out to win their friendship. The Huron, on the contrary, were at first extremely hesitant in their dealings with the French,[43] in part because they had no treaty with them and also because they regarded the French as allies of the Algonkin,

---

[39] The fact that the Huron and Algonkins both were at war with the Five Nations naturally pitted the French against these latter tribes. Presumably Champlain's decision to side with the Huron and Algonkins was based on his conviction that it was impossible to maintain satisfactory relations with both sides, as well as on the economic factors mentioned in the text. For a discussion of the origins of the hostility between the Algonkins and Five Nations, see B.G. Trigger, "Trade and Tribal Warfare on the St. Lawrence in the Sixteenth Century," in *Ethnohistory*, IX, (1962), 240-56.

[40] For Champlain's own comment on Indian expectations in this regard, see Biggar, ed., *Works of Champlain*, II, 70, 71, 110.

[41] H.A. Innis, *The Fur Trade in Canada*. (2nd ed.;Toronto,1956.), 23-6.

[42] Thwaites, ed., *Relations*, XV, 229. The first Huron chief to have dealings with the French was Atironta of the Rock tribe.

[43] Biggar, ed., *Works of Champlain*, II, 188, 189, 193. For a more general reference see II, 254.

who might become hostile if they saw the Hurons trying to establish an independent relationship with them.

The ambiguity of the Huron position can be seen in the exchange of children that was arranged in 1610. At that time the Huron gave Champlain custody of a boy, who was to go to France with him, and in exchange they received a young Frenchman. When the Huron departed, however, the French boy (probably Etienne Brûlé) did not leave with them, but stayed with Iroquet, an Algonkin chief from the lower Ottawa.[44] Iroquet, however, seems to have been one of the Algonkin who was in the habit of wintering in Huronia. Thus a three-sided exchange seems to have been arranged in which the Huron laid the basis for a friendly relationship with the French, but one that was subordinate to, and dependent upon, their relationship with the Algonkin.

As trade with the French increased, the Huron began to appreciate French goods and to want more of them. Metal awls and needles were superior to native bone ones, and iron arrowheads could penetrate the traditional shields and body armour of their enemies. Metal kettles were easier to cook in than clay pots and metal knives were much more efficient than stone ones. Clearing fields and cutting wood was easier when stone axes were replaced by iron hatchets. Luxury items, such as cloth and European beads, were soon sought after as well.[45]

The growing demand for these products no doubt made the Huron anxious to establish closer relations with the French, without, if possible, having to recognize the Ottawa River Algonkin as middlemen or to pay them tolls to pass through their lands.[46] Since the principal item that the French wanted was beaver pelts,[47] the Huron probably also began to expand their trade with the north at this time in order to secure these furs in larger quantities. In return for these furs, they carried not only corn and tobacco but also French trade goods to their northern trading partners. The tribes north of Lake Huron seem to have continued to trade exclusively with the Huron rather than seeking to obtain goods from the French. No doubt this was in part because Huronia was nearby and reaching it did not require a long and hazardous journey down the Ottawa River. Such a journey would have been time-consuming, if not impossible, for a small tribe. More importantly, however, they wanted corn for

---

[44] Ibid., II, 141; IV, 118, 119. This interpretation is reinforced by Champlain's statement that the boy was brought back by 200 Huron on June 13, 1611 (II, 186; IV, 136).

[45] For comments on the Indians' desire for European manufactured goods, see Innis, *Fur Trade*, 16-19; Hunt, *Wars of the Iroquois*, 4, 5.

[46] For examples of Algonkin harassment of Huron trade along the Ottawa River and various Algonkin attempts to imperil French-Huron relations (particularly by the Algonkin from Allumette Island) see Biggar, ed., *Works of Champlain*, V, 102; Wrong, ed., *Sagard's Long Journey*, 262; Thwaites, ed., *Relations*, V, 239; VII, 213; VIII, 83, 99; XI, 271; X, 77; XIV, 53. The Montagnais also tried to intimidate the Huron, mainly to get free corn (Wrong, ed., *Sagard's Long Journey*, 265-8).

[47] Innis, *Fur Trade*, 3 - 6, 11-15.

winter consumption which the Huron, but not the French, were able to provide. Although there is no documentary evidence to support this suggestion, it seems likely that increasing supplies of corn permitted these hunters to devote more time to trapping and relieved them of some of their day-to-day worries about survival.[48] Thus the growth of the fur trade may have led the northern groups to concentrate on trapping and the Huron to devote more of their energy to producing agricultural surpluses to trade with the north.[49] On at least one occasion, the Huron were providing even the French at Quebec with needed supplies of food.[50] In the 1640s their close friends and trading partners, the Nipissing, were travelling as far north as James Bay each year in order to collect the furs which they passed on to the Huron.[51]

In spite of the Huron desire for French goods and their ability to gather furs from the interior, the development of direct trade between Huronia and the St. Lawrence required the formation of a partnership that was expressed in terms the Indians could understand. Without continual assurances of goodwill passing between Huron and French leaders and without the exchange of gifts and people, no Huron would have travelled to Quebec without fear and trepidation. Even after many years of trade, Hurons going to Quebec felt safer if they were travelling with a Frenchman whom they knew and who could be trusted to protect their interests while they were trading.[52] Champlain understood clearly that treaties of friendship were necessary for successful trading partnerships with the Indians. For this reason he had been willing to support the Algonkin and Montagnais in their wars with the Mohawk and, since it was impossible to be friendly with both sides, had maintained his alliance with these northern tribes in spite of Iroquois overtures for peace.[53] The cementing of a treaty with the various Huron tribes was clearly the main reason he visited Huronia in 1615, a visit made in the face of considerable opposition from the Ottawa River Algonkin.[54]

---

[48] This is essentially the kind of relationship that existed between trading companies and Indian trappers in the north in more recent times.

[49] Champlain reports that the Huron produced large food surpluses which he says were meant to carry them over years of poor crops (Biggar, ed., *Works of Champlain*, III, 155-6). At least a part of these surpluses was used for trade.

[50] Le Clercq, *Establishment*, I, 298.

[51] Thwaites, ed., *Relations*, XXXV, 201. There is good evidence, however, that the Nipissing were travelling north even earlier (Biggar, ed., *Works of Champlain*, II, 255-6).

[52] Le Clercq, *Establishment*, I, 211; Wrong, ed., *Sagard's Long Journey*, 244.

[53] Biggar, ed., *Works of Champlain*, V, 73-80; Hunt, *Wars of the Iroquois*, 69.

[54] The Huron had invited Champlain to visit their country as early as 1609 (Biggar, ed.), *Works of Champlain*, II, 105). His attempt to travel up the Ottawa River in 1613 was brought to an end by the opposition of the Algonkin, among other things. Marcel Trudel, *Histoire de la Nouvelle-France. II. Le Comptoir, 1604-1627* (Montreal, 1966), 198-201, may be correct

Quite properly in Huron eyes, Champlain spent most of his time in Huronia with the Rock tribe. This had been the first of the Huron tribes to contact him on the St. Lawrence and therefore had a special relationship with the French according to Huron law. When he accompanied a Huron war party on a traditional, and what appeared to him as an ill-fated raid against the central Iroquois, Champlain was resorting to a now-familiar technique for winning the friendship of particular tribes.[55] What Champlain apparently still did not realize was that the aim of these expeditions was adventure and taking prisoners, rather than the destruction of enemy villages.[56] The Huron were undoubtedly far more pleased with the results of the expedition than Champlain was.

From 1615 on, a number of Frenchmen were living in Huronia; their main purpose in being there was to encourage the Huron to trade.[57] Many of these young men, like the coureurs de bois of later times, enjoyed their life among the Indians and, to the horror of the Catholic clergy, made love to Huron women and probably married them according to local custom. The rough and tumble ways of individuals like Etienne Brûlé endeared them to their Huron hosts and this, in turn, allowed them to inspire confidence in the Indians who came to trade. It has been suggested that the main reason these men remained in Huronia was to persuade the Huron to trade in New France rather than to take their furs south to the Dutch who had begun to trade in the Hudson Valley after 1609.[58] This explanation seems unlikely, however. Until 1629 most of the Dutch trade appears to have been confined to the Mahican.[59] Although the Dutch were apparently anxious to trade with the "French Indians" as early as 1633, the Mohawk were not willing to allow them to do so unless they were

---

[55] when he suggests that the Algonkin stirred up trouble between Champlain and Vignau in order to protect their trading interests in the interior.

Although Champlain visited all the major Huron villages, he returned repeatedly to Cahiague, a Rock village. He also spent more time there than anywhere else. Lalemant reports that in 1640 his reputation was still very much alive among the Rock (Thwaites, ed., *Relations*, XX, 19).

[56] Biggar, ed., *Works of Champlain*, III, 66, 69, 73; IV, 254-66; also Hunt, *Wars of the Iroquois*, 20.

[57] Since most of the available data about this period was recorded by priests, we have little information about these men, and practically none from a friendly source. For what there is see, Biggar, ed., *Works of Champlain*, V, 101, 108, 129, 131, 132, 207; Le Clercq, *Establishment*, I, 205; Wrong, ed., *Sagard's Long Journey*, 194-5; Thwaites, ed., *Relations*, V, 133; VI, 83; XIV, 17, 19; XVII, 45; XX, 19; XXV, 85.

[58] Trelease, A.W., *Indian Affairs in Colonial New York: The Seventeenth Century* (Ithaca, 1960),.30.

[59] Ibid., 46. Intermittent hostilities between the Mahican and Mohawk kept the latter from Fort Orange prior to the stunning defeat of the Mahican in 1628 or 1629 (p. 48).

in some way able to profit from the trade themselves.[60] This the Huron, who had a long-standing feud with the Iroquois, were unwilling to let them do.

The main job of the early coureurs de bois appears to have been to live in Huronia as visible evidence of French goodwill and as exchanges for the Huron youths who were sent to live with the French.[61] In this capacity they were able to encourage the Indians to engage in trade. Each year some of them travelled down river with the Huron to see that the Algonkin did not prevent the passage of their canoes or scare the Huron off with stories of disasters or plots against them in Quebec.[62] They also acted as interpreters for the Huron and aided them in their dealings with the traders.[63] Except for the years when the Mohawk blockaded the Ottawa River, the Huron sent an annual "fleet" or series of fleets to Quebec bearing the furs they had collected.[64] It is unfortunate that the records do not supply more information on these fleets, particularly about who organized them and what their tribal composition was. The fleets left Huronia in the spring and returned several months later. When the St. Lawrence was blocked by the Iroquois, the Hurons made their way to Quebec over the smaller waterways that led through the Laurentians.[65]

The Recollet and Jesuit missionaries who worked in Huronia between 1615 and 1629 were accepted by the Huron as part of the Franco-Huron trading alliance and as individuals whose goodwill was potentially advantageous in dealing with the traders and authorities in Quebec. That they lacked interest except as shamans is evident from Gabriel Sagard's statement that it was hard to work among any tribe that was not engaged in trade (i.e., bound by the Franco-Huron alliance).[66] The priests appear

---

[60] Ibid., 52-4; Thwaites, ed., *Relations*, VIII, 59-61; Hunt, *Wars of the Iroquois*, 34. In 1638 the Huron told the Jesuits that "Englishmen" had come as far as Montreal telling the Indians that the Jesuits were the cause of sickness in Huronia (and no doubt attempting to trade with them or divert trade to the south) (Thwaites, ed., *Relations*, XV, 31).

[61] See, e.g., Biggar, ed., *Works of Champlain*, V, 101, 207.

[62] Ibid., V, 108. on the usefulness of having Frenchmen accompany the fleet see Wrong, ed., *Sagard's Long Journey*, 262. Sagard reports that in the 1620s the Iroquois refrained from attacking Huron flotillas when they knew Frenchmen were travelling with the Indians (p. 261).

[63] These were at least the functions that the Huron expected Frenchmen who had lived in Huronia would perform. The coureurs de bois are frequently referred to as interpreters (Biggar, ed., *Works of Champlain*, III, 168-72).

[64] Wrong, ed., *Sagard's Long Journey*, 249-56.

[65] This route apparently had been used in prehistoric times as well (Biggar, ed., *Voyages of Cartier*, 200-1, as interpreted by Innis, *Fur Trade*, 22).

[66] Edwin Tross, ed.,. *Histoire du Canada et voyages que les Frères maneurs Recollets y ont faits pour la conversion des infidèles depuis l'an 1615...*, by G. Sagard (4 vols., Paris, 1866), I, 42. This statement refers to the visit Le Caron made with Champlain. On the Huron desire to have the priests act as go-betweens in their trade with the French see Wrong, ed., *Sagard's Long Journey*, 244; Le Clercq, *Establishment*, I, 211.

to have restricted their missionary activities to caring for the needs of the French traders in Huronia and trying to make some converts among the Indians. Their preaching, as far as it was understood, did not appear to present a challenge or affront to the Huron way of life, although the customs of the priests were strange to the Indians, who found these men austere and far less appealing than the easy-going coureurs de bois.[67] For obvious reasons, relations between the priests and local traders were not good and Sagard claims that among other things the latter often refused to help the missionaries learn native languages.[68] The most serious charge that the priests levelled at these traders was that their behaviour sowed confusion and doubt among the Huron and impeded the spread of the Christian faith among them.[69] These early experiences convinced the Jesuits that to run a mission in Huronia properly the priests must control those Europeans who were allowed to enter the country.

In the early part of the seventeenth century the colony of New France was nothing more than a trading post and its day-to-day existence depended upon securing an annual supply of furs.[70] Not understanding the long-standing hostility between the Huron and the Iroquois, the French were apprehensive of any move that seemed likely to divert furs from the St. Lawrence to the Hudson Valley. The French made peace with the Mohawk in 1624 and French traders did business with them, an arrangement that no doubt pleased the Mohawk as it made them for a time less dependent on the Dutch and therefore gave them more bargaining power in their dealings with Albany.[71] Nevertheless, the French became extremely alarmed about a peace treaty that the Huron negotiated with the Seneca in 1623. This appears to have

---

[67] The Indians often were reluctant to take missionaries back to Huronia with them (Thwaites, ed., *Relations*, IV, 221). Some priests, however, became personally popular with the Huron. The popularity of Father Brébeuf during his initial stay in Huronia is evidence for the welcome he received when he returned in 1634.

[68] This claim appears in the *Dictionary of Canadian Biography*. I. 1000 to 1700, (Toronto,1966), 133. It appears to be based on Sagard's comments on the behaviour of an interpreter named Nicolas Marsolet. Although Marsolet refused to teach the Montagnais language to the Recollets, he later agreed to instruct the Jesuits (Tross, ed., *Histoire du Canada*, II, 333).

[69] It is perhaps significant that the main complaint was about the sexual behaviour of these men rather than the sale of alcohol to the Indians (cf. André Vachon, "L'Eau-de-vie dans la société indienne," Canadian Historical Association, *Report*, 1960, 22-32). Alcohol does not appear to have been a serious problem in Huronia, no doubt because the Huron did not at this time feel their culture threatened by European contacts. The Jesuits' distaste for these men is reiterated in the Jesuit Relations, particularly when they are compared with the *donnés* and other men who served in Huronia under Jesuit supervision after 1634. See Thwaites, ed., *Relations*, IV, 83; XIV, 19; XV, 85; XVII, 45.

[70] Trudel, *Histoire de la Nouvelle-France*, II, 405-34.

[71] Trelease, *Indian Affairs*, 52; Hunt, *Wars of the Iroquois*, 69-70.

been one of the periodic treaties that the Huron and Iroquois negotiated in order to get back members of their respective tribes who had been taken prisoner, but not yet killed, by the enemy.[72] As such, it was probably perfectly harmless to French interest. Nevertheless the situation was judged sufficiently serious for a delegation of eleven Frenchmen, including three clerics, to be sent to the Huron country.[73] Various writers have followed Jean Charlevoix in saying that this delegation was instructed to disrupt the new treaty. Charlevoix, however, wrote long after the event took place and is not an unbiased witness.[74] It seems more likely that the expedition had as its main purpose simply the reaffirming of the alliances made between Champlain and the various Huron chiefs in 1615. In actual fact the Huron probably had no thought of trading with the Iroquois at this time. To the chagrin of the Dutch, the Mohawk were firm in their refusal to allow the northern tribes to pass through their country to trade on the Hudson. The Huron undoubtedly felt that direct trade with the French, even if they were farther from Huronia than the Dutch,[75] was preferable to trade *via* the Mohawk with the Europeans in New York State.

The very great importance that the Huron attached to their trade with the French even at this time is shown by their efforts to prevent potential rivals, such as the Petun or Neutral, from concluding any sort of formal alliance with the French. Neither group seems to have constituted much of a threat, since the Petun had to pass through Huron territory in order to paddle north along the shore of Georgian Bay[76] and the Neutral, who do not seem to have had adequate boats, would have had to travel down the St. Lawrence River to Quebec—en route the Mohawk would have

---

[72] Thwaites, ed., *Relations*, XXXIII, 121.

[73] Le Clercq, *Establishment*, I, 204; Tross, ed., *Histoire du Canada*.

[74] There is nothing in Sagard or Le Clercq that implies that the priests were instructed to disrupt this treaty, as Hunt implies. Trudel (*Histoire de la Nouvelle-France*, II, 370) says that it was necessary to send Father Le Caron and the other Frenchmen to Huronia to prevent a commercial treaty between the Huron and the Iroquois. It is my opinion that the prospect of this treaty was a figment of the imagination of the French in Quebec and never a real possibility (see text below).

[75] On the Mohawk refusal to let the French Indians pass through their country to trade with the Dutch see Trelease, *Indian Affairs*, 52-3; Hunt, *Wars of the Iroquois*, 34. Trudel's (*Histoire de la Nouvelle-France*, II, 364-6) suggestion that the Huron were about to trade with the Dutch and that the French who stayed in Huronia did so to prevent this seems unlikely in view of the traditional enmity between the Huron and the Iroquois. To reach Albany the latter would have had to travel through the tribal territory of the three eastern Iroquois tribes. Mohawk opposition to this seems to have effectively discouraged the Huron from attempting such trade.

[76] Sagard says that the Huron did not permit other tribes to pass through their territory without special permission (Wrong, ed., *Sagard's Long Journey*, 99). The Jesuits say categorically that the Huron did not permit the Petun to trade with the French (Thwaites, ed., *Relations*, XXI, 177).

either stolen their furs or forced them to divert most of the trade to the south.[77] The Huron do not seem to have minded well-known coureurs de bois occasionally visiting the Neutral or other tribes with whom they traded, but when, on his visit to the Neutral in 1626, Father de La Roche Daillon proposed an alliance between them and the French, the Huron spread rumours about the French that brought an end to the proposed treaty.[78] The ease with which the Huron did this, and repeated the manoeuvre in 1640-41,[79] is an indication both of the insecurity that tribes felt in the absence of a proper treaty with foreigners and of the importance that the Huron placed on their privileged relationship with the French. These observations reinforce our conclusion that coureurs de bois did not live in Huronia simply to dissuade the Huron from going to trade with either the Mohawk or the Dutch, but instead were a vital link in the Franco-Huron alliance and necessary intermediaries between the Huron and the French fur traders in Quebec. Such were the services for which Brûlé received a hundred pistoles each year from his employers.[80]

Franco-Huron trade increased in the years prior to 1629. Undoubtedly the Huron were growing increasingly reliant on European goods, but it is unlikely that they were ever completely dependent on trade during this period. There is no evidence that the British occupation of Quebec led them to trade with New Holland or with the Iroquois. Several renegade Frenchmen, including Brûlé, remained in Huronia and probably encouraged the Huron to trade with the British.[81] It was during this period that Brûlé was murdered by the Huron living in Toanché. Since he was given a proper burial it is unlikely that he was tortured to death and eaten as Sagard reports.[82] More likely, he was killed in a brawl with the Huron among whom he lived. That he was killed during the British occupation of New France does not, however, seem to be without significance. Until the French withdrawal he had been protected not only by his popularity but more importantly by the Franco-Huron alliance. Once the French had departed, he was on his own.

---

[77] For a reference about canoes see Hunt, *Wars of the Iroquois*, p. 51.

[78] Le Clercq, *Establishment*, I, 267. The Huron spread evil rumours about the Jesuits among the Petun when the Jesuits tried to do mission work there in 1640 (Thwaites, ed., *Relations*, XX, 47-51).

[79] Thwaites, ed., *Relations*, XXI, 207-15. At first the priests pretended to be traders. This pretence, however, failed.

[80] Thwaites, ed., *Works of Champlain*, V, 131.

[81] The French later describe him as a traitor (Thwaites, ed., *Relations*, V, 241).

[82] Tross, ed., *Histoire du Canada*, II, 431. For a description of his proposed reburial see Thwaites, ed., *Relations*, X, 307-9.

The Jesuits Take Control

The Compagnie des Cent-Associés, which took effective control of the affairs of New France after the colony was retroceded to France in 1632, was different from earlier trading companies in that its members were more interested in missionary work than their predecessors had been. At this time the Society of Jesus also managed to obtain the *de facto* monopoly over missionary activities in New France that it was to hold for many years.[83] The Jesuits brought about a number of changes in policy with regard to Huronia. In particular, they were much more anxious to evangelize the Huron *as a people* than the Recollets had been.[84] As their prime goal they sought to lead the entire confederacy toward the Christian religion, rather than to convert individuals. Moreover, as a result of the strong influence they wielded at the French court, they were in a better position to command the support of officials and fur traders.[85] For the first while after they returned to the Huron country, the Jesuits continued many of the mission practices that had been current prior to 1629, such as sending Indian children to their seminary at Quebec.[86] As their knowledge of the Huron language and of the country improved (in both cases as a result of systematic study) they gradually began to modify their work along lines that were more in keeping with their general policy.[87]

A major *bête noire* of the missionaries prior to 1629 was the French traders who lived in Huronia and set a bad example for the natives. In order to assure unity of purpose for their work, the duties that formerly had been carried out by these coureurs de bois were taken over by lay brothers, workmen, and *donnés* directly subject to

---

[83] G. Lanctot, *A History of Canada*, I (Toronto,1963), 148-9.

[84] It appears that one reason the Recollets received little support from the trading companies was that their policy of settling migratory Indians and of wanting Huron converts to settle in Quebec conflicted with the traders' own interests (Le Clercq, *Establishment*, I, 111).

[85] The support of Governor Montmagny appears to have been particularly effective (Thwaites, ed., *Relations*, XXI, 143; XXII, 309, 311).

[86] Thwaites, ed., *Relations*, X, 33; XI, 97, 109, 111, 113; XIII, 9; XIV, 125, 161, 231, 235, 255. On the discontinuation of the seminary, see XXIV, 103. During the first two years the Jesuits were back in Huronia they were struggling to orient themselves and to understand the nature of Huron society better. At first they tended to be rather patronizing. They gave advice on military matters (X, 53) and, failing to understand the nature of Huron politics, felt that their intervention was needed to mediate disputes among the different tribes (IX, 273; XIV, 17, 21). Later, when they realized how the Huron did things and that intervention was unnecessary, these efforts ceased.

[87] One example is the decision to seek to baptize older men—and especially influential ones (Thwaites, ed., *Relations*, XV, 109).

Jesuit supervision.[88] Later accusations that the Jesuits were engaged in the fur trade seem to have sprung largely from this action. The oft-repeated claim that priests were vital to the fur trade in Huronia is obviously without foundation. The coureurs de bois, who had lived in Huronia for many years, not only had functioned effectively during this period without missionary support but also appear to have been substantially more popular and more effective in their dealings with the Huron than the priests had been. The Jesuits wished to be rid of this group principally to assure that the French living in Huronia would not be working at cross-purposes. The trading companies apparently were willing to allow the Jesuits to have their own way in this matter, but in return it was necessary that the laymen attached to the Jesuit mission discharge at least the most vital functions of organizing the annual trade which the coureurs de bois had done heretofore.[89] The reasons that the Jesuits had for wanting to be rid of the coureurs de bois were clearly religious, not economic.

The Jesuits' connections with the fur trade did not arise, however, simply from their desire to be rid of the coureurs de bois; they also depended on it not only to get into Huronia but also for their personal safety so long as they remained there. The Huron were obviously not at all interested in what the Jesuits had to teach, and on several occasions after 1634 they made it clear that they preferred the former coureurs de bois to the Jesuits and their assistants.[90] In 1633, and again in 1634, they offered a whole series of excuses, including the hostility of the Algonkin from Allumette Island, as reasons for not taking the Jesuits home with them.[91] Moreover, fearing revenge for the death of Brûlé, they were unwilling to allow their children to remain as seminarians at Quebec.[92] In 1634 Champlain made the official French position clear when he informed the Huron that he regarded the Jesuits' presence in their country as a vital part of a renewed Franco-Huron alliance, at the same time

---

[88] For Jesuit policy regarding lay assistants in Huronia, see Thwaites, ed., *Relations*, XXI, 293-303. See also VI, 81, 83; XV, 157; XVII, 45; XX, 99; XXV, 85; XXVII, 91.

[89] Parkman, *Jesuits in North America*, 465-7. Concerning early charges of Jesuit participation in the fur trade and a declaration by the directors of the Company of New France concerning their innocence, see Thwaites, ed., *Relations*, XXV, 75.

[90] Thwaites, ed., *Relations*, XIV, 17-19. For a clear statement that the Jesuits were aware that their presence in Huronia depended on the traders' ability to coerce the Huron to let them stay, see XXXIV, 205. Soon after the Jesuits returned to Huronia, Brébeuf wrote that they won the esteem of the Indians by giving them arrowheads and helping them to defend their forts (XXXIV, 53). He hoped that the confidence won by these actions would permit the Jesuits eventually to "advance the glory of God."

[91] The main reason seems to have been that the French had detained a Huron who was implicated in killing a Frenchman in Huronia (*ibid.*, VI, 19). It is interesting to note that the Huron also made it clear they wanted Frenchmen with guns instead of, or at least alongside, the priests (VII, 217).

[92] *Ibid.*, IX, 287.

expressing the hope that they would someday agree to become Christians.[93] Since the Huron wanted to renew their former trading relationship with the French, they agreed to accept the priests as a token of this alliance. Henceforth they were bound by treaty to allow the Jesuits to live among them and to protect the priests from harm. The thought of having these individuals who were so respected by the French in Huronia and under their control must also have given the Huron confidence in their dealings with the French who remained in Quebec.

Although the Jesuits travelled to Huronia in 1635 in canoes that belonged to members of the Cord and Rock tribes, they were put ashore rather unceremoniously in the territory of the Bear tribe, where Brébeuf had worked previously and where Brûlé had been murdered.[94] It is not clear whether the Jesuits had wanted to go to this region or were left there by their Rock and Cord hosts, who did not want to take them to their own villages. It is possible that the Bear, who were the most powerful of the Huron tribes, exerted their influence to have the Jesuits left among them. In this regard it is perhaps not without meaning that the Jesuits previously had discussed with the Indians the possibility of their settling in Ossossané, the chief town of the Bear nation.[95] Brébeuf was welcomed by the villagers of Ihonitiria, among whom he had lived before, and the Jesuits decided to settle in that village both because it was close to the canoe route to New France and also in order to persuade the villagers that they bore them no ill will for having murdered Brûlé. The latter, the Jesuits said, was regarded by the French as a traitor and debauched renegade.[96] Nevertheless, his murder haunted the Huron, and even some neighbouring tribes,[97] who feared that it might lead to war with the French. Such fears may have been responsible for the dispute that the Jesuits observed between certain villages of the Bear tribe shortly after their arrival in Huronia.[98]

---

[93] Ibid., VII, 47. The officials in Quebec continued to exhort the Huron to become Christians (XVII, 171).

[94] Ibid., VIII, 71, 91, 99.

[95] That was in July 1633 (Ibid., V, 259). The people of Ossossané continued to press the Jesuits to move there.

[96] Ibid., VIII, 99, 103-5. They also stayed at Ihonitiria because they felt it better to start work in a small village rather than a large and important one (VIII, 103). Ossossané was also unsatisfactory as its inhabitants were planning to relocate the village the next spring (VIII, 101).

[97] Ibid., V, 239, VIII, 99; X, 309; XIV, 99-103.

[98] For an account of this dispute and the Jesuits' attempts to resolve it, see *ibid.*, X, 279-81, 307; XIV, 21. No mention is made of the dispute after 1637, so presumably it was patched up. Brébeuf mentions elsewhere that, as a result of Brûlé's murder, other Huron were threatening the people of Toanché (the village where he was killed) with death (VIII, 99). The bad relations between Ossossané and the village of Ihonitiria (which was inhabited by Toanchéans) were exacerbated in 1633 when the latter became angry at the efforts of the chiefs of Ossossané to persuade all the Jesuits to settle in their village (V, 263).

It would appear that according to native custom the Jesuits coming to Huronia had a right to expect they would receive free food and lodgings. This would have been in return for similar care given by the French to the young seminarists in Quebec.[99] In Huron eyes the latter had been exchanged as tokens of good faith in return for the Jesuits and their assistants.[100] In fact, the Huron provided food and shelter for the Jesuits only rarely. The missionaries had to purchase or provide these things for themselves and found the Huron demanding payment of some sort for most of their services.[101]

For a time after their return to Huronia the Jesuits were the objects of friendly public interest and their presence and goodwill were sought after, in part because individual Hurons sought to obtain favours in Quebec through their commendation, in part because the services people performed for the Jesuits, and even attendance at religious instruction, were rewarded with presents of trade goods and tobacco. The latter, although a native product, was scarce in Huronia at the time.[102] Since all of the priests (except perhaps Brébeuf) were struggling to learn the Huron language, most of the missionary activities during the first few years were confined to the Bear country. Only a few trips were made into more distant areas of Huronia.[103]

The Epidemics of 1635 to 1640

The first serious trial for the Jesuits, and for the Franco-Huron alliance, occurred between the years 1635 and 1640. An unspecified disease, either measles or smallpox, was present in Quebec the year the Jesuits returned to Huronia and it followed the Huron fleet up river. This was the beginning of a series of epidemics which swept away more than half the Huron population in the next six years.[104] These new maladies were especially fatal to children and old people. Because they were fatal to the latter group, many of the most skilful Huron leaders and craftsmen,

---

[99] Presents were also given to the Huron both as tokens of goodwill and to ensure the good treatment of the Jesuits.

[100] For a discussion of the financial help the Jesuits expected to receive from the trading company see Thwaites, ed., *Relations* VI, 81-3. The financial support of the mission is discussed in Parkman, *Jesuits in North America*, 465-7.

[101] Thwaites, ed., *Relations*, X, 249; XIII, 141; XVII, 95; XVIII, 19, 97.

[102] Ibid., X, 301.

[103] One of these trips was to visit the father of a young convert named Amantacha who lived at St. Joseph (Ibid., VIII, 139). A careful tabulation by Miss Clark of the places the Jesuits mention visiting each year and the amount of attention given to each village in Huronia shows clearly that prior to 1640 their activities were confined to the Bear nation and particularly to the Penetang Peninsula. After that time their mission work spread into all parts of Huronia.

[104] To less than twelve thousand.

as well as the people most familiar with native religious lore, perished.[105] The loss of children may well have meant that the proportion of men of fighting age in the Huron population was below normal by the end of the next decade.

The Jesuits, who wished to save the souls of dying children, frequently baptized them, both with and without their parents' permission. The Huron, being unclear about the Jesuits' intention in doing this, observed that children tended to die soon after baptism and came to suspect that the Jesuits were practising a deadly form of witchcraft.[106] The rumour revived that the Jesuits had been sent to Huronia to seek revenge for Brûlé's murder,[107] a rumour which gained credence from pictures of the torments of hell that the Jesuits displayed in their chapel and from the ritual of the mass (which the Huron understood had something to do with eating a corpse).[108] According to Huron law, sorcerers could be killed without a trial, and in times of crisis extensive pogroms appear to have been unleashed against persons suspected of this crime.[109] Nevertheless, while individuals threatened to murder the Jesuits and on one occasion a council of the confederacy met to try the Jesuits on a charge of witchcraft,[110] none of the Frenchmen in Huronia was killed.

Although the majority of the people were frightened of the Jesuits and believed that they were working to destroy the country, their leaders repeatedly stressed that they could not afford to rupture the Franco-Huron alliance by killing the French priests.[111] One well-placed chief said that if the Huron did not go down river to trade with the French for even two years, they would be lucky if they found themselves as well off as the [despised] Algonkins.[112] While this statement was a bit of rhetoric, it stresses the importance of the fur trade to the Huron at this time and their growing reliance on French trade goods. During the entire course of the epidemics only one village, apparently a small one, was willing to give up the use of trade goods, and hence presumably to sever relations with the French.[113] Instead, the Huron resorted to indirect means to persuade the Jesuits to leave Huronia *voluntarily*. Children were encouraged to annoy them, their religious objects were befouled, and occasionally

---

[105] Thwaites, ed., *Relations*, XIX, 123, 127; VIII, 145-7. The high mortality rate among children is an overall impression gained from reading the relations of the years 1636-40. It also corresponds with what is known about similar epidemics among other Indian groups.

[106] Ibid., XIX, 223.

[107] Ibid., XIV, 17, 53, 99-103.

[108] Ibid., XXXIX, 129.

[109] Ibid., XIX, 179.

[110] Ibid., XV, 59-67.

[111] At all times the Huron leaders appear to have been convinced that killing a priest or one of their assistants would terminate the Franco-Huron alliance.

[112] Thwaites, ed., *Relations*, XIII, 215, 217. For a French statement emphasizing the Huron dependence on trade goods see XXXII, 179 (1646-48).

[113] Ibid., XV, 21.

they were personally threatened or mistreated.[114] The Jesuits noted, rather significantly, that these persecutions diminished before the annual trip down river or after the return of a successful fleet.[115] The French officials in Quebec were aware of the dangerous situation in which the Jesuits found themselves, but as long as feelings ran high in Huronia, these authorities could do no more than to try to spare them from the worst excesses of Huron anger. They did this by threatening to cut off trade if the Jesuits were killed.

By 1640 the serious epidemics in Huronia were over. That summer, the new governor of Canada, Charles Huault de Montmagny, took action to "punish" the Huron who came to Quebec for their bad treatment of the Jesuits.[116] It is not clear what form this punishment took, but it appears that in the course of his dealings with them he made it clear that he considered their bad treatment of the Jesuits had terminated the existing alliance. At the same time he offered to renew the alliance, but only on the clear understanding that the Jesuits would continue to live in Huronia and work there unmolested. This is the first time, to our knowledge, that French officials had injected a positive element of threat into their dealings with the Huron. Presumably, the great losses in manpower and skills that the Huron had suffered and their consequent increasing dependence on trade and French support made such action possible. The Huron were in good health and expecting an abundant harvest; hence, many of the anxieties that had plagued them in recent years were dispelled. Because of this they were once more in a good mood and, hence, under the protection of a renewed Franco-Huron alliance the Jesuits found themselves free not only to continue the mission work among them but also to intensify their efforts.[117]

Already during the final crisis of 1639, the Jesuits had decided to establish a permanent centre for their missionary work in the Huron area. This centre was foreseen as serving various functions. Not only would it provide a refuge in time of danger (such as they lacked in 1639), but it also would allow them to put up buildings of European design. It had not been economical to construct these in the Huron villages, which shifted their location about once every decade. The Jesuits' centre was thus designed to be a further example of European culture in the heart of Huronia, a focus from which new ideas could diffuse to the local population. Gradually, pigs, fowl, and young cattle were brought up river from Quebec and European crops were grown in the fields nearby.[118] The residence of Ste. Marie acquired a hospital and a burial ground and became a place where Christian Indians could come for spiritual retreats and assemble on feast days.[119] Being located apart

---

114   Ibid., XV, 51.
115   Ibid., XV, 55; XVII, 115.
116   Ibid., XXI, 143; XXII, 310.
117   Ibid., XXI, 131.
118   One heifer and a small cannon arrived in 1648 (Ibid., XXXII, 99).
119   Ibid., XXVI, 201.

from any one village, and near the geographical centre of the confederacy, it was better able, both from a political and a geographical point of view, to serve as a mission centre for all Huronia. (During the worst years of the epidemics the Jesuits had remained for the most part in the northwest corner of Huronia.) In 1639 the Jesuits also made a survey and census of the country prior to setting up a system of missions that would carry the Christian message to all of the Huron tribes and, as far as possible, to other tribes as well.[120]

The Jesuits had thus weathered a difficult period. It is clear that they had been allowed to enter Huronia and to continue there only because of the Franco-Huron alliance. That they were not killed or expelled from Huronia at the height of the epidemics is an indication of how dependent the Hurons were becoming on the fur trade and how much the alliance with the French meant to them. It also indicates that the Huron leaders were able to restrain their unruly followers in order to preserve good relations with New France.[121] Evidence of lingering malice towards the priests can be seen in the events that came to light on the visit of Fathers Brébeuf and Chaumonot to the Neutral country in the winter of 1640-41. There the priests learned that the Huron had offered the Neutral rich presents, if they would kill the missionaries.[122] In this way the Huron hoped to destroy two of the "sorcerers" who had been tormenting their nation without endangering the French alliance. They also had other motives, however. The proposed murder, so long as it was not traced back to the Huron, would put the Neutral in a bad light and would prevent Brébeuf from pursuing any dealings with the Seneca. Although there is no evidence that Brébeuf planned to visit the Seneca, a rumour had spread that having failed to kill the Huron with witchcraft he now was seeking to turn their enemies loose upon them.[123]

A Crisis in Huron-Iroquois Relations

If the year 1640 marked the end of the persecution of the Jesuits in Huronia, unknown to them and to their Huron hosts, it also marked the beginning of a crisis that was to destroy Huronia. Beaver had become rare in the Huron country and most of the skins they traded with the French came from neighbouring tribes to the

---

[120] Concerning the establishment of Ste Marie and the mission system see Ibid., XXIX, 123-65.

[121] There is a considerable amount of other evidence concerning the coercive power of Huron chiefs. See B.G. Trigger, "Order and Freedom in Huron Society," in *Anthropologica*, N.S., V (1963), 151-69.

[122] Thwaites, ed., *Relations*, XXI, 213. About the same time the Huron were spreading bad reports concerning the Jesuits among the Petun (XX,54) with whom they had recently made a new treaty of friendship (XX, 43). These rumours were spread by Huron traders.

[123] Ibid., XXX, 75-7. So bitter was the Huron opposition to Brébeuf after he returned to Huronia that the Huron mission was compelled to send him down to Quebec until the situation quieted down (XXIII, 35).

north.[124] A similar decline in the beaver population of New York State seems to have reached a point of crisis by 1640. That year the number of pelts traded at Fort Orange is reported to have dropped sharply.[125] While it is possible that at least part of the decline was the result of clandestine traders cutting into official trade, most commentators agree that it was basically related to the exhaustion of the supply of beaver in the Iroquois' home territory.[126]

While this hypothesis is not well enough documented that it can be regarded as certain, it seems a useful one for explaining Iroquois behaviour during the next few years. There is little doubt that after 1640 the Iroquois were preoccupied with securing new sources of pelts. The main controversy concerning their relations with their neighbours during this period centres on whether they were seeking to obtain furs by forcing the Huron to share their trade with them[127] or were attacking their neighbours in order to secure new hunting territories. Although Trelease[128] supports the latter theory, the data he uses apply for the most part to a later period and come mainly from sources in New York State and New England. Contemporary Canadian evidence definitely seems to rule out his claims; indeed if his hypothesis were true, the events leading to the destruction of Huronia would make little sense at all.

Trelease's theory finds its main support in claims made by the Iroquois in the early part of the eighteenth century that they had conquered Ontario and adjacent regions as beaver hunting grounds. In the treaty of 1701, in which the Iroquois placed their "Beaver ground" under the protection of the King of England, the Iroquois said explicitly that they had driven the indigenous tribes from this area in order to hunt there.[129] Trelease errs, however, in assuming that the reasons the Iroquois gave for conquering this territory in 1701 were the same as those they actually had for doing so half a century earlier. There is no doubt that in 1701 the Iroquois (mainly the Seneca) were hunting beaver in Ontario, but since the Huron country was reported in the 1630s to be as hunted out as their own it is illogical to assume that they attacked this region in 1649 in order to secure more hunting territory. The Huron beaver supplies they sought to capture were those coming by trade from the north. Only after their attacks failed to capture the western fur trade and after Ontario was deserted for a time, allowing the restoration of the local beaver

---

[124] The Jesuit Relation of 1635 records that the beaver was already totally extinct in the Huron country and that all the skins they traded with the French were obtained elsewhere (Ibid., VIII, 57).

[125] Trelease, *Indian Affairs*, 118-20; Hunt, *Wars of the Iroquois*, 32-4. For a later source see Jean Talon cited in Hunt, *Wars of the Iroquois*, 137.

[126] Hunt, *Wars of the Iroquois*, 32-4; Trelease, *Indian Affairs*, 118.

[127] This theory was first advanced by C.H. McIlwain in 1915. It was taken up in Innis, *Fur Trade*, 34-6 and Hunt, *Wars of the Iroquois*, 32-7, 74.

[128] Trelease, *Indian Affairs*, 120.

[129] E.B. O'Callaghan, ed., *Documents Relative to the Colonial History of the State of New York* (15 vols.; Albany, 1853-87), IV, 908.

population, did the Iroquois begin to hunt there. Since they lacked historical records, it is not surprising that by 1701 the Iroquois believed the use that they were making of Ontario at the present time was the same reason they had for attacking the tribes there long before. The attacks that the Iroquois launched against the Petun and Neutral, following their attack on the Huron, offer no opposition to this theory. Although these groups had not participated in the fur trade prior to 1649, there was considerable danger that with the Huron gone they would attempt to do so. Hence, their dispersal was also necessary.

Trelease's theory thus fails to provide an acceptable explanation of events in Canada in the middle of the seventeenth century. It seems much more likely that the Iroquois, and mainly the Mohawk, began by trying to force the Huron to trade with them and that only latterly, when their efforts in this direction were unsuccessful, did they decide to destroy the Huron (and their neighbours) as an intermediary group.

The Mohawk began to intimidate the Huron by harassing those travelling along the Ottawa River—a tactic that had the additional advantage of providing a supply of captured furs. In 1642 Iroquois raiders spread fear and terror throughout all of the Huron villages,[130] and in 1644 they succeeded in preventing contact between Quebec and Huronia.[131] The increasing number of guns that the Iroquois were acquiring from the Dutch, English, and Swedish colonies along the Atlantic seaboard gradually gave them military superiority over the Huron, among whom the French had limited and controlled the sale of guns.[132] In 1644 the French despatched more than twenty soldiers to Huronia to protect the Huron over the winter and assure the arrival of their furs in Quebec the next spring.[133] The Mohawk were also harassing the French in the St. Lawrence Valley, who were moved the next spring to discuss peace, both to assure their own safety and to re-open the river to trade. Although the subsequent treaty of 1645 was with the French, the Mohawk seem to have interpreted it as involving a commitment that in the future the Huron would trade with them as well as with the French.[134] The Huron, however, had no intention of doing this, and the French, who may not have perceived clearly what the Mohawk wanted, did not want to encourage them to divert trade. The main French reason for the treaty with the Mohawk was the short-term one of opening the river. The French had little to offer the Iroquois in return and refused to sell them guns, the one item they wanted.[135] When it became clear to the Mohawk that the Huron did not intend to trade with them, they renewed their attack on Huronia and on the Huron fleet.

---

[130] Thwaites, ed., *Relations*, XXIII, 105.
[131] Hunt, *Wars of the Iroquois*, 76.
[132] Tooker, "Defeat of the Huron," 117-18. Thwaites, ed., *Relations*, XXVI, 71; XXVII, 89, 277. Brébeuf returned to Huronia at this time.
[133] Thwaites, ed., *Relations*, XXVI, 71; XXVII, 89, 277. Brébeuf returned to Huronia at this time
[134] Hunt, *Wars of the Iroquois*, 77-8.
[135] For the Iroquois desire to obtain French guns, see the evidence presented in Hunt, *Wars of the Iroquois*, 74.

The Development of a Christian Faction

While this dangerous crisis in intertribal relations was boiling up, a situation was developing in Huronia that put a new strain on the Franco-Huron alliance.

Prior to 1640, most Christian converts were Hurons on the point of death, many of whom knew nothing about Christian theology but who hoped that baptism would save their lives.[136] At one point during the epidemics a Huron version of the rite of baptism became part of a native healing cult that was said to be inspired by a native deity who had revealed himself as the real Jesus.[137] In these rites the sick were sprinkled with water as part of an orgiastic ceremony typical of traditional Huron healing rituals. After 1640, however, the Jesuits began to convert increasing numbers of people who were in good health. Many were men of importance, whose conversions made that of their families, friends, and tribesmen easier.[138] In order to prevent backsliding, the Jesuits at first made it a policy to baptise (except in cases of extreme ill health) only adults who had provided substantial proof of their devotion to Christianity and whose family life seemed to be stable.[139]

Many factors seem to have induced people to convert: some admired the bravery of the Jesuits, others wished to be able to follow a Christian friend to heaven, still others noted in their names a theological term that the Jesuits were using.[140]

Although economic motives were not the only ones involved in conversion, it is noteworthy that at least a few Huron became Christians to avoid participation in pagan feasts, which required them to give away considerable amounts of property in the form of presents and entertainment.[141] A far larger number of people hoped through conversion to receive preferential treatment in their dealings with traders and officials in New France.[142] In 1648, when only 15 per cent of the Huron were Christian, half of the men in the Huron fleet were either converts or were preparing for baptism.[143] Those who traded with the French in Quebec not only were more exposed to French culture and to Christianity than were those who remained at home but also had more to gain from good relations with the French. Commercial considerations may also explain why the Jesuits generally found it easier to convert men than women.

While stressing the practical economic motives that certainly motivated many conversions, personal and cultural factors should not be ignored. The Huron were increasingly dependent on French culture and in the eyes of many, but (as we shall

---

[136] Thwaites, ed., *Relations*, X, 13; XIII, 171.
[137] Ibid., XX, 27-31.
[138] Ibid., XX, 225; XXVI, 275.
[139] Ibid., XV, 109. For the later relaxation of these requirements see XXXIII, 145-7.
[140] Ibid., XIX, 191.
[141] Ibid., XVII, 111; XXIII, 129.
[142] Ibid., Concerning this preferential treatment see Ibid., XX, 225, 227.
[143] Ibid., XXXII, 179.

see) certainly not all of the Huron, the priest was coming to replace the native sorcerer as an object of awe and respect. This did not, however, lead the Huron to lose faith in themselves or in their culture, as it did many other tribes.[144] Supported by the respect shown by the Jesuits for the Huron people and for much of their culture, many Huron converts appear to have been imbued with a sincere zeal to change and reform their own culture. No doubt the size of the Huron confederacy and its isolation from unsupervised contact with the Europeans did much to prevent the deterioration in self-confidence that is obvious among many weaker tribes. Had other circumstances not been adverse, I think it would have been possible for the Jesuits to have transformed Huronia successfully into a nation that was both Christian and Indian.

For a time the growing number of Huron converts posed no serious problems for the rest of the society, although individual converts were frequently taunted and sometimes expelled from their longhouses with much resulting personal hardship.[145] (A woman who had been a member of a pagan healing society was threatened with death when after conversion she refused to perform in the society.[146]) Threats and assassination no doubt were the fate of other converts. The Jesuits and their assistants, however, were no longer attacked or molested in any way.[147] It appears that at least some headmen surrendered their political office on becoming Christians, since they felt that the obligation to participate in Huron festivals which these offices entailed was contrary to their new faith.[148] In this and in other ways the nascent Christian community avoided for a time the possibility of an open clash with the large pagan majority.

Gradually, however, a rift began. Some Christians refused, for example, to be buried in their tribal ossuaries, which in effect was to deny membership in their village or tribe.[149] They also refused to fight alongside pagans in the war parties but instead formed their own detachments, no doubt because of the religious implications of traditional Iroquoian warfare.[150] As the number of converts grew, men retained their political offices after conversion, but appointed deputies to handle the religious functions traditionally associated with them.[151] As the number of Christians who

---

144 Vachon, "L'Eau-de-vie."
145 Thwaites, ed., *Relations*, XXIII, 67, 127; XXVI, 229. Pagan women also attempted to seduce Christian men to persuade them to give up their faith (XXX, 33). The Relation of 1643 mentions that some converts lived for six months at Quebec to avoid facing temptation in their homeland (XXIV, 121).
146 Ibid., XXX, 23.
147 Ibid., XXI, 131.
148 Ibid., XXIII, 185.
149 Ibid., XXIII, 31.
150 For another reference to the Huron-pagan rift see Ibid., XXIII, 267.
151 Ibid., XXVIII, 89. For other acts of Christian assertiveness around this time see XXIX, 263-9; XXX, 63.

held these important offices continued to grow, the split between pagans and Christians became increasingly a political issue.

The Jesuits, for their part, now set as their immediate goal the Christianizing of an entire village.[152] Significantly the most promising town was Ossossané, where the Jesuits had been working for a long time. This town, belonging to the Bear tribe, was also the political centre of the Huron confederacy.[153] In 1648 they achieved their objective. By then the majority of people in Ossossané were converts. And that winter the chiefs of the village refused to allow the people who remained pagan to celebrate the traditional festivals, and they appointed a Jesuit as the chief headman of the village, with the right to act as a censor of public morals.[154]

The Pagan Reaction and the Destruction of Huronia

Although in 1645 such social revolutions were still several years in the future, many of the pagans had already begun to fear for the survival of their traditional customs and beliefs.[155] Undoubtedly a large number of these people were genuinely attached to the old ways and for this reason alone resented the growth of Christianity. It is also possible that many chiefs who wished to remain pagan began to fear a decline in their own influence as Christians began to play a stronger role in the life of the country. They probably resented the closer contacts that Christian chiefs had with the French and feared that these contacts would be used as a source of power. As a result of these fears and rivalries, pagan and Christian factions began to develop within the various tribes and villages throughout Huronia.[156]

Although the documentation in the Jesuit Relations is scanty, there appears to have been a considerable variation in attitude towards the Jesuits and Christianity among the different Huron tribes. The Bear, among whom the Jesuits had lived for the longest time and whose main town, Ossossané, had a large and rapidly growing Christian community, seem to have been the most pro-Christian and pro-French.[157]

---

[152] Ibid., XXV, 85.

[153] Tross, ed., *Histoire du Canada*, I, 200; Ibid., V, 259.

[154] Thwaites, ed., *Relations*, XXXIV, 105, 217.

[155] For one incident see Ibid., XXX, 61-3. Various cults also arose that appear to have been aimed at organizing ideological resistance to Christianity. One was the cult of a forest monster (XXX, 27); the second was more explicitly anti-Christian (XXX, 29-31).

[156] As one Huron put it, "I am more attached to the church than to my country or relatives" (Ibid., XXIII, 137). The Jesuits also observed that it was hard to be a good Christian and a good Huron (XXVIII, 53).

[157] Ibid., XXVI, 217. The Jesuits had noted the special inclination of the Bear tribe to receive Christianity as early as 1636 (X, 31).

The Cord probably had much the same sort of attitude.[158] The Rock and Deer tribes, however, seem to have been considerably less friendly. The Jesuits report that the former tribe, being the easternmost, had suffered most from the attacks of the Iroquois and was therefore the most inclined to seek peace with their traditional enemies. The Rock were also described, however, as a tribe with a strong aversion to the faith who never had been converted.[159] The Deer had a reputation among the Jesuits for being sorcerers,[160] and one assumes from this that they gave the missionaries a bad time. Both of these tribes joined the Iroquois of their own free will after the break-up of Huronia in 1649.[161] Despite this variation, however, there were people in all the Huron tribes who were starting to have misgivings about the future of Huronia and who resented the changes that the French alliance was bringing about.

After 1645 these sentiments seem to have led to the formation of a sizable anti-French party, which apparently found a certain amount of support everywhere in Huronia, except perhaps in Ossossané. This marked a new development in French-Huron relations, all previous opposition having been to the priests resident in Huronia rather than to the French in general. Supporters of this party seem to have reasoned that Christianity was a threat to Huronia, that Christianity flourished because the Jesuits were able to work there under the terms of the Franco-Huron alliance, and that the best way to save the country (and enhance the power of the pagan chiefs at the expense of their Christian rivals) was therefore to expel the Jesuits, break off the alliance, and begin trading with the Iroquois. In this way, not only would the traditional culture of Huronia be saved, but the attacks of the Iroquois, which had been growing in intensity,[162] would be brought to an end. Thus for the first time a respectable body of opinion in Huronia came to believe that an alliance with enemies who shared similar beliefs and culture was preferable to one with strangers seeking to change the Huron way of life. The threat that was facing the traditionalists made the thought of trading with their old enemies and rivals seem much less unpleasant than it had been a few years previously.

The first plan for a rapprochement with the Iroquois was well conceived and sought to exploit internal differences within the Iroquois confederacy for the Hurons'

---

158 After the destruction of Huronia the Cord were very loyal to the French. They were the only Huron tribe that refused to leave Quebec to go and live with the Iroquois (Ibid., XLIII, 191). Prior to 1640, the Cord were not at all friendly with the Jesuits (XVII, 59); their change in attitude seems to have come about soon after (XXI, 285; XXIII, 151; XXVI, 265).

159 Ibid., XLII, 73. Concerning their early desire for peace with the Iroquois see XXXIII, 119-21.

160 Ibid., XVII, 89.

161 Ibid., XXXVI, 179. The Deer lived among the Seneca in their own village and on good terms with their hosts (XLIV, 21). Many Rock people, including the Indians of Contarea, lived among the Onondaga (XLII, 73).

162 For evidence of incipient deterioration in morale and the beginning of the abandonment of Huronia in the face of Iroquois attack, see Ibid., XXX, 87; XXXIII, 83-9.

own advantage. Since the treaty of 1645 had failed to obtain the furs they wanted, the Mohawk were likely to be suspicious of, if not hostile to, further Huron blandishments. The Seneca likewise were unfriendly because of recent Huron attacks on them.[163] The Onondaga, however, had long enjoyed the position of being the chief tribe in the confederacy and were increasingly jealous of the Mohawk, who were exploiting their close contacts with the Dutch and the English in an effort to dominate the league.[164] It is therefore no surprise that it was through the Onondaga that the Huron attempted to make peace with the Iroquois.

The Jesuits did not record, and may not have known, the exact nature of the treaty that the Huron were trying to negotiate. The presence of a clause promising that the Huron would trade furs with the Iroquois is suggested by a remark, attributed to the Andaste or Susquehannock (who were allies of the Huron and sent ambassadors to the Onondaga to argue on their behalf), that such a treaty would promote the trade of all these tribes with one another.[165] It is also significant that among the Huron the Bear tribe was the one most opposed to this treaty.[166] The Jesuits said this was because the Bear had suffered less from Iroquois raids than had the other Huron tribes, but a second reason could be that the Christians, who were more numerous in this tribe than in the others, saw in these negotiations a clear threat to the Franco-Huron alliance and to their own power and well-being. Negotiations continued for some time, but were terminated in January 1648, when a party of Mohawk warriors slew a Huron embassy on its way to the chief Onondaga town to arrange the final terms of the treaty.[167] A distinguished Onondaga chief, who had remained in Huronia as a hostage, committed suicide when he learned what the Mohawk had done.[168]

There seems little reason to doubt the honesty of the Onondaga in these negotiations. The Mohawk probably attacked the Huron embassy because they were angry that negotiations were being conducted with the Onondaga rather than with them. The Mohawk may also have believed that the Huron were trying to deceive the Onondaga and that the only way of dealing with the Huron confederacy was to destroy it. In any case, the Mohawk managed to bring the first major political offensive of the anti-French faction in Huronia to an ignominious conclusion.

---

163   Ibid., XXXIII, 125. Hunt (*Wars of the Iroquois*, 72) notes that in 1637 the Huron had broken a peace treaty with the Seneca.
164   Thwaites, ed., *Relations*, XXXIII, 71, 123.
165   Ibid., XXXIII, 131.
166   Ibid., XXXIII, 119-21.
167   Ibid., XXXIII, 125.
168   Ibid., XXXIII, 125-7. He probably did this through anger at his allies and to show the innocence of the Onondaga. He might also have committed suicide to avoid Huron vengeance directed against his person, but this would have been construed as an act of cowardice. It is unlikely that the Onondaga would have exposed an important chief to almost certain death had they not been negotiating in good faith.

Even though this first effort had failed, at least some Huron apparently believed that a rapprochement with the Iroquois still was possible. Indeed, either because they were totally convinced of the necessity of appeasing the Iroquois or because of their extreme hatred of the Christians, a minority seems to have become convinced that a break with the French was a precondition for further negotiation. The group responsible for the next move was led by six, apparently distinguished, chiefs from three villages.[169] Unfortunately, these villages are unnamed. The chiefs decided to make a public issue of the question of a continued Franco-Huron alliance through the simple expedient of killing a Frenchman. They do not appear to have designated any particular victim and their henchmen slew Jacques Douart, a *donné* whom they encountered not far from Ste Marie. Once Douart was slain, the conspirators issued a proclamation calling for the banishment from Huronia of the French and all of the Huron who insisted on remaining Christian.[170] An emergency council was convened (apparently from all over the country) and for several days these proposals were debated. On the one side were the Christians and those pagans who felt that the Franco-Huron alliance should continue; on the other the traditionalists who had stirred up the trouble and no doubt some other Hurons who hated neither Christianity nor the French, but who felt that a peace treaty with the Iroquois was important enough to be worth the termination of the French alliance. Among the latter must have been many refugees from the Rock tribe, which had been forced to abandon its villages as a result of Iroquois attacks only a short time before.[171] The pro-French party finally won the debate and the Jesuits in turn agreed to accept the traditional Huron compensation for a murder, in this case one hundred beaver skins.[172] The ritual presentation of this settlement made clear that it was designed to reaffirm and protect the Franco-Huron alliance, which the unprecedented actions of these chiefs had endangered. Thus ended what appears to have been the last attempt to rupture the Franco-Huron alliance.

During the summer of 1648 the Seneca attacked and destroyed the large town of St. Joseph. As the situation grew more serious the Huron turned increasingly to the French for help and the number of conversions increased sharply.[173] As in 1644, a few French soldiers were sent to winter in Huronia. These soldiers, so long as they remained in Huronia, were believed sufficient to hold off the Iroquois, but they had been instructed to return to Quebec with the Huron fleet in the spring.[174] As the military situation in Huronia grew more desperate, the French in Quebec became increasingly anxious to profit as much as possible while they still could. In the

---

[169] Ibid., XXXIII, 229.
[170] Ibid., XXXIII, 231.
[171] Ibid., XXXIII, 81.
[172] Ibid., XXXIII, 233-49.
[173] Ibid., XXXIV, 227.
[174] Ibid., XXXIV, 83.

summer of 1649, a party of over thirty coureurs de bois made a flying trip to Huronia and returned to Quebec, bringing with them 5000 pounds of beaver.[175]

In the spring of 1649 the Iroquois unleashed the attack that resulted in the death of Fathers Lalemant and Brébeuf and brought about the dispersal of the Huron confederacy. Many factors contributed to the Iroquois victory, but their superior number of guns was undoubtedly the most important.[176] Hunt has suggested that the Huron were so given over to trading by 1649 that virtually all of their food was imported from the Neutral and Petun tribes and that the main factor in their defeat was therefore the cutting of their supply routes.[177] This suggestion is entirely without foundation. Agriculture was a woman's occupation and little affected by increasing trade. While men may have spent more time trading, the importation of iron axes made it easier to cut trees and hence there was no problem clearing the forests for agriculture. There are frequent references to the Huron as engaged in agricultural activities in the years prior to 1649, and one of the reasons the Iroquois returned to Huronia in the spring of 1650 was to prevent the planting of crops.[178] Driven from their homes and deprived of food, the Hurons scattered and their trading monopoly came to an end. It is interesting that large numbers of Huron, particularly from the Rock and Deer tribes, migrated to the Iroquois country and settled there. The latter tribe settled *en masse* among the Seneca, where they lived in their own village and retained their separate customs for a long time.[179] Their tribal affiliations suggest that these refugees were for the most part traditionalists and probably among them were many of the people who had been the most hostile to the French during the last years of the Jesuit mission. This hostility explains how these groups were so easily adopted by the people who had destroyed their homeland.

For the Jesuits the destruction of Huronia was the end of their first dream of leading a nation to Christianity in the heart of the Canadian forest. At least once in the Relations they mentioned the work their colleagues were accomplishing in Paraguay and compared this work with their own.[180] The chance had been lost of converting a people to Christianity while allowing them to retain their language and those institutions and customs that were not incompatible with their new faith.

---

[175] Lanctot, *History of Canada*, I, 194, based on Ibid., XXXIV, 59-61.

[176] Tooker, "Defeat of the Hurons," 117-18; Innis, *Fur Trade*, 35-6. For the effective use of firearms by the Iroquois see Thwaites, ed., *Relations*, XXII, 307. The Jesuits saw the danger of growing Iroquois firepower as early as 1642 (XXII, 307) but the French officials in Quebec never developed a policy to counteract it. The restiveness of the Huron pagans may be one reason why the French did not want too many guns in Huron hands, even if they were being sold only to Christians.

[177] Hunt, *Wars of the iroquois*, 59.

[178] Thwaites, ed., *Relations*, XXXV, 191.

[179] Ibid., XXXVI, 179; XLIV, 21; XLV, 243. Many of the Rock nation, particularly from Contarea, were later found living with the Onondaga (XLII, 73).

[180] Ibid., XII, 221. The work of Paraguay is also mentioned in XV, 127.

Because they were writing for a patriotic French audience, the Jesuits have little to say about the constitutional status of the Huronia they wished to create. Nevertheless, it seems clear that what they aimed at was not so much a French colony as an Indian state, which under Jesuit leadership could blend the good things of Europe with those already in the native culture. A Catholic Huronia would of necessity have been allied with France, the only Catholic power in eastern North America. Years later Louis de Buade de Frontenac probably came closer to a basic truth than he realized when he accused the Jesuits at Quebec of disloyalty because they kept the Indians apart from the French and taught them in their own language.[181]

The fur trade was the one means by which the Jesuits could gain admittance to Huronia and the only protection they had while working there. Ties with fur traders and government officials in Quebec were thus vital for the success of the Huron mission, but these ties do not seem to have prevented the Jesuits from seeking to serve the best interests of their Huron converts and Huronia at large—as they perceived these interests. To reverse the equation and say that the Jesuits were in Huronia mainly *for the purpose* of serving either the fur trade or the French government does not accord with anything we know about their activities.

In the short run the destruction of Huronia was a serious setback for New France. For a time the fur trade, on which the well-being of the colony depended, was cut to practically nothing. The Iroquois, on the other hand, seem to have achieved less than they hoped for from the destruction of Huronia. The western tribes soon became involved in a protracted war with the Erie[182] and tribal jealousies rent the confederacy. As a result of these jealousies the four western tribes began to trade with the French to avoid travelling through Mohawk towns to reach the Dutch.[183] By 1654 the French were starting to put together the rudiments of a new trading network north of the Great Lakes.[184] The remnants of the Huron and Petun who had remained in this area, and more importantly the Ottawa, an Algonkin tribe, played a major role in pushing this trading network to the west in the years that followed.[185] As the population of New France increased, the young men of the colony, with or without official permission, joined in this trade. Thus the destruction of Huronia was neither a total nor a permanent disaster for New France and certainly it did not help to save North America for Protestantism and the Anglo-Saxons, as at least one eminent historian has suggested.[186]

---

[181] G. Lanctot, *A History of Canada*, II. (Toronto, 1964), 63.

[182] Hunt, *Wars of the Iroquois*, 100-2.

[183] Thwaites, ed., *Relations*, XLI, 201-3, and XLIV, 151; Hunt, *Wars of the Iroquois*, 99, 100.

[184] Thwaites, ed., *Relations*, XL, 215; Lanctot, *History of Canada*, I, 212-13. On the lack of furs in Montreal in 1652-3 see Thwaites, ed., *Relations*, XL, 211.

[185] Hunt, *Wars of the Iroquois*, 102-3.

[186] Parkman, *Jesuits in North America*, 550-3.

A more serious question is what would have happened had the anti-French party in Huronia been successful. Had they been able to organize an effective resistance to the Huron Christians and conclude a treaty with the Iroquois, the trade from the north might have been diverted permanently from the St. Lawrence into the Hudson Valley. Had that happened (and as Sagard and Le Clercq indicate, the people in Quebec knew it well[187]) the chances of the infant French colony surviving even for a short time would have been slim. Instead of the destruction of Huronia tipping the balance of power in favour of the English, its survival might well have led to a Huron-Iroquois alliance that would have resulted in the destruction of New France and the end of the French presence in North America.

---

[187] Tross, ed., *Histoire du Canada*, III, 811; Le Clercq, *Establishment*, I, 204.

French Sovereignty and Native Nationhood During the French Regime[1]

Cornelius J. Jaenen

Our generation has become aware of the fact that the Vikings and the early European fishermen, who preceded such adventurers as John Cabot and Jacques Cartier, were not the "discoverers" of North America. This paper will concern itself with the French intrusion and colonization in the context of Amerindian occupation and exploitation of the Americas. In other words we shall examine how in this early colonial period concepts of French sovereignty and Native nationhood were reconciled. Europeans, of course, had a long-established experience with colonization and the occupation of new lands. Ancient and medieval history are replete with instances of conquest and annexation.

The first historical fact that must be kept in mind in dealing with the matter of sovereignty and nationhood is that the early whalers, walrus hunters, and cod fishers from the French Atlantic ports did not find an uninhabited New World. Virtually from the moment of first contacts those in authority, both civil and ecclesiastical, were aware of the Native peoples, or "new men," of the Western hemisphere. The first record of Amerindians being taken to France for official presentation and public display dates from a fishing expedition undertaken by Thomas Aubert of Dieppe in 1508.

Presumably, the Amerindians had migrated into *terra nullius* and as first occupants had established undisputed possession of North America, at least so it now appears in terms of international law as subsequently canonized by European jurists. There is no archaeological evidence, or corroborating scientific evidence, to suggest that the remains of earliest humans on this continent are not of Mongoloid origin and predecessors of the Native peoples "discovered" by Europeans in the tenth and following centuries. Whether the *Skraelings* contacted by the Norsemen or the *sauvages* encountered by the crews of fishing vessels were lineal descendants of the first peoples to inhabit northeastern America is problematical. Oral tradition and archaeological research point to major displacements of Amerindian cultural and ethnic groups before European contact. Major migrations and traumatic demographic shifts occurred both at the time of and subsequent to first French contact. The disappearance of the Laurentian Iroquois, between Cartier's departure in 1542 and the reappearance of his nephews at the sites of Quebec and Montreal in the 1580s, is probably the best known example of such important demographic change. Important territorial redistributions render unreliable even so basic a cultural boundary as the

---

[1] Revised version of a public lecture given at the Native Studies Department, University of Saskatchewan, 4 October 1984.

demarcation between the territories of the nomadic Algonkian hunting bands and the sedentary Iroquoian tribes.

The second historical fact which will need to be kept in mind in dealing with the matter of sovereignty and nationhood is that the French established beachheads for settlement in largely unoccupied lands. The valleys of the St. Lawrence and the Annapolis, where they started settlements in the early seventeenth century, were not at that time inhabited. The presumed annihilation, or adoption and assimilation following conquest, of the Iroquoian peoples who had met with Cartier and Roberval's expeditions in the 1530s and 1540s, and shunning by Algonkian Micmac bands of the salty marshlands along the Bay of Fundy which attracted de Monts and Champlain, gave initial French colonization a unique and important characteristic. In these restricted areas, the French, not unlike the Amerindians who had migrated from Asia to North America, were able to move into *terra nullius* from another continent. The immediate consequence of this rather unique situation was that from the outset there was no question of displacement of aboriginal residents or of concern about legitimate title to lands appropriated. The colonization of New France, therefore, began without evident concern about territorial occupancy as a factor in French-Amerindian relations. Hospitality, sharing of possessions, and exchange of gifts—all Amerindian cultural qualities—marked the initial French intrusion into Amerindian America. Even when pursuit of trade and missionary work resulted in deep penetration into the heartland of North America, neither was associated with land acquisition.

The objectives of French intrusion into North America are well documented. By contrast, we know virtually nothing of the Amerindian motives for migration to this continent, the pressures that may have been exerted upon them to leave Asia, or the circumstances of their arrival. The French came in the first instance in search of walrus, whale and cod, then of fabulous riches similar to those found by the Spaniards in Central and South America, and of the route to the exotic Orient. None of these necessitated extensive settlement. Religious motivation developed only later in the French contact. Cartier's third commission, that of 1541, ordered him to penetrate inland and "converse with the said peoples thereof and live among them, if need be" in order to facilitate the spread of the Christian religion.[2] Yet none of the French expeditions to the New World was accompanied by missionaries before 1610.

By the late 1690s, however, it was becoming clear that France's chief interest in North America was no longer commercial but rather strategic. The priority given military matters in Europe during the closing decades of Louis XIV's reign was mirrored in New France. This significant shift in colonial policy placed new emphasis on holding the *pays d'en haut*, conciliating Native inhabitants, associating the fur trade with military operations, and opening career opportunities to the

---

[2] H.P. Biggar, ed., *A Collection of Documents relating to Jacques Cartier and the Sieur de Roberval* (Ottawa, 1930), p. 128.

Canadian nobility in the Marine contingents. In this context the need to reconcile Native self-government with French claims remained imperative...[3]

By what right did France come into possession of New France? Her invasion of America, to employ a term popularized by Francis Jennings, seemed justified by a European tradition that evolved out of classical Roman, medieval Christian and feudal concepts. Roman civil law clearly set forth the rules to be observed in settling disputes between individuals over ownership of lands previously unclaimed. Hugo Grotius in 1625 applied this Roman legal concept of lands previously unclaimed to nations: "as to things without a master, if we follow nature alone, they belong to him who discovers and occupies them." On the basis of this argument in *Droit de la Guerre et de la Paix* the "vacant lands" of America could legally be claimed by the nation which first discovered and took possession of them. Colonization was seen as a normal expansion of European law and government into a legal vacuum and of European peoples into vacant lands.[4]

Roman civil law seemed to uphold the occupation and appropriation of newly discovered territory that was virtually uninhabited and not extensively cultivated. Europeans did not believe that nomadic, loosely organized Native societies with communal land-sharing constituted sovereign states which could be recognized as such in international diplomacy. Northeastern America was "vacant land" either in the Roman sense of *vacuum domicilium*, or the sixteenth-century term *terra nullius* for lands unoccupied by any other sovereign state, concepts which in our day Robert Berkhofer has described as lands devoid of extensive human occupation and cultivation and which Olive Dickason calls "lands not already under Christian control."[5] In other words, the European powers adopted the concept that the "laws of nature" permit a nation to settle an unoccupied territory and to develop its own society. This would have been the Amerindian claim to North America had it been made in European juridical terms.

That the argument to justify European occupation of the Americas could also be used to affirm the prior rights of the Amerindians had not passed unnoticed. Francisco de Vitoria, a theologian at the University of Salamanaca in the mid-

---

[3] Cornelius J. Jaenen, *The French Relationship with the Native Peoples of New France* (Ottawa, 1984), pp. 158-212.

[4] Cited in Walter B. Scaife, "The Development of International Law as to Newly Discovered Territory," *Papers of the American Historical Association*, 4, No. 3 (July 1890); Hugo Grotius, *Droit de Guerre et de la Paix* (Paris, 1867), II, ch. 2, art, ii, 5; Christopher C. Joyne, "The Historical Status of American Indians under International Law," *The Indian Historian*, 2, No. 4 (1978), 30-36; James Simsarian, "The Acquisition of Legal Title to *Terra Nullium*," *Political Science Quarterly*, 53, No. 1 (1938), 111-128.

[5] Robert F. Berkhofer Jr., *The White Man's Indian* (New York, 1978), p. 120; Olive P. Dickason, "Europeans and Amerindians: Some Comparative Aspects of Early Contact," Canadian Historical Association, *Historical Papers/Communications historiques, 1979* (Ottawa, 1980), p. 192.

sixteenth century, argued in two famous treatises entitled *De Indis* and *De Jure Belli* that the Amerindians were the true possessors of the Americas by virtue of their occupation of these lands from time immemorial. This was the initial statement of aboriginal rights. However, he qualified it with the judgment that all nations had the right of visiting, sojourning and trading in newly discovered lands and that the high seas were open to all nations. There was emerging a concept of international law, which Victoria described as "having been established by the authority of the whole world."[6] It was a view that a number of Catholic theologians at the time, and later, employed to decry the exploitation and despoiling of Native peoples.

Christian theology and medieval musings about the rights of infidel and non-Christian populations, nevertheless, contributed a second element to European justifications for taking possession of America. While Pope Innocent IV had opined in the early thirteenth century that non-Christian states enjoyed the same rights and authority as Christian states, and Thomas Aquinas taught that legitimacy of dominion did not depend on the religious beliefs of those exercising authority, the church undertook Crusades and used the Ostiensian thesis to justify its actions. Henry of Susa, Cardinal of Ostia (d. 1271), held that infidel nations were not legitimate, their rulers lacked recognized jurisdiction, and the lands of such states could be appropriated without compensation...[7]

Feudalism held that the acquisition of a territory presupposed the possibility of holding it effectively, so that if "positive rule and legal authority" were not exercised all legitimate claim was lost. On such grounds Francis I had challenged the papal division of the New World between Portugal and Spain with the celebrated phrase "Show me Adam's will!" The royal commission to Roberval in 1541 commanded him to take possession of regions "uninhabited and not possessed or ruled by any other Christian princes."[8] Effective occupation was the only recognized claim to possession. International law eventually pronounced in favour of such an

---

[6] Francisco de Vitoria, *Leçons sur les Indiens et sur les Droits de Guerre* (Geneva, 1966), pp. 82-84; James B. Scott, *The Catholic Conception of International Law*, (Washington, 1984), p. 89.

[7] Olive P. Dickason, "Renaissance Europe's View of Amerindian Sovereignty and Territoriality," *Plural Societies*, VIII, 3-4 (1977), 97-107; Olive P. Dickason, *The Myth of the Savage and the Beginnings of French Colonialism in the Americas* (Edmonton, 1984), pp. 127-132; Neville Figgis, *The Divine Right of Kings* (Cambridge, 1914), pp. 45-64; Lewis Hanke, *The Spanish Struggle for Justice in Conquest of America* (Philadelphia, 1944), *passim;* Fred H. Kimney, "Christianity and Indian Lands," *Ethnohistory*, 7 (1960), 44; James Muldoon, *Popes, Lawyers and Infidels. The Church and the Non-Christian World, 1250-1550* (London, 1979), *passim;* Kenneth J. Pennington Jr., "Bartolome de Las Casas and the Tradition of Medieval Law," *Church History* 39 (June, 1970), 149-161; Walter Ullmann, *Medieval Papalism. The Political Theories of the Medieval Canonists* (London, 1949), pp. 129-137.

[8] Biggar, *Collection of Documents*, p. 178.

interpretation. In 1672, Pufendorf expanded on Grotius' concept of the rights of discovery to include physical appropriation because "'twould be in vain for you to claim as your own, [that] which you can by no means hinder others from sharing with you." The Swiss legal scholar, Emmerich de Vattel, in *Le Droit des Gens (The Law of Nations)* held that it was not ancient occupation of the land, as consecrated in the phrase "from time immemorial," that was the basis of title and right, but the use made of the land which was the ultimate justification for its possession.[9]

Emmerich de Vattel thought that the majority of the Native peoples of "those vast tracts of land rather roamed over them than inhabited them" and by pursuing "this idle mode of life, usurp more extensive territories than, with a reasonable share of labour, they would have occasion for;" therefore, it was just "if other nations more industrious and too closely confined, come to take possession of a part of those lands..." He concluded of the Native inhabitants of New France that "their unsettled habitation in those immense regions cannot be countered a true and legal possession," whereas Europeans "were lawfully entitled to take possession of it, and settle it with colonies."[10] This view represented the culmination of conceptualization, based on Roman, Christian and feudal principles, regarding the European right to colonize. The philosopher-encyclopedist Diderot could not help but wonder if his compatriots would defend the thesis had some Amerindians by chance landed on French soil and "had written on the sand of your beaches or on the bark of your trees: This land belongs to us."[11]

By what means did France establish and proclaim her sovereignty over New France? The official view of the French administration in the eighteenth century was that Jean da Verrazano had taken possession for Francis I in 1523 and Jacques Cartier had reaffirmed this *prise de possession* in 1535.[12] The formal taking possession of a territory was usually expressed through some symbolic act such as erecting a cross, posting the King's arms, burying inscribed lead plates, and reading a proclamation in the name of God and the King. The French did not read a *requerimiento* as did the Spaniards on approaching new lands, but it has been stated that they erected crosses in Brazil with the intention of imposing French laws and customs and the Catholic religion, as well as laying formal claim to the land. Cartier planted many crosses on his journeys to North America but most of these, as Brian Slattery has demonstrated,

---

[9] Samuel Pufendorf, *De Jure Naturae et Gentium* (Oxford, 1934), pp. 600-601; Emmerich de Vattel, *Le Droit des Gens; ou, Principes de la Loi Naturelle* (Washington, 1916), III, 38.

[10] Emmerich de Vattel, *The Law of Nations or the Principles of Natural Law* (London, 1758), I, 35-36, 98-100.

[11] Yves Benot, *Diderot: De l'athéisme à l'anticolonialisme* (Paris, 1970), p. 197.

[12] Public Archives of Canada, MG4, C-1, Article 14, Vol. I, No. 6 "Droits de France sur le Canada," (1755), 41-42.

were markers or navigational aids, religious symbols, or commemorative pillars without any symbolic taking of possession of the country.[13]

Nevertheless, as Slattery has also noted, there were formal French claims in the sixteenth century which tended to support the view that New France was acquired through right of conquest. The royal commission to Roberval, dated 15 January 1541, said explicitly that he was to "descend and enter these lands and put them in our possession, by means of friendship and amicable agreements, if that can be done, or by force of arms, strong handed and all other hostile means," to destroy its strongholds and establish French control. Roberval was instructed to acquire the region either through voluntary cession or "consent and tuition of the said countries."[14] These instructions must be understood in the light of Cartier's rather troubled relations with the Laurentian peoples during the six previous years and the fact that settlement was going to be undertaken in an inhabited region.

This aggressive approach continued throughout the remaining years of the sixteenth century. The Marquis de la Roche received authority in 1577 to "invest and make his all lands which he can make himself master of" and not previously claimed by other Europeans. The following year he was named governor of "new found lands and countries which he shall take and conquer from the said barbarians." In the letters-patent of 1588 to those who had inherited Jacques Cartier's privileges in New France "conquests under our name and authority by all due and licit means" were authorized. The commission to La Roche for Sable Island in 1598 authorized him to acquire possession "by means of friendship and amicable means" and failing that "by force of arms, strong handed and all other hostile means" as had been the directive to Roberval.[15] Fortunately for French-Amerindian relations, these early colonization attempts failed.

The seventeenth century witnessed a very different approach. The planting of a trading post at Tadoussac in 1600, the founding of "habitations" at Port Royal (1605) and Quebec (1608), and the inauguration of missionary work in Acadia (1611) and Canada (1615) were accompanied by a policy of pacification and reconciliation. De Mont's commission of 8 November 1603 did stipulate that he was "to establish, extend and make known our (royal) name, power and authority" but there was no longer any mention of coercive measures. The commissions of 1612 and 1625 for

---

[13] Arthur S. Keller *et al.*, *Creation of the Rights of Sovereignty through Symbolic Acts, 1400-1800* (New York, 1938), p. 148; Joyne, pp. 30-36; Scaife, *passim*; Simsarian, pp. 111-128; Friedrich A.F. Von de Heydte, "Discovery, Symbolic Annexation and Virtual Effectiveness in International Law," *American Journal of International Law*, 29 (1935), 448-471; and for the initial discovery period especially Brian Slattery, *French Claims in North America, 1500-59* (Saskatoon, 1980), pp. 8-13.

[14] Biggar, *Collection of Documents*, p. 180.

[15] M. Michelant & M. Rame, eds., *Relation originale du Voyage de Jacques Cartier* (Paris, 1867), II, 6, 8, 41-42; *Edits, ordonnances royaux, déclarations et arrêts concernant le Canada* (Quebec, 1854-56), III, 8-9.

Champlain employed the same conciliatory tone, and the articles establishing the Company of New France in April 1627, with full title to the "property, justice and seigneury" of the colony, made no mention of acquisition of title, or imposition of French sovereignty, but contented itself with granting converted Amerindians the same rights as natural-born French subjects when in metropolitan France.[16] Thus, under royal charter company rule (1627-1663), as drawn up by Cardinal Richelieu for Louis XIII, it would appear that those Natives who accepted the King's religion (and by extension his sovereignty?) were granted the same status as other colonial subjects.

What knowledge the Native inhabitants had of these European legalities is uncertain. Although missionaries interpreted actions such as presenting gifts to the King as "paying homage," when Amerindians were presented at Court, their own reception in Iroquois country suggested a different perspective. The successful diplomatic mission, so-called, of Jean Bourdon and Father Isaac Jogues to the Mohawk in May 1646, for example, extracted only the promise that the French would always have "an assured dwelling place" among them and that the missionary personally "will always find his mat ready to receive him." The continued hostility of the Iroquois in the 1660s, however, resulted in several military raids on their villages, described by the colonial bishop at one point as a kind of crusade. The several Iroquoian tribes found themselves obliged to adhere to a series of peace treaties in 1665-66 by which Louis XIV was acknowledged "from this time as their Sovereign," the Huron and Algonkian allies of the King as being "not only under his protection but also as his proper subjects" and with whom they pledged "to live fraternally for their mutual defense under the common protection of the said Lord the King." This treaty, which ended a war regarded somewhat as a baronial struggle and which involved no territorial appropriation, also provided for exchanges of families between the French colonists and the Five Nations and explicitly provided that the Iroquois should provide French exchange families with agricultural land and hunting and fishing rights in their territory.[17] The language of the treaties would appear to substantiate the interpretation that the Iroquois, under the protection of His Most Christian Majesty, were bound by fealty and allegiance, while enjoying seigneurial rights under the Crown.

The charter of the Compagnie des Indes Occidentales, issued in May 1664, reflected the troubled relations with the Iroquois. The company was instructed to establish its commercial activities "by chasing or submitting the natives or natural inhabitants of the said countries" who were not allies of the Crown, to develop "all

---

[16] Marc Lescarbot, *Histoire de la Nouvelle-France* (Paris 1618), II, 490; E.H. Gosselin, ed., *Documents authentiques et inédits pour servir à l'histoire de la Marine normande et du Commerce rouennais pendant les XVIe et XVIIe siècles* (Rouen, 1876), 18-19; *Edits et ordannances*, III, II and 13,; I, 5.

[17] E.B. O'Callaghan, ed., *Documents relating to the Colonial History of the State of New York* (Albany, 1855-77), I, 51-52; IX, 46; Vol. III, 121, does not give the text of the treaty.

lands it shall be able to conquer and inhabit," and to enter into negotiations with "the kings and princes of the country" for "peace and alliances in our name." As it turned out, the Crown assumed direct control of the colony and limited the opportunities for its corporate subjects to exploit the Native peoples.[18]

In the interior of the country, as exploration, missions and trade progressed, more formal claims of possession through symbolic acts occurred. Saint-Lusson's *prise de possession* at Sault Ste-Marie on 14 June 1671 is probably the best known ceremony. As the representative of Louis XIV and special envoy of the Intendant Jean Talon, Saint-Lusson with Nicholas Perrot as chief interpreter and in the presence of four Jesuit missionaries, fourteen Native chieftains and about two thousand spectators took formal possession of the upper country "bounded on the one side by the oceans of the north and west, and on the other side by the South Sea." He did so "declaring to all nations therein that from this time henceforth they are subjects of His Majesty, bound to obey his laws and follow his customs." In return for what the French called a submission to the King of France, the assembled "nations" were promised "all succour and protection against their enemies." A great wooden cross had been planted, and Saint-Lusson made the declaration with sword drawn in one hand and a symbolic handful of soil in the other. A religious celebration followed and in the evening the fourteen "nations" were treated to a large bonfire, the distribution of the "King's presents," and a *Te Deum* sung in their name to thank God for having made them "the subjects of so great and powerful a Monarch." No dissenting voices were recorded as the Native people joined in a celebration which cemented commercial and military relations.[19]

Formal claims appear to have been directed more at European competitors than at Amerindians who were theoretically becoming French subjects. When Sieur de Villieu was sent in 1693 "to post the King's coat of arms along a line separating new France from New England," he underscored the fact that the Iroquois insisted they had never been subjects of Britain and he opined that such a categorical statement should be kept in the French archives for use at an appropriate time. Sieur de Louvigny, in concluding a treaty with the Fox in 1716, gave them "a copy on a sheet of paper as an authentic testimonial of our convention and the taking possession of a conquered land by the King's arms" for the benefit of the English, whom he described as "ever jealous of the success of French arms" and liable to

---

18   PAC., MG 1, Series C11A, Vol. L., "Extrait de diverses relations qui peut servir à établir le droit de la France sur le pays des Iroquois, 1646 à 1681," 427; *Edits et Ordannances*, III, 41, 46.

19   R.G. Thwaites, ed., *The Jesuit Relations and Allied Documents* (New York, 1959), LV, 104-114; J. Tailhan, ed., *Mémoire sur les Moeurs, coutumes et religion des sauvages de l'Amérique septentrionale de Nicolas Perrot* (Paris, 1864), pp. 126-128; *Collection de Manuscrits contenant lettres, mémoires et autres documents historiques relatifs à la Nouvelle-France* (Quebec, 1883-85), I, 213, 217-218; PAC, MG 4, C-I, Article 14, Vol. I, No. 5, "Droits de France sur le Canada," 32-33.

challenge the French claim to the western interior. In 1732, Joseph Normandin undertook to mark the boundary along the height of land north of Lac St-Jean separating the French territory from that of the Hudson's Bay Company. He made a formal claim of possession for Louis XV, placing four *fleurs de lys* on four trees and in the middle of a portage three crosses on the largest red pine. In 1743, Louis Fornel erected two large crosses on a promontory at Baie St-Louis in Labrador, kneeled before them singing hymns of thanksgiving, and then raised a royal standard as a sign of "the Taking of possession which we make in the name of the King and the French nation of land which has never yet been inhabited by any nation and among whom we are the first to take possession thereof."[20]

Sometimes the French were challenged when they sought to take formal possession of a region. La Vérendrye the elder, among the Mandan, gave a chief a flag and an inscribed lead tablet decorated with ribbons. He recorded that "this tablet was placed in a box, so that it might be kept forever, in memory of my having taken possession of their lands in the name of the King." But in the explanation he offered the Mandans concerning its significance he merely said "I made them understand as best I could that I was leaving this token in memory of the visit of the French to their country." His son penetrated even farther westwards to the Arikaras where he erected a pyramid of stones, as he told them "in memory of the fact that we had been in their country" but under which he had managed to deposit secretly a lead table "bearing the arms and inscription of the King." In 1749, in order to forestall British claims to the Ohio valley, Céloron de Blainville buried a series of six lead plates asserting French claims to the region, as well as posting the King's arms on prominent trees along the river bank. The Native people, even those allied with the French, wondered about the significance of these objects, removed them and asked the English about their meaning.[21]

It seems evident that the French never doubted their right to acquire lands not already under Christian control. In asserting their sovereignty, they directed their claims against European rivals in particular, while with Native nations they formed alliances and observed many traditional ceremonies in cementing good relations. The role of the King's presents was an important component of this special relationship.[22] Only with the Iroquois and Fox in the *pay d'en haut*, both of whom were regarded as being under British influence and against whom they waged war, did

---

[20] PAC, MG 5, Vol. 6, Extracts from a letter of Sieur de Villieu, 16 October 1700, 205-206; PAC, MG 1, Series C11A, Vol. 37, Lovigny to Comte de Toulouse, 1 October 1717, 387; PAC MG 7, I, A-3, Nouv. acq. fr., Vol. 9275, Journal de Joseph Normandin, 1732, 149-150; ibid., Journal of Louis Forhel, 1743, 368.

[21] C. Hubert Smith, *The Explorations of the La Vérendryes in the Northern Plains, 1738-43*, (Lincoln, 1980), pp. 49, 63, 113; PAC MG I, Series F3, Vol. 13, Pt. 2, Campaign journal of Céloron, November 1749, 472; PAC, MG 21, Egerton MSS Vol. 2694, 11.

[22] Cornelius J. Jaenen, "The Role of Presents in French-Amerindian Trade," in Duncan Cameron, ed., *Explorations in Canadian Economic History* (Ottawa, 1985), pp. 231-250.

they sign treaties. Relations in the lower Mississippi region, emanating from the government of Louisiana, were of a different order, marked notably by military action directed at the Chickasaws and the Natchez. This region of French America, characterized by plantation agriculture, slavery and the intermingling of French colonists with slaves and indigenous peoples, in terms of relations with the Amerindians should be studied in the context of the French Antilles and Guiana, not Acadia, Canada and the *pays d'en haut*.

How did the French view the status of Amerindian "nations" and how did they reconcile Native nationhood and self-government with their own claims of sovereignty in North America? There seems to have been no conceptual problem for the French because they distinguished between nationhood as understood in the international family of nations, where *states* were organized under sovereign governments possessing coercive powers to maintain order in their communities, and nationhood as understood locally, where collectivities organized as bands and tribes could conclude agreements, enter into alliances and wage wars.

Thus, while the French claimed sovereignty in terms of international law, they conceded self-determination to Native "nations." Native "nations" were seen as independent in the sense of retaining their own forms of social and political organization, customs and practices. The intention was to restrict French settlement in Canada to the St. Lawrence valley, where some domiciled Natives might come voluntarily to live on reserves under missionary guidance, and to permit only small French communities at trading posts, military forts and mission stations in the vast Amerindian territory. There was, in other words, a French area with limited Native settlement, and there was a Native area with limited French settlement. Royal instructions in 1716 not only required leaving the Native peoples to govern themselves but also forbade the French from settling and clearing land above the Montreal seigneuries.[23] This dualism had far reaching consequences and moved a Lower Canadian judge to make the following observation in his judgment in the famous *Connolly v. Woolrich and Johnson et al.* case:

> Neither the French Government, nor any of its colonists or their trading associations, ever attempted, during an intercourse of over two hundred years, to subvert or modify the laws and usages of the aboriginal tribes, except where they had established colonies and permanent settlements, and, then only by persuasion...

In answer to the rhetorical question whether "the territorial rights, political organization such as it was, or the laws and usages of the Indian tribes, were abrogated," he opined:

---

[23] PAC, MG 1, Series C11A, Vol. 36, "Mémoire instructif," 1716, 38-39; see also J. Clinebell J. Thompson, "Sovereignty and Self-Determination; The Rights of Native Americans under International Law," *Buffalo Law Review*, 27 (1978), 713.

> In my opinion, it is beyond controversy that they did not—that so far from being abolished, they were left in full force, and were not even modified in the slightest degree in regard to the civil rights of the natives.[24]

Royal policy was outlined for Governor Courcelle soon after the Crown abrogated government by charter companies in 1663. He was reminded that although the primary objective remained the Indians' rapid conversion to Catholicism, it was imperative that "the officers, soldiers, and all his adult subjects treat the Indians with kindness, justice and equity, without ever causing them any hurt or violence." The second objective was the Indians' eventual assimilation into French civil and commercial life provided "all this be carried out in goodwill and that these Indians take it up out of their own interest."[25]

This innovative dualism of Native self-determination under French sovereignty was remarked upon by an observant Spanish visitor to eighteenth-century Louisbourg. He wrote:

> These natives, whom the French term savages, were not absolutely subjects of the King of France, nor entirely independent of him. They acknowledged him lord of the country, but without any alteration in their way of living; or submitting themselves to his laws; and so far were they from paying any tribute, that they received annually from the King of France a quantity of apparel, gunpowder and muskets, brandy and several kinds of tools, in order to keep them quiet and attached to the French interest; and this has also been the political practice of the crown with regard to the savages of Canada.[26]

It was not merely a European interpretation of the unique French relationship with the Amerindians but the Native peoples themselves were explicit in their declarations. When British officers tried to get Micmac headmen to swear allegiance to King George I in 1715, they consulted their councils and concluded that "they did not want any king to say that he had taken possession of their land." They affirmed that the French could not have ceded their rights to Britain by the Treaty of Utrecht since they had always been allies and "brothers" of the French and independent.[27] The Abenakis made the same affirmations ten years later, and as late as 1752 responded to the official delegate of the Governor at Boston in these terms:

---

[24] Cited in Brian Slattery, *Canadian Native Law Cases* (Saskatoon, 1980), I, 77.
[25] *Collection de Manuscrits*, I, 125.
[26] Jorge Juan y Antonio d'Ulloa, *A Voyage to South America* (London, 1806), pp. 376-377, as cited in Dickason, "Europeans and Amerindians," p. 193.
[27] PAC, MG 1, Series C11A, Vol. 35, Ramezay to Governor, 16 September 1715, 120.

We are entirely free; we are allies of the King of France, from whom we have received the Faith and all sorts of assistance in our necessities; we love that Monarch, and we are strongly attached to his interests.[28]

In the autumn of 1748, Governor La Galissonière and intendant François Bigot met with eighty Iroquois delegates in the audience hall of the Chateau St-Louis in Quebec. As a result of this conference, officials at Versailles could reaffirm their belief that "these Indians claim to be and in effect are independent of all nations, and their lands incontestably belong to them." La Galissonière was congratulated for having "induced them to maintain their rights" against British claims. "These nations govern themselves alone," said a report noting that they were becoming "more friends and allies of the French." In fact a number of Iroquois did choose to leave their territory to take up residence in the French colony at that time.[29]

The other side of this coin, so to speak, was well illustrated by an incident which occurred at the reserve at La Présentation (Ogdensburg). The abbé Picquet had had to obtain "the consent necessary from the Iroquois nations" to proceed with his project to found this reserve in 1748. The grant was made without any thought of alienation of lands but with the idea simply of extending the rights and privileges to others which they themselves enjoyed on ancestral lands given them by the Great Spirit. No payment was made for such lands. When Governor Vaudreuil made the mistake of recognizing as "chief of the cabin" at La Présentation a certain Onondaga who had not been chosen in the traditional way, the abbé Picquet went with a delegation of sixty Iroquois to wait on the Governor and protest an action "which seemed to them to be contrary to the rights of a free and warlike people, which recognizes as chiefs only those they give themselves and for the term they wish." Vaudreuil backed down hurriedly, said there had been a "misunderstanding," reaffirmed the Native council's authority, and made suitable presents of pikes and stiff collars to the seven war chiefs to wash away the stain of his momentary lapse of good judgment.[30]

While it seems clear that the French had succeeded in having their sovereignty in New France recognized in international circles, and never having it seriously contested by the Amerindians, the right to Native self-determination was never denied by Versailles. Recognition of French sovereignty was usually expressed in terms of

---

[28] E.B. O'Callaghan, ed., *Documents relative to the Colonial History of the State of New York* (Albany, 1855), X, 5 July 1752, 253.

[29] *Rapport de l'Archiviste de la Province de Quebec pour 1921-22* (Quebec, 1922), "Acte authentique des Six nations Iroquoises sur leur Indépendance," 2 novembre 1748, p. 108; AC (Paris), Series B, Vol. 89, Rouillé to La Jonquière, 4 May 1749, f. 67; PAC, MG 5, B-1, Vol. 24, "Discussions sur les limites du Canada," 9 mai 1755, 354.

[30] PAC, MG 18, G-1, La Jonquière Papers, King to La Jonquière, 30 April 1749, p. 12; AC (Paris), Series B. Vol. 87, Maurepas to La Galissonière, 23 June 1748, f. 7; André Chagny, *François Picquet Le Canadien (1708-1781)* (Paris, 1913), pp. 304-307.

receiving the French as "brothers," the Governor-General as Onontio, and His Most Christian Majesty as Onontio-Goa, their "Father." The acceptance of missionaries, the concluding of military pacts and the conduct of trade were intertwined aspects of mutually beneficial and mutually binding relations from which it became almost impossible for either the French or the Amerindians to extricate themselves. Although the French never doubted that sovereignty resided in their Crown, they sensed that Amerindian independence and self-esteem would never permit a political relationship that went beyond voluntary association. In exchange for the recognition of their nationhood, Native collectivities submitted to what European nations considered to be French sovereignty.

This dualistic approach was not unique in European dealings with an expanding known world. Two different treaty systems evolved: a European continental system in which the Great Powers dealt among themselves, and an extended treaty system in which they dealt with the rest of the world using "a different timetable than the strictly European system."[31]

Finally, one might ask what was the status of Native possessory and territorial rights under the sovereignty-association arrangement just described. Even if the French recognized and legitimized existing Native customs and practices in this domain, there remains much obscurity. Little is known about the diverse and flexible patterns and concepts of Amerindian property rights, hunting territories and territorial delimitation. Although various clans, bands, tribes and confederacies differentiated themselves from one another in their occupancy of land, all seem to have recognized some territorial limits. Hunting territories and traditional homelands each had their boundaries. From the days of Jacques Cartier's crossing the "boundary" between the Stadaconans and Hochelagans, and the exacting of tribute by Algonkin bands from Huron and French canoe brigades passing on the Ottawa River, through to the end of the French regime, care was taken about crossing various frontiers.

All Native peoples allocated resources within their territory among themselves, whether in terms of horticultural plots or hunting ranges. Since there are no modern survivals of the aboriginal systems of tenure, or of the social and ecological conditions which formed their historical context, we are obliged to rely on Native oral tradition and scholarly reconstructions. For the Algonkian hunters it may even be that the game animals were reckoned to be the true "owners" of the hunting grounds. Land was no more "owned" by human beings than was the air or the sea. Whether exclusive hunting territories were aboriginal in origin or traced their beginnings to European intrusion and the advent of the fur trade with its demands, a matter of continuing debate among anthropologists, the fact remains that a spiritual relationship to an area as well as practical concerns (sometimes even economic) regulated behaviour. Scholars seem agreed that ownership was not conceived in terms

---

[31] Dorothy V. Jones, *License for Empire. Colonialism by Treaty in Early America* (Chicago, 1982), pp. 5-18.

of modern land tenure; therefore, modern courts have sometimes refused to recognize any Native proprietary rights.[32]

The French administration has been depicted by W.J. Eccles and L.F.S. Upton, among others, as avoiding all definition of Native property and territorial rights, as well as avoiding the Dutch and British ambiguity of purchase. Slattery argued, on the contrary, that recognition of Native possessory and territorial rights was the keystone of French sovereignty. He stressed the fact that France's primary concern was to extend its dominions in North America and it did this by incorporating Native nations under its rule rather than by acquiring lands for European settlement or attempting to extinguish aboriginal title. Through alliances and trading arrangements the French hoped "to attach the Indian nations to the French Crown as subjects and vassals, and thereby obtain dominion over their territories." Consequently, he concluded,

> The Crown's rights to the soil were to be held, not to the exclusion of the indigenous peoples, but through them. This approach was consonant with the economic gains initially sought for the establishment of French colonies in America, which centred upon the fur trade, and depended upon the Indians' retention of their hunting territories.[33]

Property has two aspects. There are first of all the privileges and benefits which derive from the exclusive use of property. Secondly, there is the power which control of property puts into the hands of a seigneur or feudal owner. In the area of French settlement the seigneurs enjoyed both revenues from their *censitaires* and privileges and honours under the Crown. In the Native regions, however, the aspects of property were separated with the Amerindians retaining their territories and enjoying the fruits of their property, yet remaining theoretically subject to the rights of the King of France as superior lord. This relationship flowed naturally from Samuel Pufendorf's definition of usufruct, "a right in a thing which belongs to another," in *De Jure Naturae et Gentium* (1688). He wrote:

---

[32] Ralph Linton, "Land Tenure in Aboriginal America," in O. Lafarge, ed., *The Changing Indian* (Norman, 1943), pp. 53-54; John C. McManus, "An Economic Analysis of Indian Behaviour in the North American Fur Trade," *Journal of Economic History*, 32, No. 1 (March 1972), pp. 39, 43, 49; Adrian Tanner, *Bringing Home Animals* (St. John's, 1979), pp. 182, 187, 190; Daniel Francis & Toby Morantz, *Partners in Furs* (Montreal, 1983), pp. 95-97, 120, 126-7, 170; A.H. Snow, *The Question of Aborigines in the Law and Practice of Nations* (Northbrook, 1972), pp. 72-75.

[33] Brian Slattery, "The Land Rights of Indigenous Canadian peoples, as affected by the Crown's acquisition of their Territories," Diss. Oxford University 1979, pp. 91-92.

> For although whoever is the owner of a thing is regularly the owner of its fruits, yet nothing prevents the separation of these two, so that dominion lies with one, and the right to enjoy the fruits with another.[34]

Pufendorf, on the other hand, had also observed that although "usufruct cannot be alienated" it terminated with the death of the usufructuary, or if it had been "left in legacy to a state" Roman law had ruled that "it should terminate after one hundred years."

Among the many affirmations made by French officials two important declarations, one made during the early years of Royal government in Canada and the other in the closing years of the French regime, stand out. The royal instructions to Governor Courcelle in 1665 said that no one was to "take the lands on which they are living under pretext that it would be better and more suitable if they were French." In 1755, the Ministry of War issued a directive governing relations with the "allied nations" of America. It said: "The natives are jealous of their liberty, and one could not without committing an injustice take away from them the primitive right of property to the Lands on which Providence has given them birth and located them."[35]

Access to food resources for Algonkian bands often required the mobility offered only by nomadism. Royal instructions in 1755 repeated views which had been expressed when the French first established forts in the hinterland. The pertinent passage said:

> The allied Natives must be deemed well everywhere...and Sieur de Vaudreuil must leave to certain nations the liberty to wander and go about the lands of the colony, provided that they do not receive foreigners, for that last point is the most essential.[36]

When the Amerindians, like the French inhabitants of Canada, came under British rule in 1760 the French did not forget their "brothers." Article 40 of the Articles of Capitulation of Montreal stated:

> The Savages or Indian allies of his most Christian Majesty, shall be maintained in the Lands they inhabit; if they chose to remain there; they shall not be molested on any pretence whatsoever, for having carried arms, and served his most Christian Majesty; they shall have, as

---

[34] Pufendrod, *De Jure naturae et Gentium*, p. 600.

[35] *Collection de Manuscrits*, I, 175; PAC, MG4, C-1, Article 14, Vol. I, No. 8, "Moyens pratiques pour concilier la France et l'Amérique," (1755), 72.

[36] H.R. Casgrain, ed., *Extrait des Archives* (Quebec, 1890), Instructions to Vaudreuil, 1755, p. 33.

well as the French, liberty of religion, and shall keep their missionaries.[37]

Article 4 of the definitive Treaty of Paris (1763) permitted the inhabitants of Canada, "French and others," to emigrate and protected their property rights. The laws and customs by which the Amerindians had been governed in New France would remain in force until specifically abrogated or changed by the new Sovereign.

It was a well established principle of international law by 1763 that the laws and civil rights of subjects acquired by conquest or cession continued in force unless repugnant to the Crown's sovereignty. In other words, the ancestral rights of Canada's Native peoples were protected as much as the laws and private rights of the French Canadian "new subjects." Just as the Canadian seigneurs and censitaires continued to possess and use their land under their customary law, so the Native peoples as agriculturalists, hunters and fishermen continued to possess and use their ancestral territory according to their group customs under the French regime. The Royal Proclamation of 1763 was the British Crown's formal declaration of adoption of a policy similar to French imperial policy regarding the Native peoples of the upper Canadian region. Just as the French had restricted seigneurial tenure to the St. Lawrence lowlands, with the Crown through its Marine officers regulating all French acquisition of property in the hinterland which had no western boundary, so the British declared a virtually identical area "reserved" to "the several Nations or Tribes of Indians, with whom We are connected, and who live under Our Protection," and closed to European settlement except when voluntarily ceded to the Crown and opened to colonization.[38]

Royal instructions sent to Governor James Murray in December 1763 directed him to gather information concerning the several bodies of Native peoples, "of the manner of their lives, and the Rules and Constitutions by which they are governed and regulated." There was some recognition that under the French regime they had enjoyed a generous measure of independence and non-interference with their indigenous system of internal order. Murray was instructed as follows:

> And You are on no Account to molest or disturb them in the Possession of such Parts of the said Province, as they at present occupy or possess; but to use the best means You can for conciliating their Affections, and uniting them to our Government...[39]

---

[37] Adam Shortt & Arthur G. Doughty, eds., *Documents relative to the Constitutional History of Canada, 1759-1791* (Ottawa, 1918), I, 2, 25-30; PAC, MG17, A-24, Vol. 4, Articles of Capitulation, 1760, 288.

[38] *The Royal Proclamation of 7 October 1763* (London, 1763), *passim*.

[39] PAC, MG17, A-4, Vol. 4, "Mémoire du Canada, 1745-60," 288; Shortt & Doughty, *Documents*, I, 2, 25, 27, 199.

In 1765 the Montagnais asked their missionary, Father Coquart, who had served them since 1746, to intervene with the British authorities to assure that the Royal Domain would not be broken up and lands parcelled out to private owners and that Native hunting and trapping rights not be permitted to lapse. They said, "we have always been a free nation, and we would become slaves, which would be very difficult after having rejoiced for so long in our liberty." General Amherst ordered that matters should "continue on the same footing as previously" under the French regime.[40]

Similarly, the chiefs of the Wabash peoples agreed to the British "taking possession of the Posts in our Country" in 1765 but warned that "we have been informed that the English wherever they settle make the Country their own." They dispute the claim that "when you Conquered the French they gave you this country." Instead, said they:

> That no difference may happen hereafter, we tell you now the French never Conquered [us] neither did they purchase a foot of our Country, nor have [they a right] to give it to you. We gave them liberty to settle for which they always rewarded us & treated us with great Civility while they had it in their power, but as they are become your People, if you expect to keep those Posts, we will expect to have proper returns from you.[41]

A few years later the Hurons of Detroit made similar statements asserting they had previously informed Sir William Johnson at Niagara that the lands on which the French were settled there belonged to the Native people and "they never had sold it to the French."

The British interpretation seems to have been, as it had been earlier in Nova Scotia following the cession of 1713, that all lands had belonged to the French Crown and that the Native "nations" had enjoyed a usufructuary and personal interest in the land.[42] The French had done all they could to guarantee a continuation under British rule of their special relationship with the Amerindians. The transfer of

---

[40] Lorenzo Angers, *Chicoutimi, Poste de Traite (1676-1856)* (Montreal, 1971), 60.

[41] Clarence V. Alvord, ed., *Collections of the Illinois State Historical Library*, Vol. XI: *The New Regime, 1765-1767* (Springfield, 1916), Crogan's Journal, 30 August 1765, 47-48.

[42] Sir Francis Bond Head in 1836 made an assessment which indicated that the British following the Conquest had adopted a policy similar to the French relationship. He said: "Over these lands His Majesty has never exercised his paramount right, except at their request, and for their manifest advantage—within their own communities they have hitherto governed themselves by their own unwritten laws and customs. The lands and property have never been subject to tax or assessment or themselves liable to personal service. As they are not subject to such liabilities, neither do they yet possess the political privileges of His Majesty's subjects generally." PAC, RG10, Vol. 60, Head's reply to House of Assembly, nd.

sovereignty, nevertheless, seemed to imply that legally the Native peoples could only make good such rights as the new Sovereign through his officers recognized.

In summary, the French claim to New France was based on concepts of Christian appropriation, settlement of vacant lands, and effective cultivation and "policing." The establishment of French sovereignty through symbolic acts met with little overt opposition; nevertheless, in the early decades the French did indicate a willingness to resort to the use of force if necessary to establish their claims. French claims were asserted against European rivals. They were not directed against the Native peoples because French settlement was geographically restricted to areas largely uninhabited by them. There were no spectacular confrontations which might have indicated the degree to which the Amerindians understood and accepted French concepts of sovereignty.

Instead, a type of dualism evolved as some Native people accepted the hospitality of the reserves in the French seigneurial tract of the riverine colony and as some French accepted the hospitality offered in the Amerindian hinterlands. The recognition of the independence and rights of Native "nations" under an umbrella of French sovereignty posed no major problems for either Quebec or Versailles. In seventeenth century France, sovereignty was generally deemed to be undivided and indivisible. The realm was governed by an unalterable set of fundamental rules and the monarch was sovereign by divine right. Yet in New France there emerged the concept of sovereignty being divided. In other words, an authority might have full power in one sphere and none in another. This followed closely the geographic division of the Canadian sector of New France into a Laurentian colony of European settlement and a vast *pays d'en haut* or Amerindian region claimed and exploited for commercial, strategic and missionary purposes. Three components of aboriginal rights had been recognized in this upper country: self-rule, as evidenced in the negotiation of alliances and inapplicability of French laws to Native peoples; possessory and territorial rights as evidenced in the need to acquire property for emplacements for forts, missions and a few French agriculturalists; usufructuary rights, specifically unhampered hunting and fishing rights.

The term "nation" was employed for what later would be called a "tribe," to designate an ethnic group and a geographical location. European powers were nation-states whose peoples were politically organized under sovereign governments which possessed coercive powers to maintain order, impose laws and exact dues. The French did not see the Illinois or Micmacs as possessing coercive governments, but they did envisage them as "nations" in the sense that they were ethnic identities, that they were bound by ties of consanguinity, that they thought and acted as a group in terms of defense, trade, religious observances, and that each "nation" had its own distinctive unwritten laws, customs and traditions.

The French operated on different levels of diplomacy in dealing with members of the "family of nations" and the Native "allied nations." On the international level, France like other European powers involved in colonization of America asserted her sovereign rights over a vast continental expanse. At the regional level, dealing with "independent" peoples, she refrained from interference with original territorial rights, customs and mode of life. French laws since 1664 applied only to colonists and were not imposed on Native inhabitants. The relationship with the latter was couched in terms of military alliances, trading arrangements, and the annual payments of the King's presents rather than in terms of the exercise of coercive social and legal powers, taxation and military service.

The Janus-like French position can be understood only when account is taken of the two diplomatic levels or spheres in which French statements must be situated. Sovereignty was stressed in interactions with other nation-states whereas independence was stressed in the context of continental coexistence. The genius of French Native policy was therefore that no inherent contradiction was perceived between these two positions. Nevertheless, pursuit of this line of conduct did require the French to do two things: first, to restrict Canadian settlement almost exclusively to the Lower St. Lawrence valley below the junction of the Ottawa River; secondly, to instruct its marine commandants at upper country posts to be circumspect in their statements and actions when dealing with the "allied Nations." So long as this relationship was maintained it would appear that France could assume responsibility under international law for colonists and aboriginal peoples. Native nationhood was protected by French sovereignty and French sovereignty was exercised through Native nationhood and self-government.

The Society of New France

Section 2

Just as it was necessary for the 17th-century French to come to terms with differences between their culture and that of the Indians, so we must make an effort to understand the differences between French society in 17th or 18th century Canada and Canadian society today.

The authors of these two essays are both historians who have worked extensively with sources in France as well as in Canada, and both have stressed how closely Canada was tied to France in that period. Here they examine two institutions of fundamental importance, one controlled by the French government and an integral part of the imperial structure, the other strongly influenced by the French Church and the values of French society.

Notice how the army in Eccles' essay affected every aspect of Canadian society—even people's daily lives and values. Why did it have so much influence? Notice how important authority and hierarchy were in the family as well as in the army. What would a French-regime Canadian have thought of *our* ideas of individual liberty, free enterprise, and private competition? Why is it that even in the New World, where land was abundant and seemingly free, these authoritarian institutions remained so strong?

For a more general survey of the history of New France, see W.J.Eccles, *France in America*; or Marcel Trudel, *Introduction to New France*.

The Social, Economic, and Political Significance of the Military Establishment in New France[1]

W.J. Eccles

Mirabeau remarked that the primary industry of Prussia was war. The same could as aptly be said of New France. If it were possible to have an accurate accounting—unfortunately, it is not—it likely would be found that the military establishment ran the fur trade a close second as the economic mainstay of the colony. But it was not only the economy that was affected by this establishment. The whole fabric of Canadian society was imbued with the military ethos. This in itself was in remarkable contrast to the Anglo-American colonies. Moreover, the role selected for New France in eighteenth-century French imperial policy was that of the military fortress: a small garrison tied down a much larger enemy force and so prevented it from interfering with more important military operations elsewhere.

Attempts to establish colonies in both North and South America began with Francis I in order to offset the growing power of Spain and the Hapsburgs. They were a distinct failure. French interest in North America was maintained by the fishermen of the Atlantic and Channel ports until the fur trade proved profitable enough to warrant the establishment of permanent settlements in Acadia, and at Quebec to protect and nourish the commercial bases. The religious revival in France in the early seventeenth century provided a further incentive for colonization: to aid the missionary drive as the Roman Catholic orders took up the challenge offered by the pagan Indian nations.

Within a few months of the establishment of the commercial base at Quebec, the French were thrust into military action to aid their Indian commercial partners in their perpetual war with the Iroquois. As the fury of the Iroquois attacks on the struggling French settlements mounted, the peasant-stock colonists were obliged to become soldiers. Every male capable of bearing arms, and many of the women, had to be ready to fight for their lives at a moment's notice. In 1651 Pierre Boucher, captain of Trois Rivières, formed the beleaguered settlers into militia units. Twelve years later the governor of Montreal, Paul de Chomedey, Sieur de Maisonneuve, formed the hard-pressed settlers at this frontier bastion into what he piously called the Militia of the Holy Virgin. The squads of this formation had the distinction of electing their officers, an innovation happily without consequence.[2] The commercial

---

[1] Grants by the Canada Council made it possible to carry out the research, at various times, upon which this article is based. They are herewith gratefully acknowledged.

[2] Gustave Lanctot, "Les Troupes de la Nouvelle France," *Canadian Historical Association Report*, 1926, 40-4. See also E.M. Faillon, *Histoire de la Colonie Française en Canada* (3

companies exploiting the fur trade were loath to provide troops because of the expense. They desired the maximum profit with the minimum overhead. Thus it was the Crown and the Society of Jesus that provided most of the funds to pay the handful of soldiers who were sent to the colony. In 1647 there were one hundred regular troops in garrison at the three centres of settlement: the following year their complement was reduced to sixty-eight.[3]

Eventually, to avert the destruction of the colony by the mass assaults of the Iroquois, the Crown had to intervene. In 1662 Louis XIV despatched one hundred regulars to the colony. Three years later Lieutenant-General de Tracy[4] arrived at Quebec with four companies of regular troops. Four companies of the Carignan-Salières regiment had already arrived and twenty more landed at Quebec two months later. In all, there were now approximately 1300 regular troops in the colony, at a time when the civilian population was estimated to be 2500. In other words, the military now comprised almost 35 per cent of the total European population. This military force, in a rather blundering manner, succeeded in bringing the Iroquois to terms and the colony enjoyed a twenty-year surcease from their devastating attacks.[5]

In addition to gaining security for the settlers, these regular troops brought economic prosperity to the tune of 150,000 *livres* a year for their subsistence alone.[6] The significance of this can be gauged by the fact that Colbert had decreed that the civil budget must not exceed 36,000 *livres* a year.[7] In 1665 Marie de l'Incarnation of the Ursulines commented in a letter to her son: "Money, which was rare in this country is now very common, these gentlemen having brought a great deal with them. They pay for everything they buy with money, both their food and their other necessities, which suits our habitants very well."[8]

When the regiment was recalled to France in 1668 several of the officers and 400 of the men chose to remain. Each man received a discharge grant of 100 *livres*, the

---

[3] vols., Villemarie 1866), III, 13-20, wherein is given a nominal roll of these militia companies.
Lanctot, "Les Troupes de la Nouvelle France."
[4] The importance attached to the Canadian command by Louis XIV can be gauged by the military rank of Tracy. There were four grades of general officers, maréchal de France, lieutenant-général, maréchal de camp, brigadier.
[5] See W.J. Eccles, *Canada under Louis XIV 1663-1701* (Toronto 1964), 39-44.
[6] Paris, France, Archives Nationales, Colonies, D2C, vol. 47, 102.
[7] *Rapport de l'Archiviste de la Province de Québec* 1930-1931 [RAPQ], 70; Archives du Séminaire de Québec, Lettres, Carton N, no. 482.
[8] Joyce Marshall, ed., *Word from New France: The Selected Letters of Marie de l'Incarnation.* Toronto, 1967, 314.

sergeants 150 *livres*.[9] The following year fresh military blood was added to the population when six army captains, twenty-four junior officers, and 333 soldiers arrived as a unit to take up land and settle. They too received a subsistence grant amounting to over 52,000 *livres*.[10] Thus the colony retained, all told, nearly 800 regular officers and men. This figure must have exceeded the number of adult males who were resident in the colony in 1665.[11]

At the same time as these military forces swelled the population a new administrative system was imposed on the colony by the Crown, an administration organized on distinctly military lines. Throughout the regime the governors-general and local governors were career officers in either the Troupes de Terre or the Troupes de la Marine. The office of intendant was part military in origin and still retained a great many purely military functions.[12] The civil population was not subject to military law, but with this notable exception the government of New France was, in essence, military government.

In 1669 the entire male population between the ages of sixteen and sixty was, on orders of the King, organized into militia units. In every parish a company was formed. In the more populous parishes the companies had a captain, a lieutenant, and an ensign; in those more sparsely populated a captain sufficed. In the three governmental districts a commandant of militia, a major, and an aide-major had overall command under the local governors.[13] These officers, almost all of them habitants rather than seigneurs,[14] had to muster the men periodically and ensure that

---

[9] R.G. Thwaites, ed., *Jesuit Relations and Allied Documents* (73 vols., Cleveland 1896-1901), V, 170.

[10] Archives Nationales, Colonies, B. vol. I, 105.

[11] The estimated population was 2500 in 1663, 3215 in 1666. In 1667 Jean Talon had a census taken; his total was 3918 (Dominion Bureau of Statistics, Demography Branch, "Chronological list of Canadian Censuses," 3). These figures are likely too low. See the comments on that score in Jacques Mathieu, "La vie à Québec au milieu de XVIIe siècle. Etude des sources," *Revue d'Histoire de l'Amérique française*, XXIII, 3, déc. 1969, 404-24.

[12] On the origins of the office of intendant see Edmond Esmonin, *Etudes sur la France des XVIIe et XVIIIe siècles* (Paris 1964), 13-112.

[13] RAPQ 1947-8, 278. Vaudreuil et Bégon au Ministre, Que., 20 Sept. 1714.

[14] Cameron Nish, *Les Bourgeois-gentilshommes de la Nouvelle-France 1729-1748* (Montreal 1968), 155-6, seems to imply that the seigneurial class dominated the commissioned ranks of the militia. The ranks above captain, perhaps, but the few seigneurs who were captains of militia appear to be exceptions that prove the rule. In 1712 the Minister of Marine instructed Governor-General Vaudreuil that the seigneurs were to abandon their claim that the *capitaines de milice* must communicate to them the orders they received from the governor or intendant (see RAPQ 1947-8, 146). Moreover, the *capitaines de milice* served as police officers, arresting suspected criminals on orders of the intendant, a task that a seigneur would have considered beneath his dignity. It was ordered that *capitaines de milice* had the right to occupy "le banc le plus honorable" in their parish church, after that of the seigneur. There

they had serviceable muskets and acquired a rudimentary acquaintance with discipline. Neither officers nor men were paid. The intendant Raudot appealed to the minister to grant the *capitaines* an honorarium of 100 *livres* a year and the rank of sergeant in the colonial regular troops,[15] but the Crown, always financially hard pressed, saw no reason why it should pay for what it customarily received for nothing. The captains of militia enjoyed an elevated social status; the men accepted militia service as a proper obligation, if not always cheerfully, at least willingly.[16] In addition to their purely military function the *capitaines de milice*, although appointed by the governor-general, served as agents of the intendant throughout the countryside to see to it that his *ordonnances* were carried out and law and order maintained.[17] What is particularly significant, however, is that the entire male population was armed, and could be swiftly mobilized by its habitant captains. This gave Canada a tremendous advantage in time of war over the adjacent English colonies.

In 1683, when the Iroquois reopened hostilities against the French in the west, the Minister of Marine was reluctantly persuaded to send 150 Troupes de la Marine to Quebec. These were regular troops, raised to guard the French naval bases and to serve in the colonies. They were under the authority, not of the minister of war, but

---

would have been no need for such an *ordonnance* had the seigneurs served as militia captains. See P.G. Roy, ed., *Inventaire des ordonnances des intendants de la Nouvelle-France conservées aux Archives provinciales de Québec* (Beauceville 1919), 161; and also RAPQ 1947-8, 242; RAPQ 1946-7, 385.

[15] Archives Nationales, Colonies, CIIA, vol. 27, 169. This offers additional proof that the *capitaines de milice* were not of the seigneurial class, whose members would have scorned noncommissioned rank in the regulars. A plea the preceding year, 1706, that militia men crippled on active service be paid a small pension was likewise rejected. See RAPQ 1938-9, 158; RAPQ 1939-40, 366.

[16] Only one occasion has been found when the militia objected to serving on a campaign, that of 1739 against the Chickasaws in Louisiana. Pressure had to be applied to make them go. Considering the distance, the ardours, dangers, and length of that campaign, their reluctance was not to be wondered at. See RAPQ 1922-3, 135, Hocquart au Ministre, Quebec, 30 Sept. 1739.

[17] Archives Nationales Colonies, CIIA, vol. 27, 169, Raudot au Ministre, Quebec, 10 Nov. 1707. See also Archives du Quebec, NF 13.8 Procédures judicaires IV, 1730-51, 359-2v wherein a certain Constantin, in 1737, wrote the intendant to inform him of an attempted murder in his district, and opened his letter by stating that it was his duty as *capitaine de milice* of Saint Augustin to investigate all accidents and "régler la police sur les Contestations" that might occur between habitants of the district.

of the minister of marine who guarded his prerogative very jealously.[18] The manner in which these troops were organized was a radical departure from seventeenth-century practice, reflecting Colbert's reforming zeal. They were comprised not in regiments but in independent companies of fifty men, *les compagnies franches de la Marine*, each commanded by a captain. Thus one of the more serious abuses attendant on the European regimental system was obviated. On both the Continent and in England most regiments were the private property of their colonels, bought and sold at very high prices, and expected to bring a reasonable return on the initial investment. In the better French infantry regiments in the eighteenth century the colonelcy cost some 75,000 *livres*, and cavalry regiments more. Companies also had to be purchased, and although commissions below the rank of captain were not strictly venal, a few thousand *livres* frequently had to be forthcoming before a colonel could find room in his regiment for a *lieutenant* or an *enseigne*.[19] No matter how able a junior officer might be, if he lacked money and influence there was little hope of advancement. In the Troupes de la Marine, in contrast, commissions were not purchased and promotion was based squarely on merit, as determined by the governor and the intendant, who submitted a separate annual report on each officer to the minister.

As the Iroquois menace increased, more Troupes de la Marine were sent to Canada until by 1685 they numbered over 1600,[20] at a time when the civilian population was less than 11,000. These troops did not live in barracks but were billeted on the people, and all things considered there was astonishingly little trouble.[21] Moreover, the men provided a sorely needed pool of labour for the colony, working on the land for wages, or in the towns as tradesmen, while most if not all of the officers held seigneuries.[22] They were, in short, well integrated into the colony's social and economic life.

Peter Kalm, the Swedish professor of botany who toured Canada in 1749, was struck by the general prosperity of the regulars. He noted that they were very well fed

---

[18] See the stern rebuke received by Denonville when the minister of marine, Seignelay, learned that the Governor-General had corresponded with Louvois, minister of war, on a very innocent civil matter (Transcript, Public Archives of Canada, Archives Nationales, Colonies, B, vol. 13, 209-310).

[19] Lee Kennet, *The French Armies in the Seven Years' War* (Durham, NC, 1967), 55-6.

[20] Archives Nationales, Colonies, CIIA, vol. 9, 105-7.

[21] For regulations governing the billeting of troops on the *habitants* see P.G. Roy, ed., *Ordonnances, commissions, etc., etc., des intendants et gouverneurs de la Nouvelle-France* (Québec 1924), 105-6, 126-8.

[22] Louise Dechêne, ed., *La correspondance de Vauban relative au Canada* (Ministère des Affaires culturelles, Quebec 1968), 19. In 1740 a sergeant was given permission to establish a tar works. See Roy, ed., *Inventaire des ordonnances des intendants* ... II, 293. On the general subject of the Troupes de la Marine as a source of labour, see W.J. Eccles, *Frontenac: The Courtier Governor* (Toronto 1959), ch. 12.

and clothed, paid regularly, enjoyed good relations with their officers, and were particularly well treated on discharge.[23] These conditions were in marked contrast to those of the regular troops in the adjoining colony, New York. In 1700, on the eve of war, the Lords of Trade complained that the 400 troops supposedly on strength in that province had been reduced to fewer than 200 by death and desertion; that these survivors were in a miserable condition, almost naked and about to perish "by reason of the great arrears that are due unto them."[24] Lord Bellomont, governor of the colony, reported in July 1700:

> The soldiers there in Garrison [at Albany], are in that shameful and miserable condition for the want of cloaths that the like was never seen, in so much that those parts of 'em which modesty forbids me to name, are expos'd to view; the women forced to lay their hands on their eyes as often as they pass by 'em. This sad condition of the Soldiers, does us great hurt with the Indians ...they being a very observing people, measure the greatness of our King, and the conduct of affairs, by the shameful ill plight of the Soldiers.... Some of the old crafty Sachems of the Five Nations, have ask'd ... whether they thought 'em such fools as to believe our King could protect 'em from the French, when he was not able to keep his Soldiers in a condition, as those in Canada are kept; who by the way ... are 1400 men, and duly paid every Saturday in the year.[25]

Society in New France, like virtually all societies in all places at all times, can be divided into two main segments: the mass of the people at the base, and the dominant class comprising perhaps 1 per cent of the population. In Canada the first group comprised the habitants, the artisans and urban labourers. They for the most part did not aspire to rise in the social scale. Satisfied with their status, they were concerned with maintaining their family security, their creature comforts, and simple pleasures. They made up the body of the militia and saw active service in all the colony's wars. As Ruette d'Auteuil remarked in 1715, from infancy the Canadians were accustomed to hunt and fish, to undertake long voyages by canoe, and this had made them tough. Moreover, the wars with the Iroquois, who more often than not subjected their prisoners to unspeakable torture, burning them to death by inches, "au petit feu," had conditioned the Canadians to fight with the utmost ferocity and

---

[23] Adolph B. Benson, ed., *The America of 1750: Peter Kalm's Travels in North America* (Dover edition, New York 1966), I, 381-3.

[24] E.B. O'Callaghan, ed., *Documents Relating to the Colonial History of New York* (15 vols., Albany 1856-83), IV, 701.

[25] Ibid., 681.

desperation, with little regard for their own lives.[26] A swift end was merciful; infinitely preferable to being taken alive.

Between 1608 and 1760 there were barely fifty years of peace all told in Canada. The longest uninterrupted stretch without the militia being engaged in fighting somewhere was the twenty-two years from 1666 to 1684. It is therefore likely that nearly all the able-bodied men served on at least one campaign during their lifetime. In short, with the exception of that one tranquil period, war was the norm in New France. A British observer commented in the mid-eighteenth century on the significant difference between the Canadians and the English colonials as martial men:

> Our men are nothing but a set of farmers and planters, used only to the axe and hoe. Theirs are not only well trained and disciplined, but they are used to arms from their infancy among the Indians; and are reckoned equal, if not superior in that part of the world to veteran troops. These [Canadians] are troops that fight without pay—maintain themselves in the woods without charges—march without baggage—and support themselves without stores, and magazines—we are at immense charges for those purposes.[27]

It was, however, among the dominant class, the colonial "establishment," or elite, that militarism and the military ethos took the firmest hold. Governor-General Denonville, shortly after his arrival in the colony, recommended that the sons of indigent Canadian nobles be sent to France for training as officers in the Guards. His motive was to keep what he regarded as a dangerous group of young hellions out of mischief. He subsequently succeeded in having the officer corps of the Troupes de la Marine opened to the sons of Canadian seigneurs.[28] By the end of the century, of one incomplete list of eighty-seven officers, thirty-five were Canadian born. Of the fifty-two officers born in France, several had married in the colony, acquired seigneuries, and could be regarded as colonials.[29] In addition, several Canadians

---

[26] In a paper read at the International Colloquium on colonial history held at the University of Ottawa in November 1969, Dr. Wilcomb E. Washburn of the Smithsonian Museum pointed out that the torture of prisoners was part of the Indian's ethical framework; that "the warrior represented courage and was expected to demonstrate it as effectively in being killed by his enemies as in killing them." The Canadians came to accept this as a condition of war in the North American environment.

[27] J. Mitchell, *The Contest in America between Great Britain and France* (London 1757), 137-8 [quoted in J.K. Steele, *Guerillas and Grenadiers* (Toronto 1969), 72].

[28] Archives Nationales, Colonies, CIIA, vol. 7, 94-5; vol. 9, 31; vol. 11, 143, 192-3.

[29] Archives Nationales, Colonies, D2C, vol. 47, 253, Mémoire Contenant les noms des officiers des troupes qui sont en Canada....

served as officers in the Troupes de la Marine in France and other of the colonies.[30] By 1753 the officer corps in Canada had become a caste. Commissions were reserved for the sons of Canadian serving officers.[31] In 1733 the Baron de Longueuil, in asking for a commission for one of his sons, plaintively stated that he was the only captain who did not have a son serving as an officer.[32]

Contrary to eighteenth-century custom, Canadian officers had to undergo long and arduous training in the ranks before they were commissioned. This was enough to discourage all but those who were really determined on an active military career. Before being commissioned as junior officers they served as cadets. In this capacity they were supposed to be treated as merely the senior soldiers in their respective companies, receiving the same pay and rations, the same uniforms and equipment as ordinary soldiers. They did, however, show a tendency to take advantage of their social station and their prospects to obtain better treatment than the rank an file. Governor-General Duquesne considered this a sign that the Canadians were becoming "effeminate" and he likely made himself unpopular with the cadets by ordering their officers to curb these pretensions.[33]

Each of the thirty companies was allowed two cadets and they served as such until vacancies occurred among the ensigns. They could, therefore, expect to serve in the ranks as cadets for eight to ten years.[34] In 1719 one cadet, the Sieur de Grandpré, had served for twenty-two years.[35] Moreover, in time of war they saw more than their share of the fighting. They were sent out on the small war parties to raid the English settlements, and with Indian scouting parties to take prisoners for intelligence purposes. To cite but one case, in 1746 the Intendant Hocquart wrote in his annual dispatch to the Minister: "Je ne dois pas oublier de vous parler du fils aîné du Sr. Sabrevois de Bleury, cadet à l'Eguillette, c'est un jeune homme agé de 17 à 18 ans qui depuis un an s'est trouvé dans tous les partis, il a fait de sa main plusieurs prisonniers."[36]

Despite the hazards, the very low pay,[37] and the extreme hardships on military campaigns in the North American wilderness, the members of the Canadian dominant

---

[30] The Brothers Le Moyne are good examples. So too are the three sons of Charles Legardeur de Tilly. See Bibliothèque Nationale, Collection Clairambault, vol. 849, 108.

[31] Archives du Séminaire de Québec, Fonds Verreau, Carton 5, no. 62, Duquesne à Marin, Montréal, 20 juin 1753.

[32] Archives Nationales, Colonies D2C, vol. 48, 19, 7 mars 1733, Canada. Remplacements d'officiers de guerre.

[33] Ibid., Duquesne à Marin, Montréal, 20 juin 1753.

[34] Ibid., vol. 47, 325, 333, 382. Enseignes Vacante 1719.

[35] Ibid., CIIA, vol. 50, 140, Beauharnais au Ministre, Québec, 1 Oct. 1728.

[36] Ibid., vol. 85, p. 357.

[37] Cadets were paid 6 *livres* 15 *sols* a month; *enseignes en second*, 25 *livres*; *enseignes a l'éguillette*, 40 *livres*; *lieutenants*, 60 *livres*; *capitains*, 90 *livres*. The *livre* was equal to one shilling sterling in the early eighteenth century, declining to ten pence by the 1750s.

class were avid for commissions for their sons as soon as they were big enough to handle a musket. In 1707 the Minister rebuked Governor-General Vaudreuil for appointing mere children as cadets. He ordered that in future they must be at least seventeen.[38] Vaudreuil's wife, who although Canadian born had considerable influence at Versailles,[39] pleaded with the Minister to reduce the requisite age to fifteen. The Minister remained adamant;[40] but Madame de Vaudreuil was possessed of remarkable persuasive powers and she argued her case well. "Je n'ay point d'interest Monseigneur," she wrote, "a vous representer que c'étoit un bien pour le pays de recevoir les enfans de famille cadets dans les troupes a l'age de 15 ou 16 ans, cela les forme de bonheure et les rend capables après avoir servi dans les choses aisées de servir dans les occasions les plus difficiles et d'estre de tres bons officiers."[41] By 1729 the age limit had been reduced to fifteen. The Governor and Intendant assured the Minister they would hold the line there.[42]

Given this demand for commissions, with an officer corps totalling around 130, and with the population doubling every generation, the competition among the leading families was extremely keen; in fact, bitter. Thus in the eighteenth century a new "shadow rank" was created, called the *expectative*.[43] Seniority lists were drawn up by the governor-general and intendant for every rank in each company, from cadet to lieutenant. Families pleaded to have their fourteen-year-old sons placed on the *expectative* list for cadetships. Junior cadets given the *expectative* listing acceded to the first vacancies as *cadets àl'éguillettes; expectatives* of the latter rank were next in line to be commissioned *enseignes en second,* and so on up the ranks. In 1745, however, with war raging, the Ministry of Marine ordered the abandonment of the *expectative* lists. Vacancies now had to be filled by those who had distinguished themselves in action, without regard for seniority.[44] This was an excellent means to stimulate an aggressive spirit in the officer corps, not to mention casualties, and hence accelerated promotions.

Much research must be done before definite conclusions can be drawn on the social consequences of this military caste system. Research already carried out depicts the progress of some families up the social scale. The path is clearly marked: the

---

38   RAPQ 1939-40, 375.
39   In 1709 the Marquise de Vaudreuil crossed to France to defend her husband at the Court against his critics. A remarkable woman, she quickly won the favour of the Minister and was appointed assistant governess to the children of the Duc de Berry, Louis XIV's grandson. Her influence in Canadian affairs was very great. See d'Auteuil, Mémoire de l'état présent du Canada, 1712, RAPQ 1922-3, 50.
40   RAPQ 1946-7, 376.
41   Ibid., 409.
42   Archives Nationales, Colonies, CIIA, vol. 50, 6-7, Beauharnois et d'Aigremont au Ministre, Quebec, 1 Oct. 1728; Ibid., vol. 51, 244, Hocquart au Ministre, Quebec, 25 Oct. 1729.
43   Ibid., D2C, vol. 47, 270-1, 303, 319, 405, 417, 423, 431.
44   Ibid., vol. 48, 70.

original settler comes from France as a humble soldier or indentured worker. Four generations later his great-grandson returns to France after the Conquest as an officer and a member of the nobility, holding the Croix de St. Louis for distinguished service. In between is likely a voyageur, a captain of militia, a merchant trader, a local official, a seigneur.[45] There were some 200 lay seigneuries in 1760[46] and it would seem a logical assumption that they comprised the leading colonial families, that is, the dominant class. There were 112 officers in the twenty-eight companies of Troupes de la Marine after 1700, plus several supernumerary officers, and a few Canadians commissioned in the navy proper or serving in France. In addition there were fifty-six cadetships, two per company, making a total of nearly 200 officers or potential officers. It would therefore seem likely that most of the seigneurial families had at least one member in the officer corps, or aspired to gain entry into it.[47] Thus the military ethos, with its aristocratic values, must have dominated the colonial establishment by sheer weight of numbers. The first British governor of Quebec, James Murray, who had good reason to know, commented in 1764, "the Canadians are to a man Soldiers."[48]

This absorption into the military of a goodly proportion of the available supply of brains, initiative, and ability—assuming these qualities to have been required of the officer corps to some degree—may well help to explain why the colony's economic development was not more flourishing. In this connection a brief glance at the population figures is revealing. In 1716 the population of Canada was 20,890 and in 1718, 23,325.[49] In 1717 Governor-General Vaudreuil informed the Minister that there were 4484 Canadians between the ages of fourteen and sixty fit to bear arms;[50] that is, approximately one quarter of the population. If that ratio be taken as the norm, the labour force can be assumed to have numbered one quarter of the total population at a given time. In 1726, therefore, the labour force would have been approximately 8000 of the total population of 31,169.

The next question is, of that number how many could be expected to have had the requisite education, entrepreneurial talent, drive, and adequate supply of capital required to undertake the establishment of large-scale commercial and industrial

---

[45] One has only to peruse Volume II of the *Dictionary of Canadian Biography* (Toronto 1969), to note the prevalence of this social mobility. A few random examples of families that followed the path are Le Moyne, Boucher, Charly St. Ange, Marin, Hertel, Charest.

[46] Richard Colebrook Harris, *The Seigneurial System in Early Canada* (Madison 1966), 38, 62.

[47] It is not without significance that in 1705 Governor-General Vaudreuil succeeded in obtaining royal sanction to grant the officers a month's leave in May and a month in September to allow them to oversee the seeding and harvest on their seigneuries. See RAPQ 1938-9, 42, 98, 120, 170.

[48] Adam Shortt and Arthur G. Doughty, *Documents Relating to the Constitutional History of Canada 1759-1791* (Ottawa 1918), I, 211.

[49] "Chronological List of Canadian Censuses" (Dominion Bureau of Statistics, Ottawa nd).

[50] Archives Nationales, Colonies, CIIA, vol. 36, 100, Vaudreuil au Comte de Toulouse, 1717.

capitalist enterprise? If the arbitrary figure of 1 per cent of the total population be assumed, then the group numbered some 300. Even if that figure be doubled, then the officer corps of the Troupes de la Marine absorbed one-third of the available pool of possible industrialists.[51] Perhaps this helps explain why what little heavy industry there was in New France was capitalised and directed by the state, the wholesale trade largely in the hands of French merchants, and only the retail trade in Canadian hands.[52] The military presence was by no means the only factor affecting this situation. Nor is it at all certain that had military careers not been available and so attractive to the seigneurial class its members would then have devoted their energies to developing the colonial economy on capitalist lines. But that the military option was a significant factor can hardly be doubted, much less ignored.

Another reason frequently advanced for the frailty of the Canadian economy was the dominance of the fur trade, and there is a good deal of evidence to support this thesis. Yet it requires qualification. Until 1696 the trade prospered, providing large profits for the merchant traders and some favoured officers in the Troupes de la Marine who were given command of posts in the west during King William's war, as well as relatively high wages for a few hundred salaried employees—voyageurs, blacksmiths, and *commis*. By that year, 1696, the French beaver market was bankrupt owing to over-production during the preceding years that had completely glutted the market.[53] In desperation the King and his Minister of Marine sought to restrict the beaver trade by abandoning the western posts and withdrawing from the west. For military and political reasons, however, this decision was rescinded. The Indian nations had to be retained in the French alliance, and the garrisoned fur trade posts were essential for this purpose.

In 1700, on the eve of the War of the Spanish Succession, Louis XIV embarked on his imperialist policy in North America to occupy the west from the Great Lakes to the Gulf of Mexico in order to contain the English colonies.[54] The fur trade was now not merely a means to derive commercial profit, but primarily an instrument of French imperial policy. The northern and western Indian nations had to be retained in the French alliance, and this could only be done by making it worth their while to obey French political and military directives. At all costs these allied tribes had to be kept away from the English in peacetime and induced to oppose the enemy in time of war. This required that the French provide the Indians with the goods and services

---

[51] To eliminate this guess work a quantitative and qualitative study of the colony's population will have to be made. This will require a close analysis of such sources as the notarial *greffes* and the judicial records, as well as the more obvious official correspondence. Only in this way will a reasonably accurate picture of the social fabric of the colony emerge. In this connection, see Mathieu, "La vie à Québec au milieu du XVIIe siècle."

[52] Shortt and Doughty, *Documents*, I, 79, General Murray's report of the state of the government of Quebec in Canada, 5 June 1762.

[53] See Eccles, *Frontenac: The Courtier Governor*, 273-94.

[54] Ibid., 334-7.

they demanded in both peace and war. All that the Indians could offer in return was furs in peacetime and military aid, or at least benevolent neutrality, in war. The French had to prevent the establishment by the English of trade relations with these Indian nations. this forced the French crown to subsidize the fur trade, directly and indirectly.

When in 1705, the *Compagnie de la Colonie*, which had taken over the beaver marketing monopoly, was bankrupt, the Crown had to step in and place it in the hands of the *Domaine d'Occident*.[55] At the end of the war, when the Treaty of Utrecht gave the English the right to trade in the west, the Canadian authorities had to employ every possible device to prevent them from taking advantage of this clause.[56] At the posts closest to the English traders the Crown acted as merchant-trader to keep the price of goods lower than private traders could profitably do. For a time the other, more distant, posts were leased to Canadian merchants but this was not a political success. In 1729 Governor Beauharnais had warned that it would be dangerous to lease the posts to merchants since "ces sortes de personnes" had nothing in view but profits.[57] To maintain the Indian alliances the trade was given over to the military commandants at the posts, who were expected to subordinate their private pecuniary interests to the political aims of the Crown.[58] By 1729 ten served in this capacity,[59] and the competition for the appointments was very bitter.[60]

Whether or not this militarization of the fur trade effected the desired improvement in Indian relations is a moot point. The post commandants doled out 20,000 *livres* worth of presents to the Indians, furnished by the Crown; recommended chiefs for the coveted silver and enamel medals presented by the governor-general; provided the services of a blacksmith; and acted as mediator in intertribal disputes.[61] All this cost money; in fact, it cost a lot of money. In 1717 the Council of Marine accepted Governor-General Vaudreuil's estimate of costs amounting to 50,000 *livres* to

---

[55] See Guy Frégault's article "La compagnie de la colonie" in his *Le XVIIIe siècle canadien: Etudes* (Montréal 1968).

[56] See Yves F. Zoltvany, "The Frontier Policy of Philippe de Rigaud de Vaudreuil 1713-1725," *Canadian Historical Review* XLVIII, 3, Sept. 1967.

[57] Archives Nationale, Colonies, CIIA, vol. 50, 31-3.

[58] One clause in the instructions given to Le Gardeur de St Pierre, commandant at the Mer de l'Ouest, read "... il aura pour principal objet de maintenir toutes les nations de ces postes dans les interests du Roy et de la nation française, et faira de son mieux pour les détacher du comerce et des liaisons qu'ils peuvent avoir avec les Anglois," Archives du Séminaire de Québec, Fonds Verreau, Carton 5, no. 33.

[59] Archives Nationales, Colonies, D2C, vol. 47, 402.

[60] RAPQ 1934-5, 52, 54, Mme Bégon à son gendre, Montréal, 28, 29 mars, 2 avril 1749. See also RAPQ 1927-8, 334, Mémoire sur les postes du Canada ... par le chevalier de Raymond.

[61] On these aspects of a post commandant's responsibilities see RAPQ, tome 41, 1963 Journal de Marin, fils, 1753-4; and, archives du Séminaire de Québec, Fonds Verreau, carton 5, nos. 24, 33, 54.

establish three new posts in the far west.[62] In 1754 the total cost borne by the Crown for the maintenance of the western posts was put at 183,427 *livres* a year.[63] Other costs were incurred in wartime when the governor-general and intendant found themselves obliged to raise the prices paid to the Indians for beaver by as much as 50 per cent to keep them from entering into negotiations with the English.[64] The picture was the same in Louisiana. Governor Vaudreuil-Cavagnial declared that only the Choctas post was worth leasing; that at the other posts the price of trade goods had to be subsidized by the Crown. The post at Tombocbé, he stated, had to be maintained to retain the alliance of the Choctas and eliminate English influence. Were it to be abandoned the English would flood into the region.[65] This may help explain why the Louisiana budget climbed from 322,629 *livres* in 1742 to 930,767 in 1752.[66]

Some of these post commandants were reputed to have made vast fortunes out of the fur trade. Even though the reports of the profits they realized were likely greatly exaggerated, the competition among the leading Canadian families for these appointments indicates that there were compensations for an arduous, and hazardous, existence in the distant wilderness. But whatever profits were made there is no evidence that they were invested in the economic development of the colony; rather they appear to have been spent on conspicuous consumption, after the fashion of the nobility. Although the economic climate for capitalist exploitation and development of the colony's resources was not thereby enhanced, the social ambience of the military ruling class was rendered very civilised.

When Peter Kalm visited North America in 1749 he was struck by the wealth of the Albany merchants, and also by their "avarice, selfishness and immeasurable love of money ... their sparing manner of living," and their boorishness.[67] In contrast, continuing on his way to Canada he arrived at Crown Point, where he formed a highly favourable opinion of Canadian society. The commandant of this frontier fort, Captain Paul-Louis Lusignan, is described as "a man of learning and of great politeness [who] heaped kindness upon us, and treated us with as much civility as if we had been his relations.... In short he did us more favours than we could have expected from our own countrymen, and the officers were likewise particularly obliging to us."[68] Twenty years later Captain John Knox, with Amherst's army, entered Montreal immediately after the capitulation and he was taken aback by the

---

[62] *Nouvelle France: Documents Historiques. Correspondance échangée entre les autorités françaises et les gouverneurs et intendants* (Quebec 1893), I, 148-9.
[63] RAPQ 1927-8, 353, Mémoire sur les postes du Canada ... par le chevalier de Raymond.
[64] Archives Nationales, Colonies, CIIA, vol. 85, 3-5.
[65] Guy Frégault, *Le Grand Marquis: Pierre de Rigaud de Vaudreuil et al Louisiane* (Montréal 1962), 264-5.
[66] Ibid., 406-7.
[67] Benson, ed., *The America of 1750*, I, 343-6.
[68] Ibid., 374, 392.

apparent affluence of its citizens. In his journal he noted: "The inhabitants are gay and sprightly ... and from the number of silk robes, laced coats, and powdered heads of both sexes, and almost of all ages, that are perambulating the streets from morning to night, a stranger would be induced to believe Montreal is intirely [sic] inhabited by people of independent and plentiful fortune."[69]

How may we explain that Canadians apparently enjoyed a higher standard of living than their social counterparts in France?[70] The fact that they paid no taxes, except the occasional one for local improvements, and were tithed at half the rate usual in France was one factor. A habitant could have as much land as he could till free for the clearing of it, and paid seigneurial dues—when he paid any at all—amounting to only 10 per cent of his income from the land; but obversely these low seigneurial dues meant that the seigneurs' revenue from their *censitaires* was not great.[71] Moreover, the seigneurial land-holding system precluded the concentration of capital through speculation in land.[72] These negative factors militated against the existence of a poverty-ridden proletariat, hence of concentration of capital and cheap labour; but they did not create affluence.

The colony's main exports consisted of wheat and other foodstuffs in good years, some timber, a few ships, ginseng for a time, and furs. The latter commodity was, of course, the major item. In 1715 Ruette d'Auteuil, one-time attorney-general, estimated the beaver trade to be worth 500,000 to 600,000 *livres* a year. In addition, there were hides for leather and small furs. Of the latter, 250,000 to 300,000 *livres* worth of martin pelts alone were exported. All told, the total was upwards of a million *livres* a year.[73] But from these sums the cost of trade goods, salaries, wages, commissions, freight, insurance, and storage had to be deducted. It has been asserted that between 1675 and 1760 72 per cent of the fur trade revenue went to France, 14 per cent went to Canadian merchant traders, 9 per cent was spread about the colony,

---

[69] Arthur G. Doughty, ed., *An Historical Journal of the Campaigns in North America For the Years 1757, 1758 and 1759, by Captain John Knox* (Champlain Society Publications, Toronto 1914), III, 605.

[70] A great many visitors or newcomers to the colony in the eighteenth century were struck by this phenomenon. Here, too, what is needed is a thorough study of the notarial and judicial records to establish what the living standards actually were. To put them in a clear perspective they would then have to be compared with living standards in France, and in the English colonies. Great care will have to be exercised in the analysis of this quantitative data. For example, that a man died leaving little but debts does not prove that his scale of living had been low, the reverse might well have caused the debts.

[71] See Harris, *The Seigneurial System in Early Canada*, 63-7.

[72] Cameron Nish, in his book *Les Bourgeois-gentilshommes de la Nouvelle-France*, 118-24, asserts the contrary, but in a most unconvincing fashion. Professor R.C. Harris, in contrast, produces sound arguments to demonstrate that speculation in land was virtually negligible. See *The Seigneurial System*, 56-62.

[73] RAPQ 1922-3, 59-60.

and 5 per cent went to the state.[74] In other words, if these figures be accepted then roughly 200,000 *livres* a year, at most, remained in the colony; about 140,000 *livres* of that amount being divided among perhaps twenty or thirty families.[75]

There was, however, another major source of revenue: the military establishment. Every year the Crown spent large sums for the maintenance of the regular troops in the colony, and in wartime the amounts spent on fortifications and campaigns, for goods and services, were astronomical. With money flowing into the colony to maintain the military machine there was no great need, hence little incentive, to be frugal in order to amass capital to develop the colony's resources.

Unfortunately, French government accounting practice in the eighteenth century was utterly chaotic and usually a few years in arrears.[76] In 1712, before military expenditures really soared, Ruette d'Auteuil stated that the cost of maintaining the troops in the colony amounted to 150,000 *livres*, with another 150,000 *livres* going to the civil administration an a modest 25,000 to fortifications.[77] Prior to 1730, expenditures by the Crown amounted to about 500,000 *livres* a year, about 600,000 down to 1743, and in the millions from then on. A large share of these amounts was spent on fortifications, and in providing profits and employment for merchants, habitants, and artisans. In 1710, for example, 150,000 *livres* were spent on fortifications when an English assault was expected.[78] In 1745 the extraordinary defence expenditures for Quebec and Louisiana, but mostly for Quebec, amounted—according to the Minister of Marine—to 681,408 *livres* 14 *sols*.[79] The following year the bill for military construction at Quebec alone was 186,102 *livres* 14 *sols*.[80] In 1736 the amount spent for supplies to maintain a garrison strength of seventy-two men at Crown Point for one year was 13,537 *livres* 14 *sols* 10 *deniers*;[81] and in 1745 the cost of maintaining Fort St Frédéric for the year amounted to 76,000

---

[74] Jean Hamelin, *Economie et société en Nouvelle-France* (Quebec 1960), 51-7.

[75] In 1715, thirty-two individuals hired voyageurs at Montreal to transport goods to the West. Some of them may have been French merchants, or the agents of French traders. The number of voyageurs hired and of hirers increased very rapidly over the succeeding years. See "Répertoire des engagements pour l'ouest conservés dans les archives judiciaires de Montréal (1670-1778), RAPQ 1929-30, 195-466. Unfortunately the répertoire does not give the residence of the employers or the voyageurs.

[76] See Kennet, *The French Armies in the Seven Years' War*, 89-98; and Frégault, *Le XVIIIe siècle canadien*, 289-363.

[77] RAPQ 1922-3, 43.

[78] RAPQ 1946-7, 389.

[79] R. Lamontagne, *Aperçu structural du Canada au XVIIIe siècle* (Montreal 1964), 91.

[80] Archives Nationales, Colonies, CIIA, vol. 85, 354. Extrait des payements faits au Sr Dejauniers, entrepreneur des fortifications de Québec, depuis le 20e aoust 1744, jusqu'au 21 mars 1746.

[81] Ibid., vol. 65, 203-6.

livres.[82] Colonel Bougainville commented in 1757: "La guerre enrichit le Canada." He also noted that the habitants were well provided with silver platters, bowls, and goblets, manufactured from melted-down *écus*.[83]

Not only was the economy and the social ethos of the colony dominated by the military, the political effects were also very significant. The fact that commissions in the colonial regular troops were reserved for Canadians, for the sons of serving officers, in fact[84] ensured the maintenance of close ties between the Canadian dominant class and the metropolitan government. This in turn ensured stability for the colonial administration. Entry into the officer corps, and promotion, was dependent on the recommendations of the governor-general and the intendant to the minister of marine. The annual report of the intendant on the state of the troops contained terse comments on the character, ability, and economic circumstances of each officer. Petitions from Canadians for commissions for their sons were forwarded with critical comments.[85] Without the recommendation of these two officials appointment and promotion stood little chance. But in the final analysis, the commission and promotion came from the king through the minister. This meant that the Canadian leading families looked first to the senior officials, who were the creatures of the metropolitan government, then to the senior officials in the Ministry of Marine for the realization of their hopes and ambitions. This condition was in marked contrast to the situation in the English colonies where only the governors, a handful of royal officials, and, to a lesser degree, the appointed members of the provincial councils—usually twelve in number—had ties with the metropolitan government.[86]

In Canada colonial society came to be divided into two main groups, which can be labelled Metropolitans and Provincials. The Metropolitans were the dominant force in colonial society; to use a modern colloquial term, the Establishment. Because they looked to France for the advancement of their careers, and the careers of their children, the development of anything akin to Canadian nationalism, or even particularism, was out of the question.[87] they regarded themselves primarily as

---

82 Ibid., vol. 85, 388.

83 RAPQ 1923-4, 57, 64. In his article, "Les finances canadiennes," *Le XVIIIe siècle canadien*, 336, Frégault gives statistics for military expenditures during the years 1744 to 1751, showing a climb from nearly half a million *livres* to almost a million and a quarter. In 1748 Bigot arrived at Quebec, two years later military expenditures doubled. It is doubtful if the Canadians derived much benefit from the increase, but even so, Bougainville's comment on the habitants' possession of silver utensils indicates that some of this wealth was filtering down through Canadian society. At least this data indicates that military expenditure was then a more important factor in the economy than the fur trade.

84 See note 30 above.

85 These reports are to be found in Archives Nationales, Colonies, series D2C.

86 Leonard W. Labaree, *Royal Government in America* (New York 1930), 134 ff.

87 But see George F.G. Stanley, *New France. The Last Phase 1744-1760* (Toronto 1968), 272.

citizens of France—resident overseas. The bitter resentment in the Spanish colonies of the *creoles* against the *peninsulares* was conspicuously absent in Canada. Only during the final years of the Seven Years' War did anything resembling it begin to develop, and even then it was mainly a clash of personalities at the top level; specifically, between Montcalm and Vaudreuil.[88] Lower down the scale it was manifested more by the French officers of the Troupes de Terre than by the Canadian officers and officials.

The mass of the Canadians, the Provincials—habitants, artisans, town workers, and shopkeepers—had few ties with France. Their economic existence, their peculiar mores, virtually everything in their lives was firmly rooted in Canada where, by the eighteenth century, the overwhelming majority had been born. Although they regarded themselves as Canadians and were readily distinguishable as such, without grievances—either real or imagined—social friction, propaganda, and direction from above, the virus of nationalism could not take hold amongst these Provincials. Between the Canadian habitants and the French regular soldiers recently come from France, relations appear to have been good. At least there is little evidence to the contrary, and negative evidence is significant in this case. Many of these French troops married Canadian girls and at the capitulation in 1760 some 2000 of them chose to "filer à l'Anglais." They stayed in Canada, with the connivance of the Canadians.[89]

Finally, the military role played by Canada in French imperial policy explains much that is otherwise baffling. One of the main motives for the attempts to establish a French colony in North America in the sixteenth century was to counter the growing power of Spain. In this it failed and Spanish power was eventually

---

[88] This raises an interesting point that, in passing, deserves elucidation. When the governorship of Montreal fell vacant in 1755 Vaudreuil made a strong plea that his brother, Rigaud, governor of Trois Rivières, be given the appointment since this, he claimed, had come to be regarded as the normal succession. The Minister, however, was reluctant to appoint Rigaud because in the event of the sudden demise of the governor-general it was customary for the governor of Montreal to take over in the interim, and Rigaud clearly lacked the qualities needed for the post. It was therefore proposed to appoint a young *Capitaine de Vaisseau* governor of Montreal, who would there gain the administrative experience needed to succeed Vaudreuil. Vaudreuil, however, seeing his brother's advancement in jeopardy, opposed the suggestion strongly. He declared that if Rigaud were passed over he should be granted an honourable retirement. He also argued that the Canadian upper class would thereby be greatly offended and their zeal for the service reduced. There might have been some truth in this last, or there might not. In fact, reasons could be advanced for the opposite being more likely to be true. In any event, Vaudreuil was pleading a special case, hence his statement requires corroboration from other sources.

[89] Henri-Raymond Casgrain, ed., *Collection des Manuscrits du Maréchal de Lévis en Canada de 1756 à 1760* (Montréal and Québec 1887-95), II: *Lettres du Chevalier de Lévis concernant la guerre du Canada (1756-1760)*, 387-8.

contained by other means. In the first half of the seventeenth century commercial colonies and missionary bases were established in Acadia and the St. Lawrence valley. The one was temporarily crippled by the English and Scots, the other almost destroyed by the Iroquois. In 1663 the Crown took over and consolidated both colonies; but neither lived up to the expectations of Colbert, who desired commercial and industrial expansion comparable to that of the English colonies. Here again a main aim was to counter the growing economic power of European rivals, the Netherlands and England.

At the end of the seventeenth century the Canadian beaver trade was bankrupt, the colony an economic liability, and fears were expressed that France would withdraw its support, abandoning the colonists to fend for themselves. Then, suddenly, almost overnight, New France became vitally important. During the winter of 1700-1, with the onset of the War of the Spanish Succession, Louis XIV adopted a policy of imperialism in North America to contain the English colonies and protect Mexico. From Acadia to Louisiana a fortified zone was to be established behind the English colonies.[90] The loss of part of Acadia necessitated the creation of the naval base at Louisbourg at immense cost. This line of fortifications from the Atlantic to the Gulf of Mexico was maintained and strengthened during the ensuing thirty years peace.

In the 1740s this peace was threatened by the war hawks of England who were greatly alarmed by the rapid expansion of French overseas trade. They feared that unless French commerce were curbed it would overtake that of England and drive the English out of some of their more profitable markets, as had already happened in the Levant and had begun in the Spanish empire. The ensuing war of the Austrian Succession damaged French commerce considerably, not enough to cripple it, but enough to indicate that a better conducted spoiling war would have the desired effect.[91] England therefore was determined to renew hostilities at the first opportunity, but this next time to reduce its continental commitment to the minimum and devote itself to gaining maritime supremacy in order to destroy French overseas trade.[92]

The French, fully aware of England's strategic aims, had to find some means to counter them. The policy they adopted was intended to force the English on the defensive by attacking Hanover, and by compelling them to disperse their powerful navy to protect their own colonies. This would have the desired effect of preventing the Royal Navy blockading the continental ports and scouring the Atlantic shipping

---

[90] See Eccles, *Frontenac: The Courier Governor*, 334-7.

[91] See Roland Mousnier et Ernest Labrousse, *Histoire générale des civilisations, V: Le XVIIIe siècle* (Paris 1955), 213; Paul Vaucher, *Robert Walpole et la politique de Fleury (1731-1742)* (Paris 1924), 298-302.

[92] See E.E. Rich, ed., *The Cambridge Economic History of Europe* (Cambridge 1967), IV, 536-7.

lanes. The French colonies in North America were to play a major role in the execution of this global strategy, and Canada was a key base.[93]

On the eve of the Seven Years' War France made the first move by seizing the Ohio valley, driving out the Anglo-American fur traders and land speculators. The governor-general of Canada, Galissonière, had advocated this move to force the English to send large military and naval forces to America. He was confident that the Canadians, with some help from France, could contain them by exerting strong pressure on the frontiers of the English colonies.[94] Given the superior military organization of New France, their control of the communication routes along the continent's major waterways, and the contrasting military records of the Canadians and Anglo-Americans in the previous wars, he had good cause to be confident of the outcome. Thus relatively small forces in Canada would tie down a much larger enemy force in the forthcoming global struggle.

In the early years of the war this policy enjoyed considerable success, but eventually the French forces in Canada were obliged to surrender. England was then able to withdraw the bulk of its military forces for service on other theatres. In short, Canada had failed to fulfil successfully its intended role in French imperial strategy.

This failure likely weighed heavily in the Duc de Choiseul's decision to abandon Louisiana and relinquish all thought of regaining Canada. His main concern was to obtain a peace settlement on almost any terms. The longer the war lasted, the worse the French position became. Peace was imperative in order to recuperate, rebuild, then renew the conflict five years hence. France and the other European powers were convinced that England was bent on world dominance and had already gone a long way towards achieving it. The whole aim of French foreign policy now centred on the need to strengthen the Family Compact, then rebuild the naval forces of France and Spain sufficiently to protect their own maritime trade, and cripple that of England. In this strategy it was intended that Canada would, once more, play its old fortress role—but in a markedly different fashion. The Duc de Choiseul now believed that his policy of revenge, of restoring the balance of power in Europe, would be better served were Canada retained by England and Louisiana ceded to Spain.[95] In December 1759 he had consoled himself for the inevitable loss of Canada, following on the fall of Quebec, with the thought that this would increase the strength of the Anglo-Americans and foster their latent urge to strike out for independence.[96]

As had others before him, Choiseul clearly foresaw the removal of French power in North America as leading to the revolt of England's American colonies and the

---

[93] See W.J. Eccles, *The Canadian Frontier 1534-1760* (New York 1969), 154-6.
[94] Ibid.
[95] Ministère des Affaires Etrangères, Mémoires et Documents, Espagne, vol. 574, 26-7, Choiseul au Marquis d'Ossun, à Paris, 23 fev. 1762; 149-50, à Versailles, 17 mai 1762; Ibid., Mémoires et Documents, Angleterre, vol. 445, 21-4, Choiseul à M. de Bussy, Versailles, 4 juil. 1761.
[96] Bibliothèque Nationale, Manuscrits français, Nouvelles acquisitions, vol. 1041, 44-63.

disruption of her commercial empire.[97] This is, of course, exactly what happened. Canada in the hands of the British finally fulfilled the purpose that France had long before assigned to it. Ironically, it did this at no cost to France but at immense cost to Britain. With the benefit of hindsight it would appear that England, in 1763, would have been wiser for both political and economic reasons to insist that France retain Canada.

After the Conquest the military establishment again became a major factor in the colonial economy. It was also a heavy drain on the imperial exchequer. In 1765 the merchants of Quebec and Montreal pleaded with the British government to maintain a large garrison in the province and to embark on a naval construction program to avert economic collapse. They pointed out that military expenditures had always been the mainstay of the colony.[98] In 1800 Britain's annual expenditure for the military in Upper and Lower Canada alone was estimated at £260,000, and it increased steadily.[99] The War of 1812 poured money into British north America, and the flow did not stop with the Treaty of Ghent. In 1828 the estimates for Kingston and Halifax amounted to £330,644 and by 1843 the military establishment of 9000 men was costing the British taxpayer £698,000 plus £34,000 for civil departments, including the clergy and Indians affairs.[100] In short, for the better part of two centuries war, and the threat of war, was one of the great staples of the Canadian economy. As for the influence of the military on post-conquest Canadian society, that topic is long overdue for thorough investigation.

---

[97] The abandonment of Canada to Britain to achieve this end was advocated in December 1758 by a senior official in the Ministry of Marine, the Marquis de Capellis. See Guy Frégault, *La Guerre de la Conquête* (Montréal 1955), 318-20.

[98] Fernand Ouellet, *Histoire economique et sociale du Québec 1760-1850* (Montréal 1966), 57.

[99] C.P. Stacey, *Canada and the British Army 1840-1871* (London 1936; revised edition 1963), 11.

[100] Hansard, New Series, XIX, 7 July 1828, 1628-30; ibid., 3rd Series, C, 25 July 1848, 831-2.

The Family in New France

John F. Bosher

One of the fundamental changes in Quebec since the 1940s is a marked decline in the birth rate, which has lately become the lowest in Canada.[1] The large family is quickly disappearing, but until recently it was, as is well known, characteristic of French-Canadian society. Furthermore, if we go back to the history of that century and a half before 1763, when Quebec was a French colony, we find that the family, large or small, was a stronger and more prominent group than it is now. It was, indeed, one of the main institutions in New France. The study of it may help to explain how early Canadian civilization is so different from our own.

The typical family of New France may be described in figures drawn from statistical histories, making a sort of statistical portrait.[2] In the early eighteenth century, families had an average of five or six children, but this average includes families in which one of the parents had died and so stopped its growth. Those "arrested" families had, on the average, four or five children, whereas the complete family, in which neither parent had died, had eight or nine. These averages conceal the variety, of course: some 16% of all families had from ten to fourteen children and 2.8% had no less than fifteen children. Death among the children also kept numbers down, and to a degree staggering in comparison with our present-day infant mortality. We now lose twenty or twenty-one babies out of every thousand; but in New France 246 out of every thousand died during the first year of life, and that was normal in the eighteenth century. What the figures suggest is that the small families at the bottom of the statistical scale were made so by the hazards of death, not by the habits or the wishes of the parents. If no parents or children had died, most families would have numbered a dozen or more children. These figures are for the early eighteenth century, it should be added, after the immigration from France had fallen off; and an analysis of the population in 1663 shows it at an earlier stage when four-fifths of all families had no more than from one to six children. But at every stage the family was enormous compared to the average Quebec family in 1951, which had only 2.2 children.

Taken by themselves, the statistical facts for New France may seem to confirm two common traditions about the family habits of all our ancestors: first, that

---

[1] The Canada Yearbook for 1972, 241-242.
[2] Jacques Henripin, *La Population canadienne au début du XVIIIe siècle* (Paris, 1954); Henripin, "From Acceptance of Nature to Control: The Demography of the French Canadians since the Seventeenth Century," in M. Rioux and Y. Martin, *French-Canadian Society*, vol. 1 (Toronto, 1964), 204-216; Marcel Trudel, *La Population du Canada en 1663* (Montreal, 1973); J.N. Biraben, "Le Peuplement du Canada français," *Annales de démographie historiques* (Paris, 1966), 104-139.

women married very young; and secondly, that they tended to be eternally pregnant thereafter and to have a baby every year. Yet the facts for New France—as for old France and England also—contradict both those traditions. The average age of women at their first marriage was nearly twenty-two in New France and about twenty-five in Old France. There are, of course, some well-known cases of girls being married at twelve, which was the youngest a girl might legally marry in New France. In 1637, the explorer Jean Nicollet set an extreme example by marrying an eleven-year-old girl, Marguerite Couillard, who was Champlain's god-daughter. Not many girls followed that example, it appears, because on 12 April 1670 the royal government ordered the Intendant to pay a premium—or a bounty, perhaps—to every girl under sixteen who found a husband, and to every man who married under twenty. The Crown thought it necessary to encourage people to marry younger. For the same purpose, the Crown also decided to help poor families with the dowries for their girls, and this brings to our notice one of the impediments to an early marriage: the dowry, often a struggle for a father to find for a numerous family of girls. For this and other reasons, too, no doubt, some 18% of women did not marry until they were thirty or more; 10% waited until they were thirty-five or over; and 6% until they were over forty. Women married later than tradition and a few famous examples have led us to believe. Men, too, married older—on the average at nearly twenty-seven.

As for the frequency of births in a family, we learn that in New France women tended to have babies about every two years, not every year as legend has held. The demographic effects of such a difference were, of course, enormous; and one historian has concluded that the reason for this pause between babies, a pause of some twenty-three months from birth to birth or fourteen months plus nine months of pregnancy, was that women tended to remain temporarily sterile during the period of breast-feeding.[3]

To sum up, a typical "complete" family, which had not lost a parent, might consist of a father just over forty, a mother in her middle thirties and about eight children ranging from fourteen years of age down to a few weeks old. This may seem to be a very simple conclusion, disappointingly obvious, but it has the great merit of some basis in historical fact.

It leaves us wondering how to account for the phenomenal rate of the population's growth. In 1663, there were just over 3,000 people in New France, and a century later there were perhaps 70,000.[4] The population had multiplied by more than twenty-three. During that century, it appears that less than 10,000 immigrants came from the mother country. The remaining 57,000 people had all been born to the

---

[3] Jacques Henripin, "La Fécondité des ménages canadiens au début du XVIIIe siècle," *Population*, vol. 9 (Paris, 1954), 74-84.

[4] Marcel Trudel, *op. cit.*, 11. Professor Trudel lists 3,035 people, but admits that he is not sure of 221 of them. On immigrants, see Biraben, *Op. cit.*, and Henripin, *La Population canadienne*, ch. II, quoting Georges Langlois, *Histoire de la population canadienne française de Montréal* (1934).

3,000 Canadian families or to immigrant families as they came in, in less than five generations. If the French population had multiplied at that rate during the same century there might have been some 400 million Frenchmen by 1763, whereas there were, in fact, only twenty-two or twenty-three million. Lest we should be tempted to dismiss the figures for New France as improbable, we should glance at the increase during the two centuries after 1763 which amounts to an even more staggering rise of from 70,000 to 5_ million, or an eighty-fold increase. If the French had multiplied as quickly as the French Canadians since 1763 there would be nearly two billion Frenchmen by now, or more than half the population of the entire world. In this context, the figures for the twenty-three-fold increase in New France during the century before 1763 do not seem improbable. But they are nevertheless in need of explanation.

Leaving the mathematics of the problem to the demographers, we may sum up in general terms as follows: if women did not marry so young as we thought; if they had babies half as often as we thought; if nearly one-quarter of those babies died before the age of ten; and if the annual crude death-rate for the country was somewhere between twenty and forty per thousand; then why did the population increase so quickly? Why was the crude birth-rate so much higher than the crude death-rate or from forty-eight to sixty-five per thousand? The answer (and the missing fact in the problem as I have posed it) is that the people of New France had a high propensity to marry. They were exceptionally fond of the married state.

People in Quebec today marry at an annual rate of about seven or eight per thousand, which is below our national average. The French during the eighteenth century used to marry at the rate of about 16.5 per thousand. But in the colony of New France, the marriage rate was between 17.5 and 23.5 per thousand. The result of this high marriage rate was that from 30% to 40% of the total population were married or widowed, and this proportion seemed to be increasing in the first half of the eighteenth century.[5]

In addition to this, we find a marked tendency to re-marry. Nearly one-fifth of married men married twice, and nearly one-fifth of families had fathers who had been married before. Widows were not snapped up quite so quickly as Peter Kalm and other travellers like to think, but the average widow re-married after three years of widowhood. One way or another very few women reached the age of forty without having married and even re-married. The re-marriage rate was 163 per thousand or nearly twice as high as in 1948.

Another figure that may reflect the strong propensity to marry is the low rate of illegitimacy: it seems to have been not more than ten or twelve per thousand whereas in 1969 the average in Quebec was seventy-six per thousand. We are, I think, obliged to conclude from all the evidence that Canadians were fond of the married state and that this is one reason for the high birth rate. For all that the frontier, like any frontier, had large numbers of single young men, and for all that many Canadians

---

5   Trudel finds that in 1663, the proportion was nearly 50 per cent (*op. cit.* 74).

were attracted by the adventurous life of the *coureurs de bois,* the society as a whole consisted mainly of married people with families. After all, the *coureurs de bois* were not very numerous and not many girls went into religious orders. There were forty-one women in religious orders in 1663 and in 1763 all seven of the orders of nuns numbered only 190 women altogether, a large number of them from France.

The marriage ceremony which these early Canadians went through in such large numbers left people in no doubt about what their main duty was as a couple. Immediately after the couple had been blessed by the officiating priest, the marriage bed was blessed with the sprinkling of holy water, prayers, and exorcisms. The exorcisms were intended to ward off the evil effects of an especially dangerous curse which some enemy of the couple might put on the marriage to make it barren. This curse was known as the *nouage de l'aiguillette,* and on occasion the Church would dissolve a marriage which produced no children on the grounds that this evil magic had made it barren, so important was the procreation of children in that society. And yet the bed in which children were to be conceived and born was not supposed to be a place for pleasure, as the official ceremony for Quebec, *Le rituel du diocèse de Québec,* made very clear. The priest was to say to the newlyweds,

> Remember that your wedding bed will some day be your death bed, from whence your souls will be taken to be sent before God's Tribunal...[6]

When we come to consider why the people of New France married so willingly and in such large numbers we may at first be tempted to think that the Church forced them into it. Marriage was, after all, a Christian institution, one of the seven sacraments of the Church. There was no civil marriage, nor any civil status at all, in New France. All marriages had to be Catholic marriages and priests were forbidden to marry anyone who was not a Catholic. Very few Canadians married Indians, baptized or not, and very few married Protestants. Priests had to make sure that people who wanted to marry were satisfied that God had called them to marriage; that they had been instructed of the duties and religious principles of marriage (for instance, that it was for having children and for no other purpose); that they had made a full and true confession and communion in their parishes; and that they intended to appear and to behave decently on their wedding day, not to give way to the Devil's temptation to dress vainly or to eat and drink too much. In 1682, Bishop Laval spoke out against women coming to church "in scandalous nakedness of the arms, of the shoulders and the throat or being satisfied to cover them with transparent cloth which often serves only to give more lustre to these shameful nudities."[7] We might be inclined to

---

[6] Robert-Lionel Séguin, *La Vie libertine en Nouvelle-France au XVIIe siècle,* vol. 2 (Ottawa, 1972), 365-366.

[7] Paul-André Leclerc, "Le Mariage sous le régime français," *Revenue d'Histoire de l'Amérique française,* vol. XIII (1959), 525.

conclude that it was as good and faithful Catholics in a theocracy that the people of New France were drawn to marriage.

However, we do not have to look very far to see that marriage in that society was not only a religious sacrament, but much else besides. For one thing, weddings were one of the main social events, famous for celebrations lasting several days or even weeks together. That was why most marriages were held in November, January or February, the idle months of the year between the labours of autumn and the labours of spring. Marriage was also set about with pagan customs like the *charivari*, the ritual gathering of young people who made a disturbance outside the house of a widow who had just been married soon after being widowed, or of people of very unequal ages who had married. The crowd shouted until the newlyweds came out and either explained their actions or else paid a fine.[8] Another folk custom, brought from France, like nearly all Quebec customs, was for young people who wished to marry without their parents' consent, or without a proper wedding, to attend a regular church service and announce at the end of it that they regarded themselves as married. This was called *mariage à la gaumine* and was based on a strict and (said the clergy) illegitimate interpretation of the Papal ruling that marriage required the Church's blessing. Although it died out in the eighteenth century, this custom showed that some people viewed the Church's rules as hindrances to marriage. But all these things are only small clues to the irreligious side of marriage. Much more importantly marriage was an act of the family as a business and social enterprise. It was only rarely an act of two free individuals.

In New France, and in Europe at the time, the family was truly the fundamental unit of society and not the frail and limited group we know today. But in New France, the family was particularly important because some of the other French social groups had not taken root here. The typical French peasant lived in a close-knit village with common lands, common taxes, and a collective or communal life reflected in the word "commune" still used in France more or less as a synonym for "village."[9] However, the *habitants* of New France were not peasants, for the most part, and they lived dispersed across the countryside without common lands or duties in a pattern of rural settlement known as *le rang*.[10] Again, tradesmen in France were organized in guilds or *corporations* which governed most aspects of their working lives, but in New France they worked in a much freer and more independent way. The family was therefore a relatively more important social unit.

---

[8] Ibid., 229ff. On "Mariage à la gaumine," see *Le Rapport de l'Archiviste de la Province de Québec* (henceforth cited as RAPQ), 1920-21, 366-407.

[9] Marc Bloch, *Les Caractères originaux de l'Histoire rurale française* (Paris, 1952) [first published in 1931], ch. V.

[10] Pierre Deffontaines, "The *Rang*—Pattern of Rural Settlement in French Canada," in Rioux and Martin, *French-Canadian Society*, 3-18.

In both France and New France, however, as Guy Frégault writes, "The ties of family relationship had extraordinary strength at that time."[11] Four of its basic features will show what I mean. First, the family tended to be a business or agricultural unit with every member expecting to live on the family wealth and in turn expected to take part in the family enterprise. It was also a social enterprise in which every member tried to assist in the advancement of the whole. Families climbed socially like ivy up a wall. The mentality of social advancement at the time may be glimpsed in, for instance, some statements by an eighteenth-century governor whose attitudes may be taken as exemplary in the colony. This is Vaudreuil, who wrote to the minister at Versailles on 15 November 1703: "We have chosen the Honourable Chevalier de Courcy to carry these letters...to you because he is the nephew of Monsieur de Callieres. We have been pleased to give him this honour to let him know the respect we have for the memory of his late uncle." A year later, Vaudreuil wrote to the Minister on behalf of his own children: "I have eight boys and a girl who need the honour of your protection. Three of them are ready for service. I entered the musketeers when I was as young as my oldest. I hope you will have the goodness to grant me for him the company of the Sieur de Maricourt who has died." He then discusses his wife's relations and concludes, "On my side [of the family] I have only one relation, to whom the late Sieur Chevalier de Callieres gave a small office as ensign. I beg you to grant him a lieutenancy..."[12]

Of course patronage extended beyond the family, but the strongest claims were on blood relations and for them. We cannot read very far in any official correspondence of the time without encountering such claims, for there was almost no other way of getting ahead in life. The system of patronage is revealed in a vocabulary all its own, peculiar to the *ancien regime* whether in France or in Canada: *protection* meant patronage; *grâce* referred to a post, a promotion, a pension or a title conferred by a patron or at his request; *estime* was the attitude of the patron towards his *créature* and it was the reason they both alleged for the *grâce*. And *crédit* was the power a friend or relation had to obtain a *grâce* from someone else; whereas *faveur* expressed the power he had to obtain something for himself.

A second feature of the family is that the act of marriage was in part a business event. In particular, the family had to find a dowry for a girl or else she would probably never find a husband. Trying to marry a girl off without a dowry would have been like fishing without bait on the hook. To use another image, the dowry was a sort of marriage "scholarship," and this metaphor seems all the more true when we remember that Talon gave the *filles du Roi* dowries of fifty *livres* in linen and other goods, and that in 1711 the government of New France set aside the sum of 3,000 *livres* to be distributed as dowries among sixty girls. In New France, dowries varied a good deal and they reflect roughly the social level of the family. Here is an

---

[11] Guy Frégault, *Le XVIIIe siècle canadien* (Montreal, 1968), 179.
[12] RAPQ, 1938—39, 21-22 and 49-50.

example of a modest dowry which Magdeleine Boucher brought to her husband, Urbain Baudry Lamarche:

> Two hundred *livres* in silver; four sheets; two table-cloths; six cloth and hemp napkins; a mattress and a blanket; two plates; six pewter spoons and six pewter plates; a pot and a cauldron; a table and two benches; a flour bin; a chest with a lock and key; one cow; two pigs, male and female. The parents gave the bride a suit of clothes and as much underwear as she wanted.[13]

This was a *habitant* family affair, of course. A rich shipping merchant's daughter, at the other end of the scale of commoners, might bring thousands of *livres* to her marriage: Denis Goguet, who retired to La Rochelle after making his fortune in Canada, put up dowries of 50,000 *livres* for his daughters.[14]

The main point about such dowries is that they were family property transferred by legal contract. At the time of the marriage a contract was drawn up before a notary stating this transfer of property and other business terms pertaining to the marriage. Marriage thus had a business side to it and the business negotiations were usually between the families rather than the betrothed couple. As a rule, the families signed these contracts in large numbers; we find the signatures of uncles, aunts, cousins and so on scrawled on the last page. One of the interesting effects of this system is that the wife, represented by her family and bringing considerable property to the marriage, tended to have a greater material equality with her husband than most wives in our time.

Needless to say, therefore, both families were very much interested in arranging the marriage in the first place, and this brings up my third point about the family as enterprise: marriage was a major theatre of the family struggle for social advancement or for security. To marry above the family station was a triumph, a step upward for the entire family. The new link with a grander or more noble family was a source of benefit through the influence it afforded. If the daughter of a successful merchant married a government official or his son, the assumption was likely to be that henceforth they were allies in a common struggle for advancement.

Why, we may wonder, would a family ever allow a marriage with a lesser family? The answer is that wealth attracted the poor but respectable; and respectability attracted the rich but low-born. Or else a powerful merchant or clerical family might be glad to marry into a large family of military officers with strong connections in the army. The benefit would still be mutual. Professor Cameron Nish has shown with many examples how the various social spheres intermarried in New France,

---

[13] Leclerc, *op. cit.*, 59.
[14] Archives départementales de la Charente maritime (La Rochelle), minutes of the notary Delavergne, 10 December 1760 and 4 June 1770.

there being only one ruling class and no such thing as purely military, purely seigneurial or purely administrative families.[15]

The fourth feature of the family was its hierarchy with the father in command, captain of the family enterprise. It is all too easy these days to imagine that paternal authority was merely a rank injustice or a quaint superstition. Far from it. Every enterprise in a competitive world must be under the command of someone or some group with authority to make decisions: a manager, a president, a ship's captain, a general in the army, a board in a company, and so on. The family enterprise in New France and Old France was nearly always under the father, though there were no impediments to a widow taking over her husband's family firm. In France, especially, there were many firms with "widow" in their titles: *La Veuve Charly* of La Rochelle, *La Veuve Augier et fils aîné* of Tonnay-Charente; *La Veuve Courrejolles et fils* of Bayonne, and so on.

It has been said that circumstances in Canada tended to put women and children much higher in the social scheme of things than French women and children and to make them more equal with the husband and father.[16] Yet such a difference was not sanctioned either by custom or by law, and normally the father's authority extended to most things, unless he died, in which case his widow might assume some, though by no means all, of his authority. Parental authority over children may be seen very clearly in the field of marriage. No child could marry without his father's or widowed mother's consent until the age of twenty-five for girls and thirty for men. Until those ages, the children were considered minors. And in a world where life was shorter than it is now, we must add several years to those ages in order to appreciate the significance of that law. Marriage was primarily the family's business and by law as well as by custom the children were expected to make their marriages according to the best interests of the family.

French law provided that if a son, for example, wanted to marry a girl of whom his father did not approve, he might draw up three "respectful applications" (*sommations respectueuses*) at a notary's office, one after the other at a few weeks' intervals. Let me read to you the first respectful application that a certain Jean-Claude Louet made to his father in January 1733. He was then thirty years old and wanted to marry a shoemaker's daughter, but the father did not approve of the marriage.[17]

> My Very Dear Father,
> I am in the throes of misery at finding myself deprived of the kindnesses that I was used to receiving from you. I am extremely pained that your tender impulses which have moved me so often and so deeply are entirely extinct. However, dear father, if I withdraw the obedience and submission that I owe

---

[15] Cameron Nish, *Les Bourgeois-Gentilshommes de la Nouvelle-France*, 1729-1748 (Montreal and Paris, 1968), ch. X, "La Bourgeoisie et le mariage."
[16] Philippe Garigue, *La Vie familiale des canadiens français* (Montreal and Paris, 1962), 16-17.
[17] RAPQ, 1921-22, 60-63.

you it is out of an indispensable obligation to restore the reputation of the one whom I have lost, without which there is no salvation for me.

Finally, dear father, I entreat you in your paternal love, and by all that is dearest to you of your own blood, to let yourself be touched and persuaded by the pitiable fate of the poor girl and the lamentable state to which I have been reduced for so long. You have spoken, I have obeyed. You have sent me away to a place where I have nothing but tears and sighs to console me and keep me company.

I believe, however, that today you will be moved by my woes and will grant me the favour I am asking of you.

From he who is,
My Dear Father,
Your most humble and submissive son,
C. Louet

After the third such letter, the son was then legally entitled to marry because he was thirty years old. Under thirty, if his father still refused to consent the son would have had to wait.

We see in all this that the family was engaged in a collective struggle for survival or advancement, and children could not usually please themselves as individuals but had to act as members of the family team. This state of affairs was not merely a quaint custom, but enforced by the law of the kingdom. The law in New France, as in Old France, was prepared to punish children who disobeyed and defied their fathers; for the government, the Church and the society saw the family in that age as though it were itself a tiny kingdom in which the father, like a king, had almost total authority to rule, reward and punish. In other words, in that society the family appeared as the smallest political cell in the kingdom, modelled on the kingdom itself.

This metaphor is, however, reversible, and if we reverse it we find that the family in that eighteenth-century society served as a general pattern of organization and authority. The Church, for example, appeared to the people as a sort of family because God was presented as a father to be obeyed as one obeyed one's own father. The letter of Claude Louet above reads a little like a prayer. And not only was God a father-like figure, but beneath him there was a whole hierarchy of fathers in authority: the archbishops, the bishops and the priests. Catholic priests were addressed as "father" while the lay brothers were "brothers." The head of an order of nuns was, of course, a "mother superior," and the nuns were either "mother" or "sister." Girls first entering religious orders were expected to bring dowries as though they were being married, and a nun's dowry was not merely a symbol but a substantial sum of money, a piece of land or a parcel of goods. Records of dowries brought to Quebec orders are a useful guide to the wealth of the girls' families: some brought several thousand *livres* in cash, others came with a dowry of annuities or planks, barrels of wine, linen, furniture, wheat and so on.[18] When a Canadian girl chose to go into a monastery, she and her family prepared for the event in somewhat the same way as if she were going to be married, for they saw her as marrying into the church. She joined the church just as she might have joined a husband's family. Of course there were differences, but the similarities are striking.

Listen to the following ecstasies of love written by a woman who spent most of her life in New France: "Oh, beloved of my soul! Where are you and when shall I possess you? When shall I have you for myself and entirely for myself? Ah, I want you, but I do not want only half of you. I want all of you, my Love and my Life...come, then, come Oh my Love! The door of my heart is open to you..." and so on. Now who was this passionate woman? And who was the fortunate man to whom she was so passionately drawn? She was none other than Marie de l'Incarnation, a nun in the seventeenth century and now a saint in the Canadian Catholic calendar; and all these emotional outpourings were addressed to God. She was expressing her vocation, her call to a life in New France in God's service to which she devoted herself passionately. The point is that as these and other such passages show she saw herself as in some sense married to God or to Jesus and in her writings often referred to him as "my dear Husband."[19]

The image of the family was also present in the army. When a soldier wanted to marry, he needed the consent of his captain or other senior officer and of the Governor of New France. These two consents, which were not merely perfunctory, were duly registered by the officiating clergy. Military authority was thus in some measure paternal authority. But all authority which is not defined by clear regulations must inevitably appear as paternal in the sense that it has no limits and may extend, like a father's authority, into personal and family matters.

The political hierarchy, too, was organized on the family plan. What was the King in the Bourbon kingdom but a great father with paternal care of his subjects and paternal authority over them? Under him, the Governor and Intendant were also father figures expected to enforce not the law, but the King's paternal will. They themselves had paternal rights and duties; and this explains why they used their authority in many matters great and small which astonish us. Paternal authority had very different limits from those of men in authority in our world. "You must maintain good order and peace in families," the minister at Versailles wrote to one Canadian governor, "refrain from joining in private discussions except to bring them to an end and not join in them if you cannot settle them, never listen to women's talk, never allow anyone to speak ill of someone else in front of you and never do so yourself..." As the Intendant Raudot said, the colony was supposed to be managed

---

[18] Micheline d'Allaire, "L'Origine sociale des religieuses de l'Hôpital-général de Québec," *La Revue d'Histoire de l'Amérique française* 23 (March 1970): 559-583.

[19] Dom Albert Jamet, ed., *Le Témoignage de Marie de l'Incarnation, Ursuline de Tours et de Québec* (Paris, 1932), 70-72.

"as a good father of a family would manage his estate."[20] When, for instance, the Minister happened to hear of an officer who was not supporting his impoverished mother, he arranged to have the officer punished and part of his pay withheld for the mother.[21]

There were, then, a number of hierarchies of authority in Canada all patterned on the family and all helping to reinforce one another in the Canadian mind. To introduce the rule of law into such a society, as the British tried to do after 1763, was a difficult task. How could it be introduced in a society where all authority was regarded as personal and paternal? Still, under British rule, the change began in New France a quarter of a century before it began in Old France during the French Revolution. Since then the French have reverted frequently to the paternal authority of a father figure such as the Bonaparte emperors and General de Gaulle, not to mention Maréchal Pétain, whose regime used the motto, *Famille, Patrie, Travail*. Let us hope that in Quebec the rule of law has taken a firmer hold on the minds of the people during the past two hundred years, and that the ancient vision of the polity as a family has faded away.

---

20   Guy Frégault, *Le XVIIIe siècle canadien*, 162-163.
21   Ibid., 163-164.

The Conquest

Section 3

The Conquest was obviously a decisive turning-point in French-Canadian history, and it's not surprising that many French-Canadians have seen it as a catastrophic event which seriously harmed their society. According to one very influential but much debated theory, the Conquest virtually destroyed French Canada's business class by depriving it of its familiar financial and commercial relations in France and forcing it to compete against English rivals in a new and unfamiliar empire where it was at a decisive disadvantage.

The implications of this theory were tremendous: they suggested that the Conquest, by forcing the French-Canadians to operate in an English context, had deprived them of the chance for normal economic development and forced a future of poverty and backwardness upon them.

These ideas were worked out by historians at the Université de Montréal in the late 1940s and 50s, and the essay here by Michel Brunet is probably the best known study to present them. Can you tell from this essay why students who took history with Brunet and his colleagues in the 1950s and 60s usually became ardent nationalists and often militant separatists? How, exactly, did the conquest hurt Canadian businessmen, according to Brunet? Where does he look for evidence that they were hurt?

José Igartua, who had studied in the United States and was teaching in Ontario when he wrote his essay, represents a younger generation of historians taking another look at Brunet's ideas. How much does he accept and how much does he reject of Brunet's argument? It has been said that each generation has to write history over again. Is Igartua doing that or is he refining and adding to what had been done before? The most famous attack on Brunet's theory is in Fernand Ouellet, *Economic and Social History of Quebec, 1760-1850*. For a general survey of the post-Conquest period, see Hilda Neatby, *Quebec: The Revolutionary Age*.

The British Conquest and the Decline of the French-Canadian Bourgeoisie

Michel Brunet

For Marxist historians, the bourgeoisie is the ruling class that has been arranging man's exploitation of man for its own benefit ever since the feudal world disappeared. This is a simplistic explanation of the complexities of modern societies.

Another historical school, which we may call idealist, has all but ignored the part played by this middle class in the Western world's development in the past four centuries, and most particularly in the nineteenth. The work of these historians leaves us believing that modern nations and states emerged by chance, in spontaneous generation. Underestimating the importance of economics, these students have laid no stress on the close relations between those controlling a country's economy and those wielding its political power. They forget the constant, intentional influence of the bourgeois elite in all areas of social life.

The idealist and Marxist schools elicited an inevitable reaction. Some historians have attempted to produce a synthesis between these divergent views of contemporary history. Rejecting all determinism, economic or otherwise, the historians of the realist school have sought to give as precise a description as possible of how our modern society was assembled. Maintaining a strictly scientific approach, they have drawn on the development of economic science and sociology.

Their conclusion is unanimous. The capitalist bourgeoisie has been the ruling class in the modern West. From the medieval commune to the New York Skyscraper, without forgetting Montreal's St James Street, this dynamic class has dominated the Atlantic world. In the sixteenth and seventeenth centuries it waxed wealthy in trade and industry. It was the bourgeoisie that gave monarchs their jurists and top civil servants. A number of its sons won distinction in the Church, the magistracy, the sciences, arts, and letters, It played an active part in all artistic and intellectual movements. In its circle, painters, musicians, poets, and writers found patrons as well as a public; without these, they would have been unable to produce their masterworks. Under middle-class influence, political institutions were transformed. This was the class that founded the banks and organized the system of credit. It assumed the leadership of the industrial revolution when it placed science at the disposal of technology, built factories, canals, and railways. The universities, libraries, museums, and research laboratories received its financial support. To Atlantic societies the bourgeoisie gave leaders and orientation.

We can praise or criticize the role of this ruling class in our Western world. No one has the right to deny or downgrade it. Without this elite, no nineteenth-century society was able to develop naturally.

The Bourgeoisie of New France

New France had its bourgeoisie. It filled the positions of command in commerce, industry, the army and the administration. It was composed of noblemen and commoners, of Frenchmen and Canadians. The creation and expansion of the French empire in America cannot be explained without the presence of a ruling class interested in exploiting the wealth of the continent.

The St Lawrence colony, Great Lakes region, and Louisiana were not constituted exclusively of agricultural societies with traditional patriarchal customs. The Canadians of the seventeenth and eighteenth centuries, masters of a rich commercial empire which they exploited themselves, did not believe themselves to have a particularly agricultural vocation. They only discovered that on the day when they were eliminated from the economic life of their country....

During the eighteenth century, the Canadian bourgeoisie consolidated its power and its wealth. The American historian Bernard De Voto gives it this deserved homage: "Only the French knew the fur country thoroughly, the routes to the interior, and the Indians. The most efficient methods of carrying on the commerce, the tricks of the trade, the art of transportation, the systems of exchange and credit were all of French origin."[1] Are we the last to recognize the creative boldness and the success of the Canadian bourgeoisie in the period of New France? In 1717 the metropolitan government gave the merchants of Quebec and Montreal permission to assemble daily to discuss their affairs. Such were the origins of the stock market in Canada....

The Conquest and the Ruling Class

In 1760, then, Canada, like any other Western society which has evolved under normal conditions, had a secular ruling class composed of administrators, military officers, and businessmen. This elite, while perhaps not deserving to be called a grand bourgeoisie, nevertheless satisfied the needs of a modest colonial society of some 60,000 inhabitants. It provided the necessary leadership. Over time, this naturally ambitious elite would have grown and would have played an ever more important role in the development of the country. The Conquest changed all that.

---

[1] Bernard De Voto, *The Course of Empire* (Boston, 1952), quotation given by Arthur Schlesinger, Jr. in a review of De Voto's book, in *The New England Quarterly*, 26 (June 1953), 259.

How did the Conquest affect the fate of the Canadian bourgeoisie?[2] This question has provoked a considerable amount of discussion, some of it even polemical. Such discussion has arisen, however, from a misunderstanding born of inexact and incomplete information. the present study attempts to contribute some clarity to the debate by showing how the defeated side of 1763 lost its bourgeoisie.

Michel Bibaud, F.-X. Garneau and J.-B.-A. Ferland, the first French-Canadian historians, noted that to a degree their fellow countrymen, unlike the other nations whose historical development had been unmarked by an irreparable split, did not have an elite of businessmen, statesmen, administrators, intellectuals and scientists; in a word, they lacked a bourgeoisie. Admittedly, these historians would have had a great deal of difficulty defining the term "bourgeoisie." The absence of this class in French Canada accounts for the very special meaning long assigned to the word by our sociologists and historians, who have used it to identify doctors, notaries, lawyers, and even farmers. The members of these different professions, participating in the creation of wealth and in the country's economic and political leadership, may belong to the capitalist bourgeoisie, but do not in themselves constitute the bourgeoisie.

These historians and their successors, along with the foreigners who have studied the history of Canada since the English Conquest, are unanimous in emphasizing, for example, the leading part played in *Canadien* society after 1760 by the clergy. The Church role had not been as important in the days of New France, however, especially from the late seventeenth century onwards. The colony then had its secular leaders. Pressing their investigations no further, historians, sociologists, and observers have not told us why the conquered *Canadiens* had to rely almost exclusively on their priests for the leadership necessary to any human society. Leadership that was unfortunately improvised and inevitably incomplete. The church had been forced into an unnatural expansion of its substitute role. What had happened to the secular leaders of *Canadien* society?....

It was not until 1899 that Judge Louis-François-Georges Baby issued a thorough study in which he proved with figures that no massive emigration of the ruling classes had occurred.[3] Since that time it has been echoed with a sigh of relief that the Conquest did not deprive the *Canadiens* of their natural leaders.

A reassuring statement which has unfortunately led us to pass over the wretched post-Conquest fortunes of the *Canadien* bourgeoisie. Were the natural leaders of the *Canadien* people free to function in the fullest sense? Did not the Conquest reduce their numbers? Were they not relegated by it to a second-class role? These are the questions we must consider before claiming that the conquered *Canadiens* preserved the structures of their society.

---

[2] By bourgeoisie we mean that elite of wealthy merchants and businessmen, seigneurs, officers and administrators who provided the natural and indispensable leadership for the pre-1760 colonial society.

[3] Louis-F. Baby, "L'exode des classes dirigeantes à la cession du Canada," in *The Canadian Antiquarian and Numismatic Journal*, 3rd. series, 2 (1899), 97-141.

The Business Bourgeoisie and the New Economic Order

In the *Canadien* elite it seems to have been the businessmen who nourished the greatest illusions. They went as far as to see an actual benefit in the Conquest. To comprehend this somewhat arresting reaction we must recall that the businessmen who stayed in the country were among the most impecunious. They did not belong to the group of big businessmen, monopolists and war profiteers. Most of them formed the second stratum of the Canadian capitalist middle class at the end of the French regime, the class of the small entrepreneurs of modest income and ambition. Their limited financial resources and their more or less mediocre personal talents had prevented them from reaching the first rank in the business world. Moreover, not being from the privileged camp, they had received no official protection. They were the noisiest spokesmen for the mass of malcontents. The Bigot administration, and the shocking coups of their more fortunate competitors who were associated with or protected by the intendant, had no severer critics than these men. Let us admit that they were not completely objective. They had long envied the good luck of the Cadets, Péans, and Varins. They rejoiced at their fall, hoping it would benefit them. This selfish hope indicated great naïvety.

Their signs of relief when the conqueror announced that trade would be free may be imagined. This word "freedom" had a fascinating quality for them. One of them, a Monsieur Hervieux, who was a militia captain and a merchant, displayed great enthusiasm. As early as September 25, 1761, when the country's fate had not yet been decided, he told a correspondent in France: "Cease this compassion for us, Monsieur; our fate is less unfortunate than before."[4] He went on to explain that trade no longer depended on the will of a single man, that the farmers were no longer being forced to surrender their produce, and that inflation had stopped. Haldimand hastened to inform Amherst that the colony's middle class seemed to be highly satisfied.[5] The citizens of Montreal—priests, nobles, and bourgeois—showed no reticence as early as February of 1763 in recalling the abuses of a French colonial administration which, according to them, had reduced "the traders of the country" to the role of "silent onlookers of a trade that should be their own."[6] From this petition, signed by 52 members of the "trading Body," we may assume that its signatories had not shared in the lavish contracts of the Seven Years' War. The bourgeois of Quebec, in their docile acceptance of the "decrees of the Supreme Being"

---

[4] Letter quoted in Guy Frégault, *François Bigot, administrateur français*, (Montreal, 1948), II, 334.

[5] Haldimand to Amherst, 26 Dec. 1762, in Public Archives of Canada (PAC), B I: 262.

[6] "Pétition des citoyens de la ville de Montréal à Sa Majesté Britannique," 12 Feb. 1763, in *Documents relatifs à la monnaie, au change et aux finances du Canada sous le régime français* (Ottawa, 1925), II, 970.

that made them "subjects of our new monarch," were confident that the latter would pour his grace and bounty on them. Had they not "experienced, as conquered subjects, in the most marked manner, the mildness, justice, and moderation of his government?"[7]

A memorandum from the new subjects, dated May 1, 1764, accused the French government of having held back the colony's development by refusing to use "tolerance [freedom]." The petitioners envied the "neighbouring colonies" that had been the beneficiaries of a policy inspired by "love of the general good." It was their hope that "this love will be showered on this province."[8] Three traders from Quebec and Montreal, though disappointed in their initial hopes, were confident that England would aid the colony, and that it would prosper along with the mother country. The colony would become a new "Spain," and London "the centre of the trade and wealth of the universe." Their mouths were watering: "Our newly English hearts already experience the purest pleasure at the very thought of this great design.... We are bold to believe that we will be treated as beloved children. We choose to assure ourselves of this in advance."[9]

The illusion persisted. Becoming members of a rich and powerful empire, the *Canadien* businessmen who stayed in the country believed that they were bound to make alluring profits. With Bigot and his cronies gone, they imagined that the country's trade would thenceforth belong to them, and that the new colonial government, with their counsel, would keep a paternal eye on the furthering of their interests. They refused to realize that the Conquest had put them into an even more painfully inferior position than they had suffered in the last years of French rule. Great disappointments were in store for them.

The colony was not long in prospering, but the biggest profits did not go to the *Canadiens*. As early as the capitulation of Montreal, Amherst had invited the merchants of England and the American colonies to settle in the conquest. About a hundred responded to the appeal from 1760 to 1770. The newcomers did not intend to be last in line. After a struggle of more than 70 years New France had finally been taken. The rich commercial empire of the St. Lawrence Valley, the Great Lakes and the Mississippi would henceforth belong to the conquerors. They had not made their conquest to let the *Canadiens* exploit it....

A series of misfortunes fell upon [the *Canadien* traders]. The French government's bankruptcy partly ruined the businessmen of Canada. The bills of exchange on the public treasury and paper notes represented virtually all their liquid assets. They would recover only a small percentage. It is not known exactly how much they lost in that unhappy adventure. Nobody will deny, in any case, that the losses they

---

[7] "Adresse des bourgeois de Québec à l'occasion du Traité de paix," 4 June 1763, in Auguste Gosselin, *L'Eglise du Canada après la conquête* (Quebec, 1916-17), I, 59-60.
[8] "Mémoire par les principaux des nouveaux sujets," 1 May 1765, in PAC, Q 2: 434-461.
[9] Levesque, Lemoine and Porlier to Henry Guinaud, merchant of London, 27 Sept. 1765, in PAC, Dartmouth Papers, 1: 123-133 (M383).

suffered served to aggravate their already precarious situation. Their correspondence with their European suppliers[10] and their petitions to the British government[11] reveal all their anxiety at the thought that they would not be fully reimbursed. Learning of the decision of the French authorities, Mother d'Youville, even if she was ready to "bear her cross," nevertheless lamented: "It is another fire [the month before several houses in Montreal, including the General Hospital itself, had been destroyed by fire] for our poor people and for ourselves."[12]

Ill fortune continued to dog the merchants of Canada. A number of them had placed large orders in France during the war. These goods had not arrived. At the time trade resumed its normal course after the capitulation of Montreal, their warehouses were empty. They made desperate attempts to get the British authorities' permission to take delivery of the goods they had ordered before the end of hostilities in America.[13] These commitments had frozen the little credit they had. With nothing to sell, they could not resume the business that war had interrupted. A truly alarming situation....

The Conquest had reoriented the economic life of the colony. And it was not to the benefit of the new subjects of His Britannic Majesty. Partly ruined by the bankruptcy of the French treasury, unable to receive goods they had ordered before the end of the war, cut off from their previous sources of supply, the Canadian traders

---

[10] Havy, merchant at La Rochelle, to the chevalier d'Ailleboust at Montreal, 28 Feb. 1761, in PAC, Baby Collection (5001); Simon Jauge, merchant of Bordeaux, to F. Baby, 25 Jan., 4 Feb. & 15 May 1763, Lamaletie, Latuilière & Co., of Bordeaux, to M. La Naudière, 5 Apr. 1763, D. Goguet of La Rochelle to M. Pierre Guy, 12 Apr. 1763, Goguet to Mme Veuve Guy, 1 May 1763, Jos. & Henry Guinaud of London to F. Baby, 10 Dec. 1763, M. de Ponthieu & Co. of London to M. La Naudière, 10 Dec. 1763, same to Pierre Guy, 10 Dec. 1763, J. Thouron & Brothers of La Rochelle to M. de La Naudière, 4 Jan. 1764, M. de Ponthieu & Co. to Pierre Guy, 14 Jan. 1764, D. Goguet to same, 29 Feb. 1764, Havy to MM. Baby Frères, 7 Mar. 1764, J. Thouron Frères to Baby Frères, 15 Mar. 1765, all in Baby Collection (5233, 5234, 5247, 5239, 5242, 5246, 3944, 3946, 3947, 3950, 3951, 3952, 3953, 4144).

[11] "Pétition des citoyens de la ville de Montréal à Sa Majesté Britannique," 12 Feb. 1763, in *Documents relatifs à la monnaie*, II, 968-70; Haldimand to Amherst, 12 Feb. 1763, in PAC, B, 1: 266; Murray to Halifax, 17 Nov. 1764, in PAC, Q 2: 352.

[12] Madame d'Youville to Savarie, 18 Sept. 1765, in A. Ferland-Angers, *Mère d'Youville, première fondatrice canadienne* (Montreal, 1945), 231.

[13] "Pétition des citoyens de la ville de Montréal à Sa Majesté Britannique," 12 Feb. 1763, in *Documents relatifs à la monnaie*, II, 970; Simon Jauge to F. Baby, 25 Jan., 4 Feb., 15 May & 14 June 1763, Jacquelin, merchant of La Rochelle, to Pierre Guy, 16 Apr. 1763, D. Goguet to Mme Guy, 1 May 1763, Dhenin to F. Baby, 1 July 1763, D. Goguet to Pierre Guy, 29 Feb. 1764, Thouron & Frères to de La Naudière, 22 Apr. 1764, same to Baby & Frères, 15 Mar. 1765 & 21 Mar. 1766, all in PAC, Baby Collection (5233-4, 5247, 3942, 5244, 5246, 3943, 3952, 4143-5).

found themselves completely at a loss. Their situation was not without a tragic element. The colonial traders were generally unable to pay cash for the goods they did import. Their European suppliers had to extend generous terms. Moreover, no trading activity of any significance can be imagined without the use of credit. By the Conquest, the former markets where they had obtained credit as well as the merchandise they needed were closed to the *Canadien* businessmen. It took them some time to realize what was happening, since for a while they kept trying to re-open trade relations with France. They were in a totally confused state. Weeks after the signing of the Treaty of Paris, François Baby was again attempting to place an order in France. His former supplier wrote him at some length to make him understand how hard it was to continue their business contact:

> I have received your favour of the 7th of this month [Baby was then in Europe]. I foresee numerous difficulties as to your proposed dispatch of a ship of 100 to 120 tons for Quebec. It is not possible to find French ships to charter for that country since French ships would be impounded with their cargoes. I think you are not unaware that entry to Canada is prohibited for all the goods of French factories, as well as wines, brandy, and other beverages. And if these are brought in at present, it is by smuggling, unless they leave directly from England with their duties paid.[14]

One by one, the French exporters took leave of their *Canadien* correspondents,[15] who asked them to recommend them to London traders and transfer to London the meagre credits remaining to them in France.[16] The Montreal merchant Etienne Augé parted regretfully with one of his suppliers, and told him he would like "to be in a position to continue the French business."[17] A letter from François Baby to Simon Jauge sums up the difficulties that had to be faced by every *Canadien* trader:

---

[14] Simon Jauge, merchant of Bordeaux, to F. Baby, 14 June 1763, in PAC, Baby Collection (3942).

[15] Paillet & Meynardie of La Rochelle to Mme Guy, 15 Mar. 1763, Lamaletie, Latuilière & Co. of Bordeaux to de La Naudière, 5 Apr. 1763, Havy of Bordeaux to MM. Baby, 16 Apr. 1763, ibid., (5238-9, 5243).

[16] Simon Jauge to F. Baby, 25 Jan. 1763, Lamaletie, Latuilière & Co. to de La Naudière, 5 Apr. 1763, Daniel Vialars, merchant of London, to Pierre Guy, 11 Apr. 1763, D. Goguet to same, 12 Apr. 1763, M. de Ponthieu & Co. to de La Naudière, 10 Dec. 1763, same to Pierre Guy, 10 Dec. 1763, Etienne Augé, Montreal, to D. Goguet, 6 Apr. 1766, ibid., (5233, 5239, 5241-2, 3946-7, 5696).

[17] Etienne Augé to M. Meynardie of La Rochelle, 18 Oct. 1766, ibid., (5699).

I repeat the request I made to you last year, to have the goodness to send me news of you. You must realize that it is an absolute necessity for me to know the state of my accounts with you. I have reason to expect you to extend to me the benefit of the privileges of a British subject. For heaven's sake, Monsieur, send me through Messrs. Guinaud & Hankey of London a general and detailed accounting of the funds I left with you as well as those I authorized you to withdraw from M. Havy [a La Rochelle merchant]. My family, involved with all this business, has been pressing me for two years to give them an accounting, and I am not in a position to do so, and in consequence am obliged to face many difficult moments.[18]

Advised and recommended by their French correspondents, the *Canadien* merchants approached London businessmen: Joseph and Henry Guinaud, Daniel and Antoine Vialars, Ponthieu & Co., Isidore and Thomas Lynch, Robert Hankey. A number of them were Frenchmen who had settled in England. They appeared well disposed to their new customers.[19] It did not take them long to discover, however, that these were nothing but very small fry in business, without contacts or credit, and with no influence in their own country. And the London merchants with whom the *Canadiens* corresponded were not among the most important in the City. These modest businessmen—those of London and those of the colony—were not substantial enough to compete with their English rivals. For example, Henry Guinaud, the London merchant to whom three *Canadien* dealers unfolded their ambitious future plans in 1765,[20] declared bankruptcy four years later.[21]

The *Canadien* bourgeois abandoned their earlier optimism. Some Montreal businessmen upbraided Daniel Vialars for taking too high a commission. The accused retorted that these Montrealers were moved by "rancour," and gave them to understand that he set very little store by continued relations with them.[22] Etienne Augé appeared more or less discontented with his London suppliers.[23] It must be noted that they had had the unfortunate idea of asking him for a payment.[24] He

---

[18] F. Baby to Simon Jauge, 13 Nov. 1766, ibid., (3836).
[19] Daniel Vialars to Perrault, 25 Feb. 1763, in Archives du Séminaire de Québec (ASQ), Lettres-Carton P: 94; same to Pierre Guy, 11 Apr. 1763, in PAC, Collection Baby (5242); Joseph & Henry Guinaud to F. Baby, 10 Dec. 1763, Ponthieu & Co. to de la Naudière, 10 Dec. 1763, same to Pierre Guy, 10 Dec. 1763 & 14 Jan. 1764, ibid., (3944, 3946-7, 3951).
[20] Levesque, Lemoine and Porlier to Henry Guinaud, 27 Sept. 1765, in PAC, Dartmouth Papers, 1: 126-133.
[21] Henry Guinaud to F. Baby, 5 Dec. 1769, in PAC, Baby Collection (6120).
[22] Daniel Vialars to Pierre Guy, 10 Dec. 1763, ibid., (3945).
[23] I. Lynch & Co. to Etienne Augé, 12 Oct. 1765, ibid., (4927).
[24] Same to same, 6 May 1765, ibid., (4926).

thought he would be better to choose Daniel and Antoine Vialars as correspondents.[25] Relations between the new partners rapidly soured.[26] Augé went knocking at another door.[27] Pierre Guy too approached Thomas Lynch.[28] François Baby learned that one of his former Bordeaux contacts could not advance him the funds he needed to pay one of his creditors.[29] Another refused to honour a bill of exchange drawn on him.[30] The Quebec merchant deplored the general situation: "Business is moving very slowly in the country. Money is scarcer than ever, and bad faith is everywhere."[31] He complained of having received trade goods his customers did not want. He had a surplus in his warehouse and was afraid of not being able to unload it. He begged his suppliers to follow his instructions.[32] M. de La Naudière was dissatisfied with "the Sieur Vialars," who had not filled the order sent to him: "I am waiting to deal with him as he deserves on my arrival in London."[33] Saint-Georges Dupré, a Montreal trader, made no secret of his disappointment on receiving the account for the sale of his furs in London: "I have received your letter, my good friend, with the accounting of the balance of my furs, which you may have found, as I did, sold extremely badly, with a set of charges that swallow a good third of the miserable sale."[34] François Baby came to believe that a certain Mr. Robinson, a fur broker on the London market, favoured a few privileged vendors to the detriment of the others. His London correspondent tried to prove to him that his accusation was unfounded.[35] When a businessman does not succeed while his competitors are prospering, he easily believes himself the victim of a conspiracy.

The *Canadien* merchants saw their profits fall. Several became unable to meet their obligation. A Montreal merchant given the job of recovering the money owing to François Baby did not have an easy time of it.[36] Certain traders became embittered towards their more favoured English rivals. The Montreal dealer Adhémar reported to François Baby: "They tell me that Duperron and Saint-Martin do nothing but curse the Londoners [English merchants] and are always at loggerheads with the notorious

---

[25] Etienne Augé to D. Goguet, 6 Aug. 1766, same to M. Meynardie, 18 Oct. 1766, Antoine Vialars to Etienne Augé, 1 Mar. 1772, ibid., (5696, 5699, 5667).

[26] Antoine Vialars to Etienne Augé, 30 Sept. 1772, Etienne Augé to Antoine Vialars, 31 Jan. 1773, ibid., (5671, 5674).

[27] Thomas Lynch to Etienne Augé, 2 May 1772, ibid., (5670); same to same, 6 Jan. 1773, ibid., (5672).

[28] Thomas Lynch to Pierre Guy, 6 Jan. 1773, ibid., (5673).

[29] Havy to MM. Baby, 7 Mar. 1764, ibid., (3953).

[30] Dhenin of La Rochelle to same, 24 May 1765, ibid., (3958).

[31] F. Baby to Henry Guinaud, 27 June 1765, ibid., (1507).

[32] Same to same, 28 June 1766, ibid., (3834).

[33] La Naudière Jr. to his cousin, 1770, ibid., (1838).

[34] Saint-Georges Dupré to F. Baby, 8 Sept. 1771, ibid., (5602).

[35] Robert Hankey to F. Baby, 4 Dec. 1771, ibid., (6128).

[36] Hervieux Jr. to F. Baby, 27 Feb. & 6 Mar. 1769, ibid., (2946-7).

trader at their post."[37] Hervieux, Pierre Guy, François Baby and Saint-Georges Dupré were deep in lamentation. In their view, economic conditions had never been so bad. Saint-Georges Dupré was in a black mood: "If God abandons me, I'll soon put an end to this most unhappy life."[38]

Was the colony going through a depression? Quite the reverse. From 1765 to 1771, the trade of Canada experienced years of plenty. The end of Pontiac's war lent new impetus to the fur trade. The American colonies' agitation against the Stamp Act and the Townshend duties benefited the traders of Canada, especially those of Montreal. The American patriots' boycott of English goods had the result of increasing British exports to Canada. Montreal replaced Albany as the storage and distribution centre for English products sold in the north of the continent. From Montreal, this merchandise took the trail of the trading posts and even headed for the American colonies. The boycott called by the "Sons of Liberty" was not always effective. Most Americans had not given up the products of England. Farm prices held at an excellent level. As early as 1771, Quebec exports of food began to rise.[39] Even the price of furs was going up; Saint-Georges Dupré, who would contemplate suicide in October of 1771, had informed his cousin of this that same summer.[40]

The *Canadien* businessmen had shown themselves incapable of holding their own against their English competitors. The Conquest had forced them to compete with unequal weapons. This fact dominates the whole of the economic history of French Canada since the Conquest. While La Naudière, François Baby, Pierre Guy, Etienne Augé, Saint-Georges Dupré and their colleagues fought desperately to obtain credit and merchandise, the newcomers had no difficulty tapping the English market. The importers and exporters from England and the American colonies were quite naturally more inclined to do business with their fellow countrymen than with impecunious foreigners, yesterday's enemies and the vanquished of today. In business, only the rich can borrow. The *Canadiens* had to locate new suppliers. These were not always reliable in filling orders placed with them. Often they simply could not do so. The *Canadien* merchants were forced to change their business patterns, to learn new methods, familiarize themselves with English products. The time of groping and uncertainty lasted a number of years.

The financial losses they had suffered had in addition made them extremely timid. When a businessman's capital is limited, the slightest risk makes him afraid. Little by little, the *Canadien* merchants chose to buy from their English competitors in

---

[37] Adhémar to F. Baby, 23 July 1770, ibid., (6129).

[38] Hervieux Jr. to F. Baby, 27 Feb. & 6 Mar. 1769, F. Baby to Pierre Guy, 8 Oct. 1770 & 28 Mar. 1771, Pierre Guy to F. Baby, 16 Jan. 1771, Saint-Georges Dupré to F. Baby, 15 Oct. 1771, ibid., (2946-7, 3839, 3842, 2955, 5603).

[39] See Isabel Craig, "Economic Conditions in Canada, 1763-1783" (unpublished MA thesis, McGill University, 1937), 197-9.

[40] Saint-Georges Dupré to François Baby, 11 Aug. & 2 Sept. 1771, in Baby Collection (5600-1).

Montreal and Quebec. A number of their own customers had been going to the English stores for a long time. The traders decided it was wiser to sell their furs on the local market. The profits might be more modest, but they seemed less risky. A great number looked for safe, gilt-edged investments. They dared not expose their meagre economies to losses in profitable but chancy speculation. Moreover, they knew that the most lucrative speculation was not for them. Saint-Georges Dupré would be happy to invest his money at five or even at four per cent. He advised Baby to do the same.[41] The *Canadien* businessmen had had to give up the great export-import trade, the only significant road to wealth in that period. They left the large profits to others, and sought refuge in an honest mediocrity.

Obliged to abandon external commerce to the English merchants, the *Canadiens* also lost control of the fur trade. The two formed a whole. The fur trade was still the great wealth of the colony. It would be so until the end of the 18th century and into the first years of the 19th, when great Anglo-Canadian fortunes would be built in the timber business. On their arrival, the conquerors showed their interest in the fur trade. For a long time they had been bent on seizing the monopoly from New France. At last they could fulfil their ambitions, satisfy their desires! They were not found wanting. As early as 1762, Malcolm Fraser obtained the monopoly for the Murray Bay posts. In the same year, the officer commanding at Michilimackinac gave Alexander Henry the exclusive fur-trading privilege west of Lake Superior. Also in 1762, Dunn was granted the King's posts of the Saguenay, and Grant acquired the tract that had been Vaudreuil's.[42]

The sequel is really not hard to understand. The fur trade called for large money commitments. The canoes sent to the interior had to be fitted out, the men paddling them paid. Almost totally cut off from credit, the *Canadien* dealers were gradually ousted from the trade. They had to accept the limited role of small traders, providing they were allowed even this by a not over-brutal competition. As for the *Canadien* boatmen and voyageurs, whose frugality, obedience, and working spirit were so admired by the English explorers and businessmen, their brawn belonged to those with the cash to pay.[43] In 1767, the first year in which the trade was totally open, 121 canoes left Michilimackinac between July 7 and September 12. They carried goods to the value of £39,000 Sterling. Of 80 traders, 70 were *Canadien*; yet the list of businessmen who gave their guarantees for the good conduct of traders and hired men contained only 23 French names in a total of 40.[44]

---

[41] La Naudière Jr. to his cousin Verchères, 1770, 24 Apr. & 24 July 1773, Saint-Georges Dupré to François Baby, 11 Aug. & 8 Sept. 1771, ibid., (1838, 1840-1, 5600, 5602).

[42] Documentation from Brother Dominique-Marie, "Les Canadiens français et le commerce des fourrures, 1760-1793" (seminar report, Institute d'histoire, Université de Montréal, 1952), 12.

[43] See Benoît Brouillette, *La Pénétration du continent américain par les Canadiens français, 1763-1846* (Montreal, 1939), 73-112.

[44] Ibid., 51.

Canadian fur exporters registered big profits in 1772. That year the price of beaver rose considerably on the London market. A French house had placed orders with four different London brokers to buy large quantities of beaver, and these orders set off a wave of speculation.[45] Fur exporters profited from this sudden rise in prices. But very few French-Canadian merchants were among these privileged ones. They had acquired the habit of selling to exporters in Canada. La Naudière admitted to his associate: "We've missed out on the opportunity, my good friend."[46] The news from London excited the French-Canadian traders, and some of them tried exporting their furs themselves the following year. Unfortunately for them, prices dropped by a third that year as the speculative fever had passed.[47] La Naudière sought to raise Verchères' morale, offering as a consolation: "At least we no longer risk ruining ourselves."[48]

The careers of La Naudière, Saint-Georges Dupré and François Baby deserve a close look. These *Canadien* dealers and traders managed to maintain a higher standard of living than the farming folk by becoming civil servants of the conqueror. In his letter of 24 July 1773, La Naudière told his cousin that his father had given him the seigneurie of Ste-Anne-de-la-Pérade as part of his inheritance. He was proposing to develop it. There was beginning to be talk of a return to the land. Agriculture offered itself as a refuge for *Canadiens* cut out of their country's trade. Numerous former dealers and merchants became farmers out of necessity, not by vocation. Those searching their family trees have often noted this phenomenon: in the 18th century several members of their family were in trade; in the 19th, the vast majority were on the farm. Do not suppose that they had freely chosen that existence. It had been imposed upon them by the Conquest.

During the American Revolution the young La Naudière tried playing the loyalism game.[49] His business affairs continued in jeopardy.[50] He attempted to obtain compensation from the British government by invoking losses supposedly suffered during the American invasion.[51] He asked to be appointed a councillor.[52] Not to be discouraged, he laid siege to his official protectors.[53] Carleton's return brought him luck: he became an official surveyor and a member of the Council.

---

45 B. Comte to [?], 25 Apr. 1772, Antoine Vialars to Etienne Augé, 30 Sept. 1772, in Baby Collection (5669, 5671).
46 La Naudière Jr. to Verchères, 24 July 1773, ibid., (1841).
47 Same to same, 24 Apr. 1773, ibid., (1840).
48 Ibid. Also see note 46.
49 La Naudière to F. Baby, 17 Sept. 1776, ibid., (1848); same to Haldimand, 23 Jan. 1781, in PAC, B 74: 8.
50 Same to Lavaltrie, 2 & 7 July 1783, in PAC, Baby Collection (1853 & 1854).
51 Memorial of La Naudière, 1783, in PAC, C.O. 42-15: 8, 242.
52 La Naudière to [?], 15 June 1783, ibid., 268; La Corne Saint-Luc to [?], 3 Oct. 1783, ibid., 236.
53 La Naudière to Townshend, 6 May 1784, in PAC, C.O. 42-16: 252; same to [?], 8 May 1784 & 17 June 1785, ibid., 254 & 305.

These two sinecures yielded £600.[54] Saint-Georges Dupré, whose qualities as a businessman La Naudière praised, went through a succession of lean years after the Conquest. Until the day when he was made commissioner of militia and put in charge of organizing the forced labour for military transport.[55] His obedience and loyalty to the conquerors had brought dividends. He had made a good investment. François Baby, a member of the two Councils, official surveyor and adjutant-general, was also to bask in Carleton's and Haldimand's bounty.

These *Canadien* bourgeois had managed to find their niche. They were part of the very small minority, the favourites of the regime. But all the rest? To imagine their painful condition, we have only to scan the hundreds of petitions and appeals in the archives.[56] Conquered in the economy because their native land had been defeated on the field of battle and then occupied by the victors, cut off from the vital influence of their motherland, most *Canadien* businessmen had sunk into wretchedness or mediocrity. A scant few stayed afloat, veritable islets exposed to the all-powerful influence of their English competitors, who were the unchallengeable masters of the colony's economic life.

The forming of the North-West Company indicates how modest the *Canadien* share of the country's business was. In 1780, two of the 16 company shares belonged to French-speaking entrepreneurs in partnership, Wadin & Cie. Jean-Etienne Wadin was in fact a Swiss merchant who had settled in Canada after the Conquest. His associate was called Venant Saint-Germain. In 1783, Nicolas Montour was the only *Canadien* shareholder, with two shares only. Wadin had died in the previous year, and Venant Saint-Germain was vegetating as an ordinary company agent. The Gregory, McLeod Company, which gave hard competition to the North-West Company from 1783 to 1787, had not a single French-speaking shareholder. French names are found only among the minor employees.[57]

The businessmen of English origin did not restrict themselves to furs and the external trade. They invaded every area. Stephen Moore and Hugh Finlay, who was destined to play an important part in the colony's economic and political life, asked the government for grants of land in the Lower Town of Quebec. John Collins, Benjamin Price and Thomas Dunn made a request for land at the water's edge in Quebec, with the purpose of building wharves. Some competitors had the same plan.

---

[54] Nepean to Dorchester, 25 Aug. 1786, in PAC, Q 26-2: 515; Dorchester to Nepean, ibid., 518; list of civil servants, 30 Apr. 1788, in Q 38: 240.

[55] La Naudière to Verchères, 1770, in PAC, Baby Collection (1838); Saint-Georges Dupré to F. Baby, 21 Apr., 10 July & 29 Aug. 1777, ibid., (5617, 5618, 5622).

[56] See PAC, B 218 and B 219. These two volumes, of more than 700 pages, contain all sorts of petitions addressed to Haldimand from 1778 to 1784. The collections C.O. 42 and Q are filled with memorials, petitions, and supplications of the same sort.

[57] Brouillette, *Pénétration du continent*, 73-75.

John Gray and William Grant too needed land in the Lower Town.[58] A company was formed to obtain the leases on the King's Posts.[59] Needless to say, it included no *Canadiens*. A certain John Marteilhe was interested in the St. Maurice Forges, and disclosed his ambitions to the Board of Trade.[60] Murray seems to have preferred Simon Mackenzie.[61] In 1767 Carleton would rent the forges to a company of nine shareholders for a period of 16 years. Among these shareholders were three with French names.[62]

The grain and flour trades brought rich profits for the colony's exporters from 1771 to 1775. In 1770, Canada had exported 51,822 bushels of wheat. Exports rose to 460,818 bushels in 1774. In 1776, they returned to normal.[63] Scarcity of wheat had forced the British Parliament to lower duties on imports in 1773.[64] The price of the product doubled on the Quebec market.[65] The peasants profited from this unexpected manna. It helped create a feeling of satisfaction in the mass of the population that served the English propagandists admirably well. Events seemed to vindicate those who claimed that the conqueror had brought prosperity. His business sense and concern for the general good were supposed to be its causes! Freed from a mother country and colonial administrators who had exploited it, the colony could finally develop!

This myth arose during the first 15 years that followed the Conquest. On a pastoral visit, Bishop Briand had noted the happiness of his flock: "Everything here [in Montreal] seems very quiet to me, and since leaving Quebec I do not recall having heard a single expression of discontent with the government. The people and in general everyone strike me as being as satisfied as if they had never known any other."[66] Henry Caldwell assured Lord Shelburne of the same.[67] The bishop would recall these prosperous years when, during the American invasion, he criticized the *Canadiens*, and especially the peasants, for their lack of loyalty: "No one at the time of the revolt was feeling the misfortunes of the late war; whatever confusion it may at first have produced in our affairs, was not only repaired, but in fact you had much

---

[58] Petitions of 30 Dec. 1763, 8 Dec. 1764, 6 Nov. 1764, 20 Nov. & 12 Dec. 1764, 3 Jan. 1765, in PAC, C.O. 42-3: 46, 48, 41, 43, 49, 51.

[59] Petition of John Gray, Richard Murray & Thomas Dunn, 21 Jan. 1764, in PAC, C.O. 42-1: 166, 169, and C.O. 42-2: 359.

[60] Memorial read on 21 June 1764 to the Board of Trade, in PAC, C.O. 42-1: 159.

[61] Murray to Board of Trade, 20 Oct. 1764, in PAC, C.O. 42-2: 129.

[62] Lease for the forges, 9 June 1767, in PAC, B 27: 122-128.

[63] Statistics given in Craig, "Economic Conditions," 85.

[64] Thomas Lynch to E. Augé, 6 Jan. 1773, in PAC, Baby Collection (5672).

[65] Pierre Guy to F. Baby, 27 Nov. 1773 & 16 Mar. 1775, F. Baby to Pierre Guy, 20 Mar. 1774, Hervieux to F. Baby, 16 Mar. 1775, in Baby Collection (2962, 2965, 4952, 2966).

[66] Briand to Cramahé, 29 Oct. 1772, in Report of the Archivist of the Province of Quebec (RAPQ), 1929-30, 96.

[67] Henry Caldwell to Shelburne, May 1775, in PAC, Shelburne Papers, 66: 36.

British Conquest and the Decline of the French-Canadian Bourgeoisie 103

increased your fortunes, and your possessions had grown considerably more lucrative and rich."[68]

The farmers had sold their wheat well. They were all pleased about that. A few woollen socks contained a few extra coins. However, who had skimmed off the biggest profits? The wheat producers? We must doubt that. Would it not rather be the merchants and exporters? These were not *Canadien*. A certain Jacob Jordan, a Montreal businessman who was closely involved in a number of profitable transactions during the American Revolution, made a fortune as a wheat and flour broker. He had had the necessary capital and contacts to take advantage of the windfall. The *Canadien* merchants had been satisfied to follow his successful operations admiringly.[69] Jordan was not the only English merchant to specialize in the export of agricultural products. It must be recalled that external trade had passed into the hands of the newcomers. They also controlled the timber and fishing industries.[70]

In 15 years their network had extended through all sectors of economic life. Henry Caldwell could write to Lord Shelburne that the English, as well as holding landed property, "include a good number of merchants who, either on commission or on their own account, conduct all the affairs of the country, except for the peddling trade and the interior commerce with the savages."[71] The memorial of the London merchants against the Quebec Act attributed to the English businessmen of Canada "the merit of having been the principal promoters of the progress which has recently been achieved in that province."[72] In a petition printed in London in 1778, twenty-four English merchants of Quebec and Montreal affirmed that they and their British colleagues controlled four-fifths of the interior and exterior trade of the colony and that the English-origin population owned half of the moveable and landed wealth of the country, except for the religious holdings.[73] These spokesmen of the colony's English minority—numerical minority, but economic majority—were not just boasting vainly; they were telling the sad truth. A truth that hasn't changed, either. The historian Edgar McInnis has nicely summed up this inevitable invasion of the conquered colony by English businessmen:

---

[68] "Pastoral letter to the rebellions subjects during the American war," 1776, in *Mandements, lettres pastorales et circulaires des évêques de Québec*, II, 271.

[69] F. Baby to P. Guy, 20 Mar. 1774, Jacob Jordan to M. de La Corne, seigneur of Terrebonne, 10 & 16 Nov. 1774, in Baby collection (4952, 3279, 3281).

[70] Craig, "Economic Conditions," 23, 51-86.

[71] Caldwell to Shelburne, 9 Jan. 1775, Shelburne Papers, 66: 31.

[72] Memorial of the London merchants engaged in the Quebec trade, in *Documents constitutionnels*, I, 500.

[73] Draft of a petition to Lord Germain, London, Mar. 1778, in ASQ, Documents Faribault, no. 268.

The influx was not large. [The historian is speaking of those merchants who came in response to Gen. Amherst's invitation.] The substantial merchants, as distinct from small shopkeepers, probably numbered less than 100 during the decade after the conquest. But their importance was out of all proportion to their numbers. The existing commercial life of the colony had been stricken at its roots. The French merchants had lost the connection with Europe on which they relied for their supply of goods. The conquest transferred Canada's commercial dependence from Paris to London, and it was the British merchants with their connections in England who were the essential instruments of trade and prosperity. They stepped right into the key positions in the economic life of the province of Quebec, and that fact made them of salient importance in political affairs as well.[74]

Time consolidated this domination. The American Revolution (like all the wars in which the country has participated since the British Conquest) brought great prosperity to Canada. The supply and transport of troops, provisioning of military hospitals, prisoners, and loyalist refugees, touched off a surge in economic activity. Improved circulation of money facilitated trade and stimulated local commerce. By the end of the war the colony was in the midst of an inflationary spiral. This inflation, encouraged by some of Governor Haldimand's councillors,[75] meant profits for speculators and military provisioners. On the other hand, it meant ruin for people on fixed incomes, particularly French-Canadian seigneurs living on their seigneurial dues.

Most of the population, however, profited from this wartime prosperity. The *habitants* continued to sell their agricultural products advantageously. Small French-Canadian merchants saw their sales and their profits rise. The state of euphoria created by the prosperous years 1771-5 continued. All this must be taken into account in order to understand the enthusiasm of the French-Canadian leaders of that period, an enthusiasm that has communicated itself to several historians.

Yet who were the principal beneficiaries of this wartime prosperity? We'll find them among the army's suppliers. Everyone knows that military contracts constitute the greatest source of rapid enrichment. Of course, we won't be surprised to note that these suppliers came almost exclusively from among the English businessmen. Jacob Jordan did not confine himself only to wheat and flour sales. In 1777 General Burgoyne gave him the contract to supply his army with the horses, waggons, and drivers needed to transport artillery, munitions, and supplies—a contract worth

---

[74] Edgar McInnis, *Canada: A Political and Social History* (Toronto, 1947), 131.
[75] A.L. Burt, *The Old Province of Quebec* (Toronto, 1933), 312, 401.

British Conquest and the Decline of the French-Canadian Bourgeoisie 105

£45,000![76] It's interesting to recall that Saint-Georges Dupré had been named commissioner of transport at a salary of 10 shillings a day. Carleton had already chosen this former trader as commissioner of militia. Jordan saw in him the perfect man to provide him with the cheap labour, waggons, and horses that he needed. Dupré ended up organizing forced transport labour for the profit of this man who had hired him.[77] As we can see, it was not French Canadians who got the big profits from this contract. As for Dupré, he wasn't thinking about suicide any more; his double salary had given him a new taste for living. He offered himself the luxury of two barrels of good wine, "my throat being unable to do without it."[78] He must have drunk that wine to the health of the government and of Mr. Jordan! Did he even spare a thought for the French-Canadian militiamen who had worked on the forced labour details for a few pennies a day?....

Very few French Canadians profited from the military contracts. French names are extremely rare in the correspondence of Nathaniel Day [the commissioner-general for military supplies]. The few French Canadians who did manage to pick up orders had to content themselves with crumbs from the tables of the favoured ones. A certain Pillet of Lachine rented his house and store to Commissioner Day for £100 a year. Any repairs to these buildings rented as storehouses for the Crown were to be at his expense.[79] From time to time one finds a French name lost among those of the English suppliers. From 25 June to 24 December 1778, beef and mutton were purchased on the local market to the value of £1,585. A certain Charles Canouche sold £80's worth. A statement of extraordinary expenses of the army from 24 June to 24 December 1778, amounting to £16,650 in all, contains only one French name among the suppliers mentioned: M. Pierréville of Laprairie. He had received the enormous sum of £6 7s. 9d....[80]

Those were real years of abundance for the English merchants who controlled the colony's external trade. R. Meredith travelled to London to supervise the shipment of exports bound for Canada. These amounted to almost £600,000 in value in 1778. Learning of the Franco-American alliance of that year, Meredith foresaw that the war would be a long one and would stimulate Canadian commerce. He practically licked his lips at the thought that the British government would have to send more troops to the colony: "If that happens, the Canadian trade will prosper...."[81] Wars have

---

[76] Gen. W. Philipps to the Lords of the Treasury, 30 May 1779, W.M. Collier to Jacob Jordan, June 1779 & Jan. 1780, D.A. Geddes to same, 18 June 1779, in Baby Collection (5955, 5956, 5958, 5957).

[77] Saint-Georges Dupré to F. Baby, 21 Apr., 10 & 28 July, 4 & 29 Aug. 1777, in Baby Collection (5617, 5618, 5620, 5621, 5622).

[78] Same to same, 10 July 1777.

[79] Contract of 5 Feb. 1780, in PAC, B 191: 81.

[80] PAC, B 194: 6-8.

[81] R. Meredith to F. Baby, 10 Apr. 1778, Baby Collection (2401).

always been a good deal for the countries of America—in the 18th century as in the 20th.

And what were the French Canadian businessmen doing? They certainly weren't enjoying the good graces of those who distributed government contracts. They remained "spectators" of a trade which they had hoped to be able to control thanks to the freedom of trade which the conqueror had promised. The least unfortunate had to content themselves with being modest middlemen. Several thought it would be a good idea to associate themselves with Englishmen. A lot of them just closed up shop. The documents indicate clearly that French-Canadians just didn't count any more in the economic life of their country. In 1782, Jérôme Bédard, who owned a sloop engaged in the transport of military supplies, addressed a petition to the governor: the ship had been lost and he asked for an indemnity. A certificate of recommendation accompanied this request; Bédard had been careful to have it signed by the twelve most influential merchants in Quebec, men who regularly used his services. Only one French name, Michel Cornud, is to be found on this list.[82] When the docks and other property of John Fraser, a Quebec importer, were auctioned off, two French-Canadian businessmen, Dunière and Perrault, acted as straw men to boost the prices.[83] Not a very splendid role! The Quebec city directory published in 1790 is revealing. The capital had 37 merchants or dealers, of whom only four were *Canadien* or French. Their names are worth noting: Louis Chaperon, Michel Cornud, Louis Dunière and Jérôme Martineau. This Louis Chaperon had been assistant commissioner for military supplies in Quebec City. His association with the department of Commissioner-General Daly certainly hadn't hurt his business! He was part of that minority of French Canadians who benefited from the regime's favours. The 1790 city directory indicates that by the end of the 18th century, the only consolation available to the French Canadians was that they were still a majority among the small shopkeepers: 47 French names out of a total of 70.

And what was the situation at Montreal? In the absence of a city directory dating from the same period, we may yet affirm without fear of error that it was the same as at Quebec. The enterprise and good fortune of Montreal's English merchants were not limited to the fur trade. By the last quarter of the 18th century, the names of the men who dominated the economic life of the future metropolis of English Canada had no French ring to them: the three McGill brothers, Edward Chinn, Ezekiel Solomon, Benjamin and Joseph Frobisher, Todd, Patterson, Charles Grant, Peter Pond, Jacob Jordan, Alexander Mackenzie, Simon McTavish. John Molson settled there in 1782 with a capital of £5,000. It never hurts to start out in business with a sum like that; right from the start it gives one an advantage over less privileged competitors.

---

[82] Certificate of recommendation in favour of Jérôme Bédard, 15 June 1782, in PAC, B 194: 185.

[83] George Allsopp to his wife, 20 & 21 Sept. 1786, in Archives de la Province du Québec (APQ), Allsopp letters, 69-71.

In one generation the conquered French Canadians had been eliminated from major business. Or almost. This sociological fact is not to be attributed to any ill will on the part of the conqueror. It would be childish to see in this the result of any Machiavellian plots. This social decapitation and economic subjection of the French Canadians under a foreign power had come about quite naturally, with no violence or difficulty. Such were the inevitable consequences of the Conquest. Without support from France, its motherland and sustaining metropolis, French-Canadian society could not continue to develop along normal lines. British colonization had replaced the French. An English society was now establishing itself on the ruins of the first Canada. It was not the responsibility of the victor to protect the defeated French Canadians or to build an economic order specially suited to their interest. But simply by his presence he inevitably prevented the defeated side from establishing a business elite with the initiative needed to exploit the province's resources. The important bourgeoisie would be English from now on.

The Canadien Bourgeoisie and the New Political Order

The *Canadien* nobility made up an important part of the colonial bourgeoisie, as we have previously defined this class. Its fate was no more enviable than that of the *Canadien* businessmen. Will we ever be able to assess the humiliation heaped on these representatives and witnesses of a past that had been brutally ended by the Conquest? The majority of the nobles were not rich. The few noble families who possessed fortunes had won them in trade. Their future was the same as for the other *Canadien* merchants. Another career was open to the colonial nobles: the King's service. This ruling class, even among those holding seigneuries, could not exist independently of the political power—unless they accepted a lower standard of living. For these servants of the Crown, the Conquest appeared as a true catastrophe. They fell less easily into the illusions cherished by the *Canadien* merchants from 1761 to 1765. Haldimand saw clearly: "The nobility of this country, that class of persons who lived here at the King's expense, cannot imagine that France wishes to cede Canada."[84]

The conqueror was not anxious to keep these unemployed blades in the country. Murray and Haldimand ardently wished for the departure of the "Crosses of St Louis."[85] These leaders, decorated for their bravery and their services by the King of France, recalled a glorious past that the vanquished had to learn to forget. Their exit would simplify the occupation of the conquered colony. Worried about their land holdings and anxious not to compromise themselves before the colony's fate was definitely decided, most *Canadien* nobles maintained a prudent silence at the

---

84   Haldimand to Amherst, 26 Dec. 1762, in PAC, B I: 262.
85   Murray to Burton, 17 Nov. 1763, Murray to Amherst, 4 Dec. 1763, in PAC, Murray Papers, M. 898 B; Haldimand to Gage, 15 Apr. 1764, in PAC, B 2-2: 9.

beginning of the conquest. This is why the clergy, knowing they would stay in the country at all events, acted as the chief and almost the sole spokesmen for the conquered population from 1760 to 1763. A number of nobles went to France. Those who found jobs and pensions settled there. A few, disappointed at their reception by the French authorities, decided to return to Canada, where in any case most noblemen had stayed. M. de Lotbinière had warned one of his *Canadien* correspondents that the French King's court "would not be sorry to see all of us in Canada."[86]

The story of Gaspard-Joseph Chaussegros de Lery (1721-1797) is a good illustration of the wretched fate of the *Canadien* nobility in the wake of the Conquest.[87] A military engineer and a Knight of St Louis, De Lery went to France in the spring of 1762. He was forgotten in the ante-rooms of Versailles and Paris. "Fearing to find myself and my family in the most critical situation,"[88] he took steps to return to Canada. This nobleman, with no job and no resources, felt no pangs of conscience at switching his allegiance. "Since the distinguished services I had rendered the King [of France] in Canada, and those of my ancestors, could not secure the welfare of my family.... I became a subject of His Britannic Majesty." These career officers of the 18th century sincerely believed they could continue to serve the *Canadien* nation under the orders of a foreign monarch.

Our distinguished beggar knocked at the door of England's embassy in Paris: "A few days later, Mr. Neville replied on behalf of His Excellency the Duke of Bedford that he had received favourable reports of my character, and that if I wished to be an English subject, as the first *Canadien* gentleman who would return to the colony, I could be assured that I would also be the first recipient of His Majesty's favour. From that time I regarded myself as an English subject."

Thus, De Lery returned to Canada. There began a long career filled with carefully veiled humiliations. Murray's reception of him was apparently rather chilly. The governor was suspicious, seeing the French army officers remaining in the colony as so many spies. He particularly criticized De Lery for having left two of his children in France. His Britannic Majesty's new subject waited for Murray's departure to appeal for justice. Carleton appeared more sympathetic, and got his protégé a pension.[89] In 1775, on the governor's suggestion, the imperial authorities appointed him a member of the Council.[90] Henry Caldwell accused him of winning Carleton's favours by "his slavish adulation."[91] To allay the British government's suspicions, he tried to bring his two sons back from Paris, where they were living. However, his

---

[86] Lotbinière to [?], Paris, 9 June 1762, in ASQ, Polygraph 30: 22.
[87] See François Daniel, *Le Vicomte C. de Lery et sa famille* (Montreal, 1867).
[88] "Mémoire de Chaussegros de Lery," sent by Carleton to Shelburne, 24 Sept. 1767, in PAC, Q 84: 276ff.
[89] Carleton to Hillsborough, 18 Jan. 1769, in PAC, Q 6: 9; Hillsborough to Carleton, 13 May 1769, ibid., 12.
[90] Instructions to Governor Carleton, 3 Jan. 1775, in *Documents constitutionnels*, 2: 579.
[91] Caldwell to Shelburne, May 1775, in PAC, Shelburne Papers, 66: 36.

French friends and relations persuaded him not to oblige François-Joseph, the elder, to leave the mother country and a predicted brilliant military career. In fact, he was to become a baron of the Empire, commander-in-chief of engineers in the Napoleonic army, and a viscount under the Restoration. His name is engraved on the Arc de Triomphe.

The younger son, Louis-René, reached Quebec in 1770. His father sent him to study at the Quebec seminary. In 1774, he vainly sought a lieutenancy in the English artillery for his heir. Eight years later the young man was still looking for a job. Haldimand told his persistent father that he would give his son a place as soon as he could. In the meantime, he advised him to learn English. The young De Lery, ambitious and full of good will, did study the language of the conqueror. His father again tried Haldimand, who promised nothing. Hearing that a place had become vacant and been given to another aspirant, De Lery could not hide his dissatisfaction. He asked the governor to let his son go to France, where he could enter military service. Haldimand defended himself with the assertion that before he could interest himself in young De Lery's fate, he had to think of the candidates who had served the King of England faithfully in other colonies and came to Canada for the reward for their loyal services. Louis-René went into French exile and served in the royal bodyguard. When the Revolution began, he was in Germany with the Army of the Princes. Returning to this country in 1794, he would wait until 1798 before being admitted to the English army as captain of the second battalion of the Royal Canadian Volunteers. His patience had been rewarded! As for his father, he died before being able to find his son a job in Canada.

There was not much future in the conquered colony for ambitious young *Canadiens*. If a member of the Council and a favourite of the regime could not find places for his children, what could the other fathers do? Let us recall that Gaspard-Joseph Chaussegros de Lery had seven children to look after. Most of them had to go into exile to carve themselves a future....

The Conquest had sentenced the *Canadiens* of the nobility and those who had held important positions in the administration to be the thurifèrs of a regime that would use them for its own purposes. Carleton had foreseen that these hungry nobles would be useful: "Moreover, if it pleases His Majesty to grant his petition [the Chevalier de Lery's], it would prove to the gentlemen of Canada that they will not forever be excluded from the service of their present sovereign. I have tried to uproot this opinion, for I am entirely persuaded that it is advantageous for British interest on this continent to employ the Canadians."[92] Lord Shelburne approved the clever policy suggested by the governor: "Your observations ... quite show the appropriateness and the necessity of having these brave and faithful people take a reasonable part in the institutions that are to be the basis of the government of Quebec."[93]....

---

[92] Carleton to Shelburne, 24 Sept. 1767, in PAC, Q 4: 273.
[93] Hillsborough to Carleton, 4 Jan. 1769, in PAC, Q 6: 3.

But *Canadien* participation in public affairs was limited, in Lord Shelburne's expression, to "a reasonable part." Moreover, Carleton had been precise about the line of action to be taken. It was a question of not systematically excluding the *Canadiens* "from places of trust to which incomes are attached." Their national pride would thus be handled. It would be enough to grant three or four conspicuous *Canadiens* the honour of calling themselves councillors. There their functions would stop. In addition, the governor suggested the "conferring of three or four unimportant places in the civil administration." With these minimal dispensations, "we would at least manage to divide the Canadians."[94] The recommendations Carleton made in 1768 were to serve as a guide to all the governors. Parsimoniously, calculatedly, they dispensed their favour to the new subjects of His Majesty....

A few figures on the distribution of civil service jobs will illustrate the extremely modest *Canadien* presence in the political life of their country. In 1779 the customs and postal service had 13 civil servants, of whom one was *Canadien*.[95] In 1781, a list of 22 senior government employees includes only one *Canadien* name, that of surveyor Picotté de Bellestre. Of a total of 38 justices of the peace, we find only 16 *Canadiens*. In the Council there were but six *Canadiens* in a membership of 22.[96] From 1764 to 1791, 48 individuals served as councillors, 33 English-speaking and 15 French-speaking. The average tenure of English councillors was ten years; for the *Canadiens* it was seven years.[97] The list of civil officers in the province for the year 1784 runs to some 136 names. *Canadiens* occupied only 36 posts, or 26.4 per cent of the total, including the humblest ones. In 1788, *Canadiens* took 22.7 per cent of the salaries and pensions paid by the government.[98] It was impossible for the *Canadiens* to build up an administrative tradition. Moreover, we must not forget that those securing the hotly disputed jobs had merited them far more by their servility than by their competence.[99] Excluded from the top echelons of business, the former *Canadien* ruling class had been excluded from political life as well....

Conclusion

The French Canadians of 1790 knew that they were subject to a foreign political authority and recognized the commercial superiority of the new inhabitants that the

---

[94] Carleton to Shelburne, 20 Jan. 1768, in *Documents constitutionnels*, I, 269.
[95] *Almanach de Québec pour 1780*, 45.
[96] *Almanach de Québec pour 1782*, 43-6.
[97] See Elizabeth Arthur, "Adam Mabane and the French Party in Canada, 1760-1791" (unpublished MA thesis, McGill University, 1947), v.
[98] See *Almanach de Québec pour l'année 1785*, 17ff; also PAC, Q 38: 240.
[99] Cf the opinion of Elizabeth Arthur, "French-Canadian Participation in the Government of Canada, 1775-85" in *CHR*, XXXII (Dec. 1951), 303-14.

Conquest had brought to their country. Still, they could not foresee the ultimate consequences of such a situation. They had a vague sense of dependence. Some of them were consciously suffering from it. Nevertheless, it was impossible for them to understand the significance of their incorporation into a foreign empire and the social decapitation of which they had been the victims. The country's material prosperity, due to the initiative of the English bourgeoisie, kept them in a general state of contentment. Of course, they had learned to be content with little. What's more, knowing themselves to be the numerical majority, they truly believed that time was working for them.

The contemporary historian of French Canada sees what the late 18th-century French-Canadian leaders did not see. It is his duty. Unless he is willingly or involuntarily blind, he must see that the French Canadians, eliminated from major commerce, were unable to develop habits necessary for carrying on important business. Allowed only a small portion of subordinate posts in the public administration, they were deprived of government men and political traditions. Thirty years after the Conquest, French-Canadian society no longer had the leadership required by any society of the Atlantic world to develop normally.

This was one of the results of the Conquest: a sociological phenomenon, and in no way due to the malignity of men. This colonial people had prematurely lost its supporting metropolis. Reduced to its own resources, it was doomed to an anaemic collective survival. It no longer had the benefit of the enlightened and dynamic leadership of an economically independent bourgeoisie totally devoted to its interest as an ethnic group and capable of establishing a political, social, and cultural order suited to it. It had nothing left but a few institutions of secondary importance and the relative and inert force of numbers and social instinct. French Canada's demographic growth in the province of Quebec would be its only victory—a victory made derisory by the industrial revolution and the massive transformation of French Canadians into a proletariat in the service of a socio-economic order which they did not create.

The absence of this lay bourgeois ruling class, whose role has been so important in the evolution of the other Atlantic societies, remains the decisive factor in the history of French Canada since the Conquest....

(This essay was originally published under the title *La conquête anglaise et al déchéance de la bourgeoisie canadienne*. The translation is taken from Dale Miquelon, ed., *Society and Conquest*, and is used here with Prof. Miquelon's permission. Most of Prof. Brunet's footnotes have been restored, as have sections of the original essay not included in the published translation.)

A Change in Climate: The Conquest and the Marchands of Montreal

José Igartua

When the British government issued the Royal Proclamation of 1763, it assumed that the promised establishment of "British institutions" in the "Province of Quebec" would be sufficient to entice American settlers to move north and overwhelm the indigenous French-speaking and Papist population. These were naïve hopes. Until the outbreak of the American Revolution, British newcomers merely trickled into Quebec, leading Governor Carleton to prophesy in 1767 that "barring a catastrophe shocking to think of, this Country must, to the end of Time, be peopled by the Canadian Race...."[1] But the British newcomers, few though they were, had to be reckoned with. By 1765 they were powerful enough to have Governor Murray recalled and by 1777 they would be strong enough to command the majority of investments in the fur trade.[2] Did their success stem from superior abilities? Did the British take advantage of the situation of submission and dependence into which the Canadians had been driven by the Conquest? Did the newcomers gain their predominance from previous experience with the sort of political and economic conditions created in post-Conquest Quebec?

Historians of Quebec have chosen various ways to answer these questions. Francis Parkman was fond of exhibiting the superiority of the Anglo-Saxon race over the "French Celt."[3] More recently the studies of W.S. Wallace, E.E. Rich, and D.G. Creighton took similar, if less overt, positions.[4] One of the best students of the North West fur trade, Wayne E. Stevens, concluded: "The British merchants ... were men of great enterprise and ability and they began gradually to crowd out the French traders who had been their predecessors in the field."[5]

---

[1] Public Archives of Canada [hereafter PAC], C.O. 42, vol. 27, f. 66, Carleton to Shelburne, Quebec, 25 November 1767; quoted in A.L. Burt, *The Old Province of Quebec* (2 vols. Toronto, 1968), I, 142.

[2] See Burt, *Old Province*, I, Ch. VI; Dale B. Miquelon, "The Baby Family in the Trade of Canada, 1750-1820" (Unpublished Master's thesis, Carleton University, 1966), 145-146.

[3] Francis Parkman, *The Old Regime in Canada* (27th ed. Boston, 1892), Ch. XXI, especially 397-398.

[4] W. Stewart Wallace, ed., *Documents Relating to the North West Company* (Toronto, 1934); Wallace, *The Pedlars From Quebec and Other Papers on the Nor'Westers* (Toronto, 1954); E.E. Rich, *The Fur Trade and the Northwest to 1857* (Toronto, 1967); Rich, *The History of the Hudson's Bay Company*, II (London, 1959); D.G. Creighton, *The Empire of the St. Lawrence* (Toronto, 1956).

[5] Wayne E. Stevens, *The Northwest Fur Trade 1763-1800* (Urbana, Ill, 1928), 25.

A Change in Climate: The Conquest and the Marchands of Montreal 113

The French-Canadian historian Fernand Ouellet attributed the rise of the British merchants to the weaknesses of the Canadian trading bourgeoisie: "Son attachement à la petite entreprise individuelle, sa répugnance à la concentration, son goût du luxe de même que son attrait irrésistible pour les placements assurés étaient des principaux handicaps." No evidence is given for this characterization and the author hastens to concede that before 1775 "le problème de la concentration ne se pose pas avec acuité." But for him it is clear that the economic displacement of the Canadians resulted from their conservative, "ancien Régime" frame of mind, bred into them by the clergy and the nobility.[6] Ouellet painted British merchants in a more flattering light as the agents of economic progress.[7]

Michel Brunet has depicted the commercial competition between the British newcomers and the Canadian merchants as an uneven contest between two national groups, one of which had been deprived of the nourishing blood of its metropolis while the other was being assiduously nurtured. For Brunet the normal and natural outcome of that inequality was the domination of the conqueror, a situation which he sees as prevailing to the present day.[8]

Dale B. Miquelon's study of one merchant family, the Babys, shed new light on the question of British penetration of Canadian trade. It outlined the growth of British investments in the fur trade and the increasing concentration of British capital. The author concluded:

> The French-Canadians dominated the Canadian fur trade until the upheaval of the American Revolution. At that time they were overwhelmed by an influx of capital and trading personnel. English investment in the top ranks of investors jumped by 679% and was never significantly to decline. Even without explanations involving the difference between the French and English commercial mentalities, it is difficult to believe that any body of merchants could recover from an inundation of such size and swiftness.[9]

This conclusion had the obvious merit of staying out of the murky waters of psychological interpretations. But Miquelon's own evidence suggests that the "flood theory" is not sufficient to account for the Canadians' effacement; even before the inundation of 1775-1783, British investment in the fur trade was growing more rapidly than Canadian. By 1772, to quote Miquelon, the "English [had] made more

---

[6] Fernand Ouellet, *Histoire économique et sociale du Québec 1760-1850* (Montreal, 1966), 77.
[7] Ibid., 104-106.
[8] Michel Brunet, *Les Canadiens après Conquête, 1759-1775* (Montreal, 1969), 173-174, 177-180.
[9] Miquelon, "The Baby Family," 158.

impressive increases in the size of their investments than [had] the French, and for the first time [had] larger average investments in all categories."[10]

It is difficult not to note the ascendancy of the British in the fur trade of Canada even before the American Revolution. The success of the British merchants, therefore, was rooted in something more than mere numbers. It was not simply the outcome of an ethnic struggle between two nationalities of a similar nature; it was not only the natural consequence of the Canadians' conservative frame of mind. It arose out of a more complex series of causes, some of them a product of the animosities between Canadians and British, others inherent in the differences in the socio-economic structures of the French and British Empires; together, they amounted to a radical transformation of the societal climate of the colony.

The aim of this paper is to gauge the impact of the Conquest upon a well-defined segment of that elusive group called the "bourgeoisie" of New France. It focuses on Montreal and its Canadian merchants. Montreal was the centre of the fur trade and its merchants managed it. Historians of New France have traditionally seen the fur trade as the most dynamic sector of the colony's economy; by implication it is generally believed that the fur trade provided the likeliest opportunities for getting rich quickly and maintaining a "bourgeois" standard of living.[11] It is not yet possible to evaluate the validity of this notion with any precision, for too little is known about other sectors of the economy which, in the eighteenth century at least, may have generated as much or more profit. Research on the merchants of Quebec should provide new information on the wealth to be made from the fisheries, from wholesale merchandising, and from trade with Louisbourg and the West Indies. But if one is concerned with the fate of Canadian merchants after the Conquest, one should examine the fate of men involved in the sector of the economy of Quebec which was the most dynamic *after* the Conquest, the fur trade. The paper examines the impact of the arrival of (relatively) large numbers of merchants on the Montreal mercantile community, the attitude of British officials towards the Canadians, and the changing political climate of the colony. It is suggested that it was the simultaneous conjunction of these changes to the "world" of the Montreal merchants, rather than the effect of any one of them, which doomed the Canadian merchants of Montreal.[12]

---

10   Ibid., 142.

11   The implication is unwarranted. A given economic sector can be dynamic and even produce the largest share of marketable commodities and still provide individual entrepreneurs with meagre profits. The macro-economic level of analysis should not be confused with the micro-economic level. Jean Hamelin showed that only around 28 per cent of the profits from the beaver trade remained in Canada. Since the Canadians had an assured market for beaver, one can wonder how much more profitable it was for them to deal in other peltries. See Hamelin, *Economie et Société en Nouvelle-France* (Quebec, 1960), 54-56.

12   The obvious economic explanation for the downfall of the Canadian merchants after the Conquest has to be dismissed. The liquidation of Canadian paper money by France hurt most of all those British merchants who bought it from Canadians for speculation. Canadian

The Montreal Merchants at the End of the French Regime

In 1752 a French Royal engineer passing through Montreal remarked that "la plupart des habitants y sont adonnés au commerce principalement à celui connu sous le nom des pays d'en haut."[13] It was only a slight exaggeration. By the last year of the French regime one could count over one hundred *négociants*, merchants, outfitters, traders, and shopkeepers in Montreal. The overwhelming majority of them had been in business for some years and would remain in business after the Conquest. Over half were outfitters for the fur trade at some time or other between 1750 and 1775; these men comprised the body of the merchant community of Montreal. Above them in wealth and stature stood a handful of import merchants who did a comfortable business of importing merchandise from France and selling it in Montreal to other merchants or directly to customers in their retail stores. Below the outfitters a motley group of independent fur traders, shopkeepers, and artisans managed to subsist without leaving more than a trace of their existence for posterity.[14]

The fur trade, as it was conducted by the merchants of Montreal before 1760, had little to do with the glamorous picture it sometimes calls to mind. For the outfitter who remained in Montreal, it was not physically a risky occupation; its management was fairly simple and the profits which it produced quite meagre. For the last years of the French regime the fur trade followed a three-tier system. Fort Frontenac (present-day Kingston) and Fort Niagara were King's posts; they were not lucrative and had to be subsidized to meet English competition. The trade of Detroit and Michilimackinac, as well as that of the posts to the southwest, was open to licensees whose numbers were limited. Some *coureurs de bois* (traders without a licence) also roamed in the area. The richest posts, Green Bay and the posts to the northwest past Sault Sainte-Marie, were monopolies leased by the Crown to merchants or military

---

merchants had already compensated in part for the anticipated liquidation by raising prices during the last years of the Seven Years' War. Those Montreal merchants who had the greatest quantity of French paper were not driven out of business; on the contrary the most prominent merchants were able to open accounts with British suppliers soon after the Conquest without too much difficulty. See José E. Igartua, "The Merchants and *Négociants* of Montreal, 1750-1775: A Study in Socio-Economic History" (unpublished Ph.D. thesis, Michigan State University, 1974), Ch. VI.

[13] Franquet, *Voyages et mémoires sur le Canada en 1752-1753* (Toronto, 1968), 56.

[14] For a more elaborate description of the size and the socio-economic characteristics of the Montreal merchant community at this time, see Igartua, "The Merchants and *Négociants* of Montreal," Ch. II.

officers.[15] The export of beaver was undertaken by the French *Compagnie des Indes*, which had the monopoly of beaver sales on the home market. Other furs were on the open market.

The system worked tolerably well in peace time: there was a stable supply of furs, prices paid to the Indians had been set by custom, the prices paid by the *compagnie des Indes* were regulated by the Crown, and the prices of trade goods imported from France were fairly steady. There was competition from the Americans at Albany and from the English on the Hudson Bay, to be sure, but it appeared to be a competition heavily influenced by military considerations and compliance with Indian customs.[16]

The system faltered in war time. Beaver shipments to France and the importation of trade goods became risky because of British naval power. Shipping and insurance costs raised the Canadian traders' overhead, but the Indians refused to have the increase passed on to them. This was the most obvious effect of war, but it also produced general economic and administrative dislocations which led H.A. Innis to conclude that it " ... seriously weakened the position of the French in the fur trade and contributed to the downfall of the French *régime* in Canada."[17]

Nevertheless, outside of war-time crises, the fur trade of New France was conducted with a fair dose of traditionalism. This traditionalism resulted from two concurrent impulses: Indian attitudes towards trade, which were untouched by the mechanism of supply and demand and by distinctions between commercial, military, political or religious activities; and the mercantilist policies of France, which tried to control the supply of furs by limiting the number of traders and regulating beaver prices on the French market. While the fur trade structure of New France had an inherent tendency towards geographic expansion, as Innis argued, it also had to be oligopolistic in nature, if investments in Indian alliances, explorations, and military support were to be maximized. Open competition could not be allowed because it would lead to the collapse of the structure.[18]

---

15   See H.A. Innis, *The Fur Trade in Canada* (Rev. ed. Toronto, 1956), 107-113.

16   See Abraham Rotstein, "Fur Trade and Empire: An Institutional Analysis" (unpublished Ph.D. thesis, University of Toronto, 1967), 72.

17   Innis, *Fur Trade*, 117. For his discussion of the impact of war on the fur trade and on New France, see 114-118.

18   In theory, the French licensing system set up to restrict the trade remained in operation from its re-establishment in 1728 to the end of the French regime; only twenty-five *congés* were to be sold each year. In practice, military officers in the upper country could also acquire for a modest fee exclusive trade privileges for their particular area. With some care, concluded one author, they could make an easy fortune. See Emile Salone, *La Colonisation de la Nouvelle-France* (Trois-Rivières, 1970), 390, 392-393. No clear official description of the licensing system was found for the period from 1750 to 1760, but the precise way in which the fur trade was restricted matters less than the fact of restriction.

It is not surprising, therefore, that most outfitters dabbled in the fur trade only occasionally. On the average, between 1750 and 1775, the Canadian merchants of Montreal invested in the trade only four times and signed up about eleven *engagés* each time, not quite enough to man two canoes. Few merchants outfitted fur trade ventures with any regularity and only six men hired an average of twelve or more *engagés*, more than twice before 1761 (see Table 1).

Table 1

LARGEST CANADIAN FUR TRADE OUTFITTERS IN MONTREAL, 1750-1760

Name	Total No. of Years	Total No. of Hirings	Yearly Average
CHARLY, Louis Saint-Ange	6	85	14.1
GODET, Dominique	5	85	17.0
LECHELLE, Jean	4	130	32.5
LEMOINE MONIERE, Alexis	7	300	42.8
L'HUILLIER CHEVALIER, François	7	90	12.6
TROTIER DESAUNIERS, Thomas Ignace "Dufy"	5	129	25.8

Source: "Répertoire des engagements pour l'ouest conservés dans les Archives judiciaires de Montréal," *Rapport de l'Archiviste de la province de Québec*, 1930-31, 353-453; 1931-32, 242-365; 1932-33, 245-304.

Three of these were unquestionably wealthy: Louis Saint-Ange Charly, an import merchant who, unlike his colleagues, had a large stake in the fur trade, realized 100,000 *livres* on his land holdings alone when he left the colony for France in 1764; Thomas-Ignace Trotier Desauniers "Dufy," who in a will drawn up in 1760, bequeathed 28,000 *livres* to the Sulpicians; the illiterate Dominique Godet, who in a similar document of 1768, mentioned 5,000 *livres* in cash in hand, land in three parishes in the vicinity of Montreal, "Batiment & Bateaux qui en dependent," around 5,000 *livres* in active debts, and two black slaves.[19] Two other large outfitters left relatively few belongings at the time of their death: Alexis Lemoine Monière left

---

[19] On Charly see PAC, RG 4 B58, vol. 15, 19 September 1764, pass by Governor Murray to "Monsr. Louis Saint-Ange Charly [and his family] to London, in their way to France agreeable to the Treaty of Peace..."; Archives Nationales du Québec à Montreal [formerly Archives judiciaires de Montréal; hereafter ANQ-M], Greffe de Pierre Panet, 16 août 1764, no. 2190. Trotier Desauniers "Dufy's" will is in ibid., 29 juillet 1760, no. 1168, and Godet's will is in ibid., 28 décembre 1768, no. 3140.

less than 1,000 *livres*, all of it in household goods, and François L'Huillier Chevalier just slightly more.[20] Little is known about the sixth man, Jean Léchelle.

If the fur trade made few wealthy men among those who invested heavily in it, it would be hard to argue that less considerable investors were more successful. It is not unreasonable to conclude that the fur trade was not very profitable for the overwhelming majority of outfitters and that it only sustained a very limited number of them each year. Yet the French had reduced costly competition to a minimum and had few worries about price fluctuations. How would Canadian outfitters fare under a different system?

The Advent of the British Merchants

With the arrival in Montreal of British traders, the workings of the fur trade were disrupted. At first, the licensing system was maintained and some areas were left to the exclusive trade of particular traders.[21] But from the very beginning the trade was said to be open to all who wanted to secure a licence, and the result could only be price competition. With individual traders going into the fur trade, the organization of the trade regressed. The previous division of labour between the *compagnie des Indes*, the import merchants and outfitters, the traders, the voyageurs, and the *engagés* was abandoned and during the first years of British rule the individual trader filled all of the functions previously spread among many "specialists."

The story of Alexander Henry, one of the first British merchants to venture into the upper country, illustrates the new pattern of trade. A young man from New Jersey, Alexander Henry came to Canada in 1760 with General Amherst's troops.[22] With the fall of Montreal Henry saw the opening of a "new market" and became acquainted with the prospects of the fur trade. The following year, he set out for Michilimackinac with a Montreal outfitter, Etienne Campion, whom he called his "assistant," and who took charge of the routine aspects of the trip.[23] Henry wintered at Michilimackinac. There he was urged by the local inhabitants to go back to Detroit as soon as possible, for they claimed to fear for his safety. Their fears were not without foundation, but Henry stayed on. His partner Campion reassured him: " ... the Canadian inhabitants of the fort were more hostile than the Indians, as being jealous of British traders, who ... were penetrating into the country."[24] At least

---

[20] The inventory of Monière's estate is in ibid., 28 décembre 1768, no. 3141; that of L'Huillier Chevalier's in ibid., 15[?] juin 1772, no. 3867.

[21] See Alexander Henry, *Travels and Adventures in Canada* (Ann Arbor University Microfilms, 1966), 191-192.

[22] W.S. Wallace, *Documents Relating to the North West Company*, Appendix A ("A Biographical Dictionary of the Nor'Westers"), 456.

[23] See Henry, *Travels*, 1-11, 34.

[24] Ibid., 39.

A Change in Climate: The Conquest and the Marchands of Montreal 119

some of the Canadians resented the British traders from the outset and a few tried to use the Indians to frighten them away.[25]

Henry proceeded to Sault Sainte-Marie the following year. In the spring of 1763, he returned to Michilimackinac and witnessed the massacre of the British garrison during Pontiac's revolt.[26] He was eventually captured by the Indians and adopted into an Indian family with whom he lived, in the Indian style, until late June 1764. Undaunted, Henry set out for the fur trade again, exploring the Lake Superior area. He was on the Saskatchewan River in 1776, tapping fur resources which the French had seldom reached.[27] Finally he settled down in Montreal in 1781, and while he did join the North West Company after its formation, he seldom returned to the upper country himself.[28]

Henry was not the first British merchant to reach the upper country. Henry Bostwick had obtained a licence from General Gage before him in 1761,[29] and the traders Goddard and Solomons had followed Henry into Michilimackinac in 1761. By early 1763 there were at least two more British merchants in the area.[30] In Montreal alone there were close to fifty new merchants by 1765. Governor Murray's list of the Protestants in the district of Montreal gives the names, the origins, and the "former callings" of forty-five.[31] Over half of them came from England and Scotland and 20 per cent were from Ireland. Only 13 per cent came from the American colonies and an equal number came from various countries (Switzerland, Germany, France, Guernsey). In the proportion of more than three to one, the newcomers had been merchants in their "former calling." The others had been soldiers and clerks. Many of the newcomers were men of experience and enterprise. Among them were Isaac Todd, Thomas Walker, Lawrence Ermatinger, Richard Dobie, Edward Chinn, John Porteous, William Grant, Benjamin Frobisher, James Finlay, Alexander Paterson, Forrest Oakes, and the Jewish merchants Ezekiel and Levy Solomons, all of whom became substantial traders.[32]

The arrival of so many merchants could only mean one thing: strenuous competition in the fur trade. Competition ruthlessly drove out those with less secure financial resources or with no taste for sharp practices. Among the British as among the French, few resisted the pressures. The story of the trader Hamback is not

---

[25] Ibid., 50. Cf. the rosier picture painted by Creighton, *The Empire of the St. Lawrence*, 33.
[26] Henry, *Travels*, 77-84. The Indians killed the British soldiers but ransomed the British traders, giving to each according to his profession.
[27] Henry, *Travels*, 264-292.
[28] See Wallace, *Documents*, 456; Milo M. Quaife, ed., *Alexander Henry's Travels and Adventures in the Years 1760-1776* (Chicago, 1921), xvi-xvii.
[29] Henry, *Travels*, 11; Quaife, *Henry's Travels*, 12 n. 6.
[30] Rich, *History of the Hudson's Bay Company*, II, 9.
[31] See PAC, C.O. 42, vol. 5, ff. 30-31, Murray's "List of Protestants in the District of Montreal," dated Quebec, 7 November 1765.
[32] See Miquelon, "The Baby Family," 181-187.

untypical. Out on the Miami River in 1766 and 1767, he found that competition left him with few returns to make to his creditor William Edgar of Detroit. "I live the life of a downright exile," he complained, "no company but a Barrel of drunken infamous fugitives, and no other Comfort of Life."[33]

The Canadian merchants of Montreal had competition not only from British merchants in their town, but also from American merchants moving into Detroit and Michilimackinac. William Edgar, a New York merchant, was at Niagara in late 1761.[34] In 1763 he was established at Detroit, where he conducted a brisk trade supplying individual traders at Michilimackinac and in the South West District.[35] From Schenectady, the partnership of Phyn and Ellice also carried on a profitable supply trade for the fur traders of the interior.[36]

Competition also came from the French on the Mississippi, who were trading in the Illinois country and the Lake Superior region. These French traders could all too easily link up with French-speaking traders from Canada, whose help, it was feared, they could enlist in subverting the Indians against British rule.[37] This always troubled Sir William Johnson, the Superintendent for Indian Affairs, who refused to abandon his suspicions of the French-speaking traders from Canada.

This many-sided competition produced a climate to which the Canadian merchants were not accustomed. The increased numbers of fur traders led to frictions with the Indians, smaller returns for some of the traders, and unsavoury trade practices.[38] Even the retail trade was affected. Merchants from England flooded the market at Quebec "with their manufactures, so much so that they are daily sold here at Vendue Twenty per Cent. below prime Cost."[39] In 1760 alone, the first year of British

---

[33] PAC, MG 19 A1, 1, William Edgar Papers, vol. 1, 97, F. Hamback to W. Edgar, 2 November 1766. See also ibid., 95, Hamback to D. Edgar, 29 October 1766, and 104-106, same to Edgar, 23 March 1767.

[34] Ibid., vol. 1, 12.

[35] See Ibid., vols, 1 and 2.

[36] R.H. Fleming, "Phyn, Ellice and Company of Schenectady," *Contributions to Canadian Economics*, IV (1932), 7-41.

[37] See Marjorie G. Jackson, "The Beginnings of British Trade at Michilimackinac," *Minnesota History* XI (September, 1930), 252; C.W. Alvord and C.E. Carter, eds., *The New Regime 1765-1767* (Collection of the Illinois State Historical Library, XI), 300-301; Alvord and Carter, eds., *Trade and Politics 1767-1769* (Collections of the Illinois State Historical Library, XVI), 382-453.

[38] See "Extract of a Letter from Michilimackinac, to a Gentleman in this City, dated 30th June," in *Quebec Gazette*, 18 August 1768; see also Rich, *History of the Hudson's Bay Company*, II, 26: "The suspicions between the Pedlars [from Quebec], and their encouragements of the Indians to trick and defraud their trade rivals, especially by defaulting on payments of debt, were widespread and continuous."

[39] *Quebec Gazette*, 7 January 1768.

A Change in Climate: The Conquest and the Marchands of Montreal 121

occupation, £60,000 worth of trade goods had been brought into Canada.[40] From 1765 to 1768 the pages of the *Quebec Gazette* were filled with notices of auctions by merchants returning to England and disposing of their wares after unsuccessful attempts to establish themselves in the trade of the colony.[41]

By 1768 some thought the Canadians still had the advantage in the fur trade, even though there was "Competition" and a "strong Jealousy" between Canadian and English. The Canadians' "long Connections with those Indians," wrote General Gage, "and their better Knowledge of their Language and Customs, must naturally for a long time give the Canadians an Advantage over the English...."[42] Sir William Johnson had expressed a similar opinion the previous year and had deplored the British merchants' tactics: "The English were compelled to make use of Low, Selfish Agents, French, or English as Factors, who at the Expense of honesty and sound policy, took care of themselves whatever became of their employers."[43]

Another observer, the Hudson's Bay Company trader at Moose Factory, complained of "Interlopers who will be more Destructive to our trade than the French was." The French had conducted a less aggressive trade: they "were in a manner Settled, their Trade fixed, their Standards moderate and Themselves under particular regulations and restrictions, which I doubt is not the Case now."[44] Competition was forcing the British merchants in Montreal into ruthless tactics, a development which upset the Hudson's Bay Company man and which would unsettle the Canadians.

The pattern of British domination of the fur trade began to emerge as early as 1767. Trading ventures out of Michilimackinac into the North West were conducted by Canadians, but British merchants supplied the financial backing. The North West expeditions demanded the lengthiest periods of capital outlay, lasting two or three years. British merchants, it seems, had better resources. Of the fifteen outfitters at Michilimackinac who sent canoes to the North West in 1767, nine were British and six were Canadian; the total value of canoes outfitted by the British came to £10,812.17, while the Canadians' canoes were worth only £3,061.10. The British outfitters—most notably Alexander Henry, Isaac Todd, James McGill, Benjamin Frobisher, Forrest Oakes—invested on the average £1,351.12 and the Canadians only £510.5. The average value of goods invested in each canoe stood at £415.17 for the British and £278.6 for the Canadians.[45] The Canadians' investment per canoe was

---

[40] Burt, *Old Province*, I, 92.

[41] The flooding of the Quebec market by British merchants was part of a larger invasion of the colonial trade in North America. See Marc Egnal and Joseph A. Ernst, "An Economic Interpretation of the American Revolution," *William and Mary Quarterly*, Third Series, XXIX (1972), 3-32.

[42] Quoted in Alvord and Carter, eds., *Trade and Politics*, 288.

[43] Ibid., 38.

[44] Quoted in E.E. Rich, *Montreal and the Fur Trade* (Montreal, 1966), 44.

[45] These figures are somewhat distorted by the inclusion of a single large British investor, Alexander Henry, who outfitted seven canoes worth £3,400 in all. See Charles E. Lart, ed.,

only two-thirds that of the British and the Canadians were already outnumbered as outfitters in what would become the most important region of the fur trade.[46]

Open competition was not conducive to the expansion of the fur trade and an oligopolistic structure reminiscent of the French system soon reappeared as the only solution.[47] This led to the formation of the North West Company in the 1780s but already in 1775, those Montreal merchants who had extended their operations as far as the Saskatchewan felt the need for collaboration rather than competition. Again developments in the more remote frontiers of the fur trade foretold of events to occur later in the whole of the trade: the traders on the Saskatchewan were almost all of British origin.[48] The fur trade was returning to the structures developed by the French, but during the period of competition which followed the Conquest the Canadians were gradually crowded out. There was some irony in that. Why had the Canadians fared so badly?

The Attitude of Government Officials

Much has been made of the natural sympathies of Murray and Carleton towards the Canadians and their antipathies towards the traders of their own nation. Yet for all their ideological inclinations there is no evidence that the governors turned their sentiments into policies of benevolence for Canadians in trade matters. Rather, it is easier to discover, among the lesser officials and some of the more important ones as well, an understandable patronizing of British rather than Canadian merchants. Colonial administrators may not have set a deliberate pattern of preference in favour of British merchants. But the Canadian merchants of Montreal, who put great store by official patronage, cared not whether the policy was deliberate or accidental; the result was the same.

Official preferences played against the Canadian traders in many ways. First, the lucrative trade of supplying the military posts was given to British and American merchants as a matter of course, and this occasion for profit was lost to the Canadians. Under the French regime some of the Montreal merchants, notably the

---

"Fur-Trade Returns, 1767," *Canadian Historical Review*, III (December, 1922), 351-358. The definition of the North West as including Lake Huron, Lake Superior, and "the northwest by way of Lake Superior" given in Rich, *Montreal and the Fur Trade*, 36-37, was used in making these compilations. The French traders were "Deriviere," "Chenville," St. Clair, Laselle, "Guillaid [Guillet]," and "Outlass [Houtelas]."

[46] See Rich, *Montreal and the Fur Trade*, 36-37.
[47] Jackson, *Minnesota History*, XI, 268-269.
[48] Rich, *History of the Hudson's Bay Company*, II, 68.

A Change in Climate: The Conquest and the Marchands of Montreal 123

Monières and the Gamelins, had profited from that trade.[49] Now it fell out of Canadian hands. This advantage did not shift to the sole favour of the British merchants of Quebec. New York and Pennsylvania traders were also awarded their share of the trade. The firms of Phyn, Ellice of Schenectady and Baynton, Wharton, and Morgan of Philadelphia received the lion's share of that business while the upper country was under the jurisdiction of Sir William Johnson.[50] But this was of little comfort to the Canadians.

Less tangible by-products of the British occupation of the former fur trading areas of New France are more difficult to assess than the loss of the supply trade; they were, however, quite real. One was the British military's attitude towards Canadians. The military were wary of French-speaking traders in Illinois and on the Mississippi. Although the French from Canada had been vanquished, French traders in the interior could still deal with France through New Orleans. No regulations, no boundaries could restrain French traders operating out of Louisiana from dealing with the Indians, and the Canadians who were confined to the posts protested against the advantage held by the French traders.[51] But who were these French traders? Did they not include Canadian *coureurs de bois* and wintering merchants? How could one really tell a French-speaking trader from Canada from a French-speaking trader out of New Orleans? Were not all of them suspect of exciting the Indians against the British, promising and perhaps hoping for France's return to America?[52] As late as 1768, when Indian discontent in the West threatened another uprising, General Gage failed to see any difference between French-speaking Canadians and the French from New Orleans:

> There is the greatest reason to suspect that the French are Endeavouring to engross the Trade, and that the Indians have acted thro' their Instigation, in the Murders they have committed, and the Resolutions we are told they have taken, to suffer no Englishman to trade with them. And in this they have rather been Assisted by the English Traders, who having no Consideration but that of a present

---

[49] On the Monières, see Igartua, "The Merchants and *Négociants* of Montreal," Ch. II. On the Gamelins, see Antoine Champagne, *Les La Vérendrye et les postes de l'ouest* (Quebec, 1968), *passim*.

[50] See R.H. Fleming, *Contributions to Canadian Economics*, IV, 13; on Baynton, Wharton and Morgan, see *The Papers of Sir William Johnson* [hereafter *Johnson Papers*], 14 vols. (Albany, 1921-1965), V, VI, XII, *passim*.

[51] PAC, C.O. 42, vol. 2, ff. 277-280, petition of the "Merchants and Traders of Montreal" to Murray and the Council, Montreal, 20 February 1765: *Johnson Papers*, V, 807-815, memorial and petition of Detroit traders to Johnson, 22 November 1767; XII, 409-414, 1768 trade regulations with the merchants' objections.

[52] See Alvord and Carter, eds., *The New Regime*, 118-119, and *Trade and Politics*, 39, 287; see also Stevens, *The Northwest Fur Trade*, 44.

gain, have thro' fear of exposing their own Persons, or hopes of obtaining greater influence with the Indians, continually employed French Commissarys or Agents, whom they have trusted with Goods for them to Sell at an Advanced price in the Indian Villages.[53]

Gage's suspicions of the French traders were nurtured by Sir William Johnson, who had to keep the Indians on peaceful terms with one another and with the British. It was part of Johnson's function, of course, to worry about possible uprisings and about subversive individuals. His job would be made easier if he could confine all traders to military posts where they could be kept under surveillance. But the traders had little concern for Sir William's preoccupations. If British traders were irresponsible in their desires of "present gain," the Canadian traders' vices were compounded by the uncertainty of their allegiance to the British Crown:

> Since the Reduction of that country [Canada], we have seen so many Instances of their [the Canadian traders'] Perfidy false Stories & C^a. Interested Views in Trade that prudence forbids us to suffer them or any others to range at Will without being under the Inspection of the proper Officers agreeable to His Majesty's Appointment....[54]

Johnson's attitude spread to the officers under him, even though Carleton had found nothing reprehensible in the Canadians' behaviour.[55] Johnson's deputy, George Croghan, believed there was collusion between the French from Canada and the French from Louisiana.[56] In 1763 the commandant at Michilimackinac, Major Etherington, had displayed a similar mistrust of the Canadians.[57] Major Robert Rogers, a later commandant at Michilimackinac, checked the Canadians by trading on his own account.[58]

---

[53] *Johnson Papers*, XII, 517, Thomas Gage to Guy Johnson, New York 29 May 1768.
[54] Ibid., V, 481. See also Alvord and Carter, eds., *The New Regime*, 118-119; *Johnson Papers*, V, 362; Alvord and Carter, eds., *Trade and Politics*, 39; *Johnson Papers*, V, 762-764; XII, 486-487; Stevens, *The Northwest Fur Trade*, 28.
[55] PAC, C.O. 42, vol. 27, ff. 81-85, Carleton to Johnson, Quebec, 27 March 1767.
[56] *Johnson Papers*, XII, 372-375, Croghan to Johnson, 18 October 1767.
[57] Henry, *Travels*, 71-72.
[58] See PAC, C.O. 42, vol. 26, f. 13, Court of St. James, Conway [Secretary of State] to the Commandants of Detroit and Michilimackinac, 27 March 1766. See also Alvord and Carter, (Eds.), *Trade and Politics*, 207-208, Gage to Shelburne, 12 March 1768; 239, Johnson to Gage, 8 April 1768; 375, Gage to Johnson, 14 August 1768; 378, Gage to Hillsborough, 17 August 1768; 384, Johnson to Gage, 24 August 1768; 599, Gage to Hillsborough, 9 September 1769. More than trading on his own account, Rogers was suspected of setting up an independent Illinois territory. He was eventually cleared. See "Robert Rogers," *Dictionary*

The British military's mistrust of the French traders from Canada was understandable. Before 1760, one of the major reasons for the American colonials' antagonism towards New France had been the French ability to press the Indians into their service to terrorize the western fringes of American settlement. Thus there was a historical as well as a tactical basis for the military's attitude towards the Canadians. But British officers failed to recognize that not all Canadian traders were potential troublemakers and that there was indeed very little tangible evidence, as Carleton had reminded Johnson, of any mischief on their part. The military's attitude was directed as much by ethnic prejudice as by military necessity.

The Canadian traders could not fail to perceive this prejudice, and it dampened their spirits. Perhaps the military's attitude, as much as competition, forced the Canadians into partnerships with British merchants. (The express purpose of the bonds required for the fur trade was to ensure loyal conduct; what better token of loyalty could there be for a Canadian trader than a bond taken out in his name by a British partner?) The military's mistrust of the Canadian traders did not lessen with time. The advantage which this prejudice gave British traders would continue for some twenty years after the Conquest, as the American Revolution rekindled the military's fears of treasonable conduct by the Canadians.

Other patronage relationships between British military officials and British traders also deprived the Canadians of an equal chance in the competition for furs. It is hard to evaluate precisely the effect of such patronage; only glimpses of it may be caught. Late in 1763 a Philadelphia merchant who had lost heavily because of Pontiac's uprising wrote to William Edgar in Detroit that Croghan was in England, where he was to "represent the Case of the Traders to his Majesty," and that General Amherst had "given us his faithful promise that he will do everything in his power in our behalf."[59] In 1765 Alexander Henry was granted the exclusive trade of Lake Superior by Major Howard, the military commandant at Michilimackinac. Nine years later Henry received the support of such patrons as the Duke of Gloucester, the consul of the Empress of Russia in England, and of Sir William Johnson in an ill-fated attempt to mine the iron ore of the Lake Superior area.[60]

These were obvious examples of patronage; other forms of cooperation were less visible. Another correspondent of William Edgar, Thomas Shipboy, asked Edgar to represent him in settling the affairs of a correspondent at Detroit and at Michilimackinac where, he added, "if you find any Difficulty in procuring his effects I dare say the Commanding officer will be of Service to you if you inform him in

---

of American Biography, XVI (New York, 1935), 108-109, and *Johnson Papers*, V. VI, XII, XIII, *passim*.

[59] PAC, William Edgar Papers, vol. 1, 43-44, Callender to Edgar, n.p., 31 December 1763.
[60] Henry, *Travels*, 191-192, 235.

whose [sic] behalf you are acting...."[61] Benjamin Frobisher also asked Edgar to "use your Interest with Capt. Robinson" to put a shipment of corn aboard the government vessel which sailed from Detroit to Michilimackinac.[62] Such shipping space was scarce and was only available through the courtesy of military officers or the ships' captains. Here again British traders put their social connections to good use. A last resort was sheer military force. Out on the Miami River, the trader Hamback saw "little hope of getting anything from [Fort] St. Joseph at all, if I don't get protected, by the Commanding Officer, who might easily get those [Canadian] rascals fetch'd down to Detroit if He would...."[63]

None of this patronage appears to have been available to Canadians. It is impossible to ascertain the degree to which military suspicions and patronage lessened the Canadians' chances in the fur trade. But more important, perhaps, than the actual loss of opportunities was the psychological handicap imposed upon the Canadians. What heart could they put in the game when the dice were so obviously loaded?

The Merchants' Political Activities

The enmity between British merchants and the military, the merchants' growing agitation in favour of "British liberties" and their sentiments of political self-importance have been ably told by others and need not be retold here.[64] What needs to be underlined is that political agitation was unfamiliar to the Canadians. They had no experience in these matters under French rule. Only on rare occasions during the pre-conquest years had the Canadian merchants engaged in collective political representations; such representations were elicited by the governor or the intendant to obtain the merchants' advice on specific issues.[65] As French subjects, the Canadian merchants of Montreal had lacked the power to foster their economic interests through collective political action.

After 1760, the Canadian merchants would gradually lose their political innocence under the influence of the British merchants. During the thirty years which followed the Conquest they would make "l'apprentissage des libertés anglaises" and in 1792 they would take their place in the newly created legislative assembly, more cognizant

---

[61] PAC, William Edgar Papers, vol. 1, 90, Thos. Shipboy to Rankin and Edgar, Albany, 21 August 1766.

[62] Ibid., 201, Benjamin Frobisher to Rankin and Edgar, Michilimackinac, 23 June 1769.

[63] Ibid., 104-106, F. Hamback to Edgar, 23 March 1767.

[64] The most detailed account is given in Burt, *Old Province*, I, Ch. VI and VII. See also Creighton, *Empire of the St. Lawrence*, 40-48.

[65] See for instance E.-Z. Massicotte, "La Bourse de Montréal sous le régime français," *The Canadian Antiquarian and Numismatic Journal*, Third Series, XII (1915), 26-32.

A Change in Climate: The Conquest and the Marchands of Montreal 127

of the workings of the British constitution than the British had expected.[66] But that is beyond the concern here. In the years preceding the American Revolution the Montreal merchants were still looking for bearings. They showed their growing political awareness by following in the *Quebec Gazette* the political and constitutional debates which were rocking the British Empire. The merchants also began to voice their concerns in petitions and memorials to the authorities in the colony and in London.

The *Quebec Gazette* was the province's official gazette and its only newspaper before 1778. The paper published public notices for the Montreal district and occasional advertisements sent in by Montrealers as well as matters of concern to Quebec residents. It also made an effort to publish Canadian news of a general character. It closely followed the debates raging across the Atlantic over the Stamp Act and the general issues of colonial taxation. It reported on changes in the Imperial government and on contemporary political issues in England, notably the Wilkes affair.[67]

The pages of the *Gazette* also served on occasion as a forum for political discussion. In September 1765 a "Civis Canadiensis" declared his puzzlement at all the talk of "British liberties" and asked for enlightenment. The following year, a Quebec resident wrote a series of letters arguing that the colony should not be taxed.[68] In 1767, a debate arose on the British laws relating to bankruptcy and their applicability in Quebec.[69] Because of the pressures of Governor Carleton the *Gazette* stifled its reporting of controversial issues after 1770 and thereafter had little to print about American affairs.[70] In 1775 the *Gazette*'s political outpourings were directed against the American rebels and towards securing the loyalty of those Canadians who might be seduced by revolutionary propaganda.[71] The paper had become more conservative in its selection of the news but those Canadians who read the *Gazette* had been made familiar with the concepts of personal liberty, of "no taxation without representation," of the limited powers of the sovereign, and of the rights of the people. The *Gazette*'s readers most probably included the leading merchants of Montreal.

The *Gazette* was not the only instrument for the learning of British liberties. Anxious to give the appearance of a unanimous disposition among all merchants in Montreal, the British merchants often called on their Canadian confrères to add their

---

[66] See Pierre Tousignant, "La Genèse et l'avènement de la Constitution de 1791" (unpublished Ph.D. thesis, Université de Montréal, 1971).

[67] See the *Quebec Gazette* of 15 September 1766 and the issues from June to September 1768.

[68] See *Quebec Gazette*, 26 September 1765. Tousignant, "La Genèse," 21-39, points out the political significance of this letter.

[69] See texts by "A MERCHANT" in the 10 and 17 December 1767 issues, and rebuttals in the 24 and 31 December 1767 and 7 and 21 January 1768 issues.

[70] Tousignant, "La Genèse," 39.

[71] See issues of 13 and 27 July, and 5 October 1775.

names to various memorials and petitions dealing with the political and the economic state of the colony. The Canadian merchants who signed these petitions and memorials represented the top layer of the Canadian mercantile group in Montreal. Those who signed most often were the import merchants and the busy outfitters.

These Canadian merchants followed the political leadership of the British merchants. From 1763 to 1772 their petitions were either literal translations or paraphrased equivalents of petitions drafted by British merchants. It was only in December 1773 that they asserted views different from those of their British counterparts.[72] They petitioned the King that their "ancient laws, privileges, and customs" be restored, that the province be extended to its "former boundaries," that some Canadians be taken into the King's service, and that "the rights and privileges of citizens of England" be granted to all.[73]

The Canadians were becoming aware of their own position and were seeking to consolidate it against the attacks of the British element. The demand for the maintenance of the "ancient laws" was designed to counter British demands for British laws and representative institutions. The Canadians opposed the latter since, in their view, the colony was "not as yet in a condition to defray the expenses of its own civil government, and consequently not in a condition to admit of a general assembly."[74] The demand for "a share of the civil and military employments under his majesty's government" came naturally to those who had lived under the French system of patronage. The Canadians had been accustomed to seek official patronage as the main avenue of upward mobility. The prospect of being denied such patronage was "frightful" to them, since they had little familiarity with alternate patterns of social promotion.[75]

In style as well as in content the Canadian merchants' petitions and memorials revealed differences in attitudes between Canadians and British. British memorials and

---

[72] Canadian notables of Quebec broke with the "Old Subjects" earlier: a petition, thought to date from 1770 and signed by leading Canadians of that city, asked for the restoration of Canadian institutions. See Adam Shortt and Arthur G. Doughty, *Documents Relating to the Constitutional History of Canada* (2nd. ed. Ottawa, 1918) [hereafter *Docs. Const. Hist. Can.*], I, 419-421.

[73] The petition and the memorial are reproduced in *Docs. Const. Hist. Can.*, I, 504-506, 508-510.

[74] Ibid., I, 511. The British merchants of Montreal signed a counter-petition in January 1774, requesting the introduction of an assembly and of the laws of England. See ibid., I, 501-502.

[75] Recent historians have highlighted the influence of the military and civil administrations as sources of economic and social betterment in New France. See Guy Frégault, *Le XVIIIe siècle canadien* (Montreal, 1968), 382-384; W.J. Eccles, "The Social, Economic, and Political Significance of the Military Establishment in New France," *Canadian Historical Review*, LII (March, 1971), 17-19; and Cameron Nish, *Les Bourgeois-Gentilshommes de la Nouvelle-France* (Montreal, 1968), *passim*.

petitions were rarely prefaced by more than the customary "Humbly showeth" and went directly to the point. In their own memorials and petitions, the Canadians first took "the liberty to prostrate themselves at the foot" of the royal throne and surrendered themselves to the "paternal care" of their sovereign. They often appealed to the wisdom, justice, and magnanimity of the King.[76] Their formal posture of meekness contrasted sharply with the self-assertion of the British. The Canadians' "Habits of Respect and Submission," as one British official put it,[77] may well have endeared them to Murray and Carleton, but those habits constituted a psychological obstacle against their making full use of their new-found "British liberties" to foster their own economic interest.

Conclusion

With the fall of Montreal to British arms in September 1760 something was irrevocably lost to the Canadian merchants of that city. More than the evil effects of the war, the tribulations over the fate of the Canada paper, or the post-war commercial readjustments, the most unsettling consequence of the Conquest was the disappearance of a familiar business climate. As New France passed into the British Empire, the Montreal outfitters were thrown into a new system of business competition, brought about by the very numbers of newly arrived merchants, unloading goods in the conquered French colony and going after its enticing fur trade. In opening up the trade of the colony to competition, the British presence transformed Canadian commercial practices. The change negated the Canadian merchants' initial advantage of experience in the fur trade and created a novel business climate around them.

Competition in trade, the new political regime, the Canadian merchants' inability to obtain the favours of the military, all these crated a mood of uncertainty and pessimism among the Montreal merchants. The merchants could only conclude from what was happening around them that the new business climate of the post-Conquest period favoured British traders at their expense. They can be understood if they were not eager to adapt their ways to the new situation.

It may be argued, of course, that the changes which produced the new situation are subsumed under the notion of "conquest" and that the previous pages only make more explicit the "decapitation" interpretation advanced by the historians of the "Montreal school."[78] It is true enough that the new business climate described here

---

[76] See PAC, C.O. 42, vol. 24, ff. 72-73v; ibid., vol. 3, f. 262; *Docs. Const. Hist. Can.*, I, 504-508.

[77] See *Docs. Const. Hist. Can.*, I, 504.

[78] Maurice Séguin, of the History Department of the Université de Montréal, was the first to present a systematic interpretation of the Conquest as societal decapitation. His book, *L'Idée d'indépendance au Québec: genèse et historique* (Trois-Rivières, 1968), which contains a

might not have been created after the Seven Years' War had Canada remained a French possession. But there is no guarantee that other changes would not have affected the Montreal merchants. During the last years of the French regime they had reaped few profits from the fur trade. After the Conquest they continued in the fur trade much on the same scale as before. The Montreal merchants were not "decapitated" by the Conquest; rather, they were faced in very short succession with a series of transformations in the socio-economic structure of the colony to which they might have been able to adapt had these transformations been spread over a longer period of time.

This paper has attempted to show that the fate of the Canadian merchants of Montreal after the Conquest followed from the nature of trade before the Conquest and from the rate at which new circumstances required the merchants to alter their business behaviour. But it should be remembered that the decapitation hypothesis still remains to be tested in the area of the colony's economy which was most heavily dependent upon the control of the metropolis, the import-export trade of the Quebec merchants. Only a detailed examination of the role and the activities of the Quebec merchants, both before and after the Conquest, will fully put the decapitation hypothesis to the test.

---

summary of his thought, was published twenty years after its author first sketched out his thesis. Guy Frégault's *Histoire de la Nouvelle-France, IX, La guerre de la Conquête, 1754-1760*, (Montreal, 1955) is a masterful rendition of that conflict, cast as the *affrontement* of two civilizations. Michel Brunet, the most voluble of the "Montreal school" historians, has assumed the task of popularizing Séguin's thought. See Brunet, "La Conquête anglaise et la déchéance de la bourgeoisie canadienne (1760-1793)," in his *La Présence anglaise et les Canadiens* (Montreal, 1964), 48-112. Brunet developed the point further in *Les Canadiens après la Conquête, I: 1759-1775* (Montreal, 1969). An abridged version of Brunet's position is provided in his *French Canada and the Early Decades of British Rule, 1760-1791* (Ottawa, 1963). For a review of French-Canadian historiography on the Conquest up to 1966, see Ramsay Cook, "Some French-Canadian Interpretations of the British Conquest: une quatrième dominante de la pensée canadienne-française," Canadian Historical Association *Historical Papers*, 1966, 70-83.

Loyalism and Conservatism in Early British North America

Section 4

Canadians like to think that they are different from Americans, and those looking for a distinctive Canadian identity have frequently pointed to a certain conservatism in this country—a resepct for authority, order, and community rather than individual rights—which seems to contrast with the democratic individualism of the United States. This conservatism is often traced back to the United Empire Loyalists—people born in the American colonies who opposed the American Revolution and left the United States when the Revolution triumphed. It is supposed that the Loyalists—often thought of as coming from the well-to-do and privileged sections of American society—brought anti-revolutionary and conservative values with them when they came to Canada and Nova Scotia.

In the first of these essays, Neil MacKinnon looks at the Loyalists who went to Nova Scotia and describes their early experiences and responses to that province. Does his account seem consistent with the traditional image of the Loyalists? Were his Loyalists particularly conservative? Did they all come from privileged classes? Did they share many political or social values in common?

S.F.Wise examines a different source of conservatism in British North America: the Churches. Why did the world view of late-18th and early-19th century religion—especially Anglicanism—lead it to stress order, authority, and hierarchy? What is there in the traditional Christian view of how mankind and human society came to exist that stands in the way of individual human freedom, i.e. of the idea that people should be free to run their own lives as they see fit? How did the religious message of Anglican clergymen encourage a loyalist tradition that was independent of the Loyalists themselves?

For a survey of early Maritime history, see W.S.McNutt, *The Atlantic Provinces, 1712-1857*. The view of the Loyalists as a source of Canadian conservatism—and later of socialism!—is presented in Gad Horowitz, "Conservatism, Liberalism, Socialism," in *Canadian Journal of Economics and Political Science*, May 1966.

Nova Scotia Loyalists 1783-1785

Neil MacKinnon[1]

They had lost more than a war. They had lost their homes and property. They had lost their birthright, their place in history and, long before the official peace, they had lost their faith in their cause. This loss of faith and sense of betrayal enveloped the Loyalists as they set sail for Nova Scotia in "this hour of Darkness, Calamity & Confusion."[2]

> Was there ever an instance, my dear Cousin, can any history produce one, where such a number of the best of human beings were deserted by the government they have sacrificed their all for?[3]

There were brave epithets cast over their shoulders about quitting "this damned country with pleasure."[4] But they were not leaving because of an abhorrence for Republican principles. They were leaving because they could not stay. They were "wretched outcasts of America and Britain."[5] They would react to the elements of their exile with common instincts and a common rhetoric shaped in the crucible of revolution, and significantly tempered by this sense of desertion. But the bond of allegiance encompassed many types. These Loyalists had fought the war for varied, complex and personal reasons. The post-war release from the centripetal force of their loyalty would allow the differences among them to emerge, and the harsh environment of "Nova Scarcity" would accentuate them.

They came to Nova Scotia because they had little other choice. It was the most accessible land in which to re-settle. Canada was a distant interior wilderness, inhabited by people of a different faith and language. Some had gone to the West Indies, but most considered it an alien land of excessive heat and yellow fever. For different reasons, Britain was also an alien land. It was too grand, and without money

---

[1] The author would here like to thank Prof. G.A. Rawlick for his criticism, suggestions, and encouragement.

[2] Public Archives of Canada, A-170, Society for the Propagation of the Gospel: "C" Series, Box 1/1, Nova Scotia, 1752-1791, No. 39. Isaac Browne to Dr. Maurice, September 26, 1783.

[3] *The Winslow Papers*, ed. W.O. Raymond (St. John, N.B., 1901), p. 79. Sarah Winslow to Benjamin Marston, April 10, 1783.

[4] Public Archives of Nova Scotia, The White Collection, Vol. III, No. 193. C. Clopper to Charles Whitworth, April 18, 1783.

[5] Jacob Bailey, quoted in A.W.H. Eaton, *The History of King's County, Nova Scotia* (Salem Press, 1910), p. 107.

and connections, "the Man is lost—he is Nothing—less than Nothing and Vanity—& his Contemplation of his own comparative Littleness, is Vexation of Spirit."[6] Moreover, they were Americans, marked by the land in many subtle ways. And to the northeast there was Nova Scotia, a short journey by sea, where rumour had it good land was available. It was on the periphery of the world they had known, with the promise that only a colony can have, but a Royal colony, in a temperate clime. They had little time to study this land of fog and exile, and yet because they were being expelled there was a certain bravado in their attitude to the land. Loyalists who had gone earlier, and agents of various groups who had come to scout the colony, sent back encouraging reports. The land was good, the cattle plentiful, the taxes few, the government cheap and loyal. The country was strategically located for the fisheries, the West Indies trade and the British market, protected from the Americans by a Royal government, and with great potential. Joseph Pynchon, writing his report as agent to the Port Roseway Associates of New York in January of 1783, discussed in some detail the tremendous advantages of Port Roseway over both Halifax and New England.[7] "The Governor and Sir Andrew are both of the same opinion, that it will be one of the *Capital ports* in America."[8] There was, moreover, some small consolation in the fact that so many Loyalists were going to Nova Scotia. Part of the promise of the land lay in these people who would settle it, for "every body, all the World moves on to Nova Scotia."[9]

Letters from Loyalists in England seemed to confirm their wisdom in choosing Nova Scotia. The disillusionment of two friends of Timothy Ruggles concerning their plight in England had induced him to come to Nova Scotia.[10] A friend of Jacob Bailey had written him concerning his appointment to the mission in Annapolis. "You are now on *good bottom* and must be much more happy than tho' you were here, dancing attendance for an uncertain pittance."[11]

To many Nova Scotia was a mixed blessing, with the present discomfort outweighed by the promise of the future. Timothy Ruggles, in the Annapolis Valley, was very much impressed with the fertility of the soil and was actually boastful of the apples and other produce he was growing.[12] Gideon White spoke as

---

[6] *The Winslow Papers*, p. 14. Jonathan Sewall to Edward Winslow.

[7] P.A.C., M.G. 9, B6, pp. 60-61. Joseph Pynchon to Port Roseway Associates, in Minute Book of the Port Roseway Associates.

[8] Ibid., p. 60.

[9] *The Winslow Papers*, p. 124. Major Upham to Edward Winslow, August 21, 1783.

[10] R.S. Longley, "An Annapolis County Loyalist," *Collections of the Nova Scotia Historical Society*, XXXI (1957), 89.

[11] P.A.N.S., The Bailey Papers, Vol. III.—to Jacob Bailey, February 13, 1782. N.B. *All references to Jacob Bailey, other than quotations from secondary sources, come from the research and generosity of Ron Macdonald, of Halifax.*

[12] *The Winslow Papers*, pp. 106-107. Gen. Timothy Ruggles to Edward Winslow, Sr., July 17, 1783.

favourably of Chedabucto. "That situation is one of the best in this country."[13] Edward Winslow found the country crowded, expensive and miserable, and yet a place of opportunity for a man—like himself—of talent and ambition.[14] Jason Courtney was very discouraged on his arrival at Shelburne, yet again he perceived the considerable potential. The fish "never was more plenty nor easeyer come at, than from this place," the land "far preferable to any about Halifax" and the harbour was one of the "best in the World exceeding easey of access."[15]

The reality could be lost amidst the promises of both the colony and the people settling it, and what sometimes emerged was a loser's wishful thinking that it would eclipse the republic they had left. They might be "laying the foundations of a new Empire," and establishing "a *place chosen by the Lords elect.*"[16]

But this sense of mission seemed limited to a few, and threatened by the harsh reality of re-settlement. Most Loyalists were not so sanguine and would not have argued with the reference to "Nova Scarcity."

> All our golden promises have vanished. We were taught to believe this place was not barren and foggy, as had been represented, but we find it ten times worse.... It is the most inhospitable climate that ever mortal set foot on. The winter is of insupportable length and coldness, only a few spots fit to cultivate, and the land is covered with a cold, spongy moss, instead of grass, and the entire country is wrapt in the gloom of perpetual fog.[17]

The letters going back to the United States begin to echo this assessment. A Philadelphia newspaper in 1783 gives some idea of the changing picture of Nova Scotia. "Many of the refugees who have settled at Port Roseway have wrote their friends in New York by no means to come to that place."[18] The New York group of Loyalists for whom Amos Botsford was agent were disillusioned quite early. In May of 1783 they had written to say they were "both sorry and surprized that our affairs in your province are in so unpleasant a situation."[19] Captain Callbeck could not congratulate Edward Winslow on his arrival in Halifax, for that would be "a very

---

13   P.A.N.S., White Collection, Vol. III, No. 300. Gideon White to Thomas Melish, August 3, 1784.
14   *The Winslow Papers*, p. 97. Edward Winslow to Ward Chipman, July 7, 1783.
15   P.A.N.S., White Collection, Vol. III, No. 210. James Courtney to Archibald Cunningham, July 1, 1783.
16   White Collection, Vol. III, No. 283. William Parker to Charles Whitworth, June 8, 1784.
17   James S. Macdonald, "Memoirs of Governor John Parr," *Coll. N.S.H.S.*, XIV (1910), 51.
18   W.O. Raymond, "The Founding of Shelburne; Benjamin Marston at Halifax, Shelburne and Miramichi," *Collections of the New Brunswick Historical Society*, No. 8 (1909), 250.
19   P.A.C., M.G. 23, D.4, Vol. I, No. 11. New York Agents to Amos Botsford *et al.*, May 31, 1783.

chilly and unmeaning compliment, the Country you have left is in every respect (but as to Loyalty) a Paradise in comparison."[20] Joshua Chandler, in writing from the United States in July of 1783, expected to see all of his people back within three months, for "Nova Scotia is not the place for Happiness, or I am greatly deceived."[21] And at Shelburne, especially, the dream of the Loyalists was being shouldered aside by reality.

> I am told most Horrid accounts of the place that many people have ruined themselves by building large & spacious Houses that the Land is most Intolerably bad and Totaly unfit for Cultivation at these Accounts I am Exceedingly distressed for many of the poor Suffering Loyalists who have Emigrated thither if this is True must be ruined why was not the place Sufficiently Explored before the people went this Surely was bad management Indeed if what I hear is true.[22]

Nor was their attitude to the Nova Scotian any better. It was one of contempt, sometimes patronizing, and always self-righteous. The Nova Scotians were lazy, "languid wretches" who had been forced into some industry through shame of the Loyalists' accomplishments and energies.[23] A Loyalist traveller through Nova Scotia in the summer of 1783 found that "the people seem to live and let tomorrow provide for itself. You see a sameness in the countenance of everyone except the Refugees who are quite a Different set of people."[24] They were also shrewd to the point of greediness, and willing to turn the refugees' tragedy to their own advantage. To S.S. Blowers, they were "accumulating wealth at a great rate by the exorbitant prices which they extort from the Strangers."[25] Jacob Bailey also found that they "have enriched themselves by selling their produce by no means at a moderate price to these unfortunate adventurers."[26] This alleged greed had been detrimental to the growth of Annapolis, for the landowners had demanded such extravagant prices of the Loyalists that the more affluent had been driven to Shelburne, Halifax and the Digby area.[27]

Occasionally, however, beneath this aura of persecution, more general impressions of the Nova Scotian and his particular character can be found. In a

---

[20] *The Winslow Papers*, p. 149. Capt. Callbeck to Edward Winslow, November 21, 1783.
[21] P.A.C., M.G. 23, D.4, Vol. I, No. 13. Joshua Chandler to Amos Botsford, July 1783.
[22] P.A.N.S., White Collection, Vol. III, N.. 310. Thomas Milledge to Gideon White, September 4, 1784.
[23] *The Winslow Papers*, p. 251. Edward Winslow to Sir John Wentworth, November 27, 1784.
[24] P.A.N.S., White Collection, Vol. XV, No. 1539. Diary of an unnamed Loyalist, August 18, 1783.
[25] *The Winslow Papers*, p. 135.
[26] P.A.N.S., Bailey Papers, Vol. XIV. Jacob Bailey to Dr. Maurice, October 28, 1785.
[27] Same to same, May 12, 1786.

journal kept by Mather Byles III, there is a description of a brief visit among some natives of Yarmouth "to see their manner of living," a description which tells something of both Bluenose and Loyalist.

> The houses, or rather huts, are very miserable, some thing like those inhabited by the French people on the road to Birch Cove—I stopped at four different cottages to see their manner of living, and amuse myself with a little *right down Yankeyism*—In one of them liv'd a New England shoemaker, who immediately after the first salutations began to question me *conserning the faith*—He told me he had been putting up his petition for rain "And I dare say" says he "we shall have a *spurt* before to morrow evening."—He asked my opinion of Allan's treatise, said he begun it: but finding it was not *right sound doctrine* he *hove* it by again. Allan, he says, died in New England last spring. His wife was receiving a visit from a young lady of about twenty, who had travelled from a back country settlement called Zebouge for her education—She goes to school, and *larns all fine sort of work and sich-like*.[28]

Byles' superior tone in amusing himself with a simple yet shrewd Yankee tells us less of the typical Nova Scotian than of those characteristics which the Loyalist was beginning to classify as typically Nova Scotian. Yet this type of description is not frequent, for the Loyalist at this time could not, without difficulty, measure anyone except by the yardstick of the rebellion and its tragic consequences. It was thought that because of the particular attitude of the Nova Scotian towards the rebellion, "their envy and malignity will induce 'em to throw every obstacle and impediment in your way. I am astonished that they have not art to conceal the principles by which they are actuated."[29] As much as any of the rebelling states, during the late war they had been "King Killers,"[30] and had lived with "loyalty upon the tip of their tongues and rebellion in their hearts."[31] Nor had the cessation of hostilities weakened this feeling, for they were still "inclined to favour the Americans in other words are Rebells,"[32] and Halifax was "that source of Republicanism" that nourished the rest of the colony.[33]

---

[28] P.A.N.S., The Byles Papers, Vol. I, Folder 2, p. 14. Journal of Mather Byles III.
[29] *The Winslow Papers*, p. 291. Edward Winslow to Ward Chipman, April 4, 1785.
[30] Church Historical Society, Austin, Texas, Papers Relating to the Rev. Jacob Bailey (Microfilm). Jacob Bailey to ——, May 4, 1780.
[31] P.A.N.S., Bailey Papers, Vol. XIII. Jacob Bailey to Mrs. Rachel Barlow, November 8, 1779.
[32] P.A.N.S., White Collection, Vol. XV, No. 1539, Diary of an unnamed Loyalist, August 22, 1783.
[33] John Garner, "The Electoral Franchise in Colonial Nova Scotia" (unpublished M.A. Thesis, University of Toronto, 1948), p. 52.

The people in this Country having catched the Contagion early and indeed I wonder it has remain'd in the stamp of Government as 7/8ths of the people are Bigotted to the American Cause.... The people in this country don't deny their principles and are in general like the same class of N. England from which they ransome for Debt.[34]

Yet the Bluenose Nova Scotian was merely an incidental factor in the early struggle for survival among the Loyalists. On the other hand the British government and its efforts were all important and loomed far larger in the Loyalist mind. The attitude of the Loyalist towards the Crown in these early years was one of utter dependence and great distrust. They feared not receiving what they would treat with contempt when received. Because of the repetitious petulance of many of their requests and comments it is easy to forget the prevailing mood of desperation. It was there before they left New York, upon the initial announcement of receiving only six months provisions.[35] And it was there in the initial period in Nova Scotia. Although there were complaints about receiving "nothing here by His Majesties' rotten pork and unbaked flour,"[36] the fear was in not receiving the rotten pork at all. Although provisions were continued for three years or more, the Loyalists were never really certain or assured as to how long the provisions would continue, and thus memorials such as that of the magistrates of Shelburne in January of 1784, for a continuance, are common.[37] That it was often inadequate or unequally distributed was the crux of many Loyalist complaints throughout the colony. Charles Morris, the Surveyor General, writing to Amos Botsford of Digby in September of 1783, referred to the discouragement of the people concerning the promises of supplies not being kept by the government.[38] And as late as 1785, Mather Byles had "an abundance of distressful stories from Shelburne, Passamaquoddy, St. Mary's Bay, &c, complaining of the shortness of provisions & the danger they are in of starving."[39] To harried officialdom they appeared as insatiable ingrates. They complained loud and long about the promises delayed or not kept, and yet met extra concessions with something bordering disdain.

---

[34] P.A.N.S., White Collection, Vol. XV, No. 1539. Diary of an unnamed Loyalist, September 5, 1783.
[35] P.A.C., M.G. 9, B.6, pp. 193-194. Minute Book of the Port Roseway Associates.
[36] Macdonald, "Memoir of Governor Parr," p. 51.
[37] Col. Cor. N.S., Vol. 12, p. 30, from *Report of the Public Archives of Canada*, 1894 (Ottawa, 1895), p. 412. Memorial of the Magistrates of Shelburne to Parr, January 3, 1784.
[38] P.A.C., M.G. 23, D.4, Vol. I., No. 4. Charles Morris to Amos Botsford, September 3, 1783.
[39] *The Winslow Papers*, p. 264. Mather Byles, Jr., to Edward Winslow, January 25, 1785.

It is but a few weeks ago I heard of your Regiment being fixed on the British Establishment; I sincerely congratulate you on the event; Yet I confess it is no more than what equity and justice demanded.[40]

And yet their attitude of ingratitude should be understood in the context of their claims, and their weighing of what they had sacrificed with what they had received for that sacrifice. If they were to be too grateful, they would be selling short the only marketable commodity they really had, their loyalty. The Loyalists believed that Britain had sacrificed them for the sake of peace, and in Nova Scotia they were filled with a strong fear that Britain would sacrifice them again, for the sake of economy. Britain might thus be moved less by gratitude than by guilt, and if this were so, it would be necessary to keep before Britain the uniqueness of their loyalty and the price they had paid for it. Perhaps there was a trace of this pragmatism in their self-consciously strenuous celebration of such Loyalist holy days as the King's birthday,[41] and "the anniversary of the glorious and ever memorable TWELTH of APRIL, 1782," the day on which Admiral Rodney had defeated a French fleet in the West Indies and a day celebrated, at least in Shelburne, "with all the Joyous mirth due, from every loyal subject, on so great an occasion."[42] Perhaps there was also a slightly pragmatic as well as emotional basis for their hostility to the Nova Scotians, for their rebellious tendencies made an excellent foil for the loyalty of the refugees.

This stress was to be found in almost every letter to or concerning government officials, whether it was Charles Inglis' reference to "that sovereign for whom they had sacrificed everything but a good conscience,"[43] or the memorial to Parr from the Port Roseway Associates, "who have been great Sufferers in the present Unhappy Contest."[44] The appeal was to be found most clearly expressed in the briefs drawn up for indemnification of the Loyalists, in which the nobility of the Loyalists stands in stark contrast to the quibbling of the British government over indemnification of fortunes that "have been sacrificed by the State itself to the public peace and safety."[45]

If the Loyalists' anger towards the Crown had to be controlled, and expressed only indirectly through agents in London, their attitude towards local officials could be shown more directly. And it was. To the Loyalists, the officials in local control of the King's generosity were indifferent to their plight, or interested in it only as a

---

[40] P.A.N.S., White Collection, Vol. III, No. 326. Charles Whitworth to Messrs. Geo. & Geo. Debloise, October 21, 1784.

[41] *Port Roseway Gazeteer and Shelburne Advertiser*, June 9, 1785, p. 3, col. 2.

[42] *Royal American Gazette* (Shelburne), April 18, 1785, p. 3, col. 3.

[43] P.A.C., M.G., 23, C.6, Pt. I, p. 4. Correspondence to Charles Inglis.

[44] P.A.C., M.G. 9, B6, pp. 34-35. Memorial to Governor Parr, December 21, 1782, in Minute Book of the Port Roseway Associates.

[45] *Royal American Gazette* (Shelburne), June 13, 1785, p. 2, col. 2.

source of exploitation. At quite an early stage, the spokesmen for the Port Roseway Associates were bitterly complaining of the treatment received and obstacles placed in the way of settlement.[46] Governor Parr was early accused of being unwilling to escheat,[47] and faulted for both the shortage and the incompetence of his surveyors. In defending himself to the home government against such charges, he simply underlined the wide extent of them.[48] There were constant clashes between surveyor and loyalist,[49] in which "the Surveyors (poor devils we are) are reflected upon in the Grossest Manner."[50]

Moreover, government officials were frequently charged with procuring fees, specifically against the King's orders. Charles Morris, except for some minor and borderline nepotism, could refute such charges.[51] But others could not. Richard Gibbons, who was Attorney-General until 1784, never hesitated to charge fees of the Loyalists whether he had the right or not.[52] Loyalists complained of John Wentworth who, as Surveyor General of the King's woods, charged fees against the King's regulations.[53] Benjamin Marston, who rarely praised the Loyalists of Shelburne, had as little use for Halifax officialdom. He commented on the arrival of a customs man from Halifax, "Mr. Binney was sent there to pick a little money out of the people's pockets under pretense of entering their vessels."[54] That few government officials were exempt from the hostility of the Loyalists is indicated by Charles Morris in commenting on the "unmerited ungenerous complaints which have been made against all the officers of Government without Exception."[55]

Nor did the Loyalists feel it was any part of their function to help the surveyor in any way, unless for money. This refusal to help was a frequent complaint in Marston's diary, and a regular litany in the letterbook of Charles Morris.[56] By 1785 the government was reduced to threatening the Loyalists with the loss of their lots to

---

[46] Esther C. Wright, *The Loyalists of new Brunswick* (Fredericton, 1955), p. 35.
[47] W.S. MacNutt, *New Brunswick, A History: 1784-1867* (Toronto, 1963), p. 34. This reference is to land in the St. John valley.
[48] Beamish Murdoch, *A History of Nova Scotia or Acadie* (Halifax, 1865), III, 31.
[49] P.A.N.S., White Collection, Vol. III, No. 274. John McPherson to Gideon White, May 16, 1784.
[50] P.A.N.S., Vol. 395, letterbook of Surveyor General Charles Morris. Charles Morris to Robert Gray, January 2, 1785.
[51] Charles Morris to Robert Gray, February 6, 1785.
[52] Mr. Justice Doull, "The First Five Attorneys-General of Nova Scotia," *Coll. N.S.H.S.*, XXVI (1952), 41-42.
[53] Murdoch, *History of Nova Scotia*, III, 44; W.S. MacNutt, *The Atlantic Provinces* (Toronto, 1965), p. 108.
[54] Raymond, "The Founding of Shelburne," p. 213.
[55] P.A.N.S., Letterbook of Charles Morris. Charles Morris to Major Studholm, November 12, 1784.
[56] Charles Morris to Rev. Edward Brudenell, March 24, 1785.

more willing refugees if they did not furnish the necessary assistance of axe and chain men.[57] Moreover, there appeared to be a double standard among many of the Loyalists. If the government was obliged to be honest and conscientious towards them, it did not necessarily mean that they had also to be honest and conscientious towards the government. Benjamin Marston was, from the earliest days of Shelburne, concerned with the threat of speculators and adventurers.[58] One of the simplest and favourite ploys was for the captains to have minors and servants included in the application for lots.[59] General Campbell was forced to set up a new board to check into the many abuses and frauds in relation to the provisions.[60] Loyalists were claiming for families that had long since departed, and Campbell finally had to order a complete muster of Loyalists and soldiers in the colony to stop such abuses. This did not solve the problem, for many refugees left in the following spring, the frauds increased, and Campbell had to order another muster.[61] Nor had the speculation in the land been deterred, for in 1785 Morris noted, "we are well assured the People in every District are disposing of their land for much less than it has cost Gov^t for laying out and never mean to settle in the country but to make the most of us."[62]

Behind the surveyor stood the shadowy presence of the government at Halifax, and the Loyalists distrusted both its power and its motives. Antill Gallop expressed some reservations concerning its impartiality. "From such d___md G___rs, S___ys', Courtiers and brothers in Law God Lord deliver us."[63] Edward Winslow referred to the Halifax clique which controlled government and anything else worth controlling as "nabobs,"[64] and Jacob Bailey dismissed them as "a few self-interested republicans at the Metropolis."[65] The focal point for most of this contempt was Governor Parr. He had come to Nova Scotia hoping for a comfortable little niche in which to pass his waning career, only to find himself facing a horde of hungry Loyalists. There were completely unexpected demands on leadership, administration and energy, and a factious situation in which he was bound to make enemies. What the Loyalists considered his incompetence would have assured hostility. But he was also the protégé of the hated Lord Shelburne. The Loyalists felt, moreover, that part of the

---

57   *Port Roseway Gazeteer and Shelburne Advertiser*, May 12, 1785, p. 3, col. 2.
58   Raymond, "The Founding of Shelburne," p. 226.
59   Ibid., pp. 235, 240.
60   A. & W.I., Vol. 406, p. 145, from *Report of the Public Archives of Canada*, 1894, p. 417. Campbell to Sydney, April 20, 1784.
61   A. & W.I., Vol. 406, p. 432, from ibid., pp. 433-434. Same to same, June 24, 1785.
62   P.A.N.S., Letterbook of Charles Morris. Charles Morris to Rev. Edward Brudenell, February 12, 1785.
63   P.A.N.S., Bailey Papers, Vol. III. Antill Gallop to Jacob Bailey, December 19, 1783.
64   *The Winslow Papers*, p. 240. Edward Winslow to George Leonard, October 5, 1784.
65   P.A.N.S., Fort Anne Papers, Bailey Letterbooks 1784-1875 (Microfilm). Jacob Bailey to Colin Campbell, March 17, 1785.

land destined for them had been granted away by Parr to the old inhabitants.[66] On top of that he had sold out to the Halifax faction who, according to Bailey, "by artifice and profound dissimulation acquired an influence over the governor and directed him to dispose of honours and emoluments according to their sovereign pleasures."[67] Parr's great sin was not in accepting the existence of a powerful clique, but in accepting one not dominated by the leading Loyalists. He did not welcome them quickly into the seats of power. Moreover, he demanded their physical presence to claim the land, and limited the land allotments to a size suitable only for "peasants," or the humbler Loyalist. Consequently, one of their most cherished objectives was to secure the recall of John Parr, and to see the Executive Council and the Assembly then purged and replaced by "honest Loyalists."[68]

The hostility towards local officials, although not always as intense as among the elite, was nevertheless an emotion held by all Loyalists. Like their contempt for the Nova Scotian and the view of their sacrifice as a debt outstanding upon the British government, the degree to which it was held would vary widely among them. Yet, to some degree, it was held by all. Such views, shaped by their recent past, constituted a common Loyalists attitude.

As important as their common fears, frustrations, and villains, however, was their attitude to each other, for next to the republicans and nabobs of Nova Scotia what the Loyalist feared and distrusted most was another Loyalist. One can take the typical Loyalist attitude only so far, for there was no typical Loyalist. There were twenty thousand individuals, a complete spectrum of backgrounds, mores, motives and ambitions. There were the very rich and the very poor. There were ex-Governors and major placemen and there were the dregs of the port towns. There were those who had supported Britain because their livelihood or ambitions depended upon it, and there were the naive sorts who supported her out of such simplistic notions as loyalty and law. Some would carve out a career from their past misfortunes. Others would turn their backs on the past, to build their houses and clear their two hundred acres. There were those who had left early in the Revolution, and there were those who had left only when they had to. There were the Loyalists who had spent the war in the womb of New York, and those who had spent it in the dirty, dangerous campaigns of some of the provincial regiments. There were the opportunists and the desperate. And there were some "niggers" with their "black wenches,"[69] who could be hanged for stealing a bag of potatoes[70] and whose frolics and dances could be prohibited by local by-law.[71] Most came as servants, but within months reverted to their original status;

---

66   P.A.N.S., Bailey Papers, Vol. XIV. Jacob Bailey to Dr. Peter, November 16, 1785.
67   Bailey Papers, Vol. XVI. Jacob Bailey to Thomas Brown, January 31, 1784.
68   *The Winslow Papers*, p. 172. Rev. Charles Mongan to Edward Winslow, March 23, 1784.
69   P.A.N.S., Shelburne Records, Special Sessions, March 13, 1786; Raymond, "The Founding of Shelburne," p. 234.
70   Macdonald, "Memoir of Governor Parr," p. 64.
71   P.A.N.S., Shelburne Records, Special Sessions, May 12, 1785.

some of them were free, to be rented out on five-year contracts,[72] to be burned out when they became uppity and sold their labour more cheaply than the whites.[73] They were all Loyalists, and the schisms among them were as marked as the attitudes they shared towards the non-Loyalist world.

There was a world into which the common Loyalist would never be invited, a delightful world of banquets and concerts and influence. In Mather Byles' journal to his sister is portrayed a Loyalist world of relative affluence and gentility. It is marked with such comments as the buying of "a magnificent carpet for my grand Parlor: & on the 23^d had the Pleasure of entertaining a Number of my Refugee Friends from N York at Dinner."[74] He sought sympathy when he described himself, "sick, weak & dispirited, & grievously exercised with a troublesome Succession of sore Boils," dragging himself off in true Loyalist respect for the Queen's birthday, "to dinner at the Governor's & to a public Ball & splendid Supper in the Evening."[75] There is a letter from Captain Brownrigg to Gideon White describing an assembly night in Halifax and such major crises as quarrels over a partner for a minuet.[76] Sarah and Penelope Winslow give several descriptions of the gay life of the privileged. On Sarah's trip from New York, for example, Brook Watson, the Commissary General, saw to it that she had "a thousand advantages that no other family has had," including "an excellent Vessell without one passenger but those we chose ourselves."[77] Concerning the house she occupied in Halifax, "I leave you to judge whether the rooms are not very good when I tell you that this day week General Fox with sixteen of our Friends dined with us with great convenience."[78] Penelope Winslow, in a detached fashion, described the life of her friends in Halifax, "pursuing pleasure with ardour. Feasting, card playing & dancing is the great business of Life at Halifax, one eternal round.... The new Imported Ladies continue to be the Belles."[79] The fairest belle of all was a refugee, Mrs. Wentworth, in her gown of sylvan tissue with a train four yards long, and her hair and a wrist ornamented with real diamonds.[80] Yet such an exciting life could not detract from the tragedy of the late rebellion, or the courage

---

[72] Phyllis Blakeley, "Boston King: A Negro Loyalist Who Sought Refuge in Nova Scotia," *Dalhousie Review*, XLVIII (1968), 352-353.

[73] Raymond, "The Founding of Shelburne," p. 265.

[74] P.A.N.S., Byles Papers, Vol. 1, Folder 1, p. 5a. Mather Byles to his sister, February 20, 1784.

[75] Ibid., p. 3. Same to same, February 6, 1784.

[76] P.A.N.S., White Collection, Vol. III, No. 345. Capt. Brownrigg to Gideon White, January 24, 1784.

[77] *The Winslow Papers*, pp. 141-142. Sarah Winslow to Benjamin Marston, October 18, 1783.

[78] Ibid., p. 150. Same to same, November 29, 1783.

[79] Ibid., p. 288. Penelope Winslow to Ward Chipman, April 2, 1785.

[80] Ibid., p. 252. Same to same, November 28, 1784; Macdonald, "Memoir of Governor Parr," p. 56.

with which these people met it. "With becoming firmness I supported our first great reverse of fortunes," Penelope wrote. "I bid a long farewell to an elegant house, furniture, native place and all its pleasures.... The banishment to this ruder World you are a witness I submitted to with some degree of chearfulness."[81]

The humbler Loyalists were also affected by the banishment. They were perhaps not as sensitive as Miss Penelope. They were, however, very hungry. The backdrop for the social life of Sarah and Penelope was a Halifax where almost every church, shed, and outhouse was being used as a shelter for destitute refugees, and where bread lines were a prominent part of the street scene. Thousands were surviving on a diet of codfish, corn and molasses, and hundreds died from lack of sanitation, food or shelter.[82] While some were "pursuing pleasure with ardour" the ship *Clinton* lay at anchor for the winter, "crowded like a sheep-pen" with destitute southerners, chiefly women and children.[83] Nor was Halifax isolated in its misery. A child's impression of a Shelburne in which "strong, proud men wept like children, and lay down in their snow-bound tents to die"[84] is misleading, but Shelburne in the winter of 1783-84 was a city of tents.[85] A Miss Van Tyne "called on some of our friends in their tents ... I thought they did not look able to stand the coming winter, which proved a very hard one."[86] At Port Mouton, Tarleton's Legion was living in tents or huts of sod and log, with clothes too few and blankets too thin for the coming winter.[87] Annapolis was more fortunate in that there were existing buildings in which the Loyalists could seek shelter. Bailey mentioned that several hundred were packed in the church, although larger numbers could not be provided for.[88] Isaac Browne described "the daily increase of the number of distressed & Starving Loyalists" at Annapolis in the fall of 1783.[89] Throughout the colony, for the great majority of Loyalists, it was a basic matter of finding enough food and shelter to survive the first winter, and the gnawing fear that if the promised supplies were not forthcoming, "Numbers must and will inevitably perish."[90] Thus while some of the more fortunate were chiefly concerned with placement and position, most were concerned solely with survival. They were all Loyalists, but motivated by different fears and

---

[81] Ibid., p. 287. Same to same, April 2, 1785.
[82] Macdonald, "Memoir of Governor Parr," pp. 54, 56.
[83] Col. Cor. N.S., Vol. 15, p. 149, from *Report of the Public Archives of Canada*, 1894, p. 412. Parr to Lord North, January 15, 1784.
[84] T.W. Smith, "The Loyalists at Shelburne," *Coll. N.S.H.S.*, VI (1932), 66.
[85] H.C. Mathews, *The Mark of Honour* (Toronto, 1965), p. 112.
[86] J.R. Campbell, *A History of the County of Yarmouth, Nova Scotia* (St. John, 1876), p. 87.
[87] Thomas Raddall, "Tarleton's Legion," *Coll. N.S.H.S.*, XXVIII (1954), 33.
[88] C.W. Vernon, *Bicentenary Sketches and Early Days of the Church in Nova Scotia* (Halifax, 1910), p. 137.
[89] P.A.C., A-170, S.P.G.: "C" Series, Box 1/1, No. 40. Isaac Browne to the Secretary, December 31, 1783.
[90] *Nova Scotia Gazette and Weekly Chronicle*, October 28, 1783, p. 3, col. 2.

different ambitions; their attitude towards many facets of life in Nova Scotia would vary widely.

In a land peopled so quickly and with so few surveyors there were bound to be innumerable conflicts and legal squabbles over boundaries and ownership. These conflicts were inevitable and widespread,[91] but Shelburne was the major centre of strife, especially in the spring and summer of 1784.[92] Because of the "Discontents and disturbances having arisen at Shelburne," the Executive Council was forced to appoint special agents to assign the land and to hear allegations.[93] But if such conflict was inevitable, it was also the source of stress among the Loyalists, and this issue was of fundamental importance. The pent-up hostility and resentment of Loyalist grievances, instead of being channelled to the outside world, turned inward. Loyalist bickering with Loyalist over fundamental questions of property, and the ensuing tension, strained the common bond of loyalty.

In the White Collection at the Public Archives of Nova Scotia there is to be found a series of nineteen provisions for settling the land disputes in Shelburne, drawn up in August, 1784. Perhaps most significant are the supplementary comments on town and water lots, comments permeated with charges of favouritism and unfairness.[94] The land had been drawn for by lottery, and yet a favoured few had managed to subvert this fair policy by applying to the government for extra grants of three hundred acres. "And to this impolitic or rather inadvertent Conduct," it was observed, "is owing in some Measure the want of Lands in the Vicinity of Shelburne to satisfy the just demands of other Loyalists."[95] The author also spoke of grave injustices concerning water lots where, by a legal technicality of definition, "Persons who had come but newly into the settlement" managed to nullify the rights of the owners, and to usurp the claims themselves.

> Now, while these Instances of Injuries remain constantly before the Eyes of the people, their minds must be as constantly irritated, and till these injuries can be somehow or other redressed, many Subjects who would Scorn to be in the Breach of the Peace themselves, will nevertheless show much Reluctance at assisting the Magistrates when called upon, if they should even consent to assist them at all.[96]

---

[91] P.A.N.S., Letterbook of Charles Morris. Charles Morris to Jonathan Prescott, October 12, 1784.

[92] Col. Cor. N.S., Vol. 12, p. 118, from *Report of the Public Archives of Canada*, 1894, p. 418. Parr to Nepean, May 1, 1784.

[93] P.A.C., M.G. II, N.S.B. 18, p. 148. Nova Scotia, Minutes of the Executive Council, 1780-85.

[94] P.A.N.S., White Collection, Vol. III, No. 308.

[95] Ibid.

[96] Ibid.

These injuries were being committed, not by Nova Scotian Yankees, but by fellow Loyalists.

This too, in a sense, was inevitable. Twenty thousand Loyalists had descended upon a poor and insignificant colony, seeking land, office, and security. It was apparent that the market value of their loyalty was hurt in such an inflationary situation, and that oaths against the rebels and nabobs would succeed only to a certain degree, for there were twenty thousand other refugees with the same claims to the government's gratitude. There were simply not enough loaves and fishes, and often ambition had to be satisfied at the expense of other Loyalists. There was an air of *sauve qui peut*, of taking care of oneself and one's friends, devil take the hindmost. "Keep this Hint to yourself," Charles Morris advised Dugald Campbell, "let the others do as they please."[97] One could erase another Loyalist's name from a memorial and insert one's own to get the land.[98] One could claim land on behalf of his wife's loyalty, and demand the land of another Loyalist to boot, for the latter "is a person every way unworthy of your favour and who in the place of being an acquisition, to our Province as (recommended) has proved himself to be nothing more than a nuisance."[99] A man of slight influence could manage to take away the partially cleared land of a fellow Loyalist and have it put under his servant's name.[100]

There was conflict and jealousy between the various groups into which the Loyalists were organized, between the New York group, for example, and the Port Roseway Associates. This group loyalty and suspicion of outsiders tended to splinter the common Loyalist front into smaller fragments. When another Loyalist group appeared to be receiving any particular attention, "they cannot comprehend it, that others should have everything and they Nothing. The people for that Reason are discouraged and dispirited."[101] In Port Mouton, there was resentment by the veterans of Tarleton's Legion towards Brook Watson's New York staff who, having sat out the war in New York, seemed to be getting more material aid in Nova Scotia.[102]

There were the inevitable power struggles within the groups, for these people had been lifted out of their environment and placed, often with acquaintances of a short time, into a new, alien, and fluid environment, where old forms and standards meant little, and status was in a state of flux. In his letters to Gideon White, R.F. Brownrigg described the jockeying for position among the Loyalists in Chedabucto. On his arrival he had found that the early comers had seized the best of the town lots and that some had already sold their tools and rations to the local inhabitants. The

---

[97] P.A.N.S., Letterbook of Charles Morris. Charles Morris to Dugald Campbell, August 26, 1784.
[98] Letterbook of Charles Morris. Charles Morris to Dugald Campbell, August 26, 1784.
[99] P.A.N.S., Vertical Mss. File, Loyalists. Memorial of William Martin to Governor Parr.
[100] P.A.N.S., Letterbook of Charles Morris. Charles Morris to William White, March 24, 1785.
[101] P.A.C., M.G. 23, D.4, Vol. I, No. 41. Amos Botsford to Charles Morris, September 3, 1783.
[102] Raddall, "Tarleton's Legion," pp. 29-30, 34.

local Pooh-Bah appears to have been a Dr. McPherson who "seems to wish to become Dictator to the inhabitants of Chedabucto." Brownrigg and friends refused to extend such homage automatically. "Don't misconstrue me—we mean to live in perfect harmony—but to act with spirit."[103] Apparently Brownrigg was too sanguine, for in July of 1784 he wrote White from Halifax, and in mentioning the clique in this rather muted letter, simply states, "they are very troublesome, and have partly drove me hither."[104]

The conflict which arose among the Loyalists in Digby is indicative of the tensions which could split a Loyalist settlement. A board of four had been appointed by the captains and heads of classes to divide the government material among the refugees. At the request of some discontented Loyalists, the board decided to look into the accounts of Amos Botsford, the agent. With this done, they should have ceased functioning as a board, but they apparently assumed the powers of a permanent committee, "powers which the people did not intend."[105] What ensued was a contest between this board and the agents for political control of the community. As the struggle continued, the community divided behind either Botsford or the leader of the board, a Major Tempany. Both men sought aid in Halifax. A Thomas Osburn had stated that if Botsford had his way in Halifax, "he Osburn would head a mobb and Parade the Streets of Digby."[106] Isaac Bonnell, on the other hand, stated that "It is fully thought by the Better kind of people here Should Tempany Return with any Power the settlement must be Broke up. I shall for my own lot leave it notwithstanding the great Expence I have been at."[107] Although the incident was not necessarily typical, it does illustrate the division, animosity and bitterness that such a conflict could create within a Loyalist community.

There was a tendency in the summer of 1783 for a harassed and overworked government to give scant attention to the individual Loyalist. Under pressure from the associations, Charles Morris conceded "that I will to the utmost of my influence prevent any *Separates* carrying their Points, whatever Pitifull Plaints they may make."[108] With such an attitude, the government was allowing the particular organization in an area to assume responsibility for the stray Loyalists and at the same time permitting the association to assume more authority over land distribution than it had a right to.[109] It was in effect placing the fate of the individual Loyalist into the hands of a partial and competing body, and allowing that body to assume an almost monopolistic control of land grants in the area. When seven families asked

---

[103] P.A.N.S., White Collection, Vol. III, No. 284. R.F. Brownrigg to Gideon White, June 8, 1784.
[104] Ibid., No. 293. Same to same, July 11, 1784.
[105] P.A.C., M.G. 23, D.4, Vol. 2, Deposition of John Hooton, Digby, October 2, 1784.
[106] Ibid., Deposition of B..., October 7, 1784.
[107] Ibid., Isaac Bonnell to Amos Botsford, October 7, 1784.
[108] P.A.C., M.G. 23, D.4, Vol. 1, No. 20, Charles Morris to Amos Botsford, July 12, 1783.
[109] Ibid., No. 23, Same to same, July 16, 1783.

for land in the Conway area, Charles Morris ratified their request but Amos Botsford, the local agent for the New York association, evaded the issue. This action prompted a stern order from Morris and the Governor to place them on the land, "Provided it does not materially Interfere with the General Settlement of Conway."[110] A captain who came to the Conway area to draw a lot found that the new corps had usurped all the lots not yet drawn for.[111] Concerning another bank of Loyalists, Morris was demanding of Robert Gray in 1785 "why these people have not had a common chance of drawing Lands with others."[112] Benjamin Marston referred several times in his diary to the almost dictatorial power of the Port Roseway Associates at Shelburne. "The Association from New York are a curious set," he observed, "They take upon them to determine who are the proper subjects of the King's grant. They have a chosen committee of sixteen who point out who are to be admitted to draw for lots."[113] A short while later he wrote, "They wish to engross this whole grant into the hands of the few who came in the first fleet, hoping the distresses of their fellow-loyalists, who must leave New York will oblige them to make purchases."[114] Together with the struggle to survive, these conflicts among and within the groups dominated their early days in Nova Scotia. These Loyalist clusters provided the immediate sources of tension and discord, over land, provisions, and position. Under such circumstances, the native of Nova Scotia, frequently separated from him by miles of bush or coast, was often a rather nebulous enemy, known of only at second-hand.

Sometimes a part of this struggle, sometimes apart from it, but always a major factor, was the schism between the elite of the Loyalists and the so-called "rabble." The members of the elite were basically those who had been or known someone of influence before or during the Revolution, and hoped to be someone of influence again. The rabble were all those who had been nobody, and had little chance of being anything else. There were various shades of grey between, people who could not easily be fitted into either category; but there was an attempt to categorize by the two extremes, or, at best, to divide the Loyalists between the elite and the others. Strangely, the levelling factors of a bankrupting war and a province that was almost a frontier had not lessened the awareness. In a fluid situation, with neither guidelines nor assurance of influence, the elite, in their desperate scramble for position, wrapped their exclusiveness about them like a mantle. With their sense of class, status, and privilege, and their contempt for the lower classes, these Loyalists were far closer to the oligarchy in Halifax than to the more common refugee. The only major separation between the two elites was the lack of office and influence. But between

---

[110] Ibid., No. 17. Same to same, July 4, 1783.
[111] Ibid., No. 25. Same to same, July 21, 1783.
[112] P.A.N.S., Letterbook to Charles Morris. Charles Morris to Robert Gray, February 23, 1785.
[113] Raymond, "The Founding of Shelburne," pp. 213-214.
[114] Ibid., p. 221.

the elite and the masses, there were far too many barriers, and the only thing they had in common was their loyalty, a tenuous cord, frayed by many basic differences.

There was the aura of the snob in the announcement of the death of Lord Charles Montague by Mather Byles of the red carpet and boils. Montague had led a Carolinian Regiment to Nova Scotia, where he died on February 3, 1784.[115] "He died suddenly at a little hut in the Woods of Nova Scotia:" Byles writes, "& was Committed to the Earth with much military Foppery & ridiculous parade."[116] It is difficult to judge which Byles held more in contempt, the "ridiculous parade" or the death of the man in a common hut in the woods of Nova Scotia. James Gautier called the people of Shelburne "banditti."[117] N. Ford wrote of his delight in the fact that Isaac Wilkins "has got into an office now, that puts it out of the power of the rabble of Shelburne to remove."[118] Perhaps the best illustrations of the gentleman's contempt for the rabble is the journal of Benjamin Marston. Before his appointment as surveyor to Shelburne he had been staying in a Halifax tavern with Loyalist officers, "Such another set of riotous vagabonds never were."[119] The Loyalists in Shelburne he found indolent, clamorous,[120] and mutinous.[121] Their captains "are a set of fellows whom mere accident has placed in their present situations;.... Real authority can never be supported without some degree of real superiority."[122]

> They are like sheep without a shepherd. They have no men of abilities among them. Their Captains, chosen out of their boys at New York, are of the same class with themselves—most of them mechanics, some few have been shipmasters, they are the best men they have. Sir Guy Carleton did not reflect that putting sixteen illiterate men into commission, without subjecting them to one common head, was at best but contracting the mob.[123]

He found pathetic the attempts of these captains to play the role of gentlemen, while their wives and daughters were ladies "whom neither nature nor education intended for that rank."[124]

---

[115] Vernon, *Bicentenary Sketches*, p. 103.
[116] P.A.N.S., Byles Papers, Vol. I, Folder 1, p. 5C. Mather Byles to his sister, February 20, 1784.
[117] P.A.N.S., White Collection, Vol. III, No. 302. James Gautier to Gideon White, August 10, 1784.
[118] Ibid., No. 427. N. Ford to Gideon White, August 23, 1786.
[119] Raymond, "The Founding of Shelburne," p. 205.
[120] Ibid., p. 212.
[121] Ibid., pp. 212-213.
[122] Ibid., pp. 212-213.
[123] Ibid., p. 219.
[124] Ibid., pp. 219-220.

The select few believed that their compensation should be greater than their sacrifice or sufferings might warrant. They implied that the spoils of defeat should be based more upon what one had been than what one had done.

> The Merit of an American Loyalist consists, according to the Terms of the foregoing Resolves in a Compliance with the Laws, or much more in Assisting in Carrying them into Execution.... Where those Principles are found to have been uniformly profess'd and acted upon they Constitute a Degree of Merit which, independant of all consideration of Loss of Property gives the Persons who have thus acted a fair Claim to Attention and to a Support proportion'd to their Situation in Life and the disadvantages to which they have been subjected in Consequence of such their Conduct.[125]

Moreover, true reimbursement was not to be found as much in official claims and compensation as in position and appointments, and here merit was barely incidental, connections everything. *The Winslow Papers*, for example, are replete with the wielding of influence for family and friends, portraying almost a parasitic coterie trading upon one another's favours.[126] Mather Byles III, in referring to his father, summed up their expectations: "as every mortification and suffering which he has undergone, has been the effect of the purest principle, he has every reason to hope that his future prospects will brighten as they unfold, and the evening of his life be gilded with the rays of prosperity."[127] To the mass of the Loyalists, the outcome of the rebellion was a loss to be compensated. To the elite, it appeared to have been an opportunity to exploit. The petitions for land grants strengthen this impression. Most of the memorialists, although emphasizing the services rendered and the losses sustained, seek little more than "such proportion of lands ... as may be most consistent with his Majesty's most gracious intentions."[128] Memorialists like James Benview and Thomas Lockwood, "having served during the late war in The Regiment Late, the Royal Fencible Americans," were granted a hundred acres each.[129] However, one finds James Twaddle, a cripple from a wound received in the revolution, receiving fifty acres, and Nathaniel Thomas, "late one of the members of His Majesty's Council for the Province of the Massachusetts Bay," twelve hundred.[130] Stephen Skinner, who was among the fifty-five Loyalists who felt themselves entitled to especially large grants, also applied as an individual for an

---

[125] P.A.C., M.G. 23, A.4, Vol. 67, p. 144. Unsigned Memorial to Lord Shelburne, October 1782.
[126] The Winslow Papers, pp. 61-62.
[127] P.A.N.S., Byles Papers, Vol. I, Folder 2, p. 9. Mather Byles to his aunt, May 5, 1784.
[128] P.A.N.S., Land Grant Petitions, Vol. 14. Memorial of Edward Liskman, September 1785.
[129] Ibid., Vol. 15A. Memorial of Benvie, Lockwood, and Burns.
[130] Ibid., Vol. 10. Memorials of James Twaddle and Nathaniel Thomas.

extra "quantity of land as is generally given to Gentlemen in the like circumstances."[131] The New York agents could write to Amos Botsford for special allotments, for "the People will not object to our having an exclusive Choice of Lands."[132] Among his other grants, Isaac Wilkins managed to gain for himself ten of the town lots in Shelburne, and a public rebuke by the humbler Loyalists.[133] When General Ruggles was granted his ten thousand acres in Wilmot rather than Annapolis, so that it might not "prove very Injurious to the Settlement in General and very much Disgust the People,"[134] he was terribly put out by it all.[135]

The awareness of the many concerning the privileges to the few did not strengthen the fraternity of Loyalism. The petition of the fifty-five gentlemen, and the counter petition rebutting it, exemplify both the demands and philosophy of the elite, and the resentment stirred up among the majority by such demands. In July of 1783 a group of fifty-five gentlemen petitioned Sir Guy Carleton for approximately 275,000 acres in Nova Scotia. They requested to be put on the same footing as field officers, have the land chosen by their own agents, surveyed at government expense," and the Deeds delivered to us, as soon as possible."[136] Their claim to this land rested upon the fact that they were no longer living in the manner to which they had been accustomed, and "that the Settling such a Number of loyalists, of the most respectable Characters, who have Constantly had great influence in His Majesty's American Dominions—will be highly Advantageous in diffusing and supporting a Spirit of Attachment to the British Constitution as well as to His Majesty's Royal Person and Family."[137]

Carleton obviously was impressed by such a claim, for he recommended it to Parr, who actually began to survey.[138] The less respectable Loyalists, however, were not as impressed, and they reacted quickly and angrily. They had come to Nova Scotia, "little suspecting there could be found amongst their Fellow sufferers Persons ungenerous enough to attempt ingrossing to themselves so disproportionate a Share of what Government has Allotted for their common benefit." Those particular gentlemen demanding such claims were "more distinguished by the repeated favours of Government than by either the greatness of their sufferings or the importance of

---

[131] Ibid., Vol. 2. Memorial of Stephen Skinner, August 28, 1783.
[132] P.A.C., M.G. 23, D.4, Vol. 1, No. 10. New York Agents to Amos Botsford *et al.*, May 25, 1783.
[133] *Nova Scotia Gazette and Weekly Chronicle*, April 19, 1785, p. 1, col. 1. Wilkins', explanation of the affair is in p. 2, col. 1-2.
[134] P.A.C., M.G. 23, D.4, Vol. 1, No. 16. Charles Morris to Amos Botsford, July 2, 1783.
[135] R.S. Longley, "An Annapolis County Loyalist," p. 91.
[136] Marion Gilroy, *Loyalists and Land Settlement in Nova Scotia* (P.A.N.S. Publication No. 4 [Halifax, 1937]), p. 146.
[137] Ibid., p. 146.
[138] Col. Cor. N.S., Vol. 15, p. 166, from *Report of the Public Archives of Canada*, 1894, p. 414. Parr to Secretary of State, March 4, 1784.

their Services."[139] This rift increased the resentment and the cleavage between the "most respectable" Loyalist, and the others.

Religion exemplified the diversity of attitudes among the Loyalists. Benjamin Marston found the Loyalists of Shelburne an irreligious lot, in no hurry to have ministers among them.[140] Dr. Walter was not quite as critical, but he did feel that they consisted "of persons of very various characters Dispositions & religious Sentiments," and that it would be only with difficulty that one could "systemize" them under the Church of England.[141] A great many of the Loyalists in Nova Scotia were not members of the Church of England at all, but even among the large percentage who were, a slight Americanization had occurred which struck the missionaries of the Society for the Propagation of the Gospel as foreign, and perhaps dangerous. The outstanding example of how the American way might differ from that of Nova Scotia was to be found in the protracted struggle between Dr. Walter and the Rev. George Panton for control of the Church of England in Shelburne. It exposed an inherent conflict among the Loyalists between Old World and New World attitudes.

Mr. Panton had been rector of Trenton, New Jersey, and later chaplain of the Prince of Wales' American Volunteers. He had been invited by some of the leaders of the Port Roseway Associates to be minister to the refugees at Shelburne. He indicated his interest, and received both blessing and salary from the S.P.G.[142] Because of confusion over his intentions and his health, some Loyalists had assumed he was not going to take the position. Dr. William Walter, rector of Trinity Church in Boston, and later a chaplain with DeLancey's Brigade,[143] had written to the S.P.G. in July, 1783, that the people of the proposed settlement had no clergyman, and that he was offering his services as minister.[144] The ministers arrived in the community within two days of each other, both claiming to represent the Church of England in Shelburne, and each seeking support for his claim from parishioners, governor, and the S.P.G.

The Rev. Mr. Panton based his claim upon the invitation of the leading Loyalists and the S.P.G.'s approval of him as missionary. Dr. Walter displayed petitions from Shelburne to show that he was the people's choice, and had no doubt that the Society, "on knowing the affectionate agreement which subsists between the people & me," would see that his claim was recognized.[145] When neither the Governor nor the S.P.G. showed any enthusiasm for his claim, he placed greater and greater

---

[139] Gilroy, *Loyalists and Land Settlement*, p. 148.
[140] Raymond, "The Founding of Shelburne, p. 220.
[141] P.A.C., A-170, S.P.G.: "C" Series, Box 1/1, No. 50. Dr. Walter to the Secretary, July 1783.
[142] W.O. Raymond, "The Founding of the Church of England in Shelburne," *Coll. N.B.H.S.*, No. 8 (1909), p. 279.
[143] Ibid., p. 280.
[144] P.A.C., A-170, S.P.G.: "C" Series, Box 1/1, No. 50. Dr. Walter to the Secretary, July 1783.
[145] Ibid., No. 51. Same to same, October 17, 1783.

emphasis upon the necessity for popular support, insisting upon "the Privilege and Right of the Parishioners by Law to chuse their own minister."[146] His supporters insisted that he had been chosen and accepted "by the unanimous invitation of the members of the Church of England in Shelburne."[147] As for the claim that Panton was supported by the leading figures in Shelburne, it was obvious that they gave him such support "only because they conceive it will please the governor whose favour in grants of land & Public Offices they may wish."[148] Emphasis was also placed upon the fact that Mr. Panton had been one of the fifty-five," who solicited for no less, I believe, than five thousand acres each."[149]

On the other hand, Walter was accused by Mr. Panton of "opposing public authority."[150] He was also accused of encouraging a "dangerous Tendency, as Opening an Avenue for a Majority of *Sectaries* to introduce Clergymen of Obvious Principles equally dangerous to the Church and Government."[151] Panton's supporters placed more emphasis upon the need to rally 'round "King and Country,"[152] and upon the fact that "no *genuine* member of the Church of England, and principled Loyalist, can, consistently and conscientiously, oppose a public establishment, by proper authority, which interferes with no person's rights and that such opposition must arise from *sinister* views."[153]

Eventually Mr. Panton gave up the fight and retired from Shelburne, but the struggle had revealed a basic cleavage between the right of the parishioners to choose their minister, and the duty to support a public establishment, and public authority. It also illustrated another aspect of the clash between the elite and the masses, for Panton's supporters did stress the "respectability" of their members, and Walter's followers did indict both Panton's association with the fifty-five, and his supporters' desire to please the Governor. Moreover, the fight revealed a new connotation being given to the term Loyalist. It was no longer simply a term to connote past deeds and sacrifices. It was also to suggest certain present principles, such as the support of King, Country, and Authority.

Throughout Nova Scotia, the Church of England failed to make the inroads it should have among the Loyalists. Although no great number of adherents were lost to the Dissenters, the Church, by failing to touch the masses, did not make the gains

---

[146] J.L. Bumsted, "Church and State in Maritime Canada, 1749-1807," C.H.A. *Report*, 1967, p. 50.
[147] *Royal American Gazette* (Shelburne), January 24, 1785, p. 2, col. 3.
[148] P.A.C., A-170, S.P.G.: "C" Series, Box 1/1, No. 55. Dr. Walter to the Secretary, January 1785.
[149] *Royal American Gazette* (Shelburne), January 24, 1785, p. 2, col. 4.
[150] P.A.N.S., Assembly Papers, 1777-1785, Vol. 1A, No. 10. Mr. Panton to Governor Parr, December 24, 1785.
[151] Bumsted, "Church and State in Maritime Canada," p. 50.
[152] *Royal American Gazette* (Shelburne), January 24, 1785, p. 3, col. 2.
[153] *Loc. cit.*

it might have in these chaotic times. It did not change to meet the new demands of pioneering communities, and it had too many missionaries less interested in bringing the Word to isolated hamlets than in the vicious in-fighting for posts and patronage.[154]

There were many Presbyterians among the refugees. The Shelburne Presbyterians had petitioned William Pitt for government aid, because they could not carry the expense of Church and minister, "Numerous tho' they are."[155] They had a minister in Rev. Hugh Fraser who had been acting chaplain to the Seventy-First Regiment during the Revolution.[156] However, although it would retain the loyalty of the Scots, its emphasis upon a professional clergy and a more orthodox organization, and its lack of missionaries, would preclude it from winning a great many new souls among the poorer Loyalists.

Baptist churches were organized under David George, a Negro preacher who had arrived in Halifax with a body of Loyalists in 1784. He began preaching in Shelburne, "but I found the white people were against me.... The black people came from far and near; I kept on so every night in the week, and appointed a meeting for the first Lord's Day, ... and a great number of white and black people came."[157] The Baptists were not alone in preaching to the negro loyalists. Phyllis Blakely, in her article on Boston King, describes the Methodist interest in Birchtown, and a conversion of both King and his wife to Methodism.[158] William Black, the prophet of Methodism in Nova Scotia, won many adherents among the Loyalists. A large number had been influenced by Methodist teachings before coming to Nova Scotia. Some, such as Robert Barry, had served previously as preachers. He had organized a "class" shortly after Black's first visit to Shelburne.[159] Joseph Tinkham wrote to Gideon White on Black's preaching and hoped "he made some of you Shelburnites better by his Preaching there."[160] Freeborn Garettson, a missionary from the United States, could write from Shelburne in 1786, "Blessed be God, there have been many as clear and as powerful conversions in this township, as I have seen in any part of the States."[161]

Like his religion, the politics of the Loyalist was not necessarily that of the establishment. He had once been an American colonial seeking greater autonomy

---

[154] S.D. Clark, *Church and Sect in Canada* (Toronto, 1948), pp. 71-76; Bumsted, "Church and State in Maritime Canada," p. 49.
[155] Mathews, *The Mark of Honour*, p. 120.
[156] Smith, "The Loyalists at Shelburne," p. 73.
[157] Clark, *Church and Sect in Canada*, p. 49.
[158] Blakeley, "Boston King," p. 352.
[159] George Cox, "John Alexander Barry and His Times," *Coll. N.S.H.S.*, XXVIII (1954), 133-134.
[160] P.A.N.S., White Collection, Vol. III, No. 392. Joseph Tinkham to Gideon White, October 6, 1785.
[161] Clark, *Church and Sect in Canada*, p. 85.

from a growing centralization on the part of Britain, until reform had turned to rebellion, and rebellion had polarized the combatants. Yet once freed from the loyalty-rebellion decision, it is unlikely that he would have completely abandoned what was a natural American reflex, the desire for self-government. Benjamin Marston indirectly explains much of his attitude when speaking of an incident in Shelburne; "the settlers were all called upon to take the oath of allegiance to the King and subscribe a declaration acknowledging the supremacy of the British Parliament over the whole Empire, but this was explained as not to extend to taxation."[162] The fact that the explanation was needed indicates that the Loyalists in Nova Scotia were not so much Tories as Americans who had remained loyal in a polarizing situation. The organization of the refugee associations to handle the exodus was very democratic, as in the case of the New York agents, where the refugees "chuse their Captains & they appoint two lieutenants for every class."[163] Nor did the democratic element end with the choosing of their officers, for Marston was continually frustrated by it. In May of 1783, when the captains had chosen the site for Shelburne, the multitude objected to the site and decided to choose three men from each company to do it all over again. Marston complained, "This cursed republican, town-meeting spirit has been the ruin of us already, and unless checked by some stricter form of government will overset the prospect which now presents itself of retrieving our affairs."[164] Whether they were voting to seize the boards of a private saw mill and convert them to public use,[165] or were drawing for lots and "indulging their cursed republican principles,"[166] to Marston they were indistinguishable from the rebels they had fled. Governor Parr shared similar sentiments, for their manner of treating governors was one that he found neither customary nor congenial. Some time in the summer of 1783 he received a rather harsh note from Amos Botsford, in whose correspondence there are two letters referring to the matter. One is from Parr stating that he was doing all in his power for the Loyalists, had an immense amount of sympathy for them, but was not to be dictated to by Botsford. He suggested that Botsford should write less and work more.[167] The second letter, from Charles Morris, regretted Botsford's "dictatorial Style" and pointed out that Parr was "the King's Representative, and that there was a difference between him and a Governor of Connecticut—of the Peoples own making whom they may reject and chuse another when they please."[168]

---

[162] Raymond, "The Founding of Shelburne," p. 268.
[163] P.A.C., M.G. 23, D.4, Vol. I, No. 10. New York Agents to Amos Botsford *et al.*, May 25, 1783.
[164] Raymond, "The Founding of Shelburne," p. 211.
[165] Ibid., p. 213.
[166] Ibid., p. 214.
[167] P.A.C., M.G. 23, D.4, Vol. I. No. 21. Governor Parr to Amos Botsford, July 12, 1783.
[168] Ibid., No. 20. Charles Morris to Amos Botsford, July 12, 1783.

The Loyalists' knowledge of the system of government in Nova Scotia was often scant, and based on hearsay, for some believed that the legislative assembly was appointed for life.[169] They were consequently apprehensive. Moreover, they brought with them a tradition of self-government, and both fear and tradition dictated that they oppose any form of taxation by a body upon which they were not represented.[170] Such an attitude would lead them in the first years of settlement into a dual movement of seeking representation upon the provincial assembly, and of gaining as great a measure of autonomy as possible for their local governments.

> As to the internal Police of the Settlement, we must expect to be under the laws of the province—I am in hopes a Corporation may be obtained—I think it will unless the Jealousies of other parts of the province, make it necessary for the Peace and Quiet of the Governor, to be otherwise.[171]

There was a fear among the Shelburne people of seeing what money they had make its way to Halifax. It could take the form of a memorial from the magistrates of Shelburne asking that impost and licence duties remain within the town.[172] It could also be found in the protests of a man brought to court for defying the magistrates of Shelburne and serving liquor without a licence. He believed "the licence money went to support a set of people who walked the streets with their hands in their pockets, & therefore it was wrong to pay any licence money."[173] Their memorials on government often combine the demand for a new Assembly with Loyalist representation and the appeal for substantial autonomy in local administration, justice and education.[174]

The announcement that the fifth Assembly was to be dissolved after fourteen years made the Loyalists fear that the election was designed to allow the formation of a new Assembly before they could qualify as electors.[175] Their fears were not justified, for the decision to dissolve the Assembly had been made by the British government before their coming, and Parr was insistent upon their representation in the new House.[176] Even the existing Assembly expressed its desire "to see as soon as possible Representatives from the several new Settlements Joining us in such our

---

[169] Smith, "The Loyalists at Shelburne," p. 67.
[170] P.A.C., M.G. 9, B.6, p. 63. Report of B. Ross, C. Campbell, and A. Robertson, n.d.
[171] P.A.C., M.G. 9, B.6, p. 63. Report of Joseph Pynchon, January 23, 1783, in Minute Book of the Port Roseway Associates.
[172] P.A.N.S., Assembly Papers, 1777-1785, Vol. 1A. Memorial of the Magistrates of Shelburne, November 2, 1785.
[173] P.A.N.S., Shelburne Records, Special Sessions, September 15, 1785.
[174] P.A.C., M.G. 9, B.6 (2). Memorial of B. Ross, C. Campbell, and A. Robertson, n.d.
[175] Garner, "Electoral Franchise in Colonial Nova Scotia," p. 52.
[176] Ibid., p. 53.

Endeavors."[177] In December, 1784, an Act was passed creating six new seats for the Loyalist areas.[178]

The Assembly, which had existed since 1770, was dissolved on October 20, 1785, and the polls in Halifax opened on November 8.[179] It was a heated affair with nine elections contested before the House, and in certain ridings it appears to have represented the crystallizing of the Loyalist identity in his conflict with the pre-Loyalist Nova Scotian. It would definitely appear that way in the fight for Annapolis county between Loyalist David Seabury and Native Nova Scotian Captain Alexander Howe. In an election "conducted with unexampled temper and decency, considering the struggle between the former inhabitants and the new adventurers,"[179] David Seabury won. Howe, however, challenged the results on the ground that the sheriff had been extremely partial in allowing non-freeholders and Catholics to vote for Seabury and not for himself. On December 6, 1785, the Assembly declared the election null and void.[180] A new election was called, and the ensuing contest created an atmosphere in which "such a bitterness rancour and virulence prevails as exceeds all description."[181] Thomas Barclay, an elected Loyalist from Annapolis, appealed to leading Loyalists in the valley to give their all "to support our Interests, and we shall deserve our fate if we permit Capt. Howe to carry his Election."[182] The appeal must have been effective, for Seabury won; but again the House annulled the results, and Howe sat as one of the M.L.A.s for Annapolis. Moreover, when the House took up the matter of Barclay's letter accusing it of partiality, a straight Loyalist-pre-Loyalist division occurred on the motion to dismiss.[183] This same appeal to Loyalist solidarity occurs in a letter of James Clarke concerning the new House. "Blowers deserves every Attention and Mark of Respect from the real Loyalist," he had written to Gideon White. He insisted that "For political Reasons..., do not be pointed towards Uniacke nor discover any Thing that has the Appearance of Faction or the warmth of Party—Consult Wilkins in every Thing for be assured he ought to be looked up to as the Pole-Star of the Loyalists."[184]

There are factors, however, which distort slightly this portrait of Loyalist solidarity. Not all Loyalist communities, for example, put up local champions to represent them. Guysborough, recently populated by Loyalists, was represented by two Haligonians, James Putnam, Jr., a Loyalist Barrack Master, and J.M. Freke

---

177 P.A.N.S., Journals of the House of Assembly, 1784-85, p. 11. November 2, 1784.
178 Garner, *Electoral Franchise in Colonial Nova Scotia*, p. 53; Murdoch, *History of Nova Scotia*, III, 37.
179 P.A.N.S., Bailey Papers, Vol. XIV. Jacob Bailey to Mr. Sower, November 25, 1785.
180 P.A.N.S., Assembly Papers, 1777-1785, Vol. 1A. Minutes of the Council of the Whole House, December 6, 1785.
181 P.A.N.S., Bailey Papers, Vol. XIV. Jacob Bailey to Peter Fry, December 15, 1785.
182 P.A.N.S., Journals of the House of Assembly, 1786, pp. 23-24. June 23, 1786.
183 *Loc. cit.*
184 P.A.N.S., White Collection, Vol. III, No. 404. James Clark to Gideon White, March 1786.

Bulkeley, son of the Provincial Secretary. To one county historian, the Guysborough inhabitants were simply too busy in re-settling "to give any time to any except the most pressing problems."[185] Moreover, there were factors concerning the Annapolis election that might call into question the obvious conclusions drawn. Captain Howe was not a representative Nova Scotian, for although born in Annapolis, prior to 1783 he had been an officer with the Thirty-Sixth and 104th Regiments[186] Nor would David Seabury automatically win the support of the Loyalist rank and file, for he had been one of the infamous fifty-five.[187] What helped to split the community into Loyalist and pre-Loyalist camps was the sense of injustice felt by both sides. The one party felt that they had been terribly abused by the marked partiality of the House. The other party, and many members of the House, felt that the large pre-Loyalist minority should, in justice, have at least one of the four seats for the Annapolis region. And yet Jacob Bailey mentions that some native Nova Scotians who were "formerly great friends to the American Revolution have given their interest very warmly for Mr. Seabury."[188] It is doubtful that those considered by James Clarke as "real" Loyalists and Pole-stars would be accepted as such by the rank and file. Isaac Wilkins was not only another of the fifty-five, but had already earned the wrath of many in Shelburne with his greed for town lots, and the congratulations of his peers for securing a position that placed him beyond the rabble.[189] S.S. Blowers, on the other hand, would later gain the distinction of being one of the earliest to sell his fellow Loyalists out for the sake of government patronage.[190] And in the pure Loyalist soil of Shelburne the long hand of the Halifax clique was felt, for in an earlier letter to Gideon White, Clarke had stated that "Colo. Tongue connected himself with McNeil and Leckie, who availed themselves of that Connexion to serve Largin."[191] Largin had the position of Deputy Naval Officer, which White coveted. McNeil and Leckie were newly elected members of Shelburne, and Colonel Tongue was a leading pre-Loyalist power in the Assembly.

The sixth Assembly would in many ways be a reforming Assembly, and much of the impetus for that reform would come from the Loyalist members. However, it was more a matter of their adding greatly to the strength of existing reform sentiment than creating a Loyalist party of reform. Except for the issue of Barclay's letter, there was not to be a straight Loyalist-pre-Loyalist vote in the new Assembly. There would be too many combinations with pre-Loyalists and against fellow Loyalists to

---

[185] A.C. Jost, *Guysborough Sketches and Essays* (Guysborough, 1950), p. 184.
[186] C. Bruce Fergusson, *A Directory of the Members of the Legislative Assembly of Nova Scotia, 1758-1958* (Halifax, 1958), pp. 163-164.
[187] Gilroy, *Loyalists and Land Settlement*, p. 147.
[188] P.A.N.S., Bailey Papers, Vol. XIV. Jacob Bailey to Peter Fry, January 5, 1786.
[189] Gilroy, *Loyalists and Land Settlement*, p. 147.
[190] J.M. Beck, *The Government of Nova Scotia* (Toronto, 1957), p. 29.
[191] P.A.N.S., White Collection, Vol. III, No. 400. James Clarke to Gideon White, February 3, 1786.

speak easily of a Loyalist party, for they "had no platform, no consistent policy, and above all, no opposing party."[192] Yet they were still to play a dominant role in the fight for reform.[193]

They had men of outstanding ability among them, and, as important, they were able to lift reform out of the mud of sedition. Previously, the "Church and State Party" had been able to brand any attempts at local reform or any threats to their power as rebellious and republican. The Loyalists could not as easily be accused of sedition. Quite naturally, they would seek reform because they were on the outside looking in. They were represented in the Legislative Assembly, but not within the executive. They would consequently seek the supremacy of the legislature. Some among them, once invited into the realm of executive power, would quickly jettison their crusading zeal and don the attitudes of the oligarchy. But these were a very small percentage of the refugees, and the desire of the Loyalists for the supremacy of the elected branch of the government had roots other than exclusion, and as compelling. As Americans they had been nurtured on certain standards of representation, and they found the Nova Scotian government wanting.

> This is the misfortunate of Great Britain in respect to the colonies—placing in their own minds the landholders in the colonies upon a footing with those they call peasants in Britain, when really that character is scarcely to be found in the colonies.[194]

It is perhaps as Americans that their attitudes are most easily understood. They were not a right wing splinter of American society, but a broad and complex variety of types and opinions. They varied greatly in occupations and social strata, political and religious views. That they had supported a common cause and suffered a common fate conditioned their response to a new environment. This experience permitted the caricature of the Nova Scotian and his government, and shaped the love-hate relationship with Britain. It found expression in the election of 1785, with a situation in which lines could be drawn, the enemy defined, and the cry of Loyalist brought forth and exploited. But the intensity could not last, and the common bond could not dominate. There was much conflict with the Nova Scotian, yet it was neither constant nor intense enough to supply the cohesion necessary for a dynamic Loyalist attitude.

The danger from without was too weak, while the dissension within was too strong. The many refractory elements among the Loyalists inhibited the growth of a common front. Land squabbles, opportunism and group loyalties broke down

---

[192] Gene MacG. Morison, "The Evolution of Political Parties in Nova Scotia, 1758-1848" (unpublished M.A. Thesis, Dalhousie University, 1949), p. 18.
[193] Margaret Ells, "Nova Scotian 'Sparks of Liberty'," *Dalhousie Review*, XVI (1936-37), 476.
[194] Joseph Pynchon to the Committee of the Port Roseway Associates, February 1783, as quoted in Smith, "The Loyalists at Shelburne," p. 67.

Loyalist attachments, while the basic conflict between elite and the masses strengthened the fragmentation. The select were usurping the Loyalist image and shaping it to their own ends, whereas the great majority were placing greater emphasis upon the democratic principles and instincts that had been their pre-revolutionary heritage, but had lain dormant for close to a decade.

Sermon Literature
and Canadian Intellectual History

S.F. Wise

Canadian intellectual history must be concerned, almost of necessity, with the kinds of ideas that lie between the formal thought of the philosopher or the political theorist and the world of action, and probably closer to the latter. Since (to understate the matter) no connected history of formal thought in Canada is possible, the Canadian intellectual historian must be concerned primarily with the interrelationship between ideas and actions, and therefore the intellectual commonplaces of an age, its root notions, assumptions, and images, will be of more significance to him than the study of coherent bodies of abstract thought. This sort of interest, of course, applies not merely to Canada but to the history of ideas in other places at other times. The historian who wants to establish the connections between ideas and events during the Civil War period in England is much less interested in the political philosophy of Thomas Hobbes than in ideas, well-worn though they may be, to be found in the ephemeral writings of such politicians and pamphleteers as Hyde, Vane, Lilburne, Pyrnne, or Milton (the more so in this particular instance, since Hobbes' political behaviour was not even Hobbesian). But it seems necessary to state the nature of a Canadian intellectual history, because there has been so little of it written; perhaps through a conviction that nothing of the kind was possible in the absence of any vigorous tradition of original formal thought.

It is indeed true that the explicit structures of thought from which most Canadian ideas derive lie outside Canada. It can be shown, for example, that the commonplaces of political or social language by which British American Tories of the early nineteenth century justified their actions to themselves stem directly from such European thinkers, or their popularizers, as Burke, De Lolme, Montesquieu and Blackstone. No doubt the stock of Canadian ideas is replenished every generation from European and American sources; and doubtless it should be an important function of the Canadian intellectual historian to perform the sort of operations that will trace Canadian ideas to their ultimate external source. But his major task, surely, is to analyze the manner in which externally derived ideas have been adapted to a variety of local and regional environments, in such a way that a body of assumptions uniquely Canadian has been built up; and to trace the changing content of such assumptions. What, for example, are the social assumptions implicit in the early nineteenth century term "yeoman"? When is "yeoman" replaced by "farmer," and what is the significance of the change? What is the relationship between changing terminology, and hence changing social assumptions, and the actual social process? Do these changes, both intellectual and social, occur at the same time in different parts of Canada? Again, what is the content, at any given time, of such terms as "loyalty," "order," "liberty," "authority"; terms which are merely abbreviations for complex socio-political assumptions? The content of the words "respectability" and "interest" is radically different today from what it was a century and a half ago; the life history of either term would disclose a great deal about the intellectual history of Canada.

There are good grounds for saying that the content of social image terminology, or the constellation of notions inherent in a word like "orders," will vary from region to region in Canada, and not just between French- and English-speaking regions. This may be the result of varying rates of assimilation of externally derived ideas in different parts of the country, or perhaps because some are not received at all, being "filtered out" because of the nature of local institutions. Before anything convincing can be said about the possibility that life in different regions of Canada is organized around marginally different sets of assumptions, however, much work must be done in charting the history of ideological configurations. This is not to imply that an approach which employs "French and Catholic mind" and "English and Protestant mind" as its two categories is erroneous; but simply that it is inadequate, because it cannot explain Canadian variety and because it implies that the Canadian mind, of either category, is a constant. Useful statements about the Canadian mind, at last in its historical context, are likely only after a series of careful investigations of those source materials in which the dominant assumptions of any one age are chiefly to be found, used in a context which makes their current meaning plain.

In any period, political rhetoric is a good guide to the current scale of public values, and also can provide a measurement of the frequent lag between professed belief and actual behaviour through a comparison of what the politician says with what he does. Newspaper editorials, public and private correspondence, travel books by Canadians (especially about other countries), the literature of criticism in the arts: all these classes of material are of permanent value. Other kinds of material, however, are of more significance in a particular age than in any other. Institutional and corporate advertising, for example, embalms values important in the age of large-scale economic enterprise; and a study of the advertising of the Bank of Montreal, the Steel Company of Canada, or even O'Keefe Breweries, over a generation, would probably show some remarkable shifts and changes.

The main purpose of this essay is to show, through illustration, the peculiar value of sermon literature as a medium for the expression of conservative ideas in late eighteenth and early nineteenth century British America. Sermon literature as a source for the history of ideas, though untapped in Canada, has been used extensively elsewhere. Christopher Morris's *Political Thought in England: Tyndale to Hooker* (London, 1953),[1] and William Haller's brilliant study, *The Rise of Puritanism* (New York, 1938), both rely upon the exploitation of a large body of sermons to reconstruct the intellectual movements of early modern England; R.B. Perry's studies of the New England mind draw partly upon sermons. The most casual check of

---

[1] See especially the two chapters entitled "The Elizabethan assumptions."

standard bibliographies of Canadian imprints will disclose that large numbers of sermons were published in the eighteenth and early nineteenth centuries, while many more manuscript sermons of the time are preserved in libraries and archives. In the Ontario Archives, for example, are several substantial bundles of the sermons of John Strachan, covering approximately sixty years of our history. They have never been used by an historian. Yet his sermons, and those of his contemporaries, are indispensable to an understanding of the conservative mind of the age.

II

Most of the sermons printed in British North America between 1784 and 1820 were those of "churchmen," that is, clergy of the Church of England, the Church of Scotland, and the Congregational churches of Nova Scotia. Each of these churches, in the land of its origin, was an established church and a defender of the established order of things. It is hardly remarkable that the sermons of the colonial clergy of these churches were uniformly conservative in character. It might perhaps be argued that unpublished, rather than published sermons are a more valid source for the dominant ideas of the time, since they were intended only for the minister's congregation. It is true that since printed sermons were frequently those given on such public religious occasions as the opening of the legislature, days of general fast and humiliation, or days of public thanksgiving, they tended to be concerned with such public matters as the relationship between the state and its enemies, the purposes of God in times of war and revolution, or the duties of the citizen; while unpublished sermons, on the whole, seem to be less taken up with such questions. Even so reputedly political a churchman as John Strachan rarely gave an overtly political sermon to his own congregation. Moreover, the language of manuscript sermons is less studied, less formal, and less concerned with creating an impression of classical erudition. Yet there seems to be no substantial difference in the social and political assumptions which can be found running through the two classes of sermons. Whether on public occasions, or in ordinary Sunday services, the churchman preached social and political conservatism as well as the gospel.

It is the strategic position of the churchmen of the revolutionary age that lends a special importance to the content of their sermons. Accepted as members of the small colonial upper class, and accorded special respect because of their superior education in a society in which the general level was low, the clergy of the Anglican, Presbyterian and Congregational churches (and indeed those of the Catholic church as well) were well placed to exert a considerable influence upon the political outlook and behaviour of a large part of the colonial population. It has been argued[2] that social rank and education cut the established clergy off from the "people," but this is so only in a restricted sense, because their influence reached well beyond their by no

---

2   S.D. Clark, *Church and Sect in Canada*, Toronto, 1948.

means negligible congregations. In defining the public philosophy and the public morality, the conservative clergy had little competition, and that chiefly from the judges of the high courts, whose jury charges invaded, periodically, the ideological monopoly of the ministers. Legislative debates were not reported at this time, and thus the politician was virtually stifled. The day of the journalist-politician had scarcely dawned. The popular press did not exist. Society was wholly Christian; free-thinkers kept their thoughts to themselves. No challenge to the intellectual primacy of the clergy came from such dissenting denominations as the Baptists and the Methodists, who accepted the political and social, if not the ecclesiastical and theological assumptions of the churchmen.

The position of the conservative clergy in the realm of ideas was reinforced by the outbreak of the French Revolution, and by the long wars which were its aftermath. Men knew that the Revolution had brought a new age, and whether they wished it well, or were horrified by it, they followed the shifts and changes of the huge drama with absorbed fascination. Even in the little societies of British North America, a weekly budget of despatches, letters, bulletins, treaties, atrocity stories and propaganda borrowed by the infant colonial press from newspapers abroad or from the United States kept the reading public informed (a few months in arrears) of the enormous events that were shaking the old order to its foundations. The deadly antagonism between the Revolution and established ideas and institutions meant that everywhere conservatives rallied to attack it. The politician Edmund Burke, in his *Reflections on the Revolution in France*, provided both a defence of British institutions and an eloquent assault upon the Revolution and all its works, and of course his arguments made a deep impression upon British-American conservatives as well as those of Great Britain. In the colonies, however, it was the clergy, not the politicians, who bore the chief responsibility for interpreting the meaning of Europe's convulsions to society at large, and because of this, they made a lasting contribution to the nature of Canadian conservatism. It can be seen in that combination of religious and secular elements which gave to colonial Toryism one of its most marked characteristics, and perhaps its only real claim to distinctiveness. This synthesis, worked out during the long crisis of the Revolution, the French wars, and the War of 1812, proved an extraordinarily durable one. Some illustrations of its beginnings follow.

III

That the French Revolution surpassed previous revolutions in scale and in the social depths to which it reached was not questioned, even by the Loyalist clergy of British North America. To Charles Inglis, the Loyalist Bishop of Nova Scotia, it was an event without precedent.

The state of France at the present day is an occurrence wholly new in the annals of the human race. The history of mankind ...furnishes no instance ... of so general a phrenzy seizing a populous and polished nation; a phrenzy that is not confined to any particular description, but diffused through all ranks and orders of people. The high and the low, the peer and peasant, the learned and the ignorant, are equally stimulated to the perpetration of the most atrocious crimes; delighting in slaughter and unbridled cruelty; sporting with the lives and property of mankind; destroying all religion and subordination; openly avowing atheism; and sinking into a total depravation of principles and manners![3]

That it might be possible to equate the revolutions in France and America does not seem to have occurred to Inglis;[4] it was not the degree of violence or the universality of upheaval that made the French Revolution so radical a break from previous experience, but the shock of such an explosion in a nation so "populous and polished." How could so ancient and civilized a people be "suddenly transformed into a race of sanguinary barbarians and ruffians"?[5] Had the French gone spontaneously mad? Or were there deeper causes for this apparent national insanity? Could an explanation be found in the instabilities of the volatile French character, or was the Revolution a product of causes which could operate anywhere, and not exclusively in France?

The sermons of the day were attempts to answer such questions. In them is to be found an anatomy of the Revolution, and of revolutions: the false ideas from which they spring, the nature and the motivation of the men who concoct and spread inflammatory ideas, the vast deception behind the protestations of reformers. It is not really important that these sermons were couched in the terms of traditional thought, despite some flashes of insight or felicities of phrase. What is important is their contribution to the formation of a conservative political ideology. The principles hammered home from the pulpits during the long crisis with France were those which were to condemn a Gourlay, a Mackenzie or a Papineau in the years after the end of the wars, and were to endure, in modified form, long beyond the collapse of political Toryism.

According to the Reverend Andrew Brown, incumbent of the Protestant Dissenting Church in Halifax, the seeds of the French Revolution were planted by

---

[3] Charles Inglis. *A Sermon preached in the Parish Church of St. Paul at Halifax, on Friday, April 25, 1794. Being the day appointed by Proclamation for a General Fast and Humiliation in His Majesty's Province of Nova Scotia*. Halifax, 1794, p. 24.

[4] Cf. R.R. Palmer, *Age of the democratic revolution: a political history of Europe and America, 1760-1800*. Princeton, 1959, Ch. VII.

[5] Charles Inglis, *Steadfastness in Religion and Loyalty recommended, in a Sermon preached before the Legislature of His Majesty's Province of Nova Scotia; in the Parish Church of St. Paul, at Halifax on Sunday, April 7, 1793*. Halifax, 1793, p. 22n.

the free-thinking followers of Lord Herbert of Cherbury. Under the guise of defending the freedom of the press and the right of private judgment, they launched a subtle attack upon organized religion, and by degrees poisoned the arts, science and philosophy with their sceptical doctrines. In this they had the assistance of the European aristocracy, who, out of a sense of guilt for their historic crimes, sought "a commodious apology for the disorders of their conduct."[6] Aristocratic complicity was crucial:

> Abandoned by the rich and fashionable, the church continued for a season to be a refuge to the poor and afflicted. But in time the lower orders learned to despise, in their hearts, those religious observances which they saw their more enlightened superiors treat with unreserved contempt. Copying their example with perverse ingenuity, they joined in the ridicule poured upon their clergy, and regarded every scandalous story which reflected on the church or the sacred office, as an invaluable piece of history which could not be too carefully recorded.... Amidst the indifference and depravity of a degenerate age, Christianity was publicly renounced by many in the upper ranks of life, and a speculative deism, in no respect distinguishable from actual atheism, was substituted in its room.[7]

It was a cardinal principle of Tory social psychology that the example set by the upper orders would always influence decisively the conduct of the mass of mankind. This is why a relatively few aristocratic followers of "Voltaire, Rousseau, Helvetius, D'Alembert, &c." could produce a "nation of Atheists."[8] Once "Reason" was enthroned, the way was clear for the perpetration of the shocking crimes of the Revolution. But this black page of history had a moral utility, could its lesson be understood:

> ... from the general tenour of the affairs of France since its rulers abjured religion, the least instructed of mankind ... may be enabled to institute a comparison between the effects of genuine Christianity, and of that sublime Philosophy which was to regenerate the human race ... no sooner had the sceptical philosophers usurped the powers of legislation than ... strife and anarchy prevailed. The worst passions of the worst persons rioted without control.... The prisons were crowded with victims; new modes of trial and execution were invented; and

---

[6] Andrew Brown, *The Perils of the Time, and the purposes for which they are appointed. A Sermon, preached on the last Sabbath of the Year 1794.* Halifax, 1795, p. 27.
[7] Ibid., p. 28.
[8] Inglis, *Steadfastness in Religion and Loyalty*, pp. 15, 16n.

under the direful agency of a murderous tribunal blood flowed in a continual stream.[9]

The bloody events of the Revolution, then, were the natural and inevitable outcome of the abandonment of religion by the ruling classes of France. It was vain and self-deceiving to imagine that the enlightened principles of the philosophers had somehow been betrayed by weak men; the atrocities in France were, in fact "inseparable from the nature of the new principles, and would mark their rule to the world's end."[10]

Here the conservative clergy were on familiar ground: the mutually supporting nature of religion and the state. While admitting that without government man would long since have exterminated himself, Inglis argued, following Warburton,[11] that religion was necessary to rectify the imperfections of government. Secular laws, which rested upon force, could not reach "the source and spring of our actions," the conscience. Moreover, society cannot work without such "duties of imperfect obligation" as gratitude, hospitality, charity and so on. Yet social duties, without which the state of society would be "miserable," cannot possibly be legislated. Indeed, society is incapable of sufficiently rewarding its members to ensure its own preservation. Aside from the very few persons who receive rank and emolument from serving the state, society provides for the general mass of citizens only the reward of mere protection, quite insufficient to stimulate preservative civic virtues. As man grows more numerous, new problems arise: the more populous the society, the larger the cities, the wealthier their citizens, then the greater the increase in crime as "the depraved appetites of mankind" are inflamed. A rise in material prosperity and urban population does not mean progress, but merely more inducements to greater crime. A government based upon secular philosophy, no matter how benign, is powerless against the forces of evil and destructiveness latent in society itself. There is only one principle that will bind up the warring elements within peoples, and that is the "superior principle" of religion. Only religion teaches that government is ordained of God, a principle that gives the state an authority that no secular sanction can give it.[12] Only religion renders man conscious of the all-seeing eye of God and

---

9   Brown, *Perils of the Time*, pp. 29-30.
10   Ibid., p. 30.
11   Bishop William Warburton, *Alliance of Church and State*, London, 1766.
12   Inglis, *Steadfastness in Religion and Loyalty*, pp. 9-12. The Rev. John Burns, Presbyterian minister of Stamford, Upper Canada, could find no other way to express this idea than by enunciating the doctrine of the Divine Right of Kings, in words virtually those of James I! "Kings are God's deputies, or vicegerents, here upon earth. They derive their power from him, and are the instruments, which his providence has made choice of, to govern and protect the world." *True Patriotism; a Sermon Preached in the Presbyterian Church in Stamford, Upper Canada, on the 3rd day of June, 1814....* Montreal, 1814, p. 10. Upper Canada, the nursery of a variety of out-of-the-way political notions during these years, presents no more

of his own ultimate accountability to God. Without instruction in his duty towards God, man inevitably falls victim to the ever-increasing temptations that surround him, and is drawn into enormous crimes. It is therefore "the avenging terrors of Almighty God" which are "the best support of Government."[13]

Brown's argument was similar, if a little less crudely put. Any system, he held, that considered this life as the whole of existence, and thought of death as an everlasting sleep, would hold out only "safety and self-aggrandisement" as the ends of life, and since man is not accountable for his behaviour, the pursuit of these ends "by all means, even the most atrocious," is justified. But when society is Christian, then "the gospel ... moderates the passions of the rich, and supports the virtue of the poor."[14] These and other arguments concerned with the vital social and political utility of religion were to be vigorously employed by the next generation of clerical and lay conservatives in their defence of the principle of the connection between church and state, or at least the public recognition of the Christian nature of society through financial aid to churches other than the Church of England. To conservatives, the necessity of some connection between organized religion and the state had been triumphantly vindicated by the horrors which irreligion had caused in France, and by the final defeat of France herself. Andrew Brown, in the early years of the Revolution, had been confident that such would be the outcome of the great contest then beginning:

> To all the arguments in (Christianity's) favour which past ages have furnished, will be added those alarming ones derived from the bloody history of the French revolution.... Christianity will thus be restored to new credit and influence. The vain babblings of philosophy will be consigned to everlasting perdition. Men will reject with detestation all the modifications of deism, and be solicitous to establish in their country, in their houses, and in their hearts, the genuine doctrines of the Cross of Christ.[15]

Although the first concern of the conservative clergy was to explain the French Revolution in terms of the abandonment of religion for the pernicious ideas of the free-thinkers, they also addressed themselves directly to radical French politics and the dangers French radicalism posed for British North America. Much is said, for example, of the character of the political innovator. Taken together, these remarks

---

extraordinary spectacle than this revival of divine-rightism by a spiritual descendant of John Knox and the Melvilles.

13   Inglis, *Steadfastness in Religion and Loyalty*, pp. 12-13.

14   Brown, *Perils of the Time*, p. 31. A representative Catholic development of similar themes is Rev. Edmund Burke, *Letter of Instruction to the Catholic Missionaries of Nova Scotia*, Halifax, 1804.

15   Brown, *Perils of the Time*, p. 31.

form a kind of compendium of the Tory rhetoric against reform, and are an illustration of a conventional pattern of thought that was to have a long life. To the churchmen, society was delicately and precariously balanced, an entity dependent upon the maintenance of an equilibrium between the desire of all its members for security in life and property, and the desire of each for self-aggrandisement. As we have seen, it was the function of religion to "subdue this restlessness and discontent," and to teach man to be "resigned to the will of God, and thankful for his allotment in the state of life where his providence has placed us."[16] The innovator, however, had more than the ordinary share of natural restlessness. He was a person in whom "ambition, self-interest, and humour" were in dangerous combination. "Not content with (his) proper rank in the scale of beings," he schemed to advance himself by stirring up others.[17] His tactics were ever the same: he called for redress of grievances in the name of patriotism, liberty, and the public welfare; he formed clubs, circulated inflammatory publications, got up petitions, spread rumours, worked up the multitude in the name of some great cause. He was a demagogue who played upon the baser desires of the artless populace; he was a hypocrite, because "self-interest generally lies at the bottom" of the ringing ideals he professed. Such men rose on the hopes they created in the masses, and "secretly laugh at those who are the dupes of their artifices."[18] In this timeless game, the people were always deluded; indeed, doubly so: first by the deceitful demagogue who used them for his purposes, and second by their own illusion that programmes of reform could have any beneficial effect upon their condition. Just as the state of France demonstrated the horrible consequences of irreligion, so also it showed the absurdity of impracticable schemes of political reformation, launched "under the specious names of *Fraternity, Equality,* and *Liberty.*"[19] Just as the deists had had the arrogant presumption to challenge eighteen centuries of Christianity, so the political philosophers had been dreaming dreams of perfection and calling them constitutions, when the teachings of both religion and history showed that the hard lot of man was to submit to his own imperfections and to put up with the institutions he had, which represented, after all, the wisdom of countless generations. How cruel to hoodwink the masses with glittering slogans!

> To meditate the establishment of equality..., that splendid delusion of the present age, the vision of the weak, and the pretext of the wicked, is in fact to meditate war against God, and the primary laws of creation....
> In society inequality is just as natural as in the forest, but productive of much more salutary effects. Without inequality what would become of

---

16 Inglis, *Steadfastness in Religion and Loyalty*, p. 17.
17 Mather Byles, *The Victory Ascribed to God....* Saint John, N.B., 1798, p. 5.
18 Burns, *True Patriotism*, p. 15; Inglis, *Steadfastness in Religion and Loyalty*, pp. 17, 22.
19 Jacob Mountain, *Sermon Preached at Quebec January 10, 1799 ... for General Thanksgiving*, Quebec, 1799, p. 29.

the necessary distinctions of parent and child, master and scholar, the employer and the employed![20]

Most clergymen were prepared to admit that there were times when political and social changes were necessary and even desirable, and that failure to change could bring upheavals like the French Revolution. But there were some, like Bishop Inglis, who saw no need at all for change in the present state of perfection. For him, religious history had come to a stop with the salutary changes of the Protestant Reformation, and political history with that culmination of the English genius, the Glorious Revolution of 1688:

> But, blessed be God, those times are now past. We enjoy the benefits resulting from those changes; we should be thankful to heaven for them; and look back with reverence to the fortitude and virtues of our ancestors who were instruments, in the hand of Providence, of conferring those signal blessings upon us. For we live in a period, when the Religion of Jesus Christ is professed and taught in its native purity, as contained in holy Scripture. We live under the best of Civil Constitutions; where we enjoy as much Liberty as is consistent with a state of Civil Society.... In these circumstances, to think the business of changing should still go on, and never stop, must surely proceed from (the) spirit of innovation,... or from something worse.[21]

Therefore, enjoined Inglis in the words of a text no longer in fashion, but then much used: "Fear thou the Lord and the King; and meddle not with them that are given to change."

Another important theme of the sermons of this period had to do with the meaning of the great struggle in which Britain and France were engaged. How could the larger purposes of God for man be reconciled with the necessity to justify a British victory? The interpretive framework upon which these sermons were preached was the providential theology, and, like other churchmen before and since, the clergy of the day were gradually drawn to identify the purposes of God with the policies of their own nation. Preaching in the first months of the war, Andrew Brown, "a short-sighted mortal," was wary of divining God's "precise purposes," but remained confident that He "never ordained impiety and anarchy to be perpetual among men."[22] Inglis was less cautious. He declared that "the judgments of God are actually abroad," and announced his conviction that the war against France was a sacred war. Surely it was "a contest in the cause of humanity against violence and blood, of order and government against anarchy and confusion, of right and justice against lawless

---

[20] Brown, *Perils of the Time*, pp. 34-5.
[21] Inglis, *Steadfastness in Religion and Loyalty*, p. 18.
[22] Brown, *Perils of the Time*, p. 19.

rapacity, of real liberty against oppression and tyranny, of truth against falsehood, and of God against the most audacious Atheism."[23] Yet both Inglis and Brown asserted that the war was also a sore judgment of God against Britain and her allies for their transgressions, in which Godless France was the divine instrument of punishment, just as God had used such pagan idolaters as the Egyptians and Babylonians when Israel had strayed from the paths of righteousness. The war was monitory, therefore, and was to be seen as providing opportunity for a purifying repentance. Should the opportunity so presented be wasted, then Britain would be broken like a potter's vessel.[24]

But as the war went on, the emphasis upon British sinfulness became less and less strong, and more and more the clergy, especially the Anglicans, came to equate the aims of God and Great Britain. When Nelson won at Aboukir Bay, Mather Byles in Saint John adduced the victory as proof that the British people were "the favourites of God," and that France was Satan personified as a many-headed nation. Behind Great Britain was "the secret, irresistible scheme of Providence."[25] In a sermon celebrating the same victory, Bishop Mountain at Quebec nodded to conventional theology in acknowledging that God had used France to chastise a sinful world, but professed to see that the British people, having passed through the refiner's fire of adversity, were now "happily for ourselves, and for the world, made the instruments of chastising the arrogance, humbling the power of France." Who could doubt that "we are engaged against an enemy whom we may, without presumption, consider as much more wicked than ourselves"?[26]

Mountain, and many another minister of the time, fell into the classic error of accommodating Christianity to the current system of values. They persuaded themselves, and many of their hearers, that God was not merely using Britain to defeat atheistic France, but that British victories meant also Divine approval of the social, religious, and political institutions of the mother country.[27] This delusion, always latent in British nationalism, was given special strength by the zeal with which it was preached during the many years' crisis, and was permitted to take firm hold partly because there was nothing that could be called an "intellectual opposition" in colonial society. The notion that God had staged the quarter-century of destruction as a kind of massive lesson to benighted humanity of the superior virtues of the British constitution in church and state (though never stated quite so baldly), became an article of faith with British American Tories. The special religious element in colonial Toryism owed much to the inculcation, during the war years, of a crude providentialism, as did the fact that British American conservatives had no

---

[23] Inglis, *Sermon ... for a General Fast and Humiliation*, p. 31, p. 23.
[24] Ibid., 24-5, Brown, *Perils of the Time*, p. 24.
[25] Byles, *Victory Ascribed to God*, pp. 9, 12.
[26] Mountain, *Sermon ... for General Thanksgiving*, Montreal, 1814, p. 5.
[27] Ibid., pp. 25-30.

provision in their scheme of things for orderly change, but merely for the orderly acceptance of things as they were.

In the sermons of John Strachan, the "lessons" the conservative clergy thought the French wars had taught can be read plainly. Unlike the other clergy mentioned to this point, Strachan belonged essentially to the post-war period, but his ideas were formed, once for all, before 1815. This fact is of prime importance, because Strachan was teacher, mentor and minister to a whole generation of Tory politicians in Upper Canada, a central figure in the politics of his province for at least twenty-five years and a dominant influence in his church for many more years than that. His impact upon the Ontario community in this formative stage was very great, in one way or another, and yet it cannot be said that his ideas have ever been adequately analyzed. Plentiful material for such an analysis is to be found in the large body of sermons, printed and in manuscript, that he left behind him. These sermons establish clearly Strachan's intellectual debt to the clergy of the age of revolution, but also demonstrate that he was much more extreme in his conservatism than any of them.

Strachan's mind was rather like a megalithic monument: strong, crude and simple. It moved in straight lines, was impatient of subtleties and qualifications (though often itself devious and self-deceiving), and was unleavened by what might be variously described as realism, a sense of proportion or merely as a sense of the absurd. To such a mind, providentialism was heady wine, for Strachan pushed the conclusions to be drawn from it farther than did any of his contemporaries. Not for him the modest disclaimers of Brown, or even the more specious qualifications of Mountain. God's intentions could not be doubted; "never have so many unquestionable proofs of a superintending Providence appeared in so short a period."[28] The secular, egalitarian assumptions upon which the governments of the United States and France were, or had been based, had been judged and found wanting; "the two great experiments in America and France to constitute governments productive of virtues and happiness only ... have completely failed." The lesson of the war was that "no great and decided amelioration of the lower classes of society can be reasonably expected: ... that foolish perfectibility with which they have been deluded can never be realized."[29] On the other hand, Strachan was not content to depict Britain as an instrument in the hands of God, used to accomplish his purposes, as had his clerical contemporaries. Just as God had revealed his truth to the Jews, thought Strachan, so had he in a later day to another nation. "Here, My Brethren," said Strachan, "I allude to the British nation, but not in the spirit of boasting or ostentation."[30] His victory sermon of 1814, and such other sermons as the

---

[28] John Strachan, *Sermon Preached at York, Upper Canada, on the Third of June, being the Day Appointed for a General Thanksgiving*, Montreal, 1814, p. 5.

[29] Ibid., pp. 29-30.

[30] Ibid., p. 8.

Rebellion sermon of 1838,[31] disclose that his deepest beliefs were that the British were God's peculiar people, and that their order in church, state and society was providentially blessed. Among God's British, the Upper Canadians occupied a special position. This "remnant" of a once-great continental empire had been purified and united through struggle with the United States, the only country in the world to become the ally of France by free choice. The miraculous survival of tiny Upper Canada was a North American testimony to God's gracious dealings with those whom he designed specially to prosper. Strachan's sermon of 1814, preached in the first flush of victory over Napoleon and in the knowledge that Wellington's veterans were soon to be launched against the Americans, is an important document. It is a kind of manifesto of Upper Canadian Toryism, but it contains not a programme so much as an anti-programme; that is, it lays down those things—the connection between church and state, the relative perfection of the British constitution, the delusiveness of projects of reform and the suicidal dangers in listening to innovators—which the will of God as revealed in the verdict of the war had determined to be beyond challenge. Rid of her invaders, cleansed of her traitors and secure in her beliefs, Upper Canada would stand as a shining witness in North America. "Now," said Strachan, "the dawn of the happiest times is rising upon us."[32]

IV

One of the great difficulties in reconstructing the conservative mind (of any period) is the fact that the conservative is rarely explicit about his most cherished beliefs. He assumes certain things to be immutably true and established, and finds it unnecessary to explain them to his friends, and pointless to explain them to his enemies. When an Upper Canadian Tory ran for election with a strong belief in the British constitution as his only declared platform, neither he nor his sympathetic constituents found such an appeal platitudinous or ludicrously inadequate. Such phrases stood for a whole set of conservative values.

At no time was the Tory less explicit than in explaining his social values. Quite possibly this was because the standard British arguments in justification of the principle of aristocracy seemed irrelevant to the much more democratic societies of North America; more probably it was because the Tory, while retaining his belief in a graded social order, realized that he was unlikely to get a favourable hearing for his views from the community at large. At any rate, any source which supplies an exposition of what the British American conservative meant by a phrase like "due subordination in society" is valuable.

---

[31] Ontario Archives, *Strachan Papers*, Sermon on text "And thy judgments are as the light that goeth forth," Hosea 6:5, delivered Dec. 14, 1838.

[32] Strachan, *Sermon ... for a General Thanksgiving*, p. 38.

The unpublished sermons of John Strachan contain some of the most illuminating expositions of conservative social thought available, perhaps because the Doctor in his pulpit, speaking to his parishioners, felt a freedom unknown to his pupils, on the hustings, in the legislature, or in the press. As an illustration, there is his sermon on I Timothy 4:8, "But Godliness is profitable unto all things." Strachan's notations show that it was first preached at sea September 24, 1824, and that he delivered it several more times in the 1820s and 1830s. His ostensible purpose was to comment upon the relationship between the enjoyment of the pleasures of this world and the prospect of salvation. Should religion "stalk abroad with all the rigour of Egyptian Taskmasters"?[33] He concluded (predictably enough) that when not carried to excess the pursuit of pleasure, wealth and honours was natural, proper and by no means out of keeping with the religious life.

But Strachan's purpose was not primarily to justify temporal happiness, but the existence and necessity of social inequality. His argument was immeasurably old, a kind of historical pastiche of the commonplaces of social conservatism, but with some quirks which are his alone. Just as in the natural world there is an ascending order of creation, and within each species there are both weak and strong individuals, so in human society are men given an infinite variety of capacities:

> One is formed to rule, another to obey.... Subordination in the Moral World is manifest and this appearance of nature indicates the intention of its Author. The beauty and advantages of this arrangement are obvious and universally acknowledged.... The various relations of individuals and Societies require a mutual exchange of good offices.... Hence it would appear that they who labour in the inferior departments of life are not on that account the slaves of their superiors. The Magistrate requires the aid of his people—the master of his Servant. They are all dependent upon one another, as they subsist by an exchange of good offices.... The lowest order enjoys its peculiar comforts and privileges, and contributes equally with the highest to the support and dignity of Society.

Not only did the social order correspond to the different levels of ability given to men by God, but men were also allotted "different shares of sensibility," so that the pursuit of happiness became the pursuit of that degree of happiness one is capable of attaining. Because of this, only bitterness can come to the man who aspires to a place above his station. While "efforts to better our condition are laudable," the man

---

[33] Ontario Archives, *Strachan Papers*, Sermon on text "But Godliness is profitable unto all things," I Timothy 4:8, first delivered Sept. 24, 1824. All subsequent quotations are from this sermon.

who gets above himself will drink deeply of "Chagrin, Melancholy, Envy, Hatred and other wretched passions." Strachan offered as consolation for the inferiority of one's lot the perennial conservative cliché that the mighty of this world ought not to be envied their luxury and pomp; they pay for their splendours many times over with the heavy burden of care that attends high position:

> Let us not be dazzled by the opulence and splendour of the great. The delicacies of his Table would soon pall upon our sense, vitiate our taste, and perhaps enervate us by Sickness or disease. We may admire the pomp of his public appearance, when his pride, the duties of his station, the applause of a surrounding multitude, or the brilliancy of the whole scene may preserve an air of superior ease and happiness in his deportment, but let us follow him to his retirement during the season of reflexion and we may see him oppressed with cares, which neither the most delicate repast nor costly apparel nor a multitude of Friends and dependents nor all the glories of a crown can alleviate.

Not pausing to explain to his hearers how it was that the share of sensibility awarded the great did not bring them the kind of happiness commensurate with their rank, Strachan rushed on to provide a sovereign remedy for dissatisfaction with one's subordinate position in life (so long as one was not too subordinate). Instead of eating one's heart out with envy of those more fortunate, why not reverse the process?

> You compare your situation with that of your Superiors. This will turn your attention to the advantages you want rather than those you possess.... But compare it to the inferior stations of life, and the effect will be more favourable to your comfort.... You do not consider their blessings but plume yourselves as enjoying much superior. By thus contrasting your condition with those that are worse, you will see how much more unhappy you might be and thus derive satisfaction from your superiority. In this way learn to contract your desires and you will obtain all the happiness which others so anxiously pursue.

Strachan's recommendation is testimony to his sense of social psychology, if not to his grasp of Christian social ethics.

Stripped of its characteristic individual quixotries, this sermon is probably representative of early nineteenth century conservative social thought. How relevant its categories were to the social and economic realities of British North America is quite another question. Deeply held social and political assumptions change when circumstances dictate, when they have clearly ceased to have any connection with the life they purport to explain. Perhaps it was such a change that explains the superscription scrawled upon this sermon by John Strachan in old age: "Read this Sermon on 12 March 1858 and found it very inferior to what I expected."

Fur Trade Society

Section 5

The fur trade drove the Canadian economy for two centuries, and in the North-West all of society revolved around it till 1870, when Canada annexed the territory and opened the prairies to agricultural settlement. Fur trade society was in many ways distinct from that of settled and developed provinces, and central to its distinctiveness was the contact between whites and Indians—not merely commercial, but social and personal contact as well.

These two essays—the first by a University of Toronto historian and the second by an anthropologist—explore aspects of personal and social relations between whites and Indians, and in doing so they throw new light on what happens when different societies and cultures mix together. Out of these contacts whole new social classes and ethnic identities emerged, some of which were to play a dramatic role in later Canadian history.

In what ways did fur trade society's concept of marriage differ from that of more settled regions? Why were white men attracted to marriage unions with Indian women? What attracted the women to such unions? Does Trigger's article on French-Huron relations (above, first topic) help us to understand the importance which these unions might have had for white-Indian trade relations? What factors determined how durable such unions were?

Why did the children of these *mariages à la façon du pays* turn out so differently from each other? What determined whether they would be considered Indians, whites, Métis, or half-breeds when they grew up? What does Brown's essay tell us about the origins of ethnic identity? Would she accept the popular notion that our ethnicity is determined by our ancestry?

A general history of the fur trade and fur trade society can be found in E.E.Rich, *The Fur Trade and the Northwest to 1857*. On the Métis see Jacqueline Peterson and Jennifer Brown, eds., *The New Peoples: Being and Becoming Métis in North America*.

"Women in Between": Indian Women in Fur Trade Society in Western Canada

Sylvia Van Kirk

In attempting to analyze the life of the Indian woman in fur trade society in Western Canada, especially from her own point of view, one is immediately confronted by a challenging historiographical problem. Can the Indian woman's perspective be constructed from historical sources that were almost exclusively written by European men? Coming from a non-literate society, no Indian women have left us, for example, their views on the fur trade or their reasons for becoming traders' wives.[1] Yet if one amasses the sources available for fur trade social history, such as contemporary narratives, journals, correspondence and wills, a surprisingly rich store of information on Indian women emerges. One must, of course, be wary of the traders' cultural and sexual bias, but then even modern anthropologists have difficulty maintaining complete objectivity. Furthermore, the fur traders had the advantage of knowing Indian women intimately—these women became their wives, the mothers of their children. Narratives such as that of Andrew Graham in the late eighteenth century and David Thompson in the nineteenth, both of whom had native wives, comment perceptively on the implications of Indian-white social contact.[2] The key to constructing the Indian woman's perspective must lie in the kinds of questions applied to the data;[3] regrettably the picture will not be complete, but it is hoped that a careful reading of the traders' observations can result in a useful and illuminating account of the Indian woman's life in fur trade society.

The fur trade was based on the complex interaction between two different racial groups. On the one hand are the various Indian tribes, most importantly the Ojibway, the Cree and the Chipewyan. These Indians may be designated the "host"

---

[1] The lack of written Indian history is, of course, a general problem for the ethnohistorian. Indeed, all social scientists must rely heavily on the historical observations of the agents of white contact such as fur traders, explorers and missionaries. Little seems to have been done to determine if the oral tradition of the Indians is a viable source of information on Indian-white relations in the fur trade period.

[2] Glyndwr Williams, ed., *Andrew Graham's Observations on Hudson's Bay 1769-91* (London, Hudson's Bay Record Society, v. XXVII, 1969); Richard Glover, ed., *David Thompson's Narrative 1784-1812* (Toronto, Champlain Society, v. XL, 1962).

[3] A fascinating study which indicates how the application of a different perspective to the same data can produce new insights is *Women of the Forest* by Yolande and Robert Murphy (New York, 1974). Based on field work conducted twenty years earlier in Amazonian Brazil, the authors found that by looking at the life of the Mundurucu tribe from the woman's point of view, their understanding of the actual as opposed to the official functioning of that society was much enlarged.

group in that they remain within their traditional environment. On the other hand are the European traders, the "visiting" group, who enter the North-west by both the Hudson's Bay and St. Lawrence-Great Lakes routes. They are significantly different from the Indians in that they constitute only a small, all-male fragment of their own society. For a variety of factors to be discussed, this created a unique situation for the Indian women. They became the "women in between" two groups of males. Because of their sex, Indian women were able to become an integral part of fur trade society in a sense that Indian men never could. As country wives[4] of the traders, Indian women lived substantially different lives when they moved within the forts. Even within the tribes, women who acted as allies of the whites can also be observed; certain circumstances permitted individual women to gain positions of influence and act as "social brokers" between the two groups.

It is a major contention of this study that Indian women themselves were active agents in the development of Indian-white relations.[5] A major concern then must be to determine what motivated their actions. Some themes to be discussed are the extent to which the Indian woman was able to utilize her position as "woman in between" to increase her influence and status, and the extent to which the Indian woman valued the economic advantage brought by the traders. It must be emphasized, however, that Indian-white relations were by no means static during the fur trade period.[6] After assessing the positive and negative aspects of the Indian woman's life in fur trade society, the paper will conclude by discussing the reasons for the demise of her position.

I

Miscegenation was the basic social fact of the western Canadian fur trade. That this was so indicates active cooperation on both sides. From the male perspective, both white and Indian, the formation of marital alliances between Indian women and the traders had its advantages. The European traders had both social and economic reasons for taking Indian mates. Not only did they fill the sexual void created by the absence

---

[4] Marriages between European traders and Indian women were contracted according to indigenous rites derived from Indian custom. For a detailed explanation, see Sylvia Van Kirk, "'The Custom of the Country': An Examination of Fur Trade Marriage Practices" in L.H. Thomas, ed., *Essays in Western History* (Edmonton, 1976), pp. 49-70.

[5] See Murphy, *Women of the Forest*, Ch. 6 for a useful comparison. Mundurucu women actively welcomed the social change brought about by the introduction of the rubber trade into their traditional economy.

[6] An instructive study of the Indians' economic role in the fur trade is provided by Arthur Ray in *Indians in the Fur Trade* (Toronto, 1974). He shows that the Indian played a much more active, although changing role in the dynamics of the fur trade than had previously been acknowledged.

of white women,[7] but they performed such valuable economic tasks as making moccasins and netting snowshoes that they became an integral if unofficial part of the fur trade work force.[8] The traders also realized that these alliances were useful in cementing trade ties; officers in both the Hudson's Bay and North West companies often married daughters of trading captains or chiefs.[9] From the Indian point of view, the marital alliance created a reciprocal social bond which served to consolidate his economic relationship with the trader. The exchange of women was common in Indian society where it was viewed as "a reciprocal alliance and series of good offices...between the friends of both parties; each is ready to assist and protect the other."[10] It was not loose morality or even hospitality which prompted the Indians to be so generous with their offers of women. This was their way of drawing the traders into their kinship circle, and in return for giving the traders sexual and domestic rights to their women, the Indians expected equitable privileges such as free access to the posts and provisions.[11] It is evident that the traders often did not understand the Indian concept of these alliances and a flagrant violation of Indian sensibilities could lead to retaliation such as the Henley House massacre in 1755.[12]

But what of the women themselves? Were they just pawns in this exchange, passive, exploited victims? Fur trade sources do not support this view; there are numerous examples of Indian women actively seeking to become connected with the traders. according to an early Nor'wester, Cree women considered it an honour to be selected as wives by the voyageurs, and any husband who refused to lend his wife would be subject to the general condemnation of the women.[13] Alexander Ross observed that Chinook women on the Pacific coast showed a preference for living with a white man. If deserted by one husband, they would return to their tribe in a

---

[7] H.B.C. Men were prohibited from bringing women to Hudson Bay. It was not until the early nineteenth century that the first white women came to the Northwest.

[8] In 1802 H.B.C. men defended their practice of keeping indian women in the posts by informing the London Committee that they were "Virtually your Honors Servants," H.B.C. Arch., B.239/b/79, fos. 40d-41. For a discussion of the important economic role played by native women in the fur trade, see Sylvia Van Kirk, "The Role of Women in the Fur Trade Society of the Canadian West, 1700-1850," unpublished Ph.D. thesis, University of London, 1975.

[9] H.B.C. Arch., Albany Journal, 24 Jan. 1771, B3/a/63, f. 18d; "Connolly v. Woolrich, Superior Court, 9 July 1867," *Lower Canada Jurist*, vol. XI, p. 234.

[10] Charles Bishop, "The Henley House Massacres," *The Beaver* (Autumn), 1976, p. 40.

[11] Ibid., p. 39. For a more technical look at the socio-economic relationship between the Indians and the traders, see the discussion of "balanced reciprocity" in Marshall Sahlins, *Stone Age Economics* (Chicago, 1972), ch. 5.

[12] In this instance the Indian captain Woudby attacked Henley House because the master was keeping two of his female relatives but denying him access to the post and its provisions.

[13] Alexander Henry, *Travels and Adventures in Canada and the Indian Territories 1760-1776*, ed. by Jas. Bain. (Boston, 1901), p. 248.

state of widowhood to await the opportunity of marrying another fur trader.[14] Nor'wester Daniel Harmon voiced the widely-held opinion that most of the Indian women were "better pleased to remain with the White People than with their own Relations," while his contemporary George Nelson affirmed "some too would even desert to live with the white."[15] Although Alexander Henry the Younger may have exaggerated his difficulties in fending off young Indian women, his personal experiences underline the fact that the women often took the initiative. On one occasion when travelling with his brigade in the summer of 1800, Henry was confronted in his tent by a handsome woman, dressed in her best finery, who told him boldly that she had come to live with him as she did not care for her husband or any other Indian. But Henry, anxious to avoid this entanglement partly because it was not sanctioned by the husband whom he knew to be insatiably jealous, forced the woman to return to her Indian partner.[16] A year or so later in the lower Red River district, the daughter of an Ojibway chief had more luck. Henry returned form New Year's festivities to find that "Liard's daughter" had taken possession of his room and the devil could not have got her out."[17] This time, having become more acculturated to fur trade life, Henry acquiesced and "Liard's daughter" became his country wife. The trader, however, resisted his father-in-law's argument that he should also take his second daughter because all great men should have a plurality of wives.[18]

The fur traders also comment extensively on the assistance and loyalty of Indian women who remained within the tribes. An outstanding example is the young Chipewyan Thanadelthur, known to the traders as the "Slave Woman."[19] In the early eighteenth century after being captured by the Cree, Thanadelthur managed to escape to York Factory. Her knowledge of Chipewyan made her valuable to the traders, and in 1715-16, she led an H.B.C. expedition to establish peace between the Cree and the Chipewyan, a necessary prelude to the founding of Fort Churchill. Governor James Knight's journals give us a vivid picture of this woman, of whom he declared: "She was one of a Very high Spirit and of the Firmest Resolution that ever I see any Body in my Days."[20]

---

14 Alexander Ross, *The Fur Hunters of the Far West*, Vol. 1, (London, 1855), pp. 296-97.
15 W. Kaye Lamb, ed., *Sixteen Years in the Indian Country: The Journal of Daniel Williams Harmon 1800-1816* (Toronto, 1957), p. 29; Toronto Public Library, George Nelson Papers, Journal 1810-11, 24 April 1811, p. 42.
16 Elliot Coues, ed., *New Light on the Early History of the Greater North West: The Manuscript Journals of Alexander Henry and David Thompson 1799-1814*, (Minneapolis, 1965), pp. 71-73.
17 Ibid., p. 163.
18 Ibid., p. 211.
19 For a detailed account of the story of this women, see Sylvia Van Kirk, "Thanadelthur," *The Beaver*, (Spring), 1974, pp. 40-45.
20 Ibid., p. 45.

Post journals contain numerous references to Indian women warning the traders of impending treachery. In 1797, Charles Chaboillez, having been warned by an old woman that the Indians intended to pillage his post, was able to nip this intrigue in the bud.[21] George Nelson and one of his men only escaped an attack by some Indians in 1805 by being "clandestinely assisted by the women."[22] It appears that women were particularly instrumental in saving the lives of the whites among the turbulent tribes of the Lower Columbia.[23] One of the traders' most notable allies was the well-connected Chinook princess known as Lady Calpo, the wife of a Clatsop chief. In 1814, she helped restore peaceful relations after the Nor'Westers had suffered a raid on their canoes by giving them important information about Indian custom in settling disputes. Handsome rewards cemented her attachment to the traders with the result that Lady Calpo reputedly saved Fort George from several attacks by warning of the hostile plans of the Indians.[24]

The reasons for the Indian women's action are hinted at in the traders' observations. It was the generally-held opinion of the traders that the status of women in Indian society was deplorably low. As Nor'Wester Gabriel Franchère summed it up:

> Some Indian tribes think that women have no souls, but die altogether like the brutes; others assign them a different paradise from that of men, which indeed they might have reason to prefer...unless their relative condition were to be ameliorated in the next world.[25]

Whether as "social brokers" or as wives, Indian women attempted to manipulate their position as "women in between" to increase their influence and status. Certainly women such as Thanadelthur and Lady Calpo were able to work themselves into positions of real power. It is rather paradoxical that in Thanadelthur's case it was her escape from captivity that brought her into contact with the traders in the first place; if she had not been a women, she would never have been carried off by the Cree as a prize of war. Once inside the H.B.C. fort, she was able to use her position as the only Chipewyan to advantage by acting as guide and consultant to the Governor. The protection and regard she was given by the whites enabled Thanadelthur to dictate to Indian men, both Cree and Chipewyan, in a manner they would not previously have tolerated. Anxious to promote the traders' interests, she assaulted an old Chipewyan

---

[21] Public Archives of Canada (P.A.C.), Masson Collection, Journal of Charles Chaboillez, 13 Dec. 1797, p. 24.

[22] Nelson Papers, Journal and Reminiscences 1825-26, p. 66.

[23] Ross, *Fur Hunters*, Vol. 1, p. 296.

[24] Coues, *New Light*, p. 793; Frederick Merk, ed., *Fur Trade and Empire: George Simpson's Journal, 1824-25* (Cambridge, Mass., 1931), p. 104.

[25] Gabriel Franchère, *Narrative of a Voyage to the Northwest Coast of America 1811-14*, ed. R.G. Thwaites, (Cleveland, Ohio, 1904), p. 327.

on one occasion when he attempted to trade less than prime furs; she "ketcht him by the nose Push'd him backwards & call'd him fool and told him if they brought any but Such as they ware directed they would not be traded."[26] Thanadelthur did take a Chipewyan husband but was quite prepared to leave him if he would not accompany her on the arduous second journey she was planning to undertake for the Governor.[27] It is possible that the role played by Thanadelthur and subsequent "slave women" in establishing trade relations with the whites may have enhanced the status of Chipewyan women. Nearly a century later, Alexander Mackenzie noted that, in spite of their burdensome existence, Chipewyan women possessed "a very considerable influence in the traffic with Europeans."[28]

Lady Calpo retained a position of influence for a long time. When Governor Simpson visited Fort George in 1824, he found she had to be treated with respect because she was "the best News Monger in the Parish;" from her he learned "More of the Scandal, Secrets and politics both of the out & inside of the Fort than from Any other source."[29] Significantly, Lady Calpo endeavoured to further improve her rank by arranging a marriage alliance between the Governor and her carefully-raised daughter. Although Simpson declared he wished "to keep clear of the Daughter," he succumbed in order "to continue on good terms with the Mother."[30] Many years later, a friend visiting the Columbia wrote to Simpson that Lady Calpo that "'fast friend' of the Whites" was still thriving.[31]

As wives of the traders, Indian women could also manoeuvre themselves into positions of influence. In fact, a somewhat perturbed discussion emerges in fur trade literature over the excessive influence some Indian women exerted over their fur trader husbands. The young N.W.C. clerk George Nelson appears to have spent long hours contemplating the insoluble perplexities of womankind. Nelson claimed that initially Cree women when married to whites were incredibly attentive and submissive, but this did not last long. Once they had gained a little footing, they knew well "how to take advantage & what use they ought to make of it."[32] On one of his first trips into the interior, Nelson was considerably annoyed by the shenanigans of the Indian wife of Brunet, one of his voyageurs. A jealous, headstrong woman, she completely dominated her husband by a mixture of "caresses, promises & menaces." Not only did this woman render her husband a most unreliable servant, but Nelson also caught her helping herself to the Company's rum. Brunet's wife, Nelson fumed, was as great "a vixen & hussy" as the tinsmith's wife at the market place in Montreal: "I now

---

[26] Van Kirk, "Thanadelthur," p. 44.
[27] Ibid., p. 45
[28] W. Kaye Lamb, ed., *The Journals and Letters of Sir Alexander Mackenzie* (Cambridge, Eng., 1970), p. 152.
[29] Merk, *Fur Trade & Empire*, p. 104.
[30] Ibid., pp. 104-105.
[31] H.B.C. Arch., R. Crooks to G. Simpson, 15 March 1843, D.5/8, f. 147.
[32] Nelson Papers, Journal 1810-11, pp. 41-42.

began to think that women were women not only in civilized countries but elsewhere also."[33]

Another fur trader observed a paradoxical situation among the Chipewyan women. In their own society, they seemed condemned to a most servile existence, but upon becoming wives of the French-Canadian voyageurs, they assumed "an importance to themselves and instead of serving as formerly they exact submission from the descendants of the Gauls."[34] One of the most remarkable examples of a Chipewyan wife rising to prominence was the case of Madam Lamallice, the wife of the brigade guide at the H.B.C. post on Lake Athabasca. During the difficult winter of 1820-21, Madam Lamallice was accorded a favoured position because she was the post's only interpreter and possessed considerable influence with the Indians.[35] George Simpson, then experiencing his first winter in the Indian Country, felt obliged to give in to her demands for extra rations and preferred treatment in order to prevent her defection. He had observed that the Nor'Westers' strong position was partly due to the fact that "...their Women are faithful to their cause and good Interpreters whereas we have but one in the Fort that can talk Chipewyan."[36] Madam Lamallice exploited her position to such an extent that she even defied fort regulations by carrying on a private trade in provisions.[37] A few years later on a trip to the Columbia, Governor Simpson was annoyed to discover that Chinook women when married to the whites often gained such an ascendancy "that they give law to their Lords."[38] In fact, he expressed general concern about the influence of these "petticoat politicians" whose demands were "more injurious to the Companys interests than I am well able to describe."[39] The Governor deplored Chief Factor James Bird's management of Red River in the early 1820s because of his habit of discussing every matter "however trifling or important" with "his Copper Cold. Mate," who then spread the news freely around the colony.[40] Too many of his officers, Simpson declared, tended to sacrifice business for private interests. Particular expense and delay were occasioned in providing transport for families. Simpson never forgave Chief Factor John Clarke for abandoning some of the goods destined for Athabasca in 1820 to make a light canoe for his native wife and her servant.[41]

It is likely that Simpson's single-minded concern for business efficiency caused him to exaggerate the extent of the Indian women's influence. Nevertheless, they do

---

[33] Nelson Papers, Journal 1803-04, pp. 10-28 passim.
[34] Masson Collection, "An Account of the Chipwean Indians," p. 23.
[35] E.E. Rich, ed., *Simpson's Athabasca Journal and Report 1820-21* (London, H.B.R.S., v. I, 1938), p. 74.
[36] Ibid., 231.
[37] H.B.C. Arch., Fort Chipewyan Journal 1820-21, B.39/a/16, fos. 6-21d. *passim*
[38] Merk, *Fur Trade and Empire*, p. 99.
[39] Ibid., pp. 11-12, 58.
[40] H.B.C. Arch., George Simpson's Journal 1821-22. D.3/3, f. 52.
[41] Rich, *Athabasca Journal*, pp. 23-24; see also Merk, *Fur Trade & Empire*, p. 131.

seem to have attempted to take advantage of their unique position as women "in between" two groups of men. This fact is supported by the traders' observation that the choice of a husband, Indian or white, gave the Indian woman leverage to improve her lot. Now she could threaten to desert to the whites or vice-versa if she felt she were not being well-treated:

> She has always enough of policy to insinuate how well off she was while living with the white people and in like manner when with the latter she drops some hints to the same purpose.[42]

Although Chipewyan women who had lived with the voyageurs had to resume their former domestic tasks when they returned to their own people, they reputedly evinced a greater spirit of independence.[43] Considerable prestige accrued to Chinook women who had lived with the traders; upon rejoining the tribes, they remained "very friendly" to the whites and "never fail to influence their connections to the same effect."[44]

From the Indian woman's point of view, material advantage was closely tied to the question of improved influence or status. The women within the tribes had a vested interest in promoting cordial relations with the whites. While George Nelson mused that it was a universal maternal instinct which prompted the women to try to prevent clashes between Indian and white,[45] they were more likely motivated by practical, economic considerations. If the traders were driven from the country, the Indian woman would lose the source of European goods, which had revolutionized her life just as much if not more than that of the Indian man. It was much easier to boil water in a metal kettle than to have to laboriously heat it by means of dropping hot stones into a bark container. Cotton and woollen goods saved long hours of tanning hides. "Show them an awl or a strong needle," declared David Thompson, "and they will gladly give the finest Beaver or Wolf skin they have to purchase it."[46]

Furthermore, it can be argued that the tendency of the Indians to regard the fur trade post as a kind of welfare centre was of more relevance to the women than to the men. In times of scarcity, which were not infrequent in Indian society, the women

---

[42] "Account of Chipwean Indians," pp. 23-24.
[43] Ibid., p. 23.
[44] Ross, *Fur Hunters*, vol. 1, p. 297.
[45] Nelson Papers, Journal and Reminiscences 1825-26, p. 66. Nelson claimed that around 1780 some Indian women had warned the Canadian pedlars of impending attack because in their "tender & affectionate breast (for women are lovely all the world over) still lurked compassion for the mothers of those destined to be sacrificed."
[46] Glover, *Thompson's Narrative*, p. 45. Cf. the Mundurucu women's desire for European goods, Murphy, *Women of the Forest*, p. 182.

were usually the first to suffer.[47] Whereas before they would often have perished, many now sought relief at the companies' posts. To cite but one of many examples: at Albany during the winter of 1706, Governor Beale gave shelter to three starving Cree women whose husbands had sent them away as he could only provide for his two children.[48] The post was also a source of medical aid and succour. The story is told of a young Carrier woman in New Caledonia, who having been severely beaten by her husband managed to struggle to the nearest N.W.C. post. Being nearly starved, she was slowly nursed back to health and allowed to remain at the post when it became apparent that her relatives had abandoned her.[49] The desire for European goods, coupled with the assistance to be found at the fur trade posts, helps to explain why Indian women often became devoted allies of the traders.

In becoming the actual wife of a fur trader, the Indian woman was offered even greater relief from the burdens of her traditional existence. In fact, marriage to a trader offered an alternative lifestyle. The fur traders themselves had no doubt that an Indian woman was much better off with a white man. The literature presents a dreary recital of their abhorrence of the degraded, slave-like position of the Indian woman. The life of a Cree woman, declared Alexander Mackenzie, was "an uninterrupted succession of toil and pain."[50] Nor'Wester Duncan McGillivray decided that the rather singular lack of affection evinced by Plains Indian women for their mates arose from the barbarous treatment the women received.[51] Although David Thompson found the Chipewyan a good people in many ways, he considered their attitudes toward women a disgrace; he had known Chipewyan women to kill female infants as "an act of kindness" to spare them the hardships they would have to face.[52]

The extent to which the future traders' observations represent an accurate reflection of the actual status of Indian women in their own societies presents a complex dilemma which requires deeper investigation. The cultural and class biases of the traders are obvious. Their horror at the toilsome burdens imposed upon Indian women stems from their narrow, chivalrous view of women as the "frail, weaker sex." This is scarcely an appropriate description of Indian women, particularly the Chipewyan who were acknowledged to be twice as strong as their male

---

[47] Samuel Hearne, *A Journey to the Northern Ocean*, edited by Richard Glover, (Toronto, 1958), p. 190.
[48] H.B.C. Arch., Albany Journal, 23 Feb. 1706, B.3/a/l, f. 28.
[49] Ross Cox, *The Columbia River*, edited by Jane and Edgar Stewart. (Norman, Okla., 1957), p. 377.
[50] Lamb, *Journals of Mackenzie*, p. 135.
[51] A.S. Morton, *The Journal of Duncan McGillivray...at Fort George on the Saskatchewan 1794-95* (Toronto, 1929), p. 60.
[52] Glover, *Thompson's Narrative*, p. 106.

counterparts.[53] Furthermore, while the sharp sexual division of labour inflicted a burdensome role upon the women, their duties were essential and the women possessed considerable autonomy within their own sphere.[54] Some traders did think it curious that the women seemed to possess a degree of influence in spite of their degraded situation; indeed, some of the bolder ones occasionally succeeded in making themselves quite independent and "wore the breeches."[55]

A possible way of explaining the discrepancy between the women's perceived and actual status is suggested in a recent anthropological study of the Mundurucu of Amazonian Brazil. In this society, the authors discovered that while the official (male) ideology relegates women to an inferior, subservient position, in the reality of daily life, the women are able to assume considerable autonomy and influence.[56] Most significantly, however, Mundurucu women, in order to alleviate their onerous domestic duties, have actively championed the erosion of traditional village life and the concomitant blurring of economic sex roles which have come with the introduction of the rubber trade. According to the authors, the Mundurucu woman "has seen another way of life, and she has opted for it."[57]

This statement could well be applied to the Indian woman who was attracted to the easier life of the fur trade post. In the first place, she now became involved in a much more sedentary routine. With a stationary home, the Indian woman was no longer required to act as a beast of burden, hauling or carrying the accoutrements of camp from place to place. The traders often expressed astonishment and pity at the heavy loads which Indian women were obliged to transport.[58] In fur trade society, the unenviable role of carrier was assumed by the voyageur. The male servants at the fort were now responsible for providing firewood and water, although the women might help. In contrast to Indian practice, the women of the fort were not sent to fetch home the produce of the hunt.[59] The wife of an officer, benefiting from her husband's rank, enjoyed a privileged status. She herself was carried in and out of the

---

[53] Hearne, *Journey to Northern Ocean* p. 35: "Women," declared the Chipewyan chief Matonabee, "were made for labour; one of them can carry, or haul, as much as two men can do."

[54] There has been a trend in recent literature to exalt the Indian woman's status by pointing out that in spite of her labour she had more independence that the pioneer farm wife; see Nancy O. Lurie, "Indian Women: A Legacy of Freedom," *The American Way*, vol 5 (April), 1972, pp. 28-35.

[55] Morton, *McGillivray's Journal*, p. 35; L.R.F. Masson, *Les Bourgeois de la Compagnie du Nord-Ouest*, Vol. I, p. 256.

[56] Murphy, *Women of the Forest*, pp. 87, 112.

[57] Ibid., p. 202.

[58] Lamb, *Journals of Mackenzie*, p. 254; Glover, *Thompson's Narrative*, p. 125.

[59] Masson Collection, Journal of John Thomson, 15 Oct. 1798, p. 10.

Indian Women in Fur Trade Society in Western Canada 187

canoe[60] and could expect to have her baggage portaged by a voyageur. At Fond du Lac in 1804 when the wife of N.W.C. *bourgeois* John Sayer decided to go on a sugar-making expedition, four men went with her to carry her baggage and provisions and later returned to fetch home her things.[61]

While the Indian woman performed a variety of valuable economic tasks around the post, her domestic duties were relatively lighter than they had traditionally been. Now her energies were concentrated on making moccasins and snowshoes. As one Nor'Wester declared, with the whites, Indian women could lead "a comparatively easy life" in contrast to the "servile slavish mode" of their own.[62] The prospect of superior comforts reputedly motivated some Spokan women to marry voyageurs.[63] The ready supply of both finery and trinkets which *bourgeois* and voyageurs were seen to lavish on their women may also have had an appeal.[64] Rival traders noted that luxury items such as lace, ribbons, rings and vermilion, which "greatly gain the Love of the Women," were important in attracting the Indians to trade.[65] The private orders placed by H.B.C. officers and servants in the 1790s and later include a wide range of cloth goods, shawls, gartering, earrings and brooches for the women.[66] When taken by a trader *à la façon du pays*, it became common for an Indian woman to go through a ritual performed by the other women of the fort; she was scoured of grease and paint and exchanged her native garments for those of a more civilized fashion. At the N.W.C. posts, wives were clothed in "Canadian fashion" which consisted of a shirt, short gown, petticoat and leggings.[67]

The traders further thought that Indian women benefited by being freed from certain taboos and customs which they had to bear in Indian society. Among the Ojibway and other tribes, for example, the choicest part of an animal was always reserved for the men; death it was believed would come to any woman who dared to eat such sacred portions. The Nor'Westers paid little heed to such observances. As Duncan Cameron sarcastically wrote: "I have often seen several women living with the white men eat of those forbidden morsels without the least inconvenience."[68] The traders were also convinced that Indian women welcomed a monogamous as opposed to a polygamous state. Polygamy, several H.B.C. officers observed, often

---

[60] J.B. Tyrrell, *Journals of Samuel Hearne and Philip Turnor 1774-92* (Toronto, Champlain Society, vol. XXI, 1934), p. 252.

[61] Michel Curot, "A Wisconsin Fur Trader's Journal 1803-04," *Wisconsin Historical Collections*, vol. 20, pp. 449, 453.

[62] Nelson Papers, Journal 1810-11, p. 41; Reminiscences, Part 5, p. 225.

[63] Cox, *Columbia River*, p. 148.

[64] Coues, *New Light*, p. 914; Ross, *Fur Hunters*, vol. 11, p. 236.

[65] Tyrrell, *Journals of Hearne and Turnor*, p. 273.

[66] H.B.C. Arch. Book of Servants Commissions, A.16/111 and 112 *passim*.

[67] Lamb, *Sixteen Years*, pp. 28-9.

[68] Masson, *Les Bourgeois*, Vol. II, p. 263.

gave rise to jealous and sometimes murderous quarrels.[69] It is possible, however, that the traders' own cultural abhorrence of polygamy[70] made them exaggerate the women's antipathy toward it. As a practical scheme for the sharing of heavy domestic tasks, polygamy may in fact have been welcomed by the women.

II

Thus far the advantages which the fur trade brought to Indian women have been emphasized in order to help explain Indian women's reactions to it. It would be erroneous, however, to paint the life of an Indian wife as idyllic. In spite of the traders' belief in the superior benefits they offered, there is evidence that fur trade life had an adverse effect on Indian women. Certainly, a deterioration in her position over time can be detected.

First there is the paradox that the supposedly superior material culture of the fur trade had a deleterious effect on Indian women. It was as if, mused Reverend John West, the first Anglican missionary, "the habits of civilized life" exerted an injurious influence over their general constitutions.[71] Apart from being more exposed to European diseases, the Indian wives of traders suffered more in childbirth than they had in the primitive state.[72] Dr. Richardson, who accompanied the Franklin Expedition of the 1820s noted, that not only did Indian women now have children more frequently and for longer periods, but that they were more susceptible to the disorders and diseases connected with pregnancy and childbirth.[73] It was not uncommon for fur traders' wives to give birth to from eight to twelve children, whereas four children were the average in Cree society.[74]

The reasons for this dramatic rise in the birth rate deserve further investigation, but several reasons can be advanced. As recent medical research had suggested, the less fatiguing lifestyle and more regular diet offered the Indian wife could have

---

[69] Hearne, *Journey to Northern Ocean*, p. 80; Williams, *Graham's Observations*, p. 158.

[70] Alexander Ross, *Adventures of the First Settlers on the Oregon or Columbia River* (London, 1849), pp. 280-81: Glover, *Thompson's Narrative*, p. 251.

[71] John West, *The Substance of a Journal during a residence at the Red River Colony 1820-23* (London, 1827), p. 54.

[72] The traders were astonished at the little concern shown for pregnancy and childbirth in Indian society; see for example Lamb, *Journals of Mackenzie*, p. 250 and Williams, *Graham's Observations*, p. 177.

[73] John Franklin, *Narrative of a Journey to the Shores of the Polar Sea 1819-22* (London, 1824), p. 86.

[74] Ibid., 60. The Indian wives of Alexander Ross and Peter Fidler, for example, had thirteen and fourteen children respectively.

resulted in greater fecundity.[75] The daily ration for the women of the forts was four pounds of meat or fish (one half that for the men);[76] when Governor simpson jokingly remarked that the whitefish diet at Fort Chipewyan seemed conducive to procreation he may have hit upon a medical truth.[77] Furthermore sexual activity in Indian society was circumscribed by a variety of taboos, and evidence suggests that Indian men regarded their European counterparts as very licentious.[78] Not only did Indian women now have sex more often, but the attitudes of European husbands also may have interfered with traditional modes of restricting family size. The practice of infanticide was, of course, condemned by the whites, but the Europeans may also have discouraged the traditional long nursing periods of from two to four years for each child.[79] In their view this custom resulted in the premature aging of the mothers,[80] but the fact that Indian children were born at intervals of approximately three years tends to support the recent theory that lactation depresses fertility.[81]

The cultural conflict resulting over the upbringing of the children must have caused the Indian women considerable anguish. An extreme example of the tragedy which could result related to the Chinook practice of head-flattening. In Chinook society, a flat forehead, achieved by strapping a board against the baby's head when in its cradle, was a mark of class; only slaves were not so distinguished. Thus it was only natural that a Chinook woman, though married to a fur trader, would desire to bind her baby's head, but white fathers found this custom abhorrent. The insistence of some fathers that their infants' heads not be flattened resulted in the mothers murdering their babies rather than have them suffer the ignominy of looking like slaves. Gradually European preference prevailed. When Governor Simpson visited the Columbia in the early 1820s, he reported that Chinook wives were abiding by their husbands' wishes and no cases of infanticide had been reported for some years.[82]

In Indian society, children were the virtual "property" of the women who were responsible for their upbringing;[83] in fur trade society, Indian women could find themselves divested of these rights. While the traders acknowledged that Indian women were devoted and affectionate mothers, this did not prevent them from exercising patriarchal authority, particularly in sending young children to Britain or

---

[75] Jennifer Brown, "A Demographic Transition in the Fur Trade Country," *Western Canadian Journal of Anthropology*, Vol. VI, No. 1, p. 68.
[76] Cox, *Columbia River*, p. 354.
[77] J.S. Galbraith, *The Little Emperor* (Toronto, 1976), p. 68.
[78] Nelson Papers, Reminiscences, Pt. 5, p. 225
[79] Brown, "A Demographic Transition," p. 67.
[80] Margaret MacLeod, ed., *The Letters of Letitia Hargrave* (Toronto, Champlain Society, v. XXVIII, 1947), pp. 94-95; Alexander Ross, *The Red River Settlement* (Minneapolis, 1957), p. 95, 192.
[81] Brown, "A Demographic Transition," p. 65.
[82] Merk, *Fur Trade and Empire*, p. 101.
[83] Williams, *Graham's Observations*, pp. 176, 178.

Canada so that they might receive a "civilized" education.[84] It must have been nearly impossible to explain the rationale for such a decision to the Indian mothers; their grief at being separated from their children was compounded by the fact that the children, who were especially vulnerable to respiratory diseases, often died.[85]

It is difficult to know if the general treatment accorded Indian women by European traders met with the women's acceptance. How much significance should be attached to the views of outside observers in the early 1800s who did not think the Indian woman's status had been much improved? Some of the officers of the Franklin Expedition felt the fur traders had been corrupted by Indian attitudes toward women; Indian wives were not treated with "the tenderness and attention due to every female" because the Indians would despise the traders for such unmanly action.[86] The first missionaries were even stronger in denouncing fur trade marital relations. John West considered the traders' treatment of their women disgraceful: "They do not admit them as their companions, nor do they allow them to eat at their tables, but degrade them *merely* as slaves to their arbitrary inclinations."[87] Such statements invite scepticism because of the writers' limited contact with fur trade society, and in the case of the missionaries because of their avowedly hostile view of fur trade customs. Furthermore, the above statements project a European ideal about the way women should be treated, which apart from being widely violated in their own society, would have had little relevance for Indian women. It is doubtful, for example, that the Indian women themselves would have viewed the fact that they did not come to table, a custom partly dictated by the quasi-military organization of the posts, as proof of their debased position.[88] The segregation of the sexes at meals was common in Indian society, but now, at least, the women did not have to make do with the leftovers of the men.[89]

Nevertheless, there is evidence to suggest that Indian women were misused by the traders. In Indian society, women were accustomed to greater freedom of action with regard to marital relationships than the traders were prepared to accord them. It was quite within a woman's rights, for example, to institute a divorce if her marriage proved unsatisfactory.[90] In fur trade society, Indian women were more subject to arbitrary arrangements devised by the men. Upon retiring from the Indian Country, it became customary for a trader to place his country wife and family with another, a practice known as "turning off." Although there was often little they could do about it, a few cases were cited of women who tried to resist. At a post in the Peace River

---

[84] Ross, *Adventures on the Columbia*, p. 280; W.J. Healy, *Women of Red River* (Winnipeg, 1923), pp. 163-66.
[85] Lamb, *Sixteen Years*, pp. 138, 186.
[86] Franklin, *Narrative of a Journey*, pp. 101, 106.
[87] West, *Red River Journal*, p. 16.
[88] Cox, *Columbia River*, p. 360.
[89] Hearne, *Journey to the Northern Ocean*, p. 57.
[90] Williams, *Graham's Observations*, p. 176.

district in 1798, the Indian wife of an *engagé*, who was growing tired of wintering *en derouine*, absolutely rejected her husband's attempt to pass her to the man who agreed to take his place.[91] At Fort Chipewyan in 1800, the estranged wife of the voyageur Morin foiled the attempt of his *bourgeois* to find her a temporary "protector"; she stoutly refused three different prospects.[92] Indian women also did not take kindly to the long separations which fur trade life imposed on them and their European mates. Although the Indian wife of the Chief Factor Joseph Colen was to receive every attention during his absence in England in the late 1790s, Colen's successor could not dissuade her from taking an Indian lover and leaving York Factory.[93]

Indian wives seem to have been particularly victimized during the violent days of the trade war when rivals went so far as to debauch and intimidate each other's women. In 1819 at Pelican Lake, for example, H.B.C. servant Deshau took furs from a N.W.C. servant and raped his wife in retaliation for having had his own wife debauched by a Nor'Wester earlier in the season.[94] A notorious instance involved the Indian wife of H.B.C. servant Andrew Kirkness at Isle à la Crosse in 1810-11. In the late summer, this woman in a fit of pique had deserted her husband and sought refuge at the Nor'Westers' post. She soon regretted her action, however, for she was kept a virtual prisoner by the Canadians, and all efforts of the H.B.C. men to get her back failed. The upshot was that Kirkness himself deserted to the rival post, leaving the English in dire straits since he was their only fisherman. Kirkness was intimidated into remaining with the Nor'Westers until the spring with the threat that should he try to leave "every Canadian in the House would ravish his woman before his eyes." Eventually Kirkness was released, but only after his wife had been coerced into saying that she did not want to accompany him. As the H.B.C. party were evacuating their post, the woman tried to escape but was forcibly dragged back by the Nor'Westers and ultimately became the "property" of an *engagé*.[95]

Such abusive tactics were also applied to the Indians. By the turn of the century, relations between the Indians and the Nor'Westers in particular showed a marked deterioration. In what seems to have been a classic case of "familiarity breeding contempt," the Nor'Westers now retained their mastery through coercion and brute force and frequently transgressed the bounds of Indian morality. An especially flagrant case was the Nor'Westers' exploitation of Chipewyan women at their posts in the Athabasca district. By the end of the eighteenth century, they had apparently built up a nefarious traffic in these women; the *bourgeois* did not scruple at seizing Chipewyan women by force, ostensibly in lieu of trade debts, and then selling them

---

91   Thomson's Journal, 19 Nov. 1798, p. 20.
92   Masson, *Les Bourgeois*, Vol. II, pp. 384-85. We are not told whether she also escaped being sold when the brigades arrived in the spring as the *bourgeois* intended.
93   H.B.C. Arch., York Journal, 2 Dec. 1798, B.239/a/103, f. 14d.
94   H.B.C. Arch., Pelican Lake Journal, 18 Jan. 1819, D.158/a/l, f. 7d.
95   This account is derived from the Isle à la Crosse Journal, H.B.C. Arc., B.89/a/2, fos. 5-36d *passim*.

to the men for large sums.⁹⁶ The situation became so bad that the Chipewyan began leaving their women behind when they came to trade, and when Hudson's Bay traders appeared on Lake Athabasca in 1792, the Indians hoped to secure their support and drive out their rivals. The English, however, were too weak to offer any effective check to the nor'Westers who continued to assault both fathers and husbands if they tried to resist the seizure of their women. Since they were not powerful enough to mount an attack, the Chipewyan connived at the escape of their women during the summer months when most of the traders were away. Resentful of their treatment, many of the women welcomed the chance to slip back to their own people so that the summer master at Fort Chipewyan was almost solely preoccupied with keeping watch over the *engagés'* women.⁹⁷ By 1800 at least one voyageur had been killed by irate Chipewyan, and the *bourgeois* contemplated offering a reward for the hunting down of "any d—nd rascal" who caused a Frenchman's woman to desert.⁹⁸

The Indians appear to have become openly contemptuous of the white man and his so-called morality. A northern tribe called the Beaver Indians took a particularly strong stand. At first they had welcomed the Canadians but, having rapidly lost respect for them, now forbade any intercourse between their women and the traders.⁹⁹ Elsewhere individual hunters boycotted the traders owing to the maltreatment of their women.¹⁰⁰ Sporadic reprisals became more frequent. Whereas Indian women had previously played a positive role as a liaison between Indian and white, they were now becoming an increasing source of friction between the two groups. Governor Simpson summed up the deteriorating situation:

> It is a lamentable fact that almost every difficulty we have had with Indians throughout the country may be traced to our interference with their Women or their intrigues with the Women of the Forts in short 9 murders out of 10 Committed on Whites by Indians have arisen through Women.¹⁰¹

Although there is little direct evidence available, it is possible that the Indian women themselves were becoming increasingly dissatisfied with their treatment from the whites. In spite of the initiative which the women have been seen to exercise in forming and terminating relationships with the traders, there were undoubtedly times when they were the unwilling objects of a transaction between Indians and white men. Certainly not all Indian women looked upon the whites as desirable husbands, a view that was probably reinforced with experience. George Nelson did observe in

---

[96] Tyrrell, *Journals of Hearne and Turnor*, pp. 446n, 449.
[97] Ibid., 449-50.
[98] Masson, *Les Bourgeois*, Vol. II, pp. 387-88.
[99] Lamb, *Journals of Mackenzie*, p. 255; Rich, *Athabasca Journal*, p. 388.
[100] Masson Collection, Journal of Ferdinand Wentzel, 13 Jan. 1805, p. 41.
[101] Merk, *Fur Trade & Empire*, p. 127.

1811 that there were some Indian women who showed "an extraordinary predilection" for their own people and could not be prevailed upon to live with the traders.[102]

The increasing hostility of the Indians, coupled with the fact that in well-established areas marriage alliances were no longer a significant factor in trade relations, led to a decline in the practice of taking an Indian wife. In fact in 1806, the North West Company passed a ruling prohibiting any of its employees from taking a country wife from among the tribes.[103] One of the significant factors which changed the traders' attitudes toward Indian women, however, was that they were now no longer "women in between." By the turn of the century a sizeable group of mixed-blood women had emerged and for social and economic reasons, fur traders preferred mixed-blood women as wives.[104] In this way the Indian women lost their important place in fur trade society.

The introduction of the Indian woman's perspective on Indian-white relations serves to underscore the tremendous complexity of inter-cultural contact. It is argued that Indian women saw definite advantages to be gained from the fur trade, and in their unique position as "women in between," they endeavoured to manipulate the situation to improve their existence. That the limits of their influence were certainly circumscribed, and that the ultimate benefits brought by the traders were questionable does not negate the fact that the Indian women played a much more active and important role in the fur trade than has previously been acknowledged.

---

[102] Nelson Papers, Journal 1810-11, pp. 41-42.

[103] W.S. Wallace, *Documents relating to the North West Company* (Toronto, Champlain Society, v. XXII, 1934), p. 211. This ruling was not enforced in outlying districts such as the Columbia. Even after the union in 1821, Governor Simpson continued to favour the formation of marital alliances in remote regions as the best way to secure friendly relations with the Indians, see Rich, *Athabasca Journal*, p. 392.

[104] For a discussion of the role played by mixed-blood women in fur trade society, see Van Kirk, "Role of Women in Fur Trade Society."

Diverging Identities: The Presbyterian Métis of St. Gabriel Street, Montreal

Jennifer S.H. Brown

In North America of the late twentieth century, it has become fashionable and even normal to wear, more or less visibly, some label of ethnic identity and to display it by various symbolic means. Whether involuntarily or by choice, most of us become ethnics; for censuses, or with a diversity of political, economic, or psychological motives, we check ourselves into one or another ethnic pigeonhole, no matter how varied or undocumented our ancestors may have been. Ethnicity, as Karen Blu noted in her study of the Lumbee Indians of North Carolina,[1] has not only gained ground as a means of classifying people; it is also the foundation for both personal and expressive declarations about one's "roots," and for a variety of interest groups who seek power and legitimacy and need members and converts—people who elect an ethnic identity that they had formerly rejected, concealed or had been unaware of.

Ethnic movements exhibit strong tendencies to redefine the past—or better, a multiplicity of pasts—in terms provided or actively promoted in the present. The growth and cultivation of ethnic identity may be seen as a centripetal process; of the varied strands of individual and group histories, certain ones are sorted, drawn together and interwoven to form a strong core, a heart or centre that gives integrity (in all its senses) to people's lives and personalities. The Newberry Library Conference on the Métis in North America was, among other things, an expression of our times—of a dynamic present in which concerns about ethnic roots, history, survival and political and economic rights are vigorous and widely shared. Among the métis of the Canadian West, Montana, Ontario and elsewhere, such concerns have recently gained a momentum that is demonstrated in the current intensity of political, organizational and publishing activity.[2]

Métissage, or the process by which this population arose, is a term that has been used with two meanings which need to be carefully distinguished. Biologically, it is the creation of persons of mixed Indian-white parentage and the mingling of groups

---

[1] Karen I. Blu, *The Lumbee Problem: The Making of an American Indian People* (Cambridge: Cambridge University Press, 1980), 212-14.

[2] Expressions of this momentum are to be found in, for example, Duke Redbird, *We are Métis: A Métis View of the Development of a Native Canadian People* (Willowdale, Ont.: Ontario Métis and Non-Status Indian Association, 1980) which lists on p. 31 the many métis organizations founded in Canada since 1900; Joe Sawchuck, *The Métis of Manitoba: Reformulation of an Ethnic Identity* (Toronto: Peter Martin Associates, 1978); and Alberta Federation of Métis Settlement Associations, *Métisism: A Canadian Identity* (Edmonton: 1982).

characterized by distinctive traits such as blood group gene O, so widely distributed in New World aboriginal populations.³ For the purposes of this discussion, however, it is the social, cultural and political creation of persons who accept or decide to affirm that "we are métis," taking that dual aspect of their ancestry and affiliation as a central fact of life.

An effort has been made to avoid the term *mixed-blood* because of its connotations for English speakers. Although blood cannot "mix," English folk biology, reflected in language usages, suggests that it can, and uses the word as a gloss for shared genetic substance ("blood" relatives are closest and most real; "blood" is thicker than water; "blood lines" are lines of descent; a purebred animal is also a "pureblood").⁴ These unconscious and rather insidious linguistic habits tighten their hold upon us when we translate the etymologically neutral French term, *métis*, by using a term emphasizing blood, in the absence of good English alternatives.

The centripetal processes by which modern métis identities are being constructed and maintained have proved richly productive of research and synthesis, stimulating the mining of untapped sources of information, the devising of new analytical approaches, and the study of communities long neglected or misunderstood. Some of the new work has vital legal implications as it uncovers past governmental abuses and neglect, and as it attempts to chart a better course for the future under Canada's new Constitution. Data recently assembled by the Native Council of Canada, the newly founded Métis National Council and the Manitoba Métis Federation, for example, have reopened questions about the handling of "halfbreed" claims in the making of Canada's numbered Indian treaties, and about the abuses that followed upon the Manitoba Act of 1870 which specified that 1,400,000 acres were to be allotted to the children of the "halfbreeds" in that new province.⁵ The great range and variety of recent writing in other social, cultural, literary and linguistic domains are

---

3   Alfred W. Crosby, Jr., *The Columbian Exchange: Biological and Cultural Consequences of 1492* (Westport, Conn.: Greenwood Press, 1972), 28-29.

4   For discussion of this point, see David M. Schneider, *American Kinship: A Cultural Account* (Englewood Cliffs, N.J.: Prentice-Hall, 1968).

5   Native Council of Canada, *A Statement of Claim Based on Aboriginal Title of Métis and Non-Status Indians* (Ottawa: 1980); Métis National Council, *Report on Historical Research* (typescript for the federal-provincial meeting of officials on aboriginal constitutional matters, Ottawa, 1983); Manitoba Métis Federation, *Métis Anoutch: Manitoba Métis Rights Constitutional Consultations* (Winnipeg: 1983). See also: Douglas N. Sprague, "Government Lawlessness in the Administration of Manitoba Land Claims, 1870-1887" (*Manitoba Law Journal* 10 [1979-80]; 415-41); and Douglas N. Sprague and R.P. Frye, *The Genealogy of the First Métis Nation* (Winnipeg: Pemmican Publications, 1983).

reflected in a rapidly expanding number of other publications,[6] as well as in this volume.

There is always some risk, however, that historical work done in response to the perspectives and pressing concerns and needs of the present may distract us from understanding people of the past on their own terms, in all their complexity and variability. The viewpoints and interests of the living are readily projected onto the dead, who regrettably refuse to answer our queries and questionnaires or to dispute our interpretation. We cannot, for example, ask the nineteenth-century Atkinson or Richards families of James Bay or the Anglican clergyman James Settee of Manitoba (all of Hudson's Bay Company [HBC] and Cree descent), or the Connolly, Rowand or Barnston offspring in Montreal (all North West Company native families) how they felt about their mixed ancestry. We can only infer their opinions (or lack thereof) from the incomplete records that they and others have left, and try to avoid co-opting them into groups or categories that were absent from or irrelevant to their own lives and communities. One thing we have been learning, after all, is that the northern fur trade of the seventeenth to nineteenth centuries was a multiplicity of social settings, too shifting and variable to allow unitary categorization of all the biracial individuals born in its midst.[7]

In fact, in counterpoise to the understandably centripetal tendencies of much modern ethnic historiography, the fur trade is better viewed as centrifuge, that is, spawning a diversity of persons and groups who were spun off, so to speak, into numerous different niches and categories in the period from the mid-eighteenth to mid-nineteenth centuries. Rather than a unified, bounded society, the fur trade was the meeting ground of many Indian communities and two major groups of specialized, relatively transient European traders—the English HBC men with their royal charter, remote directorship, and salaried "servant" status, and the Montreal-based Scottish and French entrepreneurs who coalesced into the dominantly Scottish North West Company after 1784. Given their trade and fur-extraction orientation, neither company aimed to build a stable new society in the Northwest; there was no sponsorship of settlement and colonization by company personnel until the HBC support of efforts to found Red River in 1811-12 and thereafter. This meant that traders, whatever their degree of commitment to their native wives and children

---

[6] For another sampling besides this volume, see the thirteen papers in the 1983 special issue of the *Canadian Journal of Native Studies*, vol. 3, no. 1, on the métis since 1870, edited by Antoine S. Lussier.

[7] Daniel Francis and Toby Morantz, *Partners in Furs: A History of the Fur Trade in Eastern James Bay, 1600-1870* (Kingston and Montreal: McGill-Queen's University Press, 1983) offers important background on this point. For a wide range of other recent literature, see the annotated listings in Jacqueline Peterson and John Anfinson, "The Indian and the Fur Trade": A Review of Recent Literature: in W.R. Swagerty, ed., *Scholars and the Indian Experience: Critical Reviews of Recent Writing in the Social Sciences* (Bloomington: Indiana University Press, 1984).

acquired during their careers, were given no option for permanent, secure retirement in the places where they had worked. HBC men were shipped back to England with an occasional family member, perhaps a son, in tow, unless they found their way to the Montreal region to retire, as a few did between 1810 and 1820. Among the old Nor'Westers of the Canadian-based trade, in contrast, low-ranked employees, usually of French descent, might become "freemen" and form their own homes and ties with métis and Indian kin and friends, away from the posts where they had worked. The Scottish Nor'Westers who were typically the higher-ranked partners and clerks sooner or later withdrew to eastern Canada, perhaps with some of their children, but usually without the native mothers.

The effects of these centrifugal forces on fur-trade families were considerable. No strong company sanctions kept parents and children together in long-term co-residential units. Often, in fact, the demands of fur-trade life imposed considerable pressures against their maintenance, as for HBC men whose familial ties violated company rules in the first place, and for men travelling to different points far inland. Marriages "according to the custom of the country" were widely accepted, but the seriousness with which the ties were treated varied with individual traders' moral stances, as did the priority they were granted when conflicting with business and practical considerations.[8]

Given these varied circumstances, mixed-descent offspring of white traders and native women found and were assigned a variety of social positions and identities. Numerous eighteenth- and early-nineteenth-century HBC descendants were absorbed into the "homeguard" bands that took shape around the major HBC posts, and were classed as Indian. Others who took countless low-level jobs around the posts became known at times as "natives of Hudson's Bay," a category of persons who, although possessing close, interlocking familial ties, did not coalesce as a political force in their early days and lacked (or were spared) distinguishing labels such as métis (or halfbreed) to give focus to their uniqueness. Still others, in much smaller numbers, faded into white society outside the Indian country.

A comparable diversity of destinies awaited the progeny of the Montreal Nor'Westers and Indian women. Some disappeared into Indian societies, and some into white. Most distinctive was a third population whose members, like their French predecessors, found a semi-independent life with freemen and métis already settled in the Indian country.[9] In this particular group, more or less connected with the North West Company as the context of its most rapid growth and maturation (both demographic and political) lay the genesis of the mid-nineteenth-century métis (or in older English translation, halfbreed) sense of identity and pride, the

---

[8] For detailed discussion of company patterns and the familial patterns therein, see Jennifer S.H. Brown, *Strangers in Blood: Fur Trade Company Families in Indian Country* (Vancouver: University of British Columbia Press, 1980).

[9] See Jacqueline Peterson's essay in Peterson and Brown, eds., *The New Peoples: Being and Becoming Métis in North America*.

ramifications of which are still spreading among modern métis, and among collateral bi-racial groups whose ancestors would have found the concept of métis identity unfamiliar and foreign.

The registers of the St. Gabriel Street Presbyterian Church in Montreal provide a core of data for the study of a group of Nor'Westers' progeny—potentially métis—who experienced the fur trade as centrifuge, finding themselves cast at young ages into a new urban world remote, in most instances, from the sites of their early childhoods. For the first forty years of its existence, from 1796 to 1835, the St. Gabriel Street Church witnessed a relatively small but distinctive and continuing influx of strangers of mixed descent. During these years, the clergy of the church baptized and/or buried eighty-nine children whose parents were connected with the North West Company (or after 1821, the HBC with which it merged in that year), and had lived or were still living in what Canadian traders called the Indian country— areas west and north of the Great Lakes. A further ten baptisms were of native descendants of old (pre-1821) HBC employees who arrived in the Montreal area between 1812 and 1820.[10]

These individuals had several traits in common. With one or two exceptions, all were of partly Indian descent, given the almost complete absence of white women in the Indian county before the 1820s.[11] All were born to parents whose unions either were never regularized in accord with British law or Christian ritual, or else received only belated church and legal recognition. Although the fathers' names were invariably entered in the registers, mothers' names were lacking in the great majority (over eighty-five per cent) of cases (see table 1), with the exception of the pre-1821 HBC entries which, as we shall see, must be treated separately. The absence of maternal names (most were described simply as "a woman of the Indian Country") reflected both these women's lack of standing and the fact that most were themselves not present at the baptismal or burial rites of these offspring; enduring co-residence with both parents was not a typical attribute of most of these children's lives, particularly during their Montreal sojourns.

The register data show a pattern of temporal variation. The numbers of fur-trade offspring appearing in baptismal and burial entries rose during the 1796-1805 decade, peaked in the years between 1806 and 1815, declined somewhat between 1816 and 1825, and fell sharply between 1826 and 1835, probably for several reasons. From the late 1700s to the early 1800s, there was a tendency for traders of both Montreal

---

[10] St. Gabriel Street Presbyterian Church registers. Archives of Ontario, Toronto. Microfilm.

[11] The exceptions in question were Frederick (baptized 1818), son of Nor'Wester Charles Grant and Lizette or Elizabeth Landry who had the unique distinction of being herself a former engagée in the Company; and Ann, whose mother, Ann Foster, presented her for baptism in 1828 and whose naming of Governor George Simpson as the father was accepted without question, he being absent. The stories of some of the first white women in the Canadian Northwest are recounted and placed in context by Sylvia Van Kirk in *"Many Tender Ties": Women in Fur-Trade Society, 1670-1870* (Winnipeg: Watson and Dwyer, 1980), 175-81.

and the HBC to become more committed to and open about their family ties in the Indian country and to acknowledge paternity of their native children; and, beginning in 1796, the St. Gabriel Street Church gave Presbyterian Nor'Westers their own setting for such acknowledgement. In the years after 1820, however, several developments probably contributed to the decline in entries. Missionaries became active at Red River (Manitoba) and beyond, and some children who might otherwise have joined their siblings in the Montreal registers were instead baptized in the Northwest (for example, offspring of John George McTavish, Alexander McKay, Angus Bethune, and John Dougald Cameron: Red River Anglican entries 215, 294, 582, 285, 392 and 580, respectively). The schools that opened in Red River may also have kept more offspring there—although British Nor'Westers themselves did not favour settling in that place and remained oriented toward eastern Canada where they had roots, social standing, and kin and friends. Additionally, the rising trend of company officers to seek white wives around 1830[12] may have made some traders less anxious to acknowledge their native offspring, particularly in an eastern urban setting. And the constituency of the St. Gabriel Street Church parish itself was also changing and growing; entries after 1820 indicate a membership active in a variety of trades, with a large component of new immigrants and relatively fewer old fur-trade families, white or of mixed descent.

Who were the St. Gabriel Street fur-trade offspring of 1796 to 1835, both individually and as a category of persons assuming and being assigned identities in the changing contexts in which they matured? Names, statistics, and information regarding their fathers' occupational and company ties provide some answers. Close to three-quarters were fathered by men bearing Scottish surnames or of known Scottish ancestry—a proportion not surprising in a Presbyterian church founded in good part by the Scottish families who after the British conquest of New France had taken over leadership of the Canadian fur trade. The other fathers were of English, French or other European backgrounds (for example, Willard F. Wentzel, Charles O. Ermatinger, Peter W. Dease).

Table 1—Baptismal and burial entries, fur trade offspring*
St. Gabriel Street Presbyterian Church, 1796-1835.

Years	Baptismal Entries					Burial Entries		
	Father present	Mother present and/or named	M	F	Total	M	F	Total
1796-1805	18 (of possible 17; 1 deceased)	1	15	10	25	2	0	2

---

[12] Van Kirk, "*Many Tender Ties*," chap. 8.

1806-1815	9 (of possible 27; deceased)	5**	27	11	38	3	3	6
1816-1825	5 (of possible 15; deceased)	1	11	5	16	6	1	7
1826-1835	0 (of possible 2)	2	1	1	2	2	1	3
Total	27	9**	54	27	81	13	5	18

* Excludes entries concerning pre-1821 Hudson's Bay Company families.
** Three of these entries concern David Thompson's wife.
Note: Because more than one child at a time were sometimes presented for baptism, the total of possible occasions on which a father might have been present is lower than the total number of children baptized. Ten burials were of individuals who had been previously baptized in the church.

Ages at baptism ranged from one year and under (notably, three children of explorer David Thompson born after his retirement to Terrebonne) to thirteen, averaging about six years. The burial register indicates that they were a vulnerable population, doubtless reflecting the fact that so many were separated from one or both parents to be sent at early ages on long journeys from various parts of the Indian country to the foreign setting of Montreal. Close to one out of every eight children baptized at the church was buried there within a few days to three or four years later, and the deaths of a further eight fur-trade children not baptized there are also on record in the years from 1796 to 1835.

The ratio of males to females baptized and buried is worthy of note (see Table 1). Twice as many boys as girls were baptized, and the proportion of male to female burials was still higher. This evidence, along with data from other sources, indicates that, without doubt, sons were sent down to Montreal more commonly than were daughters. Trader fathers were more willing and anxious to invest their energies and funds in the placing and advancement of boys than of girls; the father-son bond took priority over those of father to mother or father to daughter.

For numerous of the Scottish Nor'Westers, this tie between males was also integrated at their sons' baptisms with other male-dominated kinship or friendship ties; brothers or other male associates were persuaded to take young strangers from the Indian country into their charge and witness their baptisms. On October 17, 1815, Alexander McKenzie and Roderick Mackenzie of Terrebonne were among the baptismal witnesses for four boys aged six or seven, the sons of their associates Alexander McKay (deceased), Robert Henry, Edward Smith and Thomas McMurray by women "of the Indian Country." Duncan McDougall fathered a son and daughter in the James Bay area between 1804 and 1807. On October 26, 1812, when McDougall was at Fort Astoria on the Pacific coast, Alexander McDougall presented the son, George, for baptism; the daughter remained in James Bay. On November 7, 1798, James, son of Cuthbert Grant, was baptized, the witnesses being merchants James Laing and James Grant, and on October 12, 1801, his younger brother Cuthbert was presented by Nor'Westers William McGillivray and Roderick Mackenzie, the father having died in 1799. The boys' three sisters remained unbaptized in the Indian country.[13]

For the Grant boys, as for other such offspring, the trip to Montreal was not made solely to be baptized; that rite of recognition was a prelude to being educated, particularly, as some fathers and patrons hoped, for a career in the upper echelons of the fur trade. Such hopes were usually in vain or only partially fulfilled. Cuthbert Grant, having attended school for several years, probably in Scotland, returned to the Indian country as a nineteen-year-old clerk in 1812; he was later kept on, as Governor George Simpson put it in 1832, "intirely [sic] from political motives" for "the benefit of his great influence over the halfbreeds and Indians of the neighbourhood" [Red River].[14]

Roderick, son of Daniel McKenzie, was baptized at age six in 1804 and entered the North West Company in 1818; in 1832, he was said by Simpson to be "tolerably steady considering his breed, but a man of poor abilities and of very limited education." Alexander William, son of William McKay, was baptized at age seven in 1809 (witnesses being his uncle Alexander McKay and Simon and Catharine Fraser), and acquired sufficient education to serve the HBC as a low-level clerk from 1823 to 1843. Simpson in 1832 had "a very poor opinion" of him, although admitting that he "manages a small Trading Post satisfactorily." Benjamin, son of Chief Factor Roderick McKenzie, was baptized at age ten in 1815, witnesses being Daniel and Roderick McKenzie. He joined the company in 1827, became a clerk in 1833, and died in 1837. Simpson, less dyspeptic on his character than on that of other "halfbreed" employees, admitted that he had "had the benefits of a tolerably good Education and had made a good use of the advantages he has had...Promises to become a useful Man."[15]

Not much is known about many of the other offspring named in the registers. Most sons and daughters disappeared into various niches in eastern Canadian society; unlike the fur-trade clerks and postmasters just mentioned, their names do not recur in records of the Indian country.

Yet the fur trade as centrifuge did not necessarily destroy the fragile unity of its families; Nor'Westers John Thomson, John Dougald Cameron, and a few others who

---

[13] Margaret MacLeod and W.L. Morton, *Cuthbert Grant of Grantown* (Toronto: McClelland and Stewart, 1974), 2. See also Jennifer S.H. Brown, "Duncan McDougall," *Dictionary of Canadian Biography*, ed. Francess G. Halpenny and Jean Hamlin, 11 vols. (Toronto: University of Toronto Press, 1983) 5:525-27.

[14] MacLeod and Morton, *Cuthbert Grant*, 7; Glyndwr Williams, ed., *Hudson's Bay Miscellany, 1670-1870* (Winnipeg: Hudson's Bay Record Society, 1975), 30:210.

[15] Williams, *Hudson's Bay Miscellany*, 219-33.

visited St. Gabriel Street retained their native wives. Nor'Wester and former HBC man David Thompson in fact married Charlotte Small in the church, as well as baptizing six children there. And another fur-trade cluster, the retired HBC families of Robert Longmoor and his son-in-law, James Halcro, occupied ten spaces in the baptismal register upon settling in Vaudreuil in 1813. Longmoor brought with him his wife, Sally Pink, aged about forty, from Hudson Bay; she was baptized on July 1, 1813. The Longmoor daughters, Catharine, Jane and Phoebe, were baptized earlier that year, as were Catharine's and James Halcro's four children. And on the same day that her mother was baptized, Catharine and James Halcro were married; if Robert Longmoor had not died by that time, he and Sally Pink probably would have done likewise. The unity of this family and the presence of both parents contrast, as does David Thompson's family configuration, with the residential fragmentation along sex lines that was typical of most Nor'Westers' families represented in the registers.

The St. Gabriel Street Church records, then, provide one view in microcosm of some of the varied and uncertain destinies that awaited fur-trade progeny of mixed descent. The fact of their shared Indian-white parentage and birth in the Northwest by no means cast them into a single social group or category; the differing circumstances in which they matured steered them in several different directions.

Yet amid the diversified experiences of individuals, some patterns emerged. Gender differences carried significance, as already remarked. The tendency, suggested in both the St. Gabriel Street Church and other data, of more daughters than sons to remain in the Indian country rather increased the proportion of mixed-descent women to mixed-descent men around the posts, and may have been one factor urging the North West Company partners to rule in 1806 that their employees should marry daughters of white men rather than Indians.[16] Another effect of this pattern would have been to maintain mother-daughter bonds; and the effect of these linkages as a basis for family-building and identity-formation may have been considerable in the métis communities that grew up in the nineteenth-century Northwest (see Louis Riel's statement, "It is true that our savage origin is humble, but it is meet that we honor our mothers as well as our fathers.")[17] Additionally, where maternal ties between Indian and mixed-descent women bonded them to Indian communities as well as to white communities, such women could act as important informal intermediaries in dealings with the white man's world. Some recent research has called attention to the wide distribution of what is termed *matriorganization* in subarctic Indian societies. This feature could have allowed mixed-descent women an extra degree of influence

---

[16] W.S. Wallace, ed., *Documents Relating to the North West Company* (Toronto: Champlain Society, 1934), 22:211.

[17] Joseph Kinsey Howard, *The Strange Empire of Louis Riel* (Toronto: Swan Publishing, 1965), 46.

among their Indian kin—and may also have carried over into related métis communities, reinforced by the other factors noted above.[18]

While strong Indian maternal ties were a factor in the genesis of a métis identity among fur-trade children, they were not in themselves a sufficient force. Most offspring who experienced lasting bonds only with maternal kin and whose fathers or other white male associates played no role in their lives tended to be reintegrated into Indian societies, just as the relatively few children whose fathers intervened actively and consistently in their upbringing and career placement could become assimilated into white society.

Between these two poles, however, lay a large and fertile ground in which métis identity-building and activism could flourish, particularly in the cases of the numerous North West Company sons who combined roots in the Indian country with a limited and perhaps frustrating exposure to life in eastern Canada or Europe. It is of interest that nineteenth-century métis political activity and self-consciousness arose in good part from men who were in a tension between two worlds—Cuthbert Grant, Jr., the North West Company sons involved in the Dickson Liberating Army on the Great Lakes in 1837,[19] and Louis Riel himself, schooled as a youth in Montreal. In the Canadian Northwest, as elsewhere, a recipe for ethnic political awareness was to be cast between worlds, having had enough experience of each to realize that life could be different and better. Fur-trade sons who visited Montreal but lacked enduring paternal ties and returned to the Indian country experienced a distinct back-and-forthness in their lives—abrupt removals from maternal bonds, along with intermittent or lasting isolation from fathers whose attempts to replace themselves with relatives or friend were likely to be unsuccessful. Such familial fragmentation would have spawned alienation and disillusionment. And it was particularly a North West Company phenomenon; far fewer sons of the old HBC, given its policies and travel restrictions, could travel to London and then return, to interact and combine with others of similar experience.

In conclusion, the familial data gleaned from the St. Gabriel Street registers and elsewhere suggest the uses of looking for the genesis of métis identity-building, or lack thereof, first in the microcosm of parental, parent-child, and gender roles and relationships. Métis consciousness and commitment, or their absence, were of course much affected by the political and economic conditions of fur-trade children's adult lives. But the early years of growth were formative. The relative importance and consistency of paternal and maternal ties, and the nature and strength of their attachments to the broader communities in which they were enmeshed, determined the various trajectories these children would follow, moving outward from the

---

[18] Charles A. Bishop and Shepard Krech, III, "Matriorganization: The Basis of Aboriginal Subarctic Social Organization," *Arctic Anthropology* 17(1979) 2:34-45; Jennifer S.H. Brown, "Woman as Centre and Symbol in the Emergence of Métis Communities," *Canadian Journal of Native Studies* 3(1983) I:39-46.

[19] Brown, *Strangers in Blood*, 190-92.

variable contexts of their fur-trade origins. The full story of métissage as a sociocultural and political phenomenon in northern North America involves the study and understanding of a wide range of individual and group experiences—both those that led to *la nation métisse* and those in which métissage was a potentiality denied, unrecognized, or left unfulfilled, perhaps to be discovered some generations later.

Settlement and Social Class in Upper Canada

Section 6

In the popular view of the North American past, the New World was a land of opportunity—a vast open continent of free land waiting for settlers to clear it, plough it, and win prosperity. The poor, the homeless, and the oppressed of the Old World would find the chance here to become independent. A Canadian pamphlet of the late 19th century, written to attract settlers to the West, promised that "Any man whose capital consists on his arrival of little but brawny arms and a brave heart" could, within a short time, become "the proud possessor of a valuable farm, which has cost him little but the sweat of his brow." This was a democratic promise, in which the landless would become property owners, the poor would become prosperous, and people would mix in a society of equal and independent citizens.

In the early 19th century Upper Canada was the destination of most settler immigrants to British North America. Did they find a land of promise there? Were they able to rise from poverty to independence and overcome class differences? These two essays by social historians certainly seem to raise doubts.

In the first essay David Gagan looks at the settlement of Peel County, which would eventually develop into a prosperous agricultural region. How easy was it for a poor settler to acquire land in Peel? What obstacles stood in the way of a poor immigrant who wanted to become an independent farmer? Who benefited most from the distribution of land in this region? What connexion between land and social class do we see in this essay? How might problems of land settlement help explain the appeal of William Lyon Mackenzie and the popular discontent which expressed itself in the 1837 rebellion?

In the second essay Michael Cross looks at a region where lumbering rather than agriculture drove economic development. What were the causes of the violence he describes? Why did there seem to be a link between ethnicity and class in this region? Why did poor Irish immigrants seem condemned to ongoing economic and social inferiority in the new land?

For a general survey of Upper Canadian history, see Gerald Craig, *Upper Canada: The Formative Years*.

Genesis: Settling Peel County

David Gagan

The five townships—Albion, Caledon, Chinguacousy, Toronto, and the Gore of Toronto—which constituted Peel County were integrated into Upper Canada's frontier of agricultural settlement in 1820. Until 1806, the area between Etobicoke Creek and Burlington Bay was the preserve of the Mississauga Indians, who had resisted successfully the Crown's efforts to purchase their land. An initial surrender was arranged in 1806 and at least part of the region, including what was to become the Old Survey of Toronto Township, was opened to settlement. The War of 1812-14 brought immigration to a standstill, however, and it was not until peace in Europe and America and the consequences of peace in Britain—massive social dislocation—opened the floodgates of emigration that the expansion of Upper Canada's settlement frontier became urgent. Consequently, in 1818 the Crown and the Mississaugas at last came to terms for the purchase by the government of the rest of the Mississauga Tract, and in 1819 tenders for surveying the new townships were let.[1]

Compared to most of the other forty-six counties carved out of southern Ontario, Peel was relatively small. Its 293,000 acres extended from Lake Ontario nearly forty miles northward, at first narrowly confined by the Credit River and Etobicoke Creek, then broadening to encompass the upper reaches of Mimico Creek and the Humber River. Inside this spatial rhombus, concession lines running at right angles to the lake and sideroads spanning the creeks and rivers from east to west scored the landscape in four of the five townships into perfect parallelograms, roughly three-quarters of a mile wide (66 chains) by nearly two deep, each containing five 200-acre lots. These would be divided into half lots, each fronting on a concession road. In the southern half of Toronto Township, however, the survey had squared the grid. Here, on the "front," long narrow lots four to the mile and more than a mile deep ranged along the sideroads in blocks of five, gave the appearance of a succession of seigneuries awaiting the pleasure of a landed gentry and the labour of their tenantry.

Initially, John Graves Simcoe's military road, Dundas Street, and the lake were the region's only arteries of trade, commerce, and communication with the town of York. It was the centre not only of provincial, but of regional government, for in the beginning Peel had no political identity of its own. Until 1851 the county was governed from York, later Toronto, as part of the Home District which included the counties of York, Peel, Simcoe, and Ontario. For the purposes of political representation Peel was in the West Riding of York until 1833, when its five

---

[1] Government of Ontario, Department of Planning and Development, *Credit Valley Conservation Report 1956* (Toronto 1956) 15-16, 55, 61-2.

townships were designated as the second riding of York entitled to one seat in the provincial legislative assembly. Its first representative was the future rebel, William Lyon Mackenzie. Before 1851, in any event, Peel County was merely a geographical expression for the purposes of registering property and establishing electoral districts. After 1851, when the county replaced the district as the basic unit of local government in Canada West, Peel was recognized by statute as a separate administrative unit; but in practice it was governed by a common council for the United Counties of York and Peel until 1866 when popular agitation won for Peel political independence from York.[2]

This political relationship with York/Toronto during the first half of the nineteenth century was fraught with serious implications for the social and economic development of the county in the age of settlement. If Peel was a new frontier of free or cheap land after 1819 it was, in the first place, York's frontier, and the master-servant relationship which quickly developed between the government and the vested interests at "muddy York" on the one hand, and the natural resources of Peel on the other, had a profound effect on the nature and pace of the community's growth. Land, after all, was at once the province's most bountiful asset and its most important commodity. To colonial administrators land was the vital catalyst of social and economic development, the essential source of public revenues, a sound foundation (in the form of endowments) for the principal institutions of provincial society, and even the fountain of both the imperial and the Canadian governments' largesse in rewarding their servants. To the speculator Upper Canada's backwoods offered windfall profits from a limited investment of capital if the growth of population fulfilled the predictions of the essayists and the dreams of the politicians. To the immigrants, land held the promise of independence, an existence free from the social and economic constraints of the old world which placed the private ownership of a thousand, five hundred, or even one hundred acres of land and the opportunities it afforded beyond the reach of ordinary men.[3] In Peel, as in every community in Upper Canada, the conflicting interests of government, speculator, and immigrant settler quickly surfaced to plague the orderly development of society.

---

[2] F.H. Armstrong, *Handbook of Upper Canadian Chronology and Territorial Legislation* (London 1967) 137-41; *Illustrated Atlas of Peel County*.... 1871 [reprint] (Port Elgin 1971) 56.

[3] Lillian Gates, *Land Policies of Upper Canada* (Toronto 1968), esp. conclusion; J.K. Johnson, "The Businessman as Hero: The Case of William Warren Street," *Ontario History* LXV, 5(1973) 127-9; J. Sheridan Hogan, *Canada: An Essay* (Montreal 1855) 9.

Table 1—Alienation of Crown land in Upper Canada
and Peel County 1810-40

	Upper Canada	Peel County
Total acres alienated	3,500,000*	230,200
(a) Alienated by sale	-	73,568†
Percentage of total	-	31.9
(b) Alienated by grants	3,039,000*	156,632‡
Percentage of total	85.8	68.8
(c) Free grants	1,338,800*	83,977*
Percentage of (b)	44.0	53.6
(d) Military grants	346,900*	16,855†
Percentage of (b)	11.4	10.7
(e) UEL grants	1,125,300*	43,050†
Percentage of (b)	37.0	27.5
(f) Surveyors' grants	228,000*	12,720
Percentage of (b)	7.5	8.1

* - 1804-24   † - 1826-40   ‡ - 1810-40

Source: Paterson, p. 153; Public Archives of Ontario [OA], Crown Land Papers [CLP] RG 1, C-I-8, Vols. XI and XII, Land Grants, A-M, N-Z, 1810-35

Crown land could be alienated into private hands by sale, by free grants with or without the payment of fees, and by "privileged" grants to military claimants and to United Empire Loyalists or their children. Before 1826 free grants as well as military and Loyalist land grants represented the thrust of government policy in Upper Canada. But the need for more revenue coupled with the evident failure of scores of patentees to improve their property let alone take up residence on it prompted the administration in 1826 to abolish free grants and to introduce the New South Wales system of alienation by sale at auction. The government established an "upset price," in effect a reserve bid, for each lot in advance of regularly held auctions. Successful bidders then were permitted to pay for their land in annual instalments, but they were required to take up residence within six months and to provide, within three years, a sworn affidavit testifying that settlement duties (clearing half the roadway on their frontage and erecting a dwelling) had been performed. This system obtained until 1837 when land policy was again changed by removing the option of instalment buying in favour of cash purchases only.[4]

Under these various schemes (catalogued in Table 1) approximately 230,000 acres or nearly 79 per cent of the land in Peel County was transferred from the Crown into

---

[4] Gilbert C. Paterson, *Land Settlement in Upper Canada, 1783-1840: Sixteenth Report of the Department of Archives for the Province of Ontario* (Toronto 1920) 39, 115, 131, 147, 171.

private hands between 1810 and 1840. In effect, all of the land which could be alienated was. The remaining 20 per cent represented either Crown Reserves or, particularly after 1824, Clergy Reserves which normally were leased rather than sold. (In 1824, the Crown Reserves were transferred to John Galt's Canada Company.) Of these 230,000 acres more than two-thirds were alienated by direct grants of one sort or another. Thirty-two per cent of Peel's lands designated for settlement were alienated, in the first instance, by sale. Of the more than 156,000 acres ordered for granting after 1810, 83,977 (54%) were awarded as free grants to 627 unofficial petitioners; 43,500 (27%) were assigned to 115 children of Loyalists; 16,885 acres (11%) went to 90 military claimants; and 12,720 (8%) were used to discharge the government's obligations to the five men who surveyed the county. The result of this system in Peel, as elsewhere in Upper Canada, was the distortion of the settlement process to the detriment of the ordinary settler and his aspirations.

In the first place, neither the military claimants, who received on the average 187 acres each, nor the sons and daughters of Loyalists, whose grants averaged 375 acres, were as likely to be legitimate settlers as the first generation of Loyalists or the discharged Revolutionary War veterans had been. Elizabeth Ferris Henderson is a good example. The daughter of John Ferris, UE, she resided with her father and husband David in Kingston Township. She received a location ticket for 200 acres in Caledon Township in 1828, two years later submitted an affidavit of settlement duties performed, and then retained title to the property for the next fifteen years, finally selling it in 1845 for £100.[5] She never occupied her land. It sat, idle and barely developed, an obstacle to improvement in the township. It is difficult to know precisely how many of these grantees, "privileged" and otherwise, followed Elizabeth Henderson's example; but it is certain that of the 842 individuals who received grants of Crown land in Peel between 1810 and 1835, only 161, less than 20%, were residents of the county in 1836.[6] It is entirely probable that most of the remaining four-fifths never set foot in the county.

If the total amount of land taken out of circulation by absentee grantees is a matter of speculation, the acreage deliberately closed to private ownership as a matter of policy is more definite. By statutory requirement, one-seventh of the land in each township was assigned to the Clergy Reserves Corporation as an endowment for the support of a protestant clergy. In Peel these reserves consisted of more than 40,000 acres concentrated in Albion, Caledon, Chinguacousy, and Toronto Gore townships, which had to absorb a greater than normal percentage of reserved land because the old survey of Toronto Township had none. The extent to which these reserves were a hindrance to the settlement of Upper Canada or agents of a "dynamic process" of settlement has

---

[5] OA, CLP, Township Papers, Caledon Township Conc. III E, Lots 18, 19; Peel County, Abstracts of Deeds, Caledon Township, Conc., III E, Lots 18, 19.

[6] Computed by linking the lists of patentees in OA, CLP, RGI, C-I, Vols. 11 and 12 with George Walton, *Directory of Toronto and the Home District* (Toronto 1837).

occasioned much debate.[7] Such evidence as exists for Peel County scarcely supports the view that these reserves eventually provided the means for integrating late, inexperienced immigrants into highly developed agricultural communities. For example, an official inspection of Albion's 5,000 reserved acres as late as 1845 revealed that after a quarter of a century of settlement in the township, nearly 40% of the Clergy Reserves were in the hands of absentee owners or lessees and still unimproved and unoccupied. Of the 2,900 occupied acres a little more than 50% (1,500 acres) were occupied by the owner or lessee; the remainder had been sublet and in several cases broken up into very small plots. The twenty-three families on these lots had managed to clear a mere 500 acres, less than 20% of the acreage they occupied.[8]

The government of the day also set aside 10,500 acres of land in Peel as part of the endowment for yet another institution, King's College. To be administered by and for the Church of England, the proposed college was intended as a nursery where young professionals—the future leaders of the province—could be imbued with correct political, moral, and spiritual attitudes. The scheme quickly encountered stiff political opposition, especially from the proponents of a common schools system, and had to be abandoned; but the endowment was perpetuated (and fell to King's College's successor, the University of Toronto) and together with the Clergy Reserves before 1840 effectively restricted more than 15% of Peel County's total acreage to occupation by lease only.

Finally, and most significantly, between 1810 and 1840 the vacant lands of Peel County attracted the attention of a group of men, some of whom acquired their land as free grants, others by sale, who constituted a class of great, powerful, and more or less permanent absentee landlords. They are not to be compared with the Elizabeth Hendersons, the little speculators who sought security in one or two hundred acres of bush. These men, as a group, never represented more than 3% of the total number of proprietors in the community; yet they sat, at any time between 1820 and 1840, astride a minimum of 10% of the county's vacant land (Table 2). Moreover, these speculators, whose lands were one of the principal sources of distortion in the orderly social and economic development of the county (see Map 1), not only were, for the most part, residents of Toronto, but were often the very men responsible for defining and policing the land policies of Upper Canada.

---

[7] Alan Wilson, *The Clergy Reserves of Upper Canada: A Canadian Mortmain* (Toronto 1968) 127-8; Robert Gourlay, *Statistical Account of Upper Canada*, S.R. Mealing, ed. (Toronto 1974) 240-7.

[8] OA, CLP, RGI, A-VI-9, Vol. 16, Inspection Reports, Clergy Reserves, Albion Township, 1844-5.

Table 2—Distribution of land, Peel county 1820-40

	1820	1830	1840
No. of acres alienated	56,530	131,524	229,140
Percentage of alienated acres held by proprietors of 500 acres or more	27.4	19.8	10.0
Total no. of proprietors of 500 acres or more	8	14	16
No. of non-resident proprietors of 500 acres or more	7	12	13
Total no. of different proprietors	245	855	1542
Proprietors of 500 acres or more as percentage of total	3.2	1.7	1.0
Absentee proprietors of 500 acres or more as percentage of total	2.9	1.4	0.84

This class of speculators made its appearance almost immediately after the first surveys of Toronto Township were completed, that is, before 1812. John Beikie, clerk of the Executive Council, patented 800 acres, as did Duncan Cameron, member of the Legislative Assembly for Glengarry, and Roger Loring, aide-de-camp to Sir Roger Sheaffe, who succeeded Isaac Brock as commander of the British forces in Upper Canada. Their 2,400 acres, about 8% of the old survey (excluding the Indian reservation), established the pattern that was to become a permanent characteristic of Peel after the War of 1812. Indeed, the very act of surveying the four new townships after 1818 created the first of Peel's most persistent absentee landlords—the surveyors Richard Bristol, Timothy Street, James Chewett, Samuel Ryckman, and Reuben Sherwood. They were paid in land, more than 4% of the county's total area, and still held most of their lots as late as 1840. Similarly, the King's College endowment produced what was, by any other name, a major absentee landlord controlling another 4% of the county's total acreage between 1820 and 1850.

But Peel's absentee proprietors of particular historical interest are eighteen men and their families whose names are inextricably linked to the mainstream of Upper Canadian history between 1820 and 1840. The list includes five executive councillors: John McGill, Samuel Smith, John Beverley Robinson, John Strachan, and Adam Ferrie. Ferrie, a Scottish merchant who moved his interests to Canada where he and his sons rose to prominence as entrepreneurs in the Hamilton and Galt areas, became active in provincial politics only after 1837. The others held some of the most powerful appointed offices in Upper Canada before the rebellion. Smith had been the Administrator of the province in 1819 (in effect, acting lieutenant-governor). Robinson had been Attorney-General, and was Chief Justice in 1837. "Captain" John McGill, who died in 1834, had served as Inspector-General, then

Receiver-General. The D'Arcy Boultons, father and son, one sometime Solicitor-General and the other Auditor-General of Public Accounts, were members of the same privileged circle. Two bankers, William Proudfoot and Peter McGill, were directly connected to this political establishment. Peter McGill, President of the Bank of Montreal, was John McGill's nephew and himself a member of the Legislative Council after 1840. William Proudfoot was a Scottish emigrant who enjoyed the patronage of the Boultons and through them rose to become the president of the Bank of Upper Canada on the eve of its fateful collapse in 1836. The Jarvises, too, held appointed positions of public trust in the affairs of the Home District, most notably as successive sheriffs. James Chewett, the surveyor, also falls within the compass of this colonial establishment. He was Strachan's pupil and the son of a surveyor-general of Upper Canada. Chewett soon became Deputy Surveyor-General, and his subsequent commissions included the construction of the provincial legislative building. Finally, Andrew Mercer, whose fortune endowed the Mercer Reformatory for Women, held appointments as Clerk of the Executive Council, Paymaster of the Militia, King's Printer, and Magistrate; and John Radenhurst, First Clerk of the Land Patents Office, processed, with a good deal of arbitrariness, all petitions for land to and from the Executive Council.

Not all Peel's great absentee landowners were cut from the same cloth. The Cawthra family held no offices and even tended toward neutrality in their political sentiments. Their real interest was money. Merchants and private bankers, their landholdings paled into insignificance beside the indentures of mortgage which they held against property throughout the province. W.A. Baldwin was a member of another prominent York family which produced the architect of responsible government in Upper Canada, his brother Robert. William Augustus shared his father, William Warren Baldwin's, interest in land speculation and farming, and in addition to his handsome estate in Etobicoke had extensive holdings in Peel which developed from a wedding present of 900 acres from his father-in-law, James Buchanan, the British Consul in New York.

The Cawthras and the Baldwins are the exception which prove the rule that land speculation on a grand scale in Upper Canada united the rich and the powerful, whatever their political affiliation, in a common interest. But it seems clear that in Peel County, at least, the families who played the game for the highest stakes were synonymous with York's Tory establishment of power, place, and privilege, the so-called "Family Compact." Indeed, even among the less grand speculators in this county, excluded here only by virtue of the size of their holdings in this place, the names of several more of York's leading families predominate: Denison, Carfrae, Ridout.[9] William Lyon Mackenzie coined the epithet "Family Compact" to identify

---

[9] To identify these absentee speculators I have relied on a variety of sources, namely: Armstrong, *Handbook of Upper Canadian Chronology*; Henry Scadding, *Toronto of Old*, F.H. Armstrong, ed. (Toronto 1966); *Commemorative Biographical Record of the county of York, Ontario* (Toronto 1907): *Macmillan Dictionary of Canadian Biography*, W.S. Wallace, ed.

an apparent conspiracy to use family connection, executive authority, and legislative supremacy to control the economy, society, and politics of Upper Canada in the interests of an oligarchy of Tory families. He singled out the Boultons, Robinsons, Sherwoods, Macaulays, Hagermans, Allen, Powells, Jarvises, Joneses, and the McGills as the tallest heads in this conspiracy led by John Strachan. The Denisons, the Carfraes, the Ridouts, Proudfoot, the Streets, and others all fell into the category of henchmen.[10] Their specific improprieties, which Lord Durham repeated in his famous *Report*, were that they allegedly possessed and controlled the highest offices in the province and therefore most of the powers of government; that they maintained their power by dispensing patronage through the Legislative Council, the judicial system, and the Church of England; and that they sought to achieve their social and economic objectives through their manipulation of the banks and the vacant lands of the province.[11] In particular, their open disdain for the commercial and entrepreneurial classes in the province and their readiness to promote the interests of the landed classes have been interpreted as evidence of the extent to which they identified public policy with private interest, in spite of their altruistic defence of their actions.[12]

The record of absentee landlordism in Peel County during the first twenty years of the region's history of settlement leaves little room for doubt that, whatever ideological and familial bonds held the "Family Compact" together, they shared at least one material interest—the profits to be made from the vacant lands on York's frontier of economic development. In this they were not different from their constituents for whom gambling in land, as one historian has remarked, had become a "national pastime."[13] But the acreage under their control and the way in which they acquired it are remarkable even by contemporary standards; and when their unofficial activities are linked to the results of the land policies which were their official responsibility, their effect on the social landscape of colonial Upper Canada comes into sharp relief. Toronto Township, especially the southern half, is a case in point. In the other four townships of Peel, Crown and Clergy Reserves and the lands of the largest speculators together represented, on average, about 20% of the land available for settlement. In Toronto Township they constituted about 30%. But in the southern half of the township, which attracted the most attention from speculators,

---

(Toronto 1963): OA, CLP, R.G.1, C-I-8, Vols. 11 and 12; and Township Papers for Albion, Caledon, Chinguacousy, Toronto Gore, and Toronto Townships.

10 See Alison Ewart and Julia Jarvis, "The Personnel of the Family Compact," *Canadian Historical Review* VI (Mar. 1926) 209-21; Robert E. Saunders, "What was the Family Compact," *Ontario History* XLIX (1957) 173-8.

11 Gerald Craig, ed., *Lord Durham's Report* (Toronto 1964) 78, 88-9.

12 See Hugh G.J. Aitken, "The Family Compact and the Welland Canada Company," *Canadian Journal of Economics and Political Science* XVIII (1952) 63-76.

13 J.K. Johnson, "The Businessman as Hero" 128.

their holdings alone, on the eve of the uprising of 1837, represented more than 30% of the area. As late as the 1850s much of it was still undeveloped.

Ironically, William Lyon Mackenzie, too, was an absentee proprietor in Peel in the 1820s and 1830s, albeit the owner of a very insignificant lot. It was Mackenzie who first made a public issue of the inability of legitimate settlers in Peel to secure Crown deeds to their land, while government officials openly flouted the regulations. Strachan, according to Mackenzie, had been given patents for his 2,000 acres on the pretext of defraying the costs of a journey to England on official business in 1828, land which Strachan still held, unimproved, a decade later. Meanwhile, ordinary settlers could not get patents for their lots precisely because their land remained unimproved as the result of the economic stagnation, created in part by the distortion of the settlement process by the holdings of the absentees, which in turn prevented them from acquiring the capital necessary for improvements.[14]

The facts seem to be on Mackenzie's side. Most of the public officials among the speculators do not appear to have petitioned for their grants but rather acquired their patents simply by executive order. Moreover, all the great absentee proprietors seem to have been able to secure deeds and to retain ownership of their vacant property for fifteen or twenty years before taking their profits. Ordinary settlers who were slow to improve their lots, who failed the exercise, or who were unable to meet their monetary obligations each January either waited interminably for a satisfactory inspection report or had their property auctioned out from under them. In Chinguacousy Township, which Mackenzie knew best, the elapsed time between locating and deed registration averaged thirteen years; and as late as 1842 more than 60% of the occupants of land who had been in the township at least five years still had no legal title to their farms.[15]

Some simply squatted on lots which they assumed to be rightfully theirs and defied the authorities to evict them. Others swore false oaths, with the assistance of sympathetic neighbours or larcenous magistrates, attesting to the performance of settlement duties. The practice apparently was widespread as early as 1824.[16] For most, the court of last resort was the Commissioner of Crown Lands. Thus, in June 1833, David Long, a settler in Albion Township, begged for more time to complete his settlement duties and to raise more cash. His land, he said, had already cost him

---

14   J.L.H. Henderson, ed., *John Strachan: Documents and Opinions* (Toronto 1969) 177; Leo Johnson, "Land Policy, Population Growth and Social Structure in the Home District, 1793-1851," *Ontario History* LXVII (1971) 43.

15   Computed from Peel County, Abstracts of Deeds, Chinguacousy Township, and Walton, *Directory of Toronto.*

16   *Credit Valley Conservation Report* (1956) 75. Citing the testimony of Hugh Black, DPS, before the Surveyor-General, in Province of Ontario, Dept. of Lands and Forests, Survey Records, Letters, Vol. 11, nos. 36 and 37.

$23 five journeys to York & back making 180 miles ... with loss of my toe nails & three weeks idleness it is a pity if I lost it I being prepared to go on direct, having some utensils a yoke oxen 3 cows & what is better four sons ... who are all desirous of being their own servants.... I hope you will pardon me, theres [sic] now [sic] man a greater object for land than I am at present.... I beseech you for Godalmightys [sic] sake to assist me....[17]

The petition fell on deaf ears and Long's land was put up for auction.
Ultimately, of course, these inequities, added to his infinite list of grievances against the injustices of his times and the imperialism of York's political and social élite, drove William Lyon Mackenzie to rebellion in 1837. Though relatively few of them joined his rebellion, many of the settlers of Peel counted themselves among Mackenzie's most ardent supporters, returning him as their representative in spite of repeated attempts to expel him from the Legislative Assembly. Indeed, Peel became a battleground of the contending Tory and radical factions. Mackenzie had been forced to campaign in 1836 with an armed escort, and several meetings threatened to degenerate into full-scale riots.[18] A year later Mackenzie was in exile and the fortunes of his constituents and their causes which he championed were left to the palliative effects of time and improved circumstances. Still, for the next thirty years at least the main elements in the social history of Peel County remained those which had been indelibly implanted during the first forty years of the community's development.

"What is capital but property unequally distributed?" asked Upper Canada's Chief Justice, John Elmsley, during one of the many early debates on land policy.[19] The idea that Upper Canada's public land should be used to create a society characterized by political, social, and economic inequality in the interests of stability and progress continued to inform official policy until the middle of the nineteenth century.[20] In Peel county, the practical effects of this design are to be seen in the diversion of thousands of acres of land into the hands of speculators, and especially into the control of a few highly placed families at Toronto before 1840. From this original distortion of the land-hungry immigrant's high expectations flowed the ineluctable facts of the ordinary settler's experience in the community during the next thirty years. Wave upon wave of prospective farmers pursuing the dream of equal opportunity encountered, instead, a very unequal struggle for individual and familial security.

---

[17] OA, CLP, Township Papers, Albion Township, Concession IV, Lots 34, 35.
[18] Charles Lindsey, *The Life and Times of William Lyon Mackenzie* II (2 vols., Toronto 1862) 27-9.
[19] Quoted in Gates, *Land Policies of Upper Canada* 47.
[20] Johnson, "Land Policy, Population Growth and Social Structure in the Home District, 1793-1851" 41-60.

They came—from England, Scotland, the United States of America, the older counties of Upper Canada, and especially from Ireland—until, by 1851, 3,700 families representing nearly 25,000 men, women, and children were settled in Peel county. However, the flow of migrants was not relentless. In 1828 the population stood at about 4,300, an increase of only 20% after a decade of settlement. The great migrations from the British Isles after 1828 hastened the growth of population in the county; but by the end of the troubled thirties the rate of growth had noticeably slowed and in two townships, Caledon and Toronto—one of the most remote and the other with the highest levels of absentee ownership—it had come virtually to a standstill. No census data are available for the years between 1842 and 1852, but the startling increase in Albion, Caledon, and Chinguacousy townships which nearly doubled their population, and an overall increase of 54%, were almost certainly the direct or indirect result of the Irish migrations of the late forties. In short, the relative speed with which the county was filled up had much to do with the pressures placed on Upper Canada's frontier of settlement generally by patterns of trans-Atlantic migration throughout the period, and by domestic social and economic conditions.

By 1835, more than three-quarters of all the land that would be privately owned in 1852 already had been taken up. In Toronto Township, more than 90% of the land had been alienated into private hands by 1835, in Toronto Gore nearly 85%, in Chinguacousy more than 78%, and in Albion and Caledon better than two-thirds. In all, 196,000 acres—two-thirds of the county's entire acreage—were privately owned by 1835. When the Clergy Reserves are added to this figure, to all intents and purposes there remained less than 60,000 acres—the equivalent of six hundred 100-acre farms, much of it in the least attractive townships of Albion and Caledon—open for settlement through the public auction system after 1835. (In 1840, according to the registry records, fewer than 46,000 acres remained unpatented.) These 196,000 acres were owned by approximately 1,200 landholders; yet the population of the county stood at 10,000 in 1835, perhaps 1,700 families in all.[21] With allowances for the non-agricultural population of the principal towns and villages (Streetsville, Port Credit, and Springfield) it seems plausible, then, that at least one of every four rural householders (400/1,600) was a tenant or squatter on someone else's land by 1835, either because they could not afford the upset price of unpatented land, or because they were unable to purchase land held for speculation at any price. In either case, the inference to be drawn is clear. By 1835, unless he was content with leased land, the prospective farmer in Peel required capital to get land. Even if he had capital, his ability to acquire good land was dependent on the willingness of an established owner, more often than not a speculator himself, to part with his

---

21   The 1837 *Directory of the Home District* enumerates 2,140 households in a population of 12,572, an average of 5.8 persons per household. I have used this average to calculate the number of households in 1835. The average is probably too high, however, given the number of single men reputed to have been characteristic of the pioneer populations.

property. Peel County, with only 50% of its 1852 population in place on the eve of the Rebellion of 1837, was no longer, if indeed it ever had been, a frontier of cheap land awaiting the poor, but industrious immigrant.

These developments can be illustrated best with reference to Chinguacousy Township, for which the 1842 assessment roll exists. The roll lists 741 owners or occupants of land. Of this number, 568 (77.8%) were actually residents of the township, the rest (22%) were absentee proprietors. Of the resident occupants of land, 39% owned the farms they occupied; another 24% were in the process of securing titles (which they eventually received) by completing settlement duties. The remaining 215 (37%) were effectively tenants, although they may have been in the process of buying land on the instalment plan, a common practice, through annual quit rents plus interest.[22] In any event they did not have, and never acquired, titles to the lands they occupied. Finally, in 1842 only 13% of the landowners, resident or non-resident, were the original locatees and Crown patentees of their land. The vast majority had purchased their lots from some former private owner at whatever price the traffic would bear. Most of the activity had taken place before the rebellion of 1837; less than 25% of the residents of these concessions were recent arrivals.

Thus, in just twenty years this township had undergone a complete transformation. In 1820 it had been a vast reserve of wild land freely open to settlement. In 1842, 95% of its land was in private hands and two-fifths of those private landholders were non-residents. Consequently, new arrivals increasingly faced the prospect of tenancy or, if they had capital, of using it to purchase expensive land rather than to improve cheap land. In either case, the results were the same. In Chinguacousy, as in the rest of the county, development proceeded slowly, and sometimes not at all.[23]

Figure 2 compares the rate of land alienation in Peel county to the rate at which land was improved, as reported in the annual assessment returns, which distinguished between cultivated and uncultivated land. The distinction seems to have been based on rather crude assumptions about the nature of land improvement and use, but it was vital nevertheless. As the result of legislation passed in 1819 uncultivated—that it, unimproved—land was valued for assessment purposes at four shillings per acre, improved land at £1. Taxed at the rate of one penny per pound of assessed value, 100 acres of wild land paid less than two shillings per annum when it was taxed at all, 100 acres of improved land more than four times as much.[24] Thus speculators could

---

22 An indenture of bargain and sale was executed and a deed conveyed, in such cases, only after the full amount of the transaction had been discharged. I am indebted to Professor R.C. Risk of the University of Toronto Law School for this inference.

23 These data for Chinguacousy Township were derived by linking the following sources: Chinguacousy Township, Assessment Roll, 1842 (original in Chinguacousy Library); Walton, *Directory of Toronto and the Home District, 1837* Toronto 1837; PAC, manuscript Census of the Canadas, 1851-2, Peel County; Chinguacousy Township, Abstract Index of Deeds [microfilm].

24 Gates, *Land Policies of Upper Canada* 239.

maintain vast tracts of unimproved land for years at little cost. Surrounded by underdevelopment, isolated from markets, and with little capital to improve his holdings, the so-called "improving" farmer's performance often belied his reputation. By 1830, when more than 40% of Peel's land had been taken up, less than 10% of it had been improved. Five years later, nearly a quarter of the alienated acreage had been improved, a reflection of the flurry of settlement activity in the early thirties. But over the next decade the rate of improvement abated considerably. Between 1836 and 1842, although land alienation proceeded apace, the rate of improvement remained nearly constant. Ultimately, it was the advent of better economic prospects with the appearance, first, of an American market for local wheat shipped through Port Credit, and then of a burgeoning imperial market for Canadian wheat and flour which spurred Peel's emergence after 1846 as a developed, agrarian society. In the meantime, as late as 1845, for every 600 acres of improved land in Peel County there were a thousand more of wild land awaiting the axe, the plough, and the labour of many hands....

The Shiners' War: Social Violence in the Ottawa Valley in the 1830s

Michael S. Cross

By late May of 1835, unrest in Bytown had reached unprecedented proportions. All winter the people of the town, the entrepôt of the Ottawa timber trade, had been bracing themselves, awaiting the annual visitation, the annual affliction, of the raftsmen who came each spring from high up the Valley to roister and riot in the streets of Bytown. Like the freshets in the streams, the raftsmen and social disorder arrived each April and May. But never before had their coming brought such organized violence as it did in 1835. For the Irish timberers now had a leader, and a purpose. Peter Aylen, run-away sailor, timber king, ambitious schemer, had set himself at the head of the Irish masses, had moulded them into a powerful weapon. He had given them a purpose: to drive the French Canadians off the river and thus guarantee jobs and high wages in the timber camps to the Irish.

Confident in their numbers, Aylen and his followers swaggered the streets of Bytown, brawling and drinking on the sidewalks, savagely beating anyone who dared challenge them. The town suffered under this reign of terror for weeks. The Irish mob, glorying in the name of the Shiners, seemed in complete control. But this was a stratified society; there was a class line beyond which even the Shiners went at their peril. While French-Canadian labourers were being abused, the gentry of the community shook their heads in disgust and grumbled about the Irish misbehaviour. When a respectable lawyer, Daniel McMartin of Perth, was assaulted by Peter Aylen, however, the forces of social order sprang into action. Aylen was promptly arrested.

The rule of the gentility in the town, and the aspirations of the Shiners, had come into direct conflict.[1] In 1835 the forces of order and disorder were in fine balance. The authorities were able to hold Aylen by incarcerating him in the sturdy garrison cells and then sending him overland, under heavy guard, to the district jail at Perth. However, in Bytown itself the furious raftsmen were in almost complete control. They paraded the streets, screaming threats at the magistrates, boasting they would burn down Chitty's Hotel, where the injured lawyer McMartin was in residence. Only the reading of the Riot Act and the calling-out of the garrison prevented the destruction of the hotel. Thwarted in their search for revenge on McMartin, the Irish turned to thoughts of rescuing Peter Aylen. From one unkempt raftsman to another,

---

[1] On the gentry of Bytown and the surrounding Carleton County, see Michael S. Cross, "The Age of Gentility: the Creation of an Aristocracy in the Ottawa Valley," *Canadian Historical Association, Historical Papers*, 1967. Later class conflict in the area is described in Michael S. Cross, "Stony Monday, 1849: The Rebellion Losses Riots in Bytown," *Ontario History*, LXIII, 3, Sept. 1971.

the rumour spread that their leader was to be sent to Perth by boat, along the Rideau Canal. Operating on this erroneous assumption, several hundred Shiners swarmed aboard a steamer anchored at Bytown. Furious at their failure to find Aylen, they smashed the interior of the boat and beat several crewmen who had attempted to resist them.[2]

The arrest of Aylen was only a temporary check. He was soon out of jail, and the disorder went on. G.W. Baker, a Bytown magistrate, wrote to the government on 15 June, offering his resignation in light of the futility of attempting to check the shiners with the feeble forces available to the magistrates. In his despair, Baker effectively summed up the crisis in Bytown: "I cannot Sir describe to you the situation of the town. If I could, you would deem it incredible and it is becoming daily worse.... No Person whatever can move by day without insult, or at night without risk of life—thus whole families of unoffending people are obliged to abandon the Town, and nothing except a Military Patrol will succeed in arresting the evil, and dissipating the general alarm.... I have not moved without Arms since the 14th May...."[3]

The origins of the Shiner movement are obscure, as is its pattern of organization. Even the source of the name is difficult to determine. The Shiners were Irish immigrants who, for the most part, worked in timber camps and river drives. The name has variously been described as a corruption of the French "chêneur," or cutter of oak; as a self-designation meaning they were to "shine" above others; as a nickname derived from the shiny silk hats worn by greenhorns arriving at Bytown; or as coming from the newly-minted half-crown coins with which timberers were paid. When the Shiners emerged is similarly uncertain. The date usually credited is 1828, when a St. Patrick's Day brawl at Bytown resulted in the death of an Englishman, Thomas Ford. However, even if the beginning of Shinerism is placed so early, it was not an organized force until the middle 1830s. "At first," a contemporary remarked, "these ruffians acted independently of one another, and without concert—jeering and insulting the defenceless and unprotected, and occasionally `pounding an enemy'."[4]

The Shiners' War, the period of wide-scale, organized violence, extended into the 1840s, but was at its peak from 1835 to 1837. The emergence of a leader precipitated the outbursts of these years. The leader was the self-styled "King of the Shiners," Peter Aylen. Aylen came to Canada from Ireland as a sailor. He jumped ship at Quebec, changed his name, and disappeared into the forests of the Ottawa. Entering

---

[2] The events are described in Public Archives of Canada [PAC], Upper Canada Sundries, vol. 152, George Hamilton to Lt-Col. Rowan, 1 June 1835; ibid., G.W. Baker to Rowan, 15 June 1835; *Bathurst Courier*, 5 June 1835.

[3] Upper Canada Sundries, vol. 152. Baker to Rowan, 15 June 1835.

[4] Toronto *Globe*, 25 Dec. 1856, "Chaudiere Letters".

The Shiners' War: Social Violence in the Ottawa Valley in the 1830s 221

the timber trade in 1816, he rapidly became a wealthy merchant.[5] By the time of the Shiners' War, Aylen owned property in Bytown, Nepean Township, and Horton Township, and had large timber operations on the Madawaska, Bonnechere, and Gatineau rivers.[6] He clearly was no hungry ne'er-do-well, but rather one of the wealthiest men in the district. Presumably economic motivations were not central for him. His actions seem explainable only by one of two causes: a genuine desire to aid his Irish countrymen; or a drive for personal power. As a study of the Shiner movement will show, his often cynical manipulation of his followers belies any unselfish motives on Aylen's part.

He assumed leadership of the Irish raftsmen in 1835. The lures he offered them to follow him were seductive. He gave them jobs, in his shanties and those of his friends. He promised them a complete victory over the French Canadians who competed with the Irish for jobs in the timber camps, and who had superior skills and a better reputation for reliability. With such a victory the Irish would not only be secure in employment, but they could set their own salary scales.[7]

Not the least of the things Peter Aylen offered the Shiners was sensual enjoyment. For a people all too familiar with poverty, the lavish entertainment proffered by Aylen was highly alluring. Food and drink were always available at the Shiner leader's home, as were pleasures of a more exotic nature. Women were supplied the raftsmen, to satisfy the lusts pent-up from a winter of enforced celibacy. On some occasions, it was reported, Aylen imported prostitutes from Montreal for his men. The orgies at the King's home were extended, exuberant affairs, which often combined the dual pleasures of debauchery and insult to the respectable community. For instance, after sexual appetites were satisfied, the Shiners were known to fill their women with liquor until they collapsed insensible. Then the girls were stripped naked and arranged on the public sidewalk—well illuminated with candles so they might be seen by the shocked townspeople.[8]

The Irish in the Valley were more than ready for a leader and for violence. The immediate causes of their disorder have been mentioned. But the origins go much deeper. They were conditioned by the unhappy situation of their homeland, where violence was an everyday fact of life. Even after the police reforms of the 1830s, the Irish crime rate remained perhaps the highest in Europe. On a per capita basis, there were, in 1839, thirteen times as many murder indictments in Ireland as in England,

---

[5] On Aylen, see ibid.; J.L. Gourlay, *History of the Ottawa Valley* (Ottawa 1896), pp. 52-3; Miller Stewart, "The King of the Shiners," in *Flamboyant Canadians*, ed. Ellen Stafford (Toronto 1964).

[6] *Bytown Gazette*, 8, 29 Sept., 6 Oct. 1836.

[7] The factor of wages was emphasized by the anti-Shiner timber operator George Hamilton, in a letter to Lt-Col. Rowan: Upper Canada Sundries, vol. 152, 1 June 1835. Also, PAC, Upper Canada State Papers, vol. 83, Charles Shirreff to Rowan, 11 July 1835, p. 88.

[8] Stewart, "King of the Shiners," p. 76; Toronto *Globe*, 25 Dec. 1856.

and in the same year there were 3,409 trials for riot in Ireland.[9] There clearly was not only a greater incidence but a greater tolerance of violent crime in Ireland than in most other western countries. Poverty and foreign rule combined to produce a society teetering on the edge of anarchy. Disaffection on a wide scale was particularly prevalent in those areas from which most immigrants to the Ottawa Valley were drawn. Limerick and Tipperary had unusually high crime rates, even by Irish standards. They were also centres of the activity of the Whiteboys and other agrarian terrorist societies. In the period when many who would become Shiners were leaving Ireland, between 1813 and 1823, "considerable portions of the south and west were under the domination of peasant `armies'."[10]

The Ireland from which the Shiners came was a poor and overcrowded country. The population was growing far more rapidly than the agricultural capabilities, increasing from 4,753,000 in 1791 to 7,767,000 in 1831. Conditions could only worsen for the peasants as landholdings became smaller and houses more crowded. The average number of persons per house grew from 5.65 in 1791 to 6.20 forty years later.[11] Living standards were declining, life expectancy was depressingly low. The average age of death in Ireland in the 1830s was nineteen.[12]

To these factors could be added the evident lack of an economic future, high rents and low wages, frequent famine and disease, a near chronic state of civil war, and political and religious suppression. All these conditions bred into the Irish peasantry a sullen dissatisfaction, a hatred and contempt for authority. Irish social customs emphasized these tendencies. Except for a curious puritanism regarding sexual relations, the lower classes of Ireland, contemporary observers agreed, were sunk in depravity.[13] Drunkenness was the most common Irish vice, alcoholism being prevalent among both sexes and all ages.[14] It was, of course, a vice which further encouraged violence and disorder. The family system was often another source of anti-social behaviour. Within the extended Irish family, close cooperation, "cooring," was the pattern in work as well as in social relations. However, those outside the pattern were viewed with hostility and suspicion. Friendliness was viewed as a matter

---

[9] J.G. Kohl, *Travels in Ireland* (London 1844), pp. 167-9.

[10] Galen Broeker, *Rural Disorder and Police Reform in Ireland, 1818-36* (London 1970), p. 10.

[11] K.H. Connell, *The Population of Ireland, 1760-1845* (Oxford 1950), p. 25, table 4.

[12] William Forbes Adams, *Ireland and the Irish Emigration to the New World* (New Haven, Conn. 1932), p. 337.

[13] For example, Michael Thomas Sadler, *Ireland: Its Evils and Their Remedies* (London 1828), p. 150, cited in Connell, *Population of Ireland*, p. 49.

[14] For a study of twentieth-century Irish drinking habits with insights into their historical origins, see Robert Freed Bales, "The 'Fixation Factor' in Alcohol Addiction: A Hypothesis Derived from a Comparative Study of Irish and Jewish Social Norms" (unpublished Ph.D. thesis, Harvard University, 1944).

of mutual obligation, obligation which could most easily be met within the family framework.[15]

Given such a background, the Irish were prone to ethnocentrism, to identify themselves most strongly with their nation, their group, their family. They were prone, as well, to violence, the violence of the drunken, of the desperate, of the insecure. Emigrating to Canada, removing from their familiar surroundings and from their families, it is not surprising that they should have herded together, that they should have been aggressive in defence of themselves and their way of life. They felt themselves challenged—challenged by the new conditions, challenged by economic insecurity, challenged by the other groups in Ottawa society.

The tradition of violence which they brought from Ireland was re-emphasized by the conditions they found on the Ottawa frontier. They lived in squalor amidst the festering swamps of the Rideau country. In 1828 Sir James Kempt visited the Rideau Canal works, which first brought the Irish to the Ottawa. Writing from Kingston, he breathed the sigh of relief of those lucky enough to escape the Rideau alive: "*Thank God* I am at last again in a Christian Country and not the land of Swamps and Musquitoes."[16]

Many of the Irish labourers never reached a Christian country again, instead perishing by the hundreds among the bogs.[17] Conditions in Bytown, the headquarters of the canal works, were hardly better than in the mud of Cranberry Marsh. Much of the eastern section of the village, Lower Town, had been covered by swamp until reclaimed. Even after drainage, it remained an uncomfortable and unhealthy area. Here the Irish made their adjustment to the frontier. Rather than allowing the environment to erode their traditions, to strip away their cultural shields, they, like so many other immigrant groups in Canada, drew their inherited patterns all the more tightly about themselves. A powerful illustration of this fact was provided by the living style of the Irish. Surrounded by the forest wealth of Canada's greatest lumbering region, the Irish immigrants chose to ignore the wood of their new country and instead recreated the sod huts of Ireland by burrowing their homes into the piles of dirt excavated from the canal bed.[18] What more vivid symbol could be offered of habit's resistance to nature?

The Irish formed their own community, Corktown, a huddle of ramshackle huts and moist caves along the canal banks. The contrast was sharp with the comfortable homes of Upper Town, rising in clear view along Wellington and Victoria streets. The Bytown of the gentry, a traveller enthused in 1832, was "... quite a lively, fashionable place; here are to be seen the European fashions, silks vying with muslins, the poke bonnet with the immense leghorn. Here are quadrille parties, and

---

[15] Conrad H. Arensberg, *The Irish Countryman* (New York 1950), pp. 66-8.
[16] PAC, Dalhousie Papers (microfilm), Sir James Kempt to Earl Dalhousie, 26 June 1828.
[17] See, for example, John Mactaggart, *Three Years in Canada* (2 vol.s London 1829), II, 14.
[18] Ibid., 243.

Scotch reel parties, and many other parties where mirth usually presides."[19] Corktown had little in common with this gay, genteel world. John Mactaggart, engineer and sympathetic observer, was more aware of this other community than the enthusiastic traveller. He saw the fever victims dying by the hundreds. He saw Irish labourers crushed by stones, or plummeting to their deaths in the Chaudière rapids. Most of all, he saw the abject poverty of the immigrants, the filth and misery of their lives. One in ten of the Corktown residents died in their first two years in Canada.[20]

Inherited animosities, and the reality of their poverty, were increased for the Irish by the contrast between their situation and that of the gentry of Upper Town. Bytown was a community in which the distinctions were made abundantly clear by the very topography of the village. Upper Town was separated physically from Lower Town by the Canal and by a wide strip of empty, government-owned land along the west bank of the waterway. Social distinctions added to the physical barrier. James Johnston, an Irish merchant, was not alone in his dislike of Upper Town's pretensions. In his short-lived newspaper, the Bytown *Independent*, Johnston reported in March 1836 the complaints of one "Dick Smith" who was disturbed by the "slander" so prevalent in Upper Town. Johnston replied to his correspondent: "He must be aware that the west end of all cities and villages, are made choice of by the fashionable and fain would be nobility; and back-biting, raillery, and slander, is the requisite sauce for idle conversation, in what the world calls good company, now-a-days."[21]

The ethnocentricity and truculence of the Irish was increased by the evident discrimination against them, discrimination they faced almost everywhere in British North america. Quite apart from the question of skills, employers in the timber camps preferred passive French Canadians to aggressive Irishmen. In the town, too, the immigrants felt themselves second-class citizens. Scots dominated all positions of importance. A bitter petition to the Lieutenant-Governor in 1833 from some inhabitants of Bytown showed how strained feelings were on this issue. They asked for more magistrates but insisted any new appointments should not be Scottish. Although Bytown contained a very diverse population, all four of the present magistrates were Scottish, and, the petition acidly remarked: "The natives of Scotland are not the most wealthy, best informed or most respectable."[22] James Johnston went further to charge that this apparent ethnic bias carried over into law enforcement; Scottish magistrates showed much more severity in dealing with Irish miscreants than with those of other nationalities.[23]

---

[19] George Henry Hume, *Canada, as It Is* (New York 1832), p. 60.

[20] Mactaggart, *Three Years in Canada*, II, 245.

[21] Bytown *Independent*, 10 March 1836.

[22] Upper Canada Sundries, vol. 125, Petition of Freeholders and Inhabitants of Bytown to Sir John Colborne, 9 Jan. 1833.

[23] Ibid., vol. 137, Johnston to Colborne, 23 Jan. 1834.

The Shiners' War: Social Violence in the Ottawa Valley in the 1830s   225

Events such as the cholera epidemics of 1832 and 1834 turned distinctions of rank and affluence into harsh, life-and-death realities. With the completion of the Rideau Canal, Bytown was on the main route for emigrants on their way from Lower to Upper Canada. As a result, when cholera was carried to Canada by emigrant ships it soon struck Bytown. Arriving first in the summer of 1832, the cholera devastated Lower Town. Terror spread, as the disease took its toll and the town officials appeared to be slow in reacting. While the magistrates of Bytown and its neighbour across the Ottawa, Hull, argued over whether river travel into the area should be banned and whether the Ottawa steamer, the *Shannon*, should be quarantined, the frightened Irish took matters into their own hands. Assembling in force at the Bytown docks, they threatened "... to destroy with sticks and stones, any vessel that might arrive...."[24]

The cholera returned two years later in an extended siege which lasted almost two months. Again it was Lower Town which suffered, while the residents of Upper Town remained relatively secure. In a report to the commander of the Bytown garrison, Captain Bolton, in August 1834, the Board of Health noted that all deaths from cholera had taken place in the eastern section of the town. They blamed the trouble on "... the stagnant and fetid state of the waste weir of the Rideau Canal...." and requested that the weir be cleaned. The request was in vain, Bolton replying that he had no funds available for such work.[25]

No records exist to indicate the feelings of the Irish Lower Town residents about these events—they were not a literate people. One may speculate, however, that they felt that their interests were not as important, in the eyes of the community leaders, as those of the Scots and English of Bytown's west end. To watch the unedifying spectacle of the magistrates quarrelling over a quarantine of steamers in 1832, while Irish died in the airless gloom of the Bytown hospital shed; to see the soldiers remain safe in their quarters atop Barracks Hill, in 1834, while the Irish suffered alongside the foul waste channel of the Canal: such displays were not calculated to bring greater Irish acceptance of the Bytown society-at-large or of its rules and customs.

Class lines were tightly drawn in Bytown, even within the Irish community. No "respectable" leadership offered itself to the Corktowners, to operate as a restraining influence on them. There were some Irishmen in Bytown who had talent, education, and the potential for leadership. Daniel O'Connor, for instance, was a natural leader. From a middle-class Irish background, with good manners and safe political and social opinions, O'Connor found it easy to make his way in Bytown. So, too, did John Pennyfather, contractor for excavation on the first eight locks of the Rideau Canal. These two were found in positions of prominence in Irish community organizations during the canal era. They were members of the committee formed in

---

24   Montreal *Gazette*, 24 July 1832.
25   PAC, Hill Collection, vol. 19, Charles Shirreff to Captain D. Bolton, 14 Aug. 1834, p. 4732; ibid., Bolton to Shirreff, 15 Aug. 1834, p. 4734.

1828 to superintend the construction of a Catholic church in the village.[26] When the Society of the Friends of Ireland, a group supporting the British Catholic emancipation movement, was established in February 1829, O'Connor and Pennyfather were again the leading figures.[27]

The Society died within a few months of its birth, when the Catholic Emancipation Act in Britain removed its rationale. And it represented practically the last example of leadership for the Irish masses by men such as O'Connor and Pennyfather. For they were ambitious men who made their cause with the established leadership of the community. O'Connor's quixotic spirit, which had led him to adventuring in South America with Bolivar, prepared him more for association with the prickly aristocrats than with the peasantry, as did his education. "The educated class being very few," he explained in his diary, "the excellent education that I received gave me many advantages and I soon ... became one of the prominent citizens of the town."[28] He did, indeed. He was content to accept the Upper Town orientation of Bytown leadership, to join community service agencies designed to support the community-at-large rather than ones planned to meet the peculiar needs of Lower Town. The result was that a sector of society already dislocated and dissatisfied was left without responsible leadership, was alienated even further from the general community, was made prey to any dynamic demagogue who might offer the dispossessed an answer to their problems.

In the absence of individual leadership, one institution might have been expected to reconcile the Irish to the community. That institution was the Catholic Church. But, in Bytown, the church was hardly more effective than other social institutions in influencing the Irish masses. The parish, throughout the 1830s, was torn by strife, tormented by widespread disobedience and disbelief. It was "more than enough," lamented the Catholic bishop, Alexander Macdonell, "to break my heart...."[29]

One explanation, as in the similar failure of Anglicanism, lies with the quality of the clergy sent to the Bytown mission. The letters of Bishop Macdonell are filled with anxiety over the poor calibre of priests who came to the province. The only major source of English-speaking priests was Ireland, and by and large only the most incapable of Irish clergymen would make the arduous translation to Canada; the competent had no difficulty finding suitable employment at home. Macdonell

---

[26] P. Alexis de Barbezieux, *Histoire de la Province Ecclesiastique d'Ottawa* (2 vols., Ottawa 1892), 1, 147.

[27] PAC, Daniel O'Connor Papers, minutes of meeting of Society of Friends of Ireland, 11 Feb. 1829.

[28] Daniel O'Connor, *Diary and Other Memoirs* (np. nd), p. 30.

[29] Kingston Diocesan Archives (KDA), Macdonell Letterbook, 1834-9, Macdonell to Rev. John Cullen, 19 Aug. 1834, p. 28.

summed up the situation: "The Irish clergymen who were employed in this province have indeed done much injury to the cause of Religion...."[30]

Bytown suffered from the maladministration of a series of poor priests. The first Catholic clergyman, the Rev. Patrick Horan, was much addicted to alcohol and became increasingly erratic in his behaviour. He was discovered to have been selling church land and keeping the proceeds for himself. The congregation was badly split over what to do with Horan, and Macdonell hesitated to act against him until petitioned by the church wardens for his removal in the spring of 1829.[31] Different difficulties arose with Patrick Polin, assistant curate from 1832 to 1835, who, it was discovered was a fake, with no training for the priesthood.[32] He was followed by Timothy O'Meara, who was removed within a few months of his appointment for "shameful Immoralities" and "execrable conduct" in the mission.[33]

Even apart from the low quality of priests, the Irish could not be expected to offer automatic obedience to the church. In Ireland, before the clergy re-established their leadership in the emancipation movement, there were equivocal responses to the church in the troubled areas of the country. Deeply Catholic, the masses nevertheless often resented the clergy's support of British authority. And the secret societies sometimes used terrorist tactics to resist Catholic, as well as Anglican tithes.[34] This was even more true in Upper Canada where the church, from the beginning was Scottish dominated. Even after the Irish became the majority among Upper Canadian Catholics, the church continued in the hold of Macdonell and his Scots and remained, in the view of its critics, anti-Irish in its sentiments.[35] In the inflamed atmosphere of Bytown, such an organization was suspect; even a church which attempted to be scrupulously fair to all ethnic groups would have drawn upon itself the ire of the Shiners, who operated on the assumption that anyone who was not unequivocally with them was irretrievably against them.

---

[30] Ibid., Macdonell Letterbook, 1820-9, Macdonell to Bishop Plessis, 17 Nov. 1821, p. 50. For other complaints about emigrant priests, see ibid., Macdonell to Dr. Weld, 6 May 1827, p. 156; ibid., Macdonell Letterbook, 1834-9, Macdonell to Dr. Murray, 29 Oct. 1834, pp. 43-4; ibid., Bishop Macdonell, Miscellaneous Correspondence, Envelope 4, Macdonell to Cardinal Weld, 22 June 1835.

[31] Ibid., Macdonell Letterbook, 1820-9, Macdonell to Pennyfather, 13 May 1828, pp. 263-4; Macdonell to Col. By, 2 May 1829, p. 401; Macdonell to Rev. P. Horan, 1 June 1829, p. 404.

[32] Ibid., Macdonell Letterbook, 1834-9, Macdonell to Rev. John Cullen, 16 July 1834, p. 16; Macdonell to Polin, Jan. 1835, p. 72.

[33] Ibid., Macdonell to Bishop Gaulin, 18 March 1835, p. 96; Macdonell to Rev. James Campion, 21 March 1835, p. 98.

[34] Broeker, *Rural Disorder*, p. 4.

[35] For an example, see the dispute between Macdonell and Murty Lalor, an Irish priest at Kingston. Lalor was accused of "inflaming national prejudice against your Scots superiors": KDA, Macdonell Letterbook, 1829-34, Macdonell to Lalor, 26 July 1831, p. 193.

Ethnic conflict was a subject on which the church was particularly sensitive, and as a result the documents tend to be sketchy and evasive on such disputes. That serious disagreements took place in Bytown is clear but the issues involved are difficult to establish. Two cases do stand out, however. One was the conflict between the Rev. John Cullen and an Irishman named Ryan. It appears that Ryan was angry over Cullen's sympathy with the French Canadians in their battle with the Irish. The dispute reached the stage of blows, Ryan bringing charges of assault against Cullen, and Macdonell excommunicating Ryan in 1834.[36] Another example was provided by the removal of Timothy O'Meara from the parish in 1835. O'Meara's "scandalous" behaviour appears to have involved the priest's support of the Shiners in the Bytown civil war.[37]

The O'Meara incident raises the question of what influence might have been exerted on the Shiners by a sympathetic church. But the question remains entirely speculative. Along with the other institutions of this society, the Catholic church alienated the Irish and left them little choice but to take their own form of direct action.

In the absence of social restraints and responsible leadership, the only potential check on the Irish was coercion. But this, too, was lacking. Police power was seriously deficient. At least during the canal era, the military forces engaged in the construction were available in times of particular disorder. However, in the 1830s there was no such source of authority. Indeed, at a time when pressure was building up within Bytown itself and when increasing numbers of raftsmen were invading the area, the police power was completely disintegrating. By 1833, Bytown was often without the services of a magistrate, ordinarily the only law officer in the absence of any provision for a police force. Of the four magistrates appointed for the village, one was on an extended absence in England, another spent six months of the year in Quebec, and the other two, both merchants, were frequently out of town on business.[38] Nor could the inhabitants rely on the district authorities for aid. For over a year, the office of sheriff of the District of Bathurst was void of influence owing to a degrading power struggle over the income of the office between two claimants, John A.H. Powell and John F. Berford, both of Perth in Lanark County.[39]

Even had the authorities been present and active, they would have been faced with enormous difficulties. Four part-time magistrates, middle-aged and untrained, could hardly form a very intimidating police force. They were attempting to maintain order in a border community, where criminals could slip across the river into Lower

---

36   Ibid., Macdonell to Cullen, 3 June 1833, p. 409; Macdonell to Cullen, 17 Jan. 1834, p. 457.
37   KDA, Macdonell Letterbook, 1834-9, Macdonell to Rev. P. Phelan, 6 July 1834, p. 141; Macdonell to Very Rev. W.P. MacDonald, 23 July 1835, p. 146.
38   Upper Canada Sundries, vol. 125, Petition of the Freeholders and Inhabitants of Bytown, 9 Jan. 1833.
39   Ibid., vol. 140, J.A.H. Powell to Col. Rowan, 25 April 1834; petition of J.F. Berford, 25 April 1834.

Canada and into another jurisdiction—one equally poorly policed.[40] Even if criminals were successfully arrested, the magistrates' problems were not at an end. The only jail was in Perth, forty miles away by canal or overland through the forest. The jail was remarkably porous, with a long history of successful escapes. Not untypical were the events of November 1835. John Stewart, a timberman, was arrested for assault and battery and jailed at Perth. With the aid of a friend outside, one Thomas Murphy, Stewart escaped from the prison. Murphy was subsequently arrested for his part in the jail break, but a few days later he too escaped and disappeared into the Ottawa forest.[41] A constable, who received payment for his services which hardly met his expenses in transporting a prisoner to Perth, presumably was not encouraged to run the risk when in all likelihood his prisoner would soon free himself from the rickety cells of the district jail.

The Bytown situation was one all too common in Upper Canada. With no effective local government and no provision for police forces, social order depended on the effectiveness of other institutions to restrain the population. But these institutions—churches, leadership structures, social agencies—were often as weak as the police power, especially in frontier areas. Or, as with the military, they were prevented from acting by their superior authorities. Those regions, such as the Ottawa, dependent on the timber trade or other commercial activities, lacked the full spectrum of social institutions. Churches found it difficult to provide clergymen, especially competent clergymen;[42] schools were rarely available; the upper classes were often alienated from the masses, and too often incompetent to lead the community; few charitable organizations existed. And the basic institution of social control, the family, was often weakened. One of the complaints frequently made against the timber trade was its effect on family life. A critic insisted, in 1835, that the timber trade should be discouraged, for "... by causing bodies of men to live in the woods in shantees [sic] ... [it] places them beyond the good social effects consequent upon being surrounded by women...."[43]

---

[40] PAC, Hill Collection, vol. 21, petition of the Inhabitants of Bytown to Sir F.B. Head, 1828, p. 5540.

[41] Upper Canada Sundries, vol. 159, Baker to Rowan, 17 Nov. 1835.

[42] The Anglicans, for instance, had the same problems as the Catholics with a long list of eccentric and unreliable clergymen. Between 1829 and 1837, the Bytown region suffered from the ministrations of a series of disastrous Anglican priests. One was an opium addict, one was insane, one was a heretic who left the Anglicans to become "an Angel in the Spiritual Church," and one was charged with immorality involving a female parishioner. The cases are chronicled in the Quebec Anglican Diocesan Archives, Series B, Section II, Parochial Reports; Series D, Section VII, General Correspondence.

[43] British Sessional Papers, House of Commons, 1835 (519), XIX, Select Committee on Timber Duties, testimony of Samuel Revans, p. 178.

The situation suggests a reinterpretation of the concept of the frontier.[44] The frontier has been seen as the place where a new society emerged in North America. The destruction of traditional social structures and values by the frontier environment, the social disorder it produced, allowed new forms to emerge. Our analysis has stressed other factors than the physical environment in producing disorder. Viewed this way, the physical definition loses its pre-eminent importance. The frontier ceases to be the place where civilization meets the natural wilderness, ceases to be, necessarily, a place of light population density. It can be redefined simply as a place which is distant from the forces of social order. In this definition, an urban ghetto could be a frontier as much as the wilderness, and much the same process of social breakdown would operate there.

The completion of the Rideau Canal in 1832 created an employment crisis in the Ottawa country. Hundreds of Irish were unemployed. Lacking skills and experience, they found it difficult to get work in the timber camps where French Canadians held most of the jobs. But it was also a time of vicious competition among the timber operators, struggling to exploit the best accessible tracts. Some operators began to employ Irishmen to improve their competitive position by intimidation. As the Hawkesbury timber merchant, George Hamilton, complained to the government in 1835, some employers were importing "bravoes & ruffians" to drive their rivals out of disputed territories.[45] Peter Aylen was one such employer. Another was Walter Beckwith who ruled with an iron hand at Westneath, near Pembroke. Beckwith boasted he would employ none but Shiners, and they repaid his support by brutally suppressing anyone who questioned Beckwith's right to take timber freely from crown and private lands. On one of the few occasions when the authorities attempted to intervene, in 1835, the problems of maintaining order in this region were again demonstrated. When magistrates arrived to arrest Beckwith for trespassing and illegal timbering, he simply scuttled across the river to Lower Canada, to return and resume his sway when the officers had left.[46]

By 1835 Aylen was prepared to use the Shiners for broader purposes—to seize effective control of Bytown and its region. The first shots of the Shiners' War were fired on 5 January 1835 with the daring daylight murder of a Mr McStravick on a street in Lower Bytown. The murderer, a lumberer named Curry, was arrested but like so many after him he escaped custody and fled to the United States.[47] Sporadic violence continued through the winter in Bytown; tension built up in the village, as stories came from upriver, stories of beatings and mutilations and killings. But not even the combined prayers of all the respectable citizens of Bytown could hold back the seasons. Spring came to the Ottawa, and with it the rafts.

---

[44] For a variety of opinions on the concept, see Michael S. Cross, ed., *The Frontier Thesis and the Canadas* (Toronto 1970).
[45] Upper Canada Sundries, vol. 152, Hamilton to Rowan, 1 June 1835.
[46] Ibid., vol. 158, Baker to Rowan, 20 Oct. 1835.
[47] Ibid., vol. 155, Baker to Rowan, 13 July 1835.

The Shiners' War: Social Violence in the Ottawa Valley in the 1830s

While Bytown became the centre of the disorders, they spread the length of the Valley. Aylen quickened the pace of his anti-French campaign, determined to win a rapid, total victory. In the spring of 1835, the Shiners began to stop rafts manned by French Canadians, to rout the crews, and then demolish the rafts. However, the Canadians, tired of ceaseless persecution, struck back. The first recorded resistance took place in June, at Grand Calumet, north of Pembroke. A boarding crew of Shiners was beaten off a raft when French-Canadian reinforcements joined the raftsmen.[48] The major example of French-Canadian reaction, however, came in July, when a raft manned by Shiners was ambushed in the channel behind Montreal Island.[49] The Irish were seized, beaten, and thrown to the shore. No Irishman, the Canadians declared, would be allowed in the future to pass the Long Sault. The threat was not idle. A raft owned by Peter Aylen was shot at and seized at the same spot.

But, for savagery and intimidation, the French Canadians could not match the Shiners. By the end of the season, the Irish were clearly triumphant. In October the Hull lumberman, Ruggles Wright, was deploring to George Hamilton the success of the Shiners' war effort. Business was seriously threatened, for the Shiners were impossible to work with and the French Canadians were disheartened: "... we shant [sic] be able to engage Canadiens to go into the interior of the Country at any price."[50] Nor were the attempts of the major operators to police the Ottawa any more successful than those of the French Canadians. The Ottawa Lumber Association was formed to apply collective sanctions against timberers who engaged in violence. But the effect seems to have been negligible. The association was soon spending most of its energies in improving the physical facilities for the trade, rather than in the hopeless task of attempting to control the Shiners. It was an ironic statement on the failure of the association in its original purpose, that its major cooperative effort in the summer of 1836 was the construction of slideways and dams on the Madawaska River—construction carried out under the supervision of Peter Aylen.[51] Aylen had thoughtfully taken a vacation from leading his ruffians to aid the good work of the organization set up to punish him.

It was a long summer in Bytown. Many of the Shiners stayed on there, rather than going on to Quebec with the rafts. To the traditional insolence of the raftsmen there was added this year the swagger of self-confidence. All down the Ottawa they had tasted their new-found power. The feeble forces of authority in Bytown were not likely to enjoy much success in stemming this Shiner tide. Under the leadership of magistrate George W. Baker, however, they made a valiant attempt.[52] The arrest and brief imprisonment of Peter Aylen for his assault on Daniel McMartin was one

---

[48] Upper Canada State Papers, vol. 83, Charles Shirreff to Rowan, 11 July 1835, pp. 88-9.
[49] Upper Canada Sundries, vol. 156, deposition before C.J. Bell and G.W. Baker, justices of the peace, by J. Bulger, A. Leamy, and M. Whalen, 5 Aug. 1835.
[50] PAC, Wright Papers (microfilm), Ruggles Wright to George Hamilton, 8 Oct. 1835, p. 927.
[51] Bytown *Gazette*, 21 July 1836.
[52] Baker, a half-pay officer, was postmaster of Bytown.

example. Another case occurred in mid-May 1835. Three Shiners—Jerry Ryan, John Hoolahan, and Michael Hoolahan—assaulted and raped an old Indian woman. They were arrested by Baker, but it was a real question whether the magistrates would be able to hold the prisoners. Jerry Ryan's brother, Edward, and another raftsman, Joseph Benson, boasted they would rescue their compatriots and threatened to "Blow out the brains" of the chief witness, a carpenter named William Brown.[53] Baker foiled the plan by arresting Ryan and Benson, and confining all five of them in the garrison cells, where they were secure from rescue.[54] The wisdom of his actions was proven when the prisoners were sent to Perth for trial. The five Irishmen made a nearly successful escape from the Perth jail, by digging a tunnel under the walls, an attempt thwarted at the last minute by the jailers who discovered the tunnel.[55]

But such victories were few. By the middle of June, authority had collapsed almost completely. This was the occasion of Baker's resignation as magistrate. The laws, he said, could not be enforced; he could not rely on twelve men in the whole village to aid him in time of trouble. His full exertion would have to be employed in protecting his own family in this period of chaos.[56]

The measure of control enjoyed by the Shiners, once Aylen had organized them, was demonstrated by their domination of the Union Bridge over the Ottawa River. The toll-keeper, one McClellan, established a "shibbeen" selling liquor to the raftsmen. Attracted by his wares, the Shiners took over control of the span, insulting and assaulting travellers and demanding payment for passage over it. Although the government owned the bridge, no one dared intervene to stop the outrages. All too frequently bodies were found below the bridge, victims of the playful celebrations of the Shiners above.[57]

Shiner violence became an everyday fact of life, sometimes of a spectacular nature. There was, for example, the case of Joseph Galipaut. In 1833 Peter Aylen's bodyguard, the giant Martin Hennessey, rode his horse into the tavern operated by Galipaut. The tavern was a gathering-place of French Canadians, and Hennessey's intrusion was looked upon as a hostile gesture. In the resultant dispute, Galipaut shot Hennessey, leaving him blind in one eye.[58] Galipaut was a marked man from that point on. A raftsman, Matthew Power, attempted to take the Shiners' revenge in June 1835, only to receive the same portion as Martin Hennessey; Power was felled by a shot from Galipaut's gun.[59] The fury of the Shiners was uncontrollable. The

---

[53] *Bathurst Courier*, 15 May 1835.
[54] Upper Canada Sundries, vol. 152, Baker to Rowan, 15 June 1835.
[55] *Bathurst Courier*, 20 May 1835.
[56] Upper Canada Sundries, vol. 152, Baker to Rowan, 15 June 1835.
[57] Ibid., vol. 156, petition of the grand jury of the Bathurst District to Sir John Colborne, Aug. 1835.
[58] William Pittman Lett, *Recollections of Bytown* (Ottawa 1874), p. 48.
[59] Upper Canada Sundries, vol. 155, James Johnston to Colborne, 9 July 1835; ibid., Baker to Rowan, 13 July 1835; Upper Canada State Papers, vol. 83, Shirreff to Rowan, 11 July 1835.

The Shiners' War: Social Violence in the Ottawa Valley in the 1830s   233

innkeeper and his family were forced to flee Bytown. His tavern was put to the torch, creating a spectacular blaze—which was prevented from spreading to other buildings only by the fortunate occurrence of a heavy rainstorm.[60]

What lifted the Galipaut affair above the level of other Shiner outrages was the involvement of Daniel O'Connor. This bastion of the gentility began to play an equivocal role in the Bytown civil war, splitting the front of authority and making it less effective. Moved either by ethnic feeling, or fear of the Shiners, O'Connor demonstrated clear ethnic bias. As the only available magistrate, O'Connor was called upon after the wounding of Matthew Power. According to James Johnston and George Baker, O'Connor was highly partisan in his investigation, seeking only that evidence which tended to incriminate Galipaut.[61] O'Connor had the unfortunate French Canadian incarcerated in the garrison cells, while taking no action against the burglar Power. Yet in a similar case a few weeks later, O'Connor behaved very differently. When a Shiner invaded the home of an Irishman and was wounded. O'Connor took no action against the homeowner.[62]

The Shiner tide continued to rise. Few indeed were those who would stand against them; George Baker estimated that of sixteen men deputized in the town, only four could be counted on in an emergency.[63] This was dramatized on 29 July. A constable, one Mr. Dixon, attempted to arrest a Shiner wanted for a rape charge. Dixon was beaten unmercifully by three Shiners, in full view of a large crowd of citizens.[64] The population was too frightened to take any action against the Shiners. Since law enforcement in Upper Canada depended on the efforts of amateur policemen, and operated on the assumption that the citizens would share responsibility for maintaining order, this consensus of terror brought Bytown to the verge of anarchy. As well, there were economic factors militating against vigorous action. The raftsmen represented not only violence and bloodshed, but also bread and butter. Everyone ultimately was dependent on the money brought to Bytown by the timberers. Such reliance bred a strong tolerance for the behaviour of the raftsmen and a strong reluctance to oppose them openly.[65]

Even in the summer of 1835, the Shiner movement was showing signs of growing beyond the stage of a struggle for jobs and an exercise in petty violence. The organizational talents of Peter Aylen and his dreams of power were both evident in the Shiner coup of August 1835 against the Bathurst District Agricultural Society. Few organizations were dearer to the hearts of the Carleton gentry than the

---

60   *Bathurst Courier*, 10 July 1835.
61   Upper Canada Sundries, vol. 155, Baker to Rowan, 13 July 1835; Johnston to Colborne, 9 July 1835.
62   Ibid.
63   Ibid., Baker to Rowan, 13 July 1835.
64   Ibid., vol. 156, Baker to Rowan, 6 Aug. 1835; Montreal *Gazette*, 6 Aug. 1835.
65   This factor was mentioned by George Baker: Upper Canada Sundries, vol. 173, Baker to J. Joseph, 9 Dec. 1836.

Agricultural Society, in which they paid at least lip service to the agrarian myth, so important a part of the gentle ideal as imported from Britain. The affection in which the Society was held made it a natural target for Aylen. He had declared war on the gentility and its leadership of society, and his war was one of nerves and irritation as much as one of guns and clubs.

The annual meeting of the Society for 1835 convened in Bytown in August. Peter Aylen arrived with a large body of raftsmen, each equipped with the dollar fee necessary for membership. Never had the friendly little aristocrats' club witnessed such a scene. Sprawling on the benches, swigging poteen from their bottles, roaring over coarse jokes, the Shiners turned the austere meeting room into a fair facsimile of a Lower Town tavern. Then came the moment Aylen had been awaiting—the election of officers. Vastly outnumbering the legitimate members, the Shiners voted out of office the entire executive and replaced them with timberers. Of these new officers of the Agricultural Society, not one could have distinguished a turnip from a tomato. But the crowning blow for the gentry was the election for the presidency which saw returned, as chief officer of their beloved organization, their arch-enemy—Peter Aylen. The Shiners maintained their hold on the Society for two years until, in April 1837, the frustrated community leaders of Carleton County gave up hope of recovering the original society and formed a totally new agricultural association.[66]

By the fall of 1835, the gentility recognized that its leadership was in jeopardy, that the Shiner troubles represented more than the annual disorder brought by the raftsmen. The few hundred Irishmen[67] who followed Peter Aylen threatened to bring down the aristocratic order so diligently erected in the community. The response of the gentry was the Bytown Association for the Preservation of the Peace. On the evening of 20 October 1835, a group of householders met at the court house to organize their opposition to the Shiner terror. The meeting passed a resolution calling for the creation of "... an armed association ... of the Inhabitant Householders of Bytown and its vicinity for the purpose of cooperation with and assisting the Magistrates in the Preservation of the Public Peace." A committee of management, including several leading members of the gentility, was elected. The first action of this committee was to ask the magistrates for one hundred guns to arm members of the Association.[68]

By the end of the first week of operation, the vigilante organization had a membership of two hundred and had established a system of nightly patrols by armed citizens.[69] In the spring of 1836 operations were widened. A subscription fund was started to raise money for prosecuting felons, for paying constables' fees, and for meeting any other expenses necessary to bring criminals to justice. Further, the

---

66 *Bathurst Courier*, 19 May 1837.
67 The Brockville *Recorder*, 23 Oct. 1836 estimated the fighting strength of the Shiners at 150.
68 *Bathurst Courier*, 14 Nov. 1835; Upper Canada Sundries, vol. 158, Baker to Rowan, 22 Oct. 1835, enclosing minutes of the meeting.
69 Upper Canada Sundries, vol. 158, Baker to Rowan, 27 Oct. 1835.

executive authorized Colonel George Baker to raise, as quickly as possible, an armed corps—the Bytown Rifles—whose formation already had been approved by the lieutenant governor.[70]

The Association enjoyed some measure of success. While crimes of violence were frequent in 1836, Bytown did not suffer from the same degree of organized agitation as it had the previous year. However, the effectiveness was reduced by now familiar limitations: dissension within the leadership group and lack of support from provincial authorities. The chief disturber within the ranks was Captain Baker. Authorized to form his armed corps, Baker was carried away by the grandeur of his position. On 4 June 1836 he called a muster of all men of military age to meet on Barracks Hill, and there to be introduced into the Bytown rifles. Since the captain had no power to order a general militia muster, most Bytownians ignored the order. The furious Baker threatened to punish the absentees with all penalties authorized under the Militia Act. Finally, the provincial government was forced to intervene and to explain the legalities to Baker. The only results of the affair were public humiliation for George Baker and the early demise of the Bytown Rifles.[71] The Association was forced to function without its chief coercive agency.

From the beginning, the Bytown vigilantes had received little cooperation from senior authorities. The confusing orders which led to the Bytown Rifles fiasco were echoed in the issue of the garrison cells. The Association was given to understand the cells on Barracks Hill would be available for the detention of prisoners. Unfortunately, this information had not been relayed by the government to the commander of the Bytown detachment, Captain Bolton, who refused to allow the civilians access to the military jail.[72] But the lack of cooperation with the Bytown group was only a function of the government's larger failure of responsibility: had the province been willing to supply protection to its citizens, the Bytown Association for the Preservation of the Peace need never have been formed. Many individuals and agencies had drawn to government's attention the need for military aid to suppress the Shiner bands.[73] The requests were ignored. Even if the attention of provincial authorities could be gained, action could be blocked by the lieutenant-governor, as it was by Sir Francis Bond Head in 1837. The story was told in a minute of the Executive Council: "Notwithstanding the obvious objections to the employment of a military force for the preservation of the Peace, it seems necessary that a detachment should be stationed at Bytown, to act in aid of the Magistrates in

---

[70] Hill Collection, vol. 22, minutes of meeting of the Managing Committee of the Bytown Association for the Preservation of the Peace, 30 March 1836, pp. 5830-1.
[71] Lucien Brault, *Ottawa Old & New* (Ottawa 1946), pp. 161-2.
[72] Upper Canada Sundries, vol. 158, Baker to Rowan, 27 Oct. 1835.
[73] Upper Canada State Papers, vol. 83, Shirreff to Rowan, 11 July 1835, pp. 91-2; *Brockville Recorder*, 23 Oct. 1835.

any case of extraordinary emergency." At the bottom of the page is a terse note: "I cannot at present concur in the above recommendation. FBH."[74]

That the efforts of the Association were not totally successful was demonstrated in the early months of 1837, when Peter Aylen's coup reached a climax. The annual township meeting for Nepean, in which Bytown was located, was held at Stanley's Tavern in Bytown on 2 January 1837. Aylen saw in the meeting an opportunity to repeat his success with the Agricultural Society. Leading a gang of raftsmen, he appeared at the meeting to demand the vote for his followers and to elect a council favourable to the Shiners. When he was resisted, Aylen broke up the meeting. In the resultant riot, George Patterson and James Johnston were beaten severely by the timberers.[75] Commenting on the affair, George Baker summed up the bitterness and frustration of the gentility: "How strange it seems that one man should have the power to keep the whole town and neighbourhood in disorder—but it is so...."[76]

It was a depression winter, trade languished, prices for the necessities of life were high, the Shiners were idle and frustrated and angry. The list of outrages grew with each passing day. And as the catalogue of crimes mounted, the anger of the respectable elements mounted as well. The inhabitants of the surrounding townships, less dependent than the townsfolk on the timberers, were also less tolerant of Shiner pranks. The country people reached the breaking-point over an outrage which occurred on 14 February 1837. A farmer named Hobbs had run afoul of the raftsmen. That afternoon the female members of his family had come to town to shop. Returning home in their sleigh, they were recognized by a gang of Shiners, led by one Gleeson. The Irishmen attacked the sleigh, beating the girls. Hobb's pregnant wife, terrified at the savage assault, attempted to leap from the sleigh. Her clothing caught on the side and she was dragged behind the vehicle, bumping over the frozen road, while the Shiners beat her with sticks. The women eventually escaped the raftsmen, who then turned their fury on the pair of horses drawing the sleigh. When the animals were turned loose the next morning they bore the signs of Shiner vengeance. Hobbs found them wandering, dragging their tattered harness behind them. One horse had a gaping knife wound in its side, both had been mutilated, their ears and tails cut off.[77]

The magistrates made their usual futile attempts to punish the Shiners for the affair. But it proved impossible to apprehend Gleeson and his gang. A week after the attack, on 21 February, a large company of country people arrived in Bytown. The grimfaced farmers, heavily armed with guns, pitchforks, clubs, announced to the magistrates that they had come to aid in capturing Gleeson. Bytown was faced with

---

[74] Upper Canada Sundries, vol. 174, Executive Council Minute, 16 Feb. 1837.
[75] Ibid., Baker to Hamnett Pinhey, 10 Jan. 1837; Brault, *Ottawa Old & New*, p. 68; Stewart, "King of the Shiners," p. 75.
[76] Upper Canada Sundries, vol. 174, Baker to Pinhey, 10 Jan. 1837.
[77] This account of the attack has been reconstructed from several sources: *Bytown Gazette*, 16 Feb. 1837; Brockville *Recorder*, 23 Feb. 1837; Toronto *Globe*, 25 Dec. 1856.

the threat of open warfare. Hearing of the arrival of the country people, the Shiner leaders spread rumours that Orangemen had come into the town to attack Catholics. The raftsmen were then joined by many otherwise peaceful Catholic residents, all preparing to repel the imaginary Orange invasion. However, the magistrates were able to head off the confrontation by convincing the farmers to return home and, in the Lower Town confusion, arresting Gleeson.[78]

The respite was only temporary. On 9 March 1837 the streets of Bytown were buzzing again with the warning: "The country people are coming!" A force of twenty constables was on its way from the village of Richmond to enforce a warrant against Peter Aylen, for an assault on an old man on the Richmond Road. Once again the story circulated in Lower Town that a great army of Orangemen was coming to murder Catholics. Again, however, violence was avoided. The leading citizen of Richmond, George Lyon, arrived and convinced his people to cancel their expedition.[79]

The day's excitement was far from over. James Johnston, long an enemy of the Shiners, had once more earned their enmity for opposing their raid on the Nepean council and for aiding in the arrest of Gleeson. It was now assumed he was in league with the country people. It was rumoured, that night of 9 March, that the hated Hobbs had come to town to arrest Aylen, and was staying at Johnston's home. A crowd of sixty Shiners marched to the Johnston house about 8 o'clock that evening to demand Hobbs be surrendered up to them. They left when Johnston appeared at the door, waving a brace of pistol.s Barely had the Johnstons retired, however, when they received another visitation. Led by Peter Aylen himself, a mob of drunken Shiners arrived before the house about 10:30 that night, and began to shoot through the windows and doors. When they had their fill, the Shiners went off seeking other amusements, leaving behind a frightened but uninjured Johnston family.[80]

The events of February and March 1837 uncovered new potentialities for violence in the area. The economic and ethnic struggles which had underlain the Shiners' War were buttressed by religious tensions. As the community moved into a new stage of development, in which the early enthusiasms of frontier growth were passing, and the problems of sustaining growth were emerging—problems of a debtor region, problems of unsatisfied expectations—new frustrations emerged. Not only the Shiners showed evidence of these tensions. As the *Bytown Gazette* pointed out: "... although these disturbances have been in general attributed to the Lumber-men, under the cognomen of Shiners, there have been instances in which our yeomanry have been the aggressors."[81]

Among those influenced by religious prejudice was Daniel O'Connor. He played a significant role in rallying Lower Towners against what he believed was an Orange

---

[78] Upper Canada Sundries, vol. 175, Baker *et al.*, to Joseph, 13 March 1837.
[79] Ibid.
[80] Ibid., Johnston to Head, 14 March 1837; *Bytown Gazette*, 17 March 1837.
[81] *Bytown Gazette*, 23 Feb. 1837.

invasion. The country people, he had been told, were planning to burn down some houses, O'Connor's among them.[82] The incident drove a wedge between the magistrates, on ethnic and religious lines. How serious was the breach emerged a few weeks later. A Shiner, Thomas Macaulay, committed an assault on one John Little. Pursued by three magistrates, George Baker, Daniel Fisher, and D.R. Macnab, Macaulay fled to Peter Aylen's house. Aylen attempted to bar entry to the magistrates but they pushed past him. Inside they discovered Daniel O'Connor, who supported Aylen, insisting the magistrates had no right to enter the house without a warrant. In the resultant argument, Aylen assured the justices he would make them "... sweat for it," while O'Connor insulted Macnab, calling him "that Creole."[83]

The magistrates pulled themselves together sufficiently to head off threatened trouble on St Patrick's Day. Swearing in a large number of constables, and employing the good offices of the Catholic priest, Rev. Cannon, they maintained order.[84] The impetus provided by the success on St Patrick's Day was strengthened by another outrage. On 24 March 1837 the Shiners attempted to take their long-awaited revenge on James Johnston.[85] Peter Aylen, bound over for the assizes on charges arising from three separate riots, denied himself the personal pleasure of disposing of Johnston. Instead he hired some experienced strongarms to carry out the assassination. But Johnston slipped through the Shiner patrols posted on the Sapper's Bridge over the Rideau Canal and thwarted their plans. The next afternoon, however, three raftsmen were again on the bridge. Thomas Burke, Patrick O'Brien, and James McDonald knew Johnston's movements, and ambushed him at one end of the span. Johnston, in a desperate move, leaped down the canal bank, falling twelve feet into deep snow below. Trapped in the snow he was an easy target. While two Shiners assailed him with bullets and stones from above, Tom Burke scrambled down to attack Johnston with a heavy whip. But Johnston's shouts brought help, citizens who beat off the Shiners. Johnston was pulled from the snowbank, his skull fractured in two places.

A new spirit was evident in Bytown. Angered by the attack on Johnston, the authorities reacted with unusual energy and unity. The three would-be assassins were arrested. When Aylen boasted of how easily he would free them, the garrison joined the magistrates to frustrate him. The prisoners were convoyed to Perth by thirty soldiers. Aylen did make good his boast, for during the early morning of 1 May a gang of Shiners broke into the Perth jail and freed their associates. However, the aroused authorities tracked the escapees and on 3 May recaptured them at Morristown,

---

[82] Upper Canada Sundries, vol. 175, Baker *et al.*, to Joseph, 13 March 1837.
[83] Ibid., Baker *et al.*, to Joseph, 4 April 1837.
[84] Ibid., Baker to Joseph, 30 March 1837; *Bytown Gazette*, 17 March 1837.
[85] *Bytown Gazette*, 30 March 1837; Upper Canada Sundries, vol. 175, Baker to Joseph, 28 March 1837; ibid., affidavit of James Johnston, 25 March 1837.

New York.[86] Tried in September, 1837, each received three years imprisonment at hard labour on charges of attempted murder.[87]

Shiner violence was far from over. But, increasingly, there was a new confidence in the community, a new willingness on the part of ordinary citizens to aid the authorities.[88] The Rebellion winter of 1837-8 established beyond doubt the victory of the forces of order. It was a time when disaffected elements might have been expected to rise. But, in fact, Bytown and its region remained most unnaturally tranquil during the troubles agitating so much of the Canadas. When troops were withdrawn for service elsewhere, their place was taken by civilian special constables, who had no difficulty maintaining order.[89] Obviously aware of the new mood, Peter Aylen sold his property in Bytown and moved to Aylmer, Lower Canada. There, unchecked by an already existing ruling group, he became the leading citizen of the town and a tower of respectability.

The discontents which drove the Shiners had not disappeared. Peter Aylen had not been magically reformed. But he had pushed the leadership structure too far, in the attack on the government at the Nepean council and the attempt to assassinate James Johnston. Murder in Lower Town, if deplorable, was not a direct threat to the ruling group. Assaults on middle class gentlemen, however, could not be tolerated. And when the leaders reacted strongly, they gave confidence to the community-at-large. In such a society, the solution to the problem of violence by the disadvantaged was not to meet their grievances; it was to establish authority with sufficient power that the disadvantaged did not dare to challenge it.

The Shiners' War was over. As late as 1845, communities on the Ottawa were troubled by gangs who called themselves Shiners.[90] But the organization which had marked the years 1835-7 was gone, and the troubles were only those caused by drunken and restless men anywhere. The old leaders had left: they had grown rich and respectable, like Aylen and his right-hand man, Andrew Leamy; or they were dead, like Martin Hennessey, laid low by a blow on the head in a Bytown brawl.[91] And the Shiners had enjoyed only a very partial success. The Irish did win jobs in the timber camps. But the grander purposes, of punishing the community which rejected them, of seizing power over that community, ultimately failed.

---

[86] Upper Canada Sundries, vol. 176, Baker *et al.*, to Joseph, 6 May 1837.

[87] *Bathurst Courier*, 29 Sept. 1837.

[88] In August of 1837, for example, the Shiners boasted they would free a rapist, Thomas McAuley. But the men of Bytown formed an escort for the magistrates and transported McAuley to Perth. And, in October, Shiners responsible for attacking French Canadians were hunted down and arrested: *Bytown Gazette*, 16 Aug., 18 Oct. 1837.

[89] *Bytown Gazette*, 21 Feb. 1838

[90] See the complaints of the citizens of Carillon, see PAC, Canada State Book D, 8 Sept. 1845, p. 533.

[91] Lett, *Recollections of Bytown*, p. 23.

Yet, success or failure, the Shiners' War is worth attention for what it says about the sources and nature of social violence in British North America, and for what it says about the community's response to such disorder. The Shiner movement emerged for two major reasons. One was the pattern of violence and disorder imported from Britain. As the experience of so many communities in the colonies demonstrated, the ocean voyage did not wash away old ethnic and religious hatreds, did not bleach out Orange or Green. Indeed, it often reinforced them. The insecurity of a new physical environment tended to cause people to cling even more tenaciously, in their initial period of adjustment, to certain traditional values and means of self-identification. Ethnic and religious bonds could often be tightened by the migration experience. This was especially so in areas such as the Ottawa frontier where many competing groups were thrown together, without the bonds of adequate social institutions. Lacking such institutional buffers, the groups were left to rub together, to find their security in greater emphasis on their group identities.

This points to the second major cause of the Shiner outburst. The community of Bytown and Carleton County failed to absorb the Irish and to give them a legitimate place within that community. They were denied economic security; they were the last hired and first fired. Few social organizations made any attempt to reach them, not even the Catholic church. They were rejected by a community which nursed strong anti-Irish prejudices.[92] Members of the "better" classes of Irishmen cast in their lot with the Scots and English gentility, rather than show any interest in the welfare of the Irish masses.[93] The Shiners were outsiders, outside the community-at-large. They formed their own pseudo-community, one at war with the general community. It was a community in that its members shared common sentiments, shared the same animosities. It was a community in that it had social coherence, it was organized with its own leadership. However, the qualifying "pseudo" is necessary, for it lacked a basic requirement of a true community. Its members could not live out their lives within it; they remained dependent upon a larger, outside community for their economic livelihood and for the basic social institutions. Since, in 1835-7, they could not conquer the community-at-large, the Shiners would sooner or later have to come to terms with it.

The initial violence of the Shiners was characteristic of that prevalent in British North America. It often had a "recreational" character, a simple relief from the

---

[92] The prejudice in nineteenth-century England is well described in L. Perry Curtis, Jr., *Apes and Angels: The Irishman in Victorian Caricature* (Washington 1971). For examples in Upper Canadian literature, see Mactaggart, *Three Years in Canada*, II, 242-54; John M'Gregor, *British America* (2 vols. Edinburgh 1833), II, 540; Samuel Strickland, *Twenty-Seven Years in Canada West* (2 vols., London 1853), II, 205.

[93] This was true in many areas of the colonies not only in Bytown. See the comments of Mactaggart, *Three Years in Canada*, II, 254.

frustrations of poverty.[94] And it was largely confined to conflict among the lower orders, rather than to attacks on other classes. For the Irish, the French Canadians were not only rivals for jobs. They were also a weak and identifiable group who could be abused with relative impunity. The Irish, underprivileged themselves, climbed at least a little way up the social ladder by standing on those below them. It was the psychology of the poor white in the American South who found his security in the fact that the black, at least, was below him: he felt what W.J. Cash calls the "... vast ego-warming and ego-expanding distinction between the white man and the black."[95] The anonymous "Chaudiere Letters" published in the Toronto *Globe* in 1856 described the same impulse operating in the Shiners: "'Paddy' at home is a slave; abroad, a task master; in fact he must be groaning under a load of chains, real or imaginary, it little matters which, or else he must have a `Niggar' to wallop. The poor quiet Franco-Canadian, for the time, was Paddy's `Niggar' here...."[96]

Whatever its impetus, internal violence within the lower class was expected and viewed with relative equanimity by the gentle classes of society. The lower orders were assumed to be brutal, prone to violence and disorder, and so long as they exercised their passions on one another, this was simply a fact of life. This was especially true of the Irish. Until the 1830s, then, there was relatively little excitement over evidence of this brutal passion.[97]

When such violence took on an organized nature, and began to threaten the established order or to turn to physical intimidation of the upper classes, it was treated much more seriously. A recent article has suggested that rioting was accepted in early America as an extension of the basic tendencies of democracy.[98] Rioting involved "... those incidents where a number of people group together to enforce their will immediately, by threatening or perpetrating injury to people or property outside of legal procedures but without intending to challenge the general structure of society."[99] In the absence of adequate law enforcement, such activity was accepted, if carried out by the masses, or applauded, if carried out by the respectable. As well as the normal lower-class violence, this definition would embrace the vigilante activities of the Bytown gentility. What was not acceptable, however, was insurrection: "... the uprising of people essentially excluded from political participation," or group criminality: "where people act in defiance rather than alleged

---

[94] On recreational violence, see Charles Tilly, "Collective Violence in European Perspective," in *Violence in America: Historical and Comparative Perspectives*, ed. Hugh David Graham and Ted Robert Gurr (New York 1969), p. 15.

[95] W.J. Cash, *The Mind of the South* (New York 1954), p. 51.

[96] Toronto *Globe*, 11 Dec. 1856.

[97] J. Jerald Bellomo, "Upper Canadian Attitudes Towards Crime and Punishment (1832-1851)," *Ontario History*, LXIV, 1, March 1972, p. 4-3.

[98] David Grimsted, "Rioting in its Jacksonian Setting," *American Historical Review*, LXXVII, 2, April 1972, 397.

[99] Ibid., p. 365.

support of accepted communal standards...."[100] Charles Tilly draws the same sort of distinctions between "communal" violence, the violence on a primitive level of groups interacting naturally, and "associational" violence, a more organized form exercised by groups seeking to improve their position in society.[101]

The Shiners hardened society's resistance against them when they moved from group criminality to insurrection. A similar pattern was evident elsewhere in British North America. The revolutionary activity of 1837 profoundly affected the way in which the upper classes looked at violence, it demonstrated the potential threat to their position. There was a similar preoccupation in the thought of Lord Durham, Lord Sydenham, and Robert Baldwin to establish adequate local governmental institutions as a way to control the violent potential in society. Such feelings were strengthened further by the troubles surrounding the Rebellion Losses Act in 1849, when again the politics of violence became apparent. The governor general, Lord Elgin, expressed a not-untypical reaction: "I confess I did not before know how thin is the crust of order which covers the anarchical elements that boil and toss beneath our feet."[102] It was no coincidence that the 1850s saw the establishment of police forces in many municipalities, and a much less tolerant attitude towards casual violence.

The Shiners accelerated Bytown's movement through these stages, transformed society's attitudes towards violence more rapidly than would otherwise have been the case. For they committed one major crime: they did not accept the comic role cast for them, the role of drunken, brawling Paddy. Instead, faced by a society which would make no room for them, they attempted to use their force to coerce that society into opening itself to them. But the time of the lower orders had not yet come. In the Shiners' War, the ultimate victory of the classes over the masses was a near-inevitability.

---

[100] Ibid.
[101] Tilly, "Collective Violence," pp. 14-16, 38-40.
[102] Sir Arthur G. Doughty, ed., *The Elgin-Grey Papers, 1846-1852* (4 vols., Ottawa 1937), I, Elgin to Grey, 30 April 1849, p. 350.

Political, Economic, and National Conflict in Lower Canada

Section 7

The first four decades of the 19th century seemed filled with conflict in Lower Canada. From the 1805 dispute about taxation till the rebellions of 1837-38, quarrels arose repeatedly between the legislative assembly and the governor, between merchants and landholders, between English and French Canadians. These essays look at two different aspects of the conflict and seem to offer explanations at two different levels.

In studying the opposition between the legislative assembly and the governors, Lawrence Smith looks directly at the reform leaders of the assembly and what they were saying. Where did they get their ideas about what powers an elected assembly should have? Why did their ideas conflict with those of the governor? How could leaders of the *Parti canadien* reconcile their emerging French-Canadian nationalism with their sense of themselves as British subjects? Can we get any help in understanding this from Jaenen's explanation of French sovereignty and Indian nationhood (topic #1)?

While Smith seems to see conflict as emerging from the attempt to work out the Lower Canadian constitution in the light of ideas that were current in the British intellectual world of the early 19th century—ideas about the rights of legislative assemblies, executive power, national self-determination—Fernand Ouellet argues that, underlying all that, other forces were at work: the conflicting interests of economic and social classes. What is the basic social and economic conflict which he sees in Lower Canada? What is his explanation for the origin of French-Canadian nationalism?

How valid are economic explanations for political events, the spread of ideas, or constitutional structures? Must all political and social movements or conflicts be seen as a function of economic interest?

A more complete account of the Lower Canadian conflict and its economic and social context is to be found in Fernand Ouellet, *Lower Canada, 1791-1840*.

Le Canadien and the British Constitution, 1806-1810

Lawrence A.H. Smith

"The English Constitution is...too complex a machine to be at once understood, adopted, and put in motion, by a simple and uninformed people, who have not been accustomed to political disquisitions and abstract reasoning...Rational and genuine freedom is not the child of theory." These words, which have a familiar ring for modern students of the British Empire, were in fact written in 1806 by a visitor to Lower Canada.[1] Hugh Gray's criticisms of the way in which the constitution of 1791 had been working out in the province were certainly not original. Both before and after 1791 there had been many who doubted the wisdom of a sudden grant to a people, used to autocratic rule, of a representative Assembly based on a franchise which was more liberal than even the contemporary British one. And Hugh Gray was merely echoing the feelings of those English-speaking representatives who had, from the very first session of 1791, found themselves in a continual and exasperating minority in an institution which they jealously considered that only they knew how to operate.

With the arrival of Sir James Craig as governor in 1807 the dissatisfied elements found a powerful ally. During his administration a determined effort was made to have the constitution amended or repealed, an effort which culminated in the Ryland mission to England of 1810. One of the arguments which was constantly pressed was that given above—that the French Canadians were ignorant of British constitutional practices and that therefore it was foolish to continue the constitutional experiment. Nor did this reasoning fall on unreceptive ears in England. The Secretary of State, Lord Liverpool, in a candid and friendly private letter to Craig, wrote: "I can assure you that we are all fully convinced of the Evils which have arisen from the Act of 1791, and of the absurdity of attempting to give what is falsely called the British Constitution to a People whose Education, Habits & Prejudices, render them incapable of receiving it."[2]

There were other arguments which Ryland presented to the British Government to build up his case. But this particular one merits closer study. An understanding of the political crisis which developed in the province during Craig's tenure of office depends on an understanding of the way the Assembly was seeking to work the new "British Constitution."

---

[1] Hugh Gray, *Letters from Canada, 1806-1808* (London, 1809), 85.
[2] Add. Mss. 38,323, British Museum, Liverpool Papers, Sept. 11, 1810 (private).

By 1807 the leading figures in the Assembly were a group of French-Canadian lawyers whom Craig described as a "new order of men"[3] and who, because of the declining influence of the seigneurs, had come to dominate the *habitant* members. At first ignorant of and inexperienced in the functioning of representative institutions, they had been developing through practice and study an increasing confidence in their own abilities. Some at least felt a debt to the English members. One was later to refer to them as "ceux qui nous ont montré le chemin, qui nous ont donné les premières idées de la bonne Liberté Britannique."[4] The crisis of 1809 to 1810 revealed how well they had learned their lessons. It would seem that these Canadian lawyers came to understand, adopt, and put in motion the constitutional machinery with amazing speed.[5]

The most useful source for an understanding of their political opinions is *Le Canadien*, the weekly newspaper which they founded in 1806. It is impossible to name accurately all who were instrumental in the production of the paper. Articles in it were usually written in the form of letters to the editor and signed with assumed names such as "Un Spectateur," "L'Ami de la Justice," or "Juvenis." Its founders and writers, however, certainly included Pierre Bédard, Louis Bourdages, J.B. Planté, J.A. Panet, Michel Berthelot, François Blanchet, Louis Borgia, J.T. Taschereau, and P.D. Debartzch.[6] All of these men were either advocates or notaries with the single exception of Blanchet who was a medical practitioner. The first named five were members of the Assembly in 1806 at the time of the founding of *Le Canadien* and the other four had all become members by 1809. Moreover, in 1810 when the presses of the paper were seized by the Executive Council it was discovered that at least three more members of the Assembly were also "proprietors" of the paper—François Huot, François Bellet, and Thomas Lee.[7]

Craig, then, could report with some reason that *Le Canadien* "was supported principally and almost entirely by the...Leaders of the Party."[8] This did not mean that the letters published in *Le Canadien* presented a unified front. There was room for argument. On such matters as the role of commerce in the province there was considerable controversy. A close reading of the paper would indicate that its writers

---

[3]   C.O. 42/136, Craig to Castlereagh, Aug. 4, 1808.
[4]   Address by Pierre Bédard to the electors, *Quebec Gazette*, Nov. 9, 1809.
[5]   For a similar opinion see H.T. Manning, "The Civil List in Lower Canada," *Canadian Historical Review*, XXIV (1943), 47.
[6]   F.J. Audet, "Louis Bourdages," *Proceedings and Transactions of the Royal Society of Canada*, 3d ser., XVIII (1924), sec. I, 87; Audet, "L'Honorable Pierre-Stanislas Bédard," ibid., XX (1926), sec. I, 35-7; Audet, "Joseph-Bernard Planté," ibid., XXVII (1933), sec. I, 139; N.E. Dionne, "Pierre Bédard et son temps," ibid., 2d ser., IV (1898), sec. I, 87-8; I. Caron, "Mgr. Joseph-Octave Plessis," *Le Canada français*, 2d ser., XXVIII (April, 1941), 792; C. Roy, *Nos Origines Littéraires* (Quebec, 1909), 91-5n.
[7]   C.O. 45/47, Minutes of the Executive Council of Lower Canada, March 17 and 19, 1810.
[8]   C.O. 42/136, Craig to Castlereagh, Aug. 5, 1808.

formed a loose intellectual circle rather than a tightly knit organization. Nevertheless, in political and constitutional matters there was a cohesive body of thought being developed within its pages. Here Pierre Bédard was, it would seem, the main influence; he was their deepest thinker and principal writer on such subjects.[9]

As is well known, *Le Canadien* was originally founded by these Lower Canadian lawyers to defend the character of the French Canadians against the malicious attacks of the Quebec *Mercury*.[10] The honour of the French Canadians was to be upheld under the motto of *Fiat Justitia Ruat Coelum*.[11] Soon a bitter counter-attack was launched by the paper against the so-called anti-Canadians who wanted to anglicize the province. This aspect of the newspaper's history is certainly the most famous one. There was, however, another purpose behind the founding of *Le Canadien*. The opening paragraph of its prospectus read: "Il y a déjà longtems que des personnes qui aiment leur pays et leur Gouvernement, regrettent en secret, que le trésor rare que nous possédons dans notre constitution, demeure si longtems caché, faute de l'usage de la liberté de la presse, dont l'office est de répandre la lumière sur toutes ses parties."[12] The inhabitants, then, were to be shown the glories of their new constitution and instructed in the functioning of its various parts. Those who had been teaching themselves were now to become teachers of others.

The first and basic lesson to be propounded was that which had been acted upon in the first provincial Parliament—that the intention of the King and the Imperial Parliament, in granting an Assembly, had been to give "une Grande Majorité aux Canadiens dans le Bas-Canada" so that they might be protected from the tyranny of their political opponents; and the speeches of Pitt, Fox and Burke, carefully extracted, were given to prove the point.[13] From this there followed a somewhat surprising interpretation.[14] The Assembly had been given not to an alien population but to new subjects who were just as British as any group in the United Kingdom. "Tous les habitants de la province ne sont ils pas Sujets Britanniques? Les Anglois ici ne doivent pas plus avoir le titre d'Anglois, que les Canadiens celui de François. Ne serons nous jamais connus comme un Peuple, comme Américains

---

[9] N.E. Dionne, *Pierre Bédard et ses fils* (Quebec, 1909), 78.

[10] This aspect of the paper has been described in A. Faucher, "*Le Canadien* upon the Defensive 1806-1810," *Canadian Historical Review*, XXVIII (1947), 249-65.

[11] The motto "Notre langue, nos institutions et nos lois" has often been wrongly attributed to this period.

[12] *Le Canadien*, Nov. 13, 1806.

[13] Ibid., Dec. 6, 1806.

[14] i.e. surprising as compared to the withdrawal into the shell of nationalism which took place at a later period, but not surprising for the time. See Mansfield's propositions in *Campbell v. Hall* (1774): "conquered inhabitants...become subjects; and are universally to be considered in that light, not as enemies or aliens...An Englishman in...the plantations has no privilege distinct from the natives while he continues there:" V. Harlow and F. Madden, *British Colonial Developments 1774-1834* (Oxford, 1953), 78.

Britanniques?"[15] A French-Canadian representative, on being elected, could compliment the electors on being "dignes de porter le titre glorieux de libres sujets Britanniques."[16] England was even referred to as "la mère-patrie."[17]

These assertions did not mean that *Le Canadien* wanted to see the Canadian character of the province in any way reduced; its attack on the anti-Canadians was maintained. What it did mean was that the constitution, by allowing a majority to the French Canadians in the Assembly, allowed it to a people who were no different from the Scots or Irish or English within the Empire. "Croyez-vous qu'un Irlandois fut coupable de haute trahison, s'il engageoit ses compatriotes à choisir plutôt un de leurs qu'un Ecossais de Perth...?" Why then, it was argued, did the "English" in the province maintain that colonies should be ruled by the English? Whom did they mean? Just the English? Or the Scots too? And if the Scots, then why not the French Canadians as well.[18]

Granted, therefore, that the Canadians should hold both by reason and law a majority in the Assembly, it had to be shown how this Assembly as a British institution was supposed to function within the constitution. Here the writers in *Le Canadien* were on rather difficult ground. An appeal could not be made to the Act of 1791 because it contained almost nothing descriptive of the role of the lower House. Nor had there been time to build up much constitutional precedent within the colony. Consequently lessons about its functioning had to be drawn from overseas, particularly England. And this meant that these Canadian lawyers, if they were not to be laughed to scorn by the English-born residents who believed that only they knew how the English constitution worked, had to buttress up every argument with incontestable authority. There can be little doubt that they, in their admiration for the new constitution, had made a deep study of the British political tradition so that they might be able to grasp the opportunities offered by representative government.

These "authorities" were no doubt carefully selected. References in *Le Canadien* were made to those which best backed up the political ideas of the Canadian lawyers. It would seem, however, that these sources simultaneously had a profound influence in moulding their thinking. Roughly three strands can be separated in an examination of these overseas influences: there were the individual figures representing the liberal tradition in British politics; there was the entire body of precedents and usages of the British constitution; and lastly there were the political theorists.

The first of these sources was of no distinguishable importance to *Le Canadien*. Such figures might illuminate what was considered to be the freedom and the great tradition of the British constitution, but they could not be of much use to a group of lawyers who were seeking to give legal proof to their assertions. Consequently no references were made in their paper either to English radicalism or to the movement

---

[15] *Le Canadien*, Nov. 22, 1806; also July 9, 1808.
[16] François Huot to the electors of Hampshire, *Quebec Gazette*, Nov. 9, 1809.
[17] *Le Canadien*, Sept. 23, Nov. 11, 1809.
[18] Ibid., July 9, 1808, Dec. 30, 1809.

for reform in the Imperial Parliament. Moreover, it must be remembered that the writers of the paper were always anxious that it should be well received in England. They knew full well that their enemies would immediately raise before the British Government any "passages malheureux" which might be printed.[19] They did not want to be portrayed as radicals out to change things but as respectable constitutionalists with conservative purposes. Charles James Fox, however, seems to have been taken to their hearts. Generous, flamboyant, passionate, and with an intense love of freedom, he touched a chord in the hearts of the young Canadian lawyers which made him appear "une véritable illusion." He, above all others, merited a special place in their publication.[20]

The laws and precedents of the English constitution were a much more important source of authority. A question of privilege in the Assembly often resulted in the appointment of a committee to search in the Journals of the British House of Commons for cases as similar as possible to the question under discussion.[21] Such cases could not be gainsaid. (Political opponents might maintain that British parliamentary privileges did not exist in Lower Canada, but there were few of the English party in the lower House who were willing to go to that length.) As a result, coupled with the lawyers' insistence that the "Canadian" character of the Assembly had to be preserved, there developed an equally strong desire to make the institution as "British" as possible in powers and privileges.

This stratagem had been acted upon since 1792. J.A. Panet, as speaker in the first Assembly, laid claim on behalf of the House to "the freedom of speech, and generally all the like privileges and liberties as are enjoyed by the Commons of Great Britain." Such a claim was not new in the Empire. In 1815, when Lord Bathurst asked the Law Officers of the Crown whether the Assemblies of the two Canadas had a right to such privileges, they replied that the claim had been previously made by other colonial assemblies but had never been recognized. Since the Act of 1791 had not delineated specific privileges to the Canadian lower House, they continued, those they possessed were "confined to such only as are directly and indispensably necessary to enable them to perform the functions with which they are invested, and therefore may be fairly said to be incidental to their constitution." In Lower Canada the representatives of the Crown had replied in this limited spirit from the beginning. Lieutenant-Governor Clarke had replied to Panet that the Assembly could depend on "the full exercise and enjoyment of all just Rights and Lawful Privileges."[22] The terms just and lawful thus came to have different meanings for the Assembly and for

---

[19] Ibid., March 14, 1810.

[20] Ibid., April 25, 1807, July 30, 1808. *Le Canadien* was fully aware of Fox's attitude towards the Act of 1791.

[21] See, for example, *Journals of the Legislative Assembly of Lower Canada*, Feb. 16, 29, 1808. (Referred to hereafter as *Journals of the Assembly*.)

[22] A.G. Doughty and D.A. McArthur, eds., *Documents relating to the Constitutional History of Canada, 1791-1818* (Ottawa, 1914), 162 n., 480-3.

the Government. The former continued to see itself as a replica House of Commons, while the latter tended to see differences but avoid any clear definition of what was "incidental" to the Constitutional Act.

Such theoretical problems, however, had been worked out in response to specific problems as they rose. By the time of the founding of *Le Canadien* the lower House had already had many of the demanded privileges confirmed, including freedom of debate, freedom from arrest in civil cases for members, the right of regulating internal proceedings, the right of initiating all revenue bills, taxes, and grants, the power of expelling members by resolution, the power to commit for acts of contempt of the Assembly or for attempts to "intermeddle" in the House.

Following the establishment of *Le Canadien*, the Canadian lawyers were able to appeal to British precedents in a way they could not do before. They were able, for example, to defend the privileges of the House even when it was not sitting. When, in March, 1809, Craig gave only twenty-six days notice of the summoning of Parliament,[23] *Le Canadien* announced to its readers that the Lower Canadian legislature should be entitled to the same privilege as its British counterpart and that therefore notice should be given at least forty days before the date fixed unless there were pressing circumstances. It went on to warn that in England such an abuse of prerogative could result in the impeachment of the ministers who had advised such a course.[24] When, in June, 1809, it was felt that the administration was trying to exercise an undue influence in the Assembly and over elections, *Le Canadien* published in bold capitals across the top of the front page an extract from the Bill of Rights:

> QUE L'ELECTION DES MEMBRES DU PARLEMENT DOIT ETRE LIBRE: QUE LA LIBERTE DE LA PAROLE ET DES DEBATS OU DES PROCEDURES EN PARLEMENT, NE DOIT ETRE SUJETTE A AUCUNE ACCUSATION, NI A ETRE MISE EN QUESTION DANS AUCUNE COUR, OU DANS AUCUN LIEU HORS LE PARLEMENT.[25]

Hatsell's *Precedents*,[26] too, was quickly adopted as an authority and a guide book to parliamentary procedure and privilege. It was already in the legislative library and the Assembly voted in 1806 to have it translated into French so as to be easier to read for the members.[27] In *Le Canadien*, moreover, it was used to cite British examples for political arguments advanced by the writers.[28]

---

[23] On March 14 Craig announced that the session would convene on April 10.
[24] *Le Canadien*, March 25, April 1, 1809.
[25] Ibid., June 3, 1809. This remained part of the masthead in the following issues.
[26] J. Hatsell, *Precedents of Proceedings in the House of Commons* (4 vols.; london, 1796).
[27] *Journals of the Assembly*, April 1, 1806.
[28] Dec. 27, 1806, March 25, 1809.

All these different lessons imported from England explained how the constitution actually worked, not what it ought to be. The political theory to which the leaders of the Assembly looked was of the same nature. Again the desire to preserve respectability and legality made them shun all radical political thinkers—at least in public utterance. They wrote no abstract theories about the rights of man, or social contracts, or utopian forms of government. They proclaimed to all that the constitution under which they lived was already the epitome of wisdom and freedom, "un trésor rare."[29] Sir William Blackstone and J.L. DeLolme suited their needs perfectly: the *Commentaries on the Laws of England* and the *Constitution of England* were considered to be practical guides for the student of politics. These works analyzing and explaining the working of the constitution while praising it had a wide acceptance in contemporary England. *Le Canadien* treated John Locke in the same analytical fashion. It shunned his theories about natural law and contract and concentrated on his closely reasoned arguments which sought to justify the Revolutionary Settlement and to expound the rule of law and toleration. All three of these authors were constantly used as references in *Le Canadien*, together with the sources previously mentioned, to illustrate the important functions of the lower House and the independence which was therefore necessary for it.[30]

> Ils [Blackstone and Locke] montrent que le pouvoir exécutif n'a le droit d'exercer aucune censure sur les branches de la législature; que le pouvoir exécutif, comme tel, est inférieur au pouvoir législatif, et que comme étant une des branches de la législature, quoique la première en rang et en dignité, les autres branches ne sont aucunement dans sa dépendance."[31]

The extent to which such English sources could be used to illuminate the Canadian constitution, can be seen in the issue of June 3, 1809. This edition contained the above translation from the Bill of Rights; a long section from Rapin's *History of England* wherein the author had shown that James II's flight had been due to bad councillors and judges and attempts to influence elections (all an indirect commentary on Craig's actions); extracts from chapters two and seven of the first volume of Blackstone's *Commentaries* in which the author discussed election writs and the limits to royal prerogative; part of chapter twelve of Locke's second *treatise of Civil Government* which discussed the supremacy of the legislative power; comments by the editor on all this; and a stirring translation of "Rule Britannia." It was an exceptional edition and was caused by the Governor's angry dissolution of Parliament

---

29 *Le Canadien*, Nov. 13, 1806.
30 See, for example, the issues of Jan. 31, 1807; June 25, July 2, 9, 16, 23, 1808; March 25, June 3, 24, July 29, Sept. 23, 1809. DeLolme was extensively quoted to show the role of a free press in the constitution.
31 *Le Canadien*, June 3, 1809.

two weeks earlier, but it does show how in times of censure the French-Canadian lawyers immediately looked to British precedents to substantiate their own position. This process was straightforward in matters of privilege and function. But in using Blackstone and DeLolme to prove the necessity of free elections or an independent House, the Canadian lawyers adopted more than a guide book which would give them "une idée du pouvoir et des privilèges de notre Parlement Provincial;"[32] they also inherited a political philosophy. What has been described as "the real keynote of Blackstone and DeLolme"[33] was the Montesquieu interpretation of the division and balance of powers within the British constitution. Both Blackstone and DeLolme saw the secret of political freedom as resting in a constitutional equilibrium, in a mechanical balance of power within the state. In the former this point was clearly made:

> And herein indeed consists the true excellence of the English Government, that all the parts of it form a mutual check upon each other...Thus every branch of our civil policy supports and is supported, regulates and is regulated, by the rest: for the two houses naturally drawing in two directions of opposite interest, and the prerogative in another still different from them both, they mutually keep each other from exceeding their proper limits...Like three distinct powers in mechanics, they jointly impel the machine of government in a direction...partaking of each, and formed out of all; a direction which constitutes the true line of liberty and happiness of the community.[34]

DeLolme elaborated this idea to an even greater length. His work was an exposition of how this process of check and counter-balance had made Britain a place where "Liberty has at last been able to erect herself a Temple."[35]

Now the Act of 1791, by dividing the Executive and Legislative Councils for the first time in colonial history, and by creating an Assembly, made possible the belief that the constitutions of the two Canadas had been modelled on that of Great Britain.[36] As a result an attempt was made in Lower Canada, as it had been in the United States, to apply a formula for liberty and stability which had descended from Montesquieu. Political theorists such as Pierre Bédard did not maintain that the Canadian constitution was an exact copy of the English one. It was admitted that the Governor, although the representative of the King, had only a shadow of his prerogative right, and that the Legislative Council had none of the judicial power of the Lords. But these differences were seen to lie mainly in the upper two-thirds of

---

[32] Ibid., Sept. 23, 1809.
[33] J.H. Laski, *Political Thought in England from Locke to Bentham* (London, 1927), 128.
[34] *Commentaries on the Laws of England* (9th ed., London, 1783), I, 154-5.
[35] *The Constitution of England* (London, 1775), 446.
[36] *Le Canadien*, Sept. 23, 1809.

Parliament, not in the Assembly, whose powers and privileges were similar to those of the Commons. How far this similarity extended was regarded as "une question abstraite sur laquelle il ne pouvoit être donné de décision." In a colonial assembly, as in the House of Commons, the extent of powers and privileges had to be kept indefinite so as to be kept flexible and able to meet changing circumstances; "on décide sur chaque cas particulier à mesure qu'il se présente, et cela est suffisant."[37]

In applying the British parliamentary model to the Canadian constitution, therefore, the popular leaders were chiefly concerned with how it affected the role of the Assembly. And the differences between institutions did not stop them from applying the Blackstone-DeLolme theories of equilibrium to Lower Canada. To Bédard, the province enjoyed "une Constitution où tout le monde est à sa place." The Assembly had to be independent of the other branches of the legislature in order to protect the rights of the people against any abuse of prerogative by the representative of the King, and in order to preserve the equilibrium. "C'est qu'il existe un équilibre tellement ménagé entre les droits du peuple et les siens, que s'il va au delà des bornes que la constitution lui a assignées, ou s'il fait de son autorité un usage inutile, le peuple a un moyen sûr et juste de l'arrêter dans sa marche."[38]

In legislative matters the balance was easy to perceive: the Assembly, Legislative Council, and Governor corresponded to the three parallel parts of the Imperial legislature and each could exercise the necessary checks on the other two in the passing of bills. The maintenance of the perfect equipoise, however, demanded that the Houses should be constantly on the watch to resist encroachment by the royal prerogative, for it was argued that if the executive branch gained any degree of control over the legislative Houses, then their power would be lessened and the equilibrium destroyed. Such pure theory corresponded to the actual conditions no more in Canada than it did in England. It was an essential part of the working of the eighteenth-century constitution that the King should be able to aid his ministers to gain and maintain a majority in the Commons. But the theory was a useful one for the popular leaders in Lower Canada to put forward, for it showed that if an independent Assembly was a necessary part of the constitution then it was also implicit in the 1791 Act, and hence had a legal basis. Thus for example in 1809 Bédard and Blanchet succeeded in passing a resolution in the Assembly "that every attempt of the Executive Government, and of the other branches of the Legislature, against this House, whether in dictating or censuring its proceedings...is a violation of the Statute by which this House is constituted; a breach of the privileges of this House against which it cannot forbear objecting..."[39]

From this theory of checks and counter-checks, there also sprang another belief of the Canadian lawyers in the Assembly. Blackstone and DeLolme in pointing out that the

---

[37] Ibid., June 24, 1809. N.E. Dionne (*Bédard et ses fils*, 98 ff) definitely attributed these words to Bédard.
[38] Ibid., Nov. 4, 1809.
[39] *Journals of the Assembly*, Feb. 3, 1809.

balance of the constitution could only be preserved if the executive was kept within due limits had also pointed out the proper method of doing so: "And this executive power is again checked and kept within due bounds by the two houses, through the privileges they have of inquiring into, impeaching, and punishing the conduct (not indeed of the King, which would destroy his constitutional independence; but which is more beneficial to the public) of his evil and pernicious counsellors."[40] In a similar fashion DeLolme had shown that censurable acts of the King were always to be considered as "the faults of his Ministers, or in general of those who advised him."[41] The French-Canadian leaders in the Assembly were thus faced with the problem of how the idea of the King's ministers in England was to be fitted into the parallel constitution of Lower Canada. And to *Le Canadien* it thus became a logical necessity that there had to be a ministry in the province.[42] It did not maintain that a ministry had been set up in 1791, but rather that it was implicit in the nature of the constitution. To those who replied that this maxim was ridiculous, that the Governor took his directions from England and could act without advice, *Le Canadien* retorted that such an interpretation would deprive the Canadians of an exercise of their constitutional rights.

> Car s'il est vrai (comme on ne sauroit nier) que la Personne du Représentant du Roi doive être sacrée et inviolable ici, comme l'est la personne même du Roi en Angleterre; dire que c'est le Représentant du Roi qui fait tout ici, c'est ôter aux Canadiens le droit d'examiner les actes publics du Gouvernement. A quoi leur sert alors la part qu'ils ont dans la Législation, si on leur ôte le moyen de connoître les abus auxquels il y'auroit à remédier par cette législature?

And appeals were made to both Blackstone and DeLolme in an effort to prove the point.[43]

In the Assembly, too, the lawyers put forward a strong argument of a similar nature. On April 15, 1809, when the House was drafting its return address to the Governor, Bédard and Bourdages acted together in an effort to censure the Governor's advisers. Bourdages's speech, in support of his amendment to the address, was very much in the Blackstone tradition. He first pointed out how essential it was for the Assembly to preserve its independence against attempts from above to dominate it. If one adopted, he went on, the sentiment of those who said there was no ministry in the country, then only two courses of action would be possible: either the Assembly would have to give up all hope of examining executive action, or else it would have

---

[40] Blackstone, *Commentaries*, I, 155.
[41] DeLolme, *the Constitution of England*, 436-7.
[42] The idea of a ministry received early treatment in *Le Canadien*, as, for example, in the issue of Jan. 31, 1807.
[43] *Le Canadien*, June 25, July 16, 1808.

to adopt the monstrous idea of rebuking the Governor himself, the fixture who represented in the Canadian constitution "la personne sacrée" of the King. Neither of these courses was possible. Therefore, his argument was reported to continue,"...cette idée du ministère, n'étoit pas un vain nom...mais une idée essentielle à la conservation de notre constitution."[44]

The logic of these reasoning processes in *Le Canadien* and in the Assembly which sought to prove the actual existence of a ministry through the logical necessity of a ministry is somewhat open to criticism, to say the least. Moreover, many contemporaries such as Sir James Craig viewed these arguments as little but hypocritical and dangerous clamour whereby these men wanted to force their way into office: "They either believe, or affect to believe, that there exists a Ministry here and that, in imitation of the Constitution of Britain, that Ministry is responsible to them for the Conduct of Government. It is not necessary to point out to your Lordship the steps to which such an Idea may lead them."[45] Without doubt desire for office was a strong motivating factor in the minds of the lawyers. In his speech Bourdages had gone on to show that Craig would have to change his advisers before he could become acquainted with the feelings of the inhabitants. Nevertheless, these arguments which attempted to prove the need for, or rather the existence of, a ministry in Lower Canada, do represent a serious and sincere attempt to use British traditions in order to adapt the 1791 constitution to local conditions and to make it workable. One would have to strain to see in them a precursor of responsible government. It was never implied that the Governor could not choose his advisers completely as he pleased nor that they had to have the confidence of the House. Nor was it implied that they should have a collective responsibility. The theory was a legal one, that the advisers of the Governor should not remain concealed and that they should be subject to the censure of the Houses in order to prevent abuse and maintain the balance of the constitution. In short there simply had to be someone whom the Assembly could blame for executive actions, not where the legitimate use of prerogative was concerned, but where the supposed privileges and powers of the Assembly were invaded.

As it has been seen, the basis of the constitutional theory and practice of the lawyers was English in origin. From England also came indirect influences as reflected from and modified by other parts of the Empire. In their search for lessons which could teach them how to work parliamentary institutions, the French-Canadian lawyers had not been content to look to the metropolis only.

In 1811 the library committee of the Assembly made a very interesting report to the House. It advised the purchase of, among other publications, Hume's *Essay on*

---

44   Speech of April 15, 1809, reported in *Le Canadien*, April 26, 1809. (This speech has been attributed to Bédard, but it seems clear from the account that it was made by Bourdages.)

45   C.O. 42/136, Craig to Castlereagh, Aug. 5, 1808. The passage is quoted in W.P.M. Kennedy, *Documents of the Canadian Constitution 1759-1915* (Toronto, 1918), 250, with a slight variation in text.

Taxation, Locke's *On Civil Government*, Bentham's *Principles of Legislation*, Cobbett's *Parliamentary History* and *Parliamentary Debates*, and the statutes and journals of the assemblies of Upper Canada, Jamaica, Barbados, New Brunswick, New York, and Nova Scotia.[46] As already shown above, works like those of Hume and Bentham were not well suited for the use to which the writers of *Le Canadien* wanted to put their documentary sources; they dealt too much with principles or theory and not enough with legal analysis or precedent. Consequently they could not be used publicly as authorities and the extent to which they influenced the minds of the lawyers is impossible to estimate.

But in the case of the statutes and journals of other colonies in the Empire, such objections did not exist. In fact the use which older colonies had made of representative government could be, and was, a valuable lesson. As a result, more than rum was imported from the West Indies. The conflict between the Assembly and Governor of Jamaica, which developed in 1808 following the insurrection in May of that year, was watched closely in *Le Canadien*. It published at great length the proceedings of the Jamaican Assembly and its claims to the same privileges and powers as the House of Commons, particularly to the right of investigating all acts prejudicial to the public safety and of summoning before its bar all military and civil personnel save only the Governor.[47] When it was learned in Lower Canada four months later that the Duke of Manchester had been instructed from England to take conciliatory action concerning the Jamaican Assembly, *Le Canadien* published a long article in which the lessons for Lower Canada were clearly drawn. It quoted the *New Scotsman* to show that public and official opinion in England had viewed the actions of the Jamaican Assembly as being perfectly constitutional and correct in spite of the Governor's prorogation. Such an example, then, should be a spur to the timid in the Lower Canadian Assembly. "En confrontant les résolutions de la chambre d'assemblée de la Jamaïque, qui ont été approuvées en Angleterre, avec celles de la Chambre d'assemblée du Bas-Canada, on verra si la chambre du Bas-Canada a été à la moitié des prétensions de celle de la Jamaïque."[48]

The mere amount of documentary reference in *Le Canadien* to overseas precedents and political thinkers does not and can not prove motivation. All that can be seen is that the French-Canadian lawyers who controlled the majority in the Assembly looked both directly and indirectly to Great Britain to see how the constitution should run. It would seem that the influence was deep. It must not be forgotten, however, that these were war years. The French-Canadians, under suspicion of treason and disloyalty by many of their political opponents, and therefore anxious to show their attachment to the government, would undoubtedly have used as many "British" ideas

---

[46] *Journals of the Assembly*, March 8, 1811.
[47] *Le Canadien*, Feb. 18, 1809.
[48] Ibid., June 24, 1809. Significantly, lessons were also drawn from Jamaica in the issue of July 1, 1809; from Bermuda in that of May 13, 1809; from the former Massachusetts Bay in that of June 24, 1809.

as did not endanger their way of life. Moreover, the years of war with France were accompanied by years of near-war with the United States. Sympathetic references to the constitutional history of either of these countries would have led to the immediate accusation of treason. As a result, the political idealism which led to revolution in both these countries, and which one might expect would have had a profound effect in Lower Canada (through reasons of race, language, and geographic proximity) could never be openly expressed by the young intellectuals. That there was influence to some degree from France and the United States cannot be doubted. It is possible to see traces of Voltaire even in *Le Canadien*.[49] And the story has been told of a captured French ship, containing books by eighteenth-century French writers, being brought into Quebec and its cargo sold to the eager population before the Catholic Church authorities could stop the sale.[50] Then too the provincial executive was always worried about the number of youths who were going to the United States for their education where they were suspected of picking up "pernicious principles."[51] François Blanchet, for example, who had studied medicine at Columbia College, was reported by Craig to have returned with "principles of the purest democracy."[52]

Although the revolutionary traditions of France and the United States can be expected to have made some impression on the Canadian intellectuals, it must be remembered that the English constitution in the eighteenth century was viewed by most of the world as a marvel of reason and freedom. This admiration seems to have been inherited by the Canadian lawyers. It would certainly not have been greatly damaged through a perusal of Montesquieu or Diderot or Voltaire. A deep mistrust might have come from the United States, but the French Canadians felt no great kinship with their southern neighbours. consequently, so long as a Pierre Bédard believed that British constitutional practice could be successfully applied to Lower Canada, he had little need to look to other solutions. To him French rule was a time when a governor was "un homme devant lequelle il n'étoit pas permis de lever la tête." But this was no more; the new constitution was something "dans laquelle un homme est quelque chose."[53]

These visions of liberty and freedom depended, as has been seen, on the theory that British precedents could be applied to the working of the Lower Canadian constitution. It should be remembered, however, that the arguments had not been developed in a vacuum; they had been awakened and asserted in response to the challenge of specific problems and opposing political tenets. The crisis during Craig's administration can be viewed as a time of testing for these beliefs, as a time

---

[49] M. Trudel, *L'Influence de Voltaire au Canada* (Montreal, 1945), I, 74-7.
[50] I. Caron, *La Colonisation de la Province de Québec — Les Cantons de l'Est 1791-1815* (Quebec, 1927), 300.
[51] C.O. 42/127, Milnes to Camden, July 4, 1805.
[52] C.O. 42/141, Craig to Bunbury, Feb. 21, 1810.
[53] *Le Canadien*, Nov. 4, 1809.

when the Canadian leaders in the Assembly first came to grips with the questions left unanswered in 1791 and looked to the example of the British constitution in order to formulate solutions. To their tory opponents, the application of the kind of British constitutional precedents propounded in *Le Canadien* implied the loss, not the saving, of the colony; they wished to see their own brand of British precedents applied. Thus, on many occasions, the conflict took the form of one between two different types of British "assimilation." The fact that personal interest had a great deal to do with the type of assimilation proposed did not lessen the importance of the constitutional struggle. It was a story which was to be told many times over in the ensuing twenty-five years as the extremes grew further apart and the accusations of self-interest grew more shrill.

French-Canadian Nationalism: From its Origins to the Insurrection of 1837

Fernand Ouellet

"Le nationalism canadien-français; de ses origines à l'insurrection de 1837." Reprinted from The Canadian Historical Review 45, December 1964, by permission of the author and University of Toronto Press.

Seen in terms of the traditional and even the neo-nationalist historiography, the problem of the sources of French-Canadian nationalism is one of the easiest we could consider. Indeed, Quebec's nationalist historians have argued the necessity of a national framework in any collective life. So they have confidently insisted that French-Canadian nationalism made its appearance with the founding of New France itself. Little challenged until recently, though highly challengeable, the thesis is clearly explained in Guy Frégault's *La Civilisation de la Nouvelle-France*. This historian holds that, beginning in the seventeenth century, the inhabitants of the St. Lawrence Valley had an awareness of "ethnic individuality," and, a century afterwards, truly possessed "a national consciousness." The real significance of this view is readily seen. Here, in basic outline, are the "tragedy of the Conquest" and its disastrous sequel.

In the very wake of Conquest, so far as most of the nationalist historians are concerned, the struggle for survival began, never to cease; for others, meanwhile, the same conquest ushered in an age of great decline and emasculating compromises. Formed on past triumphs and ancestral ties, the vision of Canon Groulx focuses on the struggle for *la survivance* [national survival] and the equally glorious battleground of the constitution. "As previously," he writes, "the history of the Canadian people [after 1760] would call for determined flexing, continual outstripping." On the other hand, Michel Brunet, rejecting the "vainglory of the past," comes to another view of the cataclysm of conquest, which, he claims, by cutting off the bourgeois head of the French-Canadian nation, doomed that young nationality to inferiority and degeneration. For Brunet and Séguin, this social mutilation was the thing that reduced French Canada to slavery; severing all contacts with the old motherland, the tragedy of the Conquest traumatized the still delicate Canadian nationality. If we were not dealing with pure symbolism, we might suitably raise a few questions about this excessive vulnerability in so feeble an adolescent.... And so in spite of appreciable differences between Canon Groulx's reassuring position and Michel Brunet's pessimism, they do share a common starting point: the existence before 1760 of a French-Canadian nationality. The whole of their interpretation of Canada's history logically flows from this initial observation and from their special idea of the nature of this nationality.

These interpretations have undoubtedly had the merit of awakening feelings and thus reaching people's minds. But do they reflect reality? Is emotional content a guarantee of their truthfulness? Long before me, historians have suspected not. I must say that my researches prompt me to share their uneasiness.

French-Canadian Nationalism in the Eighteenth Century: Myth or Projection?

The positing of a nationality in New France depends on an extremely thin and, in my opinion, highly unsatisfactory case, one which I think is more the product of the historian's mind than of strong evidence. Admittedly, the Canadian society of that time was not a mirror image of the mother country, and showed some original qualities; the admission is all the more easily made in that local conditions strongly affected the growing social organization. Yet even when they are given ready-made models and set out to imitate them, colonial societies never end up as exact replicas of their mother countries. Economic and geographical conditions, not to mention the free will of men, call for adaptation of any models. If as a result, the Canadians of the French regime developed attitudes that were in many respects different from those of the metropolitan French, and there were even instances of misunderstanding and actual strong opposition, this still does not necessarily produce a national sentiment. In other circumstances and in more recent times all this could have helped build a national consciousness; such was not the case in the French regime.

The population of New France was not yet aware of national principles. Its beliefs, aspirations, interests and even its weaknesses were not such as to move it in that direction. In economic terms, its dependence on France was total. The fur trade and military commitments bound the colony utterly to the motherland. Mercantilism was the philosophical background of these economic relations, and it was accepted then without restriction. Were it not that we are aware of the anaemic state of the local middle class, we should be surprised at the absence of pressure for more flexibility in the colonial system. Certainly that lower bourgeoisie experienced some frustration at the omnipotence of metropolitan merchants who dominated exchanges between France and Canada, but they lacked both the strength to assert themselves and the energy to raise objection. No real effort was made to argue the colony's own interests, even less the interests of the nation, against those of the mother country.

New France was dependent on the mother country not only from the economic viewpoint. It also needed France constantly in terms of military strength. Trade rivalries with New England, along with conflicts in Europe, meant almost unrelieved danger for the St. Lawrence Valley. There is no reason for astonishment, then, to find the colony fully appreciative of the protection owed it by the mother country. For this was no simple guarantee that could be altered according to circumstances; French military support was an essential component of the colonial system and the imperial philosophy.

In terms of politics and society, moreover, these relations were more intimate and penetrating still. The values uniting the individual citizenry were always synthesized around the monarchical ideal. And in itself this feeling had no national quality; loyalty to the monarch, with its sources in religion and politics, went beyond national membership. The inhabitant of New France shared in this value system to the fullest, all the more so in that his situation left him no choice. His social organization and his social beliefs, without exactly mirroring those of the motherland, were to some extent taken from them.

In spite of the deep affinities and ties that bound the man of the St. Lawrence to old France, then, he had affiliations within himself that could soften the blow that could come with a change of rule. As his world implied the necessary presence of a metropolitan country and a monarchy, the inhabitant of New France could have quickly adapted to the new situation. Moreover the scandals of the close of the French regime, with a deep longing for order and peace, aided the transition a great deal. The clear and understanding approach of the military commanders worked to the same end. We must not think, however, that the change in allegiance cancelled all the past without a trace; fear persisted among the farming people, particularly the fear of deportation, which we encounter again in 1775. Nonetheless, on the whole the Conquest was not the source of a trauma that can explain all the difficulties French-Canadian society would have to endure afterwards. The fact is that the economic, political, social, and judicial structures remained stable at least until 1791, so that the Conquest produced no basic change in the life of someone living in the St. Lawrence Valley. By getting rid of the profiteers of the old regime, it even brought clarification to a number of personal affairs and soothed a number of businessmen. The memorandum presented by the French-Canadian business community in 1765 proves not only their permanent awareness of the old values, but also the wholly healthy nature of their reactions to the new regime and the tasks before them. In the wake of 1760, the man of New France was not someone whose psychological forces were destroyed and whose only future was servitude. Profitable prospects lay before him; many choices were implicit in the challenges that confronted him. His destiny was, then, linked to the quality of his response.

In these circumstances, it has hard to explain why the Conquest should have launched either the famous struggle for survival or else the decline of French-Canadian society. Between 1760 and 1791, conflicts existed, but they had nothing to do with nationality. They were simply social, and set governors, civil servants, and seigneurs of all national origins at odds with the trading classes. At that time, the basic rift was not yet ethnic, but social. Professor Creighton has amply demonstrated this. For Professor Lower, however, these conflicts were of a more general kind. They originated in the varying concepts of French Canadians and Britons as to individual and collective life. The cultural variants were already occasioning misunderstandings that were liable, given suitable circumstances, to produce a conscious nationalism. These two complementary points of view, in my opinion, constitute a valid but in some respects incomplete approach to the problem of the sources of French-Canadian nationalism.

The fact is that the nationalist interpretation lives only on abstractions and projections; it is based on facts whose meaning is inadvertently exaggerated and distorted. Thus, the policy expressed in the Royal Proclamation of 1763 is held to be the main event that stimulated the defensive reflexes of the elites of the French-Canadian nation. From that time on, the clergy and seigneurs are supposed to have assumed leadership of the masses in the battle for survival and, thanks to support from good governors, obliged the London leaders to alter their position. This conception errs on the real meaning of the policy adopted in 1763, and also confuses traditionalism and nationalism, while being in obvious error as to the contemporary situation.

The policy the English leaders tried to install in 1763 had not been worked out with the aim of placing a French-Canadian majority in submission to a British minority. At the beginning, it was based rather on a dual expectation: its promoters believed that the new regime would usher in an unprecedented age of prosperity which, in a few years, would produce a society of the "mercantile" type, dominated by the bourgeoisie; moreover, they were persuaded that with the aid of new institutions and a new economic context, the colony would see massive immigration that would quickly give numerical preponderance to the British. These expectations were more dream than reality. It was very soon seen that the situation was quite different. In this sense, the crisis of 1765-66 had a salutary effect. Leaders in government and in many other areas realized that in the short term there was no major change to be expected in the economic pattern. As for immigration, a few years showed how unpromising that was.

This situation, unfavourable for assimilation, meant that the new regime would have to rely on the French-Canadian majority, with its social framework and institutions, particularly from the time when revolutionary agitation appeared in New England. In a sense, this situation validated the functions that had been assumed by the traditional elites, the seigneurie and the Coutume de Paris. There could no longer be any question of imposing on the French Canadians institutions that corresponded to the ambitions of the capitalist bourgeoisie and the British tradition. It is not difficult to understand why the 1763 policy was barely installed before it began to disintegrate. From this viewpoint, the Quebec Act seems like the consecration of this trend and not the herald of a new order. Towards 1780, Haldimand would write with conviction, "The Canadians are the people of this country...." By this he meant that the policy followed after 1765 always respected the economic, social and demographic realities.

It is perfectly obvious that this situation was not suitable for the blooming of a national consciousness, still less of a nationalist reaction, among the French Canadians. On the contrary, the elites grew more and more attached to a regime that stood by monarchical and aristocratic values, a regime that fully respected their religious convictions. Buttressed by the government-employed bourgeoisie, the seigneurs were not afraid to show open contempt for the businessmen, and even nourished some hope of seeing their old privileges restored. As for the farming folk, who had seemed to accept the new regime with a good grace, they showed a remarkable absence of zeal at the time of the American invasion of 1775. In this habitant passivity the nationalist historians have discerned a sure sign of nationalist-type reaction. In fact the farmers' attitude is easily understood without our having to invoke national feeling. Moreover, nothing was heard from them at this point. The factors best explaining the behaviour of the farming folk were a new concept of military service, the hope of profit, the fear of deportation—a flame that was fanned joyfully by the American emissaries—and memory of general exploitation during the Seven Years' War.

Post-conquest rural society in French Canada was still a colonial society that had not learned to define itself otherwise than in terms of the mother country. In spite of distinctions between "old" and "new" subjects, there were new alignments that to some extent replaced the alignments which had been lost. Agriculture tended to be conditioned by the imperial markets. Farmers benefited from this, and thus, through actual contact, better understood the necessity of the imperial base.

The fur trade itself was not conducive to ethnic confrontation. In fact, it developed along the old lines. The rivals were the same, Albany and Hudson Bay. Here nothing had changed. French Canadians and Britons went ahead side by side in the exciting adventure of the west. In the beginning, the former group enjoyed a distinct advantage in numbers and experience. In terms of capital they were in no sense inferior to the latter. Up to the American Revolution, the fur trade was not a British enterprise. The French Canadians even kept a degree of primacy. From 1774 on, however, their leadership role was reduced with every year, so that in 1783, the year of the founding of the North-West Company, primacy passed to the Scots. The social "decapitation" cited with such feeling by Michel Brunet was, then, not a direct result of the Conquest. Rather it was the result of certain deficiencies in French-Canadian business. An individualist, the French-Canadian fur trader was afraid of associating with others, of diversifying his investments; moreover his taste for conspicuous consumption often preventing him from doing so. Bound to the fur trade, he refused to involve himself in other sectors of the economy. It was only after 1783 that French-Canadian business experienced a serious decline. In truth, no one clearly understood this phenomenon or its overall significance before the beginning of the nineteenth century.

The significant demographic accident of Loyalist migration could have produced a xenophobic reaction in the people of French Canada. That natural distrust of the outsider which is especially characteristic of rural groups could in suitable circumstances have been turned into nationalism. Here again, however, the situation was not such as to generate a basic change in conflicts, which remained social ones. The influx did, of course, raise the problem of injecting a strong British minority into a society that was ill prepared to receive it in terms of leadership and institutions. The problem was ultimately resolved by London in the 1791

Constitutional Act, dividing the territory on a cultural basis. The creation of Upper Canada and the townships flowed from this view, a prelude to future nationalist conflict. The installation of the parliamentary system in 1791 was in fact the only important concession to the capitalist group.

The fact is that Loyalist immigration took place at a time when land was still extremely abundant in Quebec. It also came at a time when furs and wheat were the bases for accelerated economic growth. The quantitative development achieved from 1785 on did not mean a major change in economic pattern, however. Rather it was the result of a swell of prosperity that lent impetus to expansion in farming and the fur trade. This situation, which benefited the majority, contained nothing that could have aroused an immediate budding of national consciousness. On the contrary, it helped people appreciate the advantages of imperial solidarity. The French Revolution and its wars that began in 1793 tended to further cement ties between the French-Canadian elites and British rule, even to the point of Anglomania; and one saw an unreserved admiration for British institutions. If there was an era in Canada's history when ideological unanimity was close, this was it. The nineteenth century, however, was approaching with its many tensions; it would wreck this fragile structure.

Emergence of French-Canadian Nationalism: Its Nature and Early Development (1802-37)

With the early years of the nineteenth century came a noticeable change in atmosphere. The optimism and fatalism of the previous century now yielded to a climate of unease and aggression, producing a variety of conflicts. It was only then, in this new context, that the first French-Canadian nationalism was seen. Contrary to claim, moreover, this nationalism did not emerge among the clergy and seigneurs of the old families, but among the membership of a new social class, the bourgeoisie of the liberal professions.

The emergence of this bourgeoisie was in fact a recent phenomenon. Had it not been for the decline of French-Canadian business and the old seigneurial elite, its appearance in the society would have been delayed. As the century opened, then, the liberal professions could expect to supply the lay leadership of French-Canadian society. The weakness of the traditional ruling classes left the way open to them, while their own interests and aspirations impelled them in this sense. Within this fast-growing group a class consciousness was taking shape and stimulating them to carve a special place for themselves in society. Yet what was to be their main field of action? Would it be strictly professional, or social, or political? Certainly these educated half-country folk commanded respect in the rural areas where the masses were illiterate. It is equally obvious that their social usefulness contributed to their importance. We should add that their own rural roots kept them in relation to the people. From all these points of view, however, the parish priests were their equals if not their superiors. A long history of authority and an unrivalled moral influence, as well as their control of certain institutions gave the clergy unequalled prestige and power. Tension appeared between these newcomers and the clerics; confrontation took shape. In the minds of this lower middle class there would be room for secular, liberal thinking. But the development of such thinking would remain dependent on the development of a broader range of ideas which ultimately conflicted with liberalism.

Nor could the liberal professions depend upon their economic status for prestige. From 1800 on, their economic situation was less favourable in that their numbers were rising at a disturbing rate. Each year the classical colleges, of which several were founded after 1820, presented the public with ever-increasing numbers of young men, lacking a priestly vocation and available only to the professions. It is not surprising that poverty awaited most of those who took this route. Pierre Bédard and Norbert Morin may be taken as typical examples. The overcrowding in the liberal professions was one of the chief characteristics of this uneasy era; their massive entry into politics was another.

We can thus better understand why these members of the lower middle class took advantage of parliamentary institutions to try to find in politics the prestige they required for social recognition. Politics would even be the springboard that made the administrative posts and incomes accessible to them. The ambitions of the liberal professionals could not be fulfilled on the constitutional plane, however, unless they worked under the banner of a certain liberal philosophy. The distrust of the existing administrators and the political power of the commercial middle class consigned this new bourgeoisie to an opposition role, unless it were to accept the social leadership of the capitalists. As a result, they had to proclaim the rights of the people as loudly as they could within the parliamentary system, and secure control of the executive branch. Only from this viewpoint can we fully understand the significance of the headlong campaign for ministerial responsibility as early as 1809-10, the struggle for control of the civil list, and, after 1831, the effort to have the elective principle extended to the Legislative council. The principal objective here was mastery of the political and administrative systems. Admittedly, these reforms were demanded in the name not of special interests but of national ones. Yet even though the first French-Canadian nationalism was not simply a front for the special interests of the liberal professions, it so depended on the world of this small group that it is hard to dissociate the two.

The fact is that the deepening of a national self-consciousness among the professional men went hand in hand with that of a class consciousness. The promotion of this bourgeoisie's own interests and values seemed an impossibility without an ideological base that could rally the masses. It would be tempting to see nothing but opportunism behind these calls for the rights of the nation. And yet this nationalism was not built simply on private ambition; it drew also on collective realities and aspirations. Furthermore, it was expressing the more or less conscious French-Canadian popular reaction to the new situation of the early nineteenth century. It should not be forgotten that this lower middle class had come from the farming community. The move from the rural to the bourgeois environment had in most cases occurred without any intermediate stage, so that there was a significant lag between the actual attitudes of these newcomers and their social status. Hence, their fear and rejection of the values and beliefs offered by the capitalists. The elite of a rural society, ill-adapted to the imperatives of economic and social progress, the professional middle class showed a dangerous tendency to turn back to the past, taking their national feeling from that past and rejecting the summons to progress. Capitalism they saw as an Anglo-Saxon value system; they soon saw it also as the supreme agent of the collapse of traditional institutions. Yet it was not simply as traditional values that these were thought to deserve protection, but above all as national values. The French-Canadian politicians of the early nineteenth century were influenced by European ideologies; among them, nationalism was the one that drew the deepest response.

Thus it was on the political plane, working through a majority party (the Patriote Party), that the liberal professions attempted to launch the national struggle. From this viewpoint liberalism, that inseparable partner of nationalism, was now, like the body of democratic ideas, only a vehicle for the attainment of nationalist aims and the entrenchment of class interests. This attitude opened the way for a host of contradictions. A substantial number of anticlerical and often agnostic liberals with democratic pretentions would be seen rising to the defence of the seigneurial system, the Coutume de Paris, and the privileges of the Church, while also denouncing capitalism. The fact is that they would be truly progressive only when their liberal ideas could work for the furthering of their own class interests and national projects.

The first French-Canadian nationalism was not, then, a result of a strong growth impetus in French-Canadian society; it was the product primarily of internal uneasiness and problems experienced by that society in adjusting to the age. It was not the creation of an expanding society that needed to burst the colonial structure. On the contrary, this nationalism expressed the maladjustment of men and institutions, the fears of this society in the circumstances of the age. In this sense and despite the need for regeneration that was felt at all levels in that society, it came out of a series of defensive reflexes that were brought on by the many challenges confronting French Canada.

After a late eighteenth century characterized in many respects by normal growth and security, circumstances were becoming less and less favourable. Beginning in the first years of the nineteenth century, the fur trade, that traditional activity which had formed a way of life, entered a phase of decline that would last until that great settlement of 1821. The world that was gradually vanishing took with it the old spatial sensibilities. Loss of contact with the west and its myths had much to do with the withdrawal of many French Canadians into the St. Lawrence lowlands. This loss cut them off from various concrete ties of empire. It was not the only retreat of the period, however; the agricultural crisis, first noticeable around 1802, was a phenomenon of the highest importance.

Quebec agriculture was based traditionally on wheat, that cereal superbly suited for bread and also connecting the Canadian economy to the imperial one. Fundamental to the food supply and to staple trade, wheat was thus central to the activities of most of the French-Canadian people. Their living standards were essentially dependent on it. A bad harvest instantly brought misery to rural society and all who depended on it. After 1802, bad harvests tended to increase disturbingly; surpluses were less and less substantial. At the same time, however, demand on external markets moved in the opposite direction. Soon, Lower Canada had serious deficits to contend with; only rarely did it manage to recover its production levels. After 1832, the deficit was chronic, and with the wheat fly epidemic, tended to mount from year to year. The only factor that can really explain this unfortunate state of affairs, however, is the underdevelopment of farming technology. On this subject, William Sutherland wrote:

> I verily believe that the almost destruction of the wheat crops by the wheat fly, which was the case for 6 or 7 years, and just about the period of the rebellion in 1836 and 7, was in one respect an incidental cause of that rebellion. The French-Canadian peasantry had always been in the habit of consuming a great deal of wheaten bread in their families. But by the wheat fly they were obliged to feed up on the inferior grain, oats, and potatoes. I have myself observed among them the discontent this at first occasioned, and altho they could not blame the government on this account, still when a man is suddenly reduced to more uncomfortable circumstances than customary, he is the more ready to receive the impulse of dissatisfaction infused into him by discontented and designing demagogues and their numerous emissaries.

The depression in wheat farming on the Quebec lands not only further distanced the French-Canadian habitant from the presence of the empire, but also placed him in a fairly unhealthy atmosphere of pessimism. For the ebb in wheat production, not being the result of a voluntary decision on his part, involved both the abandonment of long-entrenched farming concepts and the collapse of farm incomes. Impoverished or in debt, the farmer found it impossible to purchase English dry goods, and was therefore obliged to make his own clothing. In these unhappy circumstances he tended now to withdraw into his own world, and cling to traditions, even those that did him injury. He grew dissatisfied with his lot in life, aggressive towards anything that posed a direct or indirect threat of even greater instability. Given his poor motivation to refurbish his farming techniques, it is not surprising to find that he looked outside for someone to blame for his wretchedness. The capitalist or the Englishman thus emerged as the object of his fears and the source of his problems. Consciously or not, moreover, the politicians did not hesitate to channel his aggressions in this sense. Through its many reverberations, the crisis in agriculture became the backdrop for the tragedy of nationalism and rebellion. It was not the sole conditioning factor, however.

Overpopulation in the seigneurial lands was another essential factor spurring unease in the rural environment. In the course of the eighteenth century the population of French Canada had risen at an extraordinary rate, with a doubling time of less than twenty-eight years. With a birth rate varying around fifty per thousand population, this performance is not surprising. Virtually everything, we may say, except for the wilderness life that took off husbands and delayed marriages, encouraged such a rise. Land was abundant, and farming paid well. After the beginning of the nineteenth century, however, this situation gradually changed. The rate of natural increase remained constant until 1850, while accessible lands began to grow scarcer. Towards 1810, parts of the province were noted as being saturated with people. Graver still at a time when the productivity of the land was sagging, the land in these areas had been parcelled out into the smallest possible lots. Still isolated, this tension nevertheless gave rise to some disquiet in the elites. The situation developed rapidly, so that in 1822 there was overpopulation throughout the seigneurial territories. The seigneurs, by trying to keep the good lands for themselves and raise the seigneurial quit-rents, were themselves partly responsible for this demographic tension. By this time, farm overpopulation had become a permanent reality. The problem was exceptionally serious. It included the emergence of a rural proletariat composed of people in search of land. The collapse in productivity on the cultivated lands, with a population increasing at a terrifying pace, produced a reduction in population densities. True, there were substantial stretches of land outside the seigneuries waiting for settlement; but it seemed at the time as if the townships stood as major obstacles to the growth of the French-Canadian population. The nationalist reaction that characterized the township as a tool of anglicization ultimately discouraged the channelling of surplus people to the township lands. When they ought to have been building and maintaining roads to colonize these lands, the politicians of French Canada were satisfied merely to insist that the townships be turned into seigneuries. From the strictly nationalist standpoint, the township question became utterly politicized. With a number of other factors, the feuds it produced meant delay in opening up the new lands. Like the immigrant groups, the French-Canadians were not really attracted to the available spaces. It was the time of the first French-Canadian emigration to the United States.

In this context of agricultural crisis and seigneurial overpopulation we can better see the reasons for habitant hostility to capitalists and immigrants. The French-Canadians were hypersensitive to the agrarian issue in all its aspects. They could lose land ownership, the symbol of their individual and collective security. To the capitalist and the immigrant, both of them with an interest in getting land, they would say: the soil is ours. Just as important was the fact that the immigrant was seen as a dangerous competitor for jobs. From that time on, most of the French-Canadian people viewed this demographic tension as a deadly menace to the future of their community. The nationalist reaction that led up to the insurrection of 1837 cannot be understood if we fail to take this central phenomenon into account.

Immigration and the Quebec agricultural crisis had occasioned a shift of centres of production to the Eastern Townships and Upper Canada. Among other adjustments, this change required new improvements in communications. At all costs freight charges must be cut, if producer incomes were to be maintained and competition run against the Americans. Yet it was another phenomenon, of more decisive importance, that finally led to these same basic imperatives. The long-term decline in prices that began in 1815 and continued up to 1850 created a general climate of hardship in Quebec which reached the whole of the society: workers, farmers, businessmen, land owners, and people in the liberal professions. Wages tended to go down, farm incomes to fall, trading profits to sag. The situation was rife with challenges for Canadian society. The revolution in farm techniques was one; another was reduction of freight costs by the building of roads and the improvement of navigable waterways. At the same time, this unfavourable situation called for far-reaching reform of French customary law and the seigneurial system. Thus, it seemed a matter of urgency to establish registry offices to aid transfers of real estate, and give this sector a capitalistic tone. This at least was the response to the problem suggested by the people of capital.

The reaction from the farming community and people in the liberal professions was not as positive. Instead of encouraging them to look for ways of solving the problems, the economic situation made them fearful, and produced defensive reflexes in these groups. The canalization of the St. Lawrence and the registry offices, to cite but two examples, were greeted as infernal devices to promote the interests of immigrants and English capitalists. Never abandoning the hope of a resurgence in wheat farming on Quebec lands, the habitant was afraid improvement of the waterway would make this return to the past a permanent impossibility.

The agricultural crisis, the demographic tensions, and the rivalries in society were the moving forces behind the nationalist crisis of the first half of the nineteenth century. Fortunately, however, the Lower-Canadian economy possessed one fully expanding sector whose role would be to soften the blow. Emerging from 1803 on, the timber trade was to be extremely important in this unfavourable context. Essentially an Anglo-Saxon enterprise, as was shipbuilding, forest exploitation was also a major source of profits and a vehicle for massive immigration. In this light the sector tends to look as if it would be a source of problems for the political leaders of French Canada. From other points of view, however, there was no doubt of the usefulness of this primary enterprise. In those difficult circumstances, it created valuable new jobs both for rural people and for the day labourers and poor immigrants of the towns. In this sense, and also because it opened up a market for farm production, the forest industry would to some degree preserve the standard of living for a fairly high percentage of the population. Certainly the peaceful attitude of Quebec City residents in the 1837 insurrection may primarily be accounted for by the relative stability of the timber trade and the shipbuilding industry.

The nationalist ideology created by the bourgeoisie of the liberal professions was thus also the product of an internalization by this elite of the misfortunes of rural French-Canadian society. The resultant desire for self-affirmation was then focused on tradition and opposed to capitalism, whether in trade, finance, or industry. As far as the clergy were concerned, they did not begin to move into nationalism until around the 1830s. It would fall to Msgr. Lartigue, the first bishop of Montreal, to free nationalism from its liberal entanglements and make it the moving force in the building of a theocratic, clerical society.

Yet if nationalism emerged as the dominant ideology in the French Canada of that age it is also because it was projected through personalities who were capable of making it obey their own fundamental objectives. It was surely not by mere chance that Pierre Bédard and L.-J. Papineau became its authentic spokesmen. A strong and realistic nationalism that was open to progress would certainly have found men who were less doctrinaire, more flexible and in the last analysis better balanced to proclaim it. The choices of the collectivity would have been represented by men who, though less brilliant and intellectual, would have been less distracted, more active.

Such are the principal factors conditioning the development of French-Canadian nationalism from its initial appearance at the beginning of the century up to the explosion of 1837. As the economic malaise took root, as capitalism worked to extend its grasp, and as demographic pressure, social tensions, and political conflicts made their appearance, so French-Canadian nationalism, under the stimulus of movements in Europe, penetrated more and more into the minds of men. Until 1830, however, the nationalist crisis did not issue in a challenge to the colonial system as such; rather, it led to a reform of parliamentary institutions based on a much more liberal interpretation of British traditions. The fact is that the nationalists believed they could achieve all their aims by remaining "reformers." However, beginning with the Union crisis of 1822, in the heart of the fight for control of supply, nationalism gradually tended to free itself from these past alliances. The "Canadian party" became the "Patriote Party," and from that time on an unconfessed republican spirit was at work behind the reform mask. It was now being realized that French-Canadian nationalism could not flourish under the protective aegis of British institutions. The political leaders recognized that attainment of political power and social leadership would be impossible for the professional people as long as the old colonial system remained in force. So it was that after 1830, the political concepts of the Patriotes relied on the American model. This is why they called for the extension of the elective principle to all areas where it seemed possible to apply. At the same time, opposition to economic, social, and judicial reform was hardening. Political obstruction, previously practised with such success, now became a permanent tactic. There were dreams of a French-Canadian republic, established with the forced cooperation of London and maintaining only vague relations with Britain. The most violent and the most realistic nationalists, however, were viewing armed revolution as the only possible route to independence. The People's Bank founded in 1835 had the funding of eventual rebellion as its secondary objective. After 1834, certainly, intensifying conflict was headed for tragedy. The aggression and intractability of the adversaries reached their peak. If one factor in the crisis were to be aggravated, it would be enough to produce an explosion.

The year 1837 was ominous in this respect. The previous year's harvest had been extremely poor, and there was no sign of imminent improvement. To top everything, financial crisis spread through England the United States to affect Canada. All classes of society were touched by uneasiness and agitation. It was in the midst of this general misery, offset to some extent by resistance in the timber trade and in shipbuilding, that news came of the passage of the notorious Russell resolutions. The glove had been flung down. The Patriotes could not forbear to pick it up.

The pitiable failure of the 1837-38 insurrections was not owing to unhappy fate. Nor should it be attributed primarily to clerical opposition; this was a factor, but certainly not the most important one. The contradictory actions of a Papineau were as decisive for the fate of the movement as the fulminations of a Msgr. Lartigue. The fact is that the insurrections were too closely bound to the immediate interests of certain individuals and groups for them to succeed. Above all, they were too closely based on passing problems whose true solutions lay elsewhere. The independence of Lower Canada would have done nothing to solve the challenge of changing farming technology. Cutting Quebec off from the imperial markets, it would rather have accentuated economic underdevelopment, and left the field open to theocracy and feudalism. The liberal and democratic ideal would certainly not have withstood such a development.

Ideological Divergence under the Union

Section 8

In his famous report on the affairs of British North America, Lord Durham argued that a political union of Upper and Lower Canada would bring English and French closer together in attitude and eventually make one people of them. He thought that the experience of working together within a single political system would gradually bring them to share common values and outlooks.

The Union of 1840 did force the two groups to work out a political partnership and a common parliamentarianism; but, as these two essays indicate, their political and social values and ideals remained far apart, and even, in some measure, moved farther apart during the Union period.

What were the main differences between the ideals which Monet shows spreading in Quebec and the ones which Careless sees as prevailing in Ontario? Why were they so different? What does Monet mean by "ultramontanism"? Why did it become more influentiual in Lower Canada during the 1840s? What does Careless mean by liberalism? How close was his 19th-century liberalism to what we would consider liberal today?

Notice that both Upper Canadian liberals and Lower Canadian ultramontanes were strongly influenced by ideas coming from other countries. The differences between them reflected an ongoing 19th-century conflict that had begun with the French Revolution and was still being worked out on both sides of the Atlantic—a conflict between the old conservative and monarchical values based on orthodox religion and the notion of a divinely ordained social and natural order (remember Wise's article in topic #5), and the modern secular values of individual liberty, equality, and popular government. Can you see from these articles how 19th-century Canadians fit into that context?

A fuller and more general account of the Union period is given in J.M.S.Careless, *The Union of the Canadas*.

French-Canadian Nationalism and the Challenge of Ultramontanism

Jacques Monet

A funny thing happened to French-Canadian nationalism on its way to responsible government. It became ultramontane.

At the end of the 1830s French Canada was in ferment. Under British domination for some 75 years, the French had succeeded in surviving, but not in developing by themselves, a full, normal, national life. They had kept the essentials: their ancestral land, their French language, their Catholic faith, their time-honoured and peculiar jurisprudence, and their long family traditions, but they needed a new life. The seigneurial system could no longer hold the growing population. The economy lagged, the problems of education had reached such an impasse that the schools were closed, and the old civil code no longer applied to modern circumstances. Above all, the upward thrust of the growing professional middle class created a serious social situation of which the rebellions of 1837-38 were only one expression. Clearly, if the struggle for national survival were to hold any meaning for the future, French-Canadian nationalists needed new solutions.

They were divided, however. Inspired by the ideology of Louis-Joseph Papineau some considered *la survivance* could be assured only by political isolation in a territory over which French-Canadians would be undisputed masters. Militant idealists, they were led by John Neilson and Denis-Benjamin Viger until Papineau returned to politics in 1847. Others, broader minded and more practical, held to a doctrine of which the Quebec editor Etienne Parent was the clearest exponent, and which Louis-Hippolyte LaFontaine translated into politics. They reasoned that it was the flexibility of the British constitutional system that could best assure not only their acquired rights, but also (by means of self-government) the certain hope of a broadening future for their language, their institutions, and their nationality.

Before achieving responsible government, however, LaFontaine needed to accomplish two things. He had to forge the unity of his people in favour of British parliamentary democracy and, along with this, form a united political party with the Upper Canadians. Neither was easy. In the years immediately following the rebellion French Canada's strongest sympathies belonged to the leaders of the Viger-Neilson group, believers neither in responsible government nor in union with Upper Canada. After the election of 1841, for instance, out of some 29 members elected by French-Canadian ridings, LaFontaine could count on only six or seven to be sympathetic to his views. By 1844, he had succeeded in persuading many more—at least he could then count on some two dozen. But not before the end of the decade could he be certain of victory, for until then Papineau, his followers, and especially his legend remained one of the strongest forces in the country. Still, after a decade of fistfights on electoral platforms, scandals, riots, and racial fury; after a brilliant, dynamic, and flexible partnership with Robert Baldwin, LaFontaine became in 1848 the first Canadian Prime Minister in the modern sense and, by means of the British Constitution, the first French-Canadian to actually express and direct the aspirations of his people.

He had also gradually, and all unwittingly perhaps, presided over the marriage of ultramontanism with the practical politics and the nationalist ideology of his party. At the beginning of the decade, the hierarchy and priests of the Roman Catholic Church in French Canada hardly conceived that practical party politics could be their concern, nor did they think of adding significantly to the nationalist theme. They worked behind the scenes; and, in 1838, for instance, after deciding to oppose the Union, they composed and signed an unpublicised petition which they sent directly to London to be presented to the Queen. But in 1848, during the crisis which consecrated the practice of responsible government, they openly took sides with LaFontaine's party, and allowed their newspapers to give approval to his administration. Likewise, at the time of the rebellions, most of the priests, and especially those among the hierarchy, had officially disassociated themselves from what seemed to be the main preoccupations of the leading French-Canadian nationalists. "Des mauvais sujets ... prétendus libéraux, attachés à détruire dans nos peuples l'amour de la religion,"[1] Bishop Jacques Lartigue of Montreal called the *Patriotes*, while Archbishop Signay of Quebec tried to explain to his flock that Colborne's devastating march against the rebels had been undertaken "pas àdessein de molester ou maltraiter personne, mais pour protéger les bons et fidèles sujets, pour éclairer ceux des autres qui sont dans l'erreur et qui se sont laissés égarer."[2] Within a decade later, however, they openly wrote and talked of the doctrine that the Catholic faith and French Canada's nationality depended one upon the other. "Tous les rapports qui nous arrivent des divers points du diocèse," the *Mélanges Religieux* reported on July 7, 1843, about the Saint-Jean-Baptiste Day celebrations, "prouvent combien sont vifs et universels les sentiments de religion et de nationalité de nos concitoyens. Partout ces deux sentiments se sont montrés inséparables dans les coeurs: la pompe et les cérémonies religieuses ont accompagné les démonstrations civiles et patriotiques.... C'est parce que nous sommes catholiques que nous sommes une nation dans ce coin de l'Amérique, que nous attirons les regards de toutes les autres contrées, l'intérêt et la sympathie de tous les peuples.... Qu'on nous dise ce que serait le Canada s'il était peuplé exclusivement d'Anglais et de Protestants?" Of course, much happened between 1838 and 1848 to change the thinking of both nationalists and Catholic clerics.

One very important thing was the advent of Ignace Bourget. A short time after succeeding to the See of Montreal in 1840, this earnest and authoritarian Bishop made it clear how much he intended to renew the face of Catholicism in French

---

[1] Archives de l'Archevêché de Montréal, Mgr. Lartigue à G.A. Belcourt, 24 avril 1838.
[2] Archives de l'Archevêché de Québec, Mgr. Signay à A. Leclerc, 25 novembre 1837.

Canada. During his first year—incidentally, after successfully reasserting in an interesting conflict with Poulett Thomson the doctrine of Papal supremacy and of episcopal independence of civil authority—he had organized a great mission through his diocese, preached by Bishop Forbin-Janson, one of France's foremost orators. Between September 1840 and December 1841, the French Bishop travelled across Lower Canada, visiting some sixty villages and preaching rousing sermons—two of which Lord Sydenham attended in state at Notre-Dame—before crowds sometimes estimated at ten thousand. Bishop Bourget thus initiated close and large-scale religious contacts with France.

Indeed, while Forbin-Janson was still in Canada, the new Bishop of Montreal left on the first of some five voyages to France and Rome, a trip from which he would return carrying with him the reawakened energies of the Catholic revival. While in Europe, he held discussions with a cluster of interesting and influential Catholic ultramontane leaders. At this time, European ultramontanes—whose intellectual roots reached as far back as the quarrels between Philippe LeBel and Boniface VIII, the pope "beyond the mountains"—had outgrown the traditional belief that the Pope held doctrinal and jurisdictional supremacy over the whole Church. Brought up on DeMaistre's *Du Pape*, a book that urged Papal dominion over temporal rulers in all Church matters, and feverish with romanticism's revival of all things medieval, they urged the subservience of civil government to the papacy, of State to Church. They had not understood that there was a difference between the surrender of all men to God's will, and the obedience of civil society to the Pope. They were mistaken—but they were, perhaps because of his, all the more dogmatic, energetic, aflame with zeal: they directed newspapers, notably Louis Veuillot's *L'Univers*, entertained crucial political polemics over education, censorship, and "secret organizations"; by the 1840s, they had founded hundreds of pious societies for desirable ends, collected a multiplication of relics from the Roman catacombs, covered Europe with imitation Gothic, and filled their churches and parlours with Roman papier-maché statuary.

Bishop Bourget fell under their spell as soon as he arrived. In Paris he had long conversations with the Abbé Desgenettes, curé of the ultramontane cenacle at Notre-Dame-Des-Victoires, and the founder of the Archconfraternity of the Most Holy and Immaculate Heart of Mary; he met Théodore de Ratisbonne, a convert from Judaism and the founder of the Daughters of Sion, Jean-Marie de Lamennais, the founder of the Brothers of the Christian schools, and the most noted of them all, Louis Veuillot, who attended a sermon of Mgr Bourget's at Notre-Dame-Des-Victoires and gave it a rave review in *l'Univers*. At Chartres, he was entertained by the compelling personality of the Abbé, later Cardinal, Louis-Edouard Pie, the future exponent of Papal infallibility at the Vatican Council. In Marseille, he was impressed by Bishop de Mazenod, another staunch defender of the Vatican; and in Rome, he was greeted by Fr. John Roothaan, the General of the Jesuits, with whom he spent eight days in retreat and meditation. Finally, several audiences with the kindly Gregory XVI crowned the series of discussions that made him the most ultramontane churchman of his generation in Canada.[3]

In Chartres, the Bishop of Montreal also had a long conversation with Bishop Clausel de Montals. The later was a strong Gallican, but nonetheless the acknowledged champion in the fight for Catholic institutions against the State University. He doubtless recited for his Canadien colleague a long list of the dangers and evils of the *école laïque*. For from that day onwards Mgr Bourget would battle tirelessly to keep the Church in control of education in Lower Canada. And all Canadian ultramontanes would follow him in this.

Back in Montreal, Mgr Bourget began injecting into the Canadien mood the full fever of his Roman creed. With a crusader's singleness of purpose, he arranged for the immigration from France of the Oblate and Jesuit Orders, of the Dames du Sacré-Coeur and the Sisters of the Good Shepherd; he founded two Canadian religious congregations of his own, established the Saint Vincent de Paul Society; carried out an extensive canonical visitation of his diocese, and pressed Rome to establish an ecclesiastical province that extended within a few years to new dioceses in Toronto, Ottawa, British Columbia, and Oregon, "une vaste chaîne de sièges épiscopaux qui doit s'étendre un jour de la mer jusqu'à la mer: a mari usque ad mare."[4] He also organized a whole series of parish revivals and religious ceremonies superbly managed to stir the emotion of all classes. At Varennes on July 26, 1842, for example, before a huge crowd of several thousand, surrounded by some sixty priests and in the full pontifical splendour of his office, he presided over the crowning of a holy picture of Saint Anne, according to "le cérémonial usité à Rome pour de semblables solennités." (The end of the day was, perhaps, more Canadien: "Tous ces feux," reported the *Mélanges*, "des salves d'artillerie ou de mousquetterie au milieu du silence d'une nuit profonde, après toutes les cérémonies de la journée, faisaient naître des émotions nouvelles inconnues."[5]) Another time, in November 1843, he presided over a huge demonstration in honour of the transferral to the chapel of the Sisters of Providence of the bones of Saint Januaria, ancient Roman relics which he had negotiated away from the custodian of one of the catacombs. At this service, the golden reliquary was carried by four canons of the cathedral surrounded by eight seminarians bearing incense, and "la foule eut peine à se retirer, tant était grande son émotion."[6] Throughout the 1840s, he ordered many more such occasions. For the blessing of the bells for the new towers of Notre-Dame church, "on exécuta parfaitement le jeu du *God Save the Queen—Dieu sauve notre reine* auquel la bande

---

[3] I want to thank Fr. Léon Pouliot, author of *Mgr Bourget et son Temps* (2 vols., Montréal, 1955-56) and of *La Réaction Catholique de Montréal* (Montréal, 1942) for pointing out to me the importance of this trip in the formation of Mgr. Bourget's thinking.

[4] *Mélanges Religieux* [henceforth *MR*], 13 mai 1842.

[5] *MR*, 28 juillet 1842.

[6] *MR*, 14 novembre 1843.

du régiment fit écho de toute la force de ses instruments."[7] (Yes, the ultramontanes were also strong royalists. The *Mélanges* often published articles on royalty, one of which began by praising "les principes d'honneur, de devoir, d'ordre, de générosité, de dévouement, qui dérivent de l'idée monarchique."[8]) A not untypical reaction to this type of demonstration was that of the politician Joseph Cauchon who wrote to a colleague about the funeral of Archbishop Signay in October 1850: "Le deuil de l'Eglise était grandiose et solennel àl'extrême. L'installation du nouvel archevêque s'est faite avec une égale solennité. Il y a quelque chose de grand, de sublime dans ce développement des cérémonies soit lugubres soit joyeuses du Catholicisme."[9]

The new Orders naturally aided Mgr Bourget with his ultramontanism—especially the Jesuits who began in 1843 to lay the foundation of Collège Sainte-Marie, an institution that would train so many energetic young nationalist Catholics. The *Mélanges Religieux* also helped. In this bi-weekly newspaper, the priests from the bishopric published over and over again long articles of praise for the papal states, and copious excerpts from the works of leading ultramontanists: speeches by the Spanish conservative Donoso Cortès, Montalembert's famous oration on the Roman question, Mgr de Bonald's pastoral letter "contre les erreurs de son temps," and long book reviews such as the one condemning Eugène Sue's salacious *Les Mystères de Paris* for trying to "répandre sur la religion et ses pratiques tout l'odieux possible."[10] They also issued vibrant appeals to Canadian youth to join in their movement: "Vous voulez être de votre siècle jeunes amis, vous voulez marcher avec lui?.... Avez-vous trouvé mieux où reposer votre âme que dans les oeuvres immortelles des DeBonald, de Maistre, de Chateaubriand, de Montalembert, du Lamartine *catholique*, de Turquety?"[11] They also gave news of Catholicism throughout the world, concentrating especially on the independence of the Papal States and the University Question in France. "Pour parvenir à remplir leur mission," the *Mélanges* noted on March 31, 1846, "les Éditeurs n'ont rien épargné; ils ont fait venir à grands frais les meilleurs journaux d'Europe, *L'Univers, L'Ami de la Religion, Le Journal des Villes et des Campagnes de France,* le *Tablet* de Londres, le *Freeman's Journal* de New York, le *Cross* d'Halifax, le *Catholic Magazine* de Baltimore, le *Catholic Herald* de Philadelphie, le *Propagateur Catholique* de la Nouvelle-Orléans." In a word, the *Mélanges* opened a window on the Catholic world. And through it there blew in the high winds of ultramontanism, which, for the Canadiens, felt so much like their own aggressive and assertive nationalism.

Through it there also came for the clergy a novel regard for the layman. Since the Restoration in Europe, the Catholic Bishops and priests had achieved some success

---

[7]   *MR*, 4 juillet 1843.
[8]   *MR*, 27 janvier 1843.
[9]   *Archives de la Province de Québec* [henceforth *APQ*], Papiers Taché A50. Joseph Cauchon àE.-P. Taché, 9 octobre 1850.
[10] *MR*, 20 novembre 1849.
[11] *MR*, 26 novembre 1842.

there in reintegrating the Church into educational life and social services. Very often they had done this with the assistance of influential laymen. Through the *Mélanges* publication of articles and speeches by these European ultramontane politicians, the Canadien priests gradually developed a fresh respect for their own lay politicians. They began to think of new ideas on how they could work with them. In fact, with the coming of responsible government the old ways which the priests had grown accustomed to were passing into history forever. The Union had marked the end of the courteous and courtly style which the Bishops and the British governors had so carefully devised over the years to fuse the good of the throne with the good of the altar. Now, effective political power was passing from the hands of the Governors-General to those of the Canadien electors. And if the Church was to exercise the influence which the priests felt in conscience it must, then the clergy must begin to deal directly with the politicians and the people.

Besides, they were finding nationalist politicians whom they liked. Indeed, by the middle of the decade, it was becoming obvious how much LaFontaine's followers and the priests seemed made to understand each other. The debate on the Union, during which they had been on opposite sides, was settled. And since then, they had forged new personal friendships. In Quebec, politicians such as René-Édouard Caron, Étienne-Pascal Taché, and especially Joseph-Édourd Cauchon, the editor of the influential *Journal de Québec*, enjoyed frequent hospitality at the Séminaire. Taché and Cauchon were also close correspondents of the Archbishop's secretary, the talented and ubiquitous abbé Charles-Félix Cazeau. In Montreal, LaFontaine's close friend, Augustin-Norbert Morin, also received a cordial welcome at the bishopric, especially from Mgr Bourget's *Grand-Vicaire*, Mgr Hyacinthe Hudon. So did other partisans like Lewis Thomas Drummond and Joseph Coursol. Indeed, as these priests and politicians grew to admire each other, a new esteem was also developing between their leaders, between the new Bishop of Montreal and the man who in 1842 became French Canada's Attorney-General. Despite initial suspicion on both their parts, Bourget and LaFontaine were by temperament made to understand each other. Both were heroes to duty, strong-willed leaders, unyielding in their principles, and expert at manoeuvring within the letter of the law. Especially they had in common that each one thought in absolute terms that he was in total possession of the truth. Neither could accept from an adversary anything but complete conversion.

Thus it was that slowly within the womb of LaFontaine's party, despite appearances, the pulse of the clerico-nationalist spirit began, faintly, to beat.

None of these things—Bishop Bourget's trip to Europe and its effects in Montreal, the historical turn in Canadian politics caused by responsible government, the new intimacy between ultramontanes and nationalists—none could weigh enough to bring the priests officially into LaFontaine's party. But they did prepare the way. Then, in 1846, the public discussion over a new Education Bill and over the funds from the Jesuit Estates revealed to the clergy which politicians were its natural allies and which were not. The Education Bill of 1845, proposed by Denis-Benjamin Papineau, the great tribune's brother, who was Commissioner of Crown Lands in the

Viger-Draper administration, did not satisfy the clergy. Although it provided for the curés being *ex officio* "visitors" to the schools, it did not give them the control they wished. They therefore began a campaign to have the project amended in their favour.

The *Mélanges* took the lead, repeatedly emphasizing the close connection between education and religion. "Nous ne comprenons pas d'éducation sans religion, et conséquemment sans morale," it had written back on November 8, 1842, in words which could easily have been inspired by Bishop Bourget's conversation with Clausel de Montals, "et nous ne voyons pas ce qui pourrait suppléer à son enseignement dans les écoles. Que sera donc l'instruction et l'éducation des enfants sans prières, sans catéchisme, sans instruction religieuse et morale quelconque?" Even as the Bill was being debated, the *Mélanges* kept up the pressure, receiving great assistance from A.-N. Morin, "ce monsieur dont le coeur est droit," as one curé wrote.[12] From his seat on the Opposition benches, with the aid of his colleagues Taché, Drummond, and Cauchon, Morin proposed amendment after amendment to bring about a system which would happily unite clerical authority on the local level with centralized control by the Superintendent at the Education department. "M. Papineau, auquel j'ai eu le plaisir d'administerer quelque dure médecine pour lui fair digérer son Bill d'Éducation, ne veut pas que l'éducation soit religieuse," Cauchon reported to the abbé Cazeau. "J'ai dit, moi votre ouaille, qu'une éducation dépouillée de l'instruction religieuse mènerait à de funestes résultats."[13] Finally, in mid-1846, Denis-Benjamin Papineau bowed to the pressure, and accepted the Morin amendments.

If the Bishops accordingly felt happy about the Act in its final form, they owed it in great part to the support of politicians like Morin and his friends. At the same time, they were receiving support from LaFontaine's friends on another critical issue: the Jesuit estates.

The problem of these lands, which had been granted by a succession of French kings and nobles to serve as an endowment for education, had definitely passed to the British Crown in 1800 at the death of the last Jesuit. Their revenues were used by the Colonial Office for any number of Government sinecures until 1832, when as a gesture of conciliation it agreed that they be administered by the Lower Canadian Assembly. Then there began another struggle with the Catholic Bishops who claimed that they and not the Assembly were the true heirs of the Jesuits. By 1846 the controversy had reached the floor of the House, and the Provincial Government, led by Denis-Benjamin Viger, refused the Bishops' claim. As in the debate over Papineau's Education Bill, LaFontaine and his party supported the priests. LaFontaine, Morin (who had been acting as confidential adviser to the clergy on the question), Drummond, and Taché each delivered an impassioned speech against the "spoliation" of French Canada's heritage; Morin himself proposing that the funds be

---

[12] *APQ*, Fonds de l'Instruction Publique. Lettres reçues. P. Davignon à J.-B. Meilleur, 23 novembre 1843.

[13] Archives de l'Archevêché de Québec, DM H-245. Joseph Cauchon à C.-F. Cazeau, 24 février 1845.

transferred entirely to the Church. Viger defended the Government's action on the grounds of precedent and Parliamentary supremacy. He won the vote. But in appealing to Parliamentary supremacy, he began a disagreeable discussion which continued in the press for over three months. At the end, it was clear how wide a division had taken place among French-Canadian nationalists: a division as explicit as the opposing doctrines of liberalism and ultramontanism.

While traditionally nationalist papers such as *Le Canadien*, and *L'Aurore des Canadas*, defending Viger, assailed the Church's position, *La Minerve*, *Le Journal de Québec*, and *La Revue Canadienne*, all LaFontaine papers, became like the *Mélanges* defenders of the Faith. In a series of articles probably written by Viger,[14] *L'Aurore* insisted that the Bishops had at most a very tenuous claim to the Jesuit funds which had never, in fact, belonged to them, and which, if the intentions of the donors were to be respected, should be applied to the whole territory of what had been New France. Since they were being spent exclusively in Lower Canada, as the Bishops themselves agreed was correct, then the revenues derived their title from the Imperial decision of 1832 which put them at the disposal of the "volontés réunies des pouvoirs exécutif, législatif, administratif" of the Lower Canadian Assembly, and hence of the Union government which was its heir. When the LaFontaine press generally replied that the taking of the property from the Church in the first place had been a sacrilege, the argument rose to a higher level.[15] Running through precedents that went back to Justinian, La Régale, and the *coutumes* of pre-Revolutionary France, *L'Aurore* retorted that since the Church's possession of property derived from the State's civil law, any change by the government could hardly be a sacrilege. To which, in best scholastic manner, the *Mélanges* retorted that since the Church possessed property by divine and natural right, civil recognition added nothing. And to this *l'Aurore*, in best liberal tradition, asserted that since nature knew only individuals, no corporate body such as the Church could claim existence by natural law.[16]

And so the controversy proceeded. It was one which could not easily be resolved. For while the *Mélanges* was reasserting the Doctrine so dear to the nineteenth-century ultramontane that the Church, by natural and divine right, was autonomous with respect to the State, Viger, brimming with the liberal's faith in the individual, denied any natural right to a corporate body. It was an argument that could not be settled for generations; indeed not until both the liberals and the ultramontanes, in the face of other problems, would come to modify their intransigence.

This was not the first difference of opinion that had brought Viger's party and the *Mélanges* into conflict. Back in 1842 they had measured paragraphs against each other over the interpretation of Bishop Lartigue's famous *Mandement* against rebellion in 1837; and at that time also they had been quarrelling from the viewpoint

---

[14] *L'Aurore des Canadas*, 3, 6, 13, 16 juin 1846.
[15] *L'Aurore des Canadas*, 13 juin 1845.
[16] *MR*, 26 juin 1846, *L'Aurore des Canadas*, 30 juin 1846.

of opposing ultramontane and liberal doctrines.[17] Yet somehow that discussion had not caused any overt split. The 1846 one did—and soon with the re-emergence of Louis-Joseph Papineau into political life, all bridges were broken between his party and the clergy. By 1849, the priests had become one of the great forces on the side of responsible government in Canada.

Having returned from his exile in liberal, anticlerical France, the great rebel found little to encourage him in Canada. He was disgusted by LaFontaine's politics, repelled by the growing power of the priests. Especially he suffered at being forced to witness his people's growing commitment to the British connection. In the late fall of 1847 he issued what Lord Elgin called "a pretty frank declaration of republicanism,"[18] reviving his dreams of the 1830s for a national republic of French Canada. Around himself he rallied Viger's followers and a group of enthusiastic young separatists who edited the radical newspaper *L'Avenir*. They shared the rebel leader's philosophy: if it only depended on them they would win through the sharpness of their minds what he had not by sharpness of sword.

What struck the ultramontanes about Papineau and *L'Avenir* was of course not so much the attacks against LaFontaine and responsible government. It was their anticlericalism. As things turned out the republicans would hurt their own cause more than they would the Church: on the subject of responsible government, Papineau might conceivably weaken LaFontaine, especially if he concentrated on nationality and the defects of the Union. But by challenging the Church, the *rouges* merely helped to cement the alliance between LaFontaine and the priests.

On March 14, 1849, *L'Avenir* created quite a stir by publishing large extracts from the European liberal press on the Roman revolution which had forced Pius IX into exile and proclaimed Mazzini's republic. The articles were bitter: and the Lower Canadian republicans left little doubt where their own sympathies lay. The *Mélanges* took up the challenge. Through several series of learned front pages, it tried to show "les Messieurs de l'Avenir" how serious were "l'injustice et la faute qu'ils ont commises."[19] But the young editors did not understand. They continued to insult the Pope; and at their Société Saint-Jean-Baptiste banquet that year, they replaced their traditional toast to the Sovereign by a defiant speech on "Rome Régénérée." "Les journaux socialistes et anti-religieux sont sans cesse à vanter les hauts faits de MM. les rouges àRome," the *Mélanges* complained,[20] adding sadly that "la manie d'aboyer contre la soutane semble être à la mode."[21]

Indeed it was. On July 21, 1849, *L'Avenir* led another attack which would lock the journalists in another discussion for two months: this time on tithing. "La

---

[17] Cf. F. Ouellet, "Le Mandement de Mgr Lartigue de 1837 et la Réaction libérale," *Bulletin des Recherches historiques,* 1952 (580), 97-104.
[18] Elgin-Grey Papers I, 102. Elgin to Grey, December 24, 1847.
[19] *MR* 30 mars 1849.
[20] *MR*, 6 juillet 1849.
[21] *MR*, 21 septembre 1849.

dîme," it pronounced, "est un abus encore bien plus grand que la tenure seigneuriale." Then later, when it began to campaign for the abolition of seigneurial tenure, the radical paper again attacked the Church for its ownership of seigneurial lands. In fact, it averred, one of the very reasons against the system was the amount of revenue which accrued from it to the Séminaire de Québec and other religious institutions.

On September 14, 1849, the *Mélanges* warned the republican youngsters at *L'Avenir*: "Nos adversaires ne doivent pas se dissimuler que par leur conduite et leurs écrits ils se font plus de tort qu'ils nous en font à nous-mêmes." True enough. For as the priests were being attacked by their own political enemies, LaFontaine's publicists naturally came to the clergy's rescue. Thus, all during 1849, the *Journal de Québec*, *Le Canadien*, and *La Minerve*, defended the Church as if they themselves had been directly concerned.

While the dispute raged about the Pope's temporal sovereignty, for instance, Cauchon's *Journal* featured a serial on the subject by the French Bishop Dupanloup of Orleans, and another series covering several instalments by "Un Canadien Catholique" assailed *L'Avenir* for "la prétention qu'il entretient de catéchiser le clergé sur ses devoirs." So also on the issue of tithing: Cauchon spread an article defending the Church over the front page of three issues in October 1849, and underlined the connection between anticlericalism and the republicans: "Ce sont les aimables procédés du passé, la haine entre le peuple et ses chefs religieux pour assurer le triomphe des doctrines pernicieuses et anti-nationales."[22] When the *rouges* criticized the clergy's role in the schools, Cauchon answered by giving the clergy credit for *la survivance*:

> D'où vient cette haute portée d'intelligence, ce caractère si beau, si noble, si grand de franchise, d'honneur, de grandeur d'âme et de religieuse honnêteté qui distingue nos premiers citoyens et qui contraste si étonnamment avec cette populace de banqueroutiers qui soudoient les incendiaires, les parjures, les voleurs et la lie des villes pour commettre en leur nom, pour eux, et à leur profit des crimes dignes de Vandales? Du clergé national, sorti des rangs du peuple, identifié avec tous ses intérêts, dévoué jusqu'à la mort, initié à tous les progrès des sciences modernes, des arts et du génie, aux tendances des sociétés actuelles.[23]

Finally, when the *rouges* hurled insults, the editor of the *Journal* answered flamboyantly:

> Détrôner le Dieu de nos pères et lui substituer l'infâme idole du sensualisme, voilà leur but; vilipender le prêtre, calomnier son enseignement, couvrir d'un noir venin ses actions les plus louables,

---

22 *Journal de Québec*, 2 octobre 1849.
23 *Journal de Québec*, 2 mars 1850.

> voilà leur moyen.... Quel but, quelle fin vous proposez-vous en livrant à l'ignominie le prêtre du Canada, votre concitoyen, votre ami d'enfance, l'ami dévoué deo notre commune patrie! Aurez-vous relevé bien haut la gloire de notre pays lorsque vous aurez avili aux yeux de l'étranger ses institutions les plus précieuses, couvert de boue ses hommes les plus éminents dans l'ordre religieux et civil, enseveli sous un noir manteau de calomnies le corps le plus respectable de la société comme un cadavre sous un drap mortuaire?[24]

Le Canadien wrote less lyrically, but like the *Journal*, it too came to the defence of the priests, and struck back at *L'Avenir*. It found that the republicans' articles "représentent trop de passion et par conséquent une notable injustice envers les hommes en qui le pays a confiance."[25] And at the height of the temporal power dispute, it noted how the same republicans who praised Mazzini had also supported those who burned down the Canadian Parliament buildings, and signed the manifesto demanding Annexation to the United States.

In return, of course, the priests supported LaFontaine. At the time of Papineau's Manifesto at the end of 1847, during the general election that swept LaFontaine to the final achievement of responsible government, reports from different parts of Lower Canada came in to Montreal that "certains prêtres, même à Montréal, ont prononcé en chaire des discours presqu' exclusivement politiques."[26] But more important still than such electoral advice was the increasing involvement in party politics of the *Mélanges Religieux* and its junior associate in Quebec, the weekly *Ami de la Religion et de la Patrie*. Edited by Jacques Crémazie, *L'Ami* first appeared in early 1848 under the interesting motto: "Le trône chancelle quand l'honneur, la religion, la bonne foi ne l'environnent pas." It endorsed LaFontaine's ideas so unequivocally that Cauchon was glad to recommend it to his party leader for patronage:

> Il ne faudra pas oublier quand vous donnez des annonces d'en donner aussi à l'*Ami de la Religion* ... qui montre de bonnes dispositions et fait tout le bien qu'il peut.[27]

As for the *Mélanges*, since mid-1847 it had practically become a LaFontaine political sheet. In July 1847, the clergy had handed over the editorship to a twenty-one-year-old law student who was articling in the offices of A.-N. Morin: Hector Langevin, whose religious orthodoxy they felt well guaranteed by his two brothers

---

[24] *Journal de Québec*, 6 décembre 1849.
[25] *Le Canadien*, 31 mai 1848.
[26] *MR*, 14 décembre 1847.
[27] Public Archives of Canada, MG 24, B-14. LaFontaine Papers. Joseph Cauchon à LaFontaine, 24 octobre 1849.

(and frequent correspondents) in Quebec: Jean, a priest professor at the Séminaire, and Edmond who in September 1847 became secretary to the Archbishop's *Grand-Vicaire* Cazeau.

With mentors like Morin, the youthful editor soon threw his paper into the thick of the political fight. In fact he became so involved that at last the priests at the Bishopric felt they had to warn him (they did so several times) to tone down his enthusiasm for LaFontaine. He did not, however. His greatest service was perhaps the publicizing of the clergy's support for LaFontaine at the time of the trouble over Rebellion losses. At the height of the crisis, on May 5, 1849, he issued the rallying call:

> En présence de cette activité des gens turbulents et ennemis de la Constitution, on se demande ce qu'ont à faire les libéraux [i.e., LaFontaine's supporters] ... regardons nos Évêques, regardons nos prêtres, regardons notre clergé; il vient de nous montrer l'example en présentant lui-même des adresses à Son Excellence Lord Elgin, et en envoyant d'autres à notre gracieuse souveraine. Après cela hésiterons-nous à agir avec vigueur, promptitude et énergie? Hésiterons-nous à suivre la route que nous trace notre épiscopat, que nous trace notre clergé tout entier?[28]

Half a year later he spelled out his full sentiments in a letter to his brother Edmond:

> Si les rouges avaient l'autorité en mains, prêtres, églises, religion, etc., devraient disparaître de la face du Canada. Le moment est critique. Il faut que le ministère continue à être libéral tel qu'à présent, ou bien on est Américain, et puis alors adieu à notre langue et à notre nationalité.[29]

Perhaps it was inevitable that during the closing years of the decade the French-Canadian clergy would come to play an increasingly political role. For with responsible government the Canadiens had, for the first time in their long national life, taken over the direction of their own destiny. And as the Catholic Church had long played an important part in fashioning their thought, it was natural for most of those on the political stage to welcome the support of the priests. Yet, would it have happened as effortlessly if Bishop Bourget had not fallen in with the *Veuillotistes*? If LaFontaine and Morin had not supported clerical schools in 1846? If Hector Langevin had not articled in Morin's office? If *L'Avenir* had not attacked the Papal states? Would it have happened at all if Denis-Benjamin Viger had won the election

---

[28] *MR*, 5 mai 1849.
[29] *APQ* Collection Chapis, 253. Hector à Edmond Langevin, 25 janvier 1850.

of 1844? If the Papineau legend had persisted? Be that as it may, the *bleu* alliance of priest and politician (since we can now give it its name) radically transformed LaFontaine's party and French-Canadian nationalism.

Except when the rights of the Church were in question, ultramontanes tended to consider politics as secondary. They concentrated rather on Church-State problems, thus gradually moving away from areas of cooperation with Upper Canada—especially at a time when the "voluntary principle" was converting Baldwin's party as ultramontanism was LaFontaine's. Gradually they came to appeal almost exclusively to ideas and feelings which were proper only to French Canada. When he began in the late 1830s LaFontaine aimed at political and economic reforms in which both Canadas would share. In his famous *Adresse aux Électeurs de Terrebonne*, he described the problems of French Canada in political and economic terms alone. As the decade moved on, however, under pressure from his opponents and his followers, he found himself becoming more and more involved with ultramontanism and a narrower nationalism. Reluctantly, it seems. Late in 1851, several weeks after his resignation, he recalled to Cauchon, who had bragged about rallying the priests, how he had cautioned him about the faith-and-nationality theme. "Je me rappelle ce que vous m'avez dit," Cauchon admitted, "par rapport à la question nationale. Mais je vous répondais que c'était le seule corde qu'il était possible de faire vibrer avec succès."[30] Later, to another admonition from the former premier, the editor of the *Journal de Québec* admitted that "la question de nationalité était délicate," but protested again that "c'était la corde qui vibrait le mieux. J'espère que vous avez en cela parfaitement compris ma pensée et que vous êtes convaincu que je n'ai pas voulu employer un moyen malhonnête pour atteindre mon but."[31] LeFontaine had wanted to break with Papineau's particularist and republican nationalism. He appealed to a more general, open point of view, founding his hopes on cooperation with Upper Canada and in the British political system. Yet, in the end, he found himself the head of a party which tended to be as particularist as Papineau's (although for different reasons).

His party also turned out to be one which did not understand parliamentary institutions. The ultramontanes were not rigid republicans like Papineau, but they were rigid Catholics, used to "refuting the errors of our time," with a doctrine which they proudly wanted as "toujours une, toujours sublime, toujours la même."[32] They were accustomed to think in an atmosphere rarified by unchanging principles. Instinctively they reacted in dogmatic terms, pushing ideas to their limits—and students of the absolute make poor parliamentarians. The ultramontanes could not really understand parliamentary practice as LaFontaine and Parent had. They lacked political flair and skill in manoeuvring. They could not adapt to the gropings and

---

30   LaFontaine Papers. Joseph Cauchon à LaFontaine, 11 novembre 1851.
31   Ibid., décembre 1851.
32   *MR*, 15 décembre 1843.

costs of conciliation. To them, "rights" were an objective reality which could not be negotiated, only acknowledged. "Toleration" could not mean respect for an opposing opinion; at best it was a necessary evil. Applied to theology, their attitude might have had some validity (although not for ecumenism!) but transferred to politics and nationalism—as inevitably it was—it could not but extinguish Lafontaine's hopes for a broadening democracy of the British type.

For years the *bleus* and their Upper Canadian colleagues supported the same men, but as the French party gradually concentrated so dogmatically on Faith and Nationality, there could be no true meeting of minds. Outwardly, LaFontaine's and Parent's wider nationalism seemed to have prevailed: responsible government and British parliamentary institutions were secured. Also, a political party uniting Upper and Lower Canadians continued to govern the country for over a generation. But this was external appearance only: in reality, the party from which LaFontaine resigned in 1851 was assiduously becoming less concerned with the larger perspective than with the particular Church-State problems of French Canada; it was becoming decreasingly parliamentarian, increasingly authoritarian.

A funny thing indeed had happened to French-Canadian nationalism on its way to responsible government.

Mid-Victorian Liberalism in Central Canadian Newspapers, 1850-67

J.M.S. Careless

It would clearly be inadequate to assess the cultural life of a modern community through its newspapers. Yet such an approach seems necessary for an understanding of the intellectual development of the English-speaking part of the Province of Canada in the mid-nineteenth century. In the eighteen-fifties and sixties Canada West was just emerging from the all-embracing pioneer struggle. A raw young community, it imported the bulk of its books and ideas and was almost without native literary expression. It did, however, have its own press. Journalism may often be a rather dubious form of literature, but the investigator must work with what is available. Hence the Central Canadian press of the Confederation era is particularly significant because there is little else with which to test the mind of the Canadians in this crucial period when the modern Canadian state was coming into existence. And the thoughts and opinions dominant in these years were vitally important in shaping the future national character.

It is also true that, although much smaller and simpler, the Canadian newspapers of this era were generally of a higher intellectual calibre and of greater influence in their community than most of our modern journals. The nineteenth century was perhaps the golden age of the press, when the reading public, undistracted by the competing charms of radio, movies, and television, gave a single-minded attention to its newspapers. This was the age of great political journalists—in Canada, of editors like William Lyon Mackenzie and George Brown—when readers hung eagerly on the word of these lords of opinion and did not escape to the sports page, the comic strips, or to a confusion of syndicated columnists. The Canadian press of a century ago was of major importance in mirroring the mind of the community, and in helping to shape it as well.

For the purpose of a paper, not a book, any discussion of this press must be drastically limited in scope. Accordingly, it is possible here to examine only the Toronto journals among the many published in Central Canada in these years. There is reason in this, however, even for non-Torontonians. It is useful to choose a complete community of newspapers for analysis, and what more suitable than that of the chief city of Canada West, its political, economic, and intellectual centre, whose principal journals had the largest circulation in the province? Furthermore, during this mid-century period the Toronto press was taking on a metropolitan character and attaining a province-wide circulation, thanks to the advent of railways, cheap postage, and the rise of Toronto itself towards metropolitan stature. The English-speaking Montreal papers could not hope to gain so wide a constituency. Leading Hamilton, London, Ottawa, or Kingston journals might each have a large local circulation. The Toronto press, however, entered all these areas, and two of its members, the *Globe* and *Leader*, stood out over all the province as the giants of Canadian journalism, quite comparable in circulation to important British and American papers of the day.

The other main newspapers in Toronto between 1850 and 1867 were, on the Reform or Liberal side, the *North American* and the *Examiner*, and, on the Conservative, the *Patriot* and the *British* or *Daily Colonist*. The *North American* was established in 1850 as the organ of the new Clear Grit radical movement. The *Examiner* was a much older paper, founded in 1838 by Francis Hincks to fight the battle for responsible government. But by the mid-century mark, its place as the chief Reform newspaper had been usurped by the *Globe*, begun in 1844 by the energetic young George Brown. Largely in retaliation, the *Examiner* tended to make common cause with the *North American* against Brown and his journal. In the early fifties the *Globe* battled hard against the alleged extremism of these Clear Grit partners. In fact, it scorned the very name "Clear Grit," until, after the shattering of the Reform party by the Liberal-Conservative coalition of 1854, the Brownite and Clear Grit groups came together to oppose the coalition ministry, and gradually accepted the name of "Grit" for a watered-down version of original Clear Grit radicalism.

The Toronto *Leader* was founded in 1852 as a moderate Liberal organ. In 1854 it followed the Hincksite Liberals into the coalition with the Conservatives, and henceforth espoused the Liberal-Conservative ministerial cause against the *Globe* and the opposition forces of Reform. Nevertheless for years the *Leader* claimed to be upholding true and pure Liberalism against the wild-eyed, factious followers of George Brown. The *British Colonist* was avowedly Conservative, but more moderate in its Conservatism than the *Patriot* which was, on the whole, the Orangemen's organ, the fervent defender of the British tie and the glorious memory of King William III.

The *Examiner* and *North American* were bought out by the *Globe* in 1855, the *Patriot* by the *Leader* in 1854. The *Colonist* died of malnutrition in 1858. For most of the period, accordingly, the *Globe* and *Leader* held the field between them. The most significant point emerging from an analysis of these two powerful newspapers, the two main organs of the opposing sides in politics, is that they shared the same general framework of ideas. They looked to British institutions and precedents, turned their backs on things American, and accepted the chief political and economic doctrines of contemporary mid-Victorian Britain. In fact, mid-Victorian Liberalism seems the best term to describe the pattern of their thought and opinions. To the left of the *Globe*, the *Examiner* and *North American* were plainly more liberal, or radical, than British. To the right of the *Leader*, the *Colonist* and *Patriot* were more British than liberal. But in general, this pattern of mid-Victorian Liberalism, though admittedly fraying at the edges, may be applied to the whole Toronto newspaper community during the Confederation era. Here was British thought deep in North

America, in the most influential press in Canada, and at a critical time in her history. Its meaning deserves investigation.

To make such an inquiry, one might follow many threads of ideas through the questions discussed in these journals, but there is room to deal with only a few main aspects of their opinions. Those most in evidence concern the value which they placed on British political institutions and ideas, their acceptance of Cobdenite economic doctrine, and the stress they laid on issues involving the relations of church and state. Turning to the first of these topics, we are immediately struck by the amount of time spent in the Toronto journals in weighing the relative merits of the British and the American political systems, to the detriment of American democracy. Since Canada had won the right to govern herself in internal affairs by 1850, the question of how to use this right naturally assumed a new importance. Was the British technique of responsible cabinet government, used to win autonomy, a sufficient end in itself or only a means to further political change? Now that Canadians governed themselves, should they adopt new political machinery?

It is true that the *North American*, at least, did accept the American version of democracy. Indeed, it was founded to press for further political change and for new democratic machinery in Canada. This paper and its early Clear Grit associates declared for complete "elective institutions"—an elected governor, upper house, and local officials, and full manhood suffrage. The "aristocratical" forms of the British constitution were deemed unsuited to North America. It was argued that without a written constitution and the separation of powers, ministries were too powerful, extravagant, and corrupt. The state governments of New York or Ohio were urged as the true models to follow.[1] The *Examiner* echoed the *North American* in this Clear Grit crusade, but with less grasp of theoretical arguments and much harking back to the good old days of the Reform party under William Lyon Mackenzie[2] Mackenzie, incidentally, was a frequent contributor to its pages during the early fifties.

The rest of the press, however, was at least equally fervent in defence of British institutions. The *Patriot* and *Colonist* boiled with indignant loyalty. The *Leader* and *Globe* set out to prove the superiority of the British system in liberty, efficiency, and honesty, and the worthlessness of American republicanism. In fact, these papers were quite ready to indict one another with the most damning charge of all: a leaning towards American ideas. Thus the *Colonist* somehow found that the "prosaic maunderings" of the *Leader* were too close to the American "ravings of ultra-republicanism,"[3] even though the *Leader* had earlier been attacking "republican equality" as a state "where all men are born free and equal, with certain black exceptions," and had characterized the position of the President of the United States

---

[1] *North American* (weekly), Oct. 30 to Nov. 22, 1850; Jan. 17, Feb. 14, 1851.
[2] *Examiner* (weekly), Sept. 5, 19, 1849; Mar. 20, 1850; May 31, 1854; Jan. 3, 1855.
[3] *Daily Colonist*, Jan. 24, 1856. The daily edition of the *Colonist* was so titled. That issued three times a week was named the *British Colonist*.

as "the slave of the Rabble."[4] And the *Patriot*, as always, expressed a most decided faith in Canadian Conservatism, "which clings to the BRITISH CONSTITUTIONAL system of Government as superior to all others, believing it to possess within itself those inherent principles of elasticity and vigour which adapt to the various circumstances of the people, and enable it to meet, with becoming vigour and suitableness, the increased intellectual and progressive knowledge of the country."[5]

Yet since the main concern of this paper is with the Liberal side, it is perhaps most significant that the Toronto *Globe* was so definite, so explicit, and so well informed in arguing the case in favour of the British system of government. This was the largest Liberal journal, the one which soon absorbed the heretical *North American* and *Examiner*, but kept no part of their doctrines; the paper which became identified with the Reform cause, but underlined the British affiliations of Liberalism in rebuilding the Reform party. During the years 1850 to 1855 the issue of elective institutions was a major one in Central Canadian politics, although one somewhat neglected by our historians. This issue was exhaustively canvassed by the *Globe*, which tirelessly upheld the British model.

It is true that later, in 1859, the year of gloom and frustration after the failure of the Brown-Dorion government, the *Globe* did toy with written constitutional checks and elected ministries as the solution to Canada's political difficulties; but it soon turned its back on these to offer a combination of responsible government and federation as the way out. And when Confederation became not a distant possibility but a definite project, George Brown's journal again insisted on the British system as the basis for a national government. In fact, it favoured the federal principle as a device which would permit Canada to retain the virtues of the British parliamentary constitution while meeting the North American problem of sectionalism.[6]

The *Globe*'s viewpoint on the constitution appears most clearly with regard to an elected upper house. At the time of Confederation, the paper strongly urged that the new federal senate be not elected but appointed, since under the British parliamentary system a second chamber should have only the minor role of amending and delaying, and should not be able to thwart the national will of the much more significant house of commons. Two elected houses on the American model, on the other hand, might both claim a popular mandate, and if opposed to each other, deadlock the constitution.[7]

This was the same stand that the *Globe* had taken in the early fifties when the campaign for an elected upper house for the Province of Canada was the main focus of the elective institutions question.[8] The paper had to fight this battle on two

---

[4] *Leader* (daily), Aug. 14, Dec. 8, 1854.
[5] *Patriot* (daily), May 24, 1853.
[6] *Globe* (daily), Sept. 14, 1859; July 15, 1864.
[7] Ibid., Oct. 8, 20, 1864.
[8] Ibid., Mar. 23, 1852.

fronts. The Clear Grit journals desired an elective legislative council as a step towards the American democratic system. The Conservative press sought it for other reasons, in part because the existing nominated council was solidly entrenched with Liberal appointees, and also because an upper house elected on a highly qualified franchise would form a stronger bulwark against dangerous radical tendencies. Denying any subservience to Americanism, the Conservative papers could claim that an elected council was not an American innovation since it had been adopted in other British colonies far from the shores of the United States. Still the *Globe* viewed it as the thin edge of the Yankee wedge.[9] A majority composed of Clear Grits and some Conservative and Liberal elements managed to carry an act for an elective council in 1855, but the *Globe* had the satisfaction of seeing the measure undone at Confederation. And it is worth noting that at this later time the *Leader*, now the chief Conservative organ, agreed that an elected council had been a mistake, although it gave as its reason the danger of too much democracy if both houses were elected. And democracy, it said, meant "the dead level of forced and false equality."[10]

It is well to keep in mind that in Canada during the mid-nineteenth century democracy was still a suspect word, with Jacobin, or at any rate American, overtones. The Conservative journals would certainly have none of it, and both the *Leader* and *Globe* pointed to the evils of rule by the masses. "Our form of government is not a democracy," said the *Leader* during the American Civil War, "unbridled and uncontrolled...completely in the hands of the mob."[11] Only the *North American* was whole-hearted in its democratic faith. The *Examiner* declared "a plague on both your houses." It condemned indeed the "flunkeyism" of British society and government, but also attacked the "tyranny and slavery of the republican Americans."[12] If Britain had noblemen, the United States had slaves. In this, one is tempted to see the reaction of Mackenzie himself, soured first with Britain and then with the United States—as indeed he said he was, on his return to Canada from his American exile.

Both the *Leader* and the *Globe* in their view of democracy expressed the central position of mid-Victorian Liberalism. Both declared for a wide, popular electorate but still wanted a qualified franchise to recognize property and intelligence, and to prevent the rule of ignorance and mere numbers. The former journal, to be sure, attacked George Brown's doctrine of representation by population as an un-British principle of numbers,[13] but the latter denied that its cherished policy implied universal suffrage.[14] The *Leader* quoted from John Stuart Mill on the tyranny of the majority and urged plural votes for "the virtue of industry and thrift which acquires and

---

[9] Ibid., Oct. 31, 1850; Apr. 13, 1852; Mar. 24, 1854.
[10] *Leader*, Oct. 3, 1864.
[11] Ibid., jan. 25, 1862.
[12] *Examiner*, July 25, 1855.
[13] *Leader*, Apr. 3, 1865.
[14] *Globe*, Apr. 12, July 24, 1861; June 23, 1864.

preserves property."[15] The *Globe* rejected "that broad and tumultuous constituency which has no restriction in residence or property," and scorned "the unwashed multitudes who boast of universal suffrage."[16] It claimed besides that a limited franchise secured the truest expression of the public mind; while, "the lower we go in the scale of suffrage the more we add to that dangerous element."[17] The *Globe* also agreed with Liberals in Britain that the franchise should be extended no faster than public education, the Liberal panacea, could proceed.[18] In short, there was in this mid-century Canadian press little of the spirit of American Jeffersonian or Jacksonian democracy with their faith in the natural worth of the common man.

The economic views of these Canadian journals approximated as closely to the pattern of British mid-Victorian Liberalism as did their political views. The *Globe* was most fully and consciously Cobdenite in endorsing the British Manchester School philosophy of free trade and the reign of natural economic laws. Cobden, Bright, and their disciple at the Chancellory of the Exchequer, Gladstone, were its economic patron saints. The paper frequently discoursed on the evil of state interference with "the laws of trade," attacking usury laws especially, lectured on sound currency with many quotations from British classical economists, and viewed tariff protection as something between stupidity and sacrilege.[19] It need hardly be said that the *Globe* regularly condemned the United States protective tariff and any heretical protectionist tendencies in Canada.

Its views on labour relations and problems of social welfare were similarly orthodox: labour unions were not to infringe on the liberal right of free contract (this was especially so in the case of strikes at the *Globe* office); strikes could not raise wages artificially, "by flying in the face of nature"; and if the masses suffered in old lands, the only solution was to educate them to understand their lot as dictated by political economy, and to urge them to emigrate in order to enable the labour market automatically to adjust itself. The state should not step in. The *Globe*'s economic individualism was indeed tempered by humanitarianism, and it deplored the doctrinaire rigidity of the more extreme followers of Jeremy Bentham. These same qualifications, however, were being made in Britain within the general context of mid-Victorian Liberalism. In sum, the *Globe* found its authorities, doctrines, and proper practice in economic matters in contemporary Liberal Britain, and condemned any American deviations from the British norm.

The other journals were less explicit and less theoretical in setting forth their economic beliefs. Yet these can be gleaned from the attitudes they assumed towards

---

[15] *Leader*, Oct. 3, 4, 1864.
[16] *Globe*, June 1, 1850; May 19, 1865.
[17] Ibid., Jan. 28, 1851; Sept. 23, 1857.
[18] Ibid., May 4, 1852.
[19] See J.M.S. Careless, "The Toronto *Globe* and Agrarian Radicalism, 1850-67" (*Canadian Historical Review*, March, 1948, 32-4) for economic doctrines of the *Globe* relevant to this and the succeeding paragraph.

practical issues in Canadian affairs. In commercial policy, for instance, the *North American* did not accept the prevalent United States model, and attacked "the antiquated notions of American Protectionists."[20] It wanted complete free trade and direct taxation, along with the abolition of customs duties. The *Examiner* shared this general position, praising Cobden, "the lion," for his sound political economy and his programme of free trade and retrenchment in Britain. At the same time it condemned the old protectionist imperial policy as a "clumsy system of mutual monopoly."[21] The *Patriot*, on the other hand, still looked back hopefully to the defunct colonial system, and, as a good old-fashioned Tory, opposed Whig-Liberal free trade in Britain or Canada. Nevertheless it used the language of current economic liberalism in advocating the repeal of usury laws in Canada. Money should be left "to flow in its natural channels." The legislator had no more power to control profit than to prevent water finding its own level. "He cannot alter the law of nature."[22]

The Conservative *Colonist* held that it was hopeless for the *Patriot* to dream of Britain returning to protection, although it praised the Tories and "honest Protectionists" in England—always excepting Disraeli, whose sudden conversion to free trade in 1852 it thought "indecent."[23] The *Colonist*, however, did think that protection was both sound and feasible in the case of Canada; but felt that the practical course lay between British free trade and the American high tariff, through a tariff designed to create revenue and offer some measure of "incidental protection" at the same time.[24] In this matter the *Colonist* was, as usual, practical in its approach and middle-of-the-road in its decisions, seemingly less concerned than the other papers with the theoretical background of its policies.

The *Leader* also took the practical view with regard to Canadian trade policy: the colony needed the revenue derived from customs duties, and these might well be arranged to offer incidental encouragement to rising Canadian manufactures. In theory, however, it claimed to adhere to the liberal doctrine of free trade and rejected "the exploded theories of protection."[25] The *Leader* thus defended Galt's tariff of 1859 as a revenue measure, and not as protectionist in character, noting that even free-trade Britain still found it necessary to raise a large revenue by customs duties on non-essential articles. Canada could not be charged with adopting "a discarded policy of protection," because she, too, could not afford absolute free trade.[26] But the journal also recognized that "a young community that has just assumed the responsibilities of a separate national existence has many temptations to violate the principles of

---

[20] *North American*, Mar. 7, 1851.
[21] *Examiner*, Jan. 30, 1850.
[22] *Patriot*, Nov. 18, 1852.
[23] *British Colonist*, Mar. 19, June 29, 1852.
[24] Ibid., Mar. 19, 23, 1852.
[25] *Leader*, Dec. 20, 1850.
[26] Ibid., Nov. 24, 25, 1859.

economic science," and so had to beware the protectionist "nonsense about the desirability of a nation doing everything for itself."[27]

The *Leader* used the proper liberal phrases on currency questions. It too paid homage to the water-level principle by pointing out that "money will go to the dearest market as sure as water flows down hill."[28] Any interference with the value of money was "absurdly injurious," as absurd as fixing food prices by state action; but "this mist of ignorance must soon go in this age of progress, of railroads and steam and sea-spanning telegraphs."[29] Yet towards the close of our period this paper still had to lament the fact that the Toronto Board of Trade was seeking to fix an "artificial" rate of discount for depreciated American silver coins in circulation in the city. Such an attempt showed "an ignorance of those economic laws which no Legislature can overrule."[30]

On labour questions the *Leader* again was orthodox liberal. Disliking the ideas and ideals of trade unionism, it agreed with the *Globe* that the cooperative movement was the true form of unionism for the working classes to pursue, one which permitted them to flourish as capitalists on their own behalf and did not lead them against the immutable laws of economic individualism. The *Leader* noted that cooperative societies were advocated by Cobden, a man "who perhaps did more for the working men of England than any statesman of his time."[31] But greater still, the *Leader* said, was the authority of John Stuart Mill. It gave long excerpts from Mill's *Political Economy* in support of cooperatives.[32] The trade union as a collective bargaining agency was not so well authorized, as far as the Toronto press was concerned, and the *Colonist*, indeed, referred to the strike of the Toronto Typographical Union of 1854 as "a gross and unreasoning assertion of power," an attempt by the strikers to assume arbitrary control for themselves.[33]

But a much more burning topic in the press of the Confederation era than the incipient Canadian labour movement, usury laws, currency questions, or even tariff problems was the half-political, half-social issue of the relations of church and state. It had many ramifications. It involved in particular, after 1850, the agitation of the secularization of the clergy reserves, the alleged Lower-Canadian Catholic domination of Canadian politics, and the perennial separate school question. The separation of church and state was far from having been achieved in Canada West during this period. The resolve to fight for that principle led George Brown into active politics, brought him and the Clear Grit originals gradually together, and greatly influenced

---

27 Ibid., Feb. 18, 1862.
28 Ibid., Jan. 2, 1857.
29 Ibid., May 20, 1857.
30 Ibid., Mar. 14, 1865.
31 Ibid., May 5, 1865.
32 Ibid.
33 *Daily Colonist*, June 3, 1854.

the character of the western Liberal party which grew under his leadership out of this alliance.

The separation of church and state was doubtless to a considerable extent a narrowly sectarian cry, leaving Brown and the *Globe* and their followers open in that day and this to charges of bigotry. It was also, however, an essential belief in the mind of English-speaking Liberalism in mid-century Canada; and it was associated, above all, not with the United States, where the separation of church and state had already been accomplished, but with the British background, where the struggles of Nonconformity with the state Church of England were very far from over.

In contemporary Britain, Nonconformity had moved on from an acceptance of religious toleration to a demand for religious equality. It was attacking the principle of establishment itself, urging against "state-churchism" the voluntary principle, that is, that churches should be voluntary organizations without state backing or recognition, so that religion might be kept out of politics and politics out of religion. The battle was joined especially in the field of education, where the "voluntaries" contended against Anglican control of state-supported schools. Voluntaryism (or voluntarism) was strong in British Liberalism, just as Nonconformity was strong in middle-class, Victorian Liberal ranks. Indeed, Edward Miall, a prominent member of the Manchester School, was editor of the powerful *Nonconformist*, a voluntaryist journal founded to work for disestablishment.

Voluntaryism was equally strong, or stronger, in Canada West. The *Globe*, in fact, observed that many of the Canadian Reformers had brought the voluntarist principle with them from Britain.[34] And, of course, George Brown and his father had themselves been vigorous exponents of voluntaryism in supporting the Free Church in Scotland on its break from the established Presbyterian body. In fact, they had come to Canada initially to found a journal (the *Banner*), in behalf of the Free Kirk party in the colony. Accordingly, in Canadian politics George Brown and the *Globe* contended against every manifestation of "state-churchism," and found many supporters.

In the eighteen-forties they worked for the removal of the University of Toronto from Anglican control, and against attempts to divide the provincial endowment among sectarian colleges. After 1850 they strove for the secularization of the clergy reserves, and to prevent the passage of an increasing number of Lower Canadian "ecclesiastical bills" which, they claimed, implied state recognition of Roman Catholic institutions. Next they plunged into the rising separate school struggle, determined to defend the secular public school system of Canada West against sectarian inroads and "state-church" designs. And whether it was right or wrong in this regard, the Brownite stand was firmly based on the linked principles of voluntaryism—that no public funds should go to church schools—and the separation of church and state—that popular education was a matter for the state alone. For

---

[34] *Globe*, Apr. 2, 1853.

these principles the *Globe* looked to Britain, and found support for them among Victorian Liberals and Nonconformists.

Brown and the *Globe* made the voluntary movement in Canada very much their own. They began to build a new Liberal party about it. Yet the *North American* and *Examiner* also endorsed voluntaryism. The former early declared for "religious equality to the fullest extent," and on occasion railed against Lower-Canadian Catholic influence in the state.[35] The latter became almost as bound up in the religious issue as the *Globe*. "Are we slaves to Popish Prelates?" it asked excitedly.[36] "Puseyite state parsons" of Anglicanism were also attacked.[37] "Let the people of this Province eschew the curse of a State-paid clergy of whatever name."[38] Indeed, the *Examiner's* motto, from its inception in 1838, was "Responsible Government and the Voluntary Principle." William Lyon Mackenzie, closely associated with the *Examiner*, worked with George Brown in parliament on his return to the house in the eighteen-fifties on at least one thing, the voluntaryist campaign. In this he was one of Brown's first parliamentary allies.

The rest of the Toronto press was not so voluntary-minded. The *Leader* approved the principle of the separation of church and state, but stressed that the stand of the *Globe* and its followers was bigoted and so, illiberal. We prefer, it said, equality with Roman Catholics to domination by bigots.[39] At the same time this journal sought the secularization of the reserves, and was distressed by separate school bills that cut away at the state education in which it believed. Yet the *Leader* recognized a need of compromise with the powerful Catholic population in the province on the separate school issue. Here it was naturally voicing the view of the Coalition between French and English-speaking elements which it supported after 1854.

The *Colonist* could hardly agree with the *Globe's* voluntaryism since it was the organ of the Church of Scotland Presbyterians who had held to the side of the established church in the old land. It also attacked the "state irreligion" of the *Leader*, and opposed the purely secular common schools that both *Globe* and *Leader* upheld, desiring some religious instruction in the curriculum.[40] The *Patriot* seemed to share the confusion on the religious issue of its Orange supporters, some of whom put "Protestant liberties" first and joined the voluntaryist Protestant Alliance, while others, stressing Tory allegiance, would have nothing to do with this Reform-inspired body. But at length the *Patriot* came down on the side of Toryism; and when Toryism and Orangism came shortly to rest in coalition with the Catholic *Bleus*, the question was closed for it. It was closed even more definitely by the sale of the *Patriot* to the *Leader* in that same year, the political *annus mirabilis*, 1854. Yet

---

[35] *North American*, May 31, June 4, Dec. 13, 1850.
[36] *Examiner*, July 11, 1855.
[37] Ibid.
[38] Ibid., June 14, 1854.
[39] *Leader*, Sept. 1, 1853.
[40] *Daily Colonist*, Jan. 9, 24, 1856.

whether opposed or friendly to voluntarism, the Conservative journals like the rest dealt fully with the question of the relations of church and state, and with frequent references to British precedents and British conditions.

Here lies the key to this major discussion in the mid-century press, to this question, as well as to those of political institutions and economic policies: the constant reference to British ideas. The same reference could be found elsewhere in the journals, on topics of social welfare, sabbatarian morality, and intellectual standards. The plain fact is that these newspapers felt very strongly the sense of belonging to a British intellectual community, no less than of belonging to a physical British empire. They were in a stream of ideas emanating from Britain at the height of her power and prestige. Nor was this incompatible with their position in North America.

It is well to make clear that no sharp distinction is intended, or really can be made, between "British" and "American" intellectual influences on Canada at this time. The United States itself was then in many ways still a cultural colony of Britain, and ideas originating in Britain might conceivably come into Canada by way of their American modifications. British and American ideas were hence much of the same kind, but the question of the degree of difference is all important. It has here been suggested that most of the newspapers under discussion received their main ideas directly from Britain, and tended to reject any American differences and modifications. No doubt this was not wholly true. In matters, say, of agrarian policy or public education, Canadian opinion owed much to American inspiration, or to general North American experience. But in regard to major problems of government, economic policy, and the relations of church and state, the influential Toronto press—and hence the mind it influenced—expressed itself mainly in British terms. This fact represents a general transfer of British ideas to Canada, to the North American scene.

Qualifications, of course, are necessary. The *North American* was certainly more American than British in its feeling, in that day, for democracy. Yet this paper also claimed that it cared not if a doctrine was British or American as long as it was useful;[41] and there is reason to think that its democratic ideas had British as well as American roots. The writer who explained the *North American*'s original programme in a series of well-considered articles was Charles Clarke, an Englishman, whose first political memories were those of Chartism; and there were other Chartist affinities in early Clear Grittism.[42] American democratic examples were usually cited; but so they were by democratic radicals in Britain herself at the time, because the United States naturally supplied the working model of democracy.

The *Examiner* also advocated a pattern of democratic government. But much of its thought here went back to the early days of Mackenzie radicalism, which was certainly open to British influences as well as American, stemming from Hume and

---

[41] *North American*, Oct. 31, 1851.
[42] Charles Clarke, *Sixty Years in Upper Canada* (Toronto, 1908), 13, 45, 58, 61.

Roebuck as well as Andrew Jackson. And the *Examiner*, incidentally, was still receiving its British parliamentary papers from Joseph Hume in the eighteen-fifties. Furthermore, in its economic and voluntaryist discussions, this journal looked to British, not American, leaders and precedents.

There seems little difficulty in linking the *Globe* and the *Leader* with British Liberal ideas, or the Conservative papers at least with British ideas. Moreover, one should recall that the radical and Tory wings of the Toronto press in this period soon declined, leaving the essentially moderate Liberalism of the *Leader*, and of the *Globe*, for all its religious zeal, as most fully expressing the public opinion of the day. Whatever advertisements may bring or clever journalists contrive, in that day at least it was the newspapers with the less popular opinions that went under.

We are left, then, with the general view of a press that transferred its main opinions from Liberal Victorian Britain. Why so? The "colonial attitude of dependence" is not an answer, but merely re-words the question. The reaction against the apparent failure of the democratic experiment in the United States, collapsing into sectionalism in the fifties and aflame in civil war in the sixties, is a better reply, but only a partial one. A more complete explanation would first deal with the fact of British immigration. The great mass movement from Britain into Central Canada in the first half of the nineteenth century had virtually inundated the earlier English-speaking population in the country, which had had deeper North American roots. By 1850 the immigrants had firmly established themselves in their new community and thanks to their numbers had risen to the fore. The extent of their ascendancy in the ensuing period may be quickly recognized by noting how many contemporary Canadian public men, party leaders or Fathers of Confederation, for instance, had been born in Britain. Canada, perhaps, never before or since has been so British.

This was particularly true in the newspaper world, where journalists educated and frequently trained in Britain readily came to lead in what was still largely a half-taught, pioneer community. George and Gordon Brown of the *Globe*, Hugh Scobie, first owner of the *Colonist*, James Lesslie, owner of the *Examiner*, were Scots; Ogle Gowan of the *Patriot* and James Beaty of the *Leader* were Irish; Samuel Thompson, later proprietor of the *Colonist*, David Lindsey, editor at different times of the *Examiner* and *Leader*, and George Sheppard, similarly editor of the *Colonist* and *Leader*, were English. Only William McDougall, owner of the *North American*, was Canadian-born. In respect to this journal, there may be something in a name, after all. But the *Globe* boasted that all its editorial staff were from the old country.[43]

Another point of explanation might lie in the fact that in the mid-nineteenth century this Canadian community was, on the whole, more effectively tied into the British imperial system than it had been before or was to be thereafter. Responsible government had removed the main grievances of colonialism. Nationalism had not yet really developed. The British tie meant liberty, and security as well against the still threatening United States. Steamships and telegraphs had cut down the barrier of

---

[43] *Globe*, Nov. 23, 1861.

distance from Britain, but transcontinentalism had not yet arisen to turn Canada's eyes inward and to the west. Central Canada was still a long, narrow settlement along the St. Lawrence system that pointed to Britain and channelled every impulse from the imperial centre deep into the Great Lakes country.

And so it was with ideas. They were channelled from Britain by steamship and telegraph, or carried with the immigrants, who so influenced their community that it kept looking to the centre of the British world for the source of its thought. This is not merely to be called dependence. Feeling a unity with Britain, English-speaking Canadians accepted the bulk of her ideas as their own. Their newspapers naturally did the same. The result was the dominance of mid-Victorian Liberalism, seen in the press that has been examined. In the period, therefore, when the modern Canadian nation was being founded, English-speaking opinion in Central Canada was tending away from the exciting extremes of both radicalism and toryism towards a moderate, and no doubt stodgy, cast of mind. Have we lost all our Victorian Liberalism yet?

There is another note to be added. The transfer of British ideas observed in the case of these newspapers suggests an hypothesis for broader use in the study of Canadian history. Such an hypothesis was elaborated some years ago for United States history by Dixon Ryan Fox.[44] He urged against the frontier thesis, which held that civilization was largely shaped in America by the influence of the West, that the major process in the development of the United States was the progressive transfer of European civilization across the Atlantic and from east to west. This concept of the "transit of civilization" is one of a number of qualifications which have been made to the frontier or native North American interpretation in United States history. One might suggest that the traditional time-lag has been operating long enough in Canadian history-writing. The North American view or stress in our history similarly needs qualifying now by a regard for the transit of civilization. This, in the case of English-speaking Canada, means largely a regard for the influence of transferred British ideas and institutions on our part of the North American scene.

If the history of Canada and the United States may be read broadly as an interaction of the American environment and imported cultures, then surely the transfer of ideas, even if a minor theme, is still more important for English-speaking Canada than for the United States. For we came into the environment later, kept our colonial ties longer; in fact, today we are largely marked off from Americans because we did so. That being the case, we largely exist as Canadians and have a separate identity because of the greater continuing influence which the transfer of ideas has exercised upon us. To such grand suppositions a paper on a few journals during a few short years may lead, though it can only suggest the hypothesis, not prove it.

---

[44] See D.R. Fox, *Ideas in Motion* (New York, 1935), and D.R. Fox, ed., *Sources of Culture in the Middle West* (New York, 1934), especially his introduction.

Society in the Union Period

Section 9

As British North America became increasingly settled and its economy developed, it seemed in many ways to be truly a land of opportunity. Canals and railroads were built, towns sprang up, industries appeared, and trade in wheat, flour, and lumber flourished. Growth and prosperity were clearly visible—and yet, as these articles show, not everyone shared equally in the benefits. Class distinctions existed, and while some flaunted wealth and wielded power, the nature of the economy—and even of the climate itself—forced others into an ongoing cycle of poverty and distress. What's more, even the wealthy could not be sure of holding on to their success. Catastrophe was a possibility in every trade or profession, and all faced the risk that they might have to pull up stakes one day and move on to someplace else.

It was Michael Katz who, in the article presented here, first pointed out the instability in mid-19th century Canadian life, the constant movement and failure to become established in one place. He did this by using previously unfamiliar methods of manipulating census data and similar sources. His techniques required the expenditure of enormous time by a large team of people and the use of computers—a new tool for historians. But was there any other way to have discovered what he refers to as "transience" in Canadian society?

Aside from the fact of transience, what else does Katz tell us about the character or structure of 19th-century Canadian society? What kind of people formed the elite? Who were more likely to succeed and who less likely?

Why did climate have such a large impact on the British North American economy in the 19th century? What does Fingard tell us about the ways in which society dealt with poverty in that age? How does her approach to the study of history compare with Katz's? Is it possible to say which approach is more valuable—or more interesting?

Both Katz and Fingard deal largely with little people—"nameless" people—the kind not mentioned in traditional histories that describe politics, wars, and the building of economies. Why is it important that this sort of study be done?

You may be interested to know that the transience which Katz found in Hamilton has been found in rural areas as well. An example can be seen in David Gagan, *Hopeful Travellers*. For more of Fingard's type of work see her book, *Jack in Port*.

The People of a Canadian City: 1851-2

Michael Katz

On an average day in 1851 about 14,000 people awoke in Hamilton, Ontario. Most of them were quite unremarkable and thoroughly ordinary. In fact, there is no reason why the historian reading books, pamphlets, newspapers, or even diaries and letters should ever encounter more than seven hundred of them. The rest, at least ninety-five out of every hundred, remain invisible. In so far as most written history is concerned, they might just as well have never lived.

One consequence of their invisibility has been that history, as it is usually written, represents the record of the articulate and prominent. We assume too easily, for example, that the speeches of politicians reflected the feelings and conditions of ordinary people. Another consequence is that we lack a foundation on which to construct historical interpretations. It was, after all, the activities, interactions, and movements of these invisible men and women that formed the very stuff of past societies. Without a knowledge of how they lived, worked, behaved, and arranged themselves in relation to each other our understanding of any place and point in time must be partial, to say the least. A third consequence is that we apply contemporary assumptions to past society. We use our everyday experience of modern social relationships to make models which we apply to the past. We believe, for instance, that we are more sophisticated than our ancestors about sex, marriage, and the spacing of children. As a result, we imagine that they must have married younger than we do today and reproduced as fast as nature would allow. Both of these assumptions, as it happens, are generally quite untrue.

The problem, of course, is evidence. How are we to write with meaning of the life of an ordinary labourer, shoemaker, or clerk in a nineteenth-century city? Or trace the most common patterns between important social features such as occupation, wealth, religion, ethnicity, family size, and school attendance? Those questions may be answered more directly and in a more straightforward manner than we have often imagined, as I hope to make clear in the rest of this essay. My purpose is twofold: first, to show the range of questions about ordinary nineteenth-century people that may be asked and answered, and second, to sketch what, at this juncture, I take to be the primary social and demographic patterns within a mid-nineteenth-century Canadian city. The two great themes of nineteenth-century urban history, I shall argue, are transiency and inequality; I shall devote a section of this paper to each and, as well, to the nature of the family and household. For differences in family and household structure reflected, in part, the broad economic distinctions within urban society.

At the beginning two caveats are necessary: the quantitative information presented here is only partial; it is drawn from a great many detailed tables.[1] Second, figures given here are approximate. Such must be the case with all historical data. However, and this is the important point, the magnitudes, the differences between groups, may be taken, I believe, as a fair representation of the situation as it existed.

The manuscript census is the most valuable source of information about people within nineteenth-century cities. Its value is enhanced by its arrangement because it provides a list of features not only for each individual but for each household as well. For individuals the census from 1851 onward lists, among other items, name, age, birthplace, religion, occupation, school attendance, and birth or death within the year. It provides a residential location for each household and a description of the kind of house occupied; it permits the differentiation of relatives from non-relatives and the rough delineation of the relationships of household members to each other. In some cases it provides information about the business of the household head by listing other property, such as a store or shop owned, and number of people employed. Assessment rolls supplement the manuscript census with detailed economic information, usually about each adult member of the workforce. The assessment lists income over a certain level, real property, personal property, and some other economic characteristics. As well, it lists the occupation of each person assessed, the owner of the dwelling, and hence, whether the individual was an owner or renter of property. (In some instances a man who rents one house or store owns another; in other cases individuals own property around the city. These bits of information about individuals may be gathered together to present a more complete economic profile.) Published city directories corroborate the information from other sources and provide, additionally, the exact residential address of people and, in the case of proprietors, the address of their business if outside the home. Directories include, additionally, listings of people in various important political, financial, and voluntary positions within the city. Many other sources which list information about ordinary people supplement the census, assessment, and directory. Newspapers are the richest of these; mined systematically they yield an enormous load of information about the activities of people within the city. There are marriage records, church records, records of voluntary societies and educational institutions, cemetery records and listings of other sorts as well. Each of these sources may be studied by itself and the patterns it presents analyzed and compared with those found in other places. It is

---

[1] For detailed quantitative information see the first two interim reports of the Candian Social History Project as well as subsequent working papers, all of which are available from the Department of History and Philosophy of Education of The Ontario Institute for Studies in Education. See also my essay, "Social Structure in Hamilton, Ontario" in Stephen Thernstrom and Richard Sennett, eds., *Nineteenth-Century Cities: Essays in the New Urban History* (New Haven and London 1969), 209-44. I have rounded all percentages in this essay to whole numbers. Considering the inexactness of historical data, this seems quite appropriate, especially when it increases ease of reading.

most exciting and rewarding, however, to join records together. By finding the same individuals listed in different records it is possible to build up rich and well-documented portraits of the lives of even the most ordinary of people.[2]

The project on which this essay rests uses all of the various records described above. Its most general purpose is to analyze the impact of industrialization on urban social structure and social mobility, using Hamilton, Ontario, as a case study. It deals with the years 1851 through, at the least, 1881; its basis is coded information about all, and not a sample, of the individuals listed in the kinds of sources described above, studied at differing intervals.

This essay discusses, primarily, the early 1850s. Its principal sources are, specifically, the manuscript census of 1851, the assessment roll of 1852 (compiled three months after the census), the city directory of 1853 (the first published within the city), the marriage registers of 1842-69, and two local newspapers, one for both 1851 and 1852 and one for 1852.[3] In some instances the analysis rests on one source alone, in others on sources combined.

The sources for Hamilton as well as studies of American cities make clear that the first great theme of a nineteenth-century city is transiency. The most careful students of transiency to date, Stephen Thernstrom and Peter Knights, conclude from their study of Boston that far more people lived within the city in the course of a year than the census taker could find present at any point in time. The census of 1880 listed the population of Boston as 363,000; that of 1890 as 448,000. However, during those ten years they estimate that about one and one-half million different people actually lived within the city. Elsewhere Knights has estimated that twice as many artisans in some crafts plied their trade within the city in the course of a year as might be found there at any given moment. Eric Hobsbawm's tramping artisans, quite obviously, were a North American as well as a British phenomenon.[4]

---

[2] Record-linkage is one of the central technical problems of all studies similar to the one described here. For a discussion of the problem, and of our approach to it, see Ian Winchester, "The Linkage of Historical Records by Man and Computer: Techniques and Problems," *Journal of Interdisciplinary History*, I, I, autumn 1970, 107-24. The hand-linkage of the 1851 census, 1852 assessment, and 1853 directory was done by Mr John Tiller, who also has done most of the coding of the 1851 census and assessment. I should like to acknowledge Mr Tiller's continued and invaluable participation in this project.

[3] The *Spectator* and the *Gazette*.

[4] Stephen Thernstrom and Peter Knights, "Men in Motion: Some Data and Speculations about Urban Population Mobility in Nineteenth Century America," in Tamara K. Hareven, ed., *Anonymous Americans Explorations in Nineteenth-Century Social History* (Englewood Cliffs, N.J. 1971), 17-47; Peter R. Knights, "Population Turnover, Persistence, and Residential Mobility in Boston, 1830-1860," in Thernstrom and Sennett, *Nineteenth-Century Cities*, 258-74; E.J. Hobsbawm, "The Tramping Artisan," in his *Labouring Men Studies in the History of Labour* (London 1964), 34-63.

The same transiency characterized the population of Hamilton. At this point it is not possible to provide exact figures or to say more than that transiency was a mass phenomenon. We do so on the following evidence. The assessment roll of 1852 listed 2552 people. Through careful linkage by hand (later replicated by computer) we have been able to join only 1955 of them to people listed on the census, which, as mentioned above, had been taken three months earlier. (There is no reason to assume that the intervening three months were unusual in any way.) Even with a generous allowance for error, large numbers of people could not be found because they had moved into the city during the intervening three months. In the same way a comparable percentage of household heads listed on the census could not be found three months later on the assessment. Most of them had left the city. Similarly, fewer than half the people on census or assessment could be found listed in the city directory compiled about a year and a half later, and there were a great many people listed on the directory and not on either census or assessment. Death records point to the same conclusion. Each household head was required to record on the census the name of any person within his household who had died during the preceding year. However, Hamilton cemetery and church records for both 1851 and 1861 reveal that the number of people who actually died within the city far exceeded the number recorded on the census. Only a few can be linked to families resident within the city at the time the census was taken.[5] In most instances the families apparently had left the city. It is difficult to estimate the number of deaths that fall into this category; certainly it is not less than a number half again as large as the number of deaths recorded on the census.

The population, this evidence suggests, contained two major groupings of people. The first consisted of relatively permanent residents who persisted within the city for at least several years. This group comprised between a third and two-fifths of the population. The remainder were transients, people passing through the city, remaining for periods lasting between a few months and a few years.

Many of the transients were heads of household, not, as we might suspect, primarily young men drifting around the countryside. The age distribution among the transient heads of household closely resembled that among the more permanent. If anything, the transients on the average were very slightly older. Nor, as one might expect, were the transients all people of little skill and low status. The percentage of labourers among the transients (15 per cent) was only slightly higher than among the more permanent residents. Indeed, there were many people with skilled or entrepreneurial jobs who moved from place to place; the transients included twenty-four merchants, fifty-eight clerks, seven lawyers, fifty-one shoemakers, twenty-eight tailors, and so on.

Although the transients approximated the rest of the population in age and occupation, they differed in one critical respect: wealth. Within every occupational

---

[5] Unpublished papers by Mrs Judy Cooke and Mr Dan Brock, OISE.

category, the people who remained within the city were wealthier.[6] Thus, it was the *poorer* merchants, shoemakers, lawyers and, even, the poorer labourers who migrated most frequently. All of this points to the coexistence of two social structures within nineteenth-century society: one relatively fixed, consisting of people successful at their work, even if that work was labouring; the other a floating social structure composed of failures, people poorer and less successful at their work, even if that work was professional, drifting from place to place in search of success.[7]

The significance of the existence of transiency as a key feature of social structure in both Boston, Massachusetts, and Hamilton, Ontario, becomes evident from considering the fundamental differences between the two cities. Late nineteenth-century Boston had become an industrial city; mid-century Hamilton remained a small, commercial, and pre-industrial one. Yet both were filled, in Knights' and Thernstrom's phrase, with "men in motion"; transiency formed an integral and international feature of nineteenth-century society and one not immediately altered by industrialization.

The relationship between workplace and residence underscores the pre-industrial nature of Hamilton. The separation of work and residence has been one of the most profound consequences of industrialization; the degree to which they remain united provides a rough guide to the extent of industrial development within a society. Contemporary sociologists contrast the organization of family and workplace by pointing to their basic structural differences in terms of authority relationships, criteria for rewards, and so on. They argue that people must play radically different roles in each setting. It becomes the task of the family and the school to teach the individual to make the transition between home and work and to learn to live with the sorts of internal switching required by a continual shifting from the personal and warm relations of the family to the impersonal, bureaucratic organization of work. This dichotomy in roles is a consequence of modern work organization. It came about as a result of the separation of residence and workplace. Its implication for the psychology of the individual person and for the functions of family and school are what make the shift of such profound significance.[8]

---

[6] The mean assessed wealth of all the people engaged in commerce was £96; of the transients in commerce, £63; of resident professionals, £71; of transient ones, £21; of resident artisans, £25; of migrants, £13; of resident labourers, £9; of migrant ones, £7.

[7] The existence of a similar phenomenon—a division of success within trades—is clearly revealed by Henry Mayhew's description of the organization of various trades in London in the middle of the nineteenth century. An example is the distinction between the "honourable" and "dishonourable" parts of the tailoring trade. See, E.P. Thompson and Eileen Yeo, *The Unknown Mayhew* (London 1971), 181-277, on tailors.

[8] Robert Dreeben, *On What is Learned in Schools* (Reading, Mass. 1968), 95, provides an example of this point. See also Talcott Parson and Robert F. Bales, *Family, Socialization and Interaction Processes* (Glencoe, Ill. 1955).

The People of a Canadian City 305

It is almost impossible to state precisely the proportion of men who were self-employed and the proportion who worked at their homes in Hamilton in the 1850s. What follows is a rough estimate of the minimum numbers in each category.[9] In 1851, 1142 male household heads were employees and 957 employers. Adding 1310 male adult boarders, almost all employees, gives a total male workforce of 3409 of which 2452 or 74 per cent were not self-employed and 26 per cent were. Given the approximate nature of the figures, it would be unwise to claim more than that between a quarter and a third of the men within the city worked for themselves. Certainly, this is evidence enough to point to a contrast with contemporary industrial society.

Of those men who were self-employed about 137 (comprising roughly half of the proprietors of businesses and attorneys) worked away from their homes. Interestingly, if the proportion had been based on the number of *businesses*, not the number of proprietors, the proportion uniting work and residence would have been much higher. For many businesses were partnerships in which one member lived at the place of business, the other elsewhere. On the basis of this estimate approximately 14 per cent of self-employed men worked away from their place of residence, as did 72 per cent of all employed males or 60 per cent of household heads. Put another way, at least four out of ten households combined the function of place of work and place of residence for some of their members. That figure clearly demonstrates the pre-industrial character of life within the city.

Even though many people had to leave home each day to go to work, few spent their time in large, formal settings. Most people, regardless of where their job was done, worked in small groups. According to the census of 1851 (which is undoubtedly an underenumeration in this respect) there were within the city 282 artisan shops, stores, offices and manufactories. The proprietors of over half of these (52 per cent) listed no employees. A further twenty-five listed one, and an additional sixty, between two and five employees. Only thirty places had between six and ten employees and but a handful had more than ten. This picture of smallness and informality is completed by the city government, which employed approximately fifteen people full-time, a few others part-time, and spent annually only about £18-20,000.[10]

The preceding discussion has described features of a nineteenth-century city that might be located almost anywhere in North America or Great Britain. There was, however, one feature of Hamilton that marked it as distinctively Canadian and, at the same time, adds more evidence to the theme of transiency; this was the birthplaces of its residents. Only about 9 per cent of Hamilton's workforce had been born in Canada

---

[9] Not all employed men necessarily worked away from their homes. As Mayhew, *The Unknown Mayhew*, points out, it was common for manufacturers of various sorts to give work to craftsmen to perform in their own homes.

[10] See, for example, Proceedings of the Council of the City of Hamilton, 22 Jan. 1851, 398-9; 19 Jan. 1805, 128-9, available on microfilm in the Public Archives of Ontario.

West. The rest were immigrants, about 29 per cent from England and Wales, 18 per cent from Scotland, 32 per cent from Ireland, 8 per cent from the United States, and the rest from elsewhere. Hamilton in 1851 was an immigrant city and so it remained for at least a decade, as the figures for the birthplace of household heads in 1861 reveal. It was, thus, in a double sense that the people of Hamilton were "men in motion." At a very basic level, the origins of their people, early Canadian cities differed fundamentally from ones in the United States and Great Britain. The consequences of this demographic difference might provide a fruitful perspective from which to begin the comparative study of national development and of national character.

The immigrants to Hamilton did not gather themselves into ghettos. On the basis of indexes of segregation used by both sociologists and historians, the degree of residential clustering by ethnicity, religion, and wealth appears slight, a feature apparently characteristic of Philadelphia and Boston in the same period as well. Nonetheless, there were some broad economic differences between regions of the city. It is possible to distinguish three zones: a core district, a district surrounding the core, and an outer district. The core zone had disproportionately few poor, 9 per cent, and disproportionately many well-to-do people, 45 per cent. In the outer district that situation was reversed: 32 per cent of the people there were poor and 24 per cent well-to-do. In the middle district over half the people were of average wealth and 18 per cent poor. This pattern reflects what other scholars have described as the typical residential patterns within a nineteenth-century city before the coming of urban transport systems, a pattern that changed when the well-to-do were able to move to the suburbs and the poor clustered in downtown ghettos.[11]

Despite these trends, people of all degrees of wealth lived in close proximity to each other, the poor and the affluent intermingling on the same streets far more, probably, than they do at present. Indeed, it is clear already the extent to which the nineteenth-century city differed from the urban environment which we know today. The transiency, the newness, and the intermingling of its population, the small scale of its enterprise, the high degree of self-employment, and the continued unity of work and residence: all define a situation which our own experience of urban life prepares us poorly to comprehend, but which, as historians, we must try to recapture.

---

[11] For a discussion of calculating the index of segregation see Karl E. Taeuber and Alma F. Taeuber, *Negroes in Cities: Residential Segregation and Neighborhood Change* (Chicago 1965), 195-245; for the application of the index, see Leo F. Schnore and Peter R. Knights, "Residence and Social Structure: Boston in the Ante-Bellum Period," in Thernstrom and Sennett, *Nineteenth-Century Cities*, 247-57, and Sam Bass Warner, Jr., *The Private City: Philadelphia in Three Periods of its Growth* (Philadelphia 1968), 13. For studies of residential patterns in nineteenth-century cities, see also two recent monographs, David Ward, *Cities and Immigrants: A Geography of Change in Nineteenth Century America* (New York 1971), and Peter Goheen, *Victorian Toronto* (Chicago 1970).

In fact, it is easy to be nostalgic about small pre-industrial cities. The absence of large-scale industry, the informality of government, and the lack of bureaucratic forms suggest an urban style both more cohesive and personal than that which we know today. We can imagine them, without too much difficulty, as filled with less tension and more warmth than contemporary cities, as stable, neighbourly, and easy places in which to live, as communities in a sense in which urban places have ceased to be. Unfortunately, the image just emerging from close, empirical study of nineteenth-century cities does not support the nostalgic vision. From one perspective it is partly contradicted by the facts of transiency, which we have already observed. The continual circulation of population prevented the formation of stable and closely integrated communities within nineteenth-century cities. At the same time, sharp inequalities in wealth and power reinforced the pressures of population mobility against cohesion and integration; together they made the nineteenth-century city, even before industrialization, a place at least as harsh, as insecure, and as overwhelming as urban environments today.

It is scarcely novel to assert that sharp inequalities existed within nineteenth-century cities or to posit a sharply graduated rank ordering of people. What should be stressed about that inequality is this: first, it may have been greater even than we have imagined; second, it underlay other social differences between people, such as household size and attitudes toward education; third, it shaped political patterns and processes. In short, the division of people on most social measures corresponded to the economic differences between them. Social, political, and economic power overlapped and interlocked, creating a sharply divided society in which a small percentage of the people retained a near monopoly on all the resources necessary to the well-being of the rest.

There are various ways with which to measure the division of wealth within a community, and each one, each scale that is adopted, yields a different result.[12] One division is property ownership: about one quarter of the population owned all the real property within the city. Roughly three-quarters of the people rented their living accommodations and owned no other real property whatsoever. The most affluent 10 per cent of the population held about 88 per cent of the wealth represented by the possession of property. From a slightly different perspective, people in the top 10 *income* percentiles (as reported on the assessment) earned nearly half the income within the city, and this figure, for a variety of reasons, is undoubtedly greatly understated. At the other extreme the poorest 40 per cent earned a little over 1 per cent of the income. Measured on a third scale, one designed to show economic ranking, the pattern of inequality is similar. On this scale "wealth" is a construct of different items and does not correspond exactly to either total income or assessed property; it is, however, the best available indicator of economic rank. On the basis

---

[12] I have discussed the construction of these scales in working paper no. 21, "The Measurement of Economic Inequality."

of this measure, the wealthiest tenth of the people controlled about 60 per cent of the wealth within the city and the poorest two-fifths about 6 per cent.

The scale of economic ranking also reveals differences between the wealth of the various sectors of the city's economy. The people engaged in building, about 14 per cent of the workforce (indicating the rapid expansion of the city), held only about 7 per cent of the city's wealth; similarly, those engaged in some form of manufacturing (primarily artisans), about one-quarter of the workforce, had only 15 per cent of the wealth. Likewise, as might be expected, the unskilled and semi-skilled labourers, about 22 per cent of the workforce, had less than 5 per cent of the wealth. At the other extreme those engaged in professions, about 4 per cent of the workforce, held over 7 per cent of the wealth, and the men in commerce, about a quarter of the workforce, controlled nearly 59 per cent of the wealth, a figure which underscores the clear commercial basis of the city.

Religious and ethnic groups, like the various sectors of the economy, shared unequally in the city's wealth. Of the various immigrant and religious groups, the Irish and the Catholics fared worst. It is fair, I have argued elsewhere, to consider as poor the people in the lowest forty economic ranks. Using this criterion, 47 per cent of the working population born in Ireland were poor, as were 54 per cent those who were Catholic. This, of course, is not a surprising finding. On the other hand it might be supposed that the English and the Anglicans were disproportionately wealthy, but this was not the case. Both groups formed a microcosm of the larger social structure, distributed quite normally among different economic categories.[13] The Free Church Presbyterians did rather better but the most affluent group, considering both numbers who were poor and numbers who were well-to-do, were the Wesleyan Methodists.[14] In terms of birthplace, the native Canadians and Americans fared best, a prosperity no doubt reflecting the problems of trans-Atlantic migration rather than inherent ethnic capacity or style. Of the Canadians 32 per cent were well-to-do, as were 31 per cent of the Americans.[15]

It is difficult to associate economic rank with standard of living and to demarcate with precision the line separating the poor from the comfortable. To say that the fortieth economic rank marks the spot at which people ceased being poor means that

---

[13] Fifty-one per cent of the working population born in England and Wales were in the middle (40-80th) economic ranks as were 46 per cent of the Anglicans.

[14] Of the Free Church Presbyterians 26 per cent were poor, compared to 16 per cent of the Wesleyan Methodists. At the same time 31 per cent of the Free Church Presbyterians were well-to-do (80-100th economic ranks) as were 29 per cent of the Wesleyan Methodists.

[15] Of the other major ethnic and religious groups, briefly: the Scottish-born were predominantly middle-income, much like the English; the adherents of the Church of Scotland, and those who called themselves simply Presbyterians, were likewise middling in terms of wealth, except that the former had few wealthy adherents. The figures for Methodists were much like those for Presbyterians; and for Baptists, much like members of the Church of Scotland.

it was the point at which they probably no longer had to struggle for and occasionally do without the necessities of life. Poverty in nineteenth-century cities did not mean the absence of luxuries, simple spartan living with good home-grown food and sturdy home-sewn clothes. Poverty meant absolute deprivation: hunger, cold, sickness, and misery, with almost no place to turn for relief. The poor within Hamilton, it is important to remember, remained quite at the mercy of the well-to-do, who controlled not only employment opportunity but dispensed what little welfare there was as a gift, not as a right. The Ladies Benevolent Society, a voluntary and paternalistic body, formed in effect the city welfare department. Financed by charitable donations and grants from the City Council, it assigned teams of gracious ladies to roam the streets, locate the worthy poor, and dispense loaves of bread, sometimes coal and groceries, even occasionally rent. The City Council coped with massive numbers of immigrants overcrowding the combination hospital and poorhouse by transporting newly arrived Irish people in wagonloads to country towns where they were summarily left. Clearly, they believed such widespread poverty was only a temporary problem, which could be solved by simple expedients that did not require the permanent and institutionalized extension of public responsibility for individual welfare.[16]

Aside from economic hardship, poverty in Hamilton meant powerlessness and invisibility. The lack of public provision for welfare reveals part of the powerlessness: the poor had no assistance on which they could draw as a right. Nor could they make their wants heard in any legal way, as the suffrage restrictions show. Less than half of the adult males in Hamilton owned or rented enough property to vote; 53 per cent of all adult men, or 43 per cent of household heads, could not meet the economic requirements for suffrage. Neither could 80 per cent of the labourers, 56 per cent of the artisans, or 59 per cent of the business employees (primarily clerks). No working class political protest could be expressed through the ballot in Hamilton; most of the working class simply lacked the vote. The invisibility that accompanied powerlessness is harder to demonstrate; its existence has come to light by comparing the records of the Ladies Benevolent Society with the manuscript census. The former contain a month by month listing of the recipients of welfare. Early checking to find these names on the census, even for the very month in which the census had been taken, located very few of them. Perhaps they were simply passed by, a blot on the city it was as well, if possible, to ignore.

Even within a relatively simple society like Hamilton's, the affluent had tangible means of demonstrating their degree of success. One was the employment of servants. It was at the 80th economic rank that a family became more likely than not

---

[16] The records of the Ladies Benevolent Society are available in manuscript at the Hamilton Public Library. For the actions of the City Council with respect to immigrants, see, e.g., Proceedings of the Council, 20 Aug. 1849, 31; 10 Sept. 1849, 149-50. On the institutionalization of poverty in the United States see the recent, provocative book by David Rothman, *The Discovery of the Asylum* (Boston 1971).

to employ domestic help, and the likelihood increased with each higher rank on the scale. Overall, about one-quarter of the families in Hamilton had a servant living with them. If Hobsbawm's assertion that the possession of a servant defined middle-class status applies to Canada as well as England, then the percentage of households without servants indicates, again, the magnitude of the working class in Hamilton.[17] Most of the servants, 60 per cent, had been born in Ireland and 47 per cent were Catholic. They were by and large young girls: slightly more than half were under twenty years old, and three-quarters were under twenty-five. Nearly nine out of ten servants were females, 93 per cent unmarried, although some of the latter had children of their own. Families that employed servants were likely to live in a brick or stone house with two or more stories surrounded by an extra-large plot of land. The first two became, like the employment of servants, more likely than not at the 80th economic rank, the latter, size of plot attached to dwelling, increased most often at the 90th.

Household size also increased quite directly with wealth: to take one example, 15 per cent of the households in the 20-40th ranks were large (eight or more members), compared to 30 per cent of those in the 60-80th, and 61 per cent of those in the top 1 per cent. There was, however, little relationship between wealth and number of children. Consequently, the presence of servants, boarders, and relatives accounted for the larger household size of the wealthy. In fact, servants, boarders, and relatives all lived more frequently with affluent than with poor families. School attendance also varied directly with economic standing. Families with no servants sent only slightly more than a third of their school age children to school; families with one servant sent just over half; families with more than one servant sent still larger proportions. Wealthier people also kept their children in school longer. Twenty-two per cent of the fourteen-year-old children from families with no servants had attended school, compared to 42 per cent of those from families with one servant and 82 per cent of those from families with two servants. The employment of servants, the occupancy of a large brick or stone house, a spacious plot of land, a large household, the steady and prolonged attendance of one's children at school: these, then, were the principal means through which the affluent demonstrated their success to their neighbours.

The affluent of the city solidified their economic control with political power. First of all, as we have already observed, property qualifications excluded most of the poor from voting. Moreover, the wealthy monopolized local political offices. Despite the fact that nearly 30 per cent of elected city officials called themselves by an artisan title, most were wealthy. They were by no means working men as we usually employ that term. Of the elected officials, nearly 70 per cent were in the top ten economic ranks; 83 per cent were in the top twenty. In the two years 1851-2, 42 per cent of the wealthiest 1 per cent of the workforce held political office.

To understand the exercise of power within the city it is necessary to grasp the extent of overlap between membership in elite positions. Measured grossly from

---

[17] E.J. Hobsbawm, *Industry and Empire* (London 1969), 157.

listings in the newspaper, the overlap between membership in three elites—people elected to city political offices, business officials, and officers of voluntary societies—is striking and, beyond question, statistically significant.[18] Of the forty-eight elected city officials, for instance, fifteen were business officials, twenty-one officers of voluntary societies, and eight jurors. Of the 130 business officials, fifteen were elected city officials, forty-one officers of voluntary societies, thirty-six petitioners (asking the city for favours), and twelve jurors. Among 196 officers of voluntary societies (a very high figure suggesting an extraordinarily important role for voluntary activity with this society), twenty-one were elected city officials, forty-one business officials, eight appointed city officials, six school trustees, and eighteen jurors. Of the seventy-four jurors who served during 1851 and 1852, eight were elected city officials, twelve were business officials, and one was an elected city official. Ten people were elected city officials, business officials, and officers of voluntary societies simultaneously.

Measures designed to test statistical significance—to see whether or not the results described above could have occurred by chance—tell the same story. The relationships were strong and real. The unmistakable overlap between elites underlines the interconnections between economic, political, and social power within this nineteenth-century city. More than that, the relation of people in elite positions with petitioners and jurors is revealing. A poor or unimportant man in Hamilton, it is quite clear, lacked the temerity to ask the city for favours, and, in fact, if he incurred its displeasure he was not even tried by a jury of his peers.[19]

Just as poverty and powerlessness brought invisibility, so did affluence and power make a man visible. On the basis of their mention in local newspapers it is possible to divide the people of the city into three groups according to their "visibility": those "invisible" (not mentioned in the newspapers at all) or about 94 per cent of the population in 1851; those moderately "visible" (mentioned once or twice); and those highly "visible," mentioned five or more times, about 1 per cent of the population. Who then were the highly visible people? They were, as might be expected from the foregoing analysis, the members of the interlocking elites. Highly visible people comprised more than half of the following categories: city and county officials, appointed city and county officials, business officials, officers of voluntary societies, school trustees, petitioners, jurors, advertisers, union members (only six were mentioned in the newspapers at all), political committee members, and people publicly honoured. Interestingly, as with the case of overlap between various sorts of officeholders, jurors and petitioners interconnect with the most powerful men within the city.[20]

---

[18] Mrs. Anne-Marie Hodes coded the 1851 and 1852 newspapers for the project.

[19] Only the top three-quarters of the assessed population were eligible to serve on the jury. I suspect that those actually chosen did not represent a cross-section of that group.

[20] For the idea of constructing a scale of visibility I am indebted to the work of Professor Walter Glazer of Cincinnati.

These interconnections between kinds of power within Hamilton pose important comparative questions. Did economic, social, and political power exist in a closer relationship at that time than they do at present? What impact did industrialization have upon their relationship to each other? Is the curve of inequality steady over time, or did it widen in the initial stages of industrialization and then diminish in the twentieth century? Whatever the answers to these questions turn out to be, the detailed examination of the distribution of income and power should help dispel any lingering nostalgia about the existence of equality and community in nineteenth-century cities.

Detailed examination of actual cases also dispels a number of common notions about families in pre-industrial society. It is often thought that the nuclear family emerged as a consequence of industrialization, that in early times people married at very young ages, and that the poor, especially, had very large families. None of these propositions are true. There were clear relations between transiency and inequality, the two great themes of the nineteenth-century city, and the domestic arrangements of its people. However, to some extent the family and household exhibited characteristics partially independent of wealth and related rather (sometimes at this stage of research inexplicably) to other measures. Thus, it is important to consider family and household structure by themselves.

We may begin with the formation of the family through marriage. The statistics are based upon the marriage registers for Wentworth County for the years 1842-69.[21] Marriage patterns within Wentworth County were endogamous. Of 5327 brides, 4443 resided in Wentworth County, as did 4026 of the same number of grooms. It is to be expected that most brides would be from Wentworth County, since marriage customarily takes place at the bride's residence. What is more notable is the small proportion of local girls who married men from outside the county. Nevertheless, the majority of marriages throughout the period involved people who had both been born outside of Ontario and, indeed, outside of Canada.

For the most part the figures for age of marriage contradict our stereotypes of early marriage among the people of pre-industrial society. The mean age of marriage for men was 27.7, the median 25.7; 61 per cent of grooms were twenty-five years old or over; 25 per cent were over 30. Brides were considerably younger, about four years on the average. Their mean marriage age was 23.2 and the median 21.8. Just over one-quarter of the girls married before they were twenty and 72 per cent had married by the time they were twenty-five.[22] Both religion and birthplace influenced marriage age, though of the two birthplace appeared strongest. Younger marriages were slightly more common among Baptists and "Protestants" and later marriages more common among Presbyterians. Similarly, the Scottish people married notably

---

[21] The marriage registers were coded by Mrs. Margaret Zieman.

[22] The figures are supported by those found for European countries, See, e.g., Peter Laslett, "Size and Structure of the Household in England Over Three Centuries," *Population Studies*, XXIII, 2, July 1969, 199-223.

later than other groups.[23] People born in Canada West married youngest by far, and there were no unusual distributions of age among brides and grooms born in England, the United States, or, contrary to what might be expected, Ireland.[24]

Figures for births, like those for marriage, do not support common notions about Catholic families. From what we can tell at this point, the birth-rate among Catholics or Irish born people was no higher than among the population as a whole. What appears striking from an analysis of the births listed in the 1851 manuscript census is the congruence between the percentage of total births in the city occurring among a particular group and that group's percentage of the total population. Thus, Catholics aged 20-29 formed 18 per cent of the household heads of that age group within the city; to them occurred 18 per cent of the births among that age group. The poor form 26 per cent of the household heads; they had 27 per cent of the births. It would be tedious to continue to present these figures; with one exception they remain the same for ethnicity, religion, and wealth. That exception, and an interesting one, is the people born in French Canada, who formed a tiny 0.4 per cent of the 20-29-year-olds but accounted for 2 per cent of the births, a disproportion consistent with trends in French-Canadian demography.[25]

This initial survey of Hamilton's demography would be incomplete without some mention of death and death rates. At this juncture it is not possible to discuss the relations between death rate, age at death, and other social variables, such as religion, ethnicity, and wealth. We do know that the infant mortality rate was staggeringly high. Of 210 people recorded as having died on the census, 106 or 51 per cent were five years old or younger; all but twenty-one, or 10 per cent, were under the age of fifty.

Figures for the number of children within a household are generally, though not completely, consistent with the statistics of marriage and birth. Among the heads of households as a whole 55 per cent had small families (0-2 children); 36 per cent had medium sized families (3-5 children), and 10 per cent had large families (6 or more children). Any discussion of family size is affected by the age distribution of the population. In order that we may have a fair basis of comparison I shall restrict the following discussion to heads of household aged 40-49, those whose families were both complete and, to the largest extent, still living together. Of the 40-49-year-old

---

[23] Only 20 per cent of Scottish grooms were less than twenty-five years old compared to 39 per cent of all grooms, while 30 per cent of Scottish grooms were in their 30s compared to 18 per cent of all grooms.

[24] Among people born in Canada West, 51 per cent of the grooms, compared to 39 per cent of all grooms, had been married before the age of twenty-five; of the brides, 82 per cent, compared to 75 per cent of all brides, had been married before they were twenty-seven years old.

[25] For an overview of Canadian population history that makes this point, see Census of Canada, 1931, Ch. 2 and 3 of the excellent monograph on the family.

household heads, 37 per cent had small families, 44 per cent medium sized ones, and 18 per cent large numbers of children.

First of all, as with births, family size among the 40-49-year-olds shows little relation to wealth.[26] The poor did not breed more quickly than the rest of the population. In fact the only discernible relation between wealth and number of children works in the other direction. Among the heads of household as a whole 0.3 per cent of the very poorest people, those in the bottom twenty economic percentiles, had a large number of children compared to 15 per cent of those in the 95-99th percentiles. Among the 40-49-year-old household heads the poorest men had no children about twice as often as most other groups; similarly, they had the smallest percentage of medium-sized families of any group. Considering all ages together, the mean number of children among the poorest 20 per cent of household heads was 0.54 and, among the wealthiest 1 per cent, 3.32. In between, however, scores are quite similar. One other difference, which relates to economic standing, shows the same trend. Transients, who were poorer than those people we consider more permanent residents, had a slightly lower mean number of children despite their similarity in age.

An examination of the mean number of children among 40-49-year-old household heads highlights some ethnic and religious distinctions generally unrelated to wealth. North Americans, natives of Canada West and the United States, had small families. The lowest mean score, 2.40, was that of the Americans, followed by the Canadians, the English, the Irish, and the Scottish in that order.[27] These figures reflect the late marriage age of Scottish people, which we observed earlier.[28] Among religious groups those with heavily Scottish membership rank high in mean number of children among 40-49-year-olds.[29] At the other end of the scale the denomination with the smallest mean family size, the Baptist, is heavily American in origin.[30] The mean size for the Catholics, it might be pointed out, was quite average for the 40-49-year-olds, although their mean for the 20-29-year-olds was the highest in the cohort, which indicates that Catholics had more of their children when they were

---

26 Of the poor, 18 per cent had a large family; so did 20 per cent of the middle-income and 21 per cent of the well-to-do. Similarly 38 per cent of the poor had a small number of children, as did 35 per cent of the middle-rank and 38 per cent of the well-to-do.

27 The means are: US born, 2.40; Canadian, 3.18; English, 3.35; Irish, 3.52; Scottish, 4.01.

28 The Scottish rank third in mean number of children among 20-29-year-olds, fifth among 30-39, and first among the 40-49-year-old group.

29 Thus the mean for members of the Church of Scotland is 4.39 and for Free Church Presbyterians, 4.62.

30 The Baptist score is 2.17.

younger, not, as is often thought, that they had a greater number in all than did other groups.[31]

The mean family size of different occupational groups reveals more systematic differences. The means for all merchants and clerks were 1.78 and 1.91. For bakers, blacksmiths, carpenters, shoemakers, tinsmiths, and labourers the means were: 2.69, 2.96, 2.78, 2.34, 2.89, and 2.89 respectively. Quite clearly, the entrepreneurial white collar groups had fewer children than men who worked with their hands. In this respect it is the line separating the people engaged in commerce from those following the trades that counts most. Distinctions between skilled and unskilled workers appear to matter but little. More than that, the difference in number of children appears more related to kind of work performed than it does to wealth. The mean number of children, as we have observed, varied but little with economic rank, and the relations between occupation and wealth were not as tidy as we might expect, as we have noticed in the case of elected city officials. In fact, there was usually a great variation in wealth between individuals in the same trades. Thus, on the basis of the evidence at hand, it is entirely reasonable to suppose that the aspiring business classes had begun to practice some form of family limitation.[32]

There were distinctions, it is critical to note, between the family size of people engaged in commerce and other non-manual workers. Relatively small family size remained more a hallmark of men with an entrepreneurial outlook than a badge separating white and blue collar workers in our modern sense. This becomes apparent from the mean family size of other, non-entrepreneurial and non-manual groups: the mean family size of teachers, for instance, 3.71, was the highest of any group; the mean for gentlemen was 2.89, the same as for labourers and tinsmiths; and the mean for lawyers fluctuated strangely with age. For lawyers in their forties it was 6.00. All of this suggests that limiting the number of his offspring had become linked in the mind of the aspiring entrepreneur with increasing his wealth. The source of that idea is particularly important to locate. For, if the facts that I have presented here are correct, he would not have learned it from the world around him where, in fact, the most successful men did not have small families.

As we have observed already, the mark of a wealthy man was the size of his household, not the number of his children. That household was composed of

---

[31] In fairness to traditional ideas it should be pointed out that very preliminary inspection of the 1861 results indicates a larger than average family size for Catholics and Irish. At this point the change is inexplicable.

[32] For comparative figures on class and birth control, see E.A. Wrigley's excellent book, *Population and History* (New York 1969), 186-7. On the method of studying birth control in past societies, see E.A. Wrigley, "Family Limitation in Pre-Industrial England," *Economic History Review*, Second Series, XIX, I, 1966, 82-109. For more on the relation between status and birth control in the nineteenth century, see J.A. Banks, *Prosperity and Parenthood: A Study of Family Planning Among the Victorian Middle Classes* (London 1954) and D.E.C. Eversley, *Social Theories of Fertility and the Malthusian Debate* (Oxford 1959).

boarders, servants, relatives, and visitors in addition to husband, wife, and children. There were fewer extended families in this pre-industrial city than we might have expected; relatives other than husband, wife, and children lived in only 15 per cent of the households. Like the families Peter Laslett and his associates have studied in England over a period of four hundred years, the ones in Hamilton were overwhelmingly nuclear. As with servants, relatives lived most frequently in the households of the well-to-do; they were present in 4 per cent of the poorest 20 per cent of the households and in 24 per cent of those in the 95-99th economic ranks.[33]

The same is true of boarders, who were found in 28 per cent of the households. They lived, however, with 8 per cent and 15 per cent respectively of the families in the 0-20th and 20-40th economic ranks and with 46 per cent of those in the 90-95th. There were boarders, in fact, in more than four out of ten households in each group above the 80th economic rank. This finding is somewhat surprising. We might suppose, offhand, that boarders would be most likely to live with poorer families, who needed the extra income they could provide. But this was not the case. It prompts us to look closely at exactly who boarders were and at their place within the household.

The presence of boarders in so many households reflects an important characteristic of social life: it was extremely unusual for people to live alone; everyone was expected to live within a family grouping. Not much more than 1 per cent of the workforce lived by themselves. Large numbers of young unmarried people living alone is clearly a modern development. This pattern of residence, moreover, constituted an informal system of social control. For young men a close supervision and a constant scrutiny of their behaviour constituted the other side of the warmth of living in a family grouping. Boarding the young men of the town provided the affluent with a convenient means of keeping a close check on their behaviour.

Most of the boarders, 71 per cent, were men; 14 per cent were married. This accounts in large part for the women and children who were listed as boarders. Like the servants, boarders were young, though not quite so young: 34 per cent were under twenty and a further 52 per cent between twenty and twenty-four years old; 84 per cent were under thirty. They came more often from Ireland than from elsewhere, in 43 per cent of the cases, but many, 19 per cent, had been born in Canada West, a disproportionately large number considering that men from Canada West made up only a bit more than 9 per cent of the workforce. These boarders were, perhaps, young migrants to the city from rural areas. A little over one-third of the boarders were Catholic, the largest single figure for any denomination, and the rest were scattered among other religious groups. Boarders followed a staggering variety of occupations. Many of them, about 54 per cent, were craftsmen of one sort or another; of the remainder, about 13 per cent were labourers and 8 per cent clerks. Spinsters, widows, and women following domestic occupations like dressmaking

---

[33] On general patterns of household size in England over four hundred years, see Laslett, "Size and Structure of the Household."

frequently boarded, as did some young professionals, nine lawyers and seven physicians probably establishing themselves in practice.

It appeared likely, from these figures, that many boarders were young men living with their employers in households that combined work and residence. However, a close comparison of the occupations of boarders and their landlords demolished that hypothesis. It is extremely difficult to determine if a boarder and a household head might have worked together. Occupational terminology is vague and sometimes misleading. But in most cases it was clear that no reasonable connection could be made. Not only occupation but class seemed to make little difference. Labourers lived with judges, physicians, attorneys, and gentlemen, as well as with fellow labourers, moulders, and widows. Widows, in fact, took in many boarders, obviously a way to make a little money. Other than that, there seems little pattern in the distribution of boarders by occupation. Overall, slightly over 9 per cent of the boarders might have been living with their employers.

Other obvious principles on which boarders might have selected their residence are religion and ethnicity. Perhaps young men coming to the city looked for families of similar ethnic and religious backgrounds with whom to live, whatever their occupation might be. In most cases this did not happen. There was some tendency for Irish and for Catholic boarders to choose landlords of the same background, and a very slight tendency for the English and the Anglicans to do the same. But in no instance did those living with people of similar religious or ethnic backgrounds constitute a majority.

In short, it appears that other factors were more important in the choice of a lodging, probably convenience, price, and the presence of some friends already living there or nearby. The population of Hamilton, we must not forget, was expanding rapidly. The estimated growth between 1850 and 1852 was from ten to fourteen thousand. The practical implication of this must have been a severe strain on housing facilities. Perhaps rooms were in such short supply that people took whatever they could find. Perhaps, too, there was great pressure on anyone with a spare bed to take someone in. This is why so many of the more affluent, with larger houses, had boarders.

It is as important to discover the behavioural patterns associated with types of families and households as it is to determine their size and structure. There are, however, fewer indexes of behaviour than of structure on which to base systematic observations. One of the most readily available, and most interesting, is school attendance. The analysis of school attendance links parental attitudes to social, demographic, and economic measures and, as our data reveal, to family size as well. It thus provides a way of joining the family and household to the large social context in which they are embedded.[34]

---

[34] There has been amazingly little written on the history of school attendance. The only monograph in English that I know to be specifically devoted to the topic is David

Of all the children in the city aged 5-16 in 1851, 50 per cent attended at each age level. Very few children entered school before the age of six. At the age of six a third began to attend, but the ages 7-13 were the period of heaviest school attendance, the proportion attending exceeding 40 per cent only in each of those years. The peaks were reached between the ages of nine and eleven, the only time when more than half of the age group attended school.

Part of the variation in school attendance can be explained by family size. It is often thought that small families provide settings conducive to education. Indeed, twentieth-century studies have shown an inverse relation between school achievement, scores on intelligence tests, and family size. If our data have anything to contribute on this point, it is that the contemporary relationship did not hold within the nineteenth century. The percentage of school-age children attending school generally increased with the number of children in the family.[35] This relationship held even for the youngest and eldest children attending school: 3 per cent of children aged 3-5 from families with two children attended school compared to 10 per cent from families with five children; 18 per cent of 15-16-year-old children from families with two children attended school compared to 23 per cent from families with five children.

The birthplace of the head of household also affected school attendance. Irish fathers were least likely to send their children to school. The percentage of Irish children aged 5-16 attending school was under one-third. For two groups, however, it was over one-half; these were the Scottish and the native Canadians. The relations between religion and attendance reinforce these findings: fewer than 30 per cent of Catholic children attended schools, compared to over 50 per cent for Church of Scotland and Wesleyan Methodist and over 60 per cent for Free Church Presbyterians. Scottish Presbyterianism should obviously be added to family size as an important factor promoting school attendance.

So should wealth, as we observed earlier. Measuring wealth by the possession of servants, the relation with school attendance was striking. That relation supports the observations of school-promoters who perceived their problem as persuading poor families to school their children. In so far as educational reform took its impetus from a perception of idle, vagrant children from poor homes wandering the streets, it was based on a very real situation.

The relations between occupation and school attendance spoil the neatness of the foregoing analysis, for they fail to adhere completely to the boundaries set by wealth,

---

Rubenstein, *School Attendance in London 1870-1904: A Social History* (Hull 1969). See also my article, "Who went to School," *History of Education Quarterly*, XII, 3, fall 1972.

[35] For families with two children it was, for instance, 42 per cent; for families with five children, 61 per cent. Similarly, the percentage of families which sent more than half their school-age children to school rose from 24 per cent for families with one child to 35 per cent for families with two, to 58 per cent for families with five children and 67 per cent for families of seven.

ethnicity, and religion. Lawyers, for instance, sent few of their children to school. It is entirely possible that they hired private tutors. Tinsmiths, on the other hand, were exceptionally conscious of schooling; 85 per cent of their school-age children attended school during 1851, a figure exceeded only by the children of teachers, 92 per cent of whom had attended. Labourers, as could be expected, were at the bottom; less than one-quarter of their school-age children went to school in 1851, compared, for instance, to 46 per cent of the children of merchants and 58 per cent of the children of physicians. Differences between artisan groups parallel those between professionals; 38 per cent of shoemakers' school-age children attended school, for instance, as did 54 per cent of the children of cabinet-makers. There are at present no explanations for most of these differences.

Although school attendance often followed economic lines, it is clear that cultural and social factors intervened to make the pattern that finally emerged quite complex. Two of these factors are noteworthy: North Americans kept their children in school somewhat longer than other groups, and the relationship between wealth, Catholicism, Irish origin, and low school attendance did *not* hold among the very youngest age groups. Perhaps school served as baby-sitting agencies for large, poor families, relieving the parents of pressure at home and permitting the mother to work. At the same time affluent parents of large families may have realized that they were unable to teach at home certain basic skills which it was traditional for children to learn before they started school at age seven. They may have used the school to remedy what, given the size of their families, would have had to be accomplished by a private tutor if their children were not to lag educationally.

But all conclusions must remain tentative at best. The most we can say is this: the people who most frequently sent children to school were well-to-do, had larger than average families, and had been born in Scotland or North America. Those sending fewest were poor, Irish Catholic, and labourers. The same groups generally kept the most and the fewest children in school past the usual school leaving age. But the figures for early school attendance revealed slightly different rankings, which indicates that early schooling served important economic functions for some poor families and important psychological ones for large families. The relations between occupation and schooling are unclear, aside from the figures for labourers. Why did the lawyers send so few children? Why did the tinsmiths send so many? We cannot answer these questions at present; like so many of the findings discussed in this essay they remain beginnings, as much questions to be answered as conclusions.

Clearly family and household patterns in Hamilton were complex; they defy simple general descriptions. Equally clearly, they contradict many commonly held assumptions about pre-industrial families. Men and women married relatively late, later probably than most people do today. In the vast majority of instances they formed nuclear families, the more wealthy adding a servant, a boarder, or, in comparatively few instances, a relative. Almost everybody lived in a family, whether they were married or not, young or old. Within families there was relatively little difference in the number of children born to parents of different economic conditions.

Ethnicity and religion, in fact, were more influential than wealth in determining age of marriage and number of children. The traditional image of the frugal, self-denying, and ambitious Scot emerges intact; the picture of the indulgent, over-breeding Irish Catholic is shattered. In fact, there were at least two types of households within the city. At one extreme was the Irish Catholic labourer living with his wife and two or three children in a one and a half storey frame house. At the other extreme, but perhaps on the same street, was the prosperous merchant living with his wife, two or three children, a servant, and a boarder in a three-storey stone house surrounded by a spacious plot of land. Most other families fell somewhere in between. It will take a good deal more analysis to isolate other widespread family types, and a good deal of imaginative research into other sorts of sources to explain the results that emerge; to answer, that is, questions such as why did American Baptists have small families?

It is also important to ask if the relations between family size and ethnicity that existed in Hamilton were present in other Canadian cities as well. That, in turn, is part of the larger issue of representativeness. How can one know that the findings from Hamilton have meaning for any other place? From one viewpoint the question is irrelevant. Every city's history is both unique and at the same time representative of larger trends and forces. More than that, the relationships we wish to study can be investigated only on the local level. Even if Hamilton turns out to be less "representative" than one might wish, the study is important because it provides a datum with which to begin an analysis of what is special and what is general within nineteenth-century cities in Canada and elsewhere.

Hamilton was not representative of some things, quite obviously: for instance, it was not like villages and rural areas. On the other hand, it should have had a number of similarities to pre-industrial cities in nineteenth-century Britain and the United States. Most of all, it was not too unlike other cities in Canada West. That is clear from studying published census figures for a number of Canadian cities. It is striking to observe the extent of similarity between Kingston, London, Toronto, and Hamilton with respect to the birthplace and religion of their residents; their age structures and sex ratios; their birth and death rates; and, even, their occupational structures. On the basis of these similarities it is obvious that Hamilton was structurally similar to other cities in Canada West. On that basis we may conclude with some general observations about the nature of a pre-industrial Canadian city.[36]

First, even in the mid-nineteenth century a relatively small commercial city was an enormously complex place. Simple general statements about its society, families, or households are inadequate to the richness of its structural patterns. Economically, even before industrialization, Canadian cities were highly differentiated. Socially, they were highly stratified.

Second, the pre-industrial family was a more rational and "modern" organization than we have often suspected. Even at this early date people clearly related decisions about marriage and often about the size of their families to other, undoubtedly

---

[36] Tables comparing these cities are in the project working paper no. 23.

economic, considerations. The difference between the pre-industrial and modern family does not rest in structure; both are nuclear. It lies, rather, in the number of children born to the average couple and in the structure of the household, which in terms of size has lost its clear relation to affluence.

Third, in no sense can we think of pre-industrial cities as communities defined by stability, integration, and egalitarianism. The problem of inequality we have touched on above; the facts of transiency destroy any further illusions about community. The population simply changed too rapidly.

Fourth, the articulation of various structures with each other produced a powerful concentration of interlocking forms of power in the hands of a very small group of people. Household structure, political power, school attendance—the privileges that this society had to offer—all related to wealth. The distribution of men by economic rank corresponded to their division on most other social measures. Looked at another way, the business elite, the political elite, and the voluntary elite overlapped to a striking and significant extent. We know already that the political elite overlapped with the top rungs of the scale of economic rank. There is every reason to believe that the others did so as well.

The group that controlled economic, political, and social power within Hamilton contained at most 10 per cent of the household heads. People within elite positions formed slightly more than 8 per cent of men aged twenty and older. This figure is quite close to the 10 per cent estimated elsewhere as wealthy. It is close, in fact, to the approximately 75 per cent of elected city officials whom we know to have been within the top ten income percentiles. Hence we can conclude that about 8 or 10 per cent of the adult men, at the very maximum, controlled virtually all the resources necessary to the health, well-being, and prosperity of the rest.

In Hamilton the rulers, the owners, and the rich were by and large the same people. They clearly headed the stratification system. At the bottom the grouping was likewise clear: poor, propertyless, powerless men made up about 40 per cent of the workforce or between a fifth and a quarter of the household heads. In between fell the rest. About 40 per cent were marginal; they owned no property, they possessed no power, but they were prosperous enough to differentiate themselves from the poorest families. Their margin seems so slim and the consequences of falling so appalling, however, that these people must have lived always with great tension and great fear. Between them and the wealthy, comprising about a fifth of the families, was a qualitatively more affluent group. Most of them employed a servant and lived in a brick house, which they owned. They were likely to vote but still not very likely to hold political office.

These four groups existed within Hamilton in the middle of the nineteenth century. Using wealth, power, and ownership as dimensions on which to rank people, they form somewhat overlapping but nonetheless distinguishable clusters of people holding a similar position on each scale. Were they classes? That depends on the definition of class, which is a subject beyond the scope of this essay. Clearly, however, by whatever definition is followed it would seem difficult to deny that class was a fundamental fact of life in mid-nineteenth-century urban Canada.[37]

---

[37] I want to include a plea that more Canadian historians undertake empirical analyses of past social structures. Those who are interested but hesitant should gain some knowledge of how to proceed from two recent books: Edward Shorter, *The Historian and the Computer: A Practical Guide* (Englewood Cliffs, N.J. 1971), and Charles M. Dollar and Richard J. Jensen, *Historian's Guide to Statistics, Quantitative Analysis and Historical Research* (New York 1971). Our team is continually developing a store of practical lore which we should be delighted to share with anyone venturing into related studies.

The Winter's Tale: The Seasonal Contours of Pre-industrial Poverty in British North America, 1815-1860[1]

Judith Fingard

Because of the seasonal fluctuations in the commercial economy, winter meant entirely different things to the inhabitants of British North America in the pre-industrial period. To the successful merchant and his family winter represented a time of entertainment, sport, cultural activity or, at worst, boredom. To his summer labourer, winter was synonymous with hardship: cold, hunger, and gloomy unemployment or underemployment until the welcome return of summer. In the towns where the extremes of wealth and destitution were most commonly found cheek by jowl, the contrast between the amusements of the well-to-do and the privations of the indigent classes was particularly stark in winter. As a representative of the relatively well-off, the editor of the *Quebec Mercury* considered the Christmas season an appropriate time for calling to the attention of his readers

> the hordes who will be pining in wretchedness and hunger, while we are gathered in social festivity, and happiness, round a well furnished and luxurious board; blest with all that can render life an elysium.... How gloomy, how dark, how fraught with shuddering sympathy, the reverse of this joyous picture, when we turn to the dwellings of the poor of Quebec, on this anniversary, this day of common and universal jubilee? Round a cold, fireless hearth, the humble child of want sits in moody despair, watching the huddled groups of his famishing family, whose blue, pinched, features, painfully index the weakening inroads of long continued and gnawing hunger; a few worn rags covering their emaciated frames, shiveringly drawn yet closer and closer around them, being their only means of warmth.[2]

---

[1] This essay is a product of a program of research supported by the Canada Council whose assistance I gratefully acknowledge.

[2] "Christmas and the Poor," *Quebec Mercury*, 22 Dec. 1842; Letter from A Well-Wisher, *British Colonist* (Saint John), 9 Dec. 1831; Speech by Nugent, Assembly Debate, 16 Jan. 1840, *Newfoundland Patriot* (St. John's), 15 Feb. 1840; *Novascotian* (Halifax), 11 Dec. 1843; *Sun* (Halifax), 24 Dec. 1850; "A Word in Season," ibid., 31 Dec. 1851; Ladies' Benevolent Society Appeal, *Weekly Observer* (Saint John), 28 Jan. 1851; *Public Ledger* (St. John's), 25 Dec. 1855; "Christmas", *Sun*, 24 Dec. 1858; "A Merry Christmas," *Evening Express* (Halifax), 23 Dec. 1859; J.J. Bigsby, *The Shoe and Canoe or Pictures of Travel in*

Yet both the sufferers and the unaffected shared the common experience of exposure to the impersonal forces of nature—the snow fell alike on the rich and the poor—and no man could be held accountable for the vagaries of the Canadian climate. As the ink froze in her pen, author Anna Jameson recorded that human character and behaviour "depend more on the influence of climate than the pride of civilized humanity would be willing to allow" and went on to pity the poor immigrants who were as "yet unprepared against the rigours of the season!"[3] Editor J.H. Crosskill rhetorically reminded his readers, "Is it not true, that our humane feelings are particularly excited by the approach of cold weather! There is not a human being, unless he has the stony heart of a German fairy tale, but must at this season feel some pity for those who are destitute and comfortless."[4] In his Saint John paper, G.E. Fenety from time to time displayed similar sensibilities:

> Winter is a terrible enemy to the destitute in this most rigorous climate. None but those who experience it, can tell the amount of suffering there is in this City, during five months in the year, among women and children. We see the pauper in the streets, in tattered garb and attenuated form, and he passes by and out of our mind in a moment. Could we follow him to his inhospitable abode, and see his little ones crouching around a single brand of fire, to keep themselves warm, and witness the scanty meal of which they are to partake, we should soon begin to learn something of the dark shades of human life, and incline towards charity.[5]

It seems that the seasonal features of colonial poverty in the nineteenth century did indeed stimulate a degree of expedient humanity towards the poor which, combined with religious motivations, largely counteracted the prevailing influences of conscious *laissez-faire* and unconscious indifference. While it would be simplistic to suggest that winter was the only cause of poverty, it intensified the underemployment of labour, aggravated illness, and attracted the destitute rural poor to the cities where sufficient wealth, self-interest, and jobbery could be found to sustain charitable relief and public asylums. By comparison, whatever poverty existed in the summer months was "more endurable than when the wintry winds

---

the Canadas, (London, 1850), vol. 1, 26; W.H.G. Kingston, *Western Wanderings or, a Pleasure Tour in the Canadas*, (London, 1856), vol. 2, 142.

[3] A. Jameson, *Winter Studies and Summer Rambles in Canada*, (London, 1838), vol. 1, 27-29; Female Benevolent Society, *Kingston Chronicle*, 14 Nov. 1829; *Patriot* (Toronto), 13 Oct. 1837; "December," *Saint John Herald*, 31 Dec. 1845.

[4] "Winter at Last," *Halifax Morning Post*, 13 Dec. 1844.

[5] "Christmas Day," *Morning News* (Saint John), 23 Dec. 1850; "Christmas and the Poor," ibid., 24 Dec. 1841.

their inability to screen themselves from the piercing blast."[6] Moreover, cruel winter plumbed the depths of utter desperation whenever it followed a summer of excessive immigration, raging epidemic, or disastrous crop or fishery failure, or when it coincided with periodic commercial depression or occasional urban conflagration. Since some of these afflictions plagued one or more of the major colonial towns during most winters of the first half of the nineteenth century, the hyperborean climate provides a useful common denominator and point of departure for examining the ramifications of colonial poverty, the characteristics of poor relief, and the attendant attitudes of society in St. John's, Halifax, Saint John, Quebec, Montreal, Kingston, and Toronto. In the pre-industrial period the long Canadian winter both determined the contours of poverty and shaped the responses of affluent and poor alike to the latter's plight.

I

The distress of the "honest" poor, whether outdoor labourers, wretched immigrants, or the helpless sick, old, young, and female, was exacerbated by the exigencies of winter in two principal ways: winter deprived the poor of their employment at the same time as it made the necessaries of life prohibitively dear; and it endangered their health by aggravating the plight of the sick and infirm, by creating dietary problems for those at or below the subsistence level, and by causing disablement or death for others through exposure.

By far the greater number of the poor suffered in winter from a paralysing interruption in their means of earning a living. The seasonal nature of economic activity based on North Atlantic shipping and on harvesting the soil and the sea entailed a total lack of job security for the lower classes. During the months of mercantile activity labourers were normally much in demand in the towns and wages were relatively attractive. This meant that steerage immigrants (usually Irish) arriving in the busy ports of the east coast or the St. Lawrence in summertime were often tempted to take jobs as day labourers since they came badly prepared for "roughing it in the bush." In addition to private employment, major public works were generally suited to summer employment and offered the immigrant no more than a few months of continuous employment. The making of roads, for example, could best be pursued in the summer when every kind of employment was operating at full capacity. Unfortunately employers failed to explain the seasonal nature of outdoor labour and the new arrivals, often grossly misinformed about the colonial environment, learned too late that summer employment seldom compensated for winter distress. In November dockwork in the ice-locked ports of the Canadas ground to a complete halt. Even in the ice-free coastal ports, the perils for North Atlantic shipping in the days of the sailing ship and the unsophisticated steamer reduced

---

[6] "Toronto House of Industry," *Christian Guardian* (Toronto), 20 Nov. 1850.

shipping in the days of the sailing ship and the unsophisticated steamer reduced waterfront activity to a trickle in the winter. Urban workers, both immigrant and resident—day labourers, mill hands, truckmen, seamen, carpenters, and other building trades workers—who were thrown out of work in the autumn thereafter encountered severe competition in their quest for the few remaining jobs and for regular or special relief, particularly from those poor agricultural labourers and fishermen able to make their way to the towns to plead for winter subsistence. These intruders must always have included a proportion of immigrants, who had been attracted during the summer to farms as labourers or servants expecting the kind of security provided by annual hirings in England. Such settlers must have found especially disconcerting the tendency of colonial farmers to hire workers by the month and thereby protect themselves against the slack and lean season.[7] At the other extreme, the shore fishermen of Newfoundland accepted regular winter unemployment as the normal state of things and gravitated towards St. John's in search of the equally regular relief to be found there.[8]

As the number of available jobs decreased during November and December and the labour market in each of the colonial towns became glutted, employed workers found themselves completely at the mercy of employers who took advantage of this surplus, as well as shorter winter hours, to reduce wages for both skilled and unskilled labourers. In Lower Canada labourers and mechanics could expect to earn one-quarter to one-half less in January than in August. House carpenters in Saint John in 1853 received 5s. a day in winter compared to 7s.6d. to 10s. a day in summer. Not only were labourers paid less per day but they also worked sporadically during the winter months.[9] At the same time, the supply of imported and locally produced goods diminished and the needy had to pay the resulting inflated prices and seldom enjoyed credit facilities beyond those available in the pawn shop. Because of the inability of the poor to buy in quantity during seasons of moderate prices, their regular dependence on the winter markets invariably meant in effect they were paying more than the non-labouring classes. With what were at best subsistence, and often

---

[7] "Immigration," *Upper Canada Herald* (Kingston), 12 Jan. 1841; *New Brunswick Courier* (Saint John), 19 June 1841; J. Taylor, *Narrative of a Voyage and Travels in Upper Canada*, (Hull, 1846), 92; J.F.W. Johnston, *Notes on North America*, (Edinburgh & London, 1851), vol. 2, 198.

[8] J. Hatton & M. Harvey, *Newfoundland: Its History, its Present Condition, and its Prospects in the Future*, (Boston, 1883), 83.

[9] *Quebec Mercury*, 21 Aug. 1832; *Morning News* 31 Jan. 1853; Letter from Peter Needy, *Quebec Mercury*, 16 Jan. 1816; Proceedings of the Provincial Association, *St. John Weekly News*, 27 Jan. 1844; *Morning Journal* (Halifax), 26 Jan. 1857. Similarly in northern American towns, S. Thernstrom, *Poverty and Progress: Social Mobility in a Nineteenth Century City*, (Cambridge, Mass., 1964), 20. For an example of a labourer's days of employment, see H.C. Pentland, "The Lachine Strike of 1843," *Canadian Historical Review*, XXIX, 1948, 268.

starvation, wages, the underemployed labourer was often forced in wintertime to purchase bread, the favoured staple in his diet, at prices inflated by as much as fifty per cent, as well as firewood at exorbitant rates in the larger towns.[10]

The poor man could seldom escape from this vicious situation. Even if he was able to save out of his summer earnings enough to provide for impending winter, he rarely had any place to store substantial quantities of potatoes or firewood or anywhere to bake bread if he managed to lay in a barrel of flour. Accordingly he still had to purchase both "HIS *Fuel* and HIS *Food*, from *hand* to *mouth* at a considerably advanced price."[11] The sufferings of the poor man's family were exceeded only by those of the widowed or helpless woman frequently with a dependent brood of children and with even less chance of finding employment. "Imagine for a moment," the St. John's branch of the St. Vincent de Paul Society suggested, "the condition of a poor widow, with a large family, young and helpless, cold and famishing, without fuel or food—without any employment whatever, during the dreary and bitter days of a protracted winter...."[12] A protracted winter usually meant that early spring was the season of greatest hardship, "the pinching season," according to the St. John's *Times*, "when every article of provision naturally advances in price and becomes by the poor almost unattainable."[13] In Saint John the situation was compounded for penniless poor tenants who customarily found themselves forced to move house on May Day when their quarterly rents became due at the very moment when their means were completely exhausted.[14]

A striking illustration of the predicament of the urban poor in winter is afforded by the difficulties they encountered in obtaining a major necessity of life—fuel. It is singularly ironic that during the decades when the British American timber trade flourished, the poor suffered severely from a lack of cheap firewood. Whilst insufficient attention to this prosaic matter might lead the twentieth-century Canadian historian to conclude that the poor man simply took his axe and felled a nearby tree, the degree of urbanization by the 1820s precluded this obvious recourse.

---

10 Letter from A Friend to the Poor, *Upper Canada Herald*, 6 Dec. 1836; *Quebec Mercury*, 12 Dec. 1844, 12 Dec. 1846; Letter from Solicitus, ibid., 23 Dec. 1847. Montreal firewood rates were considered exorbitant by the *Kingston Herald*, 5 Jan. 1847.

11 Letter from Spectator, *Acadian Recorder* (Halifax), 29 Jan. 1825; X to the Young Ladies of Halifax, *Morning Chronicle* (Halifax), 30 Oct. 1845; "Bread for the Poor," *Halifax Morning Post*, 22 Nov. 1842; "Advance in the Price of Provisions, Fuel, Rents," *Morning News*, 8 Feb. 1854.

12 Report of Proceedings of Society of St. Vincent de Paul, *Newfoundlander* (St. John's), 11 Dec. 1856; "Suffering in St. John," *Morning News*, 1 Apr. 1844; "Distress in the City—The House of Industry," *Globe* (Toronto), 11 Jan. 1860; Poor Relief Association: Appeal to the Public, *Newfoundlander*, 18 Feb. 1867.

13 *Times* (St. John's), 18 Oct. 1848; *New Brunswick Courier*, 29 May 1824; Mr. Murdoch's Speech, *Halifax Morning Post*, 29 Oct. 1840; *British Colonist* (Toronto), 15 Feb. 1854.

14 "Monstrous," *Morning News*, 6 May 1842.

Admittedly, many of the poor of St. John's and the town of Upper Canada eked out their winter subsistence by supplying the local wood markets, but even the experienced, small-scale timber cutters depended on persistent winter weather in order to prosecute their activities in the forests.[15]

For the poor of the island and near island towns of Montreal and Halifax, marketable supplies of firewood were essential, because unfenced land had long been denuded of its wood and the standing timber on private property was carefully protected. In Nova Scotia, many outports along the south shore earned a living in winter by supplying the Halifax market with firewood carried to the city by boat, so that in those bitterly cold winters when the outport harbours froze solid, the sufferings of the poor both in town and country greatly increased. Until the railway raised hopes of adequate supply in Montreal in the 1850s, the poor of that city looked for their wood to the small loads brought to town across the ice by the habitants' sleighs. At old Quebec, where the banks of the St. Lawrence were stripped of forests, firewood had to be brought down from the region of the St. Maurice and other tributaries to the north, and similarly at Saint John before rail transportation the markets relied on river traffic. The difficulty was that all these water highways froze in winter.[16]

The residents of towns surrounded by woods rather than by water could in theory supply their own needs, provided the households included healthy adults, storage space, and a sleigh. But even enterprise might be rewarded by practical obstacles. In Quebec and St. John's the local authorities, concerned for the safety of the inhabitants and their livestock, intermittently promoted measures which deprived the poor man of the dogs he needed for hauling wood. As one sympathetic observer in Quebec remarked:

> To many families the dog is almost indispensable, they depend on him for the conveyance of all their fuel, and the interdict against the use of canine carriers is one of the luxuries of the wealthy; who feeling no want of the services of these animals themselves think it quite

---

[15] *Morning News*, 14 Oct. 1840; J. McGregor, *British America*, (Edinburgh & London, 1832), vol. 1, 218; R.H. Bonnycastle, *Newfoundland in 1842*, (London, 1842), vol. 2, 122; Taylor, *Narrative of a Voyage*, 80; "The Poor," *Patriot* (St. John's), 13 Feb. 1847; ibid., 12 Feb. 1853; "The Weather," *Quebec Mercury*, 15 Jan. 1848; *Times*, 1 Mar. 1848, 14 Dec. 1850; *Newfoundland Express* (St. John's), 3 Jan. 1854.

[16] Letter from Beneficius, *Acadian Recorder*, 15 Feb. 1817; *Christian Messenger* (Halifax), 16 Jan. 1852; *Montreal Herald*, 17 Dec. 1840; "Froid-Détresse," *La Minerve* (Montreal), 29 Jan. 1844; "C'est l'Hiver," ibid., 14 Dec. 1846; *Quebec Gazette*, 10 Oct. 1851; Letter from Canadian, *Montreal Gazette*, 29 Jan. 1851; Letter from Housekeeper, "Firewood," ibid., 1 Feb. 1854; Kingston, *Western Wanderings*, vol. 2, 130; "High Price of Fire Wood," *Morning News*, 20 Sept. 1854; ibid., 21 & 28 Nov. 1855; "Cordwood on the Railway," ibid., 15 Oct. 1860.

exemplary to relieve their poorer neighbours of them also, moreover the wealthy because they only use the dog for purposes connected with sport and ostentation, are often too ignorant to think it more cruel to harness a dog than a horse, while in point of fact, man has just as good a right to use the dog for draught, and carriage, as any other beast in creation.[17]

It was an age which saw both great fear of "hydrophobia" (rabies) and experiments to protect the public health, and the authorities insistently argued that overloading the dog as a beast of burden caused the thirst and fatigue which induced distemper.[18] At the same time, fear of mad dogs and the prevalence of sheep and cattle killing in St. John's led to a regulation which sanctioned the shooting of stray dogs, a move which prompted one irate editor to point out that "The whole dependence of every poor family in the town for fuel is upon the Dog," and that an order to exterminate the dogs was tantamount to an instruction to exterminate the poor.[19]

On the other hand, many who were forced to rely on the town markets for fuel but had no storage space could not buy wood by the cord even if they had the money.

> Is it at all possible [asked one contemporary in Halifax] to crowd so much lumber into a moderate sized room, which is occupied by *five* families, the middle one of which "takes in *boarders*!" One half the houses that are occupied by the poor, have no yard room, and few have more than enough to "swing a cat in"; beside, if there were a yard to hold six cords of wood, owned by three persons, and the house is taken by half a dozen families, three of which are not prudent, is it not likely the latter would be now and then *borrowing* a stick of it while the former were asleep?[20]

Obliged to shop for two or three feet of wood at a time, the poor were forced to pay more per cord than if they had been able to purchase it by the full cord from the local depot or direct from the supplier.[21] As small-scale purchasers, the poor were

---

[17] *Quebec Mercury*, 15 Feb. 1853.

[18] Entry, 10 Dec. 1820, Lord Dalhousie's Journal, Public Archives of Canada; "Carters and Dogs," *Quebec Gazette*, 12 Feb. 1844; *Quebec Mercury*, 10 Feb. 1844, 1 Feb. 1853.

[19] "Sheep-Killing," *Patriot* (St. John's), 5 Oct. 1850; ibid., 24 June 1847; Speech by Parsons, Assembly Debate, 19 Apr. 1866, *Newfoundlander*, 14 June 1866. For less sympathetic views and information on problems caused by dogs, see "The Dogs Again!" *Times*, 18 Sept. 1847; J.F. Maguire, *The Irish in America*, (London, 1868), 174-5.

[20] Letter from Charity, "Bazaars—Fuel &c," *Acadian Recorder*, 10 Aug. 1833.

[21] Letter from Vindex, *Acadian Recorder*, 5 Feb. 1825. Similarly the poor had to buy coal in small quantities when at its highest annual prices. "Wanted—A Coal Depot in Halifax" *Morning Journal*, 9 Feb. 1859; "Wanted—A Coal Dept," ibid., 2 Nov. 1859.

also particularly vulnerable to dishonest practices and forestalling in the winter wood markets, usually perpetrated by people equally impoverished, during decades when the supplies were limited and in the absence of municipal regulations adequate for their protection. "A Friend to the Poor" in Montreal reported in 1845 that local hucksters were purchasing wood at the wood yard for resale in the market and loading it on their sleighs in one-quarter cords, "and it is so ingeniously piled on them that they bamboozle the poor man into the idea that they have at least a third of a cord on their sleighs."[22]

Contemporaries believed that the outlay for fuel represented a major, if not the greatest, expense borne by the poor city dweller in winter. In 1854 the editor of the *Montreal Gazette* estimated that factory labourers in that city were compelled to devote about 20 per cent of their wages to the purchase of wood, an expenditure which he assumed rendered wages in this northern clime far less attractive than comparable wages in the United States.[23] Indeed, another traveller in the Canadas at mid-century considered the dearness of fuel to be one of the great drawbacks to the progress of colonial settlement. When the supply of firewood eventually became exhausted as the woods rapidly receded and conservation was neglected, he reckoned that the cost of coal would bear so heavily on the poor that it would "prevent the peopling the country."[24] Although fuel was costly, fire was indispensable in a cold climate in order to preserve life itself. William Kingston, who was intrigued by the logistics of fuel supply and the technology of domestic heating in Quebec during the 1850s, reported that the poor suffered "dreadfully in the winter from want of firing, especially the poor Irish, for the first two or three years after their arrival in the colony.... Many, after their day's work is over, go to bed directly they reach home, and remain there till it is again time to be off, as the only means they possess to escape being frozen."[25]

As if these obstacles were not enough, in their struggle to obtain the necessaries of life, the poor were remorselessly haunted by the spectre of illness. Instances of

---

[22] *Montreal Gazette*, 15 Feb. 1845; *Free Press* (Halifax), 11 Nov. 1823; *Montreal Gazette*, 8 Jan. 1825; *Montreal Herald*, 31 Aug. 184; "High Price of Firewood," *Quebec Mercury*, 11 Nov. 1851; Letter from One Who Suffers, *Montreal Gazette*, 11 Nov. 1853; "The Supply of Wood," ibid., 4 Oct. 1854; Letter from R., "Fuel Wood," ibid., 6 Oct. 1854.

[23] *Montreal Gazette*, 4 Mar. 1843; W. Brown, *America: A Four Years' Residence in the United States and Canada*, (Leeds, 1849), 89; Letter from Sydney Bellingham, *Montreal Gazette*, 3 Oct. 1854; "The Supply of Firewood," ibid., 5 Oct. 1854.

[24] R. Everest, *A Journey through the United States and Part of Canada*, (London, 1855), 46-47; G.W. Warr, *Canada as it is; or, the Emigrant's Friend and Guide to Upper Canada*, (London, 1847), 84.

[25] Kingston, *Western Wanderings*, vol. 2, 167. See also "Winter," *Montreal Transcript*, 18 Oct. 1836; "Fuel," ibid., 22 Oct. 1836; "The Poor—God Help Them! Let Man think of them, too! Great Suffering in consequence of Scarcity of Fuel," *Halifax Morning Post*, 10 Mar. 1846.

malnutrition leading to starvation in winter were not uncommon, and even where relief in the shape of soup or cornmeal was available, it did not necessarily counteract illnesses caused by dietary deficiencies. Many immigrants amongst the poor were so unused to Indian meal—the staple relief provided by government—that the coarse food caused serious problems for weakened constitutions. Nor was relief provided on a sufficiently regular basis. The visitors of the St. Vincent de Paul Society of St. John's found that poor fishermen's families frequently went whole days in winter without food, and enumerated some of the results, such as the "miserable and emaciated mother" with nine freezing and starving children who was found nursing her eighteen-month old twins, and on "being asked why she continued to give them the breast so long, she said she had nothing to give them to drink, and that she had no other means of keeping life in them."[26] If the demographic patterns produced by the winters in other northern countries apply also to Canada, it is as likely that long winters caused the greatest degree of regular seasonal illnesses and considerably increased the rate of mortality, the cumulative effect of dietary deficiencies and poor health being most noticeable in the early spring of especially hard seasons.[27]

While the kinds of illness aggravated by the winter came increasingly to be treated by outdoor relief through the establishment of public visiting dispensaries, the sick poor in winter also required institutional care. The few public institutions which did exist were often unsuitable for the treatment of the sick. This was the period when the town jail or house of correction represented the colonial counterpart to the "general mixed workhouse" in Britain and was likely to fulfil welfare, protectionist, and correctional functions as well as furnishing a house for inmates of all manner of ages and sexes, mental and physical conditions. Whatever their facilities, such institutions were rarely adequate for the care of the sick, very few being endowed with an infirmary. While the healthy transient poor frequently sought admission to the town jails for shelter in winter, the buildings were seldom adequately supplied with heat. For a chronically sick poor man there was little to choose between the prospect of freezing to death in a garret or outhouse and freezing to death in the local jail. The jurors' verdict on a coroner's inquest on the death of an infirm vagrant in the Quebec house of correction in February 1827 concluded that the deceased man, after having suffered three months' incarceration in a jail lacking three-quarters of its window panes, "died from Misery, Cold, and want of Clothing."[28]

---

[26] Reports of Society of St. Vincent de Paul, *Newfoundlander*, 1 Aug. 1853, 31 July 1854.

[27] Evidence of Dr. Shea, Secretary of Poor Commissioners, *Newfoundland Express*, 18 Mar. 1852. G. Utterström, "Some Population Problems in Pre-Industrial Sweden," *Scandinavian Economic History Review*, II, 1954, 120.

[28] *Quebec Mercury*, 20 Feb. 1827; *Montreal Gazette*, 10 Dec. 1835; Report of Special Committee appointed to enquire into the circumstances which preceded and accompanied the death of John Collins, who died in the Common Gaol of the District of Montreal, *Journal of the Legislative Assembly*, Lower Canada, 1835-6, App. W.W.; Presentment of Grand Jury, *Quebec Gazette*, 20 Jan. 1836; "Sociétés de bienfaisance," *La Minerve*, 19 Feb. 1846; F.H.

While observers denounced such public squalor as scandalous, the primitive, wretched abodes of the poor were thought to constitute a far more serious, intractable problem. Benevolent citizens called for the provision of specialized refuges from the cold for the destitute and sick poor who, like a Quebec woman removed prostrate from her unheated and unprovisioned garret to the jail to die in 1846, were likely to suffer untold miseries in helpless obscurity.[29] The grand jury of Montreal in February 1847 feared that two recent deaths of children from "hunger cold and misery" represented only the beginning of deaths that winter from exposure amongst the city's "1,100" indigent families, especially when "More than 100 families have nothing but straw for their beds, and to protect them from the attacks of cold, no clothes but those rendered ragged through their poverty."[30] The deaths of helpless poor children from exposure in their ghastly dwellings were graphically described in contemporary accounts. In the severe winter of 1816-17 a jury in Quebec concluded that little Maria Louisa Beleau died of "a violent sore throat, and cold, produced by exposure to the inclemency of the weather." Like so many of the colonial poor, Maria Louisa belonged to a family without a male provider, the type of family most crippled by the lack of employment and regular poor relief. A witness at the inquest claimed that

> The hovel in which the decreased had lived, with her mother, and two sisters, IS NOT FIT FOR A STABLE. It is open in many parts of the roof, and on all sides. There is no other floor than the bare earth. It is a mere wooden shell; it has no window, nor any chimney. In the middle is a shallow hole made in the earth, in which there are marks of a fire having been made; and the smoke escaped through the open parts of the roof and sides.—When I was there on Tuesday last, there was no fire in the hole....[31]

As a result of the widely publicized distress of the poor in winter, coupled with such health hazards as epidemics, these years saw the inauspicious beginnings or faltering development of poorhouses and hospitals in the major urban centres. Nevertheless, facilities for treating the sick remained woefully inadequate. The poorhouses, catering largely to the helpless unemployable, tended to herd promiscuously together the sick and healthly. The hospitals for their part afforded

---

Armstrong, "Toronto in Transition: The Emergence of a City 1828-1838," (unpublished Ph.D. thesis, University of Toronto, 1965), 296-7.

29 Letter from One of the Jury, *Quebec Mercury*, 6 Mar. 1847; *Chronicle and Gazette* (Kingston), 24 Feb. 1841.

30 Presentment of Grand Jury, *Montreal Gazette*, 19 Feb. 1847.

31 Letter from H, *Quebec Mercury*, 3 Dec. 1816. Another case of a child's death from exposure occurred in Kingston in 1837 when an infant living in "a perfect barn" had its extremities frozen. *Montreal Gazette*, 2 Feb. 1837.

insufficient accommodation, were often discriminatory in their admissions policies, and suffered from financial uncertainty.

While existing institutions might well have been designed to protect the sick poor against the ravages of the cold, they did not always succeed in solving hibernal distress any more than did jails. In 1838 John Kent, a member of the legislature in Newfoundland, claimed that mental patients in St. John's Hospital frequently suffered frostbite in their feet so serious that amputation was required. The inmates of the Kingston House of Industry, a poorhouse, were found to be freezing from want of clothing in 1855. And the frigid, pathetic scenes in the "Camps," the apology for almshouses in St. John's, epitomized the very worst in public institutions.[32]

Although the colonial poor have themselves left little first-hand documentary evidence of their sufferings in winter, there is no reason to believe that they passively accepted their fate. The nearest they came to doing so in the popular mind was in the case of the French-Canadians, the most traditionally acclimatized residents of towns, who were said to "associate the idea of disgrace with the fact of destitution, and, with few exceptions, proudly conceal any amount of privation with a sort of Indian stoicism."[33] Arguably, this response demonstrates a full adaptation to the unrelenting realities of the climate; but the mid-century marked also the period of substantial French-Canadian emigration to the United States. Certainly the most enterprising, effective response to the climate and its rigours, as well as to the lack of jobs in general, was to leave it and migrate either permanently or at least seasonally to more congenial climes. As "Off-For-Australia" wrote to the *Newfoundland Patriot* in 1839, "in these times of great distress, the only way to relieve one's poverty is to emigrate."[34]

Indeed, as the editor of a Halifax paper observed, the climate contributed to the well-known transiency of the population of colonial towns:

> The exceedingly precarious nature of industrial pursuits with the hopelessness of looking elsewhere within a nearer distance than the American cities for employment, naturally creates a vast amount of poverty in our city.... So sensible are the poorer classes of this, that few who have undergone the privations incidental to a severe winter,

---

[32] Speech by Kent, Assembly Debate, 1 Aug. 1838, *Newfoundland Patriot*, 11 Aug. 1838; "The Camps—State of the Poor!," *Times*, 11 Jan. 1851; "The House of Industry," *Weekly British Whig* (Kingston), 7 Dec. 1855.

[33] *Quebec Mercury*, 1 Feb. 1855.

[34] *Newfoundland Patriot*, 23 Mar. 1839; Government Emigration Officer Perley to Provincial Secretary Saunders, 26 Dec. 1845; Provincial archives of New Brunswick, REX/PA, Immigration 1; *Newfoundlander*, 22 Sept. 1853; Report of Special Committee on Emigration, JLA, Canada, 1857, App. No. 47; Letter from Justice, *Quebec Mercury*, 16 Jan. 1858.

ever risk the repetition, but with the close of the year pack up their few little traps and clear out for Boston.[35]

Because of the transiency caused partly by the climate and the seasonal limits it imposed on the pre-industrial economy, the poor were ineffective in organizing protests against the tendency of colonial employers to exploit the situation to their own narrow advantage. The composition of the lower class changed too rapidly in the first half of the nineteenth century and its members were too inured to the seasonality of employment for a vigorous campaign of protest to have been successfully launched against the inequities of winter. Admittedly, individual petitioners begged government for relief and jobs. On a larger scale, "ungrateful" labourers engaged on the roads in St. John's in the early spring of 1849 collectively petitioned against scanty wages of 1s.6d. a day and remuneration in truck rather than in cash. Similarly, desperate Irish labourers on the first winter canal building at Lachine in 1842-3 struck against a seasonal cut in wages which were paid in truck.[36] The aims of these public works labourers were singularly short term and show the kind of "occasional collective outburst" to be expected from men whose sole common denominator was hardship.[37]

Even a mass meeting of 2000-3000 unemployed French-Canadian shipyard workers in Quebec in November of the severe depression year of 1857 cannot be taken as evidence of an effective show of aggressive solidarity. Hardship was also a part of their experience in an industry that formed an ancillary activity to the primary business of shipping and therefore a winter works programme writ large. Although shipbuilding was run by private enterprise to a greater extent than public works of the period, it remained overwhelmingly a winter activity, employing the labourers and farmers of the Quebec area in very large numbers, and, to the joy of the shipbuilders, at relief level wages. The shipwrights were thus not only semi-skilled, but were ruthlessly exploited and rendered politically impotent as a class by the continuing success of the deception played upon them that their work on ships in winter represented a charitable favour and not a right. Consequently, during the chronic depressions which necessarily interrupted the export-based, winter shipbuilding industry, the Quebec workers did not riot but publicly demanded

---

[35] "The Weather and the Water," *Times and Courier* (Halifax), 22 Mar. 1849. On seasonal transiency in St. John's, see J. McGregor, *Historical and Descriptive Sketches of the Maritime Colonies of British America*, (London, 1828), 237. The grand jury of Saint John in 1844 referred to "The fluctuating and ever changing population of large seaport towns." Presentment, Dec. 1844, PANB, RMU, Csj, 1/11; *Morning News*, 31 Jan. 1853.

[36] Speech by O'Brien, Assembly Debate, 2 Apr. 1849, *Newfoundlander*, 3 May 1849; *Montreal Gazette*, 25 & 28 Mar. 1843; Pentland, "The Lachine Strike of 1843," *CHR*, XXIX, 1948, 255-77.

[37] G.S. Jones, *Outcast London: A Study in the Relationship between Classes in Victorian Society*, (Oxford, 1971), 340-4.

alternative forms of winter relief.[38] In the depths of winter they constituted no more of a threat to social order than did the pathetic unemployed fishermen of St. John's. Nonetheless, the so-called benevolence of employers in winter had begun by midcentury to encourage the articulation of working-class resentment. The remarks of a Halifax carpenter in 1852 were probably typical. "He asks if it be fair, that for five months in the year able and willing mechanics are compelled to accept the alternative of walking the streets or working for wages which do not afford ample remuneration for the labour performed." Then, "after submitting to all this, with apparent resignation—after enriching their employers by the sweat of their brow, on terms which barely keep the thread of life from snapping—they are told with barefaced effrontery that they were employed in charity." The solution, according to the carpenter, lay in the organization of a trade union as a means of self-defence.[39]

As for more primitive forms of protest, observers occasionally feared or at least noted with surprise the absence of mass demonstrations and violent crimes amongst the poor during the winters of greatest suffering, but did not draw the probable conclusion that the poor had to preserve what little energy they possessed in order to sustain life itself.[40] While the anticipation of winter hardship occasionally turned starving populations into lawless banditti who threatened or raided stores or perpetrated gang robberies, winter itself was a hopeless season for protest.[41] Admittedly, poor individuals might commit misdemeanours in order to gain admission to the local jail for the coldest months.[42] But the poor were far more likely to show their spirit during the season of employment after they had "thawed

---

[38] "Shipbuilding," *Quebec Gazette*, 27 Aug. 1834; ibid., 18 Jan. 1837; "Distressed State of the Working Classes," *Quebec Mercury*, 27 Dec. 1842; *Morning News*, 5 Apr. 1847; *Quebec Gazette*, 25 Oct. 1847; Letter from Solicitus, *Quebec Mercury*, 27 Jan. 1848; "Mass meeting of the Unemployed," ibid., 17 Nov. 1857; "More Mob Demonstrations," ibid., 2 Dec. 1858; "Ship-Building in Quebec," *New Brunswick Courier*, 4 Apr. 1863; Report of A.C. Buchanan, Chief Emigration Agent, for 1860, *JLA*, Canada, 1861, Sessional Papers, vol. 3, No. 14; A Faucher, "The Decline of Shipbuilding at Quebec in the Nineteenth Century," *Canadian Journal of Economics and Political Science*, XXIII (1957), 211-12; F. Ouellet, *Histoire économique et sociale du Québec 1760-1850*, (Montreal, 1966), 500-5.

[39] *Halifax Daily Sun*, 4 Mar. 1852. And indeed it is no coincidence that prominent amongst the first groups of urban workers to organize were the victims of winter unemployment.

[40] Carroll to Jeffery, 20 June 1827, Public Archives of Nova Scotia, RG 1, vol. 309, doc. 116; *Quebec Mercury* 10 Dec. 1842; Charge of Mr. Justice Power to Grand Jury, *Quebec Gazette*, 7 Apr. 1852; "Material and Moral Conditions," *Newfoundlander*, 20 Mar. 1854; *Times*, 12 Apr. 1854; Presentment of Grand Jury, *Quebec Mercury*, 1 Feb. 1859.

[41] L.A. Anspach, *A History of the Island of Newfoundland*, (London, 1819), 266; C. Lyell, *Travels in North America, Canada, and Nova Scotia*, (London, 2nd ed., 1855), vol. 2, 118; "Dangerous State of the City," *Quebec Mercury*, 28 Nov. 1858.

[42] "Christmas Night," *British Colonist* (Toronto), 28 Dec. 1849; Police Office, *Morning News*, 12 Jan. 1857.

out" and as their expectations rose. When railway labourers in Saint John struck for higher wages and shorter hours in March 1858, despite the employment provided for them during January and February by "benevolent" contractors, the editor of the *Morning News* complained: "Do as much as you may for them in their adversity, as soon as they get upon their feet and feel that they have strength and got you in their power, they will turn upon you and wring the last copper from your pockets."[43] Town labourers and mechanics were notorious for demanding high wages in season. Who could blame them when summer employment might represent the sum total of their year's labour? To the immigrant—the uninitiated—the demand for high wages accorded with a high level of expectation produced by emigration propaganda, but to the experienced colonial labourer it reflected a primitive determination to enjoy to the full a season of plenty.[44] This disposition amongst fishermen in Newfoundland caused one newspaper editor to draw a comparison with the habits of the British sailor who "will earn his money like a horse and spend it like an ass."[45] Enjoyment invariably led to excess—a tendency to feast and be merry for four or five months of the year rather than to live frugally for twelve. Reformers also believed that a tradition of winter relief encouraged indolence and fretted that persons in Newfoundland "have been known to bask in the noon-day's sun during the very height of the fishery!"[46] Indeed, the rhythm of seasonal employment was complemented by the rhythm of seasonal relief. The seasonal labourer could not be abandoned to the savagery of winter. If no shipbuilding or stone breaking was available, the poor man, whether considered deserving or not, could usually obtain a donation of welfare provisions, a temporary refuge in an asylum, or a share of the alms doled out by private citizens and religious institutions. Such relief was never lavish or particularly attractive, but then neither were the rewards of providence and frugality.

While the poor therefore suffered through most winters with resignation, confining their protests largely to displays of summer intransigence and perennial improvidence, they did exhibit an inward-looking response to their seasonal predicament by cooperating amongst themselves. Extended families and individuals united by a common experience or nationality drew together and pooled their resources against the vicissitudes of winter. This reaction is reflected in comments by observers who often noted that the poor comprised the most charitable segment of

---

[43] "The `Poor People,'" *Morning News*, 8 Mar. 1858; "Strikes and Starvation," *Daily Leader* (Toronto), 8 May 1855.

[44] "Standing out for Wages—A Hint to the Common Council," *Morning News*, 26 Apr. 1843; Letter from A Merchant, ibid, 28 Apr. 1843; *Examiner* (Toronto), 11 Aug. 1847; P. Morris, *A Short Review of the History, Government, Constitution, Fishery and Agriculture, of Newfoundland*, (St. John's, 1847), 108; "A Strike," *Morning News* 17 May 1854; "The Weather vs House Building," *Morning Journal*, 12 Dec. 1859.

[45] Investigator No. 1, *Times*, 21 Oct. 1854.

[46] *Times*, 29 Sept. 1847, 29 July 1848; *Quebec Gazette*, 27 Oct. 1845.

the colonial population and that it was the poor who supported the poor.[47] Certainly this is how the Irish population, which comprised the majority of the urban poor, initially managed to survive through the long winters at a time when their numbers, their national characteristics, and their penury did little to endear them to established residents.

II

For their part, the well-to-do, surveying the plight of their unfortunate compatriots from the vantage point of warm houses and comfortable affluence, responded with good advice and practical proposals as well as hibernal sentimentality. Except in Upper Canada, which was not sufficiently urbanized until the 1830s, winter poverty as a public issue came to the fore in the older colonial towns during the depression following the Napoleonic Wars. The ensuing periodic debates proceeded within the context of various practices of public welfare in the colonies which were themselves much influenced by the climate.[48] In the seacoast towns voluntary assistance supplemented government aid; in the river and lake ports the reverse was the case. Nova Scotia and New Brunswick both enjoyed statutory adaptations of the English poor law, including poor-rates and poorhouses in Halifax and Saint John, while the inhabitants of Newfoundland, who hovered on the brink of pauperization throughout

---

[47] Speech by Nugent, Assembly Debate, 16 Jan. 1840, *Newfoundland Patriot* 15 Feb. 1840; *Public Ledger*, 22 Sept. 1840; Report of Charitable Committee of St. Andrew's Society, *Montreal Gazette*, 15 Nov. 1848.

[48] For example three times as much indoor and outdoor relief was reported to be given by the overseers of the poor in Saint John in winter as in summer. Letter from An Old Tax Payer, "Poor House," *Morning News*, 16 Mar. 1842. In the Halifax poorhouse the total number of inmates in January/February (the only monthly totals available) was always 15-20% higher than the average total for the year. See Record Books of Commissioners of the Poor, 1829-60, PANS, RG 25, Series C, vol. 4A; *JLA*, Nova Scotia, 1858, App. No. 31. The following table indicates that the expenditure on the casual poor in St. John's fluctuated according to the seasons.

Public Expenditure for the Relief of the Poor in St. John's District in 1861 (to the nearest £)												
	Jan.	Feb.	Mar.	Apr.	May	June	July	Aug.	Sept.	Oct.	Nov.	Dec.
Permanent Poor	121	124	124	124	122	117	110	111	110	113	115	115
Casual Poor	308	554	655	691	486	214	181	133	125	158	273	610
Poor in Sheds	99	94	95	92	91	83	85	84	85	105	121	131
(Source: *JLA*, Newfoundland, 1862, App., 118-19)												

the five decades considered here, were relieved out of colonial revenues. A system of weekly licensed begging, combined with congregational and monastic alms-giving, sustained the poor of Quebec and Montreal until the intensifying social problems of urbanization led Protestants and more especially the Catholic majority to establish separate institutions for various categories of poor, though the well respected Hôtels Dieu (hospitals) and Hôpitaux Généraux (poorhouses) dated from the French colonial period. In Upper Canada district funds were initially used for piecemeal poor relief, but in the 1820s and 1830s, welfare measures in the municipalities of Kingston and Toronto had become largely voluntary. Although the establishment of asylums in Upper Canada, beginning in the late 1830s, aimed to relieve the distress of the generality of the poor, the trend towards the polarization of Protestant and Catholic institutions soon emerged. Since the measures in all the towns rapidly came to depend on some financial aid from the legislatures and from the community at large, the period was marked by lengthy public disagreements over the categories of poverty and the methods, amounts, and responsibilities for providing relief—issues which constitute a topic in itself.

In spite of divergent political, religious, and philosophical views on poverty, the actual cause of winter distress provoked little difference of opinion. Contemporaries blamed unemployment, which the solicitor general of Newfoundland in 1855 trenchantly attributed to the seasonality and underdevelopment of the colonial economy. Poverty in Newfoundland, he explained, is caused by "the absence of employment for the labouring classes during a particular period of the year, when the prosecution of the fishery ceases; and from the fact that the fishery itself was not sufficiently fostered to enable those who prosecuted it to derive their full sustenance from it."[49] But in the absence of a transformation in their economy, townspeople and other commentators suggested one of two approaches to the problem: remove the poor from the cities or provide facilities on the spot for their relief.

Those who advocated removal were motivated either by a refusal to accept responsibility for the care of the transient poor or by an Arcadian vision of the agricultural future of the colonies. Removal sometimes meant re-emigration, especially in Newfoundland, where this recourse remained a favoured panacea for distress. Similarly in Halifax, the proposed remedy for releasing the blacks of the town's rural ghettos from their regular winter distress was to induce them "to migrate to a climate and soil better adapted to their constitution and habits."[50] In Saint John and other colonial towns, the anticipation of a winter of hardship in 1847-8 prompted the authorities to try to persuade Irish immigrants to return to their native country.[51]

---

[49] Speech by Solicitor General, Legislative Council Debate, 2 June 1855, *Newfoundland Express*, 11 July 1855; St. John's Poor Relief Association, *Newfoundlander*, 10 May 1867.

[50] W. Moorson, *Letters from Nova Scotia; Comprising Sketches of a Young Country*, (London, 1830), 127.

[51] Resolution of Common Council, 10 Nov. 1847, PANB, MSJ, Saint John Common Clerk; "Employment for the Poor," *Morning News*, 1 Dec. 1847.

In some instances removal simply amounted to a matter of passing the burden from one town to another, as in the severe winter of 1817-18, when shiploads of poor Newfoundlanders were sent from St. John's to Halifax.[52] More often these proposals involved the transfer of the poor from urban to rural areas. In Saint John this kind of resettlement was seen as a way of alleviating the poor-rate of some of its ever-increasing winter burden.[53] In Quebec, the prospect of a winter of severe unemployment prompted the editor of the *Quebec Mercury* to encourage labourers in 1855 to move westward beyond Toronto in search of harvest work, which would not only secure their short-term livelihood, but carry them so far from Quebec that its citizens would be relieved of a proportion of winter street beggars.[54] It was also the official policy of the government emigrant agent at Quebec to encourage new arrivals to remain in the towns as briefly as possible and to proceed to agricultural districts where they would "more easily procure the necessaries of life and avoid the hardships and distress which are experienced by a large portion of the poor inhabitants in the large cities, during the winter season."[55] And then there were the agrarian idealists who argued that the future independence and security of the present colonial poor could be achieved only by their settlement on the land. Farming represented the one means of attaining not only the salvation and prosperity of the country, but also the permanent cure of seasonal distress, even if agriculture could be pursued only as an ancillary activity.[56] Since farming in the British North American climate was suspended for five months of the year and confined to river valleys and other enclaves of fertile land, the successful pursuit of small-scale subsistence agriculture remained no more than a fanciful idea and evidence of an unrealistic primitivism. In actual fact removal in any shape or form represented a negative response to the rigours of seasonal poverty.

On the other hand, neither idealism nor indifference animated those who were willing to accept winter poverty as an urban responsibility. Some regarded the centralization of relief measures in the towns as an administrative necessity. The poorhouses in Halifax and St. John's (1861) were partly intended to serve the transient poor of their respective provinces. Similarly, the managers of the conventual institutions in Montreal believed they were not fulfilling their expected

---

52 *New Brunswick Courier*, 15 Nov. 1817; Hatton & Harvey, *Newfoundland*, 80.

53 "Provisions of the Poor," *New Brunswick Courier*, 30 Oct. 1841; "Charity in the City and Labor in the Country," *Daily Leader*, 2 Feb. 1855.

54 "Prospects of the Labouring Classes," *Quebec Mercury*, 11 Aug. 1855.

55 Instructions of Mr. Buchanan, Emigrant Agent at Quebec, to settlers, in J.S. Hogan, *Canada: An Essay*, (Montreal & London, 1855), 75n.

56 *Free Press*, 11 Feb. 1817; General Meeting of Halifax Poor Man's Friend Society, *Novascotian*, 18 Feb. 1826; Letter from Publico, *Star* (Quebec), 22 Apr. 1829; Report of Benevolent Irish Society, *Newfoundland Patriot*, 20 Feb. 1841; Morris, *A Short Review*, 108; J. Homer, *A Brief Sketch of the Present State of the Province of Nova-Scotia* (Halifax, 1834), 30.

function unless they attracted the infirm and needy from the surrounding countryside. Other townsmen were keen to retain the poor in the cities out of sheer self-interest. As the major employers of seasonal labourers, merchants involved in the import-export trades wanted to maintain throughout the winter the level of labour in the peak summer season in order to facilitate the ready resumption of commercial activity in the spring.[57] They did not want to see surplus town labourers dispersed to the farmlands, returned to Europe, or enticed to the United States. The fishing merchants of St. John's, for example, wanted to have a large selection of "dealers" on hand from which to choose.[58] As a correspondent to the Halifax *Acadian Recorder* explained in 1816: "In a climate like ours a very considerable number of labouring men in town, must be without employment, the greater part of the winter; otherwise the community must be very deficient of the quantity of labour required in summer."[59] For this reason the names of prominent merchants were sure to head the subscription lists of charitable societies and predominate in reports of public meetings. Michael Tobin, a merchant of Halifax, openly admitted that the merchants, governed as they were by the vagaries of the market economy, did not pay their labourers sufficient wages to see them through the winter and that the deficiency had therefore to be supplied by other means.[60] The merchants of St. John's were notorious for cutting off the accustomed "store pay" to their "slave labour" as soon as the commercial season ended and for sending the unemployed fishermen to the government for relief.[61]

In their attempt to find an urban solution for winter destitution, colonial employers, moralists, educators, and editors maintained that the most efficacious remedy lay in the promotion of individual self-reliance. Given the seasonal nature of employment, however, they could not appropriately encourage the poor to help themselves and overcome their distress by working harder: the development of a work ethic surely depended on the availability of year-round labour. Nor did common-school education as a panacea for poverty gain wide public acceptance until about the middle of the century, and even then its success in instilling the rising generation

---

[57] "Employment for the Poor," *Morning News*, 29 Jan. 1858.

[58] S. March, *The Present Condition of Newfoundland, with Suggestions for Improving its Industrial and Commercial Resources*, (St. John's 1854), 8.

[59] Letter from Beneficus, *Acadian Recorder*, 21 Dec. 1816; Proceedings of Corporation of Montreal: Council Meeting, *Montreal Gazette* 21 Dec. 1841.

[60] General Meeting of Poor Man's Friend Society, *Novascotian*, 2 Feb. 1825.

[61] Speech by Hogsett, Assembly Debate, 3 Apr. 1854, *Newfoundland Express*, 11 Apr. 1854; "Our Trade System," *Newfoundlander*, 1 Feb. 1855. Even in Montreal, which was rapidly industrializing by the 1860s and beginning for the first time to offer opportunities for regular year-round employment to the poor, the pre-industrial tradition of winter wage cuts, which had characterized seasonal poverty, persisted into the late nineteenth century. Maguire, *The Irish in America*, 99; see Royal Commission on the Relations of Capital and Labor in Canada, *Evidence—Quebec* (Ottawa, 1889), 86, 313, 680.

with the notions of self-help and social responsibility remained prospective rather than immediate.[62] In this period, therefore, believers in the value of self-help placed the major emphasis on encouraging the poor to "weather the winter" by making what scanty resources they had go further towards supplying the necessaries of life.[63] The advocacy of rigid economy included suggestions for making do with cheaper provisions. In 1849 the editor of the *Public Ledger* advised the St. John's poor to eat cods' heads in winter, "the most nutritious part of the fish, but which has hitherto been thrown out as manure."[64] Unsolicited good advice extended in full measure to the drinking habits of the poor. If the poor drank heavily, it was sometimes part of an attempt to keep warm. Rum was often used as a cheaper substitute for firewood, and the warm public house seemed more attractive than the cold and cheerless home. But to the classes who were called upon to provide relief for the poor in winter, the latter's avid consumption of rum seemed a particularly spendthrift habit. Temperance advocates therefore exhorted the poor to save for a wintry day the summer earnings which they wasted on grog, a thrifty habit which might both discourage the reliance on winter relief and thereby diminish the regrettable dependence on the tavern as a warming house.[65]

The failure of town labourers to economize in the summer in order to subsist independently through the long winters was frequently bemoaned by their self-appointed counsellors. While the more cynical observers attributed to ingrained improvidence the inability of the labourer to amass savings while in full employment, they nonetheless admitted that the poor had to have a secure place in which to lodge their meagre savings. Horrific tales circulated describing what happened to poor men who put their faith in seemingly honest friends or prosperous merchants as bankers.[66] Consequently, beginning in the 1820s and 1830s, the two modes urged by political economists for stretching the wages of the poor to cover winter exigencies caused by unemployment and by sickness were, respectively, savings banks and friendly or mutual benefit societies. To many observers high

---

[62] J. Fingard, "Attitudes towards the Education of the Poor in Colonial Halifax," *Acadiensis*, II, Spring 1973, 32-33.

[63] "The Potato Taint Again," *Times*, 23 Oct. 1847; "Business and Prospects," *Morning News*, 29 Sept. 1858.

[64] *Public Ledger*, 3 July 1849.

[65] Second Report of Committee for establishing a Poor House or House of Industry in Montreal, *Montreal Transcript*, 3 Oct. 1837; *Novascotian*, 11 Dec. 1843; "Houses for the Working Classes," *Montreal Witness*, 20 July 1846; "State of the Poor—Its Causes," *Newfoundlander*, 10 Oct. 1853; *Newfoundland Express*, 25 Oct. 1853.

[66] *Kingston Chronicle*, 22 Mar. 1822; Letter from Malthus, Poor Man's Friend Society No. 1, "On its Disadvantages," *Novascotian*, 12 Jan. 1825; Remarks by Charles R. Fairbanks, General Meeting of Poor Man's Friend Society, ibid., 2 Feb. 1825; An Essay upon Savings Banks, Nos. 4, 5, ibid., 15 & 22 June 1826; "Seasonable Benevolence," *Globe*, 26 Dec. 1859.

summer wages and winter unemployment made savings banks particularly desirable institutions for colonial communities. Although the labouring poor could not be forced to deposit their earnings, the habit might be actively encouraged.[67] Not only might the poor thus be enabled to buy provisions in winter, but the most desirable virtues would be cultivated amongst the banks' customers.

> The depositor, in order to place himself in a way to be benefited, will soon discover that he must substitute thoughtfulness for carelessness, sobriety for intemperance, thriftiness for prodigality, a manly desire of independence for a degrading and paralysing reliance on the benevolence of others....[68]

At the same time the charitable segment of the community, which included the merchant-bankers, would thereby be relieved of calls on its benevolence, and "habits of economy among the labouring classes" would eventually lead to a new accumulation of capital which would contribute to the progress of the colonies, or so the familiar story went.[69]

While savings banks, appealing to the individual, went gloriously forward with increasing numbers of small depositors, friendly and benefit societies materialized more slowly. Their upper-class promoters feared that organized cooperation amongst the labouring classes might concentrate power in the wrong hands, while the labouring classes themselves, at least until the 1850s, remained too mobile to sustain such organizations. The favoured mode by which the better-off might retain control of a benefit society was to combine it with a savings bank and dispense annuities or sick pay instead of interest.[70] National societies honouring St. George, St. Andrew, and St. Patrick, besides bestowing charity, sometimes claimed that they created an opportunity for both rich and poor to cooperate through mutual assistance, but it is doubtful that they included many members of the working class.[71] Those friendly societies which did attract labourers seem to have concentrated in this period on providing sick pay and meeting funeral expenses. Nonetheless these associations

---

[67] For example, "Bazaar," *Acadian Recorder*, 3 Oct. 1829. On savings banks for the working classes, see Letter from Franklin, *Kingston Chronicle*, 7 Nov. 1829; *Montreal Gazette*, 5 Oct. 1841; *Kingston Herald*, 8 Feb. 1842; "Bank for Small Savings," *Newfoundlander*, 2 Mar. 1854; Letter from The Poor Man's Friend, *Times*, 1 Nov. 1854; *Newfoundlander*, 8 Nov. 1855.

[68] Letter from Cato, "Quebec Savings Bank," *Quebec Mercury*, 3 Apr. 1821; Letter from Charity, "Bazaars—Fuel &c," *Acadian Recorder* 10 Aug. 1833; *Public Ledger*, 25 Apr. 1834.

[69] An Essay upon Savings Banks, No. 5, *Novascotian*, 22 June 1826.

[70] Letter from A Patriot, *Free Press*, 4 Nov. 1817; ibid., 1 Feb. 1825; Association of Newfoundland Fishermen and Shoremen, *Newfoundlander*, 19 Feb. 1829.

[71] Letter from An Englishman, *Quebec Mercury*, 16 Jan. 1849; Letter from a Member of St. George's Society, ibid., 3 Feb. 1849.

became the fledgling unions of colonial towns when they began to be organized by the workers themselves on the basis of particular trades and labouring activities, such as the longshoremen's societies formed in Saint John in 1849 and Quebec in 1857.[72]

While self-help could in time conceivably rescue some summer labourers from an undue reliance on winter relief, it represented too much of a long-term solution to obviate the need for immediate palliative measures. Faced with the foreboding prospect of winter distress, the citizenry of towns undertook to relieve the poor through special schemes of employment or charitable aid. Those who discerned winter unemployment as the crux of the problem were increasingly prone to argue that urban society would benefit from systematic employment relief—a far more radical approach than that of those with other-worldly, charitable aims who continued to grapple with winter poverty as an unexpected disaster wrought by providence. Whatever the attitude, however, labour schemes were preferred by all elements in society, because they both distinguished between the "deserving" and "undeserving" poor and benefited society at large. The work had of course to be sufficiently unattractive to discourage the regularly employed labourers in the towns and surrounding countryside from opting for subsidized winter employment. Employment was therefore always provided at a "less eligible" rate of wages than could be obtained elsewhere, earning for its beneficiaries such token payments as 1s.6d. to 2s. per day for stone breaking in Halifax in 1832. The wages paid to winter labourers in Saint John ten years later of 1s.3d. to 2s. per day, depending on the size of family, were said to be "sufficient to keep them off the parish."[73]

Not only were the wages "less eligible," but the jobs themselves were unattractively menial. Since most of the labourers in colonial towns were considered unskilled, hand labour with pick and shovel was promoted as the most suitable form of activity. Preference was most commonly given to those public works which could be pursued through most of the winter such as stone breaking for macadamizing the roads, canal building, snow removal, well digging, and laying water pipes. The success of shipbuilding as a form of winter relief in Quebec inspired Newfoundlanders to demand the establishment of that industry for the same purpose.[74] By the 1850s railroad construction in the immediate neighbourhood of

---

[72] J.R. Rice, "A History of Organized Labour in Saint John, New Brunswick 1813-1890," (unpublished Master's Thesis, University of New Brunswick, 1968), 20-28; J.I. Cooper, "The Quebec Ship Labourers' Benevolent Society," *CHR*, XXX, 1949, 339-40.

[73] Letter from An Inhabitant of Halifax, *Acadian Recorder*, 14 Dec. 1816; *Weekly Observer*, 3 Jan. 1832; Matthew, Overseer of Poor, to Mayor Black, 3 Jan. 1842, PANB, RLE/642/22/2. A maximum of 1s.8d. per day was paid in Quebec in 1842-3. "Relief of the Distressed Working Classes," *Quebec Mercury*, 31 Dec. 1842. For a discussion of cost of living and inadequacy of winter wages for family men, see Pentland, "The Lachine Strike of 1843," *CHR*, XXIX, 1948, 268-9.

[74] Speech by March, Assembly Debate, 3 Feb. 1853, *Patriot* (St. John's), 12 Feb. 1853; March, *The Present Condition of Newfoundland*, 19-20.

the towns also afforded winter jobs.[75] In order to sustain a continuity in the programmes of winter relief, the editor of the *New Brunswick Courier* asserted that the extensive preparation of materials always required for summer road building could all be done in the winter. Such public works would provide a way "in which the necessities of the labouring poor could be made to dovetail with the general interest of the whole community, so that they might be benefited by receiving work, while those who pay for it might be equally benefited by having it done."[76] Similarly, the editor of the *Quebec Gazette* suggested that for every dollar invested by the citizens in the employment of winter workers, "at least 75 per cent of it becomes permanently, and perhaps profitably, invested for public good."[77]

Outdoor winter works, however, did not readily lend themselves to an extensive system of relief. Large-scale operations such as road and canal building were normally halted by the onset of bad weather in the autumn. In Newfoundland, for example, road building was finished by the end of October and therefore afforded only two months' relief after the fishery ended.[78] Nor could such schemes involving heavy labour benefit women, the group that comprised the greatest proportion of unemployed colonial poor. In comparison with men, "To find suitable employment for females, is more difficult, but not by any means less requisite, as they abound far more than the poor of the other sex."[79] On grounds both moral and humane contemporaries thought that women as well as children had to be engaged indoors, and one of the earliest projects in the colonies was that organized in Halifax in the early 1820s whereby women and girls were employed in knitting and spinning in one of the town's free schools.[80]

The search for more economical and utilitarian methods of relief for able-bodied women and children helped to produce frequent, and sometimes successful, demands for the establishment of houses of industry in the colonial towns. While the influence of the new English poor law and fashionable ideas on social order and social control tended to predominate in discussions concerning the reform of poor relief, townsmen also specifically advocated houses of industry as a means of

---

[75] "Winter Work for the Industrious," *Morning Chronicle*, 27 Jan. 1855; "Ship Building and Saw Mills about St. John—Hard Times—The way to relieve distress," *Morning News*, 10 Dec. 1858.

[76] "Winter Employment for Outdoor Labourers," *New Brunswick Courier*, 30 Jan. 1858; see also *Times*, 9 Oct. 1847; "The Poor," *Globe*, 17 Dec. 1858.

[77] "The Present Destitution," *Quebec Gazette*, 1 Feb. 1855.

[78] Speech by Surveyor General, Assembly Debate, 10 Mar. 1858, *Newfoundlander*, 18 Mar. 1858. Similarly in the Kingston area, *Upper Canada Herald*, 27 June 1837.

[79] Letter from Homo, "Employment of the Poor," *New Brunswick Courier*, 14 Jan. 1832.

[80] Letter from Agenoria, *Acadian Recorder*, 29 Nov. 1823; J. Fingard, "English Humanitarianism and the Colonial Mind: Walter Bromley in Nova Scotia, 1813-25," *CHR*, LIV, 1973, 133-4.

providing steady employment for the poor in winter.[81] Even in Halifax, where a permanent poorhouse and a number of voluntary and denominational charities existed, the poor were often reduced to beggary in winter, and social reformers believed that although a house of industry "should not diminish the poor rate one single farthing, or lessen the demand for private charity, still we contended, that it is infinitely better for us to maintain the healthy and able-bodied poor in humble industry, although comparatively unproductive, than in entire sloth and inactivity."[82] A desire to diminish both street begging by the seasonally unemployed and the necessity for the poor to seek winter refuge in the house of correction where they were exposed to the nefarious influence of "criminals and hardened felons," inspired a group of citizens in Quebec to favour the establishment of a house of industry.[83] The grand jury of Montreal also based its demand for such an institution in 1847 on the need to abolish street begging caused by the severity of the winter and the practice of committing "petty thefts in order to obtain admission in the prison, so as to find a refuge from the severity of the winter."[84]

Not surprisingly, therefore, whether houses of industry enjoyed a very short, sporadic, or permanent existence, they usually began as seasonal institutions. A house of industry was established in Quebec in the winter of 1836-7.[85] One opened the same winter in Montreal as a seasonal institution which, while designed to force professional mendicants off the streets, was found in practice to attract mainly the seasonally unemployed.[86] A similar institution in Kingston which opened in the winter of 1847 closed in the summer.[87] The Toronto House of Industry was founded in 1837 because of the distress of the poor in previous winters and the prospect of misery during the approaching winter, and though continued on a regular basis as a

---

[81] "New House of Industry," *Montreal Gazette*, 3 Nov. 1828; Letter from C, ibid., 8 Jan. 1820; Presentment of Grand Jury, ibid., 14 Mar. 1837; Letter from H.A. Gladwin, *Novascotian*, 1 Jan. 1835.

[82] "House of Industry," *Guardian*, 20 Mar. 1839.

[83] "House of Industry," *Quebec Mercury*, 31 Dec. 1832.

[84] Presentment of Grand Jury, *Montreal Gazette*, 20 Jan. & 19 Feb. 1847. The jail was still a winter refuge in 1859. "House of Industry," *Montreal Weekly Gazette*, 8 Jan. 1859.

[85] Letter from Philanthropist, *Quebec Gazette,* 28 Oct. 1836; Report of Public Meeting, ibid., 4 Nov. 1836; "House of Industry," ibid., 14 Nov. 1836; *Quebec Mercury*, 20 Dec. 1836. The house burned down in March 1837. "Calamitous Fire," *Quebec Gazette*, 6 Mar. 1837.

[86] Second Report of Committee for establishing a Poor House or House of Industry in Montreal, *Montreal Transcript*, 3 Oct. 1837. It failed to reopen the next winter because the old jail in which it was housed was required to accommodate rebels. Until January 1843, when it reopened for four months, the committee provided soup, wood, and small-scale employment in winter. Ibid., 9 Dec. 1837; *Montreal Herald*, 23 Apr. 1840; *Montreal Gazette*, 21 Jan. 14 Feb., & 12 May 1843.

[87] "House of Industry," *Kingston Herald*, 24 Nov. 1847; Letter from a Pastor, "House of Industry," *Chronicle and News* (Kingston), 12 Apr. 1848; ibid., 22 July 1848.

year-round establishment, it was busiest by far in winter when the number of applicants for relief, particularly outdoor pensioners, significantly multiplied.[88] The privately organized and short-lived female house of industry in Saint John, designed to train domestic servants, also aimed to "afford a shelter, food and clothing to the inmates during the rigorous season of winter."[89] It would thus be misleading to assume that the existence of houses of industry fulfilled the expectations of their founders. Indeed the term remained a misnomer since these institutions were no more concerned with industry than were the public poorhouses of Halifax and Saint John; they resembled refuges from winter more than anything else.[90]

One apparent exception in the colonial period to the general pattern of institutions ostensibly designed to provide indoor winter work was the St. John's factory. Here was an establishment which supplied nothing but work and which made a real attempt to "dovetail" with the interests of the community, because it eventually concentrated on making and mending fish nets, an ancillary to the fishery and one which facilitated the employment of women and children.[91] Founded in the winter of 1832-3 through the efforts of public-spirited females, it undertook "to find employment for the destitute, and to stimulate the poorer classes to independence, by showing them the means of earning their own livelihood."[92] While the major function remained that of providing winter work for women and children, the local demand for its manufactures and the solicitations of the workers had produced a year-round institution by 1837.[93] Many of the women and children employed by the factory were the only breadwinners in their families and came to depend on the work as the sole means of support, a development which made it increasingly difficult for the committee "to curtail (as much as possible) the amount of employment during the summer months, with a view to the accumulation of means by which to deal it out more extensively in winter."[94] At the same time the factory tried to provide additional jobs in particularly bad years. During the severe winter of 1847-8, for example, between 100 and 150 extra labourers were employed daily in making and

---

[88] Report of Committee for the Relief of the Poor and Destitute of the City of Toronto, *Christian Guardian*, 15 Feb. 1837; *Patriot* (Toronto), 13 Oct. 1837; "Toronto House of Industry," *Daily Leader*, 4 May 1855.

[89] Petition of Managing Committee of the Female House of Industry, 2 Feb. 1835, PANB, RLE/835/pe/4, No. 82.

[90] "House of Industry," *Examiner*, 27 Nov. 1844; "House of Industry," *British Colonist* (Toronto), 13 Jan. & 5 Dec. 1846.

[91] Report of Factory Committee, *Newfoundlander*, 3 Aug. 1837.

[92] Report of St. John's Factory, *Public Ledger*, 16 Aug. 1836.

[93] *Newfoundlander*, 15 June 1837; Report of St. John's Factory, *Times*, 3 Aug. 1842; "The Factory," ibid., 4 Nov. 1846; Bonnycastle, *Newfoundland in 1842*, vol. 2, 232.

[94] Report of Committee of St. John's Factory, *Public Ledger*, 30 July 1841; *Times*, 23 Mar. 1849; Speeches by Warren and Shea, Assembly Debate, 8 Apr. 1853, *Newfoundland Express*, 28 Apr. 1853.

repairing nets.[95] Eventually in the 1850s the local St. Vincent de Paul Society, which concentrated a portion of its efforts on the provision of winter work for the poor, adopted the upper floor of the factory as its own site for additional employment in net making and mending and in textile handicrafts.[96] Even in these circumstances, however, the society prided itself on being able to provide a warm, comfortable workroom for its employees, in place of "exposure to cold and hardship."[97] The attraction of a glowing stove should not be underestimated. Indeed, when the factory came to be controlled completely the Catholic society in the 1860s, it reverted to its winter status of thirty years before.[98]

The relief of the poor through charity formed the alternative and supplement to employment schemes. Easier to organize and sustain, voluntary acts of benevolence by individuals or associations were particularly designed to ameliorate the distress of new immigrants and the resident disabled poor—the old and infirm, helpless women and children. While not all charitable aid was confined to the winter months and indeed immigrant societies were specifically summer-oriented, contemporaries believed that the resources for alleviating the condition of the poor in hard times should be carefully husbanded for use in winter when "real poverty is most severely felt." Relief should be applied as "the antidote at the time when the disease is most apparent."[99] Moreover, city residents were prone to warm to "thrilling and eloquent" descriptions of the poor in winter.[100] But as a result of their emphasis on winter activities, charitable organizations were likely to find themselves extending help to the seasonal poor (comprised of labouring or casual poor) as well as to the unemployable. In these circumstances voluntary agencies, whether public, national, or denominational, began to worry about the moral implications of gratuitous relief. They not only reserved unconditional aid for cases of dire emergency but also with varying degrees of assiduity substituted scientific for casual charity by investigating their clients' situations through domiciliary visits, by furnishing employment on the basis of piece-work, or by serving as informal labour exchanges.[101] Although their

---

[95] Report of St. John's Factory Committee, *Public Ledger*, 27 July 1838; Report of St. John's Factory, *Newfoundlander*, 10 Aug. 1848.

[96] Reports of Society of St. Vincent de Paul, *Newfoundland Express*, 16 Dec. 1856, 11 Dec. 1858, 10 Dec. 1861; Notice: Employment to the Poor, ibid., 24 Feb. 1858.

[97] *Newfoundlander*, 2 Apr. 1857.

[98] Reports of Society of St. Vincent de Paul, *Newfoundlander*, 7 Dec. 1865, 10 Dec. 1866, 20 Dec. 1867, 22 Dec. 1868, 4 Jan. & 30 Dec. 1870.

[99] *Newfoundlander*, 27 Nov. 1838; "The Season," *Halifax Morning Post*, 4 Dec. 1844; "Benevolence," ibid., 16 Dec. 1844.

[100] Letter from Humanitas, *Quebec Mercury*, 21 Dec. 1847; Letter from A Native, ibid., 11 Jan. 1848.

[101] Ladies charitable societies often gave winter employment in needlework to women and children. Statement of Ladies Bazaar, *Novascotian*, 17 July 1833; Female Benevolent

most active motivation remained that of Christian stewardship, the concern to obtain a *quid pro quo* in terms of labour, sobriety, or conformity to accepted norms brought the charitable elements in society close in their objectives to the political economists of the day. It was not therefore the methods for aiding the poor, nor the aims in view, that characterized the most single-minded charity workers; it was their attitude towards the role of free enterprise in social welfare. Since many charity workers were steadfast voluntarists or Catholics, they objected to government interference and compulsion in the relief of the poor as unwarranted infringement on the duties of churches and the rights of the individual and tended therefore to oppose proposals for legalized, permanent schemes of relief. While the income of private or sectarian agencies might well include grants from the legislatures and municipalities, they valued independence of state control as their source of greatest strength.[102]

Dependent primarily, though seldom exclusively, on voluntary contributions for their income, benevolent societies, churches, and *ad hoc* citizens' committees, frequently in conjunction with the obliging military, variously raised charitable funds for winter relief by means of charity sermons, benefit performances at the theatre, charity balls and concerts, public subscription campaigns launched at public meetings and completed by door-to-door canvassing, and charitable bazaars. With the funds so raised, which were appropriated by visiting committees, the poor were provided gratuitously, at cost, or conditionally, with clothing, places of refuge, food, and of course fuel.

In response to the insuperable difficulties which the poor encountered in obtaining firewood, many of the voluntary urban relief schemes concentrated on supplying the indigent with fuel. The Halifax Poor Man's Friend Society, for example, preoccupied itself in 1824-5 with securing firewood for distribution to the poor.[103] In the winter of 1828-9, the citizens of Saint John, aware of the distress suffered by a large number of newcomers and the high cost of firewood, organized a "Fuel Day" for the poor. Owners of land in the outlying districts contributed stands of "soft" timber, voluntary axemen offered their services, and the carmen of the city donated a day of work to carting the wood to a fuel yard established for the purpose. A committee then distributed the wood to the most necessitous of the poor.[104] A joint fuel committee on cooperative principles organized by the national societies or a fuel assistance society which aimed at reducing the cost of wood to the poor were schemes advocated

---

Society, *Chronicle and Gazette*, 7 Dec. 1839; St. Matthew's Church District Society, *Guardian*, 15 Nov. 1850.

[102] *La Minerve*, 1 June 1829; "Charity on Crutches," *Daily Leader*, 17 Jan. 1855; "The Poor," *True Witness* (Montreal), 23 Dec. 1859.

[103] *Acadian Recorder*, 12 Feb. 1825; General Meeting of Halifax Poor Man's Friend Society, *Novascotian*, 18 Feb. 1826.

[104] "Charity! or a Day for the Poor," *New Brunswick Courier*, 3 Jan. 1829; ibid., 10 Jan. 1829; "Fuel for the Poor," *Weekly Observer*, 3 Feb. 1829; Letter from D, *British Colonist* (Saint John), 13 Feb. 1829; Remarks by Equity on Charity, ibid., 13 Mar. 1829.

in Montreal in the mid-1830s without success.[105] More tangible results were produced in Quebec where an association known as the Young Men's Charitable Firewood Society existed for several years. Founded in 1842, its object was to collect enough subscriptions to enable it to retail firewood to the poor at about half the regular market price. In the winter of 1843-4 the society delivered free of charge and distributed at half price or less 327_ cords of wood to 314 families.[106] Most of these enterprises were, however, small-scale, ephemeral, and usually allied to other forms of eleemosynary relief.

Undoubtedly the most popular mode of economical, short-term relief came to be the ubiquitous winter soup kitchens, "those friendly resorts of famishing multitudes."[107] Not only were they promoted by doctors for the nourishment they afforded, but this form of relief was the least open to objection. As the soup kitchen committee in Montreal argued in 1841, soup represented "the better way of supplying the destitute with food, and decidedly the cheapest mode [by which] the city can support the poor, and there is no risk of the recipient making a bad use of it, as is too often the case in giving money indiscriminately, or even clothes, that find the way in many cases to the Tavern or Pawnbroker."[108] There need be no fear of debased, profligate parents selling "the bread and meat given for the support of their children, to low groggeries for whisky; whereas the soup cannot be thus bartered. It is eaten in the kitchen, or taken away in cans and kettles, and being of a highly nutritious nature and well seasoned, it is most wholesome and agreeable."[109]

This priority given to winter relief by charitable citizens meant that voluntary associations, visiting societies, and private institutions, like the erstwhile houses of

---

[105] *Montreal Herald Abstract*, 17 Mar. 1835; *Montreal Gazette*, 16 Apr. 1836.

[106] *Quebec Mercury*, 19 July 1842; Second Annual Report of Quebec Young Men's Charitable Fire Wood Society, ibid., 4 May 1844; Report of Quebec Charitable Firewood Society, ibid., 29 Apr. 1845; for the demise of the society, see Letter from One of the Four, ibid., 30 Apr. 1846. A similar subscription society was formed in Toronto in the winter of 1853-4. "Fuel for the Poor," *Daily Leader*, 10 Dec. 1835, 14 Jan. 1854. For other schemes see Letter from Trim, *Acadian Recorder*, 22 Feb. 1817; Letter from Beneficus, ibid., 18 Apr. 1840; "More Fuel," *Montreal Gazette*, 11 Feb. 1855.

[107] Letter from Solicitus, *Quebec Mercury*, 18 Jan. 1849; "The Soup Kitchen," ibid., 31 Dec. 1860; Letter from Benevolens, *Acadian Recorder*, 12 Feb. 1820; ibid., 19 Feb. 1820; "Soup House," ibid., 28 Mar. 1835; *Montreal Gazette*, 11 Feb. 1828; "The Poor," ibid., 1 Feb. 1844; *New Brunswick Courier*, 7 Jan. & 4 Feb. 1832, 1 & 8 Nov. 1834; Letter from Medicus, ibid., 6 Dec. 1834; Report of Benevolent Irish Society, *Public Ledger*, 28 Feb. 1834; "Soup House," *Morning News*, 14 Dec. 1842; Letter from A.C.D., *Quebec Gazette*, 16 Dec. 1842; House of Industry Report, *Globe*, 14 Jan. 1859. For an anti-soup kitchen article, see "Public Soup Kitchens," *Quebec Gazette*, 27 Jan. 1855.

[108] Report of Committee of Soup Kitchen of Montreal for 1839-40, *Montreal Herald*, 4 Jan. 1841; "A Charitable Suggestion," *Halifax Morning Post*, 8 Jan. 1846.

[109] City Council, *True Witness*, 23 Feb. 1855.

industry, were often set on foot at the onset of a cold winter in towns suffering also from economic depression or a surfeit of destitute immigrants, only to die a natural death each year in April, sometimes to be revived the following December or January if the need recurred. A failure on the part of historians to perceive the seasonal nature of the activities in this period of such institutions as the Quebec Sick and Destitute Strangers Society, the Halifax Poor Man's Friend Society, the Quebec Mendicity Society, the Kingston Female Benevolent Society, les Dames de la Charité of Montreal, the Montreal Strangers' United Friend Society, the Wesleyan Dorcas Society of Toronto, and the St. Vincent de Paul Societies, might lead to unnecessary speculation about their ephemeral careers or characteristic inefficiency.[110] The societies themselves, though wary of giving undue encouragement to the poor, regretted the interruption of their operations in summer, particularly the consequent

---

110   *Quebec Mercury*, 23 Mar. 1819; Minutes, 18 Jan. 1822, Proceedings of the Halifax Poor Man's Friend Society, 1820-6, PANS, MG 20, No. 180:2; Annual Meeting of Poor Man's Friend Society, *Acadian Recorder*, 8 Feb. 1823; *Free Press*, 1 Feb. 1825; Poor Man's Friend Society: To the Public, *Novascotian*, 9 Feb. 1825; Letter from Malthus, Poor Man's Friend Society No. 5, "Answer to my Opponents," ibid., 16 Feb. 1825; Petition of Committee of Poor Man's Friend Society, 4 Mar. 1825, PANS, RG 5, Series P, vol. 80; "Quebec Charitable Institution," *Quebec Mercury*, 2 June 1829; *Montreal Gazette*, 27 Nov. 1828; *Star*, 29 Nov. 1828; *La Minerve*, 29 Oct. 1832; Annual Report of Female Benevolent Society, *Kingston Chronicle*, 14 Jan. 1825; Annual Meeting of Female Benevolent Society, ibid., 4 May 1827; Letter from Humanity, *Upper Canada Herald*, 31 Aug. 1831; ibid., 9 May 1832; Letter from Charitas, *Chronicle and Gazette*, 5 Oct. 1833; Report of Female Benevolent Society, *Kingston Herald*, 24 May 1842; Ladies Benevolent Society, *Chronicle and Gazette*, 8 May 1844; Report of Female Benevolent Society, *Argus* (Kingston), 7 July 1846; M. Angus, *Kingston General Hospital A Social and Institutional History* (Montreal, 1973), 1-26 passim; Report of Strangers United Friend Society, *Montreal Gazette*, 20 Feb. 1846; *Christian Guardian*, 24 Nov. 1852, 26 Oct. 1853; "The Society of St. Vincent de Paul," *True Witness*, 23 Feb. 1855; Report of Receipts and expenditure of Society of St. Vincent de Paul, *Newfoundlander*, 29 Nov. 1855; Maguire, *The Irish in America*, 15.

Number of persons relieved by Halifax Poor Man's Friend Society, 1820-4 (Population of Halifax, c.10,000)											
	Jan.	Feb.	Mar.	Apr.	May	June	July	Aug.	Sept.	Oct.	Nov.	Dec.
1820	—	680	1279	483	192	56	70	60	46	84	153	486
1821	1228	1304	1122	382	81	80	49	38	21	30	25	129
1822	1350	1540	1140	79								
1823			1430									
1824			1326									
(Source: *Acadian Recorder*, 30 Dec. 1820; Second to Fifth *Annual Reports* of the Halifax Poor Man's Friend Society)												

inability to economize by purchasing supplies in the season of plenty. Their chequered careers depended on the seasons. For it was not normally until the howling blast of winter winds and the anguished countenances of freezing, famished children actually focused local attention on the perils of winter that sufficient interest was aroused amongst the better-off to promote and organize relief and send the subscription papers round the town.[111]

Winter, then, provided the common bond which united the well-to-do in charitable undertakings, a collective pastime to supplement sleighing, theatricals, assemblies, and parties. Winter afforded colonial employers with the convenient *raison d'être* to lay off operatives, cut wages, and acclimatize the poor to regular hardship. Winter transformed the labouring poor into a seasonally exploited class, dependent on relief and demoralized by the insecurity, distress, and drinking habits of the pre-industrial economy. Winter reduced the helpless poor to unbearable, heart-rending privations. In winter British North America most emphatically was not a "poor man's country" and, furthermore, if the cold climate produced the nineteenth-century myth of ruggedness, independence, and self-reliance, it was a myth in which the urban poor played no part and from which they drew no inspiration.

---

[111] See "The Season and the Poor," *Globe*, 6 Dec. 1858; Letter from H. Hope, "Relief of the Poor," *ibid.*, 14 Jan. 1860.

Confederation

Section 10

It seems that Canada's federal constitution is never out of the news! When the first of these essays was written, the Parti Québécois had not yet been founded, yet people were already debating constitutional issues familiar to us with as much passion as today. Decentralisation—increased autonomy for the provinces, especially Quebec—and bilingualism were already hot issues when Canada's best known historian of the time, Donald Creighton, attempted to discuss them in the light of history.

Creighton, a former head of the University of Toronto History Department, had already written a prize-winning biography of Sir John A. Macdonald and a book on the making of Confederation when he wrote this essay. He was in a good position, therefore, to speak with some authority on the intentions and the work of the fathers of Confederation. His essay is of interest, however, not only for what he tells us about those intentions and that work but also for what he says about the relation between history and present-day problems. What does he mean when he says that we must confront the past in order to make changes in the present? Does he think we should always follow slavishly the decisions of history? What is the relevance of history to our present public life?

Creighton maintains that the intentions of the fathers of Confederation were clear and unambiguous. What does he say they were? How decentralised and how bilingual did they intend Canada to be?

The second essay here, written by a University of Toronto political scientist, shows us that the intentions of the fathers of Confederation were not as unambiguous after all as Creighton claimed. According to Vipond, were they even agreed among themselves about what Confederation should be like? What groups favoured strong provincial governments, and why? How could they hope to have a confederation in which both the central and the provincial governments were strong? Why was the idea of sovereignty important in understanding what they did? (Does Jaenen's discussion of French sovereignty in 17th- 18th-century North America have any relevance here?) How is it possible for Vipond to agree that the fathers of Confederation wanted to avoid the American model of federalism and yet claim that many of them developed a model similar to that of the US "Federalists"? Does his work offer any help in dealing with our present political and constitutional difficulties?

Creighton's full-length account of the making of Confederation is called *The Road to Confederation*. Other standard historical works on the subject are P.B.Waite, *The Life and Times of Confederation*, and W.L.Morton, *The Critical Years*.

Confederation: The Use and Abuse of History

D.G. Creighton

In his speech at the laying of the cornerstone of Champlain College, Premier Jean Lesage made a remark which provides an appropriate introduction for this discussion. "To those who keep repeating `What exactly does Quebec want?'" Mr. Lesage said, "I ask, `What exactly do you want Quebec *not* to want?'" Well, I have no intention of picking up Mr. Lesage's challenge in the form in which he so dramatically flung it down. I suspect that a Canadian from any one of the other nine provinces would have as little relish for specifying what he *does not* want Quebec to want as Mr. Lesage evidently has for specifying what Quebec *does* want. But the embarrassment of being specific, which everybody feels, is not my main reason for declining to submit an itemized list of refusals to Mr. Lesage. My main reason is that his challenge appears to rest on an assumption which I do not find acceptable. His words seem to imply that Canadians are divided into two great classes: those in Quebec who have wants and those outside Quebec who want to deny those wants.

This is surely, at the very least, a very large over-simplification of the present confused and agitated state of public opinion in Canada. Obviously the "wants" of which Mr. Lesage speaks are concerned with the position of Quebec Province, and of French Canada as a whole, in Canadian Confederation; but these are not the only "wants" that are being felt in Canada today, and, equally important, they are not the only wants that imply changes in the Canadian constitution. All over the country Canadians are advocating changes, or discussing the advisability of changes, or—and this is perhaps most important of all—making demands, reaching decisions, drawing up plans which, though they realize it only partly if at all, may mean still more drastic, though indirect, changes in the future. It is not enough to examine the wants of Quebec or of French Canada in isolation; it is necessary to review the whole range of recent developments which either directly or indirectly alter the form or upset the balance of the Canadian constitution. If a "quiet revolution" has been going on in Quebec, another revolution, quieter still but just as significant, has been going on in Canada as a whole.

Revolution means the complete overthrow of an established form of government, or, more generally, of an established political and social regime; and it is obvious at once that changes on such a grand scale are not in many Canadians' minds at the present time. A considerable part of our constitution, like most of the British, is unwritten; and with these venerable conventions, by which free men are ruled in a constitutional monarchy, nobody wants to tamper seriously. When we talk about constitutional change what we almost invariably mean is change in the purely federal part of our constitution, which is, of course, set out in the *British North America Act* of 1867. This *Act* has been amended in the past; but the amendments have not been frequent and few of them are really substantial in character. In its written form, our federal constitution is thus fairly close to what it was a hundred years ago; and that brings us back to the intentions of the Fathers of Confederation, which is the subject of this paper. What I should like to do is to re-examine the intentions of the Fathers in the light of the new demands and changed circumstances of the present day. What were those intentions and why are they now regarded by some as inadequate? What arguments are advanced to justify constitutional change and how valid are they?

All revolutionaries—including "quiet" revolutionaries—have got to make up their minds about history. The past inexorably confronts all those who advocate sudden and major changes. The question of how history is to be regarded, of how it is to be interpreted so as to justify drastic reforms, is inevitably a crucially important problem for revolutionaries. They have, of course, found extremely varied solutions to it over the centuries; but, at bottom, these varied solutions are simply different expressions of two main approaches or attitudes to history. The past can either be represented as an era of misery and oppression from which society must try to escape, or it can be pictured as a lost golden age to which a defrauded people must seek to return. History can either be the "bad old times" whose harsh enactments should be abolished; or it can be the "good old times" whose wonderful spirit has been forgotten or killed by the letter of the law.

These two revolutionary attitudes to the past, here contrasted sharply for the sake of clarity, have, of course, been modified and toned down in a variety of ways. It is obviously not necessary, for example, to look back upon the past as completely evil—as nothing but the record of the crimes, follies and misfortunes of mankind. It can be, and sometimes is, dismissed just as effectively by holding it up not as the "bad old past" but simply as the past without any adjectives at all—the past which is irrelevant and useless to the present merely because it is history. This assumption comes naturally and readily to modern town and city dwellers who live in oblongs of space in high-rise apartments with not much room, no privacy, and lots of chrome, arborite and gadgets. They have been taught by journalists and television personalities that anything older than ten years is positively medieval; they have been convinced by advertisers that rapid obsolescence is the greatest principle of the good life yet discovered by man. To say—as was said a while ago by someone who ought to have known better—that the *British North America Act* is "a piece of antiquated mid-Victorian plumbing" is more than enough to damn it irretrievably in their eyes. In affluent North America, no stigma can be more humiliating than antiquated plumbing. Nothing can be done with it except remove it in disgust; it must be yanked out and replaced with what is invariably called in the advertisements a "new unit." And a truth which is valid for bathtubs and furnaces—those two supreme expressions of western civilization—must surely apply also to constitutions. If the British North America Act can be properly described as "a piece of antiquated mid-Victorian plumbing" then it must be dispatched to the junk yard without the slightest delay and a new constitutional "unit" installed in its place.

Confederation: The Use and Abuse of History

To dismiss the past as outworn and unsatisfactory for the needs of the present is a favourite revolutionary approach to history. But, as has already been noted, there is another, more sophisticated approach which may be equally effective. This is not to reject the past as completely valueless for the modern generation; but to discover in it a new meaning or significance, which has been lost or forgotten, and which fortunately happens to provide a complete justification for the revolutionary demands of the moment. In this case, history becomes the "good old times," or the "better old times," with rights and liberties which have since been violated, promises and agreements that have not been kept, and a fine generous spirit that has not been lived up to. Obviously this type of revolutionary does not want to wash his hands of the past; his aim is to reinterpret it so as to bring out its lost or forgotten meaning; and if the black letter of the historical document seems to cast doubt on this new interpretation, he is apt to appeal to something beyond it, to some unwritten agreement or unspoken major premise which underlies the bare historical record and gives it its real meaning. This "real meaning" is often just another way of stating the revolutionary demands; and history is thus made to give its authority and sanction to a major programme of change.

II

There are, of course, other approaches to history. Historians are human beings with individual biases and prejudices; and they can differ widely in their interpretations. But for the moment we are concerned with revolutionary approaches, for revolutionary approaches are more popular when great changes are under consideration; and Canadians are ill-equipped to judge their validity, for they have no great body of historical knowledge to fall back upon. Colonies, which have no clear sense of an identity separate from that of the empire to which they belong, are very apt to be indifferent to, and ignorant of, their own history. Canada ceased entirely to be a dependent entity in the British Empire-Commonwealth at a time well within the memory of many people now living; and there are many occasions now when she seems to be becoming, if she has not already become, an even more thoroughly assimilated and tractable portion of the Empire of the United States. There are signs, perhaps increasing in number during the past two decades, that Canadians are growing more interested and concerned about their history, as a result possibly of some obscure fear of the extinction of their collective personality. But it still remains true that Canadians, as they face the future, cannot rely upon any substantial body of knowledge about the past. They are confused and uncertain about the direction they should be taking, partly because they do not know whence they have come, or by what route, or with what aims and ideals as guides for the journey. Ignorance readily accepts myth and is vulnerable before propaganda.

Yet there is no real reason for this ignorance. There is, for example, a large body of records on the making of Canadian Confederation; and in the past there has never been any substantial difference of opinion as to what the intentions of the Fathers of Confederation really were. With the utmost clarity and precision, in speech after speech and resolution after resolution, the Fathers set out their purpose of establishing a great transcontinental nation in the form of a constitutional monarchy under the British Crown. Constitutional monarchy on the British model meant, of course, parliamentary sovereignty—the concentration of legislative power in a single sovereign legislature; and, if they could have had their way, most Canadians, including in all probability, a majority of the Fathers of Confederation themselves, would have preferred to see all the British North American Provinces joined in a legislative union under one common parliament. Legislative union was their first choice. But legislative union was, they realized, impossible, partly because French Canada wished to guard its distinctive culture with some measure of local autonomy, and partly because the Maritime Provinces, which had not developed municipal institutions, would have been left literally without any local government at all, if their provincial legislatures had been abolished.

For these reasons, the union could not be legislative, it would have to be federal; but though most Canadians in the years 1863-67 recognized the inevitability of federalism, they could not help regarding it with the greatest doubt and suspicion. Up to that time, there had never been a federal union in the British Empire; in the whole history of the English-speaking world the only federal union was that of the United States of America; and in 1864 when the British American union was being planned, the United States appeared to be fatally divided by a terrible civil war. In the eyes of British Americans, the explanation of that Civil War was to be found in the very large powers granted by the American constitution to the individual states and in the extravagant demands they had based upon them. As one British American journalist put it, federalism was the Guy Fawkes lurking under the structure of the American union who had eventually succeeded in blowing it to pieces. Was there not a terrible possibility, he and other British Americans asked, that history might repeat itself north of the international boundary, and that the centrifugal forces of federalism would in their turn destroy the union of British America?

The realization that federalism was necessary was therefore almost exactly balanced by the conviction that federalism was dangerous. The greatest task facing the northern Provinces was the task of preserving their separate collective identity in a continent dominated by the United States; and if they formed a union that broke up through internal weakness, it would likely mean that the fragments would be devoured at its convenience by the great republic. The only union which could ensure the survival of British America was a strong union; and if federalism had to be accepted as unavoidable, the forces of disruption latent within it must be systematically weakened and rigidly controlled. This was the sober and deliberate judgment of the Fathers assembled in the Charlottetown and Quebec Conferences; and out of it came what, it seems to me, should be regarded as the "Great Compromise" of Canadian Confederation. The union, it was admitted, would have to be federal in character; but at the same time it must also be the most strongly centralized union that was possible under federal forms. It was on this condition, and on this condition alone, that a federal framework was accepted by the architects of Confederation.

The spirit of this basic compromise pervades the whole of the seventy-two Quebec Resolutions on union. The Fathers openly declared and avowed that they proposed to correct the mistakes and remedy the weaknesses of the American constitution by reversing the decentralist federal principles upon which it was based. The American states had granted small and insufficient powers to the federal government, retaining all the rest, the so-called residuary powers, themselves; the British American Provinces, on the contrary, were to be given only the limited authority necessary for local needs, and all the remaining or residuary powers were to be held by the central government. In two crucial debates in the Quebec Conference—the debates on the residuary clause and on the federal controls over provincial legislation—these basic principles of the proposed federal scheme were challenged by a small minority of delegates, and in each case the challenge was decisively beaten. The Provinces and the Dominion were not to be coordinate in authority, as a purist definition of federalism would have required them to be; on the contrary, as John A. Macdonald openly explained, the provincial governments were to be subordinate to the central government. Their functions and responsibilities, it was generally expected, would be relatively small and unimportant, and most people hoped and believed that they should be organized in a very simple and inexpensive fashion. So important a delegate as George Brown would have preferred to give the "local" legislatures a frankly municipal organization and to have reduced them to the level of glorified county councils.

To the great disappointment of some Canadians, who cannot believe they are free men until they have tried to imitate the United States, the *British North America Act* makes no attempt to provide a complete constitution for Canada, as the American Constitution of 1787 does for the United States. The main purpose of the *British North America Act* was to establish the new federal institutions and to divide legislative power between the Provinces and the Dominion; and unlike the American constitution, it does not start out with a preamble setting forth the aims of government, nor does it include a bill of rights. In general, the liberties of the subject are assumed as part of the unwritten constitution inherited from Great Britain; and it is only in a few particular cases that the *Act* concerns itself with rights or liberties and then in a characteristically practical and empirical fashion. It provides safeguards for the distinctive Civil Code of the Province of Quebec, for the already established sectarian schools of religious minorities, and for the use of the English and French languages in the Parliament and courts of Canada, and in the legislature and courts of the Province of Quebec.

It goes no further. Canada was not declared to be a bilingual or a bicultural nation—the modern use of the latter term was unknown in 1867. Such a declaration of general principle was never even suggested. It must always be remembered that the aim of Confederation was not simply to settle the sectional rivalries of Canada East and Canada West—the future Quebec and Ontario. That problem might have been solved just as well, as George Brown wanted to solve it, by changing the legislative union of Canada into a federal union. The main aim of Confederation was to found a strong transcontinental nation; and the first great step in this enterprise, and the most difficult and decisive achievement of the Fathers, was the union of Canada with the Maritime or Atlantic Provinces. This union was also to be called Canada; but the name did not imply by any means that the rights and liberties peculiar to the Province of Canada were now to be exported to the Maritime Provinces. The new Dominion of Canada was not to be a duality, as the old Province of Canada had been; on the contrary, it was designed and organized as a triumvirate of three divisions, Ontario, Quebec, and the Atlantic Provinces, which would become fourfold with the addition of the North-West Territories and British Columbia. The rule of the Civil code and the use of the French language were confirmed in those parts of Canada in which they had already been established by law or convention. But that was all. They were not extended to the Maritime Provinces or to Ontario. Alexander Galt's original resolution on language, presented on behalf of the Coalition government to the Quebec Conference, is nothing more than a draft of Section 133 of the *British North America Act*. There is no evidence that French-speaking ministers or ordinary members of the legislature ever proposed that the French language be given legal status in Ontario or the Maritime Provinces. There is a good deal of evidence which strongly suggests that Tilley, Tupper and Brown would not have listened for a moment to such a proposal.

III

Now it is obvious from even the most casual glance at the state of the Canadian nation, that enormous changes have occurred in our federal system since 1867. In a number of important ways, the intentions of the Fathers have not been realized; some of their most confident expectations have failed of fulfilment; and the relations between the Provinces and the Dominion and between English-speaking and French-speaking Canadians have altered, shifted, veered in new directions, and taken new courses in a fashion which the Fathers of Confederation clearly never anticipated. The various aspects of this constitutional revolution, at times "quiet," at times stridently vociferous, are of course extremely numerous; but, for the sake of brevity they can be grouped in two main trends or tendencies. On the one hand, the balance of power between federal and provincial governments, which the Fathers believed should incline decisively towards the Dominion, has now fallen sharply towards the Provinces; and on the other the Province of Quebec, which the Fathers recognized as different in only a few particulars, has asserted the pervasiveness of its distinct character and has claimed a special status in Confederation as a result.

The Provinces which George Brown regarded as glorified county councils have become great and powerful states, with large resources and a wide variety of functions; and the Federal-Provincial Conference, in which they are directly represented in their own right, seems at times to have grown into a paramount legislature which may threaten to supersede the authority of the Dominion Parliament. The Province of Quebec has pointedly withdrawn from many of the enterprises in which the other Provinces and the Dominion are cooperating, insists that it must have direct superintendence over most of the activities of the Canadians living within its boundaries, affects at times to assume a kind of protective guardianship over French Canadians in other parts of Canada, and, on occasions even appears to claim that it is an international person capable of making binding agreements with foreign powers.

This, in very general terms, is the revolution that threatens to change the whole nature of Canadian federalism. And, like every other revolution, it is now confronted by history. It is confronted in the first place by the *British North America Act* of 1867, the formal embodiment of the intentions of the Fathers of Confederation. But the *British North America Act* is not the only obstacle in the path of its onward career. Its way is also impeded or embarrassed by our more general knowledge of the aims and purposes of the men of 1867 and of Sir John Macdonald in particular, by our instinctive feeling that radical changes might perilously weaken the fabric of our federal union, and finally by the haunting fear that the survival of Canada as a separate and autonomous political society in North America is still by no means assured. The past is not dead. It stands at bay, confronting the revolution with its legal barriers, its historical memories, and inherited convictions; and, if the revolutionaries are to succeed, they must overcome these obstacles, silence these fears, eradicate these inhibitions.

This is what, with increasing vigour, they have been trying to do for the past few years. This is, in part, the explanation of the revived interest in the amendment of the *British North America Act* and the drafting of what is popularly called the Favreau-Fulton amending formula. It may also turn out to be the explanation of the ultimate failure of the Favreau-Fulton formula to win acceptance and establishment as part of the constitution. In the end, the formula may be dropped as intolerably inflexible; and an attempt may be made, not to thread a difficult path through the obstacles of the *British North America Act*, but to go round the *Act* or to jump over it. The earlier belief that an informed "dialogue" on the constitution would do good, has now been followed by suggestions that an informal or formal conference would be advisable, and even by the hint that in the end a constitutional assembly or convention, specially called for the purpose, may be found necessary.

But this is only the beginning. It is not enough to devise ways and means of carrying out radical changes; it is also necessary to justify them. And it is here that the inevitable encounter with history takes place. The "quiet" revolutionaries must get rid of history or they must make it serve their purpose. They must either demonstrate that the recorded intentions of the Fathers of Confederation have been invalidated by the passage of time and are therefore obsolete; or they must prove that the recorded intentions do not constitute the whole of the great plan of Confederation, that beyond them was another and a more important general purpose, an inarticulate major premise, which underlay the whole scheme of the *British North America Act*, but never found adequate expression in it. As a result, it must be argued, the spirit which might have humanized our federal union has never been lived up to, and the implicit agreement which formed its basis had never been properly carried out.

Both these arguments have in fact been used. It has been urged, in the first place, that economic and social developments have made the intentions of the Fathers of Confederation irrelevant and their plans obsolete; and in the second place it has been contended that Confederation was not, as most people have always believed in the past, a union of several Provinces, but a union of two cultures or two nations, French and English. The evidence for the first of these propositions is stronger on the face of it than that for the second; it is always easy to make an impressive list of differences between the present and the past of a hundred years ago; and proving how much better—and how much better off—they are than their ancestors has always been a favourite indoor sport of each generation. Thus the "quiet" revolutionaries argue that the Fathers of Confederation obviously did not foresee the tremendous expansion of education, or the coming of the welfare state, with its pensions, family allowances, medical care, and various forms of insurance. The Fathers also mistakenly assigned natural resources to the Provinces under the impression that most of the best land had already been alienated and that public domain would never bring in a large revenue. These confident expectations, the "quiet" revolutionaries argue, have been largely falsified by the discovery of enormous mineral deposits in central and western Canada, by the exploitation of forest resources, and the development of hydro-electric power. Finally, it is claimed, the Fathers were also sadly mistaken in their expectation that the great public improvements of the future would be federal enterprises such as transcontinental railways. On the contrary, it is provincial and municipal public works—schools, universities, hospitals and roads—that now constitute the bigger part of the public enterprises of Canada. In short, the whole trend of modern development has placed more power and more responsibility in the hands of the Provinces; and this inevitably means such a large degree of decentralization as to make the centralist scheme of the Fathers seem obsolete.

In the meantime, while the Fathers were meeting with this frontal attack, their position was also menaced by a more subtle flanking movement. Confederation, the revisionists of Canadian history explained, was not, or not mainly, a union of Provinces; rather it was an agreement between two cultures or two nations, French and English. There was, some of the revisionists admitted, very little evidence for this thesis in the Charlottetown or Quebec Conferences, or in the proceedings that led up to the enactment of the *British North America Act*. In 1867, therefore, they say, the agreement could perhaps best be described as an extra-legal agreement, an unspoken moral commitment, which was meant to inform the whole union with its spirit. It was only when Manitoba and the Northwest Territories were incorporated in the union, that the Fathers of Confederation and their immediate successors took positive steps to ensure that this bicultural compact should prevail in the new western domain and that it should thus become the common possession of both

English-speaking and French-speaking Canadians. In this spirit, it is claimed, the first Conservative government gave legal status to the French language in Manitoba and the first Liberal government after Confederation did the same for the Northwest Territories. Finally, it is argued that this agreement between the two cultures, with which Confederation started out, has not been honoured as it should have been, and that substantial amends must now be made.

The uses to which the two nation theory can be put are manifold. It can give support to the promotion of French in the public service, or the increase of French-taught schools in areas where the character of the population requires it. But its advocates are not usually content with such modest programmes. The two-nation theory can be made to justify a bicultural senate and a bicultural Supreme Court, with equal representation for French and English-speaking Canadians. It is also the basis of the proposal that Quebec be made an associate state.

IV

Such are the two radical views of the Fathers of Confederation and their work; such are the arguments on which they are based. It is obvious at once that these interpretations have been used to support very large claims and sweeping conclusions; and this very fact invites us to examine their supporting evidence closely. As soon as we begin to do so, it is immediately clear that there are very serious weaknesses in the case for radical change.

We are deceived by the theory of inevitable decentralization. It has such an air of sweet reasonableness about it. How could the Fathers of Confederation be expected to make provision for the welfare state and the modern Canadian economy? The answer is *not* "Of course they couldn't" as the "quiet" revolutionaries assume. The answer is that the Fathers *did* make ample provision by founding a strong central government which could have coped very effectively with modern social and economic problems. And the fact that it is not now capable of playing the role which the Fathers intended it to play is not simply the result of natural social evolution and economic change, but also, and more importantly, of arbitrary human intervention—of the decisions of the courts and the arrangements of politicians. The *British North America Act*, as I have said, has not often been formally amended; but its whole character has been drastically changed, and, indeed, almost exactly reversed, by the decisions of the courts, and particularly of the Judicial Committee of the Privy council, which in effect have transferred residuary authority from the central government, where it was intended to lie, to the Provinces, which were never meant to have it. There was nothing natural or inevitable about this at all; it might, it ought, to have happened the other way. With infinitely more justification than in the United States, the trend of judicial interpretation could have favoured the central government. But it did exactly the opposite. And the tragic irony of our present plight is that the Canadian constitution, which was designed to prevent the defects of decentralization from which the United States was supposed to suffer, has in fact acquired far more of these defects than the American constitution itself.

The judges began the process of decentralization by transferring powers and responsibilities to the Provinces; the politicians have continued and hastened it by transferring vast sums of money. During the depression of the 1930s and the war of the 1940s, the Dominion Government still maintained its dominating economic and financial control; but since then provincial pressures and federal concessions have altered this state of affairs, and with accelerating rapidity. The recent financial agreements between the Provinces and the Dominion have steadily increased the provincial share of the Canadian tax dollar. The "opting out" or "contracting out" formula may give the Provinces more complete administrative and financial control over development and welfare programmes which they have previously shared with the federal government. Finally, the new Canada Pension Plan will put in the hands of the provincial governments enormous capital sums which can be used quite independently to carry out provincial economic and social projects. This huge increase in the provincial share of the public or government sector of the economy could threaten serious trouble for the future. It might weaken the Dominion's power to support its monetary and fiscal control, and hence its capacity to maintain the nation's economic well-being. It might help to break down those common minimum standards of public services and welfare which most people believe a nation ought to try to achieve.

The arguments for the theory of inevitable decentralization are certainly defective; yet its consequences may be serious. The same general comment might very well be made about the two nation theory of Canadian Confederation. The obstinate historical facts will simply not bear the weight of this massive generalization. The *Manitoba Act* of 1870, which gave provincial status, the French language, and sectarian schools to the first prairie province of Canada, was not at all the original intention of the Fathers of Confederation. Their original intention was expressed in an *Act* passed one year earlier, now generally forgotten, an *Act for the Provisional Government of Ruperts Land*, which gave the northwest the government of a territory, not of a Province, and made no mention of languages or schools. What forced the Fathers of Confederation to abandon their original plans for the northwest was, quite simply, the Riel Rising of 1869-70. It was Louis Riel, backed by five thousand *métis*, the partial support of the Red River Community, and further strengthened by British pressure and Anglo-Canadian fears of American intervention in the northwest, which compelled the Fathers of Confederation to fix the institutions of Manitoba prematurely, before the true character of the Province had declared itself.

Even if one concedes, which I do not, that the settlement of 1870 was wise, it by no means follows that the *Manitoba Act* established a bicultural pattern for the northwest which was carefully confirmed and followed thereafter. The *Northwest Territories Act* of 1875, which first set up a territorial government for the prairies beyond Manitoba, made no mention whatever of language rights; and the amendment which in 1877 gave the French language legal status in the territories was proposed, not by the Liberal government of the day, but by a private member in the Senate. Anybody who cherishes the fond delusion that these early bicultural provisions in the west were the result of a settled policy followed by both Conservative and Liberal governments, would be well advised to read the speech with which David Mills, then Minister of the Interior, greeted this Senate amendment when it was brought down to the Commons in April, 1877. He reminded the members that the prevailing language of the region was Cree. He regretted the amendment; and he reluctantly accepted it because otherwise it would be impossible to get the revised bill through before the end of the session.

The Fathers of Confederation were neither political philosophers, nor political dreamers, but hard-headed, practical, empirical statesmen. They had come through some very bitter disputes over the controversial subjects of religion, education, and language; and it was not in their nature to provoke trouble by laying down abstract declarations of general principle. On these contentious cultural matters, they contented themselves with a few provisions which were precise, definite, and limited. Yet these limitations have not prevented a liberal enlargement of the original privileges, by usage and convention, far beyond the letter of the law. The *British North America Act* merely requires that French as well as English shall be used in the records and journals of the Houses of Parliament; but what a vast extension has already taken place here, and entirely without the sanction of the theory of the two nations! The use of French as well as English on stamps and banknotes, in federal stationary, forms, and notices, in all the publicity, information and publications of a modern state, and in such national enterprises as the Canada Council, the Film Board, Air Canada, and the Canadian Broadcasting Corporation, has come about gradually but steadily, and a great advance has been made within the past twenty-five years. The Royal Commission on Bilingualism and Biculturalism may usefully help this process on its way; but it would be dangerously unwise for its members to regard themselves as the Stepfathers of Confederation and to assume that their terms of reference empower them to propose fundamental changes in the Canadian constitution. They should remember—we should all remember—that the attempt to impose a bicultural pattern by law on the Canada West was resisted with the utmost determination as soon as the West had formed its character and come of age. The resulting controversy was as prolonged and bitter as anything in Canadian history and it ended with the West's total rejection of biculturalism.

Thus the theory of natural decentralization and the theory of Confederation as a bicultural agreement, both of which have such a plausible appearance, become doubtful and suspect in the hard light of history. This realization ought to strengthen our resolve to understand and respect our past. History must be defended against attempts to abuse it in the cause of change; we should constantly be on our guard against theories which either dismiss the past or give it a drastically new interpretation. Such theories are likely to abound in an age of doubt and uncertainty about the future; and most of them, whether consciously or unconsciously, have been developed to serve the radical programmes of the moment. From this path to historical propaganda is short and easy; and as George Orwell has shown in his terrible satire, *Nineteen Eight-Four*, the systematic obliteration and recreation of the past may become the most potent instrument in the armoury of a collectivist dictatorship. A nation that repudiates or distorts its past runs a grave danger of forfeiting its future.

Confederation and the Federal Principle

Robert Vipond

If the Canadian Fathers of Confederation[1] held any truth to be self-evident, it was that the architects of the U.S. Constitution had made a fundamental constitutional mistake in 1787, the terrible consequences of which were being played out at that very moment—the mid-1860s—on the battlefield. John A. Macdonald, the central figure of the Confederation movement, argued bluntly that the Americans, in declaring "by their Constitution that each state was a sovereignty in itself," had begun "at the wrong end." Macdonald was not alone. As Peter Waite argues, "no understanding of Confederation is possible unless it be recognized that its founders, many of its supporters, and as many of its opponents were all animated by a powerful antipathy to the whole federal principle."[2] Yet what Macdonald conceived as an express attempt to overcome the "errors" of the U.S. federal constitution ended in the creation of a basic law, the British North America Act,[3] which, within a

---

[1] I adopt this conventional nomenclature in part to remind readers of the exclusive and elitist nature of mid-nineteenth-century Canadian politics. Unlike the resolutions adopted at Philadelphia in 1787, the Confederation proposal, known as the Quebec Resolutions, did not require ratification by specially designed constitutional assemblies. The resolutions themselves called only for approval by the various local parliaments, and even here there was some reluctance in some of the affected colonies to enter into a full-scale legislative debate. Moreover, even if there had been some form of official referendum on the proposals, the restrictions on the franchise would have severely limited participation. In Upper Canada (Ontario), the franchise at the time of Confederation excluded both women and those who did not hold a sizeable amount of real property. Indeed, in 1866 the Canadian Legislative Assembly actually raised the property qualification, in part as a reaction against what was perceived as the dangerously democratic tendencies at work in the U.S. This limitation on the franchise may help to explain why, with the exception of cultural questions, the theme of minority rights does not loom as large in the Canadian Confederation debates as it did in the American constitutional debates. One way of ensuring that the property-less many do not cancel debts or redistribute the property that belongs to the few is to disenfranchise those who do not possess the requisite amount of property. On the franchise in mid-nineteenth-century, see D.G.G. Kerr, "The 1867 Elections in Ontario: The Rules of the Game," Canadian Historical Review 51 (1970), 369-377.

[2] Peter B. Waite, The Life and Times of Confederation, 1864-1867 (Toronto: University of Toronto Press, 1962), 33.

[3] The Constitution Act, 1867 was formerly known as the British North America Act. For reasons of historical accuracy, I will refer to it in the text itself as the Fathers of

generation of its passage in 1867, had come to be viewed by many as the legitimate source of provincial autonomy and the embodiment of the federal principle.

The burden of this essay is to explain the constitutional bases of the Confederation settlement of 1867 with a view to understanding the apparent transformation that occurred thereafter. I say *apparent* transformation because I want to distance myself to some extent from the conventional view, encapsulated above, that generalizes from Macdonald's example and concludes that "the Fathers ... distrusted pure coordinate or classical federalism."[4] As K.C. Wheare put it in a now-famous formulation, the original constitution can best be described as "quasi-federal" because the constitutional framers included a number of provisions (like the veto power of disallowance) which rendered the regional governments "subordinate to the

---

Confederation referred to it, that is as the BNA Act. In the notes, however, I will refer to it by its present and correct name.

[4] Bruce Hodgins, "The Canadian Political Elite's Attitudes Toward the Nature of the Plan of Union," in Bruce W. Hodgins, Don Wright and W.H. Heick, eds., Federalism in Canada and Australia: The Early Years (Waterloo: Wilfrid Laurier University Press, 1978), 43. Of course, the view that the Confederation settlement was at best "quasi-federal" is no more monolithic than the views of the Confederationists themselves. Moreover, the emphasis on the Confederationists' hostility to the federal principle varies somewhat from author to author. Still, the view that, as a body, the Fathers of Confederation did not embrace the federal principle is widespread. See André Bernard, La Politique au Canada et au Québec (Montréal: Les Presses de L'Université du Québec, 1977), ch. 11; Ramsay Cook, Provincial Autonomy, Minority Rights and the Compact Theory, 1867-1921 (Ottawa: Queen's Printer, 1969), ch. 2; Donald Creighton, Dominion of the North (Toronto: Macmillan, 1957), ch. 6; Donald Creighton, The Road to Confederation (Boston: Houghton Mifflin, 1965), ch. 6; Kenneth McNaught, The Pelican History of Canada (Middlesex: Penguin, 1969), ch. 9; W.L. Morton, "Confederation, 1870-1896," in A.B. McKillop, ed., Contexts of Canada's Past (Toronto: Macmillan, 1980), 208-228; J.C. Morrison, "Oliver Mowat and the Development of Provincial Rights in Ontario: A Study in Dominion-Provincial Relations, 1867-1896," in Three History Theses (Toronto: Ontario Department of Public Records and Archives, 1961), ch. 1; J.R. Mallory, "The Five Faces of Federalism," in P.-A. Crépeau and C.B. Macpherson, eds., The Future of Canadian Federalism (Toronto: University of Toronto Press, 1965), 3-15; John T. Saywell, The Office of Lieutenant-Governor (Toronto: University of Toronto Press, 1957), ch. 1; Norman Ward, Dawson's The Government of Canada, 6th ed. (Toronto: University of Toronto Press, 1987), ch. 14. See also Gil Rémillard, Le Fédéralisme Canadien (Montréal: Québec/Amérique, 1983). Mr. Rémillard notes the view, propounded by Wheare, that the BNA Act was "quasi federal" (149). His own view seems to be closer to the one developed here, however. Thus, he says, "d'une façon générale, il semble bien que les Canadiens de l'époque aient tout simplement confondu fédéralisme, comme il était alors courant de le faire. Cependant, le Canada est bien une fédération et non une confédération" (64). Mr. Rémillard's views are of special interest because he was the Quebec minister of intergovernmental affairs at the time the Meech Lake Accord was negotiated.

general government and, not coordinate with it."[5] The fundamental problem with the conventional view, I will argue, is that it underestimates the extent to which the meaning of federalism was in flux during the period 1864-1867. It is true that the Canadian political elite was horrified by the Civil War, and it is equally true that many of the Confederationists inferred from their reading of the causes of the war that the federal principle is inherently unstable. But for a significant number of Confederationists—drawn especially from the franks of the Reform party of Upper Canada (Ontario) and the conservative Bleus of Lower Canada (Quebec)—the Civil War did not discredit the federal principle so much as it issued a challenge to place federalism on a more secure constitutional footing. The irony is that, having rejected one model of American federalism, these Canadian reformers came in their own way and on their own terms to reconceptualize federalism in a way that is strongly reminiscent of another American precedent—the Federalists' classic exposition of constitutional federalism.

These other Confederationists usually did not acknowledge explicitly the similarity between their own ideas and those of the Federalists; indeed, it is by no means clear that they appreciated the extent to which they were retracing the steps of James Madison and James Wilson. The parallel is nonetheless striking, and it suggests that the roots of constitutional federalism in Canada were put down somewhat earlier than is usually thought. While the provincial rights movement did not blossom until the 1880s, the seeds of provincial autonomy were sown in the BNA Act of 1867. It is therefore with the debate leading up to the Confederation settlement of 1867 that an account of provincial autonomy must begin.

II

Confederation came about in 1867 because the leaders of three of the four largest factions in Canadian politics at the time, George-Etienne Cartier, George Brown and John A. Macdonald, had agreed in 1864 to dedicate themselves to the establishment of a federal union in British North America.[6] The Great Coalition of 1864 is surely

---

[5] K.C. Wheare, Federal government, 4th ed. (London: Oxford University Press, 1963), 18.

[6] See W.L. Morton, The Critical Years, 1857-1873 (Toronto: McClelland and Stewart, 1964). I am dealing here only with the pre-Confederation politics in the Province of Canada, what is now Ontario and Quebec. On the politics of Confederation in the other colonies, see, for instance, Kenneth G. Pryke, Nova Scotia and Confederation, 1864-74 (Toronto: University of Toronto Press, 1979), ch. 1; G.A. Rawlyk and Doug Brown, "The Historical Framework of the Maritimes and Confederation," in G.A. Rawlyk, ed., The Atlantic Provinces and the Problems of Confederation (Breakwater, 1979), 1-47. Frederick Vaughan provides useful insights into the Atlantic debates over Confederation in "Critics of the Judicial Committee of the Privy Council: The New Orthodoxy and an Alternative Explanation," Canadian Journal of Political Science 19 (1986), 495-519, especially 511-512. See also Jennifer Smith,

one of the most curious alliances ever forged in Canadian politics. The Reformer Brown and the Conservative Macdonald had been engaged in a longstanding political rivalry, the bitterness of which had been deepened by the rhetorical exigencies of party politics and the partisan press. Brown was relentlessly anti-clerical, Cartier was associated with clericalism. Brown and Macdonald were Upper Canadian and Scots, Cartier was Lower Canadian and French. Yet whatever their differences, each had come to the conclusion that it was in his interest to support a federal union. For this brief, but crucial, moment they were united by their common desire to form a federal union. That desire brought them, and held them, together.

A number of factors combined to make a union of the British North American Colonies possible and perhaps even urgently necessary. The dismantling of the British mercantile system, the fear that the U.S. would abrogate the Reciprocity Treaty of 1854, and the prospect of turning the West both into a market for eastern goods and the supplier of raw materials made union an attractive economic option—especially for politicians with strong connections to crucial economic elites. The notion that some sort of coordinated defense was necessary to protect the colonies from American expansionism carried some weight; it probably did not hurt the cause to suggest that the real enemy was that "warlike power" to the south which, "under Mr. Lincoln" was ready to force "this universal democracy doctrine" on the rest of North America.[7] Moreover, it was patently clear to the members of the Great Coalition that the present union between Upper and Lower Canada was not working. The basic political institutions were deadlocked, ministries were created and fell with almost predictable frequency, and the tone of politics was deeply and unhelpfully confrontational. Given all of these things, some sort of basic constitutional reform appeared to Cartier, Brown and Macdonald to be necessary. The interesting question, therefore, is less why the Great Coalition came together than why they joined together to create a specifically federal form of union.

For Cartier and his Bleu party, federalism recommended itself as the best means to cultural survival. As A.I. Silver has argued, French Canadians in the 1860s "generally considered French Canada and Lower Canada to be equivalent."[8] That is, they equated their distinctive identity as a people with a specific territory in which they formed a majority. This was, admittedly, a somewhat false equation. There were, even in the mid-1860s, francophone populations beyond the borders of Quebec, in Manitoba and New Brunswick for example, but at the time of Confederation they figured only slightly in the political calculations of the French-Canadian political

---

[7] "Canadian Confederation and the Influence of American Federalism" Canadian Journal of Political Science 21 (1988), 443-463.

Canada, Legislative Assembly, Parliamentary Debates on the Confederation of the British North American Provinces (Quebec: Hunter, Rose and Company, 1865), 107 (Brown); 143, 130 (McGee).

[8] A.I. Silver, The French-Canadian Idea of Confederation, 1864-1900 (Toronto: University of Toronto Press, 1982), 33.

elite.[9] As Silver argues, most French Canadians at the time, whether for or against Confederation, considered that the future of French Canada depended on what happened in and to Lower Canada.[10] That said, it was quite natural to think that the distinctive institutions, laws and cultural values of French Canada could best be protected if decisions affecting them were made in the provincial legislature of Quebec, the one legislature in which French Canadians would be sure to dominate. Questions of importance to the country as a whole could safely be consigned to a central legislature in which French Canadians were represented but which they did not control as long as the distinctive, local subjects were left to the disposition of the provincial legislature which they did control. If there had to be constitutional change, then some form of division of powers between a national and a series of provincial legislatures was the best hope for cultural survival.[11]

George Brown's support for Confederation is slightly less self-explanatory, and must be understood in the context of the Reform party in Upper Canada. The Reform party grew from the Union Act of 1840, under the terms of which Upper and Lower Canada were given equal representation in a common legislature. This initially favoured Upper Canada, which had the smaller population, but within a short time the demographic balance had shifted such that Upper Canadians found themselves proportionately under-represented in the combined legislative assembly. What made matters worse, according to the Reformers, was that a solid phalanx of Lower Canadian Conservatives (or Bleus), together with a small number of Upper Canadian Conservatives, had been able to control the assembly without interruption since the early 1850s. Together, the Reformers claimed, this coalition legislated at the expense and against the wishes of the majority of Upper Canadians. Some Reformers protested that Lower Canada had forced sectarian schools on Upper Canada.[12] Others complained that they had been "fleeced" by Lower Canada, forced time and again to pay for what they believed was Lower Canadian profligacy.[13] Still others blamed the underdevelopment of the West on Lower Canadian indifference to the rich rewards to be won there.[14] All agreed with their leader, George Brown, that a great injustice had been visited upon the citizens of Upper Canada, and all agreed that some basic constitutional reform was necessary to redress these grievances....

---

[9] Ibid., ch. 3, 4.

[10] Ibid., ch. 2.

[11] For a survey of French-Canadian arguments for Confederation, see Silver, French-Canadian Idea, ch. 2; see also Cartier's speech in the Confederation Debates, 60, where he argues that the central government would have jurisdiction over the "large questions of general interest in which the differences of race and religion had no place."

[12] J.M.S. Careless, Brown of the Globe, 2 vols. (Toronto: Macmillan, 1959), vol. I, ch. 4.

[13] Toronto Globe, 11 November 1859, speeches of Wilkes and Brown at the Reform Convention. Also see Confederation Debates, 92 (Brown).

[14] Toronto Globe, 24 May 1859, "Federation."

One of the clearest statements of this sort was made before the Reform Convention of 1859 by Oliver Mowat, one of the most respected members of the Reform party before Confederation, and premier of Ontario and a leader of the provincial rights movement thereafter. The problem with the existing constitutional arrangement, Mowat insisted, was not merely that it effectively allowed a minority to rule the majority. The deeper problem was that it permitted a French, Catholic minority to rule an English, Protestant majority. It allowed those "of another language, another race, another country" to rule Upper Canada.[15] The fear for cultural survival dominated Lower Canadian politics before Confederation. Ironically, it dominated Upper Canadian politics as well.

Thus George Brown, leader of the Reform party, found the Confederation proposal attractive because it met both of the longstanding conditions set out by his party. First, the Confederation proposal was "a great measure of representative reform"[16] inasmuch as it provided that representation in the House of Commons would reflect population. It would simply be much more difficult for Lower Canada to "fleece" its neighbour when the latter would suddenly have "seventeen additional members in the House that holds the purse."[17] Beyond this, the Confederation plan embraced the principle that "local governments are to have control over local affairs."[18] This, too, would protect Upper Canada, for it meant that "if our friends in Lower Canada choose to be extravagant, they will have to bear the burden of it themselves."[19] Confederation thus held out the promise that Ontario would both dominate national politics and control its own affairs. It thereby offered Ontario a double indemnity against past "injustices." It is small wonder that Brown, speaking in 1865, could accept the Confederation plan "without hesitation or reservation."[20]

Macdonald's reasons for endorsing a specifically federal union were more narrowly political and his support less enthusiastic. He cheerfully admitted in the course of the debate on the Confederation proposal, held in the Canadian assembly in 1865, that he preferred a unitary to a federal government because he believed that what the country most needed—a strong defense, a continental outlook and material prosperity—could best be provided by a highly centralized regime. But he realized equally well that the various sections comprising the union would not agree to a plan that would destroy their "individuality." By 1864, he had reconciled himself to the impracticability of complete union and had given his support instead to a proposal that, he believed, would produce the next best thing: a highly centralized, but still federal, union....

---

[15] Cited in Charles R.W. Biggar, Sir Oliver Mowat, 2 vols. (Toronto: Warwick Bro's and Rutter, 1905), vol. I, 93.
[16] Confederation debates, 92 (Brown).
[17] Ibid.
[18] Ibid.
[19] Ibid.
[20] Ibid., 87 (Brown).

III

As mythic figures the Fathers of Confederation have never been as successful as their American counterparts. Despite their best efforts to portray themselves as heroic legislators, they have never been idolized and revered in the way Madison, Hamilton, Jefferson and others have been in the United States. One reason for the difference is that the Canadians were engaged in an enterprise that was simply less amenable to mythmaking. Notwithstanding their own conceits, the Fathers of Confederation were not "founding" a political state in the way it is often said the American constitution-makers were "Founders." In the Canadian case there was no self-conscious break with the past and certainly no revolution; indeed, the Fathers of Confederation went out of their way to emphasize that Confederation represented continuity and had been achieved "under the fostering care of Great Britain, and our Sovereign Lady, Queen Victoria."[21] There was, therefore, no need to expound first political principles or to weave together a set of authoritative public values in the way Publius did.[22] It was enough to say that as Canadians they wanted to inherit a "constitution similar in principle to that of the United Kingdom."[23] For much the same reason, there was no need to develop a new approach to understanding politics, a new political science if you will, to provide a new perspective on these first principles. Fundamental questions about the purposes and organization of government, with which Publius had concerned himself and on which his mythic reputation is based, simply were not raised in the debate over Confederation. The fundamental political choices had already been made, and with those implicit decisions went the best opportunity for the Canadian framers to establish themselves as self-conscious, deliberate founders.

Yet as a number of the critics of the Confederation proposal noted, the Confederation coalition was even reluctant to explain and clarify the features of the plan that were novel—especially those concerning federalism.[24] This reluctance was in part strategic. Macdonald, Cartier and Brown understood perfectly well that their coalition ran clearly against the grain of Canadian politics, and they knew that their opponents were waiting for an opportunity to rekindle the rivalries that had been set aside temporarily. They therefore went out of their way to exaggerate what they had in common and to abstract from or simply ignore their differences. Given the imperative to maintain the unity of the coalition, it was crucial to confine the discussion as much as possible to the most general level where agreement could be assured, rather than descending to a detailed examination of the proposals, where

---

21 Ibid.
22 Publius was the common pen-name used by the authors of The Federalist Papers, which advocated ratification of the U.S. constitution — Ed.
23 Constitution Act, 1867, Preamble.
24 See, for instance, the comments of M.C. Cameron and Christopher Dunkin, Confederation Debates, 459, 482.

disagreement almost certainly would have surfaced. Moreover, since the Quebec Resolutions were presented to the Canadian assembly as a fait accompli to be voted up or down, it was doubly necessary to create the impression of unity. Had the Quebec Resolutions been placed before the electorate for ratification, it might well have been in the coalition's interest to stress that this was a collaborative effort that was democratically heterogeneous and that invited a wide variety of views and interpretations. As it was, the resolutions were placed before the Canadian Legislative Assembly more in the form of a governmental measure in which differences had to be suppressed in favour of cabinet solidarity.

The debates on the Confederation proposal that were held in the Canadian Legislative Assembly in 1865 betray this strategic circumspection particularly clearly. At the most general level, the tripartite coalition agreed that federalism was the only acceptable constitutional remedy for the various ills besetting British North america. They agreed, further, that federalism meant dividing legislative jurisdiction between a national parliament, which would legislate on those matters of "general" or "national" interest, and several provincial legislatures, which would have the authority to pass laws on matters of "local" significance. But most supporters of the Confederation proposal did their best to avoid giving these general propositions substance. Most speakers were little inclined to explain how precisely the local was to be distinguished from the general; how conflicts of jurisdiction were to be resolved; whether federalism was compatible with the protection of minority rights, or other crucial matters of substance in a federation. In some cases the dogged refusal to examine the substance of the Confederation proposals became comical. C.B. de Niverville, a Bleu (or Conservative) member from Trois-Rivières, spoke in favour of Confederation even though he had not read the resolutions and even though, lacking English, he had been unable to follow the debate in the assembly.[25] Nor was the flight from substance confined to the back benches. John A. Macdonald himself avoided confronting the possibility of federal-provincial conflict by stating unequivocally (and quite absurdly) that the constitutional architects had managed to avoid "all conflict of jurisdiction and authority."[26]

It is not as if the Confederation proposal was crystal clear. The coalition's unwillingness to discuss matters of substance in any detail was especially noticeable and unsatisfying because the text of the proposal itself seemed to contradict the very federal principles that it was meant to embody. The coalition agreed, for instance, that in the proposed federation the provincial legislatures would enjoy full, indeed "exclusive," control over local affairs.[27] Yet the text that, read one way, seemed to

---

[25] Confederation Debates, 947-950.
[26] Ibid., 33.
[27] Quebec Resolutions, section 29:37, reprinted in G.P. Browne, ed., Documents on the Confederation of British North America (Toronto: McClelland and Stewart, 1969), 154-165. See Confederation debates, 30, 33. More importantly, the Constitution Act, 1867 itself enshrines the exclusivity of provincial jurisdiction. See section 92 (Preamble) and section

guarantee local self-government could be read with equal ease as a massive hedge against local control. The federal government was given a general, residual power to legislate for the "peace, order and good government" of the country, a potentially vast power illustrated, but apparently not limited, by an additional, enumerated list of legislative powers.[28] The provinces were not given the fiscal capacity to match their constitutional responsibilities; from the start they depended on federal subsidies.[29] The federal government was given the power to claim jurisdiction over "local works and undertakings" by declaring them to be "for the general advantage of Canada."[30] The power of disallowance gave the federal government the right to veto any act of a provincial legislature within one year of the act's passage.[31] The federal government was expected to appoint a lieutenant-governor in each province, which officer had the power to reserve assent from (or effectively prevent the passage of) provincial legislation.[32] Even in the crucial area of sectarian education, the constitutional settlement deviated from the principle of complete provincial control. By section 93 of the BNA Act the federal government was given the power to oversee minority educational rights in any province in which a system of separate schools existed by law at the time the province entered Confederation. Section 93 further provided that, if necessary, the federal government could impose remedial legislation upon an offending province.[33]

None of these provisions could be reconciled easily with the official claim that under the terms of the Confederation settlement each province would be utterly free to legislate on all matters of peculiar importance to it—something the many critics of Confederation repeatedly pointed out. The most perceptive and spirited of these critics were Antoine-Aimé and Jean-Baptiste-Eric Dorion, Rouge representatives from Quebec, who insisted that Confederation would become for all intents and purposes a unitary government because the provinces would be both too weak and too vulnerable to defend themselves against the imperious and meddlesome designs of the federal government. What the Dorions had wanted was a "real Federal system" in which the members states "retain their full sovereignty in everything that immediately concerns them, but submitting to the General Government questions of

---

93, where the provincial legislatures are granted the power "exclusively" to make laws in the matters listed therein.

[28] Constitution Act, 1867, section 91 (Preamble). It should be noted that this grant of power to legislate for the "peace, order and good government" of the country was meant, as Macdonald said, to avoid the errors of the American Constitution. See Confederation Debates, 33.

[29] See J.A. Maxwell, Federal Subsidies to Provincial Governments in Canada (Cambridge, Mass., 1937).

[30] Constitution Act, 1867 section 92:10:c.

[31] Ibid., section 56, 90.

[32] Ibid., section 55, 58, 90.

[33] Ibid., section 93:4.

peace, of war, of foreign relations, foreign trade, customs and postal service."[34] What had been proposed instead was "a Legislative Union in disguise" in which "the Federal Parliament will exercise sovereign power inasmuch as it can always trespass upon the rights of the local governments without there being any authority to prevent it."[35]

The great force of the Dorions' criticism was that it related the new and unfamiliar proposals for Confederation to one of the basic concepts of Anglo-American political discourse—sovereignty. Gordon Wood has shown how the debate leading to the ratification of the American Constitution was informed by Blackstone's axiom that there must be in every political system "a supreme, irresistible, absolute, uncontrolled authority, in which ... the rights of sovereignty reside."[36] And he has described brilliantly how this assumption that sovereignty is indivisible became "the most powerful obstacle" to the acceptance of the federal constitution.[37] Blackstone's axiom was no less important in the debate leading to Confederation and no less powerful an obstacle to its coherent defence. For the Dorions, as for most educated Canadians, the idea of sovereignty served as an anchor for political analysis, even if they were typically less inclined than Americans to identify this foundation explicitly.[38]

In making sovereignty the focus of their analysis of the Confederation scheme, the Dorions immediately clarified the choices and hardened the alternatives. For if Blackstone was right that sovereignty is indivisible, then, as the Dorions showed, there could really be only two ways of forming a broader political association in British North America. At one extreme, sovereignty could be lodged in some central authority which had the legislative power to make laws for all the colonies or provinces; this was what was meant by a legislative union. At the other extreme, each member of the association could remain sovereign or supreme; this was the legal description of what the Dorions called a federal union. In either case the sovereign power could "delegate" law-making authority to some "subordinate" body. In a legislative union authority could be delegated to provincial legislatures in much the same way that authority was traditionally delegated to municipal or county

---

[34] Confederation Debates, 859, 858 (J.B.E. Dorion).

[35] Ibid., 858 (J.B.E. Dorion); 690 (A.A. Dorion).

[36] William Blackstone, Commentaries on the laws of England I:ii:7.

[37] Gordon W. Wood, The Creation of the American Republic, 1776-1787 (New York: Norton, 1969), 529.

[38] See Blaine Baker, "The Reconstitution of Upper Canadian Legal Thought in the Late-Victorian Empire," Law and History Review 3, (1985), 255. Peter Waite suggests that a similar understanding of sovereignty informed Joseph Howe's opposition to Confederation. For Howe, the most prominent anti-Confederationist from Nova Scotia, "(o)ne government or another had to be supreme. Apparently both could not be." See Peter B. Waite, "Halifax Newspapers and the Federal Principle, 1864-1865," in J.M. Bumsted, ed., Canadian History Before Confederation, 2nd ed. (Georgetown: Irwin-Dorsey, 1979), 505.

councils or in the way that the imperial Parliament "delegated" power to the colonial legislatures. Conversely, in a federal union authority could be delegated in various ways from the individual sovereign states to a common congress. But in either case, the delegated power ultimately existed at the sufferance of the sovereign. Power could be withdrawn, supervised, influenced and controlled by the one supreme authority.

Judged by the criterion of sovereignty, it was clear to the Dorions that the Confederation proposal was misnamed. This was not a "real confederation, giving the largest powers to the local governments, and merely a delegated authority to the general government."[39] Rather, the various elements of the Confederation plan, taken together, established a clear pattern of national hegemony. The extraordinary, potentially limitless power to legislate for the peace, order and good government of the country; the veto powers lodged in the federal government; the creation of federally appointed governors in each province; the power to declare local works in the national interest—all of this was incontrovertible evidence that the provincial legislatures would have no real control over local affairs because they were not sovereign. In the Confederation plan "all the sovereignty is vested in the General Government;"[40] conversely, "all is weakness, insignificance, annihilation in the Local Government."[41] As another member put it, under the Confederation scheme local governments would be "nothing more than municipal councils," which, in the case of jurisdictional collision, would be "completely at the mercy of the hostile Federal majority."[42]

What was yet more damning was that the supporters of Confederation cooperated in their own indictment. Macdonald was of course particularly vulnerable to the charge of false advertising. He openly admitted that he had only grudgingly accepted the proposal to create a specifically federal union, and even then his conversion was half-hearted. Federalism was a practical or political necessity for Macdonald, not something desirable in itself, and he did his best to limit this concession by ensuring that the federal government would always be able to judge and control precisely how much "individuality"[43] the provinces should be allowed to display. For Macdonald, the constitutional model from which the Canadian proposal was derived was not the American federation (which, after all, had been discredited by the Civil War)[44] but the British empire. Expressed in the language of sovereignty, Macdonald argued that the relation between Ottawa and the provinces would replicate the relation between the sovereign imperial Parliament and the colonial legislatures; "all the powers incident to sovereignty," he argued, would be vested in the federal government while "the local governments and legislatures" would be "subordinate to the General

---

[39] Confederation Debates, 250 (A.A. Dorion).
[40] Ibid., 689 (A.A. Dorion).
[41] Ibid., 858 (J.B.E. Dorion).
[42] Ibid., 623-24 (Perrault).
[43] Ibid., 33 (Macdonald).
[44] Ibid., 33, 41.

Government and Legislature."[45] The extent of provincial autonomy or liberty would depend on the judgment of the federal government just as the extent of colonial freedom depended on the judgment of the imperial authorities. The provinces, like the colonies, might be allowed considerable room to legislate freely on those matters local in nature. But there could be no mistake, according to Macdonald, that in the final analysis the federal government was sovereign over the provinces just as the imperial Parliament was sovereign over Canada. Thus, it is no coincidence that much of the apparatus of imperial supervision—the vetoes of reservation and disallowance and the office of lieutenant-governor, for example—found their way into the Canadian constitution as tools of federal supervision. This was to be federalism on the imperial model; this is what I will call "political federalism."

The position of the Upper Canadian Reformers[46] is rather more difficult to categorize and describe, but here too there was considerable grist for the Dorions' mill. The Reformers in general and George Brown in particular were well aware of the advantages of a strong central government.[47] They were eager to develop the West, build industry and promote trade. They realized that such development would require greater central coordination than a weak, state-centred federation could provide, and they understood perfectly well that Ontario, by virtue of its greater political and economic power, would be able to dominate national affairs. Moreover, the Reformers appreciated the disadvantages associated with traditional, state-centred federalism. For most of the Upper Canadian Confederationists, traditional federalism was synonymous with American federalism—a model which in 1864 hardly invited imitation. In light of the Civil War, most Reformers simply concluded that to confer sovereignty on the states was tantamount to sowing the seeds of national dissolution. The most prominent Reform newspaper, George Brown's Toronto *Globe*, put it this way:

> The civil war ... has afforded an excellent opportunity of judging of the weak points and defects in the United States constitution. It has especially shown the evil which the "States-rights" doctrine involves. The idea of the United States constitution is that the central government is a delegated government, deriving its powers from the "sovereign" States which go to make up the Union. The

---

[45] Ibid., 42, 33.

[46] The Reform party was not monolithic in its support of the Confederation settlement. Not all Reformers supported Confederation, and a few prominent members of the party, among them John Sandfield Macdonald, were openly critical of it. Most, however, did support it, and most of the Reform press rallied behind it. On the participation of the Reform press, see Waite, Life and Times of Confederation, 126-33. On John Sandfield Macdonald and other Reform critics, see Bruce W. Hodgins, John Sandfield Macdonald (Toronto: University of Toronto Press, 1971), ch. 5.

[47] On George Brown's centralism, see Careless, Brown of the Globe, vol. II, 164-169, 232.

constitution provides that the President and Congress shall have certain powers which the States have covenanted to give up to it. All others are vested in the States. This idea, pushed to the extreme, lies at the basis of what is known as the Calhoun doctrine, and was held thirty years ago, to justify the attempt of South Carolina to "nullify" a certain Act of Congress. The same thing is now relied upon by the secessionists to justify their efforts to withdraw their States from the federal compact.[48]

The *Globe* recognized that the Civil War could not be explained in terms of these constitutional defects alone. But it had to admit that Calhoun's radicalization of the constitutional principle of state sovereignty had "served to weaken the authority of the general Government at Washington" and had furnished "the secession leaders with an exceedingly plausible argument."[49] This was not, therefore, an example to be followed.

The Reformers' aversion to state sovereignty forced a good many of them to concede that the only alternative to this state-centred federalism was to vest sovereignty squarely in the central government. As long as they remained loyal to the language of Blackstone, they had no choice but to think of federalism as "an extension of our municipal system" in which the provincial legislatures would be "subordinate" to the federal government, their powers "delegated" by the central government.[50] Indeed, lacking the attributes of sovereignty, George Brown's *Globe* argued that it would be advisable to keep "the local governments as simple and inexpensive as possible."[51] It clearly would be unnecessary to have two legislative chambers in each province, and the *Globe*, in October 1864, even cast doubt on the necessity of bothering with a truly responsible government. After all, the federally appointed "Governor" of each province would probably have a veto on the legislature's acts, and "a responsible ministry in each province would certainly not be the cheapest system which could be adopted."[52]

The Reformers put the best possible face on this situation. They argued valiantly that the federal government would understand that it was not in its interest to become embroiled in local affairs, and they maintained that the Senate would protect the

---

[48] Toronto Globe, 1 August 1864. See also Confederation Debates, 674 (Hope Mackenzie), and 807 (Walsh), for a similar line of argument based on a similar reading of the U.S. Constitution.

[49] Toronto Globe, 1 August 1864. See also Ottawa Union, 1 November 1864.

[50] Toronto Globe, 1 August 1864, 29 August 1864, 15 October 1864; St. Catharine's Journal, 27 September 1864; Ottawa Union, 12 September 1864; Confederation Debates, 433 (Alexander Mackenzie).

[51] Toronto Globe, 4 October 1864.

[52] Ibid.

smaller provinces from being bullied.[53] Yet at base these were guarantees, like Macdonald's, that depended on the good graces of a central government that was sovereign over provincial governments that were legally subordinate. The critics of Confederation could see no difference between the Reformers' understanding of "political federalism" and Macdonald's, and this remains the conventional scholarly view of the Confederation settlement as well....[54]

What this view ignores, however, is that the Reformers were clearly uncomfortable with this conception of federalism because they, too, realized that it offered insufficient protection for the autonomy of local governments. The Reformers, after all, were committed by ideology and tradition to some form of decentralized government.[55] The roots of that tradition can be traced at least as far back as the 1820s, and it had been given special force in the 1860s by their francophobia.[56] Thus, while it is perfectly true that the Reformers wanted a strong central government, especially one in which Ontario would dominate, they simply did not see that the achievement of "Rep. by Pop." and strength at the centre were incompatible with their traditional goal of local control over local affairs. What the Reformers really wanted to create was a federal system that would provide both strong, united direction at the centre together with clear constitutional protection for local government at the periphery. As the *Globe* put it: "We desire local self-government in order that the separate nationalities of which the population is composed may not quarrel. We desire at the same time a strong central authority. Is

---

[53] Toronto Globe, 8 October 1864.

[54] J.C. Morrison, "Oliver Mowat and the Development of Provincial Rights in Ontario," 11, 1. Also see Peter Waite, Life and Times of Confederation, 133, who argues that the Reformers "did not in fact concern themselves much about local government." W.L. Morton goes further when he argues that "(t)he provinces were not, in fact, expected to be self-supporting as they were not thought sovereign even in their spheres of exclusive jurisdiction. They were subordinate governments both in appearance and in fact. They had no great tasks to perform and were given no great powers." W.L. Morton, "Confederation, 1870-1896," in A.B. McKillop, ed., Contexts of Canada's Past, 209. See also Frederick Vaughan, "Critics of the Judicial Committee of the Privy Council: The New Orthodoxy and an Alternative Explanation," Canadian Journal of Political Science 19 (1986), 505.

[55] For a challenging interpretation of the political and constitutional roots of localism in Ontario, see Paul Romney, "From constitutionalism to Legalism: Trial by Jury, Responsible Government, and the Rule of Law in the Canadian Political Culture," Law and History Review 7 (1989), 121-174; and Paul Romney, "From the Rule of Law to Responsible Government: Ontario Political Culture and the Origins of Canadian Statism," Canadian Historical Association, Historical Papers 1988 Communications Historiques, 86-119.

[56] See Elwood H. Jones, "Localism and Federalism in Upper Canada to 1865," in Hodgins, Wright, and Heick, eds., Federalism in Canada and Australia, 19-41.

there anything incompatible in these two things? Cannot we have both? What is the difficulty?"[57]

The difficulty was with the traditional understanding of federalism, and as long as the Reformers accepted the doctrine of undivided sovereignty, these desiderata—central power and provincial autonomy—were indeed incompatible. But as the Reformers were pressed, especially by Lower Canadians, to provide a more solid constitutional foundation for provincial government, they began to wonder aloud whether their choices were quite as limited as traditional federal theory seemed to suggest. The Reform supporters of Confederation were neither sufficiently presumptuous nor sufficiently sophisticated to reject the conventional understanding of sovereignty outright. But in the period preceding Confederation they did begin, albeit tentatively, to offer a second description of Confederation that differed in subtle, but important, ways from Macdonald's conception of "political federalism" that I have already described. While on the one hand the Reformers cleaved to the traditional language of legislative and federal union, they asserted on the other that they were creating a new form of political organization that could be described neither as a legislative nor as a federal union but which was a "happy medium" between them, a "compromise" that would allow both for a powerful central government and legally secure provincial legislatures.[58] This is what I will call "constitutional federalism."

IV

The Reformers' attempt to reach an acceptable constitutional compromise can best be understood in light of the American precedent that anticipated both their problem and their solution.... The Reformers defended a constitutional position in 1865 that was in many ways similar to the Federalists' defence of the American Constitution some eighty years before, and it will prove helpful for understanding the pre-Confederation debate to bear in mind the American model. Like the Reformers, the Federalists were accused of creating a constitutional system that pretended to reserve an important place for the states but which in fact would lead ineluctably to their annihilation. Like the Reformers, the Federalists were told that there could be no middle ground between the loosest form of confederation and outright consolidation. And like the Reformers, only more forcefully and clearly, the Federalists attempted to demonstrate that it was possible to dissolve the tension between these two forms of political organization, to create a constitution that was a defensible, principled compromise

---

[57] Toronto Globe, 17 September 1864.
[58] Toronto Globe, 29 August 1864, 3 September 1864, 4 October 1864, 15 October 1864. See also Confederation Debates, 108 (Brown).

between them. In James Madison's famous phrase, the Constitution of 1787 was "in strictness neither a national nor a federal constitution; but a composition of both."[59]

Madison's explanation of this constitutional compromise is now taken to be the first and authoritative definition of modern, "classical" or constitutional federalism.[60] This definition turned on a reformulation of the idea of sovereignty and a qualified rejection of Blackstone's authoritative teaching. For Blackstone, the two great threats to liberty were anarchy on the one hand and kingly prerogative on the other. By defining sovereignty as the power to make laws, Blackstone provided an alternative to the traditional identification between sovereignty and the monarch's will. By locating this sovereign law-making power in one body, even one as complex as Parliament, he provided some final, ultimate political authority that would thereby foreclose the possibility of anarchy.[61] For both reasons a Parliament which could make laws, delegate limited authority to other bodies (or rescind that authority), and enforce the laws, became for Blackstone and those who followed him the central institution of British politics.

For the Federalists (as indeed for the revolutionary generation of 1776), this identification of sovereignty with legislative will was inadequate either to protect liberty or maintain stability. Put bluntly, the pre-Revolution experience with Parliament suggested to the Americans that they could hardly count on Parliament to protect their liberties. Indeed, as the authors of the Declaration of Independence understood very well, Parliament had actually cooperated in the oppression of America. Nor was this all. American experience under the Articles of Confederation suggested the still more sobering lesson that even indigenous, democratically representative legislatures could not be counted on to protect liberty—especially, but by no means exclusively, the right to accumulate and dispose of property. If Parliament, or representative assemblies more generally, threatened liberty, it would not do to allow them to be sovereign. This problem led many Americans to rethink Blackstone's doctrine and to relocate the locus of sovereignty outside of government altogether—in the people-at-large.

The Federalists were particularly quick to seize on this novel understanding of sovereignty because it helped them to see how they could create a constitutional system that would purge the "ill humours" they associated with excessively democratic government without actually abandoning democratic principles.[62] Thus, while a state legislature or the Congress might be called sovereign in some "lower"

---

[59] Alexander Hamilton, James Madison and John Jay, The Federalist Papers (New York: Bantam, 1982), 195.

[60] Wheare, Federal Government, ch. 1.

[61] For a useful analysis of various issues of concern to Americans arising from the gradual acceptance of Blackstone's doctrine of parliamentary sovereignty, see Thomas Grey, "Origins of the Unwritten Constitution: Fundamental Law in American Revolutionary Thought," Stanford Law Review 30 (1978), 865-93.

[62] Federalist Papers, #78, 397.

or "secondary" sense of legislative power, the source of this power, sovereignty in the "higher" sense, rested with "the people." The people, Publius argued, are "the only legitimate fountain of power." They are the "ultimate authority" by which governments are constituted and "the common superior" to which all duly constituted governments are answerable.[63]

This transfer of sovereignty from law-making bodies to the people-at-large had enormous implications for the theory and practice of American politics because it made it possible to conceive of a government that was derived from, but not in any immediate way controlled by, the people. As Judith Shklar has pointed out, the effect of this transfer of sovereignty was to make the people the only legitimate source of authority; but the effect was also to replace the unmediated will of the people—their sovereignty—with a complex set of political and legal processes, federalism included, that could operate without constant popular initiative.[64]

This transformation of the locus (and understanding) of sovereignty was especially important in the case of federalism because it made it possible to contemplate what had previously been unthinkable—the existence of two independent, fully constituted, sovereign governments within the same political system. The people, acting in their original, primal, constituent capacity could create two levels of government, empowered and limited by a constitution. It was no longer necessary to ensure that one level could control, and if necessary destroy, the other because both would be controlled by their "common superior," the people or the constitution framed by the people. Sovereignty remained indivisible. It was vested, in this constituent sense, in the people. But at the same time, federal and state governments could be understood to be "coequal sovereignties," as legally equal, independent governments which derived their authority from, and were protected by, a constitution; governments which were sovereign in the sense that they had full or supreme power to act within the sphere defined by the fundamental law.[65]

Madison described this new understanding as a compromise between outright nationalization and confederalism, and although it was later challenged, we recognize it quite clearly as the first description of classical or constitutional federalism. The

---

[63] These images are taken from The Federalist Papers, #49 (255) and #46 (237) respectively. My debt to Gordon Wood's presentation of the question should be obvious. See Wood, Creation, 372-383.

[64] Shklar, "The Federalist as Myth," 950.

[65] See Wood, Creation, 529 and Hamilton, Madison and Jay, The Federalist Papers, No. 39 (194). Madison did not rest the protection of state interests solely on a judicially patrolled division of powers. Jennifer Smith is quite right to point out that Madison's theory of federalism "extends beyond that to encompass" representation in national institutions. See Jennifer Smith, "Canadian Confederation and the Influence of American Federalism," Canadian Journal of Political Science 21 (1988), 446. See also Samuel H. Beer, "Federalism, Nationalism and Democracy in America," American Political Science Review 72 (1978), 9-21.

members of the Canadian Confederation elite, however, did not recognize the Federalists' project this way. They interpreted the federal provisions of the American Constitution largely in the manner of John Calhoun, and to that extent they continued to believe that the American understanding of federalism, based on the sovereignty of individual states, was misguided beyond remedy. Yet while the Canadians were doing their best to distance themselves from Calhoun's doctrine of state-based confederalism, they were simultaneously groping towards something that in crucial ways resembled the Madisonian understanding of constitutional federalism; and, as with Madison, this search began with a reconsideration of the idea of sovereignty.

The Canadians of the 1860s took Blackstone's understanding of sovereignty as their base. For them, as for Blackstone, sovereignty meant parliamentary sovereignty, and they therefore typically identified sovereignty with legislation, the power to make laws. Yet as the citizens of a largely self-governing colony, the Canadians came in their own way and through their own experience to appreciate the ambiguity of Blackstonian sovereignty. For while the imperial Parliament was sovereign over Canada, the Canadians well understood that this sovereignty did not express itself as directly or with the same bite as in Britain. At least since the time of Lord Durham, it was understood to be in the interest both of the colonies and of Britain to leave British North America to govern itself on those matters that did not directly compromise or conflict with imperial interests. By 1864, Durham's suggestion had become the basis of a well-established, if informal, proto-federal arrangement. To be sure, Parliament passed the basic laws by which the various colonial legislatures governed; it served as the ultimate appeal from colonial legislation; and it reserved the right to involve itself in Canadian affairs when its own interests—as it defined them—were at issue.

Still, by 1864 the Canadian colonists had come to expect that Britain would not as a rule interfere in colonial politics. The Canadians thus understood quite well that sovereignty and legislative power, the source of legitimacy and actual governance, need not be identical. The Toronto *Globe* insisted, as Madison had, that it would be a mistake in framing or interpreting a constitution to assume that sovereignty and legislative power were simply synonymous. As the *Globe* noted, one could easily conceive of a government that was sovereign but which exercised little legislative power, having delegated "a very wide range of duties" to some other authority.[66] Conversely, one could imagine a local government that legislated on a host of subjects even though it was not nominally sovereign. This was, after all, basically how the empire worked, and in Canadian eyes it provided a useful model.

The conceptual wedge having been driven between sovereignty and legislative power, the debate over Confederation allowed (or perhaps forced) the supporters of the proposal to push the distinction still further so as to defend the Confederation proposal against those who believed it would lead to the destruction of local

---

[66] Toronto Globe, 1 August 1864; see also the edition of 30 August 1864.

governments. In this respect the distinction between sovereignty and legislative power was important to the *Globe* for much the same reason that it was important to Madison: it allowed the supporters of Confederation to break out of the familiar pattern of federal thinking, to find a "middle ground" which would secure a firm constitutional foundation for provincial legislation without sacrificing vigorous central leadership.

The Dorions, to recall, had argued that under the terms of the Confederation proposal the federal government would be able to legislate on virtually any matter, no matter how local, and override any provincial legislation, no matter how innocuous. Armed with the distinction between sovereignty and power, the advocates of Confederation were able to respond that this misrepresented the sovereign basis of Confederation and therefore underestimated the extent of provincial security. True, the federal government would be a powerful government, but it would not be a sovereign government in the full Blackstonian sense of the term. It did not create the provincial governments and could not destroy them; it could not unilaterally change the terms of the agreement and was not the final authority to which an aggrieved party could turn for redress. Only the imperial Parliament would be sovereign in this fundamental, constituent sense of the term. In the Canadian scheme, therefore, the imperial Parliament performed much the same function and was sovereign in much the same way that the people were sovereign in the United States; it would be the source and ultimate authority over the legitimate exercise of political power. By precisely the same reasoning, the BNA Act would do in Canada what the Constitution did in the United States: it would empower and limit the various governments by law.

Of course the substance of the Reformers' understanding of sovereignty was not identical to the American, and they did not intend it to be. The Reform view maintained a world of difference between vesting ultimate sovereignty in the people and vesting it in the imperial Parliament, and guarded the difference jealously. The real beauty of the Reformers' argument, therefore, was that it allowed them to adapt their comfortable loyalty to British imperialism to the new categories of American political science, to combine the substance of British political culture with the forms of American government. Thus did the Reformers use their experience of British colonial politics to create a legal structure that in this crucial way resembled American constitutional federalism.

Already by 1864 the Reform press (and even a few Conservative papers) had begun to put together the pieces of this novel federal understanding. A month before the Quebec Conference was convened to discuss federal union of the British North American colonies, the Toronto *Globe* attempted to reassure its public, especially in Quebec, that if a federation were created it would provide adequate protection for the integrity of local government:

> When we speak of local provinces under a federal form of government, we do not mean mere county Councils, but legislatures

empowered by the Imperial Legislature and the Crown to deal with specified matters, and enjoying a prescribed authority, with which "Congress" will not be allowed to interfere. Such legislatures would be beyond the control of the central power, set apart form it, untouchable by it.[67]

Untouchable, the *Globe* pointed out, because provincial jurisdiction would be protected by what Americans—and increasingly Canadians[68]—called a constitution, a fundamental law over which neither federal nor provincial governments would have control:

> The Lower Canadians who have been apprehensive that their rights would not be fully secured will be glad to see the proposition that the distribution of power between the local and general governments shall be clearly fixed by an act of the Imperial Legislature, and shall not be the work of the federal Parliament. This removes all fear of local privileges being tampered with.[69]

Reporting on the Quebec Conference itself, the Hamilton *Weekly Times* concluded that "the functions of the general and local governments, and the subjects delegated to each, must be clearly defined in the constitution, so as to prevent collision and leave security for local interests, the whole to be embodied in an act of the Imperial Parliament."[70] For its part, the Toronto *Leader* noted that while the powers of the local government would be "defined and limited," they would be "conferred by Imperial authority" and so "practically" would not be "subject to recall."[71] The imperial Parliament, being the source of governmental power in Canada, was thus truly sovereign in the constituent sense of the term, and the BNA Act was, as in the United States, a fundamental law by which federal and provincial governments were

---

[67] Ibid., 30 August 1864.

[68] For references to a constitution in this "American" sense of a written, fundamental law, see Toronto Globe, 15 October 1864 ("Surely we can safely put into our constitution...."); 20 June 1867 ("The constitution excludes local and sectional questions from the federal Parliament.... The people of Ontario have got the absolute control of their local affairs, and they have a just representation in the Parliament which deals with the affairs of the Dominion. So far as these cardinal points in the Constitution are concerned, we have all that we asked or could ask").

[69] Toronto Globe, 4 October 1864; see also London Free Press, 26 September 1864; Hamilton Times, 12 August 1864, 7 October 1864; Toronto Leader, 27 September 1864.

[70] Hamilton Weekly Times, 30 September 1864.

[71] Toronto Leader, 27 September 1864. The Leader was in fact a Conservative newspaper, but as Peter Waite notes, it had a "liberal Conservative" slant on the Confederation proposal that brought it closer to Reform doctrine (Life and Times of Confederation, 126).

both empowered and limited. So conceived, the *Globe* could conclude that under the Confederation scheme the federal government would be "precluded from any interference with the legislation of the local bodies, so long as they keep within constitutional limits, and we shall all be quite safe."[72]

By 1867, the view that under the Confederation scheme the provinces would be able to legislate without interference from the federal government had become a standard part of Reform rhetoric. At the Reform convention held only days before the BNA Act came into effect, the first resolution recorded the delegates' "high gratification that the long and earnest contest of the Reform party for the great principles of Representation by Population and local control over local affairs, (had) at last been crowned with triumphant success."[73] Several of the delegates, in speaking to the resolution, seized on the importance of constitutionally protected non-interference. Aemilius Irving reminded the delegates of the editorialist who, at the time of the 1859 Reform Convention, had called for the creation of a federal system that would give the local legislatures "entire control over every public interest, except those and those only that are necessarily common to all parties." The BNA Act, Irving concluded, represented "the most satisfactory fulfilment of the prophecy."[74] George Brown reiterated his now well-worn view that "this Constitution gives us entire control over our own local affairs."[75] The St. Thomas *Journal* came to the same conclusion in its pre-Confederation analysis.[76] And the Toronto *Globe*, in its pre-convention exhortation to Reform delegates, interpreted the impending constitutional change thus: "The people of Ontario have got the absolute control of their local affairs, and they have a just representation in the Parliament which deals with the affairs of the Dominion. So far as these cardinal points in the Constitution are concerned, we have all that we asked or could ask."[77]

---

[72] Toronto Globe, 30 August 1864.
[73] Toronto Globe, 28 June 1867.
[74] Ibid.
[75] Ibid. See also Confederation Debates, 446-47 (Burwell).
[76] Cited and reproduced in the Toronto Globe, 22 June 1867.
[77] Toronto Globe, 20 June 1867. One of the great advantages of emphasizing the constitutional protection of local control from external interference is that the Reformers did not have to face the important intra-party differences that existed about the precise definition of "local." Bruce Hodgins has argued, for instance, that the highly centralist rhetoric that George Brown preferred between 1864 and 1866 was in many ways inconsistent with Reform traditions. Yet as he goes on to point out, there was little discussion, much less recognition of disagreement, about the scope of federal and provincial responsibilities at the time. That evidence fits with the interpretation I have advanced that the central issue for the Reformers was to find a way to insulate local governments — however powerful — from national interference. See Bruce Hodgins, "Disagreement at the Commencement: Divergent Ontario Views of Federalism, 1867-1871," in Donald Swainson, ed., Oliver Mowat's Ontario (Toronto: Macmillan, 1972), 52-59.

Many of the Quebec supporters of Confederation arrived at much the same conclusion and drew out the implications more clearly. A.I.Silver has shown through an exhaustive analysis of Bieu pamphlets and newspapers that the "moderate majority was firm in maintaining that the provinces would be in no way inferior or subordinate to the federal government, that they would be at least its equal, and that each government would be sovereign and untouchable in its own sphere of action."[78] As Joseph Blanchet put it to the Canadian Legislative Assembly: "I consider that under the present plan of Confederation the local legislatures are supreme in respect of the powers which are attributed to them, that is to say, in respect of local matters."[79]

Stung by the Dorions' criticism that the provincial legislatures would have no protection against a central government holding supervisory powers, several of the Bleus were finally moved toward the end of the Confederation Debates to demonstrate that Lower Canada would in fact have nothing to fear. Cartier interrupted A.A. Dorion's attack on the Confederation plan to explain that in the case of jurisdictional collisions the federal government would not be able to run roughshod over the provinces, but that disputes would be resolved by a third party—although he was not quite sure whether this responsibility would devolve upon the imperial authorities or the courts.[80] His colleague Paul Denis argued that the federal government would not have the unilateral power to abolish the use of French by noting that "the Imperial Act will guarantee to us the use of our language."[81]

The clearest defence of the plan, however, was provided by Joseph-Edouard Cauchon. By the time of Confederation, Cauchon was one of the most powerful Conservative figures in Quebec. He had been in public life for some twenty years, having first been elected to the combined Legislative Assembly in 1844. He had held various governmental posts in the intervening years, most notably minister of public works, and enjoyed a high public profile as the editor of the Quebec daily *Le Journal*.

Cauchon's views on federalism were complicated. When the idea of a British North American union was first discussed in the late 1850s, he opposed it because he saw no reason to shake the stability of the established order. By 1864, he had reached the conclusion that something had to be done to meet the challenge presented by American expansionism on the one hand and Anglo-Saxon preponderance on the other. The difficulty, from Cauchon's perspective, was that these threats required quite different reactions. To meet the American threat, Cauchon argued, unity was absolutely necessary; to preserve the French-Canadian nation, some form of separation was needed. The solution, therefore, was to create a centralized federation that also respected the autonomy of the provinces, and it was on this understanding that Cauchon became one of the most vigorous supporters of the Confederation

---

[78] Silver, French-Canadian Idea, 43.
[79] Confederation Debates, 547.
[80] Ibid., 690.
[81] Ibid., 876.

proposal. The Dorions maintained that the central government would have "sovereign power ... over the legislatures of the provinces." Cauchon denied it:

> There will be no absolute sovereign power, each legislature having its distinct and independent attributes, not proceeding from one or the other by delegation, either form above or from below. The Federal Parliament will have legislative sovereign power in all questions submitted to its control in the Constitution. So also the local legislatures will be sovereign in all matters which are specifically assigned to them.[82]

In the case of conflict, matters would be settled by "the judicial tribunals,...charged by the very nature of their functions to declare whether such a law of the Federal Parliament or of the local legislatures does or does not affect the Constitution."[83] And he understood that, as the ultimate source of both federal and provincial power, the Imperial Parliament—not one of the constituted governments—would have the final authority to judge on questions pertaining to the Canadian constitution.[84] This was pure Madisonian logic applied to the Canadian case.

To be sure, the Reform and Bleu understanding of federalism as it was expressed in the years 1864-1867 was inchoate, often expedient and frequently confused. Grappling with a new way to think about federalism yet unable to jettison the older conception altogether, they would often move casually from the older to the newer discourse apparently without fully realizing their incompatibility. Yet it would be wrong to dismiss their contribution to the Confederation debate simply because their thought was often obscure, self-interested or even contradictory. For one thing, if these supporters sometimes described federalism in a way that was more compatible with John A. Macdonald's vision, so Macdonald conceded something to them and, in so doing, rendered his own conception deeply ambiguous. It is an indication of the force of the new constitutional conception of federalism that despite all of the centralizing mechanisms even Macdonald was forced to accept its core principle: the principle that, within its sphere of jurisdiction, each province has the "exclusive" power to legislate. That is how he presented the proposal publicly, and that is how the BNA Act was drafted and passed.[85]

---

[82] Ibid., 697 (Cauchon).
[83] Ibid.
[84] Confederation Debates, 575-576 (Cauchon); see also Joseph Cauchon, L'Union des Provinces de L'Amérique Britannique du Nord (Quebec: A Côté, 1865), 40; and Confederation Debates, 690 (Cartier).
[85] See 27 above. Macdonald also adopted the Reform image that emphasized the novelty of the Confederation proposal, calling it a "happy medium" between a legislative and a federal union. See Confederation Debates, 33, and Toronto Globe, 15 October 1864. Compare that

Moreover, however imperfectly the federal principle was understood in 1865, it provided a foundation on which to build a more impressive and coherent constitutional doctrine. The discovery of federal theory in the years preceding Confederation played a crucial part in the subsequent struggle for provincial rights because it allowed the provincial autonomists to treat Macdonald's centralizing mechanisms as if they were impurities that had to be removed from the constitutional system. They could thus claim that, in attempting to secure the real autonomy of the provinces against Macdonaldian centralism, they were fulfilling the spirit of the constitution of 1867, not undermining it—a difference of real rhetorical importance. In short, the discovery of the federal principle allowed the autonomists to create their own founding myth around the Confederation settlement, to prosecute their political goals in the name of constitutional principle, and to dictate the terms in which the debate was carried on. As we will see, this creation of a new language of federalism in Canada was enormously advantageous to the provincial rights movement and deeply significant for Canadian constitutional discourse.

V

It did not take long before the language of constitutional federalism—of inviolable spheres of legislative autonomy—became the *lingua franca* of constitutional discourse in Canada. Before 1867 the disagreement about the role and status of the provincial governments remained latent and inoffensively general. Once the ink was dry on the BNA Act, however, these differences came into the open while the meaning and implications of the federal principle were refined into a versatile and powerful constitutional doctrine. It cannot be overstressed that the most serious and damaging criticism of John A. Macdonald's centralism came not from those who actively opposed Confederation, but from those who had been part of the coalition that engineered its passage. Three episodes—involving the privileges and immunities of the legislatures, the dual mandate and better terms for Nova Scotia—set the tone for what was to come.

In 1869, the Ontario legislature passed a bill that conferred the traditional privileges and immunities associated with parliamentary government—immunity from prosecution for slander, for example—on members of the Legislative Assembly and its employees.[86] Upon review by the federal government, however, the act was struck down (that is, "disallowed") for being beyond the power of the provincial legislature. John A. Macdonald, who served both as prime minister and attorney general in the first federal cabinet, explained that while the BNA Act expressly conferred the power to define "the privileges and immunities of the Senate and House

---

with Madison's characterization of the American Constitution as a "composition" of national and confederal elements.

[86] 32 Vict. ch. 3.

of Commons" on the Parliament of Canada, it said nothing about the provincial legislatures. Even in the absence of such clear authorization, the federal government could still argue that the definition of parliamentary privileges pertained to the "peace, order and good government" of the country. But the provincial legislatures, he noted, had no corresponding general power to legislate "for the good government of the provinces" as a whole. It must, therefore, be assumed that the Ontario act was "in excess of the power of the provincial legislature."[87]

As in many of the subsequent disputes this formal explanation of the constitutional issue barely hints at the larger, symbolic significance of the provincial action. The first premier of Ontario, John Sandfield Macdonald, was not known as a champion of provincial rights. Though of Reform stock, he had opposed Confederation and had been persuaded by John A. Macdonald to head a coalition government in Ontario.[88] Yet even Sandfield bridled at the suggestion that the provincial legislatures could not define the rules by which they governed themselves. It was "singular," Premier Macdonald wrote in reply to the disallowance report, that the provincial legislature should be allowed to "confer such privileges upon any court or municipal body" but that it "should not be able to grant them to itself."[89] More seriously, it was an affront to the "dignity" of the provincial legislature, rendering it "more feeble than a justice of the peace, who has a right to punish contempt committed at his petty sessions."[90] This was the crux of the issue, and this is why the premier took it so seriously. From John Sandfield's perspective, the disallowance of this apparently innocuous legislation conveyed the clear message that the federal government considered the provinces to be less independent, less sovereign, in short less worthy of respect even than municipal councils. What Ontario affirmed, and what the federal government apparently denied, was that the provincial legislatures were full-fledged parliaments, not municipal councils or local corporations: independent, sovereign, and as deserving of respect as any other parliament, the one in Ottawa included.

In the end and despite the veto, Ottawa acquiesced. Having disallowed both the Ontario law and a similar Quebec law in 1869, the federal government declined to strike down a repackaged version of the parliamentary privileges act when it was passed by the Quebec legislature in 1870.[91] Macdonald still had "great doubts whether the legislature had jurisdiction." But he ultimately judged it "inexpedient to interfere" when the act was thought necessary "to uphold the authority and dignity of

---

[87] W.E. Hodgins, comp., Correspondence, Reports of the Ministers of Justice, and Orders in Council upon the Subject of Dominion and Provincial Legislation, 1867-1895 (Ottawa: 1896), 83. (Hereinafter cited as Dominion and Provincial Legislation.)
[88] See Hodgins, John Sandfield Macdonald, ch. 5.
[89] Hodgins, Dominion and Provincial Legislation, 88.
[90] Ibid., 87.
[91] 33 Vict., ch. 5.

the provincial legislature."[92] Several years later, with a Liberal administration in power federally, the Ontario legislature repassed its parliamentary privileges bill without incident.

Of greater substantive importance was the abolition of the "dual mandate," the practice which allowed the same person to represent a constituency simultaneously in the provincial legislature and the federal parliament. In Ontario, for example, John Sandfield Macdonald was both premier of the province and a federal member of Parliament, while on the other side Edward Blake both led the Liberal party in the Ontario legislature and sat on the Liberal side in the House of Commons. As W.L. Morton has observed,[93] the practice of dual representation "was in many ways a continuation of the Union" that had preceded Confederation, for it supposed that "local" and "national" issues could be, and in the interests of harmony ought to be, deliberated upon by the same people. Brown Chamberlin, one of John A. Macdonald's closest political allies in Quebec, explained the purpose of dual representation this way:

> Every man who has studied history carefully, especially the history of Federal Governments, knows that the greatest danger to their stability lies in the amount of jealousy and friction likely to grow up between the Local and the General Governments. This is especially seen in the history of the United States. That country has suffered in consequence of the Powers exercised by the Local and the General Governments being ill defined, and it has resulted in imposing upon that people a constitution that their forefathers would never have assented to. We should avoid this jealousy rising up against the General Government. By having some members in the Local Legislatures, we will promote a spirit of harmony between them and the General Government. They will carry our views into the Local Legislatures, and they will bring us back some ideas acquired by mingling with their orators.

The ultimate, and salutary, effect of dual representation would thus be "to ward off continual collision between the Local and the General Governments."[94]

Chamberlin's defence of dual representation was transparently centralist; the object, as the foregoing quotation says directly, was to protect the central government rorm jealous provincial governments, not the other way around. The opposition to dual representation was led by David Mills (1831-1903), the Liberal MP for the southwestern Ontario constituency of Bothwell. Mills is one of the most

---

[92] Hodgins, Dominion and Provincial Legislation, 256.

[93] W.L. Morton, "Confederation: 1870-1896," in McKillop, ed., Contexts of Canada's Past, 227.

[94] Canada, Parliament, House of Commons Debates, 28 November 1867, 149.

remarkable, and least known, figures of late-nineteenth-century Canadian politics. Member of Parliament for some thirty years, newspaper editor, law professor, minister of justice under Laurier, associate justice of the Supreme Court—Mills was in all of this one of the leading defenders of provincial rights in the formative period of Confederation. Mills's background was quite typical of the Reform movement to which he belonged. He was born in Canada, grew up in rural, southwestern Ontario, and was given a strong religious education. Upon graduating from the local common school, Mills apparently received further private tuition, worked as a school inspector for almost a decade, then, in 1865, left the family farm to attend law school at the University of Michigan.

Mills's views about law, especially the constitutional basis of federalism, were decisively shaped at Michigan by Thomas Cooley. Cooley was one of the dominant legal minds in the U.S. in the latter part of the nineteenth century.[95] His treatise on the "Constitutional Limitations which Rest Upon the Legislative Power of the States of the American Union"[96] is considered one of the classic expositions of the period and one of the leading mid-century attempts to fashion American law into a systematic whole. Cooley's treatise was adapted from his lectures on the same subject at Michigan, lectures which Mills attended. For a Canadian, they were of special value in explaining with great clarity the sovereign basis of American federalism. Mills's notes record Cooley's words thus:

> In every country sovereign power is recognized as resting somewhere, and wherever that power is lodged there too reposes the power to amend or change the constitution. A constitution is expressive of the present will of the sovereign power. The power to change the constitution rests with the person or body that is sovereign. Here the sovereign power is with the people, not with the law making power. The legislature of the state or nation derives its power form the constitution and is subject to it.[97]

From this it followed, according to Cooley, that "both the state and national legislature are sovereign in a qualified sense." Each is sovereign in that each has "complete jurisdiction over the persons and property within its territorial limits." But this sovereignty is qualified in that this authority is limited to "a certain class of subjects"[98] as defined by the Constitution. Here, succinctly, was a description of the

---

[95] On Cooley, see Alan R. Jones, The Constitutional Conservatism of Thomas McIntyre Cooley (New York: Garland Publishing Inc., 1987).

[96] (Boston: Little Brown, 1874).

[97] Mills Papers, Box 4285, Notes on Prof. Cooley's "State Constitutional Law and Legislative Limitations," 1.

[98] Ibid., 8.

federal principle towards which the Reformers groped their way in the years preceding Confederation.

Cooley provided much more than a formal framework for understanding federalism, however, Cooley's legal universe was informed by a fundamental tension between legislative will and constitutional limitation. The object of government, Cooley stated, is "to give each person the greatest amount of security with the least curtailment of liberty." Government is necessary, but unrestrained it threatens to overwhelm the liberty or independence of those less powerful than it. It is consequently necessary, Mills recorded, to keep government from going "beyond its own legitimate province," and to keep governmental power within "its prescribed limits."[99] Specifically constitutional governments, including federal governments, "are such as not only locate the sovereign power but define the power of individuals and bodies and limit the exercise of this power with a view to protect individual rights and shield them against arbitrary action."[100] Power and the limitations on power to secure liberty—this was the theme, indeed the title, both of Cooley's course and of his treatise.

This was the understanding of federalism as a form of constitutional government that Mills applied to the question of dual representation. As Mills understood it, the BNA Act "called into existence a number of independent Legislatures with limited powers ... each having exclusive jurisdiction within the sphere assigned to it by the Constitutional Act."[101] Like Cooley, however, Mills assumed that neither federal nor provincial legislatures could be trusted to stay within the jurisdictional boundaries that were meant to separate them:

> It was a matter which the experience of men in every department of life fully justified, and one resulted from the imperfections of human nature, that if a man was placed in any position he would always attempt to arrogate to himself more power than was necessary for the discharge of the duties which devolve upon him.[102]

Considering the evident weakness of the provincial legislatures, it was especially important to ensure that the "barriers erected by the Constitution"[103] were respected by the federal government.

Federalism, like all social relations, was essentially competitive. The only way to regulate the competition, therefore, was to give both governments, but especially the provinces, the defensive capacity to "mutually check each other."[104] This

---

[99] Ibid.
[100] Ibid., 2.
[101] Canada, Parliament, House of Commons Debates, 28 April 1869, 96.
[102] Ibid., 28 February 1871, 200.
[103] Ibid., 28 November 1867, 149.
[104] Ibid., 28 February 1871, 200.

competitive premise left no room for cooperation, alliance or even divided loyalties among federal and provincial representatives. Mills explained the implications of his understanding to Parliament as follows:

> A gentleman having a seat in this House as well as in a Local Legislature was like a person who was a partner in two firms, one of which could not gain except at the expense of the other. When he found the house trespassing on the powers of the Local Legislatures, it was not his interest to object, because as a member of this house he would share in the advantage of the powers thus usurped.[105]

The object of the constitution, in other words, was quite different from what Brown Chamberlin suggested. It was not to create harmony or alliances. Rather, the object of the "federal principle" was "to enable the different Governments to carry on their functions independentally (sic) and without interference."[106] To protect this freedom within the limits of law (what Mills and others variously called independence, autonomy or sovereignty), "it is necessary that the Local Legislature be composed of persons entirely distinct from the general Government, in order to prevent the Parliament of Canada from making encroachments upon the Local Government."[107]

In 1873, after several unsuccessful attempts, Mills managed to shepherd his bill prohibiting dual representation through Parliament. One by one the provincial legislatures that had permitted the practice passed similar legislation, with the result that by 1874 dual representation had disappeared in Canada. Thereafter, as W.L. Morton has astutely observed, "two separate kinds of politicians developed, the national and the provincial,"[108] and from that ensued the very sort of competition that Mills had said was the normal state of affairs in a federation....

These...episodes suggest an important lesson. The immediate post-Confederation period was crucial for the development of Canadian federalism because it proved conclusively that the Confederation settlement, far from settling matters, had in fact lent legitimacy to two quite different visions of Canada, the one represented by the relentless centralism of Macdonald, the other dedicated to the establishment of provincial governments which were legally autonomous and independent—supreme within the sphere allotted to them by the constitution.

---

[105] Ibid., 28 April 1869, 96.
[106] Ibid., 28 November 1867, 154.
[107] Ibid., 149.
[108] W.L. Morton, "Confederation, 1870-1896," in McKillop, ed., Contexts of Canada's Past, 227.

National Development Policies

Section 11

It wasn't till more than a decade after Confederation that the Conservative party came up with its coherent programme for national economic development—an integrated plan in which the all-Canadian railroad to the Pacific, the settlement of the prairies, and a protective tariff would all contribute to the growth of a national economy based on an eastward flow of prairie wheat and a westward flow of Canadian manufactured goods. Of those three elements, the protective tariff, which Macdonald referred to as his "National Policy," became the most controversial, and in the end—after more than a century—it has been abandoned in favour of free trade with the United States and participation in the GATT.

Two of the most frequent criticisms of the National Policy during its long career were that it promoted the economic dominance of Ontario and Quebec by concentrating manufacturing in those provinces at the expense of other regions—and that it turned Canada into a mere branch plant of the United States by encouraging American companies to set up local subsidiary operations here.

These may seem to be strange results for a policy that was supposed to be "National" and that was supposed to promote *Canadian* manufacturing. How, then, did they come about? Why did people support the policy in the first place if it was going to produce such results? These are some of the questions answered in the two essays presented here. Why did Maritime businessmen support the National Policy? Did they gain any benefits from it? Why did they lose out in the end to central Canadian interests? Were promoters of the tariff unaware that it would encourage American operations in Canada? Why did that not bother them?

The origins and adoption of the protective tariff are analysed in Ben Forster, *A Conjunction of Interests: Business, Politics and Tariffs, 1825-1879.* For some modern criticism of the National Policy, see John Dales, "Protection, Immigration, and Canadian Nationalism," in Peter Russell, ed., *Nationalism in Canada.*

The National Policy and the Industrialization of the Maritimes 1880-1910

T.W. Acheson

The Maritime provinces of Canada in 1870 probably came the closest of any region to representing the classic ideal of the staple economy. Traditionally shaped by the Atlantic community, the region's industrial sector had been structured to the production and export of timber, lumber products, fish and ships. The last was of crucial significance. In terms of the balance of trade, it accounted for more than one-third of New Brunswick's exports at Confederation. In human terms, the manufacture of ships provided a number of towns with large groups of highly skilled, highly paid craftsmen who were able to contribute significantly to the quality of community life. Against this background, the constricting British market for lumber and ships after 1873 created a serious economic crisis for the area. This was not in itself unusual. Throughout the nineteenth century the region's resource-based economy had suffered a series of periodic recessions as the result of changing imperial policies and world markets. Yet, in one respect, this crisis differed from all earlier; while the lumber markets gradually returned in the late 1870s, the ship market did not. Nova Scotians continued to build their small vessels for the coasting trade, but the large ship building industry failed to revive.

In the face of this uncertain future the National Policy was embraced by much of the Maritime business community as a new mercantilism which would re-establish that stability which the region had enjoyed under the old British order. In the first years of its operation the Maritimes experienced a dramatic growth in manufacturing potential, a growth often obscured by the stagnation of both the staple industries and population growth. In fact, the decade following 1879 was characterized by a significant transfer of capital and human resources from the traditional staples into a new manufacturing base which was emerging in response to federal tariff policies. This development was so significant that between 1881 and 1891 the industrial growth rate of Nova Scotia outstripped all other provinces in eastern Canada.[1] The comparative growth of the period is perhaps best illustrated in St. John. The relative increase in industrial capital, average wages, and output in this community

---

[1] Nova Scotia's industrial output increased 66 per cent between 1880 and 1890; that of Ontario and Quebec by 51 per cent each. Canada, *Census* (1901), III, pp. 272, 283. Bertram estimates that the per capita value of Nova Scotia's industrial output rose from 57.8 per cent to 68.9 per cent of the national average during the period. Gordon Bertram, "Historical Statistics on Growth and Structure of Manufacturing in Canada 1870-1957," Canadian Political Science Association Conference on Statistics 1962 and 1963, *Report*, p. 122.

significantly surpassed that of Hamilton, the Canadian city whose growth was perhaps most directly attributable to the protective tariff.[2]

Within the Atlantic region the growth of the 1880s was most unequally distributed. It centred not so much on areas or sub-regions as upon widely scattered communities.[3] These included the traditional Atlantic ports of St. John, Halifax, and Yarmouth; lumbering and ship building towns, notably St. Stephen and New Glasgow; and newer railroad centres, such as Moncton and Amherst. The factors which produced this curious distribution of growth centres were human and historical rather than geographic. The one characteristic shared by them all was the existence in each of a group of entrepreneurs possessing the enterprise and the capital resources necessary to initiate the new industries. Strongly community-oriented, these entrepreneurs attempted, during the course of the 1880s, to create viable manufacturing enterprises in their local areas under the aegis of the protective tariff. Lacking the resources to survive the prolonged economic recessions of the period, and without a strong regional metropolis, they acquiesced in the 1890s to the industrial leadership of the Montreal business community. Only at the century's end, with the expansion of the consolidation movement, did a group of Halifax financiers join their Montreal counterparts in asserting an industrial metropolitanism over the communities of the eastern Maritimes. This paper is a study in that transition.

I

The Maritime business community in the 1870s was dominated by three groups: wholesale shippers, lumber and ship manufacturers, and the small scale manufacturers of a variety of commodities for purely local consumption. As a group they were deeply divided on the question of whether the economic salvation of their various communities was to be found in the maintenance of an Atlantic mercantile system, or in a programme of continentalist-oriented

---

[2] Canada, *Census* (1901), III, pp. 326-9. The increase between 1880 and 1890 was as follows:

	St. John	Hamilton
Population	-3%	34%
Industrial Capital	125%	69%
Industrial Workers	118%	48%
Average Annual Wage	12%	2%
Value of Output	98%	71%

[3] See Table 1.

Table I—Industrial Development in Principal Maritime Centres 1880-1890

	Population	Industrial Capital	Employees	Average Annual Wages	Output	Industry by Output (1891)
Halifax (1880)	39,886	$2,975,000	3,551	$303	$6,128,000	Sugar[**]
Dartmouth (1890)	43,132	$6,346,000	4,654	$280	$8,235,000	Rope,[*] Cotton, Confectionary, Paint and Lamps
St. John (1880)	41,353	$2,143,000	2,690	$278	$4,123,000	Lumber[**]
(1890)	39,179	$4,838,000	5,888	$311	$8,131,000	Machinery,[***] Smelting, Rope,[**] Cottons, Brass,[*] Nails[*] and Elect. Light[*]
New Glasgow(1880)	2,595	$160,000	360	$255	$313,000	Primary Steel[*]
(1890)	3,777	$1,050,000	1,117	$355	$1,512,000	Rolling Mills[**] and Glass
St. Stephen (1880)	4,002	$136,000	447	$314	$573,000	Cottons
Milltown (1890)	4,826	$1,702,000	1,197	$320	$1,494,000	Confectionary, Fish Canning, Soap and Lumber
Moncton(1880)	5,032	$530,000	603	$418	$1,719,000	Sugar
(1890)	8,765	$1,134,000	948	$333	$1,973,000	Cottons, Woolens and Rolling Stock
Fredericton(1880)	7,218[a]	$1,090,000[a]	911[a]	$221[a]	$1,031,000[a]	Cottons
Marysville(1890)	8,394	$2,133,000	1,526	$300	$1,578,000	Lumber and Foundry Product
Yarmouth(1880)	3,485	$290,000	211	$328	$284,000	Cotton Yarn[*]
(1890)	6,089	$783,000	930	$312	$1,234,000	Fish Canning and Woolens
Amherst(1880)	2,274	$81,000	288	$281	$283,000	Foundry Product
(1890)	3,781	$457,000	683	$293	$724,000	Shoes and Doors

[a] Estimates, Marysville was not an incorporated town in 1880, and totals for that date must be estimated from York County figures.
[*] Leading Canadian Producer. [**] Second. [***] Third.
Source: Canada. *Census* (1891), III, Table 1: Ibid., (1901), III, Tables XX, XXI.

industrial diversification. A wedding of the two alternatives appeared to be the ideal situation. While they had warily examined the proposed tariff of 1879, most leading businessmen accepted its philosophy and seriously attempted to adapt it to their community needs.[4]

---

[4] For a sampling of business opinion on the National Policy see K.P. Burn's reply to Peter Mitchell in the tariff debate of 1883, Canada. House of Commons, *Debates*, 1883, pp. 551-2;

For a variety of reasons the tariff held the promise of prosperity for the region's traditional commercial activities and, as well, offered the possibilities for the development of new manufacturing industry. For most Nova Scotian business leaders the West Indies market was vital to the successful functioning of the province's commercial economy. It was a major element in the region's carrying trade and also provided the principal market for the Nova Scotia fishing industry. These, in turn, were the foundations of the provincial shipbuilding industry. The successful prosecution of the West Indies trade, however, depended entirely upon the ability of the Nova Scotia merchants to dispose of the islands' sugar crop. The world depression in the 1870s had resulted in a dramatic decline in the price of refined sugar as French, German, British and American refineries dumped their surplus production on a glutted world market. By 1877 more than nine-tenths of Canadian sugar was obtained from these sources,[5] a fact which threatened the Nova Scotia carrying trade with disaster. A significant tariff on foreign sugar, it was felt, would encourage the development of a Canadian refining industry which would acquire all of its raw sugar from the British West Indies. Through this means, most Nova Scotian wholesalers and shippers saw in the new policy an opportunity both to resuscitate the coastal shipping industry of the province and to restore their primacy in the West Indies.

Of the newer industries which the National Policy offered, the future for the Maritimes seemed to lie in textiles and iron and steel products. The optimism concerning the possibilities of the former appears to have emerged out of a hope of emulating the New England experience. This expectation was fostered by the willingness of British and American cotton mill machinery manufacturers to supply on easy terms the necessary duty-free equipment, and by the feeling of local businessmen that the market provided by the tariff and the low quality labour requirements of such an enterprise would guarantee that a profitable business could be erected and maintained by the efforts of a single community. Behind such reasoning lay the general assumption that, despite major transportation problems, the Maritimes, and notably Nova Scotia, would ultimately become the industrial centre of Canada. The assumption was not unfounded. The region contained the only commercially viable coal and iron deposits in the Dominion, and had the potential, under the tariff, of controlling most of the Montreal fuel sources. Under these circumstances the development of textiles and the expansion of most iron and steel industries in the Atlantic area was perhaps not a surprising project.

Despite a cautious enthusiasm for the possibilities offered by the new federal economic dispensation, there was considerable concern about the organizational and financial problems in creating a new industrial structure. The Maritimes was a region of small family firms with limited capital capabilities. Other than chartered banks, it

---

[5] the opinion of Josiah Wood, ibid., pp. 446-8; and the view of John F. Stairs, ibid., 1885, pp. 641-9.
Quoted by J.F. Stairs in the tariff debate of 1886, Canada, House of Commons, *Debates*, 1886, p. 775.

lacked entirely the financial structure to support any large corporate industrial entity. Like the people of Massachusetts, Maritimers were traditionally given to placing their savings in government savings banks at a guaranteed 4 per cent interest rather than in investments on the open market.[6] Regional insurance, mortgage and loan, and private savings corporations were virtually unknown. The result was to throw the whole financial responsibility for undertaking most manufactories upon the resources of individual entrepreneurs.

Since most enterprises were envisioned as being of general benefit to the community at large, and since few businessmen possessed the necessary capital resources to single-handedly finance such an undertaking, most early industrial development occurred as the result of co-operative efforts by groups of community entrepreneurs. These in turn were drawn from a traditional business elite of wholesalers and lumbermen. In Halifax as early as May, 1879, a committee was formed from among the leading West Indies shippers "to solicit capital, select a site and get a manufacturing expert" for the organization of a sugar refinery.[7] Under its leadership $500,000 was raised, in individual subscriptions of $10-20,000, from among members of the Halifax business community. This procedure was repeated during the formation of the Halifax Cotton Company in 1881; more than $300,000 was subscribed in less than two weeks, most of it by thirty-two individuals.[8]

The leadership in the development of these enterprises was taken by young members of traditional mercantile families. The moving spirit in both cases was Thomas Kenny. A graduate of the Jesuit Colleges at Stonyhurst (England) and St. Gervais (Belgium), Kenny had inherited from his father, the Hon. Sir Edward Kenny, M.L.A., one of the largest wholesale shipping firms in the region. In the early 1870s the younger Kenny had invested heavily in shipyards scattered throughout five counties of Nova Scotia, and had even expanded into England with the establishment of a London branch for his firm. Following the opening of the refinery in 1881, he devoted an increasingly large portion of his time to the management of that firm.[9] Kenny was supported in his efforts by a number of leading merchants including the Hon. Robert Boak, Scottish-born president of the Legislative Council, and John F. Stairs, Manager of the Dartmouth Rope Works. Stairs, who had attended Dalhousie University, was a member of the executive council of Nova Scotia, the son of a legislative councillor, and a grandson of the founder of the shipping firm of William Stairs, Son and Morrow Limited.[10]

---

6   *Monetary Times*, 4 June, 6 September 1886. Forty-five of the fifty savings banks in the Dominion were located in the Maritimes.
7   *Monetary Times*, 16 May 1879.
8   *Monetary Times*, 20 May 1881.
9   George M. Rose, ed., *Cyclopedia of Canadian Biography* (Toronto, 1886-9), II. pp. 729-31, henceforth cited as CCB).
10 *Encyclopedia of Canadian Biography* (Montreal, 1904-7), I, p. 86; CCB, II. p. 155; W.J. Stairs, *History of Stairs Morrow* (Halifax, 1906), pp. 5-6.

In contrast to Halifax, St. John had always been much more a manufacturing community and rivalled Ottawa as the principal lumber manufacturing centre in the Dominion. Development in the New Brunswick city occurred as new growth on an existing industrial structure and centred on cotton cloth and iron and steel products. The New Brunswick Cotton Mill had been erected in 1861 by an Ulster-born St. John shipper, William Parks, and his son, John H. Parks. The latter, who had been trained as a civil engineer under the tutelage of the chief engineer of the European and North American Railroad, assumed the sole proprietorship of the mill in 1870.[11] In 1881 he led the movement among the city's dry goods wholesalers to establish a second cotton mill which was incorporated as the St. John Cotton Company.

The principal St. John iron business was the firm of James Harris. Trained as a blacksmith, the Annapolis-born Harris had established a small machine shop in the city in 1828, and had expanded into the foundry business some twenty-three years later. In 1883, in consequence of the new tariff, he determined to develop a completely integrated secondary iron industry including a rolling mill and a railway car plant. To provide the resources for the expansion, the firm was reorganized as a joint stock company with a $300,000 capital most of which was raised by St. John businessmen. The New Brunswick Foundry Rolling Mills and Car Works, with a plant covering some five acres of land, emerged as the largest industrial employer in the Maritimes.[12] The success of the Harris firm induced a group of wholesale hardware manufacturers under the leadership of the Hon. Isaac Burpee, a former member of the Mackenzie Government, to re-establish the Coldbrook Rolling Mills near the city.

Yet, despite the development of sugar and cotton industries and the expansion of iron and rope manufactories, the participation of the St. John and Halifax business communities in the industrial impulse which characterized the early 1880s can only be described as marginal. Each group played the role of participant within its locality but neither provided any positive leadership to its hinterland area. Even in terms of industrial expansion, the performance of many small town manufacturers was more impressive than that of their city counterparts.

At the little railway centre of Moncton, nearly $1,000,000 was raised under the leadership of John and Christopher Harris, John Humphrey, and Josiah Woods, to permit the construction of a sugar refinery, a cotton mill, a gas light and power plant, and several smaller iron and textile enterprises. The Harris brothers, sons of an Annapolis ship builder of Loyalist extraction, had established a shipbuilding and shipping firm at Moncton in 1856.[13] Under the aegis of their firm they organized the new enterprises with the assistance of their brother-in-law John Humphrey, scion of Yorkshire Methodist settlers of the Tantramar, longtime M.L.A. for

---

[11] *Canadian Biographical Dictionary* (Montreal, 1880-1), II, pp. 684-5 (henceforth cited as CBD); Parks Family Papers, F. no. 1, New Brunswick Museum.

[12] *CBD*, II, pp. 684-5; *Monetary Times*, 27 April 1883, 22 June 1888.

[13] *CCB*, II, pp. 186-7, 86.

Westmoreland, and proprietor of the Moncton flour and woollen mills. They were financially assisted in their efforts by Josiah Wood (Later Senator) of nearby Sackville. The son of a Loyalist wholesaler, Wood first completed his degrees (B.A., M.A.) at Mount Allison, was later admitted to the New Brunswick bar, and finally entered his father's shipping and private banking business.[14] The leadership of the Moncton group was so effective that the owner of the *Monetary Times*, in a journey through the region in 1882, singled out the community for praise:

> Moncton has industrialized ... business people only in moderate circumstances but have united their energies ... persons who have always invested their surplus funds in mortgages are now cheerfully subscribing capital for the Moncton Cotton Co. Unfortunately for industrial progress, there are too many persons [in this region] who are quite content with receiving 5 or 6% for their money so long as they know it is safe, rather than risk it in manufactures, even supposing it yielded double the profit.[15]

At St. Stephen the septuagenarian lumber barons and bankers, James Murchie and Freeman Todd, joined the Annapolis-born ship builder, Zechariah Chipman, who was father-in-law to the Minister of Finance, Sir Leonard Tilley, in promoting an immense cotton concern, the St. Croix, second largest in the Dominion at the time. The son of a local farmer, Murchie, whose holdings included more than 200,000 acres of timber lands—half of it in Quebec—also developed a number of smaller local manufactories.[16] At the same time two young brothers, Gilbert and James Ganong, grandsons of a Loyalist farmer from the St. John Valley, began the expansion of their small confectionery firm,[17] and shortly initiated construction of a soap enterprise in the town.

At Yarmouth a group of ship builders and West Indies merchants led by the Hon. Loran Baker, M.L.C., a shipper and private banker, and John Lovitt, a shipbuilder and member of the Howland Syndicate, succeeded in promoting the Yarmouth Woolen Mill, the Yarmouth Cotton Manufacturing, the Yarmouth Duck Yarn Company, two major foundries, and a furniture enterprise.[18] The development was entirely an internal community effort—virtually all the leading business figures were

---

14   *CCB*, II, pp. 354-5; *CBD*, II, p. 693; Henry J. Morgan, ed., *Canadian Men and Women of the Time* (Toronto, 1898), p. 1000.
15   *Monetary Times*, 16 December 1882.
16   *CCB*, II, pp. 221-2; *CBD*, II, pp. 674-5; Harold Davis, *An International Community on the St. Croix (1604-1930)* (Orono, 1950), chapter 18; *Monetary Times*, 1 August 1890.
17   Canada. *Sessional Papers*, 1885, no. 37, pp. 174-97.
18   *Monetary Times*, 11 December 1885; *Canadian Journal of Commerce*, 3 June 1881; *CBD*, II, pp. 409-10, 510; *Canadian Men and Women of the Time* (1898), p. 44.

third generation Nova Scotians of pre-Loyalist American origins. A similar development was discernible in the founding of the Windsor Cotton Company.[19]

A somewhat different pattern emerged at New Glasgow, the centre of the Nova Scotia coal industry. Attempts at the manufacture of primary iron and steel had been made with indifferent results ever since Confederation.[20] In 1872, a New Glasgow blacksmith, Graham Fraser, founded the Hope Iron Works with an initial capital of $160,000.[21] As the tariff on iron and steel products increased in the 1880s so did the vertical expansion of the firm. In 1889, when it was amalgamated with Fraser's other enterprise, the Nova Scotia Forge Company, more than two-thirds of the $280,000 capital stock of the resulting Nova Scotia Steel and Coal Company was held by the citizens of New Glasgow.[22] Fraser remained as president and managing director of the corporation until 1904,[23] during which time it produced most of the primary steel in the Dominion,[24] and remained one of the largest industrial corporations in the country.[25]

Fraser was seconded in his industrial efforts by James Carmichael of new Glasgow and John F. Stairs of Halifax. Carmichael, son of a prominent New Glasgow merchant and a descendant of the Scottish founders of Pictou, had established one of the largest ship building and shipping firms in the province.[26] Stair's investment in the New Glasgow iron and steel enterprise represented one of the few examples of inter-community industrial activity in this period.

The most unusual pattern of manufacturing development in the region was that initiated at Fredericton by Alexander Gibson. Gibson's distinctiveness lay in his ability to impose the tradition and structure of an earlier semi-industrial society onto a changing pattern of development. A St. Stephen native and the son of Ulster immigrants, he had begun his career as a sawyer, and later operated a small lumber firm at Lepreau. In 1865 he bought from the Anti-Confederationist government of A.J. Smith extensive timber reserves on the headwaters of the Nashwaak River,[27] and at the mouth of that river, near Fredericton, built his own mill-town of Marysville. Freed from stumpage fees by his fortunate purchase, the "lumber king of

---

[19] *Canadian Journal of Commerce*, 10 June 1881.

[20] W.J.A. Donald. *The Canadian Iron and Steel Industry* (Boston, 1915), chapter 3.

[21] *Monetary Times*, 28 April 1882.

[22] *The Canadian Manufacturer and Industrial World*, 3 May 1889 (henceforth cited as *Canadian Manufacturer*).

[23] Henry J. Morgan, ed., *Canadian Men and Women of the Time* (Toronto, 1912), p. 419; C.W. Parker, ed., *Who's Who and Why* (Vancouver, 1916), VI & VII, p. 259 (hereafter cited as *WWW*).

[24] *Canadian Manufacturer*, 1 April 1892.

[25] Ibid., 7 March 1890.

[26] *CBD*, II, pp. 534-5.

[27] A.G. Bailey, "The Basis and Persistence of Opposition to Confederation in New Brunswick," *Canadian Historical Review*, XXIII (1942), p. 394.

New Brunswick" was producing as much as 100,000,000 feet of lumber annually by the 1880s—about one third of the provincial output. His lumber exports at times comprised half the export commerce of the port of St. John.[28]

One of the wealthiest industrial entrepreneurs in the Dominion, Gibson determined in 1883 to undertake the erection of a major cotton enterprise entirely under his own auspices.[29] He erected one of the largest brick-yards in the Dominion and personally supervised the construction of the plant which was opened in 1885.[30] In that same year he employed nearly 2,000 people in his sundry enterprises.[31] By 1888 his sales of cotton cloth totalled nearly $500,000.[32] That same year the Gibson empire, comprising the cotton mill, timber lands, saw mills, lath mills, the town of Marysville, and the Northern and Western Railroad, was formed into a joint stock company, its $3,000,000 capital controlled by Gibson, his brother, sons and son-in-law.

Several common characteristics distinguished the men who initiated the industrial expansion of the 1880s. They were, on the whole, men of substance gained in traditional trades and staples. They sought a substantial, more secure future for themselves within the framework of the traditional community through the instrumentality of the new industrial mercantilism. Averaging fifty-four years of age, they were old men to be embarking upon new careers.[33] Coupled with this factor of age was their ignorance of both the technical skills and the complexities of the financial and marketing structures involved in the new enterprises.

The problem of technical skill was overcome largely by the importation of management and skilled labour, mainly from England and Scotland.[34] The problem of finance was more serious. The resources of the community entrepreneurs were limited; the costs of the proposed industry were almost always far greater than had been anticipated. Moreover, most businessmen had only the vaguest idea of the quantity of capital required to operate a large manufacturing corporation. Promoters generally followed the normal mercantile practice and raised only sufficient capital to construct and equip the physical plant, preferring to finance operating costs through

---

[28] *Monetary Times*, 9 January 1885.

[29] Ibid., 11 May 1883.

[30] *Our Dominion. Historical and Other Sketches of the Mercantile Interests of Fredericton, Marysville, Woodstock, Moncton, Yarmouth, etc.* (Toronto, 1889), pp. 48-54.

[31] Canada, *Sessional Papers*, 1885, no. 37, pp. 174-97.

[32] Canada, Royal Commission on the Relations of Labour and Capital (1889), *Evidence*, II, p. 448.

[33] American industrial leaders of the same period averaged 45 years. See W.F. Gregory and I.D. New, "The American Industrial Elite in the 1870s: Their Social Origins," in William Miller, ed. *Men in Business* (Cambridge, 1952), p. 197.

[34] Canada, Royal Commission of the Relations of Labour and Capital, *Evidence*, II, pp. 256, 458, and III, pp. 78, 238, 249; *Canadian Manufacturer*, 24 August 1883; *Monetary Times*, 17 June 1887.

bank loans—a costly and inefficient process. The Halifax Sugar Refinery perhaps best illustrated these problems. When first proposed in 1879 it was to have been capitalized at $300,000. Before its completion in 1881 it was re-capitalized twice to a value of $500,000.[35] Even this figure left no operating capital, and the refinery management was forced to secure these funds by loans from the Merchants Bank of Halifax. At the end of its first year of operation the bank debt of the corporation totalled $460,000,[36] which immediately became a fixed charge on the revenues of the infant industry. Fearing bankruptcy, the stockholders increased their subscriptions and kept the business functioning until 1885 when they attempted a solution to the problem by issuing debenture stock to a value of $350,000 of which the bank was to receive $200,000 in stock and $50,000 cash in settlement of debts still owed to it.[37]

While many industries received their initial financing entirely from local capitalists, some projects proved to be such ambitious undertakings that aid had to be sought from other sources. The St. Croix Cotton Company at St. Stephen, for example, was forced to borrow $300,000 from Rhode Island interests to complete their huge plant.[38] Some industries came to rely so heavily on small community banks for perpetual loans for operating expenses that any general economic crisis toppled both the industries and the banks simultaneously. The financing of James Domville's enterprises, including the Coldbrook Rolling Mills, was a contributing factor in the temporary suspension of the Maritime Bank of St. John in 1880,[39] while such industrial loans ultimately brought down the Bank of Yarmouth in 1905.[40]

II

The problem of industrial finance was intricately tied to a whole crisis of confidence in the new order which began to develop as the first enthusiastic flush of industrial expansion paled in the face of the general business downturn which wraked the Canadian economy in the mid-1880s. At the heart of this problem was a gradual deterioration of the British lumber market, and the continued shift from sea borne to railroad commerce. Under the influence of an increasingly prohibitive tariff and an extended railroad building programme a two cycle inter-regional trading pattern was gradually emerging. The westward cycle, by rail into the St. Lawrence basin, left the region with a heavy trade imbalance as the central Canadians rapidly replaced British and American produce in the Maritime market with their own flour and manufactured

---

35 *Monetary Times*, 18 March 1881.
36 Ibid., 17 February 1882.
37 Ibid., 19 March 1886.
38 *Canadian Journal of Commerce*, 26 October 1883.
39 *Monetary Times*, 18 October 1880.
40 Ibid., 10 May 1905.

materials.[41] In return, the region shipped to Montreal quantities of primary and primary manufactured products of both local and imported origins. The secretaries of the Montreal and St. John boards of trade estimated the extent of this inter-regional commerce at about $15,711,000 in 1885, more than 70 per cent of which represented central Canadian exports to the Maritimes.[42] By contrast the external trade cycle moved in traditional fashion by ship from the principal Maritime ports to Great Britain and the West Indies. Heavily balanced in favour of the Maritimes, it consumed most of the output of the region's resource industries. The two cycles were crucially interdependent; the Maritime business community used the credits earned in the external cycle to meet the gaping deficits incurred in the central Canadian trade. The system worked as long as the equilibrium between the two could be maintained. Unfortunately, as the decade progressed, this balance was seriously threatened by a declining English lumber market.[43]

In the face of this increasingly serious trade imbalance, the Maritime business community became more and more critical of what they regarded as the subversion of the National Policy by central Canadian interests. The argument was based upon two propositions. If Canadian transportation policy was dedicated to creating an all-Canadian commercial system, then this system should extend not from the Pacific to Montreal, but from the Pacific to the Atlantic. How, in all justice, could the Montreal interests insist on the construction, at a staggering cost, of an all-Canadian route west of that city and then demand the right to export through Portland or Boston rather than using the Maritime route? This argument was implicit in almost every resolution of the Halifax and St. John boards of trade from 1880 onward.[44]

The second proposition maintained that, as vehicles of nationhood, the railways must be considered as a means of promoting national economic integration rather than as commercial institutions. The timing of this doctrine is significant. Before 1885 most Maritime manufacturers were competitive both with Canadian and foreign producers. Nails, confectionery, woolens, leather, glass, steel and machinery manufactured in the Maritimes normally had large markets in both central Canada and the West.[45] The recession of 1885 reached a trough in 1886.[46] Diminishing demand

---

[41] Ibid., 8 January 1886.

[42] *Monetary Times*, 30 January 1885, Principal Maritime imports from Central Canada included flour, shoes, clothing, textiles, alcoholic beverages and hardware; exports to Quebec and Ontario centred on sugar, coal, cotton cloth, iron and fish.

[43] Exports of New Brunswick lumber declined from 404,000,000 board feet in 1883 to 250,000,000 feet in 1887. *Monetary Times*, 9 January 1885, 2 and 7 January 1887, 21 January 1898.

[44] See particularly, *Proceedings of the Ninth Annual Meeting* of the Dominion Board of Trade (1879), pp. 65-73; *Monetary Times*, 27 January 1882; Minute Book of the St. John Board of Trade (1879-87), 14 October 1887, New Brunswick Museum.

[45] Canada, *Sessional Papers*, 1885, no. 34, pp. 86-125.

[46] Bertram, p. 131.

coupled with over-production, particularly in the cotton cloth and sugar industries, resulted in falling prices, and made it increasingly difficult for many Maritime manufacturers to retain their central Canadian markets. The *bête noir* was seen as the relatively high freight rates charged by the Intercolonial Railway. The issue came to a head late in 1885 with the closing of the Moncton and the two Halifax sugar refineries. The response of the Halifax manufacturers was immediate and decisive. Writing to the Minister of Railways, John F. Stairs enunciated the Maritime interpretation of the National Policy:

> Four refineries have been set in operation in the Lower Provinces by the policy of the Government. This was right; but trade having changed so that it is now impossible for them to work prosperously it is the duty of the Government to accommodate its policy to the change. The reduction in freight rates asked for is necessary to this.... If in answer to this you plead that you must manage so that no loss occur running the I.C.R., we will reply, we do not, and will not accept this as a valid plea from the Government ... and to it we say that the people of Nova Scotia, nor should those of Ontario and Quebec, for they are as much interested, even admit it is essential to make both ends meet in the finance of the railroad, when it can only be done at the expense of inter-provincial trade, and the manufacturers of Nova Scotia.... How can the National Policy succeed in Canada where such great distances exist between the provinces unless the Government who control the National Railway meet the requirements of trade....[47]

At stake, as Stairs later pointed out in a confidential memorandum to Macdonald, was the whole West Indies trade of Nova Scotia.[48] Equally as important and also at stake was the entire industrial structure which had been created in the region under the aegis of the National Policy.

The Maritimes by 1885 provided a striking illustration of the success of that policy. With less than one-fifth of the population of the Dominion, the region contained eight of the twenty-three Canadian cotton mills—including seven of the nineteen erected after 1879[49]—three of five sugar refineries, two of seven rope factories, one of three glass works, both of the Canadian steel mills, and six of the nation's twelve rolling mills.

---

[47] J.F. Stairs to J.M. Pope, 10 September 1885, Macdonald Papers, 50080-5, Public Archives of Canada.

[48] J.F. Stairs to Macdonald, 5 February 1886, ibid., volume 155.

[49] *Monetary Times*, 5 October 1888.

Although Stairs succeeded in his efforts to have the I.C.R. sugar freight rates reduced,[50] the problem facing the Maritime entrepreneur was not one which could be solved simply by easier access to the larger central Canadian market; its cause was much more complex. In the cotton industry, for example, the Canadian business community had created industrial units with a production potential sufficient to supply the entire national market. In periods of recession many American cloth manufacturers were prepared to cut prices on exports to a level which vitiated the Canadian tariff; this enabled them to gain control of a considerable portion of the Canadian market. The problems of the cotton cloth manufacturers could have been solved by a further increase in the tariff—a politically undesirable answer—by control of railway rates, or by a regulated industrial output.

From a Maritime regional viewpoint the second of these alternatives appeared to be the most advantageous; the limitations of the tariff could then be accepted and, having attained geographic equality with Montreal through a regulated freight rate, the more efficient Maritime mills would soon control the Montreal market. Such was the hope; there was little possibility of its realization. Such a general alteration in railway policy would have required subsidization of certain geographic areas—districts constituting political minorities—at the expense of the dominant political areas of the country, a prospect which the business community of Montreal and environs could hardly be expected to view with equanimity. Apart from the political difficulties of the situation, most Maritime manufactories suffered from two major organizational problems: the continued difficulty faced by community corporations in securing financing in the frequent periods of marginal business activity,[51] and the fact that most firms depended upon Montreal wholesale houses to dispose of their extra-regional exports.[52] Short of a major shift in government railway or tariff policy, the only solution to the problem of markets which seemed to have any chance for success appeared to be the regulation of industrial production, a technique which was to bring into the Maritimes the Montreal interests which already controlled the major part of the distributive function in eastern Canada.

III

The entry of Montreal into the Maritime region was not a new phenomenon. With the completion of the Intercolonial Railway and the imposition of coal duties in 1879, Montreal railway entrepreneurs moved to control both the major rail systems of New Brunswick and the Nova Scotia coal fields. A syndicate headed by George Stephen and Donald Smith had purchased the New Brunswick Railroad from

---

50 Ibid., 12 February 1886.
51 See the problems faced by John Parks and the N.B. Cotton Mills. Parks Family Papers, F. New Brunswick Museum.
52 *Montreal Herald*, 15 October 1883.

Alexander Gibson and the Hon. Isaac Burpee in 1880,[53] with the intention of extending it to Rivière du Loup. This system was expanded two years later by the purchase of the New Brunswick and Canada Railroad with the ultimate view of making St. John the winter port for Montreal.

In the same year, another Montreal group headed by John McDougall, David Morrice and L.-A. Sénécal acquired from fifteen St. John bondholders, four-fifths of the bonds of the Springhill and Parrsboro Railroad and Mining Company,[54] and followed this up in 1883 with the purchase of the Springhill Mining Company, the largest coal producer in Canada.[55] The following year another syndicate acquired the International Mine at Sydney.[56] The coal mine takeovers were designed to control and expand the output of this fuel source, partially in an effort to free the Canadian Pacific Railways from dependence upon the strike-prone American coal industry. By contrast, the entry of Montreal interests into the manufacturing life of the Maritimes aimed to restrict output and limit expansion.

The first serious attempts to regulate production occurred in the cotton industry. Although informal meetings of manufacturers had been held throughout the mid-1880s, the business depression of 1886 and the threatened failure of several mills resulted in the organization of the first formal national trade association. Meeting in Montreal in the summer of 1886, representatives of sixteen mills, including four from the Maritimes, agreed to regulate production and to set standard minimum prices for commodities. The agreement was to be renegotiated yearly and each mill provided a bond as proof of good faith.[57] The arrangement at least stabilized the industry and the agreement was renewed in 1887.

The collapse of the association the following year was precipitated by a standing feud between the two largest Maritime mills, the St. Croix at St. Stephen and the Gibson at Marysville. Alexander Gibson had long been the maverick of the organization, having refused to subscribe to the agreement in 1886 and 1887. During this period he had severely injured his larger St. Stephen competitor in the Maritime market. By the time Gibson agreed to enter the association in 1888, the St. Croix mill, faced with bankruptcy, dropped out and reduced prices in an effort to dispose of its huge inventory. The Gibson mill followed suit. With two of the largest coloured cotton mills in the Dominion selling without regulation, the controlled market system dissolved into chaos, and the association, both coloured and grey sections, disintegrated.[58] The return to an unregulated market in the cotton industry continued for more than two years. A business upswing in 1889 mercifully saved the industry from what many manufacturers feared would be a general financial collapse. Even so,

---

[53] *Monetary Times*, 8 October 1880.
[54] Ibid., 15 December 1882.
[55] Ibid., 8 June 1883.
[56] Ibid., 16 November 1884.
[57] Ibid., 13 August 1886; *Canadian Manufacturer*, 20 August 1887.
[58] *Canadian Journal of Commerce*, 7 September 1888.

only the mills with the largest production potential, regardless of geographic location, escaped unscathed; most of the smaller plants were forced to close temporarily.

In the summer of 1890 a Montreal group headed by A.F. Gault and David Morrice prepared the second attempt to regulate the cotton market. The technique was to be the corporate monopoly. The Dominion Cotton Mills Company, with a $5,000,000 authorized capital, was to bring all of the grey cotton producers under the control of a single directorate. In January 1891, David Morrice set out on a tour of Maritime cotton centres. On his first stop, at Halifax, he accepted transfer of the Nova Scotia Cotton Mill to the syndicate, the shareholders receiving $101,000 cash and $101,000 in bonds in the new corporation, a return of 25 cents on the dollar of their initial investment.[59] The following day Morrice proceeded to Windsor, "to consummate the transfer of the factory there,"[60] and from there moved on to repeat the performance at Moncton. Fearful of total bankruptcy and hopeful that this stronger organization would provide the stability that earlier efforts had failed to achieve, stockholders of the smaller community-oriented mills readily acquiesced to the new order. Although they lost heavily on their original investment, most owners accepted bonds in the new corporation in partial payment for their old stock.

The first determined opposition to the cotton consolidation movement appeared in St. John. Here, John H. Parks, founder and operator of the thirty-year old New Brunswick Cotton Mill, had bought the bankrupt St. John Cotton firm in 1886 and had proceeded to operate both mills. Despite the perennial problem of financing, the Parks Mills represented one of the most efficient industrial operations in the Dominion, one which had won an international reputation for the quality of its product. The company's major markets were found in western Ontario, a fact which made the continued independence of the firm a particular menace to the combination. The firm's major weakness was its financial structure. Dependent upon the Bank of Montreal for his operating capital, Parks had found it necessary to borrow more heavily than usual during the winter of 1889-90. By mid-1890 his debts totalled $122,000.[61]

At this point two events occurred almost simultaneously: Parks refused to consider sale of the St. John Mills to the new corporation, and the Bank of Montreal, having ascertained that the Montreal syndicate would buy the mills from any seller, demanded immediate payment in full of the outstanding debts of the company[62]—a most unusual procedure. Claiming a Montreal conspiracy to seize the company, Parks replied with an open letter to the dry goods merchants of greater St. John.

---

59 Thomas Kenny in Canada, House of Commons, *Debates*, 1893, p. 2522.
60 *Monetary Times*, 16 January 1891.
61 St. John *Globe*, 1 May 1891.
62 E.S. Clouston to Jones, 25 April 1891, Bank of Montreal, General Managers Letterbooks, vol. 8, Public Archives of Canada.

>...I have made arrangements by which the mills of our company will be run to their fullest extent.
>
>These arrangements have been made in the face of the most determined efforts to have our business stopped, and our property sold out to the Montreal syndicate which is endeavouring to control the Cotton Trade of Canada...I now propose to continue to keep our mills in operation as a St. John industry, free from all outside control. I would therefore ask you gentlemen, as far as your power, to support me in this undertaking —
>
>It remains with you to assist the Wholesale Houses in distributing the goods made in St. John in preference to those of outside manufacture so long as the quality and price of the home goods is satisfactory.
>
>The closing of our mills...would be a serious calamity to the community, and you, by your support can assist materially in preventing it. I believe you will.[63]

Park's appeal to community loyalty saved his firm. When the bank foreclosed the mortgage which it held as security for its loans, Mr. Justice A.L. Palmer of the New Brunswick Supreme Court placed the firm in receivership under his control until the case was resolved. Over the strongest objections of the bank, and on one legal pretext after another, the judge kept the mill in receivership for nearly two years.[64] In the meantime he forced the bank of continue the provision of operating capital for the mill's operations, and in conjunction with the receiver, a young Fredericton lawyer, H.H. McLean, proceeded to run an efficient and highly profitable business. When the decision was finally rendered in December 192, the firm was found to have cleared profits of $150,000 during the period of the receivership. Parks was able to use the funds to repay the bank debts and the mill continued under local control.[65]

The St. John experience was unique. Gault and Morrice organized the Canadian Coloured Cotton Company, sister consolidation to the Dominion Cotton Mills, in 1891. The St. Croix Mill entered the new organization without protest early in 1892,[66] and even the Gibson Mill, while retaining its separate corporate structure, agreed to market its entire output through the new consolidation. By 1893 only the St. John Mills and the small Yarmouth plant remained in the hands of regional entrepreneurs.

The fate of the Maritime cotton mills was parallelled in the sugar industry. In 1890 a syndicate of Scottish merchants, incorporated under English laws as the

---

[63] 15 December 1890, Parks Papers, Scrapbook 2, New Brunswick Museum.
[64] Clouston to Jones, 13, 22 April, 23 May 1891, Bank of Montreal, General Managers Letterbooks, vol. 8, Public Archives of Canada.
[65] St. John *Sun*, 28 December 1891.
[66] *Monetary Times*, 18 March 1892.

Halifax Sugar Refinery Ltd., bought up the English-owned Woodside Refinery of Halifax.[67] The ultimate aim of the Scottish group was to consolidate the sugar industry into a single corporate entity similar to Dominion Cotton. Failing in this effort because of the parliamentary outcry against combines, they turned their efforts to regional consolidation. With the assistance of John F. Stairs, M.P., they were able, in 1894, to secure an act of incorporation as the Acadia Sugar Refineries which was to amalgamate the three Maritime firms. Unlike the Cotton Union, the new consolidation worked in the interests of the regional entrepreneurs, the stock holders of all three refineries receiving full value for their holdings. Equally important, the management of the new concern remained in the hands of Thomas Kenny, M.P.

The consolidation movement of the early 1890s swept most of the other major Maritime manufactories. In some cases local entrepreneurs managed to retain a voice in the direction of the new mergers—John Stairs, for example, played a prominent role on the directorate of the Consumers Cordage Company which swept the Halifax and St. John rope concerns into a new seven-company amalgamation in 1890.[68] On the other hand, the Nova Scotia Glass Company of New Glasgow disappeared entirely in the Diamond Glass consolidation of that same year.[69] On the whole, saving only the iron and steel products, the confectionery and the staple export industries, control of all mass consumption industries in the Maritimes had passed to outside interests by 1895. Thus, in large measure the community manufactory which had dominated the industrial growth of the 1880s ceased to exist in the 1890s. Given the nature of the market of the period, some degree of central control probably was inevitable. The only question at stake was whether it would be a control effected by political or financial means, and if the latter, from which centre it would emanate.

The failure of any Maritime metropolis to achieve this control was partly a result of geography and partly a failure of entrepreneurial leadership. The fear of being left on the fringes of a national marketing system had been amply illustrated by the frenetic efforts of the St. John and Halifax business communities to promote political policies which would link the Canadian marketing system to an Atlantic structure with the Maritime ports serving as the connecting points.[70]

The question of entrepreneurial failure is more difficult to document. In part the great burst of industrial activity which marked the early 1880s was the last flowering of an older generation of lumbermen and wholesale shippers. Having failed to achieve their position as the link between central Canada and Europe, and faced with the dominant marketing and financial apparatus of the Montreal community, they drew back and even participated in the transfer of control. This failure is understandable in the smaller communities; it is more difficult to explain in the larger. In the latter

---

67 Ibid., 24 October 1890.
68 *Canadian Journal of Commerce*, 22 March 1895.
69 *Monetary Times*, 24 October 1890.
70 Ibid., 12 June 1885, 22 April 1887, 22 August 1902; Minutes of the St. John Board of Trade, 1 December 1879, 8 November 1886, New Brunswick Museum.

case it may well be attributable to the perennial failure of most Maritime communities to maintain a continuity of industrial elites. The manufacturing experience of most families was limited to a single generation: Thomas Kenny's father was a wholesale merchant, his son a stock broker. John F. Stairs was the son of a merchant and the father of a lawyer. Even in such a distinguished industrial family as that of John Parks, a second generation manufacturer, the son attended the Royal Military College and then entered the Imperial service. Commerce and the professions provided a much more stable milieu, and while many participants in both of these activities were prepared to make the occasional excursion into manufacturing, usually as part of a dual role, few were willing to make a permanent and sole commitment to an industrial vocation.

IV

The lesson brought home to the Maritime entrepreneur by the industrial experience between 1879 and 1895 was that geography would defeat any attempt to compete at parity with a central Canadian enterprise. In response to this lesson, the truncated industrial community of the region turned increasingly to those resource industries in which geography gave them a natural advantage over their central Canadian counterparts. In the 1890s the thrust of Maritime industrial growth was directed toward the processing and manufacturing of primary steel and of iron and steel products. In part, since these enterprises constituted much of the industrial machinery remaining in the hands of regional entrepreneurs, there was little choice in this development. At the same time, Nova Scotia contained most of the active coal and iron deposits in the Dominion and had easy access to the rich iron ore deposits at Belle Isle. In any event, most competition in these industries came from western Ontario rather than Montreal, and the latter was thus a potential market.

Iron and steel development was not new to the region. Efforts at primary steel making had been undertaken successfully at New Glasgow since 1882. Yet production there was limited and would continue so until a more favourable tariff policy guaranteed a stable market for potential output. Such a policy was begun in 1887 with the passage of the "iron" tariff. Generally labelled as a Nova Scotia tariff designed to make that province "the Pennsylvania of Canada"[71] and New Glasgow "the Birmingham of the country,"[72] the act provided an effective protection of $3.50 a ton for Canadian-made iron, and imposed heavy duties on a variety of iron and steel products.[73] Protection for the industry was completed in 1894 when the duty on scrap iron, considered a raw material by secondary iron manufacturers, was raised

---

71 *Monetary Times*, 20 May 1887.
72 *The Canadian Journal of Commerce*, 29 April 1887.
73 Canada, Statutes, 50-1 Victoria C. 39.

from $2 to $4 a ton, and most rolling mills were forced to use Nova Scotia-made bar iron rather than imported scrap.[74]

The growth of the New Glasgow industries parallelled this tariff development. In 1889 the nova Scotia Steel Company was united with the Nova Scotia Forge Company to form a corporation capable of manufacturing both primary steel and iron and steel products. In the same year, to provide the community with its own source of pig iron, a group of Nova Scotia Steel shareholders organized the New Glasgow Iron, Coal and Railroad Company with a capital of $1,000,000.[75] Five years later, following the enactment of the scrap iron duty, New Glasgow acquired the rich Wabana iron ore deposits at Belle Isle—some eighty-three acres covered with ore deposits so thick they could be cut from the surface. This was followed the next year by the union of the Nova Scotia Steel and Forge and the New Glasgow Iron companies into a $2,060,000 corporation, the Nova Scotia Steel Company. Containing its own blast and open hearth furnaces, rolling mills, forges, foundries, and machine shops, the firm represented the most fully integrated industrial complex in the country. The process was completed in 1900 when the company acquired the Sydney Coal Mines on Cape Breton Island, developed new steel mills in that area and reorganized as the Nova Scotia Steel and Coal Company with a $7,000,000 capital.[76]

The development of the Nova Scotia Steel and Coal corporation had begun under the direction of a cabal of Pictou County Scottish Nova Scotians, a group which was later enlarged to include a few prominent Halifax businessmen Aside from Graham Fraser, its leading members included James D. McGregor, James C. MacGregor, Colonel Thomas Cantley, and John F. Stairs. All four were third generation Nova Scotians, the first three from New Glasgow. Saving only Cantley, all were members of old mercantile families. Senator McGregor, a merchant, was a grandson of the Rev. Dr. James McGregor, one of the founders of the Presbyterian Church in Nova Scotia; MacGregor was a partner in the large shipbuilding concern of Senator J.W. Carmichael, a prominent promoter of Nova Scotia Steel. Cantley was the only member of the group of proletarian origins. Like Graham Fraser, he spent a lifetime in the active service of the company, having entered the newly established Nova Scotia Forge Company in 1873 at the age of sixteen. Promoted to sales manager of the amalgamated Nova Scotia Steel Company in 1885, he had been responsible for the introduction of Wabana ore into England and Germany. In 1902 he succeeded Graham Fraser as general manager of the corporation.[77]

Aside from its value to the New Glasgow area, the Nova Scotia Steel Company was of even greater significance as a supplier of iron and steel to a variety of

---

[74] Simon J. MacLean, *The Tariff History of Canada* (Toronto, 1895), p. 37.
[75] *Nova Scotia's Industrial Centre: New Glasgow, Stellarton, Westville, Trenton. The Birthplace of Steel in Canada* (n.p., 1916), pp. 45-6.
[76] *Monetary Times*, 9 March 1900; *Industrial Canada*, 20 July 1901.
[77] *WWW*, VI & VII, pp. 927, 1075-6.

foundries, car works and machine mills in the region. Because of its unique ability to provide primary, secondary and tertiary steel and iron manufactures, it was supplying most of the Maritime iron and steel needs by 1892.[78] In this respect, the industrial experience of the 1890s differed considerably from that of the previous decade. It was not characterized by the development of new industrial structures, but rather by the expansion of older firms which had served purely local markets for some time and expanded in response to the demand created by the tariff changes of the period.[79]

The centres of the movement were at New Glasgow, Amherst and St. John, all on the main lines of the Intercolonial or Canadian Pacific railroads. At New Glasgow, the forge and foundry facilities of the Nova Scotia Steel Company consumed half the company's iron and steel output. At Amherst, Nathaniel Curry (later Senator) and his brother-in-law, John Rhodes, continued the expansion of the small woodworking firm they had established in 1877, gradually adding a door factory, a rolling mill, a railroad car plant and an axle factory, and in 1893 bought out the Harris Car Works and Foundry of St. John.[80] At the time of its incorporation in 1902, Rhodes, Curry & Company was one of the largest secondary iron manufacturing complexes in the Dominion.[81] Curry's industrial neighbour at Amherst was David Robb. Son of an Amherst foundry owner, Robb had been trained in engineering at the Stevens Institute of New Jersey and then had entered his father's foundry. Specializing in the development of precision machinery, he expanded his activities into Massachusetts in the 1890s and finally merged his firm into the International Engineering Works of South Framingham of which he remained managing director.[82]

If under the aegis of a protective government policy the iron and steel industry of the Maritimes was rapidly becoming a viable proposition for local entrepreneurs, it was also increasingly attracting the interest of both Boston and Montreal business interests. There was a growing feeling that, once a reciprocal coal agreement was made between Canada and the United States, Nova Scotia coal would replace the more expensive Pennsylvania product in the New England market. Added to this inducement was the fact that Nova Scotia provided the major fuel source on the Montreal market—the city actually consumed most of the coal produced in the Cape Breton fields.[83] With its almost unlimited access routes and its strategic water

---

[78] R.M. Guy, "Industrial Development and Urbanization of Pictou Co., N.S. to 1900" (unpublished M.A. thesis, Acadia University, 1962), pp. 120-3.

[79] *Canadian Manufacturer*, 20 April 1894.

[80] *Monetary Times*, 30 June 1893.

[81] *Industrial Canada*, March 1910; *Canadian Men and Women of the Time* (1912), p. 290.

[82] *CCB*, II, p. 183; *CBD*, II, pp. 506-7; *WWW*, VI & VII, p. 997; *Canadian Men and Women of the Time* (1912), p. 947.

[83] *Monetary Times*, 26 November 1896. The St. Lawrence ports imported 88,000 tons of British and American coal in 1896, and 706,000 tons of Nova Scotia coal. The transport of this commodity provided the basis for the Nova Scotia merchant marine of the period.

position midway between Boston and Montreal, Nova Scotia seemed an excellent area for investment.

In 1893 a syndicate headed by H.M. Whitney of Boston and composed of Boston, New York and Montreal businessmen, including Donald Smith, W.C. Van Horne and Hugh McLennan, negotiated a 119-year lease with the Nova Scotia government for most of the existing coal fields on Cape Breton Island.[84] The new Dominion Coal Company came into formal being in March of that year, with David MacKeen (later Senator) as director and general manager, and John S. McLennan (later Senator) as director and treasurer. The son of a Scottish-born mine owner and member of the legislative council, MacKeen had been an official and principal stockholder in the Caledonia Coal Company which had been absorbed in the new consolidation.[85] McLennan was the second son of Hugh McLennan of Montreal, a graduate of Trinity College, Cambridge, and one of the very few entrepreneurs who made the inter-regional transfer in this period.[86] The success of the Dominion Coal syndicate and the growing feeling that the Canadian government was determined to create a major Canadian primary steel industry led Whitney in 1899 to organize the Dominion Iron & Steel Company. The date was significant. Less than two years earlier the government had announced its intention to extend bounty payments to steel made from imported ores.[87] The $15,000,000 capital of the new company was easily raised, largely on the Canadian stock market,[88] and by 1902 the company was employing 4,000 men in its four blast and ten steel furnace works.[89] Graham Fraser was induced to leave Nova Scotia Steel to become general manager of the new corporation,[90] and J.J. Plummer, assistant general manager of the Bank of Commerce, was brought from Toronto as president.

The primacy of American interests in both the Dominion Steel and Dominion Coal companies was rapidly replaced by those of Montreal and Toronto after 1900. The sale of stocks added a strong Toronto delegation to the directorate of the steel company in 1901.[91] In that same year James Ross, the Montreal street railway

---

[84] Ibid., 3 February 1893.

[85] *Canadian Men and Women of the Time* (1912), pp. 689-9; *WWW*, VI & VII, p. 1118.

[86] *WWW*, VI & VII, p. 1322.

[87] Donald, however, argues that Whitney had been determined to go into steel production even if no bounty had been granted. See Donald, *The Canadian Iron and Steel Industry*, p. 203.

[88] Partly, the *Canadian Journal of Commerce* (15 March 1901) suggested, on the promise of the promoters that the Company would receive bonuses of $8,000,000 in its first six years of operation.

[89] *Industrial Canada*, May, 1902.

[90] J.H. Plummer to B.F. Walker, 3 December 1903, Walker Papers, University of Toronto Archives.

[91] *Annual Financial Review*, I (1901), p. 92; III (1903), pp. 158-160.

magnate, bought heavily into the coal corporation, re-organized its management and retained control of the firm until 1910.[92]

V

The increasing reliance on the stock market as a technique for promoting and securing the necessary financial support to develop the massive Nova Scotia steel corporations emphasized the growing shift from industrial to financial capitalism. Centred on the Montreal stock market, the new movement brought to the control of industrial corporations men who had neither a communal nor a vocational interest in the concern.

In emulation of, and possibly in reaction to the Montreal experience, a group within the Halifax business and professional communities scrambled to erect the financial structure necessary to this undertaking. The city already possessed some of the elements of this structure. The Halifax stock exchange had existed on an informal basis since before Confederation.[93] The city's four major banking institutions—the Nova Scotia, the Union, the Merchants (which subsequently became the Royal Bank of Canada) and the Peoples—were among the soundest in the Dominion. The development of Halifax as a major centre for industrial finance began in 1894, at the height of the first Montreal-based merger movement, when a syndicate headed by J.F. Stairs founded the Eastern Trust Company.[94] The membership of this group was indicative of the change that was occurring in the Halifax business elite. Although it contained representatives of the older mercantile group, such as Stairs, T.E. Kenny and Adam Burns, it also included manufacturers and coalmen, notably J.W. Allison and David MacKeen, a stockbroker, J.C. MacKintosh, and lawyers such as Robert L. Borden and Robert E. Harris.

Until his death in 1904, the personification of the new Halifax finance capitalism was John Stairs. It was Stairs who arranged the organization of Acadia Sugar in 1894, who initiated the merger of the Union bank of Halifax with the Bank of Windsor in 1899, and who led the Halifax business community back into its traditional imperium in the Caribbean with the organization of the Trinidad Electric and Demerara Electric corporations.[95] After 1900, it was Stairs who demonstrated to this same group the possibilities for industrial finance existing within the Maritimes. With the assistance of his young secretary, Max Aitken, and through the medium of his own holding company, Royal Securities, he undertook the re-organization of a number of firms in the region, most notably the Alexander Gibson

---

[92] *Monetary Times*, 3 August 1907.
[93] Ibid., 17 April 1903.
[94] Ibid., 23 February 1894.
[95] *Annual Financial Review*, XXIII (1923), pp. 682, 736.

Railroad and Manufacturing Company which was re-capitalized at $6,000,000.[96] The scope of his interests, and the changes which had been wrought in the Maritime business community in the previous twenty-five years, were perhaps best illustrated in the six corporation presidencies which Stairs held in his lifetime, five of them at his death in 1904: Consumers Cordage, Nova Scotia Steel, Eastern Trust, Trinidad Electric, Royal Securities, and Dalhousie University.

Yet, while promotion of firms such as Stanfield's Woollens of Truro constituted a fertile field of endeavour,[97] the major industrial interest of the Halifax finance capitalists was the Nova Scotia Steel Company. In its search for additional capital resources after 1900, the entrepreneurial strength of this firm was rapidly broadened from its New Glasgow base. The principal new promoters of the company were Halifaxmen, notably James Allison, George Campbell and Robert Harris. The New Brunswick-born nephew of the founder of Mount Allison University, Allison had entered the chocolate and spice manufactory of John Mott & Company of Halifax in 1871, and had eventually been admitted to a partnership in the firm. He had invested heavily in several Nova Scotia industries and sat on the directorates of Stanfield's Woollens, the Eastern Trust, and the Bank of Nova Scotia in addition to Nova Scotia Steel.[98] George Campbell, the son of a Scottish gentleman, had entered the service of a Halifax steamship agency as a young man and ultimately became its head. Like Allison he was deeply involved in a number of Nova Scotian firms including Stanfield's, the Silliker Car of Amherst, the Eastern Trust and the Bank of Nova Scotia.[99]

By far the most significant figure in the Nova Scotia Steel Corporation after Stairs' death was Mr. Justice Robert Harris. The Annapolis-born scion of a Loyalist family, Harris shared the same antecedents as the Moncton and St. John entrepreneurs of the same name. After reading law with Sir John Thompson, he was called to the Nova Scotia bar in 1882 and rapidly became one of the leading legal figures in the province. In 1892 he moved his practice to Halifax and there became intimately involved in the corporate promotions of the period, ultimately serving on the directorates of thirteen major corporations including the Eastern Trust, Eastern Car, Bank of Nova Scotia, Maritime Telegraph and Telephone, Acadia Sugar, Robb Engineering, Brandram-Henderson Paint, and held the presidencies of Nova Scotia Steel, Eastern Trust, Demerara Electric, and Trinidad Electric.[100]

Despite the continuing need for additional capital, the Nova Scotia Steel Company found little difficulty obtaining most of this support from the Halifax

---

96 *Monetary Times*, 5 December 1902.
97 Ibid., 22 April 1911.
98 *Canadian Men and Women of the Time* (1912), p. 192; *WWW*, VI & VII, p. 762; *Annual Financial Review*, III (1903), pp. 174-6.
99 *Canadian Men and Women of the Time* (1912), p. 192; *WWW*, VI & VII, p. 803.
100 *Canadian Men and Women of the Time* (1912), p. 505; *WWW*, VI & VII, p. 1107; *Annual Financial Review* III (1903), pp. 176-6.

business community.[101] In turn, the corporation remained one of the most efficiently organized industrial firms in the country. In striking contrast to the larger Dominion Steel enterprise, Nova Scotia Steel's financial position remained strong, its performance solid and its earnings continuous. It was generally credited with being the only major steel company which could have maintained its dividend payments without the aid of federal bounties.[102]

As the first decade of the twentieth century wore to a close, the Halifax business elite appeared to have succeeded in establishing a financial hegemony in the industrial life of an area centred in eastern Nova Scotia and extending outward into both southern New Brunswick and peninsular Nova Scotia. Yet, increasingly, that hegemony was being challenged by the burgeoning consolidation movement emanating from Montreal. The most serious threat was posed in 1909 when Max Aitken, with Montreal now as the centre for his Royal Securities Corporation, arranged the amalgamation of the Rhodes, Curry Company of Amherst with the Canada Car, and the Dominion Car and Foundry companies of Montreal to form the Canadian Car and Foundry Company. The union marked a triumph as much for Nathaniel Curry as for Aitken—he emerged with the presidency and with nearly $3,000,000 of the $8,500,000 capital stock of the new corporation.[103] The move was a blow to the Halifax capitalists, however, as it placed the largest car manufactory in the country, an Amherst plant employing 1,300 men and annually producing $5,000,000 in iron and steel products,[104] firmly in the Montreal orbit of the Drummonds and the Dominion Steel and Coal Corporation. Tension was heightened by the feeling that this manoeuvre was a prelude to the creation of a railroad car monopoly. The reaction was swift. To prevent the takeover of the other Amherst car works, the Silliker Company, a Halifax-based syndicate bought up most of the Silliker stock and organized a greatly expanded company, Nova Scotia Car Works, with a $2,625,000 capital.[105] The following year Nova Scotia Steel organized its own $2,000,000 car subsidiary, the Eastern Car Company.

The contest between Montreal and Halifax finance capitalism reached its climax at the annual meeting of the Nova Scotia Steel Company of New Glasgow in April, 1910. Fresh from the triumph of the Dominion Coal and Steel merger, Montreal stockbrokers Rodolphe Forget and Max Aitken determined to extend the union to include the smaller steel firm, a proposal which the Scotia Steel president, Robert Harris, flatly refused to consider. Arguing that the firm was stagnating and that a more dynamic leadership in a reorganized corporation would yield greater returns,

---

[101] Most of the stock in this concern was held by Nova Scotians who also bought up two-thirds of the $1,500,000 bond which the company put out in 1904. L.M. Jones to B.E. Walker, 5 August 1904, Walker Papers; *Monetary Times*, 15 August 1902.
[102] *Monetary Times*, 9 March 1907.
[103] Ibid., 8 January 1910.
[104] *Industrial Canada*, August, 1913.
[105] *Monetary Times*, 29 October 1910.

Forget launched a major effort to acquire proxies with a view to taking control from the Nova Scotia directors. Using the facilities of the Montreal Stock Exchange, he bought large quantities of Scotia stock at increasingly higher prices, an example followed by Robert Harris and his associates at Halifax. At the April meeting, Harris offered Forget a minority of the seats on the directorate; Forget refused. In the voting which followed, the Montreal interests were narrowly beaten. The *Monetary Times*, in a masterpiece of distortion, described this victory as the triumph of "the law ... over the market place,"[106] and proclaimed that "New Glasgow prefers coal dust to that of the stock exchange floor."[107] In fact, it marked a victory, albeit a temporary one, for New Glasgow industrial capitalism and Halifax financial capitalism. More important, it marked the high point of a late-developing effort on the part of the Halifax business community to create an industrial region structured on that Atlantic metropolis. It was a short-lived triumph. By 1920 the Halifax group made common cause with their Montreal and London Counterparts in the organization of the British Empire Steel Corporation, a gigantic consolidation containing both the Dominion and the Nova Scotia Steel companies. This event marked both the final nationalization of the region's major industrial potential and the failure of its entrepreneurs to maintain control of any significant element in the industrial section of the regional economy.

VI

The Maritimes had entered Canada very much as a foreign colony. As the least integrated part of the Canadian economy, it was the region most dependent upon and most influenced by those policies designated to create an integrated national state. The entrepreneurs of the 1880s were capable men, vividly aware of the problems involved in the transition from an Atlantic to a continental economy. The tragedy of the industrial experiment in the Maritimes was that the transportation lines which linked the region to its new metropolis altered the communal arrangement of the entire area; they did not merely establish a new external frame of reference, they recast the entire internal structure. The Maritimes had never been a single integrated organic unit; it was, in fact, not a "region" at all, but a number of British communities clustered on the Atlantic fringe, each with its separate lines of communication and its several metropolises—lines that were water-borne, flexible and changing. In this sense the railroad with its implications of organic unity, its inflexibility, and its assumption that there was a metropolitan point at which it could end, provided an experience entirely alien to the Maritime tradition. The magnitude of this problem was demonstrated in the initial attempts at industrialization; they all occurred in traditional communities ideally located for the

---

[106] Ibid., 2 April 1910.
[107] Ibid., 9 April 1910.

Atlantic market, but in the most disadvantaged positions possible for a continental one.

Central to the experience was the failure of a viable regional metropolis to arise to provide the financial leadership and market alternative. With its powerful mercantile interests and its impressive banking institutions Halifax could most easily have adapted to this role, but its merchants preferred, like their Boston counterparts, to invest their large fortunes in banks and American railroad stocks rather than to venture them on building a new order. Only later, with the advent of regional resource industries, did that city play the role of financial metropolis.

Lacking any strong regional economic centre, the Maritime entrepreneur inevitably sought political solutions to the structural problems created by the National Policy; he consistently looked to the federal government for aid against all external threats and to his local governments for aid against Canadians. Since the regional politician was more able to influence a hostile environment than was the regional businessman, the latter frequently became both. In many respects the National Policy simply represented to the entrepreneur a transfer from a British to a Canadian commercial empire. Inherent in most of his activities was the colonial assumption that he could not really control his own destiny, that, of necessity, he would be manipulated by forces beyond his control. Thus he produced cotton cloth for the central Canadian metropolis in precisely the same manner as he had produced timber and ships for the British. In so doing he demonstrated considerable initiative and considerable courage, for the truly surprising aspect of the whole performance was that he was able, using his limited community resources, to produce such a complex and diversified industrial potential during the last two decades of the nineteenth century. The inability of the Canadian market to consume his output was as much a failure of the system as of the entrepreneur; the spectacle of a metropolis which devoured its own children had been alien to the Maritime colonial experience. Ultimately, perhaps inevitably, the regional entrepreneur lost control to external forces which he could rarely comprehend, much less master.

Canadianizing American Business: The Roots of the Branch Plant

Michael Bliss

Was there a Golden Age of Canadian economic nationalism? Did Canadians implement a national economic policy in the era of Sir John A. Macdonald that protected Canada and its resources from the United States? Can those salad days of energetic nation-building before the long liberal sell-out be held up by modern nationalists, or nationalist-socialists, as an example of what anti-American (or pro-Canadian) economic nationalism should be trying to achieve now?

No.

In the light of present issues, the Canadian National Policy of tariff protection was a very limited form of economic nationalism. Its effect was to resist only certain kinds of potential foreign domination of Canadian economic life, while encouraging exactly those other forms of outside penetration that are now, according to economic nationalists, our most serious economic problem. There was nothing accidental about this apparent contradiction. The old economic nationalism was based on premises about the needs of the Canadian people that transcended the simple black and white attitudes towards Americans familiar to readers of this book. These premises have continued to operate, virtually without regard to the political labels of governments in power, as the underlying consensus shaping much of Canadian economic strategy.

The 1911 election seems to have been the apogee of classic Canadian economic nationalism. Laurier's relatively innocuous reciprocity agreement with the United States roused Canadian protectionists to one last spirited defence of the old National Policy. Once again, as in the 1891 campaign, the issue of Canada's commercial relations with the United States was transfigured into a plebiscite on the future of the Canadian nationality. Reciprocity, it was argued, would subvert the economic foundations of Canada (an industrialized central Canada servicing a dynamic agrarian West through a developed east-west communications network), leading inevitably first to economic integration and then to political integration with the United States. More important, the Canadian attempt to preserve a distinctive identity in the northern half of the continent would be abandoned. Imperialists and nationalists—who were never very distinguishable—agreed that continued tariff protection for Canadian industries equalled Canadian patriotism and *vice versa*. This compelling equation split the Liberal party as its protectionist wing rallied round the flag, drove protectionist business organizations like the Canadian Manufacturers' Association into active politics in the comfortable role of national guardians, and doomed Laurier's desperate gamble for one final mandate for his crumbling regime. The election campaign was characterized by anti-Americanism ranging from the rational to the paranoid. John Diefenbaker tried but failed to resurrect its spirit in 1963; one wing of the NDP keeps trying.

But one of the minor themes of the Conservative-protectionist argument in 1911 illustrates the paradox of the "nationalism" of the National Policy. By 1911 there were already enough American branch plants in Canada to arouse concern when Canadians considered tariff policy. That concern, though, was not to limit what had already been called an American "invasion" of Canada,[1] but rather to sustain and encourage the branch-plant phenomenon. Branch plants were obviously a creation of the tariff, and it was equally obvious that tariff reductions under reciprocity might lead to an American withdrawal back across the border. According to the *Financial Post*, the possibility of such an *undesirable* situation developing was already worrying the Laurier government in 1910:

> Now our ministers at Ottawa have not the slightest desire to do anything, or to agree to anything, that will have any tendency whatever to check the movement of United States manufacturers to establish large plants in this country. These American establishments operate importantly to build our population and trade, and to build up a good market for the produce of our farms. And it seems that the existence of our moderate tariff against United States manufactured goods has been instrumental in many cases in bringing us these industries. Hence a strong argument exists for not meddling overmuch with the duties.[2]

When the government nonetheless pushed on with an agreement that raised the prospect of lower duties on manufactures, Canadian nationalist-protectionists made the branch-plant issue a minor but significant part of their campaign. In his landmark speech to the House of Commons, when he finally broke with the Liberal party, Clifford Sifton specifically pointed to the good effects the Quaker Oats Company was having on the economy of Peterborough, cited an interview in which its president had announced the company's intention to return to the United States under reciprocity, and worried that reciprocity would put an end generally to the beneficial development of American branch plants in Canada.[3] Lloyd Harris, another renegade Liberal, read to the House of Commons letters from American manufacturers threatening to withdraw from Canada and/or refusing to expand. Harris spelled out the branch-plant creating effect of the tariff, and concluded: "That is exactly what I want the Canadian policy to do. I want the American manufacturers to be forced to establish plants on this side of the line and provide work for our Canadian workmen if they want to have the advantage of supplying our home markets."[4]

---

1   *Financial Post*, June 11, 1910.
2   Ibid., June 4, 1910.
3   *House of Commons Debates*, Feb. 28, 1911, pp. 4394-6.
4   Ibid., March 8, 1911, p. 4905.

Still another defecting Liberal MP, William German of Welland, was moved by exactly the same consideration. He pointed out that the tariff had caused seven or eight million dollars of American capital to be invested in branch plants in his constituency, had given employment to thousands of workers, and had created a home market for agricultural products. Reciprocity likely would destroy all of this and ruin the economy of the Welland area.[5] German supported the National Policy because it fostered American economic expansion into his constituency.

Canada's leading protectionist publications similarly were worried about the inhibiting effects of reciprocity on the branch-plant movement. The *Montreal Star* compiled lists of the American branch plants in Canada, and the Toronto *News* asked, "Why ratify a reciprocity agreement that will largely remove this necessity for American industries to establish branch factories in this country? Why do anything that may stop the influx of United States capital for industrial enterprises in Canada?"[6] The *Monetary Times* headlined an anti-reciprocity article, "Americans Will Not Establish Branches."[7] *Industrial Canada*, the organ of the Canadian Manufacturers' Association, worried about branch plants in every issue during the campaign; once its cartoonist depicted an American manufacturer standing on the Canadian side of the tariff barrier meditating, "I'd build a factory here if I was sure they wouldn't destroy the dam."[8]

All the while, of course, protectionists were branding Americans as monopolistic marauders lusting to exploit Canada's resources and ravish her political nationality. But it was only American Americans to whom these phrases applied. Let an American move across the border and locate his business in Canada and he immediately became a useful economic citizen whose presence should be appreciated and encouraged. Geography, it seemed, had marvellous pacifying qualities.

The branch-plant-creating effect of the protective tariff was not new in 1911, only a bit more obvious. The 1858 tariff on agricultural implements had caused at least one implement firm to pole-vault into Canada. This was noticed and used in 1875 as an argument for further protection.[9] Although Macdonald did not rely on the investment-creating argument in his speeches defending the National Policy, his supporters were quite conscious of it (one Conservative in 1879 claimed the protective tariff "would bring capital into the country, that that was one of its chief attributes."[10]) As early as 1880, in fact, MPs were read a communication from the

---

[5] Ibid., March 2, 1911, pp. 4486-7.
[6] Reprinted in *Industrial Canada*, XI, 10 (May 1911), p. 1072.
[7] March 4, 1911, p. 918.
[8] XI, 7 (Feb. 1911), p. 729. For the issue of branch plants and reciprocity in the United States, see Ronald Radosh, "American Manufacturers, Canadian Reciprocity, and the Origins of the Branch Factory System," *C.A.A.S. Bulletin*, III, 1 (Spring/Summer 1967).
[9] William Dewart, "Fallacies of Reciprocity," *Canadian Illustrated News*, Feb. 13, 1875.
[10] *House of Commons Debates*, March 28, 1879, p. 791. Mr. John Weiler brought this and the letter cited in the next footnote to my attention.

manager of a branch-plant-child of the tariff: "Tell the members of the House of Commons that the St. Catharines Cotton Batting Company would not be in Canada today had it not been for the National Policy, and if the duty is taken off they will take the machinery back to the other side, as we can get cotton cheaper and save freight, which is quite a consideration ... we sell more cotton batting in this part of Canada than all the factories combined. We would ask for a further increase in duty."[11]

Throughout the 1880s and 1890s the establishment of branch plants was noticed in the Canadian press and hailed as one of the finest achievements of the National Policy. From 1882 to 1896, for example, various issues of the *Canadian Manufacturer* (the first organ of the Canadian Manufacturers' Association) contain sixty-nine references to branch plants being considered by Americans, negotiations being carried on towards the establishment of branch plants, branch plants being established, and the benefits of branch plants. Invariably the phenomenon is explained as a result of the protective tariff; the notices often end with comments like "Score another for the N.P.," "the N.P. does it," "more fruit from the N.P. tree," and "another monument to the glory and success of our National Policy." The need to protect American branch plants was used as an argument against unrestricted reciprocity in the 1880s; and the fear that Americans would withdraw from Canada was used as an argument in favour of the Conservative National Policy in both the 1891 and 1896 elections.[12] By the early 1900s it was common knowledge that Canada's protective tariff had encouraged such major American companies as Singer Sewing Machine, Edison Electric, American Tobacco, Westinghouse, Gillette, and International Harvester to establish Canadian subsidiaries. By 1913 it was estimated that 450 off-shoots of American companies were operating in Canada with a total investment of $135,000,000; the triumph of the National Policy in 1911 had greatly encouraged the branch-plant movement.[13] But as early as 1887 a federal royal commission had been told by the secretary of the CMA that there was scarcely a town of importance in Ontario that did not contain at least one branch of some American business.[14]

As economists have long recognized and historians long ignored, the roots of the branch-plant economic structure in North America must clearly be traced to the operations of the National Policy of tariff protection. The situation could hardly have been otherwise; for in an integrated continentalist economy, a branch-plant structure

---

11 Ibid., March 23, 1880, pp. 836-7.

12 See *Canadian Manufacturer*, May 6, 1887, p. 263; April 17, 1891, p. 198; June 5, 1896, p. 468.

13 Fred W. Field, *Capital Investments in Canada* (Toronto, 1914), p. 25. For another account of early American investments see Herbert Marshall *et al.*, *Canadian-American Industry* (Toronto, 1936), chap. 1.

14 Royal Commission on the Relations of Capital and Labour in Canada, *Evidence - Ontario* (Ottawa, 1889), p. 179.

designed for anything but regional economies would have been inefficient and superfluous. The economic nationalism of the late nineteenth century, then, operated and was known to operate to induce Americans to enter Canada and participate directly in the Canadian economy. Accordingly, the National Policy sowed many of the seeds of our present problem with foreign ownership. Possibly it caused more American manufacturing penetration than completely continentalist or free trade policies would have encouraged. From the perspective of the late 1960s it now appears to have been a peculiarly self-defeating kind of economic nationalism. The funny thing about our tariff walls was that we always wanted the enemy to jump over them. Some walls!

The paradox dissolves once the real nature of traditional Canadian economic nationalism is clarified. The impulse behind the National Policy and the whole complex of policies comprising our strategy for national development was not simply or even basically anti-American. It was rather a kind of neo-mercantilism designed above all to secure the maximum utilization in Canada of a maximum of Canadian resources. The nationality of foreigners competing to manufacture Canadian resources in their own countries or to supply Canadians with foreign resources was quite irrelevant. In the early years our tariffs shut out foreign products without regard to their national origin. They probably had a much more negative impact on trade with England than on trade with the United States, and the economic nationalism of Canadian producing classes supplied much of the resistance to any serious system of imperial preferences in the twentieth century.

Similarly, massive inputs of foreign capital were seen to be absolutely central for this concept of national economic development. Outside money was wooed without regard for either nationality or modern distinctions between direct and portfolio investment. Few people in the half-century after Confederation questioned Canada's absolute reliance on foreign capital. Aside from worrying now and then about our ever being able to pay off our debts, no one was seriously upset about the ultimate consequences of a high percentage of foreign ownership—either British or American—of our resources. Least of all were they worried about the flow of interest and profits to foreign countries. As *Industrial Canada* lamented in 1908, "That a portion of the profits made on the development of our latent resources has to be paid out in interest is no hardship, since without the capital there would have been no profits at all."[15]

If the Canadian tariff policy was consciously designed to attract foreign capital to Canada in whatever form it chose to come, there were other more precise policies to encourage the same migration. The applications of export duties on saw-logs in the 1890s and then again on pulpwood in the early 1900s were deliberate and successful attempts to force American lumber and pulp manufacturers across the border to set up

---

[15] VIII, 10 (May 1908), p. 763.

their mills in Canada.[16] Intermittently throughout the 1890s and early 1900s both the Dominion and the Ontario governments blustered, cajoled, and legislated in an unsuccessful attempt to force the International Nickel Company to move its main refinery to Canada.[17] And the most important of all of these efforts to induce direct foreign investment has been the least noticed: every Canadian province, every Canadian city, every Canadian hamlet pursued its own "national policy" of offering all possible incentives to capitalists and developers to come into its territory and establish manufacturing enterprises. The practice of granting bonuses to industries in the form of free sites, free utilities, tax concessions, loans, and outright cash grants was universal and persistent, despite the vehement objections of established capitalists. It was responsible for the attraction of countless American branch plants to specific cities as well as for the occasional municipal bankruptcy.[18] The federal government led the way in "bonusing" with its subsidies to the CPR and the general subsidy to manufacturing industries inherent in the tariff. On an even grander scale it conducted an astonishing alienation of public resources by "bonusing" every farmer who came to the Canadian West, regardless of his nationality, with 160 acres of free land. Many American farmers came; and there was more concern about their effect on Canadian national life in the early twentieth century than about all the branch plants combined (in a way every American-owned homestead that had family connections to the United States was a little branch plant).[19]

The basic assumption underlying all of this activity was the conviction that foreign capital and business enterprise should be Canadianized, that is, that they should be put to work inside Canada on Canadian resources and thereby produce the maximum benefit for the Canadian people and the Canadian nation. This explains precisely why Americans in the United States were competitors and economic

---

[16] H.G.J. Aitken, ed., *The American Economic Impact on Canada* (Durham, NC, 1959), chap. 1; Aitken, "Defensive Expansionism: The State and Economic Growth in Canada," in W.T. Easterbrook and M.H. Watkins, eds., *Approaches to Canadian Economic History* (Toronto, 1967). It is significant that the federal government, not the provinces, first began the use of export duties on saw-logs as a means of inducing manufacture in Canada.

[17] O.W. Main, *The Canadian Nickel Industry* (Toronto, 1955), chap. 4.

[18] For "Bonusing" see any Canadian business periodical for any year between Confederation and 1914, but especially the note beginning "Belleville ... has organized a little National Policy of its own," *Canadian Manufacturer*, May 17, 1889, p. 329; also ibid., July 19, 1895, p. 69, "American firms of every description ... have only to make public their designs and be inundated by letters from Canadian municipal authorities."

[19] In a paper read at the 1969 meeting of the Canadian Historical Association, "The Decline and Fall of the Empire of the St. Lawrence," Donald Creighton argues that the chief subversion of the National Policy came only after the rise to prominence of provincially controlled resources in the 1920s. He implies that the federal government shepherded resources under its control more responsibly, or at least more nationalistically, than the provinces did. My argument may suggest a reconsideration of Creighton's thesis.

enemies, but were invaluable allies once they had crossed the border with their money and skills, The bare fact of their crossing the border Canadianized them. In this sense the Canadianization of foreign business was one of the basic themes of economic nationalism, at least until the First World War.

Vague dreams of a "Big Canada," of population growth, wealth, status, and power undoubtedly all motivated Canadian National Policy-makers.[20] But there was one significant specific variation of these themes that deserves more attention. After defence and public order the most important function of government in nineteenth century Canada was the provision of more and better jobs. Hamlets, towns, cities, provinces, and the nation all assumed that they had a duty to promote jobs for their citizens and for incoming future citizens. They rightly knew that jobless citizens left depressed communities and that such emigration was a sign of communal failure in the most basic way. Particularly in bad times this explains the desire on the part of every political unit to promote industrial development (in good times the "bigness" theme became predominant). The argument of development to create employment was especially important on the national level in the depression of the 1870s. Macdonald's concern for the emigrating unemployed echoes (with only a touch of hyperbole) through his great 1878 speech demanding a National Policy:

> We have no manufactures here. We have no work-people; our work-people have gone off to the United States. They are to be found employed in the Western States, in Pittsburg, and, in fact, in every place where manufactures are going on. These Canadian artizans are adding to the strength, to the power, and to the wealth of a foreign nation instead of adding to ours. Our work-people in this country, on the other hand, are suffering for want of employment. Have not their cries risen to Heaven? Has not the Hon. the Premier been surrounded and besieged, even in his own Department, and on his way to his daily duties, by suffering artizans who keep crying out: "We are not beggars, we only want an opportunity of helping to support ourselves and our families"? Is not such the case also in Montreal and in Quebec? In fact, is not that the state of things which exists in every part of Canada....?
>
> ... if these men cannot find an opportunity in their own country to develop the skill and genius with which God has gifted them, they will go to a country where their abilities can be employed, as they have gone from Canada to the United States.... The hon. gentleman opposite sneered at the statement that thousands of our people had left this country to seek for employment in the United States. Why,

---

20   R. Craig Brown, "The Nationalism of the National Policy," and John Dales, "Protection, Immigration and Canadian Nationalism," both in Peter Russell, ed., *Nationalism in Canada* (Toronto, 1966).

the fact is notorious that the Government of the Province of Quebec have been taking steps to bring back their people.

... if Canada had had a judicious system of taxation [a protective tariff] they would be toiling and doing well in their own country.[21]

By fostering home industries, protection would give these artisans the jobs they were going to the States to find. It was only a small step to the realization that protection would also draw American manufacturers across the border to provide even more jobs for Canadian artisans. And once this was realized, good nationalists—nationalists concerned with protecting the Canadian community from emigration through unemployment—could only encourage the process. Whether or not this whole argument made or makes sense theoretically is irrelevant; it was the economic theory that Canadians acted upon.

French Canadians faced the same problem even more dramatically. The greatest threat to the French-Canadian nationality in the late nineteenth century was emigration to the textile mills of New England. Quebec governments had to create jobs to preserve the national identity of their overpopulated community. The colonization programmes that were begun in the 1840s were serious attempts to create employment in agriculture—far more serious and sophisticated than historians have credited them with being. But there were also significant French-Canadian attempts to encourage industrial development of all kinds in the province of Quebec from at least the 1880s. Thanks to William F. Ryan's *The Clergy and Economic Growth in Quebec (1896-1914)*, we now know that French Canadians at many levels of society understood the potential benefits of industrialism to their community and deliberately encouraged manufacturing and resource-development as job-creating alternatives to emigration. Anglophones, usually Americans, were entirely welcome in Quebec because of the ultimate value they had for preserving the French-Canadian nationality. Ryan's discussion of the role of Laurentide Pulp in the community of Grand-Mère summarizes volumes of French-Canadian social and economic history: "Jamais de mémoire d'homme on n'avait vu tant d'argent dans la région et dans la paroisse," comments a native about the early years of the pulp mill; "Owing to the new prosperity the curé of Sainte-Flore was able to complete his new church in 1897," remarks Ryan; and a succeeding curé tells the American manager of Laurentide, "Mr. Chahood, you and I are partners—I look after the spiritual welfare of my people while you are responsible for their bodily well-being.[22]

Extreme dependence on capitalists—often foreigners—for initiating crucial economic development with its accompanying employment explains much of the respect for "captains of industry" before the great depression. Capitalists created jobs; they spent money; they enabled curés to build churches. Even when they behaved

---

[21] *House of Commons Debates*, (March 7, 1878); pp. 857, 859.

[22] Ryan, *The Clergy and Economic Growth in Quebec (1896-1914)* (Quebec City, 1966), pp. 62, 64, 67.

badly, as the capitalists of the International Nickel Company did before the First World War, the jobs they provided were so critical that neither Ontario nor Canada wanted to stand up to them.[23] The leaders of the province of Quebec often had to genuflect to capitalists by urging deference and docility upon the working class for fear that a militant labour movement would discourage investment in Quebec and thereby create even more desperate poverty leading to emigration and denationalization.

The nineteenth century economy created the role of the capitalist as hero, as nation-builder.[24] When the foreign capitalist's work led to the development of Canadian resources he too qualified as a builder of the Canadian nation, whether or not he repatriated his profits. Van Horne of the CPR is the most famous Canadianized American (C.D. Howe seems to have won more notoriety than fame, although his contributions to Canada vastly exceeded Van Horne's); but perhaps the most exciting in his day was Frank Clergue, a semi-respectable American promoter who in the late 1890s created the multi-million dollar industrial complex at Sault Ste Marie. Clergue's remarkable ability to turn the wasteland of northern Ontario into a seeming El Dorado amazed, delighted, and shamed Canadians who marvelled at a man with more faith in their country than they had themselves. For a time, in fact, Clergue became a stronger Canadian nationalist than the Canadians, urging them to have confidence in their own country and its resources and campaigning at all levels of government for extensions of Canadian mercantilism (which would, of course, benefit his industries). Clergue's activities aroused concern about the participation of Americans in Canadian development, but only in the form of exhortations to native Canadians to be as enterprising and dynamic as this American and his Philadelphia backers.[25] Here was a fully Canadianized American businessman, right down to the refurbished Hudson's Bay Company blockhouse he lived in, communing with the spirits of the builders of the empire of the St. Lawrence. Despite the spectacular bankruptcy in 1903 that effectively ended his Canadian career, Clergue has been the only "Canadian" businessman to live on in our fiction, the subject of our most prolonged hymn to capitalist enterprise.[26]

---

23 Main, *The Canadian Nickel Industry*, chap. 4.

24 This is recognized in our historiography in the popularity of the "Laurentian thesis" and in the interpretation of the construction of the CPR as a national epic. Frank Underhill has been the only major historian to promote a "robber baron" approach to nineteenth century Canadian businessmen.

25 For Clergue's career, see Margaret Van Every, "Francis Hector Clergue and the Rise of Sault Ste. Marie as an Industrial Centre," *Ontario History*, LVI, 3 (Sept. 1964); for his exhortations to Canadians, see Francis H. Clergue, *An Instance of Industrial Evolution in Northern Ontario, Dominion of Canada; Address Delivered to the Toronto Board of Trade, April 2nd, 1900* (Toronto, 1900); for reaction to Clergue see *Monetary Times*, April 6, 1900, p. 1323; Feb. 1, 1901, p. 987; March 8, 1901, p. 1160.

26 Allan Sullivan, *The Rapids* (Toronto, 1922).

In a 1901 speech to the citizens of Sault Ste. Marie, Clergue spelled out the ultimate arguments for the American economic penetration of Canada:

> Let me summarize the conditions which the captious critic would discover here. He would find in the different lines of industry we had expended here in the neighbourhood of nine millions of dollars, cash, all of which has been foreign money injected into the circulating medium of Canada, to remain forever to the everlasting blessing of thousands of its inhabitants; that the completion and successful operation of our undertaking will require the expenditure of a sum nearly as large; that several thousands of inhabitants had found new employment in these undertakings at a higher scale of wages than had ever before prevailed in Canada ... that our works sent over $300,000 in cash to Georgian Bay ports last year for purchases; that we sent nearly as much to Hamilton, and nearly as much to Toronto; that the machinery and electrical supplies that we have purchased from Peterborough have amounted to over $100,000; that Brantford, Galt, Dundas and every other Ontario town engaged in mechanical manufactures had received from twenty-five thousand to two hundred thousand dollars of patronage from us; that our requirements had advanced the price of horses and nearly all the farm products in that part of Ontario tributary to Sault Ste. Marie.... Looking over our office staff he would find scientific and classical graduates from every college in Canada, clerks from nearly every bank in Canada and accountants from almost every city in Ontario. Among the artisans, mechanics and labourers he will find nearly every town and city in Ontario represented, and all of these people have assembled here because they found the rewards of labour greater here than elsewhere.[27]

To Canadians of the day these were unanswerable arguments. The citizens of Sault Ste. Marie had literally danced at the opening of Clergue's works.

Could things have happened differently in the two or three generations after Confederation? Could a more foresighted and active Canadian government or a more dynamic entrepreneurial class have perceived the ultimate American threat to Canadian society and thwarted it before serious inroads were made? Even if Canadians had recognized an American threat—unlikely inasmuch as Canadianizing American business was integral to Canadian nationalism—there would have been no acceptable alternative to reliance on foreign capital and capitalists for national development. Mel Watkins has suggested that a more thorough-going state capitalism, including a

---

[27] *Address by Francis H. Clergue At a Banquet Given in His Honour by the Citizens of Sault Ste. Marie, Ont. Feb. 15, 1901* (n.p.), 29-30.

national investment bank, would have obviated dependence on outsiders.[28] In the context of the late nineteenth century this is utopian: Canadian governments were barely competent to run a post office efficiently or anything honestly, let alone be entrusted with hundreds of millions of dollars for national development; the Canadian people fiercely resisted all forms of public appropriation of their incomes; the safety-valve of emigration to the United States put firm limits on the extent to which Canadian development policies could diverge from American, or the Canadian standard of living could fall below that of the United States. Recently Watkins has also argued that a weak and timid entrepreneurial class abdicated from its crucial role as moulder of a natively Canadian economic policy.[29] Such a Schumpeterian or proto-Marxist approach to economic development is probably inadequate in theory. It is at least unproven in fact, for we know virtually nothing about the actual entrepreneurial activities of native Canadians in the formative years of industrialism. My suspicion is that Canadian businessmen did meet ordinary standards of entrepreneurial prowess and that in areas like industrial education they were frustrated by the conservatism and élitism of the cultural establishment, notably professors of the humanities.

This argument has no more implications for present policy than any historical study. It does, I hope, do something to save the past record from the distortions of the present-minded. The economic nationalism of the National Policy was clearly inadequate as a defence against American penetration of the Canadian economy. On the contrary, it encouraged the commencement of American penetration in the form that most worries modern nationalists, and it did this with a fair measure of purposefulness. The great "sell-out" did not begin with Mackenzie King in the 1920s or with C.D. Howe in the 1940s. If anything it was a consistent policy about which there was an extraordinarily broad consensus. If King and Howe are to be criticized for not perceiving that Americans were the "real" threat to Canadian independence, surely Macdonald also must be censured either for not perceiving the future course of North American economic development or for wilfully promulgating a policy that encouraged American economic migration to this country. In all three cases it is much more fruitful to emphasize the force of their desire to create a community of prosperous and happy Canadians (largely happy because prosperous) and their willingness to import outside resources to that end.

Discussions of the role of élites in Canadian history have so far had little to do with historical reality. If élite theory must be used to explain Canadian economic development, some of the points raised in this essay should lead to a reconsideration of the interaction of élites in the late nineteenth century. Insofar as industrial employment depended on the existence of capitalists, the industrial worker had a

---

[28] "The 'American System' and Canada's National Policy," *C.A.A.S. Bulletin*, III, 2 (Winter 1967).

[29] "A New National Policy," in Trevor Lloyd and Jack McLeod, eds., *Agenda 1970; Proposals for a Creative Politics* (Toronto, 1968).

profound common interest with his employer—in the preservation of his job. The benefits of tariff protection in sustaining and encouraging manufacturing, including branch plants, were distributed to the industrial working class in much the same proportion as to the industrial employing class. Instead of a working class being oppressed by a capitalist élite, there was, at least on issues of high commercial policy, a single "industrial élite" which perceived itself as the beneficiary of the National Policy and all its consequences. By the 1890s a few union leaders had developed a working-class consciousness that led them away from paternalism and conventional Canadian economic wisdom. The mass of Canadian industrial workers, though, were still protectionist. The tariff, they thought, protected their jobs and created new jobs in industrial production. After all, the working class supplied the Canadian content of the American branch plants.

Some of the problems and attitudes reviewed here are still directly relevant. The Canadianization of Texas Gulf Sulphur takes another step forward as the Robarts government is egged on by the NDP to force it to transfer its refinery to Canada—creating jobs in Timmins by sacrificing the possibility of native Canadians some day building their own refinery. Joey Smallwood offers to deal with the devil if he has the capital to produce jobs for Newfoundlanders through industrial development (and what are a few Erco-poisoned fish compared to the wages that ex-fishermen can get in factories?); his alternative is the depopulation of the island. Anglophone control of the Quebec economy is despised, but its withdrawal threatens to destroy the economic base of the French-Canadian nationality. In Manitoba Ed Schreyer finds out as the head of an NDP provincial government that he must take capital where he finds it whatever his theoretical doubts about the extent of American investment in Canada. On the whole Canadians continue to believe—wisely, I think—that a limited but prosperous national existence is preferable to a pure, poor nationality.

In 1909 the Canadian Manufacturers' Association launched another crusade for the support of Canadian home industries. One of the first companies proudly advertising its product as "Made in Canada" was Coca-Cola. Things went better....

The North-West Rebellion 1885

Section 12

Canada's settlement of the prairies was twice interrupted by native uprisings—once at Red River, in 1869-70, at the moment when the West was being annexed, and once in Saskatchewan, in 1885, as settlement was well under way.

Both these uprisings were led by the same man, Louis Riel, and both depended on the armed action of French Métis (though there was support from English Métis at Red River and some Indian participation in 1885).

Modern scholarship on these uprisings has long been influenced by the work of G.F.G. Stanley, who argued that both insurrections represented native resistance against the advance onto the prairies of agricultural settlement. Métis and Indians alike, he wrote, had depended on the buffalo hunt and the fur trade for their livelihood and way of life, and these were threatened by the advance of whites, who would destroy the buffalo and plough up the land. This interpretation identified the Métis with the Indians as aboriginal peoples of the West and seemed to explain the participation of Indians as well as Métis in the rebellion of 1885.

In recent years, much of Stanley's interpretation has been called into question—by the authors of these two essays among others.

The first essay suggests that prairie Indians could have been helped to meet the crisis in their economy and way of life by adopting agriculture and thus participating in the development of the new western economy. Were the Indians willing to participate in such a programme? What obstacles stood in its way? How serious was the government about making it work? Despite their difficulties, why did so few Indians participate in the 1885 rebellion? How did that rebellion affect the government's treatment of western Indians?

The second essay is drawn from Thomas Flanagan's book, *Riel and the Rebellion*, in which Métis grievances are examined. Flanagan argues that in fact the Saskatchewan Métis were able to acquire land and establish farms, and that the federal government, though slow, did respond positively to the difficulties they complained of. "Why then did the North-West Rebellion occur at all?" he asks at the beginning of this paper. What is his answer to that question? How important is the personality of Louis Riel himself in Flanagan's interpretation? Is it reasonable to see the ideas and temperament of a single person as able to shape major historical events, or must we always look to impersonal social or economic forces?

G. F. G. Stanley's classic work on the western uprisings is *The Birth of Western Canada*. Some more recent work on the 1885 rebellion is collected in F. L. Barron & J. Waldram, eds., *1885 and After: Native Society in Transition*.

An Opportunity Lost: The Initiative of the Reserve Agricultural Programme in the Prairie West

Noel Dyck

Western Canadians generally regard the development of the prairie West between 1870 and 1905 as a proud chapter in the building of this nation. The many centennial anniversaries commemorated in the region in the last fifteen years or planned for the next twenty bear witness to the popularity of heroic interpretations of this earlier period. Yet these tributes to the history of nation-building and pioneering on the prairies tend to overlook that the achievements registered by some of our forefathers during this period were offset by the losses borne by others. One as yet little-recognized cost of the settlement period was the federal government's mishandling of prairie Indians' attempts to take up agricultural pursuits following the disappearance of the buffalo from the Canadian plains in 1879. Rather than aiding Indians to make the transition to new forms of self-sufficiency, the so-called "humanitarian" policies pursued by the federal government actually sabotaged Indians' efforts to preserve their autonomy and make a viable transition to new ways of life.

This paper examines the social, political and economic forces that led to the implementation of the reserve agricultural programme in the prairie West prior to 1885. It questions the cultural determinism implicit in the commonly held notion that the programme failed mainly because aboriginal culture and personality types were unequal to the demands of a settled, agricultural way of life.[1] The disappearance of the buffalo from the Canadian prairies did not in itself doom Indians to become subordinate figures in a coercive system of reserve administration. There is evidence not only of the willingness of prairie Indians to embark upon an agricultural way of life,[2] but also of their continuing concern from the time of the negotiation of the treaties in the mid-1870s to prepare for this eventuality. How and why did the reserve agricultural programme mounted between 1880 and 1885 frustrate this objective?

Far from being historically inevitable, this outcome was primarily the product of the arbitrary political relationship imposed upon Indians by government officials. The opportunity that existed in the 1870s and early 1880s to build a cooperative relationship between Indians and government, a relationship that could have fostered

---

[1] See George F.G. Stanley, *The Birth of Western Canada: A History of the Riel Rebellions* (Toronto: University of Toronto Press, 1960) for an early and influential statement of this position.

[2] Noel Dyck, "The Administration of Federal Indian Aid in the North-West Territories, 1879-1885" (M.A. thesis, University of Saskatchewan, 1970) and Sarah Carter, "Agriculture and Agitation on the Oak River Reserve, 1875-95," *Manitoba History* no. 6 (Fall 1983): 2-9.

the establishment of self-supporting and self-governing Indian communities, was lost for want of commitment on the part of government officials to these objectives. The events of 1885 sealed the fate of the reserve agricultural programme and provided the pretext for the imposition of a coercive system of reserve administration that lasted well into the twentieth century. Federal officials' power to manage outsiders' access to and understandings of this sphere of relations comprised another essential element of this destructive system of control, the effects of which have still not been clearly recognized, let alone satisfactorily resolved. This was not the arrangement that either Indians or government representatives sought when the treaties were signed. Why did it occur?

II

The transfer of Rupert's Land and the North-West Territories to the Dominion of Canada in 1870 marked the first step towards the integration of this vast area into the new nation. A major portion of the young country's energies in the remaining decades of the nineteenth century would be absorbed by the demands of Euro-Canadian settlement of the region. Throughout this period relations between Native peoples and the growing non-Native population comprised a fundamental concern for federal authorities.

Ottawa's dealings with prairie Indians reflected a number of factors, only a few of which can be mentioned here. To begin with, the federal government inherited from the pre-confederation period in eastern Canada a comprehensive Indian policy that promoted "protection, civilization and assimilation."[3] The main features of the policy applied in the prairie West were already well developed in 1870: the practice of the Crown alone accepting the surrender of Indian lands; the establishment of Indian reserves as a means of transforming Indians into settled and self-sufficient agriculturalists; and the eventual goal of eliminating Indian reserves and communities through the process of enfranchisement and individual allotment of Indian lands. A second factor was officials' desire to escape what were seen as the unnecessary expenses and excesses of the American government's dealings with its western Indians. The substantial costs incurred by the American army in fighting a series of protracted and expensive Indian wars horrified Canadian government leaders who were determined to adopt a more "humanitarian" and economically prudent approach to western settlement. Third, a far-reaching ecological transformation took place on the prairies in the latter half of the nineteenth century, and this was to have dramatic effects upon Indian-government relations. By 1870 it was recognized that the buffalo herds were declining rapidly; year by year increasing numbers of Indians came to accept that agricultural settlement of the prairie West would eventually overtake and

---

[3] John L. Tobias, "Protection, Civilization, Assimilation: An Outline History of Canada's Indian Policy," *Western Canadian Journal of Anthropology* 6 (1976): 13-30.

displace the buffalo-based economy. What was not appreciated, especially by the federal government, was just how abruptly this would happen. A fourth factor that influenced the conduct of Indian administration throughout this period, but particularly in the 1880s, was the federal government's already problematic pattern of dealing with the Métis.

The negotiation of the prairie treaties, that vital first stage in Indian-government dealings, indicated just how substantially the government's and the Indians' interests differed. The initiative for treaty-making came from Indian leaders whose people were determined to prevent Euro-Canadian settlement of their lands until their rights had been recognized.[4] While the federal government intended the "numbered" treaties to serve primarily as instruments for the surrender of Indian lands to the Crown, Indians approached these proceedings as the preliminary step in a longer-term process of developing a workable relationship with newcomers whom they would allow into their territories under certain conditions. Federal leaders viewed settlement of the prairie West as a means of accomplishing the economic integration of Canada as a nation. Railway construction and large-scale settlement depended, however, upon the fabrication of a political and administrative infrastructure which, in turn, awaited the forging of a viable relationship between the new government and indigenous peoples. On the other hand, prairie Indians sought to build formal links with federal authorities so they might begin to prepare for the future. From their perspective, an integral part of treaty-making would be to achieve a commitment from government to assist them when they would no longer be able to support themselves from the hunt and would have to become farmers.

Beginning with these quite different interests and assumptions and conducting their consultations usually in a matter of days through interpreters, it is easy to see how different interpretations of what had been agreed upon in these sessions might have emerged.[5] Even within government circles the signing of treaties could be construed as involving quite different options, as was indicated by Commissioner Provencher in a report to the Secretary of State:

> Treaties may be made with them simply with a view to the extinction of their rights, by agreeing to pay them a sum and afterwards abandon them to themselves. On the other side, they may be instructed, civilized and led to a mode of life more in conformity with the new position of this country, and accordingly make them good, industrious and useful citizens.

---

[4] John L. Tobias, "Canada's Subjugation of the Plains Cree, 1879-1885," *Canadian Historical Review* 64 (1983): 520-21.

[5] John L. Taylor, "Two Views on the Meaning of Treaties Six and Seven," in Richard Price, ed., *The Spirit of the Alberta Indian Treaties* (Halifax: The Institute for Research on Public Policy, 1979).

> Under the first system the Indians will remain in their condition of ignorance and inferiority, and as soon as the facilities for hunting and fishing disappear, they will become mendicants, or be obliged to seek refuge in localities inaccessible to immigration or cultivation. Under the second system, on the contrary, they will learn sufficient for themselves, and to enable them to pass from a state of tutelage, and to do without assistance from the government.[6]

Yet statements such as this one, phrased in the emerging rhetoric of federal Indian administration, suggested a straightforwardness of approach and a purity of motives that were sometimes conspicuously absent from federal actions.

Indian leaders had definite ideas about what they expected of government. The Cree who negotiated Treaty Six refused to sign the document until government commissioners agreed to a number of conditions, including an undertaking:

> That in the event hereafter of the Indians comprised within this treaty being overtaken by any pestilence, or by a general famine, the Queen ... will grant to the Indians assistance of such character and to such an extent as her Chief Superintendent of Indian Affairs shall deem necessary and sufficient to relieve the Indians from the calamity that shall have befallen them.[7]

This clause, along with another stipulating that the government would grant provisions to Indians during the initial period when they would settle on reserves and begin cultivation, underlined Indian leaders' determination to establish ground rules for the world as it would be without buffalo. The treaty negotiations did not, however, resolve the concerns of several Cree leaders who were determined to obtain more substantial recognition from government representatives of Indians' right to autonomy. Thus, a number of bands remained outside the treaties, although government representatives doggedly sought their adhesion to the treaties in subsequent years. In the meantime the buffalo still existed, albeit in ever-declining numbers. Federal officials showed as little interest in preparing for the agricultural experiment that lay ahead as they did in responding to requests form Indians and other prairie residents that steps be taken to conserve the buffalo as a subsistence resource for as long as possible.[8]

In spite of constant warnings regarding the precipitous decline of the buffalo, the suddenness and finality of their disappearance from the Canadian prairies in 1879

---

[6] Canada, House of Commons, *Sessional Papers*, 1875, Vol. VII, 56.
[7] Alexander Morris, *The Treaties of Canada with the Indians of Manitoba and the North-West Territories* (Toronto: Belford Clarke and Co., 1880), 354.
[8] Dyck, "Administration of Federal Indian Aid," 22-25.

surprised local observers and federal officials alike.[9] Both the Cree and the Blackfeet had been reported to be in a starving condition during the spring and summer of 1878. By the next summer their state had become desperate. One government official reported that the Blackfeet were:

> ...selling their Horses for a mere song, eating gophers, mice, and for the first time have hunted the Antelope and nearly killed them all off.... Strong young men were now so weak that some of them could hardly walk. Others who last winter were fat and hearty were mere skin and bone.[10]

The critical situation facing prairie Indians generated anxiety throughout the territory concerning how they would respond to this calamity. While remarking upon the amazing restraint exercised by Indians, reports from settlers and officials on the prairies left no doubt that Indians expected federal authorities to honour the obligations entered into only a few years earlier. The time for government action had arrived.

The necessity of supplying prairie Indians with at least limited provisions had been recognized in March 1879 when the government expended ten thousand dollars to provide temporary relief to Indians at Battleford, Duck Lake and Qu'Appelle.[11] The situation steadily worsened during the spring and summer, prompting the convening of council of regional representatives of various agencies in August. This "starvation council" agreed that fears of a general famine were only too well founded and recommended that unless Indians were rationed by government during the coming winter, there would be dire consequences not only for the Indians but also for the settlers scattered throughout the prairie West. Under the circumstances the government had little choice but to accept this advice and incur a large and curiously unanticipated expenditure. Alarmed by the prospect of footing a burgeoning appropriation for feeding the Indians of the North-West, the government eagerly took up its treaty commitments to help Indians to turn to agricultural pursuits. Federal officials spoke bravely of mounting a reserve agricultural programme that would make prairie Indians self-sufficient in a few years.

---

[9] While small herds of buffalo did occasionally slip into the North-West Territories following 1879, they were quickly taken by impoverished Indian bands; see Frank Gilbert Roe, *The North American Buffalo: A Critical Study of the Species in Its Wild State* (Toronto: University of Toronto Press, 1951), 480-81.

[10] Glenbow-Alberta Institute, *Dewdney Papers*, Vol. IV, Dewdney's Journal for 1879, 17 July (hereafter cited as Dewdney Papers).

[11] Dyck, "Administration of Federal Indian Aid," 31-33.

III

Before turning to the specifics of the agricultural programme mounted in the early 1880s, it may be useful to identify some of the factors that might have been expected to limit its success. To begin with, agriculture was still in its infancy in the prairie West. Outside of the Red River settlement there had been only limited agricultural experimentation by fur traders, missionaries, Indians and settlers. Detailed practical knowledge about soils and growing conditions simply did not exist; seed types and cultivation practices suited to the prairie West would not become readily available until the turn of the century. Moreover, the Department of Indian Affairs was ill-prepared, either in terms of administrative infrastructure or of practical experience, for the demands of overseeing a large-scale development programme. The expense of the programme, including the cost of provisioning Indians as they turned their hands to ploughing, was further increased by the high charges involved in transporting goods and implements into the area.

Closely related to these factors were a pair of ideological considerations that conspired to plague the operation of the reserve agricultural programme from the outset. On the one hand there was an enormous reluctance among Canadian politicians during this age of neo-mercantilist economic policy to provide support of any kind to needy individuals.[12] Charity was reckoned to be the responsibility of families and churches, not of governments. It was essentially the possibility of an armed rising in the prairie West—a risk that threatened state-supported investments in railway construction and western development—that compelled federal authorities to supply rations to starving Indians. Yet throughout the early years of the programme, government officials sought to resolve their abiding moral qualms by assuring themselves and the public that Indians would be made to work for every pound of rations they received.

On the other hand, federal leaders from time to time expressed fundamental doubts about the programme that was supposed to make prairie Indians self-sufficient in a few years. Even in the course of promoting the programme in Parliament the Prime Minister expressed misgivings about whether Indians could suddenly be converted from a nomadic, hunting way of life to a sedentary, agrarian existence.[13] To assuage these doubts federal officials referred to the reserve agricultural programme as an act of Christian humanitarianism, implying that it ought to be judged in terms of its motives rather than its results.

In light of these constraints and misgivings, the initial results of the programme were cautiously favourable. During the summer of 1880 over 11,000 Indians settled upon reserves, built houses and broke some 4,600 acres of land for cultivation. The

---

[12] See Kenneth McNaught, *The Pelican History of Canada* (Harmondsworth: Penguin, 1969), 173 ff. for a discussion of federal economic policy during this period.

[13] Canada, House of Commons, *Debates*, 23 April 1880 and 5 May 1880.

harvest that year yielded moderate though promising quantities of wheat, oats, barley and potatoes. Included in the Indian commissioner's report was an extract that described the progress achieved that summer on Red Pheasant's reserve near Battleford:

> The crop on this reserve was magnificent. The potato yield was very heavy....The barley and wheat I am happy to say came to maturity. The turnips and beets cannot be surpassed, but the carrots, owing to not being thinned in time are in some cases small. These Indians are intelligent, peacefully inclined and good workers.[14]

Yet in spite of the optimism generated by initial farming operations, there was no question of discontinuing the rationing of bands settled on reserves. Though a few of the bands were in a position to eke out an existence, Commissioner Dewdney reported that eight-tenths of the Indians of the North-West were helpless.[15] Nevertheless, opposition criticism in Parliament of expenditures on Indians made the government acutely sensitive to the political desirability of maintaining economy.

This concern with economy, combined with misgivings about the merit of the government granting "charity" to Indians, often gave rise to conflicting purposes within federal Indian administration. As early as 1881 the Minister of Finance recommended that Indians be employed in the construction of the Canadian Pacific Railway in order to offset ration expenditures.[16] Although this measure was not adopted, rations for Indians were initially restricted on average to three-quarters of a pound of meat and three-quarters of a pound of flour per person per day for a per capita daily cost of eight cents.[17] This was significantly less than the fifty cents per day allowed by the Department for the feeding of each of its white farm labourers.[18] Moreover, the Department insisted that Indians not be given something for nothing: "The system pursued in affording relief to the Indians is calculated to accustom them to habits of industry and at the same time to teach them to depend on their own efforts of subsistence."[19]

---

[14] Canada, House of Commons, *Sessional Papers*, 1881, Vol. 14, Report of the Department of Indian Affairs for 1880: 83, Order to Dewdney, 18 November 1880.

[15] Public Archives of Canada, Manuscript Group 26A, John A. Macdonald Papers, Vol. 210: 89450-89462, Dewdney to Macdonald, 19 June 1881 (hereafter cited as PAC, MG 26A, letters).

[16] PAC, MG 26A, Vol. 210: 89418, Tilley to Macdonald, 7 May 1881.

[17] PAC, RG 10 Indian Affairs Files, File 22367, Estimate for Indian Expenditures in the North-West Territories, 1881-82, n.d. (hereafter cited as PAC, RG 10, file, letter).

[18] Ibid.

[19] Canada, House of Commons, *Sessional Papers*, 1881, No. 14, Report of the Department of Indian Affairs, 2.

Government spokesmen steadfastly maintained that while the rationing of the Indians in the North-West would initially incur great expenditure, the Indians would within two or three years achieve some degree of self-sufficiency. For instance, in an application to the Privy council in 1881 for a supplementary grant to meet departmental over-expenditures in the North-West, the Prime Minister predicted that that year's harvest would be sufficient to feed Indians settled on reserves for three, if not four, months of the coming year.[20] Yet departmental officials privately observed that ration expenses and overall costs would not soon decrease, but would in all probability rise during the next few years with the settlement of more bands on reserves.[21] These less sunny projections were, in effect, ignored in official pronouncements which indicated that the programme was for the most part proceeding satisfactorily in the North-West.

Prior to 1882 participation in the reserve farming programme was largely restricted to bands residing within the boundaries of Treaty Six and in the eastern section of Treaty Four. There remained in the southern and western sections of the North-West a substantial Indian population—including the followers of Big Bear in the Cypress Hills region and, further west, the Blackfeet—whose involvement in agricultural pursuits was either limited or non-existent. The Commissioner of Indian Affairs in the North-West Territories actively encouraged the Blackfeet to continue hunting in American territory for several years after the buffalo had disappeared from the Canadian plains. By offering them rations to supplement their returns from hunting, the Commissioner estimated that he had saved the government at least $100,000 over a two-year period. In the meantime, government efforts and resources were to be concentrated on developing existing Indian reserves.

Eventually the many Indians who had gathered in the Cypress Hills region in order to mount periodic hunting forays into the United States while maintaining pressure upon the Canadian government to grant them what would have amounted to an Indian territory were compelled to settle on geographically dispersed reserves in the northern and eastern sections of the Territories.[22] Yet even on established reserves, the farming programme was not proceeding according to plan. In spite of promising efforts in Treaties Four and Six, the Indians there were far from being self-sufficient by 1883. In Treaty Seven agricultural development had only been half-heartedly attempted by the Department with the result that the ration expenditures there were more than twice as large as in the other two treaties combined.[23] Although agricultural reports for the North-West superintendency indicated progress

---

20   PAC, RG 10, 30249 Black, Macdonald to the Privy Council, 27 June 1881.
21   PAC, RG 10, Private Letterbooks, Vol. 1082, Vankoughnet to Dewdney, 10 November 1882.
22   See Tobias, "Canada's Subjugation of the Plains Cree," 526-32, for details of how this was accomplished.
23   This may also have reflected the greater fear of the Blackfeet held by government officials.

both in terms of the amount of new land being cultivated and in crop returns, the necessity of providing rations to Indians settled on reserves remained.[24]

It has been suggested that the "failure" of the government's agricultural policy to meet its original objectives was due to the "restlessness...inherent in the Indian disposition" and to Indians' "dislike of uncongenial work."[25] In fact, agents and instructors generally reported favourably on the efforts shown by bands that had undertaken to farm; to cite but one example, a farming instructor in the File Hills Agency reported to Commissioner Dewdney in the spring of 1884 that "the men kept the oxen steadily at work and three families who came last fall have broken up enough land with their hoes for gardens and potatoes."[26] Their efforts were in sharp contrast to the short rations and reneging on treaty commitments that became characteristic of federal Indian administration.[27] Considering that prairie agriculture was then in its infancy, that the development of suitable crops, farming techniques and agricultural equipment for the northern climate still lay ahead,[28] and that the Department had not provided Indians with sufficient implements and supplies to serve all those who were prepared to farm, the progress realized was not inconsiderable. Yet the drive for economy in Indian administration systematically retarded agricultural development. For instance, departmental officials spent three years considering the cheapest method of constructing a grist mill in the western district of Treaty Six. In the meantime Indians in the area remained over a hundred miles from the nearest mill where their grain could be milled into flour.

The Conservative government's fixation with economy in Indian administration was not, however, unrepresentative of Canadian political thinking of that day. Indeed, according to the Liberal opposition, which maintained that the Crown's responsibilities extended only to meeting the narrowly stated specific terms of the treaties, the Conservative programme was generous. In any case, Prime Minister Macdonald assured the House of Commons that the government was doing its best to keep expenditures low, reducing Indians to one-half and one-quarter rations and "refusing food until the Indians are on the verge of starvation."[29] The enforcement of

---

[24] Dyck, "Administration of Federal Indian Aid," Appendix A.
[25] Stanley, *Birth of Western Canada*, 239.
[26] PAC, RG 10, 13642 Black, Nichol to Dewdney, 13 May 1884.
[27] Tobias, "Canada's Subjugation of the Plains Cree," 542, notes that Indian Commissioner Dewdney admitted privately that government had violated the treaties and took steps in February 1885 to rectify this and to increase rations to forestall the convening of further Indian political councils that summer.
[28] Frost damaged crops in large sections of the North-West each year between 1880 and 1884.
[29] Canada, House of Commons, *Debates*, 27 April 1882, Vol. II: 1186.

this policy resulted in starvation[30] and a rapidly increasing mortality rate among prairie Indians.

Other measures taken to achieve economies in federal Indian administration required more elaborate explanations by government officials. One of the Liberals' long-standing targets had been the supply farms established to produce as large as possible a portion of the food supplies needed to ration Indians. These units were not, however, able to feed even the white labourers who operated them, let alone produce a surplus. Curiously, the conclusion that if white farmers had not yet come to terms with prairie agricultural conditions, then Indian farmers could hardly be expected to have done so did not seem to occur to either the government or the opposition. The eventual closure of the supply farms was justified on the basis that these units had really been intended to demonstrate proper field husbandry techniques and that Indians on nearby reserves had by now had sufficient opportunity to see how farming should be conducted.[31]

In 1882 and 1883 criticism of expenditures on Indians increased as the country slid into economic recession. A decline in government revenues that began in the last quarter of 1882 marked a turning point in the reserve agricultural programme. Expenditures on Indian affairs in the North-West that had reached a peak of $1,106,961 in 1882 were reduced to $1,099,796 the following year and to $1,025,575 in 1884,[32] even though the number of Indians residing on reserves increased in each of these years. As a result of these cutbacks and an accompanying reshuffling of departmental spending, provisions for destitute Indians in the North-West Territories were reduced by more than $90,000 or 15 per cent between 1882 and 1884.[33] There was a surprising lack of hesitation within the upper echelons of government in making this reduction, so crucial to the state of affairs in the North-West. In September 1883 the Prime Minister instructed Commissioner Dewdney that expenses in the North-West were to be kept down as much as possible, although "life and property must be protected."[34] Dewdney's willingness to comply with Macdonald's request marked a complete reversal of the stand he had taken two years earlier when he had confidently predicted that, although expenditures would be high, the final results of the reserve agricultural programme would justify their cost.[35]

---

[30] Isabel Andrews, "Indian Protest Against Starvation: The Yellow Calf Incident of 1884," *Saskatchewan History* 28 (1975): 41-51.

[31] PAC, RG 10, Private Letterbooks, Vol. 1085, Vankoughnet Memorandum, 31 January 1884.

[32] Stanley, *Birth of Western Canada*, 273.

[33] Dyck, "Administration of Federal Indian Aid," Appendix A2.

[34] Dewdney Papers, Vol. III, Macdonald to Dewdney, 17 September 1883, 445-46.

[35] PAC, MG 26A, Vol. 210: 89486, Dewdney to Macdonald, 4 July 1881.

IV

The response of Indians in the North-West Territories to the reserve agricultural programme reflected the geographical and cultural diversity of the region as well as the leaders' differing views of what would be best for their people in the present and the future. Crowfoot, a Blackfoot chief, pursued a policy of cooperating with the government from the signing of the treaties. When he first met Dewdney in the summer of 1879, Crowfoot greatly impressed the newly appointed Indian Commissioner, who noted that Crowfoot had spoken "very well, and reasonably."[36] Although Crowfoot declared a willingness to farm, he informed Dewdney that unless the government could bring back the buffalo, it would have to feed the Blackfeet. The Commissioner encouraged Crowfoot and his people to continue hunting in American territory for the next two years. When the Blackfeet did settle on reserves in 1881, Crowfoot once again stated his readiness to take up farming as long as his people were provided sufficient assistance by the government.

Other Indian leaders pursued less patient courses of action. The Cree chief Poundmaker had been among the first to settle on a reserve in 1879. In the following two years he and his band made considerable progress in breaking land and constructing buildings, working "like Trojans," their farming instructor reported.[37] Nevertheless, the government's ration policy, balanced as it was between keeping the Indians from starvation, on the one hand, and maintaining economy, on the other, offered scant encouragement for their efforts. Discouraged by the treatment accorded his people, Poundmaker in the spring of 1881 sent out messengers to different parts of the North-West, inviting the chiefs to gather in Battleford that summer so they might press the government for better terms.[38] Bands in the Battleford district refused to seed crops that year and the agent was told that unless he issued rations they would take the cattle out on the plains and kill them for food. In June, Poundmaker and part of his band left their reserve and headed south to confer with Indians in the Cypress Hills. When Indians were granted an opportunity to discuss their grievances with the Governor-General during his tour of the North-West later that summer, Poundmaker outlined the difficulties and hardships they were encountering on the reserves:

> Ever since the white man made the Treaty the white man always talks of how they are to make their living. I am striving hard to work on my farm that my children may benefit but, I am not accustomed to work on a farm and am short of implements. I mean

---

[36] PAC, RG 10, 15266 Black, Dewdney to Dennis, 22 July 1879.

[37] Canada, House of Commons, *Sessional Papers*, 1881, No. 14, Report of the Department of Indian Affairs for 1880, 84.

[38] PAC, RG 10, 29548 Black, Reed to Dewdney, 8 May 1881.

the same things used by the white man. A reaper, mower, that is what we want.... We cannot work in the winter. It is cold and we are naked. There is much sickness on my reserve and I would like a Doctor there.[39]

In the fall of 1881 Poundmaker returned to his reserve and once again engaged in farming. Taking this as a sign of submission, the authorities largely ignored his requests. In 1883 Poundmaker again left his reserve to meet with other Indian leaders, an action that Assistant Indian Commissioner Reed explained as part of an effort by Poundmaker to make himself "a great man" in the eyes of the other Indians.[40] Reed's suggestion that Poundmaker be deposed as chief of his band if he did not set a better example to his people demonstrated no more understanding of Cree political processes than of the reasons for Poundmaker's discontent with reserve life.

While Crowfoot and Poundmaker worked from within the treaty structure to achieve improved conditions for their people, Big Bear, the Cree chief whom Dewdney considered the most influential Indian on the prairies,[41] chose to remain outside of the treaty for six years while conducting a campaign to obtain greater autonomy for Indians. His efforts were not in vain, for as long as he remained on the plains, demanding more liberal terms from the government officials who regularly sought his adhesion to Treaty Six, he demonstrated to those Indians already settled on reserves that they were not obliged to leave their fate in the hands of the Department of Indian Affairs. Nor could the government afford to ignore Big Bear. Year after year officials sought his acceptance of the treaty, and with equal persistence, Big Bear refused to give it. Meeting with Lieutenant-Governor Laird in 1878, Big Bear, who acted as a spokesman for both treaty and non-treaty Indians, reiterated that the treaty did not furnish enough for the people to live on.[42] The following year Big Bear held conferences in the southern part of the territories with both Crowfoot and the Sioux chief, Sitting Bull.

Between 1879 and 1882, Big Bear and his band travelled between the Cypress Hills and the Judith Basin in Montana in pursuit of the buffalo. But as the herds dwindled and the Cypress Hill Indians faced starvation, leaders such as Piapot, Little Pine and Lucky Man fell victim to Dewdney's relentless campaign to drive them and their followers to settle on reserves. Eventually Big Bear, too, succumbed to these pressures and signed an adhesion to Treaty Six, although he did not pick a reserve until 1884. While he failed in his efforts to locate his reserve adjacent to other Cree reserves in the Battleford area, a proposal that would have created a substantial Indian

---

[39] PAC, RG 10, 33642 Black, Minutes of the Governor-General's tour of the North-West Territories, n.d. [probably August 1881].

[40] PAC, RG 10, 10644 Black, Reed to Dewdney, 28 December 1883.

[41] PAC, MG 26A, Vol. 210: 89477-90, Dewdney to Macdonald, 4 July 1881.

[42] PAC, RG 10, 10771 Black, Laird to Mills, 12 November 1878.

territory with a concentrated, politically significant Indian population, his opposition to government policies continued. During these years he travelled from district to district, discussing with chiefs in different areas how government might be forced to respond to Indian demands. Officials took considerable care in handling Big Bear and even broke the "no work, no food" rule in the case of his band.[43]

Late in 1883 the Department learned that Big Bear and other Cree leaders were organizing a large gathering of Indians to be held in the Battleford district in 1884. This council took on even greater significance as the reduction of government expenditures for the North-West began to take effect. The immigration of the southern Indians into the reserve agricultural programme during the summer of 1883 should have resulted in a proportionately larger appropriation for the Department of Indian Affairs. Instead, a general reduction in costs was initiated and rations were cut back. Reaction in the North-West to the reduced ration issues came swiftly. The farming instructor at Fort Pitt was threatened at knife point when he refused to grant rations to an Indian who had just returned from an unsuccessful hunting expedition. Indians in the Crooked Lakes district seized a government storehouse and distributed the rations it contained. Their leader, Yellow Calf, explained to a police officer that, "when they stole the provisions their women and children were starving ... and that they were well armed and might just as well die as be starved by the Government."[44] A police patrol sent to the reserve encountered a gathering of Indians determined to protect those who had taken food that they considered to be properly their own. Bloodshed was only narrowly averted.[45]

The Crooked Lakes incident and the threat of further Indian agitation alarmed Department officials both in Ottawa and in the North-West. Officials in the North-West informed the Prime Minister that Indians would probably congregate in large numbers in the southern area as well as in the Battleford district that summer,[46] and predicted that there would be a strong inclination for the Indians to kill their cattle if the "no work, no food" rule was adhered to. It was recommended that every effort be taken to prevent these gatherings, including arresting some of the leaders:

> ...the law might have to be strained a little to meet a particular case, but in the interests of the country at large as well as the Indians themselves such a course I think would be advisable.
> A magistrate before whom these Indians might appear, if at all conversant with Indian character could readily discern his proper course.[47]

---

[43] PAC, RG 10, 309A Black, Rae to Dewdney, 11 March 1884.
[44] PAC, RG 10, 10181 Black, Herchmer to White, 26 February 1884.
[45] See Andrews, "Indian Protest Against Starvation," 45, for an account of this incident.
[46] PAC, RG 10, 10648 Black, Reed to Macdonald, 12 April 1884.
[47] Ibid.

It was decided in Ottawa to adopt a dual policy of issuing somewhat more liberal rations to those Indians working on the reserves, while at the same time strengthening the Mounted Police.[48]

The long awaited Indian councils, held in 1884 in both the northern and southern areas, amply demonstrated the inadequacy of this response as a means of keeping Indians working on the reserves, let alone for satisfying their demands. A police patrol sent to arrest Piapot, the chief organizer of the council to be held in the South, found itself surrounded by armed warriors. Police and government representatives were forced to permit the planned council and thirst dance to proceed as planned.[49] In the course of another council, staged several weeks later on Poundmaker's reserve, the matter of rationing policy came to the fore when a farming instructor refused to grant provisions to an Indian from a visiting band. This provoked an incident that almost ended in a pitched battle between the North-West Mounted Police and the assembled Indians.[50] According to police reports, except for the efforts of Big Bear and several other chiefs to avoid trouble, the showdown would almost certainly have sparked the massacre of the police party.[51]

The interruption of this council by the incident delayed the working out of a coordinated plan for further political agitation. Nevertheless, Big Bear persevered in his efforts to unite the Cree in opposition to the government's administration of the reserve agricultural programme. The next month he and chiefs in the Carlton district met with the recently returned Métis leader, Louis Riel. This council, held near Duck Lake, marked a crucial stage in the development of a unified Indian political movement in the North-West. Big Bear presented the Indians' reasons for dissatisfaction with government: His people had surrendered their lands and settled on reserves in response to the government's promise that they would achieve a better way of life through farming; the government had not kept its promises and therefore, a new and more generous settlement would have to be negotiated. It was also agreed that a council including bands from every section of the North-West would meet the following summer to demand better terms from the government. Differences between the political aims of the Indians and the Métis, however, limited the council to achieving only an exchange of general statements of sympathy between the Cree leaders and Riel.[52]

That same summer Crowfoot and several other chiefs from Treaty Seven travelled to Regina to present the Commissioner with various requests, including one that the

---

[48] PAC, RG 10, Private Letterbooks, Vol. 1085: 535, Vankoughnet to Reed, 19 March 1884.
[49] Tobias, "Canada's Subjugation of the Plains Cree," 534-35.
[50] Ibid., 535-36.
[51] PAC, RG 10, 309A Black, Crozier to Irvine, 25 June 1884.
[52] Stanley, *Birth of Western Canada*, 290-91.

flour ration not be further reduced.[53] Although Dewdney suggested in a letter to the Prime Minister that these Indians had "no substantial grievances," he endeavoured to appease Crowfoot through a number of inexpensive measures. Crowfoot visited the North-West Territorial Council in session and was awarded fifty dollars by it "as a mark of the esteem in which his nation is held." The chiefs were then taken to Winnipeg on the newly constructed railway in an effort to demonstrate to them "the supremacy of the white man and the utter impossibility of contending against his power." The solution Dewdney proposed to the Prime Minister to resolve ration grievances in Treaty Seven was that greater allowances of tea and tobacco be issued to working Indians. The cost of the tea could, he suggested, be made up by a corresponding reduction from other rations. In the meantime, the rations issued in Treaty Seven remained inadequate as the Department provided a daily per capita ration of less than five ounces of flour.[54]

An unusual calm fell over Indian administration in the North-West following the turbulent summer of 1884. Although there had been a near total crop failure in the North-West that year, the autumn annuity payments were carried out without difficulty. Still, the Department received numerous warnings throughout the winter of 1884-85 that a settlement with Indian and Métis peoples should be sought without delay. The government was not, however, prepared to renegotiate the terms of the treaties nor to allow the creation of the large Indian territory sought by Big Bear and his allies. In an attempt to head off a further series of Indian councils planned for the summer of 1885, Dewdney sought to placate the Cree with increased rations and by finally supplying all of the goods stipulated in the treaties.[55] If these measures failed, then he would order the arrest of key Cree leaders under charges of incitement to insurrection, even though neither he nor the police anticipated violence from the Cree political movement.[56] These plans were in place when armed conflict erupted between the Métis and government forces.

V

The most remarkable aspect of Indian involvement in the North-West Rebellion of 1885 was that it was so limited.[57] A much detested Indian agent and eight other men were killed by a few dissident members of Big Bear's band; two farming instructors

---

[53] PAC, MG 26A, Vol. 210: 42864-71, Dewdney to Macdonald, 5 September 1884.
[54] PAC, RG 10, 15040 Black, Wadsworth to Dewdney, 14 August 1884.
[55] Tobias, "Canada's Subjugation of the Plains Cree," 542.
[56] Ibid.
[57] For further detail see Desmond Morton, *The Last War Drum* (Toronto: Hakkert, 1972) and Bob Beal and Rod Macleod, *Prairie Fire: The 1885 North-West Rebellion* (Edmonton: Hurtig, 1984).

in the Battleford District were also murdered in a settling of personal scores.[58] The only major action Indian forces took part in was the Battle of Cut Knife Hill where government forces, fearful of missing out on military action and glory, attacked the group that had gathered around Poundmaker. Only the remarkable restraint shown by Cree leaders saved the government force from being massacred. Elsewhere in the North-West a number of bands left their reserves and killed their cattle for food.

Government officials chose to construe these events as comprising an attempted insurrection by "rebel" Indians, thus providing themselves with the means to prosecute the leaders of the Cree political movement despite ample evidence of the efforts of these leaders to prevent violence. In addition to the eight Indians convicted of murder and hanged at Battleford, Big Bear and Poundmaker were sentenced to prison terms after being tried in a politically expedient fashion.[59] So ended the Cree movement to renegotiate the treaties.

During the summer and fall of 1885 the Department considered a number of proposals for the future management of Indian affairs in the North-West Territories. A memorandum submitted to Dewdney by Assistant Indian Commissioner Reed was illustrative of the repressive stance assumed by the Department;[60] Indian agents, he suggested, should ensure that "rebel" Indians understand that they had forfeited every claim "as a matter of right." A policy of rewarding "loyal" Indians was adopted, and blankets, cattle and ponies that had been confiscated from "rebel" Indians were distributed to those bands that had distinguished themselves during the Rebellion by inaction.[61] To guard against further trouble, the Indian appropriation for the North-West was raised to its 1882 level. Although expenditures in Treaties Four, Six and Seven fell off in the late 1880s, this reflected a sizeable drop in population following the Rebellion. By the end of the decade there was an annual ratio of 41.71 births per thousand Indians as compared to a death rate of 46.38 in the North-West.[62] A sharply declining Indian population made it much easier to maintain economy in Indian administration, at least in the short run. The staggering social and human costs triggered by the decision to sacrifice a co-partnered reserve agricultural programme to a rigid and arbitrarily defined political position would not become apparent until the next century.

The reserve agricultural programme initiated prior to 1885 fell short of achieving government expectations not only because unrealistic short-term goals had been set for it, but also because the purposes of this programme took second place to federal

---

[58] Tobias, "Canada's Subjugation of the Plains Cree," 543-46.

[59] For accounts of these trials see Sandra Estlin Bingaman, "The Trials of Poundmaker and Big Bear," *Saskatchewan History* 28 (1975): 81-94.

[60] Dewdney Papers, Vol. 6: 1414-20, Reed to Dewdney, 20 July 1885.

[61] Glenbow-Alberta Institute, Memorandum of rewards to Indians especially distinguished for loyalty during the late rebellion, n.d.

[62] PAC, RG 10, 63912 Black, Vankoughnet to Reed, 3 January 1890.

officials' determination to bring Big Bear and other activists under control. Moreover, the compulsion to observe the strictest possible economy that echoed through almost every facet of government operations proved to be a major stumbling block in officials' dealings with Indians. Although the Department of Indian Affairs continued its programme to develop farming on reserves, the initial premise of the reserve agricultural programme—at least as it had been conceived of by Indians—was lost. The farming conducted on prairie reserves after 1885 was no longer the achievement of Indians who were seeking to become self-sufficient members of a new society; instead, it comprised the carefully supervised activities of a people who had become the involuntary wards of government.

In the wake of the Rebellion, Indian agents came to exercise administrative control over almost every aspect of reserve life. Reserves became highly regulated units within a closed system of federal Indian administration. Access to Indians and to information about Indian administration was closely controlled by federal authorities who attributed the slow progress made in reserve agriculture in subsequent years to the nature of Indians as an uncivilized, non-Christian people. In time the Department's self-serving characterization of Indians as being dependent upon government became a self-fulfilling prophecy. Eighteen eighty-five signalled the loss of Indians' ability to affect in any direct or significant fashion the conditions under which they lived. Henceforth their choices were limited to deciding whether to take an active part in reserve agriculture and to place themselves under the unrelenting tutelage of government personnel or whether to adopt a course of circumspect but determined passive resistance. In either case they would remain dependent figures, subject to the ideological presumptions and instrumental power relations of the Canadian Indian administration. By the turn of the century, the Minister in charge of Indian Affairs, Clifford Sifton, would champion a policy of transferring unused Indian reserve lands into the hands of speculators and Euro-Canadian settlers.[63]

The policies and actions that served to undermine Indians' initial efforts to respond positively to the disappearance of the buffalo represent an historical indulgence that succeeding generations of Indians have had to endure. A century later Canadians have become willing at least to listen to Indian leaders' proposals for achieving self-reliance and greater autonomy for their communities. To accomplish these ends it will be necessary to come to terms with the unfortunate legacy of a hundred years of tutelage and enforced dependency. A small but essential step towards this objective will be to recognize that the virtual exclusion of Indians from the history of prairie development tells us a great deal more about government than it does about Indians.

---

[63] See D.J. Hall, "Clifford Sifton and the Administration of Indian Affairs, 1896-1905," *Prairie Forum* 2 (1977): 127-51.

Aboriginal Title

Thomas Flanagan

Why then did the North-West Rebellion occur at all, if the objective grievances of the *Métis* were remedied by the government? In this connection, it must be remembered that many other factors contributed to the *Métis'* sense of alienation. They were still bitter over the events in Manitoba, which, in spite of the seeming success of the movement of 1869-70, had left them a marginal minority in their own homeland. Having moved farther west to escape this status, they could see themselves once again faced with being outnumbered by white settlers. Another long-range consideration was the decline of the *Métis* economy. The buffalo withdrew from the Canadian prairies during the 1870s and vanished altogether after 1878, adversely affecting numerous trades in which the *Métis* had been prominent: buffalo hunting, trading with the Indians for pemmican and robes, and transporting these goods to market. The *Métis* cart trains and boat brigades also suffered from the advent of railways and steamboats in the Canadian West. Deprived of much of the income from traditional occupations, the *Métis* had to rely more on agriculture. As they began to make this transition, they were struck, as were all western farmers, by the economic depression and a fall in grain prices which began in 1883. For the *Métis* of St. Laurent, this economic malaise was aggravated by the decision to build the Canadian Pacific Railway along the southern route through Regina instead of along the northern route through Prince Albert. The *Métis* lost out on the jobs and contracts that would have been created by a construction boom in northern Saskatchewan.

All these factors help to explain the prevailing mood in St. Laurent, yet none really accounts for the outbreak of the Rebellion; for similar factors were equally at work in other *Métis* settlements which did not turn to violence. The unique fact about St. Laurent was the presence of Louis Riel. His great prestige made him a prism through which all information from the outside world was refracted to the *Métis*. His interpretation of the government's concessions made them seem like provocations. Any explanation of why the rising occurred must focus on Riel. What motivated him to take up arms? Such questions can never be answered with total certainty, but one can make a reasonable estimation of the forces at work in his mind at this time.

First was Riel's brooding resentment over the aftermath of 1869-70. Thinking himself the natural leader of his people, he had expected a quick amnesty followed by a successful career in politics. Instead he received exile, loss of his Commons seat, and penniless obscurity. His own misfortunes paralleled those of the *Métis* as they were submerged in Manitoba politics and went into voluntary emigration. Riel's bitterness lay behind the efforts he would make in the winter of 1884-85 to obtain a cash payment from the federal government. In his mind, this was fair compensation for the wrongs he had suffered. The failure of these efforts to show any tangible result must have strengthened his readiness to undertake extreme measures.

A second factor was Riel's religious "mission." As I have shown at length in *Louis "David" Riel: "Prophet of the New World,"* he believed himself to be a divinely inspired prophet, even after his "cure" in the insane asylums of Quebec. His mission of religious reform was only in abeyance, awaiting a signal from God to be made public. The longer he stayed with the *Métis*, the more ostentatious became Riel's piety. He began to argue with the Oblate missionaries over points of politics and theology, until the exasperated priests threatened him with excommunication. The notebook of prayers he kept over the winter of 1884-85 shows an ascending curve of spiritual confidence culminating in readiness for action. Riel launched the Rebellion convinced it was the occasion to reveal his new religion to the world. That is why he began his first major speech to the *Métis* with the words, "Rome has fallen."

In spite of this religious dimension, Riel's rising was a political phenomenon whose causes must also be sought at the political level. If the *Métis* grievances over river lots and land scrip do not furnish an adequate explanation, more insight can be found through examining Riel's views on aboriginal rights. For reasons explained below, he held that the *Métis* were the true owners of the North-West; that their entry into Confederation had been conditional upon fulfilment of the Manitoba "treaty;" and that they were legally and morally free to secede from Canada since (in his view) the "treaty" had not been kept by Canada. In this sweeping perspective, the grievances of river lots and scrip were petty complaints, useful in mobilizing local support but peripheral to the real issues. Study of the course of the agitation, from July 1884, when Riel arrived at St. Laurent, to February 1885, the eve of the Rebellion, demonstrates that his strategy was built upon his radical view of aboriginal rights. Pre-existing local grievances were only pawns in a complex series of manoeuvres aimed at vindicating *Métis* ownership of the North-West as a whole. To understand this is to explain the apparent paradox that the *Métis* launched an insurrection immediately after the government granted their demands. Under Riel's leadership, they were fighting for stakes which far transcended river lots and scrip. They may have only dimly perceived what the real goals were, but these are plain enough in Riel's writings.

Conflicting Views of Aboriginal Rights

Riel's political views can only be appreciated against the background of the events of 1869-70 and their aftermath. In his interpretation of these events he was quite different from official circles in Ottawa or London. To see the magnitude of this difference, we must first sketch the official view. Here, a word of caution is required. What I call the "official view" was not articulated until the *St. Catherine's Milling*

Case, decided in 1889. But the theory of aboriginal rights developed in this case was, I believe, implicit in the practice of the previous decades, including the acquisition of Rupert's Land by Canada and subsequent dealings with Indians and halfbreeds in that territory. Naturally, there is room for debate over the exact contours of an implicit, unarticulated view.

To the rulers of Britain and Canada as well as to the proprietors of the Hudson's Bay Company, the acquisition by Canada of Rupert's Land and the Northwestern Territories was a complicated real estate conveyance. In return for compensation from Canada, the Company surrendered its land to the Crown, which in turn passed it to Canada by Act of Parliament and Royal Proclamation. The transaction was founded on the property rights conferred on the Company by the royal charter of 1670:

> ...the sole trade and commerce of all those seas, straights, bays, rivers, creeks and sounds in whatsoever latitude they shall be that lie within the entrance of the straights commonly called Hudson's Straights together with all the lands and territories upon the countries, coasts, and confines of the seas, bays, lakes, rivers, creeks, and sounds aforesaid that are not already actually possessed by or granted to any of our subjects or possessed by the subjects of any other Christian prince or state.[1]

It is true that Canada had accepted the Company's ownership rights only reluctantly and after years of protest, putting forward the different theory that most of Rupert's Land ought to belong to Canada because of the explorations undertaken from New France. But the Colonial Office refused any measures that might diminish the Company's rights, and in the end the sale went through on the assumption that the Company was the rightful owner of this immense territory.

When the *Métis* of Red River, who had never been consulted about the sale, showed signs of resistance, the Canadian government refused to take possession, much as a purchaser might refuse to take possession of a house which had undergone damage in the period between signing of contract and date of transfer. The Imperial government doubted the legality of Canada's position but did not force the issue. Canada invited the inhabitants of Red River to send a delegation to Ottawa to make their concerns known. Having discussed matters with the three delegates (Father N.-J. Ritchot, Alfred Scott, John Black), the Canadian government drafted the Manitoba Act to respond to the desires of Red River: provincial status, responsible government, official bilingualism, protection of customary land rights, etc. Importantly, the Manitoba Act was a unilateral action of the Canadian Parliament, not a treaty between independent partners (although it was probably *ultra vires* of the Canadian Parliament and had later to be confirmed by Imperial statute). Payment for

---

[1] Cited in Peter A. Cumming and Neil H. Mickenberg, *Native Rights in Canada* (Toronto: General Publishing, 1972; second edition), p. 138. I have modernized the orthography.

Rupert's Land was made in London after the Company delivered the Deed of Surrender to the Colonial Office; and the Imperial government, by Order-In-Council of 23 June, 1870, annexed Rupert's Land to Canada, effective 15 July.

It was always assumed by both governments that aboriginal rights of the Indians would be respected. Indeed section 14 of the Order-In-Council of 23 June, 1870 specified that "any claims of Indians to compensation for lands required for purposes of settlement shall be disposed of by the Canadian Government in communication with the Imperial Government."[2] The *Métis* were not explicitly mentioned, but the Canadian government had already recognized their aboriginal rights in the Manitoba Act.

Native title was not seen as sovereignty in the European sense. Only a state could claim sovereignty, and the North American Indian tribes had never been organized as states. Hence, the validity of claims to sovereignty made by European states on the basis of discovery, settlement, and conquest. Nor was Indian title understood as ownership in fee simple, for the nomadic tribes of North America had never marked off plots of land in a way compatible with European notions of private property. Indian title was interpreted as an encumbrance upon the underlying title to the land held by the sovereign. Indians had a real and enforceable right to support themselves on this land as they had from time immemorial. This right could be surrendered only to the sovereign, not to private parties; and compensation had to be paid for surrender, according to the ancient principle of common law that there should be no expropriation without compensation.

This understanding was legally articulated in the *St. Catherine's Milling Case*, decided by the Supreme Court of Canada in 1887 and the Judicial Committee of the Privy Council in 1889. There, aboriginal title was defined in the context of a dispute between the governments of Ontario and Canada over who owned the lands ceded by the Ojibway in Treaty No. 3:—the Crown in right of Canada or the Crown in right of Ontario? We can ignore this aspect of the dispute to concentrate on the issue of aboriginal title. To explain this concept, the judges resorted to the concept of usufruct, which in Roman law was the right to use and enjoy the fruits of property— usually slaves or a landed estate—without actually owning it. The holder of usufructuary rights could enjoy the property undisturbed during the life of those rights, but could not sell or otherwise alienate the property. At the expiration of the usufruct, the property reverted to the owner. The Canadian and British courts, seeking to interpret aboriginal title as it had developed over the centuries, used the concept of usufruct as an analogy. They cast the sovereign in the role of owner and the natives in the role of holders of "a personal and usufructuary right"[3] to occupy the land and support themselves from its produce. This limited right stemmed from the benevolence of the sovereign, who had not yet chosen to make use of the land in

---

2 Ibid., p. 148.
3 See ibid., pp. 13-50.

other ways. It was an internal concession made by the sovereign as part of Indian policy; it was not a right to be claimed under the law of nations by Indian tribes as if they were sovereign nations.

Title, thus, was vested in the Crown. The aboriginal right to use the land was an encumbrance on that title which had to be extinguished before the Crown could alienate the land to private owners. Extinguishment required compensation, which might take the form of land reserves, money payments, educational or medical services, etc. Logically, the situation was not different from other real estate conveyances where an encumbrance existed upon a title, as from mortgage or other debt. Title had to be cleared before alienation through sale or donation was possible.

The Canadian government acted on this basis to extinguish aboriginal rights in Rupert's Land. The Indians were dealt with in the numbered treaties of the 1870s, and a land grant of 1,400,000 acres was divided among the *Métis* of Manitoba. The only anomaly concerned the *Métis* of the North-West Territories, where delay had ensued for various reasons. But on the eve of the Rebellion, the government announced that it would also deal with them, although the precise form that compensation would take was apparently still undecided. This sequence of actions should have wiped the slate clean, according to the official view. All encumbrances to title should have been removed, all aboriginal rights extinguished. Without injustice to Indian or *Métis*, the government could open the land for homesteading, make land grants to railways or colonization companies, and in general act as a landlord with a clear title.

It is crucial to appreciate the intellectual framework within which the government acted. From offer to purchase through taking possession and finally clearing title, everything was based on the validity of the Hudson's Bay Company's charter and on the contemporary understanding of aboriginal rights. The quarrel with Riel arose in large part because he had a view of the situation which diverged at fundamental points. This view was never expressed completely and systematically, but it may be put together from various writings and utterances. Since many of these statements come from the months after the Rebellion was put down, there may be some question as to whether they adequately represent Riel's earlier ideas. We must presume they do; otherwise there is not enough material to analyze Riel's thinking at the pivotal moment of the Rebellion's outbreak. Apart from this one assumption, we will try not to impose an artificial consistency upon the thoughts of a man who was not a political philosopher.

Riel explicitly denied the validity of the Hudson's Bay charter because of its monopolistic provisions. The Company's sole right to trade "unjustly deprived the Northwest of the advantages of international trade and the rest of humanity, especially neighbouring peoples, of the benefit of the commercial relations with the North-West to which they were entitled."[4] The result was impoverishment and oppression of the native inhabitants, both Indians and *Métis*. Riel coined the term

---

[4] Louis Riel, [Mémoire sur les troubles du Nord-Ouest], *Le Canadien*, 26 December, 1885. Ms. Missing.

haute trahison internationale[5] to describe the situation which we might translate into today's idiom as "a crime against humanity." The charter was void, as was any sale based upon it; for the Company could not sell what it did not own. The most Riel would admit was that the Company had an interest in the land which it had sold to Canada;[6] but that transaction did not affect the natives, who were the true owners of the land. Aboriginal rights were clearly in Riel's mind not a mere encumbrance on the title but actual ownership—not individual ownership in fee simple, perhaps, but a collective ownership by the *Métis* as a nation and by the Indians as tribes. In effect, he reversed the official view according to which the Hudson's Bay Company was the true owner of lands in which the natives possessed an interest consisting of the usufructuary right of subsistence. Riel made the natives the owners of the lands in which the Company possessed the interest of being allowed to trade. They owned their land in the same way as all other nations owned their lands under the law of nations; their title was not merely a limited right of occupancy dependent on the grace of the sovereign. He stood in the tradition of *Métis* nationalism which stretched back to the conflict with the Hudson's Bay Company about the Selkirk Settlement. Traders of the Northwest Company had suggested to the *Métis* that the land was theirs, not the Company's, and the idea had persisted across the generations.

Riel had argued in a slightly different way when he established the Provisional Government on 8 December, 1869. He issued a Declaration which somewhat grudgingly conceded the legitimacy of the Company's regime while remaining silent about the question of ownership:

> This Company consisting of many persons required a certain constitution. But as there was a question of commerce only their constitution was framed in reference thereto. Yet since there was at that time no government to see to the interests of a people already existing in the country, it became necessary for judicial affairs to have recourse to the officers of the Hudson's Bay Company. Thus inaugurated that species of government which, slightly modified by subsequent circumstances, ruled this country up to a recent date.

Although this government "was far from answering to the wants of the people," the *Métis* "had generously supported" it. But now the Company was abandoning its people by "subjugat[ing] it without its consent to a foreign power," and according to the law of nations, a people abandoned by its government "is at liberty to establish any form of government it may consider suitable to its wants."[7] Thus the

---

[5] Ibid.

[6] Interview with C.B. Pitblado, *Winnipeg Sun*, 3 July, 1885.

[7] Thomas Flanagan, ed., "Political Theory of the Red River Resistance: The Declaration of December 8, 1869," *Canadian Journal of Political Science* 11 (1978): 154.

Provisional Government was legitimate according to the law of nations, and the Hudson's Bay Company had no right to transfer to Canada the land and people it had abandoned. Canada would have to deal with the Provisional Government if it was going to annex Rupert's Land.

Riel's original position of 1869 was that it violated that law of nations (or "international law" as we would say today) to transfer a population without seeking its consent. In 1885 he added the argument that the Company did not own Rupert's Land because its charter was void. Both arguments led to the same conclusions, that the sale to Canada was invalid until the inhabitants of Rupert's Land gave their consent, and that, living in a political vacuum, they certainly had the right to form their own government to negotiate the terms of sale on their behalf.

Riel not only sought to demonstrate the legitimacy of the Provisional Government through abstract reasoning, but also tried to show that the Provisional Government had been recognized by both Britain and Canada. He formulated the facts slightly differently on various occasions, but the main line of argument was always the same; ministers of the Canadian government had invited the insurgents to send delegates to Ottawa and had conducted negotiations with them. An amnesty had been promised by the Governor General himself, both directly and through intermediaries. Thus, both Canada and Britain had recognized the Provisional Government *de facto*, even if there had not been a formal exchange of ambassadors according to international protocol.[8]

The legitimacy of the Provisional Government was essential to Riel because it determined his interpretation of the Manitoba Act and of the entry of Manitoba into Confederation. His frame of reference was the law of nations (*droit des gens*), because negotiations had been carried out between independent entities, Canada and Red River. Rupert's Land had not been purchased; rather its inhabitants, acting through their government, had decided to join Canada. Union with Canada was not the result of unilateral action in Ottawa; it had required the assent of the Provisional Government, which was formally given after Father Ritchot returned from Ottawa to report on the terms offered by Canada. After the vote, Riel's "secretary of state" wrote to Canada's secretary of state to inform him that

> ...the Provisional Government and the Legislative Assembly, in the name of the people of the North-West, do accept the "Manitoba Act," and consent to enter into Confederation on the terms entered into with our delegates.... The Provisional Government and the Legislative Assembly have consented to enter into Confederation in

---

[8] *Le Canadien*, 26 December, 1885; and Petition "To His Excellency [Grover] Cleveland...," [August-September, 1885], NARS, Despatches from U.S. Consuls in Winnipeg, No. 44.

the belief, and on the understanding, that in the above mentioned terms a general amnesty is contemplated.[9]

The arrangement was a "treaty" in the sense of an international agreement between states. The treaty had two parts: the written text of the Manitoba Act and the oral promise of amnesty for all actions committed over the winter of 1869-70. This explains the final lines of Riel's pamphlet on the amnesty question:

> Ce que nous demandons, c'est l'amnistie: c'est l'exécution loyale de l'acte de Manitoba. Rien de plus, mais aussi rien de moins. [What we demand is amnesty—the fulfilment in good faith of the Manitoba Act—nothing more, but also nothing less.][10]

Riel literally meant that the annexation of Rupert's Land was the result of a "solemn treaty"[11] which, like all treaties, would become void if it were not observed. Ergo the annexation was reversible. The people of Rupert's Land, which had become the Province of Manitoba and the North-West Territories, could remove themselves from Canada if the treaty was broken in either of its branches: the amnesty or the Manitoba Act.

In Riel's view, Canada had betrayed its obligations under both headings. We will not go into the amnesty question here. It was certainly never far from Riel's mind, but it would not have sufficed to raise the flag of revolt among the *Métis* in 1885. This purpose was served by Riel's interpretation of the Manitoba Act, particularly of section 31, which authorized the half-breed land grant. At its time of entry into Confederation, Manitoba consisted of approximately 9,500,000 acres. With the 1,400,000 acres set aside by section 31 for the "children of half breed heads of families," the government clearly thought to equip each young *Métis* with enough land to make him economically self-sufficient. It was the same principle as the one by which Indian reserves were calculated at the rate of a quarter-section of land per family of five. The government was thinking in terms of the future needs of a special group among the population.

Riel, on the contrary, viewed the 1,400,000 acres as the sale price of the 9,500,000 acres comprised in Manitoba. This ratio set a precedent for the rest of the land of the North-West. As subsequent acres were opened for settlement, the *Métis* of those areas should receive a similar price, in order to extinguish their aboriginal title, namely one-seventh of the land or the financial value of the one-seventh. This would

---

[9] Cited in Stanley, *Birth of Western Canada*, p. 124.
[10] Louis Riel, *L'Amnistie* (Montréal: Bureau du "Nouveau Monde," 1874), p. 22.
[11] Ibid.

amount to about 176,000,000 acres for the North-West outside the original boundaries of Manitoba.[12]

Riel's single best explanation of this theory was given in his final trial speech. It must be read carefully, for his phrasing in English is sometimes awkward, even though the ideas are clear and logically developed:

> But somebody will say, on what grounds do you ask one-seventh of the lands? In England, in France, the French and the English have lands, the first was in England, they were the owners of the soil and they transmitted to generations. Now, by the soil they have had their start as a nation. Who starts the nations? The very one who creates them, God. God is the master of the universe, our planet is his land, and the nation and the tribes are members of His family, and as a good father, he gives a portion of his lands to that nation, to that tribe, to everyone, that is his heritage, that is his share of the inheritance, of the people, or nation or tribe. Now, here is a nation strong as it may be, it has its inheritance from God. When they have crowded their country because they had no room to stay anymore at home, it does not give them the right to come and take the share of all tribes besides them. When they come they ought to say, well, my little sister, the Cree tribe, you have a great territory, but that territory has been given to you as our own land, it has been given to our fathers in England or in France and of course you cannot exist without having that spot of land. This is the principle God cannot create a tribe without locating it. We are not birds. We have to walk on the ground, and that ground is encircled of many things, which besides its own value, increases its value in another manner, and when we cultivate it we still increase that value. Well, on what principle can it be that the Canadian Government have given one-seventh to the half-breeds of Manitoba? I say it must be on this ground, civilization has the means of improving life that Indians or half-breeds have not. So when they come in our savage country, in our uncultivated land, they come and help us with their civilization, but we helped them with our lands, so the question comes: Your land, you Cree or you half-breed, your land is worth to-day one-seventh of what it will be when the civilization will have opened it? Your country unopened is worth to you only one-seventh of what it will be when opened. I think it is a fair share to acknowledge the genius of civilization to such an extent as to give, when I have

---

[12] Louis Riel to J.W. Taylor, [2-3 August, 1885] NARS, Despatches from U.S. Consuls in Winnipeg, 1869-1906, No. 433; [Manifeste à ses concitoyens américains], [August-November, 1885], PAC, MG 27 IC4, 2150-56, 2159-60.

seven pair of socks, six, to keep one. They made the treaty with us. As they made the treaty, I say they have to observe it, and did they observe the treaty? No.[13]

The statement accepts and justifies the surrender of land by aboriginal peoples in return for compensation. To that extent, it is compatible with the official Indian policy of Britain and Canada. Beyond that, however, lie some marked differences. Riel seems to challenge the unilateral assumption of sovereignty which was the foundation of British rule in North America. (I say "seems to challenge" because his language is ambiguous; he does not distinguish between sovereignty and ownership). In any case, he certainly does not accept the principle of unilateral extinguishment of aboriginal title through legislation. The land grant of section 31 was valid compensation for surrender of land only inasmuch as it was part of a treaty approved by both sides. Furthermore, the basis of compensation was a *quid pro quo* as in any sale. Because the advantages of civilization could multiply the value of land seven times or more, the *Métis* would be at least as well off by surrendering six-sevenths of their land and adopting civilized ways while retaining one-seventh (or its money equivalent). It was most decidedly not a matter of government allocating a certain amount of land to each *Métis* individual. In another text, Riel derided this approach as a "sophism" designed to let the government "evade its obligations" and "frustrate the *Métis*, as a group or nationality, of their seventh of the lands."[14]

Riel's insistence on the principle of "the seventh" nicely illustrates the theoretical difference between his position and the official view. According to the latter, aboriginal title was only a "personal and usufructuary right" of the natives to gather subsistence from the land. If it was to be extinguished, it was logical to compute the compensation on the basis of the number of persons who would now have to subsist in other ways. Riel, however, maintained that the natives were the true proprietors of the soil in the full sense of ownership. Thus compensation for expropriation should be based on the value of the land, not on the number of people affected. To use a modern analogy, if a provincial government has to expropriate land for, say, a hydroelectric transmission line, it would compensate owners according to the fair market value of the asset, not according to the size of their families. Riel's understanding of the nature of aboriginal title drove him to demand analogous treatment for the *Métis*.

The government grudgingly agreed to a new issue of scrip to provide for the relatively few *Métis* who had not participated in the Manitoba land grant. But in Riel's mind, the whole North-West outside Manitoba still belonged to the *Métis*. The Hudson's Bay Company had sold whatever interest it had, and the Indians, at

---

[13] Desmond Morton, ed., *The Queen v. Louis Riel* (Toronto: University of Toronto press, 1974), pp. 358-59.

[14] Riel [Manifeste à ses concitoyens américains], 2150-56, 2159-60.

least in the fertile belt, had signed land surrender treaties. It was still necessary to extinguish the *Métis* title, and that could not be done with a few pieces of scrip. It would require payment of the value of one-seventh of the whole North-West, following the precedent solemnly established in the "Manitoba Treaty." And if that treaty continued to be broken, the *Métis* would no longer be part of Canada. According to the law of nations, they could once again form a Provisional Government and undertake negotiations with other governments. There might be a new treaty with Canada, or perhaps the North-West would become a separate colony within the Empire, or perhaps it would even ask for annexation to the United States, as Riel did after his trial. Everything was possible. It is this train of thought, and only this, which makes the North-West Rebellion intelligible.

The Agitation

When Riel came to Saskatchewan on 1 July, 1884, it was expected that his work would last only a brief time. The people knew what they wanted; all they needed from Riel was advice on the best way of pressing their demands within constitutional limits. But nothing was sent to the government until 16 December, 1884, and that petition was only a preliminary draft. Work on further declarations continued well into February, 1885. Why did things drag on for such a long time? Probably because Riel was trying to unite several incompatible points of view:

1) His own radical theory that the North-West Territories were free to leave Confederation if Canada continued to refuse large-scale compensation for extinguishment of *Métis* aboriginal rights.
2) The desire of the *Métis* for an issue of scrip and settlement of their disputes with the Department of the Interior. Their aims were moderate; but, as events would show, many of them were willing to resort to arms to achieve their goals.
3) The desire of the English half-breeds for the same goals as the *Métis*. The difference was that the half-breeds were not willing to take up arms.
4) The intention of a group of white businessmen in Prince Albert, mostly allied to the Liberal Party, to win provincial status and responsible government for the North-West. Their most active figure, William Henry Jackson, was willing to consider separation from Canada, but it is not known whether there was much support for his extreme position.
5) The demand of the more militant Indians, whose most prominent spokesman was Big Bear, for a renegotiation of treaties on more favourable terms.

Riel tried to coalesce all these groups around his own views, but irreconcilable differences made the coalition unstable. The *Métis* were willing to follow him, except for those, particularly of the merchant class, who disapproved of armed force. The English half-breeds could accept his demand for a massive settlement of aboriginal rights, but they also disapproved of force. William Henry Jackson and perhaps others among the whites were willing to consider a rupture with Canada, but they were put off by Riel's ideas on aboriginal rights, which would have enriched the *Métis*, half-breeds, and Indians at the expense of the white community.

In the nine months between his return to Canada and the outbreak of the Rebellion, Riel grappled with this political problem. He wrote or collaborated on the writing of several documents, but none were completed. Those which expressed his own views could not command universal support among the different groups, while those which could be supported did not express his own radical theory. Thus no single text was produced which adequately expressed all the demands which led to the Rebellion.

Let us now follow the course of the agitation from Riel's return to Canada up to the eve of the Rebellion. This is not a general history of these months, which has been well written by Stanley and others. It is a study of the intellectual difficulties faced by Riel in melding his own views with those of the groups he hoped to organize under his leadership. The analysis is sometimes speculative because very little written by Riel during the period of the agitation has been found. However, there is abundant material in the papers of Riel's collaborator, William Henry Jackson, with which to fill the gaps.[15]

Riel was received at Fish Creek on 1 July. He made public appearances to the *Métis* and half-breeds within the next two weeks, but we do not know what he said. His first major appearance was a speech in Prince Albert, 19 July. His own notes, and the various transcripts of the speech, show that he stressed provincial status and responsible government, themes dear to that audience. "Let the people of Assiniboia, of Alberta, of Saskatchewan petition in the proper manner for immediat[e] admission as provinces in the confederation." Riel also admonished his listeners to insist on provincial control of public lands, which had been denied Manitoba. But they were to strive for all this strictly "within the bonds of constitutional energy."[16] One account reports a brief reference to aboriginal rights;[17] but the reporter garbled what Riel said, and probably its full significance was not apparent to the audience.

---

[15] I am indebted to the new research on Jackson carried out by Donald B. Smith and Miriam Carey, although my interpretation differs somewhat from theirs. See Smith, "William Henry Jackson: Riel's Secretary," *The Beaver* 311 (Spring, 1981): 10-19; *idem*, "Honoré Joseph Jaxon: A Man Who Lived for Others," *Saskatchewan History* 34 (Autumn, 1981): 81-101; Carey, "The Role of W.H. Jackson in the North-West Agitation of 1884-85," Honours Thesis, University of Calgary, Political Science, 1980.

[16] [Notes for Speech in Prince Albert], [19 July, 1885], PAC, RG 13 B2, 2359, 2345.

[17] Prince Albert *Times*, 25 July, 1885.

Shortly after this meeting Jackson circulated an open letter to residents of Prince Albert and the surrounding area. It began: "We are starting a movement in this settlement with a view to attaining Provincial Legislatures for the North-West Territories and if possible the control of our own resources, that we may build our railroads and other works to aid our own interests rather than those of the Eastern Provinces." Readers were asked to send delegates to the executive committee, "which will be called together in a few days to put our own statement of rights in final shape." The petition would be sent to Ottawa for action by the Canadian government, though Jackson also mentioned a more radical option: "Possibly we may settle up with the East and form a separate Federation of our own in direct connection with the crown." There was no mention of the *Métis*, except to say that Riel had united them "solidly in our favour;" nor was there mention of Riel's special theories.[18]

Jackson's reference to "a few days" shows he was thinking of quick action. This is confirmed by a letter he wrote to Riel the same day: "Today I shall finish up work in town and tomorrow start for the Lower Flat, etc. I will try and get out to your place toward end of week. Please be working up the petition into shape and we will get it in neat form before the committee is called to endorse or alter it."[19] This sense of urgency was apparently shared by Riel, for he wrote at this time that he intended to return to Montana around September.

The petition which Jackson expected to finish in a few days has been preserved among his papers. It chided the British government for having permitted the North-West Territories to be governed by men "chosen by and responsible to not the people of the said Territories but the people of the Eastern Provinces."[20] A long list of grievances mentioned public works and services, taxation, tariffs, monopolies, and other topics of interest to local businessmen. Homestead regulations got only a few lines, and aboriginal rights were barely mentioned. It was clearly a Prince Albert document, one that would have little appeal to the *Métis* or to Riel, except that he would have been in accord with its closing demand that the Territories "be forthwith formed into Provinces, each Province having full control of its own resources and internal administration, and having power to send a just number of representatives to the Federal legislature."[21]

Another and much more radical draft seems to be connected with Jackson's idea of "settling up with the East." Alleging that the "Government of Eastern Canada hath

---

[18] W.H. Jackson to "Gentlemen," 23 July, 1884, PAC, RG 13 B2, 512-17.
[19] W.H. Jackson to Louis Riel, 23 July, 1884, PAC, RG 13 B2, 503-9.
[20] Louis Riel to Joseph Riel and Louis Lavallée, [25?] [July, 1884], PAM, MG 3 D1, No. 418.
[21] USL, A.S. Morton Mss. Collection C555/2/13.9v. Typescript, original missing. Several other typed drafts are in the same collection. None is dated, but the contents match the description of the petition given by Jackson in his letter to "Gentlemen," note 18 *supra*.

grossly exceeded and abused" its trusteeship over the North-West, it calls upon Great Britain

> to assert its suspended Guardianship and remove the Trusteeship of the said lands from the hands of the Gov't of Eastern Canada and place it in the hands of a council composed partly of members elected by the actual residents to protect interests of actual settlers, and partly of members nominated by Brit. Gov't. to protect interests of future settlers.[22]

August brought two reasons for delay. When a visit from Minister of Public Works Sir Hector Langevin was announced, it was decided to present a list of grievances to him; but he cancelled his trip late in the month. The second reason for delay was a broadening of the movement to include the Indians. In the first ten days of August there was a council of several Cree bands at the Duck Lake reserve. Several speakers denounced the treaties and called for renegotiation. Jackson seems to have been present and taken notes, for the speeches are recorded in his hand. Riel apparently did not attend, but he was in contact with the chiefs through intermediaries. Later in August, Riel and Big Bear met at Jackson's house in Prince Albert.[23] These delays caused resentment among the English half-breeds. James Isbister wrote to Riel on 4 September: "I cannot for a moment, understand what is your delay, in not having our Committee meeting, sitting and working.... I must say we the people of the Ridge, Red Deer Hill, Halcro's Settlement, and St. Catherine Parish find you are too slow, or does the delay rest with W. Jackson and his people?"[24] Isbister, one of those who had gone to Montana to fetch Riel, had been the earliest farmer around Prince Albert, and his opinion carried great weight. But even as Riel received this letter, he was off on another tack, this time particularly concerned with the *Métis*.

On 5 September the *Métis* held a large meeting at St. Laurent to discuss their grievances with Bishop Grandin, who was making a pastoral visit. Riel read aloud a memorandum of eleven points. Two days later, as Grandin left for Regina, Riel gave him a slightly abridged written version containing eight items.

It is not clear why the list was reduced from eleven to eight. Perhaps it was only because Riel was writing in haste under awkward conditions. One of the three omitted points was a demand for better rations for the Indians. Riel, complaining that the *Métis* and other settlers were forced to support the Indians, had called on the government to "make the Indians work as Pharaoh had made the Jews work"—a proposal that may lift some eyebrows among those who now regard him as a humanitarian. A second point was a request that the government should pay a

---

22   Ibid., C555/2/13.9q.
23   Sgt. W.A. Brooks to L.N.F. Crozier, 21 August, 1884, PAC, RG 13 B2, 522-23. Typed copy.
24   James Isbister to Louis Riel, 4 September, 1885, PAM, MG 3 D1, No. 412.

thousand dollars to build a convent wherever there were enough *Métis* to justify the nuns in coming to found a school. The third point was a demand for provincial status for the districts of the North-West as soon as their populations equalled that of Manitoba in 1870. Provincial status "should be accompanied by all the advantages of responsible government, including the administration of public lands."[25] The first two of the omitted points were rather peripheral to the agitation and to Riel's long-term goals, but the third was absolutely fundamental, so its omission is curious.

Its main idea was, however, partially included in the first item of the eight-point list given to Grandin, which called for "the inauguration of responsible government." Four other points on the list covered long-standing grievances of the local *Métis*. Riel wanted "the same guarantees ... as those accorded to the old settlers of Manitoba," which implied several things such as river lots, hay and wood privilege, and squatter's rights. He demanded patents for the plots of land along the Saskatchewan on which the *Métis* had settled, often in disregard of homestead rules. A land grant similar to that in Manitoba would of course be required. Finally, Riel requested that more contracts for public works be let to local inhabitants. These were all old items of complaint, and Riel's document added nothing new to their formulation.

The list did, however, contain three points, stemming directly from Riel, which added a whole new dimension to the *Métis* demands.

> 5. That two million acres be set apart by the government for the benefit of the half breeds, both Protestant and Catholic. That the government sell these lands; that it deposit the money in the bank, and that the interest on that money serve for the support of schools, for the construction of orphanages and hospitals, for the support of institutions of this type already constructed, and to obtain carts for poor half breeds as well as seed for the annual spring planting.
> 6. That a hundred townships, selected from swampy lands which do not appear habitable at the moment, be set aside by the government and that every eighteen years there take place a distribution of these lands to the half breed children of the new generation. This to last 120 years.
> 7. The Province of Manitoba has been enlarged since 1870. The half breed title to the lands by which it was enlarged has not yet been extinguished. Let that title be extinguished in favour of the half breed children born in the province since the transfer [i.e. since 15

---

[25] A copy of the memorandum in the hand of Louis Schmidt is included in his "Notes: Mouvement des Métis à St-Laurent Sask. TNO en 1885," AASB, T 29799-80. The original has not been found.

July, 1870] and in favour of the children born there for the next four generations.[26]

Item 5 amounted to a *Métis* trust fund designed to promote their economic and social advancement, while item 6 would have insured the availability of land to several new generations of *Métis*. Item 7, although vague, had the most radical implications, for it hinted at Riel's theory that *Métis* ownership rights to the North-West were still alive. All these points flow from his idea of collective ownership of the North-West by the *Métis* nation. Riel was asking for a two million acre reserve, plus a hundred townships (2,304,000 acres), plus something for the expansion of Manitoba: a considerable amount in all, but far less than one-seventh of the North-West. These demands were moderate because they were only a first instalment, as shown by Riel's postscript to the document: "This is what we ask while we wait for Canada to become able to pay us the annual interest on the sum that our land is worth and while we wait for public opinion to agree to recognize our rights to the land in their fullest extent (*dans toute leur étendue*).[27] Grandin gave a copy of Riel's text to Governor Dewdney, who forwarded an English translation to Sir John A. Macdonald. The bishop stated that he supported the traditional demands of the *Métis* but that he could not speak to the political questions of responsible government and aboriginal title.[28] Macdonald received additional information about Riel's postscript from A.-E. Forget, who had accompanied Grandin. Forget reported that Riel's document

> only purports to contain such requests as need an immediate settlement. In addition to these advantages, they claim that their right to land can only be fully extinguished by the annual payment of the interest on a capital representing the value of land in the Territories estimated to be worth at the time of transfer twenty-five cents an acre for the halfbreeds and fifteen cents for the Indians. This is the claim alluded to in the post-scriptum of Riel's memo to His Lordship.[29]

Forget added that the *Métis* were planning to draw up a memorial on this basis and send it to the House of Commons. He tried to persuade them to direct it to the governor general in council through Governor Dewdney.

A draft of such a memorial exists in Riel's hand, addressed to "Your Excellency in Council." The heading suggests it was written out after the conversation with Forget

---

[26] Louis Riel to J.-V. Grandin, [7 September 1884], ACAE, Correspondence of Vital Grandin.
[27] Ibid.
[28] Edgar Dewdney to J.A. Macdonald, 19 September, 1884, PAC, MG 26 A, 42897-905. The English translations are in ibid., 42935-41.
[29] A.-E. Forget to Edgar Dewdney, 18 September, 1884. Ibid., 42921-34.

on 7 September, although earlier drafts must have preceded this neatly written text. Unaccountably long overlooked, this document is an invaluable statement of Riel's true objectives.[30]

The text began by denouncing the Indian treaties as a swindle because they "are not based on a reasonable estimation of the value of their lands." The Indians would not be content until they receive this value. "It is the opinion of your humble petitioners that the land in its uncultivated state, with its natural wealth of game, fish, and berries cannot be worth less to the Indian than twelve and a half cents per acre." The same principle applied to the *Métis*, except that the land was worth twenty-five cents an acre to them because their usage of it was "fairly civilized." Then followed some calculations, based on certain assumptions:

—1,100,000,000 acres of land in the North-West
—100,000 Indians
—100,000 *Métis*
—5% interest rate

The result of these assumptions was an annuity of $68.75 for each Indian and $137.50 for each *Métis*. However, not too much importance was attached to these calculations, which were "only approximate." They were offered only to give "a fair idea" of *Métis* rights and to suggest "the profound distress in which the Dominion of Canada plunges us by taking possession of our lands and not giving us the adequate compensation we expect of it."[31]

The line of reasoning embodied in this petition was not a temporary aberration on Riel's part. He reproduced exactly the same argument in his last major piece of writing, published posthumously as "Les Métis du Nord-Ouest," except that he used figures of fifteen cents an acre for the Indians and thirty cents an acre for the *Métis*.[32] Furthermore, the total amounts of money involved were of the same magnitude as the value of the one-seventh of the North-West demanded at the trial.[33] The notion of a trust fund based on the value of the land surrendered flowed directly from Riel's conception of aboriginal title as collective ownership, not a mere encumbrance on the sovereign's title, and was in direct contrast to the official policy of calculating compensation proportionally to numbers of individuals rather than to the area of land involved.

---

[30] Gilles Martel, "Le Messianisme de Louis Riel (1844-1885)," Thèse de doctorat, Paris, 1976, p. 393.

[31] Pétition à "votre excellence en conseil," [September, 1884], PAC, RG. 13 B2, 42-43.

[32] "Les Métis du Nord-Ouest," Montreal *Daily Star*, 28 November, 1885.

[33] Riel's petition requested a total compensation to natives of 37_¢ per acre, slightly more than one-seventh of the current preemption price of $2.00 per acre.

Why this petition dropped completely from sight is one of the riddles of the agitation. One may conjecture that its radical theory of aboriginal rights was unacceptable to the white settlers whose support was indispensable to a joint movement. Collaboration with the white settlers and English half-breeds became very active in September. An important meeting was held 10 September at the home of Andrew Spence of Red Deer Hill. A brief minute of that meeting in the hand of Jackson shows the internal strains to which the movement was subject: "Committee met at Red Deer Hill, Andrew Spence's residence Wednesday afternoon, dispute whether Bill of Rights or petition. Committee appointed to prepare samples of both."[34]

As will be shown below, the "petition" was to be a list of grievances submitted to the government for redress. Compiling such a document was a purely constitutional action. The "Bill of Rights" was to be a more sweeping statement of the right of the people of the North-West to self-determination. To speak in such terms would at least be to border on sedition, and the committee was still undecided whether to go that far.

Not surprisingly, it was easier to compile the petition than the Bill of Rights. A draft seems to have been completed as early as 22 September,[35] and two days later a copy was sent to Archbishop Taché.[36] Further copies were mailed on 1 October to Father Constantine Scollen, an Oblate missionary in Alberta, and to J.W. Taylor, American Consul in Winnipeg.[37]

Of the three copies sent out, the only one to have been found is Taylor's. Written entirely in Riel's hand, it is very little different from the later draft sent to the secretary of state on 16 December. It was mostly concerned with the redress of specific grievances without challenging the government's authority. But the final paragraph showed a larger strategy:

> Your humble petitioners are of the opinion that the shortest and most effectual methods of remedying these grievances would be to grant the N.W.T. responsible government with control of its own resources [sic] and just representation in the federal Parliament and

---

[34] W.H. Jackson, [Note], [September, 1884], PAC, RG 13 B2, 159. The date of the meeting is taken from Jackson to J. Isbister, 8 September, 1884, PAC, RG 13 B2, 528.

[35] Louis Riel to W.H. Jackson, 22 September, 1884. USL, A.D. Morton Mss. Collection C555/2/13.7d.

[36] Enclosed in Louis Riel to A.-A Taché, 24 September, 1884. AD, W206.M62F, No. 744, p. 7. Microfilm; the original, once at AASB, is now lost.

[37] There are two drafts of a letter from Riel to Scollen, 1 October, 1884, PAC, RG 13 B2, 77 and 531-32. The final letter has not been recovered. The letter to Taylor, 1 October, 1884, is in DAMMHS, J.W. Taylor Papers, A partial draft, [1 October, 1884], is in PAC, RG 13 B2, 74-76.

> Cabinet. Wherefor[e] your petitioners humbly pray that your excellency in council would be pleased to cause the introduction, at the coming session of Parliament, of a measure providing for the complete organization of the District of Saskatchewan as a province; and that they be allowed, as in 70, to send delegates to Ottawa with their Bill of Rights, whereby an understanding may be arrived at as to their entry into confederation with the constitution of a free Province.[38]

The dispute over whether to prepare a petition or a Bill of Rights had been resolved by deciding to submit the petition first, followed by a Bill of Rights.

The document's meaning is not fully apparent until one recalls Riel's interpretation of the events of 1870. He was not merely calling for the government to hear and act upon complaints; he was proposing a new "treaty" in the international framework of the law of nations. This analysis is confirmed by Riel's covering letter to Taylor, which made the point emphatically:

> The people of the Northwest are poor. They are not happy under the Canadian rule; not only because their public affairs are improperly administered by the federal government, but because they are practically denied by that government the enjoyment *of the right of people*. [Riel's emphasis] That is principally what is ruining them.[39]

Another mystery of the agitation is that nothing further happened for two and a half months after this burst of activity in September. It may be that Riel and the others were waiting for signatures to be gathered. We know little about this, but efforts to obtain signatures in other parts of the Territories seem to have been made.[40] It may also be that they were waiting for reactions to the copies they had sent out.

Taché's reply was not slow in coming, nor was it encouraging. He told Riel to "give up useless agitation, give up certain ambiguities of language whose true meaning would not escape those who reflect."[41] He had obviously divined the implications of allusions to a Bill of Rights. Father Scollen, less politically sophisticated, was more positive. He passed the petition on to Dan Maloney, a

---

[38] Petition "To His Excellency the Governor General in Council, etc." [1 October, 1884] DAMMHS, J.W. Taylor Papers.

[39] Louis Riel to J.W. Taylor, 1 October, 1884, DAMMHS, J.W. Taylor Papers.

[40] A trip to Battleford is mentioned in Louis Riel to T.E. Jackson, 29 September, 1884. USL, A.S. Morton Mss. Collection, C555/2/13.73.

[41] A.-A. Taché to Louis Riel, 4 October, 1884. AASB, T 29742.

political figure of St. Albert who had befriended the *Métis* on other occasions. Maloney promised to do what he could to intercede with the government on their behalf.[42]

The final version of the petition, hardly changed from the text of late September, was sent on 16 December to the Secretary of State. There were several odd things about the submission which could not but detract from the impression it made in Ottawa. Although the petition was written out in longhand by Riel, his name did not appear anywhere. The petition in fact is unsigned, although earlier researchers, confusing the petition with the covering letter, have claimed it bore the names of W.H. Jackson and Andrew Spence.[43] There certainly is no long list of signatures of the kind one would expect to accompany such a petition. It seems that this submission was only preliminary, for Jackson was occupied after the New Year in collecting signatures. Apparently he intended to resubmit the signed petition directly to the Governor General. A covering letter, rather bold in tone, was provided by Jackson, who signed himself "Secretary General Committee," without explaining the nature of the committee:

> the petition is an extremely moderate one ... to the Canadian and English wing of the movement a more searching exposition of the situation would have been much more satisfactory. The opinion has been freely expressed that our appeal should be directed to the Privy council of England and to the general public rather than to the federal authorities.[44]

Jackson's choice of words was deliberately disingenuous. He admitted elsewhere that the petition "was purposely made weak, as a blind," because the agitators were not yet ready to show their hand to the government.[45] The petition gave the impression that it was one last attempt at moderation, which might be followed by more extreme measures if concessions were not made immediately; yet Jackson and Riel were already preparing their next steps even before the petition could have

---

[42] Constantine Scollen to Louis Riel, 10 November, 1884. PAM, MG 3 D1, No. 415; Dan Maloney to Louis Riel, 17 November, 1884, ibid., No. 416.

[43] Petition "To His Excellency the Governor General in Council," [16 December, 1884]. PAC, RG 15, Dominion Lands Branch Correspondence, File 83808. Assertions that the petition was signed by Andrew Spence and W.H. Jackson are made by Stanley, *Louis Riel*, p. 291; and Lewis H. Thomas, "Louis Riel's Petition of Rights, 1884," *Saskatchewan History* 23 (1970): 16-26.

[44] W.H. Jackson to J.A. Chapleau, 16 December, 1884. PAC, RG 15, Dominion Lands Branch Correspondence, File 83808.

[45] W.H. Jackson to Frank Oliver, 21 January, 1885. USL, A.S. Morton Mss Collection, C555/2/13.9e. Typescript, original not found.

reached its target. On 18 December, Jackson, back in Prince Albert, wrote to Riel that he would be down to see him in ten days or so, adding, "In the meantime please work away at your proclamation," probably a reference to the Bill of Rights.[46]

It cannot be emphasized too strongly that this petition was only secondarily an appeal to the Canadian government for redress of grievances, although it has generally been presented that way in the historical literature. It was primarily a step in a bigger campaign whose objectives, although not absolutely certain, were on a grand scale. Immediate provincial status, control of natural resources, renegotiation of the terms of Confederation, separation from Canada, and a vast settlement of aboriginal claims were all possible outcomes. The concrete grievances of the *Métis* had become merely a means to these ends.

The petition's ulterior purpose helps explain its peculiar structure. It was divided into two parts of roughly equal size: sixteen particular items of complaint, followed by a seventeenth item of great length rehearsing the events of 1870 and the government's subsequent failure to observe the "treaty." The sixteen points corresponded to specific grievances; the seventeenth laid the foundation of a demand for self-determination under the law of nations.

The specific grievances fell into several categories. One demand called for better rations for the Indians. Another called for a half-breed land grant as in Manitoba. Eight items concerned the complicated issues of survey and homestead requirements. The remaining six are readily identifiable as standard tenets of western Liberalism: greater efficiency and economy in public works and buildings, a Hudson's Bay railway, strict liquor laws, secret ballot, and free trade. This part of the petition was truly a comprehensive, if miscellaneous, catalog of local dissatisfactions.

The seventeenth point was in contrast a long, tightly reasoned chain of argument: the people of the North-West in 1870 had sent representatives to Ottawa who were recognized "as the Delegates of the North-West." Even as Canada negotiated with them, she was preparing a military expedition. Promises of amnesty were made and not fulfilled. The Imperial Order-in-Council annexing Rupert's Land to Canada was passed before the people of the North-West had a chance to ratify the agreement. Since that time Canada had continued to violate the "treaty" by denying provincial status to the North-West, by excluding Westerners from the cabinet, and by retaining control of natural resources. Riel did not openly state the conclusion of the argument, namely that the broken "treaty" had released the people of the North-West from allegiance to Canada, but he hinted at it obliquely, stating that inhabitants of the North-West "are treated neither according to their privileges as British subjects nor according to the rights of people." The implication is clear to anyone familiar with Riel's thinking. The petition closed with virtually the same words as those of the draft of October, calling for delegates to take a Bill of Rights to Ottawa and negotiate entry into Confederation.

---

[46] W.H. Jackson to Louis Riel, 18 December, 1885. PAM, MG 3D1, No. 417.

Not much came of this petition. A formal acknowledgement was sent to Jackson, while the document was sent to William Pearce for comment. In a point-by-point analysis, he argued that the specific grievances were based on misconceptions or were being dealt with.[47] Indeed the government had already made an inquiry into the homestead problems of St. Laurent and had decided to do something about scrip. Ironically, the petition had arrived after the major problems of the *Métis* were on the way to resolution.

However, the long-range plans of Riel and Jackson were very much alive, as we may deduce from a letter of 27 January. Having received a formal acknowledgement of the petition, Jackson wrote:

> I think with you [Riel] that the mere fact of an answer is a very good sign considering the bold tone of my letter and our audacious assumption that we are not yet in Confederation, an assumption which it seems to me, they have conceded in their letter.[48]

This was surely building on air, for the acknowledgement had only stated that "the matter will receive due consideration." But Jackson was looking for favourable signs for his work. His letter spoke rather confusingly of several documents he had drawn up. There was a reference to a petition for which he was collecting signatures, probably the petition which had already been submitted without signatures to the secretary of state. He may have planned to get it signed and resubmit it with more publicity. Also mentioned were

> a memorial suitable to catch the [Parliamentary] opposition in case the Council [i.e. cabinet] pay no attention—a stronger memorial for the Imperial sec'y of state for the Colonies in case the Federal Parliament pays no attention—and the Declaration of Rights for private circulation, and use if necessary. I will get all these documents signed along with the petition.[49]

The order of the documents suggests a strategy of appeals to cabinet, Parliament, and Great Britain, followed by a unilateral declaration of independence, if necessary. Jackson anticipated quick action as the parliamentary session was about to open, but he was also prepared for delays: "I will have the councillors in good heart for an unlimited period of quietness if found unavoidable. They must learn that quietness does not necessarily mean stagnation."

---

[47] H.J. Morgan to W.H. Jackson, 5 January, 1885; memo by William Pearce, n.d.; PAC, RG 15, Dominion Lands Branch Correspondence, File 83808.

[48] W.H. Jackson to Louis Riel, 27 January, 1885. PAC, RG 13 B2, 568-79.

[49] Ibid.

The description of the strategy was amplified in an undated note by Jackson. The plan was

> to organize every settlement & the N.W.T. convene a central congress in about two months and take our case direct to the throne. In the meantime we will send down a softly worded petition which will leave them under the impression that if they remove some of our present grievances, we will cease to agitate for the power to prevent other grievances. They will therefore ease the present situation by giving us a greater share of grain contract and an order to float cash among us, and we will then have the sinews of war to go for stronger measures. The Bill of Rights is composed so as to cover the whole North West. The various examples of the resolution of those rights will be collected in each settlement, and we will then have a clear case for the Privy Council.[50]

And more radical still:

Platform

1. In regard to Government:
   Petition Brit. Govt. to appoint Commit. & transfer Govt. to council.
   In case of refusal declare Independence and appoint Council & assume control.[51]

The most interesting document to recover would be the Bill of Rights, but it was deliberately burnt shortly before the battle of Duck Lake.[52] No one has stated why it was destroyed, but perhaps Riel felt it to be incriminating. His explanation of the revolt was that the *Métis* had taken up arms in self-defence, fearing they were about to be attacked by the Mounted Police.[53] That theory would have been seriously compromised by a Bill of Rights showing that an uprising had long been posited as a possible last step if other measures failed.

Some idea of the Bill of Rights can be gleaned from Jackson's letter of 27 January. As the Bill was an English document, Riel had left the writing to Jackson, who had looked up precedents in law books; but the thought came from Riel. His central principle was that "the world is governed by justice." It was unjust "that the

---

[50] W.H. Jackson, "Summary," n.d. USL, A.S. Morton Mss. Collection, C555/2/13.9o. Typescript, original missing.
[51] W.H. Jackson, "Platform," ibid.
[52] W.H. Jackson to "Dear Michel," 6 September, 1886. AASB, T53009-11.
[53] Louis Riel to Romuald Fiset, 16 June, 1885. PAC, RG 13 B2, 1036-43.

inhabitants of any section of the Globe should possess the right of irresponsible and infallible authority over the inhabitants of some other section of the Globe." Such rule from afar would spoil its subjects, subjecting them to injustice. The aboriginal inhabitants had self-government, and this "consistency between their institutions and natural law ... resulted in fair play & prosperity to each member of the community." But the introduction by the colonial powers of "irresponsible authority" had led to general misery. The declaration concluded "with the assertion of the natural right of self-government thus proven." It was obviously meant not as a theoretical statement but a call to action; Jackson was putting it "into such a simple shape that any ordinary man could catch the main drift of the argument at first reading."[54]

Although Riel and Jackson seemed agreed on strategy, signs of strain were already beginning to show in their alliance. A bizarre episode took place on 14 or 15 January when Riel was having dinner at the Jackson home in Prince Albert. He was served an end cut of roast beef, rather heavily seasoned with salt and pepper. After he tasted it, he ran outside and made himself vomit. Then he went to Father André's residence to fetch Charles Nolin, whom he mysteriously informed that attempts were being made to poison him. The incident, improbable as it sounds, is attested in several independent sources.[55] A few days later, Jackson wrote to the Edmonton newspaperman Frank Oliver: "Efforts are being made to separate Riel and myself, but though we differ on certain theoretical points we have too much confidence in each other's honesty of purpose for such attempts to succeed."[56]

In the first two weeks of February Jackson made the round of the English settlements, collecting signatures for the petition, memorials, and Bill of Rights. According to one report, he also had people sign an authorization for him to be their delegate to Canada.[57] On 14 February, he went upriver to the French parishes to collect more signatures. It was on this trip that he and Riel came into open conflict. According to the subsequent account of T. Eastwood Jackson, William's brother, "[Riel] opposed the petition, attacking it on the basis of Halfbreed ownership, and my brother being equally determined on the other side, the argument lasted all night, and became so fierce that Riel lost his self-control"[58] If Eastwood may be believed, William was kept under house arrest, from which he twice tried unsuccessfully to

---

[54] W.H. Jackson to Louis Riel, 27 January, 1885. PAC, RG 13 B2, 568-79.
[55] Louis Schmidt "Notes," AASB T 29811. It was described in very similar terms by Cicely Jackson to A.S. Morton, 25 June, 1932; USL, A.S. Morton Mss. Collection, C555/2/13.5 W.H. Jackson obliquely refers to it in his letter to Riel, 27 January 1885; PAC, RG 13 B2, 579. It is also mentioned in Louis Riel to Julie Riel, 9 June, 1885; PAM MG 3 D1, No. 420.
[56] W.H. Jackson to Frank Oliver, 21 January, 1885. USL, A.S. Morton Mss. Collection, C555/2/13.9e.
[57] Affidavit of John Slater, 28 July, 1885. USL, A.S. Morton Mss. Collection, C555/2/13.9h.
[58] T.E. Jackson, Letter to the Editor, Toronto *Globe*, 2 July, 1885.

escape. Whatever the precise details, it was definitely the end of the collaboration between Riel and Jackson as equal partners.

After the Rebellion was over and Jackson had been sent to a lunatic asylum, he briefly explained what had caused the argument. He had maintained his conviction

> that the particles of matter composing the Earth were the property of whosoever first chose to develop them into articles of utility except in case of the express allocation of land as in the case of Canaan, while Mr. Riel was, if I remember, pursuing the argument which I see he advanced on the occasion of his trial of Regina—that *every nation is allotted its means of existence in the shape of a land.*[59]

Since it hinges on the idea of uniting one's labour to the land to form property, Jackson's view may loosely be called Lockean. His report of his opinions corresponds substantially to a letter he wrote on 2 February, 1885 to Albert Monkman, a leader of the agitation who moved in both the *Métis* and English half-breed communities.

> Let this be our aim. Let us sink all distinctions of race and religion. Let the white man delight in seeing the Indian helped forward to fill his place as a producer of wealth, and let the Indian and Halfbreed scorn to charge a rent for the soil which God has given to man, upon the settler who comes in to help to build up the country ... and let both unite in seeing that the fur country be managed for the benefit of the Indians who live by hunting, not for the good of a grasping company. Direct the attention of the Indian to the H.B.Co. monopoly, and to the necessity of providing schools for those who wish to learn productive arts, and turn them aside from the idea of being landlords. Why should God give a whole continent to 40,000 Indians and coop up 40,000,000 Englishmen in on a little island? The Indians are the same race; they, too, once lived in Europe. America was once without a man in it, why should a part of the human race go into that empty continent, and as soon as they have got there, turn round and forbid any more to come in, unless they pay for the privilege?[60]

It is not hard to see why Riel would have been enraged by such a cogent critique of the very idea of aboriginal title. It contradicted the basis of the agitation as he saw it.

---

[59] W.H. Jackson to "My dear Family," 19 September, 1885. PAM, Selkirk Asylum Medical Records, MG 3 C20.

[60] Cited in T.E. Jackson to the Toronto *Globe*, 2 July, 1885. Original missing.

The agreement between Jackson and Riel on provincial status and responsible government was superficial compared to this profound disagreement about who really owned the North-West.

Riel began to assume a belligerent stance in public from 24 February onwards. Did the recent break with Jackson help steer him in that direction? Perhaps it made him feel that, if he continued the collaboration with the English, he would never be able to make his theory of aboriginal rights prevail.

Absence of documents, particularly on Riel's side, makes it likely that much will always remain obscure about the North-West agitation. But we know enough to realize how false is the naive version of events so often found in the contemporary literature. It would be more nearly true to tell the story thus: Riel saw in the grievances of the *Métis* an opportunity to implement his theory that the Manitoba "treaty" had been broken; that the *Métis* were the real owners of the North-West; that they could renegotiate entry into Confederation; that they must receive a seventh of the value of the land of the North-West as compensation for letting others live there; and that they could seek an independent political destiny if these terms were not met. Collaborating with white agitators like Jackson who were chiefly interested in provincial status and responsible government, he embarked upon a complex and deliberately deceptive strategy of making successively more radical demands. A Bill of Rights amounting to a Declaration of Independence was envisioned almost from the beginning. Finally, when Riel realized there was an unbridgeable gap between himself and Jackson, he determined to go it alone, as he had in 1869. The *Métis* would take the lead, rise in arms, and carry the English half-breeds and white settlers with them.

Labour and Industrialisation

Section 13

Perhaps the most dramatic transformation in 19th-century Canadian life was that produced by industrialisation and the rise of big cities. This not only changed methods of production but altered the organisation of work and the lives of workers and their families. Industrialisation threatened skilled craftsmen especially with loss of control over how they worked and in what conditions. For working class families, the rise of the industrial city meant a growing dependence on employers for the means to stay alive. As work concentrated increasingly in crowded cities, it became impossible to combine seasonal labour with farming or to supplement low and occasional wages by raising a few pigs or chickens or growing some vegetables in the yard.

These two articles describe some of the ways in which workers and their families responded to those threats. Both the authors are historical pioneers, Kealey as one of the founders of modern labour history in Canada, with its emphasis on workers' *experience* of their condition, and Bradbury for her part in bringing women and children to the centre of Canadian working class history.

What enabled pre-industrial craftsmen to have independence and control over their work? How did industrialisation threaten these? Why is it that some workers were able to organise themselves effectively to keep control, while others were not? How did families manage to cope with the problems of inadequate wages and unstable employment in an age when there was no unemployment insurance, public health, or other government welfare support? Many critics of industrialisation feared that impoverished and unstable conditions would destroy the family and weaken the influence of religion in working class lives. Does that appear to be the case from Bradbury's essay?

Students wanting a more general history of Canadian labour might be interested in Bryan Palmer, *Working Class Experience*.

"The Honest Workingman" and Workers' Control: The Experience of Toronto Skilled Workers 1860-1892[1]

Gregory S. Kealey

And now Canadian workingmen,
Arise and do your duty;
Behold these massive towers of stone,
In all their wondrous beauty.
Who builds those lovely marble towers,
Who works and makes the plans?
'Tis he who sleepless thinks for hours—
the honest workingman.

From "The Toilers" written for
The Ontario Workman, 17 July 1873.

Skilled workers in the nineteenth century exercised far more power than we have previously realized. Well on into the industrial period craftsmen through their trade unions played important roles in community affairs, in the world of politics and especially on the job. In Toronto workplaces, craftsmen employed their monopoly on skill and experience to dictate terms to their employers in a wide array of areas which, in modern parlance, gave to these late nineteenth century craftsmen a high degree of workers' control of production. In this paper I will describe the practice of three Toronto unions from the 1860s to the early 1890s to illustrate the extent of this power.

The three unions under discussion have been chosen to exemplify significant variants of trade union power in Toronto. They include: the relatively little known Coopers International Union, Ontario No. 3, which played an important role in the Nine Hour Movement and the establishment of the Toronto Trades Assembly; the extensively studied International Typographical Union No. 91; and the Iron Molders International Union No. 28, employed in Toronto's heavily capitalized stove,

---

[1] This is a revised version of "Workers' Control and Mechanization: The Experience of Toronto Skilled Workers, 1860-1892," a paper delivered at the McGill Colloquium on "Canadian Society in the Late Nineteenth Century" in January 1975. I would like to thank David Frank, Craig Heron and Bryan Palmer for their comments on that paper. The Dalhousie History Department North American Studies Seminar also gave the earlier version a useful critique.

machinery and agricultural implements industry. This great diversity of experience demonstrates that the crafts analyzed here, although each unique, are nevertheless not atypical of other Toronto skilled unions of this period. Other crafts could have been chosen and although the details would differ the overall patterns would remain much the same.

To date most discussion of artisanal resistance to the arrival of industrial capitalism has focused on the maintenance of pre-industrial work habits, the tenacious hold of ethnic cultural ties, and on the deep suspicion craft workers felt for "the new rules of the game" demanded by the advent of the market economy.[2] This analysis applies to workers undergoing the process of industrialization and will account for the Coopers' early Toronto experience but in studying the history of Toronto moulders and printers we will need other explanations.

David Montgomery has suggested that we must look beyond pre-industrial cultural forms if we are to understand the behaviour of skilled workers in late nineteenth century America. These workers often were "veterans of industrial life" who "had internalized the industrial sense of time, were highly disciplined in both individual and collective behaviour, and regarded both an extensive division of labour and machine production as their natural environment."[3] This was the world of Toronto moulders; Toronto printers, or rather Toronto compositors, occupied a position somewhere between the experience of the cooper and that of the moulder. The world of moulders and printers certainly drew on old craft traditions but it also transcended them. Although drawing on "residual" cultural categories there was much about their world that was "emergent," if we can borrow the important theoretical distinction drawn by Raymond Williams.[4] In the late nineteenth century Toronto skilled workers came to terms with the new industrial society but the terms they arrived at were those of constant resistance and struggle. The success that they and

---

[2] See Herbert Gutman, "Class, Status and the Gilded Age Radical: A Reconsideration" in Gutman and Kealey, eds., *Many Pasts: Readings in American Social History*, Vol. 2, (Englewood Cliffs 1973), 125-151 and his "Work, Culture, and Society in Industrializing America, 1815-1919," *American Historical Review*, 78(1973), 531-588; see also E.J. Hobsbawm, "Custom, Wages and Work-load," in *Labouring Men: Studies in the History of Labour*, (London 1964), 344-370.

[3] David Montgomery, "Workers' Control of Machine Production in the Nineteenth Century," *Labor History*, forthcoming. See also his "Trade Union Practice and the Origins of Syndicalist Theory in the United States," unpublished paper, and his "The 'New Unionism' and the Transformation of Workers' Consciousness in America, 1909-1922," *Journal of Social History*, 7 (1974), 509-529. All these are part of Montgomery's ongoing study, tentatively titled *The Rise and Fall of the House of Labor, 1880-1920*.

[4] Raymond Williams, "Base and Super-structure in Marxist Cultural Theory," *New Left Review*, 82 (Nov.-Dec. 1973), 3-16. For an application of these categories to U.S. working class history see Leon Fink, "Class Conflict and Class Consciousness in the Gilded Age: The Figure and the Phantom," *Radical History Review*, (Winter 1975).

other workers achieved forced management and government to devise entirely new strategies which have become commonly known as "scientific management" and "progressivism." Those innovations remain, however, subjects for other papers; here we will limit ourselves to an analysis of how the workers struggled, often successfully, for control of the workplace.[5]

I

The experience of coopers in Toronto and throughout Ontario in the late 1860s and early 1870s provides a classic case of the artisan response to industrial capitalism. Elsewhere I have described the confrontation that occurred between Toronto shoe manufacturers and the Knights of St. Crispin.[6] Although less dramatic in their response than the Crispins' Luddism, the coopers shared with the shoemakers the unfortunate fate of watching the destruction of their craft by a combination of mechanization, the rise of factory production, the depression of the 1870s, and an all-out employer offensive.

Originally organized on a shop basis, coopers enjoyed all the prerogatives of the skilled artisan. One vivid description of the old-time cooper's lifestyle follows:

> Early on Saturday morning, the big brewery wagon would drive up to the shop. Several of the coopers would club together, each paying his proper share, and one of them would call out the window to the driver,.'Bring me a goose egg,' meaning a half-barrel of beer. Then others would buy 'Goose Eggs' and there would be a merry time all around.... Saturday night was a big night for the old time cooper. It meant going out, strolling around town, meeting friends usually at a local saloon, and having a good time generally after a hard week's work. Usually the good time continued over Sunday, so that on the

---

[5] On scientific management in the U.S. see Milton Nadworny, *Scientific Management and the Unions*, (Cambridge, Mass. 1955); Katherine Stone, "The Origin of Job Structures in the Steel Industry," *Radical America*, 7 (1973), 19-66 and Bryan Palmer, "Class, Conception and Class Conflict: The Thrust for Efficiency, Managerial Views of Labor and the Working Class Rebellion, 1903-1922," *The Review of Radical Political Economics*, 7 (1975), 31-49. For Canada see Bradley Rubin, "Mackenzie King and the Writing of Canada's (Anti)Labour Laws," *Canadian Dimensions*, 8 (Jan. 1972); Michael Piva, "The Decline of the Trade Union Movement in Toronto, 1900-1915," unpublished paper, CHA, 1975; and Craig Heron and Bryan Palmer, "Through the Prism of the Strike: The Contours and Context of Industrial Unrest in Southern Ontario, 1901-1914," forthcoming.

[6] Gregory S. Kealey, "Artisans Respond to Industrialism: Shoemakers, Shoe Factories and the Knights of St. Crispin in Toronto," Canadian Historical Association, *Historical Papers*, (1973), 137-157.

following day he usually was not in the best condition to settle down to the regular day's work. Many coopers used to spend this day sharpening up their tools, carrying in stock, discussing current events and in getting things in shape for the big day of work on the morrow. Thus Blue Monday was something of a tradition with the coopers, and the day was also more or less lost as far as production was concerned. 'Can't do much today, but I'll give her hell tomorrow,' seemed to be the Monday slogan. But bright and early Tuesday morning 'Give her hell' they would, banging away lustily for the rest of the week until Saturday, which was pay day again, and new thoughts of the 'Goose Eggs.'[7]

However these older artisanal traditions were coming under attack at mid-century from trade unionists as well as efficiency-minded manufacturers. A St. Louis cooper's 1871 letter depicts both the tenacity of the old tradition and the new attitudes of skilled workers:

The shops are paid off every two weeks, on which occasion one of these shops is sure to celebrate that time-honoured festival, Blue Monday. When Blue Monday falls it usually lasts for three days. And the man who succeeds in working during the continuance of this carnival is a man of strong nerve and indomitable will. Mr. Editor, did you ever hear of Black Monday? Perhaps not. But I tell you wherever Blue Monday is kept, there also is kept Black Monday. The only difference is, Blue Monday is celebrated at the shop, while Black Monday is observed at the cooper's home. The man celebrates Blue Monday, but the wife and family observe Black Monday.[8]

In 1870 craftsmen created the Coopers International Union in order, as the Chicago *Workingman's Advocate* so aptly put it, to avoid the fate of the ship caulkers and ship carpenters, artisanal victims of the new age of iron and steam.[9] The new union with head offices in Cleveland was "in many ways the model of a successful organization of skilled mid-nineteenth century American craftsmen."[10] Its leaders were deeply embedded in the labour reform tradition which found its organizational expression through the National Labor Union in the U.S. In Canada the Cooper's International Vice-President, John Hewitt, played an active role in

---

[7] Franklin E. Coyne, *The Development of the Cooperage Industry in the United States, 1620-1940*, (Chicago 1940), 24.

[8] *Coopers' Journal* [henceforth *CJ*] May 1871, 210-211.

[9] *Chicago Workingman's Advocate*, March 19, 1870.

[10] H.G. Gutman, "The Labor Policies of the Large Corporation in the Gilded Age: The Case of the Standard Oil Company," unpublished paper, October 1966, 10.

organizing the Toronto Trades Assembly and the Canadian Labor Union, and was one of the major theorists of the Nine Hour Movement of 1872. The C.I.U. created a union structure which provided sick and death benefits, an international strike fund, and a card system for tramping members. Entering Canada in 1870 the union organized 24 branches in the first two years of its existence.[11] In early 1872 on a visit to Chicago John Hewitt announced that "the coopers in Canada were alive and active and increasing their organization rapidly."[12] Their decline was to be equally precipitous, but let us first examine the basis of their strength.

Coopers, like most skilled workers in the late nineteenth century, can best be described as "autonomous workmen." This term, usefully defined by Benson Soffer, describes workers who possess:

> Some significant degree of control over the quantity and quality of the product; the choice and maintenance of equipment; the methods of wage payment and the determination of individual wages and hours; the scheduling and assignment of work; recruitment, hiring, lay-off and transfer; training and promotion of personnel; and other related conditions of work.[13]

A reading of *The Coopers' Journal*, the excellent newspaper of the C.I.U., provides copious evidence that Canadian coopers enjoyed most of these prerogatives.

As was the case with most unions of skilled workers in the nineteenth century wages were not the subject of collective bargaining. The union met together, arrived at the "price" of its labour, informed management of its decision and either accepted the new rate with gratitude or struck if the boss refused. Local unions had no trouble dictating terms in prosperous times, as can be seen in the report of the Brantford local of August 1871, which simply notes that they had imposed a new price list and expected no trouble.[14] In January of 1872 representatives from seven of the fifteen existing Ontario C.I.U. locals met in Toronto to arrive at a province-wide price list.[15] This document imposed not only prices but also called for a maximum ten-hour day province-wide. It dictated prices for 37 different categories of piece work and added a day rate of $1.75 for work not included on the list.

---

[11] Organizational data is drawn from *CJ*, 1870-1875; Coopers' International Union of North America, *Proceedings*, 1871 and 1873; and Coopers' International Union of North America, Executive Department, *Names and Addresses of the Co[rresponding] Secretaries of all the Unions,* (Cleveland 1873).

[12] *Workingman's Advocate*, Jan. 20, 1872.

[13] Benson Soffer, "A Theory of Trade Union Development: The Role of the Autonomous Workman," *Labor History*, 1 (1960), 141.

[14] *CJ*, August 1871, 319.

[15] Ibid., April 1872, 254 and Coopers' International Union of North America, Executive Board, *Price List*, (Cleveland 1872), 32-33.

In addition to assuming control of hours and wages coopers also restricted production, especially when work was short. In this way they could spread the work around and also prevent speed-ups or other infringements of their shop-floor control. In the Ontario reports stints are mentioned by locals in St. Catharines, Seaforth, Oshawa and London.[16] This union-dictated restriction of output was of course the greatest evil in the eyes of the manufacturer. Coopers also struggled to control the methods of production as in this Brantford case:

> H.W. Read, a boss cooper of this place, has shown his dirty, mean spirit by discharging three flour bbl.[barrel] makers from his shop; they were making bbls. at nine cts. jointed staves and circled heading. The boss took the jointer boy away, so that the hands had to join their own staves, which they did until noon, when they refused to make any more barrels, unless the staves were jointed for them or they were paid extra. For thus demanding their rights, Boss Read discharged them.... But we fear him not, for no respectable cooper will take a berth in his shop under the circumstances.[17]

The union also enforced personnel decisions in the shop. The monitor of each shop assured that new workers' union cards were clear if members and that "nons" would abide by the shop rules. "Nons" who refused often found themselves moving on to the next town sooner than anticipated. In Brantford in 1871 for example:

> A scab in one of our shops, by the name of David Clawson, made himself very obnoxious to our men by his persistent abuse of the Union. At our last meeting it was ordered that the shop should strike against him, which was accordingly done, the consequence of which was that the mean tool of a man tramped and our men were out but half a day.[18]

One year later in Seaforth:

> J. Carter (who was suspended in Jan. 1872) got a berth at Ament's shop.... The monitor of the shop immediately went to him and asked him to pay up his dues.... And also that if he did not pay up, either he or they should not work there. [After he refused] the monitor of the shop went to the boss and told him that he must either sack

---

[16] *CJ*, October 1872, 633; March 1873, 133-134; June 1873, 278.
[17] Ibid., , Sept. 1872, 566.
[18] Ibid., June 1871, 248.

Carter or they would take their tools out of the shop ... [When he refused] they did instantly.[19]

Equally the coopers controlled admission to the craft and their ritual pledged them to "allow no one to teach a new hand" in order "to control the supply of help."[20] Use of helpers and apprenticeship rules were tightly supervised by the union.[21]

But perhaps more striking even than the presence of workers' control is the pervasiveness of appeals to manliness evidenced throughout the coopers' materials. David Montgomery has argued that this was a crucial component of "the craftsmen's ethical code."[22] Skilled workers carried themselves with pride and felt themselves to be the equal of their boss. C.I.U. President Martin Foran's novel, *The Other Side*,[23] illustrates this theme well. The hero is a proud and respectable workman surrounded by unscrupulous capitalists and unmanly workers who have given up their self-respect in order to carry out the evil tasks of the monopolistic bosses. Foran in discussing his didactic novel claimed that:

> The main incidents of this story are founded upon `notorious fact,' so notorious that anyone wishing it can be furnished with irrefragable, incontestable proofs in support of all the charges made against the typical employer, Revalson; that working men have been—because being trade unionists—discharged, photographed on street corners, driven from their homes, hounded like convicted felons, prevented from obtaining work elsewhere, arrested at the beck of employers, thrown into loathsome prisons on ex parte evidence, or held to bail in sums beyond their reach by subsidized, prejudiced, bigoted dispensers of injustice, & in every mean dishonourable manner imaginable, inhumanly victimized and made to feel that public opinion, law & justice were Utopian `unreal mockeries' except to men of position and money....[24]

Canadian coopers saw "manliness" as the keystone of their struggle and for them honour and pride were sacrosanct. "Owls" or "nons" who broke pledges or violated oaths were less than men:

---

[19] Ibid., June 1872, 373.
[20] *Coopers' Ritual*, (Cleveland 1870), 8-9.
[21] *CJ*, May 1871, 211.
[22] Montgomery, "Workers' Control of Machine Production," 7-9.
[23] Martin Foran, *The Other Side: A Social Study Based on Fact*, (Washington 1886). The novel originally appeared in serial form in *CJ* commencing in December 1871 and was reprinted in the *Ontario Workman* in 1872.
[24] *CJ*, July 1872, 426-429.

> At our last monthly meeting, the name of George Morrow was erased from our books, it having been proven beyond a shadow of doubt that he had violated his obligation by making known the business of our meetings to his boss. This thing Morrow, for I cannot call him a man, has never been of any use to us, he has not only betrayed us, but degraded himself in the estimation of every good man in our community.[25]

The Hamilton corresponding secretary went on to describe Morrow as a "compromise between man and beast."[26]

The traditions of autonomous work and the culture which grew from it made the coopers men to be reckoned with. Yet if the rise of the C.I.U. was rapid its decline was even more precipitous.

By late 1873 only seventeen locals remained and by 1875 this number had plummeted to approximately five.[27] The Canadian case was in no way unique, and from a peak membership of over 8000 in 1872 the union's total membership had declined to 1500 by 1876. In that year *The Coopers' Journal* suspended publication.

This disastrous decline was related both to the depression of the mid-1870s and to a concerted employers' assault on the trade. The best account of the coopers' demise describes the displacement of the hand cooper by machines in the Standard Oil works in New York and Cleveland. These cities, which contained the largest concentrations of coopers in North America, saw an epic struggle as Standard Oil moved to crush the C.I.U., the one remaining obstacle in its path to modernization and total monopoly.[28]

A similar process took place in Ontario. Coopering began to break out of its artisanal mould in the late 1860s in Ontario when the need for well-made, tight oil barrels in western Ontario led the London firm of R.W. and A. Burrows to introduce stave making and stave dressing machinery.[29] Until then the entire process had been performed by hand. This innovation was adopted by larger cooperages in the province such as those at distilleries in Windsor and Toronto. These three shops, Burrows', Walker's and Gooderham's, also differed from the old-time cooper's shop due to their larger size; they resembled small manufactories far more than artisans' shops.

---

[25] Ibid., March 1871, 153.
[26] Ibid.
[27] Ibid., and *Proceedings*.
[28] Gutman, "Standard Oil."
[29] H.B. Small, *The Products and Manufactures of the New Dominion*, (Ottawa 1868), 139-141. For a good description of hand production see T.A. Meister, *The Apple Barrel Industry in Nova Scotia*, (Nova Scotia Museum, Halifax n.d.).

Gooderham, for example, employed forty coopers in Toronto while the next biggest Toronto shop in 1871 held only seven.[30]

Although creating some problems for the C.I.U. these early machines did not abolish the need for skilled workers. Skill and knowledge were still important components of barrel making. Thus as late as 1871, Martin Foran was taking consolidation in the cooper's skill:

> Many of our members place far too much significance on machinery as a substitute for their labour. I have given the subject much thought and consideration, and am unable to see any serious cause for apprehension in barrel machinery.... Ours is a trade that cannot be reduced to the thumbrule of unfailing uniformity. To make a general marketable piece of work, of any kind peculiar to our trade, it requires tact, judgment and discrimination on the part of the maker ... when the friends of barrel machinery succeed in inventing a thinking machine they will succeed in making a success.[31]

Within two years of this statement Standard Oil's version of "a thinking machine" was a complete success.

The process was less revolutionary in Ontario but the effects of increased mechanization can be seen in the reports of the Toronto local. Gooderham's defeated the union between 1870,[32] when hours and wages were dictated by the workers and C.I.U. President Martin Foran acclaimed "Gooderman's [sic] shop as without exception the finest cooper shop [he had] ever seen,"[33] and late 1872 when John Hewitt reported that the shop:

> contained the most inveterate set of owls to be found on this continent and the few good men we have there, not being able to control the shop, have concluded to sacrifice their principles and work on for whatever price the great Gooderham chooses to pay.[34]

At its peak strength in March of 1872 the Toronto local had had complete control over the trade.[35] The ability of the coopers to dictate terms was seriously undermined

---

[30] For Gooderham's see *CJ*, Oct.-Nov. 1870, 25; July 1871, 268; April 1872, 235; August 1872, 500; September 1872, 566; December 1872, 741; March 1873, 133; Toronto *Mail*, April 23, 1872. For Walker's see *CJ*, January 1872, 47-48. For other Toronto shops see Canada, *Census*, 1872, Industrial Mss.

[31] C.I.U., *Proceedings*, 1871.

[32] *CJ*, Oct.-Nov. 1870, 25.

[33] Ibid., July 1871, 268.

[34] Ibid., December 1872, 741.

[35] Ibid., March 1872, 182.

elsewhere in Ontario by the advent of machinery. In 1874 the Seaforth local noted that the installation of two barrel machines would throw a great number of coopers out of work.[36] Six months later they reported their failure to control the machines due to non-union coopers taking their jobs at low rates.[37] By the 1880s the struggle was over; the cooper's craft was dead. In 1887 a Windsor cooper argued before the Labour Commission that machinery had "killed the trade" and that there no longer was "a man in the world who would send his son to be a cooper."[38]

The power that coopers had possessed as artisans they tried to adapt to the industrial age. Old models of the trade practices of independent craftsmen were transformed into union rules and struggled over with new-style bosses. However one base of their power was disappearing rapidly in the 1870s as technological innovation stripped them of "their monopoly of particular technical and managerial skills."[39]

Yet we should always be careful in positing technological change as the crucial factor, for other workers, as we shall see here, were more successful than the coopers. A Seaforth cooper, P. Klinkhammer, recognized this only too clearly:

> The men here have much to say about the barrel machine. The machine is not to blame. If the union men had been supported by the nons last fall and the latter had not taken the berths vacated by the union men and worked at 4 cents the machine would not be making barrels now.[40]

Their one real hope was to ally with other workers as Klinkhammer suggested. Their important role in the U.S. National Labor Union and the Toronto Trades Assembly, the Canadian Labour Union, and the Nine Hour Movement were steps in the right direction, but craft particularism remained very strong in the 1870s. However unionism did not disappear totally from the barrel factory with the demise of the C.I.U. Like the shoemakers, the coopers learned from their experience. Toronto coopers retained an independent union after the demise of the C.I.U. and were successful in raising their rates in the spring of 1882.[41] The next year they participated in attempts to create a new International.[42] In 1886 the Toronto local joined the Knights of Labor as "Energy Assembly," LA 5742.[43] This path was followed by many other coopers' locals throughout Canada and the U.S.

---

[36] Ibid., December 1874.
[37] Ibid., June 1875.
[38] Greg Kealey, ed., *Canada Investigates Industrialism*, (Toronto 1973), 113-116.
[39] B. Soffer, "The `Autonomous Workman'," 148.
[40] *CJ*, June 1875.
[41] *Globe*, April 15, 24, 1882.
[42] *Iron Molders' Journal*, August 1883.
[43] G.S. Kealey, "The Knights of Labor in Toronto," unpublished paper, 1974.

II

Workshop control traditions were extremely strong in foundry work. Late nineteenth century moulders displayed all the characteristics that Soffer and Montgomery identify as typical of "autonomous workmen." Two things distinguish them from the coopers. First is their impressive success in tenaciously maintaining these traditions on into the twentieth century. Second was their presence from the start of this period at the centre of the industrial capitalist world. Moulders were not artisans working in small shops reminiscent of pre-industrial society. In Toronto, Hamilton and throughout Ontario, moulders worked in the important stove, machinery and agricultural implements industries. These firms, among the largest in nineteenth century Ontario, led Canadian industry in attempting to fix prices and later to create multi-plant firms. Not surprisingly, these companies were also continually in the forefront of managerial innovations regarding labour.

Moulders in Toronto were first organized into a local union in 1857.[44] This local joined the Iron Molders International Union, organized in 1859, some-time in 1860.[45] The International made clear its position on questions of shop floor control from its inception. The original constitution claimed for the union the power "to determine the customs and usages in regard to all matters pertaining to the craft."[46] This gave the union control over the price of the moulders' labour. In stove shops, the union shop committee would meet and discuss the price to charge for moulding new patterns as the boss brought them in. The committee would meet with the boss or foreman and arrive at a mutually acceptable overall price for the whole stove, but as there were always a number of pieces involved in the assembly of any stove the committee would then decide amongst itself how to split this price among its members working on the different castings. This "board price" once established was considered to be almost non-negotiable, and these prices very quickly became recognized as part of the established customs and usages that were the union's sole prerogative. This price was not the only source of the moulders' wages, for there was a second element termed the "percentage," which was a supplement paid in addition to the piece rate. This percentage was negotiable, and wage conflicts in the industry

---

[44] Paul C. Appleton, "The Sunshine and the Shades: Labour Activism in Central Canada, 1850-1860," unpublished M.A. thesis, University of Calgary, 1974.

[45] The best work on the Iron Molders International Union [henceforth I.M.I.U.] in Canada is C.B. Williams, "Canadian-American Trade Union Relations: A Study of the Development of Binational Unionism," unpublished Ph.D. thesis, Cornell, 1964, chs. 3-4. Although limited in scope the discussion of the Union is insightful.

[46] I.M.I.U., *Constitution*, 1859 as cited in Williams, "Canadian-American," 105.

generally revolved around the "percentage," for very few bosses made the mistake of trying to challenge the "board price."[47]

This was one considerable area of strength for the union but there were others. The shop committee also dictated the "set" or "set day's work," which was the number of pieces that a member was allowed to produce in one day. Thus production control was also taken out of the boss's hands. It was of course in the union's self-interest to "set" a reasonable amount of work which an average craftsman could perform. Craft pride would dictate against "setting" too low, but equally craft strength could prevent any attempt at a speed-up.[48] Peterborough moulders enforced the "set" and brought charges against members who "rushed up work."[49] Generally part of each local's rules, the "set" was made a part of the International Constitution at the 1886 convention in London: "Resolved that all molders working at piece work be not allowed to make over $3.50 a day." In 1888 this was struck from the Constitution and was again left to the discretion of each local. Canadian locals continued to enforce this control over production. In Peterborough, in June 1891 "Brother Bruns brought a charge against Brother Donovan for earning over $3 a day."[50]

An additional area in which the union dictated terms was hiring. Members who made the mistake of applying to the foreman instead of to the shop committee were often fined.[51] In one such case in Toronto moulders directly recruited by stove manufacturer Edward Gurney were casually turned away by the shop committee whom they had been directed to by the workers after asking for the foreman.[52] The number of apprentices allowed in a shop was also set by the union. The Peterborough local in 1889 refused to allow "Mr. Brooks to bring in any more apprentices" and in 1891 reasserted that the union would "allow no more than the regular number of apprentices, one for every shop and one to any eight moulders."[53] The union also controlled the use of "bucks" or "berkshires" (unskilled labourers). When used they were traditionally paid directly by the moulder out of his wages, and thus were employed by the craftsman, not the employer. Later when bosses tried to use "bucks" to perform some of the work customarily performed by moulders, the

---

[47] The discussion of wages in the industry is drawn from John P. Frey and John R. Commons, "Conciliation in the Stove Industry," *Bulletin of the Bureau of Labor*, 62 (1906), 124-196, especially 125-130, and Frank T. Stockton, *The International Molders Union of North America*, (Baltimore 1921).

[48] Carroll D. Wright, "Regulation and Restriction of Output," *Eleventh Special Report of the Commissioner of Labor*, (Washington 1904), 149-185.

[49] Peterborough Iron Moulders International Union, No. 191, *Minutes*, September 4, 1882, in Gainey Collection, Trent University Archives [henceforth *Minutes no. 191*].

[50] Ibid., June 19, 1891.

[51] Jonathan Grossman, *William Sylvis, Pioneer of American Labor*, (N.Y. 1945), 153.

[52] *Globe*, January 21, 1871.

[53] *Minutes no. 191*, February 8, 1889; May 15, 1891.

latter did all in their power to prevent it.[54] This was the greatest area of contention with Toronto employers. Finally the union struggled to impose a closed shop on its employers and refused to work with non-union moulders. Thus in the moulding industry large areas of control in the setting of price, productivity and hiring resided with the union.

The extent of the control that the union established was neither won nor maintained without constant struggle. Manufacturers used every device in their power to break the moulders' shop floor control. In 1866 the newly founded employers' association in the industry passed a resolution to

> proceed at once to introduce into our shops all the apprentices or helpers we deem advisable and that we will not allow any union committees in our shops, and that we will in every way possible free our shops of all dictation or interference on the part of our employees.[55]

The "Great Lock-out of 1866" that followed the employers' posting of the above "obnoxious notice," which extended into Canada, culminated in a costly victory for the union. Canadian stove manufacturers also organized and were active in the 1870s in fixing prices, advocating increased protection and most significantly in pressing a concerted effort to deal the union a smashing defeat.[56] In this they too failed.

In the Toronto moulding industry, the union's claim to control was the central issue. Strikes were fought at least fourteen times in the years between the founding of Local No. 28 and 1895.[57] The moulders engaged in the major strikes to resist demands by the manufacturers that the customs and usages of the craft be sacrificed. Thus in 1867 McGee demanded that he be allowed to hire as many apprentices as he wished;[58] in 1870 Gurney tried to force his moulders to work with "bucks";[59] in 1890 both Gurney and Massey offered their moulders a choice of either a substantive cut in the previously unchallenged board price or accept "bucks";[60] in 1892 Gurney demanded that his moulders not only accept a reduction on the percentage rate but also commit themselves to this rate for a year, a new scheme to prevent their raising

---

[54] Frey and Commons, "Conciliation," 126-127, 176; Stockton, *International Molders Union*, 170-185.

[55] Williams, "Canadian-American," 120.

[56] *Iron Molders Journal*, August-December 1874; February 1876; May 1876.

[57] Strike data drawn from Toronto press, 1867-1892 and from *Iron Molders Journal*, 1864-1895 and I.M.I.U., *Proceedings*, 1864-1895.

[58] *Globe*, March 22, April 3, 1867.

[59] Ibid., December 21, 23, 27, 1870; January 20, 1871. I.M.I.U., *Proceedings*, 1872.

[60] *Globe*, May 24, June 2, September 26, 1890; January 10, 1891; Massey Clipping Files, Vol. 1, 1886-1891, Massey Archives, Toronto. I.M.I.U., *Proceedings*, 1890.

the "percentage" as soon as the economic climate changed.[61] The same battles were to be fought yet again in 1903-1904.[62]

These strikes were not minor struggles in the history of the Toronto working class. In the general employers' offensive of the late sixties and early seventies to counter the emergence of a strong and newly self-confident working class movement, the boss moulders used various techniques in their attempt to defeat the union. In this period they resorted most often to coercion, falling back on outmoded statutes and the power of the law. The frequently cited case of George Brown and the Toronto printers of 1872 was preceded in Toronto by numerous uses of the courts by stove manufacturers. In 1867 McGee charged six Buffalo moulders with deserting his employment. Recruited by his foreman for a one-year term they quit work when they discovered that they were being used as scabs. The magistrate claimed he was being lenient due to the implicit deception used and fined them only $6.00 each.[63] Two apprentices who left McGee's before their terms were up because of the union blacklist of the shop were not so lucky. They received fifteen days in jail for deserting his employment.[64] Three years later Gurney, a large Toronto and Hamilton stove manufacturer, made use of the courts to fight the union in a slightly different way. He had two union members charged with conspiracy and assault for trying to prevent scabs from filling his shop after he turned out the union men for refusing to work with "bucks" and a large number of apprentices. After the men were found guilty the Toronto Grand Jury commented that:

> It is with sincere regret that the Grand Jury have had before them . . . two persons charged with assault and conspiracy acting under the regulations of an association known as the Molders union and they feel it their duty to mark in the most emphatic terms their disapproval of such societies being introduced into our new country calculated as they are to interfere with capital and labour, cramp our infant manufactures and deprive the subject of his civil liberty....[65]

During another strike that same summer Beard charged ten of his apprentices with "unlawfully confederating to desert his service with the intent to injure the firm in their business." Their real offence had been seeking a wage increase and then using the traditional moulders' weapon of restricting their output to enforce their demand. On their last day on the job they all did the same limited amount of work. They were

---

61 I.M.I.U., *Proceedings*, 1895.
62 See especially *H.J. Barnett to John Robertson, Toronto, August 20, 1903 and May 30, 1904* in *I.M.I.U. no. 191*, Correspondence, Gainey Collection [henceforth *Correspondence no. 191*].
63 *Globe*, March 22, 1867.
64 Ibid., April 3, 1867.
65 Ibid., January 20, 1871. See also December 21, 23, 27, 1870; April 21, 1871.

found guilty.[66] Nevertheless the founders' tactics failed. The victory that the moulders won here was especially sweet given the force brought to bear against them. This victory was quite clearly contingent on their monopoly of skill and their ability to control the labour market. Thus it was reported that Gurney was forced to resort to employing moulders such as "John Cowie, who quit one job to go scabbing in Gurney's shop where he had never worked in before, simply because he was of so little account they would never hire him—circumstances sometimes make strange companions."[67] The union "defied anyone to produce such a lot of moulders as were in Gurney."[68] But if the victory over Gurney was pleasing, that over Beard was valued even more highly:

> It appears that for a year or two past, Beard and Co. of Toronto, have been running an independent scab shop refusing to be `dictated to by the Union as they felt competent to conduct their business in their own way'.... They found that reliable men were all union men, they found that the sober men were all union men, and what was of more importance, they found that all the good moulders were union men and they were obliged to take the off-scourings of creation, all the drunken scallawags and botch workmen, that found their way to Toronto.... Their scab foreman was not equal to the situation and they found that their trade was fast leaving them and to save themselves from utter ruin the nauseous dose had to be swallowed....[69]

The 1880s saw the maturing of the system of industrial relations that was only emerging in the 1860s and 1870s. The foundrymen mounted no challenges to the basic rights of the union in 1880s and only the percentage came under consideration. In 1880 moulders sought and gained a 10% increase, but when the economy turned in late 1883 they were forced to accept a 20% reduction. In 1886 they won a 12.5% advance, but in 1887 their request for a 10% increase was resisted by Gurney and after a nine-week strike a compromise 5% advance was accepted. In early 1887 the Ontario branches of the I.M.I.U. came together to form a District Union. The thirteen Ontario locals with over 1000 members were brought together to organize more efficiently and to run joint strikes more effectively.[70] In 1887 for example the Hamilton moulders' strike against Gurney spread to Toronto when Gurney locked out

---

[66] Ibid., July 15, 18, November 18, 1871; For the moulders' response to these legal initiatives see *Iron Molders Journal*, January 31, 1871.

[67] Ibid., February 28, 1871. For other similar cases see *IMJ*, September 30, 1871; December 31, 1870.

[68] Ibid., September 30, 1871.

[69] Ibid., December 31, 1871.

[70] *Globe*, January 8, 1887; January 6, 1888; *Canadian Labor Reformer*, January 8, 1887.

his moulders there. Later in 1890 moulders at the Massey Hamilton plant refused to mould while their Toronto brothers were locked out. But perhaps the major example of these cross-industry strikes was the Bridge and Beach Strike of 1887 in the U.S. In March of that year moulders struck the Bridge and Beach Manufacturing Co. in St. Louis with the sanction of the International. Immediately the new Stove Founders National Defense Association attempted to manufacture the required patterns for the Company. Their moulders in turn refused to work on the patterns from the struck foundry. This process spread until at its height almost 5000 moulders were locked out in fifteen centres. Finally in June, the Defense Association called the patterns in and supplied the St. Louis company with a force of non-union moulders and work resumed as before at the other shops. Both sides claimed victory, but most important was that each side had demonstrated to the other their respective strength and staying power. Almost immediately after the end of this strike negotiations were commenced which were to lead to the establishment of national conciliation in the industry through conferences of the contending parties.[71]

The Canadian industry did not take part in these conferences nor did conciliation apply to the machinery moulding branches of the trade. Until these industry-wide agreements in stove foundries the strength of the moulders depended entirely on their skill and control of the work process and their ability through their union to maintain this and to exercise some degree of control over the labour market. This labour market control was of great importance and has been admirably discussed before with reference to the moulders.[72] The importance of the union card to the moulder has been summarized: "... within the jurisdiction of his own local a union card was a man's citizenship paper; in the jurisdiction of other locals it was his passport."[73]

The early 1890s saw a new employer offensive in Hamilton and Toronto as Gurney and Massey both attempted to smash the moulders' continuing power in their plants. The Gurney strike which commenced in February 1890 lasted an amazing sixteen months before Local 28 ended it. The Massey strike covered ten months from October 1890 to July 1891.[74] In both cases the companies pursued a similar strategy. They shut down their moulding shops, ostensibly for repairs and, after a considerable lapse of time, called in the shop committees and asked them to accept either a sizeable reduction or work with "bucks."[75] In both cases the moulders refused, for "union rules did not permit `bucks' and the men thought they saw in it their eventual displacement by these labourers and a menace to their trade."[76] Both

---

[71] Frey and Commons, *Conciliation*, 104-147.
[72] Williams, "Canadian-American," *passim*.
[73] Grossman, *Sylvis*, 110.
[74] Ontario Bureau of Industry, *Annual Report, 1892*; I.M.I.U., *Proceedings*, 1892-1895.
[75] *Globe*, February 27, 1890; August 22, 1890; September 26, 1890; October 3, 1890; January 10, 1891; *News*, August 25, 1890; *Monetary Times*, October 31, 1890.
[76] *Globe*, January 10, 1891.

"The Honest Workingman" and Worker's Control 497

Gurney and Massey claimed that they could no longer afford union rates and compete successfully, but the moulders suspected "a long conceived plan in the attempt at a reduction."[77] In each case management and labour settled down for a protracted struggle. David Black, the secretary of Local 28, wrote after five months on strike:

> Our fight with Gurney still continues and bids fair to last quite a while longer, we succeed very well in relieving him of his good men, but he has plenty of money and it will take hard fighting and time to beat him.[78]

The Toronto local spared no expense or risk in this struggle and a number of their members were arrested and tried for intimidating scabs.[79] In September the local issued an appeal "To the Canadian Public" which explained they had been locked out "because they refused to make their work cheaper than for any other employer in the same line in the city; and thus assist them to destroy their competitors and monopolize the Canadian market at our expense." The public was called on to buy only union made goods since

> By this means our victory over monopoly will be assured; our right to organize and obtain fair wages for our labour will be vindicated; while the superior quality of your purchase will amply repay your preference.[80]

The union lost both these struggles but the cost to capital was also high. Gurney, in early 1891, when his victory seemed sure brayed triumphantly that "the only change resulting from the strike is that he now controlled his shop." However when he continued to claim that things were excellent, the *Globe* reporter noted that, faced with the open incredulity of the union representatives present, Gurney modified his statement mentioning "that of course the whole year had not been as smooth." The key in these struggles in the early 1890s was control. As capital entered a new stage where it recognized the necessity of supervising more closely the process of production, it had to confront and defeat its "autonomous workmen." This gives Gurney's parting chortle added significance:

> The men must work for someone else until they come to one of my proposals. I do not think (with a smile) that there is any likelihood

---

[77] Ibid., August 22, 1890.
[78] David Black to F.W. Parkes, Peterborough, June 29, 1890, *Correspondence, no. 191.*
[79] *Globe*, May 24, June 2, 1890.
[80] "To the Canadian Public," Toronto, September 1, 1890, *Correspondence, no. 191.*

of my going to local union 28 and asking them to come and take control of my foundry.[81]

Gurney's last laugh was too precipitous, however, for the I.M.I.U. came back strong in Toronto in the late 1890s and a new wave of struggle broke over the foundry business in 1902-1904.[82] It is not the purpose of this paper to detail that struggle, but it is important to emphasize that the power of the moulders was not broken in the struggles of 1890-1892. Gurney and Massey delivered only a partial defeat and the moulders came back strong. J.H. Barnett, Toronto I.M.I.U. secretary, described one 1903 struggle:

> Just after adjourning the meeting this afternoon the foreman of the Inglis shop, R. Goods, came to the hall and informed us that he had discharged all the scabs in his shop and that he wanted the union men in on Monday, that the firm was tired of the scabs and was willing to give the nine hours....[83]

One year later, in yet another struggle with Toronto foundrymen now supported by the National Foundry Association, Barnett wrote again of the continued monopoly on skill that the moulders enjoyed:

> They are having greater losses in the foundry now than when they first started. They have been trying to make a big condenser and can't make it. They have started the old St. Lawrence shop with some of the old country moulders who refused to work with Ersig, the NFA foreman up in the new shop. Jas Gillmore and Fred McGill is instruction [sic] them but ain't doing any better.[84]

Iron moulders then, unlike coopers, maintained a high degree of workplace control on into the twentieth century. This was primarily due to their strong organization, but was also partially contingent on the slowness with which technology replaced their skill. Machines for moulding were experimented with in the mid-1880s but

---

81 *Globe*, January 10, 1891. Encouraged by his temporary victory in Toronto Gurney attacked his Hamilton moulders the next year. For this bitter struggle see I.M.I.U., *Proceedings*, 1895; Fred Walters to F.W. Parkes, Peterborough, March 20, 1892; Executive Board I.M.I.U., "Circular letter," March 3, 1892; Hamilton I.M.I.U. Local No. 26, "Labor Struggle against Capital," March 28, 1892. The last three items are in *Correspondence, no. 191*.

82 For general material on the employee offensive see works cited in note 4, *supra*.

83 J.H. Barnett to John Robertson, Jr., Peterborough, August 20, 1903, *Correspondence, no. 191*.

84 Barnett to Robertson, May 30, 1904, *ibid*.

were an extremely expensive failure.[85] Massey imported its first machines in 1889.[86] Thus, unlike the coopers and shoemakers, the moulders had time to perfect their organization before their major contest with machinery.

Moulders also developed an early understanding of the need for solidarity with their unskilled co-workers. Thus, when the Knights of Labor struck the huge Massey works in Toronto in 1886, moulders left the job in their support. Peterborough I.M.I.U. Local no. 191 also cooperated with the Lindsay Knights of Labor.[87]

III

The workers' control enjoyed by Toronto moulders, and their struggle to retain it, was more than equalled by the experiences of Toronto printers. The printers' control of the shop floor demonstrates extremely well early union power. In the 1890s the President of the Toronto local of the I.T.U. insisted:

> The work of the composing room is our business. To no one else can we depute it. It is absolutely ours. The talk of running another man's business will not hold. It is ours; we learned it and must control it.[88]

Unionism among the Toronto Printers owed much to the customs and traditions of the craft. Organized first in 1832 the Society lapsed in 1836 but was refounded in 1844 to resist a new Toronto employer's departure from the "settled usages of the trade."[89] In 1845, when forced again to fight the initiatives taken by George Brown, the printers issued a circular to the Toronto public demanding only "to maintain that which is considered by all the respectable proprietors as a fair and just reward, for our labour and toil—'the labourer is worthy of his hire'."[90] Here the tenacity of

---

[85] Robert Ozanne, *A Century of Labour-Management Relations at McCormick and International Harvester*, (Madison 1967), ch. 1.

[86] Massey Account Books, Massey Archives, Toronto. For the best discussion of technological innovation in the moulding industry see James Cooke Mills, *Searchlights on Some American Industries*, (Chicago 1911), ch. 7.

[87] For Massey Strike see Kealey, "Knights of Labor," 23-27; for Peterborough-Lindsay connection see *Minutes no. 191*, 1886-1887. Ozanne, *A Century*, provides similar evidence of cooperation between Chicago moulders and the Knights.

[88] From William Powell's address to the fifty-first annual convention of the I.T.U. cited in Wayne Roberts, "The Last Artisans: Toronto Printers, 1896-1914," in Kealey and Warrian, eds., *Essays in Working Class History*, (Toronto 1976).

[89] Toronto Typographical Union, *Minutes*, March 5, 1845 [henceforth T.T.U., *Minutes*].

[90] Ibid., July 2, 1845.

preindustrial notions of traditional wages can be seen. Customary usage dictated wages—not any abstract notion of what the market might bear. Employers as well as workers had to learn the new rules of a market economy, and the disruptions caused by the Browns' arrival in the Toronto printing trades in the 1840s suggest that until then wages had been "largely a customary and not a market calculation."[91]

The printers possessed a strong tradition of craft pride and identification. In their 1845 statement to the Toronto public they resolved "to maintain by all legitimate means in their power their just rights and privileges as one of the most important and useful groups in the industrious community."[92]

Members of the "art preservative", they saw themselves as the main carriers of rationalism and the enlightenment. No trade dinner or ball, and these were frequent, was complete without a set of toasts to the printers' patron, Benjamin Franklin, and to Gutenberg and other famous printers. Franklin replaced the older European craft tradition of saints and his rationalism fitted very well with the printers' disdain for other societies who had recourse to secret signs and fiery oaths. The printers prided themselves on the fact that:

> initiation ceremonies, melo-dramatic oaths, passwords, signs, grips, etc., though advocated by many worthy representatives, and repeatedly considered by the national union, never found a place in the national or subordinate constitutions.[93]

The printers saw their craft as crucial in maintaining all that was best in the western literary tradition. As one printer toasted in an 1849 Anniversary Dinner: "To the art of printing—under whose powerful influence the mind of fallen and degraded man is raised from nature up to nature's God."[94] Thus printer's shop committees were "chapels" and the shop steward was "the father of the chapel." This pride in craft was manifested time and time again throughout the nineteenth century.

In 1869 the executive recommended the initiation of a reading room and library:

> where the members of the craft can have access in leisure hours for the enjoyment of study and mental recreation and where may be ever within their reach increasing facilities for the acquisition of whatever in our art it may be of advantage to know.... It is a laudable

---

[91] Hobsbawm, "Custom, Wages and Work-load," 347. See also Sally Zerker, "The Development of Collective Bargaining in the Toronto Printing Industry in the Nineteenth Century, *Industrial Relations*, 30 (1975), 83-97.
[92] T.T.U., *Minutes*, July 2, 1845.
[93] George E. McNeill, *The Labor Movement*, (Boston 1887), 185.
[94] T.T.U., *Minutes*, March 7, 1849.

endeavour to support one's calling which two centuries ago was deemed the most honourable of all professions....[95]

The union seal depicted a printing press with light emanating from all around it.[96]

The Toronto printers had a strong sense of the history of their craft and their union. They were particularly proud of being the oldest Toronto union and parts of their frequent fêtes were often spent on these themes. The 1888 picnic programme, for example, contained original histories of both the art of printing and of the Toronto Typographical Union.[97] All these traditions were put to use by the printers and they brought the craft lore together in stirring addresses invoking custom in the struggle against oppression:

> Fellow-workingmen, knights of the stick and rule, preservers of "the art preservative,"—ye whose honourable calling is to make forever imperishable the noblest, truest, and most sublime thoughts of the statesman, the philosopher, and the poet,—to you is committed the mightiest agent for good or ill which has yet been pressed into the service of humanity. The printing press, the power mightier than kings, more powerful than armies, armaments, or navies, which shall yet overthrow ignorance and oppression and emancipate labour, is your slave. Without your consent, without the untiring labour of your skillful fingers and busy brain, this mighty giant, with his million tongued voices speeding on wings of steam all over this broad earth of ours, would be dumb. Shorn of his strength which your skill imparts, his throbbing sides and iron sinews might pant and strain in vain; no voice or cry of his or your oppressors could ever reach or be heard among men. Realizing this my friends it is easy to determine our proper station in the grand struggle that is now in progress all over the civilized world, the effort of the masses to throw off oppression's yoke.... We belong in the front rank, at the head of this column. Since the discovery of printing humanity has made great progress and already we see the dawn of the coming day when light and knowledge shall illuminate all lands and man shall no longer oppress his fellow-man.[98]

---

[95] Ibid., January 1869.
[96] Ibid., June 6, 1891.
[97] *Globe*, July 27, 1888. The extensive historical interests of printers are also evidenced by two early official I.T.U. histories: John McVicar, *Origins and Progress of the Typographical Union, 1850-1891*, (Lansing, Mich. 1891) and George A. Tracey, *History of the Typographical Union*, (Indianapolis 1913).
[98] International Typographical Union, [henceforth I.T.U.] *Proceedings*, 1881, 46.

Central to the power of the International Typographical Union was the extent to which each local maintained its control over production. The composing room was the preserve of the printer. Management's only representative there, the foreman, was a union member and subject to the discipline of his brothers. This was true in Toronto from the inception of the T.T.U. and was very important because the union also demanded that all hiring be done through the foreman.[99] In 1858 the I.T.U. convention had ruled that:

> The foreman of an office is the proper person to whom application should be made for employment; and it is enjoined upon subordinate unions that they disapprove of any other mode of application.[100]

The new I.T.U. constitution of 1867 fined members who applied for jobs to anyone other than the foreman. Four years later this control was reasserted but foremen were also warned:

> It is the opinion of your humble servant that the foreman of an office belongs to the union under which he works and the union does not belong to the foreman ... and that no foreman has the right to discharge a regular hand ... on any other ground than that of shortness of work or wilfull neglect of duty....[101]

In an extraordinary 1873 case the I.T.U. ruled that the Ottawa local was correct to strike against J.C. Boyce, the proprietor of *The Citizen*, when he took over operation of his own composing room. Only if Boyce submitted a clear card from the London (Eng.) Trades Society would he "be allowed to work under the jurisdiction of the Ottawa Union."[102]

This effective union control of the hiring practice was augmented by the role the foreman played in enforcing the printer's right to divide work. In newspaper offices each regular employee had a "sit" and with this place came the right to choose a replacement any time the regular wanted time off. Although not technically employed by the regular printer, that was actually what the practice amounted to. In Toronto the *Mail* paid the money to the regular who then paid the subs from his salary.[103] When bosses tried to regulate this custom by utilizing "sub-lists" which delineated the substitutes from whom regulars were forced to choose, the International roundly condemned the practice and refused to allow locals to cooperate

---

[99] Carroll Wright, "Restriction of Output," 88-91.
[100] National Typographical Union, *Proceedings*, 1858, 45-46.
[101] I.T.U., *Proceedings*, 1871, 47.
[102] Ibid., 1873 and Elizabeth Baker, *Printers and Technology: A History of the Printing Pressmen and Assistants' Union*, (New York 1957), 215.
[103] *Globe*, July 21, 1884.

with it.[104] The union claimed ever more interest in the hiring process. In 1888 a resolution was introduced at the I.T.U. convention "that would have placed the regulation of hiring and discharging of employees entirely in the hands of the local unions."[105] In 1890 "the priority law" was passed by which the grounds upon which foremen could discharge were even more tightly circumscribed. Only incompetency, violation of rules, neglect of duty or decrease of labour force were acceptable causes for firing and on discharge a member was entitled to a written statement of cause. In addition the final part of the law ruled that "subs" in an office had priority when positions became available.[106] The power of the union, then, in controlling the selection of printers, was almost total.

The union also retained a strong position in bargaining. The union would first arrive at an approved scale of prices unilaterally and would then take it to the employers.[107] Some negotiation was possible but much of the scale was regarded as non-negotiable. For example after the strike of 1872 for the nine hour day never again were hours subject to consideration; having been won once they were off limits for further discussion.[108] The scale was a complex document divided into three major sections: time work; piece work, news and magazines; and piece work, books. Time work was not the traditional method of payment in the printing industry but throughout the late nineteenth century more and more job shops adopted it. However the time rate was closely tied to the piece rate. In Toronto, where the piece rate was 33 1/3 cents per 1000 ems, the time rate was 33 1/3 cents an hour—the general assumption being that a hand compositor averaged 1000 ems an hour. In newspaper offices the usual method of payment was by the piece which in the compositor's case was measured by the area of type that he composed and expressed in "ems." Printers were thus paid per 1000 ems of matter. There were a number of areas of conflict implicit in this type of payment. Rates were set for the newspaper as a whole, but special rates were set for material classified as difficult such as foreign languages or tables or even for illegible copy.[109] As the century progressed, more and more newspaper work consisted of advertising, which contained far more blank space than regular material. This copy became known as "fat" matter and was the most lucrative for the printer. The printers insisted that rates were set for the paper as a whole, thus

---

[104] George A. Barnett, "The Printers: A Study in American Trade Unionism," *American Economic Association Quarterly*, 3rd series, X (1909), esp. 218-221.

[105] Ibid., 230.

[106] Ibid., 228-242 and *Typographical Journal*, July 15, 1890.

[107] Zerker, "Development of Collective Bargaining," 84-88.

[108] Sally Zerker, "George Brown and the Printers' Union," *Journal of Canadian Studies*, 10, 1 (1975), 47.

[109] A humorous example of the last was the Vancouver "cap `I' strike" of 1889. The printers struck the *World* for two days when management refused to pay for corrections in faulty copy. See George Bartley, *An Outline History of Typographical Union, no. 226, Vancouver, B.C., 1887-1938*, (Vancouver 1938), 8.

retaining the higher rate for fat matter as well. The traditional way of distributing the material was that all copy was hung on the "hook" as it arrived in the composing room and the compositors picked it up in order, thus insuring an even distribution of the "fat." Bosses began to object to this and tried to create "departments" by which specific printers did the special composing. This the union resisted strenuously and forbade locals from accepting "departments." They offered, as a compromise, to allow members to bid for the "fat" matter. The successful bidder who gained the ads then paid back to the union the amount of his bid, usually a percent of his earnings, which was then used to buy things in common for all the printers, to hire a person to clean everybody's type, or was distributed equally among the members.[110] The Toronto local, however, resisted all employer incursions in this area. Toronto employers certainly tried. In 1882 the *Mail* offered its printers an advance but in return demanded the return of the ads. Instead the new scale of 1883 reiterated that "where weekly and piece hands are employed the piece hands shall have their proportionate share of 'fat' matter."[111] Seven years later another new scale still insisted that "compositors on newspapers were entitled to equal distribution of any 'phat'."[112] The complexity of the Toronto printer's scale is suggested by the 39 sections of the 1883 and 35 sections of the 1890 contracts.[113] All this led one managerial strategist named DeVinne, who was later to play a major role in the United Typothetae, to moan that "It is the composition room that is the great sinkhole. It is in type and the wages of compositors that the profits of the house are lost.[114]

So far we have spoken entirely of only one branch of printing—the compositors. Until the middle of the century in the cities and until much later in small shops, a printer ran the press as well as composing. With the rise of power presses, the pressman's role became more and more complex and increasingly the old time printer who did both jobs disappeared and new specialists took over. By 1869 the Toronto local had special piece rates for pressmen and the job definition of the compositor prevented him from performing press work. The pressmen's new consciousness led the I.T.U. to begin to charter Pressmen's locals separately in 1873 and ten years later the Toronto Pressmen set up their own local. Disputes with Local 91 however led them to join the new International Printing Pressmen's Union in 1889. This splintering of the printing crafts caused many problems but the pressmen as an equally skilled group carried with them the traditions of printers' unionism. Time

---

[110] Barnett, "The Printers," 108-142, and Sally Zerker, "A History of the Toronto Typographical Union," unpublished Ph.D. thesis, University of Toronto, 1972, 1-14.

[111] T.T.U., "Scale of prices" in *Minutes*, March 17, 1883.

[112] Ibid., December 20, 1890.

[113] Ibid., March 17, 1883; December 6, 20, 1890; March 28, December 5, 1891.

[114] Baker, *Printers and Technology*, 69. For a discussion of the historical roots of I.T.U. strength and for contemporary twentieth century examples see S.M. Lipset, M.S. Trow, J.S. Coleman, *Union Democracy: The Internal Politics of the I.T.U.*, (Glencoe, Ill., 1956), ch. 2.

was spent at meetings, for example, in designing outfits for the various marches and parades that were so much a part of working class life in Toronto in the 1880s.[115]

Although the major focus of this paper is the skilled worker's power on the job, one cannot discuss the Toronto printers without alluding also to their political strength in the city, in provincial and even in national politics. They provided the Toronto working class community and movement with important leadership. It was natural for these literate, working class intellectuals to play key political roles but the extent of their dominance is striking nevertheless. Although not the initiators of the Toronto Trades Assembly (this honour belongs to John Hewitt of the Coopers International Union) they did play an important part in this organization and in the Canadian Labour Union. In the 1880s they helped found the Toronto Trades and Labor Council after the meeting of the I.T.U. in Toronto in 1881 and later were quite active in the meetings of the Trades and Labor Congress. Moreover of the six labour papers published in Toronto between 1872 and 1892 three of them were published and edited by printers—*The Ontario Workman* under J.S. Williams, J.C. McMillan, and David Sleeth, all prominent members of Local 91; *The Trade Union Advocate/Wage Worker* of Eugene Donavon; and D.J. O'Donoghue's *Labor Record*. Other members of Local 91 also enjoyed prominent careers in labour reform—John Armstrong, a former International President of the I.T.U. (1878-9) was appointed to Macdonald's Royal Commission on the Relations of Labour and Capital in 1886; D.J. O'Donoghue, prominent as an MPP, leading Canadian Knight of Labor and later collector of labour statistics for the Ontario Bureau of Industries; E.F. Clarke, arrested in 1872 and later Mayor of Toronto, MPP and MP; and W.B. Prescott, International President of the I.T.U. from 1891 to 1898. This was just one generation of Local 91's membership, the next was to include two mayors of Toronto and a senator.[116]

Local 91's political role stemmed from its union activities. Toronto printers, for example, had little use for George Brown's brand of Liberalism. As early as 1845 they had noted the irony implicit in his labour relations policies:

> A person from the neighbouring Republic commenced business here and has ever since been unremitting in his Liberal endeavour to reduce as low as possible that justly considered fair and equitable rate of remuneration due to the humble operatives.[117]

---

[115] Toronto Printing Pressmen's Union, No. 10, [henceforth T.P.P.U.] *Minutes*, March 1883-December 1890, P.A.C. and Baker, *Printers and Technology, passim.*

[116] Roberts, "Toronto Printers" and Ross Harkness, *J.E. Atkinson of the Star*, (Toronto 1963), 28.

[117] T.T.U., *Minutes*, July 2, 1845.

His "Liberal" endeavours were to lead him into conflict with the printers, time and time again culminating in the Printer's Strike for the nine hour day in 1872.[118] Brown's use of antiquated British laws against combination to arrest the leaders of the I.T.U. was turned against him by Macdonald's passage of the Trade Union Act. The Torys controlled Toronto working class politics for a number of years following, until D.J. O'Donoghue, the Knights of Labor, and the legislative responsiveness of the Mowat Ontario government started a swing towards the Liberals.

The political expertise of the printers had of course grown throughout their various struggles and the tactics perfected in 1872 were used again in the 1880s. Thus when John Ross Robertson's *Telegram* came under union attack in 1882 the union first turned to the boycott to bring pressure on the owner. They decided that in this way they could expose

> the treatment which union printers have received at the hands of JRR for many years past, and the manner in which that gentleman (?) invariably casts aspersions upon the union mechanics of this city generally through the columns of his vasculating [sic] paper.[119]

John Armstrong and D.J. O'Donoghue were appointed to visit the merchants who advertised in the *Telegram* and convince them to place their ads elsewhere. The next year when I.T.U. No. 91 passed a new scale of prices they struck the *Telegram*, pulling most of the compositors out on strike. They then received the endorsement of the whole Toronto Trades and Labor Council for the boycott and late in March held a mass meeting at which speeches were delivered by most of the prominent Toronto labour leaders pledging support for Local 91.[120]

The strikes the following year against the *Mail* and the *Globe* were even more eventful and suggestive of the printers' political acumen. The papers united with other Toronto publishers and print shops to demand a 10% reduction on the printers' wages and gave only a week for consideration. The printers refused and struck. The union was successful in forcing job offices and smaller papers to withdraw the reduction but the *Globe* and the *Mail* held out. The *Globe* insisted that it had never become a union shop because "the boss needed absolute control in a newspaper office."[121] The morning papers after a hard fight won the reduction to 30 cents per 1000 ems down from 33 1/3 cents but their victory was short lived. In 1885 the *Globe* reversed its position of a year before and the political game of the 1870s by becoming a union shop for the first time. This left only the Tory *Mail* holding out against the typos. The *Mail* succumbed in February of 1886 and became a union

---

[118] Zerker, "George Brown," *passim* and for greater detail on T.T.U. struggles in the 1850s see Appleton, "The Sunshine and the Shade," 103-116.
[119] T.T.U., *Minutes*, June 3, 1882.
[120] *Globe*, March 21, 23, 30, 1882.
[121] Ibid., July 5, 1884.

shop, withdrawing the iron-clad contract that it had adopted after the troubles in 1884.

What tactics had the I.T.U. used to win these long-range victories after their apparent defeat in 1884? The printers had employed their usual measures against the papers. They first withdrew all their members from the shops and when they failed to prevent the shops' filling up with the much despised "country-mice," non-union printers from small towns, they turned to the boycott and mass demonstrations of workingmen.[122] But this time they also requested all workingmen to boycott any candidates supported by the *Mail* in the municipal election campaigns of the winter of 1885-6.[123] Local 91 passed a resolution: "that this union will oppose to its utmost any candidate for municipal honours who may be supported by the *Mail* newspaper."[124] The following weeks saw union after union endorse the I.T.U. motion and also saw a number of Tory ward heelers running for cover and abandoning the *Mail*. The union issued a circular exposing its dealings with the *Mail* since 1872 and then placed advertisements in the Toronto papers in January of 1886 strongly attacking Manning, the *Mail's* candidate for Mayor:

> Resolved that this union consider Mr. Manning a nominee of the Mail, he having advertised in that paper ... and having been editorially supported by it, particularly so on Saturday morning January 1; and therefore we call on all workingmen and those in sympathy with organized labour to VOTE AGAINST MANNING, THE NOMINEE OF THE MAIL.[125]

The same Local 91 meeting also decided to blacklist aldermanic candidates who had not broken with the *Mail* and decided to issue 10,000 circulars denouncing Manning and these candidates. After Howland's stunning election as mayor, widely regarded as a working class victory, the I.T.U. issued this statement:

> To the Trades and Labour organizations of Toronto—Fellow unionists: Toronto Typographical Union No. 91 takes this opportunity of thanking the labour organizations of this city and their friends who so nobly supported us at the polls in our effort to defeat the Mail. To the workingmen of Toronto who have had the honour and manhood to rise above party ties in the cause of labour, the heartiest thanks of the 300 members of the TTU are due.... At a time when we needed your assistance you have shown that the motto

---

[122] Ibid., July 5, 6, 21, 22, 1884 and I.T.U., *Proceedings*, 1885, 1886.
[123] T.P.P.U., *Minutes*, December 11, 1885.
[124] *Globe*, December 8, 11, 15, 16, 19, 22, 1885.
[125] Ibid., January 4, 1886. Emphasis in original.

of our union 'United to support not combined to injure' is the guiding stone of the honest toiler everywhere....[126]

This electoral defeat led to the *Mail's* total reversal in February 1886 when it surrendered to the Union. Local 91 had had to prove its strength at the polls, however, for as early as 1884 leading Tory printers had warned Macdonald of the possible repercussions of the *Mail's* adventure. J.S. Williams had written in August, 1884:

> Not only will the matter complained of [Mail lock-out] alienate a very large proportion of the working men who have hitherto nobly supported the party, but it places a barrier in the way of any prominent or representative workingman actively working or speaking in the future.

Moreover he predicted that the *Mail's* reactionary policies could cost the Tories two to three seats in Toronto and perhaps seats in other urban centres as well. E.F. Clarke, a prominent politician and member of Local 91, wrote to the same effect:

> A reduction of wages at a week's notice and a refusal of the Mail to leave the settlement of the question to arbitration will alienate the sympathies of a large number of workingmen who have hitherto supported the Conservative cause, and will weaken the influence of the journal with the masses....

A non-working class Tory politico wrote that the labour friends of the party were now in an impossible position since they "cannot support the party that treats them so shabbily" and expressed the fear that the loss of the whole Toronto Trades and Labor Council might result in electoral defeat in the city.[127] Nevertheless these warnings were ignored until the humiliating defeats of January 1886. Then the party rushed in to settle the matter once and for all. Harry Piper, a Tory ward heeler, wrote to Macdonald in February to inform him that the I.T.U.-*Mail* fight "had of late assumed a very serious aspect" since a number of old party workers had clearly transferred their allegiance in the election. As a result he arranged a meeting with John Armstrong, a Tory leader of Local 91 who had lost his own job at the *Mail* during the strike. Piper convinced Armstrong that "the Union was *killing our Party* and the Grit were reaping the benefit of the trouble and using our own friends." Armstrong promised to help if the iron-clad was removed. Piper then arranged with the manager and directors of the *Mail* that the document be ceremoniously burned

---

[126] Ibid., January 5, 1886.

[127] J.S. Williams to John A. Macdonald, Toronto, August 4, 1884, 196352-55; E.F. Clarke to Macdonald, Toronto, August 5, 1884, 196358-60; John Small to Macdonald, Toronto, August 5, 1884, 196369-70. *Macdonald Papers*, P.A.C.

before the printers and Armstrong agreed to have the union lift the boycott.[128] Thus the seeming defeat of the summer of 1884 had been translated by political means into a striking victory for Local 91. Neither the *Globe* nor the *Mail* was to cause the union difficulty again in the late nineteenth century.

Similar tactics were employed successfully against J.H. Maclean of the *World* in 1888 when he tried to defeat the union's control of "fat" matter. The struggle was precipitated by a fight over the price to be paid for an advertisement that was inserted twice. The union rule was that if the advertisement was run in an identical manner then the compositor was only paid once but that if any changes were made the compositor was paid again for the whole advertisement. The foreman supported the printers' case but the Macleans, after paying the money owed, locked out the union. The I.T.U. then reiterated its position on "fat" matter:

> Only by the getting of the advertisements and other "fat" matter are the men able to make anything like living wages, and this fact is recognized by all fair-minded employers as well as the men.[129]

In late July, after filling his shop with "country-mice," Maclean sought an injunction against the I.T.U.'s boycott of the *World*. It was granted on an interim basis and then made permanent in mid-August.[130] The inunction did not solve Maclean's problems:

> The World is in sore straights as a result of the law compelling union men not to buy it or patronize merchants who advertise therein. Internal storms are of such common occurrence that a couple of weeks ago the vermin employed there went out on strike even but returned to the nest again.[131]

A few months later Maclean again sought to make his paper a union shop. Again the political dimensions of the settlement are clear. W.B. Prescott, the President of Local 91, wrote John A. Macdonald and sought his intervention with Maclean to ensure that the *World* came around. Prescott pointed out that "the cheap labour policies of the *World* antagonized organized labour."[132] Perhaps one reason that Maclean and the *World* felt the pressure was the Local had quickly found a way to circumvent the injunction by promoting union papers rather than naming those boycotted. They continued to use this technique especially in a political context. In the municipal campaigns of 1891-2, for example, they issued the following circular:

---

[128] Harry Piper to Macdonald, February 2, February 3, 1886, 2-5474-6, *Macdonald Papers*.
[129] *Globe*, July 18, 1888.
[130] Ibid., July 26, 27, August 8, 15, 1888.
[131] *Typographical Journal*, September 15, 1889.
[132] W.B. Prescott to Macdonald, Toronto, May 5, 1890, 241968, *Macdonald Papers*.

> Having been informed that you are seeking municipal honours, we desire to call your attention to the fact that there are a few printing and publishing houses in this city who do not employ union labour, and we, believing it would be to your advantage to patronize only those who do employ such, request you to place your patronage and advertising in union offices only, as we can assure you that from past experience, your chances of election are greater by so doing.[133]

The circular then listed the dailies that were union shops which by 1891 included all but the *Telegram*, which was shortly to enter the fold. In March 1892 the T.T.U. also began to use the union label.[134] Thus the power of the Toronto printers continued to grow throughout the late nineteenth century and a larger proportion of Toronto printers were unionized in the early 1890s than had been at any previous date.[135]

The initial encounter with mechanization served to strengthen their position. Until the invention of linotype and monotype machines in the late 1880s, typesetting had remained unchanged from the sixteenth century.[136] In Toronto the *News* introduced the Rogers typography machine in 1892 and offered the printer-operators 14 cents/1000 ems. The I.T.U. had recommended in 1888 "that subordinate unions ... take speedy action looking to their [linotype machines] recognition and regulation, endeavouring everywhere to secure their operation by union men upon a scale of wages which shall secure compensation equal to that paid hand compositors."[137] This was amended in 1889[138] to demand that in all union offices only practical printers could run the machines and that the rates on the machines would be governed by the local unions.[139] In Toronto the union's right to control the operation of the machine was not challenged initially and their *Typographical Journal* correspondent reported in March of 1892 "that so far we have not suffered from their use." However that summer the *News*, appealing to the craft custom of piece rates, refused to pay operators by the day. After a seven week strike the union won its demand that the printers be paid by time. They were to receive $12.00 a week for six weeks while learning the machine operation and then $14.00 after they

---

[133] T.T.U., *Minutes*, December 5, 1891.
[134] Ibid., March 5, 1892.
[135] Zerker, "A History," ch. 3.
[136] For the best discussion of the effects of mechanization on printers see George E. Barnett, "The Introduction of the Linotype," *Yale Review*, (Nov. 1904) 251-273. A good summary of all the literature on printers and mechanization is Harry Kalber and Carl Schlesinger, *Union Printers and Controlled Automation*, (N.Y. 1967), especially ch. 1.
[137] I.T.U., *Proceedings*, 1888 and Barnett, "The Printers," 197.
[138] I.T.U., *Proceedings*, 1889. For the struggle in New York which set the continental pattern see Kalber and Schlesinger, *Union Printers*, ch. 1.
[139] I.T.U., *Proceedings*, 1891.

demonstrated their competency, which was set at 2000 ems per hour or 100,000 ems per week. This settlement brought the union not only control of the machine and the wage style it sought but also implicitly recognized the printers' right to limit production since the rate of competency set was far below the actual capabilities of the machine, which were estimated to be anywhere from 3 to 8 times as fast as hand composition.[140] The International was also concerned to prevent any proliferation of speed-ups with the new machine and ruled that "no member shall be allowed to accept work ... where a task, stint, or deadline is imposed by the employer on operators of typesetting devices."[141] The union later successfully resisted any attempts by employers to speed up work totals. The victory over the *News* and the union's previous success with Robertson's *Telegram* also brought Local 91 control of all Toronto newspapers for the first time in its history.[142] The printers had learned their lessons well. They left the century not only with their traditions intact but also with their power actually augmented. They had met the machine and triumphed.[143]

IV

What ramifications did shop floor power have in terms of how workers thought about their society, how it was changing and their own role in it? David Montgomery has argued that the major impact of this early workers' control was the skilled workers' growing awareness that the key institution for the transformation of society was the trade union.[144] From their understanding that they, through their unions, controlled production, it was a relatively easy step to the belief that all the capitalist brought to the process was capital. Thus an alternative source of capital would transform the society, ending the inequities of capitalist production and creating the producer's society that they all dreamed of. This ideology looked to cooperation administered through the trade union as the major agent of change. All the unions we have discussed favoured cooperation.

John Monteith, President of Toronto I.M.I.U. Local 28, wrote *Fincher's Trades Review* in 1863 to describe the work of Canada West members in discussing and

---

[140] For a similar success in Vancouver see Bartley, *Outline History*, 12.

[141] I.T.U., *Proceedings*, 1893.

[142] Zerker, "A History," 160-165; 202-207; Harkness, *Atkinson*, 25-26; Barnett, "The Printers," ch. 11 and Wright, "Restriction of Output," 35-55.

[143] For the English response to typesetting machines see Ellic Howe, ed., *The London Compositor*, (London 1947), ch. 19. For an excellent autobiographical account of an Edwardian British compositor which illustrates many of the themes discussed here see John Burnett ed., *The Annals of Labour: Autobiographies of British Working Class People 1820-1920*, (London 1974), 330-340.

[144] David Montgomery, "Trade Union Practice," 16-25.

investigating cooperation. A union moulders' committee had contacted Rochdale and now recommended both producers and consumers co-ops to their local unions. They sought cooperation because "our present organization does not accomplish what we want. That is to take us from under the hand of our employers and place us on an equal footing."[145] Cooperation of course would accomplish this very end. Five years later another Toronto moulder complained that "We are but little better off than our forefathers who were serfs to the feudal barons We are serfs to the capitalists of the present day...." His solution:

> Let the next convention create a co-op fund to be devoted entirely to cooperation.... We have been cooperating all our lives, but it has been to make someone else rich. We have been the busy bees in the hives while the drones have run away with the honey and left us to slave in the day of adversity.... Day after day the wealth of the land is concentrating in the hands of a few persons. The little streams of wealth created and put in motion by the hard hands of labour gravitate into one vast reservoir, out of which but a few individuals drink from golden cups; while labour, poor, degraded and despised labour, must live in unhealthy hovels and feed upon scanty, unhealthy food from rusty dishes....[146]

The I.M.I.U. founded as many as twenty cooperative foundries in the 1860s.[147]

Toronto printers started three cooperative newspapers. At the height of the nine hour struggle in 1872 *The Ontario Workman* was started as a cooperative venture, as was D.J. O'Donoghue's *Labor Record* of 1886. In 1892 during the strike at the *News* a group of printers banded together and founded the *Star*.[148] The *Ontario Workman* operated as a co-op paper for only six months and the *Labor Record* and the *Star* each lasted about a year. Capital for the *Star* was raised from the T.T.U. and T.T.L.C. They initially used the presses of the *World* since W.F. Maclean offered them his facilities in return for 51% of the operation. This "Paper for the People" enjoyed quick success in winning the readership of the *News*, which had from its inception in 1882 posed as the paper for Toronto workers.[149] Riordan, the owner of the *News*, attempted to buy the operation and Maclean tried to merge it with the *World*, but the printers refused both offers and instead bought a press. However they failed to make a

---

145 *Fincher's Trades Review*, August 15, 1863.
146 *Iron Molders Journal*, February 1868.
147 James C. Sylvis, *The Life, Speeches, Labors and Essays of William H. Sylvis*, (Philadelphia 1872), 390.
148 For similar events in Vancouver see Bartley, *Outline History*, 11. There, during a strike in 1892, the printers founded *The New World*.
149 Russel Hann, "Brainworkers and the Knights of Labor: E.E. Sheppard, Phillips Thompson and the Toronto *News*," in Kealey and Warrian, eds., *Essays*.

go of it and the paper suspended publication in June of 1893. It was continued after its purchase as a pro-labour paper but control had passed out of the printers' hands.[150]

Machinists and blacksmiths organized a cooperative foundry early in 1872 after losing a strike at the Soho works.[151] Six years later Toronto cigar makers established the Toronto Cooperative Cigar Manufactory Association. Here, as with the moulders in the 1860s, the push for cooperation came as a logical extension of their knowledge of the trade and their refusal to accept management's reduction of wages. Alf Jury, a Toronto tailor and labour reformer, denounced "the wage system as a modified form of slavery" and demonstrated that there could be "no fraternal feeling between capital and labour" at a cigar makers' strike meeting that year. Jury then cited production statistics to repudiate the employers' claims that the reduction was necessary. A number of bosses who had agreed to pay union rates supported this assertion. Jury's logical solution was the great aim of working class struggle: "to do away with the capitalists while using the capital ourselves"—the establishment of a cooperative factory.[152] An association was founded, shares were issued, a charter was obtained and the factory opened for business in March 1879. About a year later the Toronto local of the C.M.I.U. reported that the cooperative was "progressing finely" and "doing a good trade."[153] Stratford cigar makers also founded a cooperative factory in 1886 which was owned by the Knights of Labor and run under C.M.I.U. rules. It employed between 20 and 30 men and produced a brand known as "The Little Knight."[154] Toronto Bakers Assembly LA 3499 also set up a cooperative bakery which lasted about two years in the mid-1880s.[155]

The successes or failures of these cooperative ventures are of less importance than the ideological assumptions on which they were based. Often originated only in crisis situations, they, nevertheless, flowed directly from the shop floor experience of skilled workers and the practices of their unions in struggling to control production. It was a relatively easy step from there to envisioning a system that was free of the boss who did so very little. A Chatham moulder wrote in 1864:

> This then shows both classes in their just relations towards each other—the capitalist and the mechanic; the one, the mechanic, is the moving power—the capitalist bearing about the same relation to him that the cart does to the horse which draws it—differing in this respect, that the mechanic makes the capitalist and the horse does not

---

[150] Harkness, *Atkinson*, 25-47.
[151] *Machinists and Blacksmiths' Journal*, December 1871, 451; January 1872, 486.
[152] *Globe*, October 30, November 5, 18, 27, December 14, 1878.
[153] *Cigar Makers Journal*, March 1879; April 1880.
[154] *Palladium of Labor*, May 29, July 3, 10, 1886.
[155] *Globe*, January 30, 31, February 5, 8, 22, 25, 28, March 17, April 28, May 9, 15, 1884; see also *Journal of United Labor*, Oct. 25, 1885.

> make the cart; the capitalist without the mechanic being about as useful as the cart without the horse. The capitalist no doubt at times increases the sphere of usefulness of the mechanic; so does the cart that of the horse, and enables him to do more for his owner than otherwise he could do; but deprive him of it, and there is little that he can do with it that he could not accomplish without it. In short the workingman is the cause the capitalist the effect.[156]

The syntax may be confused but the moulder's meaning comes through clearly. In 1882 at the time of a Toronto carpenters' strike, during discussion of a cooperative planing mill, a reporter asked union leader Thomas Moor if the carpenters had the requisite skills. Moor's response was simple but profound: "If the men can manage a mill and make it a success for their employers, surely they can do the same thing for an institution in which they have an interest."[157]

Cooperation was one extension of workers' control, socialism was to be another.[158] Capital, however, also began to respond to the challenges raised by the growing tradition of workers' control. F.W. Taylor, capital's main work-place ideologue, understood very well the power of the "autonomous workman":

> Now, in the best of the ordinary types of management, the managers recognize the fact that the 500 or 1000 workmen, included in the 20 or 30 trades, who are under them, possess this mass of traditional knowledge, a large part of which is not in the possession of management.... The foremen and superintendents know, better than anyone else, that their own knowledge and personal skill falls far short of the combined knowledge and dexterity of all the workingmen under them.[159]

Taylor also reminisced at length about his first job experience in a machine shop of the Midvale Steel Company in the late 1870s:

> As was usual then, and in fact as is still usual in most of the shops in this country [1912], the shop was really run by the workmen, and not by the bosses. The workmen together had carefully planned just how fast each job should be done, and they had set a pace for each

---

[156] *Fincher's Trades Review*, April 23, 1864.

[157] *Globe*, April 5, 1882.

[158] David Frank, "Class Conflict in the Coal Industry: Cape Breton 1922," in Kealey and Warrian, eds., *Essays*.

[159] F.W. Taylor, *The Principles of Scientific Management*, (New York 1967), 32. For a brilliant discussion of modern management strategies see Harry Braverman, *Labor and Monopoly Capital*, (N.Y. 1974).

machine throughout the shop, which was limited to about one-third of a good day's work. Every new workman who came into the shop was told at once by the other men exactly how much of each kind of work he was to do, and unless he obeyed these instructions he was sure before long to be driven out of the place by the men.[160]

After his appointment as foreman Taylor set out to increase production. He fired some of the men, lowered others' wages, hired "green" hands, lowered the piece rate—in general engaged in what he described as a "war." His limited success in this "bitter struggle" he attributed to not being of working class origin. His middle class status enabled him to convince management that worker sabotage, not the speed-up, was responsible for a sudden rash of machine breakdowns.[161]

The new popularity of Taylor and the other proponents of "scientific management" in the early twentieth century was indicative of capital's new attempt to rationalize production.[162] This, combined with the rise of the large corporation, the rapid growth of multi-plant firms, and the ever-increasing extension of labour-saving machinery, challenged directly not only workers' control traditions but also the very existence of the labour movement.

Toronto workers, who had struggled throughout the late nineteenth century for shop floor control, were about to face new, more virulent battles. The custom of workers' control, widely regarded as a right, had become deeply embedded in working class culture. The fight, initially to maintain and later to extend this control, became the major locus of class struggle in the opening decades of the twentieth century.

Thus even in the cases where craft unions abandoned the traditional practices of the "autonomous workman" in return for concessions or out of weakness, the leadership could not always assure management that the membership would follow union dictates. As one investigator noted about the foundry business:

> The customs of the trade ... do not always vanish with the omission of any recognition of "the standard day's work" in wage agreements. Nor can it be expected that the entire membership of an organization will at once respond to the removal of limitations on output by a national convention of that organization. Trade customs, shop practices, grow; they become as much a part of the man as his skill as a molder....[163]

---

[160] Taylor, *Principles*, 49.
[161] Ibid., 53.
[162] Palmer, "Class, Conception and Conflict," 31-33.
[163] Wright, "Restriction of output," 174.

Written in 1904, these cautions were as true of other skilled workers as they were of moulders. Customs of control, established by struggle, would not vanish; they had to be vanquished by persistent management assault.

The Fragmented Family: Family Strategies in the Face of Death, Illness, and Poverty, Montreal, 1860-1885

Bettina Bradbury

Working-class families in mid- to late-nineteenth-century Montreal lived in fairly constant contact with disease, poverty, and death. The newborn children of the poor were almost as likely to die as to live. Many families were fragmented by the death of a mother or father. Many more experienced periods when one or both parents or children were sick, perhaps hovering on death. The high incidence of disease coupled with the fragility of many a family's earning power presented constant challenges to basic survival and to family coherence and stability.[1]

As the city industrialized, families were increasingly dependent upon an uncertain and very seasonal labour market. Fathers were usually the primary wage-earners. In all but the most skilled of working-class households, however, additional wage-earners were necessary. Only seldom did a wife and mother work for wages. It was to their children that working-class parents turned for the necessary extra income. In addition, the family required the labour of the mother and, often, daughters in the home to make the necessary purchases, cook, sew, and clean to replenish the working members.[2]

Their family economy was a fragile one, changing over the life cycle, but always subject to sudden challenges. If either wage-earner or mother became sick, families faced a temporary crisis. If either died, the crisis was more fundamental. Even at such times as pregnancy or childbirth the delicate balance of incoming wages and household management could be shattered. Only when both parents survived and several children reached working age was a degree of financial security ensured. While sons and daughters were too young to work parents had to seek other ways of

---

[1] Philip Carpenter, "On Some of the Causes of the Excessive Mortality of Young Children in the City of Montreal," *The Canadian Naturalist*, New Series, Vol. 4 (1869), 198. Paul André Linteau, René Durocher et Jean-Claude Robert, *Histoire du Québec Contemporain* (Montréal: Boréal Express, 1979), especially Chapter 7 and pp. 175-9; Fernand Harvey, *Révolution industrielle et travailleurs, Une enquête sur les rapports entre le capital et le travail au Québec àla fin du 19ᵉ siècle* (Montréal: Boréal Express, 1978); Bettina Bradbury, "The Family Economy and Work in An Industrializing City, Montreal in the 1870s," Canadian Historical Association, *Historical Papers* (1979). On the need for several family members to work in a different city, see Frances H. Early, "The French Canadian Family Economy and Standard of Living in Lowell, Massachusetts, 1870," paper presented at the Canadian Historical Association Meetings, Montreal, June, 1980.

[2] Bradbury, "The Family Economy," 77-8, 86.

stretching their incomes or minimizing necessary expenditures. When sickness, death, or loss of work shattered a family's precarious material security, help had to be sought from neighbours, kin, or charity.[3]

Working-class families dealt with such crises in a variety of ways. Some, when the future seemed particularly bleak and impossible, gave up their children permanently to kin, orphanages, or other institutions. Some shared housing with relatives or strangers. A few mothers took jobs that could be done at home; still fewer went out to work. Charity tided others over difficult times, while some placed their children temporarily in orphanages, taking them home again when the particular crisis had passed or when they were old enough to work.[4]

It is particularly with this latter strategy that this paper is concerned. The history of the use that parents made of one Montreal orphanage, L'Orphelinat St. Alexis, in St. Jacques ward, shows how some families responded to poverty, sickness, and death. The experiences of these children shed light more generally on family survival strategies.

The impact of poverty, sickness, and death upon working-class families cannot be understood apart from the context within which they lived. Throughout the nineteenth century, but especially after 1850, Montreal changed rapidly, if unevenly, from a city dominated by commerce to one in which industry held a central and increasingly important position. Children grew up in a world that was visibly changing and very different from that of their parents' youth. Parents raising their families in an industrializing city had to draw on both old traditions and new resources.

Since the 1850s industrial capitalists had persistently reshaped the nature of production and work. Their factories employed hundreds of workers, drawing on an increasing proportion of the city's growing population. The pace and speed of change varied from trade to trade. Its fundamental result was the divorce of an ever-growing number of workers from ownership of their own productive units and from control over their work. The sons and daughters of both rural and urban producers became an urban proletariat. They formed families with no capital and no land to fall back on in times of crisis. Their survival depended on their ability to sell their labour power in an impersonal and changing labour market.[5]

---

[3]   Jane Humphries, "Class Struggle and the Persistence of the Working Class Family," *Cambridge Journal of Economics*, 1 (1977), 248-9.

[4]   Bradbury, "The Family Economy," 92, 86. On the semi-permanent giving up of children to orphanages in England, see Joy Parr, *Labouring children* (London: Croom Helm, 1980), especially Chapter 4, "Family Strategy and Philanthropic Abduction."

[5]   Gerald J.J. Tulchinsky, *The River Barons. Montreal Businessmen and the Growth of Industry and Transportation, 1837-1853* (Toronto: University of Toronto Press, 1977), especially Chapter 12; Linteau *et al.*, *Histoire du Québec*, especially Chapter 7; Joanne Burgess, "L'industrie de la chaussure à Montréal, 1840-1870—Le Passage de l'artisanat à la fabrique," *Revue d'histoire de l'Amérique française*, 31 (septembre, 1977).

The Fragmented Family

The reorganization of work coincident with factory production was rendering old skills obsolete. "There is a considerable feeling of depression," explained a shoemaker in 1888, "because the working man has been replaced by a machine." Apprentices no longer learned how to make a commodity from beginning to end. They had become cheap sources of labour for employers interested only in maximum, rapid production. Women and children as well as men were drawn into the new and usually tedious kinds of jobs created by the mechanization of old processes. Skilled workers faced competition from unskilled workers and from women and children in jobs that might retain their old names but were fundamentally altered in their content.[6]

These changes in the nature of production had contradictory effects upon the families of the growing proletariat. Skilled workers chances of being unemployed increased. A swelling body of unskilled workers would compete for jobs and depress wages, or at least prevent them from rising. On the other hand, with the growing demand for female and child labour, some other family members were more likely able to find work. While work by sons, daughters, or wives sustained the family income, it also perpetuated the low-wage system. The desire of capital for cheap workers, and of families for extra income, were thus inextricably linked. An economy built on wage dependence would be a shaky and unstable one for many families.

The growth of industry reshaped the geography of the city as it did people's work and lives. Areas took on specific characteristics. Ste. Anne in the west and Ste. Marie in the east became predominantly industrial, working-class districts. The old city became a centre of commerce, its residents gradually moving out to the old suburbs and to the newer wards. In St. Jacques ward in the east this transition was particularly evident. Artisanal workshops and small stores, often with dwellings above them, were interspersed among workers housing. While most productive units in the area were small workshops with under five employees, the ward's three large factories employed more people than all other manufacturing units combined.[7]

In St. Jacques old and new were mixed, but newcomers and new ways were rapidly affecting the old. Migrants to the city mingled with established city dwellers. St. Jacques' population rose by over 12,000 between 1861 and 1881, an increase of 94 percent compared to the 55 percent by which Montreal as a whole grew over the same period. The 2,000 houses built in the ward during these two decades were not sufficient to keep up with the influx. The demand for cheap workers housing was a

---

[6] The Royal Commission on the Relations of Labour and Capital, *Quebec Evidence*, 1889, 369. These testimonies are particularly eloquent and explicit on the nature and meaning of these changes to the workers. On the work of women during this period, see Suzanne Cross, "The Neglected Majority: The Changing Role of Women in 19th Century Montreal," in Susan M. Trofimenkoff and Alison Prentice, eds., *The Neglected Majority: Essays in Canadian Women's History* (Toronto: McClelland and Stewart, 1977).

[7] Industrial Schedules, Manuscript Census, 1861, 1871, St. Jacques Ward.

boon to the owners of land and to builders and construction companies. Proprietors took advantage of the great increase in the value of land by cramming houses as close together as possible. Houses were rapidly and carelessly constructed. City regulations aimed to prevent fire hazards were avoided more frequently in St. Jacques than in any other city ward. Wooden houses, sheds, and stables remained unbricked despite a city by-law requiring the end of wooden housing. The building of houses neither kept up with population growth nor provided space at rates that the poorer families could afford. Families shared houses, Sometimes four to five families resided in "one small tenement house." Under half of the unskilled families of the area had a dwelling to themselves. St. Jacques had the highest population density of any area of town, with over 150 people per acre in 1877, 168 in 1884, and 235 by 1896. The increased density represented an increase in the number of people sharing houses, from 1.35 families per house in 1871 to 1.65 in 1881.[8]

Crowding and high death rates went hand in hand. Throughout this period St. Jacques and Ste. Marie wards consistently had the highest death rates in the city. City records placed St. Jacques' rate at between 35 and 39 per 1,000 in the 1870s and around 30 in the 1880s. However, as a Dr. Fenwick pointed out in the 1870s, aggregate rates hide vast variations. He suggested that, "in certain unhealthy and overcrowded courts, or in certain crowded districts of this city" mortality rose "to 40, 50, 60 or 70 per 1,000" while "in the other more open, airy and well ventilated localities the death rate" fell to 10 or 20 per 1,000. Such an overcrowded area lay in the southeastern corner of St. Jacques ward, stretching east into Ste. Marie. There, where once there had been a swamp, the "largest proportion of deaths" in the city were found.[9]

The city's medical officer had no hesitation in attributing high death rates to overcrowding. In such parts of town the isolation necessary to prevent the spread of smallpox was impossible. The disease spread within the "most over-crowded parts of the city, among poor families located in small badly lighted and ill ventilated rooms." Certainly overcrowding, dirt, malnutrition, and ignorance were important factors. But these were the results of poor wages and lack of steady work, and

---

[8] Montreal's population increased from 90,323 in 1861 to 140,747 in 1881. In the same period that of St. Jacques increased from 13,104 to 25,398. On the nature of this part of town, see Bradbury, "The Family Economy," 74; *Census of Canada*, 1861, 1871, 1881; "Mayor's Valedictory," *Reports on the Accounts of the Corporation of the City of Montreal*, 1870 (hereafter *Montreal Annual Reports*), 90; "Report of the Inspector of Buildings," *Montreal Annual Reports*, 1873; "Report of the Medical Health Officer," *Montreal Annual Reports*, 1876, 10; Bradbury, "The Family Economy," 92; Jacques Bernier, "La condition des travailleurs, 1851-1896," in Noel Bélanger et al, *Les Travailleurs Québécois 1851-1896* (Montréal: Les Presses de l'Université du Québec, 1975), 47.

[9] "Report of the Medical Health Officer," 1876-79; "Mayor's Valedictory," 1874, 15-16; 10; "Report of the Medical Health Officer," 1879, 11.

The Fragmented Family

especially of the poor condition of the housing built by the speculators of the city. "It is the duty of Council," Dr. Philip Carpenter argued in 1859,

> to see that the wages of death are no longer wrung form the hard earnings of the poor, but that all who undertake to let houses shall be compelled to put them and their surroundings into a condition favourable to health and life.

Housing continued, however, to be expensive, poorly constructed, and unsanitary.[10]

Death hit unequally. It was the children who were dying in greatest numbers and especially the children of the working class and poor French Canadians. Of the babies born in Montreal in 1867, for instance, "two out of every five died within the year." Used to death, some parents attributed "disease and misery to the Divinity which are rather the consequence of ignorance and often of unpardonable neglect. Children are exposed to a contagious disease, they become affected and it is said that God ordained it so."[11] In the first year of life intestinal diseases and diarrhoea were the major killers. These ailments were often the result of adulterated milk to which "chalk, starch and the brains of sheep" were added to increase the specific gravity. Mothers and producers added water to make milk go further, diluting away its nourishment. Had infants been breast-fed in the early months, many of these deaths might have been avoided. But weary, malnourished mothers make poor breast-feeders. "The majority of mothers living in cities" were reported to "believe themselves incapable of nursing their infants and have recourse to artificial alimentation which is one of the principal causes of the excessive mortality of children under 1 year of age."[12]

For children over one year of age, smallpox was the major cause of death. St. Jacques and Ste. Marie were areas where resistance to inoculation was especially strong. This opposition was not mere backwardness and suspicion on the part of the people. Some vaccines had been contaminated, and even with good vaccine the experience of inoculation was gruesome and did not guarantee immunity. Families hid their children and made a variety of excuses to avoid it. In 1878, 594 people refused or avoided inoculation. In these two wards were concentrated over half of the city's smallpox deaths, but only one-third of its population.[13]

---

10   "Report of the Medical Officer," 1879, 10; Philip Carpenter, *On the Relative Value of Human Life in Different Parts of Canada* (Montreal: Lovell's, 1859), 15; "Report of the Medical Officer," 1879, 11.

11   Carpenter, "Excessive Mortality," 198.

12   "Report of the Medical Officer," 1879, 19; 1876, 65; Georges Genier, *Quelques Considérations sur les causes de la Mortalité dans Enfants contenant des conseils aux méres sur les soins à donner aux enfants* (Montréal: Senécal, 1871), 9-10.

13   "Report of the Medical Officer," 1878, 24, 18. It should be noted that such parents were not as remiss as we might think. Smallpox inoculations were gruesome and often dangerous during this period.

Among adults and especially women between the ages of twenty and forty, phthisis or tuberculosis was the leading killer. Predisposition to phthisis was acquired, the city's medial officer explained, "by want of exercise, by occupations which confine the thorax, by impure air, and by insufficiency and bad quality of nourishment and above all anything that lowers morale." Childbearing, depriving themselves to feed the rest of the family better, and the exhaustion of child-rearing made mothers especially vulnerable to such disease. The sickness of a mother presented special problems to wage-earning families unable to pay for assistance.[14]

In this changing, growing, and probably bewildering city, keeping a family sheltered, clothed, healthy, and together was a difficult task. Some parents just could not cope. At all stages of a family's life cycle a few, seeing no way out, deserted their children or their spouse. Some parents, married or single, abandoned their newborn children at the doors of the city's foundling hospital. These babies' chance in life was minimal. Of the more than 600 abandoned in 1863, for instance, only 10 percent survived. Many were already dead by the time the Grey Nuns found them. Other parents relinquished all moral control over their older sons and daughters, allowing them to roam the streets by night and day, to the consternation of the upper classes. Such children moved effortlessly and almost naturally into delinquency and crime. In 1869 the Inspector of Prisons argued that abandoned children constituted the nursery from which three-quarters of the prison population sprung. It was hoped that schools of reform and industry would offer shelter to the "many poor, unhappy infants without parents, protectors or shelter." That year nearly 2,000 children under sixteen went to prison.[15]

Other parents relinquished their sons and daughters permanently to city orphanages, hoping that, there, the children might escape their meagre and disorganized beginnings. By the 1860s at least twelve institutions run by six orders of nuns and various lay and Protestant groups cared for 750 orphaned youngsters annually. Some orphanages placed children out as apprentices, others had them adopted by good families. Still others retained them in the institution, giving them the education and skills necessary to make it on their own.[16]

---

[14] "Report of the Medical Officer," 1877, 65.

[15] L.A. Huguet-Latour, *L'Annuaire de Ville Marie* (Montreal, 1863), 63. On a later period see J. Germano, "Histoire de la Charité à Montréal," *Revue Canadienne*, 32 (1896), 423-38; see also *The Municipal Loan Funds and the Hospitals and Charities of the Province of Canada (Morning Chronicle*, Quebec, 1864), 5; *The Saturday Reader*, Montreal, IV (1867), 22; "Rapport des Inspecteurs des Prisons," *Quebec Sessional Papers*, 1869, 2-3.

[16] Figures on the numbers of orphans were derived from institutions listed in Huguet-Latour, *Annuaire*, 57-103. The number (750) refers only to those in Catholic institutions; the real number, therefore, would have been considerably higher. For information on other orphanages see their annual reports, e.g., Boys' Home Montreal, *Annual Reports, 1890*; Protestant Orphan Asylum, *Annual Reports, 1858-1869*; Protestant Infants' Home, *Annual Reports, 1870-1895*. See also Alfred Sandham, *Ville Marie, or Sketches of Montreal Past and*

But not all orphanages took children for indefinite periods. And not all demanded or expected parents to abandon their young. Several of the city's institutions consciously provided a short-term shelter where families could place their children during difficult times. Still others, while ostensibly caring for real orphans, welcomed youngsters who would sooner or later return to their own families. The St. Alexis Orphanage, located in St. Jacques ward, the area described above, was one such institution. The parents and children who used St. Alexis are interesting because they are typical or working-class families that fragmented temporarily in crisis, yet stayed together in the longer term.[17]

The St. Alexis Orphanage was officially founded in 1853. It was run by the Sisters of providence, one of many orders created by Bishop Bourget. The mid-nineteenth century was a period when the Catholic Church throughout Quebec expanded its power, increased its personnel, and began to deal specifically with the problems of poverty and secularization accompanying industrial capitalist production. The Sisters had begun their work among the widows and the elderly. Their tasks rapidly expanded to include visiting the poor and sick in their homes, providing food for the hungry, teaching, and providing institutional care for orphans, widows, and elderly priests.[18]

Speaking in 1867 to the lay women who helped the Sisters raise money and visit the poor, Bourget pointed with evident fear to the rapid population growth and the miseries that would accompany it. He stressed that charitable institutions would have to be prepared to care for the existing wretchedness, for if they did not he believed they would be overwhelmed by it and it would recur in even more hideous form. Home visiting in the poorest neighbourhoods could prevent demoralization from

---

Present (Montreal: Georges Bishop and Co.; 1870), 302-3; Marie-Claire Daveluy, *L'Orphelinat Catholique de Montréal, 1832-1932* (Montréal: Editions Levesque, 1933); *A History of the Montreal Ladies Benevolent Society, 1815-1920* (Montreal, 1920); Janice Harvey, "Upper Class Reaction to Poverty in Mid-Nineteenth Century Montreal: A Protestant Example" (M.A. thesis, McGill, 1978), 88-100.

[17] The Protestant Infants' Home (founded 1870), the Montreal Protestant Orphan Asylum, and the St. Patrick's Asylum run by the Grey Nuns also took children on a short-term basis, returning them to their parents. More research is required to tell which other institutions did the same.

[18] Nive Voisine, *L'Histoire de l'Eglise au Québec, 1608-1970* (Montréal: Editions Fides, 1971); Huguette Lapointe Roy, "Paupérisme et Assistance Sociale à Montréal, 1832-1865" (M.A. thesis, McGill University, 1972); Serge Gagnon, "Le diocèse de Montréal durant les années 1860," in Pierre Hurtubise et al., *Le Laïc Dans L'Eglise Canadienne-Français de 1830 à Nos Jours* (Montréal: Fides, 1972); Leon Pouliot, "L'impulsion donnée par Mgr Bourget à la pratique religieuse," *Revue d'histoire de l'Amérique Française*, 16 (juin, 1962); l'Institut de la Providence, *Histoire des Filles de la Charité. Servants des Pauvres dites soeurs de la Providence*, Vols. II, IV, VI (Providence: Maison Mere, 1940).

devastating the lowest classes.[19] The Sisters and their lay helpers would help to regulate families and keep the peace in households. They could thus instruct the ignorant, correct vices, suppress scandals, and encourage attendance at the sacraments and industry and economy among the poor.[20]

The Sisters' work in the orphanage thus blended with their work in the homes of the poor. Some families took their daughters to Sisters they had met through household visits. Sisters suggested that certain girls, especially those not receiving a Catholic upbringing at home, be sent to them. Père Gauvin called upon the Dames de la Charité to help the Sisters to give youngsters spiritual guidance. Quoting Christ's "suffer the little children to come unto me," he suggested that the women assiduously seek out abandoned or deserted children for care by the consecrated daughters of the church.[21]

The proliferation of orphanages, schools, day nurseries, and kindergartens during this period brought more and more children into close and sustained contact with nuns and priests. They hoped through saving children to preserve the family and broaden Catholic social values. The orphanage and other charitable works were to counteract the evils of a rapidly secularizing city. Youngsters sheltered for a time in church institutions gained a religious education and the force of example to help them resist temptation when they returned home.[22]

To families, such orphanages offered pragmatic advantages. The placement of their girls temporarily in the orphanage offered parents the chance to recover from sickness, bereavement, or unemployment secure in the knowledge that their children were being fed, clothed, and cared for.

Over 1,000 girls passed through the St. Alexis orphanage between 1860 and 1889. At first, parents from both rural and urban areas sheltered their children there. Increasingly over the period, however, the institution came to serve the people of Montreal and especially the families of the surrounding district of St. Jacques. By the 1880s over 80 percent of the girls entering St. Alexis had parents who lived in Montreal.[23]

Nearly all these girls came from working-class families. Labourers, whose work was always temporary and poorly paid, were especially likely to send their daughters to St. Alexis. So, too, were shoemakers, men whose trade was rapidly being undermined by the reorganization of the work process, the elaboration of putting out, and the employment of women and children that accompanied industrial capitalism.

---

[19] *Histoire des Filles de la Charité*, VI, 168.
[20] *Histoire des Filles de la Charité*, VI, 191.
[21] Association des Dames de Charité de l'Asile de la Providence (Montreal: n.d.), 1.
[22] On schools, see Marta Danylewycz, "Through Women's Eyes: The Family in Late Nineteenth Century Quebec," paper presented at the Canadian Historical Association meetings, Montreal, June, 1980.
[23] "Registre pour les orphelines de l'orphelinat St. Alexis" (handwritten register), Archives of the Sisters of Providence (hereafter ASP).

The other girls' fathers were also from trades in which the pay was low, the work seasonal and especially vulnerable to cyclical variations in the economy. They were from families completely dependent on wages so low they allowed for no savings against crisis.[24]

Eighty percent of the girls were first taken to St. Alexis when they were between the ages of four and eleven. The average age of entry was around eight, an age when children might cost as much to support in food and clothes as an adult yet were unlikely to contribute to the family income. Most children did not spend many years at the St. Alexis orphanage. The orphanage was, like the nineteenth-century city, a place of great mobility with children continually arriving and leaving. Ten percent of the girls stayed one month or less, half for under one year. Between 1860 and 1885 the length of the girls' stays grew shorter. Increasingly, parents seem to have used the orphanage to solve short-term rather than long-term family crises. Thus in the 1860s, only one-third of the girls stayed under one year; in the 1870s 58 percent, and between 1880 and 1885, 65 percent. The mobility of the girls reflected that of their parents. Some were placed with the Sisters while their father or mother sought work away from Montreal. Nineteen percent returned to families who had moved elsewhere in Quebec, three percent to families in the United States, and one percent to households in Ontario. Thus, of those who originally came form Montreal, a quarter did not return there.[25]

Some of the girls came to the orphanage for a second term, a few for a third. Charlotte Bolduc's stays in the orphanage, for instance, spanned eight years. She arrived first at age four in early 1873 and stayed for four months. Her mother then came and took her home but returned her a year later, this time for three years. At the age of eight she went home for five months but then returned to the orphanage for another four years. She left St. Alexis in 1881, old enough to be a valuable helper at home or to go out to work for wages.[26]

Of the 538 girls from Montreal who entered the orphanage between 1860 and 1885, half were accompanied, followed, or preceded by a sister. Most sisters came to the orphanage together (70 percent), but some were brought at different times, perhaps years apart, sometimes only after an older sister had been taken home. The

---

24   One hundred parents' occupations were found in the manuscript censuses and in the parish registers. 23 percent were labourers, 19 percent shoemakers, 9 percent carpenters or joiners. 90 percent were in working-class occupations.

25   This and following sections are based on the information given in the register on the 538 girls from the Montreal area who entered St. Alexis between 1860 and 1884. The register listed the child's name, her father's name, and her mother's maiden name as well as her age at entry, the dates of arrival and departure, and the person who collected her.

26   The individual family histories were built up by matching the children to their families in the manuscript censuses of 1861, 1871, and 1881. Parish death registers were also checked to see whether their parents had died. The families of 104 girls (66 families) were found in the three censuses. "Registre" nos. 617, 675, 814.

Feliatrault sisters, daughters of a blacksmith, present an extreme example. Albina, Alphonsine, and Maria were taken to St. Alexis by their mother, Emelie, on the 5th of January, 1871. They were aged 11_, 9 and 6. Their older sister Fredoline, who was old enough to be helpful around the house, remained at home with her parents. Two years after the mother returned for Albina, six months later for Alphonsine, and finally three years later for Marie, now eleven years old. Maria had by then spent five years in the orphanage. In 1881 the four girls, then aged sixteen to twenty-eight, were still living with their parents, two of them working as seamstresses. Apparently their placement in the orphanage had not made them resentful of their parents or eager to leave home. With three members at work, the family probably lived better in these years than it ever had before.[27]

The experience of the four Crepeau sisters was less happy. Their mother Celina died on the 22nd of March, 1870. That very day their father, Jerome, a forty-one-year-old labourer, took his two middle daughters to the orphanage. Seven-year-old Ernestine died there a year later. Undeterred by this sad event, Jerome took his oldest daughter to St. Alexis in 1872. She was soon apprenticed out, probably as a servant in St. Denis. Eight years later the youngest daughter came to the orphanage and was placed with a lawyer in St. Athanase. After the death of his wife, Jerome obviously tried to bring up his daughters but was forced to relinquish them one by one, until his family was scattered.[28]

Few of the St. Alexis girls were true orphans. Parents brought them to the orphanage, parents returned to take them home again. Over half of the girls whose families were found in the censuses of the St. Jacques area had two living parents at the time they entered St. Alexis. Probably one-third had only one parent. Three-quarters of the girls would be reclaimed by one of their parents, others were called for by kin. Only 16 percent were adopted or apprenticed out to strangers.[29]

The death of a spouse was a common feature of married life in Montreal but a very different experience for men and women. For men it meant, indeed necessitated if there were children, hasty remarriage. For women, loss of a spouse was usually followed by years of struggle to bring up a family alone. Remarriage for widows was less likely than for widowers. If they did remarry, it was seldom soon after their first husband's death. As a result, at any one time widows always predominated over

---

[27] "Registre," nos. 543, 544, 545; 1881 mss. census, St. Jacques Ward, HH no. 187, Fam. no. 221.

[28] "Registre," nos. 509, 510, 608, 943; 1861 mss. census, St. Jacques Ward, no. 7865; 1871 mss. census, St. Jacques, 6, HH no. 109, Fam. no. 166.

[29] Estimates on how many children had one or two parents are based, first, on the families found in the three censuses and, second, on scrutiny of the parish registers between 1850 and 1875. The names of both parents of the girl were checked in the death registers. As the name of the spouse was given on death it was easy to be definite about matches. This method obviously missed any parents dying outside Montreal, thus underestimating the numbers with one or two dead parents. The fractions should be viewed only as reasonable approximations.

widowers. Thus, in St. Jacques ward in 1871, there were 565 widows, but only 177 widowers. Together they represented 13 percent of all people over twenty years old. One-third of women over sixty-one were widows. Some of these lived in institutions, most tended to live alone or board with children or non-related families.[30]

For widows with young children, survival was especially precarious. Nearly all those under fifty began looking for work. Sickness or unemployment made continued care of the children extremely difficult. At least 15 percent (thirty-four) of the girls arriving at St. Alexis had mothers who were widowed. Another three lost their fathers soon after, suggesting that their mothers had brought them to the Sisters during family illness.[31]

It was not the loss of a spouse that precipitated admission. Mothers did not place their girls in the orphanage immediately after the father's death. Rather, the death of a husband made survival more difficult for women lacking both skills and capital. Widows usually looked after their children for some time following their husband's death. They struggled to survive as best they could, working as seamstresses, charwomen, or washerwomen. These jobs usually allowed them to work with their young children at hand. The girls were only placed in the orphanage when this new and more fragile family economy was upset by illness or loss of work. Most widows returned for their children. Indeed, widows' daughters stayed in the orphanage for less time and were more likely to be reclaimed than the girls of the orphanage as a whole. This was because widows needed help from their children. Such youngsters were much more likely than those with two parents to be sent out to work under the age of 15. They also appear to have stayed at home longer, supporting their mothers until they were late into their twenties.[32]

The fragility of a widow's survival is clear from the histories of widows Josephine Brousseau and Angelique Fauteux. Josephine lived on Amherst St., sharing a dwelling with a couple, a twenty-four-year-old widower and his one-year-old child. She worked as a washerwoman. In 1868 she placed eight-year-old Clara in the orphanage for a year. By the time Clara was twelve she was working with her ten- and fourteen-year-old brothers in the Macdonald's tobacco factory, the largest employer of the area.[33]

---

30   For a recent review of widowhood and remarriage, set in one particular place, see Alain Bideau, "A Demographic and Social Analysis of Widowhood and Remarriage: The Example of the Castellany of Thoissey-en-Dombes, 1670-1840," *Journal of Family History*, 5 (Spring, 1980); *Census of Canada*, 1871. Material on living arrangements is based on analysis of a 10 percent random sample of families living in St. Jacques, 1871.

31   Ten percent sample of St. Jacques, 1871. Orphans linked to death registers.

32   These two latter statements are impressions gained from material collected from the 1861, 1871, and 1881 mss. censuses but not yet statistically analyzed.

33   "Registre," no. 455; mss. census, 1871, St. Jacques, 6 HH no. 265, Fam. no. 446.

Angelique Fauteux had three daughters. In 1875 she took her nine-year-old Emelie to the Sisters. A year later she took her home but left the younger sister Eugenie there. Eugenie, in turn, was taken home twice, then went back to the orphanage, the second time with younger sister Victoria. Finally in 1881, when Eugenie was thirteen and Victoria eleven, they all returned home. By then the girls were old enough to work or to provide vital help around the home.[34]

If it was difficult economically for widows to survive, the problems that faced widowers were of a different order. The sexual division of labour made men the wage-earners, and women, even when they worked for wages, the socializers and nurturers of children. Reproductive work—providing meals, shopping, doing housework, and raising children—was women's work. The death of a wife, therefore, thrust upon a man's shoulders a whole range of new experiences, ones that were difficult to perform while working. Those with a steady and reasonable income could engage a housekeeper. Those without sought alternate strategies. Relatives might help by taking the children or doing housework. Not surprisingly, more widowers than widows appear to have taken their daughters to the orphanage at some point after their spouses' deaths.

About 20 percent of the girls had only a father when they were placed in the orphanage, two more lost their mother three to four months later. More widowers than widows placed their daughters with the Sisters within a week of their spouses' deaths, others waited a month. Some supported them or had help from relatives and friends for up to seven years.

Widowers were somewhat less likely to return for their daughters than were other parents or widows. Men probably felt particularly inadequate for the task of raising daughters. For instance, Ubalde Mazurette, a watchman, kept his sons with him, following his wife's death, but relinquished charge of his daughters, first to the Sisters and subsequently to strangers elsewhere in the province.[35]

No record can be found of remarriages among the widowed mothers of orphans. At least seven of the twenty-eight identified widowers definitely remarried, usually within two years of their spouses' deaths. Remarriage does not seem to have led to the automatic withdrawal of the children. Some girls were taken home before their father remarried, more returned home between a month and two years afterwards. Eugene Laroche, for instance, lost his wife Priscille in August, 1862. This left him with one-year-old Elie and four-year-old Adelaide to look after. He managed somehow for seven months, then in March, 1863, placed his daughter at St. Alexis. She returned home two years later. In 1871 Elie, now aged ten, was working with his father as a shoemaker. Adelaide, now aged thirteen, was at home helping her stepmother keep house and looking after her new one- and two-year-old siblings.[36]

---

[34] "Registre," nos. 736, 774, 812, 921, 922.

[35] "Registre," nos. 575, 576, 577, 578; mss. census, 1881, St. Jacques, *Lovell's City Directory*, 1878.

[36] "Registre," no. 326; mss. census, 1871, St. Jacques, 5 HH no. 165, Fam. no. 220.

For couples, as well as for widows and widowers, poverty was probably a major reason for temporarily relinquishing children. This inability to provide for a family might result from the economic ups and downs characterizing the emerging world industrial capitalist system; from life-cycle-based poverty in families where children were too young to work and the father's wage insufficient and irregular; or from misspent wages, especially earnings dissipated on alcohol. In other families parents may simply have been fed up, exhausted, or temporarily unable to cope and so taken advantage of the service offered by the nuns to get a few days or months respite from care of some of their children.

The economic depression that hit Quebec between 1874 and 1879 was soon felt by the families of St. Jacques. The Sisters running the local Salle D'Asile St. Vincent De Paul, a daycare for working mothers, reported an increase in the number of parents who could no longer pay for their children's care. In 1876 they commented on the arrival on Monday mornings of small boys, trembling with weakness, who had not eaten over the weekend. In the school within the orphanage the numbers of non-paying students who took advantage of free lunches offered by the Sisters increased. So, too, did the numbers of girls entering the orphanage. Thirty-five girls entered in 1873 compared to fifty-one in 1874. The numbers fluctuated but remained high until 1881, when the request for some payment deterred the most needy parents. That year the poorest children were refused admission and only those whose parents could pay the $2 to $3 a month were taken. This regulation was probably relaxed by 1887 when the numbers increased dramatically.[37]

Some parents had always sent a few dollars a year to contribute toward their daughters' upkeep. Most payments came from parents outside Montreal, from those who had apparently consciously given up their children forever, or from widowers, glad to contribute to their daughters' upkeep.[38]

Most parents did not and could not pay for their daughters, for the girls came from the class most subject to unemployment and low wages. Furthermore, they came from families at a stage of the life cycle when their children were in need of much care but too young to work for pay. Half the girls came from homes where all the children were under the age of eleven. Another one-quarter of the families had no youngsters over fifteen. This was clearly the critical stage of the life cycle. Families were at their largest but had the smallest number of wage-earners. In St. Jacques in 1871, 25 percent of families in this situation shared with other families, more took in boarders. Unskilled workers were especially likely to share space. The girls at St. Alexis came from dwellings where up to four families resided. The placement of

---

[37] "Notes pour less Chroniques de L'Asile St. Vincent" (handwritten), ASP, 1876, 30; "Chroniques de l'Orphelinat St. Alexis depuis l'Année 1854" (handwritten chronicles), ASP.

[38] "Recettes—Orphelinat St. Alexis," ASP. These list the names of orphans whose parents paid pensions for their daughters between 1869 and 1874.

children in the orphanage was another method of dealing with poverty and, especially, with this difficult period of the family life cycle.[39]

A complex variety of factors determined when parents reclaimed their daughters. The age of the girls, the time of year, the re-establishment of stability after sickness or loss of a job were all important. When life-cycle-related poverty had been a major reason for surrendering a daughter, arrival at working age might mean she would return home. Eliza Masson, for instance, spent just over four years in the orphanage between the ages of eight and twelve. When she was fifteen the census enumerator found her back with her family. She was working as a seamstress, adding to the shaky wages of her shoemaker father, while her younger sisters went to school. Eliza St. Germain, whose father was a barber, left the orphanage at the age of thirteen and joined her mother working as a seamstress, probably at home in the crowded building that they shared with three other families.[40]

Many of Montreal's leading industries relied on young workers, and wage labour by girls under sixteen was not uncommon. About 20 percent of girls and 28 percent of boys under sixteen years old worked in manufacturing establishments in 1871. More would have worked in commerce and especially as domestic servants. It is hard to know exactly why parents placed their daughters in the orphanage and even more difficult to determine why they took them home again. The immediate future of some girls can be examined. Of those found living with their parents after leaving St. Alexis, about one-quarter were working, mostly as seamstresses and factory hands. The Sisters tried to counteract the tendency of parents to reclaim girls the order considered too young to work or not ready for the world. In 1886 they established a workshop to give those over fourteen an apprenticeship in dressmaking. This program aimed to give girls a useful skill and to encourage them to remain longer in the convent "because the parents had been taking them out to send them to work for their profit."[41]

When parents did withdraw girls of working age their action was not merely mercenary. The placement of one or several daughters with the Sisters had reduced family expenditures during a troubled period. Once children had grown old enough to work they no longer needed to be separated from the rest of the family. They might pay for their keep and perhaps contribute additionally to the family income. If parents were exploiting children for their wages, the reasons lay in the structure of an economy in which one worker's wage was insufficient to support a family. That many of the girls remained at home with their parents for many years after their period in the orphanage suggests that they did not think themselves exploited by the family they rejoined.

---

[39] Mss. census, 1861, 1871, 1881, Linked families, St. Jacques; Bradbury, "The Family Economy," 23-4.

[40] "Registre," nos. 278, 464; mss. census, 1871, St. Jacques, 5 HH no. 309, Fam. no. 363; "Registre," no. 456; mss. census, 1871, St. Jacques, 5 HH no. 27, Fam. no. 50.

[41] "Chroniques de l'Orphelinat," 184.

More children, it seems, returned home because particular family crises had passed. With some sort of family equilibrium re-established, daughters returned to school or to housework. More of them went to school after leaving than went to work. There they extended the education they had received in the orphanage, kept out of the mothers' way during the day, but were free to help at home at night. Other girls returned home and became their mothers' household help, especially when there were many younger siblings to be looked after.[42]

While some girls came from homes torn apart permanently by the death of a parent and others from families that fragmented through the difficult period of the family life cycle, yet others came to the orphanage because of sickness at home. Ill health, in this area of high morbidity and mortality rates, posed a constant problem, especially for those unable to pay for assistance. The high birth and infant mortality rates meant that mothers were pregnant almost every second year. Pregnancy, childbirth, and associated illnesses thus posed recurring challenges to family management. At the Protestant Infants' Home, the sickness of mothers was a major reason for children's entry. Its 1895 report stated of the children's families that "Many are too poor to pay anything—out of work—wife sick—seeking the benefits of the home for their little ones until such times as they can provide a home for them." In that home, 21 percent of the 1895 "orphans" were sent to the home because their mothers were sick. Sick fathers explained only 2 percent of the entries.[43]

These figures underline the importance of a mother's role in such working-class families. Where the mother was ill, care of the children, cooking, and housekeeping would not get done unless there were children of an age to help. Similarly, when a mother was sick during pregnancy or after childbirth, or when a new and demanding and often sick child arrived, care of older children became a problem. The relationship between the Masson family and the St. Alexis orphanage illustrates this dilemma well.

Louis Masson was a shoemaker. He lived, in 1871, with his wife Delphine at 456 Jacques Cartier, a few blocks away from the orphanage on St. Denis Street. In May, 1861, their oldest child, Eliza, then aged eight, was placed in the orphanage. She stayed there four years, returning home with her mother in 1865. Three years later, the third girl of this family of girls, Roseanne, went to the orphanage for five years. When she returned home Eliza was twenty and had been working for at least two years as a seamstress. The orphanage relieved this family of care of two of their five daughters at critical periods. Eliza's first stay coincided with the births of the

---

[42] *Census of Canada*, 1871. Montreal had 6,117 girls between the ages of eleven and fifteen; 1,262 or 20 percent of them worked in industrial establishments; only twenty-seven girls have been found in the manuscript censuses of 1871 and 1881 living with their families *after* their stay in the orphanage. Of these, eleven were at school, six were listed as working, and ten were not listed as doing either. The latter were all of an age to do odd jobs or to help with care of younger children or with shopping and housework.

[43] Protestant Infants' Home, *Annual Reports, 1895*, 6.

third girl in 1861 and another the following year. When brought home at the age of twelve, Eliza was probably able to help look after the younger girls, until at some point she began to work as a seamstress, thus contributing to the family income. Roseanne's time in the orphanage coincided with the birth of the youngest child, Marie. While Roseanne was in the orphanage her two nearest sisters in age were able to attend school. Any equilibrium this family briefly attained was shattered shortly after the 1871 census had been taken by the death of the father. Roseanne remained in the orphanage for several years after his death. When she returned home, she, too, was old enough to work. The family at that time moved, probably to cheaper lodgings.[44]

Putting the children in the orphanage may well have been a last resort—something that was done only after kin had been turned to for help. Kin regularly took children who had been in the orphanage for some period of time, as in the case of Hélène Girouard. The Girouard family lived in the same building as the Massons in 1871. André was a labourer and, like many of his neighbours, was illiterate. In 1865 their eight-year-old daughter, Hélène, joined her neighbour Eliza in the orphanage, leaving her fourteen-year-old brother and two younger sisters at home. Six years later, her brother was working as a domestic servant, possibly contributing some money to the family or at least receiving support for himself. Hélène, however, left the orphanage, not to live with her parents but with an aunt.[45]

Hélène's experience was important. For some of the children, kin evidently took the place of parents, even when parents were living. While 70 percent of girls whose future is known returned home with one of their parents, 5 percent were taken home by an aunt or uncle and 4 percent by a grandparent or older sibling.[46]

Children truly orphaned were often taken into the families of kin. Widows frequently lived with married children. Young married couples moved in with their parents, and related people doubled up in the houses of St. Jacques. Living together they could provide support in times of need and share costs. Thus, the family in Montreal, as elsewhere, acted as a major source of welfare in a time before the state directly provided any such services. The church both complemented and competed with the family in this sphere, especially among the poor.[47]

---

44   "Registre," nos. 278, 464; mss. census, 1871, St. Jacques, 5, HH no. 309, Fam. no. 363, *Lovell's,* 1871-2, 1873-74.

45   "Registre," no. 366; mss. census, 1871, St. Jacques, 5, HH no. 307, Fam. no. 361.

46   These figures are based on the 484 girls for whom the nuns recorded information about their future. For another fifty-four no information was available. Where girls returned several times only their final experience was counted. 16 percent went to non-relatives; 6 percent died while resident in the orphanage.

47   Bradbury, "The Family Economy," 23. Priests, bishops, and sisters seem to have encouraged familial support only as long as the people involved were considered good practising Catholics. Where there was any question of Protestant influence or of slipping from Catholic principles, church institutions were seen as preferable to familial aid.

The Fragmented Family 533

For the church, orphanages and schools offered a chance to raise a new generation in the Catholic faith. Bourget's speeches and the actions of the Sisters suggest that their view of the family was similar to that held by reformers in Ontario in the same period. Children were to be taken from homes that did not offer a suitable, in this case, Catholic, environment. Orphanages were seen not simply as alternatives to the family, but as places where the omissions and failings of the family could be countered. Where family situations appeared inimical to a Christian and Catholic upbringing, the Sisters were only too happy to keep the children with them. The story of Céleste Bacon, who died in 1887 after eight years in the orphanage, is especially poignant. "Several hours after her death," wrote the Sister in the Chronicles,

> ...we received a telegram from her father who, not believing she was gravely ill, was asking her to rejoin him in the United States. We thanked God...for having preserved this dear child from such a danger...The father could not raise her decently or in Christianity, because of defects in his character.[48]

Where parents were poor, but devoted, they were to be assisted in every way possible. The Sisters tried to help keep worthy families together. Occasionally mothers were taken in as residents in the orphanage so that they could be near their daughters. An unemployed father was given work repairing the buildings while his daughters were housed there. The line between the church and the family was thus flexible. Did not the Sisters and the church offer a spiritual family for the girls? Care of the girls, in turn, offered the Sisters a chance to mother the young, a role they clearly enjoyed and fulfilled with compassion.[49]

For the girls themselves, their parents' decision meant that for varying periods they were separated from their family of origin. Instead, they lived with up to 100 other girls in the two large dormitories of the orphanage. There, they slept, took classes, helped with the housework, and learned to sew and knit. There they received, if they remained long enough, a solid grounding in the Catholic faith, a habit of deference to the givers of alms and charity, and a free education. They were taught what girls of their class were expected to know as workers and mothers. Some of the girls became very fond of the nuns and the priests who served the orphanage and returned later to visit them. While in the orphanage, girls were probably better fed, clothed, and cared for than they would have been at home in a time of crisis. Life in the orphanage offered not only education, housekeeping, and religious duties but also entertainments that most working-class families could not have afforded. The girls went on occasional trips to the country and for day-time excursions, and they

---

[48] "Chroniques de l'Orphelinat," 174.
[49] Ibid., 57, 65, 67.

celebrated Christmas and the New Year with festive dinners provided by their patroness.⁵⁰

L'Orphelinat St. Alexis and similar institutions clearly served primarily working-class families. They were probably a last resort for those lacking either the money or the family and friends to enable them to deal with crises in some other way. Obviously not all working-class families placed their children temporarily or permanently in orphanages.⁵¹ Highly skilled workers earned enough to support their families adequately. Some families managed better on meagre incomes than others. Some had friends and relatives more affluent than themselves to whom they could turn. That some did need to place their children in orphanages highlights the fragility of the family economy based on wage labour. Such orphanages were not a temporary or purely local phenomenon. Nor were they limited to St. Jacques ward or parish or to the French-Canadian working class. Both the Protestant Infants' Home and the Orphan Asylum run by the Grey Nuns provided mostly for Irish Catholic boys and girls. Parents made similar use of institutions in eighteenth-century France and in nineteenth-century Ontario. Well into the twentieth century many of the Grey Nuns' day nurseries were still very much like St. Alexis. Sociologist Arthur St. Pierre suggested in the 1930s that true orphans constituted only a small body of the children in Quebec's institutions. Orphanages, he argued, helped to preserve the family "by giving shelter for a time to one whom it helps and who will later return to his home." Discussions of orphanages during that decade show social workers and Sisters aware that most of their charges had parents who used the institutions when they could not cope. Proponents of mothers' allowances in the 1920s argued that such payments would ease burdened institutions by enabling mothers and widows to support their children at home. Clearly, the orphanages of the recent past served both parentless children and those with living parents and thus acted as a prop to the families of the poor.⁵²

---

50 Ibid., 1860-89.

51 Cap. XIII, 35 Vict., 1871, allowed "any incorporated orphan asylum" to "apprentice or place out under indenture to any respectable and trustworthy person, any child or juvenile offender under their control...During the whole term of any placing out...the rights, power and authority of the parents over...such child, shall cease."

52 Susan E. Houston, 'The Impetus to Reform': Urban Crime, Poverty and Ignorance, 1850-1875" (Ph.D. dissertation, University of Toronto, 1974), 281-5, 304-6; Cissie C. Fairchilds, *Poverty and Charity in Aix-en-Provence, 1640-1789* (Baltimore: Johns Hopkins University Press, 1976), 86-8; Micheline Dumont-Johnson, "Des garderies au XIXᵉ siecle: Les Salles d'asiles des Soeurs Grises à Montréal," *Revue d'Histoire de l'Amérique Française*, 34 (juin 1980), 52-3; Terry Copp, *The Anatomy of Poverty: The Condition of the Working Class in Montreal, 1897-1929* (Toronto: McClelland and Stewart, 1974), 122; L'Ecole Sociale Populaire, *Nos Orphelinats* (Montréal, 1930), 3-4; Veronica Strong-Boag, "'Wages for Housework': Mothers' Allowances and the Beginnings of Social Security in Canada," *Journal of Canadian Studies*, 14 (Spring, 1979), 32.

In nineteenth-century Montreal, death, illness, and poverty regularly threatened working-class households. The temporary placement of children in institutions that separated parent and child, sister and brother, fragmented the kin group for a time, but in many cases ensured the family's survival.

Note

My thanks to the Social Sciences and Humanities Research Council for a doctoral fellowship, which helped me research this paper, and to Concordia University for a graduate fellowship.

Immigration in the Laurier Period

Section 14

Canada has always been a country of immigrants, but the wave of immigration during the period of the so-called "Laurier boom" was particularly spectacular. The numbers of newcomers were unprecedentedly high; they helped to settle whole new regions and shift the geographical balance of population in Canada over a very brief period. They also changed the country's ethnic composition, because so many of them came from countries that had not previously been significant sources of emigrants to Canada.

Then as now, immigrants were wanted because they stimulated economic growth. They would establish new farms and contribute to Canada's wheat exports; they would increase the market for Canadian manufactured goods and make business for railroads and manufacturers, storekeepers and professionals. Laurier's first minister of immigration, Clifford Sifton, was particularly interested in attracting farmers to settle the prairies—and he was glad when it became possible to bring large numbers of Ukrainian and other east European farmers to the Canadian West, even though they would form the first large group of non-British population to come here since the founding of English Canada itself. "A stalwart peasant in a sheepskin coat," he said, "is good quality."

But the stalwart peasants of eastern and southern Europe did not all become independent farmers in Canada, nor were they always very well received or respected by Canadians.

Donald Avery's essay draws attention to another kind of immigrant—one that was particularly sought out in non-French, non-English-speaking countries. Why did the railroads and certain other businesses promote immigration? What sort of immigrant did they particularly want—and why? Why were they not anxious to see newcomers assimilated? Was it from a sense of multiculturalism? In fact, what sort of attitude toward eastern and southern European cultures is reflected in the treatment of the "foreign navvy" question?

Dislike or contempt for members of other ethnic groups is often associated with prejudices or "stereotypes", in which all members of a group are thought to be alike in sharing some undesirable characteristics. These stereotypes, which are often formed on the basis of first contact with members of another group, are very hard to change, since we are always more apt to notice cases that conform to our stereotypes than ones which do not.

Naturally, Ukrainians and other non-British, non-French immigrants met prejudice and stereotyping among already-established Canadians—just as they formed prejudices and stereotypes of their own about English and French Canadians. For the newcomers, already at a disadvantage in having to adjust to a new country, facing hostile prejudice could be an even more severe handicap. It is important to ask, therefore, how widespread prejudices were and how they affected those Canadians with whom immigrants came most into contact.

In the second article here, John Lehr looks at those government officials who received immigrants in the West and assigned land to them for settlement. How did these people view the Ukrainians with whom they dealt? Did they see them only through ethnic stereotypes or were they able to recognise individuality and differences among them? How did stereotypical views of Ukrainians originate? How far did they affect the treatment of newcomers by government officials?

A general introduction to Canadian immigration and ethnic history can be found in Jean Burnet and Howard Palmer, *Coming Canadians*.

Canadian Immigration Policy and the "Foreign" Navvy 1896-1914

Donald Avery

Two of the most important factors determining the rate and pattern of Canadian economic growth during the period from 1896 to 1914 were the expansion of the railway system and the massive influx of immigrants. Throughout both the Laurier and Borden era, the agricultural and industrial sectors of the economy required abundant new supplies of labour, both skilled and unskilled. As a result there was a strong commitment to the idea of an "open door" immigration policy, particularly on the part of the entrepreneur. But the question of labour supply was not simply economic; it had had consequential and, at times, explosive cultural and racial overtones. Indeed the debate over which groups should be admitted to the country constituted one of the most important aspects of the social history of this entire period. Whose influence would prove to be decisive in determining the character of the Canadian population—the big businessman, driven by the logic of economic growth and power, or the Canadian nationalist, determined to admit only those immigrants capable of easy assimilation into the existing population?

Nowhere was the clash of ideologies more pronounced than in the question of wholesale importation of immigrant railroad labourers commonly referred to as "navvies." By exploring the social and economic conditions connected with the employment of navvies, the underlying attitudes of the Anglo-Canadian, particularly those of the managerial class, towards the unskilled immigrant worker are revealed.

There is no doubt that the connection between the railroad construction and immigration was direct and immediate. The opening up of the prairies, and the resultant demand not only for feeder lines but additional transcontinentals to move the bountiful harvests, acted as a tremendous catalyst for railway building.[1] This was, of course, a process that worked both ways. As has so frequently been the case in Canadian history, railway construction preceded settlement.[2] During the period under review, the railway aspect of the railway-settlement symbiosis took precedence.

---

[1] Morris Zaslow, *Canadian North*, pp. 199-223: O.D. Skelton, *The Life and Letters of Sir Wilfrid Laurier* (Toronto, 1921), pp. 415-418; W.L. Morton, *Manitoba: A History* (Toronto, 1957), pp. 275-278, 298-300; James B. Hedges, *Building the Canadian West: the land and colonization policies of the Canadian Pacific Railway* (New York, 1939), pp. 34, 47, 129-130, 140-142, 390-391; G.R. Stevens, *Canadian National Railways*, vol. II (Toronto, 1963), pp. 12-19, 54-55.

[2] H.G.J. Aitken, "Defensive Expansionism: The State and Economic Growth in Canada," in W.T. Easterbrook and M.H. Watkin, *Approaches to Canadian Economic History* (Toronto, 1967), pp. 203-210.

Colonization railroads were clearly seen as a means of placing settlers in developing regions.[3] In this process immigrants would satisfy several needs: they would serve as a source of labour in the construction of the roads; their crops would provide an additional revenue base; and ultimately their labour could be utilized in developing industries.[4] Moreover, from the point of view of immigration policy, work on railroad construction gangs would be a means of initiation whereby the newcomers could adapt to the Canadian environment.[5]

In their stated policies, both the Laurier and Borden governments clearly gave priority to the recruitment of agricultural settlers.[6] This meant that immigration officials tended to see the recruitment of foreign labourers to work on railway construction as an aspect of the settlement process. But while the federal policy may have given priority to agricultural immigrants of an "acceptable" ethnic group, the urgent demands of the railroads for cheap and readily available labour created a serious problem. If the immigrant settler was only interested in railway construction work until he became established, if he was, in consequence, only a temporary member of the industrial labour force until a better opportunity presented itself, then the unskilled labour market would be very unstable. Yet one of the vital ingredients of rapid industrialization is the existence of what Professor H.C. Pentland has called a capitalistic labour market:

> By a capitalistic market is meant one in which the actions of workers and employers are governed and linked by impersonal considerations of immediate pecuniary advantage. In this market the employer is confident that workers will be available whenever he wants them; so he feels free to hire them on a short term basis, and to dismiss them whenever there is a monetary advantage in doing so ... labour to the employer is a variable cost.... From a broader point

---

[3] Morris Zaslow, *Canadian North*, pp. 167-171, 180-181, 187-194, 215-222; James B. Hedges, *Building the Canadian West*, pp. 129-130, 140-141.

[4] This point has been developed by the authors cited in fn. 1.

[5] Immigration Branch, Public Archives of Canada (hereafter, I.B.), file 39145, W.F. McCreary, Commissioner of Immigration, Wpg. to Andrew G. Blair, Minister of Railways and Canals, June 21, 1897; *Sessional Papers*, 1900, no. 25, pt. 2, pp. 111, 147; ibid., 1902, no. 25, pt. 2, pp. 122, 139; ibid., 1903, no. 25, pt. 2, p. 111; ibid., 1904, no. 25, pt. 2, pp. 98-100.

[6] *Canada—A Handbook of Information for Intending Emigrants* (Ottawa, 1874); *Sessional Papers*, 1896, no. 13, pt. 7, Annual Report of the High Commissioner, Sir Charles Tupper; House of Commons, *Debates*, 1897, p. 4067 (hereafter *Debates*); *Sessional Papers*, 1913, no. 25, pt. 2, p. 77; ibid., 1914, no. 25, pt. 2, pp. 80, 106; *Debates*, 1914, p. 161; Norman Macdonald, *Canada: Immigration and Colonization 1841-1903* (Toronto, 1968), pp. 148, 197; John W. Dafoe, *Clifford Sifton in Relation to His Times* (Toronto, 1931), pp. 132-144; W.T.R. Preston, *My Generation of Politics and Politicians* (Toronto, 1972), pp. 216-217; O.D. Skelton, Life of Laurier, pp. 46-47; Karl Bicha, "The Plains Farmer ...", pp. 414-435.

of view, the capitalistic labour market represents a pooling of the labour supplies and labour needs of many employers, so that all may benefit by economizing on labour reserves.[7]

To maintain such a market in Canada, it was necessary to do much more than import large numbers of unskilled immigrants. In addition, these immigrants had to be of a type prepared to seek employment in the low paying, exacting jobs associated with labour intensive industries. Implicit in this argument was the idea that a permanent proletariat might not be a bad thing.

The ethnic composition of the railroad proletariat was to change substantially during the 1896-1914 period. The Irish Catholic navvies, who had been so important in building the railroads of the 19th century, were no longer available in sufficient quantity. The great wave of Irish immigration had subsided. Indeed, during the period 1901-1911, the number of Irish immigrants coming to Canada numbered only 10% of those coming from England and 25% of those coming from Scotland.[8] It is also worth noting that in occupational terms, during this period there were more farmers, farm labourers, and mechanics coming from Ireland than there were general labourers.

In terms of numbers, English and Scottish immigrants could have provided the necessary replacement for the Irish navvies.[9] This was particularly true between 1904 and 1914 when approximately 995,107 immigrants, or 41% of the total number of emigrants leaving Great Britain came to Canada.[10] This alteration of the pattern of British emigration flow away from the United States and towards Canada was greeted with considerable enthusiasm by immigration officials.[11] This favourable reaction was magnified by the belief that the quality of the British immigrants was improving.[12] But if these immigrants were attractive to government officials, large employers of unskilled labour were not so impressed. Few of these British immigrants were in the category of unskilled labour — only 15.6% as compared to

---

[7] H.C. Pentland, "The Development of a Capitalistic Labour Market in Canada," *Canadian Journal of Economics and Political Science*, XXV (November, 1959), pp. 450, 460.

[8] Lloyd Reynolds, *The British Immigrant*, pp. 32-45; *Sessional Papers*, 1902-1915. Report of the Superintendent of Immigration.

[9] Immigration from France is not discussed in this paper for two reasons. In the first place, the total number of French immigrants between the years 1900 and 1914 was only 25, 273. Moreover, in terms of occupation, only 15% of the male immigrants arriving in the period 1906-1914 were placed in the general labourer category. (*Report of the Royal Commission on Bilingualism and Biculturalism*, Book IV, pp. 238-239; *Sessional Papers*, 1907-1908 to 1915, Report of the Superintendent of Immigration).

[10] Rowland Berthoff, *British Immigration in Industrial America, 1790-1950* (Cambridge, 1953), p. 21; Lloyd Reynolds, *The British Immigrant*, p. 299.

[11] Lloyd Reynolds, *The British Immigrant*, p. 21; *Sessional Papers*, 1907-1908, no. 25, pt. 2, pp. 67, 85; ibid., 1911, no. 25, pt. 2, pp. 75, 95; ibid., 1912, no. 25, pt. 2, pp. 70, 94.

[12] Ibid.

51.5% for the European immigrants who arrived in the same decade, 1901-1911.[13] Moreover, many of the British immigrants who came over as navvies proved to be very troublesome.

One of the most celebrated incidents of this nature occurred in 1897 when the Canadian Pacific Railway was preparing to expand its Crow's Nest Pass line, an endeavour for which it required a large supply of labour. On this occasion, an attempt was made by Immigration officials to find work on the Crow's Nest Railway for some one thousand Welsh farmers and farm labourers who wanted to settle in western Canada.[14] The project was very much in keeping with the settlement-railroad arrangement. The initial income of the immigrants would be supplemented, and the railway companies would be provided with a large pool of unskilled labour. The C.P.R. was immediately interested.[15]

But the arrangement was not a success, largely because the Welsh workers were not prepared to tolerate the low wages or the camp conditions. Their ability to focus public attention on their plight proved embarrassing to both the C.P.R. and the Canadian government.[16] Indeed, the incident created such a stir in Britain that James A. Smart, Deputy Minister of the Interior, warned the C.P.R. President that unless the situation was rectified. "... immigration to Canada could be very materially checked."[17] But Thomas Shaughnessy, the President of the C.P.R., was not a man easily cowed or intimidated. In a very blunt letter, he rejected the validity of the complaints and expressed his disdain for the British labourer:

> Men who seek employment on railway construction are, as a rule, a class accustomed to roughing it. They know when they go to the work that they must put up with the most primitive kind of camp accommodation ... I feel very strongly that it would be a huge mistake to send out any more of these men from Wales, Scotland or England ... it is only prejudicial to the cause of immigration to import men who come here expecting to get high wages, a feather bed and a bath tub.[18]

The sentiments that Shaughnessy expressed were shared by many Canadian entrepreneurs; they wanted hardy, malleable labourers whose salary requests would be

---

[13] Lloyd Reynolds, *The British Immigrant*, p. 46.
[14] I.B., file no. 39501, Memorandum, James A. Smart (Deputy Minister of the Interior), 1897, n.d.
[15] Ibid.
[16] Ibid., James A. Smart to Thomas Shaughnessy, October 26, 1897.
[17] Ibid. In October, 1897, the Canadian Agent in Cardiff, Wales, W.L. Griffith, informed Smart that as a result of the statements appearing in the press "matters are very ugly here. The people are prepared to mob me...." W.L. Griffith to J.A. Smart, October 25, 1897.
[18] Ibid., Thomas Shaughnessy to James A. Stewart, October 27, 1897.

"reasonable," who were not unionized, and who could not use the English-Canadian language press to focus public attention on their grievances.[19] Shaughnessy also articulated a certain bias held by many Canadian entrepreneurs, and many western Canadians, that the British labourer was not suited either physically or psychologically to the conditions on the frontier.[20]

Even many of the Immigration officials manifested distinct reservations about recruiting British labourers. In 1897, for instance, when the matter of bringing British navvies into the country to aid in the construction of the Crow's Nest Railway was first being discussed, W.F. McCreary, the Winnipeg Commissioner of Immigration, indicated his objection to the project: "The English are no use whatever on the railroad, or, in fact, for that matter, almost any place else."[21]

It is evident that many employers discriminated against British immigrants, a situation which disturbed many in the Old Country.[22] In 1907, the editor of the *East Anglian Daily Times* complained to Sir Wilfrid Laurier that the Grant Trunk Railway had refused jobs to several immigrants 'because they were Englishmen.'[23] Although Laurier denied that such discrimination existed, studies of the employment practices of railroad construction companies have revealed that the charge had appreciable substance.[24]

The source of labour supply which would most perfectly accommodate the capitalistic labour market was to be found in the Orient. In this region the supply of

---

[19] Martin Robin, "British Columbia: The Politics of Class Conflict," in Martin Robin (ed.). *Canadian Provincial Politics* (Scarborough, 1972), pp. 29-30. Similar American studies have revealed the same trend: Neil Betten, "The Origins of Ethnic Radicalism in Northern Minnesota, 1900-1920," *International Migration Review,* IV, no. 2 (Summer, 1970), pp. 51, 55; Melvyn Dubofsky, *We Shall Be All: A History of the Industrial Workers of the World* (Chicago, 1969), pp. 320-321. This trend has also been described from the ethnic perspective by Joseph Kirschbaum, *Slovacs in Canada* (Toronto, 1967), pp. 69-76.

[20] John W. Dafoe, *Clifford Sifton,* pp. 148-152, 322; Lloyd Reynolds, *The British Immigrant,* pp. 41-45, 72-73; Carl Berger, *A Sense of Power,* pp. 181, 260; Edmund Bradwin, *The Bunkhouse Man,* pp. 94, 211.

[21] Basil Stewart, *'No English Need Apply'* or, *Canada as a Field for the Emigrant* (London, 1909), pp. 25-40; G.F. Plant, *Overseas Settlement: Migration from the United Kingdom to the Dominions* (London, 1951), pp. 59-60; *Special Report on Immigration, dealing mainly with co-operation between the Dominion and Provincial Governments and the movement of people from the United Kingdom to Canada,* Arthur Hawkes, Commissioner (Ottawa, 1913), pp. 10, 20-22.

[22] Sir Wilfrid Laurier Papers, Public Archives of Canada (hereafter, Laurier Papers), 125151, Editor, *East Anglian Daily Times,* Ipswich, to Laurier, May 8, 1907.

[23] Ibid., 125152, Laurier to Editor, *East Anglian Daily Times,* May 10, 1907; Edmund Bradwin, *The Bunkhouse Man,* pp. 94, 211; G.R. Stevens, *Canadian National Railways,* vol. II. pp. 194-195; *I.B.,* file 571672, no. 1, W.D. Scott to Lord Strathcona, January 11, 1907.

[24] I.B. file 39501, W.F. McCreary to James A. Smart, October 30, 1897.

unskilled labourers was unlimited. Asiatics, moreover, of all immigrant groups, could be cast most easily into the role of a permanent proletariat.[25] There had, of course, always been a direct connection between transcontinental railroads and the importation of Oriental labourers. Sir John A. Macdonald had been prepared to override the sustained and vociferous objections of British Columbia that no Chinese be employed on the road gangs building the C.P.R.[26] According to Macdonald, the shortage of white construction workers necessitated a choice for the people of British Columbia: "either you must have this labour or you cannot have a railway."[27] To make the decision more acceptable the Prime Minister emphasized that these Chinese navvies were only a temporary addition to the labour force. Hence there need be "... no fear of a permanent degradation of the country by a mongrel race."[28] Yet it is significant that, contrary to this prediction, most of the Chinese remained in British Columbia. By 1891 they constituted about one-tenth of the total population of the coast province.[29]

The Oriental worker was regarded by many businessmen associated with labour intensive industries as the ideal worker for an expanding economy.[30] But from the point of view of both Canadian workers and Canadian racial nationalists, the Chinese immigrant in particular was regarded as highly undesirable.[31] Both groups agreed that the social behaviour of the Chinese was deplorable, that they lived in overcrowded and filthy conditions, and that they were "a non-assimilating race."[32] To organized labour, however, the matter was even more crucial; not only would the Chinese presence create a mongrelized nation, but it would also produce an autocratic economic and political system:

> They [the Chinese] are thus fitted to become all too dangerous competitors in the labour market, while their docile servility, the

---

[25] "Evidence," *Royal Commission on Chinese Immigration*, 1885, pp. 55-57, 85, 95; Report (Gray's Section), p. lxix; Carl Berger, *The Sense of Power*, p. 231; Charles J. Woodsworth, *Canada and the Orient*, pp. 35-38.

[26] Charles Woodsworth, *Canada and the Orient*, p. 29; Margaret Ormsby, *British Columbia: A History*, p. 280.

[27] *Debates*, 1882, 1477; Andrew Onderdonk, the chief contractor of the British Columbia section had informed Macdonald in 1882 that unless he was allowed to import Chinese coolies, the C.P.R. would not be finished for another twelve years. *Macdonald Papers*, 144771. A. Onderdonk to John A. Macdonald, June 14, 1882. Eventually Onderdonk brought over 10,000 Chinese into British Columbia. Pierre Berton, *The Last Spike*, p. 204.

[28] *Debates*, 1883, 1905.

[29] Charles Woodsworth, *Canada and the Orient*, p. 41.

[30] See fn. 25.

[31] "Evidence," *Royal Commission on Chinese Immigration*, 1885, pp. 48, 83, 125, 140; *Debates*, 1883, 904; ibid., 1884, 975-976.

[32] "Evidence," *Royal Commission on Chinese Immigration*, 1885, p. 46.

natural outcome of centuries of grinding poverty and humble submission to a most oppressive system of government, renders them doubly dangerous as the willing tools whereby grasping and tyrannical employers grind down all labour to the lowest living point.[33]

What is important about the involved subject of Chinese immigration is that even as the exclusionist forces were gaining in strength, the voice of the business groups was still heard loudly and clearly in Ottawa.[34]

The C.P.R. and other railroad companies continued to agitate for an "open door" arrangement allowing Asiatic labourers into the country, and strenuously opposed any increase in the head tax.[35] It is also apparent that the C.P.R. continued to employ a considerable number of orientals, and established arrangements with emigration organizations such as the Canadian Nippon Supply Company not only to import Japanese labourers, but also to control them while they were in the employ of the railway company.[36] But perhaps of even greater significance was the fact that the state-supported Grand Trunk Pacific was also seriously contemplating importing Oriental labour. In December, 1906, a tentative agreement was made between the representatives of the Canadian Nippon Company and E.G. Russell Purchasing Agent of the Grant Trunk Pacific.[37] Public statements by prominent officials of the G.T.P. served to confirm the belief that the railway company intended to import Asiatic workers. In March, 1907, Frank Morse, Vice President and General Manager, was quoted as saying that "no transcontinental had yet been constructed without the assistance of Oriental labour."[38] In September, while the ashes of Vancouver's Chinatown smouldered, the General Manager of the Grand Trunk, Charles M. Hays, gave a provocative analysis of the labour requirements of the transcontinental:

---

[33] Ibid., p. 156.

[34] The Laurier government received numerous letters from large employers of labour, both agricultural and industrial, particularly when in 1903 it was proposed to increase the head tax to $500.00.

[35] Laurier Papers, 5749, Sir William Van Horne, President of C.P.R. to J.C. McLagan, Editor of Vancouver *World*, July 17, 1896; ibid., 41460, Thomas Shaughnessy to Laurier, January 26, 1900; ibid., 71362, D. McNicoll, General Manager, to Laurier, March 31, 1903.

[36] *Report of the Royal Commission Appointed to Inquire into the Methods by which Oriental Labourers have been induced to Come to Canada* (Ottawa, 1908), pp. 5, 13, 18, 54. Mackenzie King Papers (King Papers, P.A.C.), C-29731, C-29478.

[37] *Report of the Royal Commission ... Oriental Labourers*, pp. 15, 19; *Sessional Papers*, 1909, no. 36. Report of the Deputy Minister of Labour, pp. 111-112; *King Papers*, C-30258-30259.

[38] The *Bruce Times*, March 7, 1907; *I.B.* file 594511, no. 1.

We will employ the kind of immigrants on the line that the Government allows into the country. Am I opposed to the entrance of Oriental labour, you ask? Well, you need cheap labour, don't you, and why should we reject the Oriental if we cannot get the supply we require from any other source?[39]

Hays might also have added that the rising cost of labour was a major consideration for the Grand Trunk. Indeed, with the extensive industrial activity, particularly the appreciable railway construction, wages for unskilled labour had soared. Between 1903 and 1907, the daily wage of white navvies in British Columbia had increased from $1.50 to as high as $3.00. The advance was even more spectacular for oriental navvies; for this group the daily wage had advanced from $1.00 to $2.50.[40] According to the *Royal Commission Appointed to inquire into the methods by which Oriental Labourers have been induced to come to Canada* (1908), the impact of these high wages was to render ineffective the hitherto prohibitive head tax.[41] The situation had been, therefore, very conducive for Asiatic immigration.[42]

Naturally the railway companies welcomed this state of affairs; for the Laurier government, however, the situation was fraught with grave danger. This was dramatically shown by the Vancouver riots of September, 1907, and the subsequent growth of the Asiatic Exclusion League.[43] In 1908, the Dominion government responded to the protests emanating from British Columbia with two Orders-in-Council: the first excluded immigrants from coming to Canada other than by continuous journey from their country of birth, or citizenship; the second stipulated that immigrants from India had to have $200.00 in their possession upon landing in Canada.[44] These Orders-in-Council complemented the celebrated Gentleman's Agreement between Canada and Japan of December, 1907. This arrangement had

---

[39] Montreal *Daily Herald*, September 28, 1907; *I.B.*, file 594511, no. 2. For an account of the anti-Asiatic riots see Margaret Ormsby, *British Columbia: A History*, pp. 350-351.

[40] *The Labour Gazette*, vol. VII, 1906-1907, p. 261; *Sessional Papers*, 1911, no. 36. Reports of the Deputy Minister of Labour, p. 95.

[41] *Sessional papers*, 1911, no. 36, p. 95.

[42] Ibid.

[43] Margaret Ormsby, *British Columbia: A History*, pp. 350-351. Extensive correspondence on the activities of the Asiatic Exclusion League are to be found in the correspondence between W.W.B. McInnes and Laurier during 1907 and 1980. *Laurier Papers*, 129162, 131593, 131596, 134026, 136303, 136615.

[44] John Duncan Cameron, "The Law Relating to Immigration to Canada, 1867-1942," unpublished Ph.D. thesis, Department of Law, University of Toronto, 1942, pp. 265-269; R. MacGregor Dawson, *William Lyon Mackenzie King*, 1874-1923 (Toronto, 1958), p. 164; Charles Woodsworth, *Canada and the Orient*, pp. 82-94, 103, 289; Khushwant Singh, *A History of the Sikhs*, 1839-1964 (Princeton, 1966), pp. 160-175.

provided that control of Japanese immigration, especially from the labouring classes, would rest with the Japanese government.[45]

These developments, however, did not mean that railroad entrepreneurs such as Charles M. Hays had discarded the notion that Oriental labourers should be imported; nor did the arrangements of 1907-1908 mean that the Laurier Government would be unresponsive to future suggestions that the regulations be relaxed. This was illustrated in 1909 when Charles Hays once again proposed an "open door" immigration policy.[46] Laurier's rationale for rejecting this overture was neither racial nor economic. He took his stand on purely political grounds:

> The condition of things in British Columbia is now such that riots are to be feared if Oriental labour were to be brought in. You remember that in our last conversation upon this subject I told you that if the matter could be arranged so that you could have an absolute consensus of McBride, the dangers would probably be averted, but with the local government in active sympathy with the agitators the peace of the province would be really in danger and that consideration is paramount with me.[47]

The fact that in the 1908 federal election the Liberals had lost five out of the seven seats they had previously held in British Columbia clearly weighed heavily with Laurier.[48] He was also no doubt influenced by the mounting evidence that both the federal and provincial Conservatives would in the future make even greater use of the "yellow peril."[49]

By 1907, therefore, the Canadian railroad companies had reached an impasse with regard to a cheap labour supply. British workers were clearly unsuitable as an industrial proletariat, while oriental labourers could not be imported in sufficient

---

[45] The negotiations associated with the "Gentleman's Agreement" are fully documented in the Laurier Papers, the King Papers, and the Rodolphe Lemieux Papers (P.A.C.).

[46] Laurier Papers, 160620-160621, Charles Hays to Laurier, October 4, 1909; ibid., Hays to Laurier, November 10, 1090; G.R. Stevens, *Canadian National Railways*, vol. II, pp. 226-227.

[47] Laurier Papers, 161983. Laurier to Hays, November 12, 1909. There are indications that in 1912 the G.T.P. approached the British Columbia government requesting their assent to the importation of Chinese navvies. The McBride government refused. A.W. Currie, *The Grand Trunk Railway in Canada* (Toronto, 1957), p. 412.

[48] Charles Woodsworth, *Canada and the Orient*, p. 94. Although Laurier's biographer, O.D. Skelton, stressed the fact that "Laurier sacrificed British Columbia's seats rather than compete with Mr. Borden in concessions to the exclusionists...." it was quite apparent that there were limits to this sacrifice. O.D. Skelton, *Sir Wilfrid Laurier*, p. 348.

[49] Charles Woodsworth, *Canada and the Orient*, pp. 96-99; Ottawa *Free Press*, September 23, 1910; *Vancouver Province*, October 6, 1910; *Debates*, 1911, 286, 9815-9850.

quantities for ethnic and cultural reasons. The response of the Canadian "captains of industry" to the situation was to turn increasingly towards central and southern Europe for their "coolie labour." Yet, this approach also embarrassed the Dominion government; by 1907 the idea had become popular in Canada that southern Europeans were of "inferior stock," inclined towards crime and immorality.[50] A distinction was made, however, between southern Europeans and central Europeans; the latter group, it was widely believed, were superior in a racial sense, as well as having preferable cultural qualities which were derived from their agrarian way of life.[51]

This bias against southern Europeans had been evident in the immigration priorities established during Clifford Sifton's term as Minister of the Interior, 1896-1905.[52] In 1897, for example, W.F. McCreary, Commissioner of Immigration, had prevailed upon the Minister of Railways, Andrew Blair, to exert "mild" pressure on the C.P.R. to desist from importing Italian navvies from the United States.[53] According to McCreary, the Italians and many other southern Europeans were birds of passage, coming into the country with no intention of settling on the land or making any positive contribution.

In contrast, encouragement had been given to railway companies by the Dominion government to employ central European settlers. The railway companies had found this group appealing because "they ask no light-handed work ... they have been obedient and industrious."[54] This docility was perhaps not surprising, for in 1900 James A. Smart, the Deputy Minister of the Interior, had made it very clear to his subordinates that the central European settler-labourer should be discouraged from adopting collective bargaining tactics. "They should be told when they need work they had better take the wages they are offered."[55]

The 1901 strike of the maintenance-of-way employees, "the humble and unlettered trackmen," provided an example of how the foreign worker was regarded by the

---

[50] Allan Smith, "Metaphor and Nationality in North America," Canadian Historical Review (CHR), LI. no. 3, (September, 1970), p. 250. J.S. Woodsworth, *Strangers Within Our Gates*, p. 159. John Higham, *Strangers in the Land: Patterns of American Nativism*, 1860-1925 (New Brunswick, N.J., 1955) has provided an excellent study of American bias towards southern European immigrants.

[51] This point was made in countless letters from Immigration officials, especially in I.B., file 594511, nos. 1-6.

[52] Sifton appears to have had a very low opinion of Italian immigration. Clifford Sifton Papers, Public Archives of Canada (hereafter, Sifton Papers), 89315, Sifton to Smart, November 16, 1901.

[53] I.B., file 39145, no. 1, W.F. McCreary to A.G. Blair, June 21, 1897.

[54] I.B., file 60868, no. 1. C.W. Speers, Travelling Immigration Inspector to Frank Pedley, Superintendent of Immigration, January 24, 1900.

[55] I.B., file 39145, no. 1. James A. Smart to W.F. McCreary, June 5, 1900.

C.P.R.[56] The strike also revealed the extent to which the Dominion government was willing to accommodate the company.

The C.P.R. was bent on smashing the strike; it refused to cooperate with representatives of the strikers, and denounced the President of the Brotherhood of Railway Trackmen as a "foreign agitator."[57] It also set about recruiting strike breakers both in Canada and from the United States. These tactics placed the Laurier government in a very awkward position.

The attempt by the Canadian Pacific to use the Winnipeg immigration officers "not only to recruit scabs...," but to coerce the Galician and Doukhobor workers, threatened to destroy the credibility of the Immigration Branch with both the immigrants and organized labour.[58] But Commissioner J. Obed Smith of the office refused to accommodate the Company despite pressure from the C.P.R.[59] His predecessor, W.F. McCreary, however, held a different view. He informed Clifford Sifton that the consequences of strained relations with the C.P.R. "would be disastrous for Canadian immigration ventures."[60]

Ultimately it was the McCreary attitude which prevailed. The C.P.R. was allowed to import "four or five hundred pauperized Italians" from the United States in contravention of the Alien Labour Law.[61] This Act, passed in 1897, forbade companies from bringing contract labour into Canada, or in any way encouraging or assisting the importation of alien workers.[62] By the time of the strike, however, the Dominion government was not directly responsible for the enforcement of this legislation; rather enforcement depended upon individual action before the courts.[63] Mackenzie King, the Deputy Minister of Labour, brought the Alien Labour Act to the attention of the C.P.R. President, but the Dominion government otherwise

---

[56] John Wilson, *The Calcium Light: Turned on by a Railway Trackman* (St. Louis, 1902), introduction.

[57] Ibid., p. 42.

[58] I.B., file 39145, no. 1. J. Obed Smith, Commissioner, to Frank Pedley, June 24, 1901; ibid., Smith to J.W. Leonard, General Superintendent Western Division, C.P.R., June 25, 1901; *Inland Sentinel*, cited John Wilson, *The Calcium Light*, p. 51; The *Voice*, cited ibid., p. 51.

[59] I.B., file 39145, no. 1. U. Obed Smith to Frank Pedley, June 26, 1901.

[60] Sifton Papers, 83178. W.F. McCreary to Clifford Sifton, July 3, 1901. McCreary was a Winnipeg lawyer who had been very active in civic affairs during the 1880s and 1890s. After three years as Commissioner of Immigration (1897-1900) he was elected for the federal constituency of Selkirk. *The Canadian Guide*, 1903 (Ottawa, 1903), p. 111. It does appear from both his stand in 1901, and his previous attempts to work in a cooperative fashion with the C.P.R., that McCreary regarded the support of the C.P.R. as very important to the cause of the Liberal Party.

[61] Ibid., J. Obed Smith to Frank Pedley, June 26.

[62] W.D. Atkinson, "Organized Labour and the Laurier Administration," pp. 20-35; Martin Robin, *Radical Labour*, pp. 54-55.

[63] Martin Robin, *Radical Labour*, p. 55; H.A. Logan, *Trade Unions in Canada*, pp. 483, 488.

ignored the situation.[64] During the next three years, the Canadian Pacific not only continued to import Italian navvies from the United States, but actually developed a scheme whereby these men were supplied on a regular basis by an organization operating out of Montreal.[65]

By 1904 there were between six and eight thousand destitute Italian labourers in Montreal. Urged by Montreal civic officials, the Montreal Trades and Labour Council, the Montreal Italian Immigration Society and the Italian Consul in the city, the Laurier government was finally forced to act.[66] A Royal Commission was established under the chairmanship of Judge John Winchester, which ultimately indicted the C.P.R. in a scathing fashion.[67] Yet no attempt was subsequently made to strengthen the Alien Labour Law.[68] If anything, the trend was in the opposite direction.

Between 1906 and 1908 actual construction on the various sections of the Grand Trunk Pacific and the National Transcontinental was initiated: the "new" railway boom was about to begin.[69] In keeping with the optimism of the period, in 1907, Frank Morse, the Vice president and General Manager of the Grand Trunk Pacific, stated that his company needed 20,000 navvies, and suggested that the Laurier government consider advancing the fares of these men in order to expedite recruitment.[70] Given the attitude which had developed towards British and Oriental

---

[64] Mackenzie King to Thomas Shaughnessy, July 3, 1901, cited, John Wilson, *The Calcium Light*, p. 46.

[65] I.B., file 39145, no. 1. J. Obed Smith to W.D. Scott (the new Superintendent of Immigration), May 7, 1903; *Report, Royal Commission to Inquire into the Immigration of Italian labourers to Montreal, and alleged fraudulent practices employment agencies* (Ottawa, 1904), p. 19.

[66] I.B., file 28885, no. 2, Chevalier Honore Catelli, President, Montreal Italian Immigration Society to Dr. A.D. Stewart, April 15, 1904; Catelli to Stewart, April 29, 1904; Dr. Peter Bryce, Immigration Medical Inspector, to James A. Smart, April 23, 1904; *Sessional Papers*, 1906, no. 36. Report of the Deputy Minister, p. 88.

[67] *Royal Commission to Inquire into the Immigration of Italian Labourers* ..., p. 72.

[68] H.A. Logan, *Trade Unions in Canada*, pp. 483, 488.

[69] G.R. Stevens, *Canadian National Railways*, vol. II, pp. 159-163, 172-183, 214-217.

[70] *The Bruce Times*, March 7, 1907; *I.B.*, file 594511, no. 2. Frank Morse to Acting Superintendent of Immigration, L.M. Fortier, October 15, 1907. Morse had been hired as General Manager of the G.T.P. by Charles Hays, and apparently the choice was disastrous. G.R. Stevens, *Canadian National Railways*, vol. II, p. 224. Peter Veregin, the Doukhobor Leader, publicly announced his intention to try and recruit 10,000 Russian railway labourers as an illustration of his good will towards The Canadian Government, James Mavor Papers, University of Toronto Archives (hereafter Mavor Papers), James Mavor to George Cox, Toronto, April 12, 1907. It is significant that by the period 1910-1914 some 50,000 navvies were also required annually. *Labour Gazette*, July, 1911—June, 1912, XII, p. 721. See also Monthly Reports Pertaining to Railroad Construction, 1910-1914.

navvies, it is not surprising that in this situation the contractors of the Grand Trunk Pacific and National Transcontinental now turned towards southern Europe for the fulfilment of their labour needs. Their recruitment programme, however, ran counter to the prejudices which had developed among Immigration officials, and in the country at large, against the admission of immigrants from this region. The Immigration Branch was primarily interested in agricultural immigrants who could be temporarily utilized in railroad construction work. They were prepared to adopt a tough line against the indiscriminate entry of "inferior" immigrants simply to meet the short-term needs of railway contractors. Hence, they attempted to enforce rigorously the continuous journey and money reserves regulations.[71]

From the point of view of railroad contractors, the Scandinavian and Galician settler-labourers favoured by the Immigration officials had several disadvantages.[72] In the first place, these settler-labourers would only be available during the late spring and summer, quitting in August in order to harvest their crops.[73] Moreover, these immigrants were sufficiently thrifty that they quickly established themselves full time on the land, and so moved out of the labour market. In contrast, the Italian labourers were not interested in settling on the land; in fact, many of them returned at the end of the construction season to the United States or to Italy. The Italians also preferred to remain aloof from other ethnic groups, "to form companies and board themselves, building little camps for that purpose, as they can do so for less than $4.50 per week."[74] They also often followed the practice of working with the contractor through headmen or *padroni*.[75] Both the *padrone* system and the isolation of the camps held advantages for the contractor. Their internal discipline made the Italian labourers a reliable group, while their lack of contact with Canadian workers,

---

[71] Extensive correspondence by Immigration officials on this problem of restriction is located in I.B., file 594511, nos. 2-6; *Sessional Papers*, 1911, no. 25, pt. 2, p. 104; ibid., 1914, no. 25, pt. 2, p. 144. What also troubled Canadian Immigration officials was the difficulty of deporting "undesirable" non-naturalized Slavic and Italian labourers who entered Canada from the United States. I.B., file 594511, no. 3, F.H. Larned, Acting Commissioner-General, Immigration and Naturalization, to W.D. Scott, June 16, 1906.

[72] In 1908, W.D. Scott had taken considerable exception to the ethnic groups which the Grand Trunk Pacific was attempting to import into Canada. I.B., file 594511, no. 2. W.D. Scott to J.T. Davis, May 4, 1908.

[73] I.B., file 571672, no. 1, Blake Robertson, Immigration Special Inspector, to Frank Oliver, October 10, 1907.

[74] Ibid.

[75] Ibid. The *padrone* system has been extensively discussed by American studies on the subject of Italian immigration. Maldwyn Jones, *American Immigration* (Chicago, 1961), pp. 190-192, provided a very succinct explanation of how the system worked. The *Royal Commission to Inquire into the Immigration of Italian Labourers...*, p. 19, provides a vivid description of how the *padrone* Herocle Cordasco operated.

especially with Canadian trade unions, tended to minimize the danger of a strike occurring.[76]

In the clash between the Immigration Branch and the Railroad companies, the federal politicians were inclined more often than not to support the interests of the companies. When the need arose, the "open door" could usually be achieved by the large employers of labour through their political leverage. This was clearly indicated in the period 1910-1913 when Liberal and Conservative ministers acceded to the demands of the railway contractors for a relaxation of regulations pertaining to the immigration of navvies. During 1910, both the C.P.R. and the Grand Trunk Pacific exerted pressure on the government to admit "railroad labourers ... irrespective of nationality...." The Grand Trunk Pacific contractors further insisted that they had to have southern Europeans who were "peculiarly suited for the work...."[77] After Laurier had been approached by Duncan Ross, a lobbyist for the construction firm of Foley, Welch & Stewart, during his "famous" 1910 tour of western Canada, the Dominion government capitulated on the issue.[78] By this time, of course, the prestige of the Laurier government was riding on the rapid completion of the Grand Trunk Pacific.[79] In this situation, neither the cause of Canadian racial purity, nor the opposition of organized labour, nor the objections of the Immigration Branch, nor the combined opposition of Frank Oliver, the Minister of the Interior, and William Lyon Mackenzie King, the Minister of Labour, could offset the influence of the railway contractors. Mackenzie King vividly described the mood of the Laurier cabinet:

> Oliver is strong in his opposition to labour being brought into the country for work on railroads that ultimately is not going to be of service for settlement and favours making restrictions on virtually all save northern people of Europe. I agree with him, but we are about alone in this, others preferring to see railroad work hurried.[80]

---

[76] Edmund Bradwin, *The Bunkhouse Man*, pp. 110-111; *Proceedings before the Royal Commission on Industrial Relations*, 1919 (Department of Labour, Library, Ottawa), Edmonton Hearings, pp. 12, 52; ibid., Cobalt Hearings, pp. 1757, 1764.

[77] I.B., file 594511, no. 3, W.D. Scott to D. McNicoll, Vice President, July 6, 1910; ibid., J.O. Reddie, G.T.P., to W.D. Scott, April 1, 1910.

[78] Laurier Papers, 182131, Duncan Ross to Laurier, February 27, 1911; I.B., file 594511, no. 3, W.W. Cory, Deputy Minister of the Interior, to W.D. Scott, July 16, 1910.

[79] I.B., file 594511, no. 3. W.J. Bartless, Secretary, Winnipeg Trades and Labour Council to Frank Oliver, Minister of the Interior, August 3, 1910. Attorney General, W.J. Bowser, of the British Columbia government, in September, 1911, charged the Immigration Branch with consciously violating the Alien Labour Law by allowing railway companies to import navvies from the United States (Montreal *Daily Star*, September 5, 1911; Vancouver *News Advertiser*, September 7, 19110.

[80] The King Diary, January 10, 1911, *P.A.C.*

The coming to power of the Conservatives in 1911 did not significantly disrupt the government-contractor relationship; indeed, the ability of the business lobby to influence immigration policy decisions was again clearly revealed in 1912. In that year the Immigration officials resumed their attempts to limit the number of southern Europeans entering Canada as railway navvies in response to increasing public complaints that those immigrants "constituted a serious menace to the community."[81] However, the Minister of the Interior, Robert Rogers, was too good a politician to offend powerful vested interests. When it was brought to his attention by both Donald Mann of the Canadian Northern, and Timothy Foley, one of the leading contractors of the Grand Trunk Pacific, that the restrictions were unnecessary and indeed harmful, Rogers overruled his subordinates.[82] The result was the free entry of alien navvies.[83]

The admission of large numbers of southern Europeans, particularly Italian labourers, showed that the long standing goal of bringing into the country only the settler-labourer type of immigrant had been displaced by a policy of importing an industrial proletariat. Immigration statistics reveal that the percentage of unskilled labourers, as compared to the total male immigrants entering Canada, had increased from 31% in 1907 to 43% in 1913-1914.[84] In contrast, the percentage of agriculturalists decreased from 38% in 1907 to 28% in 1914.[85] Similarly, the ethnic aspects of immigration policy revealed that there was a steady advance in the percentages of central and southern European immigrants from 29% in 1907 to 48% in 1913-1914.[86]

---

[81] I.B., file 594511, no. 3, Report, J.M. Langley, Chief of Police, to Mayor Alderman, City of Victoria, B.C., August 28, 1911; ibid., no. 5, J. Bruce Walker, Commissioner of Immigration, to W.D. Scott, March 12, 1912.

[82] Ibid., no. 5, Donald Mann to W.D. Scott, August 26, 1912; ibid., Timothy Foley to Robert Rogers, March 27, 1912. Three quarters of the total construction mileage was awarded to Foley Brothers in their many different partnerships. They were an American contracting company which had had considerable experience with both the C.P.R. and the Canadian Northern. G.R. Stevens, *Canadian National Railways*, vol. II, p. 176.

[83] I.B., file 594511, no. 5, Memorandum, Office of the Minister of the Interior to W.W. Cory, Deputy Minister of the Interior, April 2, 1912. John D. Cameron, *The Law Relating to Immigration*, p. 278.

[84] Statistics tabulated from *Sessional Papers*, 1907-1908, no. 25, pt. 2, Report of the Superintendent of Immigration; ibid., 1915, no. 25, pt. 2, Report of the Superintendent of Immigration.

[85] Ibid.

[86] Ibid. For the railway contractors the outbreak of conflict in the Balkans meant that many of their Bulgarian navvies rapidly returned to Europe. *The Christian Guardian*, November 12, 1912, Ed.

Economic priorities were paramount in determining the attitude of the successive Dominion governments towards the industrial utilization of the immigrant navvy. Completion of the Grand Trunk Pacific and the Canadian Northern was of such crucial importance that the Ottawa authorities seemed prepared to allow railroad contractors a free hand in the operation of the construction camps. This *laissez-faire* stance was adopted despite abundant evidence that working conditions were not only unsanitary but also hazardous.[87] The *Annual Reports* of the Department of Labour showed that the number of fatal accidents associated with the operation and construction of railroads was unusually high. Between 1904 and 1911, for example, out of a total of 9,340 fatal industrial accidents in Canada, 23% were related to the railway industry.[88] Even these statistics do not tell the true story. It was not until 1912 that the Dominion government required contractors receiving public funds to register fatalities occurring in their camps.[89] Even with this provision there was some question as to whether the number of recorded deaths of foreign labourers were always accurate: "'Oh, some Russian is buried there' was the passing remark that commonly designated an unkempt plot in the vicinity of an erstwhile camp."[90] The human and economic consequences of the high rate of accidents connected with railroad construction were also illustrated in a report written by J. Bruce Walker, Commissioner of Immigration, in 1910. Walker reported that one of the reasons for the shortage of labour in the National Transcontinental construction camps around Fort William was that many Galician and Polish labourers would not accept construction jobs because "the majority of men now engaged in rock work are afraid of it on account of the numerous accidents...."[91]

The contractors were also given a free hand with respect to the standards of accommodation provided in the construction camps. Although there was an obligation on the part of the head contractor, who accepted federal funds, to provide for the basic needs of the men, contractual arrangements and actual practice seemed often to have been at variance.[92] Controversy over unsanitary conditions in navvy

---

[87] There was quite a difference of opinion between the account included in labour newspapers such as the *Voice* and the official reports of investigators sent out by the Department of Labour and the Immigration Branch.

[88] Statistics tabulated from *Sessional Papers*, 1913, no. 36, Report of the Deputy Minister of Labour, p. 72.

[89] Ibid., p. 12.

[90] Edmund Bradwin, *The Bunkhouse Man*, pp. 153, 200, 212.

[91] *I.B.*, file 594511, no. 3. J. Bruce Walker to W.D. Scott, February 16, 1910.

[92] Edmund Bradwin, *The Bunkhouse Man*, pp. 81, 144-153, 200, 206. The Department of Labour had the responsibility of enforcing the Fair Wages Regulation (1900) which established certain employment practices applicable to employers who were receiving either a federal subsidy or guarantee. MacGregor Dawson, *William Lyon Mackenzie King* pp. 70-71; *Sessional Papers*, 1907, no. 36, Report of the Deputy Minister of Labour, pp. 64-67.

camps, of course, has had a long history in Canadian railway construction.[93] In 1897 the C.P.R. had been charged with mistreating a group of Welsh navvies, and complaints continued to reach the attention of the federal government throughout the period under review.[94] In October, 1910, the Edmonton Trades and Labour Council made representation to the Minister of Labour about the improper treatment of construction workers employed by the Grand Trunk Pacific.[95] The Council pointed out the disgraceful condition of the camps; the prevalence of typhoid fever within the camps; the inadequacy of the food and accommodation supplied to the men while on route to the job site; and the delays which were occurring in the payment of wages. Frank Plant, an official of the Department of Labour, was dispatched to Alberta to investigate the charges and submit a report. Plant noted some abuses, but, in general, he exonerated the Company and its leading contractors, especially Foley, Welch & Stewart, from the charges.[96] With respect to the living conditions within the camps, Plant noted that the accommodation was adequate, and the food generally wholesome. None of those interviewed, he optimistically reported, had had "any grievance as to treatment, food or accommodation."[97]

Critics of the contracting companies were not so easily satisfied. It was alleged in labour circles that the government inspectors visited the bush camps only infrequently, and spent most of their time "at the end of steel," close to civilization.[98] It was further alleged that the men were often intimidated by the power of the head contractor who "... along the grade ... is supreme ... not unlike a Tartar chieftain."[99] The prospect of being dismissed, miles from settlement, was enough to deter most men.[100] And for the foreign worker, who was often unable to communicate in English, who was manipulated by an "ethnic straw-boss," and who had a basic mistrust of state officials, the government inspector simply did not offer a viable channel of protest.[101]

Conditions in the railroad construction camps of the Grand Trunk Pacific and the National Transcontinental continued to be an issue until the outbreak of war. In

---

[93] Partial accounts of camp conditions are included in Pierre Berton, *The Last Spike*, pp. 110, 194-205, 275-279; Terry Coleman, *The Railway Navvies*, pp. 66, 80; A.W. Currie, *The Grand Trunk*, pp. 28-29.

[94] I.B., file 39501, no. 1, James A. Smart to Thomas Shaughnessy, October 26, 1897. Also see pages 9-10. In 1906 a series of complaints were submitted by a party of Scottish navvies concerning the construction camps of the Grand Trunk Pacific. I.B., file 751672, no. 1. Lord Strathcona, High Commissioner, to Frank Oliver, December 5, 1906.

[95] *Sessional Papers*, 1912, no. 36, pp. 88-100.

[96] Ibid.

[97] Ibid.

[98] Edmund Bradwin, *The Bunkhouse Man*, pp. 206, 216.

[99] Ibid., pp. 198, 206-213.

[100] Ibid.

[101] Ibid.

1913, for example, another raft of complaints led to an investigation of the Foley, Welch & Stewart camps. Once again, however, the company was exonerated.[102] This conclusion brought an angry response from militant elements in the labour movement. According to the *Eastern Labour News* "...the false statements made as to living conditions ... and given wide publicity in the capitalist press, will wisen up the workmen so that they will vote for a man to represent themselves, and not for the lying parasites who will always be against them."[103]

The failure of government officials to redress their grievances turned many alien construction workers in the direction of radical labour. By 1912, the growing labour radicalism in the construction camps was a source of concern to many of those who had immediate contact with these foreign workers.[104] What made it appear even more ominous was the fact that neither the companies involved, nor the federal or provincial governments, nor the institutionalized churches, nor even the Trades and Labour Congress seemed prepared to assume responsibility for the physical and spiritual needs of the alien navvy.

The problem faced by the churches in relation to the foreign workers stemmed from insufficient resources and faulty organization.[105] The energies of the Presbyterian and Methodist churches, in particular, were consumed by the thousands of immigrants who were located in homesteads, or in urban ghettos.[106] The failure of the established churches in coping with the foreign workers was responsible for the formation of the Reading Camp Association, in 1899, by a young Presbyterian minister, the Reverend Alfred Fitzpatrick.[107] Fitzpatrick's concern was not specifically religious; rather, he was interested in Canadianizing the men by teaching them the English language and introducing them to the native "ideals of citizenship,

---

[102] *Sessional Papers*, 1914, no. 36, p. 58.

[103] *Eastern Labour News*, May 24, 1913

[104] Edmund Bradwin, *The Bunkhouse Man*, p. 234

[105] Ibid., pp. 219-220. In this study the author has restricted his analysis to the Methodists and Presbyterians. Certainly the role of the Catholic Church in the bush camps among the Roman Catholic and Greek Catholic navvies would be a study of considerable importance.

[106] Apparently the Methodist Church spent about a quarter of a million dollars on their missions among the foreigners between 1896 and 1914. George Emery, "Methodist on the Canadian Prairies, 1896-1914," unpublished PhD. thesis, Department of History, University of British Columbia, 1970, p. 346. The Presbyterians were also very much committed. See Presbyterian Church in Canada, 'Report of the Board of Home Missions,' *Acts and Proceedings of the General Assembly* (hereafter cited as Presbyterian Acts and Proceedings), 1900-1914, (United Church Archives). W.G. Smith, *Building the Nation: The Churches' Relation to the Immigrants* (Toronto, 1920), pp. 65-77, 122-123, 176, 193.

[107] Frontier College Papers, 1919, *P.A.C.* (known as the Reading Camp Association until 1919). A. Fitzpatrick to H.H. Fudger, President, Robert Simpson Co., November, 191; Alfred Fitzpatrick, *University in Overalls*, pp. x, 13; Edmund Bradwin, *The Bunkhouse Man*, pp. 14-17.

and ... life."[108] The Reading Camp Association attempted to elicit the support of the businessman-philanthropist, especially those associated with railways and mining operations. By 1912, the Association was supported financially by all three transcontinental railways, as well as by leading members of the Toronto business community.[109] Writing in 1919, one business contributor rationalized his support for the Association in these words:

> I am not very strong on Religious matters but my business training tells me that the work you are doing will go a long way to educate foreigners and rough fellows out on our Frontier and after all that is where the trouble in the Industrial World is most ready to break out or I might say that it is amongst men of this type that the I.W.W. and Bolsheviki find their ground for sewing [sic] their seed, therefore I am pleased to help support the work.[110]

While a segment of the business community out of enlightened self-interest were prepared to support at least some basic Canadianization work among the alien labourers, appeals by the Association to the federal government had failed. The Association was "slapped ... over the back with the British North America Act, and referred ... back to the provinces."[111] Most of the provinces were likewise indifferent to the appeals of the Association, assuming, perhaps, that responsibility for these workers rested with the Dominion government.[112] From Fitzpatrick's perspective, this rejection was all the more frustrating because neither level of government, federal or provincial, had implemented Canadianization programmes among the immigrant workers in the industrial camps.[113]

---

[108] Frontier College Papers, 1912, A. Fitzpatrick to Dr. M.E. Church, December 2, 1912; Ibid., 1912, A. Fitzpatrick to H.H. Fudger, November 19, 1919.

[109] Ibid., 1912, A. Fitzpatrick to James Hales, July 31, 1912; ibid., Fitzpatrick to J.B. Skeaff, Manager, Bank of Toronto, July 29, 1912.

[110] Ibid., 1919, Wallace Robb, President of the Cannuck Supply Co., Montreal, November 14, 1919.

[111] Ibid., A. Fitzpatrick to R.H. Grant, Minister of Education, Government of Ontario, December 17, 1919.

[112] Ontario had been the first province to provide financial assistance, with amounts ranging from $25.00 in 1900 to $1,750,000 in 1912. Ibid., A Fitzpatrick to R.H. Grant, December 17, 1919. In 1919 both Saskatchewan and Alberta indicated that they would provide $250.00 each; ibid., August Ball, Deputy Minister of Education, Government of Saskatchewan, to Fitzpatrick, November 5, 1919; ibid., John Ross, Deputy Minister of Education, Alberta, to Fitzpatrick, February 1, 1919.

[113] Numerous authors urged government to move in this direction, most notably, J.S. Woodsworth, *Strangers Within Our Gates*, J.T.M. Anderson, *The Education of the New*

The Canadian Trades and Labour Congress also seemed quite unconcerned about the plight of the foreign navvy during most of the period under study. The Congress seems to have concerned itself mainly with the introduction of restrictive immigration measures designed to safeguard the job security of Canadian workers.[114] But even in this effort the T.L.C. directed its efforts mainly against British- killed mechanics and Orientals. In 1911, however, the Congress began to display a greater interest in the problems of the alien worker. A resolution was passed at the Annual Convention calling for the services of the T.L.C. solicitor to be extended to the unskilled labourers in the construction camps "so as to prevent these workers from being intimidated by contractors and local law enforcement agencies."[115]

One explanation for the greater interest shown by the T.L.C. at this stage was to be found in the growing influence of the Industrial Workers of the World among the unskilled workers.[116] The I.W.W. threat revealed itself in various strikes among the construction workers employed by contractors of the Grand Trunk Pacific and the Canadian Northern.[117] One of the most serious strikes occurred in 1912 among the 7,000 navvies engaged in the construction of the Canadian Northern Railway.

Although the strike only directly affected one company, and did not extend beyond the borders of British Columbia, the incident had a number of wide-reaching implications. An article in the *British Columbia Federationist* of April 5, 1912, hailed the walkout as "an object lesson as to what a movement animated by an uncompromising spirit of revolt ... can accomplish among the most heterogeneous army of slaves that any system of production ever assembled together."[118] In a later edition, the *Federationist* noted that the ethnic antagonisms which the railway contractors had utilized in dividing the men had been laid aside: "Canadians, Americans, Italians, Austrians, Swedes, Norwegians, French and Old Countrymen all on strike ... a hint to King Capital to look for some other country more healthy for

---

Canadian, W.G. Smith, *Building the Nation: The Churches in Relation to the Immigrant*, Edmund Bradwin, *The Bunkhouse Man*, and of course Fitzpatrick, *University in Overalls*.

[114] Edmund Bradwin, *The Bunkhouse Man*, p. 134; *Proceedings of the Twenty-sixth Annual Session of the Trades and Labour Congress of Canada* (1910), p. 41. I.B., file 594511, no. 3. L.M. Fortier, Acting Superintendent of Immigration to P.M. Draper. September 1, 1910.

[115] *Proceedings of the Twenty-seventh Annual Session of the Trades and Labour Congress of Canada (1911)*, p. 83.

[116] Edmund Bradwin, *The Bunkhouse Man*, p. 234; H.A. Logan, *Trade Unions in Canada*, p. 299. An excellent account of the success achieved by the I.W.W. among the unskilled labourers is by Melvyn Dubofsky, *We Shall Be All: A History of the International Workers of the World*, pp. 24, 26, 151.

[117] G.F. Stevens, *The Canadian National Railways*, vol II, pp. 194-195.

[118] *British Columbia Federationist*, April 5, 1912, p. 1.

him to exploit labourers in than this."[119] Initially there seemed to be a reasonable chance for an I.W.W. victory, but increasingly the position of the employers improved as the power of both provincial and federal governments was brought to bear on the dispute. The high degree of class unity exhibited by the workers in the early stages of the strike was eroded by the ability of the contractor to hire "scab" labour from employment agencies in Vancouver and Seattle.[120]

The *British Columbia Federationist* alleged that the McBride government had rushed detachments of provincial police to the railway camps not only to protect the strike breakers, but also to arrest the strike leaders on trumped up charges.[121] There certainly appeared to be little evidence that the police had been dispatched to protect the strikers from the violence of professional thugs employed by the contractors.[122] The Borden government soon revealed its willingness to cooperate with management. Despite the objections of organized labour, few contractors had difficulties circumventing the Alien Labour Law in their efforts to import navvies from the United States. There is evidence that Donald Mann of the Canadian northern and Timothy Foley, one of the principal contractors, had prevailed upon Robert Rogers, the Minister of the Interior, to issue instructions allowing certain regulations to be waived by officials of the Immigration Department.[123] Furthermore, the Dominion government refused to consider a union request that a conciliation and arbitration board be established. The official reason given for this refusal was that railroad construction belonged to a "class of labour to which the provisions of the Industrial Disputes Investigation Act would only be applied by the mutual consent of the employers and employees."[124]

Time worked against the strikers. As the *Federationist* so succinctly stated, "the threat of hunger makes cowards of us all."[125] That the strike had been broken was clearly indicated in September when the Canadian Northern announced that most of the men had returned to work, and "the places of the others had been filled."[126]

In the peak years between 1911 and 1914, an estimated 50,000 workers were engaged annually in the construction of the various transcontinentals and provincially-chartered railways.[127] The abrupt cessation of most of these projects, due to the unsettled international situation of 1914, meant that a high percentage of

---

[119] Ibid., June 8, 1912, p. 1.
[120] Ibid. *The Western Wage Earner*, April 1909, p. 4.
[121] *British Columbia Federationist*, June 29, 1912, p. 1., ibid., June 22, 1912, p. 1.
[122] Ibid.
[123] I.B., file 594511, no. 3. Donald Mann to W.D. Scott, August 26, 1912; ibid., Timothy Foley to Robert Rogers, March 27, 1912. See discussion on page.
[124] *The Labour Gazette*, August, 1912, p. 191.
[125] *British Columbia Federationist*, May 6, 1912.
[126] *The Labour Gazette*, July, 1912, p. 79.
[127] Ibid., February, 1912, p. 721. See monthly reports, *The Labour Gazette*, July, 1910—July, 1914.

these labourers became unemployed.[128] The foreign navvy, whom the railroads had relied upon to supply the cyclical demands for construction labour, found the transition most difficult. Many navvies emigrated to the United States but large numbers of destitute men, unfamiliar with Canadian society, drifted into the cities and towns. Hence they became a focal point of racial tension and labour radicalism. Under the banner of economic growth, the Laurier and Borden governments had given a high priority to railroad construction. The amount of new track laid was impressive but the social costs were high.[129]

---

[128] In September, 1914, *The Labour Gazette* reported that railway construction had "somewhat halted upon the advent of war...." Ibid., September, 1914, p. 332. Throughout the next twelve months continual reports were made on the number of unemployed navvies who had gravitated to cities such as Winnipeg, Edmonton, and Vancouver. Ibid., October, 1914—September, 1915. Ibid., *Passim*.

[129] The amount of railway mileage in Canada more than doubled between 1896 and 1914. By 1921, only taking the Canadian Pacific system and the railways owned by the Dominion government, there were 35,452 miles of track. G.R. Stevens, *Canadian National Railways*, vol. II, pp. 17, 519.

Government Perceptions of Ukrainian Immigrants to Western Canada 1896-1902

John C. Lehr

Within the short space of approximately thirty years the prairie provinces of Western Canada were transformed from the wilderness of the fur trade frontier to a settled agricultural territory, raw and crude, perhaps, but firmly linked to the industrial-urban structure of the metropolitan heartland and increasingly European in population, language and values. Immigrants from the peasant heartland of Europe played a major role in this transformation. Although never the dominant group, they were a vital ingredient in the European settlement of the West. Most of these peasants were Ukrainians from Galicia [Halychyna] and Bukovyna, at that time a part of the Austro-Hungarian empire.

Although the geographical, social, and political effects of this massive Ukrainian immigration into the West have received attention from scholars in a variety of disciplines, the attitudes of Crown agents involved in settlement have not yet undergone detailed consideration.[1] This paper is intended as a step towards filling this lacuna by assessing official perceptions of, and attitudes towards, Ukrainian immigrants as they homesteaded in Western Canada in the closing years of the nineteenth century.

Ukrainian Immigration into Canada

Until 1896, the Canadian government displayed little interest in, or awareness of, the trickle of Ukrainian immigrants who, even after four years, totalled barely 1000 souls. Most came from the Kalush district, were more or less related by ties of blood and marriage, and chose to settle in the Star district of Alberta, about 35 miles northeast of Edmonton.[2]

Geographically and linguistically isolated, they attracted little attention until 1895 when they received government notice when Dr. Joseph Oleskow of L'viv, Galicia, sought information on settlement opportunity in the Canadian West for Ukrainian peasants to include in his widely read pamphlet, *Pro Vilni Zemli* [About Free

---

[1] The question of general Canadian perception of immigrants to the Canadian West is treated at length by Marilyn Jean Barber, "The Assimilation of Immigrants in the Canadian Prairie Provinces, 1896-1918: Canadian Perception and Canadian Policies," unpublished Ph.D. thesis, University of London, 1975.

[2] V.J. Kaye, *Early Ukrainian Settlements in Canada 1895-1900* (Toronto: University of Toronto Press for the Ukrainian Canadian Research Foundation, 1964), pp. 318-321.

Lands].[3] Before this contact with Oleskow, Ottawa was ignorant of the true nature of the "Austrian" settlement in Alberta. Invited to visit the West to experience frontier conditions and assess settlement opportunities, Oleskow and a peasant delegate toured Western Canada, visiting Ukrainian and German settlements in the Edmonton district. Impressed by the potential of Western Canada, he published a detailed report of his findings in a lengthy pamphlet, *O Emigratsii* [On Emigration], which circulated widely in Galicia and Bukovyna. These, and subsequent publications, were largely responsible for the initiation of mass migration from the Western Ukraine to the homestead lands of Western Canada.[4]

The immigration movement popularized by Oleskow's writings coincided with the change of government in Canada in 1896. Clifford Sifton, Minister of the Interior responsible for immigration and settlement in the new Liberal government, introduced an unusually aggressive immigration policy, seeking out experienced agriculturalists to pioneer the West.

Sifton's actions and statements indicate that he regarded any Caucasian agriculturalist as a valuable acquisition for Canada.[5] If he were well endowed with capital, Protestant, English-speaking, and imbued with traditions of loyalty to the British Crown, so much the better, but Sifton rated agricultural skill as most important. As a result of Oleskow's initial efforts (from 1896 to 1900) and Sifton's encouragement during his tenure as minister, Ukrainians poured into Western Canada in the thousands, until the outbreak of war in Europe in 1914 halted immigration.[6] Sifton welcomed this rapid increase in immigration, although his Department came under considerable pressure and found itself at the centre of an often virulent debate centring on the character of these Slav immigrants.

Although the government had changed in 1896, and the usual round of patronage appointments had been made within the Department of the Interior, most officials kept their jobs. Continuity was maintained, and most new Liberal party appointees were well qualified for their new tasks. For example, William F. McCreary, Sifton's appointee as Commissioner for Immigration in Winnipeg, the man responsible for settling thousands of Ukrainians in the West, was an experienced administrator, a former alderman and mayor of Winnipeg, and was highly regarded in his day. James A. Smart, Sifton's Deputy Minister, was formerly mayor of Brandon, Manitoba, and had been Provincial Secretary, and a member of the Provincial Cabinet. Frank Pedley, Superintendent for Immigration, was a successful Toronto lawyer before

---

[3]   Dr. Josef Oleskow, *Pro Vilni Zemli* [About Free Lands](L'viv: Prosvita Society, 1895).

[4]   Dr. Josef Oleskow, *O Emigratsii* [On Emigration](L'viv: Michael Kachkowskyi Society, 1895).

[5]   Sifton's best known statement on his immigration policies was published long after his tenure as Minister of the Interior. Clifford Sifton, "The Immigrants Canada Wants," *Maclean's Magazine*, April 1, 1922, pp. 16, 33-35.

[6]   W. Darcovich ed.,. *A Statistical Compendium of the Ukrainians in Canada 1891-1976* (Ottawa: University of Ottawa Press, 1980), pp. 500-502.

assuming his duties with the Department.[7] While administrative ability was not lacking within the Department, few of its members had experience with Slavic immigrants.

The Immigration Controversy

The debate surrounding the immigration movement and the settlement of the west struck to the very heart of Canadian national identity. The various parties disagreed violently on who were desirable immigrants but were united in their conviction that assimilation of alien groups into the matrix of Britannic culture was vital for the survival of Canadian identity. They differed as to which people would assimilate rapidly and disagreed as to whether those without the cultural paraphernalia of the English or Western European peoples would successfully integrate into Canadian life. Not surprisingly, there was a consensus in the strongly nativist Anglophone culture that non-white, non-Christian peoples should be discouraged from entering Canada, but the Liberals under Laurier and the Conservative opposition disagreed on the merits, or otherwise, of the Slav immigrant.[8]

Sensing the political capital which could be generated by an emotional appeal to nativist sentiments, the Tory Party and its press engaged in a shrill campaign of vituperation against Ukrainian immigrants and the administration which was settling them on homesteads in the West. Throughout this debate immigrants were most often described in terms of stereotyped images, implying all members of an ethnic group resembled each other in fundamental patterns of belief, conduct, ability and economic circumstance. For example, Italians were not farmers and were too fond of saints' days and knife fighting; Scottish artisans were riotous and turbulent, with an

---

[7] William Forsythe McCreary was born in 1855 in Ontario. He was a law student together with Sifton in Winnipeg and from 1883 to 1884, served as alderman in Winnipeg. In 1895-96 and in 1897 he served as mayor. Appointed as Commissioner for Immigration by Sifton in 1897 he served until 1900 when he was elected to the House of Commons for the Selkirk constituency. Known affectionately as "Doukhobor Bill" he was the one man who most closely influenced settlement in the West at a time when the social and geographical personality was being transformed by a massive influx of settlers. He died in 1904. See, Kaye, *Ukrainian Settlements*, p. 383; *Manitoba Free Press* and *Winnipeg Telegram*, May 5, 1904.

[8] John C. Lehr and D. Wayne Moodie, "The Polemics of Pioneer Settlement: Ukrainian Immigration and the Winnipeg Press," *Canadian Ethnic Studies* 12 (2:1980):88-101. For examples of the more extreme views on the qualities and merits of the Slav immigrants, see *The Mail and Empire* [Toronto] July 14, 1899; *Ottawa Daily Free Press*, July 27, 1899; and Clive Phillips Wolley, "Mr. Sifton's Anglo-Saxondom" *The Anglo Saxon* XII (9:1899):1-4; and the *Halifax Herald*, March 18, 1899.

insatiable appetite for whisky; Doukhobors were dirty and illiterate. Even the English were categorized as lazy complainers.[9]

The Ukrainians, because of their numbers, visibility, and obviously alien ways of dress and language, became a focus of attention in the Conservative press, which described them as ignorant, dirty, priest-ridden moral degenerates, unfit to become citizens of a democratic state.[10] While it is clear that not all shared this assessment, to say that established Anglophone society accepted a stereotypical image of the Ukrainians as poor, ignorant foreigners of marginal desirability would probably not be too wide off the mark, since in some sectors of Canadian society, "Galician" was, and still is, considered a negative appellation.

This, then, was the cultural and social milieu of which the department's personnel were a part, and within which they worked.

Formation of Opinion

In the early years of settlement before 1905 most Ukrainian immigrants were peasant farmers. Many were illiterate. By Canadian standards, most were poor when they arrived in the West. Their picturesque peasant garb, demeanour, and unfamiliar tongue set them apart from immigrants coming from North America and Western Europe. After a trans-Atlantic and transcontinental journey, many Ukrainian immigrants arriving in Winnipeg did not look impressive.[11] On the homestead, frontier conditions made it difficult to maintain appearances, and isolation removed the social controls of village opinion. Even the father of Ukrainian emigration to Canada, Dr. Josef Oleskow, was appalled at the change wrought upon the social demeanour of some Ukrainian settlers in Alberta by a few years of frontier hardship and isolation.

> Our people can live in Canada on an equal footing with others, yet they let themselves go from the viewpoint of both their clothes and personal cleanliness and often look worse than the Indians. The shame and damage done by our *Boykos* [Ukrainians from the Kalush district on the western slopes of the Carpathians] who arrived in Canada last spring, are a painful souvenir (our immigrants are accepted unwillingly because of this). Imagine people covered with spots of scab over their entire body, scratching incessantly,

---

[9] *Winnipeg Tribune*, February 6, 1894, and October 2, 1906; Sifton, "Immigrants," p. 16; *Winnipeg Telegram*, November 2, 1899, October 3, 1902, November 13, 1909, and December 17, 1909.

[10] Lehr and Moodie, "Polemics of Pioneer Settlement," p. 93.

[11] Canada, Parliament, Sessional Papers XXXIV, No. 10, 1900, Part II, Paper No. 13, Report No. 2, 16-19, W.T.R. Preston to Lord Strathcona, London.

unwashed for several weeks and wearing underwear which they keep on until it disintegrates! Their children are dressed in filthy rags instead of shirts, while their women wear no blouses at all and are clad in some sort of a coat opening in front.

"For Heaven's sake, how could you let yourselves go like this?"—said I during a visit to the farm of Ruthenian colonists.

"And why not?"—replied the woman, "there is no one here to dress for...."

Yet there are colonies of Germans from Galicia all around them. Only then did I understand why local people made such funny faces when I inquired about the Ruthenian settlers.[12]

Oleskow's concern was that all subsequent immigrants from Western Ukraine would be prejudged by the example of those in the vanguard of immigration. His explicit instructions to intending immigrants in his widely read pamphlet, *O Emigratsii*, regarding maintenance of personal hygiene, the adoption of a North American social demeanour, and standards of dress, indicated his recognition of the importance of appearances to the acceptance of Ukrainians by the Canadian public.[13]

The first impression made upon officials of the Department of the Interior by Ukrainian arrivals was not good. In official published reports, such as the Parliamentary *Sessional Papers*, officials noted the Ukrainians' capacity for work and expressed a cautious optimism about their assimilative qualities and agricultural potential. A.M. Burgess, then Deputy Minister for Immigration, reported that the Ukrainians, "although apparently frugal and industrious, are miserably poor" but displayed "a disposition to settle down to work and become independent."[14] In departmental correspondence, however, officials revealed that they were clearly taken aback by their first encounters with them. Alfred Akerlindh, a Government immigration officer, reported that the incoming parties of Ukrainians were physically impressive but were "very filthy in their habits and very dirty about their clothing and their persons," and were ignorant of the use of the toilet facilities within the colonist cars.[15] The Ukrainians were initially regarded as a second class grade of immigrant by Crown agents stationed in Winnipeg. William McCreary, commissioner of Immigration in Winnipeg, initially remarked that the Ukrainians

---

[12] Oleskow, *O Emigratsii*, pp. 43-4. See also, Rev. Nestor Dmytriw, "Kanadiyska Rus'" [Canadian Ruthenia] *Svoboda* 1897, in Harry Piniuta (trans. and ed.), *Land of Pain, Land of Promise: First Person Accounts by Ukrainian Pioneers 1891-1914* (Saskatoon: Western Producer Prairie Books, 1978), pp. 37-40.

[13] Oleskow, *O Emigratsii*, pp. 9-15.

[14] Canada, Parliament, *Sessional Papers* Vol. XXXI, No. 11, 1897, "Interior" Report of A.M. Burgess, Deputy Minister, xxxvii.

[15] Alfred Akerlindh, Winnipeg, to L.M. Fortier, Ottawa, March 11, 1897 and May 8, 1897. P.A.C., R.G. 76, Vol. 144, File 34214, pt. 1.

were of "a low illiterate, ignorant class..."[16] but such private assessments were not reflected in the published parliamentary reports of the Department personnel.

Communication problems, reflecting the paucity of proficient Ukrainian interpreters, caused Crown officials to evaluate Ukrainian immigrants on the basis of superficial visual criteria, although all immigrants were officially judged by the qualities thought to have the greatest bearing upon success in agricultural settlement: amount of capital, physique, assimilative potential, and co-operative spirit. Nevertheless, superficial criteria like peasant garb, tonsorial style, foreign concepts of social distance, and misunderstood behavioural norms, all received unfavourable comments.

Hand kissing, bowing, and failure to look a perceived superior in the eye, were examples of normal behaviour for many Eastern European peasants. Oleskow was in no doubt as to the way in which these behaviours would be perceived if practised in North America, and in *O Emigratsii* he specifically cautioned against them.[17] There were many reasons why his urgings were not always heeded. For example, Thomas McNutt, an employee of the Department of the Interior, witnessed a Crown interpreter of Eastern European background using a whip to direct a party of Ukrainian immigrants. McNutt, who had the employee dismissed, was outraged but amazed that none of the immigrants had objected, although the interpreter was "a little runt" who could have easily been overpowered by any one of the immigrants.[18]

Although the immigrants' tolerance of such harsh treatment may be explained by their prior experiences with the gendarmerie of Austria and their dread of being deported, their stoic behaviour was categorized as serf-like by their detractors.

A critical measure of success in the immigration debate was the government's ability to secure European or American settlers "well endowed with capital." Naturally, the government was always highly sensitive to charges that the Ukrainians were "pauper immigrants" likely to become a burden upon the nation's treasury, for this was the damaging allegation most frequently levelled against the Ukrainians by the Conservative party and its press.[19] Yet, despite the charges of the opposition, it is clear that by no means all Ukrainian immigrants were destitute upon arrival. Indeed, those immigrants selected and dispatched to Canada by Professor Josef Oleskow were reported to be relatively well endowed with capital. For example, of 172 families of Ukrainian settlers who arrived at Strathcona [Edmonton] in May 1899, twenty had over $300.00, and sixty-seven had between $50.00 and $100.00. Only thirty-eight families had less than $50.00. The minimum amount was

---

[16] William F. McCreary, Winnipeg, to James A. Smart, Ottawa, May 13, 1897; P.A.C., R.G. 76, Vol. 144, File 34214, pt. 1.

[17] Oleskow, *O Emigratsii*, pp. 10-15.

[18] Thomas McNutt, "Galicians and Bukowinians," in John Hawkes, ed., *Saskatchewan and its People* (Chicago-Regina: S.J. Clarke Publishing Co., 1924), pp. 731-2.

[19] Lehr and Moodie, "Polemics of Pioneer Settlement," p. 94.

$10.00.[20] Nevertheless, a few families arrived in such a destitute condition that Government interpreters were obliged to purchase bread and milk for them,[21] and many Ukrainian settlers certainly *became* destitute after settlement, when their limited capital failed to provide for basic agricultural needs and supplies to sustain them through their first winter. Some starved, many suffered, while others, more judicious and better provided, experienced no unusual hardship.[22]

Crown agents occasionally suspected that some groups possessed more than they declared, but officials were still obliged to take the word of the immigrant and act accordingly, even when they suspected immigrants concealed cash to claim destitution and get governmental assistance.[23] The stereotype of the destitute Ukrainian was thus reinforced. This was expressed geographically in the settlement arena because Crown agents always directed "destitute" groups towards locations which afforded opportunities for work off the homestead or for the generation of capital *in situ* by the cutting and sale of cordwood.[24] The great concern was that destitute settlers would become charges upon the state, a severe political embarrassment for the government since the opposition used such incidents to ridicule the government's "pauper immigration." Thus settlement locations for Ukrainian immigrants were generally evaluated in terms of provision for short term survival rather than provision for agricultural progress in the long term.[25]

Immigrants were also judged by their physical appearance. Although mostly impressed with the physique of the Ukrainians, the Crown agents were not impressed

---

[20] List of immigrants arrived at Strathcona [Edmonton, Alberta] May 1899. P.A.C., R.G. 76, Vol. 24, File 531, pt. 1. Although it would seem logical for the Department of the Interior to record the means of each incoming settler few of these records survived. Records of the means of settlers after one or two years of farming provide little indication of their cash on hand at arrival, but suggest that this record might not be atypical.

[21] Alfred Akerlindh to L.M. Fortier, Ottawa, May 8, 1897. P.A.C., R.G. 76, Vol. 144, File 34214, pt. 1.

[22] For details of the condition of Ukrainian settlers during the first two years of settlement see Kaye, *Ukrainian Settlements*, pp. 322-346.

[23] W.F. McCreary, Winnipeg, to James A. Smart, Ottawa, June 2, 1897; William Anderson, Winnipeg, to the Secretary, Department of the Interior, Ottawa, May 5, 1897; Alfred Akerlindh, Winnipeg, to Frank Pedley, Ottawa, May 3, 1898; P.A.C., R.G. 76, Vol. 144, File 34214, pts. 1 & 2; W. Boardman, Winnipeg, to Frank Pedley, Ottawa, January 18, 1900. P.A.C., R.G. 76, Vol. 61, File 2614, pt. 2; and E. Denville, Ottawa, to James A. Smart, Ottawa, February 9, 1899. Archives of Saskatchewan, Regina, File 19 (C.F. Aylsworth).

[24] John W. Wendelbo to H.H. Smith, August 8, 1896, P.A.C., R.G. 15, File 410595; Canada, Parliament, *Sessional Papers* XXXII, No. 10, 1898, Report of the Department of the Interior, pp. 170-172.

[25] This contention has been argued at length in John C. Lehr, "The Government and the Immigrant: Perspectives on Ukrainian Block Settlement in the Canadian West," *Canadian Ethnic Studies*, (2: 1977):42-52.

with their personal grooming. During the arduous trans-Atlantic journey as steerage passengers many immigrants picked up vermin. Sea-sickness and lack of proper washing facilities also left their mark.[26] Furthermore, peasant social mores did not sit well with middle class English-speaking immigrants accustomed to Victorian manners and affectations and so, prior to taking up land, Slavic immigrants were physically segregated during their residence in Immigration sheds.[27]

The Department of the Interior never clearly articulated any policy of segregating Ukrainians from other settlers when placing them on the land, but departmental concern to avoid confrontation in settlement was evident in departmental correspondence if not in the carefully edited reports published in the *Sessional Papers*. There can be little doubt that the Crown was not averse to giving tacit encouragement to those wishing to settle on the agricultural margins, away from English-speaking or Western European settlers, on land which should have properly been reserved from settlement, if criticism of the Government's Slavic immigration policy was reduced. The development of closely knit blocks of Ukrainian settlement in relatively isolated locations on the northern margins cannot be attributed solely to public stereotyping of Ukrainians as "uncouth" or "unhygienic", but such stereotyping arguably affected the actions of Crown agents shaping the geography of Ukrainian settlement in the West.

Intra-Group Stereotypes

In 1896, Government attitudes to Ukrainian immigrants were clouded by ignorance. The Ukrainians' Austrian citizenship confused Canadian officials who assumed that all Austrian nationals were German-speaking. The numerous terms employed to describe Ukrainians—Ruthenians, Galicians, Bukowinians, Little Russians and Austrians—perplexed even experienced immigration officers: "a number of settlers from Austria called Ruthenians, have come out recently ... they appear to be closely allied with the Galicians.... They speak a language difficult to interpret, very few strangers having heard it."[28]

Yet within a year practical experience of the new immigrants allowed Crown agents stationed in Western Canada to develop a fairly sophisticated understanding of the characteristics of the group, even to the extent of distinguishing between those who came from the province of Galicia and those who came from the province of

---

[26] Alfred Akerlindh to L.M. Fortier, Ottawa, March 11, 1897. P.A.C., R.G. 76, Vol. 144, File 34214, pt. 1.

[27] Thomas Bennet, Strathcona, to Frank Pedley, Ottawa, December 5, 1900; Frank Pedley to James A. Smart, Ottawa, September 26, 1901; and J. Obed Smith, Winnipeg, to Frank Pedley, Ottawa, June 20, 1902. P.A.C., R.G. 76, Vol. 24, File 531 pts. 1 and 2.

[28] Canada, Parliament, *Sessional Papers* XXXI, No. 11, 1897, Interior, Report No. 1. Commissioner of Dominion Lands, p. 13.

Bukovyna. "Galician" continued to be used as an umbrella term to describe all Ukrainians. But in departmental correspondence, the context generally made clear whether the term was being used generically, as a synonym for Ruthenian or Ukrainian, or in the specific sense of "originating from Galicia." In 1896, W.F. McCreary, Commissioner of Immigration at Winnipeg, claimed that the Bukovynians were:

> ... somewhat different from *regular Galicians* [my italics]; their chief difference, however, being in their religious persuasion. They do not affiliate, and, in fact, are detested by the Galicians; they are a lower class, more destitute and more awkward to handle.[29]

C.W. Sutter, immigration agent at Edmonton, was similarly confused by the ethnological terminology, but he shared McCreary's assessment of the Bukovynian immigrants:

> Among them [a party of Ukrainians from Galicia] were a small number of Bukowinians, from the adjacent Grand Duchy of Bukowina. They are in dress and language very similar to Ruthenians, but are lazy and shiftless and are not calculated to do well here, although the rising generation may improve.[30]

The Bukovynians were also generally thought to be poorer than the Galicians. They came to be regarded as less sophisticated and more deeply imbued with a peasant philosophy than those from Galicia. They were also regarded as less adaptive, less familiar with tools and implements, less self-reliant in settlement, and yet, perversely, more intractable and obstinate in their dealings with immigration officials.[31]

It is unlikely that these perceptions of the Galicians and Bukovynians resulted in any major differences in patterns of land occupation, but official awareness of cultural differences between the Galicians and the Bukovynians certainly facilitated the growth of separate settlements of the two groups. Colonization agent Thomas McNutt

---

29 William F. McCreary, Winnipeg, to James A. Smart, Ottawa, May 15, 1897. P.A.C., R.G. 76, Vol. 144, File 34214 pt. 1.

30 Canada, Parliament, *Sessional Papers* XXXII, No. 10, 1898, "Interior," Report of C.W. Sutter, Immigration Agent at Edmonton, p. 205.

31 J.S. Woodsworth, "Ukrainian Rural Communities: Report of Investigation by Bureau of Social Research. Governments of Manitoba, Saskatchewan and Alberta" (typewritten). Winnipeg, January 25, 1917; "Placing Galician Immigrants," Department of the Interior, May 19, 1897; William F. McCreary, Winnipeg, to James A. Smart, Ottawa, May 20, 1897, P.A.C., R.G. 76, Vol. 144, File 34214 pt. 1; and E.H. Taylor, Yorkton, to W.F. McCreary, Winnipeg, August 24, 1898. P.A.C., R.G. 76, Vol. 110, File 21103 pt. 2.

reported that he had "to put the Bukowinians and Galicians in two separate groups as they were not friendly with each other ... there was some religious difference between them which appeared to cause friction."[32]

Crown agents were initially surprised by the intensity of feeling associated with religious differences between the Orthodox Bukovynians and the Uniate (Greek Catholic) Galicians. To many Ukrainian peasants, religious affiliation meant more than adherence to a style of worship, it was the cornerstone of life. It carried strong national and political overtones.[33] The Galicians feared Russophile sympathies by the Orthodox Bukovynians who, in turn, were suspicious of Roman Catholic and Polish dominance of the Uniate church. This rift was exacerbated by differences in folk culture between Galicia and Bukovyna, and by the mental images which each group had of the other. To some Bukovynians the Galicians were miserly and without compassion, whereas to the Galicians the Bukovynians were unsophisticated bucolic "hayseeds."[34] Indeed, the intensity of their mutual antipathy was remarked upon by many officials of the Department of the Interior who worked with the two groups, and who, like Thomas McNutt, segregated them in settlement, placed them in distinct areas within the Ukrainian blocks, and, on occasion, segregated them while in transit to their homesteads.[35]

Correspondence between the Commissioner of Immigration and the Deputy Minister of the Department of the Interior suggests that officials in the West placed the Ukrainians into three general categories. In order of preference they were: 1) the settlers organized and dispatched by Professor Josef Oleskow in Galicia, who were regarded as cooperative and judged to possess adequate capital for settlement, 2) others from Galicia, and 3) those from Bukovyna. Each group was approached and handled slightly differently. For example, Departmental correspondence implies that the Bukovynians, generally thought to be more stubborn and intractable, were treated with greater firmness by Crown agents.

---

[32] McNutt, "Galicians and Bukowinians," pp. 731-732.

[33] A good indication of the intensity of feeling which accompanied religious affiliation among Ukrainian immigrants in the early years of settlement is given by J.G. McGregor in his discussion of the conflicts between the Orthodox and Uniates in Alberta. J.G. McGregor, *Vilni Zemli—Free Lands: The Ukrainian Settlement of Alberta* (Toronto: McClelland and Stewart, 1969), pp. 164-182.

[34] Insight into the perceptions which each group had of the other was gained by extensive fieldwork and interviewing of pioneers and their descendants undertaken in Alberta (1971-72) and Manitoba (1974-76). To a limited degree these stereotypes survive today.

[35] Anton Keyz, "Diary," (handwritten, in Ukrainian, n.p.).

Matching Land to the Settler

As knowledge of the Ukrainians increased, opinions appeared to change, generally to a more favourable assessment of their qualities. There is a shift from cautious optimism to enthusiastic endorsement in the Reports of the Department of the Interior published in the Sessional papers. In his report of 1902, W.T.R. Preston hinted that the continental European immigrant made a better settler than the Englishman. J. Obed Smith, McCreary's successor as Commissioner of Immigration in Winnipeg, described the Ukrainian settlement as: "surprisingly successful ... singularly free from serious crimes, or even misdemeanours of the ordinary sort, and ... practically immune from epidemics of disease" such as were encountered with other settlers.[36] Smith contended that the initial prejudice against the Ukrainians was "entirely dissipated, except amongst a few implacable persons, who can see no merit in any nationality save their own."[37]

In a sense Smith was quite correct, in that public expression of anti-Ukrainian sentiment by the Conservative party and its press had virtually ceased by 1902, but the attitudes so harshly expressed a few years earlier had merely gone underground.[38] Their expression had become politically counter-productive because newly enfranchised settlers constituted a significant force in provincial and territorial elections. Within a few years the Conservatives were seeking to woo the Ukrainian vote, charging Liberal duplicity and unfair treatment of Ukrainians![39]

Within the Department of the Interior the early stereotyping of the Ukrainians bore a legacy which persisted for some years, despite a deepening awareness of the diverse characteristics of the group, namely the practice of classifying types of land according to the perceived needs of the various nationalities.

Just how Crown officials arrived at their conclusions as to what properties rendered an area "well adapted for German settlement," or made it "suitable for Finnish settlement," is unclear. It seems that the type of lands selected by the first settlers of an ethnic group was important in influencing official attitudes. There was general agreement, moreover, that it was desirable to locate immigrants in the type

---

[36] *Canada*, Parliament, *Sessional Papers* XXXVI, No. 10, 1902, "Interior," Report of J. Obed Smith, Commissioner of Immigration, Winnipeg, p. 119.

[37] *Ibid.*

[38] See Lehr and Moodie, "Polemics of Pioneer Settlement," fig. 4, p. 96. After 1902 the Tory *Winnipeg Telegram* continued its campaign against undesirable foreign immigration but seldom specified any group as the target of its remarks. The Ukrainians were no longer referred to as "Slav scum" but were still deemed to be "far less satisfactory" than English speaking settlers. The barbs were oblique, but still present.

[39] For example, *Winnipeg Telegram*, April 1, 1911; December 6, 1911; May 31, 1913; and June 23, 1913.

of environment with which they were familiar, for example, to locate Finns in areas with abundant hay and large stands of coniferous timber.[40]

Given the imperfect understanding of the prairie environment even in the late 1890s this rationale had its merits. Certain environmental myths enjoyed wide popularity, contributing in some cases to what later proved to be unwise decisions in settlement.[41] There were few long-standing climatological records of any reliability and the attractions of various localities were shamelessly promoted by boosters and land speculators alike. Crown agents seeking the best for incoming settlers had to rely upon often sketchy and sometimes inaccurate survey traverse notes and their own experiences of the way in which settlers from different ethnic groups adapted to different environments.[42]

Given the remarkable state of ignorance about the Ukrainian people and their homeland among Dominion officials at the turn of the century, it is unlikely that they attempted to match the Ukrainians with a topography reminiscent of Galicia or Bukovyna. But they were convinced that the rough bush country along the northern and eastern margins of the aspen parkland provided an appropriate environment for immigrants lacking capital. There the immigrant found a wide resource base; timber, water, meadow, herbs, roots, and berries, fish and game. Short term survival was possible even if long term agricultural progress would be extremely difficult. On the other hand, to place settlers stereotyped as penurious on the open prairie was inconceivable, for, without capital and without knowledge of the appropriate farming techniques, they would soon become charges of the state.

It is not surprising, therefore, that by 1898 the correspondence of the Department of the Interior abounded in references to land "well adapted to Galician settlement," or, more commonly, "land fit for Galicians." The pejorative implication of the latter phrase is somewhat deceiving, for in their characterization of land Crown agents were wholly pragmatic. Nevertheless, once some Ukrainians showed a desire, or perhaps simply a willingness, to settle the northern marginal areas of the aspen parkland, agents appeared to interpret this as an expression of a uniform group desire. Those Ukrainian settlers well endowed with capital were either encouraged to settle, or at

---

[40] James A. Smart, Ottawa to W.H. Cottingham, Red Deer, February 13, 1901. P.A.C.,R.G. 76, Vol. 238, File 141288, pt. 1.

[41] Typical of such beliefs were that "rain follows the plow," or that the grassland climate could be changed by progressive farming techniques. See, for example, *Manitoba Free Press*, April 11, 1901, and March 29, 1902; *Winnipeg Telegram*, July 20, 1898, and January 4, 1905; and *Winnipeg Tribune*, September 11, 1899, and March 29, 1901.

[42] A contemporary newspaper account indicates that these decisions were based on subjective assessments of topography, vegetation, and climate, and were sometimes made by delegates of the groups concerned. *Manitoba Free Press*, March 7, 1900.

least were not dissuaded from settling, amongst their fellows in the northern parkland because that environment could best support poor immigrants.[43]

In 1901 the Department of the Interior compiled a map showing areas of the West then considered to be suitable for settlement. Areas of settlement were demarcated and annotated as to the groups which the government expected to be able to settle in each region. Significantly, there was no apparent discrimination in allocation of lands. Although the areas marked as suitable for Ukrainians were on the parkland's northern fringe similar areas were also demarcated as suitable for at least some English and American settlers.[44]

It seems, therefore, that although some degree of stereotyping was prevalent among Crown agents, deliberate discrimination did not occur. If it did have an effect, however, it was in encouraging all Ukrainians into the same types of environments.

Conclusion

The remarkable aspect of governmental treatment of Ukrainian immigrants is that although the personnel of the Department of the Interior, at the executive level, at least, were a part of the established Anglo-Saxon and generally strongly nativist culture, their assessments of the Ukrainian immigrants appear to have been reasonably balanced and even moderate. They were always a far cry from the invective of the Anglophile press and Conservative politicians, and certainly they were far less condemning than the prevailing opinion of the surrounding society.

The perception of the Ukrainian immigrants by officials of the Crown working in the settlement field did have some geographical effects. Their realization that an apparently homogenous group was rent by religious differences based upon their province of origin contributed to the geographic separation of settlers from Galicia and Bukovyna, a separation which has lasting implications for landscape evolution and the survival of folk culture.

It could be argued that the settlement of many Ukrainian immigrants on marginal lands in isolated locations was a reflection of their assigned socio-economic position in Canadian society, a position with which the officers of the Department of the Interior were supposedly in sympathy. It is suggested here, however, that the evaluation by these officials, based on firsthand experience, was perceptive and was free of much of the nativist bias found in Canadian society as a whole. Unfortunately, when placing immigrants in the West, the Crown did not operate in a social vacuum. The officials were a part of, and had to function within, a larger society. They, through their political masters, were sensitive to public opinion, but

---

[43] That some Ukrainians arrived in Canada with sufficient capital to contemplate farming on the prairie grasslands is suggested by information contained in Michael Ewanchuk. *Spruce, Swamp and Stone* (Winnipeg: By the author, 1979), pp. 24, 62-65.

[44] This map, untitled, is found in P.A.C., R.G. 76, Vol. 238, File 141288.

it was not always only the opinions of the majority Anglo-Saxon culture to which they responded. Other European nationalities held strong negative opinions about the Ukrainians and were well able to stir up political controversy over the government's immigration policies.[45] What is surprising is that the officials of the Department of the Interior treated the Ukrainians as well as they did, given the nature of Canadian opinion and the social and political pressures which surrounded them during this crucial formative period of the Canadian West.

Acknowledgements

I wish to thank Dr. James M. Richtik of the Department of Geography at the University of Winnipeg and two anonymous referees for their helpful criticism of earlier versions of this paper.

---

[45] See, for example, the correspondence regarding complaints to the Canadian Pacific Railway from non-English settlers upset that the CPR was carrying Ukrainian settlers into their districts near Edmonton and Rosthern. A.M. Stanton, Calgary and Edmonton Railway Co., Winnipeg, to William Whyte, CPR Manager, Winnipeg, August 4, 1898. CPR Archives, Montreal, File 49761.

World War I

Section 15

From any point of view, the first world war was a major crisis in Canadian life. Never before had the country been mobilised in such a massive way for a single national purpose, especially one with such dramatic consequences. The number of Canadian soldiers who lost their lives was just about equivalent to the entire population of Canada at the time of the Conquest. The war broke thousands of Canadian families, radically changed Canada's relations with Great Britain, and provoked a major confrontation between French and English. The introduction of compulsory military service in 1917 led to the formation of a government from which all French-Canadian representation was excluded, to rioting in Quebec in which troops opened fire, killing five civilians in the streets, and to the discussion of a resolution in the Quebec parliament calling for separation from confederation.

Why did Canada participate in this war? Why were English Canadians, at any rate, willing to make such tremendous sacrifices, and why was the government so sure they were necessary that it was willing to risk the complete alienation of Quebec to ensure the maintenance of an all-out war effort?

Some answers to these questions will be found in the article of R.C.Brown. According to it, what issues did prime minister Robert Borden consider to be at stake in the war, and why did he believe it deserved Canada's total commitment? Did he see Canada as participating in the war as a British colony or as a separate nation? What effect did this have on Anglo-Canadian relations?

Desmond Morton, a military historian, is, like Craig Brown, a member of the University of Toronto history department. According to what his essay shows us, why was in more difficult for French than for English Canadians to commit themselves to the military effort? How did the Canadian army come to be organised in such a way that French Canadians felt out of place in it?

In reading Morton's essay, you should keep in mind the general history of French-English relations since Confederation. Remember the Riel affair, the New Brunswick and Manitoba schools crises, the disestablishment of the French language in Manitoba, Saskatchewan, and Alberta, and the implementation of Regulation 17 in Ontario. How did these affect the feelings of French Canadians about the place being allotted to them in Canadian society? How would Morton's point about the army fit into that context, and how would all this affect French Canadians' attitudes toward participation in the kind of war that Borden thought Canada was fighting?

For more on Canada's military history since Confederation, see Desmond Morton, *Canada and War*. For a general history of the Laurier-Borden period, covering the last two topics as well as the Great War and its impact on Canada, see R.C. Brown & G.R. Cook, *Canada, 1896-1921: A Nation Transformed*.

Sir Robert Borden, the Great War and Anglo-Canadian Relations

Robert Craig Brown

Historians of modern Canada are agreed that the Dominion's participation in the great war resulted in a fundamental change in the Anglo-Canadian relationship. And though they may argue over the precise nature of the change they credit Sir Robert Borden with responsibility for the transition which took place. Borden was at once the instrument and the embodiment of the transition. Before the First World War, with the exception of Canada's direct relations with the United States, at no time was Canadian advice crucial, or even influential, in the determination of imperial foreign policy. But in the winter of 1918-19 Borden, representing Canada, sat in the highest councils of the Empire-Commonwealth, contributing to decisions on imperial foreign policy. That was indeed a far cry from the state of affairs when Sir Robert had first gone to London to speak for his country in discussions about naval policy just six years earlier. Then, in the summer of 1912, all he secured in return for a promise of a contribution to the imperial navy was the privilege of wistful participation in an advisory committee with a grandiose title but increasingly less influence over foreign policy. Significantly, Asquith and Harcourt pointed out to Borden this negative interpretation of Canada's participation in the Committee of Imperial Defence both at the time and in retrospect.[1] Strangely, Borden seemed to ignore the cautionary advice of the British prime minister and the colonial secretary. He chose to interpret the concession more positively: "No important step in foreign policy would be undertaken without consultation with such a representative of Canada," he told the House of Commons on his return.[2] He regarded it as an important initiative towards Canadian responsibility in foreign policy, temporarily sufficient though not the

---

[1] Participation in the C.I.D. discussions was based on the 1911 Imperial Conference resolution which included the phrase, "when questions of naval and military defence affecting the Oversea Dominions are under consideration." Harcourt's despatch of December 10, 1912 noted that "We [Asquith and Harcourt] pointed out to him [Borden] that the Committee of Imperial Defence is a purely advisory body and is not and cannot under any circumstances become a body deciding on policy...." See Department of External Affairs, *Documents on Canadian External Relations, I, 1909-1918* (Ottawa, 1967), no. 390, p. 276 and no. 401, pp. 276-77. (Hereafter referred to as DCER). I would like to thank Mr. Robert Bothwell, who was my research assistant in the summers of 1968 and 1969, for his assistance and suggestions in the preparation of this paper. Mr. Bothwell is preparing a study of Loring Christie for his doctoral thesis at Harvard University.

[2] See his speech of December 5, 1912, on Naval defence. Canada, House of Commons Debates, 1912-13, cols. 692-693.

ultimate goal. Of course, many "important steps" were taken without consultation with Canada, or, for that matter, with the C.I.D. In Canada, between the 1912 visit and the beginning of the war, the Senate quashed the Canadian part of the bargain by rejecting Borden's naval bill. Attitudes to policy had been expressed in the inconclusive naval bill. Attitudes to policy had been expressed in the inconclusive naval debate, but no opportunity presented itself for their transformation and practice.

In mid-December 1913 Loring Christie, recently recruited by Borden as legal advisor to the Department of External Affairs and governmental factotum, pointed out the inconclusiveness of Canadian foreign policy in a memorandum for the prime minister. "The Canadian people must sooner or later assume a control over foreign policy (i.e. over the issues of peace and war) no less effective than that now exercised by the people of Britain or by the U.S.A." Reflecting on the crystallization of attitudes that had come out of the naval debate, and over-simplifying them, Christie saw only two routes for Canada:

> (a) by separating their own foreign policy from that of the Empire and by controlling it through their own Dominion Government;
> (b) or by insisting that the foreign policy of the Empire be separated from the domestic affairs of Britain and entrusted to a government responsible no less to Canadian than to British voters ... it follows that in assuming control of foreign affairs, Canadians will either commit their country to final separation from the Empire or to becoming an organic part of it....

He added that most Canadians, however, "do not grasp the reality of these two alternatives, neither of which is palatable, nor do they understand that it is impossible to evade one or the other."[3]

It is the purpose of this paper to suggest that Canada's participation in World War I and the consequent strains it produced in the Anglo-Canadian relationship provided the opportunity to clarify the objectives of Canadian foreign policy and to achieve responsibility in foreign affairs without having to accept either of the "unpalatable alternatives" presupposed by Loring Christie.

The first step in the process was to articulate Canadian justification for participating in the war at Great Britain's side. Once done, the Canadian statement became both the background and the framework for the Canadian case in subsequent disputes with the British government and, with constant reiteration, a statement of Canadian war aims. Significantly, Canada's enunciation of explicit war aims was unique among the autonomous Dominions. No other Dominion government spent as

---

[3] Public Archives of Canada, Borden Papers, Memo from L.C., December 10, 1913, no. 67875.

much time and effort elaborating what were defined as national war aims as did the Canadian. As early as August 6, 1914, Borden instructed Christie to draw up the initial statement. Sir Robert believed it was imperative to "justify the action of Great Britain"[4] and, more important, establish why Canada should follow the British lead. Canada did not participate in the war simply because when Britain was at war Canada was at war. Rather, Canada was involved in "a struggle in which we have taken part of our own free will and because we realize the world-compelling considerations which its issues involve." Those considerations were larger than the Anglo-Canadian relationship, larger than the welfare of the Empire. What the Kaiser had called into question was "the future destiny of civilization and humanity" and "the cause of freedom."[5]

For Borden this was more than pious rhetoric. Like a good prosecuting attorney, he wanted to establish his texts and marshall the facts necessary to his brief. He referred Christie to Oppenheim's volume on international law, specifically to his concept of the "community of interests" of "civilized states." He asked Christie to

> lay particular stress upon the refusal of the.... Emperor to accept the mediation which was so earnestly sought by.... Grey and which doubtless would have prevented the war. Emphasize also the weakness of the excuses which the Emperor offers and ... the violation of the treaty ... guaranteeing the neutrality of Belgium.

Borden's use of the word "justify" was deliberate. The Emperor had violated the norms of conduct of "civilized states" and it was necessary to apportion blame. Germany and, at least at this stage of the war, more particularly the Kaiser, was being arraigned. Justification was to be established or discredited by a process not dissimilar to that of a trial, and then enforced by the united action of Canada in fulfilment of its "duty to the world."

Canadian war aims, couched in the terminology of legal moralism, were constantly stressed by Borden. The war was a struggle to punish the German "military aristocracy" for disturbing the peace of the world and to prevent it from doing so again. The war was just; being just it had to be pursued—and here lies an important distinction from the later attitudes of Smuts and Sir Henry Wilson—until the objective was unequivocally attained. "Probably no part of the Britannic Commonwealth was more disinterested in reaching a decision as to its duty," Borden wrote in 1918. "We are ready to fight to the last for the cause as we understand it, for every reasonable safeguard against German aggression and for the peace of the world."[6]

---

[4] P.A.C., Christie Papers, II, file 6, Borden to Christie, August 6, 1914.
[5] "Canada at War," A Speech ... by ... Borden," November 18, 1916, pp. 7-9.
[6] Department of External Affairs, Borden Papers, Peace Conference, file 18, Borden to L.S. Amery, August 22, 1918.

At the heart of Borden's concept of Canadian war aims was the assumption that the law must be used as an instrument of war, as the basic rationale for Canadian participation in the war. The law was the bedrock of civilization—"the chief insignia of a civilized nation are orderly government and respect for the law."[7] The law must be protected if civilization was to endure; it must be the active agent in the prosecution of a just war. In the past it had been the most suitable instrument used by civilized men to eliminate inequality and bondage. Now that inequality and bondage under the Kaiser threatened the civilized states, the purposefulness of the law must be reasserted. Borden told the Lawyers Club in New York City that "the purpose of the law must be found in some help which law brings towards reaching a social end."[8] During the war that social end was the punishment of the Kaiser's Germany, the salvation of the "civilized states" and the eventual establishment of a higher international order.

Total involvement in the war, of course, meant the acceptance of great sacrifices for Canada and its people. But because the call to duty was based upon the righteousness of the cause there would be attendant benefits to the participants. At the front the humdrum life of the average young man would be enlivened by a sense of commitment, an exercise of mind, spirit and morality which was tested in physical endeavour and sacrifice. It all could be, the English scholar Gilbert Murray observed, "one form at least of very high happiness."[9] Borden believed that the beneficial social effects of making war extended to all Canadians.

> They have learned that self sacrifice in a just cause is at once a duty and a blessing, and this lesson has both inspired and ennobled the men and women of Canada. It was indeed worth a great sacrifice to know that beneath eagerness for wealth and apparent absorption in material development there still burned the flame of that spirit upon which alone a nation's permanence be founded. One must move among our people to realize their overmastering conviction that the justness and greatness of our cause overpower all other considerations and to comprehend the intensity of the spirit which permeates and quickens every Canadian community.[10]

He was convinced that out of Canada's commitment to what Arthur Marwick has called "a deeply felt sense of moral purpose" would come a better Canada and a better world. "The character of a nation is not only tested but formed in stress and trial, through sacrifice and consecration to duty," he told a London Opera House audience

---

[7] Speech to New England Society. New York, December 22, 1915. Borden Papers, no. 175538.
[8] "Canada at War," *op. cit.*, p. 5.
[9] Cited, Arthur Marwick, *The Deluge* (London, 1967), p. 48.
[10] "Canada at War, *op. cit.*, p. 8.

in August, 1915.[11] A month later the Canadian Club in Ottawa heard the prime minister suggest that the war would "prove to be the death of much that marred and hindered the progress and development of civilization and democracy. Shall we not hope and indeed believe, that this war may prove the birth pang attending the nativity of a nobler and truer civilization."[12]

Loring Christie, reflecting his, as distinct from Borden's, close connections with the Round Tablers, was more specific in his hopes for Canadian war aims. In a burst of imperial enthusiasm he told Charles Magrath that the war offered "the greatest opportunity ever held out to a young nation," "a chance at least to save our soul of Canada." The path to salvation was through recognition by Canadians of "this crying need of coming together," of the necessity of the "members of the British Commonwealth" to "deliberately join their destinies."[13] But Borden refused to follow his adviser's lead. Mention of imperial consolidation is seldom found in his speeches and, when present, is clearly stated as cooperation rather than consolidation. Indeed, on occasion, the prime minister even deleted "British Dominions" from a Christie draft and inserted "Canada" in the final address.[14] Again and again he placed more stress on Canada's duty to civilization at large than did Christie. Christie hoped for the "coming together" of the British Empire; time and again in his speeches Borden looked to a "noble and truer civilization," the "regeneration of civilization."

Canada's war aims were nationally defined, general, moral and unselfish. They provided the high-minded purposefulness which Sir Robert believed was the necessary answer to critics of Canada's war effort. They convinced him of the purity of his and his country's motives in pursuing the war. They convinced him, further, of the superiority of the morality and earnestness of Canada's contribution. This point was brought into sharp relief by the inevitably increased intimacy of the Anglo-Canadian relationship during the war and the resultant conflicts over priorities among the contending partners, both in everyday operations and in ultimate objectives. "So far as Canada is concerned," Borden loftily proclaimed to his fellow members of the Imperial War Cabinet, "she did not go into the war in order to add territory to the British Empire."[15] Behind all of Borden's stormy complaints about the British war effort and Canada's part in it rested the "first principles" of Canada's own war aims.

One matter of continual concern to Borden and his colleagues in Ottawa was the apparent incompetence of the British High Command. Hughes reported in the late spring of 1915 that "complacency is observed on every hand." Though mobilization in Canada was certainly a triumph of luck rather than the consequence of rational

---

11   Borden Papers, no. 175500-07.
12   Ibid., no. 175510.
13   Christie Papers, II, file 3, Christie to Magrath, n.d.
14   Compare, for example, the draft of "Canada at War" in Christie Papers, II, no. 1385-92, with the copy of the text in Borden Papers, no. 175560-6 and the printed pamphlet cited above.
15   DCER, II, no. 14, pp. 13-14.

planning, Borden did not hesitate to complain to Perley about the "apparent lack of system in the War Office touching the measures being taken here."[16] Perhaps the evidence from the mercurial Minister of Defence, by itself, could be dismissed or heavily discounted. But it did fit with the general impression of discord and disillusionment in 1915 that accompanied the long-delayed realization that the war was a conflict of uncertain duration and scope. On June 16 Borden received a letter from Colonel J.A. Currie "complaining of lack of foresight and incompetence of British. 'They send us on every forlorn hope.'" The following week Sir Richard McBride returned from England and reported that he was "not optimistic as to result of war. He thinks England did not take it seriously enough at first. He doubts competency of some English generals." The total neglect of the Dominion by the Asquith government meant that there was no opportunity to get evidence to the contrary and only reinforced Canadian doubts. And what Borden saw and heard during his visit to London in the summer of 1915 confirmed his worst fears. "The efforts which Great Britain is making to provide the necessary war material, such as guns, machine guns, ammunitions, etc." were hardly, he told his cousin, Sir Frederick Borden, "characterized by reasonable efficiency." Almost desperately, he sought reliable information on the military situation. To his dismay he discovered on the eve of his departure for Canada that Kitchener "had forgotten the preparation of the memo he had undertaken."[17]

Nor was there any improvement as the war dragged on. One observer attributed the disastrous defeat on the western front in the spring of 1918 to the "blundering stupidity of the whisky and soda British Headquarters Staff", and Borden replied that there was "some ground for that impression."[18] At the War Cabinet meeting of June 11, called to consider the implications of the spring's events, Lloyd George "gave no explanation of how Germans can drive our forces back and inflict greater losses than they incur." But the same day Sir Clifford Sifton, "who is greatly disturbed," did have an answer: "says many British divisions useless and men disorganized." The next day General Currie arrived and "gave an awful picture of the war situation among the British. Says incompetent officers not removed, officers too casual, too cocksure. No foresight."[19]

At another meeting of the War Cabinet on the 13th Borden was scheduled to make a statement on the war activities of the Dominion. After a summary of Canadian war statistics he angrily turned to the subject of the British defeat in France. "There must be a cause for our failure," he observed, adding that "it seems apparent, having regard to the material of which the British Army is composed, that the unfortunate results

---

[16] Borden Papers, "Memo on the War Situation" by Hughes, no. 31706-21; Hughes to Borden, May 28, 1915, no. 31777-9; Borden to Perley, June 4, 1915, no. 31698-9.

[17] Borden Papers, Private, Diary, June 16 and 25, August 23, 1915, Borden to Sir Frederick Borden, September 9, 1915. R.L.B. Series, folder 929.

[18] Borden Papers, Memoir Notes, no. 2382.

[19] Diary, June 11 and 12, 1918.

which have obtained during the past year, and especially during the past three months, are due to lack of foresight, lack of preparation, and to defects of system and organization." He cited Currie's comments comparing Canadian and British troops and leadership, with examples pointedly taken from Passchendaele. There and elsewhere routine and stupidity had frustrated sound planning. British intelligence was invariably worthless. British preparations were inadequate. A British officer had "told [Currie] that in his corps they had nothing comparable [to the Canadian barbed wire] and that in his particular battalion the men were engaged in preparing lawn tennis courts last autumn while the Canadians were erecting barbed wire entanglements."[20]

"Curzon, Lloyd George, my colleagues, the other overseas Ministers, Long etc. gave me very warm congratulations," Borden noted afterward in his diary.[21] And later in the day Lloyd George confessed that so far as the Flanders offensive of the previous summer was concerned, "the Government felt considerable misgivings ... but were not prepared to overrule their military advisers in regard to the strategy of the war."[22] The explanation was hardly sufficient. Borden believed that "if the British Army Corps had made the same preparation to meet the German offensive as did General Currie and the officers and men of the Canadian Forces, the German offensive could not possibly have succeeded as it did." "One could almost weep," he concluded, "over the inability of the War Office and even of the Admiralty to utilize the brains of a nation at a time when brains are most needed."[23] Until the very end the contrast between the efficiency and success of the Canadian Corps and the incompetence and relative lack of success of British armies remained constantly in Borden's mind. To him it was both evidence and proof of the higher quality and character of the Canadian war effort.

The incompetence of the British High Command, Borden believed, was but a particular manifestation of a more general problem, the persistence of inefficiency and procrastination in the whole British war effort.[24] Another special problem related to this, Borden found on his 1915 visit, was the munitions crisis of that summer. On the first anniversary of the war Borden pointedly told a London audience that "in Canada we began to organize our industries for the production of munitions of war as

---

20 Borden Papers, no. 2484-96, Imperial War Cabinet 16, Shorthand notes.
21 Diary, June 13, 1918.
22 DCER, I, no. 340, p. 201.
23 Ibid., no. 341, pp. 201-03.
24 Lord Beaverbrook, who was one of the Borden's few sources of information, later described Asquith's "own way of looking at a world at war" in words Borden would have heartily seconded: "His complete detachment from the spirit of the struggle; his instability of purpose, his refusal to make up his mind on grave and urgent issues of policy; his balancing of one adviser against another till the net result was nil; his fundamental desire to have a peaceful tenure of office in the midst of war...." *Politicians and the War, 1914-1916* (London, 1960), p. 226.

far back as the end of August, 1914."[25] A few days later at a conference with Bonar Law, Churchill and F.E. Smith, the "grave" munitions crisis was discussed with discouraging results. Borden asked when there would be an ample supply of munitions. Bonar Law said within five months but Churchill "says middle of next year." "Told them I must have definite information."[26] More discouraging was the opinion Borden received at a luncheon with Bonar Law and Lloyd George.

> I had told Law that unless I received definite information as to munitions etc. we should stay our hand. L. George delivered statement as to munitions, guns, etc. Damning indictment of Department negligence. Said Great Britain would not be ready to exert full force for year or 18 months.[27]

Borden's feelings were best expressed in a letter to Perley some months later. "Procrastination, indecision, inertia, doubt, hesitation and many other undesirable qualities have made themselves entirely too conspicuous in this war." He recalled his August luncheon with Lloyd George who "in speaking of the officers of another Department said that he did not call them traitors but he asserted that they could not have acted differently if they had been traitors. They are still doing duty and five months have elapsed."[28]

Many of the production problems were solved as time went on. Rationalization of the supply of Canadian munitions for the British war effort, for example, was achieved in November of 1915 with the disbandment of the Shell Committee and the establishment of the Imperial Munitions Board. But the "undesirable qualities" seemed to persist, even to increase their manifestations. So far as Borden could see, the most important result of the 1918 German spring offensive was Sir Henry Wilson's reaction to it; to turn tail and run. Assessing the results of the offensive, Wilson gloomily reported to the War Cabinet on July 31 that "It must be realized that all enthusiasm for the war is dead," and that, though he had no positive recommendation to make, the Allies must, somehow, resolve "to strike in 1919 or stop the war."[29] Wilson was not alone. As early as April of 1917 Smuts reported to the war Office that a military victory was neither desirable nor necessarily expected. Now, on August 14, he told the War Cabinet that he was "very much against fighting [the war] to the absolute end, because I think that, although the end will be fatal to the enemy, it may possibly be fatal to us too." "Complete military victory

---

[25] Borden Papers, no. 175500-07.
[26] Diary, August 21, 1915.
[27] Diary, August 24, 1915.
[28] DCER, I, no. 184, p. 104, Borden to Perley, January 4, 1916.
[29] Borden Papers, no. 66395-426. Years later Borden contemptuously wrote of Wilson, "Indeed he was the man most faint-hearted, more than any other." Borden Memoirs, II, 815.

may be attainable," he added, "but the risks that we are running are too great and we have to take a more moderate line."[30]

Smuts' speech, Borden thought, "left [him] open to serious attack."[31] Both Wilson's report and Smuts' comments were, at best, wrong-headed. This was no time to counsel compromise or admit of defeat. He had given Canada's answer a month before.

> Canada will fight it out to the end.... Let the past bury its dead, but for God's sake let us get down to earnest endeavour and hold this line until the Americans can come in and help us to sustain it till the end.[32]

Looking back, Borden's criticism of the British war effort can easily be matched with uncomplimentary references to much of Canada's own effort. The record, both on the home front and in the Canadian command structure, especially in England, contained more than a little of inefficiency, personal bickering and jealousy, and corruption.[33] And these too played their part in the disruption of Anglo-Canadian relations during the war. But two points can be made in reply. First, the record of the Borden governments in attempting to solve these problems as they came to light was generally creditable, especially so after the formation of the Union Government. More important, such an attack on the Canadian war effort misses Borden's fundamental point. His critique was more of attitudes than of any one or any combination of specific actions. The British, in his terms, were measured for earnestness and commitment to duty and found wanting. Of Borden's own commitment, of his earnestness, and, he believed, of his country's, there could be no doubt. If anything, the opposite was more true. Borden was, perhaps, too "earnest," too committed to winning the war to see, as Smuts did, the long-term consequences of the total defeat of Germany.

British "traitors" on the home front, incompetence in the field, and wavering in the High Command all served to aggravate even more the third general problem in Anglo-Canadian relations, the political treatment accorded to the Dominion's contribution to the war effort. Until 1917 the British government appeared to treat Canada more like a Crown Colony than the full-fledged nation it deemed itself to be. The Canadian reaction was entirely predictable. It found expression in Borden's famous "toy automata" letter to Perley on January 4, 1916. Two paragraphs bear repeating:

---

30   Borden Papers, no. 2660-72, Imperial War Cabinet 31, Shorthand notes.
31   Diary, August 14, 1918.
32   Borden Papers, no. 2484-96, Imperial War Cabinet 16, Shorthand notes.
33   A portion of this story is very well told in John Swettenham, *To Seize The Victory, The Canadian Corps in World War I*, (Toronto, 1965).

> During the past four months since my return from Great Britain, the Canadian Government (except for an occasional telegram from you or Sir Max Aitken) have had just what information could be gleaned from the daily Press and no more. As to consultation, plans of campaign have been made and unmade, measures adopted and apparently abandoned and generally speaking steps of the most important and even vital character have been taken, postponed or rejected without the slightest consultation with the authorities of this Dominion.
>
> It can hardly be expected that we shall put 400,000 or 500,000 men in the field and willingly accept the position of having no more voice and receiving no more consideration than if we were toy automata. Any person cherishing such an expectation harbours an unfortunate and even dangerous delusion. Is this war being waged by the United Kingdom alone, or is it a war waged by the whole Empire? If I am correct in supposing that the second hypothesis must be accepted then why do the statesmen of the British Isles arrogate to themselves solely the methods by which it shall be carried on in the various spheres of warlike activity and the steps which shall be taken to assure victory and a lasting peace?[34]

This letter was in response to an exchange of correspondence in late October and early November which opened with a complaint from Borden. He granted the "necessity of central control of Empire armies," he told Perley, "but governments of overseas Dominions have large responsibilities to their people for conduct of War and we deem ourselves entitled to fuller information and to consultation respecting general policy in War operations." Perley had taken the complaint to Bonar Law but found the colonial secretary's response discouraging. He feigned acceptance of the rightness of Borden's demand but then shifted the responsibility for doing something about it back on the Canadian prime minister—"it is our desire to give him the fullest information and if there is any way which occurs to him ... in which this can be done I shall be delighted to carry it out." As to consultation on war policy, Bonar Law continued,

> here again I fully recognise the right of the Canadian Government to have some share of the control in a war in which Canada is playing so big a part. I am, however, not able to see any way in which this

---

[34] DCER, I, no. 184, p. 104. Eight days after it was written, Borden instructed Perley not to pass the letter on to the British government. Perhaps Perley at some stage conveyed its general sense to Bonar Law and others but they would hardly have needed to be reminded of Borden's opinions on the subject. I use it here because I think it is an accurate summation of his consistent attitude towards the problems of consultation.

could be practically done. I wish, therefore, that you [Perley] would communicate my view to Sir Robert Borden, telling him how gladly we would do it if it is practicable and at the same time I should like you to repeat to him what I have said to you—that if no scheme is practicable then it is very undesirable that the question should be raised.[35]

Here, indeed, was the true meaning of the British government's attitude to consultation in high policy. It had been implicit in the words of caution that Asquith and Harcourt had given Borden in 1912. Now, when the matter was being put to the test, when the lives of thousands of young Canadian men were being determined behind closed doors in London, and when the Canadian government had to answer for their destinies to the Canadian people, Sir Robert and his colleagues had to rely upon the tidbits of information gleaned by Perley and Aitken supplemented by press reports. More than this was not possible, at least it could not "be practically done." The onus for correcting this unsatisfactory state of affairs appeared, moreover, to be on the Dominions. But even here it was clear that the colonial secretary was in no mood to encourage a Canadian initiative; Bonar Law had made that quite plain by his suggestion that "it is very undesirable that the question should be raised."

The "toy automata" letter was neither a momentary outburst of temper by the prime minister, nor was it solely concerned with high policy, as important as that might be. Rather it crystallized the accumulated grievances of Borden and his government over the whole range of inadequate consultation and cooperation since August 1914. For Borden, as we have seen, Canadian participation in the Great War was a domestic as much as it was an external affair; it was a matter of contracts for munitions and supplies as much as it was a matter of maintaining the Canadian Corps at strength. The Canadian involvement was, or at least should be, total. But the procurement and fulfilment of war contracts was as dependent upon consultation and cooperation with the British government as was the deployment of Canadian troops at the front. And in this sphere the British government had been singularly negligent.

The trouble began early in the war with a complaint over the letting of contracts for wagons for the British and French armies in the United States. Borden cabled Perley that "our manufacturers ask consideration only in cases where they can supply articles of equal quality at the same cost ... [but] can obtain no answer from either government except refusal unaccompanied by any reason." "Not only the people of Canada as a whole but individuals are making sacrifices hitherto undreamed of to support Empire in this war. A very painful and even bitter feeling is being aroused throughout the Dominion," he continued. "Men are going without bread in Canada while those across the line are receiving good wages for work that could be done as

---

35 Ibid., no. 165, pp. 93-94, no. 172, p. 96.

efficiently and as cheaply in this country."[36] When orders did come, when work was finally to be done in Canada, as with the building of submarines in Montreal, the Canadian government only found out about it when Vickers, the company concerned, put aside work on a previously ordered Canadian government icebreaker. The polite language of the governor general's dispatch covering the matter did not hide the dismay of the Canadian government over the way in which it had been arranged. Connaught observed that his government would "be grateful if a somewhat earlier intimation could be given to them as to the intention of His Majesty's Government in such matters as it seemed inappropriate that an arrangement ... which involved interference with work undertaken by the company for my Government should in the first instance be communication to my advisers by the company itself."[37]

Orders for war material eventually came in abundance. In April 1915, the Canadian Pacific Railway was appointed the British government's purchasing agent in Canada. The following month Borden appointed a War Purchasing Commission to coordinate and control Canadian and British war contracts (the Shell Committee was specifically exempted from the Commission's purview). And in November, as noted, the Imperial Munitions Board, responsible to the British government, acting in Canada under the chairmanship of Sir Joseph Flavelle in close cooperation with the Borden government, was established. But getting the contracts was only half the problem. Being able to fill them was another matter. Here Canadian shipping was crucial to Canadian war production. At the same time, Canadian shipping was subject to the requisitioning authority of the Admiralty. and the Admiralty exercised their powers with callous disregard of Canadian interests.

After a long series of requests for and then complaints about the lack of consultation with Canada, Borden told Perley that "it is entirely within the mark to say that no such principle has been accepted" by the Admiralty. Most recently they had requisitioned a DOSCO coaster, impairing the supply of Canadian steel for Canadian munitions plants and forcing the latter to buy their raw materials in the United States. The Admiralty "without any consultation with us have felt themselves competent and have taken it on themselves at such a distance to judge the conflicting needs and interests involved." "It should be clearly recognized, whatever the registry of the ships concerned, if they are regularly engaged by charter or otherwise in what may be distinguished as the local or coasting trade of Canada no action disturbing them should ever be initiated by the Admiralty without consulting us or carried on without our consent." Upon what principle, Borden asked, "is it claimed that the Canadian Government should not be recognized in considering Canadian needs and conditions?"[38] Clearly, upon none whatsoever. As Doherty noted in a January 1917 order-in-council, the Admiralty doubtless had the legal power to requisition the ships,

---

[36] Ibid., no. 93, p. 59.

[37] Ibid., no. 106, p. 64. This affair, a classic illustration of the point, is carefully related in Gaddis Smith, *Britain's Clandestine Submarines, 1914-1915* (New Haven, 1964).

[38] Ibid., no. 251, pp. 144-47.

but each exercise of that power violated Canada's constitutional rights. "It is the Parliament of Canada alone which constitutionally can determine and prescribe the burdens to be borne by this Dominion or by any of its citizens for the purpose of this or any other war ...this prerogative must be exercised upon the advice of Your Excellency's Ministers and not upon the advice of the Government of the United Kingdom."[39]

The problem of consultation was, of course, largely resolved with the formation of the Imperial War Cabinet. Reacting to the increasingly harsh complaints from Canada and the other Dominions, and of the even greater burdens they were going to be asked to bear, the initiative came from Lloyd George and his advisers.[40] Lloyd George's motives were decidedly mixed. The first he revealed to Walter Long in December 1916. Because "we must have even more substantial support from them before we can hope to pull through," he wrote, "it is important that they should feel that they have a share in our councils as well as our burdens."[41] But the British prime minister also wished to use the War Cabinet, an *ad hoc* committee under his control, as an instrument against his foes amongst his colleagues, especially the High Command. In July 1918 he told Borden "that for eight months he had been boiling with impotent rage against higher command, they had affiliations and roots everywhere." "It was for the purpose of strengthening his hand in dealing with the situation that he had summoned the Dominion Ministers and the Imperial War Cabinet."[42]

Once the War Cabinet assembled, consultation on all matters of high policy, of war aims and, eventually, of peace terms and conditions took place. Perhaps even Bonar Law would have admitted that it was practical. Hankey later observed to Lloyd George that "the Governments of the Dominions were associated with the work of laying the foundations of the Peace Treaty, which was really begun at the Imperial War Cabinet of 1917."[43] It was in the War Cabinet that Borden's angry attack on the High Command took place in 1918. As a result, Lloyd George established a Prime Ministers' Committee to report back to the War Cabinet on the whole scope of military policy. After careful deliberation the Committee reasserted the necessity for greater control over military policy by the civilian government. "The Government," the Committee concluded, "is in the position of a Board of Directors who have to insist that before committing the resources of the Company in some great enterprise, they shall be fully appraised of its prospects, cost, and consequences."[44]

---

[39] Ibid., no. 277, pp. 158-59. See documents no. 278, p. 163 and no. 285, p. 167 for the resolution of this particular problem.

[40] See Thomas Jones, *Whitehall Diary, Volume I, 1916-1925* (London, 1969), p. 12.

[41] Lloyd George, *War Memoirs*, IV, (London, 1934), 1733.

[42] Diary, July 14, 1918, and Borden, *Memoirs*, II, 827.

[43] Beaverbrook Library, Lloyd George Papers, Hankey to Lloyd George, July 11, 1938, G/8/18/39.

[44] Borden Papers, Memoir Notes, Report of the Prime Ministers Committee, ff. no. 2484, p. 9.

In addition, Resolution IX of the Imperial War Conference of 1917 emanated from the meetings of the Imperial War Cabinet. Professor Hancock has written that it was "a resolution of the greatest historical importance which Smuts drafted, and carried through the Imperial War Conference."[45] Hancock's point, Smuts' singular role, is overstated. Writing to R.M. Dawson in 1935, Borden noted that "Smuts and Borden did the drafting; Austin Chamberlain suggested the reference to India. The Resolution was submitted to Long and then to Lloyd George who gave it unqualified approval before it was moved."[46] Sir Robert's diary generally accords with his later letter to Dawson. On March 19 Borden met Smuts for the first time—"He impresses one as a strong and straightforward man." On the 21st the two were joined by Massey on a committee to prepare an agenda for the Imperial War Conference. The next day the three met to discuss the agenda and a resolution regarding constitutional relations. Here an important difference of opinion between Borden and Smuts arose over a critical point in the eventual resolution. Borden's diary entries tell the remainder of the story.

> 22 March, 1917: ... I insisted on a clause declaring our right to an adequate voice in foreign policy. Smuts fears this may involve responsibility for financial aid in defence etc....
>
> 27 March, 1917: ... important interview with Long ... showed him resol^{ns} as to const^1 relations & he thought my draft most suitable. In the evening discussed them with Smuts Massey and Morris & they all agreed.
>
> 28 March, 1917: ... Then War Confer. Gave notice of my res^n on Const^1 relations, having first seen Ward who raised no question....
>
> 16 April, 1917: ... went to Impl. War Confce at 11 and moved res^n respecting con relations. Spoke 15 minutes. Referred to King's position etc. Massey Smuts followed. ... Sinha [here the account differs with the letter to Dawson] proposed amend^t including India in a qualified manner. I accepted. Ward made a long rambling speech 50 minutes no logical idea running through it.[47]

---

[45] Hancock, *Smuts*, I, 429. Hancock's reference reads: "Amery (*My Political Life*, II, 109) says that Smuts was 'the main author' of this historic resolution" (p. 586). We might conclude that there are no Smuts papers relating to the resolution and that Professor Hancock either ignored or discounted the account of the incident in Borden's *Memoirs*, II, 667-77.

[46] Borden Papers, no. 149889, Borden to Dawson, January 12, 1935.

[47] Diary, March 19, 21, 22, 27 and 28 April 16, 1917. The account in Borden's *Memoirs* also credits Austin Chamberlain with the suggestion for the reference to India. *Memoirs*, II 668.

Apparently, then, there were at least two drafts of the resolution, one by Smuts and one by Borden. They were probably much the same regarding the general matter of consultation. In its final form the resolution stated that the Dominions and India should have "effective arrangements for continuous consultation in all important matters of common Imperial concern, and for such necessary concerted action, founded upon consultation, as the several Governments may determine." But it is equally apparent that this statement did not go far enough for Borden. The experience of the preceding war years had convinced him that consultation upon "matters of common Imperial concern," was too ambiguous. It might be left up to the British government to determine what were and what were not "matters of common Imperial concern." They might or might not include "the right ... to an adequate voice in foreign policy and in foreign relations,"[48] and it was this clause which differentiated his draft from Smuts'. The simple fact was that the British Foreign Office had the power to commit Canada, legally, to war or to peace. And there was no greater matter of "common Imperial concern" than that. At the same time, as the order-in-council of the previous January had stated, the Parliament of Canada "alone ... constitutionally can determine and prescribe the burdens to be borne by this Dominion or by any of its citizens for the purpose of this or any other war." It was therefore necessary to include the clause to which Smuts objected at the March 22nd meeting.

"Foreign policy and foreign relations," Borden said in his speech moving the resolution,

> with which is intimately connected the question of the common defence of the Empire, have been under the immediate control of the Government of the United Kingdom, responsible to the Parliament of the United Kingdom ... this condition ... has proceeded on a theory of trusteeship which, whatever may be said of it in the past, is certain to prove not only entirely inadequate to the needs of the

---

However, the record of the Imperial War Conference proceedings matches Borden's diary references. The resolution, as originally moved by Borden, contained no reference to India. After a seconding speech by Massey and remarks by Smuts and Morris, Sir Satyendra Sinha suggested the inclusion of India in the resolution and Borden accepted it. See M. Ollivier, ed., *The Colonial and Imperial Conferences from 1887 to 1937*, II, Part I, (Ottawa, 1954), 203-4.

[48] Borden, *Memoirs*, II, 668.

Empire but incompatible with the aspirations of the people of the Dominions in the future.[49]

Later in the discussion Borden reminded his colleagues of the distinction between the legal powers of the British Parliament and the constitutional rights of Canada. The British Parliament had the legal power to impost a foreign policy upon Canada just as it had the legal power to repeal the British North America Act. "But there is no constitutional right to do so without our assent, and therefore, while there is the theory of predominance, there is not the constitutional right of predominance in practice, even at present." Perhaps thinking back to the quarrel over ship-requisitioning, he added that

> Questions, however, do arise with regard to it from time to time. We have had, even since the War began, a question as to the exercise of the prerogative, and a question as to advice upon which the prerogative under certain conditions shall be exercised—upon the advice of the Government of the United Kingdom, or upon the advice of the Government of Canada? Doubtless, [upon] the basis which is established by this Resolution they are less likely to arise in the future.[50]

Borden returned from the first series of Imperial War Cabinet meetings full of enthusiasm for the arrangement. Canada, he had said in London, "has raised herself to the full rank and dignity of nationhood."[51] Canada's place at the cabinet table signalled the fact while side-stepping the danger of centralization. It reconciled the apparently contradictory aspiration for autonomy of which Canada was "rightly jealous" and the "necessity of consultation and cooperation." More important, the Imperial War Cabinet "arose out of the necessity imposed by events, and I am thoroughly convinced that it was not premeditated or designed."[52] Borden had told Lloyd George in a letter of April 26 that it was desirable that "the policy under which the Imperial War Cabinet has been assembled shall be continued until after the conclusion of the war."[53] In another letter he went further, expressing confidence that "the usage thus initiated will gradually but surely develop into a recognized convention."[54] Elaborating on this point in his report to the House of Commons, he expressed the hope "that annually at least, and, if necessity should arise, oftener,

---

[49] Ollivier, *Colonial and Imperial conferences*, II, Part I, 194.
[50] Ibid., p. 214.
[51] Christie Papers, II, file 3. Speech of May 2, 1917.
[52] Borden Papers, no. 175653-87. Speech to House of Commons, May 18, 1917.
[53] Ibid., no. 88280.
[54] Ibid., no. 175664.

there should assemble in London an Imperial Cabinet to deal with matters of common concern to the Empire."⁵⁵

The enthusiasm was premature. In the interval between the 1917 and 1918 meetings of the Imperial War Cabinet it became clear that Borden's voice in the determination of imperial policy was predicated on his continuous presence in London, not in Ottawa. That was both practically and politically impossible. But while the Dominion prime ministers were at home, the assistant secretary of the War Cabinet, L.S. Amery, explained, their governments had "to revert to the old system of communication through the Colonial Office." Meanwhile, the 1917 decisions regarding war policy were totally undercut by events. Nivelle's offensive failed; so did the Russian offensive. The British War Cabinet sanctioned the Flanders offensive without consultation and with disastrous results. And the German drive in the spring of 1918 was all too successful. One side of the problem was that the British government "had to shoulder that responsibility for decision-making alone;" the other was that continuous consultation was short-circuited by reliance upon the cumbersome formalized channels of communication between the Colonial Office and the Dominions. They may have been entirely adequate for relations with a nineteenth-century colony in peacetime. But Canada was a twentieth-century nation at war and, as Amery defined the use of those channels, "This is absurd."⁵⁶

Various schemes of improvement were mooted at the 1918 Cabinet and Conference. In the latter Hughes carried through a general resolution calling for administrative changes to facilitate communications. In the cabinet he urged continuous and direct links between the prime ministers and was supported by Borden. Sir Robert added the threat that if Canada did not have "that voice in the foreign relations of the Empire as a whole, she would before long have an independent voice in her own foreign relations outside the Empire."⁵⁷

Amery circulated a long memorandum on the "Future of the Imperial Cabinet-System," advocating an elaborate institutionalization of the War Cabinet scheme and the appointment of "certain Imperial Ministers of State" including imperial Ministries of Defence and Finance.⁵⁸ Lloyd George accepted the idea of direct communication between the prime ministers and suggested the appointment of Dominion ministers resident in London to sit in the cabinet when the prime ministers were in their home countries. Further, he wondered if the members of the cabinet might not immediately discuss the constitutional changes which Resolution IX called for after the war. "As regards the wider question of the permanent machinery of Imperial organization, he agreed with Mr. Churchill that it would be easier to set up some machinery during the war than after," and suggested a cabinet committee

---

55 Ibid., no, 175660.
56 DCER, no. 497, p. 338. Memo by L.S. Amery, "The Future of the Imperial Cabinet System," June 29, 1918.
57 Borden Papers, No. 2582, Imperial War Cabinet 26.
58 DCER, no. 497, pp. 332-44.

"investigate the machinery for carrying on the business of the Empire after the war." The Dominion representatives, however, "were not prepared to agree in the desirability of setting up even an informal Committee."[59]

Even that, let alone Amery's scheme, smacked of enough centralization to frighten them off. With direct continuous consultation agreed to, it was better to let well enough alone and allow the future to provide for itself. Borden clearly recognized that the Imperial War Cabinet was an *ad hoc* body specially designed to meet the demands upon the imperial government in wartime and, even more, the particular political necessities of the Lloyd George government. Neither was it the appropriate place nor the appropriate time to tinker with the constitution. The important business at hand was winning the war. For that purpose, he told Lloyd George, "I see no better method of attaining cooperation between the nations of the Empire or of giving adequate voice to the Overseas Governments."[60]

Direct communication with Lloyd George proved satisfactory after Sir Robert returned to Ottawa. Borden vacillated over the appointment of a resident Dominion minister in London, probably because of lack of confidence that either Sir George Perley or Sir Edward Kemp, who were both there, could adequately represent his views in the War Cabinet. And, as in 1917, events overtook planning. The strategy mapped out by the Prime Ministers Committee was rendered obsolete by the collapse of the enemy war effort. Within weeks Borden was back in London attending meetings of the War Cabinet to discuss peace and peace terms. Hughes fought for separate representation at the forthcoming Peace Conference with Borden's support.[61] When the War Cabinet moved to Paris in January 1919, under the new name of the British Empire Delegation, the continuity of consultation in foreign relations was maintained.

When war was declared in August 1914, Canada's foreign policy and Canada's role in the determination of imperial foreign policy were conspicuous only in their ambiguity. Only one point was clear. That was that the Borden government was as convinced as was John Dafoe in Winnipeg that it was going to be "Canada's war."[62] Even that was more a posture enunciated in innumerable speeches on war aims than a policy. But the inevitably more intimate Anglo-Canadian relationship during the war contributed directly to the transformation of "Canada's war" from an attitude to policy decisions and demands. The lack of either information from or consultation with the British government, the arbitrary interference by the Admiralty in the Canadian war effort on the home front and the apparently futile and endless slaughter of Canada's brave youth because of a mindless and inefficient British High Command induced a very real sense of bitterness about the relationship with Britain on the part of Borden

---

[59] Borden Papers, no. 2595, Imperial War Cabinet 27, no. 2603, Imperial War Cabinet 28.
[60] DCER, no. 496, p. 331. Borden to Lloyd George, June 28, 1918.
[61] See L.F. Fitzhardinge, "Hughes, Borden, and Dominion Representation at the Paris Peace Conference," *Canadian Historical Review*, XLIX, no. 2, June, 1968, 160-69.
[62] See Ramsay Cook, *The Politics of John W. Dafoe and the Free Press*, (Toronto, 1963), p. 66.

and many of his Ottawa colleagues. All of these factors forced them to think more about *their* war effort, to restate and re-emphasize *Canadian* war aims and to reflect on the British obstacles placed in the path of their fulfilment.

Rightly or wrongly, objectively or otherwise, the Canadians convinced themselves that their part in the whole, whether at home or at the front, was always a little purer than that of the others. Canada, Borden said, did not come back to the Old World to aggrandize the fortunes of the British Empire. Her civilian soldiers were more efficient, their planning was better and more successful. On the home front, after 1917, the money-changers had been driven out, the councils of government had been cleansed and Borden spoke with a fresh and united mandate—English-speaking section—to carry on to victory. There would be no procrastination. Canada's voice was that of the "bitter-enders." Unlike Smuts, or General Wilson, Borden regarded a partial peace as incomprehensible and unacceptable. It accorded neither with his nation's professed war aims nor with his nation's response to his appeal in 1917.

The creation of the Imperial War Cabinet averted a serious breach in the Anglo-Canadian relationship during the Great War. Properly, Borden thought, the initiative came from the senior partner in the alliance; not because Britain was senior—*primus inter pares*—but because it was her system, or lack of it, that was deficient and needed to be reformed. Gradually the War Cabinet became an adequate instrument for information and consultation. Through it and its 1918 Prime Minsters Committee Borden and his Dominion colleagues exerted influence on the highest policy decisions for waging war and making peace.

Resolution IX symbolized the change in the relationship. For Borden it was not a statement of Canada's aspirations but of her deeds accomplished; full nationhood and the responsibilities that went therewith were not going to be achieved in 1921 or 1923 or later, they already had been. "Full recognition of the Dominions as autonomous nations" took place in 1917. A postwar imperial conference to consider "the readjustment of the constitutional relations of the component parts of the Empire" would be just that—a conference to tidy up the constitution of the Empire-Commonwealth. There was no time to do that during the war. Beyond that, Borden was always suspicious of grand schemes like Amery's or of the visionary planners in the Round Table groups. The experience of the war, the constant necessity to accommodate to events made him the more suspicious. He went out of his way to remind the House of Commons that the Imperial War Cabinet was "not premeditated or designed." As he had told a Winnipeg audience in 1914, constitutional changes "have been usually gradual and always practical; and they have been taken rather by instinct than upon any carefully considered theory."[63] Flexibility and adjustment to circumstances would be necessary at Paris and in the post-Peace Conference world. Elaborate constitutional designs were as likely to impede Canada's evolving nationhood and its attendant responsibilities as to enhance them.

---

63 See Borden, *The War and The Future*, (Toronto, 1917), pp. 126-28.

Sir Robert Borden's role in the Anglo-Canadian relationship during the Great War has often been characterized as a dramatic shift from "imperialism" to "nationalism."[64] Probably no one would have been more surprised by that characterization than Borden. It presumes an ideological dichotomy between "imperialism" and "nationalism" and assumes that Canada's national interests were "opposed to the imperial" interests of both Canada and Britain. For Borden no such dichotomy existed. Moreover, the "national" interests of Canada and the "imperial" interests of Canada during the Great War were demonstrably the same. The point at issue was at once more subtle and more simple: what kind of relationship *did exist* and what kind of relationship *should exist* between two nation states within the Empire. World War I provided an opportunity and a catalyst for clarification of the ambiguities in the international relationship between two states whose "chief tie," Borden told the King in April 1917, was "the Crown." Certainly Borden would have agreed that the process of clarification was not complete in December of 1918. Nor, indeed, would it be after the Peace Conference. After all, he had always argued that it was and should be an ever-evolving process. Still, when the Imperial War Cabinet meetings came to an end and he packed his bags for the trip to Paris, Sir Robert was satisfied that his colleagues recognized that the Great War had been Canada's war.

---

[64] See especially Harold A. Wilson, *The Imperial Policy of Sir Robert Borden*, (Gainesville, 1966), pp. 30, 33.

French Canada and War, 1868-1917: The Military Background to the Conscription Crisis of 1917

Desmond Morton

A few days after war broke out in 1914, George Perley, the acting Canadian High Commissioner in London, received a suggestion through the Colonial Secretary. Why not raise a "Royal Montcalm" regiment in Canada "to associate the name of Montcalm & the Province of Quebec specifically with an Empire War?"[1] Transmitting the notion to the Prime Minister in Ottawa, Perley added no endorsement: " ... personally doubt wisdom of doing anything to accentuate different races as all are Canadian."[2]

At the outset of the war, Perley seemed to be right. There was remarkable unity in Canada in the face of news from Europe, and popular excitement was reported to be even greater in Montreal and Quebec than in Toronto. The French-Canadian press was almost as unanimous as the English-speaking papers in supporting the war effort. From the beginning Sir Wilfrid Laurier, leader of the Opposition and French Canada's leading politician, declared a truce in party conflict.[3] Even Henri Bourassa, who had barely escaped internment in Germany, was not immune from the early mood of solidarity.[4]

That solidarity between French- and English-speaking Canadians soon disintegrated. By 1917 the gulf could no longer be bridged. Fundamental differences in history and outlook, old grievances and some new ones, such as Ontario's attempt to eliminate French-language schools, helped to divide Canadians on linguistic and cultural grounds.[5] After their initial hesitation, Bourassa and other nationalist leaders threw themselves into a fearless and tireless campaign against the war effort, but

---

[1] Austen Chamberlain to Lewis Harcourt, August 6, 1914, P.A.C., Perley Papers, vol. I, f. 12.
[2] Perley to Borden, August 8, 1914, Ibid.
[3] O.D. Skelton, *The Life and Letters of Sir Wilfrid Laurier* (Toronto, 1921), II, 425. On other French-Canadian reactions, see Mason Wade, *The French-Canadians* (Toronto, 1968, rev. ed.), II, 643; Elizabeth Armstrong, *The Crisis of Quebec, 1914-1918* (New York, 1937), pp. 61-77.
[4] Henri Bourassa, *Le Devoir et la Guerre* (Montreal, 1916), pp. 16-20.
[5] In addition to Armstrong, *Crisis*, see Robert Rumilly, *Histoire de la Province de Québec* (Montreal, n.d.), vols. XIX-XXI; André Siegfried, *Canada: puissance internationale* (Paris 1936); and the more interesting reply, Jacques Michel, *La Participation des Canadiens Français à la grande guerre* (Montreal, 1938). On the Ontario school dispute, see Margaret Prang, "Clerics, Politicians and the Bilingual Schools Issue in Ontario, 1910-1917," *Canadian Historical Review* XLI (December, 1960).

their participation was more catalyst than cause. If war is one of those shared experiences which transform a people into a nation, Canada indeed became a country of two nations.[6]

Against this tide of feeling, the Borden government proved largely ineffective. Bourassa and other opponents of the war effort were, after all, only amplifying arguments which had helped win Conservative seats in Quebec in 1911. Uninspired and often ill-advised in dealing with French Canada,[7] the Borden government had full control over only one area which might have influenced public attitudes: military policy and administration. It would be absurd to argue that brilliant management of this aspect of the war could have overcome the resistance of Quebec; it is reasonable to suggest that it might have helped. It is therefore worth considering why the Canadian military system operated as it did and to understand the consequences. Military policy was by no means the most important factor in producing the conscription crisis of 1917, but it played a significant part. It is also an aspect of the problem which has been the least explored and the worst understood.[8]

Few of the problems of French-Canadian recruiting or service at the time of the First World War were new. The formation of French-speaking units, senior appointments for French Canadians, the language of command and instruction, even the development of special symbols and traditions which might command the loyalty of French Canadians—all of these had been recurrent preoccupations of military policy in Canada since before Confederation. Unfortunately, although the Militia as a whole had never been more efficient or healthy than in 1914, these particular problems were further than ever from a satisfactory solution.[9]

To Sir George-Etienne Cartier, the Dominion's first Minister of Militia, this would have been a grave disappointment. When he introduced his first Militia Bill in 1868, he emphasized that the new institution would be an essential part of the new Canadian nationality: "Aucun peuple ne saurait prétendre au titre de nation s'il n'a

---

[6] See, for example, the comments of C.P. Stacey, "Nationality: The Canadian Experience," *Canadian Historical Association Report, 1967,* 12.

[7] Rumilly's comment deserves repetition: "Or les Anglo-Canadiens restaient sur cette conception simpliste du Canada Français: un peuple ignorant, arriéré, soumis en toutes choses à son clergé, l'unique et facile moyen de faire marcher les Canadiens-français est d'obtenir le concours du clergé, lui-même tres hiérarchisé. C'est auprès des évêques qu'il faut agir." (*Québec*, vol. XIX, p. 58.)

[8] A work in this area which proves to be only a worthy follower of Benjamin Sulte, the prolific 19th century French-Canadian historian, is Charles-Marie Boissonault, *Histoire Politico-Militaire des Canadiens-Français (1763-1945)* (Trois-Rivières, 1969).

[9] The problem is dealt with more fully in Desmond Morton, "French Canada and the Canadian Militia," *Histoire Sociale/Social History,* III (April, 1969).

chez lui un élément militaire des moyens de défense." His introductory speech took five hours because he took the exceptional step of repeating much of it in French.[10]

Cartier's militia was not really new. From the former United Province he inherited a British-model military force with English as the language of command. However, both structure and staff respected bilingualism. The Deputy Adjutant-General for Lower Canada was invariably French-speaking. When a volunteer militia was authorized in 1856, the first unit was a French-speaking field artillery battery from Quebec, and thereafter corps were either French- or English-speaking.[11] If orders had to be given in English, explanations could be offered in French. None of this was altered by Confederation. Two of the three new military districts in Quebec were designed to include virtually all the French-speaking units and to provide vacancies for French-speaking staff officers. French-speaking instructors were employed for militia training courses and in 1872, when a tiny permanent force was created to replace the departed British garrison, the French fact was borne in mind. Most of the officers and half of the other ranks in the artillery battery organized at Quebec were French-Canadian. In 1883, when the permanent force was expanded, one of the three new infantry schools was designed for the French-speaking militia. Moreover, in Sir John A. Macdonald's cabinets, the militia portfolio was normally held by a French-Canadian minister while the Militia Department's deputy minister was a French Canadian until after the Second World War.

Cultural considerations were not forgotten when the militia went on active service. One of the two militia battalions in the Red River Expedition of 1870 was officered by French Canadians and recruited in Quebec, while in 1885 two French-Canadian battalions were included in the force sent to the North-West to quell the Métis and Indian rebellion. In 1899 a French Canadian was included among the three senior officers of the First Contingent, and one of the eight companies was commanded by French-Canadian officers—though only a small handful of French-speaking recruits actually served in the ranks.

In fact, representation in the higher appointments was no guarantee of real participation. In 1870, only 77 of the 350 men in the ranks of the Quebec Battalion were French-speaking, while one of the French-Canadian battalions called out in 1885 had to recruit most of its men from the streets of Montreal.[12] Of course, it is not hard to explain French-Canadian reluctance to go to the North-West or South

---

[10] Joseph Tassé, *Discours de Sir Georges Cartier, Baronnet, accompagnés de notices* (Montreal, 1893), p. 566.

[11] Province of Canada, *Report on the State of the Militia of the Province*, 1857, para. 39.

[12] Lt. Gen. James Lindsay to Sir John Young, August 4, 1870, Canadian Forces Historical Section, mfm. W.O. 32/815/058/316; C.R. Daoust, *Cent-vingt jours de service actif: Récit historique très complet de la campagne du 65e au nord-ouest* (Montreal, 1886), pp. 215-7. On the French Canadians on active service, see Desmond Morton, "Des Canadiens Errants: French-Canadian Troops in the North-West Campaign of 1885," *Journal of Canadian Studies*, (August, 1970).

Africa; it is less obvious why the militia should have been so weak in Quebec itself. In 1870, when three French-Canadian battalions were called out to protect their homeland from Fenian invaders, only 358 of a nominal strength of 1,005 appeared.[13] In Montreal, where there were five battalions of English-speaking militia, only one, the Carabiniers Mont-Royal, represented the French-Canadian half of the population. In Quebec City there was one battalion for each language group, while in rural Quebec there were fourteen French-speaking battalions to ten English-speaking units.[14]

Both French- and English-speaking militiamen shared many of the same problems across Canada. Until the eve of the South African War, interest in the force was often limited to polite ridicule. Government defence spending was tightly limited, and rural battalions really only existed for a few days in alternate years when they were assembled in camp. City corps could train throughout the year but their efficiency and growth depended on generous contributions of cash and enthusiasm from officers and friends. Money was essential to buy smart uniforms, finance the band and provide the lively social life which attracted recruits. When money and enthusiasm were scarce, as they often were in French-Canadian units, there was little else to attract new men or persuade would-be officers to go to the expense of buying uniforms or qualifying for their rank.[15]

One explanation of the tribulations of the militia which proved popular among its officers was Cartier's insistence on a volunteer basis for the force, even when sufficient suitable recruits were not forthcoming. While English-speaking officers argued that the restoration of the ballot and compulsory service were a practical necessity to help captains recruit their companies and enforce discipline, there were French-speaking advocates of compulsion who maintained that it was an inherent part of French culture and tradition. In 1867 a staff officer explained the failure of local people to enlist by reporting that they were waiting for the "French system" to be invoked.[16] Sir Etienne Taché, veteran of the War of 1812, former staff officer, and Macdonald's titular head in the Great Coalition, argued from experience that the voluntary system was "un système nouveau, impraticable dans les campagnes, étranger à nos habitudes, à nos souvenirs, et qui a besoin d'être soumis au creuset de l'expérience avant que l'on puisse en parler avec assurance."[17]

---

[13] Lindsay to Young, *op. cit.*

[14] Based on *Militia List*, 1885.

[15] The problems of militia life and organization are dealt with more fully in Desmond Morton, *Ministers and Generals:Politics and the Canadian Militia, 1868-1904* (Toronto, 1970), esp. chs. II-IV.

[16] Canada Department of Militia and Defence, *Annual Report*, 1867.

[17] "Un vétéran de 1812" (Sir E-P. Taché), *Quelques réflexions sur l'organisation des volontaires et de la milice de cette province* (Quebec, 1863), p. 5. See also Benjamin Sulte, *Histoire de la milice Canadienne-Française, 1769-1897* (Montreal, n.d.), p. 65.

By insisting on a volunteer militia, Cartier undoubtedly respected the wishes of civilian politicians in both English and French Canada, but his claim that the militia was a success without compulsion was only partially true. In places like Toronto, where enthusiasm for military pursuits was high, the ranks of local battalions were kept full; it was much harder where the spirit was lacking. "Several well-do-do people have told me they would willingly shoulder the musket were they obliged to do so," reported the staff officer for one of the French-speaking districts, "but their occupations would not allow them to voluntarily neglect their businesses and impair their fortunes...."[18]

Since men were not to be compelled to serve in the militia, something had to be done to make it attractive. In English-speaking districts the close imitation of British military uniforms, customs and values could exercise an appeal for many, but there was little corresponding patriotic evocation from scarlet tunics or British mess etiquette in the French-speaking counties of Quebec. One distinct attempt was made to capitalize on an authentic French-Canadian military achievement, the recruiting and despatch of more than five hundred young men between 1868 and 1870 to serve in the ranks of the Papal Zouaves. Although this particular display of ultramontanism had been criticized by Quebec *Rouges* and denounced by Ontario Protestants, the service of the Zouaves constituted as legitimate a part of Canadian military tradition as the artificially inseminated customs of British line regiments. Unfortunately, neither Canadian nor British officials saw it that way. When an attempt was made to commemorate the Zouaves by organizing a new French-Canadian militia battalion, wearing a similar, Algerian-style uniform, it was frustrated by a combination of British military objections and Sir John A. Macdonald's renowned capacity for a politically judicious delay. As British Commander-in-Chief, the Duke of Cambridge noted that he could not allow any of Her Majesty's forces to be arrayed in foreign fancy dress.[19] Doubtless the decision struck the Duke as trivial but it ended the one significant attempt to adapt the Canadian militia to its bicultural setting. Lieutenant Colonel Gustave d'Odet d'Orsonnens, a militia staff officer who had helped organize both the original Zouave contingents and the proposed regiment, made the point:

> Les canadiens-français n'ont pas tous oublié qu'ils portent l'uniforme du vainqueur, non pas que je veuille dire que notre dévouement à la cause anglaise en souffre, point du tout; mais sous le point de vue de la valeur du soldat, je prétends qu'un canadien-français avec un uniforme de zouave sur les épaules, est un homme fanatisé par la

---

[18] *Militia Report*, 1871, appendices, p. 27.
[19] On the Zouaves, see Leopold Lamontagne, "Habits gris et chemises rouges," *Canadian Historical Association Report, 1950*, and "The Ninth Crusade," *Canadian Historical Review* XXXII (September, 1959). Morton, "French Canada and the Militia," pp. 37-8.

gloire; l'orgeuil, autant que l'honneur national, le fera tuer deux fois plutôt que de le voir reculer.[20]

In the absence of military traditions, real or synthetic, or of any external threat which they could have recognized,French Canadians could still find some reasons for joining the militia. Throughout the Dominion there were modest political advantages in being a militia officer. There was prestige, prominence and a chance to distribute small favours. In the formative years of the force, many militia colonels represented their county in Parliament or Provincial Legislatures. In the long period of depression in Quebec, humbler citizens could welcome a chance to spend a few weeks in camp, even at the meagre wage of fifty cents a day. To the indignation of the commandant of the military school at St-Jean, militia commanding officers used vacancies in the school as political patronage, sending illiterates, ne'er-do-wells and other social misfits for a winter's lodging at public expense.

All across Canada political considerations impregnated militia administration. In 1891, when the Minister of Militia secured the nomination in the remote lower-St. Lawrence riding of Rimouski, the site of the district militia camp went down river with him.[21] A legitimate concern for maintaining racial balance in militia appointments sometimes meant purely political selection. In 1869 Antoine de Lotbinière Harwood (who later acknowledged "I never was a military man before") was persuaded to resign his seat in the Quebec Legislature to become a lieutenant colonel and Deputy Adjutant General for the French-speaking militia in the Montreal area.[22] It was notorious that he never did learn drill. Although such abuses occurred throughout post-Confederation militia administration, French Canada offered few of the pressures for efficiency which came from militia enthusiasts in English Canada. Instead of securing the French-Canadian position in the force as a matter of deliberate policy, it existed as a result of highly informal, *ad hoc* political arrangements.

In large part, that was why the serious reform of the militia, which began with the appointment of Major General I.J.C. Herbert in 1890, eventually proved so devastating to the French-Canadian role in the militia. Despite French-Canadian ministers and senior officers, despite linguistic enclaves, a British model had persisted. By statute, the General Officer Commanding was British. So were the training, the administration and the official set of values. These values, of course, explicitly repudiated the kind of political arrangements which overlooked limitations of knowledge or efficiency for the sake of representation and partisan satisfaction. There was nothing in the British model which intentionally excluded French Canadians. The British took a keen pride in producing soldiers of the Queen from

---

[20] Gustave d'Orsonnens, *Considérations sur l'organisation militaire de la Confederation Canadienne* (Montréal, 1874), p. 50.

[21] Canada, House of Commons, *Debates*, September 25, 1891, p. 6182; April 8, 1892, p. 1178.

[22] A.C. de Lotbinière Harwood to Sir John A. Macdonald, June 12, 1887, Public Archives of Canada, Caron Papers, vol. 194, ff. 5775-6.

every race and creed. What unified the Imperial forces was that the officers were white, spoke English and shared British values. If, like the renowned Colonel Sir Percy Girouard, they were also French-Canadian, that could even be an advantage. What British officers and their Canadian disciples rarely asked themselves was how far their criteria of military efficiency were relevant to Canada.

The reforming General Herbert was a case in point. A strong Catholic with a perfect command of French, he seemed ideally suited to winning genuine French-Canadian involvement in the force. He certainly tried. He attended camps in Quebec, lectured the troops in their own language, and largely won their affection. At the same time, he routed out inefficient officers, unearthed minor peculations, and enforced discipline without regard to politics. He concentrated much of his energy on the sadly neglected permanent force, reorganizing it, insisting on more rational attitudes to discipline, and sending the better officers, including some French Canadians, to England for further training.[23] However, the scourge of Herbert's reforms seemed to fall more heavily on the French-speaking than the English-speaking units if only because there were more old, unqualified and unsuitable officers to be removed and fewer young enthusiasts to take their place. The fact that permanent force officers were now obliged to acquire a professional competence meant that they had to go to British military schools. In turn, this meant barriers against young French Canadians who might consider a military career but not if it meant divorce from their cultural and linguistic roots.

The more able and reform-minded of Herbert's successors, Major General Edward Hutton and Lord Dundonald, were also bilingual and also concerned to recognize their French-speaking subordinates. Hutton, in particular, set an officer to the task of translating the drill book into French, and issued a highly unpopular order that staff officers would henceforth have to learn French if they expected to be promoted.[24] While Hutton made a deliberate play for the support of French Canadians in his campaign to build a Canadian force to Imperial military specifications, there was little underlying sympathy. As he explained to a British colleague, he believed that Quebec would only really catch the spirit of the imperial crusade " ... when the more energetic and professionally educated English-speaking officers should get at the French-Canadians."[25]

After the South African War the progress of reform in the militia accelerated. Many Canadian officers had added wartime experience to a rising level of professional knowledge. In 1904 the militia Act was changed to open command of the force to Canadian officers, and in 1905 Canada's assumption of responsibility for the two imperial fortresses at Halifax and Esquimalt allowed a considerable expansion of the

---

[23] O.C.C. Pelletier, *Mémoires, souvenirs de famille et récits* (Quebec, 1940), pp. 275-300 describes the experience of one such French-Canadian officer.

[24] Militia General Order (12), February 14, 1899.

[25] Hutton to Lt. Col. Gerald Kitson, January 7, 1899, British Museum, Hutton Papers, add. 50079.

permanent fore. This meant increased responsibility for officers who had taken their profession seriously. Only two of these rising professionals were French-Canadian, Colonel Oscar Pelletier and Colonel François Lessard. Even with these two officers, the effects of professionalism were apparent. While Pelletier, son of the Liberal Speaker of the Senate, retained his roots in Quebec, Lessard had virtually cut his ties with French Canada and was best known in equestrian circles in Toronto where he had spent much of his service.

One institution which contributed to military efficiency and professionalism was the Royal Military College, opened at Kingston in 1876. For the first time a military institution had been created in Canada which paid no attention to French-Canadian needs. Its first commandant, a highly competent British officer, firmly refused to compromise standards for young candidates whose first language was French. One result was that of the first thousand cadets who passed through the college, only thirty-nine were French-Canadian.[26] However, the RMC was only one example of how institutions and innovations which brought greater efficiency to the militia as a whole worked against French-Canadian influence as well. By 1914 the Militia could look back on almost a quarter-century of continuous reform but, in many respects, the French-Canadian part of the force had been left behind. In 1870 there had been fifteen French-Canadian infantry battalions and sixty-four comparable English-speaking units. In 1914 there were now eighty-five English-speaking battalions and still only fifteen French. (The relative size of the two language groups had changed very little during the period from 1870 to 1914). Since 1899 a militia staff course had been training officers for senior appointments in time of war. By 1913 there were fifty-eight graduates; only seven were French-speaking. In 1912 one of the four brigadier-generals and three of the twelve full colonels in the Canadian permanent force were French-Canadian—but only 27 of a total 254 officers. It was in the middle ranks, where wartime advancement would come, that French-Canadian representation was proportionately weakest. When it came to making policy and filling appointments, their absence would be felt.

The advent of Colonel Sam Hughes as the new Conservative Minister of Militia in 1911 altered many of the settled policies of his Liberal predecessor. Borden's choice for the militia portfolio was to have major consequences, precipitating problems which had previously been almost imperceptible. Personally, Hughes always maintained that he bore French-Canadians no ill-will. After all, some of his own ancestors had been Huguenots and two of them had fought under Napoleon at Waterloo. It was characteristic of Hughes's insensitivity that he assumed that these facts would win him friends in French Canada. His past record made that improbable. In 1894, when General Herbert had delivered a speech praising the Papal Zouaves, Hughes, as an Ontario Orangeman, had demanded his dismissal.[27] Four years later he

---

[26] R.A. Preston, *Canada's R.M.C.: A History of the Royal Military College* (Toronto, 1969), p. 70.

[27] Canada, House of Commons, *Debates, May 14, 1894, pp. 2733-4.*

denounced the government for allowing troops to attend the funeral of Cardinal Taschereau. The new Minister had always been much more explicit in his detestation of the permanent force. As a militia officer he had repeatedly tangled with the red tape generated by the professionals, and now he could have his revenge. As many as possible of the older officers, Pelletier among them, were retired. Others, including Lessard, were posted where Hughes could watch them, and militia officers were brought in to fill the vacancies. Some of them were personal cronies of the minister's, others owed their advancement to politics. At Quebec City Pelletier was replaced by Lieutenant Colonel J.P. Landry, former commanding officer of the 61st Regiment and son of the new Conservative Speaker in the Senate. Landry's appointment brought no peace in the Quebec militia. In June 1914, there was a minor explosion when Hughes forbade the Carabiniers Mont-Royal to march in Montreal's traditional Corpus Christi procession, finally relenting enough to permit them to parade without arms.[28] A few weeks later there was another storm when the 17th Régiment de Lévis was refused permission to provide an escort for the newly consecrated Cardinal Bégin.

Both incidents demonstrated Hughes's complete incomprehension of French Canada: both also demonstrated his insistence on controlling every aspect of his department's activities according to a highly personal and impetuous whim. In peacetime Hughes could do his party little good and his country no irreparable harm. In wartime it was different.

The Minister's detestation of professionalism and his absolute confidence in himself were never more in evidence than at the moment war broke out in 1914. Some years earlier, a mobilization plan had been prepared for Canada by British and Canadian staff officers. It projected a regionally and racially balanced force based on the existing militia organization.[29] Hughes had known of the plan, taken little interest in it and, now that it was needed, scrapped it. Mobilization was organized his way, by means of hundreds of telegrams to commanding officers and personal friends. Almost as if it were a principle of life, everything was to be improvised.

In Montreal, the commanding officer of the Carabiniers was invited to meet with senior officers of two English-speaking regiments. The result was the formation of the Royal Montreal Regiment, with the Carabiniers responsible for recruiting two of the eight companies.[30] This was managed with little difficulty and the new unit soon left for the Canadian contingent's brand new staging centre, Valcartier, where

---

[28] *La Presse*, June 18, 1914; Public Archives of Canada, R.L. Borden Papers, o.c. 190, vol. 17, pp. 15614-19.

[29] On the mobilization plan, see Col. A. Fortescue Duguid, *Official History of the Canadian Forces in the Great War, 1914-1919*, General Series, vol. I, *Appendices etc.* (Ottawa, 1938), appx. 11, p. 12. In 1912, Colonel Pelletier proposed one of the few changes in the plan, reducing the contingent from his district from two infantry battalions to one "with full knowledge of local conditions and sentiment."

[30] R.C. Featherstonehaugh, The Royal Montreal Regiment (Montreal, 1927), pp. 4-7.

Hughes was personally engaged in sorting order out of the chaos he had created. The Montreal regiment became the 14th Battalion of the First Contingent. Volunteers from other French-speaking militia units were clustered in the 12th Battalion, together with men from New Brunswick and Prince Edward Island. Of the 36,000 men who appeared at Valcartier, 1,245 claimed French origin, and just over seven hundred came from French-speaking units.[31] They were now divided, minorities in two battalions, with individuals scattered elsewhere in the contingent. Although Hughes could hardly have cared, for the first time a Canadian military force was being organized without apparent thought about providing for adequate French-Canadian representation. To be fair, there was no specific battalion from the Maritimes either.

By the time the First Canadian Division had finished its training and was ready to move on from England to France, its French-Canadian representation was limited to a single company of the 14th Battalion, one forty-eighth of the divisional infantry. The 12th Battalion was left in England to provide reinforcements. Within weeks of entering the line, the First Division had won enormous prestige from its role in the crucial Second Battle of Ypres. From its ranks were to come most of the commanders who led the subsequent Canadian divisions and brigades and, eventually, the Canadian Corps itself. The qualifications of men who had actually won their experience in battle had usually to take precedence over those of men whose rank had been won in peacetime manoeuvres or through friendship with the Minister. The few French-Canadian officers in the First Division gained advancement like the others, although the fate of most of them was to return to Quebec for the hopeless and humiliating struggle to recruit their compatriots for the front.[32]

Responsibility for the failure to provide a sufficient and distinctive French-Canadian representation in the Canadian Expeditionary Force belongs to Hughes alone. There were just sufficient suitable French Canadians at Valcartier to complete a battalion. However, not realizing how much of their opportunity was now irrevocably lost, French Canadians began to organize to ensure that they would be more adequately represented in the second Canadian contingent. Arthur Mignault, a French-Canadian industrialist and military enthusiast, offered $50,000 to meet the cost of raising a French-Canadian battalion. A delegation of fifty-eight prominent Quebec politicians, businessmen and professionals travelled to Ottawa to lobby Sir Robert Borden. Perhaps because Hughes was absent in England, their campaign was successful. Authority was granted for the organization of a "Royal French-Canadian Regiment" as the 22nd Battalion of the C.E.F. Lieutenant-Colonel F.M. Gaudet, an

---

31   Duguid, *Official History, Appendices*, pp. 56-8.
32   The most senior French-Canadian officer in the First Contingent was Lt. Col. H.A. Panet, a permanent force officer who commanded the Royal Canadian Horse Artillery Brigade in 1914 and, by 1916, was commanding the 2nd Divisional Artillery. Another former RMC cadet, Thomas L. Tremblay, began the war as an artillery major, commanded the 22nd Battalion for a time, and ended the war as a brigadier general.

RMC graduate who had been managing the Dominion Arsenal at Quebec, was made available as the commanding officer. On October 15, 1914, 15,000 Montrealers gathered in the Parc Sohmer to see a galaxy of politicians and publicists of all political persuasions and to hear Laurier cry: "If there are still a few drops of the blood of Dollard and his companions in the veins of the Canadians who are present at this meeting, you will enlist in a body for this cause is just as sacred as the one for which Dollard and his companions gave their lives."[33]

Bourassa scornfully denounced the meeting as an "explosion of empty and sterile chauvinism,"[34] and, in fact, the response was a little less than electric. Twelve days after the Parc Sohmer meeting, the newspapers were claiming that more than nine hundred men had enlisted in the 22nd; in fact, the regimental rolls showed only 27 officers and 575 other ranks. French Canadians were diverted from other battalions recruiting in the province and a final draft of a hundred was needed to bring the unit up to strength before it could go overseas.[35] However, on May 20, 1915, the 22nd Battalion left Halifax for England, and by September 20 it had entered the front line, the first French-Canadian battalion in the Canadian Corps—and the last.

For the first time French Canadians could feel that they were represented among the fighting troops. They also felt entitled to be represented among the senior commanders. Having failed to get a major appointment in the First Contingent, Colonel J.P. Landry was given command of a brigade in the Second Division. However, shortly before the formation was transferred to France, the divisional commander, Major General Sir Sam Steele, and two of the three brigadiers, including Landry, were relieved, to be replaced by officers who had served with the First Division. It was almost inevitable. Steele and his officers were too old or inexperienced to take their men into action. However, in many French-Canadian newspapers Landry's removal was simply interpreted as a spiteful blow at one of their own, the son, moreover, of a man who was leading the struggle of the Franco-Ontarians against Regulation 17.[36]

Having sent off two complete divisions, the Minister of Militia came to the conclusion that the easiest way to find recruits for the Canadian Expeditionary Force was to invite prominent men to accept commissions and to raise their own battalions. The North had tried a similar technique during the American Civil War, with particularly unfortunate results, and now Canada followed suit. There was little

---

[33] Skelton, *Laurier*, II, 437; Laurier-Borden, September 23, 1914, Public Archives of Canada, R.L. Borden Papers, O.C. 209, f. 21272.

[34] Rumilly, *Québec*, XXIX, 112.

[35] On recruiting the 22nd Battalion, see Duguid, *Official History, Appendices*, no. 711, pp. 344-5; Col. J-H. Chabelle, *Histoire du 22ᵉ Bataillon Canadien Français*, tome I, *1914-1919* (Montreal, 1952), pp. 20-26.

[36] Wade, *French-Canadians*, II, 169; Landry to Borden, n.d., R.L. Borden Papers, O.C., 4141, ff. 43456 ff; Perley to Borden, June 14, 1915, Perley Papers, vol. IV, f. 89. (Regulation 17 ended public Francophone education in Ontario.)

recognition of the necessity of finding replacements for casualties in battalions already in France, nor was there any firm decision on the size of the eventual Canadian contribution, a subject on which Hughes held characteristically grandiose ideas. Instead, men were simply promised that they could go to war with their own friends and neighbours, under the command of the trusted and highly popular gentlemen who addressed them from the recruiting platforms. Politicians, would-be politicians, contractors, businessmen, all blossomed forth as khaki-clad colonels. Battalions of Scotsmen and Irishmen, of sportsmen, Orangemen, Methodists and Bantams—men so short they did not reach the officially authorized minimum height of 5'2"—were all authorized.[37]

To spur on the efforts to find volunteers, recruiting leagues and committees were formed, frequently headed by clergymen, convincing others as ever that they were doing the work of the Lord. In Montreal the local military commander, Major-General E.W. Wilson, sought to launch his recruiting drive under the joint sponsorship of a Catholic priest and a Protestant clergyman. He found his clergyman without difficulty, the Rev. C.A. Williams, a Methodist minister of unfashionably broad-minded views. Unfortunately, the French-speaking community did not produce a suitable priest and, as a result, Williams became an acting major and the only Director of Recruiting for the Montreal area. This was the basis for the charge, uttered with some embellishment by Rodolphe Lemieux and other Liberals, that Hughes had handed over recruiting in Quebec to an Orangeman.[38]

Although the legend of Hughes and the Methodist recruiting officer was based on an unfair distortion, it was a mild offence compared with the confidence trick, realized or not, which Hughes was playing on his would-be battalion commanders and the men they recruited. It was a trick involving many influential men, not least the Prime Minister himself, who gave his name and considerable money to the task of raising an impressive Nova Scotia brigade of four complete battalions. In fact, almost none of the specially raised battalions ever reached France as a unit. By August 1916, the Canadian Corps was complete, and all of its forty-eight battalions were in France. Most of them had been sent to England early in 1915 and a few had been organized there. Meanwhile, more than two hundred battalions were being recruited in Canada in the full conviction that they would be going into action as units. They didn't. Many never even reached England. Some that did were posted to the Fifth Canadian Division, a formation kept to defend England against German invasion and to provide a dignified command for Hughes's son, Garnet. The great majority of the battalions were simply broken up, with the senior officers left to fill time and the junior officers and men shipped to France as reinforcements. By the time Hughes had been dismissed as Minister of Militia in November 1916, the damage had been done. The accumulation of disgruntled senior officers in England,

---

[37] Col. G.W.L. Nicholson, *Canadian Expeditionary Force, 1914-1919* (Ottawa, 1962), pp. 212-4.

[38] On Williams, see Ibid., p. 221 and Borden Papers, O.C. 310.

discontent among the would-be recruits, and the general disorder and mismanagement of Hughes's recruiting methods were unpleasant legacies for his harried successors.[39]

All of this is necessary background to understand the sad fate of efforts to raise more French-Canadian battalions to take their place beside the 22nd Battalion in France and, as many French Canadians hoped, to form a complete French-Canadian brigade of four battalions. Early in 1915 authority was granted to raise additional French-speaking battalions. By the end of 1915, a 41st Battalion had been sent to England to serve as a reinforcement depot for the 22nd, and five other units were still recruiting. The most interesting was the 163rd.

Armand Lavergne had rapidly become one of the most outspoken Nationalist critics of the war. He was also a militia officer, indeed the successor of Landry in command of the 61st Régiment de Montmagny. For some reason, Hughes retained a warm affection for Lavergne and in October 1915, he invited his friend to raise a battalion. Bluntly and publicly, Lavergne refused the offer, dismissing the war as "a somewhat interesting adventure in a foreign country."[40] To general astonishment, the offer was taken up by an even more tempestuous battler in the Nationalist cause, Olivar Asselin. His reasons were complex and not totally convincing. The facts were, as his biographer has pointed out, that Asselin loved France and ached to see action.[41] Although he insisted that the actual command of his battalion, the 163rd, must go to a more seasoned officer, Asselin became a major and threw himself, with all his notable energy, into the task of finding recruits. No sooner had he collected two-thirds of his men than he discovered that another political colonel, Tancrède Pagnuelo, had been authorized to raise a battalion in the same area. A furious Asselin sped to Ottawa and extracted authority to transfer his fledgling battalion to Bermuda. As a further revenge, recruits in the rival battalion were transferred to the 163rd. Quite beside himself at his fancied injustice, the unhappy Pagnuelo virtually told his men to desert, an outburst which won him court martial and a six months prison sentence.[42]

By the summer of 1916 a total of eleven battalions had been authorized in French Canada. One was in France, two were in England, one was training in Nova Scotia, and the 163rd was in Bermuda. There was one at Quebec City, providing reinforcements for overseas, and the remaining battalions were collected at Valcartier. As military units they barely existed, undisciplined, weak in numbers, and plagued by bad officers and desertion. However, for many in French Canada this agglomeration of military ineffectives represented a fresh hope of forming a distinct

---

[39] On the confusion in England, see D.M.A.R. Vince, "The Acting Overseas Sub-Militia Council and the Resignation of Sir Sam Hughes," *Canadian Historical Review*, XXXI (March, 1950). For the experience of a victim of the recruiting methods, see Leslie M. Frost, *Fighting Men* (Toronto, 1967).

[40] *Le Devoir*, November 2, 1915.

[41] Marcel A. Gagnon, *La vie orageuse d'Olivar Asselin* (Montreal, 1962), p. 174.

[42] *Canadian Annual Review, 1916*, p. 353.

French-Canadian brigade. Such was the advice which poured in on Sir Robert Borden and his colleagues, some of its from Gustave Lanctot, a future historian and at that time an officer in the 163rd. Like those of others, Lanctot's arguments blended political and military considerations. Creating the new brigade would give French Canadians representation on the higher staff and would convince the men in the ranks that they would be properly understood. "It will thus satisfy the province at large, civilians and military men, with the result of increasing the goodwill in all spheres and of disposing better the people for the party in power who will grant this proposal."[43]

There was not much possibility. The senior officers of the Canadian Corps were unenthusiastic about upsetting their increasingly effective military machine to insert a politically inspired brigade. Nor did the government look kindly on suggestions, even from Lord Atholstan of the Montreal *Star*, that French Canadians might be recruited for the French army if they were reluctant to fight for Britain. In any event, there was sufficient difficulty in finding enough men to fill the ranks of the one battalion of French Canadians actually at the front. On September 15-18, 1916, the 22nd Battalion won great distinction and lost a third of its men in capturing Courcelette. Two weeks later another third were lost at Regina Trench. It proved enormously difficult to fill the gaps. Two of the Valcartier battalions were shipped to England as reinforcements, another was transferred to the forestry corps. In November the 163rd sailed from Bermuda for England and, after only a month's reprieve, it, too, was broken up.

By then the possibilities of voluntary recruiting in Quebec were long past. In July 1916, the government had arranged for wide publication of a letter from Captain Talbot Papineau to his cousin, Henri Bourassa. It was an eloquent appeal, but Papineau, an officer in Princess Patricia's Canadian Light Infantry, and who was then writing news stories for the Canadian War Records Office, had little but his name to use to appeal to French Canada. Bourassa's reply, a cool but impressive summary of his arguments against the Canadian war effort, was an expression of what a majority of his compatriots were now feeling. Throughout Quebec and particularly in the major centres, the influence of the Nationalist leaders was in the ascendant in the summer of 1916. French Canada was no longer listening quietly to its established leaders. In August there were anti-recruiting riots in Montreal. In the spring of 1917, P.-E. Blondin, one of Borden's last remaining French-Canadian cabinet ministers, resigned his portfolio and, aided by the aged General Lessard, tried to raise a 258th Battalion. A series of meetings, sometimes disrupted, a cold response from the village curés, and a total of 92 recruits were all the two men could show for their efforts.

The period of voluntary recruiting was over. The government would now turn to conscription. French Canadians, who had been converted from sympathy through

---

[43] Lanctot to Borden, March 17, 1916, R.L. Borden Papers, O.C. 209, ff. 21285-88.

neutrality to hostility to their fellow countrymen's war, would now be compelled to go along. Canada, for generations to come, would pay the price.

After the war, at least one French Canadian was converted to the merits of conscription: "le volontariat tel qu'il est pratiqué chez nous est pour plusieurs raisons un mode d'enrôlement à la fois inéquitable et ruineux," wrote Olivar Asselin.[44] It was a conclusion which Sir Etienne Taché, at least, would have acknowledged with a sense of vindication. The voluntary nature of the Canadian war effort until 1917 was inevitable. The kind of foresight that could anticipate the dimensions of the eventual Canadian military commitment would not have been politically influential in 1914. However, the frenzied patriotism, frequently from non-combatants of both sexes, which accompanied voluntary recruiting, the headcounting and the comparisons, the contradictions about whether or not French Canada was playing her part, all tied in with the completely emotional debate about Ontario French-language schools, were what really drove Canada apart in 1915 and 1916. By 1917 conscription could seem to many in English-speaking Canada as a vengeance which, with its carefully adjusted exemptions, would fall exclusively on Quebec.

There was also division within French Canada between those who moved to Bourassa's position of standing apart from the war and those who, like Laurier, the higher clergy and even Talbot Papineau, were terrified of the consequences for Quebec of isolating herself and who therefore struggled, by making speeches, trying to raise troops and, in the case of Papineau, actually fighting and dying, to prove that French Canada was really playing her part.

In all of this, the military institutions of Canada really gave very little help. By 1914 French-Canadian representation in the Militia was a mere formality. Thanks to Sam Hughes, even the formality was forgotten when the moment of crisis came. A weak prime minister, a minister of militia who behaved like a stage generalissimo, a recruiting campaign based on confusion and deception, these were no instruments for persuading French Canadians to enlist in a war for which they had little basic inclination.

---

[44] Gagnon, *Asselin*, p. 193.

Social Reform and the Great War

Section 16

One effect of Canadians' feeling of commitment to the war effort was to strengthen demands for social reform within Canada itself. Late 19th century industrialisation had created new social problems and made old ones more visible in the new large urban concentrations. At first, people had responded in traditional ways, with Christian charity and voluntary welfare work. Gradually, though, many came to feel that such approaches were inadequate, and that government would have to act to reform society itself, to make it healthier, safer, and fairer.

Of these two articles, Mitchinson's throws particular light on the origins and evolution of the reform movement, while Thompson's discusses the connexion between the world war and the accomplishment of some reform goals in Canada.

Why were women so actively involved in the reform movement? Why did they see alcohol as such an important social problem? Why did they come to feel that government action was necessary to solve such problems? Why did the WCTU come to support the enfranchisement of women? Did it want to "liberate" women—to revolutionise the role of women in society? How did the war help to bring about both prohibition and women's suffrage?

Notice how important traditional Christian morality was in inspiring early 20th century reformers. Both these articles stress the sense of moral fervour that reform attracted. How was that related to the spirit which the war inspired?

This subject, like the preceding ones, is covered in the general survey of the period by R.C.Brown & G.R.Cook, *Canada, 1896-1921: A Nation Transformed*. A survey of Canadian women's history can be found in Alison Prentice et al, *Canadian Women: A History*.

The WCTU: "For God, Home and Native Land": A Study in Nineteenth-Century Feminism

Wendy Mitchinson

The organizational woman is a familiar phenomenon today whether she belongs to a feminist group, a church society or one of a myriad of other women's organizations. But this was not always the case. In the early part of the nineteenth century women were seldom organized, prevented by distance, poor transportation facilities and lack of time. Only the more privileged could overcome these obstacles and those who did tended to form local church and benevolent societies. By 1900, however, this situation had altered greatly. Women's organizations had increased in number: many continued the work of the church and benevolent societies which had formed earlier in the century; others formed to provide new expressive outlets for women; still others organized to reform what women saw as problems in society. All represented the ability and desire of many Canadian women to become active outside the domestic sphere.[1]

Several reasons account for this extraordinary expansion of women's activities: transportation had improved, making it easier for groups of women to meet together; towns and cities were growing in size, thus enlarging the membership potential of women's groups; and the increasing affluence of Canadian society meant that more middle-class women had leisure time to devote to women's organizations. In 1871, 81.2 per cent of the Canadian population lived in areas classed as rural. By 1901 this had declined to 62.5 per cent. The greater population density of cities heightened the need for institutional responses on the part of society—orphanages, refuge homes and hospitals—philanthropic areas in which women had long been involved. Cities also

---

[1] The following is only a partial list of the women's clubs which were formed in the latter part of the last century: the Woman's Auxiliary to the Board of the Domestic and Foreign Missionary Society of the Church of England in Canada, (1885); The Woman's Baptist Missionary Union of the Maritime Provinces, (1885); The Woman's Foreign Missionary Society of the Presbyterian Church in Canada, Eastern and Western Division, (1876); The Woman's Missionary Society of the Methodist Church, (1881); The Woman's Art Association of Canada, (1890); the National Council of Women, (1893); the Woman's Christian Temperance Union of Canada, (1885); the Young Women's Christian Association, (1893); the Dominion Order of the King's Daughters (1891); the Victorian Order of Nurses, (1898); the National Home Reading Union, (1895); the Aberdeen Association, (1897); the Girls' Friendly Society of Canada, (1882); the Imperial Order of the Daughters of the Empire, (1900); the Dominion Women's Enfranchisement Association, (1889); plus numerous local musical clubs, historical societies, literary societies, dramatic, athletic and charitable associations.

accentuated the problems of poverty, crime and intemperance. Many Canadian women realized such problems could not be offset through traditional benevolent activities and responded by searching for the causes of these problems. The result was the formation of reform organizations designed to eradicate the source of a specific social ill and not simply to ameliorate its symptoms. The willingness of many women to become so involved reflected an important change that was occurring in their lives.[2]

Through the latter half of the nineteenth century, Canada was slowly emerging from a commercial to an industrialized society. At the same time it was becoming more urbanized. As both these processes occurred, the workplace became separated from the home, where women were increasingly isolated. The domestic isolation of women was complemented by what historians have referred to as the "cult of domesticity", the dominating image of which was "woman as mother". Ironically, as woman's prestige in society was being enhanced by her maternal role, the actual fertility of women was declining. In 1871 the registered legitimate fertility rate in Canada was similar to what it had been in the eighteenth century, 378 births per 1,000 women aged 15 to 49 years. By 1891, however, it had declined by 24 per cent to 285 births per 1,000 women aged 15 to 49 years. This decline was especially extreme in urban areas. Although women were having fewer children than had been the case earlier in the century this did not necessarily lessen women's commitment to the domestic sphere; indeed, through an intensification of the mother-child relationship it may have increased it. Women were becoming, in fact as well as in ideal, the emotional centre of the home and family.[3]

Women may have had influence within the home but the ideal of domesticity certainly limited them outside it. The emergence of women from the domestic sphere through women's organizations was a response to their dissatisfaction with this situation. Many women wanted to preserve their status within and control of the family by becoming active in society. As well, the seeming increase in power and prestige that women had gained through the rise of the domestic ideal led to a desire to publicly assert and extend that power outside the home. The easiest way to

---

[2] In Ontario and Quebec, the most populated provinces, 22.8 per cent of the population lived in centres classed as urban in 1881. By 1891 this had increased to 33.2 per cent and 29.2 per cent respectively. No province, however, matched British Columbia, whose urban population increased by 30.6 per cent between 1881 and 1891. *Census of Canada 1890-1891*, Vol. 4, p. 401; *Sixth Census of Canada*, 1921, Vol. 1, p. 346.

[3] Barbara Welter, "The Cult of True Womanhood 1820-1860," *American Quarterly*, Vol. 18 (Summer 1966), pp. 258-71; Jacques Henripin, *Trends and Factors of Fertility in Canada* (Ottawa: Statistics Canada, 1972), pp. 39, 36. See Ann D. Gordon and Mari Jo Buhle, "Sex and Class in Colonial and Nineteenth-Century American," in Bernice Carroll, ed. *Liberating Women's History* (Chicago: University of Illinois Press, 1976), p. 286, for a discussion of the intensification of the mother-child relationship in the American context.

accomplish this, given the context of Canadian society at the time, was to rationalize it by an appeal to domesticity.[4]

Women's reform organizations were one way in which Canadian women hoped to protect the family and assert themselves in an acceptable way. Each organization was initially formed to right a specific wrong, but once formed, each tended to involve itself in a number of reform enterprises. The Woman's Christian Temperance Union was such an organization. It provides an example of the emergence of women from the domestic sphere to an active participation in society.

Formation and Platform

The first local WCTU was formed in Ontario in 1874, the first provincial union in 1877 in Ontario and the Dominion Union in 1883. By 1900, the Woman's Christian Temperance Union had approximately 10,000 members. This made the WCTU one of the largest women's organizations of the time and certainly much larger than any of the suffrage societies. As well, the WCTU was a truly national organization and was located in both small towns and urban centres across Canada, whereas the Dominion Women's Enfranchisement Association, the one national suffrage organization, was essentially based in Toronto.

The Union very early adopted prohibition as its main platform. While most reform organizations in the nineteenth century emphasized the importance of adjusting the individual to the existing norms of society, temperance organizations emphasized the adjustment of society to create an atmosphere of temperance for the individual. By mid-century, temperance advocates had concluded that voluntary appeal did not work. When the state of Main introduced a compulsory temperance law—that is, prohibition—Canadian temperance advocates quickly followed its lead. Consequently, by the time the WCTU was formed in 1874, prohibition had become *the* weapon against intemperance. But because it depended on government support, its adoption by the WCTU paved the way to an eventual confrontation between the temperance union and the elected representatives of male society, if and when the latter refused to adopt prohibition.[5]

---

[4] The second hypothesis has been suggested by Daniel Scott Smith's concept of domestic feminism. See Daniel Scott Smith, "Family Limitation, Sexual Control, and Domestic Feminism in Victorian America," in Mary Hartman, Lois W. Banner, eds. *Clio's Consciousness Raised* (New York: Harper & Row, 1974), pp. 119-37.

[5] For a discussion of the early temperance movement in Canada and the way in which it was influenced by the American, see J.K. Chapman, "The Mid-19th Century Temperance Movements in New Brunswick and Main," *Canadian Historical Review,* XXXV (1954), pp. 43-60. The confrontation with government was experienced by other women's organizations much later since few advocated such controversial reforms. Eventually, however, most women's groups were faced with government reluctance to implement their reforms.

The WCTU had few qualms about supporting prohibition. Its members believed it to be a radical reform but an essential one. The atrocities of war were negligible beside the atrocities of the liquor trade. As a foe of morality "it turns men into demons, and makes women an easy prey to lust." Because the majority of convicted criminals were known to drink, the WCTU concluded that alcohol caused crime and argued that supporting such a criminal population was uneconomical. Intemperance was ruining the physical health of Canadians as well, one member of the WCTU even linking the spread of cholera with the consumption of alcohol. The statistics of alcohol consumption served only to increase these fears. In 1871 the total alcohol consumption per capita, 15 years of age and older, was 1.19 imperial gallons, rising to 1.29 in 1873 and in 1874, the year in which the WCTU formed, to 1.42. WCTU members were convinced something had to be done to prevent the terrible toll in human suffering that this increase represented to them.[6]

They believed women, as innocent victims of an invasion of alcohol into their homes, suffered most from the liquor trade, and they exploited this appeal to the fullest. "How can Christian women sit still and be quiet while women's cries for help are in their ears?" they asked. Children's cries were also heard. The Children's Aid Society in Vancouver noted in its first annual report that, with one exception, "Every case which has been brought before us had been brought about through drink." Temperance women felt they had a special duty as women to protect these children. Certainly men did not seem willing to do anything about alcohol abuse, perhaps because they were the main consumers of alcohol and profiteers from the liquor trade. The WCTU believed most women did not drink. Where men were seemingly unable to act, then, women could and would. A social ill such as intemperance could not be kept isolated; it reached out and affected temperate and intemperate alike. It had to be stopped.[7]

The WCTU was not particularly concerned about the individual inebriate—the union had neither the resources nor the time to help individuals. They were more concerned with the effects of intemperance on society, the way in which the inebriate hurt innocent people such as his wife and children, and the way in which he undermined the strength of society.

Blaming alcohol for society's ills was a comfortable belief. It did not threaten the economic status of the temperance women or their families because they did not talk about intemperance in personal terms. In fact, their belief in prohibition was a reflection of their class status. Most executive members of the WCTU were married to lawyers, businessmen, doctors, journalists and clergymen. Considering the connection temperance women made between intemperance, crime and sexual

---

[6] Annual Report, Woman's Christian Temperance Union of Ontario, 1898, p. 96; ibid., 1899, pp. 50-51; Robert Popham, Wolfgang Schmidt, *Statistics of Alcohol Use and Alcoholism in Canada 1871-1956* (Toronto: University of Toronto Press, 1958), pp. 15-25.

[7] Annual Report, WCTU, Ontario, 1882, pp. 5-6; Anne Angus, *Children's Aid Society of Vancouver 1901-1951* (Vancouver: Children's Aid Society, 1951), p. 5.

immorality, it is not surprising that they saw in intemperance a challenge to their middle-class way of life. It was the foreign element in an otherwise ordered society.[8]

The Politicization Process

Only the state, through legislation, could ensure a temperate society. To persuade the various levels of government to respond, the WCTU became actively involved in the public sphere. Its members believed they had a responsibility as *women* to protect not only their own but all homes.[9]

One of the WCTU's methods was the use of petitions. They were circulated for signatures, then forwarded to the appropriate level of government in the hope that once officials realized there was a good deal of support for prohibition, they would act. This naive view of the democratic process assumed a common morality for all and, in fact, the existence of an absolute "right" in society, a notion which derived from a fundamentalist interpretation of Christian morality and the members' own political inexperience.[10]

These petitions did have limited success. Through them, governments became aware of the demand for prohibition, and usually responded by granting a plebiscite on the question. The plebiscite was a good tactic, for it allowed Canadians to inform the government of their views on a controversial problem on which the government was hesitant to act. If supported by an overwhelming majority, plebiscites permitted the government to act with few fears of political reprisals. Prohibition was undoubtedly a controversial question. It not only attracted opposition from the liquor interests, but also from those opposed to government intervention in the day-to-day lives of individuals, especially in a practice that was as widespread as drinking was in the nineteenth century.

Petitions and plebiscites were the high points in the preventive public work of the WCTU. They both legitimized temperance work and forced Canadians to consider

---

[8] The percentage of the WCTU executive who were traceable was small, only 38 per cent.

WCTU *Executive 1890-1901; Occupation of Husband:*

	Traceable	%
Business	8	19
Law	6	14
Ministry	9	21
Medicine	4	9.5
Journalism	5	12

(These figures represent only the professions with the largest representations.)

[9] State intervention was gradually adopted by most women's reform organizations. It was the method by which they could cope with an increasingly complex society.

[10] The importance of religious faith for the WCTU will be examined later.

the question of control. Generally the WCTU's activity was more mundane. Members painstakingly distributed literature and called on electors to vote for temperance advocates. They appealed to "their fathers, husbands, brothers, sons and friends who possessed the right of suffrage to exercise this right in the interest of temperance and total abstinence." The WCTU approached clergymen, church members, teachers of Sunday schools and public schools and heads of organizations such as the Knights of Labor, requesting them to use their influence to dissuade people from drinking. It asked doctors to stop prescribing liquor as medicine. Members tried to persuade anyone in a position of prestige to recognize their work, or any part of it, thus using their influence as women in a very traditional way, that is, through moral suasion.[11]

Yet they did not limit themselves to this tactic. The WCTU was so determined to achieve prohibition that it even gave guarded support to a new political party. In March 1888, through the efforts of male temperance organizations, Canada's New Party was formed. Soon afterwards, in the WCTU publication, the *Woman's Journal*, Mrs. Rockwell, a prominent member of the union, appealed to her readers to use their "influence with husbands, fathers and brothers, for the first and only Political Party committed to the accomplishment of the prohibition of the liquor traffic." The Dominion WCTU resolved to give "individual support to the party which will unequivocally put the plan of Prohibition in its platform". This resolution could only apply to the New Party; however, the party foundered. Old party loyalties remained entrenched and, as the corresponding secretary of the Ontario WCTU reported, "Politics first, politics last, politics everytime, each party afraid of the temperance question."[12]

This was proven again and again. In provincial plebiscites in Manitoba, Prince Edward Island, Ontario and Nova Scotia, prohibition seemed, to the WCTU, overwhelmingly endorsed; yet the respective governments did nothing. Unfortunately for the temperance women, greater disillusionment lay ahead.

In 1896 the Liberal Party under Wilfrid Laurier promised a national plebiscite on prohibition. Great excitement pervaded the temperance forces. As the president of the Nova Scotia WCTU declared,

> The question of Prohibition is at last a Political issue. Not as a weak, struggling Third Party, but a live question with which both parties feel that they must deal whether they will or not.... The world is turning to our country today, with great interest for a

---

[11] Annual Report, WCTU, Ontario, Oct. 24, 1878, Resolutions; Annual Report, Woman's Christian Temperance Union of British Columbia, 1889, p. 18.

[12] Ruth Spence, *Prohibition in Canada* (Toronto: Ontario Branch of the Dominion Alliance, 1919), p. 144; Annual Report, WCTU of the Dominion of Canada, 1889, p. 3; ibid., p. 18; ibid., 1891, 0. 43.

solution of the Liquor Question. It is nearer a solution with us than anywhere else on earth.[13]

The women naturally felt they should be able to vote in the plebiscite. When this was refused, even the Nova Scotia WCTU, usually more quiescent than others about the enfranchisement of women, showed its exasperation.

> Dear women, are we free and intelligent citizens of a civilized country, or are we the irresponsible nonentities that our government reckons us? If the former in the name of all that is just and right in the name of all that is pure and lovely and of good report; in the name of God and home and humanity, let us rise and claim the citizen's heritage—the right of self-government! If the latter then may we write "failure," not only of the cause of prohibition, but of every other righteous reform for the stream never rises above the mothers of men. If they be "small, slight ...miserable," how shall we grow?

Once again the women argued that they should be allowed to enter society in order to protect their homes; moreover, as the domestic force in society they should be encouraged to do so. Many of these women were becoming increasingly frustrated and bitter about being dependent on men to determine the nature of the society in which they lived. They used all the power they had as women to obtain a favourable result, but in the end they could only watch while men voted. The plebiscite took place on September 28, 1898. Every province with the exception of Quebec voted for prohibition, for a net majority of 13,687. The temperance forces felt this was a victory; the government, whose support lay in the province of Quebec, did not.[14]

With this defeat the women of the WCTU lost their faith that governments act in the best interests of the people. In their eyes, prohibition was never a question of individual rights but of moral rights, and it believed no government had the power to make what was morally wrong a legal right. The state was an active agent in society and as such had a responsibility to do "not what shall punish wrong-doing so much as what shall tend to right doing." The Canadian government legalized the liquor trade and, "for a price, for revenue, makes the whole nation, women and all, party to its own degradation." The only solution was for temperance women to have representation at all levels of government.[15]

One reform essential to this process was the enfranchisement of women. Appealing to the good will of men in power had failed. The alternative, then, was for women to represent themselves. By supporting a controversial reform, the WCTU

---

[13] Annual Report, WCTU, Nova Scotia, 1896, p. 27.
[14] Ibid., 1897, p. 3; Rev. W. Peck, *A Short History of the Liquor Traffic* (n.p., 1929), p. 14.
[15] Annual Report, WCTU N.S., 1897, p. 24; Annual Report, WCTU Canada, 1892, p. 53.

women had confronted their own lack of power as women. With their espousal of suffrage they went on record as supporting two of the most controversial reforms of nineteenth-century Canada. From a desire to protect their homes through the protection of society, these Canadian temperance women had come far. One way in which they met the challenge was to hold fast to the traditional concept of themselves as women, that is, they did not support suffrage as a right owed to them as individuals, but as a useful means by which to meet their feminine responsibility—the care of the family.

The WCTU, Women's Suffrage and a Sense of Identity

The WCTU had not always supported the enfranchisement of women. In the early years of organization Letitia Youmans, WCTU president, deliberately avoided the issue of women's rights and stressed the protection of home and children. In this way she hoped to gain support for the union.

> So strong was the opposition in Canada to what was commonly termed "women's rights," that I had good reason to believe that should I advocate the ballot for women in connection with my temperance work, it would most effectively block the way, and it was already uphill work for a woman to appear on a public platform.[16]

In the 1870s, the suffrage question had been a divisive issue. By the 1890s, after the WCTU had come face to face with government intransigence, it was acknowledged as *the* weapon against the liquor interests.

The WCTU stressed the good that would result if women were given the vote. Mrs. Jacob Spence, first superintendent of the Ontario WCTU's Franchise Department and mother of Canadian temperance leader F.S. Spence, explained the reasons best:

> It is not the clamor of ambition, ignorance or frivolity trying to gain position. It is the prayer of earnest, thoughtful, Christian women in behalf of their children and their children's children. It is in the interest of our homes, our divinely-appointed place, to protect the home against the licensed evil which is the enemy of the home, and also to aid in our efforts to advance God's kingdom beyond the bounds of our homes.
> It is only by legislation that the roots of great evils can be touched, and for want of the ballot we stand powerless in face of our most

---

[16] Letitia Youmans, *Campaign Echoes* (Toronto: William Briggs, 1893), pp. 206-207.

terrible foe, the legalized liquor traffic. The liquor sellers are not afraid of our conventions, but they are afraid of our ballots.

The appeal to woman's maternal role attracted many women who might otherwise have rejected such a reform. Home and family were the cornerstones of society; an attack on one was an attack on the other.[17]

The connection between prohibition and votes for women was made clear. Where it was not, support for the franchise was weakened. In the Maritimes, for example, there seemed to be little concern over the ballot except among the WCTU unions, and even this was negligible when compared to other provincial unions. One reason was that the Maritimes, more than the other provinces, took advantage of the *Scott Act*, the local option law, with the result that they had the lowest per capital alcohol consumption in Canada. Because of this virtual prohibition in the Maritimes, the connection between temperance and the enfranchisement of women could not be easily made. There, only the justice argument for suffrage remained. It was a political appeal, one that suggested a challenge to the established order that would force women out from behind their concerns of home and family into the world. Few women in the nineteenth century identified with this concept, for it negated the altruism which was seen as the source of their influence in Canadian society.

The struggle for the franchise was the epitome of the temperance women's confidence in themselves, a confidence which had emerged only slowly. In the early years they were very hesitant, even to the point of discussing whether a woman should lead a public prayer unless careful scrutiny of the audience revealed the absence of men. Such timidity was understandable. The WCTU had formed at a time when women were not used to speaking in public, and although this timidity lessened as the women learned to run meetings and publicly express themselves, it never disappeared. Certainly their attitude toward working with men remained ambivalent. On the one hand, they encouraged men's support through honourary memberships and the occasional men's auxiliaries. On the other hand, men were not allowed to vote in their meetings. There were other men's-only and mixed temperance organizations, but there was only one *Woman's* Christian Temperance Union. Its members formed a wholly female society in which they were comfortable and in which their individual efforts were recognized.[18]

The campaign for prohibition was a significant one for the temperance women. The liquor interests represented "the heaviest monied monopoly on the continent. It has an outpost in every town. It cows legislation. Its grip is upon the throttle valve of all political enginery." To counter such evil, the women of the WCTU had to be strong. Their special mission allowed no compromise, even to attract new members.

---

[17] Annual Report, WCTU Ontario, 1880, p. 10. For further information on the suffrage movement in Canada and the role the WCTU played, see Catherine Cleverdon, *The Woman Suffrage Movement in Canada*, 2nd ed. (Toronto: University of Toronto Press, 1974).

[18] *The Templar Quarterly*, (Aug. 1897), p. 28.

> I have heard it hinted some, both within and without our fold, that our burning need was an influx of the upper tendom, "to give tone to the movement," to popularize it. If the money and influence secured in this way were not counter-balanced by some shrinkage of our principles, to accommodate the less rigid notions of those educated to a polite tolerance of wrong, we would doubtless be the gainers. Yet, the "if" is a large and serious one. It is to be feared that the Dons would have more to get than to give. The common people have ever been the bond and sinew of successful revolutions, whether in morals or estates.[19]

The revolution they wanted was one of morals and attitudes. It was a world where their position as leaders would be recognized and where they would receive the accolades which normally went to "society" women. As one member explained, "While we believe there are many good women leading a social life, yet we believe no true woman whose spiritual sensibilities have not been benumbed by habit and custom, finds in this a satisfying portion." A woman was to be admired for what she did herself and not for her husband or family connections. This belief provided these organizational women with a feeling of unity and devotion to one another and to their leaders.[20]

This feeling of solidarity is evident in the following description of Frances Willard, president of the American and World WCTU. One member of the Canadian WCTU recalled with quiet reverence her first contact with Miss Willard.

> At the first appearance of her calm sweet face, I was enraptured and before she had closed, her thrilling words and the spirit within her had so filled my heart that I would have been more than willing to have left all and followed her.... As I look back through the vista of years to this first knowledge of Miss Willard, I think I have a dim realization of the feelings of the disciples when our Master and Saviour stood revealed to them in all purity and truth of His manhood and called to them "come and follow me."

---

[19] Annual Report, WCTU New Brunswick, 1899, p. 26; Annual Report, WCTU Ontario, 1898, p. 66.

[20] Annual Report, WCTU Manitoba, 1890-92, pp. 43-44; Scott Smith, op. cit., p. 125. There is a suggestion in Alison Prentice, "Education and the Metaphor of the Family: the Upper Canadian Example," *History of Education Quarterly*, XII, No. 3 (1972), p. 286, that the family as a source of identification in mid-nineteenth-century Canadian society was declining, due to the discredit brought upon the concept by the Family Compact.

Feminine friendships were particularly strong in the nineteenth century because women were expected to remain within their own, separate sphere. In the rarefied atmosphere of women's organizations, women could find congenial company and develop friendships which, as revealed by the love shown to Frances Willard, were very deep. Such devotion and trust in one another and their leaders was also necessary. WCTU members faced great opposition to their advocacy of prohibition and suffrage and they undoubtedly found needed support in these friendships.[21]

The Struggle for a Moral Society

Support for women's suffrage did not negate the belief in separate spheres for men and women. Temperance women made it clear that their espousal of suffrage did not make them "new" women. "A man is to a woman and a woman is to a man, a stronghold; a completeness such as no two women or two men ever can be to one another," they declared. Mothers were urged to train their daughters in the duties of housekeeping. The Union stressed the adoption of manual training in schools to ensure that children received the practical skills requisite for their future careers; in the case of girls this meant domestic science. Better fulfilment of the domestic role even justified support for higher education. The WCTU also advocated the appointment of female school trustees, factory inspectors, physicians at girls' reformatories, matrons, bailiffs and police matrons. The limited acceptance of these demands resulted in the creation of new work roles that extended women's participation and involvement in society and did so on a premise which most could accept, that is, the domestic ideal of woman.[22]

The women of the WCTU also wanted to protect children. The British Columbia WCTU endeavoured to secure a Children's Protection Act similar to the one in Ontario; the Dominion WCTU supported the establishment of cottage homes as reformatories for boys and girls so that juvenile offenders could be reformed in a home atmosphere; and several provincial WCTUs tried to institute curfew bells which would ring at a certain hour, usually nine o'clock, after which time no child was to be on the street unless accompanied by parent or guardian. The WCTU hoped a curfew would prevent late hours, "that most subtle of stimulants," and thus lessen the number of children who would be tempted to drink. It began to realize, however, that curfew bells only controlled the actions of children to a limited extent, whereas education encouraged them to voluntarily restrain their actions, and in 1896 the women of the New Brunswick WCTU supported compulsory education for this

---

[21] Scrapbook, WCTU, 1898, lent to the author by Mrs. Harris Magog, Quebec. For information on feminine friendships in the United States, see Carroll Smith-Rosenberg, "The Female World of Love and Ritual: Relations Between Women in Nineteenth-Century America," *Signs* *1* (Autumn 1975), pp. 1-31.

[22] Annual Report, WCTU of the Maritime Provinces, 1890, p. 43.

reason. Education for its own sake was not their goal, but it could offset a bad home influence and teach children to be well-behaved.[23]

The WCTU was equally concerned about young girls and women. Its members felt that all girls did not have the advantages of a decent home life and a loving and protecting mother, and as mothers themselves they wanted to help them. They believed that young girls kept ignorant about the beginnings of life were especially vulnerable and urged that mothers and educators be honest about sex, arguing that ignorance was not a protector of purity but a weapon against it. Society was seen by them as dangerous to women; man was the seducer, woman his victim, and unfortunately, the law favoured the former. The WCTU of British Columbia pointed out that the law did not appear concerned with the protection of girls since it allowed them to give sexual consent at the age of sixteen, yet did not prosecute the seducer until the age of twenty-one. The WCTU protested that when police raided houses of ill fame only the names of the prostitutes were published. It demanded that the names of the men be published as well, so that respectable women would know which men to shun.[24]

In many areas the WCTU was over-zealous, its members responding in a drastic way to what appeared harmless to most Canadians at the time. Concern for the moral health of society led them to condemn certain styles of evening dress, round dances, nude art, gambling, theatre, prize fights and the use of women as bar maids. For members of the WCTU these were serious problems which had dire consequences.

> What has produced the almost numberless bands of young thieves, murderers, and train-wreckers, of whom we read in every day's paper? Dime novels, indiscriminately sold....
>
> Why are there so many divorces among young married people, now-a-days, where they have not the Bible ground of excuse to plead. Distorted views of life gathered from the trashy novel, where the heroes are all strong, tender and wealthy, and the heroines are beautiful, pure, and loving. Real life proves a different thing, and there is no strength of character to meet and bear the common discipline of plain human nature.

The WCTU invited confrontation in its advocacy of prohibition and suffrage. Because of the continued rejection by the majority of Canadians of their two central reforms, WCTU members developed a siege mentality. They saw the foundations of their world—that is, the sanctity of the home—attacked on all sides. As a result, they became more entrenched in their own principles.[25]

---

[23] Annual Report, WCTU Ontario, 1893, p. 117; Annual Report, WCTU B.C., 1899, p. 58.
[24] Annual Report, WCTU B.C., 1897, p. 32; Annual Report, WCTU Ontario, 1894, p. 140.
[25] Annual Report, WCTU Maritimes, 1890, p. 49.

Any compromise in the struggle for a moral society was unthinkable. The WCTU protested vehemently when the British government reintroduced the *Contagious Diseases Act*, whereby brothels were legally licensed. When Isabella Somerset, vice-president of the World WCTU, apparently approved of the Act, she was criticized severely. At the quarterly meeting on February 4, 1898, the Stanstead County WCTU resolved, "That we have no sympathy with the propositions of Lady Henry Somerset in relation to the C.D. Act and we reaffirm that the first plank in our platform is no compromise with sin." Dr. Amelia Yeomans, a vice-president of the Dominion WCTU, condemned the re-election of Somerset by the World WCTU and urged the Canadian union to resign from the international body. By this time, however, Somerset had recanted and the Dominion executive, with the exception of Dr. Yeomans, voted full confidence in her.[26]

The WCTU accepted the view that woman was and should be the moral guardian of society and so took a particular interest in the campaign for purity. Its campaign emphasized a single standard of sexual morality for both men and women, the standard being that dictated to women—control. This standard would not only help individuals, but would safeguard the future of the race. "Impure living," whether represented in sexual promiscuity, reading licentious novels (any novels) or the "secret vice" (masturbation) had, the WCTU believed, horrendous results on subsequent generations. The WCTU held that a mother's thoughts could influence her child before birth, warning that "sensuality may be transmitted to the yet unborn child by ... want of care in this respect." The new science of eugenics confirmed it. Heredity was important physically and morally and therefore men and women had a responsibility to choose their spouses wisely. Intemperance itself was hereditary, they thought, and its consequences reached out to maim the innocent, as the 1892 Report of the Department of Heredity and Hygiene was meant to illustrate.

> Recently a friend of mine was urging a little boy two years of age to joint the Band of Hope, when he startled her by saying, "You don't know what you are asking of me. *Never drink any more liquor?* I love it better than my life, I could not live without it." Think you that was an acquired taste with that child? No, no; his parents are responsible for it. `A corrupt tree cannot bring forth good fruit.'

The purpose of this obviously fantastic story is clear.[27]

The belief in heredity created a problem. If intemperance was inherited, the WCTU could do little to prevent it, and this would mean defeat, a negation of its

---

[26] Scrapbook, Stanstead County WCTU, 1898.

[27] Annual Report, WCTU B.C., 1899, p. 60; Annual Report, WCTU Canada, 1892, p. 76. This emphasis on heredity was common in the latter nineteenth century. See Michael Bliss, "Pure Books on Avoided Subjects," Canadian Historical Association, *Historical Papers*, 1970, pp. 89-108.

entire educational and preventive program. Fortunately, the members of the WCTU had a strong belief in the spiritual power of man. As upholders of morality they were upholders of the Christian faith. The two were inseparable in their eyes and so to fully understand their determination it is important to understand the source of it.

The WCTU and the Church

The WCTU wanted a Protestant Christian society. For most of its members, faith and temperance went hand in hand. The fight for prohibition was part of a religious battle, and one which women were determined to win. In the early years of its existence this religious strain probably did much to attract the initial WCTU membership and make it a respectable organization. Certainly the WCTU was closely aligned with those churches which endorsed prohibition, as revealed by the religious affiliation of its executive. Forty-three per cent of its executive were Methodist, 18 percent were Presbyterians and only 10 percent were adherents to the Church of England. Methodists had long disapproved of the consumption of alcohol and had been active in condemning it, although Presbyterians had not. Except for the more evangelical among them, Church of England supporters were uncomfortable in an organization which disapproved strongly of their church's use of wine as part of its religious service. The WCTU, then, was aligned to the church most active in its social involvement and strongest in its encouragement to women to become involved, to accept personal responsibility and to follow Christ's teachings.[28]

The Union patterned itself after the church. Its meetings opened with a prayer and a hymn and ended with a benediction. During the meeting there was more hymn singing, a collection and often an address by a minister. The WCTU believed that religious faith was the cornerstone of a temperate society and supported anything which strengthened the church. It firmly endorsed the movement to maintain Sabbath Observance and devoted a department to this end. Sunday law allowed families to be united by granting workers one day of rest, but Sunday laws also made it difficult for the working man and his family to have outings together. In the same way that

---

[28] WCTU *Executive*:

	Number	%
Presbyterian	7	18
Church of England	4	10
Catholic	--	--
Methodist	17	43-44
Baptist	6	15
Congregational	5	13

curfew bells limited the freedom of children, Sunday laws limited the freedom of working men on the one day they had to call their own.[29]

The WCTU's religious faith was strong. Uppermost in its members' minds was the spiritual welfare of the people they were trying to help, for although they rejected the denominational exclusiveness of missionary societies, they still retained the "spirit of Faith and Prayer" which characterized them. They believed that they could help men stop drinking if they could only bring them back to the Christian faith. They did not advocate temperance as simply a rational economic philosophy, but as a moral ethical one which was necessary if man was to live through Christ. Because reform of men's temporal state came only through Christ, the WCTU wanted "to carry the Gospel cure to the drinking classes." Its only approach to the individual inebriate, then, came through an evangelical commitment.[30]

Many work departments reflected this evangelical tendency: Flower Mission, Work Among Sailors (Immigrants, Lumbermen, Railwaymen), Sabbath Observance and Sabbath Schools, and Work in Jails. The women attempted to comfort those in need with the solace of religion. They often visited the inmates of prisons, hoping to win these men and women away from their former intemperate habits by bringing them the word of God. Yet when faced with prison conditions, they were led to demand prison reform. They became the advocates of prisoner classification, work for the incarcerated, the indeterminate sentence (an open-ended sentence which would terminate only when the individual had reformed), the parole system and schoolrooms within the jail. However, the women of the WCTU were worried that prison reform might take the spotlight away from their evangelical work and so continually stressed the need to remember the power of prayer and maintained a vigilance over their own spiritual well-being.

The church was the one institution in which women had been permitted and encouraged to work, even if only in a subordinate role. More importantly, the women of the WCTU believed a common Christianity bound them together as women, allowing them the freedom to think and act. They were convinced that Christianity and its handmaiden, the Protestant church, recognized women as being equal to men. Believing this, their involvement in public agitation to support prohibition and suffrage was not a denial of their proper sphere but a fulfilment of it. Their activism was justified by faith.

WCTU members were part of a movement to rectify wrong. As individuals they counted for little; as part of a great crusade they believed they became worthy of Christ.

> The Woman's Christian Temperance Union is no accident, but one of God's special creations. Throughout the ages since the fall of man

---

[29] Annual Report, WCTU Canada, 1891, p. 93.
[30] Annual Report, WCTU Ontario, Oct. 23, 1878, Resolutions; Annual Report, WCTU Quebec, 1884-85, p. 70.

Divine Love has been raising up instrumentalities for the restoration of our race to its original standard of moral rectitude.[31]

Conclusion

The Woman's Christian Temperance Union played a significant role in the lives of many Canadian women in the nineteenth century. Its advocacy of prohibition necessitated state intervention, which meant the WCTU was forced to appeal to the public in order to persuade the government to implement such a controversial policy. This made the union much more visible than most other women's organizations and hastened the time when its members would be faced with their own powerlessness as women. Through this politicization process the members of the WCTU confronted the reality of their lives in nineteenth-century Canada—they had little concrete power. As a solution they advocated women's suffrage, not so they could represent themselves as individuals, but so they could extend their domestic power as women in their effort to protect their homes by protecting society from the problems within it that could undermine both. They did not reject society's view of women, but argued that what made them different from men and what made them the centre of domestic life necessitated their involvement in temporal society. Their belief in an active Christianity supported them in this endeavour. That their actions and beliefs might appear contradictory did not concern them. They were practical women; they did what they felt had to be done and rationalized it by any means possible.

The rationales they used were the domestic ideal of woman and Christian duty. These were successful because the members really believed in them and these were also two supports which could not be attacked by those disapproving of women's activism. There were limits to what women could do using the ideal of domesticity to justify their actions. It meant an acknowledgement that woman's role was to care for the home. However, few Canadian women in the nineteenth century perceived this as a limitation. For them there was no contradiction between their actions and belief. Their interpretation of the domestic ideal of womanhood was a dynamic one, one that could and did encompass the women's rights movement. They were social feminists, not feminists.

As a precursor for the experience of other women's groups the WCTU's significance is great. It exposed the importance of the domestic ideal and Christian duty for women in the nineteenth century and demonstrated how Canadian women were able to use what some historians have seen as restrictive concepts to extend and exert their power in society.[32]

---

[31] Annual Report, WCTU B.C., 1893, p. 23.

[32] See Jill Conway, "Women Reformers and American Culture," *Journal of Social History*, 5, No. 2 (Winter 1971-73), pp. 164-77, for an expression of this phenomenon in the American Context.

"The Beginning of our Regeneration":
The Great War and Western Canadian Reform Movements

John H. Thompson

> *I know nothing about Germany. But I do know something about our own people. I know how selfish and individualistic and sordid and money-grabbing we have been; how slothful and incompetent and self-satisfied we have been, and I fear it will take a long war and sacrifices and tragedies altogether beyond our present imagination to make us unselfish and public-spirited and clean and generous; it will take the strain and emergency of war to make us vigourous and efficient; it will take the sting of many defeats to impose that humility which will be **the beginning of our regeneration**.*[1]

The Western Canadian reform movement was not created by the enthusiasm released by the Great War. Associations advocating prohibition, women's suffrage, and economic reform had existed in Manitoba and the Northwest Territories before the turn of the century. After 1900, the problems of immigration, rapid urban growth, and an expanding wheat economy gave the political, social, and economic dimensions of reformism increasing relevance. In the decade before the war, reform causes won new supporters, and became an important theme in Western Canadian life. The "reform movement" which espoused this theme was not a monolith. It was composed of a variety of pressure groups, dedicated to such diverse objectives as tariff reform, the single tax, direct legislation, prohibition, and women's suffrage. The movement's members belonged to no particular political party, and only in Manitoba did they find it necessary to capture a party to gain their ends. The movement's common philosophical denominator was the social gospel, which swept North American protestantism at the close of the nineteenth century.[2]

By 1914, Western reformers felt that they had made considerable progress toward their goals. Each Prairie Province had an active Social Service Council, committed to the eradication of the liquor traffic and prostitution, and to the amelioration of social conditions in Western cities. The Women's Christian Temperance Union also spoke for prohibition, and was the leading force in demands for women's suffrage. Direct Legislation Leagues promised to purify political life by using the initiative, referendum, and recall to make the governments more responsive to their electorates.

---

[1] Edith Duncan to Dave Elden, R.J.C. Stead, *The Cow Puncher*, 1918.
[2] A. Richard Allen, *The Social Passion* (Toronto, 1971) Chapter 1, *passim*.

Grain Growers' Associations used their voice, *The Grain Growers' Guide*, to support these reforms and to promote tariff and tax reform as well.

But as of August, 1914, none of these causes had enjoyed significant success. No Western province had enfranchised its women or introduced prohibition.[3] Direct legislation had been partially implemented in Saskatchewan in 1912 and Alberta in 1913, but Saskatchewan's electorate had failed to endorse the Direct Legislation Act in a referendum.[4] In January, 1914, the *bête noire* of Western reformers, Premier R.P. Roblin of Manitoba, observed sanctimoniously to his Attorney General that "seemingly crime does not decrease, seemingly the world is getting no better, seemingly the efforts of social and moral reformers is [*sic*] not as effective as we would like."[5]

It was on Premier Roblin that reform eyes were fixed in July 1914. The Manitoba Liberal Party, in the grip of the provincial reform movement, was challenging Roblin's fifteen year old Conservative government. The Liberal Platform was a reformer's banquet, with direct legislation as an appetizer, women's suffrage as the entrée, and a promised referendum on prohibition to conclude the meal. Roblin opposed each of these items, and, for the first time, reform and the status quo were presented to a Western electorate as clear-cut alternatives. C.W. Gordon of the Social Service council described the significance of the confrontation for Western reformers:

> On the one side are the Christian Churches, various [reform] organizations, social workers, and all the decent citizens, on the other the Roblin Government, the Liquor traffic, and every form of organized vice and crime.[6]

But "decent citizens" were apparently not a majority in Manitoba, for the Roblin Government was returned for a fifth consecutive term.

The defeat in Manitoba did not mean that reformers throughout the West faced a hopeless situation. The Liberals made significant gains in terms of seats and in their percentage of the popular vote. But the defeat did suggest that in a head to head confrontation with "the forces of reaction" (as Nellie McClung described those who opposed reform), reform ideas did not enjoy the support of a clear majority of the electorate. Although the reform movement had increased both in size and vigour, it

---

[3] In Saskatchewan, for example, only six of the twenty-six local option referenda conducted in December, 1913, resulted in prohibitionist victories. Erhard Pinno, "Temperance and Prohibition in Saskatchewan," (unpub. M.A. Thesis, University of Saskatchewan, 1971) p. 29.

[4] E.J. Chambers, "The Plebiscite and Referendum in Saskatchewan," (unpub. M.A. Thesis, University of Saskatchewan, 1965) Chapter 1.

[5] Provincial Archives of Manitoba (P.A.M.) Colin H. Campbell Papers, R.P. Roblin to Colin H. Campbell, 9.1.14.

[6] *Canadian Annual Review* (C.A.R.), 1914, p. 598.

had not succeeded in winning the enthusiastic endorsement of the general public. This endorsement was necessary if such reform objectives as prohibition and women's suffrage were to be effectively implemented. It was in their quest for this broad public support that reformers were aided by the Great War.

A modern democracy with a literate population cannot engage in a major war without soliciting an enthusiastic mandate from its citizens. For this reason, the Great War was interpreted and described in terms very different from those applied to wars of the past. The Canadian Expeditionary Force was not fighting for territorial gain, but "in maintenance of those ideals of Liberty and Justice which are the common and sacred cause of the Allies" and for "the freedom of the world."[7] Although "there may have been wars in the history of the British Empire that have not been justifiable," "there never was a juster cause" than the war against German autocracy.[8]

But if Canadian soldiers were giving their lives for "Liberty and Justice" in Flanders, was it not the duty of those who remained behind to see to it that these same things existed in Canada? Reformers argued that the Great War was an opportunity to accomplish this very thing, a sign given to Canada in order that "the national sins which are responsible for this awful carnage may be eradicated so righteousness and peace may be established."[9] As Mrs. Nellie McClung told her many readers, the war was necessary for national regeneration, for "without the shedding of blood, there is no remission of sin."[10] If the sacrifice was not to be wasted, the reform programme had to be implemented. Even Clifford Sifton, hardly an ardent reformer, recognized that the Great War made it necessary for both Eastern and Western Canada to "cast out everything that threatens its moral health." The war produced a transformation in public attitudes to reformism, changing them to the point that "men who scoffed a few years ago are the foremost now to demand reform."[11] The transformation was particularly pronounced in Western Canada. As Mrs. Irene Parlby told the Saskatchewan Grain Growers, "before the war the real spirit of the West had been smothered in materialism," and public action had been

---

[7] The first phrase is from a resolution passed by the Manitoba Legislature on the third anniversary of the War's declaration, while the second is included in a circular written by W.R. Motherwell on behalf of the 1918 Victory Loan. P.A.M., Norris Papers, Box 2. Archives of Saskatchewan (A.S.), Motherwell Papers, p. 26267.

[8] Rev. Canon Murray, "Canada's Place in the War," in Canadian Club of Winnipeg, *Annual Report 1913-14*, p. 71.

[9] Mrs. Louis McKinney, "President's Address," in Alberta W.C.T.U. *Report of the Annual Convention 1915*.

[10] Nellie L. McClung, *In Times Like These* (New York, 1915), p. 161.

[11] Clifford Sifton, "Foundations of the New Era," in J.O. Miller, *The New Era in Canada* (Toronto, 1918), pp. 37-38.

difficult. Because of the common goal of victory, "the big broad free spirit is beginning to emerge again."[12]

In addition to changing public attitudes to the idea of reform, the wartime experience changed attitudes to the role of the state as the enforcer of reform measures. Many reform objectives, most notably prohibition and changes in the system of taxation, called for a previously unacceptable degree of state intervention into the lives of its citizens. The expansion of governmental power necessary to meet the wartime emergency gave government intervention a sanction which it had not had before 1914. The state became "more than a mere tax-collector or polling clerk," it became an organization capable of vigorous, positive activities.[13] An Alberta prohibitionist noted that "the European War has taught us that the State has a right to take such action as will best conserve its forces for the national good."[14] Because of the demands of war, no truly patriotic citizen could react to such action with "resentment or resistance;" the correct course was "a new and affectionate loyalty".[15] This new willingness to grant a more active role to government combined with the wartime ideal of redeeming Canadian society to produce a climate of opinion favourable to reform. It was this climate that the reform movement exploited to gain its ends, in some facets of the movement more successfully than in others.

The reform objective which received the greatest impetus from the wartime atmosphere was the prohibition of alcoholic liquors. Despite the social problems which liquor created in the rapidly expanding West, prohibitionists had been unable to convince the Western public or their provincial governments that prohibition was the necessary cure. The events of August, 1914, introduced a new factor into the equation. The Great War provided the necessary catalyst in the public reaction which brought about prohibitory liquor legislation, not only in Western Canada, but throughout North America. More than any other reform group, prohibitionists were able to use the exigencies of the wartime situation to lend new credence to their arguments and to exploit the desire to purify society which emerged as part of the domestic side of the war effort.

Prohibitionists had long been fond of military metaphors to describe their struggle. The cause itself was "*warfare* waged against ignorance, selfishness, darkness, prejudice and cruelty," while a successful referendum campaign might be compared to Wellington's victory at Waterloo.[16] Sara Rowell Wright of the W.C.T.U. liked to speak of her years as "a private in the rear ranks of the

---

12   A.S., Saskatchewan Grain Growers Association, *Convention Report*, 12.2.17.
13   Mrs. H.V. Plumptre, "Some Thought on the Suffrage," in Miller, *New Era*, p. 328-9.
14   Archives of the Glenbow Foundation (Glenbow) Alberta W.C.T.U. Collection no. 1, f. 35, *Report of the Annual Convention, 1915*, p. 30.
15   Plumptre, *op. cit.*, p. 329.
16   McClung, *In Times Like These*, p. 5, R.E. Spence, *Prohibition in Canada* (Toronto, 1919), p. 71.

movement," and a book of temperance poems and songs was called *The Gatling*, a reference to the way its contents were to be deployed against the liquor traffic.[17] The war made these rhetorical flourishes a mainstay of temperance propaganda. The liquor traffic was clearly identified with the Kaiser and his brutal hordes as a force blocking the way to a more perfect society. Since a Westerner would "despise the Kaiser for dropping bombs on defenceless people, and shooting down innocent people," he should also despise the liquor traffic, since it had "waged war on women and children all down the centuries."[18] The techniques to be employed in the eradication of both the Kaiser and the liquor traffic were made to seem exactly the same. Rev. J.E. Hughson of Winnipeg urged Westerners to "use ballots for bullets and shoot straight and strong in order that the demon of drink might be driven from the haunts of men."[19] A cartoon in the *Grain Growers' Guide* carried on the analogy pictorially, depicting a "war" on the entrenched liquor interests, with "votes" being loaded into a field piece by the forces under the banner of "Temperance and Righteousness."[20]

It was not only the tone of prohibitionist rhetoric that was adapted to suit the Great War, its content was modified as well. The war provided the temperance movement with two important new arguments with which to influence public opinion. The first concerned the moral and physical health of the thousands of young Westerners who had entered the army, many of whom were leaving home for the first time. What would happen to the decent boys from prairie farms when, befuddled by unfamiliar liquor, they fell victim to the prostitutes who haunted military camps in Canada and overseas? Blighted by horrible unnamed diseases, "thousands of clean-minded innocent young boys who would otherwise have been decent upright citizens will now be nothing but a scourge to their country when they return."[21]

One way to avoid such a result was to keep liquor out of the hands of soldiers. As the Medical Officer of Ralph Connor's *Sky Pilot* in *No Man's Land* pointed out, "Cut out the damned beer. Cut out the beer and ninety *per cent* of the venereal disease goes ... [Soldier's] mothers have given them up, to death, if need be, but not to this rotten damnable disease."[22] To "cut out the beer," women's groups and W.C.T. Unions bombarded legislators and commanding officers with resolutions demanding that bars and "wet" canteens be closed "for the sake of our soldiers."[23] It was not enough to restrict such protection to the period when they were in uniform, only to

---

17   Sara Rowell Wright, "The W.C.T.U. Program" in *The Social Service Congress of Canada* (Ottawa, 1914), p. 322.
18   McClung, *In Times Like These*, p. 165.
19   *Manitoba Free Press*, 6.3.16.
20   *Grain Growers' Guide*, 16.6.15.
21   Frances M. Beynon in *Ibid.*, 30.5.17.
22   Ralph Connor, *The Sky Pilot* in *No Man's Land* (New York, 1917), pp. 149-50.
23   A.S. Martin Papers, Ladies of North Battleford Methodist Church to W.M. Martin, 7.11.16, p. 31654. See also Alberta W.C.T.U. Minute Book, 2.1.15: and P.A.M. Manitoba W.C.T.U. Collection, Winnipeg District Minute Book, 9.12.14.

allow them to become victims of the liquor traffic once they were civilians again. It was the responsibility of every Westerner to see that the veterans found "a clean pure Province for them when they return to us, in which they may rest their shattered nerves and poor wounded bodies."[24] This could only be guaranteed if prohibition became a reality.

No one thought to ask the "clean minded innocent young boys" if they wanted to be rescued from the clutches of temptation. Evidence about the soldiers' opinion on the prohibition question is contradictory. During referenda on prohibition in Manitoba, Saskatchewan, and Alberta polls in military camps returned "dry" majorities, and one Saskatchewan officer wrote Premier Scott to praise the provincial government's decision to make the liquor trade a public monopoly.[25] After prohibition was in force, however, a Calgary private wrote A.E. Cross of the Calgary Brewing and Malting Company that his comrades "would be solid for to have it back to the good old days again" on their return.[26] Soldier poets poked rude fun at both "dry" canteens and prohibitionists. One particularly piquant rhyme entitled "From the Trenches," derided

> Preachers over in Canada
> Who rave about Kingdom Come
> Ain't pleased with our ability
> And wanted to stop our rum.
> Water they say would be better
> Water! Great Scott! Out here
> We're up to our knees in water
> Do they think we're standing in beer?[27]

Thus it would seem that soldiers were as divided in their opinions of prohibition as most Westerners had been before 1914. But among the public as a whole, the prohibitionist movement was rapidly making converts, and producing a consensus in favour of prohibition.

An important factor in producing this consensus was a second new temperance argument, again one peculiar to the wartime situation. Canadians were told constantly by their governments that efficiency was a prerequisite for victory over

---

[24] Motherwell Papers, Mrs. W.R. Motherwell, Address at Lemberg, Sask. 5.12.16. f. 123.

[25] A.S., Walter Scott Papers, Capt. J.L.R. Parsons to Scott, 25.3.15, p. 59695. See also Pinno, *op. cit.*, p. 121; John H. Thompson "The Prohibition Question in Manitoba, 1892-1928," (unpub. M.A. Thesis University of Manitoba, 1969), p. 2; and R.I. McLean, "Temperance and Prohibition in Alberta, 1875-1915," (unpub. M.A. Thesis, University of Calgary, 1970); p. 134.

[26] Glenbow, Calgary Brewing and Malting Collection, W. Towers to A.E. Cross, 1.1.18, f. 577.

[27] *Manitoba Free Press*, 7.3.16.

Germany. Prohibitionists quickly capitalized on this theme, pointing to the production and consumption of liquor as a drain on Canada's ability to wage war. Not only did drunkenness squander the nation's human resources, it wasted its physical resources as well. A drunken soldier was unfit to fight, an alcoholic worker was unable to produce, and grain distilled into whisky could not be used to feed starving Allies. Newspapers sympathetic to the war effort put this argument forcefully before the public, demanding that

> the bar must be closed [because] the national existence is at stake. The ship must be stripped for action. All dead weight must go by the boards if we are to win.[28]

As well as providing prohibitionists with two new important arguments, the situation created by the Great War gave them new answers to two of the most effective defences of the liquor traffic. With thousands of Westerners dying in France to serve their country, criticism of prohibition as a violation of individual liberty lost most of its impact. *Manitoba Free Press* editor John W. Dafoe reflected the popular mood when he pointed out that "the propriety of subordinating individual desires to the general good need not be elaborated at this moment, when millions of men, representing the cream of British citizenship have put aside all their individual inclinations and ambitions."[29] Nellie McClung was even more blunt. "We have before us," she wrote, "a perfect example of a man who is exercising personal liberty to the full ... a man by the name of William Hohenzollern."[30] The second anti-prohibitionist argument routed by the Great War was the claim that prohibition would produce widespread unemployment by wiping out the liquor industry and its associated outlets. The wartime demand for manpower created a labour shortage that made this contention ridiculous.

With their own rhetoric refurbished to suit the wartime situation, and with their opponents' most effective weapons temporarily silent, prohibitionist organizations intensified their efforts to put their case to the public and to the provincial governments. The traditional mainstays of the movement, the W.C.T.U. and the Social Service Councils, were joined in their campaign by groups which had not formerly been associated with prohibition. The Orange Lodge, the I.O.D.E., the Anglican Church, the Winnipeg Canadian Club; all came to the conclusion that prohibition was "the best way of dealing with the liquor traffic *at the present time*," and became war converts to the cause.[31] These new allies meant that prohibitionists could apply increased pressure on Western governments, and the movement began to gain concessions rapidly.

---

28   *Edmonton Bulletin*, 20.7.15. See also *Regina Leader*, 24.2.15.
29   *Manitoba Free Press*, 7.3.16.
30   McClung, *In Times Like These*, p. 170.
31   R.I. McLean, *op. cit.*, p. 135.

In Manitoba, for example, the antiprohibitionist Roblin government raised the legal drinking age from sixteen to eighteen and suspended the licenses of seventy-two establishments found to be flouting the liquor laws.[32] The Liberal government of Saskatchewan engaged in the same sort of short term measures, but Premier Scott and his colleagues began to realize that the public was demanding more and that "the time [was] high ripe for action." The step on which they decided fell short of prohibition. In March, 1915, the government announced that the liquor trade in Saskatchewan was to become a state monopoly. Liquor was to be available only in provincially operated dispensaries, and all bars, saloons, and stores were to be closed. Scott viewed the decision as a frank concession to wartime public opinion, and confided to Senator James H. Ross that this opinion was so strong that "to stand still any longer meant suicide for this government."[33] Scott and his cabinet regarded their dispensary system as a radical step in the direction of prohibition. J.A. Calder considered introducing the dispensaries as "having decided to go the limit," and expressed "very grave doubts" as to whether a referendum on prohibition could ever be successful in Saskatchewan.[34] The events of the next two years were to show how rapidly the war could change public attitudes to prohibition, and make a mockery of the prediction of as astute a politician as Calder.

In July 1915, with the Saskatchewan dispensary system scarcely in operation, the voters of Alberta gave a solid endorsement to a prohibition referendum. All but sixteen of the fifty-eight provincial constituencies returned prohibitionist majorities, with "wet" victories coming only in "primarily mining or remote northern areas", beyond reach of prohibitionist propaganda.[35] Manitobans followed suit seven months later, with an even larger majority. Only three constituencies remained "wet" in a prohibitionist landslide.

Saskatchewan, which had been so proud of its system of government control, suddenly found itself to the rear of temperance sentiment on the Prairies. One prohibitionist warned W.R. Motherwell that the situation had changed, and that the public was

> not satisfied with the working out of the Liquor Dispencery [sic] System. It is true that we are tremendously better off ... this

---

[32] Motherwell Papers, T.A. Mitchell to Motherwell, 22.1.16, f. 71(2).

[33] *The Western Prairie* (Cypress River, Manitoba), 2.3.16.

[34] Calder to Bulyea, 23.3.15, Calder Papers, G. 4, p. 11. Opposition to prohibition during wartime was notable among those of German birth or descent. The German language *Der Courier, Der Nordwesten*, and *St. Peters Bote* all editorialized against prohibition, and the German Canadian Alliance of Saskatchewan publicly denounced the "aggressive and unscrupulous agitation" of the prohibitionists. See Erhard Pinno, *op. cit.*, pp. 121-3, Thompson, *op cit.*, pp. 28-9, and *C.A.R.*., 1914, p. 630.

[35] *Manitoba Free Press*, 6.3.16; *Canadian Farmer*, November, 1916, translation in Martin Papers, pp. 31616-8.

however does not alter the fact that more is needed. This is a matter which is receiving a good deal of unfavourable comment at this time. The people are ready for a total prohibition measure at this very time, let us have it.[36]

The Saskatchewan Liberal government responded once again to public demands, and Saskatchewan became the third Western Province to endorse prohibition by referendum, in December, 1916. The Saskatchewan majority was the largest of the three, demonstrating again that as the war against Germany became longer and more bitter, the war against booze enlisted more and more recruits.

There are several revealing similarities among the three referenda, in addition to the fact that all were resounding prohibitionist victories. In each campaign the Great War played an important rhetorical role, and temperance workers succeeded completely in convincing the Western public that prohibition and patriotism were synonymous. The referenda themselves were treated as an opportunity for those truly behind the war effort to stand up and be counted. As the Cypress River *Western Prairie* warned on the eve of the Manitoba balloting, "anyone who will vote in favour of liquor might as well enlist under the Kaiser as far as patriotism goes."[37]

This identification helped prohibitionists overcome opposition among a traditionally hostile group, the Catholic immigrants from Central and Eastern Europe. It had been "this very heavy foreign population" which J.A. Calder had thought would prevent a "dry" Saskatchewan, and much of the opposition faced by prohibitionists during the war did come from this quarter.[38] But many of these people saw the prohibition referendum as a kind of loyalty test, through which they could prove that they were good Canadian citizens, even during this time of crisis. Prohibitionists encouraged this belief, and actively sought non-Anglo-Saxon votes. For the first time, their efforts were rewarded. In Manitoba, the Ruthenian Catholic Political Club and the Slavonic Independent Society "spoke fervently in favour of temperance," while *The Canadian Farmer*, a Western Ukrainian weekly, urged its Saskatchewan readers to "get organized and vote against the [Liquor] stores!"[39] Not

---

[36] This quotation is from a resolution of the Manitoba Rural Deanery of the Church of England, *Manitoba Free Press*, 1.3.16. The Anglican conversion to prohibition is discussed in McLean, *op. cit.*, pp. 111-112. For the Orange Order's opinion see *C.A.R.*, 1915, p. 665 and P.A.M., R.P. Roblin Papers, J.J. Stitt to R.P. Roblin, 3.3.15. For an I.O.D.E. attitude see Provincial Archives of Alberta (P.A.A.). Beaverhouse I.O.D.E. Minute Book, 1.10.14. The Winnipeg Canadian Club's views are expressed in its *Annual Report*, 1913-14, pp, 6-7.

[37] Lionel Orlikow, "A Survey of the Reform Movement in Manitoba, 1910-1920," (unpub. M.A. Thesis, U. of Manitoba, 1955), p. 150.

[38] Scott Papers, Scott to Willoughby, 1.12.14, p. 48455; Levi Thomson to Scott, 8.4.15, p. 48503; Motherwell to Scott, 18.12.14, p. 12889; Scott to S.G. Hill, 1.7.15, p. 13300; Scott to J.H. Ross, 12.4.15, p. 13650.

[39] A.S., J.A. Calder Papers, Calder to G.H.V. Bulyea, 23.3.15, G4, p. 11.

all non-Anglo-Saxons were converted, but enough voted for prohibition in each of the three provinces to largely neutralize the ballots of their wet countrymen. After the Alberta referendum, the W.C.T.U.'s Superintendent of Work Among Foreigners "knelt in thanksgiving to our Heavenly Father that not all foreign-speaking people voted wet, but that right prevailed and carried the day, even in several of their own district communities."[40] North Winnipeg, perhaps the most aggressively "foreign" community in the West, rejected prohibition by only sixty-five votes. The *Manitoba Free Press* made an observation which applied throughout the West when it noted with satisfaction that "the greatest disappointment of all to the wets was the foreign vote."[41]

The only group completely untouched by wartime arguments on behalf of prohibition was Western Canada's French Canadians. French Canadians and prohibitionists had never enjoyed cordial relations, partly because of the movement's Protestant character, and partly because of its wholehearted support for unilingual education. Since most French Canadians had centuries of North American ancestry, the idea that they needed to prove their loyalty by accepting prohibition did not occur to them. As the French language *Le Manitoba* was careful to point out, this did not mean that French Canadians were "plus intémperants que les autres", simply that they resented the totalitarian techniques of prohibition and prohibitionists. In each Western Province, Francophones rejected prohibition in the referenda of 1915-16.[42]

The second important similarity between the referenda campaigns in Manitoba, Saskatchewan, and Alberta was the demoralization of the traditional opponents of prohibition. The Great War not only defused the arguments used by the defenders of liquor, it sapped the strength of the defenders themselves. In Alberta, liquor dealers had "very little success" in raising funds to oppose prohibition during wartime.[43] In both Manitoba and Alberta, the Licensed Victuallers' Association had to turn to the United States for antiprohibitionist speakers. The Manitoba Association cooperated with the Bartenders Union to obtain Clarence Darrow, who received an enthusiastic reception from "wet" faithful, but an icy one from the general public. The Alberta Victuallers did no better with A.C. Windle, an anti-war editor from Chicago. Windle's outspoken opposition to the Great War allowed prohibitionists to

---

40 Alberta W.C.T.U., *Annual Report*, 1915, p. 60.
41 *Manitoba Free Press*, 14.3.16.
42 Pinno, *op. cit.*, p. 122; *Le Courier de l'Ouest* (Edmonton), 1.7.16; *Le Manitoba*, 13.4.16. The comparative effectiveness of patriotic arguments for prohibition on French-Canadians and non-Anglo Saxon immigrants can be demonstrated by an examination of referendum results in the Alberta Constituencies of Victoria, Whitford, St. Albert, and Beaver River. All four rejected prohibition, but Victoria and Whitford, with heavy Ukrainian populations, did so by the relatively narrow margin of 1392 to 1022. St. Albert and Beaver River, with largely French-Canadian electorates, recorded a combined majority of 889 against prohibition, 1484 to 595.
43 Calgary Brewing and Malting Collection, A.E. Cross to D.R. Ker, 24.3.15, f. 550.

reemphasize their argument that "wet" sympathy meant a lack of patriotism, and that booze and Kaiserism were inextricably intertwined.[44] In Saskatchewan's referendum campaign of 1916, there simply was no opposition to the prohibitionists. The Government Dispensary system, in effect for more than a year, had decimated the ranks of hotel keepers, who generally provided the "anti" leadership.

Because of a combination of new factors, all of them attributable to the Great War, the Prairie Provinces adopted prohibitory liquor legislation during the first two full years of the war. Provincial prohibition was not total prohibition, however, The right to restrict interprovincial trade belonged to the Dominion Government, and for this reason provincial Temperance Acts could not prevent individuals from importing liquor from another province for home consumption. A thriving interprovincial export business rapidly developed. Liquor dealers like William Ferguson of Brandon informed customers in the neighbouring province that "having decided to remain in business, and having still a large stock of draught Brandies, Scotch and Irish Whiskies, Rum, Holland Gin, Port and Sherries, [I] will continue to fill orders for Saskatchewan."[45] So much liquor came into Alberta across the British Columbia border that Bob Edwards' *Calgary Eye Opener* included the satirical "Society Note" that

> Percy M. Winslow, one of our most popular and dissipated young men, left Monday morning for Field, B.C., where he has accepted a lucrative position as shipping clerk in one of the wholesale liquor houses. We predict a bright future for Percy.[46]

Western prohibitionists were determined not to stop short of the ultimate goal. To plug the loopholes in provincial legislation, they turned to Ottawa. Petitions, letters, and resolutions reminded Members of Parliament of the gravity of the situation, and urged them to introduce measures to "abolish the sale and manufacture of alcoholic liquors during wartime."[47] Prohibitionists gave enthusiastic support to Unionist candidates throughout the West during the election of 1917. Dominion prohibition was one of the many reforms which they expected to emanate from Unionism, and the Union Government's bipartisan character and crusading style appealed to the prohibitionist mind. Many influential prohibitionists campaigned on behalf of Union Government, among them Dr. Salem Bland, Rev. C.W. Gordon, and Mrs. Nellie McClung. Their work was rewarded, for shortly after they took office the Unionists introduced federal prohibition as an Order in Council under the War Measures Act, to come into effect April 1, 1918.

---

[44] *Edmonton Bulletin*, 6.7.15.
[45] Advertisement in Motherwell Papers, f. 71(2).
[46] *Calgary Eye Opener*, 8.7.16.
[47] Manitoba W.C.T.U. Collection, Recording Secretary's Book, 15.2.16.

This made the prohibitionist victory in theory complete. All that remained was the task of making certain that the hard won legislation was enforced. The war aided prohibitionists in this respect as well, and 1917-18 became the most effective years of the prohibition experiment. Even before the Dominion Government put an end to importation, Manitoba could report that "drunkenness had been reduced 87% for the first seven months of the operation of the (Prohibition) Act ... all other crime has been reduced by 32%" and that "the support accorded the Act has surpassed the most sanguine expectations of its friends."[48] A jubilant Saskatchewan farm wife wrote to Premier Martin that "our little town, which was formerly a drunkard's paradise, since the banishment of the bars and dispensaries has assumed an air of thrift and sobriety."[49] Alberta's Chief Inspector under the Temperance Act claimed that under prohibition arrests of drunks were reduced by ninety *per cent*, and drinking, crime, and drunkenness decreased in each Prairie Province during the last two years of the War.[50] Once the war ended, however, the prohibitionist solution to society's problems became increasingly less effective.[51] The assault on prohibition began almost as soon as the war ended, and prohibitionists no longer had the wartime situation to interest the public in their programme. By 1924 all three Western Provinces had replaced prohibition with government operated liquor stores.

How much of the prohibitionists' fleeting success can be attributed to the Great War? To describe the imposition of prohibition as a purely wartime phenomenon would do an injustice to the work done before 1914 to convince Westerners of the need for liquor restriction. The foundations laid before the war began were a vital factor in the eventual success. But it was the emotional atmosphere of wartime which completed the prohibitionists' work, and which allowed prohibition to operate reasonably effectively for two short years. It was the Great War's accompanying national reappraisal which made once indifferent citizens listen to temperance arguments for the first time. Once this was accomplished, the majoritarian zeal which marked the domestic war effort ensured the right "psychological moment to strike the blow."[52] The *Saskatoon Phoenix* understood this process completely. "The temperance party," said an editorial, "has the war to thank for bringing public opinion *to a focus* on the matter of temperance reform."[53]

---

48 Province of Manitoba, *Annual Report on the Temperance Act*, Sessional Paper no. 13, 1917.

49 Martin Papers, Mrs. G.V. Jewett to Martin, 23.4.17, p. 31759.

50 R.E. Popham and W. Schmit, *Statistics of Alcohol Use and Alcoholism in Canada* (Toronto, 1958), pp. 48-53. See also James H. Gray, *The Boy from Winnipeg* (Toronto, 1970), p. 126 and *Red Lights on the Prairies* (Toronto, 1971), pp. 149-151.

51 Alberta W.C.T.U. Collection no. 1, Social Service Council Convention Minutes, 18.2.19, f. 7.

52 Scott Papers, Levi Thomson to Scott, 8.4.15, p. 48503.

53 *Saskatoon Phoenix*, 19.3.15. Richard Allen has suggested that prohibition was "almost predictable" in Manitoba and Saskatchewan before the war began in 1914, (*Social Passion*, p. 22). This judgment seems exaggerated, given the lack of success of local option ballots,

The second reformist group aided significantly by the Great War was the movement for women's suffrage. The prohibition and suffrage movements were so closely intertwined in both programme and personnel that what advanced one cause almost automatically had the same effect on the other. In the three Western Provinces, the W.C.T.U. played a leading role in both movements and an ardent prohibitionist was usually an ardent suffragette as well. In many parts of the Prairies, the pre-war suffrage movement was the Equal Franchise Department of the local W.C.T.U.[54]

The war's favourable effect on the achievement of women's suffrage is paradoxical, for prior to 1914, the women's movement had thought of itself as pacifistic, and regarded war as one of women's greatest enemies. War was part of the scheme of masculine domination which denied women an effective voice in society. "History, romance, legend, and tradition," wrote Nellie McClung, "have shown the masculine aspect of war and have surrounded it with a false glory and have sought to throw the veil of glamour over its hideous face." It was for the "false glory" that men went to war, abandoning women to face the true responsibilities of life alone.[55]

The Great War challenged these pacifistic assumptions. The wars which women had so roundly condemned had been the wars with which they themselves were familiar; the South African War, the Spanish American War, and colonial wars in Africa or the Far East. This new war was something very different. Germany was not the tiny Transvaal Republic, but an aggressive modern industrial power. Canada was not fighting for colonial conquest, but for "liberty", "justice", her very survival. Had it not been "the Kaiser and his brutal warlords" who had decided to "plunge all Europe into bloodshed"? And what about Belgium, gallant little Belgium where "the German soldiers made a shield of Belgium women and children in front of their Army; no child was too young, no woman too old, to escape their cruelty; no mother's prayers no child's appeal could stay their fury!"[56] Surely such inhumanity had to be checked lest it dominate first Europe, then the world.

As with the prohibitionist movement, the Great War's first effect on the suffrage movement was on its rhetoric. As Aileen S. Kraditor has pointed out, pre-war suffrage arguments can be divided into two categories, those based on justice and those based on expediency. The older, justice-oriented theme contended that women had a natural right to vote, as did all citizens. Arguments which emphasized

---

the defeat of the Norris Liberals in Manitoba, and comments such as those of Calder and Scott cited above, p. 10.

[54] See June Menzies, "Votes for Saskatchewan's Women," in N. Ward, ed., *Politics in Saskatchewan* (Don Mills, 1968), p. 90, Thomson, *op. cit.*, pp. 59-60 and C.L. Cleverdon, *The Women's Suffrage Movement in Canada* (Toronto, 1950), pp. 49-64.

[55] McClung, *In Times Like These*, p. 14. See also Carol Lee Bacchi Ferraro, "The Ideas of the Canadian Suffragists, 1890-1920," (unpub. M.A. Thesis, McGill University, 1970) pp. 109-111.

[56] McClung, *op. cit.*, p. 27.

expediency stressed instead the good effects that women's vote could accomplish in society.[57] Both types of argument were suitable to adaptation to the wartime atmosphere.

The new significance which the Great War gave to arguments based on justice is obvious. If the war were really "the greatest fight for liberty since the Dutch and English broke the power of Spain in the 16th Century," why, women asked, could they not enjoy in Canada the same liberty for which their sons were fighting and dying? Since the war was to be the "vindication of democracy," should not the democratic rights of millions of Canadian women be vindicated at the same time? Men who indulged in such descriptions of the war found themselves caught on the hook of their own eloquence.[58] As W.L. Morton has succinctly pointed out, "those who would carry democracy abroad must see that it is without reproach at home."[59]

Arguments based on expediency gained more power in wartime as well. The public came to accept the idea that the war could be used to redeem Western Canada from her pre-war materialism. This might be accomplished without women's votes, but what would happen when the war ended, and reforming zeal dissipated? Women's votes were necessary to prevent backsliding, and a return to evil in the post-war era. If this should happen, all the sacrifice, all the bloodshed, would be in vain. As a "war widow" told R.J.G. Stead,

> We women, we women of the war—we have nothing left to be selfish for. But we have the whole world to be unselfish for. It's all different, and it can never go back. *We won't let it go back. We've paid too much to let it go back.*[60]

To prevent this "going back," women demanded the vote.

Not only the rhetoric, but the organization of the women's movement was profoundly changed by the war. Initially, suffragists thought that the war would postpone the achievement of their goal, since it would force them to devote less time to suffrage activities. In reality, however, women's war work proved to be the greatest organizational aid the movement had ever been blessed with. The motivation provided by patriotic work increased the membership of existing women's groups, such as the United Farm Women of Alberta and Manitoba, and the I.O.D.E. Groups not formerly concerned with suffrage were brought into contact with their more

---

[57] Aileen S. Kraditor, *The Ideas of the Women's Suffrage Movement* (New York, 1965), p. 38-63.

[58] The first phrase is from P.A.C., Dafoe Papers, Clifford Sifton to J.W. Dafoe, 21.9.14. The second is from Stephen Leacock, "Democracy and Social Progress," in J.O. Miller, *New Era*, p. 13.

[59] W.L. Morton, "The Extension of the Franchise in Canada: A Study in Democratic Nationalism," *Canadian Historical Association Report*, 1943, p. 79.

[60] R.J.C. Stead, *The Cow Puncher* (Toronto, 1918), p. 342.

activistic sisters in associations like the W.C.T.U. As these women gathered to produce incredible quantities of towels and toques, socks and shirts, balaclavas and bandages, they did not sit mute. Quiet housewives conversed with ardent advocates of equal suffrage, and while

> the nimble fingers of the knitting women are transforming balls of wool into socks and comforters, even a greater change is being wrought in their own hearts. Into their gentle souls have come bitter thoughts of rebellion.... They realize now something of what is back of all the opposition to the women's advancement into all lines of activity and a share in government.[61]

In their Annual Report of 1918, the United Farm Women at Manitoba credited "war relief and patriotic work" with the formative role in the development of "a spirit of national sisterhood".[62]

It was not knitting for the Red Cross alone which produced this new frame of mind. The Census of 1911 had already revealed a tendency for increasing numbers of women to seek employment outside their homes, a tendency accentuated by the wartime shortage of manpower. More important, Western women were entering fields which had formerly tended to employ men. The number of women engaged in professional occupations, mainly teaching, increased 130% between 1911 and 1921. Alberta employed 630 more female teachers in 1916 than in 1914. Wartime vacancies also gave women an opportunity in Government Service, and Western governments employed four times as many in 1921 as they had ten years earlier.[63] New opportunities for women did not stop with employment. Women began to infiltrate other areas regarded once as *de facto* male preserves. At the University of Manitoba, for example, the "two major honours", student presidency and newspaper editorship, went to women in 1917.[64]

---

[61] McClung, *In Times Like These*, pp. 28-29. For some examples of the effects of the war in increasing the membership of women's organizations, see Glenbow, United Farmers of Alberta Collection, f. 35; Scott Papers, Eva Sherrock to Scott, 14.2.16, p. 59505; *Manitoba Free Press*, 27.2.15. For a good example of the cooperation among organizations promoted by the war, see Alberta W.C.T.U. collection no. 2, North West Calgary Union, Minutes, 4.11.15, f. 5.

[62] P.A.M., United Farmers of Manitoba Collection, United Farm Women Report, 1918.

[63] The Census of 1921 revealed a sixty-three *per cent* increase in the number of women in the western provinces employed outside their homes. For comparative figures see Canada, *Fifth Census*, 1911, vol. VI, p. 10, passim, and *Sixth Census*, 1921, vol. IV, p. 10 passim. The statistics on women teachers in Alberta are taken from Alberta Department of Education, *Annual Report*, 1916, pp. 16-17.

[64] *Manitoba Free Press*, 4.10.17.

In addition to this role as men's replacements, women pointed to the fact that they bore much of the war's real suffering. They were the ones who struggled to keep farms working and families together in their husbands' absence. They were also the ones who had to carry on after husbands and sons were killed or maimed in France. Wilson Macdonald caught this sense of sacrifice in verse:

> Ah! the battlefield is wider than the cannon's sullen roar;
> And the women weep o'er battles lost or won.
> For the man a cross of honour; but the crepe upon the door
> For the girl behind the man behind the gun.[65]

Suffragists enjoyed this image of the noble woman, quietly continuing with her duty and bearing her grief in silence. In reality, however, everything done for the war effort by woman was given the widest possible publicity and described in the most heroic terms possible. Women's pages of western dailies were filled with stories on patriotic service done by women. The caption accompanying a series of pictures featured in the *Winnipeg Tribune* provides an example:

> It is the men warriors who reap all the material rewards of war; it is the men who have medals pinned upon their breasts; it is the men whom the world lauds as heroes. What of the women who labor and suffer at home in the cause of justice and freedom? In Winnipeg there are thousands of women who are doing as much to win battles as their soldier fathers, brothers, husbands and sons. There are women who are devoting every waking hour to the provision of comforts for boys at the front, and to planning for their care when they return.[66]

Magazine articles publicized the female side of the war effort, making it clear that women "count it an honour to engage in an occupation that strengthens the hands of our Empire."[67] Politicians especially were not allowed to forget women's contributions to the struggle with Germany. Letters reminded them how "truly and nobly our women have shown themselves equal to any emergency," and urged that women be given still greater responsibilities.[68]

---

[65] Wilson Macdonald, "The Girl Behind the Man Behind the Gun," in *Song of the Prairie Land* (Toronto, 1918), pp. 124-6.

[66] *Winnipeg Tribune*, 9.10.15.

[67] P.A.A., Miriam Elston Scrapbooks, "The Home Shall be an Honoured Place," *Everywoman's World*, November 1916.

[68] Scott Papers, Ella B. Carroll to Scott, 1.2.16, p. 59492; Norris Papers, W.R. Wood to T.C. Norris, 26.1.18, Box 2. In his work on the domestic impact of the war on Great Britain, Arthur Marwick describes British Women as "a gigantic mutual-admiration circle" during wartime. Marwick, *The Deluge* (London, 1965), p. 96. Marwick's comment can be applied to their Canadian counterparts as well.

Because of this surge of publicity, and partly by direct contact with the new woman, the image men held of women began to change. Some resented the fact that the Red Cross and other activities fell largely into female hands. F.W. Rolt, secretary of the Edmonton Red Cross, found women's new assertiveness so alarming that he resigned his position, claiming that although "I don't wish to control the ladies, still less do I wish to be controlled by them."[69] But most men, even if they shared Rolt's fears about female domination, were grudgingly forced to concede that women were proving that they deserved equal citizenship. When the Dominion Parliament debated the question in 1917, for example, R.B. Bennett reversed his former opposition to women's suffrage. Since women during the war were "discharging their full duties with respect to service," he felt that they must be admitted, "side by side with the male population ... to exercise the highest rights and highest functions of citizenship." Two Western members from the other side of the House voiced enthusiasm for Bennett's conversion. W.A. Buchanan stated simply that he was "in favour of women [sic] suffrage ... because I believe the women have earned the right to that franchise since the war commenced." Michael Clark added that Bennett's opinion would be well received in the West, since it was "in accordance with the opinions of the vast majority of the people of Western Canada."[70]

It was the provincial governments, however, which acted first on the suffrage question. During the opening months of 1916, each Western Province granted its women the provincial franchise. Manitoba came first in January, and in March Alberta and Saskatchewan followed suit. Only one vote was cast against women's suffrage in all three provinces, that by a French-Canadian member of the Alberta House. Albertans made up for this by returning Mrs. Louise McKinney to the Legislature in the provincial election of the following year, and by naming Mrs. Emily Murphy as the first woman magistrate in the British Empire.[71]

The federal franchise was not to come as suddenly or as completely. The Dominion Government's grant of women's suffrage came in stages. It was established in principle by the Military Voters Act, which gave the vote to women serving in the Armed Forces, or as nurses. The controversial Wartime Elections Act, enfranchising close female relatives of men serving overseas, established it further, but still not completely. Those women who gained the ballot, especially those in Western Canada, used it to vote for the government which had given it to them. Complete women's suffrage, like prohibition, was one of the many things reformers hoped for from the newly elected Unionists. Suffragists were not disappointed. Prime Minister Borden personally introduced a franchise bill in April, 1918, and parliamentary assent followed rapidly. On January 1, 1919, less than two months

---

69   University of Alberta Archives, Henry Marshall Tory Papers, F.W. Rolt to H.M. Tory, 15.15.15, f. 14082A.
70   Canada, House of Commons, *Debates*, 1917, vol. II, pp. 1515-19.
71   L.G. Thomas, *The Liberal Party in Alberta* (Toronto, 1959), p. 165. For a detailed description of the passage of each suffrage act, see Cleverdon, *op. cit.*, pp. 46-83.

after the war ended, the crusade for women's suffrage was over, as far as the Prairie Provinces were concerned.

Women's suffrage would have come without the Great War. There can be little doubt that the women of the Western Provinces would have gained the provincial franchise before too many years had passed, and the federal franchise would have followed eventually, although probably after a much longer struggle. But the Great War, with its impact on the suffragists' rationale, organization and public image, speeded the victory at both levels. Perhaps, however, the war's real importance to the women's movement extends beyond the primary question of the right to vote. The dislocations of war won for women a foothold in fields of endeavour formerly reserved for men, and the traditional pattern of domestic service as the working woman's principal occupation. With these new opportunities came a new self-respect. By changing the average woman's image of herself and her position in a world dominated by men, the war advanced the cause of women in ways not simply political.

No other reform group was able to exploit the wartime situation as successfully as were the advocates of women's suffrage and prohibition. The direct legislation movement enjoyed a brief moment of elation in 1916, when Manitoba's Norris government introduced an Initiative and Referendum Act. The Act was not accompanied by any large-scale campaign based on the mid-war enthusiasm for democracy, but was the fulfilment of a commitment Norris had made while Leader of the Opposition. The Saskatchewan Conservative Party attempted to resurrect the direct democracy issue during the 1917 Provincial Election, but were unable to use it to gain any political advantage.[72] This was in part because of the fact that a substantial number of those who had originally supported the initiative and referendum had done so as a means to obtain prohibition, not because of a strong belief in direct legislation for its own sake. By 1917 these people were satisfied, and saw no need to campaign for a tool they no longer needed to use.

The economic reforms sought by Western reformers proved even more difficult to obtain. Unlike prohibition, women's suffrage, and direct legislation, most of these had to come from the Dominion Parliament, a body not as easily influenced as a provincial government. The war did pave the way for some specific objectives. During 1917 the first Canadian tax on incomes was imposed, and the principle of railway nationalization as exemplified by the case of the Canadian Northern was also well received in the West. Western support for Union Government was based on the assumption that more such action would be forthcoming, most particularly a reduction in the tariff. In this respect, and on the question of economic reform in general, Westerners were to be sadly disillusioned during the final year of war.

---

[72] Chambers, "Plebiscite and Referendum," p. 63.

The Great Depression

Section 17

The Great Depression of the 1930s was an international phenomenon, but Canadian society and Canadian governments still had to face it and come up with their own solutions to it. Unemployment and distress appeared to exist on a never-before-imagined scale, and governments just didn't seem able to deal with them. Consequently, discontent spread and began to express itself in support for new parties thrown up by the depression and promising radical new solutions to society's problems.

In 1933, the CCF was formed with a programme that proposed to replace capitalism by co-operation. In 1935, the newly founded Social Credit party swept to power in Alberta with a combination of Christian fundamentalism and esoteric economic theory—and the following year, another new party, the Union Nationale, won power in Quebec, ending the Liberals' 39-year rule of that province. Even the Communists gained adherents, organising in the streets, the work camps, and the unions. In the 1935 federal elections, there were almost as many CCF, Social Credit, and independent MPs elected as Conservatives.

Why was there so much disillusionment with the traditional parties? Were they really unable to come to grips with the depression?

The first of these two articles looks at the federal Conservative government. The Conservatives, under R.B.Bennett, came to power months after the depression began, when voters got the impression that the Liberal prime minister, W.L.Mackenzie King, wasn't taking it seriously enough. But five years later, Bennett was repudiated and his party humiliated at the polls.

How did Bennett attempt to deal with the problem of unemployment? How different were his attitudes toward relief from those of the mid-19th century described by Judith Fingard (in topic #9)? Why did welfare seem dangerous or unadvisable to so many people even in a time of such depression?

How did the depression and Bennett's handling of it affect the rise of the CCF? Was this a mere reaction to the problems of the 1930s or did it have roots in the past? Why was the West so much a region of radicalism in general and so important to the CCF in particular?

For a general survey of the 1920s and 30s, see John H.Thompson, *Canada, 1922-1939: Decades of Discord*.

Two Depressions:
Bennett, Trudeau and the Unemployed

James Struthers

Recent changes in Canada's unemployment insurance programme seem to defy logic and common sense. At a time when unemployment has reached a level unprecedented since the Great Depression, the government is *reducing* benefits and *stiffening* eligibility requirements. "Do you know what this means," Toronto's chairman points out. "It means we'll have 2,500 more people a month looking for money at the worst possible time of the year—a time when virtually all seasonal workers are out of a job."[1]

Why is the federal government cutting its support to the unemployed precisely when the problem has reached critical proportions? Why, as Paul Godfrey accurately observes, is it "shifting the burden...to the provinces and municipalities?"[2] The prime minister claims the cuts are justified because the unemployed have become "too fussy about what jobs they'll take,"[3] a simplified version of the Economic Council of Canada's argument that unemployment insurance itself has "increase[d] the incentive to be unemployed or remain unemployed."[4]

But is the unemployment insurance programme itself to blame for our record level of joblessness? Are the unemployed themselves the authors of their plight? One way of finding an answer and clarifying much of the current confusion over whether unemployment is real or "insurance-induced"[5] is to examine how another prime minister treated the unemployed during our last great economic crisis—the Depression of the 1930s. That was the decade which produced our original unemployment insurance programme. It was also the decade in which many of the current contradictions surrounding unemployment policy in a market society first became apparent.

We usually think the Depression produced a straightforward, clearcut unemployment problem. Surely if ever there was a time Canadians could agree that the unemployed were out of work through no fault of their own it was in 1933 when

---

1 *Toronto Star*, September 2, 1978.
2 Ibid.
3 Ibid., August 17, 1978.
4 C. Green and J.M. Cousineau, *Unemployment in Canada: The Impact of Unemployment Insurance* (Ottawa: 1976), p. 115.
5 Herbert G. Grubel, Dennis Maki and Shelley Sax, "Real and Insurance-Induced Unemployment in Canada," *Canadian Journal of Political Science*, VIII, no. 2, May 1975.

the jobless rate reached the record level of almost 30%.[6] Yet, as will be shown later, such was not the case. To understand why first requires an understanding of what the Depression meant in social as well as economic terms.

Between 1926 and 1929 the Canadian economy and the Canadian labour force expanded at a phenomenal rate. During these three years 537,000 people entered the work force for the first time, expanding it by twenty-five percent.[7] Most of this growth occurred within cities, which absorbed seventy-seven per cent of Canada's population increase during the 1920s. While agricultural income between 1926 and 1929 remained about the same, manufacturing, mining and construction income grew by 30%, 35% and 45% respectively.[8] In short, the creation of high-paying jobs, particularly in the durable goods industries, attracted hundreds of thousands of new workers into Canada's cities during the second half of the 1920s.

Most came from the countryside or abroad. Another large proportion were women.[9] For all of them, the entry into urban, wage-paying occupations was a form of social mobility, especially since the five years before 1926 were characterized by high unemployment.[10] Farm labourers got factory jobs for the first time; women moved out of the household into wage-paying occupations, and hundreds of thousands of immigrants rejected the lure of the "last, best West" for the more lucrative attractions of city living.

By 1931 their hopes had been shattered. Between 1929 and that year, the volume of employment contracted by exactly twenty-five per cent and by 1933 it had shrunk by thirty-two per cent, while national income as a whole was forty per cent below 1929 levels.[11] In large part, the first to be thrown out of work by this collapse were those with the most tenuous attachment to the labour market, that is, those who got their jobs after 1926. Their numbers swelled rapidly. By January 1933, 718,000 were without work[12] and all governments, as well as the unemployed themselves, were

---

[6] *Census of Canada*, 1931, vol. XIII, Monograph on Unemployment, p. 274. S.A. Cudmore of the D.B.S. put the rate at 33% in his January, 1934 "Report on Unemployment," Bennett Papers (PAC), vol. 782.

[7] Bennett Papers, vol. 782, S.A. Cudmore, "Report on Unemployment," Jan. 4, 1934.

[8] A.E. Safarian, *The Canadian Economy in the Great Depression* (Toronto: 1970), pp. 34-7.

[9] The number of women in the labour force increased by 36% in the 1920s. Mary Vipond, "The Image of Women in Mass Circulation Magazines in the 1920s" in S. Trofimenkoff and A. Prentice, eds., *The Neglected Majority* (Toronto: 1977), p. 117.

[10] In the winters of 1921 and 1922 unemployment rose to over 12% of the work force. As late as 1925 it was still rising to over 10% in the winter. *Census of Canada*, 1931, vol. XIII, Monograph on Unemployment, pp. 275-6. For Ottawa's response to this problem see my "Prelude to Depression: The Federal Government and Unemployment, 1918-1929," *Canadian Historical Review*, September 1977.

[11] Bennett Papers, vol. 782. S.A. Cudmore, "Report on Unemployment," Jan. 4, 1934; Leonard Marsh, *Canadians In and Out of Work* (1940), p. 260.

[12] *Census of Canada*, 1931, vol. XIII, Monograph on Unemployment, p. 274.

faced with an agonizing moral dilemma. Did those who had entered the labour force for the first time in the late twenties have the right to work?

Almost 300,000 said no. They simply disappeared from the work force by 1933, either leaving the country, going back to housework or returning as unpaid labourers to their family farms.[13] But another 300,000 disagreed. That was the approximate number of individuals and heads of families who were collecting direct relief in the nation's cities by May 1933, pending a return of work.[14] "Under past conditions," the Dominion Bureau of Statistics pointed out a year later, "this surplus population would have emigrated on the depression; under a system of relief they remained."[15] And the question they raised for the employers who had lured them there in the first place, as well as for the governments who were responsible for their care, was simply this: how long should the state underwrite their hopes for social mobility by providing either work or relief in the cities until prosperity returned?

The first answer was provided by Mackenzie King. Faced with fighting an election during the first year of the crisis, he quickly discovered that one of the principal issues of the campaign was whether the federal government should provide unemployment relief for the jobless. King said no. Reasoning that "the men who are working are not going to worry particularly over some of those who are not,"[16] he refused either to call a conference on unemployment or to provide a federal contribution to municipal relief efforts as Ottawa had done during the last depression of 1920-22.

His opponent adopted the opposite position. R.B. Bennett promised that if elected he would "end unemployment" by providing jobs "for all who can and will work." "Someone is responsible for unemployment," Bennett argued, "not individuals, but governments." If given power, he would "abolish the dole" and provide "work and wages" for the unemployed.[17] An electorate uneasy over the growing numbers of idle men naturally preferred this more positive approach and rewarded Bennett with office in 1930. However, as King's defeated labour minister pointed out, they also gave him "a mandate to look after employment and unemployment, and no matter what the written word of the Constitution may be, the Canadian people have now placed this matter in the lap of the Federal Government."[18]

At first, Bennett did not shy away from this burden. Stiff hikes in the tariff, he was convinced, would soon give work in protected industries to all who needed it. In the meantime, to tide the jobless over the upcoming winter until these changes had had a chance to take effect, Bennett also provided $20,000,000 for unemployment relief—ten times more than Ottawa spent on this problem during the entire decade of

---

[13] Marsh, *op. cit.*, p. 281.
[14] *Report of the Dominion Director of Unemployment Relief*, March 31, 1941, p. 36.
[15] Bennett Papers, vol. 782, S.A. Cudmore, "Report on Unemployment," Jan. 4, 1934.
[16] King Diary (PAC), June 14, 1930.
[17] Canada, House of Commons, *Debates*, Sept. 9, 1930, pp. 21-7.
[18] King Papers (PAC), J-4 series, vol. 141, Peter Heenan to King, July, 1930.

the twenties. True to his pledge of giving work, not doles to the unemployed, Bennett also set aside $16,000,000 of this grant for support to municipal public works in order to provide jobs. Only $4,000,000 was to go for direct relief.

Though the amount was unprecedented, the method of distribution was not. The care of the unemployed was still "primarily a provincial and municipal responsibility," the 1930 relief act pointed out. Bennett's government was not assuming any "new constitutional obligations."[19] It was simply helping the provinces and cities tide the unemployed over the winter. These governments would administer the grant, contribute their own equal share, and decide how the money should be spent. Ottawa's help was financial only.

The help was also temporary, for the act expired at the end of March 1931 and was not renewed. Yet the number of jobless, contrary to expectations, did not decline over the summer months. By July 1931, usually one of the busiest times of the year, 18% of the work force was still unemployed.[20] Most worrisome among this group were the thousands of seasonal labourers or "bunkhouse men", who usually resided in the cities over the slack winter months and departed for work on the nation's farms, railways and lumber camps in the spring. In 1931 they did not move out for there was nowhere for them to go. Yet since they were not municipal residents, the cities denied they had a claim for relief. As one social worker put it, "any humane treatment of these men...[would] make it impossible to eliminate the number."[21]

As a result, thousands began "riding the rods" looking for work or at least a meal and shelter for the night. Their "constantly increasing" numbers soon appeared to represent a "menace to ... peace and...safety" in the eyes of Bennett's labour minister, Gideon Robertson, especially since few seemed "very anxious to obtain work" and "communist agitators and advocates [were] utilizing this method of travel to spread their propaganda." Consequently, in July he recommended that the first priority of any new relief legislation should be the "removal of thousands of transients from urban centres." They should be placed in relief camps constructed along the route of the proposed Trans-Canada highway and "put to work promptly under supervision equivalent to semi-military control." If they refused to go they would "forfeit their right to State Assistance."[22] For these men, at least, there could be no right to urban relief.

The new relief act introduced in late July incorporated Robertson's suggestions. To get the men out of the cities, Bennett provided financial support to provincial

---

[19] *Statutes of Canada*, 21 George V, p. 1: "An Act for the granting of aid for the Relief of Unemployment," Sept. 22, 1930; Canada, House of Commons, *Debates*, Sept. 12, 1930, p. 174.

[20] *Census of Canada*, 1931, vol. XIII, Monograph on Unemployment, p. 274.

[21] Canadian Council on Social Development Papers (PAC), vol. 14, file 56, Ethel Parker to Charlotte Whitton, March 6, 1931.

[22] Bennett Papers, vol. 778, Gideon Robertson to Bennett, June 19, 1931.

highway programmes and to ensure they would go, he pointed out that *"where* there is work there will be pay and...if an individual is capable of work and will not work, there will be no benefits."[23] More ominously, the 1931 relief act also gave the federal government sweeping powers under the "peace, order and good government" clause of the constitution to fine or imprison anyone disobeying orders or regulations issued under its terms.[24] It was the first sign that coercion might be necessary to provide work for all who were capable of doing it.

Nor was Bennett even sure, by 1931, that he could live up to that pledge. Instead, he would only promise that "no-one will be asked to accept direct relief for whom suitable work can be procured."[25] What constituted "suitable" work was unstated.

Once Britain went off the gold standard on September 21, even this limited commitment was abandoned. Since the value of the Canadian dollar was pegged to British sterling, the initial effect of this decision was to depreciate it in terms of American currency, thus raising the cost of paying back debts owed to U.S. creditors. Terrified that the nation's credit was now in peril, Bennett determined upon a policy of "most rigid economy" for his administration.[26] Before the British move, he had talked in terms of a $50,000,000 relief programme for the winter of 1931-32. Instead, he spent only $28,000,000. It was not enough to provide most of the unemployed with more than two weeks' work or a meagre $68 in earnings over that year.[27]

When the 1931 act expired in the spring, Bennett abandoned public works altogether. The new relief act, introduced in April, for the first time provided funds for unemployment relief over the summer months, but for direct relief only. Stung by business criticism that his relief programme was endangering the nation's credit and "holding back normal...development,"[28] and perplexed by the failure of his tariff hikes to create jobs, Bennett gave up his attempt to provide work for the unemployed. It was the ultimate irony. Having won office by promising to "abolish the dole," he was now forced to rely on it as the sole remaining unemployment policy of his administration.

However, more than financial reasons lay behind this decision. Once it became clear that the unemployment problem was more permanent than most had thought, attitudes towards it and towards the unemployed began to change. Bennett, for example, could accept the fact that most of the unemployed had lost their jobs through no fault of their own. What he could not understand was why so many had

---

[23] Canada, House of Commons, *Debates*, July 29, 1931, p. 4278 (my emphasis).
[24] *Statutes of Canada*, 21-22 George V, Chapter 58, p. 429.
[25] Canada, House of Commons *Debates*, July 29, 1931, p. 4277.
[26] Bennett Papers, vol. 798, Bennett to R.B. Hanson, Oct. 22, 1931.
[27] Ibid., vol. 778, R.J. Manion to Bennett, July 1, 1931; *Report of the Dominion Director of Unemployment Relief*, March 30, 1935, p. 32; Harry Cassidy, *Unemployment and Relief in Ontario, 1929-1932* (Toronto: 1932), p. 145.
[28] *Financial Post*, November 14, 1931.

to depend upon the government to survive. "The people are not bearing their share of the load," he complained in October 1931. "Half a century ago people would work their way out of their difficulties rather than look to a government to take care of them. The fibre of some of our people has grown softer and they are not willing to turn in and save themselves."[29]

One reason, perhaps, was the existence of relief work itself. The wages were low, but not humiliating, and useful labour was performed in return. By working on such projects, men could still feel they had "earned" their living. As one M.P. noted, "many men who would never ask for direct relief will, without any feelings of humiliation, take a quota of relief work."[30] By abandoning such work projects, the government could reduce its responsibilities to only the genuinely needy. Direct relief, as one relief administrator pointed out years later,

> was a disgrace. Men would say that never in the history of their family—and they'd usually mention something about the British Empire Loyalists or coming West with the first C.P.R. trains—never had they had to go on relief... I've seen tears in men's eyes, as though they were signing away their manhood, their right to be a husband and sit at the head of the table and carve the roast. It was a very emotional time, that first time when a man came in and went up to the counter.[31]

It was meant to be, for direct relief in most Canadian cities—true to the poor law tradition of "less eligibility"—was related not to need, but to the lowest wages for unskilled labour in the surrounding area. The stigma and humiliation of a degrading level of existence were the traditional tactics used for making it less appealing than the most brutal and unremunerative form of manual work. Now these tactics would be applied to all the unemployed in an effort to ensure that any kind of work in any part of the country would remain preferable to the "dole."

To underline this point, Bennett made two important modifications to his 1932 relief act. The first was to provide five dollars a month for unemployed men willing to work on farms in the four western provinces over the upcoming winter. The second was to establish a relief settlement programme. It provided $600 ($200 in grants and $400 in loans) to any unemployed urban family on relief with previous agricultural experience that was willing to resettle on one of the nation's 33,000 abandoned farms. It was strictly "a relief measure and not...a colonization scheme," Bennett's new labour minister, W.A. Gordon, pointed out, whose object was to "get...people back on the land...where they can...keep themselves...The question of

---

29   Bennett Papers, vol. 794, Bennett to J.G. Bennett, Oct. 21, 1931.
30   Ibid., vol. 793, undated, unsigned letter (*circa* March 1932) from a Saskatchewan M.P. to Bennett, p. 489188.
31   Barry Broadfoot, *Ten Lost Years* (Toronto: 1973), p. 70.

selling...their surplus produce will have to come later on." Moreover, with a bushel of wheat going for the lowest price in recorded history, even Gordon was "at a loss to know whether today a man should be on a farm or in a city...no matter where [he] may be...he is in a very bad way."[32] Nevertheless, the programme carried a clear implication. Even the most miserable form of rural subsistence should be preferable to urban relief.

More tangible evidence of this hardening attitude towards the unemployed came that autumn. Over the summer. Bennett had appointed Charlotte Whitton, head of the Canadian Council on Child and Family Welfare, to investigate the soaring numbers dependent upon the dole in western Canada. Her October report was apocalyptic. The West, Whitton wrote, was not merely impoverished, it was becoming "pauperized." The widespread provision of direct relief had been taken up, not by the "emergency" unemployed but by the "permanently" jobless—that is, the hundreds of thousands of casual, unskilled farm labourers who were normally without work during winter months. As a result, it had succeeded only in "raising...the standard of employment and living of the great volume of the under-employed," and the whole problem was drifting towards "the inauguration of a system of permanent poor relief in the Dominion of Canada."[33]

Whitton went to great lengths to document how this was taking place. Farmers and their sons, for example, had been employed on relief projects in great numbers "when there was no actual question of the need of food, fuel, clothing or shelter for themselves and...when ordinarily the winter was a period of idleness." In southern Alberta, the large-scale provision of direct relief had "arrested...any natural disintegration" of dying mining communities and "served to `suspend' them on direct relief." The same argument applied to "dead communities" in the northern and rural fringes of all provinces which were composed of "small packets of people, generally those with the least initiative and thrift" who had been "swept back or left behind as settlements moved elsewhere."

Unemployed women fell into the same category. Theirs was "not solely nor essentially an unemployment problem." Rather, it was a "social problem" arising from desertion, death, or illegitimacy and, as such, did "not form a justifiable charge on the [relief] legislation." Direct relief had also raised the standard of living of unemployed single men and immigrant families. Too many of the former who could have stayed on farms during the winter were "going to the cities where `they could get two good meals and a bed a day on relief' and `have a real rest for the winter.'" As for immigrants, the support they received from the dole was in many cases higher than what they could get while working. Whitton argued it was "neither just nor efficient to provide supplies on a scale neither attained nor desired by these people

---

[32] Bennett Papers, vol. 783, memo to W.A. Gordon on "Unemployment Relief — Land Settlement," March 29, 1932; W.A. Gordon to Bennett, April 6, 1932.

[33] Ibid., vols. 779-780, memo from Whitton to Bennett on "Unemployment and Relief in Western Canada, Summer 1932," pp. 478800-1, 478928-30, 478847.

from their own resources or efforts." If the present system of subsidizing the existence of the marginally employed continued, she warned, "it becomes only a matter of time until the uninterrupted increase in all forms of social dependency becomes so great a burden on public funds that the whole substructure of public finance is undermined."[34] As a solution, she recommended the total reorganization of the relief system, under strict federal "leadership" (and employing the expertise of the social work profession) so that the casually unemployed could be taken off the dole before they became "permanently dependent at a scale of living which they never had and never will be able to provide for themselves."[35]

Whitton's report—the only one Bennett ever commissioned on unemployment relief—could not have been more tailored to confirm his own fears that widespread abuse of the dole was the real reason behind its rapidly increasing costs. However, the result was not what she intended. Rather than demanding that its administration be turned over to the social work profession through more rigid conditional grant legislation, Bennett instead resolved to get his government out of relief altogether. If the provinces and municipalities were wasting federal money, the solution was not to press for stricter standards through legislation, but simply to give them less money to waste. In short, by emphasizing the abuse rather than the inadequacy of direct relief, Whitton destroyed any chance that it might be reformed.

Only one of her recommendations was adopted. In October 1932, Ottawa began the takeover of direct administration of relief to single homeless men "so that discipline may be enforced."[36] The department of national defence launched a pilot relief camp scheme employing 2,000 men clearing airfields along the proposed route of the Trans-Canada Airway. The cost of their care could not exceed $1.00 a day, Bennet told General Andrew McNaughton, the principal author of the scheme; therefore, the men themselves received the princely "allowance" of twenty cents for their daily labours.[37] From Ottawa's point of view, the experiment was a great success and a year later the camps were caring for 20,000 single men working across the country on a wide variety of projects demanding unskilled, menial work.

The relief camp scheme has usually been viewed as a strictly cynical attempt to get the most dangerous class of unemployed out of the cities and under military supervision so that unrest could be avoided. Certainly, this was one principal object of the plan. Without the camps, McNaughton argued, it was "only a question of time until we had to resort to arms to restore and maintain order."[38]

Just as important, however, was the camps' function as a "Workhouse test". Before they were established, single homeless men, especially in the West, had been

---

[34] Ibid., pp. 478093-4, 478096-9, 478105, 478823, 478858-9.
[35] Ibid., pp. 478848-55, 478812.
[36] Ibid., vol. 793, Bennett to G.A. Sylte, October 5, 1932.
[37] James Eayrs, *In Defence of Canada*, vol. 1, pp. 125-6.
[38] McNaughton Papers (PAC), vol. 37, memo of meeting between W.A. Gordon and McNaughton, Oct. 3, 1933.

receiving relief through government-funded hostels and subsistence relief camps operated by the provinces. As a result, by 1932, federal officials fretted that a "dole mentality was creeping into the minds of the single unemployed" and that many had "acquired the mental attitude that such assistance from the State was their inherent right."[39] The "moral purpose" of the DND camps, according to McNaughton, was to cure this "state of mind diseased by the demoralizing effect of compulsory idleness" by subjecting the men to the influence of "steady work, wholesome food and congenial surroundings."[40] In short, it was an attempt to preserve the work ethic among Canada's bunkhouse men until jobs returned. As Bennett's labour minister pointed out, if their "usefulness" was to be maintained, it was "essential" to demand that "work...be performed by those in receipt of relief from the State."[41]

Precisely because they were a "workhouse test" rather than a means of providing work, the wages had to be kept at the extremely low rate of twenty cents a day in order to "encourage" the men, in McNaughton's words, to "return to normal industry as soon as opportunity offers."[42] From the men's point of view, however, this was ridiculous. Only the fact that they had been cut off from relief in the cities in the first place had forced them into the camps and once there they were forced to "work...to get what they obtained from the B.C. Government for nothing"—that is, subsistence.[43] As one man put it in 1933, "you come in broke, work all winter and still you are broke. It looks like they want to keep us bums all our lives."[44] It was just this contradiction that produced the "On-to-Ottawa" trek two years later.

Although flawed in conception, the camps represented Bennett's only extension of federal responsibility for the unemployed before his "New Deal" reforms of 1935. The remainder of his unemployment policy proceeded in exactly the opposite direction—towards reducing Ottawa's link with the jobless. Again, one reason was the soaring cost of relief. By April 1933, over 1,500,000 people were dependent upon the dole for survival and it was costing Bennett's government over $31,000,000 a year in direct grants for their care. In addition, Ottawa had been forced to loan another $38,000,000 to the four bankrupt western provinces to keep them solvent. By abandoning public works for direct relief Bennett had hoped to move towards a

---

39 Ibid., vol. 37, W.A. Gordon to F.J. McManus, Sept. 26, 1933.
40 Bennett Papers, vol. 783, memo by McNaughton on "The department of National Defence Unemployment Relief Scheme with some observations concerning the United States Civilian Conservation Corps," October 1933.
41 McNaughton Papers, vol. 37, W.A. Gordon to F.J. McManus, Sept. 26, 1933.
42 Dept. of National Defence Records (PAC), vol. 2965. Memo of meeting between Harry Hereford, Andrew McNaughton and William Finlayson, July 6, 1933.
43 McNaughton Papers, vol. 44, file 319, H.H. Matthews (D.O.C.B.C.) to McNaughton, June 16, 1933.
44 Dept. of National Defence Records, vol. 3181, quote from *Winnipeg Free Press*, Oct. 28, 1933.

balanced budget. Instead, by 1933 between a quarter and a third of the work force was unemployed and the federal deficit had ballooned to almost $160,000,000.[45]

Federal officials were not convinced that need alone explained these soaring expenditures. "Sufficient emphasis was not being placed upon the responsibility of the individual to maintain himself," Bennett's labour minister told the provincial premiers at a 1933 conference. "Wherever a province relieves the municipality of a share of the cost [of direct relief] the barriers are to that extent let down" and the same argument applied to Ottawa's share of the dole. If it were expanded, as the provinces demanded, relief administration would be "without restraint". Instead, W.A. Gordon put forward a different solution. "The land offers the best prospect for maintenance and independence of those who cannot find employment in the cities." To ensure the western provincial governments would pass this message on to their unemployed, Ottawa demanded that their deficits be kept below $1,000,000 a year as a condition for further federal loans.[46] In this way, perhaps, they might encourage the jobless more directly to take advantage of the relief settlement and farm placement schemes, and thus "assist...in the restoration of the balance between [the] urban and rural population which is so necessary."[47]

If Whitton's 1932 report were correct, it would be relief itself that was attracting casual labourers from the country into the cities, and thus adding to Ottawa's already staggering deficit. This trend had to be reversed. The provinces would have to be forced to push the unemployed back to the land where they could become "self-sustaining", even if that land was plagued by grasshoppers and drought. As Gordon warned the House in March 1933, only with the "gradual turn towards other vocations than those which have afforded a certain sense of security to our people in the past" could relief be phased out.[48]

C.C.F. critics put it differently. Gordon's real intention, in their view, was to create a Canadian "peasantry" that would "form a labour reserve to be called upon at a time when working conditions in the cities improve."[49] One thing at least was clear. By 1933, "Back to the Land" was the Bennett government's only long-range solution to the unemployment crisis. It was to be achieved by forcing the unemployed out of the cities.

There were two ways of implementing this strategy, one administrative, the other financial. As it had done with single men, Ottawa could simply take over the administration of direct relief itself for all the unemployed and in this way ensure that

---

[45] *Report of the Dominion Director of Unemployment Relief*, March 31, 1936, pp. 36, 33; Ibid., March 31, 1933, p. 25; *Census of Canada*, 1931, vol. XIII, Monograph on Unemployment, p. 274.

[46] Bennett Papers, vol. 561, "Minutes of the Dominion-Provincial Conference, Jan. 17-19, 1933," pp. 346894-955; vol. 566, Bennett to the four western premiers, March 9, 1933.

[47] Ibid., vol. 561, "Memoranda Regarding Questions on the Agenda," Jan. 17, 1933.

[48] Canada, House of Commons, *Debates*, Feb. 24, 1933, p. 2464.

[49] Ibid., March 2, 1933, p. 2657.

their support was kept low enough to make subsistence farming attractive. This was never seriously considered. Apart from its constitutional ambiguities, it would necessitate creating a vast federal relief structure—something Bennett was loath to do when he still believed the Depression was an emergency and that Ottawa's responsibility for the unemployed was only temporary.

More importantly, direct federal administration of the dole posed an enormous threat to the "less eligibility" principle upon which poor relief was based. As a Department of Labour memo on the subject pointed out, Canada was a "country of such widely varied conditions" that unemployment relief could not be administered "with any standardized methods across the Dominion." Instead, it had to be "met on the basis of need existing in each district" and for this reason municipal administration of the dole was best suited for "adopt[ing] different and varying means to cope with the situation."[50] Ottawa could not provide one standard of support for Gloucester, New Brunswick and another for Toronto. The municipalities could, and that was why they had to be held responsible for relief, even if they were financially unable to bear the burden. Local variations in relief scales were not an unfortunate byproduct of this policy, they were the reason for it. To abandon this approach might court disaster.

Hence Bennett opted for a financial solution. If Ottawa cut off all support for relief, the provinces and municipalities would be so financially hard-pressed that they would have no alternative but to impose rigorous relief standards upon the unemployed and weed out all those who, as Whitton claimed, were using the dole to improve their standard of living. In short, "less eligibility" could be enforced by shifting the burden of depression entirely onto the shoulders of the provinces, the municipalities and ultimately, the unemployed themselves. As the deputy minister of labour put it at the height of the crisis in May 1933, "there was the utmost need of impressing upon the municipalities that relief must be curtailed and the fact brought home to the individual that responsibility for caring for himself and his dependents devolved *solely upon himself*."[51]

Paradoxically, unemployment insurance appeared as one of the best ways of implementing this strategy. With so many out of work, it would be politically impossible for Ottawa to disavow all responsibility for the unemployed, especially after Bennett's extravagant promises in 1930. But, with the relief camp scheme, a modest programme of public works *and* a system of unemployment insurance, Bennett's principal advisor, Rod Finlayson, pointed out in 1933, "the administration of direct relief could then be entirely decentralized and its responsibility relegated to the provinces." In this way, Bennett's administration could "escape the charge that it has accepted a policy of dole."[52]

---

[50] Bennett Papers, vol. 781, "Memorandum *re* Heaps Motion," Nov. 16, 1932.
[51] Ibid., vol. 794, W.M. Dickson to A.E. Millar, May 29, 1933 (my emphasis).
[52] Ibid., vol. 813, memo from Finlayson to Bennett, n.d. (*circa* Dec. 1932-Jan. 1933).

Deputy finance minister W.C. Clark agreed. "If you segregated...unemployment relief from the insurance scheme," he advised Bennett on the eve of the 1933 dominion-provincial conference,

> you will make it much easier for your provinces to give you the new constitutional powers for which you are asking. Today, they are naturally hesitant about accepting a share in the cost of unemployment relief when the size of that burden is entirely uncertain. If you merely say to them that you will take care of the unemployment insurance programme, but that they must not expect such an insurance programme to do everything...they will, I think, be prepared to accept the major responsibility which they now have for unemployment relief.[53]

In short, accepting national responsibility for unemployment insurance would provide the perfect cover for abandoning all responsibility for direct relief.

Moreover, such a scheme need not be expensive. Benefits would be related to previous contributions, not need, and "insurance principles" would provide an effective ceiling to ensure they would not get out of hand. More importantly, Ottawa would only have to finance a minor share of the burden. Its major cost would be paid for by employers and the workers themselves.

It was powerful logic and by early 1934 it had won Bennett over. At another dominion-provincial conference in January, Gordon told the premiers that all federal support for relief would be phased out in the spring. In its place, Ottawa would launch a programme of "useful" public works and relief would be "restored" to the municipalities. At the same time, Bennett gave Finlayson the green light to prepare a draft unemployment insurance scheme.[54]

Over the winter, with the help of two actuaries and a British government official, Finlayson drafted the legislation, based largely upon the scheme in force in Great Britain. It was a highly conservative piece of work designed to preserve the "less eligibility" principle. Since the "heaviest incidence of unemployment," labour department officials noted, was among "manual and unskilled workers," they were largely left out of the plan by exempting most seasonal workers from contributions. Moreover, a uniform "flat-rate" of benefit was established at the miserable level of six dollars a week. "Unemployment insurance in itself increases...unemployment," Canada's chief actuary argued, and "this shows how dangerous and undesirable anything like generous unemployment benefits would be."[55]

---

53   Ibid., vol. 810, W.C. Clark to Bennett, Jan. 18, 1933.
54   Ibid., vol. 181, "Minutes of Dominion-Provincial Conference, Jan. 17, 1934;" vol. 813, R.H. Coats to Rod Finlayson, Feb. 2, 1934.
55   Dept. of Insurance Records (PAC), vol. 1, A.D. Watson to R.K. Finlayson, April 11, 1934; memo on "Rates of Benefit," n.d. but *circa* April 1934.

The six dollar weekly payment did not pose such a threat. Even supplemented by dependents' benefits that would bring it up to $11.40 a week for a family of five, it was still well below the minimum budget of $17.30 which the Montreal Council of Social Agencies recommended was necessary to maintain health and decency for that same household in 1933.[56] However, just to make sure the work "incentive" was maintained, a further clause was added that benefits could in no case exceed 80% of wages, no matter how low. Although unemployment insurance would have a ceiling, there would be no floor. Finally, the stipulation that forty weeks' contributions over two years would be needed before benefits could be paid guaranteed that the scheme would only care for the most regularly employed, that is, those who needed it least. It also ensured no benefits would be paid for at least a year. The total cost of the plan, the actuaries estimated, might well come to $50,000,000 a year but Ottawa's share would only be one fifth of this amount.[57]

The bill was ready for Parliament by June and Finlayson urged immediate action. The longer Bennett delayed bringing down the legislation, "the more difficult it will become as a political undertaking." Modern social thinking now held that unemployment insurance was "only a first line of defence and that a well-organized national form of relief must be established as a last line." At the moment, however, relief was "repulsive" to the country. Thus, if Bennett brought down his public works bill

> followed by insurance legislation, you have selected the most opportune time to get this job behind you as far as the political values are concerned. *This spring it could be done...without raising the relief question.* A year from now I am not quite sure that it could.[58]

Instead, Bennett ignored Finlayson's advice. His $40,000,000 Public Works Construction Act was introduced into Parliament in June. But there was no insurance bill. Nevertheless, at the same time Bennett announced that Ottawa would terminate its contributions to direct relief by June 15. The people had become "more or less relief-conscious," he argued two months later, "and were determined to get out of the Government, whether it be municipal, provincial or federal, all they could."[59] The time had come when it was necessary to draw the line.

The announcement provoked a storm of criticism. Provincial premiers claimed Bennett was trying to do something "that cannot be done." Mayors argued their

---

[56] Ibid., memo on "Rates of Benefit."
[57] Ibid., vol. 1, Watson to H. Wolfenden, Jan. 12, 1935; G.D. Finlayson to A.D. Watson, "Memo on Coverage, Exclusions and Exemptions, Eligibility Conditions, etc.," April 6, 1934.
[58] Bennett Papers, vol. 812, R.K. Finlayson to Bennett, May 25, 1934 (my emphasis).
[59] Ibid., vol. 790, Bennett to W.J. McCully, August 6, 1934.

already "meagre" relief scales could not be lowered. The R.C.M.P. requested an extra reserve in the West to deal with the anticipated unrest. Even within his own party, backbench M.P.s argued that Bennett's decision was a "neglect of duty" that would "spell disaster."[60] As a result, Bennett modified his stand. Instead of abandoning all support for relief, he only changed the policy of making a one-third percentage contribution. From August 15 onwards, fixed monthly grants-in-aid to the provinces based on need would replace percentage payments. And Ottawa alone would determine the need.

The premiers understandably were outraged by this arbitrary cut in federal support when over 1,100,000 were still on the dole, but Bennett remained unmoved. Relief had become a "racket," he told them at a hastily convened conference at the end of July. Adopting Whitton's views, he argued that at least twenty per cent of the expenditure was going to "partially employed" workers whose wages were as high as before the Depression. Ottawa would not continue to "pay a subsidy" for these low-wage labourers who were now enjoying a "hitherto unknown" standard of living.

Nor would it permit the provinces to "scrap the constitution" by packing relief rolls with indigent unemployables who were normally a municipal responsibility. Up to now, Bennett pointed out, local governments had "not taken any steps to prevent abuses."[61] Limited to a fixed federal grant, they might. As the *Edmonton Journal* concluded, "the fixed budget plan...will have a tendency to make cities think twice before they increase relief scales for, hereafter, the whole burden of such increases is likely to fall on their own taxpayers."[62]

After totally alienating the premiers by these high-handed tactics, Bennett then asked them, one month later, whether they were "prepared to surrender their *exclusive jurisdiction* over...unemployment insurance."[63] His political timing could not have been worse. While the financially beleaguered western provinces could hardly refuse, Ontario and Quebec were in no mood to make any concessions after Bennett's ruthless cut in support for relief.

Realizing that agreement was impossible, the Tory leader soon abandoned his enthusiasm for another conference and by November it had been called off. Instead, he decided simply to seize the authority he needed for his insurance legislation and worry about the constitutional implications after the election. Thus, the Employment and

---

[60] Ibid., vol. 792, L.A. Taschereau to Gordon, June 1, 1934; J. Bracken to Gordon, June 27, 1934; vol. 785, Angus Macdonald to Gordon, June 1, 1934; vol. 795, J.E. Brownlee to Bennett, May 9, 1934; vol. 797, T.D. Pattullo to Bennett, June 1, 1934; vol. 790, E. Wilton to Bennett, July 13, 1934; vol. 795, D.O.C., R.C.M.P., Edmonton, June 5, 1934; vol. 792 Jimmy Stitt to Bennett, June 5, 1934.

[61] Ibid., vol. 182, "Minutes of the July 31, 1934 Dominion-Provincial Conference," Bennett to Jimmy Stitt, July 30, 1934.

[62] Ibid., Vol. 798, editorial from the *Edmonton Journal*, Aug. 16, 1934.

[63] Ibid., vol. 182, draft letter by Bennett to all provincial premiers, Aug. 31, 1934 (my emphasis).

Social Insurance Act, which had originally been designed as part of an unemployment package for the spring of 1934, instead went down in history as part of Bennett's "New Deal."

As a result, unemployment insurance has been mistakenly interpreted as an attempt to *expand* Ottawa's responsibilities in response to the crisis of the Depression.[64] As is evident from the previous analysis, this was not the case. Instead, it was part of a political strategy designed to *reduce* the existing and quite expensive federal obligation for direct relief. The reason was as much social as financial. Simply put, Bennett and his advisers were convinced, after 1932, that the dole itself was creating unemployment. As Gordon put it to the premiers in 1934, too many people had developed the attitude that "the state owed them a living." The more Ottawa paid for relief, the more

> those unemployed would increase in numbers. To keep these numbers down, the essential thing, responsibility should rest first on the individual and secondly on the municipalities; even if at times this might result...in individual hardship.[65]

In other words, the only way of reducing unemployment was to reduce the level of support provided to the unemployed. By cutting back its own spending on the dole, Ottawa could ensure the effect would be passed on down the line. And unemployment insurance legislation could provide the perfect political cover for this retreat.

Behind this thinking lay the poor law principle of "less eligibility." As Frances Fox Piven and Richard Cloward have pointed out, relief arrangements in any society "are ancillary to economic arrangements. Their chief function is to regulate labour.... To demean and punish those who do not work is to exalt by contrast even the meanest labor at the meanest wages."[66] Since depressions produce "meaner" wages, this function becomes more important as more people are thrown out of work. The result is a paradox. The claims of human decency and need are placed in conflict with those of a self-regulating labour market.

Rod Finlayson saw the point clearly. After the last round of federal cuts in relief in August 1934, one of his closest friends from Winnipeg pointed out that a transient family of four on relief in that city received only 5¢ per person per meal. "How is it humanly possible," he asked Bennett's adviser, "to raise a family under such conditions and what can we possibly expect from the rising generation when we are trying to bring up the children at the rate of 15¢ per day apiece?" Finlayson answered:

---

[64] See, for example, Richard Wilbur, "R.B. Bennett as a Reformer," Canadian Historical Association, *Annual Report*, 1969.

[65] Bennett Papers, vol. 181, "Minutes of the Dominion-Provincial Conference, Jan. 17, 1934."

[66] Frances Fox Piven and Richard Cloward, *Regulating the Poor: The Functions of Public Welfare* (New York: 1971), p. 3.

> The basic problem is this. On the one hand, you have social economists, dieticians and others prescribing what people have to receive in order to live decently, and on the other hand, you have those who estimate what industry can pay, or in short, when you have a large proportion of your population unemployed, how much can those who have jobs pay toward the livelihood of those who have not?[67]

The answer, it seemed, was no more than would make relief more attractive than the worst-paid form of unskilled work. And to get people to take up subsistence agriculture on abandoned farms or to work for five dollars a month in rural Canada, this had to be low indeed.

Although living standards for the unskilled and unemployment benefits have increased substantially since the Bennett era, this basic moral problem remains. It is embodied in the recent cutbacks to the unemployment insurance programme. Once again an economic crisis has boosted the number of jobless and cut into the pay packets of the working poor. Once again, Ottawa has responded by reducing its level of support for the unemployed on the grounds that they have become too "fussy" about work.

At stake in this debate is not simply a difference of opinion over *whether* jobs are available. Equally important is what *kind* of jobs at what rate of pay. In short, in the 1970s as in the 1930s, unemployment policy is above all a struggle over downward mobility, a conflict between the expectations of workers and the reality of what the labour market has to offer. In the 1930s this meant an attempt to force the urban unemployed "Back to the Land". In the 1970s, it has meant pushing women back into unpaid housework and college graduates into minimum wage jobs.

In both cases, the basic tactic remains the same. The unemployed, government and business spokesmen claim, hold "unrealistic" expectations and feel "the state owes them a living." As a result, they must be punished by having their living standards reduced so that they will develop a proper "incentive" to work. "Less eligibility" thus remains as important to unemployment policy in the 1970s as it was in the 1930s or for that matter the 1830s. It can never be otherwise as long as penalizing the jobless remains our principal means of motivating people to work.

---

[67] Bennett Papers, vol. 792, E. Browne-Wilkinson to R.K. Finlayson, Aug. 17, 1934; Finlayson to E. Browne-Wilkinson, Aug. 21, 1934.

The Great Depression and the CCF

Walter D. Young

The Response to Depression

The Federal Government, to put it mildly, was unaccustomed to such widespread dislocation and hardship. Its initial reaction was to leave the provision of welfare and relief in the hands of the provinces, and municipalities, agencies that were just as unaccustomed to the role and far less able to deal with the problems created by the depression. The federal government did provide most of the funds for relief but with little oversight or control. Consequently, there were glaring and unjustifiable variations in the standards of relief available across the country. Those on relief were subjected to a bewildering array of regulations and to notorious examples of graft and patronage. The whole situation compounded despair and appeared to be designed to do anything but alleviate distress.

If the farmers and the single unemployed were the hardest hit by the depression, there were some who did not experience any economic hardship. While wages did drop and salaries were cut, prices fell drastically so that people with jobs were, in many cases, actually better off. But, as Professor Neatby indicates, the depression touched everyone, unemployed or not:

> It was impossible to live in Canada without absorbing the depression mentality. No matter how secure a person might be there were always relatives or friends whose plight brought home the reality of the depression. And no matter how secure a job might be there was always some apprehension; businesses which had once seemed as solid as the Precambrian Shield were going bankrupt. Wage-earners were aware that in the ranks of the unemployed there were men who could probably replace them and would be delighted to do so at half the salary. Couple this with the growing pessimism as hard times continued year after year, with the fear that things could and would get worse, and it is easier to understand why the survivors still remember.[1]

The depression not only affected the lives of people in the thirties, it affected the ideas and attitudes of a generation, instilling both caution and pessimism. Things would never be the same again.

---

[1] Neatby, *op. cit.* p. 22.

For those already convinced of the inequity—if not, indeed, the iniquity—of the capitalist system, the depression deepened their conviction and spurred their determination to take more direct action. The men and women in the several socialist and labour parties in the west had begun to move towards concerted action as early as 1929. The farmers, many of whom regretted the failure of the Progressive party and were anxious to try again, were joined by others as the fluctuations of the world market and crop conditions revealed once more their vulnerable position.

Uniting for the Cooperative Commonwealth

There were many labour and socialist parties in Western Canada at this time, each with a different name and most with their own preferred socialist doctrine. In British Columbia there was a Canadian Labour party and a Socialist Party of Canada. In Alberta there were branches of the Canadian Labour party and the Dominion Labour party. There was an Independent Labour Party in Saskatchewan and one in Manitoba—the one for which J.S. Woodsworth was M.P. In 1929 delegates from these parties and from several trade unions, some of which held radical political views, met in Regina to "correlate the activities of the several labour political parties in western Canada."[2] The Manitoba *Free Press* saw the conference as the beginning of a Western Canadian Labour Party, but it was not quite that. The groups did not amalgamate, they merely passed resolutions of a radical nature and agreed to meet again the following year in Medicine Hat.

The second meeting of what became known as the Conference of Western Labour Political Parties was more radical than the first, and with reason. The effects of the depression were being felt. It was not until the third gathering, in Winnipeg in July of 1931, that delegates undertook to form a national labour party. Several of the farmers' organizations were invited to that conference. It was recognized that the plight of farmers and workers was similar and that from concerted action results satisfactory to both could be achieved. There was no disagreement on policy; the farmers' groups had been moving further from the reformist doctrines of the Progressives toward a more distinctly socialist position. All the delegates at Winnipeg in 1931 agreed that, "capitalism must go and socialism be established."[3] Their aim was the establishment of a "cooperative commonwealth".

Formal steps were to be taken to build a new political movement at the fourth meeting of the Labour Conference. As the labour parties moved closer together, submerging philosophical differences in a common cause, so too the farmers' groups, as they moved leftward, moved together and came to accept more fully the need for direct political action. The decision of the labour parties to unite coincided with a similar decision on the part of the United Farmers of Alberta to invite all groups

---

[2] P.A.C., CCF Papers, Minutes, 1929 Conference, Western Labour Political Parties.
[3] Ibid., 1931 Conference.

sharing a faith in the ideal of the cooperative commonwealth to attend a conference in Calgary in 1932.

The United Farmers of Alberta (UFA) had formed the government of Alberta in 1925 but had resisted the call of federal politics, largely because of the anti-party philosophy of their leader, Henry Wise Wood. Wood retired in 1931 and was succeeded by Robert Gardiner, a member of the Ginger Group in the federal House of Commons. Gardiner was determined to put together a national political party and consequently led the UFA to the point where their convention called for the formation of a party to fight for the rights of farmers and workers alike. The cooperative commonwealth they, and the other groups, were seeking was defined as:

> A community freed from the domination of irresponsible financial and economic power, in which all social means of production and distribution, including land, are socially owned and controlled either by voluntarily organized groups of producers and consumers, or ... by public corporations responsible to the peoples' elected representatives.[4]

In Saskatchewan the Independent Labour Party, formed by M.J. Coldwell, a school principal and Regina alderman, had been working with the Farmers' Political Association led by George Williams. The two had collaborated as the Farmer-Labour party in provincial elections and both groups were active in organizing farmers and workers into local groups of one or other of these organizations. One such group was formed in Weyburn in 1932 by a young Baptist clergyman, T.C. Douglas. That same year the farmers and city workers agreed to present a single joint program and to undertake joint political action, creating in effect a Saskatchewan farmer-labour party, although both groups retained their identity. As the leader of the agrarian side of the new movement put it, the philosophy of the farmer-labour alliance was "fundamentally socialistic."[5]

The Manitoba ILP, with headquarters in Winnipeg and active branches in the smaller towns like Brandon and Souris, assumed responsibility for the development of the movement towards a new political party. The United Farmers of Manitoba were not hostile to the activities of the labour party but were not prepared to officially endorse their activities. Rural Manitoba was more in the Liberal-Progressive tradition and there was less agrarian support for the socialism of the ILP. In Winnipeg itself, however, with its large proportion of industrial workers, many of whom were immigrants, there was a lot of support.

In eastern Canada there was considerable activity among the labour and socialist parties, but it was disorganized and sporadic. There were more than a dozen labour

---

4   P.A.C., CCF Papers, *Declaration of Ultimate Objectives*, passed by UFA Convention, 1932.
5   W.L. Morton, *The Progressive Party in Canada* (Toronto: University of Toronto Press, 1950), p. 280.

and socialist parties of various colorations in Toronto alone. What organized political activity there was occurred largely through the efforts of the United Farmers of Ontario, a farmers' organization that was closer to the old Progressives in outlook than to the radical UFA or the Saskatchewan Farmers' Political Association. Nevertheless, the presence of these bodies did indicate that a national party of the left might find some support in Ontario.

There was some support in the intellectual community as well. In 1931 two university professors, one from McGill and the other from the University of Toronto, agreed that Canada needed a new political party, one which would not share the fate of the Progressives and be devoured by Mackenzie King's Liberals. The two, Frank Scott and Frank Underhill, established a society to provide such a party with a doctrine that would prove unpalatable to Mr. King. The society was known as the League for Social Reconstruction and soon had branches in Montreal, Toronto, Winnipeg and Vancouver. In many respects it was like the British Fabian Society, and, like it, hoped to become the intellectual wing of a Canadian socialist party.

The farm and labour MPs in the House of Commons were not unaware of the activities of the farm and labour groups across the country. Woodsworth had attended the conferences of the Western Labour Political Parties, had been in touch with Coldwell and Williams in Saskatchewan, and was honourary president of the League for Social Reconstruction. Robert Gardiner was president of the UFA. Miss Agnes Macphail was in the United Farmers of Ontario. On May 26, 1932, the members of the cooperating groups in the House of Commons met in the office of William Irvine and decided to bring all these strands together in a single political movement, which they tentatively called the "Commonwealth Party". Each member was given specific organizational responsibilities and all were to take every opportunity to organize support for the new party. Each one had, so to speak, grown up in the tradition of radical protest. The fact that they were meeting together as representatives of the farm and labour groups was evidence of a fundamental unity that had always existed but which had required the stress of the depression to become manifest across the land. Each had learned the lessons taught by the failure of the Progressive party and all were determined to avoid these mistakes.

The new venture they were beginning had a considerable advantage over the Progressive movement in that there was one obvious leader in the figure of J.S. Woodsworth. A man of heroic determination and devotion to principle, Woodsworth was accepted by farmer and worker alike as the symbol of the emerging movement. He had been a Methodist minister earlier in his career but had resigned from his church because of its failure to apply the teaching of the gospels to all men, and because of its attitude toward free speech. He had worked as a longshoreman in British Columbia, had travelled through the prairies on behalf of the Non-Partisan League and had edited the *Western Labor News* during the Winnipeg general strike.

In his own actions as well as in his statements on the public platform and in parliament, Woodsworth symbolized the aspirations of the men and women who were working through the farm and labour movements to bring about a better society. He spoke for all these when he moved in the House of Commons the first of what became annual resolutions:

> That in the opinion of his House the government should immediately take measures looking to the setting up of a cooperative commonwealth in which all the natural resources and socially necessary machinery of production will be used in the interest of the people and not for the benefit of the few.[6]

The submerging of political division and animosity in creating a federation of the diverse groups in Calgary in 1932 was a tribute to the symbolic and actual leadership of J.S. Woodsworth. He was subsequently described by a Liberal journalist as "a saint in politics".[7]

Outside the circle of his own followers and those commentators of a fairly liberal outlook, Woodsworth was seen almost as the devil incarnate, corrupting young minds when he spoke to university students, and preaching revolution and totalitarianism in his speeches in the House of Commons. It would have been surprising had the reaction to Woodsworth and his colleagues been anything else, for what they proposed constituted, at that time, a major reallocation of the nation's economic resources—and that was gross interference with the rights of private property.

Those who believed that private property and free enterprise—the capitalist system—formed the basis of individual freedom could not accept the proposals of the socialists despite the evidence of the depression that the system was clearly not working well for all the people. A majority of Canadians believed that socialism was evil and that property and unemployment were the result of bad luck or poor management. They were unwilling to accept the arguments of Woodsworth that the economic system was stacked against the many in the interest of the few. Proposals for unemployment insurance were scoffed at as subsidizing laziness; public ownership was said to be a form of theft that led to dictatorship.

It was characteristic of Woodsworth that despite the criticism of his ideas, he persisted when lesser men would have withdrawn from the struggle. As many of his ideas and the policies of the party he helped create were adopted and enacted by the Liberal government, many of his critics recognized the essentially noble character of the man. Pacifist, humanitarian and socialist, he was a key factor in knitting together the various strands that emerged as the fabric of a new political party, the Cooperative Commonwealth Federation or, as it was usually called, the CCF.

---

[6] Cited in K.W. McNaught, *A Prophet in Politics: A Biography of J.S. Woodsworth* (Toronto: University of Toronto Press, 1959), p. 249, from House of Commons *Debates*, 1932, pp. 226 *et seq.*

[7] The Liberal journalist was Bruce Hutchison, cited in G. MacInnis, *J.S. Woodsworth: A Man to Remember* (Toronto: Macmillan, 1953), p. 320.

The depression, acting as a catalyst, hastened the growth of the CCF but it did not, in the strict sense, cause it. By 1929 radicals in the cities and on the farms had already seen the need for a broader and more united base. The depression served to validate this belief, for it was proof of both the inadequacies of the capitalist economy and the insensitivity of the "old line" parties. Furthermore, despite the prevalence of hardship in western Canada, the depression would not bring immediate victory to the new party in the 1935 election. This was largely because the CCF was very new and, paradoxically, because its "revolutionary" character, in comparison to the other parties, had no direct appeal to those who were down and out. Socialism was to receive its greatest support at a time when prosperity had returned and those enjoying it were prepared to adopt a radical stance in order to retain it. As Professor Lipset has pointed out, support for radical movements on a large scale comes on the flood tide of rising expectations, not on the ebb of desolation and depression.

Woodsworth, Irvine and the Ginger Group had a foothold in parliament. The formation of the CCF gave them the beginnings of a nation-wide organization based on an alliance of what were essentially movements—bodies of like-minded people, dedicated to reform and prepared to make remarkable sacrifices to achieve their goals of social and political reform. As politicians, the leaders of the CCF recognized the need to weld the groups together into a democratic party that would aim for power. As participants in a movement, they could, as well, draw satisfaction from the achievement of any of their goals, whether they were in power themselves or not. In this regard they were soon able to see the results of their efforts as Mackenzie King reacted to their presence and edged his party leftward.

The tragic consequences of the depression and the ineptitude of governments in dealing with it hardened the determination of men like Woodsworth to do their utmost to ensure that it never happened again.

The CCF, 1932-1945

The conference in Calgary in August of 1932 brought together for the first time delegates from most of the major farm and labour groups in the west. Their purpose was the founding of a new political party, but it was not to be a duplicate of the "old line parties", nor was it to be like the Progressive party. The new organization was to be a federation of the existing labour and farm groups; it was also to have a clearly defined political philosophy—socialism. Its purpose was spelled out in the formal resolution passed unanimously by the delegates:

> The establishment in Canada of a cooperative commonwealth in which the basic principle regulating production, distribution, and

exchange, will be the supplying of human needs instead of the making of profits.[8]

The name of the new party was to be The Co-operative Commonwealth Federation (Farmer, Labour, Socialist).

The three words included parenthetically at the end of the name indicated that while all the delegates accepted the ideal of the cooperative commonwealth, not all would call themselves socialists; even among those who did, there was some disagreement about what socialism really was. Among the delegates from British Columbia, for example, were those who thought of socialism as the doctrine formulated by Karl Marx. Others had learned their socialism from the writings of the members of the British Fabian Society or from other English socialists. And for some socialism was just a general term that meant they were against the government and the existing economic system because it had reduced them to poverty.

Because all shared the same misgivings about the capitalist system and the working of Canadian politics, they were able to forget their doctrinal differences and agree to work together to bring about changes that would improve their lot and that of Canadians in general. In their enthusiasm for change they could unite behind a program that was more radical than anything ever advocated by the Progressives, one which declared that "social ownership and cooperative production for use is the only sound economic system."[9]

Goals and a Program

The new organization was not simply a political party, it was a political movement as well. The purpose of the CCF as it emerged from the Calgary conference was not just to win the next election, it was to bring about radical changes in the nature of Canadian society. What the members wanted was to replace the profit motive with that of service to the community and to others. It was a noble ideal. As one observer of the Calgary meeting commented, the delegates "oozed idealism to the detriment of practical experience."[10] The purpose of the movement was to win converts to a new way of thinking. Activity in the House of Commons and on the hustings in election campaigns were two ways of doing this, but not the only ones.

During the winter of 1932-33 the members of the new party devoted themselves to the problems of organizing. The provisional executive invited the League for

---

[8] W.L. Morton, *The Progressive Party in Canada* (Toronto: University of Toronto Press, 1950), p. 282.

[9] *The Co-operative Commonwealth Federation, An Outline of Its Origins, Organization and Objectives* (Calgary, 1932).

[10] Cited in B. Borsook, "The Workers Hold a Conference," from *Canadian Forum*, XXV, September, 1932.

Social Reconstruction to prepare a statement of the party's principles, a Manifesto. This task was performed largely by Frank Underhill, who wrote the first draft of what became the Regina Manifesto at his summer home in June of 1933. It was discussed by other members of the League and then presented to the first convention of the CCF, which met during August, 1933, in Regina.

Some changes were made but the Manifesto that the convention adopted with enthusiastic cheers was essentially as it had been prepared by Underhill and his colleagues. It remained the basic statement of CCF ideology until 1956 and constituted the most specific statement of Canadian socialism.

The aim of the CCF was made very clear in the opening paragraphs of the Manifesto:

> We aim to replace the present capitalist system, with its inherent injustice and inhumanity, by a social order from which the domination and exploitation of one class by another will be eliminated, in which economic planning will supersede unregulated private enterprise and competition, and in which genuine democratic self-government, based on economic equality will be possible.[11]

The Manifesto proposed the public ownership of all financial machinery—banks, insurance companies, trust companies and the like—as well as public ownership of public utilities and "all other industries and services essential to social planning." Emphasis was laid on the development of cooperatives, and particular attention was given to the problems of the farmers. There were, as well, proposals for medicare, hospital and dental insurance schemes to be run by the state. The Manifesto closed with a ringing declaration:

> No CCF Government will rest content until it has eradicated capitalism and put into operation the full programme of socialized planning which will lead to the establishment in Canada of the Cooperative Commonwealth.

The program of the new party was most assuredly socialist. It was more socialistic than some of its founders had expected or, in a few instances, were prepared to accept. Farm and labour groups had proposed similar measures before but there had never been such a specific and deliberate program as the Regina Manifesto. The guardians of the sacred institutions of Canadian capitalism declared the program preposterous. The Press and opposition politicians saw it as naked communism.

At Regina J.S. Woodsworth was elected National Chairman—in effect the party leader. But he was not a leader in the traditional sense. The CCF was a federation of

---

[11] The Regina Manifesto is appended to K.W. McNaught *A Prophet in Politics: A Biography of J.S. Woodsworth* (Toronto: University of Toronto Press, 1959).

smaller parties and movements and it was deliberately designed to ensure the fullest participation by all members in making policy and in directing the affairs of the party. One of the chief criticisms western radicals had of the old parties was that they were undemocratic, controlled by a small clique that was dominated by eastern businessmen. No such state of affairs would be allowed to prevail in the CCF. There would be annual conventions, annual elections of officers, and the party platform would be prepared by the delegates at the annual conventions.

Reaction to the New Party

Despite its democratic structure, critics and opponents of the CCF saw it as a totalitarian and alien force. Few of them understood socialism; most of them equated it with communism. Yet the CCF was clearly a direct descendent of the British Labour Party, at least as far as its ideology was concerned. The program of the CCF advocated radical changes in the Canadian economy and attacked the principle of competition and free enterprise. For many observers this was evidence enough that it was a serious threat to "the Canadian way of life". It was ironic that the CCF soon built up an enviable record in defence of individual liberties and parliamentary democracy.

The opponents of the CCF saw a revolutionary force when they looked at the new party. They feared for their property and their privileges. Some members of the CCF found the party philosophy too radical, while others complained that it was not radical enough. Short of having no political philosophy at all, such disagreement was inevitable. So, too, was the opposition of many people in Canada inevitable, for the kinds of change advocated by the CCF were sweeping and bound to arouse serious disagreement.

Because it stood for radical change, because it proposed to reshape sectors of the Canadian economy and reform aspects of Canadian society, the CCF attracted to its ranks people who were deeply concerned about the nature of the Canadian economic and political systems. Many were convinced that future depressions were certain and would remain incurable unless changes were made. The CCF also attracted people whose own situation drove them away from the old parties into the new movement in search of a satisfactory explanation of a poverty that was not of their making. The commitment of all these people to radical change meant that the CCF was able to succeed where an ordinary party could not. It had little money, only a sketchy organization and no political foothold in any legislature, but it had a growing membership of dedicated people prepared to sacrifice their time and what money they had in the cause of reform.

Typical of this kind of dedicated enthusiasm was that shown by M.J. Coldwell. A school principal in Regina when the party was founded, he seldom turned down an invitation to speak about the CCF. This often meant travelling in freezing weather by sleigh to a distant farm. Sympathetic farmers along the way would supply fresh horses, coffee and hot water bottles. In good weather he would hire a plane, leave after school, fly perhaps a hundred miles to speak and then spend the night at a farm. The next morning he would return to start the school day at nine. Money was scarce but farmers would contribute what produce they could spare: a sack of grain here, a bushel of potatoes there.

The CCF stimulated dedication because it offered an explanation of what had gone wrong and proposed what seemed to be a sensible way of preventing the same thing from happening again. In addition, it was a party that clearly belonged to the members. It provided a social focal point, bringing together men and women with similar problems and similar points of view. On the prairie the party meetings were social activities, as were the fund raising efforts—socials, picnics, and the like. In the cities the CCF groups provided a congenial social nucleus for the unemployed, helping many to overcome the feeling that they were Canada's forgotten people. It helped combat the loneliness of the underdog. The character of the CCF as a movement gave it strength and determination far beyond its numbers and financial resources.

The Struggle for Political Success

Despite its strengths, however, the CCF did not ride the crest of a wave to political success; it achieved office in only one province, and even there not until 1944. At the beginning there was public suspicion to overcome, as well as the internal divisions and inconsistencies of the movement. The CCF was not a united party; it was a federation of provincial movements and parties, each with a fairly high degree of autonomy of both action and viewpoint. In the three prairie provinces there was a good deal of consistency of philosophy. But British Columbia socialism was more militant and more highly spiced with Marxist or "scientific socialism." Some members in that province had little use for the farmers. The Ontario wing was troubled with discontent resulting from the willingness of some members and some CCF clubs to enter into an alliance with the Communist party. In 1934 Woodsworth had to reorganize the Ontario party to overcome these problems.

The lack of unity was not surprising. Ideology invites dispute, and there were members of the CCF whose main interest was argument rather than political organization. The movement also had a different character in different regions. For example, on the prairie it was growing as part of the rural community. The active leaders of the wheat pools and the cooperative movement were virtually all active in the CCF. On the other hand, in British Columbia, and to a slightly lesser extent in Ontario, the militants were more the "outsiders" of society, the determined non-conformists. Thus, although the CCF was growing, it was growing slowly and not without some internal discomfort.

The national party faced its first serious test in the 1935 federal election. It nominated 119 candidates but only seven were elected: two in Manitoba, two in Saskatchewan and three in British Columbia. This was not an auspicious beginning.

The Great Depression and the CCF

The Ginger Group had been wiped out and there were no CCF members at all from Alberta. In that province an even newer political phenomenon, Social Credit, had swept all before it. In all, the CCF got only 9 per cent of the total popular vote and only 2 per cent of the seats in the House of Commons.

The election of 1935 was a confusing one for the voter. In many constituencies there were five and occasionally six candidates. A former Conservative cabinet minister, H.H. Stevens, had created a new party, the Reconstruction party. It ran 174 candidates but elected only one. Nevertheless, it attracted close to 400,000 votes. Social Credit, in winning every seat in Alberta, cut heavily into support that might otherwise have gone to the CCF. It is likely that some of those who voted Reconstruction and Social Credit would have voted CCF, although it is impossible to say how many. However it was explained, though, the result of the election was a blow to the CCF.

The party fought a vigorous and direct campaign. Party literature pulled no punches; if anything, it was a bit too sharp in its criticism of capitalism. One CCF pamphlet read:

> Bank Robbers Get Millions, but the BIG SHOT BANKER IS A BIGGER CRIMINAL THAN THE GUNMAN because the banker's greed hurts all the people all the time.[12]

Another urged voters to "Smash the Big Shots' Slave Camps and Sweat Shops."[13] From the CCF point of view capitalism had caused the depression; but this was not quite the same things as accusing bankers of criminal greed. For the active members of the CCF the enemy was plain to see—the men who controlled the financial structure of Canada, those who suffered little during the depression. Rid the economy of their unwholesome influence, place the public in control, and the problem would be solved. There was some truth in their analysis, and their vehemence was understandable, but it did not attract many voters who were not already socialists. Indeed, it repelled many.

With only six members in a House of Commons composed of 254, the CCF seemed to be of little consequence when the new parliament opened. But as session followed session it became clear that Woodsworth and his colleagues were the real opposition to Mackenzie King's Liberal administration. After the departure of R.B. Bennett, the Conservatives groped for leadership and policy; they were to stumble in the darkness of opposition for twenty-two years. The CCF, however, did have a leader of considerable ability and a clearly defined policy. The members of the small group were dedicated to their cause and managed to do the work of a caucus at least thrice their size. In the first session, for example, T.C Douglas spoke sixty times, more than most members and as much as most cabinet ministers.

---

[12] P.A.C., CCF Papers, CCF Pamphlet, 1940.
[13] Ibid.

The role the CCF played was that of the conscience of the House of Commons, speaking out on behalf of those whose interests seemed to be ignored by the government, and championing the cause of civil rights. In the latter cause the small band was able to bring about the repeal of section 98 of the Criminal Code, the infamous section that had first made its appearance during the Winnipeg general strike in 1919, permitting the arrest and deportation of "aliens". In 1937 the CCF led a concerted attack on the inroads being made into civil liberties by provincial governments, notably those of Premier Mitchell Hepburn of Ontario and Premier Duplessis of Quebec. In both cases the police power of the state was being used to interfere with the legitimate activities of trade unions in strikes and union organization. In particular, the CCF attack was directed against the Padlock Law in Quebec, a law that enabled the arbitrary arrest of individuals who, contrary to established procedure, were then required to prove their innocence. While the CCF could not change these laws, by bringing them to the attention of the nation through debate in the House of Commons they were able to arouse public opinion and, on occasion, force the government to act.

In 1939 Woodsworth had the satisfaction of seeing the government introduce legislation guaranteeing the right of employees to form and join trade unions. He had been advocating such a bill for three years. By standing firmly on principle, by raising issues again and again and by patient and carefully prepared argument, the CCF members were able to induce the government to introduce reforms that would otherwise have been much longer in coming. Their very presence in the House of Commons was a constant reminder to the Liberal government of the sizeable body of the electorate that were in favour of broad and far-reaching reform. Political commentators may not have supported the CCF philosophy, but they were forced to admit time and again that the six CCF MPs were an efficient and formidable opposition to the government.

During this early period the members of the CCF were active across the country, bringing in new members, organizing clubs and constituency associations and eagerly looking toward the day when a CCF government would be in power. In Saskatchewan in 1934 the Farmer-Labour party had become the official opposition in the provincial legislature winning five seats—the Liberal government held the other fifty. In 1938 the CCF increased this standing to ten seats. In British Columbia the CCF became the official opposition in 1941, winning more votes than any other party. Membership in the party grew, but not as quickly as party leaders had hoped. Despite its British ancestry, Canadian socialism remained a strange and, for many, a sinful doctrine. The fact that opponents of the CCF constantly referred to it as a communist "front" did not help. Nor did the repeated public invitations of the Communist party to join forces help the CCF image.

The CCF During the War

The outbreak of war in 1939 found the CCF stronger than it had been in 1933, but not as strong as its founders had expected. The war brought a more prosperous economy. The production of war materials took up the slack in industry, the prices of farm produce improved, and the army offered employment for many who had spent the previous three or four years on relief. The war also brought a crisis in the CCF.

As a man of deep religious faith and strict adherence to principle, Woodsworth had opposed war all his life. For him the organized slaughter of one's fellow men, regardless of the cause, was not an acceptable policy. He could not support Canada's entry into the war. A majority of his fellow party members, however, did not take this position. Most were opposed to war in principle, but at the same time they accepted the fact of Hitler's ambitions in Europe and the unfortunate necessity of resisting him with force. From the day of its foundation the CCF had officially opposed war. The crisis of 1939 brought about an agonizing reappraisal of that policy.

At a long and emotionally charged meeting of the party's National Council, it was decided that Woodsworth would stand alone, stating his opposition to the war while M.J. Coldwell would speak for the party and support Canada's entry at Britain's side. In his speech to parliament Woodsworth said:

> I have every respect for the man who, with a sincere conviction, goes out to give his life if necessary in a cause which he believes to be right; but I have just as much respect for the man who refuses to enlist to kill his fellow men and, as under modern conditions, to kill women and children as well....[14]

The point was, he insisted, that "brute force" was being allowed to overcome "moral force."

During the debate Prime Minister Mackenzie King said:

> There are few men in this parliament for whom, in some particulars, I have greater respect than the leader of the Co-operative Commonwealth Federation. I admire him in my heart because time and again he has had the courage to say what lay on his conscience regardless of what the world might think of him. A man of that calibre is an ornament to any Parliament....[15]

---

[14] McNaught, *op. cit.* p. 311.
[15] Ibid., p. 309.

It was a fitting tribute to Woodsworth at a time when, his health failing and the party he had led opposing him, he stood firmly on those principles that his intellect and his conscience had told him were right and just.

The CCF entered the wartime parliament after the 1940 election with eight seats, only two more than before; but this time five were from Saskatchewan. They had lost one seat in Manitoba and two in British Columbia. There had been little change in the popular vote received. There was one ray of hope—the party had an MP from Nova Scotia, Clarence Gillis. His election was a direct result of the affiliation with the party, in 1938, of the Cape Breton local of the United Mine Workers Union. From 1936 on the party had made a determined effort to interest trade unions in providing support. The case they made was a good one: the CCF was the only party in the House of Commons that supported all the demands of organized labour. The election of Gillis was the first dividend from that policy.

The role of opposition in wartime is awkward and difficult. The government of the day tends to seek refuge in the cloak of patriotism or the spurious caves of secrecy. The CCF entered the war uneasily, with an ailing and alienated leader and little hope of improving its political position. As it turned out, during the period 1940-1945 the CCF was to reach the highwater mark in its fortunes.

The period of "the dirty thirties" passed and war, relief measures, and the gradual institution of Keynesian[16] economic policies pulled the country out of the chasm of the depression. Despite dire predictions, there had been no revolution, socialism had not swept the land, and the thousands of unemployed and economically deprived did not rise up and overthrow established authority. But in western Canada notice had been clearly given that the politics of the traditional parties had been weighed, found wanting and rejected. The spectre of a socialist take-over remained to haunt the leaders of the Liberal and Conservative parties. Many people were also surprised by the remarkable surge to power of the Social Credit Party—which was something quite different again.

The depression had demonstrated with tragic clarity the need for direct government intervention in the economy on a permanent basis. There would be no returning to the "good old days" of the free economy. The depression had also demonstrated the efficacy of government activity, something which the war further emphasized. It was during the depression—and under the aegis of a Conservative government—that the CBC, the Bank of Canada and the basis for Trans Canada Airlines had been

---

[16] John Maynard Keynes (1883-1946) was a British economist whose theories challenged the orthodox views of the day and had profound significance throughout the western world. One of his major works, *The General Theory of Employment, Interest and Money* (1936), attacked traditional fatalism in regard to mass unemployment. Keynes argued that public (government) spending should be timed for maximum effect. At the onset of recession, he suggested, government expenditure should be increased so as to increase employment and thus through the payment of wages, raise spending power and stimulate business investment.

established. As prosperity returned to those who had known the despair of poverty, it brought with it a determination to ensure that poverty would never return. Thus it was, ironically, that the CCF did not ride to great prominence and to power in Saskatchewan in the trough of despondency, but on the crest of rising expectations that grew during the war.

Foreign Relations and the Second World War

Section 18

The 1930s were marked not only by depression but by growing international tension, as groups of countries faced off against each other with increasing hostility. First Japan, then Italy, then Germany engaged in open aggression, seizing territory from other countries, spreading anti-democratic rule, and finally provoking a world war which had catastrophic consequences for Britain and Europe and which drastically altered Canada's own position in the world.

Western powers were generally slow to react to fascist aggression, but Canada seemed most particularly reluctant to become involved in any commitment to stop them. Her premier from 1935 onward, William Lyon Mackenzie King, seemed determined to avoid foreign commitments in order to protect Canada's autonomy, still newly won from the United Kingdom. For this he has been much criticised, as Blair Neatby observes in the first of these essays. Does Neatby think that King deserves the criticism? How did King view Canada's relationship with Britain, according to Neatby? Why was he unwilling to co-operate more openly with the UK? Why was national unity a problem for foreign policy? Did King successfully overcome that problem?

When the second world war began, Canada participated from the beginning, suggesting that her ties with Britain were still strong. Yet historians have seen the second world war as the point at which Canada broke away from Britain and became (as some would say) a virtual satellite of the United States. For this too Mackenzie King has been much blamed. What defence of him does J.L. Granatstein give in his essay? Did Canada have any real choice about moving into the arms of the Americans? Why not? Why was Britain no longer able to balance US influence in Canada?

For a general history of Canadian foreign relations in this period see C.P.Stacey, *Canada in the Age of Conflict* (Vol. 2: 1921-1948). The most vigorous attack on King's wartime and postwar policies is in Donald Creighton, *The Forked Road*.

Mackenzie King and National Unity

H. Blair Neatby

Mackenzie King talked a great deal about Canadian autonomy and national unity between the two world wars. His critics were not impressed. They argued that behind the platitudes there lurked an unprincipled politician for whom the only consistent national policy was the desire to win the next election. Even sympathetic observers who were not blindly partisan were sometimes uneasy because King's references to autonomy or unity seemed designed more to justify inaction than to defend a positive decision. Canadian autonomy, he had said, did not define Canada's Commonwealth commitments but left them to be determined "in the light of circumstances as they may arise at the time," and his appeals to national unity frequently seemed to be a technique to leave controversial issues undisturbed and unresolved. Even historians writing after the Second World War have reacted to Mackenzie King's career in much the same way. They are more ready to concede that King was an adept politician, but they are still inclined to deplore his obfuscations and his indecision. King seemed to avoid confronting issues in an era which demanded courage and forthright leadership.

The 1920s and 1930s were not an heroic age, and there is no angle from which Mackenzie King can be pictured as a hero. It is nonetheless surprising that Canadian scholars still react with such intensity to his career. They show little evidence of historical detachment; the more sympathetic historians are qualified in their praise, the critics are almost venomous. The emotional overtones suggest that the shadow of King still hovers over the land and that the issues which are linked with his name are still contemporary issues. Canadian history is national history by definition, and most Canadian historians have strong national feelings. Inevitably they judge King in the light of their own view of what Canada is or ought to be.

Historians who stress the North American character of Canada approve of King's emphasis on autonomy. They see the development of Canadian autonomy as the central theme of our history, in the long ascent from colony to nation, and King is credited with completing the process during the 1920s. According to A.R.M. Lower, "Until the second world war became imminent, the vital aspect of external relations was not foreign policy but the extension and completion of Canadian autonomy," and "the evolution of imperial relations, if it bears the imprint of any one personality, must bear his [Mackenzie King's]."[1] J.M.S. Careless also argues that "in external affairs, at least, King pursued a very definite policy"—that of achieving the status of nationhood for Canada—and that this was virtually accomplished by 1931.[2]

---

[1] *Colony to Nation*, 3rd ed. (London, 1957), 481-3.
[2] *Canada: A Story of Challenge*, 2nd ed. (Toronto, 1963), 344-9.

Mackenzie King's critics are more inclined to see his policy as a continuing effort to end the British connection, with anti-British sentiments influencing his policies even after the passage of the Statute of Westminster. This does not mean that they minimize the results of his policy of Canadian autonomy; on the contrary they view them as having even greater significance than the historians who are more sympathetic to King's career. It is true that Donald Creighton's *Dominion of the North*, in what can only be described as a *tour de force*, manages to make Dominion status inevitable by the end of the First World War and so denies any credit whatsoever to Mackenzie King. "Macdonald, Laurier and Borden," Professor Creighton writes, "had helped to work out the various principles of the new relationship; and the war and the post-war period served to bring the system they had devised into a working reality. All that remained to do was to give formal acknowledgement to the new Imperial association."[3] Elsewhere, however, Creighton is more willing to admit that King had some influence on events. In his presidential address to the Canadian historical Association in 1957 he declared:

> The 1920s and 1930s were the decades, above all others, in which Canadian national policy, and its supporters and interpreters, required a simple-minded, anti-imperialist doctrine which could be used against Western Europe in general and West-European and British imperialism in particular. Mackenzie King was revolutionizing the Commonwealth through the implementation of Dominion autonomy ... and Canada, for what was really the first time in its history, was luxuriating to the full in that sense of physical and spiritual isolation from the rest of the world, that moral superiority to the unfortunate remainder of mankind, which is one of the chief characteristics of North American continentalism.[4]

W.L. Morton sees the same continuing—and nefarious—influence of King's policies between the wars. In a review of a biography of Mackenzie King covering the years from 1923 to 1932 he reproves the author for not showing that "the persistent extension of Canadian autonomy without any positive counter-undertaking was in effect to destroy that European counterpoise, once military and next moral, by which Canada had balanced, or offset, the influence of the United States. King thus prepared the present condition of Canada, in which the country is so irradiated by the American presence that it sickens and threatens to dissolve in cancerous slime."[5]

These conflicting appreciations of King's version of Canadian autonomy clearly reflect different views of what Canada's relations with Great Britain—and the United States—should be. Nonetheless, all of these historians do agree that Canadian

---

[3] *Dominion of the North*, new ed. (Toronto, 1962), 481.
[4] *Canadian Historical Association Annual Report*, 1957.
[5] *Canadian Historical Review*, XLV (December 1964), 320-1.

autonomy was extended during these years and that Mackenzie King contributed significantly to this extension. They may applaud or deplore the results but they link King's name with the achievement of autonomy.

The real test of this autonomy came in 1939 when Great Britain became involved in a European war. An autonomous Canada could conceivably have remained on the sidelines. Every other country in North and South America chose neutrality at the time and, as North Americans, Canadians might have been expected to do likewise. Ten days did elapse between the British and Canadian declarations of war, but the final decision was never in doubt. In 1937 King had privately told Hitler that the Dominions would be involved if Great Britain was drawn into a European war, and in March of 1939 he told the Canadian House of Commons that Canada would go to war "if bombers rained death on London." It is also suggestive that a volume of his wartime speeches, published in 1941, was entitled *Canada at Britain's Side*. Autonomy or no autonomy, Mackenzie King decided to follow Britain into war in 1939.

It is surprising that Canadian historians have not been more puzzled by this apparent inconsistency. The significant changes in the nature of the Commonwealth which they have attributed to King's policies suddenly seem insignificant, and Mackenzie King, instead of determining or even affecting the course of events, is described as merely recording the loyal response of the Canadian people. It is never suggested that all Canadians reacted in the same way or for the same reasons, but, in the final analysis, historians seem to agree that the bonds of empire were decisive. A.R.M. Lower sees Canadians as reluctant and uncertain about the war until the fall of France, but then "the inescapable bonds of blood were sealed again and when to them was joined the eloquence of Mr. Churchill, English Canadians, casting aside whatever elements of national individuality they had acquired, merged their fate once more with England."[6] J.M.S. Careless is more impressed with the relevance of national interests in determining the decision, but he too agrees that "undoubtedly sentiment for Great Britain still played a large part."[7] Even for historians who see King as having single-mindedly destroyed our traditional links with Great Britain, these links seem to have had a remarkable resilience. According to Donald Creighton:

> As the sky over Europe darkened with menace, as the very safety of the motherland itself became imperilled, the Canadian consciousness of the reality—and the vitality—of this ancient tie steadily strengthened; and the visit of King George and Queen Elizabeth, in the early summer of 1939, confirmed, though it had no need to inspire, this realization of the values and vital interests which were bound up in the old partnership of the British people.... In the first

---

[6] *Colony to Nation*, 553.
[7] *Canada: A Story of Challenge*, 375.

ten days of September, 1939 ... the British Commonwealth took its stand and prepared to fight.[8]

W.L. Morton also sees the British connection as the decisive factor although perhaps less from sentiment than from an aversion to closer links with the United States, with "the balance towards fighting to maintain the United Kingdom, simply because an alliance with the United States to defend America without a European offset meant absorption to an unpredictable degree into the American power system."[9] In no case does Mackenzie King receive either credit or blame for the momentous decision.

When historians agree that the ties with Great Britain were strong enough to bring Canada into the war in 1939, they arouse serious doubts about the significance of King's contribution to Canadian autonomy. Formal constitutional changes mean little if they do not reflect reality; the sequence of precedents in the 1920s leading to the enshrinement of the principle of autonomy in the Statute of Westminster becomes irrelevant if the emotional attachment to Great Britain survived unscathed. It seems unfair either to applaud or to vilify Mackenzie King for his obsession with autonomy when that policy apparently counted for so little.

Mackenzie King was naturally inclined to take some personal credit for the Canadian consensus in 1939. At the same time he did not see any contradiction between autonomy for Canada and her participation in the war at Britain's side; he believed that the decision to go to war had only been possible because he had firmly established Canada's claim to autonomy. On 8 September 1939, at the special session of Parliament, he insisted that participation was a voluntary decision: "not because of any colonial or inferior status vis-à-vis Great Britain, but because of equality of status. We are a nation in the fullest sense, a member of the British commonwealth of Nations, sharing like freedom with Great Britain herself, a freedom which we believe we must all combine to save." Without this sense of autonomy, he argued, there could have been no general agreement among Canadians to go to war.[10] In an election broadcast in February 1940 he claimed that Canadian unity had been preserved by his insistence on Canadian autonomy: "My task was to see that no false step, no extreme policies or measures, no hasty action should be allowed to destroy, in advance, either the clearness of vision of our people, or its powers of action. I was determined that, if the moment for decision ever came, no cleavages of opinion, in parliament or in the country, should frustrate Canada's power to put forth her utmost effort." Pointing out that Parliament and the nation were united when the momentous decision had to be made, King then asked whether his policy had not been "the right, and, indeed, the only wise and proper one."[11]

---

8   *Dominion of the North*, 504.
9   *The Kingdom of Canada* (Toronto, 1963), 474.
10 *House of Commons Debates*, Second Session, 1939, p. 30.
11 W.L. Mackenzie King, *Canada at Britain's Side* (Toronto, 1941), 77-8.

King's interpretation of events should not be casually ignored. As a politician he may have exaggerated his omniscience, but he had in fact consistently linked autonomy with national unity long before 1939. He had repeatedly described Canadian autonomy as a prerequisite for any major commitment in external affairs. Without autonomy he believed that national agreement on such a commitment would be virtually impossible; only with autonomy would a national consensus be feasible. It was this connection between autonomy and national unity which lay behind his external policy in the 1930s. To comprehend this policy, however, one must first understand what he meant by autonomy and by national unity, for he had his own special definition of these concepts, and the meaning he gave to them coloured all his decisions.

Historians have tended to equate autonomy with independence from Great Britain. For some the corollary to this has been the achievement of a distinctive national identity, for others the corollary has been succumbing to domination of the United States; but whatever the final result, autonomy has been seen as a diminution of British influence. Autonomy for Mackenzie King, however, did not mean independence. He defined autonomy as self-government but saw no inconsistency in a completely self-governing Dominion which nonetheless had inescapable obligations to Great Britain. Indeed, for King these obligations would become more acceptable and so more secure as self-government became more complete. He used the analogy of the family to explain his concept of autonomy, but in his version the children did not grow indifferent to family interests when they became adults. The family bonds survived, and collective responsibility and collective action was not only feasible but inevitable whenever the interests of the family or of one of its members were at stake. This was a natural assumption for one who came from a closely knit family and for whom the family ties could even extend beyond the grave. Autonomy was essential to this family group, because without it the family bonds might be severed. If parents imposed too many restraints on their children, the normal family relationship could be endangered, and the children, by rejecting parental authority, might reject their filial responsibilities. This to King was independence. Autonomy was the means by which this unnatural and undesirable breakdown of family ties could be averted.[12]

This version of Canada's relations with Great Britain was based on sentiment rather than on formal commitments. At heart Mackenzie King was a nineteenth-century romantic. But policies based on sentiment are as real as policies based on calculation and are likely to be more consistently pursued over the years. Certainly King was consistent. He resented any restraint on Canadian self-government, premeditated or accidental, imagined or real, because of his conviction that autonomy was essential. In the 1920s he at least contributed to the acceptance of this principle. In the 1930s, with formal autonomy conceded, the issue became one of Canadian

---

[12] For King's use of this analogy see H. Blair Neatby, *William Lyon Mackenzie King*, II (Toronto, 1963), 176-7.

support for Great Britain in time of crisis, and here again King's version of the family relationship was consistently applied. He took it for granted that Canada should be at Britain's side in a major European war.

National unity was easier to define than to achieve. For King it meant that each major national decision should have the support—or at least the acquiescence—of people from each cultural group and from each geographical region. National policies would usually be compromises, because the different cultural and regional interests would not be identical. Compromises, however, are never popular; a tariff policy acceptable to both central Canada and the prairies would not arouse much enthusiasm in either region. Political leadership under these circumstances required much circumspection and educational effort. Differing groups or regions had to be made aware of their conflicting interest before they would accept the half-loaf which any compromise involves. Until a compromise was possible, the government could either impose a policy, at the risk of alienating a cultural group or a region, or it could procrastinate. No government, however, can postpone decisions indefinitely and remain in power. Delay, when resorted to, must be used to convince the affected groups of the necessity of compromise. Mackenzie King's insistence on the need for a national consensus on major national decisions was often discounted as an attempt to justify inaction. His alleged lack of political leadership has been exaggerated, however. He was not always waiting for a problem to disappear. Often he was trying to prepare the ground for a compromise which he had already formulated.

National policies which fitted King's definition were not easily devised in the decade of the 1930s. Observers could seldom find any issue on which there was a clear national consensus. F.H. Soward, writing shortly after the outbreak of war, believed that "in the troubled thirties Canadian unity was more seriously disturbed than at any time since Confederation."[13] The depression had exacerbated the regional and cultural divisions which had always existed. Profound discontent had sired three new political parties for the federal election of 1935, and these parties had won the support of one out of every five Canadian voters. Seemingly stable provincial governments had been unseated by new parties or by old parties with new leaders; new provincial premiers such as Duplessis, Hepburn, Aberhart, and Patullo were deliberately defying traditional party loyalties and the middle class decorum of their predecessors. At the same time industrial unions were disrupting the structure of organized labour and spreading fears of a radical social revolution. Fascist and communist groups attracted new followers, and many saw these extremists as the tip of an iceberg of disaffection and alienation.

Mackenzie King could see all the signs of national disruption in microcosm within the Liberal party itself. T.D. Patullo was behaving like a socialist in Liberal clothing, Gerry McGeer was huckstering social credit, J.T. Thorson was an unreconstructed Progressive, Mitchell Hepburn was busy denouncing Mackenzie King Liberals when he was not conspiring with Duplessis to weaken federal

---

[13] F.H. Soward, et al., *Canada in World Affairs: The Pre-War Years* (Toronto, 1941), 14.

authority, Jean-François Pouliot was fully occupied fighting communism. Liberals debated the politics of party survival, because the survival of the party was a prerequisite for any constructive government measures. In the turmoil of the thirties, party unity, like national unity, required political sensitivity and sound judgment.

External policy in the 1930s had to be devised within the context of this domestic turmoil. A foreign policy which proved unpopular in one sector of Canadian society would aggravate already existing cultural or regional jealousies. In any case, external affairs could not be isolated from the domestic situation because the bitter memories of the cultural clash during the First World War were still fresh, and because the recognition of Canadian autonomy now posed directly the question of a distinctive Canadian foreign policy. External affairs added a new and significant dimension to the problem of achieving national unity.

French Canadians usually opposed any foreign commitments. This apparent isolationism, however, did not mean that they had no interest in the outside world. They were strongly opposed to any association with communist countries and they had some sympathy for a country like Italy which, at least in theory, was Roman Catholic and corporatist. If French Canadians wanted to isolate Canada from foreign affairs it was not because they were neutral. Rather it was because they harboured deep suspicions of British influence on Canadian policies and feared that English-Canadian loyalties to Great Britain might draw Canada into a war in which Canadian interests were not directly involved. Isolationism would at least ensure that Canada would not be used as a tool of British imperialism.

Any generalization about English-Canadian attitudes is likely to be an oversimplification. So great was the diversity of opinions that contemporary observers delighted in the parlour game of trying to define categories into which public men could be pigeon-holed. It was easy to talk of collectivists who supported the League of Nations, of imperialists who backed Great Britain, and of isolationists who opposed any commitments. Unfortunately few men fitted into these simple categories. How could one classify J.S. Woodsworth, a pacifist, a leader of a party opposed to any participation in "imperialist" wars, and yet a prominent spokesman for the League of Nations? J.W. Dafoe was usually labelled a collectivist, while O.D. Skelton was considered an isolationist, and yet both of these men might better be described as autonomists. Dafoe's objection to a Canadian policy made in London led him to advocate collective security through the League, whereas a similar sentiment led Skelton to oppose any commitments. Some observers coined hyphenated refinements to describe the complex attitudes of English Canadians, but the absurdity of such categories as collectivist-isolationist or nationalist-imperialist only underlined the difficulty of labelling men who were themselves not always clear or consistent. J.H. Blackmore spoke for many when he plaintively told the House of

Commons that he was an ardent advocate of collective security but didn't know with whom to collect.[14]

Mackenzie King, as his version of Canadian autonomy suggests, believed that in time of crisis Canada would "collect" with the Commonwealth. He believed that Canadian interest were linked with those of Great Britain and that most Canadians would realize this when the time for decision came. The first problem was to avoid the crystallization of conflicting attitudes which would make an eventual consensus impossible. But public opinion must also be guided and shaped so that if Britain did become involved in a major war, most Canadians would be prepared to accept the policy of participation. King was not a passive attendant upon events. Although he avoided debates on abstract questions of principle between 1935 and 1939, he made decisions which narrowed the range of choice and channelled Canadians towards this ultimate decision.

The first major step was the elimination of the League of Nations as a significant factor in Canadian external policy. Mackenzie King, like so many well-meaning men of the era, had first seen the League as a symbol of civilized diplomacy. Another world war seemed unthinkable, and he assumed that major international disputes would be settled by negotiations. The League not only provided the necessary machinery for negotiation but it could also provide the sanction of world public opinion to ensure that negotiations would be effective. He believed that world opinion would be an effective deterrent and that any would-be aggressor would recoil from the threat of being branded as an international outlaw. Japan's aggression against China raised doubts about the effectiveness of this deterrent but it was not until Italian aggression in Ethiopia that King realized that some aggressors would not be coerced by world opinion. In such cases, should the League deplore the aggression but take no further action, or should League members declare war on the aggressor? King made his position clear after the Ethiopian crisis. He bluntly rejected the idea of a coercive League because he realized that Canadians were not prepared to fight for the principle of collective security.

When King took office in 1935 he supported the League to the extent of imposing economic sanctions against Italy; economic sanctions seemed the most effective way of expressing disapproval of aggression. He made it clear in his first public statement on the issue as prime minister that this did not imply any commitment to impose military sanctions. The repudiation of Riddell did not involve any change in this policy. King expressed his readiness to extend economic sanctions to include such items as oil, if the Committee of Eighteen and the League

---

[14] Cited in ibid., 87. Soward's chapters in this book are still the best study of the public debate on Canadian external policy in these years. A.R.M. Lower, *Canada: Nation and Neighbour* (Toronto, 1952), provides a select bibliography on "The Great Debate" and also offers his labels for a number of prominent Canadians during the decade.

itself agreed to such an extension, although he was not prepared to take the initiative. At this stage the League was still a focus of Canadian external policy.[15]

The Ethiopian crisis was significant because it made King realize more clearly the implications of League membership. World opinion had not deterred Mussolini. Disapproval, in the form of economic sanctions, had had no effect. On the other hand, if economic sanctions had been extended and had threatened to thwart Mussolini's ambitions, he might have retaliated and involved League members in a war. Italy would doubtless have been defeated, but in the meantime Canada would have faced a dangerous internal crisis. Canadian participation would have been opposed by Canadian isolationists and by Canadians who suspected that British imperial interest lay behind the opposition to Mussolini's aim of creating an African empire. This would have meant an open clash with Canadians who supported the idea of collective security through the League and with those who wanted to be at Britain side. In his diary King recorded a revealing discussion with Ernest Lapointe soon after the government took office:

> If the Government was to decide for military sanctions, he [Lapointe] would resign at once. He also said that if we did not, and the question came to be one which we had to decide, he believed that Illsley [sic] and one or two others would immediately resign. In other words, if the question of military sanctions comes we shall have the old war situation over again, with the party divided as it was at the time of conscription. My own feeling is that, if Canada carries out her part with respect to the economic sanctions, we should not be expected to go further.... Our own domestic situation must be considered first, and what will serve to keep Canada united. To be obliged to go into war would force an issue that might become a battle between imperialism and independence. At all costs, this must, if at all possible, be avoided.[16]

The issue was avoided for the moment—the Italian army conquered Ethiopia while the question of further economic sanctions was still under discussion at Geneva—but King could not afford to risk another incident in the future in which the League might insist on showing some teeth. War was inevitable if some country was intent on aggression but it need not be a large-scale war involving a number of major world powers. The principle of collective security was dangerous because it could transform a local incident into a war involving all League members. Not all Canadians,

---

[15] James Eayrs, *In Defence of Canada*, II (Toronto, 1965), provides the best account of this and of subsequent incidents in external affairs, although his interpretation of Mackenzie King's policies does not always coincide with mine.

[16] W.L. Mackenzie King, Diary, 29 October 1935.

however, would be prepared to fight for the principle of collective security and the country would be divided. Rather than hope for the best King decided to forestall this danger. He told the League Assembly in 1936 that it should rely solely on mediation and conciliation and on the influence of world opinion to preserve world peace. Canada, at least, he explained, was not prepared to accept "automatic commitments to the application of force."[17] The speech was a clear and unequivocal rejection of the principle of collective security.

The speech cut through the fuzzy sentimentality with which many Canadians had shrouded the League. Now that the distinction had been made between the League as a kind of military alliance against aggressors and the League as an international forum for discussion, it became clear that few Canadians really wanted a military alliance.[18] They might speak hopefully of the power of reason at Geneva or nostalgically of the League that might have been, but after 1936 the discussions of Canadian policy were not muddled by confusion between the two possible roles of the League or by uncertainty about the government's position. Most Canadians apparently shared King's preference for conciliation rather than collective security. In effect the League was eliminated as a significant factor in the debate over Canada's external relations.

With the League eliminated, the debate was thus focused on the crucial question of Canada's relations with Great Britain. If Britain went to war should Canada go to war? Such a hypothetical question had no easy answer. Extreme imperialists would have replied with a prompt affirmative, and extreme isolationists would have been equally prompt with a negative answer, but most Canadians would have given a qualified response. It would depend on circumstances. For many it would depend on whether Canadian interests were at stake, although even the definition of Canadian interests would have offered ample scope for prolonged arguments. For many Canadians, however, there was a preliminary question which had not yet been resolved. Was there any assurance that the question of Canadian participation would be decided on the basis of Canadian interests, however they were defined? What of the possibility that the decision might be determined by the bonds of empire—a combination of British pressure and colonial subservience—and that Canada would be drawn into Britain's war whether or not Canadian interests were at stake?

This was not an academic question. King himself saw no significant divergence between British and Canadian interests. Both the British and Canadian people wanted peace; if circumstances forced the British to fight, he assumed that Canadians would react in much the same way to these same circumstances. He believed that Britain was Canada's first line of defence and also that in any war Britain's cause would be the cause of liberty and democracy. The fortunate conjuncture of Britain and the side of right would mean that a consensus favouring Canadian participation was possible.

---

[17] The speech is printed in R.A. Mackay and E.G. Rogers, *Canada Looks Abroad* (London, 1938), 363-9.

[18] For Canadian reaction to the speech see Eayrs, *In Defence of Canada*, II, 39.

The major obstacle was psychological. Champions of Canadian autonomy would be blind to any arguments for participation if they believed that the decision had really been imposed on Canada because of the British connection. In order to assert Canadian autonomy they would oppose participation. A national consensus would only be possible if these autonomists could be convinced that the decision had been made by Canada and for Canada. A sense of autonomy was thus a prerequisite for national unity if war came.

Mackenzie King would naturally have preferred to avoid any decision on participation. He had been through the wartime crisis of 1917 and knew the destructive emotions which a war could rouse. An impassioned debate over participation, added to the internal divisions of the 1930s, could be disastrous. He therefore supported appeasement at the Imperial Conference of 1937. He was not so naïve, however, as to think that a European war could be easily averted. Like many of his contemporaries, he oscillated between cautious optimism and dark despair as one crisis was passed, only to be followed by another. Thus King's desperate hope for peace did not blind him to the possibility of war and to the need to prepare Canadian public opinion to face a decision on participation. For King this meant that Canadian autonomy had to be made credible and convincing. For the years from 1936 to 1939 every aspect of external policy was dominated by this aim.

The formal assurance of autonomy was summed up in King's oft-repeated assurance that Parliament would decide. This was not an attempt to deny personal responsibility for a decision which might be unpopular. He knew that the initiative would have to come from the government and, as he told the House of Commons, his government would first have to propose a course of action which Parliament could then approve or reject.[19] "Parliament will decide" was nonetheless a salutary reminder that the members of Parliament had the power of veto. The government could not secretly commit Canada to be at Britain's side if war came. Nor could a hasty but final decision be made by Order-in-Council. Canadians, through their representatives in Parliament, would have the opportunity to revoke any government decision. King was reminding his listeners that the Canadian Parliament was one of the guarantees of Canadian autonomy.

The doubters also had to be reassured that the government looked on the outside world through Canadian spectacles. King's speeches on foreign affairs were intended to give this reassurance. They almost invariably began with a summary of the various Canadian attitudes and showed a sympathetic understanding and appreciation of the different and often conflicting points of view. Whatever the final decision of the government might be, all Canadians at least knew that their point of view had not been ignored or summarily dismissed. E.J. Tarr compared King's performance in the House of Commons in 1937 to that of a juggler keeping the balls of Isolationism, North Americanism, Imperialism, and Collectivism in the air at once. "One sees them going up and coming down with rhythmic regularity, and suddenly

---

[19] *House of Commons Debates*, 30 March 1939, p. 2418.

they are lost in the polished phrases of a platitudinous peroration—the magician's handkerchief." It was not a satisfying performance for those who wanted the government to seize one ball with both hands and let the others drop, but at least all groups knew that their position was receiving consideration. It was, as Tarr concluded, "statesmanship honestly striving for national unity."[20]

Speeches were not enough. Actions would speak louder than words, and any action which implied that Canada would inevitably be at Britain's side of war came would convince the sceptical that the vaunted autonomy of Canada was a myth. By the end of 1936 King felt that Canadian defence expenditures had to be increased. War might come and Canada must be prepared. The decision was bound to be unpopular among isolationists, but it would also be denounced by autonomists if defence expenditures seemed designed for cooperation with Great Britain in case of war. Spending money on the army would be interpreted as preparing an expeditionary force and would imply that the die was already cast. The defence estimates introduced in 1937 directed most of the increased expenditures towards the air force and were defended as being necessary for the defence of Canada and Canadian coastal waters. There was no implication of cooperation with Great Britain. King knew that an air force would be the most useful contribution Canada could make if it did become involved in a European war, so the expenditures were also justified on these grounds, but he emphasized the aspect of home defence because this would not provoke the suspicions of autonomists.

It was not always possible to find a compromise which would make future cooperation with Great Britain possible and yet would not commit Canada to such cooperation. In the summer of 1938 the British government asked to train pilots in Canada for the Royal Air Force. Surely Canada would allow the mother country to take advantage of its vast open spaces? Mackenzie King, however, rejected the proposal and refused to yield in spite of bitter criticism by the Conservative opposition.[21] It was obvious that permission once given could not be withdrawn if Britain went to war—one of the aims of the scheme was to establish training areas safe from enemy attack—and that Canada would thus have the status of a belligerent. Committing Canada to cooperate in the training of British pilots, as King commented in his diary, "would do the Empire more harm than good by, first of all, creating disunion in Canada, and secondly, prejudicing in advance the position that might be taken at a later time.[22]

The Bren gun contract posed the same problem. As early as 1936 the British government wanted to place an order for Bren guns in Canada and asked the Canadian government to suggest a manufacturer. The contract would mean jobs for Canadians. More important, Canada had also adopted the Bren as its infantry machine gun, and a joint contract would reduce the cost of equipping the Canadian army. The objection

---

[20] Quoted in Soward *et al., Canada in World Affairs*, 57.
[21] For details see Eayrs, *In Defence of Canada*, II, 91-103.
[22] Diary, 13 May 1938.

to such an arrangement was that it would implicitly commit Canada to supplying munitions to Great Britain in time of war, and again the possibility of Canadian neutrality would be compromised. King procrastinated, and it was not until 1938, when the British insisted on an immediate decision, that he finally agreed. Even then the appearance of autonomy was maintained. The British and Canadian governments signed separate contracts with the John Inglis Company, even though the terms were the same and the price per gun depended upon both contracts being signed.[23] For two years King had run the risk of criticism for indecision and for lack of cooperation with Great Britain because a decision might prejudice his claim that Canada was autonomous. Fortunately for him George Drew misguidedly accused the government of corruption over the Bren contract[24] and so lost the chance to convict the government of the lesser fault of prolonged indecision.

King himself was not entirely satisfied with this policy of refusing to make any commitments until the outbreak of war, and explained his dilemma frankly in the House of Commons in 1938. "It must be recognized," he admitted, "that this policy is not wholly satisfactory, not a completely logical position. Like many other policies it is not an ideal solution; it is only the best of the available solutions." But the problem of national unity could not be ignored. "It should be plain to everyone ... that to force an issue like this upon the country would bring out deep and in some cases fundamental differences of opinion, would lead to further strain upon the unity of a country already strained by economic depression and other consequences of the last war and its aftermath."[25] The need to prove that Canada was not committed in advance to support Great Britain left King no alternative.

The Munich crisis in September 1938 was a turning point in King's external policy. Munich had ended with peace, but the narrow margin between peace and war showed that war might come at any time. It was no longer enough to be all things to all men, in the sense of showing an understanding of all shades of Canadian opinion. The sense of autonomy must still be preserved, but Canadians must now be prepared for the imminent possibility of participation in a European war.

King still could not risk an open commitment to be at Britain's side during the Munich crisis. He knew that his government would support Britain if Chamberlain's negotiations failed and war broke out. He also knew that he would then be blamed by his critics for not having helped to deter Hitler by showing that Chamberlain had Canada's support. A public declaration during the negotiations, however, would have meant that Chamberlain, and not the Canadian government, would openly be deciding Canada's fate. King did discuss the possibility of such an announcement with his cabinet. Various opinions were expressed, but Lapointe's reaction was probably decisive. Lapointe was in Geneva, but he cabled that in his opinion the

---

[23] For details see *Report of the Royal Commission on the Bren Machine Gun Contract* (Ottawa, 1939).

[24] George A. Drew, "Canada's Armament Mystery," *Maclean's Magazine*, 1 September 1938.

[25] *House of Commons Debates*, 24 May 1938, p. 3184.

situation in Canada was still delicate. "Submit that Parliament should be summoned, if war declared and no definite commitments made meanwhile ... I do not see how I could advise any course of action that would not only be opposed to personal convictions and sacred pledges to my own people but would destroy all their confidence and prevent me from carrying weight and influence with them for what might be essential actions."[26] For the French-Canadians, at least, support for participation would depend on avoiding any pledge before war broke out.

In the session of 1939, however, King carefully tried to tell Canadians that war might be unavoidable. He began in January by reminding the House of Commons that in case of a European war Canada could not avoid being involved to some extent, repeating Sir Wilfrid Laurier's phrase that "if England was at war we are at war and liable to attack."[27] Two months later he made an even more positive statement: "If there were a prospect of an aggressor launching an attack on Britain with bombers raining death on London, I have no doubt what the decision of the Canadian people will be. We would regard it as an act of aggression, menacing freedom in all parts of the British Commonwealth."[28] He went on to say that a war fought "over trade or prestige in some far corner of the world" would be a different matter but it was clear that the Canadian government intended to support Great Britain in case of a major European war.

Now more than ever national unity depended on convincing doubting Canadians that this would be the necessary and proper decision. In another foreign policy speech at the end of March, King repeated his opinion that "the destruction of Britain would be a menace to the freedom of every nation of the British Commonwealth,"[29] but he also made it clear that the decision to participate would be made with regret. In one sentence he captured the sense of futility shared by so many Canadians: "The idea that every twenty years the country should automatically and as a matter of course take part in a war overseas for democracy or self-determination of other nations, that a country which has all it can do to run itself should feel called upon to save, periodically, a continent that cannot run itself, and to these ends risk the lives of its people, or risk bankruptcy and political disunion, seems to many a nightmare and sheer madness."[30] A nightmare it might be, but King was pleading with his compatriots to realize that they could not exorcize this nightmare by hiding themselves under the blanket of isolation.

Even more important was his solemn promise that, if war came, there would be no conscription. He felt safe in making this promise because, as he explained, the days of large-scale infantry battles were gone. But his aim was clearly to reassure French Canadians that the bitter controversies of 1917 would never be repeated.

---

[26] Lapointe Papers, Lapointe to King, 24 September 1938.
[27] *House of Commons Debates*, 16 January 1939, p. 52.
[28] Ibid., 20 March 1939, p. 2043.
[29] Ibid., 31 March 1939, p. 2422.
[30] Ibid., 2419.

Lapointe followed King by promising that he himself would never support conscription, but he went on to argue that neutrality would be impossible if Britain was involved in a major war. No government could enforce impartial treatment of all belligerents, interning British vessels, and forbidding enlistment in Canada: "I ask any one of my fellow countrymen whether they believe seriously that this could be done without a civil war in Canada."[31] In the debate that followed English-Canadian spokesmen for the opposition parties showed a sober recognition of the need to preserve national unity and many French-Canadian speakers expressed confidence in the government's guarantee that war would not mean conscription. Mackenzie King could take some credit for the remarkable moderation of the debate and the even more remarkable support for the government's position from all sides of the House.

The moment of decision came in September 1939. By then it was a foregone conclusion. The government introduced a declaration of war in a special session and Parliament did decide—and without the necessity of a recorded vote. Even at this late date, however, many members consented with reluctance. Ernest Lapointe made a moving appeal to his compatriots to accept the inevitable, but even so three French-Canadian members spoke against participation. The CCF party was almost split over the issue. The National Council of the CCF, at an emergency meeting, reversed its previous policy of neutrality by a majority vote, but this majority was only achieved by a compromise which would limit Canada's contribution to food and munitions.[32] J.S. Woodsworth, leader of the party, resigned because he could not accept even this limited degree of participation.

National unity had been preserved. A national consensus had been achieved, reluctantly and with scattered opposition, but nonetheless a national consensus which had the support of representatives from each cultural group and from every region of Canada. Events in Europe had helped to make Canadians aware of the seriousness of the crisis and had strengthened the sympathy and support for Great Britain. Within Canada the solemn promise not to introduce conscription had had its effect. But there can be no doubt that the degree of support for participation was made possible by Mackenzie King's consistent efforts to convince Canadians that now, when the decision was being made, it was being made by an autonomous Canada. Freed from the suspicion that Canada was a British puppet, many accepted the decision who would otherwise have opposed it. King was more than the leader who divided Canada least.[33] He was also the leader who united Canadians on the fateful decision to go to war.

---

[31] Ibid., 2467.
[32] Kenneth McNaught, *A Prophet in Politics* (Toronto, 1959), 305-7.
[33] The phrase comes from F.H. Underhill, *In Search of Canadian Liberalism* (Toronto, 1960), 135.

Staring into the Abyss

J.L. Granatstein

"History repeats itself." That is a popular view of the past, but it is not, I suspect, a view shared by most historians. The differences in personalities, in context, in subtleties and shadings usually combine to persuade historians that the crisis of one decade or century is different in class and kind from that of another. But, sometimes, history really does seem to repeat itself.

In the First World War, the United Kingdom's weakened financial condition led Whitehall to pressure Canada to turn to the United States to raise money At the same time, Britain proved unable or unwilling to take all the food and munitions produced by Canada unless Ottawa picked up a greater share of the costs, and the Canadian government had little choice other than to agree. In an effort, both politically and economically inspired, to keep munitions factories working at full blast in Canada, the Imperial Munitions Board, a Canadian-operated imperial procurement and production agency, actively sought contracts from the U.S. War Department. At the same time, other arms of the Canadian government lobbied in Washington to get their share of scarce raw materials. The net effect of the First World War on Canadian-American relations was to strengthen the links across the border and to increase the number and complexity of the ties of economics, politics, and sentiment that bound the two North American nations together. The defeat of reciprocity in the 1911 election, therefore, seemed only a temporary check, one virtually nullified by the greater necessity of wartime integration and cooperation.

It should have been no surprise, then, that Canada entered the 1920s with Conservative Prime Minister Arthur Meighen urging Britain to seek an accommodation with the United States and not to renew the Anglo-Japanese Alliance.[1] Nor was it a surprise that Canada welcomed more investment from the United States while, despite repeated efforts by the Liberal governments of Mackenzie King to enhance trade with the United Kingdom, its commerce with its neighbour continued to increase.[2] The Great Depression and the massive increases in

---

[1] See Philip Wigley, *Canada and the Transition to Commonwealth: British-Canadian Relations 1917-1926* (Cambridge 1977), 129 ff. D.C. Watt erroneously saw "geographical or racialist factors" responsible for "the pro-American orientation" of Canadian foreign policy, and he argued that British actions here were taken "for the sake of keeping Canada in the Empire." *Succeeding John Bull: America in Britain's Place 1900-1975* (Cambridge 1984), 50, 52.

[2] King expressed strong support for the effort to widen imperial preferences at the Imperial Economic Conference of 1923. See R.M Dawson, *William Lyon Mackenzie King*, vol. I: *A Political Biography 1874-1923* (Toronto 1958), 469 ff. The 1930 Liberal budget lowered the duties on 270 British goods exported to Canada and threatened countervailing duties against

the American tariff put in place by a protectionist Congress and then matched by Canadian governments, however, temporarily cut into Canadian-American trade.

While these restrictions led many Canadians to look overseas with renewed imperial fervour, some Britons nonetheless feared for Canada's survival as a British nation in the face of the power of the United States. One example of the first tendency was Harry Stevens, soon to be minister of trade and commerce in R.B. Bennett's government, who told the voters in 1930 that "My ambition for Canada is that she may become a unit of the Empire and concerned not with a few petty tariff items, but with all the great problems confronting the Home Government." No worse fate could have befallen Canadians! In contrast, Leo Amery, the dominions secretary in 1928, returned from a trip to Canada worried that "the din and glare of the great American orchestra" might drown out Canada. His hopes were bolstered, however, by the conviction that there was "no deeper fundamental instinct of the Canadian national character than dislike of the United States as belonging to an inferior political civilisation."[3] For their part, officials of the United States government, as Peter Kasurak has noted, began "from a single point of view in the area of Canadian affairs—fear that Britain was forging its Empire into an international colossus which would dominate world trade."[4] To Washington, that fear seemed to be realized after the Ottawa Conference of 1932.[5]

But not even the Imperial Economic Conference and the imperial preferences agreed on at Ottawa could truly reverse the historic trend towards North American continentalism that had accelerated during the Great War. The two "hermit kingdoms," to use Charles Stacey's phrase uttered from this platform a dozen years ago,[6] had a great deal in common in an era when British trade as a percentage of world trade continued its decline and Britain's overall military power ebbed. Mackenzie King had begun the transformation of the empire into the Commonwealth during the Chanak affair of 1922 and at the Imperial Conference of 1923, where "the decisive nature of the English defeat at Mackenzie King's hands" was nothing less

---

the United States. See H.B. Neatby, *William Lyon Mackenzie King*, vol. II: *The Lonely Heights* (Toronto 1963), 323-4. On reaction to U.S. investment in this period and after see Peter Kresl, "Before the Deluge: Canadians on Foreign Ownership, 1920-1955," *American Review of Canadian Studies 6* (spring 1976), 65 ff.

3 Quoted in Norman Hillmer, "Personalities and Problems in Anglo-Canadian Economic Relations between the Two World Wars," *Bulletin of Canadian Studies 3* (June 1979), 5, 8.

4 Peter Kasurak, "American Foreign Policy Officials and Canada, 1927-1941: A Look through Bureaucratic Glasses," *International Journal* 32 (summer 1977), 548.

5 The best study of the Ottawa Conference, including its origins and aftermath, is in Ian Drummond, *Imperial Economic Policy 1917-1939* (London 1974), chap. 5 ff.

6 C.P. Stacey, *Mackenzie King and the North Atlantic Triangle* (Toronto 1976), chap. 2.

than a "surrender, which changed the course of the history of the empire."[7] Those apocalyptic phrases were the considered judgment of Correlli Barnett, "the Jeremiah of British historians," or so Noel Annan has recently called him.[8] They sound very similar in tone to the words of Donald Creighton, the Jeremiah of Canadian historians, who wrote that King, "a stocky barrel-like figure, with an audible wheeze when in full voice," was no "bulky St. George confronting a slavering imperial dragon." He was "a citizen of North America ... determined to destroy" the Commonwealth.[9]

When Mackenzie King came back to power in the middle of the Great Depression in 1935, the Ottawa agreements had demonstrably not restored Canada's economic health. Prime Minister Bennett had seemingly recognized the failure of the imperial initiative by launching his own somewhat desultory efforts to strike a trade agreement with Washington, but his attempt at an accommodation with the United States could not come to fruition before the voters eagerly dispensed with the Tory government's services.[10] It fell to the new prime minister, choosing what he described to the United States minister in Canada as "the American road," to negotiate that trade agreement with the Roosevelt administration.[11] Mackenzie King reinforced it with another trade pact with the United States three years later.[12] Simultaneously, King and his advisers in the Department of External Affairs looked with dismay at the wide-ranging rivalry between London and Washington, most pronounced in the Pacific where the two English-speaking powers jostled for economic and political dominance with each other and an aggressive Japan. Conflict between Canada's mother country and its nearest neighbour held out only the

---

[7] Correlli Barnett, *The Collapse of British Power* (London 1972), 195. Barnett's index reference under Mackenzie King refers to this episode as "destroys imperial alliance." Stacey's judgment is more sensible and accurate: King "challenged this idea of a common foreign policy and, essentially, destroyed it." Stacey, *Mackenzie King*, 33.

[8] "Gentlemen v. Players," *New York Review of Books* (29 Sept, 1988), 63.

[9] Donald Creighton, "The Decline and Fall of the Empire of the St. Lawrence," *Historical Papers 1969*, 21.

[10] Within a year of giving up the Conservative party leadership, Bennett left Canada to live in England. "It's grand to be going home," the New Brunswick-born Bennett said as he left for the mother country. That may have been the most revealing comment ever made about Canadian Conservatism prior to the Second World War. Bennett soon violated Canadian law by accepting a peerage.

[11] F.D. Roosevelt Library, Roosevelt Papers, PSF, box 33, Armour to Phillips, 22 Oct. 1935.

[12] On the decline in British trade see Paul Kennedy, *The Rise and Fall of the Great Powers* (Toronto 1987), 316. On the Canadian-American trade agreements see J.L. Granatstein, *A Man of Influence* (Ottawa 1981), chap. 3, and R.N. Kottman, *Reciprocity and the North Atlantic Triangle, 1932-1938* (Ithaca 1968).

prospect of terrible divisiveness in Canada.[13] Nonetheless, the prime minister gladly accepted and immediately reciprocated President Franklin Roosevelt's assurances, delivered at Queen's University in Kingston on 18 August 1938, "that the people of the United States will not stand idly by" if Canada were ever threatened.[14] That guarantee had to be called upon just two years later.

By 1939, as the Nazis prepared to plunge Europe into the war that was to ensure America's half century of world economic hegemony, U.S. companies and investors and the American market had already established their pre-eminence in Canada. The United States provided 60 per cent of the foreign capital invested in Canada while British sources put up only 36 per cent. In 1914 the figures had been 23 and 72 per cent, respectively. In terms of Canadian exports, shipments to the United States in 1939 exceeded those to Britain by 20 per cent; in 1914 exports to Britain had been 10 per cent higher than those to the United States. Similarly, in 1914 Canada had imported three times as much from the United States as from the United Kingdom; in 1939 Canada imported four times as much.[15] The years of the Great War had provided the impetus for Canada's shift from the British to the American economic sphere.

During the Second World War, the events of the Great War were repeated with a stunning similarity. To be sure, different men from different political parties were in charge in Canada. Mackenzie King, that most unadmired of Canadian leaders, was at the helm in Ottawa, and his attitudes and prejudices were certainly far different from those of Sir Robert Borden.

Ramsay Cook predicted almost two decades ago that King was certain to become the subject of a book of readings for students under the title "Mackenzie King: Hero or Fink?" Cook knew that the fink side of the debate would be easy to document. He suggested that King had become the central figure in the Canadian mythology, the most convenient one of all, because he was the "cause of all our failings," including

---

[13] This is the subject of Gregory Johnson's York University doctoral dissertation in progress on the relations of Canada, the United States, and the United Kingdom in the Pacific from 1935 to 1950.

[14] R.F. Swanson, *Canadian-American Summit Diplomacy, 1923-1973* (Toronto 1975), 52 ff. According to D.C. Watt, Mackenzie King was "yet another channel by which disguised isolationist ideas could be fed to the president." *Succeeding John Bull*, 78.

[15] M.C. Urquhart and K.A.H. Buckley, eds., *Historical Statistics of Canada* (Toronto 1965), F345-56; F.H. Leacy, ed., *Historical Statistics of Canada* (Ottawa 1983), G188-202. I have used 1939 data, though Canada's trade with the United States was higher then than throughout the rest of the decade since that was the fist year that showed the impact of the 1938 trade agreement. In other words, had the Second World War not distorted trade patterns, the 1939 trends would likely have continued.

the decline and fall of the British Empire in Canada.[16] Cook was certainly correct in assessing the little man's place, and few have yet come forward to argue that Mackenzie King was a great Canadian hero. Charles Stacey, in the last words of his Joanne Goodman lectures in 1976, however, did say—and I expect he was only half-jesting—that he would "not be altogether surprised if he turned up, one of these days, as the patron saint of the new nationalism."[17]

Still, King is difficult to elevate to sainthood. Even (or especially) those who observed or worked intimately with him had scant admiration for him. Tom Blacklock, a Press Gallery member in the 1920s, complained that King was "such a pompous ass that an orang-outang that would flatter him could choose its own reward."[18] Leonard Brockington wrote speeches for King for a time during the early years of the Second World War, and when he quit in exasperation he told a friend that he was "sick and tired of being mid-wife to an intellectual virgin."[19] Senator Norman Lambert ran elections for the Liberal leader, and Mackenzie King gratefully elevated him to the Upper Chamber. Nonetheless, Lambert told Grant Dexter of the *Winnipeg Free Press* that "he simply can't stand the worm at close quarters—bad breath, a fetid, unhealthy, sinister atmosphere like living close to some filthy object.... But," the senator added, "get off a piece and he looks better and better."[20]

That last comment on Mackenzie King I have always thought the nearly definite one. Up close, there was little that was admirable about the Liberal leader, much that was slippery and sleazy. But acquire some distance, get off a piece, as Lambert said, and the dumpy little laird of Kingsmere—and Canada—began to look not unlike a giant. To bring us back to Earth, I might point out that the fine Canadian novelist Hugh Hood has his main character in *The Swing in the Garden* note, "I think always of W.C. Fields when I think of Mackenzie King."[21] That may be *the* definitive description.

I have no intention of trying to paint Mackenzie King as a superhero here, though, despite years of reading Donald Creighton and W.L. Morton, I cannot yet bring myself to see him as a filthy object or even as a fink. For me, the crucial factor in assessing the common charge that Mackenzie King sold us out to the Americans is that the prime minister during the Second World War faced similar, but greater, problems to those Sir Robert Borden had had to confront a quarter century before. But though he had more resources at his disposal than his predecessor in the

---

[16] *Globe Magazine*, 15 Aug. 1970, quoted in Norman Hillmer, "'The Outstanding Imperialist': Mackenzie King and the British," Part I of *Britain and Canada in the Age of Mackenzie King*, Canada House Lecture Series No. 4 [1979], 3-4.

[17] Stacey, *Mackenzie King*, 68.

[18] National Archives of Canada (NA), Robert Borden Papers, Note by Loring Christie, nd., f. 148398.

[19] L.L.L. Golden interview, 3 Oct. 1965.

[20] NA, John W. Dafoe Papers, Grant Dexter to Dafoe, 18 April 1941.

[21] Hugh Hood, *The Swing in the Garden* (Toronto 1975), 165.

Prime Minister's office, King had no greater freedom of action when British military and economic weakness forced his country into grave difficulties. When it came to directing the weak corner of the North Atlantic Triangle in its efforts to stay safe and secure in a world suddenly unstable, King, much like Borden before him, had to turn to the United States for assistance.

One major factor was different in the Second World War. In the Great War, Britain and France lost battles but they did not suffer catastrophic defeats that placed their survival as nation-states at stake. In May and June 1940, of course, Hitler's astonishingly effective armies defeated Britain and France in the Low Countries and in France, the French capitulated, and the British Army, without equipment, found its way home thanks only to a miracle at Dunkirk.

For Canada in that terrible summer of defeat and despair, the changes in the military balance of power were catastrophic. The country had gone to war with the idea that it could fight as a junior partner with "limited liability." The government had hoped that its war effort could be small, balanced, and relatively cheap, and Quebec and the country had been promised that there would be no conscription for overseas service. Now, the planning of late 1939 had to be scrapped. Canada, with its population of eleven million and suddenly Britain's ranking ally, was in the war to the utmost—except for conscription, which was still politically unacceptable. Moreover, a huge proportion of this country's under-equipped and partially trained air, army, and naval forces was already in the United Kingdom, and if—or when—Britain fell they were certain to be completely lost. The Royal Navy had its hands full in trying to protect home waters and block the expected Nazi invasion. The aircraft necessary to operate the centrepiece of the Canadian war effort, the British Commonwealth Air Training plan, had been scheduled to come from Great Britain, but now would not arrive. If Britain fell and, especially, if the Royal Navy passed into German hands, Canada was likely to be subject to Nazi attack.[22] Britain's military weakness in July and August 1940 was exposed for all to see; so too was Canada's.[23]

The military weakness of the United States was also apparent, but there can be no doubt that President Franklin Roosevelt's country was the only hope of the Allies—

---

[22] The fate of the Royal Navy naturally concerned the United States and involved Mackenzie King in an excruciating role between Churchill and Roosevelt. See David Reynolds, *The Creation of the Anglo-American Alliance 1937-1941* (Chapel Hill, NC 1982), 115 ff., for an American historian's view.

[23] Barnett nonetheless argues that the presence of a Canadian corps in England did not make up for the dispatch of British troops to the Middle and Far East. "The nations of the empire were true `daughters' of the Mother Country in that at no time during the war did their contributions defray the cost of their own strategic keep." Barnett, *Collapse*, 586. In his later book, *The Audit of War* (London 1986), 3, he adds that the empire produced only 10 per cent of the munitions of war supplied to British and imperial forces. So much for Canada's unstinted contribution to the war.

and of Canada. Many in Canada recognized this truth in the days after Dunkirk, and they realized the new obligations this would force on the dominion. Donald Creighton, writing years later, noted that for many Canadians—and he had his despised colleague Frank Underhill in mind—the war's course "hastened the growth" of Canada's "new North American nationality by proving that ... Great Britain ... could no longer act as Canada's main defence against danger from abroad."[24]

At the time, the bureaucratic response to the new state of affairs came from Hugh Keenleyside of the Department of External Affairs, who set out the fullest statement of the likely Canadian situation as France surrendered to Hitler. It was improbable, he wrote, that the United States would protect Canada without "demanding a measure of active cooperation in return. It is a reasonable expectation that the United States will expect, and if necessary demand, Canadian assistance in the defence of this continent and this Hemisphere." Canada, he noted, would feel some obligation to participate; "thus the negotiation of a specific offensive-defensive alliance is likely to become inevitable."[25]

President Roosevelt himself was thinking along these lines. In August, Loring Christie, the Canadian minister in Washington, reported to Mackenzie King that the president "had been thinking of proposing to you to send to Ottawa 3 staff officers ... to discuss defence problems.... He had in mind their surveying [the] situation from [the]Bay of Fundy around to the Gulf of St. Lawrence. They might explore [the] question of base facilities for United States use."[26] But on 16 August Roosevelt asked King to meet him at Ogdensburg, NY, the next day to discuss "the matter of [the] mutual defence of our coasts on the Atlantic."[27]

What the president wanted was the creation of a Permanent Joint Board on Defence with equal representation from each country and a mandate limited to the study of common defence problems and the making of recommendations to both governments on how to resolve them. Delighted at the prospect of forging a military alliance with the United States, King queried only Roosevelt's desire that the board be "permanent." "I said I was not questioning the wisdom of it," King noted, "but was anxious to get what he had in mind." According to King's diary, Roosevelt replied that he wanted "to help secure the continent for the future."[28] The Canadian leader sometimes suffered from "the idea," in the superb Australian novelist Thomas

---

[24] D.G. Creighton, "The Ogdensburg Agreement and F.H. Underhill," in C. Berger and R. Cook, eds., *The West and the Nation* (Toronto 1976), 303.

[25] NA, Department of External Affairs Records (EAR), vol. 781, file 394, "An Outline Synopsis," 17 June 1940.

[26] NA, W.L.M. King Papers, Black Binders, vol. 19, Christie to King, 15 Aug. 1940. Reynolds, *Creation*, 118, describes FDR's request for the Ogdensburg meeting as being necessary to formulate "contingency plans in case Britain lost control of the North Atlantic." See also Reynolds, *Creation*, 132, 183.

[27] J.W. Pickersgill, ed., *The Mackenzie King Record*, vol. I: 1939-44 (Toronto 1960), 130-1.

[28] Ibid., 14.

Keneally's phrase, "that the only empire you need to suspect is the British."[29] Mackenzie King probably ought to have asked whose empire and whose future, but in August 1940 that question was virtually impossible even to raise—when the fear was that it might be Adolf Hitler's empire and Germany's future if no action were taken.

The decision to create the PJBD was an important one. The board sprang into existence within two weeks and began surveying defences on both the Atlantic and the Pacific coasts. A Joint Canadian-United States Basic Defence Plan, produced by the board's military members, aimed to meet the situation that would arise if Britain were overrun. In that event, strategic control of Canadian forces was to pass to the United States. A second plan, produced in the spring of 1941 and called ABC-22, looked at Canadian-American cooperation in a war in which the United States was actively engaged on the side of the Allies. The Americans again sought strategic control of Canadian forces and to integrate the Canadian east and west coast regions directly into their military commands. It was one thing to agree to American military direction in a war that saw North America standing virtually alone; it was another thing entirely in a war where Britain remained unoccupied and the United States was a partner. "The American officers," to use Keneally again, "listened ... with that omnivorous American politeness ... we poor hayseeds would come to know so well and mistrust, perhaps, not enough."[30] Nonetheless, Canada refused to accept Washington's aims for ABC-22 and won its point, thereby demonstrating that Mackenzie King's government could and would fight for its freedom of action.[31] Whether such independence could have survived a German or Japanese invasion happily never had to be tested.

The significance of the PJBD in its context of August 1940 was that a still-neutral United States had struck an alliance with Canada, a belligerent power. That had to be seen as a gain for Britain—and for Canada, too. Important as that was for the war, the true meaning of the Ogdensburg meeting was that it marked Canada's definitive move from the British military sphere to the American. The British had lost whatever capacity they might have had to defend Canada, and in August 1940 their ability even to defend the British Isles successfully was very much in doubt.[32]

---

[29] Thomas Keneally, *The Cut-Rate Kingdom* (London 1984), 125. This novel of Australia's experience with, among other things, the United States in the Second World War has some useful and suggestive parallels for the Canadian case.

[30] Ibid.

[31] J.L. Granatstein, *Canada's War: The Politics of the Mackenzie King Government, 1939-45* (Toronto 1975), 131-2.

[32] Gerard S. Vano has suggested that there had been a reversal of military obligation within the empire by this period. No longer was Canada under the British military shield, but "Britain was, to a degree, falling under a Canadian shield." *Canada: The Strategic and Military Pawn* (New York 1988), 87. Reynolds, *Creation*, 136, notes that Australia and New Zealand, as well as Canada, were forced closer to the United States by the events of the summer of 1940.

In the circumstances, Canada had no choice at all. Canada had to seek help where help was to be found, and that meant Washington.

Few people truly realized the significance of the Permanent Joint Board on Defence and the Ogdensburg Agreement that had created it in the summer of 1940. Some Conservatives grumbled at Mackenzie King's actions, former Prime Minister Arthur Meighen being the most caustic. He had noted that "I lost my breakfast when I read the account this morning and gazed on the disgusting picture of these potentates"—that is, King and Roosevelt—"posing like monkeys in the very middle of the blackest crisis of this Empire."[33] Most Tories and almost all the Canadian press showed more sense.[34]

The one critic who shook Mackenzie King, however, was Winston Churchill. The new British prime minister, in office only since 10 May 1940, had replied to King's telegram on the Ogdensburg meeting by stating "there may be two opinions on some of the points mentioned. Supposing Mr. Hitler cannot invade us ... all these transactions will be judged in a mood different to that prevailing while the issue still hangs in the balance."[35] Churchill, disgustedly seeing Canada scurrying for shelter under the eagle's wing, evidently realized that a major shift had occurred. What he would have had Canada do, what he would have done differently had he been Canadian prime minister, was never stated. Certainly he failed to recognize that with its security now guaranteed by the United States, Canada could send every man and weapon possible to defend Britain, something it dutifully and willingly did.

As for me, no matter how often I try to appraise the situation, I cannot see any other option for Mackenzie King. The issue potentially was the survival of the Canadian nation in face of an apparently defeated Great Britain and a victorious Nazi Germany. King did what he had to do to secure Canada's security. The reason Mackenzie King had to strike his arrangement with Roosevelt was the military weakness of great Britain in the summer of 1940.[36]

---

[33] NA, R.B. Hanson Papers, file S-175-M-1, Meighen to Hanson, 19 Aug. 1940.

[34] Professor Underhill, who spoke the truth about the changed Canadian relationships produced by the war, almost lost his job at the University of Toronto as a result. See Creighton, "Ogdensburg Agreement," 300 ff., and Douglas Francis, *F.H. Underhill: Intellectual Provocateur* (Toronto 1986), chap. 10.

[35] NA, Privy Council Office Records, Cabinet War Committee Records, Documents, Churchill to King, 22 Aug. 1940.

[36] Even the usually shrewd observer of Canadian-American relations, Gordon Stewart, has missed this key point. He noted that in the 1940s, Canada "participated willingly in military and defense integration ... it is inaccurate to regard American policy as being imposed on an unwilling and unknowing country. If the United States is judged guilty of imperialism, then Canada must accept a ruling of contributory negligence." "'A Special Contiguous Country Economic Regime': An Overview of America's Canada Policy," *Diplomatic History 6* (fall 1982), 354-5. True enough, but Britain aided and abetted the process. John Warnock in *Free Trade and the New Right Agenda* (Vancouver 1988), 255, notes similarly that "The

The immediate result of the Ogdensburg Agreement was wholly beneficial to Canada and Canadian interests. But we can see now that the long-term implications included the construction of major American installations and the presence in substantial numbers of American troops in the Canadian Northwest from 1942,[37] the 1947 military agreement with the United States that continued joint defence cooperation, the North American Air Defence Agreement of 1957-8, and eventually even Cruise missile testing and the possibility of Star Wars installations in the Canadian North.

Many Canadians may be less than happy with the way matters turned out. In his *Lament for a Nation*, George Grant wrote:

> In 1940, it was necessary for Canada to throw in her lot with continental defence. The whole of Eurasia might have fallen into the hands of Germany and Japan. The British Empire was collapsing once and for all as an international force. Canada and the United States of America had to be unequivocally united for the defence of this hemisphere. But it is surprising how little the politicians and officials seem to have realized that this new situation would have to be manipulated with great wisdom if any Canadian independence was to survive. Perhaps nothing could have been done; perhaps the collapse of nineteenth-century Europe automatically entailed the collapse of Canada. Nonetheless, it is extraordinary that King and his associates in External Affairs did not seem to recognize the perilous situation that the new circumstances entailed. In all eras, wise politicians have to play a balancing game. How little the American alliance was balanced by any defence of national independence![38]

Much of Grant's assessment is correct. Certainly, Canada had no choice in August 1940 in the situation in which it found itself. But to me, Mackenzie King's actions in August 1940 were an attempt to protect Canadian independence—and ensure Canada's survival—in a world that had been turned upside down in a few months by the defeat of Britain and France. Grant, writing a quarter century after the event, does

---

Mackenzie King government chose to conduct the war effort on a continental basis" and thus "greatly undermined Canadian sovereignty." Some choice in August 1940!

[37] The King government was slow to recognize the dangers posed to Canadian sovereignty by the U.S. presence. But once it was alerted to the problem (by the British high commissioner to Canada!), it moved quickly to appoint a special commissioner in the northwest and, at war's end, Canada paid the United States in full for all facilities built in Canada—quite consciously in an effort to ensure that its rights were fully protected. See Department of External Affairs, Records [DEA], documents on files 52-B(s), 5221-40C, the records of the special commissioner (NA, RG 36-7), and Granatstein, *A Man of Influence*, 120 ff.

[38] George Grant, *Lament for a Nation* (Toronto 1965), 50.

not say what King might have done after Ogdensburg to achieve a balance to the American alliance. Nor did Churchill in 1940. In the remainder of this essay, I will try to show how King successfully struggled to preserve at least a measure of financial independence for Canada.

Those who believe, like George Grant and Donald Creighton, that the Ogdensburg Agreement and its aftermath were a virtual sell-out to the United States have an obligation to offer an alternative vision. If there was "a forked road" in August 1940 and if Canada went in the wrong direction, where might the other road have led? What should Mackenzie King and his government have done that they did not do? I await the response.

The Ogdensburg Agreement had secured Canada's physical defences, but it had done nothing to resolve the country's economic difficulties. As in the Great War, the problem came about because Canada was caught between a strong United States and its desire to help an economically weak Great Britain. Indeed, Britain was weak. The ambassador in Washington, Lord Lothian, summed it up when he told a group of reporters: "Boys, Britain's broke. It's your money we want."[39] It was soon to be Canada's money that London wanted too.

Britain had begun the war in 1939 convinced that purchases had to be switched away from North America to conserve scarce dollar exchange. That laudable goal threatened Canadian tobacco, fruit, and wheat exports and provoked extraordinary outrage in Ottawa and threats that such a policy might hurt what Mackenzie King delicately called "our ability to render assistance." Similarly, British munitions orders in the Phoney War months were less than expected; that too angered the King government. But the same German victories that forced Canada to seek assistance to the south also obliged London to look to Canada for more—more money, more food, more munitions, more of everything.[40]

By February 1941, therefore, the Department of Finance in Ottawa estimated that the British deficit with Canada was $795 million, an amount that had been covered by transfers of gold, debt repatriation, and a large sterling accumulation in London.[41] Ottawa also predicted that war expenditures for the year would amount to $1.4 billion and that $433 million was needed for civil expenditure. A further $400 million would be required to repatriate additional Canadian securities held in Britain, in effect a way of giving Britain additional Canadian dollars with which to pay for the goods it bought in Canada. At the same time, the mandarins in Finance estimated that the provincial and municipal governments would spend $575 million for a total

---

[39] Cited in David Dilks, "Appeasement Revisited," *University of Leeds Review* 15 (May 1972), 51.

[40] Based on Hector Mackenzie, "Sinews of War: Aspects of Canadian Decisions to Finance British Requirements in Canada during the Second World War," Canadian Historical Association paper, 1983, 3.

[41] King Papers, W.C. Clark to King, 9 April 1941, ff. 288021 ff.

governmental expenditure of almost half Canada's Gross National Income.[42] Could the country function, they asked, if half of all production were devoted to government operations?

Historically, Canada's economic position had depended on the maintenance of a "bilateral unbalance within a balanced `North Atlantic Triangle.'"[43] That meant, in effect, that our chronic trade deficit with the United States was covered by a surplus with Britain. Pounds earned in London were readily converted to American dollars, and thus the bills could be paid. But now sterling was inconvertible, and as Canada built up large balances in London, these could no longer be used to cover the trade deficit with the United States.

Compounding the problem was that as Canada strained to produce greater quantities of war material and food for Britain, more components and raw materials had to be imported from the United States. Every time, for example, that a truck, built in Canada by General Motors or Ford, went to Britain, it contained an imported engine, specialty steels, and a variety of parts brought in from south of the border. Almost a third of the value of a tank, ship, or artillery piece had to be imported. The result was a classic squeeze. Canadian goods went to Great Britain where the British could pay for them only in sterling, which was of little use to Canada outside the British Isles (though we could buy New Zealand lamb or Malayan tin, for example, with it). In effect, Canada was financing the British trade deficit. But at the same time and as a result of war production for Britain, Canadian imports from the United States were expanding rapidly, far more so than exports to the United States. The result was a huge trade deficit with the United States, one that grew worse the more Canada tried to help Britain. In April 1941 Ottawa's estimates of the deficit for that fiscal year were $478 million; by June, officials argued that imports from the United States had risen by $400 million a year while exports to the south had increased by only half that sum.[44]

---

[42] H.D. Hall, *North American Supply* (London 1955), 230. Later, more accurate assessments put war spending in 1941-42 at $1.45 billion, aid to the United Kingdom at $1.15 billion, and civil expenditures at $1 billion With a national income of $5.95 billion, public expenditure amounted to 60.5 per cent. King Papers, "Canada's War Effort," 4 April 1941, ff. 288088 ff.

[43] The phrase is R.S. Sayers's in *Financial Policy, 1939-45* (London 1956), 322-3. The balance, however, was less than real for the British. They had large peacetime trade deficits with the United States and could pay Canada in U.S. dollars only because they received them from the other parties in a pattern of multilateral settlement that ended with the outbreak of war. I am indebted to Professor Ian Drummond for this information.

[44] King Papers, Clark to King, 9 April 1941, 288014 ff. The actual figures were even worse than these estimates. See Urquhart and Buckley, eds., *Historical Statistics*, F334-47. But whether the situation was as bleak as government officials believed at the time is less certain. Although munitions exports to Britain did stimulate the growth of imports from the United States, still more came from the war effort itself, which stimulated imports directly (in the

Canada had been trying to grapple with this problem for some time. Efforts had been made since September 1939 to control foreign exchange, to promote Canada as a tourist mecca for Americans ("Ski in a country at war," the advertisements could have said), and by devaluing the dollar to 90 cents U.S. to restrict imports from and encourage exports sales to the United States. Each measure had some positive results, but together they amounted to very little against the flood of components pouring over the border for an expanding war industry. Soon, Ottawa slapped stringent controls on the U.S. dollars Canadian travellers could acquire, and a wide range of import prohibitions were put in place in December 1940 on unnecessary imports. Those measures, strong enough to anger the American government and American exporters, also failed completely to reverse the steady growth in the deficit with the United States.[45]

What else remained? A loan from the United States government? O.D. Skelton, the undersecretary of state for external affairs until his death in January 1941, told Pierrepont Moffat, the very able American minister in Canada, that "it would be disastrous to face a future of making heavy interest payments to the United States year after year in perpetuity, or alternatively having a war debt controversy."[46] Canada was physically too close to the United States to owe debt directly to Washington, or so Skelton and his colleagues in the Ottawa mandarinate believed. What then? Could Canadian investments in the United States, estimated at $275 million to $1 billion in worth, be sold off to raise American dollars? They could, but those investments cushioned Canada from the strain of her foreign indebtedness, and there were obvious political problems in forcing private investors to sell their holdings at wartime fire-sale prices.[47] That was not a feasible route for the Mackenzie King government.

At this point, the situation altered dramatically. The United States congress accepted President Roosevelt's proposal for Lend-Lease, a scheme to permit the United States to give the Allies war materiel effectively free of monetary cost, though there were political costs of which the British were all too aware.[48] The

---

form of components) and indirectly (by increasing consumer demand and domestic investment in plant and equipment). I am again indebted to Professor Drummond.

[45] Granatstein, *Canada's War*, 135-6; Granatstein, *A Man of Influence*, 94 ff.

[46] EAR, vol. 35, "United States Exchange Discussions," 20 Nov. 1940.

[47] Urquhart and Buckley, eds., *Historical Statistics*, F164-92; King Papers, Clark to King, 9 April 1941, ff. 288018 ff; Queen's University Archives, Grant Dexter Papers, Memorandum, 11 March 1941.

[48] On the costs to the United Kingdom see Barnett, *Collapse*, 591 ff. Churchill was asked if Britain would be able to repay the United States for its aid: "I shall say, yes by all means let us have an account if we can get it reasonably accurate, but I shall have my account to put in too, and my account is for holding the baby alone for eighteen months, and it was a very rough brutal baby." Quoted in David Dilks's introduction to Dilks, ed., *Retreat from Power*, vol. II: *After 1939* (London 1981), 14.

initial appropriation accompanying the bill was $7 billion. This was, as Churchill called it, "the most unsordid act," an extraordinarily generous step by the still-neutral United States. But Lend-Lease posed terrible problems for Ottawa. First, the Canadian government did not want to take charity from the United States—"the psychological risk," two historians noted, "of becoming a pensioner of the United States was too great."[49] Second, if Britain could get war materiel from the United States free of charge, what was to happen to the orders it had placed in Canada and for which it had to pay, even if only with inconvertible sterling? C.D. Howe, presiding over Canada's war production as the minister of munitions and supply, told the Cabinet War Committee that he was "gravely concerned" that those orders might be shifted to the United States.[50] If that happened, what would the impact be on Canada's war employment and wartime prosperity?

The British characteristically and quickly saw the advantages offered by the situation and began to press Canada. Although junior ministers in Churchill's cabinet bemoaned what they saw as Canada's accelerating drift out of the empire,[51] the hard-headed officials at the Treasury knew what they wanted. Cut purchases of non-essential goods in the United States, Ottawa was told. Accept Lend-Lease. Sell off Canadian securities held in the United States. Such a regimen meant higher taxes and inflation for the Canadians, the British knew, but as the Treasury officials said, "It is as much in their interests as in ours to act along these lines, seeing that our only alternative, if we are unable to pay for our orders in Canada, is to place them instead in the United States in cases in which we should be able to obtain the goods under the `Lease and Lend' Act."[52]

Thus Canada's problem. Some way had to be found to keep the British orders, so essential for wartime prosperity, without selling the country lock, stock, and barrel to the United States. Though the Liberal government faced no immediate election, as had Borden in 1917 in similar circumstances, the retention of prosperity was every bit as much a political necessity. At the same time, and again the parallel with Sir Thomas White's refusal to borrow from the U.S. government is clear, the King government was adamant in its refusal to take Lend-Lease. That was little better than a loan and, while relations with Franklin Roosevelt's Washington were very good,

---

[49] Robert Bothwell and John English, "Canadian Trade Policy in the Age of American Dominance and British Decline, 1943-1947," *Canadian Review of American Studies* 8 (spring 1977), 54 ff. A.F.W. Plumptre commented that "Ottawa apparently believed that it is well to keep Canada as independent as possible and to avoid borrowing or begging as long as may be." *Mobilizing Canada's Resources for War* (Toronto 1941), 80. Cf R.W. James, *Wartime Economic Cooperation* (Toronto 1949), 32.

[50] Cabinet War Committee Records, Minutes, 18, 26 Feb. 1941.

[51] Public Record Office (PRO), London, Prime Minister's Office Records, PREM4/43B/2, Cranborne to Churchill, 5 March 1941; ibid., Treasury Records, T160/1340, Amery to Kingsley Wood, 10 May 1941.

[52] Ibid., T160/1054, "Canadian Financial Assistance to this Country," nd [14 March 1941].

no one wanted to be quite so indebted to the great nation with which Canada shared the continent. The Americans, as Clifford Clark, deputy minister of finance, noted fearfully, might later drive a very hard bargain on tariffs.[53] Nonetheless, Canada's trade with the United States somehow had to be brought into balance.

The ideal solution, as Canadian officials came to realize in the spring of 1941, was an arrangement that would see the United States increase its purchases in Canada and, in addition, supply the components and raw materials Canada needed to produce munitions for the United Kingdom. Those components could be charged to Britain's Lend-Lease account, a clever device that could let Canada keep its war economy going at full blast without bankrupting itself in the process. In the meantime, desperate to ensure the continuation of orders in Canada, Ottawa agreed to finance the British deficit with Canada.[54] That was again a repetition of the events of 1917. Though there is no sign in the files that anyone realized this parallel, so too was the Canadian proposal to the United States.

The Hyde Park Declaration, signed by Mackenzie King and Franklin Roosevelt on "a grand Sunday" in April, put the seal on the Canadian proposal. The United States agreed to spend $200-$300 million more in Canada, largely for raw materials and aluminum. "Why not buy from Canada as much as Canada is buying from the United States," Mackenzie King said he had told the president, "—just balance the accounts. Roosevelt thought this was a swell idea."[55] In addition, the president agreed that Britain's Lend-Lease account could be charged with the materials and components Canada needed to produce munitions for export.[56] That too dealt the trade deficit a mighty blow.

The declaration signed at Hyde Park was a splendid achievement for Canada. Howe told Mackenzie King that he was "the greatest negotiator the country had or something about being the world's best negotiator," the prime minister recorded.[57] Howe soon created War Supplies Limited, a crown corporation with E.P. Taylor as its head, to sell Canadian-manufactured war equipment and raw materials in the United States.[58]

The Hyde Park Declaration allowed Canada to do its utmost for Britain without fear of financial collapse. Most important, King had won Roosevelt's agreement without having to give up anything tangible—in the short-run. Unlike Great Britain, Canada was not obliged to sell off its investments prior to receiving U.S. aid; nor

---

[53] Granatstein, *Canada's War*, 139.
[54] Cabinet War Committee Records, Minutes, 12, 13 March 1941; Sayers, *Financial Policy*, 338 ff.
[55] Dexter Papers, Memo, 21 April 1941.
[56] The text of the Hyde Park Agreement is printed as an appendix to R.D. Cuff and J.L. Granatstein, *Canadian-American Relations in Wartime* (Toronto 1975), 165-6.
[57] Pickersgill, ed., *Mackenzie King Record*, I, 202.
[58] C.P. Stacey, *Arms, Men and Governments* (Ottawa 1970), 490; Richard Rohmer, *E.P. Taylor* (Toronto 1978), 106.

was Canada to be required to take Lend-Lease, both measures that the government sought to avoid.[59] Knowing that the desperate plight of the British had forced him to seek assistance for Canada from the United States, Mackenzie King had secured that help on the very best terms. For his part, Roosevelt could agree to King's proposals (incidentally, entirely on his own without any consultation with Congress or the State Department) because they cost the United States almost nothing, because he was friendly to Canada, and because he considered that his country's long-term interests would be best served by having an amicable and prosperous Canada on his northern border, a nation tightly linked to the United States. Undoubtedly, Roosevelt was correct. He served his country's interests well.

In retrospect, however, we can see that the inextricable linkages created or strengthened by the Second World War were the key long-term results of the 1941 agreement. The Hyde Park Declaration effectively wiped out the border for war purposes, allowing raw materials to pour south while munitions components came north. To help the war effort, to produce the goods for a desperate Great Britain, Mackenzie King's Canada tied itself to the United States for the war's duration. There is no point in complaining about this almost a half century later. The Hyde Park Declaration was one of many actions that were necessary to win the war against Hitler, and everything done to further that end was proper and right. But neither is there any point in blinking at the facts. Canada tied itself to the United States in 1941, just as it had done in 1917, because Britain was economically weak. That weakness forced Canada to look to Washington for assistance, and the Americans provided it, freely and willingly. It served Washington's interests; it served Canada's immediate interests; above all, it served the cause of victory.

The short-term results of the Hyde Park Declaration were much as the Canadian government had hoped. American purchases in Canada rose rapidly, and Canada's dollar shortage came to an end in 1942; indeed, the next year controls had to be put in place to prevent Canada's holdings of U.S. dollars from growing too large. The wartime prosperity that Hyde Park solidified was such that in 1942 Canada could offer Great Britain a gift of $1 billion, and the next year Canada created a Mutual Aid program that eventually gave Britain an additional $2 billion in munitions and foodstuffs. The total of Canadian aid to Great Britain during the war was $3.468 billion[60]—and a billion then was really worth a billion. That was help to a valued ally and friend, of course, just as much as it was an investment in continued high employment at home. As an official in the Dominions Office in London noted, "Per head of population the Canadian gifts will cost Canada about five times what lend lease costs the United States. Canada's income tax is already as high as ours; it may have to go higher.... Canada is devoting as large a proportion of her national income to defence expenditure as any other country; in no other country is the proportion of

---

[59] This was seen as a virtual miracle. See *Financial Post*, 26 April 1941.
[60] See J.L. Granatstein, "Settling the Accounts: Anglo-Canadian War Finance, 1943-1945," *Queen's Quarterly*, 83 (summer 1976), 246.

defence expenditure which is given away in the form of free supplies anywhere near so high as in Canada."[61] The war had cost Canada about $18 billion, and almost one-fifth of that staggering total was given to Britain in the form of gifts. That Canada could offer such assistance freely was the best proof possible that Mackenzie King's policy in 1941 had been correct and successful.

Still, there can be no doubt that the Hyde Park Declaration reinforced the trends that had begun to take form during the Great War. Some of those were psychological. Two bureaucrats who dealt with the United States regularly during the war had gushed fellowship in an article they published in the *Canadian Journal of Economics and Political Science* at the end of the war. "There has been the open exchange of confidence between the Americans and Canadians, the warm welcome, the freedom from formality, the plain speaking and the all-pervading friendship," Sydney Pierce and A.F.W. Plumptre wrote. This was the result of "our common background of language and culture, and to the close trade and industrial relationship: in part it is due to the fact that our approach to problems is similar."[62] That was all true, too.

Other trends were financial and commercial. By 1945 American investment had risen to 70 per cent of the total foreign capital invested in Canada. Exports to the United States were more than three times what they had been in 1939 and were 25 per cent greater than war-swollen Canadian exports to Britain. Imports from the United States were now ten times those from Britain.[63] The war undoubtedly had distorted Canada's trade figures, but the direction was clear and it would be confirmed by the events of the reconstruction period.

By 1945 Canada was part and parcel of the continental economy. It was a two-way North American street now, and the North Atlantic Triangle, if it still existed at all, was a casualty of the world wars....

---

[61] PRO, Dominions Office Records, D035/1218, Minute by A.W. Snelling, 26 Jan. 1943; Sayers, *Financial Policy*, 350 ff.

[62] S.D. Pierce and A.F.W. Plumptre, "Canada's Relations with War-Time Agencies in Washington," *Canadian Journal of Economics and Political Science* II (1945), 410-11.

[63] Urquhart and Buckley, eds., *Historical Statistics*, F345-56; Leacy, ed., *Historical Statistics*, G188-202.

Modern Quebec

Section 19

As we saw in Jacques Monet's article on ultramontanism and French-Canadian nationalism, (topic #8), French Canada became, in important ways, more conservative, more influenced by Catholic traditionalism from the 1840s onward. It certainly seemed to outsiders throughout the 19th and much of the 20th century that Quebec remained quaint, traditional, and more Catholic than the Vatican, while the rest of Canada modernised, secularised, and devoted itself to economic and social progress and material prosperity.

It was true that the clergy retained a significant influence over schools, culture, and social action in Quebec, while literature and public discourse in French Canada promoted traditional values and religion, and seemed to repudiate capitalism, materialism, and economic motives. It was also true that French Canadians remained under-represented in positions of economic power, while Quebec's own economy was largely run by anglophones and anglophone corporations.

After the second world war things changed dramatically. So rapid and so spectacular was the wave of modernising and secularising reforms during the 1960s, that people began to speak of it as a "Quiet Revolution". The State replaced the Church in the spheres of public education, health, and welfare administration. Government moved to invest in French-Canadian business, to create a vigorous, French-speaking public sector, and to make it possible for francophones to rise to the top in private corporations as well.

At the same time, Quebec, which had always seemed to live contentedly in the Canadian confederation (save for exceptional moments like the Riel affair and the conscription crises) became more and more openly insistent on changing its relationship with the rest of Canada by drawing away from the centralised system which English Canadians considered a single, united Canadian nation.

In his essay below Ramsay Cook explores the origins, character, and consequences of the "Quiet Revolution". How had economic and social developments in the 1940s and 50s paved the way for the dramatic changes of the 60s and 70s? What elements in Quebec society were most insistent on change—particularly on seeing a more active Quebec government—and why? Why did nationalism emerge stronger than ever in the new Quebec?

In the second essay Richard Jones describes the movement to strengthen the French language in Quebec since the 1960s. Why was it that, at a time when the

Trudeau government was busy promoting bilingualism in the other provinces, Quebeckers were moving more and more toward French unilingualism? Why did they feel that government action to impose French was necessary? What determined the rate and extent to which parties responded to this demand?

Students interested in a good general survey of modern Quebec should see Kenneth McRoberts, *Quebec: Social Change and Political Crisis.*

"Au Diable avec le Goupillon et la Tuque":
The Quiet Revolution and the New Nationalism

Ramsay Cook

"Borduas was the first to break radically....
He risked everything. Modern French Canada begins with him.
He taught us the lesson which had been lacking.
He let loose the liberty on us."

Pierre Vadeboncoeur
La Ligne du Risque (1963)

I

"La Révolution silencieuse," the Quiet Revolution, is a phrase that conjures up nothing so much as contradiction. Can a revolution occur silently? Did Quebec experience a revolution in the 1960s? Was Quebec quiet in the 1960s? Only the last question can be answered unambiguously—and negatively. Quebec was a tumultuous and noisy place in the 1960s. Much of the noise was the sound of steam escaping an overheated society: nationalists, students, workers, peace activists, even ecologists. Much the same as elsewhere in the industrialized world. But some of the noise in Quebec was the sound of builders renovating, if not wholly reconstructing, a society. The rhetoric of these renovators was, in many ways, familiar. It was nationalism, a central doctrine of Quebec intellectual and emotional life since the early nineteenth century. But it was not merely the same old nationalism, though it had identifiable roots in the past. Indeed, it was perhaps even more radically new than its exponents realized.

What made the nationalism of the 1960s new and different, even radically different, were the socio-economic changes that had overtaken Quebec and Quebecers since about 1940. A profound change in both the social order and the value system of Quebec was well begun by the early 1950s, moved into a turbulent phase in the 1960s, and gradually settled into the accepted consensus. Out of these changes came a new self-image formulated in a nationalism that, while related to the past, was the expression of a new set of social values, a new public philosophy.

The transformation that Quebec experienced after 1940 can be reduced to the shorthand abstractions, urban and industrial growth. What they meant in human terms can best be seen in Gabrielle Roy's classic *Bonheur d'Occasion* (1945), the tale of Maria Chapdelaine in the city. From the 1880s, when 73 percent of French-speaking Quebecers lived in the countryside, until 1951, when 67 percent resided in an urban setting, an inexorable transformation had been taking place. But after 1940 the process accelerated to a rate exceeded only by British Columbia and Alberta, and Quebec rapidly became the most urbanized province in Canada. By 1951, 34 percent of all Quebecers lived in Montreal. The 1971 census classified the 4,759,000 French-speaking Quebecers as follows: rural farm: 6 percent; rural non-farm: 16 percent; urban: 78 percent.[1]

Despite the continuous character of this socio-economic transformation, neither public authorities nor most of those who defined the society's values willingly accepted the new reality. Or, even if they did, only minimum steps were taken to adjust public policies to new needs—perhaps because some thought the new reality only temporary, or capable of being reversed. In 1927, when more than 60 percent of Quebecers were already urbanites, Henri Bourassa, still an important nationalist leader and politician, could express the hope that changes in Canadian tariff policy would "put a brake on the orgy of industrialism which disturbs the country and re-establish the preponderance of the rural life, the only guarantee of the health and the *sanity* of peoples."[2]

But in the post-war years the new reality could no longer be ignored, though there was much disagreement about the kind of response required. The nature of the problem was dramatically highlighted in a strike by some 5,000 miners in the asbestos industry lasting for three months in the spring of 1949. There, Quebec workers found themselves arrayed against an American corporation, a provincial government that called itself nationalist, and most of the important voices in a church that had always claimed to be the front-line defender of French-Canadian interests. The support of Monsignor Charbonneau, Bishop of Montreal, the nationalist daily *Le Devoir*, and a small but important group of younger intellectuals was not enough. The workers lost the battle, though the war was to last much longer, and the outcome was far more complicated. Monsignor Charbonneau's reward was exile in Victoria, British Columbia.[3]

If the Asbestos strike marked the rite of passage of a union movement growing up, it was also a revelation that the old values defended by traditional politicians, traditional churchmen, and traditional nationalists were, at best, ill-suited to the needs of an industrial society and, at worst, merely justification for a reactionary and repressive élite in both state and church. A new society was emerging, one whose size and shape ensured that the old institutions and ideologies could neither define nor confine it.

---

[1] These figures are found in Kenneth McRoberts and Dale Posgate, *Quebec: Social Change and Political Crisis* (Toronto, 1980), p. 51; and Pierre E. Trudeau, ed., *La Grève de l'Amiante* (Montréal, 1956), pp. 4-5.

[2] *Le Devoir*, 1 juillet, 1927.

[3] Trudeau, *La Grève*, pp. 165-212; Renaude Lapointe, *l'Histoire bouleversante de Mgr. Charbonneau* (Montréal, 1962).

Even before the workers, the middle class, or for that matter the social scientists, social critics, or politicians realized fully what was transpiring, there was at least one visionary who did. His name was Paul-Emile Borduas, Quebec's most imaginative and radical artist. Because he was a visionary and an artist he was easily dismissed. So he departed first for New York and finally to Paris, never to return to his beloved Sainte Hilaire. But Borduas's life and work epitomize better than any other example what was happening to Quebec: he was the *avant garde*, not just as an artist. Borduas, his biographer tells us, was a young French-Canadian painter who, during his youth in the 1920s, deviated in no way from orthodoxy. He wanted to follow a career as a church decorator. His talents were recognized by Monsignor Olivier Maurault, who sent him to study at les Ateliers d'Art sacrés in Paris in 1928. When the economic crisis struck he was forced to give up his studies and return home, where he hoped that his friend, the church artist Ozias Leduc, would help him find work. But the churches, like the economy, were in financial trouble and could not afford new religious art. Eventually Borduas found employment as a teacher in a state-supported school. Thus, unconsciously, he took the first step along the road to secularism, to a view of the world that led to the creation of his magnificent *automatiste* paintings from which all conventional religious significance disappeared.[4] It led also, in 1948, to his famous manifesto, *Refus global*. That revolutionary document, signed by Borduas and fifteen young associates, attacked the values of Quebec society uncompromisingly. Beginning with a capsule history of this "petit peuple"—the rural settlements, the conquest, the Church, the story of *la survivance*, the fear of modern ideas, of *les poètes maudits*—the manifesto rose to a crescendo first as a challenge—"the frontiers of our dreams are no longer what they were," then denunciation—to hell with the holy-water-sprinkler and the tuque," and finally aspiration—"we will follow our primitive need for liberation."[5] *Le goupillon et la tuque*—the holy-water-sprinkler and the tuque, the symbols of traditional culture, the centrepieces of traditional nationalist ideology, these had to be unmasked and rejected. Quebec had to become a modern society like the others—the United States, France, English Canada—just as Borduas and his followers would shift their talents away from crucifixes, stations of the cross, rural landscape, and habitant families, toward modern, abstract, international art.

To concentrate on one individual, however talented, and to insist that his career symbolizes the transformation of a whole society may seem perverse. But the symbolism is there, one that provides an invaluable insight into what has happened in Quebec and the new self-image, the new nationalism that developed during the years of the Quiet Revolution. Let me explain what I mean.

---

[4] François-Marc Gagnon, *Paul-Emile Borduas* (Montréal, 1978), pp. 4-64; see also André-G. Bourassa, *Surrealism and Quebec Literature* (Toronto, 1984), pp. 80-155.

[5] Paul-Emile Borduas, *Ecrits* 1942-1958 (Halifax, 1978), pp. 45-54.

II

Traditional French-Canadian nationalism was the dominant ideology of Quebec's leading classes from the second quarter of the nineteenth century until the 1950s. Though its exponents varied somewhat in their outlook, and there were significant challenges to its dominance at least from the 1930s onwards, certain fundamental ideas had a remarkable capacity to endure. Together these ideas and values described an idealized nation, one that had existed in the past, was often threatened in the present, but which, given inspired leadership and correct doctrine, would again materialize in the future. This nation was French in culture (though that meant the culture of pre-revolutionary France, the France "qui prie," not the one "qui blasphème), Catholic in religion, and agricultural in socio-economic organization. The church, the parish, and the family were its essential institutions. The state, the very idea of which implied secularism, played only a marginal role in this conception of the nation, for the society's civilizing mission was much more intimately related to the religious state: the Church.[6] Here was "l'église-nation," advocated, praised, blessed, and only rarely and softly cursed—in the speeches and writings of nationalist clergy, politicians, journalists, novelists, poets, and educators. It can be found fully and systematically formulated in Monsignor L.A. Laflèche's *Quelques considérations sur les rapports de la societé civile avec la religion et la famille* (1866), most fantastically in Jules-Paul Tardivel's *Pour la Patrie* (1895), oratorically in Monsignor L.-A. Paquêt's frequently reprinted "Sermon sur la Vocation de la Race française en Amérique" (1902), and in the voluminous historical and polemical writings of abbé Lionel Groulx, of which *L'Appel de la Race* (1922) and the essays collected in *Dix Ans d'action française* (1926) serve as the best examples. Even those organs of opinion like the mass circulation daily, *La Presse*, which favoured the industrial development of Quebec, can be found expressing similar stereotypes. On the occasion of the sixtieth anniversary of Confederation in 1927, *La Presse* pointed to Place d'Armes in Montreal as exemplifying Canadian virtues. On one side stood the Church of Notre Dame facing the Bank of Montreal with a statue of de Maisonneuve, the city's founder, in the centre. "It is the image of the Fatherland, with all that signifies. On the one hand, the contribution of the first Canadians, of those who were the first and who have guarded their faith, their virtues and everything which explains their survival and can contribute to the greatness of the nation. On the other hand, the material contribution of our English-speaking compatriots with their eminent practical qualities."[7] Here was a convenient ethnic division of labour that

---

[6] Christian Morissonneau, *La Terre promise: Le Myth du nord québécois* (Montréal, 1978); Maurice Tremblay, "Orientations de la Pensée sociale," in Jean-Charles Falardeau, ed., *Essais sur le Québec contemporain* (Québec, 1953), pp. 193-208.

[7] *La Presse*, 1 juillet 1972, cited in Geoffrey Kelley, "Developing a Canadian National Feeling: The Diamond Jubilee Celebrations of 1927" (M.A. thesis, McGill University, 1984), p. 76.

gave spirituality and virtue to the French Canadians, leaving to the English materialism, practicality, and, of course, control of the economy.

This traditional nationalism forged in the crucible of the Catholic religion focused not on politics and economics, but on culture and religion. Usually it was most clearly articulated when cultural and religious rights were threatened: when French-language, Roman Catholic schools were abolished by the provinces of Manitoba or Ontario and when the English-speaking majority attempted to drag French Canadians into the defence of the British Empire.[8] Only occasionally, and ineffectually, did these nationalists concern themselves with the problems created by the burgeoning industrialism, which produced the conditions Lord Durham had predicted in the 1840s: the French Canadians were becoming a proletariat in an Anglo-Saxon capitalist world.[9]

This traditional nationalism was expressed lucidly, if somewhat nervously, in the *Rapport de la Commission royale d'enquête sur les problèmes constitutionels*, or Tremblay Commission, which reported to the Quebec government in 1956. It is the philosophical rather than the constitutional portions of the Report that are relevant here. The definition it gave to French-Canadian culture was traditional—"Christian inspiration and French genius," as was its insistence on the fundamental differences between the French and English "confronting cultures." So, too, its account of the perilous historical conditions through which French Canadians had lived drew on the standard nationalist history as expounded from F.X. Garneau to abbé Groulx. French and English, the Report observed, "since 1760, live in competition in Canada; with one desiring despite military defeat and political subjection, to preserve its particularism and, with that end in view, seeking to take back into its own hands, and as extensively as possible, the conduct of its own life; the other, resolved to install its institutions and to organize the country according to its ideas and its interests and to have its culture everywhere predominate."[10]

But the Tremblay Report was more than just a systematic statement of conventional wisdom. It recognized that something new had been added to the old French-English equation: industrialism. "If the Conquest put the French Canadians out of tune with the political institutions," the Commission concluded, "the industrial revolution put them out of harmony with the social institutions." Here was a threat of the most demanding character. Now the Commission harked back to

---

For examples of traditional nationalism, see Ramsay Cook, ed., *French-Canadian Nationalism: An Anthology* (Toronto, 1966).

8   For example, Henri Bourassa, *Que devons-nous à l'Angleterre?* (Montréal, 1915); Henri Bourassa, *Les Ecoles du Nord-Ouest* (Montréal, 1905).

9   Joseph Levitt, *Henri Bourassa and the Golden Calf* (Ottawa, 1969).

10 René Durocher et Michèle Jean, "Duplessis et la, Commission royale d'enquête sur les problèmes constitutionels, 1953-1956," *Revue d'histoire de l'Amérique française*, 25, 3 (décembre 1971), pp. 237-64; *Royal Commission of Enquiry on Constitutional Problems, Quebec* (Quebec, 1956), II, pp. 33, 67, 44.

earlier nationalists who had warned against urban-industrial society and sang the praises of agriculture. Industrial capitalism, the commissioners warned, "is in complete disaccord with the Catholic French-Canadian culture": materialist rather than spiritual, scientific and technical rather than humanist, individualistic rather than communal. Here was the basic challenge: "We have to choose between the Christian concept and materialism, either in its pragmatic or philosophic form"—by which the commissioners meant that both North American capitalism and Marxian communism were antithetical to Christianity.[11]

Having identified the threat of secularism, though the Commission preferred the term "materialism," it could only urge a renewed defence of Quebec's autonomy as a province that, because of its Francophone and Catholic majority, had to be recognized as a province "pas comme les autres." But it only hinted at new strategies that might be required to defend the values that made French Canada a distinct "nation." "The whole institutional system which, up to now has been the broadest and most sympathetic expression of French Canada's special culture, must be completely remade along new lines."[12] The authors of that prophetic sentence little realized how extensive the remaking would prove to be. Nor could they have foreseen how the remaking of institutions would hasten the acceptance of the secular values that were so inimical to the traditional conception of the nation.

III

During the 1950s Premier Maurice Duplessis's conservative, even reactionary, Union Nationale government managed to dominate Quebec political life through a combination of nationalist rhetoric, a corrupt political machine, a gerrymandered electoral map, and good economic times. But in these same years a vigorous debate about Quebec's past and future developed. In this debate the validity of traditional nationalism was questioned from at least four fairly distinct perspectives. First there were the members of Père Georges-Henri Lévesque's recently founded school of social sciences at Laval University who, having adopted an empirical approach to social analysis, questioned the a priori character of social thought in Quebec. These sociologists, economists, and industrial relations experts urged a more inductive, social science approach to the province's social problems. Whether they were professors like Maurice Lamontagne and Maurice Tremblay, or trade union activists like Jean Marchand, they agreed that social thought and social action had to begin by accepting Quebec's urban-industrial condition. Nationalism, at least as traditionally preached, was condemned as an obstacle to a clear perception of Quebec realities.[13]

---

[11] *Ibid.*, pp. 61, 85, 87.
[12] *Ibid.*, pp. 65, 72.
[13] Robert Parisé, *Georges-Henri Lévesque* (Montréal, 1976); Michael Behiels, "Le Père Georges-Henri Lévesque et l'établissement des sciences sociales à Laval, 1938-1955," *Revue*

That view was taken a long step further by the young social scientists, lawyers, journalists, and trade unionists who founded the magazine *Cité libre* in 1950. Led by Pierre E. Trudeau and Gérard Pelletier, both of whom had supported the workers at Asbestos, they developed a forceful and well-documented polemic against traditional nationalists and nationalism generally, arguing for what they called a "functional" analysis of social problems and social reform. Like the Laval social scientists, the *Cité libristes* argued that nationalism—all nationalism—was unacceptable for it was merely the rhetoric of vested interests who opposed social change. Nationalists identified imaginary enemies outside the fortress walls, when the real enemies were within. Home rule was less important than who ruled at home. Nationalist thought, in Trudeau's words, "can only be a timid and reactionary thought." In this critique of traditional ideology, Trudeau and his friends were often sharply anti-clerical, though never anti-Catholic. But their anti-clericalism, or liberalism, and their concern for a more equitably ordered, industrial society led them to insist that the state had to accept a positive role in social and industrial development, for "some state planning has become an absolute necessity...."[14]

The re-evaluation of the role that the state should play in Quebec was one of the main themes in Quebec social thought in the 1950s. For most, though by no means all,[15] that meant the provincial state. *Le Devoir*, the most important nationalist newspaper, began to advocate a more positive role for the state after Gérard Filion and André Laurendeau took charge of the newspaper in the 1950s. These two modern nationalists began to transform the old message preached by Henri Bourassa and his disciples into a new social doctrine that accepted industrial society without any hint of nostalgia for the old agrarianism. *Le Devoir* expounded liberal Catholic social views and argued that the state had responsibility both for social justice and as the defender of French-Canadian society. In 1959 Filion wrote that "French Canadians will remain drawers of water and hewers of wood, small storekeepers and small investors, with a few millionaires here and there, as long as they will not make the only government they have under their control serve in the elaboration and realization of a large-scale economic policy."[16]

More nationalist, focusing almost exclusively on Quebec as the one place where French Canadians had a chance, more controversial than *Le Devoir*, were the views of a new school of historians who came into prominence at the University of Montreal in the 1950s. The most visible and audible of these young scholar-polemicists was Professor Michel Brunet, son of a small businessman whose post-graduate training had been in the United States, where he was attracted to the economic interpretation

---

de l'Université d'Ottawa, 52, 3 (octobre-décembre 1982), pp. 355-76; Falardeau, ed., *Essais*; Maurice Tremblay, "Reflexions sur le Nationalisme," *Ecrits du Canada français*, V (Montréal, 1959), pp. 9-44.

14 Trudeau, *La Grève*, pp. 14, 403.
15 Maurice Lamontagne, *Le Fédéralisme canadien* (Québec, 1954).
16 *Le Devoir*, 6 mai 1959.

of history. In a series of speeches and essays, in which he developed a thesis originated by his colleague, Professor Maurice Séguin, Brunet argued that traditional Quebec nationalism was nothing more than a rationalization of French-Canadian economic inferiority and a justification for clerical power. It was not the Church that had ensured French-Canadian survival but rather a high birth rate and isolation in the seigneurial system, away from the Conqueror. The society was nevertheless feeble because its entrepreneurial middle class had been decapitated by the Conquest, leaving the economy in the hands of the British. Whatever the validity of the Séguin-Brunet thesis as history, its contemporary implications were clear. The old clerical nationalism with its emphasis on agriculture, its illusions about French Canada's civilizing mission, and its fear of the state had to be banished. In its place Quebecers should concentrate on building a new entrepreneurial class, make use of the state to defend Francophone interests, and forget about the minorities living outside the province. For Brunet there were Canadians and *Canadiens*, the latter group, the minority, being under constant threat of assimilation, had only one, fleeting hope, and that lay in building a strong provincial state into a national state.[17]

Like *Le Devoir*, and utterly unlike *Cité libre*, the Montreal historians were nationalist. But they, like all the other groups considered here, shared the conviction that the old, religion-centred, rural, anti-statist nationalism had outlived its usefulness, if it had ever had any. In its place Quebec needed a new value system, a public philosophy that welcomed the industrial order, assimilated the new social sciences as a replacement for moral exhortation, and willingly used the state for economic and social development, including educational reform. Implicitly or explicitly, each of these groups—and others—were advocating a secular social philosophy, nationalist or non-nationalist.[18] Some attacked the Church for its historic role; others merely concluded that its role in the new society would have to be a diminished one. The church recognized the threat of these developments. In 1953 the Church hierarchy noted that "a wind of bad-quality liberation seems at present to blow on certain groups. According to these people, it is necessary to free the people from the hold of the Church.... It is, in a new form, pure and simple Protestantism."[19]

The fact is, as Jean Hamelin's recent history of the Church in Quebec demonstrates brilliantly, the Church was already in retreat in the 1950s, though it engaged in a strenuous rearguard action. New recruits declined in number and, of

---

[17] Michel Brunet, *Canadians et canadiens* (Montréal, 1954); *La présence anglaise et les Canadiens* (Montréal, 1958); Ramsay Cook, "L'Historien et le Nationalisme," *Cité libre*, XV, 73 (janvier 1965), pp. 5-14; Serge Gagnon, "Pour une conscience historique de la révolution québécoise," *Cité libre*, XVI, 83 (janvier 1966), pp. 4-19.

[18] Michael Behiels, *Prelude to Quebec's Quiet Revolution: Liberalism versus Neo-Nationalism, 1940-1960* (Montréal, 1985).

[19] Jean Hamelin, *Histoire du catholicisme québécois: Le XXe Siècle*, Tome 2 (Montréal, 1984), p. 139.

those who entered, fewer stayed the course. The deconfessionalization of some institutions, most notably the Catholic trade unions, was under way. Church attendance declined notably, and by the sixties a declining birth rate demonstrated the ineffectiveness of the Church's teaching about birth control. In 1956 a Church commission concluded that "our people no longer have a Christian life, they have not even the natural virtues.... Our Christians ignore their religion and the Bible." The urban-industrial order was having exactly the impact on the Catholic population of Quebec that the clerical nationalists had long prophesied. By 1970 a church-appointed inquiry described the Church as "en crise" and documented the claim with statistics such as these: where 2,000 young Quebecers had taken up religious vocations in 1946, only about 100 followed that path in 1970.[20]

The mighty army of the Church, once more numerous in proportion to population than in any country outside of Latin America, had fallen into irreversible decline. It could no longer defend the ramparts against an advancing secularism promoted by a new élite connected with the universities, the mass media, and such social organizations as the trade unions. These were the people who, in Quebec as elsewhere, led the "ethnic revival" that touched many parts of the world by the 1970s. These "secular intellectuals," as Anthony Smith calls them, espoused an "enlightened" rationalism of the sort found in Pierre Trudeau's writings advocating a secular, pluralistic, democratic society in place of the *ancien régime*. In Quebec the growing acceptance of these new ideas, and the socio-economic changes they reflected, opened the way for the collapse of Maurice Duplessis's Union Nationale government and the election of Jean Lesage's Liberals with their promise of reform and modernization. That new regime, the product of the socio-economic and intellectual evolution that had preceded it, gradually brought Quebec's public institutions more fully into conformity with social and intellectual reality. In short, it built a Quebec welfare state accompanied by a new nationalist ideology that defined the society's changed self-image.[21]

IV

Though the Lesage Liberals were elected on a platform that promised both to defend Quebec's autonomy in the Canadian federal system and to make fuller use of provincial powers than Duplessis had done, the party was not explicitly nationalist.

---

[20] *Ibid.*, p. 134; *commission d'Etude sur les Laïcs et l'Eglise* (Montréal, 1972), p. 23.

[21] Louis-Edmond Hamelin, "Evolution Numérique Séculaire du Clergé Catholique dans le Québec," *Recherches Sociographiques*, 2, 2 (1961), pp. 189-242; J. Hamelin, *Histoire*, p. 135; Anthony D. Smith, *The Ethnic Revival in the Modern World* (London, 1981) p. 104; Pierre E. Trudeau, "Some Obstacles to Democracy in Quebec," in Trudeau, *Federalism and the French-Canadians* (Toronto, 1968), pp. 103-21; and Trudeau, *Les Cheminements de la Politique* (Montréal, 1970).

Lesage himself had begun his political career in Ottawa and returned to Quebec only after the federal Liberals lost power in 1956. Moreover, the Duplessis regime had given nationalism such a bad name that many of its opponents—except perhaps *Le Devoir*—identified nationalism with reaction. What the Liberals were committed to—reforming education, the public service, the labour laws, and, more generally, the promotion of economic development—had, at least superficially, little to do with nationalism. In the process of implementing these policies, the politicians and their allies among the new élites found that nationalism was a useful weapon on the battle to overcome some of the obstacles that stood in the path of change. Yet it was not the old nationalist rhetoric of Duplessis but rather a new ideology that focused on, and legitimized, state action. Three examples, among many, will illustrate this argument: educational reform, the expansion of state control over hydroelectricity, and the establishment of the Quebec Pension Plan.[22]

The new ideology and its goals are very clearly revealed in the Report of the royal commission the Lesage government appointed to examine the province's educational system. Despite its chairmanship—Monsignor Alphonse-Marie Parent—the thrust of the Report was unambiguously secular. This is to say that the commissioners argued that the function of education in a democratic, industrial society was to equip citizens with the knowledge and skills necessary to achieve worldly success: "to afford everyone the opportunity to learn; to make available to each the type of education best suited to his aptitudes and interests; to prepare the individual for life in society." While the commissioners were aware of it, in failing to include among the goals the orthodox Catholic claim that education and religion cannot be separated, they simply skirted the issue. Moreover, and this was the main point of the Report's first volume, they contended that while education had once been the preserve of private organizations and churches, "now the state has become the principal agent for organizing, co-ordinating and financing all education." Though the nationalist note was very muted, the Report did remark that an effective educational system was "a condition of progress and survival of any country."[23]

From these propositions flowed logically the Commission's first, and perhaps most important, recommendation: the appointment of a Minister of Education. Since the last Minister of Education had been abolished in 1875 the absence of a political head of the educational system had always been viewed as a recognition of the Church's primacy in the field. As the leaders of the Church perceived instantly, the state was now being called upon to terminate that primacy. The struggle over Bill 60, which the government introduced in 1963 to implement the Parent Commission's first recommendation, was, on the whole, a decorous one conducted

---

[22] For a detailed account of the policies of the Lesage government, see Dale C. Thomson, *Jean Lesage and the Quiet Revolution* (Toronto, 1984); and McRoberts and Posgate, *Quebec*, pp. 94-123.

[23] *Report of the Royal Commission of Enquiry on Education, Quebec* (Quebec, 1963), 1, pp. 75, 81, 72, 64.

for the most part behind closed doors. The Church asserted its traditional position but rather than challenging the principle of the new proposal merely demanded, and obtained, a guarantee that confessional schools would still be allowed under the proposed scheme. A new "concordat" was established between church and state, in Professor Léon Dion's view, but it was one under which the state's supremacy in education was recognized as a fact. The secular goals of education would soon be dominant. By 1980 even the Catholic school committee admitted that schools operated "according to a pedagogical and administrative rationality that is clearly not to be found in the gospel."[24]

At least two conclusions can be drawn from the education reforms implemented during the 1960s. The first is that, since control of education has always been regarded as fundamental to the defence of Quebec's distinctive culture, after 1963 the state, and not the Church, obviously had assumed that onerous responsibility. As the aims of education would now be defined more in relation to the needs of the state than the needs of the Church, the definition of the nature of Quebec's distinctiveness would be altered inevitably. The educational system, and this is the second conclusion, as defined by successive volumes of the Parent Report, was to be centralized, bureaucratized, and, essentially, secular, one designed to prepare young Quebecers for life in the urban-industrial world. As such it would differ only in detail—and language—from the educational systems of New York, California, Ontario, or British Columbia. Insofar as the educational reforms reflected the spirit of the Quiet Revolution and the new nationalism that accompanied it, one of its paradoxical consequences was the replacement of a distinctive educational system by one that was essentially North American in spirit and function.

In the debate over educational reform the nationalist argument was more implicit than explicit. In the almost concurrent debate over a proposal to bring the remaining privately owned power companies under the publicly owned Hydro-Québec system established in 1944, the nationalist theme was utterly explicit. While the economic and administrative advantages of a unified hydroelectric system and the costs and benefits of the heavy expenditures required to complete the takeover were debated, the decisive political issue was expressed in the campaign slogan: *Maîtres chez nous*. René Lévesque, Minister of Natural Resources and chief architect of the nationalization plan, put the case in this manner: "The state must not be absent from the economic scene, for in our particular case that would be equivalent to pure and simple abandonment of the most effective instrument of economic liberation that we possess." And he continued explaining that while it was not desirable for the state to control the whole economy, it was necessary to "ally the dynamism of private enterprise with the advantages of concerted action by the whole nation." Here, then, the conflict was presented as one between the Quebec state, representing "la nation entière," and the Anglo-Canadians who were majority owners of the private power

---

[24] Léon Dion, *le bill 60 et la société québécoise* (Montréal, 1967), pp. 144-45; Thomson, *Jean Lesage*, p. 310.

companies. Nothing more graphically reveals the outcome of that struggle than a photograph in Clarence Hogue's celebratory study of Hydro-Québec depicting the strained faces of Shawinigan Water and Power Company employees "attending a French lesson in 1964." Hydro was now completely in the hands of what one of its propagandists called "the national state of French Canada," where the operational language was, quite naturally, French.[25]

Whether the costs and benefits of hydro nationalization were shared equitably by the members of "la nation entière" is a controversial question.[26] What is obvious, however, is that the new nationalism used to legitimize the hydro policy emphasized the issue of French-Canadian economic inferiority as the source of cultural weakness. Both hydro nationalization and educational reform were based on that assumption and were designed, in part, to correct it. Moreover, the new nationalism accepted without hesitation the urban-industrial society. Hydro-Québec, and especially the new developments carried out by Francophone engineers, technicians, and workers at places like Manicouagan, came to symbolize the new industrial man who stood at the heart of the new Quebec. The chansonnier Gilles Vigneault turned a prosaic industrial achievement—and ecological calamity[27]—into a popular, nationalist folk song. Where once politicians dreamed that perhaps a school or a bridge would carry their names into posterity, after the 1960s only a power dam sufficed!

The third, and most important, observation is that in this new nationalist ideology the state was again the leading actor. If Church and Nation had once been natural partners, the campaigns for educational reform and hydro nationalization had forged a new partnership of State and Nation, revealed in the growing usage of the phrase "L'Etat du Québec." And state policy in hydro, as in education, meant the centralization and standardization of a system that had once been decentralized and somewhat chaotic. Quebec would now have a hydro system very like that which existed in other Canadian provinces and American states. It would have it because it was necessary, or at least desirable, for the promotion of an industrial economy of the sort found in New York and Ontario.

If the Lesage government's policies in education can be seen as an extension of state power where once the Church reigned, and over the economy into areas traditionally dominated by Anglo-Canadians, the conflict over pensions brings the struggle to the inter-state level. Since the 1940s the federal government had been developing policies in the social security field that sometimes infringed on provincial jurisdiction or, at least, touched on disputed areas of jurisdiction. The Duplessis government had regularly protested these policies both on grounds of jurisdiction and because the Church in Quebec, viewing social security as a form of charity, opposed

---

25 Clarence Hogue, *Québec un siècle d'électricité* (Montréal, 1979), pp. 269, 386; Paul Sauriol, *La Nationalisation de l'électricité* (Montréal, 1962), p. 86.

26 Albert Breton, "The Economics of Nationalism," *Journal of Political Economy*, LXXII, 4 (August, 1964), pp. 376-86.

27 Boyce Richardson, *James Bay* (Toronto, 1972).

state intervention in this area.[28] The Lesage government intended not only to defend provincial jurisdiction but also to devise social security measures that would be run by the state. Consequently, in 1963, when the federal government announced its intention to establish a universal, portable, contributory pension scheme, the Quebec government objected that it intended to implement its own plan. One reason for the Quebec government's decision, in addition to the jurisdictional question, was the scheme devised by a group of talented, nationalistic technocrats to use pension-plan funds for public investments that would assist Francophone participation in the economy. *Maîtres chez nous* had many dimensions.

The struggle between Quebec and Ottawa was dramatic and very public, and both politicians and the media presented it as involving stakes high enough to destroy Confederation. And it is at least arguable that during this conflict Quebec was as close to moving toward independence as it has been at any subsequent time. In the end the crisis was surmounted. Quebec had a demonstrably superior plan, and a government that was far more determined and clear-minded than Ottawa. Quebec won the battle and thus gained control over its plan and its vast financial resources together with an alteration in federal-provincial tax-sharing agreements that significantly increased Quebec's tax room and revenues. Lesage had insisted that since Quebec was the homeland of the majority of French-Canadians it needed a pension plan tailored to its needs. He had used the nationalist argument effectively, flexed the muscles of the Quebec state, and won an impressive, if not total, victory.[29]

From this abbreviated account of a complex issue, a few conclusions may be drawn. First, what might have been a slightly sordid haggle over the division of public funds was converted into a nationalist cause. It was the national homeland of Francophones against Ottawa, where Francophones, always a minority, were hardly visible between 1957 and 1965. Second, the Lesage Liberals had taken a traditional Quebec position and transformed it into a modern cause; it was not the right of the Church in the social field that was being defended, but rather the determination of the Quebec state to move into an area once claimed by the Church and the federal government. Finally, again as in the examples of education and electricity, the new welfare state, of which the pension plan was only one piece, would provide centralized, rationalized, and standardized services to replace the patchwork of haphazardly organized, often patronage-ridden institutions. In this the Quebec government was taking a course already marked out in other industrial societies, though, as the Caisse des Dépôts et Placements illustrated, Quebecers were willing to make important innovations.

---

[28] Antonin Dupont, *Les relations entre l'Eglise et l'Etat sous Louis-Alexandre Taschereau 1920-1936* (Montréal, 1972).

[29] Thomson, *Jean Lesage*, pp. 184-89.

V

The essence of the new nationalism was invoked to justify the developments that have come to be known as the Quiet Revolution. Where traditionally the Quebecer's self-image, his nationalism, focused on language, religion, and the land, the new ideology was articulated by a society for which rural life was only a memory, often a bad one. For members of an urban-industrial society, the concern was with new questions that traditional religious and social teachings seemed incapable of answering. And if traditional socio-religious answers were inadequate, then the Church as an institution was less and less relevant. As new ideas, founded on economics and sociology more than theology and moral philosophy, were explored, so, too, a new institution had to be found or created to implement these ideas. That institution already existed: the provincial state provided by Canadian federalism. An "église-nation" became an "état-nation" with the only question being the degree of autonomy that the new *état* might want.

The principal remaining similarity between the old and the new nationalism was language. Yet on closer examination even that similarity is limited. Like the old nationalists, the new were determined to defend the French language as a sheet anchor of Quebec's distinctiveness. But traditional nationalists invariably identified language with religion: *la langue gardienne de la foi, la foi guardienne de la langue*.[30] Language questions often meant purity of language, language as a vehicle of a literary culture, and perhaps above all, language as a medium of education for French and Catholic students everywhere in Canada. Language was protected and preserved by the Church and the educational system and, of course, the two were actually one.

For the new nationalists language came to have a different, or at least, an additional significance. Indeed, language became even more important than in the past, for the simple reason that, as Quebec became more like the rest of North America socio-economically, language became its principal distinguishing characteristic. Thus, during the Quiet Revolution language became a growing preoccupation and a source of increasing tensions as the cry for French unilingualism developed.[31] But the issue was almost totally divorced from religious concerns. Nor was it predominantly a literary or narrowly cultural one. Instead it was socio-economic. Quebecers had come to the conclusion that it was the language of the economy, not the language of the Church, that determined both individual and collective destinies—at least in this world. An economy where corporate managers operated in English was an economy where French-Canadians rarely became corporate managers. How could this be changed? The response to this, as to so many other questions, was state intervention. It began, haltingly, with the Lesage government's establishment of a Department of Cultural Affairs. It continued wherever the state

---

[30] Henri Bourassa, *Religion, Langue, Nationalité* (Montréal, 1910); and Bourassa, *La Langue Gardienne de la Foi* (Montréal, 1918).

[31] Raymond Barbeau, *Le Québec Bientôt Unilingue?* (Montréal, 1965).

moved into the economy and French was made the operational language. It reached its culmination in the work of the Gendron Commission on the situation of the French language in Quebec[32] and in legislation by the Bourassa and Lévesque governments designed to make French the dominant or exclusive language in all sectors of Quebec life. What lay behind these acts, and the surrounding controversy, was expressed very forthrightly in the White Paper on Language Policy that preceded Bill 101 in 1977. It stated:

> The Quebec that we wish to build will be essentially French. The fact that the majority of the population is French will be distinctly visible: at work, in communications, in the country. *It is also a country where the traditional division of powers, especially in matters concerning the economy, will be modified*: the use of French will not be generalized simply to hide the predominance of foreign powers over Francophones; this usage will accompany, will symbolize a reconquest by the Francophone majority of Quebec of the hold on the levers of the economy to which it is entitled[33]

Once again, then, the principal characteristics of the new nationalism are crystal clear. In language policy as elsewhere, the state replaced the Church; the values served are secular rather than sacred; the outcome is centralization and homogenization. Though the appeal to traditional values is evident, the thrust is toward the present and future, even at the expense of past distinctiveness.[34]

VI

The rapidity of change in Quebec in the 1960s, and the vigour with which Quebecers asserted their desire for new social and constitutional arrangements, was often startling, especially to English-speaking Canadians and to outsiders. Yet what was happening in that society was far from unique. There has been an "ethnic revival" in almost every part of the world during the last quarter century. Punjabis, Ibos, Catalans, Basques, Serbs, Croats, Walloons, Occitanians, Bretons, perhaps even Bavarians have, with varying degrees of assertiveness, joined with Québécois in their determination to retain their distinctiveness in an homogenizing world. A variety of hypotheses have been advanced in an attempt to understand this phenomenon. The British social philosopher Ernest Gellner has contended that nationalism is the product of an industrializing society, the glue that holds the society together when

---

[32] *Rapport de la Commission d'Enquête sur la Situation de la Langue française et sur les Droits linguistiques au Québec* (Québec, 1972), 3 vols. See especially vol. I, *La Langue de Travail*.
[33] "La Politique québécoise de la langue française," *Le Devoir*, 2 avril 1977.
[34] William D. Coleman, *The Independence Movement in Quebec* (Toronto, 1984), p. 182.

old loyalties and obligations based on regions, families, and religion are eroded by socio-economic change. Nationalism imposes a common literacy, what he calls a "high culture," on a society in order to unify it and fit its citizens for the needs of industrial activities. "It means the generalized diffusion of a school mediated, academy supervised idiom, codified for the requirements of reasonably precise bureaucratic and technological communication." While nationalist rhetoric is advanced as an appeal to preserve a society's uniqueness, it is in reality a justification for profound change. "It preaches and defends continuity, but owes everything to a decisive and utterly profound break in human history."[35]

There is much to be said for this hypothesis when applied to Quebec. As I have argued, the new nationalism of the Quiet Revolution, while appealing to certain historic hopes and fears, was in fact the ideological component of a qualitatively different society.[36] So, too, this nationalism legitimated policies whose thrust was toward a more homogeneous, bureaucratized, and centralized society, drawn together by a new educational system, a more centralized economy, and a common welfare and social security system.[37] Thus, Gellner's contention that nationalism propels the transition from a "culture-religion" to a "culture-state" is appealing.

In Quebec in the 1960s there were certainly those who suspected that their nation was being destroyed consciously by the very people who claimed to be saving it. In 1964 abbé Groulx published what he thought would be his last book. Entitled *Chemin de l'Avenir* this cri-de-coeur was a long lament for a nation suffering "the social sickness of a disruptive industrialism."[38] He pointed to youthful unbelief and moral laxity, a creeping secularism nourished by American materialism, and the anti-clericalism of *Cité libre* and Radio-Canada. For him the Quiet Revolution was a "denial of history, of traditions, a turning of the back on the past; an attack more than cunning against all of the elements that constitute the French-Canadian man, even of the foundations which had until now formed the basis of his life."[39] No wonder he was astonished to receive a letter of congratulations from Premier Lesage, who, evidently not being a very careful reader, was following a quite contrary road to the future.

Yet Lesage's instinct may not have been entirely misguided for he, or his advisers, recognized that not everything about the Quiet Revolution was new. It had connections with the past. Gellner's exclusive emphasis on the relationship between

---

[35] Ernest Gellner, *Nations and Nationalism* (Ithaca, N.Y., 1983), pp. 57, 125.

[36] Charles Taylor, "Nationalism and the Political Intelligentsia," *Queen's Quarterly*, LXXII, I (Spring, 1965), p. 152.

[37] In *Entre l'Eden et l'Utopie* (Montréal, 1984), Luc Bureau offers a satirical and humorous account of the failures of planning. See especially pp. 200-03.

[38] Lionel Groulx, *Chemins de l'Avenir* (Montréal, 1964), p. 22. The following year the conservative philosopher George Grant offered a similar reflection on Canada as a whole in his *Lament for a Nation* (Toronto, 1965).

[39] Lionel Groulx, *Mes Mémoires* (Montréal, 1974), pp. 4, 298.

industrialization and nationalism fails to account for nationalism's earlier history in Quebec and elsewhere. Anthony Smith offers a more balanced perspective, one that can fit abbé Groulx and Premier Lesage on the same continuum. The ethnic revival, he writes, is "at one and the same time an attempt to preserve the past, and to transform it into something new, to create a new type upon ancient foundations, to create a new man and society through the revival of old identities and the preservation of the 'links in the chain' of generations."[40] Nationalism, then, is more than outward symbols; it is also the articulated will of a community to preserve its distinctiveness. That will has a long history in Quebec; it has been persistent and moderate. It has never completely disappeared, though it has changed with the changing needs of society, and especially the changing aspirations of Quebec's leading classes. "Imagined by successive petites bourgeoisies—the liberal professions, the clergy, the new middle class—the nation, as a concept, offers this ideological plasticity that allows it to be associated with the most varied projects," André-J. Bélanger has written. "The nation, like liberty, that of Mme. Roland and others ... what interests can be served in its name![41]

During the Quiet Revolution, then, a new nationalism evolved that, like the old, expressed the aspirations of Quebec's leading classes. A transformed society required a new self-image: modern, urban, industrial, and secular. Paul-Emile Borduas's angry challenge had been met: the holy-water-sprinklers and the tuques, those relics of traditional Quebec, almost vanished, replaced by micro-computers and hard hats. Borduas might have judged the change a mixed blessing.

---

40   Smith, *Ethnic Revival*, p. 25.
41   André J. Bélanger, "Le Nationalisme au Québec: Histoire en Cinq Temps d'un Imaginaire," *critère*, 28 (printemps 1980), p. 58. See also Maurice Pinard and Richard Hamilton, "The Class Basis of Quebec's Independence Movement," *Ethnic and Racial Studies*, 7, 1 (January, 1984), pp. 19-54; Kenneth McRoberts, "The Sources of Neo-Nationalism in Quebec," *ibid.*, 57-85.

Politics and the Reinforcement of the French Language in Canada and Quebec, 1960-1986

Richard Jones

It is commonplace to affirm that language has been a political issue in Canada ever since 1760 when the British completed their conquest of New France, and the colony's approximately 70,000 French-speaking inhabitants came under British domination. The new masters hoped that time would enable them to transform the French Canadians into good English-speaking members of the Church of England[1] or that British immigration would eventually swamp them. Although the English language rapidly assumed a privileged place in Quebec and in Canada, the French did not disappear; indeed they multiplied prolifically.[2] When Canada assumed Dominion status with a federal form of government in 1867, Quebec, the territory inhabited largely by Francophones, became a separate province.[3]

Confederation did not open an era of linguistic harmony in Canada. Indeed, bitter language conflict burst forth frequently as French-speaking minorities outside Quebec saw their few linguistic rights, particularly in the area of education, curtailed or eradicated by English-speaking majorities.[4]

Until 1960, it could be said that the status of the French language in Canada was at best stagnating and that citizens who spoke French or were of French ethnic origin were clearly disadvantaged compared to those who spoke English or were of British

---

[1] The secret instructions accompanying the Quebec Act of 1774 are eloquent in this regard. For historian Hilda Neatby, the act and the instructions taken together signified "gentle but steady and determined anglicization." See her *Quebec: The Revolutionary Age, 1760-1791* (Toronto: McClelland and Stewart, 1966), 139.

[2] Historian Fernand Ouellet calculated the birth rate at a very respectable 50 to 55 per thousand during the century following the Conquest. See *Histoire économique et sociale du Québec, 1760-1850* (Montreal: Fides, 1966), 142, 197, 46.

[3] In 1851, 75.2 percent of Quebec's population was French-speaking. By 1901, this figure had climbed to 80.3 percent: *Annuaire de Québec, 1968-1969* (Quebec: Bureau de la Statistique du Québec, 1968), 179.

[4] For a generally good study of English-French relations in the nineteenth century, see A.I. Silver, *The French-Canadian Idea of Confederation, 1864-1900* (Toronto: University of Toronto Press, 1982). On the Manitoba School Question, Paul Crunican's *Priests and Politicians: Manitoba Schools and the Election of 1869* (Toronto: University of Toronto Press, 1974), is excellent. As for Ontario's attempts to suppress French-language education, consult Robert Choquette, *Language and Religion: A History of English-French Conflict in Ontario* (Ottawa: University of Ottawa Press, 1975).

ethnic origin.[5] This article seeks to show that, since 1960, the status of the French language in Canada, as well as the position of Francophones in Canadian society, has, in many ways, improved markedly. Governments, at both the federal and provincial levels, have played a major role in this evolution; they intervened because of powerful political pressures applied by Canada's French-speaking population.[6] Yet many of the changes at the federal level and in the provinces with English-speaking majorities have been cosmetic or at least not very far-reaching. The really significant transformation has occurred in the province of Quebec.

The Federal Government and the English-Speaking Provinces

The Royal Commission on Bilingualism and Biculturalism was established by the federal government in 1963 in response to demands for greater linguistic equality that were being formulated by French-Canadians. According to its terms of reference, the Commission was expected to "recommend what steps should be taken to develop the Canadian Confederation on the basis of an equal partnership between the two founding races."[7] During the 1968 federal election campaign, linguistic equality was one of the themes developed by Liberal Prime Minister Pierre Elliott Trudeau. Trudeau was convinced that the federal government had to demonstrate to French-Canadians that it was the government of all Canadians, not of English-speaking Canadians alone. Trudeau's concern was that the government of Quebec would succeed in portraying itself as the real representative of French-Canadians; this

---

[5] The Royal Commission on Bilingualism and Biculturalism, in an oft-quoted and abundantly discussed table, showed that French Canadians in Quebec placed twelfth among fourteen ethnic groups by average labour income of male salary- and wage-earners in 1961. Those of British origin placed first, at a level 55 percent higher than that of the French. Even bilingualism did not appear a significant economic asset. Looking specifically at language, unilingual Anglophones were at the top of the ladder, well ahead of bilingual Francophones: *Report*, Book III: *The Work World* (Ottawa: Queen's Printer, 1969), 22-24. It should be mentioned, though, that by the 1980s the French had achieved virtual economic parity with the British in Canada: Jac-André Boulet and Laval Lavallée, *L'evolution des disparités linguistiques de revenues de travail au Canada de 1970 à 1980* (Ottawa: Conseil économique du Canada, October 1983).

[6] Canadians whose mother tongue (i.e., the first language learned and still understood) was French accounted for 28.1 percent of the population in 1961, and for 25.7 percent in 1981: Statistics Canada, 1961 and 1981 Censuses and tables furnished in *Language and Society* (Spring 1983), 20-21. Also, 24.6 percent of Canadians told government census-takers in 1981 that the language they most often spoke at home was French. This question, more indicative of the actual strength of the French language in Canada, was first asked in 1971.

[7] Royal Commission on Bilingualism and Biculturalism, Report. Book 1: *The Official Languages* (Ottawa: Queen's Printer, 1967), 173.

situation could only undermine national unity.[8] The following year, Parliament adopted the Official Languages Act whose objective was to increase the percentage of French-speaking civil servants, augment the use of French within the civil service, and make French-language services at the federal level available for most French-speaking Canadians.[9] Finally, in 1982, linguistic rights were enshrined in the Canadian Charter of Rights and Freedoms,[10] an integral part of the Canadian Constitution.

Fifteen years after its adoption, the Official Languages Act had, in the words of Language Commissioner d'Iberville Fortier, produced some remarkable achievements but fallen far short of creating the equality between the two official languages that, after all, was the stated objective of the legislation. In his opinion, Canada had reached a "kind of watershed between the solid accomplishments of the past and new challenges which will take us beyond mere statements of principle."[11]

Since the late 1960s, most of the nine Canadian provinces with English-speaking majorities, and particularly New Brunswick and Ontario, have taken measures to assist their French-language minorities. New Brunswick, approximately one-third of whose population is French-speaking, adopted its own largely symbolic Official Languages Act in 1969. Ontario, with nearly half a million citizens of French mother tongue,[12] has also extended French-language rights in areas such as education and the courts though, probably to avoid a backlash, it has refused to become officially bilingual. Other provinces have also taken initiatives although, in some important cases, they have acted only under judicial pressure.[13]

---

[8] Daniel Johnson, premier of Quebec from 1966 to 1968, promoted the Two Nations concept. In this regard, he asserted: "French Canadians seek to identify themselves with the State of Quebec, the only state in which they claim to be masters of their destiny, the only one that they can utilize to promote the development of their community." On the other hand, English Canadians tend, for their part, to "consider Ottawa as their national state": Daniel Johnson, *Egalité ou indépendance* (Montreal: Éditions Renaissance, 1965), 24, 50.

[9] S.C. 1969, c. 54, "An act respecting the status of the official languages of Canada." The text and comments may be found in Commissioner of Official Languages, *First Annual Report, 1970-1971* (Ottawa: Information Canada, 1971), 105-14 and 1-11.

[10] Sections 16 to 23 of the Constitution Act, 1982, specify language rights.

[11] Commissioner of Official Languages, Annual Report 1984 (Ottawa: Minister of Supply and Services Canada, 1985), preface.

[12] This figure, however, represents a mere 5.5 percent of the total population of Canada's most populous province; Francophones tend to be concentrated in the eastern and northern portions of the province.

[13] Such is the case of Manitoba, now obliged by the Supreme Court to translate its laws into French. The Francophones of that province proposed that, instead of translating thousands of laws, many of them inoperative, the provincial government offer certain services in French. In 1984, after having accepted the proposition, the government yielded to widespread Anglophone opposition and backed down from its commitment.

This flurry of linguistic activity in Canada has had no effect on the relatively rapid assimilation, into the English-speaking majority, of Francophones living in the eight provinces that are massively Anglophone. The Task Force on Canadian Unity, created in 1977 with a broad mandate to obtain and publicize the views of Canadians regarding the sate of their country, waxed pessimistic in this regard. Attributing the phenomenon to, among other factors, relatively high rates of intermarriage of Francophones with Anglophones, the Commission concluded: "The rate of linguistic assimilation of French-speaking minorities is quite high, and appears to be accelerating in all English-speaking provinces other than New Brunswick."[14]

The 1981 census figures confirmed this sombre diagnosis, showing that 32.8 percent of Canadians of French mother tongue, living outside Quebec, had shifted to English as the main language of the home. The 1971 figure had been 29.6 percent. Thus, the French mother tongue group now represents only 5.3 percent of Canada's population outside Quebec, and the group for which French is the language spoken in the home constitutes an almost negligible 3.8 percent of the population.[15]

There can be no doubt that, without the presence of the province of Quebec, the situation of the French language in Canada would be bleak indeed.[16] Although the Francophone minorities outside Quebec have long been agitating for better treatment, the pressures they could exert on their respective provincial governments as well as on the federal government have been relatively modest. In addition to lacking economic clout, the group has been simply too small, too widely dispersed geographically and, until recently, too disorganized to wield much weight.

Quebec's presence, then, has been decisive for the French in Canada. Four out of five French-speaking Canadians live in that province, Canada's second largest in terms of population. Just as the rest of Canada has become relatively more English-speaking as the Francophone minorities retreat, Quebec has, in recent years, become increasingly French-speaking. The 1981 census showed that 82.4 percent of Quebecers were of French mother tongue and that virtually the same proportion generally spoke French in the home.[17] In other words, languages in Canada seem to be undergoing a territorialization whereby Quebec becomes more French while the

---

[14] Task Force on Canadian Unity, *A Future Together: Observations and Recommendations* (Ottawa: Minister of Supply and Services Canada, 1979), 51.

[15] Statistics Canada, 1981 census and tables furnished in Robert Bourbeau, "Canada's Language Transfer Phenomenon," *Language and Society* 11 (Autumn 1983): 14-22.

[16] The most recent Statistics Canada report affirms that the French have maintained their positions, in relative terms, only in Quebec (figures quoted in *La Presse*, 26 janvier 1985).

[17] Bourbeau, "Canada's Language Transfer Phenomenon," 15.

rest of Canada registers consistent gains for the English language.[18] Ultimately, this phenomenon could strengthen division within Canada.

The Beginnings of the Language Debate in Quebec

Respecting the reinforcement of the French language in Canada since 1960, Quebec has been a theatre of dramatic activity, and state intervention has been constant and has had measurable impact. The undeniable result has been to strengthen the position of the French language in that province, though the extent of that improvement and particularly its durability remain subjects of rather acrimonious debate.

By the late 1960s, the major political parties in Quebec were all debating the language question and attempting to conceive policies that would not only satisfy their members but also ensure wide support at the polls. The context, as we shall see, favoured the most nationalistic of the three major parties, the Parti Québécois, ideologically committed to a French Quebec. Although after coming to power in 1976 it had to contend with realities that it could neither change nor ignore, it was able to accomplish its objectives in matters of language to a considerable degree.

A series of factors contributed to transforming the issue of language into an increasingly controversial subject in Quebec and finally to forcing the government to legislate. From 1944, the very conservative rural-based Union Nationale had been maintained in power under the firm and, according to his foes, dictatorial hand of Maurice Duplessis.[19] Duplessis died in 1959 and, the following year, the Liberals under Jean Lesage gained power, promising to modernize Quebec. The pace of change became so breathless that a journalist soon baptized the new era the "Quiet Revolution."[20]

The reforms of the Quiet Revolution aimed at modernizing the institutions, developing the economy, and furthering the welfare state. But they also had considerable nationalistic content since they were designed to improve the lot of Francophones as well as the position of Quebec in Confederation. The nationalization of the private Anglo-Canadian and American hydro-electric power

---

[18] This phenomenon was first convincingly documented by Richard J. Joy in *Languages in Conflict* (Toronto: McClelland and Stewart, Carleton Library no. 61, 1972). Davidson Dunton, co-chairman of the Royal Commission on Bilingualism and Biculturalism, has remarked on the popularity of the "two unilingualisms" solutions to the Canadian language question: "The Muddy Waters of Bilingualism," *Language and Society* 1 (Autumn 1979), 7.

[19] See Richard Jones, *Duplessis and the Union Nationale Administration* (Ottawa: Canadian Historical Association, booklet no. 35, 1983)

[20] This era has recently been chronicled by political scientist Dale C. Thomson in *Jean Lesage and the Quiet Revolution* (Toronto: Macmillan of Canada, 1984).

utilities,[21] Quebec's epic confrontations with the federal government over questions of money and power, and the province's ventures into the domain of international relations, notably with France, were at least partly based upon nationalist considerations.

The educational system, revamped at least structurally by the reformers of the Quiet Revolution, began turning out more and more graduates seeking employment. Certainly the expansion of the provincial government during these years created many new jobs for Francophones. In other fields, though, Anglo-dominated structures blocked opportunities. The federal civil service as yet offered few possibilities to Francophones unwilling to do virtually all their work in English. In addition, private enterprise, particularly the upper echelons, remained an Anglophone preserve that French-Canadians had great difficulty penetrating. Social scientists have abundantly described the rise of this new Francophone middle class.[22] For its members, tangible and intangible objectives of an individual character linked to self-interest, questions of jobs, money and social status, were not the only motivations. Aspirations of a collective nature were also important. Many Francophones were less and less disposed, after the "cultural mutation"[23] of these years, to continue to accept what they perceived as second-class citizenship. This group would be the standard-bearer of the new nationalism.

Nationalists in Quebec were highly sensitive to the nationalist currents that in the early 1960s were sweeping parts of Europe and the newly-emancipated states of Africa and Asia. Some Quebecers saw their province's status as akin to that of a colonized state and they began preaching Quebec's independence.[24] Naturally, an independent Quebec was to be a French state.[25]

The Quiet Revolution can be said to have marked the demise of the traditional Quebec, a Quebec whose identity was based on Catholicism, French language and

---

[21] "Masters in our own house" was the theme of the Liberal election campaign in 1962. The major issue of the campaign was the nationalization of the private electrical power companies (*Manifeste du parti libéral du Québec* 1962, 1).

[22] For example, Hubert Guindon, "Social Unrest, Social Class, and Quebec's Bureaucratic Revolution," *Queen's Quarterly* LXXI, 2 (Summer 1964): 150-62; Roch Denis, *Luttes de classes et question nationale au Québec, 1948-1968* (Montreal: Presses Socialistes Internationales, 1979).

[23] The expression is from Université de Montréal sociologist Guy Rocher, *Le Québec en mutation* (Montreal: Éditions Hurtubise HMH 1973).

[24] The titles of some of the separatist books published in these years are revealing: Raymond Barbeau, *La libération économique du Québec* (Montreal: Les Éditions de l'Homme, 1963); Andrew D'Allemagne, *Le colonialisme au Québec* (Montreal: Les Éditions R-B, 1966).

[25] The major independentist group of the early 1960s, the Rassemblement pour l'indépendance nationale, vigorously denounced bilingualism and objected to any legislative recognition of rights for Quebec's English-speaking linguistic minority (*Programme du R.I.N.*, octobre 1962, 2).

culture, and ruralism. Of course, since the early twentieth century, the traditional society had been in decline; indeed, by 1921, Quebec's population was half urban. By the mid-1960s, Quebec was rapidly becoming a secular society as the Church withdrew from its temporal preoccupations. What remained to distinguish French-Canadians from other North Americans?[26] Language and culture, no doubt, and the nationalists would give the promotion of these traits their full attention.

The preoccupation with language also stemmed from profound feelings of insecurity among Francophones. For example, the decline of the birth rate could have potentially disastrous effects on the proportion of the French population in Canada as well as in Quebec. As late as 1947, some observers, like Paul Sauriol, a journalist at the nationalist daily *Le Devoir*, foresaw the day when French-speaking Canadians would form the largest linguistic group in Canada.[27] Traditionally, a high birth rate was seen as a means of counterbalancing the influx of immigrants into Canada few of whom spoke French or learned that language. But, by the late 1950s and early 1960s, the birth rate began to decline precipitously. In 1954, the rate was still 30.4 per thousand. By 1965, it had dropped to 21.3.[28] The dream of the "revenge of the cradle" was apparently over.

Another worrisome trend was the fact that the great majority of immigrants settling in Quebec chose to send their children to English-language schools[29] and to integrate into the English-speaking minority. For them, English was simply the most "attractive" language. Should they leave Quebec, they would obviously require an excellent knowledge of English. Within Quebec, it did not appear essential for them to learn French, particularly for those living in the Montreal area. Some demographers hypothesized that Montreal would be close to having an English-speaking majority by the year 2000.[30] Not surprisingly, the increasingly vocal nationalist lobby urged that French be established, to a much greater degree, as the language of work and of education. Only the government could bring about the desired changes.

---

[26] Université Laval sociologist Fernand Dumont was one of those asking this question. See: "Y a-t-il un avenir pour l'homme canadien-français?" in *La vigile du Québec* (Montreal: Éditions Hurtubise-HMH, 1971), 57-76.

[27] "Programme d'immigration au service d'une politique raciste," editorial, *Le Devoir*, 7 octobre 1947, 1.

[28] *Annuaire du Québec 1968-1969*, 255.

[29] The percentage of New Canadians enroled in French schools fell from 52 in 1931-32 to 25 in 1962-63, then to 11 by 1972-73: Gary Caldwell, "Assimilation and the Demographic Future of Quebec" in *Quebec's Language Policies: Background and Response*, edited by John R. Mallea (Quebec: Centre international de recherche sur le bilinguisme, Presses de l'Université Laval, 1977), 57.

[30] Jacques Henripin saw Montreal as being between 53 and 60 percent French-speaking by 2000, a decline of between 6 and 13 percent, in "Quebec and the Demographic Dilemma of French-Canadian Society," *Quebec's Language Policies*, 43, 48.

But the government, regardless of what party was in power, had to be forced to act. The nationalists suspected that, without powerful popular pressure, the parties committed to federalism, specifically the Liberals and the Union Nationale, would not dare adopt the bold pro-French measures that they deemed necessary. But there was another more attractive possibility. Perhaps the nationalists, now more and more favourable to independence for Quebec, could themselves ride to power within a party whose backbone they would form. Then they could write and apply the language legislation. This, precisely, was to come about.

Before studying the ways in which the three major political formations dealt with the language issue, a brief description of each is necessary. The Liberal Party, largely urban-based, was the force behind Quebec's modernization in the early 1960s. It was quite willing to promote nationalist causes; still, there were limits beyond which a party committed to maintaining Quebec within Confederation could not go. In addition to widespread backing among Francophones, the party enjoyed the support of big enterprise, mostly Anglophone, and of the Anglophone minority in general.

On the specific issue of language, the Liberals were disposed to taking modest steps to strengthen the position of French. They were, however, unwilling to risk alienating those groups relatively satisfied with the status quo, particularly their English-speaking supporters and the business community. Nor, in the years from 1960 to 1966 when the Liberals held power, was the nationalist lobby sufficiently strong to force it to go further. In their 1960 election program, the Liberals promised to take measures to assist the French language and culture and notably create an Office de la langue française.[31] Few could feel threatened by these proposals. In 1966, the Liberals went somewhat further, declaring themselves willing to make French "the main language of work and of communication in Quebec" in order to "guarantee the vitality of the language and at the same time enable the majority of [Quebec's] population to live in French." Reassuring the hesitant, they declared that this objective was to be accomplished "with full respect for the undeniable rights of the Anglophone minority."[32]

The Union Nationale, in power from 1966 until 1970, might have been expected to produce bolder policies than the Liberals. During the Duplessis years, had it not boasted of being the vehicle of nationalism and the ardent defender of Quebec's autonomy?[33] Moreover, it was less beholden to the English-speaking minority from which it received relatively few votes. Yet it was perhaps more the flag-bearer of an old-style nationalism in which the defence of language through government intervention was not judged necessary. Nor did it desire to rouse English-speaking Canada against it. Thus, in 1966, the party devoted just a single line in a twenty-page program to the subject, vaguely promising to give French the status of

---

[31] *Programme politique du Parti libéral du Québec*, 1960, 2.

[32] *Québec en marche. Le programme politique du Parti libéral du Québec*, 1966, 5.

[33] The best history of the party is Herbert F. Quinn's *The Union Nationale: Quebec Nationalism from Duplessis to Lévesque*, 2nd ed. (Toronto: University of Toronto Press, 1979).

"national language."[34] Clearly, the nationalist lobby could not hope for satisfaction from this party!

The impetus for movement on the language question was to come from a new party, established in October 1968, called the Parti Québécois. This left-of-centre political formation was the vehicle of the nationalist aspirations of Quebec's new middle class, the intelligentsia that had come of age during the Quiet Revolution. Teachers, professors, professionals, students, and elements of the working class formed the backbone of the new group.[35] It proposed a modified form of independence of Quebec called "sovereignty-association," a sort of hybrid formula implying political sovereignty for the province coupled with an economic association with the rest of Canada.

The language policy of the Parti Québécois reflected both its orientation toward independence and its middle-class composition. The independentist option meant that it viewed Quebec as a separate entity. The Anglophone minority in Quebec was thus not perceived as part of a Canadian majority, a position that, in the eyes of the Liberals and the Union Nationale, justified special status for that group. Rather, Quebec Anglophones were simply another minority that would have to learn to participate in the life of a French Quebec. As for the party's middle-class power base, it implied that employers' views risked being given short shrift. Still, it should be noted that the Parti Québécois, mainly because of the powerful influence exerted by its charismatic leader, René Lévesque, did not purpose to abolish the English-language school system. Its position on this question would provoke considerable tension within the party.

Language Legislation: From Bill 85 to Bill 22

All three parties ultimately had to wrestle with the language issue, both in opposition and in power. It was during the Union Nationale's mandate from 1966 until 1970 that pressures heated up considerably. In 1968, a local school council in the town of St. Léonard on Montreal Island voted the gradual elimination of schooling in English for the large number of Italian children enroled in the district. The Italian community protested vehemently while the nationalist camp welcomed the commission's decision. "What we need are ten, twenty, fifty St. Leonards," contended *Le Devoir* editorialist Jean-Marc Léger, echoing the campaign of the group

---

[34] *Objectifs 1966 de l'Union Nationale, un programme d'action pour une jeune nation. Québec d'abord*, 3.

[35] Of the nearly 90,000 members of the Parti Québécois in 1971, nearly 40 percent belonged to the liberal professions, including a very large number of teachers, nearly 25 percent were white-collar workers, mainly office employees and service workers, and 15 percent were students: *Le Parti québécois en bref* (Montreal: Les Éditions du Parti québécois, 1971), 21.

that was spearheading the movement for obligatory French schooling.[36] The English-language community demanded that the government intervene to guarantee by law unimpeded access to English-language schools for any Quebec child. Obviously, Anglophones were concerned that this isolated incident could snowball into a powerful and dangerous trend and that the English-language school sector would be deprived of the not inconsiderable reinforcements furnished by the "allophone" community.[37]

The Union Nationale government was thus obliged to come to grips with this very volatile issue. Many of its members in the National Assembly,[38] conservatives from rural districts, had little interest in this question that concerned mainly Montreal and they were primarily concerned with preserving social peace. Pressures from the powerful Anglophone community urged legislative action to guarantee what it contended were its rights.[39] But the Union Nationale also counted a few nationalists who were convinced that action was needed to defend the French language. The premier would have to arbitrate these differences.

Daniel Johnson, Quebec's premier from 1966 until September 1968, was assuredly a nationalist. He had frequently criticized the lack of rights of the French-speaking minorities in the other provinces, demanding "Equality or Independence" as well as additional legislative powers for Quebec in the framework of a new constitution.[40] Still, he was a shrewd politician and he found the subject of St. Leonard a slippery banana peel indeed. At a press conference held a few hours before his sudden death, he responded ambiguously to English-speaking journalists who queried him repeatedly on the affair. "We will take all useful measures, not by legislation but by other means, to make non-French-speaking Quebecers part of Quebec so that they feel at home and learn French, the dominant language of Quebec." But he went on to say that language rights had to be protected and that it was inadmissible that local school commissions have the power to define them.[41] Just like the celebrated Marquess of Plaza-Toro, Johnson seemed to want to mount

---

[36] Jean-Marc Léger, "Il faut créer dix, vingt, cinquante St.-Léonard," *Le Devoir*, 4 septembre 1968.

[37] "Allophone," in the Canadian context, is the term used to describe persons whose mother tongue is neither English nor French.

[38] Since 1968, Quebec's unicameral legislature has been called the "National Assembly", an appellation of obvious symbolical value. The other Canadian provinces use the term "Legislative Assembly".

[39] From Toronto, a *Globe and Mail* editorial denounced what it saw as "cultural protectionism": "Turning Back the Clock," 2 Sept. 1968.

[40] See, for example, Johnson's speech at the first meeting of the Constitutional conference in Ottawa in February, 1968. Constitutional Conference, First Meeting, *Proceedings* (Ottawa: Queen's Printer, 1968), 53-71.

[41] Text of press conference quoted in Paul Gros d'Aillon, *Daniel Johnson, l'égalité avant l'indépendance* (Montreal: Les Éditions internationales Stanké, 1979), 230-34.

his horse and ride off in all directions at once. He certainly feared the political consequences of any action his government might take.

Johnson's successor, Jean-Jacques Bertrand, desired a rapid solution. A convinced federalist, he represented a rural district one quarter of whose population was English-speaking. Perhaps for those reasons he was less given to pushing nationalist themes. In any case, he indicated his intention to legislate "freer choice" in respect to the language of instruction, hoping thus, vainly as it turned out, to gain Anglophone support in a by-election held to fill a vacancy in the Assembly.[42] Nationalist groups objected strenuously as did several Union Nationale legislators, and Bertrand decided to withdraw the proposed bill.[43] With the objective of gaining time, he also decided, in the tried and true Canadian manner, to have a study done. He thus set up the Gendron Committee whose mandate was to "make an inquiry into and submit a report on the position of French as the language of usage in Quebec."[44]

September 1969 brought riots opposing French and Italians in St. Léonard where the school commission struggled to find a solution acceptable to all sides. The Prime Minister's office was besieged with letters and telegrams, and the English-language press urged: "Mr. Bertrand must act."[45] In the Assembly, the opposition Liberal Party also applied pressure, signifying that, although the Union Nationale appeared divided on the issue, the Liberals would support Bertrand.[46] Disorders in Montreal linked to illegal strikes provoked a veritable panic within the government, forcing it to move to repress the troubles, linguistic and otherwise.[47]

With the support of most of his Cabinet and the elected members of his party, Bertrand decided upon what he hoped would be perceived as a middle-of-the-road course. He presented Bill 63, entitled An Act to Promote the French Language in

---

[42] This was the interpretation of journalists and even Bertrand admitted that there did seem to be a coincidence ("Des groupes francophones protestent: le bill sur les droits scolaires sera présenté aujourd'hui," *Le Devoir*, 26 novembre 1968). The election theme in the district of Notre-Dame-de-Grâce, an English-speaking constituency in Montreal, was "Remember St. Leonard" (*The Montreal Star*, editorial, 20 Nov. 1968).

[43] This is the interpretation of Jérôme Proulx, a Union Nationale deputy, in his book, *Le panier de crabes* (Montreal: Éditions Parti Pris, 1971), 111-24. Journalists agreed ("Le bill sur les droits scolaires: l'opposition du caucus fait reculer Bertrand," *Le Devoir*, 27 novembre 1968, headline; Vincent Prince, "Le bill Bertrand renvoyé à un Comité," editorial, *Le Devoir*, 14 décembre 1968).

[44] Order in Council no. 3958, 9 Dec. 1968, quoted in Commission of Inquiry on the Position of the French Language and on Language Rights in Quebec, *Report: The Position of the French Language in Quebec, II: Language Rights* (Montreal, 1972), v.

[45] Robert J. Macdonald, "In Search of a Language Policy: Francophone Reactions to Bills 85 and 63" in *Quebec's Language Policies*, 219-42.

[46] Pierre Laporte's speech in Débats de l'Assemblée nationale du Québec, 10 octobre 1969, 3152.

[47] Proulx, *Le panier de crabes*, 152-53.

Quebec,[48] which proposed to give all new arrivals in Quebec a knowledge of the French language. But the really important part of the new law, the one relevant to the St. Leonard affair, was the clause dealing with the language of instruction: it recognized the right of any Quebecer to enrol his or her child in an English-language school.

In general, English-speaking Quebecers were satisfied with this new law. The Liberals, with the evident intention of embarrassing the Union Nationale, criticized the bill on the grounds that it did not really make French the "priority language" of Quebec.[49] As for the nationalists, many of whom were already supporting the fledgling Parti Québécois, they were furious at what they perceived as a "linguistic Munich," an ignominious surrender on the part of the Bertrand government, a powerful encouragement to the anglicization of Quebecers. Immediately, they began urging repeal of the law. Thousands of demonstrators converged upon the National assembly in Quebec City to express their opposition. Strikes erupted in the colleges and universities. When the next provincial elections were called in 1970, the Union Nationale was defeated handily by the Liberals but the two-year-old Parti Québécois managed to garner one-quarter of the vote. It is difficult to judge the role of the language question in the Union Nationale's defeat but the relative success of the Parti Québécois indicated that nationalist sentiment was rising.[50]

Now it was the turn of the Liberals to open Pandora's box. After the Gendron Commission finally published its report in 1973 recommending strong measures in favour of French, they could no longer refrain from moving. Fearful of the rapidly improving fortunes of the Parti Québécois (which had obtained nearly one vote in three in the 1973 elections), the Liberals had to make proposals that would conserve the support of at least the less extreme nationalists. The nationalist camp was simply becoming too important to be neglected. Yet the Liberals also represented the non-French-speaking community in Quebec and business had considerable influence

---

[48] The bill closely resembled Bill 85, presented a year earlier and withdrawn.

[49] Opposition Leader Jean Lesage's speech in *Débats de l'Assemblée nationale du Québec*, 28 octobre 1969, 3376-78.

[50] In the opinion of Jérôme Proulx, who resigned as a Union Nationale deputy to vote against Bill 63, the law destroyed the party. See *Le panier de crabes*, 153-54 and 193-94. A poll done for the Quebec City daily, *Le Soleil*, showed that the Union Nationale's stand on the language of education won it no support among Anglophones, 71.9 percent of whom proposed to vote for the Liberals while only 9.4 percent preferred the Union Nationale (*Le Soleil*, 18 avril 1970, 12). Other polling, done by political scientist Peter Regenstreif, showed that at least a small majority of Quebecers were satisfied with the government's record on language while large majorities were dissatisfied with its record on issues like strikes, taxes, and unemployment. Quoted in Vincent Lemieux, Marcel Gilbert, and André Blais, *Une élection de réalignement: l'élection générale du 29 avril 1970 au Québec* (Montreal: Éditions du Jour, 1970), 86.

in the party. How could the Liberals hope to harmonize the rapidly polarizing positions on the language question?

Bill 22 was the Liberals' attempt to find a solution to the dilemma.[51] It clearly demonstrated their conviction that most French-speaking Quebecers were now prepared to take strong measures to reinforce the position of the French language. Bill 22 thus proposed a series of measures designed to make French, at least to a greater degree, the language of work and of communication within Quebec. The means to bring this about were persuasive rather than coercive. More radically, though, the bill restricted access to schools in the English sector to Anglophones and to Allophones who had a sufficient knowledge of English, a level that was to be verified by tests. Moreover, a cap was placed on the size of enrolment in the English-language sector.

This measure showed that the Liberals were now willing to risk provoking the ire of the party's non-French-speaking supporters. Undoubtedly, they calculated that non-Francophones, even though unhappy, constituted a captive electorate. After all, they had never backed the Union Nationale in the past and there was certainly no possibility of their supporting the independentist Parti Québécois.

But the Liberals gravely miscalculated the extent of Anglophone discontent. A marathon radio program on the English-language station CFCF in Montreal brought 600,000 Quebecers, mostly Anglophones, to sign a telegram-petition to Prime Minister Trudeau urging abolition of the law.[52]

Nationalists bitterly attacked Bill 22 because of numerous loopholes; they insisted that it would do little to bring immigrants into the French-language stream, and the statistics ultimately showed that they were right in this regard. Indeed, in 1976-77, the last year of operation of Bill 22, the percentage of Allophone children attending English schools actually increased by 6.4 percent.[53] Still, the Anglophone and Allophone communities were even more adamant in their opposition to the law, particularly the stipulations regarding the language of education. When, in 1976, the Union Nationale, traditionally the voice of Quebec nationalism, made the sensational promise that, if elected, it would restore free choice of the language of schooling,

---

51 Official Language Act, Statutes of Quebec, 1974, c. 6.

52 William Tetley, "The English and Language Legislation: A Personal History" in *The English of Quebec: From Majority to Minority Status*, edited by Gary Caldwell and Eric Waddell (Quebec: Institut québécois de recherche sur la culture, 1982), 381-97. Tetley was an Anglophone minister in the Bourassa cabinet that adopted Bill 22. For an informative study of Anglophone opinion, see Michael B. Stein, "Bill 22 and the Non-Francophone Population in Quebec: A Case Study of Minority Group Attitudes on Language Legislation" in *Quebec's Language Policies*, 243-65.

53 Michel Paillé, "The Impact of Language Policies on Enrolment in Public Schools in Quebec" in *Contribution à la démolinguistique du Québec* (Quebec: Conseil de la langue française, avril 1985), 139-40; Claude St. Germain, *La situation linguistique dans les écoles primaires et secondaires, 1971-72 à 1978-79* (Quebec: Conseil de la langue française, 1979), 12, 24.

large numbers of non-Francophones rallied to it, deserting the now detested Liberal Party and its despised leader, Robert Bourassa.[54] For numerous other reasons unrelated to this paper, the Liberals lost ground while the Parti Québécois gained sufficient support to win the election and form the next government.

Bill 101: The Charter of the French Language

Contrary to the other two parties, the Parti Québécois had made no secret of its policy on language nor of the priority that it gave that question.[55] After all, the notion of an independent Quebec was predicated on the existence of a Quebec nation, of a separate identity, of a "personality at whose core is the fact that we speak French."[56] An independent Quebec would "make French the country's only official language," the party's 1971 program asserted. French would be the language of governmental institutions, it would be the working language of all enterprises, all new immigrants would be required to pass a French fluency test as a condition for obtaining a permanent visa or Quebec citizenship.[57] Since language was the fundamental value championed by the party, it was only natural that "Péquistes" be intensely concerned with the dangers faced by the French language in Quebec and committed to taking strong corrective measures. As befitted left-of-centre believers in a strongly-interventionist government, laws would be adopted to solve linguistic problems.

Parti Québécois adherents were undoubtedly far more united on language policy than were the supporters of the two rival parties. Nevertheless, the Parti Québécois was on several occasions racked by acrimonious disputes concerning what rights or privileges, if any, would be accorded the province's English-speaking community.[58] For example, would there be a publicly-financed English-language school sector? Radicals within the party who favoured unilingualism, many of whom had been members of the separatist Rassemblement pour l'indépendance nationale, wanted the

---

[54] Quinn, *The Union Nationale*, 279-80.

[55] The party's "political action program", adopted during its third congress in February 1971, specifically promised to mount a campaign to fight for the repeal of Bill 63 (Parti Québécois, *Le programme—l'action politique—les status et réglements, édition 1971*, 35).

[56] René Lévesque, *Option Québec* (Montreal: Les Éditions de l'Homme, 1968), 19.

[57] Parti Québécois, *Le programme*, 21.

[58] For Vera Murray, the Parti Québécois, even while in opposition, was rife with tension on virtually all aspects of its ideology. She sees the battles as pitting a "technocratic" wing, more moderate, emphasizing efficiency and planning, and controlling the party's executive, against a more radical "participationist" wing, representing a minority of the party's members, but very vigorous and noisy in the defence of its left-wing social-democratic positions: *Le Parti Québécois, de la fondation à la prise du pouvoir* (Montreal: Éditions Hurtubise HMH, 1976), 29-30.

demise of English schools; indeed, during the 1971 congress, party president René Lévesque had to threaten to resign in order to have his more moderate position prevail. Again, in February 1973, the party's executive had to take a harder line on public financing of English schools, agreeing to place a permanent ceiling on funding, in order to convince party members to accept simply the principle of the existence of schools for the English minority.[59]

The party program, on language as on all other questions, was defined with impressive democracy by elected delegates during frequent annual or biennial congresses; it certainly reflected the membership's aspirations, though generally tempered by the leadership's more moderate positions. It did not necessarily constitute a shrewd and sound appreciation of the Quebec context in general and of political realities in particular. Thus, after its election in 1976, the Parti Québécois quickly came to realize that designing a general policy was much easier than drawing up specific regulations and applying them to everyday situations. Like the other two parties, the Parti Québécois faced numerous constraints in dealing with language. Specifically, the need to take account of certain pressure made it impossible to build a Quebec as unilingually French as the party had originally intended.

Shortly after its arrival in power, the Parti Québécois government issued a White Paper detailing the language policy that it intended to implement.[60] This policy was soon set out in proposed legislation, the symbolically numbered Bill 1. The bill proposed vigorous measures to make French the language of the workplace and backed these up with threats of fines and other penalties for non-compliance. It also proposed that, generally, only French could appear on signs in public and that hitherto English-language institutions would have to communicate with the government and among themselves in French. The English-speaking school sector was to be maintained but, in most cases, only children with at least one parent who had had his or her primary schooling in Quebec in the English language were eligible. It was clear that the English sector was doomed to atrophy.

Reaction of Quebec's Anglophones was uniformly negative although, contrarily to what they had said of the Liberals, they could not pretend that the Parti Québécois had abandoned them.[61] English-speaking Quebeckers had shown only negligible

---

[59] *Le Devoir*, 26 février 1973.

[60] Camille Laurin, *La politique québécois de la langue française* (Quebec: Éditeur officiel, 1977).

[61] Many Anglophone organizations and firms testified during government hearings on Bill 1 (Assemblée nationale, Journal des Débats, Commission permanente de l'éducation, des affaires culturelles et des communications, *Délibérations*, juin-juillet 1977). One Anglophone pressure group, the Positive Action Committee, sarcastically commented on the bill: "The Anglophone collectivity has a place in Quebec on the condition that it is invisible and silent and progressively diminished in number" (Alison d'Anglejan, "Language Planning in Quebec: An Historical Overview and Future Trends" in *Conflict and Language Planning in Quebec*, edited by Richard Y. Bourhis (Clevedon, England: Multilingual Matters Ltd., 1984), 29-52.

support for the Parti Québécois, the party of separatism.[62] On language, the party's platform had always been quite clear—and quite unacceptable from the point of view of the English-speaking minority.[63]

In particular, business circles denounced certain aspects of Bill 1 linked to the language of the workplace. Essentially, they maintained that the law's requirements would increase costs and put Quebec enterprises at a comparative disadvantage in relation to firms elsewhere in North America. They also contended that the law gave too much power to workers and unions. Finally, the clauses that severely limited enrolment in English-language schools caused deep concern: would recruiting efforts and transfers from outside the province not be hampered?

Certainly the Parti Québécois numbered few adherents in the business world. Business thus had to make special efforts to make its weight felt once the Parti Québécois came into office. In many respects, its remonstrances were successful in that the modified version of Bill 1, called Bill 101 (in particular, its final version) took heed of business criticism. Of course, the Parti Québécois could not, even had it so wished, have abandoned the key stipulations of its language project; closely surveyed by the party's membership, the government had to remain within bounds. On the other hand, the Parti Québécois could not afford to alienate irreparably the business world. A referendum on sovereignty-association had to be held during its first mandate in office and it was reasonable to assume that, if Quebec's economy floundered during this period, the electors would spurn the project.

Even with the amendments, Anglophone businesses clearly did not like the law. Many enterprises, particularly head offices, left Quebec, often blaming the language legislation. Sun Life was a noisy and well-publicized example of this exodus. Yet it is very difficult to evaluate the actual causes of these departures. For some, higher Quebec taxes were the important issue. For others, militant unionism made Quebec a difficult place in which to do business. For still others, it was important to be where the action was, and that meant moving west, to Toronto, or to Alberta during the oil boom of the late 1970s.

The Parti Québécois was thus forced to moderate its language legislation and to apply it less rigorously than might otherwise have been the case. For example, head offices and research centres were exempted from the law's provisions. Professionals who had no contact with the public would not have to pass a test of French

---

[62] Only 9.5 percent of non-Francophones proposed to support the Parti Québécois in 1976; 22 percent intended to vote for the Union Nationale and its policy of "free choice"; 40 percent refused to answer, proposed to abstain, or did not know which party they would support (poll figures quoted in André Bernard, *Québec: élections 1976* (Montreal: Éditions Hurtubise-HMH, 1976), 49.

[63] Anglophone reactions are analyzed in Nadia Assimopoulous and Michel Laferrière, *Législation et perceptions ethniques: une étude du contenu de la presse anglaise de Montréal au vote de la loi 101* (Montreal: Office de la langue française, 1980).

proficiency.[64] Moreover, it was common knowledge that hundreds of students were illegally enroled in the English Protestant schools; while denouncing the situation frequently, the government preferred that the law be flouted rather than use force to expel these students.[65]

The courts ultimately constituted an additional constraint. They declared unconstitutional certain sections of the language legislation, thus weakening Bill 101.[66] Since Quebec remains a part of Canada, the Supreme Court of Canada is the court of last appeal, a situation that the Parti Québécois did not foresee or did not want to imagine in the heady days of 1977. In addition, the new Canadian constitution, adopted without Quebec's consent in 1982, contains certain language guarantees with which Quebec is not in agreement but which nevertheless apply.

One new element that could well have an impact on the language question is the return to power, in December 1985, of the Liberals under their reincarnated leader, Robert Bourassa. The party has again become the advocate of the English-speaking minority, which counts four ministers in the provincial Cabinet. Yet interestingly—and this is surely an indication of the very considerable evolution that Quebec has undergone in matters of language since the early 1970s—the Liberals have indicated that, while they may make certain concessions and adjust Bill 101 to make it more flexible, they will not abrogate the law. Among the modifications envisaged should be mentioned the softening of the requirement that signs be in French only. Public opinion polls show an increasing percentage of Quebecers willing to accept bilingualism on signs.[67] Still, it is apparent that Quebec has adapted to the law and

---

[64] These adaptations are examined in William D. Coleman, "From Bill 22 to Bill 101: The Politics of Language under the parti Québécois," *Canadian Journal of Political Science* XIV, 3 (Sept. 1981), 459-485, and reprinted in this volume; also in William D. Coleman, "A Comparative Study of Language Policy in Quebec: A Political Economy Approach" in *The Politics of Canadian Public Policy*, edited by Michael M. Atkinson and Marsha A. Chandler (Toronto: University of Toronto Press, 1983), 21-42.

[65] Claude Ryan, minister of education in the new Bourassa Liberal government (elected on 2 December 1985), stated that he would prefer to settle the problem of the estimated 1800 "illegals" on a case-by-case basis (*Le Devoir*, 28 et 29 janvier 1986). The government decided nevertheless on a general amnesty decried by critics because it rewarded those who disobeyed the law.

[66] Gilles Rhéaume, president of two nationalist organizations, the Société Saint-Jean-Baptiste de Montréal and the Mouvement national des Québécois, declared that the courts had riddled Bill 101 with so many holes that it was beginning to look like a piece of Swiss cheese (*The Gazette*, 5 Jan. 1985).

[67] In 1979, fewer than one of three Francophone Quebecers thought that English should be allowed on public signs. A 1981 poll showed that two in three French-speaking Montrealers agreed with bilingualism on signs. By 1984, 80 percent of Francophone Quebecers disagreed with the French unilingualism imposed by the sign stipulations in Bill 101 (Commissioner of Official Languages, *Annual Report 1984*, 37). 1985 polls conducted by the Centre de

that the law has changed Quebec. More than half of all Allophone children are now enroled in schools in the French sector.[68] The proportion of workers who say they work in French has increased significantly.[69] Enterprises under French control now furnish more than sixty percent of all jobs in Quebec, up from forty-seven percent in 1960.[70] Even the English-speaking minority, which has undergone a veritable revolution since 1970, seems able to live with the law.[71]

It was inevitable that the changes that occurred in Quebec in the early 1960s would eventually have an impact on language, a highly emotional issue. Within the federal government and the English-speaking provinces, these changes have certainly had some effect. The proportion of French-speakers in the federal civil service has increased and now approaches the proportion of Francophones in the total population.[72] French-language services have become more widely available. Bilingualism has become more popular among Canada's English-speaking population.[73] Still, a command of English remains a virtual necessity for

---

Recherches sur l'Opinion publique showed similar findings (*La Presse*, 20 janvier and 27 avril 1985).

[68] The figure increased from 30 percent in 1976-77 to 57 percent in 1974-85 (Michel Paillé, "Conséquences des politiques linguistiques québécois sur les effectifs scolaires selon la langue d'enseignement," *Le Devoir*, 29 mai 1985).

[69] Numerous surveys have been conducted on this question. The Gendron Commission prepared a lengthy study of the question as it stood in the early 1970s. Sixty-four percent of Francophones declared that they worked almost solely in French (Commission d'enquête sur la situation de la langue française et sur les droits linguistiques au Québec, *Rapport*, Livre I: *La langue de travail* (Quebec, décembre 1972, 16-19). According to recent findings, 70 percent of Francophones now work only in French, and another 20 percent generally in French ("A Linguistic Scarecrow," editorial, *The Gazette*, 9 Jan. 1985).

[70] André Raynauld and François Vaillancourt, *L'appartenance des entreprises: le cas cu Québec en 1978* (Montreal: Office de la langue française, 1985).

[71] One-half of Quebec's Anglophones (two-thirds of those under 30) are bilingual. The population of Anglo-Quebecers, however, declined by 10 percent during the 1970s because of significant out-migration. Not surprisingly, research has shown that Anglophones who left tended to speak only English while Anglophones who remained tended to be bilingual (Statistics Canada, *Language in Canada*, quoted in *The Gazette* and *Le Devoir*, 26 Jan. 1985).

[72] Commissioner of Official Languages, *Annual Report 1984*, 60. However, over half of all Francophone employees are in non-officer positions, including clerks, secretaries, and similar occupations.

[73] Fifteen percent of Canadians class themselves as bilingual. Between 1971 and 1981, their number grew at double the rate of population increase. Only 7.6 percent of English Canadians are bilingual as compared to 36.2 percent of French-Canadians. Considering only the English-speaking provinces, 5.4 percent of the English speak French while 78.9 percent of the French know English. Quebec boasts by far the highest proportion of bilinguals: Statistics Canada, *Language in Canada* (Ottawa: Supply and Services Canada, Jan. 185).

Francophones outside Quebec since, with some exceptions, the concentrations of French-speaking population are insufficient to allow daily activities, notably work, to be carried out in French. It is thus not surprising that assimilation takes a large toll among the French-speaking minorities and that even the awakening of the federal and, at least, some provincial governments to the French fact does not seem to have stemmed linguistic losses.

The Quebec case is very different since that province has always had a strong French-speaking majority that controls the provincial government. Nevertheless, until very recently, the English-speaking minority in Quebec has wielded enormous economic power (and to a somewhat lesser extent still does)[74] and, in addition, has benefited immensely from the prestige accruing to speakers of Canada's and North America's major language. The Quiet Revolution of the early 1960s made Francophones aware of a linguistic disequilibrium that disadvantaged them.[75] But it was inevitable that any attempt to modify fundamentally the balance between the two languages in Quebec would provoke bitter disputes between the majority and the minority.

Three political parties faced the challenge of enhancing the status of the French language within Quebec and of improving opportunities for Francophones. Each party's actions in this regard were affected by particular constraints. For the two old parties, the Liberals and the Union Nationale, the language issue caused internecine strife within party ranks as well as considerable harm at the polls. In particular, the Liberals had to deal with the fact that their supporters included virtually the entire non-Francophone minority, a group whose conception of Quebec society was markedly different from that of most Francophones.

The Parti Québécois, as we have seen, proceeded differently. Far from trying to shy away from the issue and to seek some middle ground that would not alienate important factions, the party placed language reform in the forefront of its program and it hoped that its promise of a strong stand in favour of the French language would generate support among a majority of French-speaking Quebecers. That hope proved realistic enough although, once in power, the Parti Québécois could no longer ignore key sectors of opinion that had opposed its language policy.

---

74 French immersion programs in the English-speaking provinces have recently become extremely popular (Commissioner of Official Languages, *Annual Report 1984*, 25-29).
Sixty-nine percent of managers in Quebec, in the public and private sectors, are now French-speaking. French-speaking managers even have a slight majority in English-Canadian and in foreign firms established in the province (Arnaud Sales, *Décideurs et gestionnaires: étude sur la direction et l'ancadrement des secteurs privé et public* (Quebec: Éditeur officiel, 1985), 177-202.

75 Language situations in which dominance is not based on demographic supremacy can easily produce social tensions. Such has been the case of Quebec. See Pierre E. Laporte, "Status Language Planning in Quebec: An Evaluation" in *Conflict and Language Planning in Quebec*, 57.

Politics and the Reinforcement of the French Language 749

What does the future bode for the French language in Quebec? The heroic exploits of the knights of language are now fading rapidly into the past. There are many indications that the younger generation of Quebecers, those who did not fight the battles of the 1960s and 1970s, believe that the question has been permanently resolved and that French is now secure in the province.[76] This phenomenon is perhaps an indication of the relative success of Bill 101 in changing the face of Quebec. Other observers, perhaps more perspicacious, see continued dangers for the French language, regardless of the language legislation. The Conseil de la langue française, charged with advising the government on matters of language, affirms that French has still not become the "normal, habitual language of work, of teaching, of communications, of commere and business."[77] The English language continues to surround and to penetrate Quebec. Communications, and notably cable television, have made English-language stations more numerous for most subscribers than French-language stations.[78] American culture and cultural practices will undoubtedly have a growing impact on Quebec as an open society. In addition, the tremendous advances of computer science since the late 1970s, a phenomenon entirely unforeseen by the writers of Bill 101, have been largely in English, whether it be manufacturers' manuals or software. Indeed, the three offices concerned with the application of Bill 101 see the francization of this sector as the major challenge of the near future.[79]

Other problems, though having no relation to Bill 101, certainly affect the future of the French language in Quebec. Education critics have decried poor teaching of French in schools.[80] Even business leaders have protested against graduates' insufficient mastery of the French language. Finally, demographic projections for Quebec indicate that the province's population will begin to diminish shortly after the year 2000. Declining births (the Quebec fertility rate now stands at 1.42, considerably below the Canadian average of 1.68), minimal immigration from foreign countries and, since the mid-1970s, a negative balance in population

---

[76] Polls conducted by the Conseil de la langue française, one of the organisms created by Bill 101, showed, in the opinion of the Conseil, that the young live "with the peacefulness of security brought about by the French language Charter." (Quoted in *The Gazette*, 22 April 1985). The Conseil expressed shock when 40 percent of high school students queried affirmed that "living in French" was not necessary for their personal development!" (*La situation linguistique actuelle* [Quebec, Conseil de la langue française, janvier 1985] 27.)

[77] La situation linguistique actuelle, 18.

[78] A study commissioned by the Conseil showed that Francophones spend about one-third of their television time watching English-language stations. *Ibid.*, 12.

[79] Jean-Pierre Proulx, "La question linguistique: la révolution informatique constitue le défi de l'heure," *Le Devoir*, 12 décembre 1985.

[80] "Un constat de piètre qualité: l'apprentissage de la langue maternelle à l'école," *Le Soleil*, 17 janvier 1985; "L'apprentissage de la langue maternelle est en crise," *Le Devoir*, 16 janvier 1985.

exchanges with other Canadian provinces, explain this phenomenon, the repercussions of which could be dramatic.[81]

Language legislation in Canada, and particularly in Quebec, has undoubtedly had significant effects. Still, it appears certain that legislation alone cannot solve the major challenges that the French language must face if it is to maintain what has been acquired over the past twenty years.

---

[81] Assemblée nationale du Québec, Commission parlementaire de la culture, *Le Québec à la croisés des chemins démographiques*, septembre 1985; Albert Juneau, "La défaite des berceaux," *Le Devoir*, 7 juin 1985; Jean-Claude Leclerc, "L'effondrement démographique: le réveil risque d'être tardif," *Le Devoir*, 8 novembre 1985; Georges Mathews, "La crise démographique au Québec," *Le Devoir*, 18 and 19 novembre 1985.